THE ROUGH GUIDE

There are more than one hundred Rough Guide titles
covering destinations from Amsterdam to Zimbabwe

Forthcoming titles include
Central America • Chile • Maya World
Indonesia • Japan • New Orleans

Rough Guide Reference Series
Classical Music • European Football • The Internet • Jazz
Opera • Reggae • Rock Music • World Music

Rough Guide Phrasebooks
Czech • Egyptian Arabic • French • German • Greek • Hindi & Urdu
Hungarian • Indonesian • Italian • Japanese • Mandarin Chinese
Mexican Spanish • Polish • Portuguese • Russian • Spanish
Swahili • Thai • Turkish • Vietnamese

Rough Guides on the Internet
www.roughguides.com

ROUGH GUIDE CREDITS

Text editor: Olivia Eccleshall
Series editor: Mark Ellingham
Editorial: Martin Dunford, Jonathan Buckley, Samantha Cook, Jo Mead, Amanda Tomlin, Kate Berens, Ann-Marie Shaw, Paul Gray, Chris Schüler, Helena Smith, Kieran Falconer, Judith Bamber, Orla Duane, Ruth Blackmore, Sophie Martin, Jennifer Dempsey, Sue Jackson, Geoff Howard (UK); Andrew Rosenberg, Andrew Taber (US)
Picture research: Eleanor Hill

Production: Susanne Hillen, Andy Hilliard, Link Hall, Helen Ostick, James Morris, Julia Bovis, Michelle Draycott
Cartography: Melissa Flack, Maxine Burke, Nichola Goodliffe
Online editors: Alan Spicer, Kate Hands (UK); Geronimo Madrid (US)
Finance: John Fisher, Celia Crowley, Neeta Mistry
Marketing & Publicity: Richard Trillo, Simon Carloss, Niki Smith (UK); Jean-Marie Kelly, SoRelle Braun (US)
Administration: Tania Hummel, Alexander Mark Rogers

ACKNOWLEDGEMENTS

The author, researchers and editor would all like to thank Helen Ostick, Susanne Hillen and Michelle Draycott for smooth production; Nichola Goodliffe for producing fine maps; Matthew Teller for careful proofing; and Lisa Pusey and Eleanor Hill for picture research. Thanks also to Yvonne Jones and Silke Kerwood for Basics research.

John: Thanks to Pete and the rest of the team for a great job; Olivia, for getting through it despite everything; Kate for looking after it all; and, as always, A and the two Js.

Peter: Thanks to Ana Lara Aguilar, Lupita Ayala and Irma Medellin at the Mexican Tourist Office in London for their invaluable advice and enthusiastic help; and many thanks to Cathy and Joanna Matos of Cathy Matos Mexican Tours, and everyone at JLA, especially Charlie Shepherd, for answering numerous queries speedily and accurately. In Mexico I can honestly say that everyone I met, from hotel receptionists and bus drivers, to directors of tourism and immigration officials, was unfailingly helpful, making months of travel and research a real pleasure. I'd like to thank everyone in tourist offices throughout Chiapas for even more enthusiasm and practical help, particularly Mercedes Cerdio de Gutiérrez and Lorena Villanueva Montserrosa in Tuxtla; Dawn Kauffman Baker and Germán García Martínez in San

Cristóbal; and Consuelo Bermúdez in Comitán. Also in San Cristóbal, I'm very grateful to Dana Burton of La Pared, for her good advice and some fine reading material while I was there, and for her amazingly swift email responses to queries from the UK.

Alex: Thanks to Gardenia D'Almeida Franca – for constant patience and inspiration; David Stott; Daniel Roznovjak; Herve Misserey; Peter at the Pantera Negra in Mérida; Martin Pimentel in Tlapacoyan; Alejandro Martinez, his wife and parents, in Rancho Paraíso, Bacalar; Karina and Manuel at the Campeche Tourist Office; Leti and Lazaro in Oaxaca; Sandra and Dan in Puerto Morelos; the Amar Inn; the people of Santa Ana del Valle, Oaxaca, particularly Macario; the Chief of Police in Huamelulpan, Oaxaca; everyone at Deep Blue, Cozumel, especially Deborah and Luiz the world's most professional diving instructor; Amigos de Si'an Ka'an; Vivienne Heller; and Amanda Rickard at Karrimor.

Daniel: Thanks to Armida Durán Aguilar.

Matt: Thanks to Alison Bigg.

Finally, this edition would have been much the poorer without all the readers who sent in their comments, advice, criticisms and recommendations: the full roll of honour (barring those whose signatures defeated us) appears on p.v.

PUBLISHING INFORMATION

This fourth edition published January 1999 by Rough Guides Ltd, 62–70 Shorts Gardens, London WC2H 9AB.
Distributed by the Penguin Group:
Penguin Books Ltd, 27 Wrights Lane, London W8 5TZ
Penguin Books USA Inc., 375 Hudson Street, New York 10014, USA
Penguin Books Australia Ltd, 487 Maroondah Highway, PO Box 257, Ringwood, Victoria 3134, Australia
Penguin Books Canada Ltd, 10 Alcorn Avenue, Toronto, Ontario, Canada M4V 1E4
Penguin Books (NZ) Ltd, 182–190 Wairau Road, Auckland 10, New Zealand
Typeset in Linotron Univers and Century Old Style to an original design by Andrew Oliver.
Printed in the USA by R.R. Donnelley & Sons.
Illustrations in Part One and Part Three by Edward Briant.

Illustrations on p.1 & p.581 by Henry Iles.
© John Fisher 1998.
No part of this book may be reproduced in any form without permission from the publisher except for the quotation of brief passages in reviews.
672pp – Includes index
A catalogue record for this book is available from the British Library.
ISBN 1-85828-342-6

Mexico

THE ROUGH GUIDE

written and researched by

John Fisher

with additional contributions by

Peter Eltringham

and

Mary Farquharson, Matthew Gardner, Daniel Jacobs
Chris Overington, Alex Robinson and Paul Whitfield

THE ROUGH GUIDES

We set out to do something different when the first Rough Guide was published in 1982. Mark Ellingham, just out of university, was travelling in Greece. He brought along the popular guides of the day, but found they were all lacking in some way. They were either strong on ruins and museums but went on for pages without mentioning a beach or taverna. Or they were so conscious of the need to save money that they lost sight of Greece's cultural and historical significance. Also, none of the books told him anything about Greece's contemporary life – its politics, its culture, its people, and how they lived.

So with no job in prospect, Mark decided to write his own guidebook, one which aimed to provide practical information that was second to none, detailing the best beaches and the hottest clubs and restaurants, while also giving hard-hitting accounts of every sight, both famous and obscure, and providing up-to-the-minute information on contemporary culture. It was a guide that encouraged independent travellers to find the best of Greece, and was a great success, getting shortlisted for the Thomas Cook travel guide award,

and encouraging Mark, along with three friends, to expand the series.

The Rough Guide list grew rapidly and the letters flooded in, indicating a much broader readership than had been anticipated, but one which uniformly appreciated the Rough Guide mix of practical detail and humour, irreverence and enthusiasm. Things haven't changed. The same four friends who began the series are still the caretakers of the Rough Guide mission today: to provide the most reliable, up-to-date and entertaining information to independent-minded travellers of all ages, on all budgets.

We now publish 100 titles and have offices in London and New York. The travel guides are written and researched by a dedicated team of more than 100 authors, based in Britain, Europe, the USA and Australia. We have also created a unique series of phrasebooks to accompany the travel series, along with an acclaimed series of music guides, and a best-selling pocket guide to the Internet and World Wide Web. We also publish comprehensive travel information on our Web site:

www.roughguides.com

HELP US UPDATE

We've gone to a lot of effort to ensure that this new edition of *The Rough Guide to Mexico* is accurate and up to date. However, things change — places get "discovered", opening hours are notoriously fickle, restaurants and rooms raise prices or lower standards, extra buses are laid on or off. If you feel we've got it wrong or left something out, we'd like to know, and if you can remember the address, the price, the time, the phone number, so much the better.

We'll credit all contributions, and send a copy of the next edition (or any other Rough Guide if you prefer) for the best letters. Please mark letters: "Rough Guide Mexico Update" and send to:
Rough Guides, 62–70 Shorts Gardens, London WC2H 9AB or Rough Guides, 375 Hudson St, 9th floor, New York NY 10014. Or send email to: mail@roughguides.co.uk
Online updates about this book can be found on Rough Guides' Web site at www.roughguides.com

THE AUTHOR

John Fisher was one of the authors of the first ever Rough Guide – in 1982 – and has been inextricably involved with the series ever since. Mexico, though, was what inspired his travelling, and to be paid to return was too good to be true. These days, John can normally be found chained to a desk at Rough Guide HQ in London, where work takes up far too much time that could be spent in a hammock. He lives in South London with his wife and two young sons.

READERS' LETTERS

We'd like to thank the **readers** of previous editions who took the time to write in with comments and suggestions. For this edition, we were helped by letters from:

Helen Bough, Joanna Bending, D.C. Bloxham, Jean Pierre Boivin, Dietmar Bothe, Astrid Braün, Annette Brenner and Jan Truöll, Gerardo Celis-Toussaint, Sarah Chenery, Rupert Cocke, Pamela Cooper, Tom Crow, Thurlow Cunliffe, Pablo DaCosta, Craig Dietz, Jon Dunbar, Joyce Edling, Stefan Ehrhardt, Fulvio Fabris and Elisabetta Ravizza, Christina Feit, Martin Fiechtner, John Ford, Miriam Forster and Guido Felstermann, Anja and Markus Gimmel, Martin R. Hansen, Jan Jenkins and Catrina Flynn, Jon C. Jones, Tom Josephs, Julia Kammann, Roland Keilwerth, Jeanine Kitchel, Andrea Knaf, Robert Krauser, Matthias Krill, Catherine Kumar, Mindaugas Labanauskas, Michal Lavi and Aviv Fried, Lucy Lay, Christian Ludwig, Jenny Lunnon, Dina Marshall, Sophia Matheson, J., R. and J.S. Moilliet, Harold Mondol, Adrian Newton, Antonio Ortega, Valerie Pacini, Robert Pangburn, Marc Patry, Sarah Penny, Angélica Pérez, Anette Pfeiffer, Michael Prest, Julie Sadigursky, Brigitta Schrapp and Michael Helbing-Schrapp, Phoebe Schultz, Petra Schütz, Steve Scott, Laura Scuriatti, Ken Shaw, Richard Shelton, Kim Smith and Simon Zisman, Michael Smith, Monica S. Staaf, Ali Stirland and Lauren Bloch, Mike Stroud, Brooke Tuthill, Tom Vanderbilt, Libby Waugh, Esther Whitby and Robert Harbison, M.V. White, Steve and Karen Williams, Brian and Jennifer Wright, C.A. Wright, Monika Woltering, George Xuereb.

CONTENTS

PART THREE CONTEXTS   581

LIST OF MAPS

MAP SYMBOLS

Railway		Airport
Highway		Hot spring
Road		Church (regional maps)
Pedestrianized street		Lighthouse
Steps		Building
Fortified wall		Cathedral/church
River		Christian cemetery
Ferry route		Park
International boundary		National Park
State boundary		Beach
Chapter division boundary		Tourist office
Mountains		Bus station
Peak		Metro station
Ancient site		Coral reef
Cave		Hill shading
Waterfall		

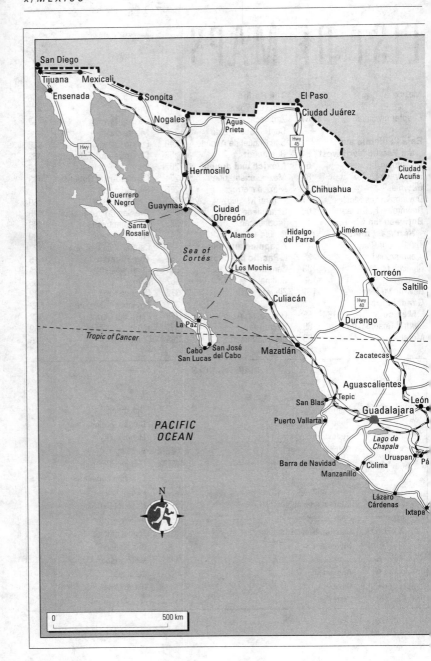

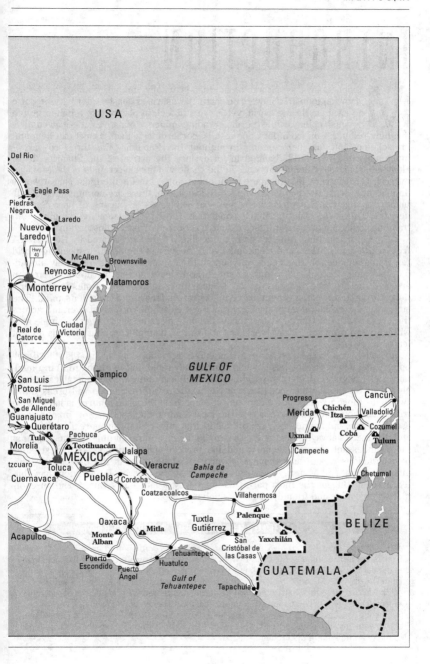

INTRODUCTION

Mexico enjoys a cultural blend that is wholly unique: among the fastest growing industrial powers on earth, its vast cities boast modern architecture to rival any in the world, yet it can still feel, in places, like a half-forgotten Spanish colony, while the all-pervading influence of native American culture, five hundred years on from the Conquest, is extraordinary. Each aspect can be found in isolation, but far more often, throughout the Republic, the three co-exist – indigenous markets, little changed in form since the arrival of the Spanish, thrive alongside elaborate colonial churches in the shadow of the skyscrapers of the Mexican miracle. Occasionally, the marriage is an uneasy one, but for the most part it works unbelievably well. The people of Mexico reflect it, too; there are communities of full-blooded *indígenas*, and there are a few – a very few – Mexicans of pure Spanish descent. The great majority of the population, though, is *mestizo*, combining both traditions and, to a greater or lesser extent, a veneer of urban sophistication.

Despite encroaching Americanism, a tide likely to be accelerated by the **NAFTA free trade agreement**, and close links with the rest of the Spanish-speaking world (an avid audience for Mexican soap operas), the country remains resolutely individual. Its music, its look, its sound, its smell rarely leave you in any doubt where you are, and the thought "only in Mexico" – sometimes in awe, sometimes in exasperation, most often in simple bemusement – is rarely far from a traveller's mind. The strength of Mexican identity perhaps hits most clearly if you travel overland across the border with the United States: this is the only place on earth where a single step will take you from the "First" world to the "Third", a small step that really is a giant leap.

Obviously you have be prepared to adapt to travel in any country that is still "developing", and where change has been so dramatically rapid. Although the **mañana** mentality is largely an outsiders' myth, Mexico is still a country where timetables are not always to be entirely trusted, where anything that can break down will break down (when it's most needed), and where any attempt to do things in a hurry is liable to be frustrated. You simply have to accept the local temperament – that work may be necessary to live, but it's not life's central focus, that minor annoyances really are minor, and that there's always something else to do in the meantime. At times it can seem that there's incessant, inescapable noise and dirt; more deeply disturbing are the extremes of ostentatious wealth and absolute poverty, most poignant in the big cities where unemployment and austerity measures imposed by the massive foreign debt have bitten hardest. But for the most part, this is an easy, a fabulously varied, and an enormously enjoyable and friendly place in which to travel.

MÉXICO? I THOUGHT WE WERE THERE ALREADY

The name of the capital of Mexico is a source of infinite confusion to travellers. **Mexico City** is not a place on any Mexican map or a name that's ever used: as far as a Mexican is concerned it's **México**, or possibly El DF (El "day effé"). The country took its name from the city and México, in conversation, almost always means the latter (in writing it's often México DF – the Distrito Federal being the administrative zone that contains most of the urban areas). The nation is La Republica, or in speeches La Patria.

Throughout this book, the capital is referred to as México, the term you'll have to use if you want anyone to understand: where we refer to the country, we've left the accent off to make some kind of distinction.

Physically, Mexico resembles a vast horn, curving away south and east from the US border with its final tip bent right back round to the north. It is an extremely mountainous country: two great ranges, the Sierra Madre Occidental in the west and the Sierra Madre Oriental in the east, run down parallel to the coasts, enclosing a high, semi-desert plateau. About halfway down they are crossed by the volcanic highland area in which stand México (ie Mexico City; see box opposite) and the major centres of population. Beyond, the mountains run together as a single range through the southern states of Oaxaca and Chiapas. Only the eastern tip – the Yucatán peninsula – is consistently low-lying and flat.

Where to go

The **north of Mexico**, relatively speaking, is a dull land, arid and sparsely populated outside of a few **industrial cities** – like Monterrey – which are heavily American influenced. The **Baja California** wilderness has its devotees, the **border cities** can be exciting in a rather sleazy way, and there are **beach resorts** on the Pacific, but most of the excitement lies in central and southeastern Mexico.

It's in **the highlands** north of and around the capital that the first really worthwhile stops come, with the bulk of the historic colonial towns and an enticingly spring-like climate year-round. Coming through the heart of the country, you'll pass the silver-mining towns of **Zacatecas** and **Guanajuato**, the historic centres of **San Miguel de Allende** and **Querétaro**, and many smaller places with a legacy of superb colonial architecture. **México** itself is a choking nightmare of urban sprawl, but totally fascinating, and in every way – artistic, political, cultural – the capital of the nation. Around the city lie the chief relics of the pre-Hispanic cultures of central Mexico – the massive pyramids of **Teotihuacán**; the main Toltec site at **Tula**; and **Tenochtitlan**, heart of the Aztec empire, in the capital itself. **Guadalajara**, to the west, is a city on a more human scale, capital of the state of **Jalisco** and in easy reach of **Michoacán**: between them, these states share some of the most gently scenic country in Mexico – thickly forested hills, studded with lakes and ancient villages – and a reputation for producing some of the finest crafts in a country renowned for them.

South of the capital, the states of Oaxaca and Chiapas are mountainous and beautiful, too, but in a far wilder way. The city of **Oaxaca**, especially, is one of the most enticing destinations in the country, with an extraordinary mix of colonial and indigenous life, superb markets and fascinating archeological sites. **Chiapas** was the centre of the **Zapatista** uprising, though visitors are little affected these days, and the strength of indigenous traditions in and around the market town of **San Cristóbal de las Casas**, together with the opening-up of a number of lesser-known Maya cities, continue to make it a big travellers' centre. East into the **Yucatán** there is also traditional indigenous life, side by side with a tourist industry based around the magnificent **Maya cities** – Palenque, Chichén Itzá and Uxmal above all, but also scores of others – and the burgeoning new Caribbean resorts that surround **Cancún**. The capital, **Mérida**, continues its provincial life remarkably unaffected by the crowds all around.

On the **Pacific coast**, **Acapulco** is just the best known of the destinations. Northwards, big resorts like **Mazatlán** and **Puerto Vallarta** are interspersed with hundreds of miles of empty beaches; to the south there is still less development, and in the state of Oaxaca are some equally enticing shores. Few tourists venture over to the **Gulf Coast**, despite the attractions of **Veracruz** and its mysterious ruins. The scene is largely dominated by oil, the weather too humid most of the time, and the beaches, on the whole, a disappointment.

Climate

To a great extent, the physical terrain in Mexico determines the **climate** – certainly far more than the expected indicators of latitude and longitude. You can drive down the coast all day without conditions changing noticeably, but turn inland, to the mountains, and the contrast is immediate: in temperature, scenery, vegetation, even the mood and mould of the people around you. So generalizations are difficult.

Summer, from June to October, is in theory the **rainy season**, but just how wet it is varies wildly from place to place. In the heart of the country you can expect a heavy but shortlived downpour virtually every afternoon; in the north hardly any rain falls, ever. Chiapas is the wettest state, with many minor roads washed out in the autumn, and in the south and low-lying coastal areas summer is stickily humid too, with occasional spectacular tropical storms. Winter is the traditional **tourist season**, and in the big beach resorts like Acapulco and Cancún, December is the busiest month of the year. Mountain areas, though, can get very cold then: indeed nights in the mountains can be extremely cold at any time of year, so carry a sweater.

In effect there are now tourists all year round – sticking on the whole to the highlands in summer and the coasts in winter. Given a totally free choice, November is probably the **ideal time to visit**, with the rains over, the land still fresh, and the peak season not yet begun. Overall, though, the climate is so benign that any time of year will do, so long as you're prepared for some rain in the summer, some cold in winter, and for sudden changes which go with the altitude at any time.

	JAN			MAR			MAY			JULY			SEPT			NOV		
	°F Max	Min	Rain inch	°F Max	Min	Rain inch	°F Max	Min	Rain inch	°F Max	Min	Rain inch	°F Max	Min	Rain inch	°F Max	Min	Rain inch
Acapulco	88	72	.5	88	72	.2	90	77	0	91	77	8	90	77	11	90	75	.6
Guadalajara	73	45	.5	82	48	.3	88	57	1	79	59	7	79	59	7	77	50	.5
La Paz	73	55	.3	79	55	0	91	63	0	97	73	1	95	73	1	84	63	.5
Mérida	82	64	1	90	68	.5	93	70	3	91	73	5	90	73	7	84	66	1
México	72	43	.5	81	50	.5	81	55	3	75	55	6	73	55	5	73	48	.5
Monterrey	68	48	1	79	55	1	88	68	2	93	72	3	93	72	4	73	54	1
Oaxaca	82	46	2	90	54	1	90	59	5	82	59	8	81	59	11	82	50	2
San Cristóbal	68	41	2	72	45	2	72	48	7	72	50	7	70	50	14	68	45	3
Tijuana	68	43	2	70	46	1	73	54	.2	81	61	0	81	61	.5	73	50	1
Veracruz	77	64	1	79	70	1	86	77	4	88	75	9	88	77	12	82	70	2

AVERAGE TEMPERATURE AND RAINFALL

To convert Fahrenheit to Centigrade, subtract 32, multiply by 5 and divide by 9.

PART ONE

THE
BASICS

GETTING THERE FROM THE USA AND CANADA

The quickest and easiest way to get to Mexico from Canada and most of the USA is to fly. Going by land won't save you much money, if any, but becomes rather more convenient the nearer you live to the border. Unless you've got your own boat, getting there by water is only normally possible on a cruise ship.

BY AIR

There are **flights to Mexico** from just about every major US city, but the cheapest and most frequent depart from "gateway" cities in the south and west, most commonly **LA**, **Dallas**, **Houston** and **Miami**.

If you live close to the border, it's usually cheaper to cross into Mexico and take an **internal flight** (which you can arrange through your local travel agent). If it's a resort that you want, you'll probably find that at least one of the airlines offers an attractive deal including a few nights' lodging (see "Packages and organized tours" on p.6).

SHOPPING FOR TICKETS

Barring special offers and **airpasses** (for more on which, see box on p.5), the cheapest fare is usually an **Apex** ticket, although this will carry certain restrictions: you have to book – and pay – at least fourteen days before departure, spend at least seven days abroad (maximum stay three months), and there's a probable penalty charge if you change your schedule. There are also **Super**

Apex tickets available in winter, slightly cheaper than an ordinary Apex, but limiting your stay to between 7 and 21 days. Some airlines also issue **Special Apex** tickets to people under the age of 24, often extending the maximum stay to a year. Many airlines offer youth or student fares to **under-25s**; a passport or driving licence are sufficient proof of age, though these tickets are subject to availability and can have eccentric booking conditions. It's worth remembering that most cheap round-trip fares involve spending at least one Saturday night away and that many will only give a percentage refund if you need to cancel or alter your journey.

You can normally cut costs by going through a **specialist flight agent** – either a consolidator, who buys up blocks of tickets from the airlines and sells them at a discount, or a discount agent, who wheels and deals in blocks of tickets offloaded by the airlines, and often has special student and youth fares and a range of other travel-related services, such as travel insurance, car rental, tours and the like. Bear in mind, though, that once again penalties for changing your plans can be stiff. Remember, too, that these companies make their money by dealing in bulk – don't expect them to answer lots of questions. Some agents specialize in **charter flights**, which may be cheaper than scheduled flights, but again departure dates are fixed and withdrawal penalties are high (check the refund policy). If you travel a lot, **discount travel clubs** are another option – the annual membership fee may be worth it for benefits such as cut-price air tickets and car rental.

To some extent, the **fare** will depend on the season. Though prices to México (Mexico City, also referred to as "El DF") and non-resort destinations show little if any fluctuation, fares to Mexico are otherwise highest around Easter (when most colleges have their spring break), from early June to mid-September and at Christmas and New Year, when prices – especially to the resort areas – may run as much as US$200 higher than in low season. Prices drop during the "shoulder" seasons – mid-September to early November and mid-April to early June – and you'll get the best deals during the low season, November through April (excluding Christmas and New Year, of course). Note also that flying at weekends adds

AIRLINES IN THE USA AND CANADA

Aero California ☎1-800/237-6225. *LA to Cabo San Lucas, Guadalajara, La Paz, Laredo, Mazatlán and México.*

Aeroméxico ☎1-800/237-6639 or ☎713/939-7535; *www.wotw.com/aeromexico. Atlanta, Dallas, LA, Miami, New Orleans, New York, Phoenix, San Antonio, San Diego and Tucson to all Mexican destinations.*

Air Canada ☎1-800/776-3000; *www.aircanada.ca. To México.*

Alaska Airlines ☎1-800/426-0333; *www.alaska-air.com. Los Angeles, Phoenix, San Francisco and Seattle to Cabo San Lucas, Mazatlán, Puerto Vallarta.*

American Airlines ☎1-800/433-7300 (domestic), ☎1-800/624-6262 (international); *www.americanair.com. Dallas and Miami to Acapulco, Cancún, León, México, Monterrey, Puerto Vallarta.*

America West Airlines ☎1-800/235-9292; *www.americawest.com. Phoenix to Cabo San Lucas, Mazatlán and México.*

Canadian Airlines ☎1-800/665-1177 (in Canada), ☎1-800/426-7000 (in USA); *www.cdnair.ca. Toronto to México.*

Continental Airlines ☎1-800/525-0280 (domestic), ☎1-800/231-0856 (international); *www.fly-continental.com. Newark, Houston and San Francisco to Acapulco, Cancún, Cozumel, Guadalajara, León, México, Monterrey, Puerto Vallarta.*

Delta Airlines ☎1-800/221-1212 (domestic), ☎1-800/241-4141 or 404/765-5000 (international); *www.delta-air.com. Atlanta, Los Angeles, New York, Newark and Orlando to México; Los Angeles to Acapulco, Guadalajara, Ixtapa, Mazatlán, Puerto Vallarta.*

Lacsa Costa Rica ☎1-800/225-2272. *Houston, Los Angeles, Miami, New York and Washington DC to México; New Orleans to Cancún and Merida.*

Mexicana ☎1-800/531-7921; *www.mexicana.com. Denver, Chicago, Los Angeles, Miami, Newark, San Antonio, San Francisco, San Jose, Montréal and Toronto to all Mexican destinations.*

Taesa ☎1-800/328-2372; *www.wotw.com/wow/ mexico/city/taesa.html. Chicago and Oakland to Aguascalientes, Durango, Guadalajara, México, Morelia and Zacatecas.*

United Airlines ☎1-800/241-6522 (domestic) ☎1-800/538-2929 (international); *www.ual.com. Chicago, Los Angeles, Miami and San Francisco to México.*

US Airways ☎1-800/428-4322 (domestic), ☎1-800/622-1015 (international); *www. usair-*

DISCOUNT TRAVEL COMPANIES IN THE USA AND CANADA

ways.com. New York, Newark and Pittsburgh to Cancún.

Air Courier Association ☎1-800/282-1202 or ☎303/215-9000; *www.aircourier.org. Courier flight broker. Annual fee US$28, plus US$30 initiation. Only accepts 150 new members per month.*

Council Travel ☎1-800/226-8624, fax 212/822-2699; *www.ciee.org. Student/budget travel agency with branches in many US cities.*

eXito ☎1-800/655-4053 or 510/655-2154; *exito@wonderlink.com, www.wonderlink. com/ exito. Latin American independent travel specialists. Their webpage has a particularly useful airfare finder and much other invaluable information.*

International Association of Air Travel Couriers ☎561/582-8320, fax 582-1581; *www.courier.org. Courier flight broker. Membership US$45 per year.*

Last Minute Club ☎1-800-563-CLUB; *www. lastminuteclub.com. Travel club specializing in standby flights and packages.*

Now Voyager ☎212/431-1616, fax 219-1753; *www.nowvoyagertravel.com. Courier flight broker and consolidator.*

STA Travel ☎1-800/781-4040 or ☎212/627-3111; *www.sta-travel.com. Worldwide discount travel firm specializing in student/youth fares, with branches in the New York, Los Angeles, San Francisco and Boston areas; also student IDs, travel insurance, car rental, rail passes and so on.*

Travel Avenue ☎1-800/333-3335 or ☎312/876-6866; *www.travelavenue.com. Full-service travel agent that offers discounts in the form of rebates.*

Travel CUTS ☎1-800/667-2887 (Canada only) or ☎416/979-2406 or ☎1-888/838-CUTS; *www. travelcuts.com. Organization specializing in student fares, IDs and other travel services, with*

AIRPASSES IN MEXICO

If you want to visit several destinations in Mexico in a fairly short time (and even travel onwards to Central or South America), then there are a few **airpasses** worth considering – these can be especially useful if combined with the flexibility of an **open-jaw ticket**.

The "MexiPass" consists of pre-booked and pre-paid coupons for internal flights on Mexicana and Aeroméxico (including subsidiaries Aerocaribe and Aerocozumel, serving Yucatán) at discount prices for travellers from outside Mexico. Travel into Mexico can be on any airline, but discounts are slightly better if you book with the Mexican carriers, or with Delta, United, Lufthansa or Air France. The pass is valid for ninety days, and you'll need to purchase a minimum of two coupons and book routes and dates in advance. Date (but not route) changes can be made without paying a penalty, provided space is available on the flight you want. Prices are for one-way flights, based on zones, increasing the further you fly, and do not include domestic departure taxes (currently US$12 per flight): México to Acapulco, for example, is US$70; México to Cancún US$145; Oaxaca to Mérida US$115. The "MexiPass Inter" is similar, but also includes international flights on the Mexican carriers between the USA, Canada and South America, and you need to buy at least three coupons. It offers real advantages on the longer flights: for example, Miami–México–Oaxaca–Cancún–Miami will cost US$560; and Toronto–México–San Cristóbal–Flores (in Guatemala)–Cancún–México–Toronto costs US$830.

Aerocalifornia, mainly serving routes between México and the northwest, also has a zone-based airpass, with a two-coupon minimum; prices start at US$40, rising to US$120 for México to Tijuana.

If you're travelling to Mexico and also want to fly to Central America, then Taca's "Visit Central America Airpass" is worth thinking about. The pass links North American gateways, including cities in Mexico, with all the capitals and some other cities in Central America, as well as with some destinations in South America and the Caribbean. For example, a routing México–Guatemala City–Flores–Belize–San José will be around US$485, saving almost one-third on flying the same route without the pass.

The potential permutations are mind-boggling, but the savings can be considerable; you need to think seriously about what you want to see, and in what order, before you go. The best way to find out how (or if) an airpass will benefit you is either to call the airlines concerned, or call a specialist flight agent.

US$20–60 to the round-trip fare; the typical lowest round-trip Apex prices quoted below assume midweek travel in high season.

FLIGHTS FROM THE US

Aeroméxico and Mexicana fly direct to dozens of destinations in Mexico, and can make connections to many others; the bigger **US airlines** have connections to México and the more popular resorts. Fares are most competitive from **Dallas** and **Houston**, where round-trip flights to México start at US$280, rising to US$490 to Acapulco and Cancún and US$515 to Mérida. From **LA**, figure on US$450 to México, US$430 to Acapulco and US$630 to Mérida or Cancún. Flights from **Miami** to Mérida or Cancún are also good value, hovering between US$360 and US$390 round-trip, as is Mexicana's night service from **San Francisco** and **LA** to Guadalajara and México, in a similar price range. Adding a feeder flight from any other city to one of the gateways is easy; from New York, a round-trip flight to México or Acapulco should cost around US$350, rising to US$540 for Merida and Cancún.

Charter, promotional, student/youth and other **discounted fares** routinely run US$100–200 lower than the above.

flights FROM CANADA

There are few direct scheduled flights from Canada to anywhere in Mexico, although charters are plentiful in the winter. Your options expand greatly if you fly via the USA.

Typical lowest round-trip Apex fares are: Montréal to México Can$500, to Cancún

LEAVING MEXICO: A NOTE

If you're **flying out** of Mexico, remember that there's an airport departure tax, equivalent to about US$13 payable in pesos or dollars, though if you bought your air ticket outside Mexico, the tax may well have been included in the ticket price. Remember to check when you buy your ticket.

Can$600 and to Acapulco Can$820; Toronto to México Can$430, to Cancún Can$550 and to Acapulco Can$730; and from Vancouver to México Can$500, to Acapulco or Cancún Can$700.

PACKAGES AND ORGANIZED TOURS

Hundreds of independent companies offer good-value **package tours** to Mexican resorts, as do the tour arms of most major North American airlines. Packages are generally only available for the more commercialized destinations, such as Cabo San Lucas, Mazatlán, Puerto Vallarta, Acapulco, Ixtapa or Cancún, and travel agents usually only give you one or two weeks. If, however, what you want is a week on a Mexican beach, your best bet is to comb the Sunday newspaper travel sections for the latest bargains and then see if your local travel agent can turn up anything better.

Prices vary tremendously by resort, season and style of accommodation, but one week in a good hotel in any of the resorts above will generally start at US$500 per person. Prices may be

less than that on last-minute deals, available a week or two before the departure date. The busiest times for North Americans travelling to Mexican resorts are during Christmas and college spring break, when you'll be less likely to get the flight or the fare you want.

In addition, literally hundreds of **specialist companies** offer tours of Mexico based around hiking, biking, diving, birdwatching and the like. See the box for just a few of the possibilities; a travel agent should be able to point out others. Remember that bookings made through a travel agent cost no more than going through the tour operator – indeed, many tour companies only sell through agents. For operators that run trips exclusively for travellers with disabilities see p.48.

More counter-cultural, and perhaps better value, are overland routes covered by **Green Tortoise Adventure Travel**. Converted school buses provide reasonably comfortable transport and sleeping space for up to 35 people; the clientele comes from all over the world, and communal cookouts are the rule. Most of their tours depart from the San Francisco headquar-

US AND CANADIAN PACKAGE TOUR OPERATORS

American Express Vacations ☎1-800-241-1700; www.americanexpress.com/travel. Resort packages, sightseeing tours. Branches across the USA and Canada and worldwide, so best to phone the above toll-free number to find your nearest office.

Friendly Holidays, 1983 Marcus Avenue, Suite C130, Lake Success, NY 11042 (☎1-800/221-9748, fax 516/358-1319; trav.org/friendly, friendly@ten-io.com. Resort packages to thirteen Mexican cities including Oaxaca and Cozumel.

Globus and Cosmos, 5301 South Federal Circle, Littleton, CO 80123-2980 (☎1-800/221-0090, fax 303/347-2080; www.globusandcosmos.com). First-class and budget sightseeing tours, ranging from US$1200 to US$1500 for nine days.

International Student Tours, 6902 Roosevelt Way NE, Seattle, WA 98115 (☎1-888/524-4408, fax 206/522-7960; www.istours.com). Student group travel company offering tours to Mazatlán and Puerto Vallarta.

Majestic Mexico Tours, PO Box 3038, Fort Walton Beach, FL 32547 (☎850/301-0045, fax 301-0046; www.mexico-tours.com). First-class

sightseeing tours celebrating colonial Mexico, from US$600 for three- or four-day tours, to US$800 and up for eight days.

Pleasant Holidays – Mexico, 2404 Townsgate Road, Westlake Village, CA 91361 (☎1-800/448-3333, fax 888-329-3774; www.2mexico.com). Getaways to various beach resorts including Acapulco, Cancún, Cozumel, Ixtapa, Los Cabos, Mazatlán and Puerto Vallarta.

Saga Holidays, 222 Berkeley Street, Boston, MA 02116 (☎1-800/343-0273, fax 617/375-5953; www.sagaholidays.com). Fourteen-day tour through Mexico's Copper Canyon by coach and rail for people over the age of fifty.

Suntrips, 2350 Paragon Drive, San Jose, CA 95131 (☎1-800/SUN-TRIP, fax 1-800-SUN-FAXE; www.suntrips.com). Wholesale travel company offering resort packages to Puerto Vallarta, Cancún and Cozumel from Denver and San Francisco.

Vantage Travel, 111 Cypress Street, Boston, MA 02146 (☎1-800/322-6677, fax 617/731-6312; www.vantagetravel.com). Package tours for mature adults to Copper Canyon.

SPECIALIST TOUR OPERATORS IN THE USA AND CANADA

Adventure Center, 1311 63rd Street, Suite 200, Emeryville, CA 94608 (☎1-800/227-8747, fax 510/654-4200; *www.adventure-center.com*). *Specializes in ecologically sound adventure travel. A two-week trek through the Sierra Madres, for example, starts at US$1100.*

Adventures Abroad, 2148 Westminster Highway, Richmond, BC VCV 2W3 (☎1-800/665-3998, fax 604/303-1076; *www.adventures-abroad.com*). *Canada-based travel planners providing small-group tours.*

Air California Adventure, 2800–2835 Scenic Drive, La Jolla, CA 92037 (☎619/452-9858, fax 592-9983; *www.flytorrey.com*). *Tours include paragliding in Baja California from US$50 to US$125 per day.*

Backroads, 801 Cedar Street, Berkeley, CA 94710 (☎1-800/GO-ACTIVE, fax 510/527-1444; *www.backroads.com*). *Hiking and biking tours to San Miguel and the Yucatán, starting around US$900 per person.*

Baja Expeditions, 2625 Garnet Ave, San Diego, CA 92109 (☎1-800/843-6967, fax 619/581-6542; *www.bajaex.com*). *Sea kayaking, birdwatching and snorkelling, among other tours.*

Ecosummer Expeditions, 1516 Dranleau Street, Vancouver, BC VCH 3S4 (☎1-800/465-8884 or 604/669-7741, fax 604/669-3244; *www.ecosummer.com*). *Sea kayaking and whale-watching in Baja.*

Gap Adventures, 266 Dupont St, Toronto, ON M5R 1V7 (☎1-800/465-5600 or 416/922-8899, fax 416/922-0822; *adventure@gap.org*, *www.gap.ca*). *Good guided group-trips (some camping) through Yucatán, Chiapas, Guatemala and Belize; C$1900 for three weeks excluding flights and meals.*

Global Exchange, 2017 Mission Street #303, San Francisco, CA 94110 (☎415/255-7296, fax 255-7498; *www.globalexchange.org*). *Offers "Reality Tours" to increase American travellers' awareness of real life in other countries, costing US$850 on average.*

Mountain Travel-Sobek, 6420 Fairmount Avenue, El Cerrito, CA 94530 (☎1-800/227-2384 in US, ☎1-800/282-8747 in Canada, fax 510/525-7710; *www.mtsobek.com*). *One- or two-week sea kayaking and whale-watching tours to Baja, ranging from US$1200 to US$1800.*

Questers Worldwide Nature Tours, 381 Park Ave South, Suite 1201, New York, NY 10016 (☎1-800/468-8668, fax 212/251-0890; *www.questers.com*). *Offer small-group, eleven-day overland tours exploring the natural history of Copper Canyon for US$2195.*

Smithsonian Odyssey Tours, 1100 Jefferson Dr SW, Rm 3077, MRC702, Washington, DC 20560 (☎202/357-4700, fax 633-9250; *www.si.edu/tsa/sst/start.htm, tours@tsa.si.edu*). *Nine-to thirteen-day educational tours of Mexico's Copper Canyon, ranging from US$2500 to US$3300.*

S&S Tours, 865 El Camino Real, Sierra Vista, AZ 85635 (☎1-800/499-5685 or 520/458-6365, fax 520/458-5258; *www.ss-tours.com*). *Personalized natural and cultural history adventure tours of Copper Canyon, Day of the Dead celebrations and various colonial cities. Eight- or nine-day tours range from US$1495 to US$2000.*

Suntrek, PO Box 1190, Rohnert Park, CA 94927 (☎1-800/SUNTREK, fax 707/523-1911; *www.suntrek.com*). *Three- to six-week overland adventure tours tailor-made to suit your group.*

Tropical Adventures Travel, 111 Second Ave North, Seattle, WA 98109 (☎1-800/247-3483, fax 206/441-5431; *www.divetropical.com*). *Well-organized three- to seven-day scuba vacations in the Caribbean and Sea of Cortés, ranging from US$200 to US$1295.*

Wilderness Travel, 1102 Ninth St, Berkeley, CA 94710 (☎1-800/368-2794, fax 510/558-2488; *www.wildernesstravel.com*). *Overland mountaineering and archeological exploration of "La Ruta Maya", and seven- to twelve-day sea kayaking tours of Baja. Price ranges from US$1100 to US$2995.*

ters, but add-on journeys from Boston, New York and many points along the Pacific Coast are easily arranged on one of Green Tortoise's cross-country services. The only routes that currently include Mexico are the nine- and fourteen-day overland adventures through Baja from November to April (US$350–500); there are also longer trips through Mexico to Guatemala (US$450–850). For more information, contact their **main office** at 494 Broadway, San Francisco, CA 94133 (☎415/956-7500 or 1-800-TORTOISE; *www.greentortoise.com*).

BY LAND FROM THE USA

There are more than twenty **frontier posts** along the US–Mexican border. Many of them, however, are only open during the day, and more-or-less inaccessible without your own transport. The main ones, **open 24 hours** a day, seven days a week, are, from west to east:

- San Diego, California – Tijuana, Baja California Norte
- Calexico, California – Mexicali, Baja California Norte
- Nogales, Arizona – Nogales, Sonora
- Douglas, Arizona – Agua Prieta, Sonora
- El Paso, Texas – Ciudad Juárez, Chihuahua
- Laredo, Texas – Nuevo Laredo, Tamaulipas
- Brownsville, Texas – Matamoros, Tamaulipas.

BY BUS

North American bus travel is pretty grim compared to the relative comfort of Amtrak, but you have a wider range of US border posts to choose from. Count on at least sixty hours' journey time from New York to a Texas frontier post (US$175), fifteen hours from San Francisco to the Baja border (US$90) – and at least a further day's travel from either point to México.

Since the NAFTA agreement, many Mexican bus companies now also cross the border into the USA, so that you can pick up a bus back into Mexico as far north as Houston or LA.

Greyhound runs regularly to all the major **border crossings**, and some of their buses will take you over the frontier and into the Mexican bus station, which saves a lot of hassle. For routes and times, plus phone numbers and addresses of local terminals, call ☎1-800/231-2222 or check their Web site, *www.greyhound.com*; for Greyhound agents abroad, see the box below. They should also be able to reserve you through tickets with their Mexican counterparts, which is even more convenient but involves a lot of pre-planning. Some Mexican buses similarly cross the border into US bus stations.

A cheap and cheerful alternative to the rigours of Greyhound travel is an overland tour in one of Green Tortoise's summer-of-love style buses (see "Packages and organized tours" on p.6).

BY RAIL

There is no direct connection between US and Mexican passenger **train services** and neither service crosses the border. The nearest they get to each other is at the **El Paso–Ciudad Juárez** crossing, where there are stations in the border towns on both sides. El Paso is on the LA–Dallas line, and is connected by Amtrak's Texas Eagle and Sunset Limited services to Dallas, Houston, New Orleans, Miami, Phoenix, LA, St Louis and Chicago. The overnight journey takes 16 hours from Houston, 25 from Miami, 18 from LA, and 44 from Chicago.

Afternoon arrivals on these services give you plenty of time to get across the frontier, have supper in Ciudad Juárez, and board the first-class-only Division del Norte, which will in theory get you to **México** in 36 hours.

Other **Mexican services** run from **Nogales** to México, and from **Piedras Negras**, **Nuevo Laredo** and **Matamoros** to Monterrey, San Luís Potosí and México respectively. However, travelling like this is nothing like as convenient as the bus – and frankly you'd have to be a real train fanatic to go this way (for more on Mexican trains, see "Getting around" on p.32).

Check current **timetables** with Amtrak (☎1-800/USA-RAIL; *www.amtrak.com*). Note that Amtrak does not sell tickets for Mexican trains.

GREYHOUND AGENTS ABROAD

UK Sussex House, London Rd, East Grinstead, W Sussex RH19 1LD (☎01342/317317).

IRELAND c/o USIT, Aston Quay, O'Connell Bridge, Dublin 2 (☎01/679-8833).

AUSTRALIA c/o North American Travel Specialists, Suite 478, High St, Maitland NSW 2320 (☎049/342088).

NEW ZEALAND Greyhound Australia Pty Ltd, Ward Building, cnr Hastings St and Beach St, Mairangi Bay, Auckland 10 (☎09/479 6555).

BORDER FORMALITIES

Crossing the border, especially on foot, it's easy to go straight past the **immigration and customs checks**. There's a free zone south of the frontier, and you can cross at will and stay for up to three days. Make sure you do get your tourist card stamped and your bags checked though, or when you try to continue south you'll be stopped after some 20km and sent back to complete the formalities.

BY CAR

Taking **your own car** into Mexico will obviously give you a great deal more freedom, but it has to be said that it's an option fraught with complications. Aside from the border formalities, you'll have to contend with the state of the roads, the style of driving and the quality of the fuel – these considerations are dealt with in more detail on p.33.

US **driving licences** are valid in Mexico, but it's a good idea to arm yourself with an International Driving Licence – available for a nominal fee from the American Automobile Association (☎1-800/222-4357; www.aaa.com). If you run afoul of a Mexican traffic cop for any reason, show that first, and if they abscond with it you at least still have your own (more difficult to replace) licence. If you're a visitor to the US driving into Mexico, note that Canadian, British, Irish, Australian, New Zealand and most European driving licences are all valid both in the US and Mexico.

As a rule, you can drive in **Baja and the Zona Libre** (the border area extending roughly fifteen miles, 24km, into Mexico) without any special formalities. To drive elsewhere in Mexico, however, you must obtain a **vehicle permit** (US$10) from the Departemento de Migracíon at the border. This must be paid for using a major credit card, otherwise you'll be asked for a minimum US$500 refundable bond plus non-refundable tax and commission. You'll need to show registration and title for the car, plus your driving licence, passport and birth certificate. The permits are good for six months. To make sure you **don't sell the car in Mexico** or a neighbouring country, you'll also be required either to post a cash bond equal to the vehicle's book value or give an imprint of a major credit card (Visa, Mastercard, Diners Club or Amex). Plastic is obviously preferable, although it carries an US$11.50 fee, especially as you can only get a refund of a cash deposit at the same border post where you paid the bond.

With few exceptions, US **auto insurance** policies don't cover mishaps in Mexico. Take out a Mexican policy, available from numerous agencies on either side of every border post. Rates depend on the value of the vehicle, but figure on US$10 or so a day. To arrange a policy **before leaving the US**, call Instant Mexico Insurance Services (☎1-800/345-4701); International Gateways (☎1-800/423-2646); Oscar Padilla Mexican Insurance (☎1-800/258-8600); or **Sanborn's** Insurance (☎1-800/222-0158). The last is the acknowledged leader in the field.

To get **discounts** on insurance, it might be worthwhile joining a **travel club**, such as Club Mex (☎619/585-3033), Discover Baja Travel Club (☎1-800/727-BAJA) or Sanborn's Mexico Club (☎1-800/222-0158). These clubs typically also offer discounts on accommodation and free travel advice. Annual dues are US$35–40. For more on general insurance policies, see p.27.

The **American Automobile Association** and **Canadian Automobile Association** produce road maps and route planners for travel to Mexico, and members may qualify for discounted insurance at affiliated border agencies. However, emergency/breakdown services apply only in the US and Canada.

CRUISES

Several lines offer seven-day **cruises** between LA and Acapulco, stopping at Los Cabos, Mazatlán, Puerto Vallarta and Zihuatanejo. Others ply the Caribbean side out of Miami, taking in Cozumel, Playa del Carmen and other Mexican destinations. Prices start at US$600 per person (plus airfare to the starting point), and go (way) up from there.

Agencies specializing in cruises include Cruise Adventures (☎1-800/545-8118) and Cruise World (☎1-800/994-7447).

NORTH AMERICAN CRUISE LINES

Carnival Cruise Lines ☎1-800/327-9501; www.carnival.com

Clipper Cruise Lines ☎1-800/325-0010; www.clippercruise.com

Commodore Cruise Lines ☎1-800/227-4759; www.commodorecruise.com

Norwegian Cruise Lines ☎1-800/327-7030.

Royal Caribbean Cruises ☎1-800/327-6700; www.rccl.com

GETTING THERE FROM THE UK AND IRELAND

The only direct flights from Britain are with British Airways, three times weekly from London Gatwick to México (Mexico City) and weekly to Cancún. From Ireland, Aeroflot fly weekly to México (via Miami) from Shannon. Flying from anywhere else, or to any other destination in Mexico, means you have to change planes somewhere.

Another possibility is to fly to the States and either continue **overland** or buy an onward flight over there. New York is usually the cheapest place to get to from London, but it's only halfway to México. LA or Houston are logical points from which to set off overland. Both of these cities, and Miami, also have reasonably priced onward flights to a number of Mexican destinations. For more on getting to Mexico from North America, see p.3.

SHOPPING FOR TICKETS

Ticket prices to Mexico are usually lower than to other Latin American destinations, and competition is such that there are often bargains available, especially if you can be flexible with dates. **High season** for fares are the months of July and August, as well as Easter and the run up to Christmas, with the lowest fares generally in October and November. Flying mid-week will also usually save you money.

If you simply want a straightforward return ticket, the best deal you'll get is usually an **Apex**, which means booking at least two weeks ahead

and committing yourself to flight dates that you cannot change without paying a hefty penalty charge. There are often deals available for young people or students, with return tickets frequently under £400. You may need to prove full-time student status, and the upper age limit is usually 26, though requirements vary. If you qualify, you'll save perhaps eight to ten percent, but you'll need to book as far in advance as you can, as seat availability at these prices is limited.

Tickets are usually valid for between three and six months, sometimes up to one year (though you may have to pay around ten percent more for a budget ticket that allows you to do this); some tickets work out cheaper if you're away less than thirty days.

If you want to fly into one city and out of another, travel to different destinations in Mexico, or even other countries in the region, then it's worth considering an **open-jaw ticket**, perhaps in conjuction with an **airpass** (see box on p.5).

Official fares, quoted by the airlines, are generally more expensive than those booked through a flight or travel agent. To find discount agents, check the travel pages of the broadsheet papers or listings magazines, Teletext or the Net. Web sites in the UK, however, are not so directly geared to finding Mexican destinations as their US counterparts, but a check through *www.cheapflights.co.uk* or *www.airtickets.co.uk* will allow some comparisons on fares to México and Cancún from various UK airports, and there are good links to travel agents and other sources of information. Campus Travel and STA's web-pages (see box opposite) have reasonable fare-finders. Deciding which flight option is best for you can be a little complex; as always, a good **flight specialist** – such as Campus, Journey Latin America, or Trailfinders (see "Specialist Flight Agents" box opposite) – is the best first call to weed through the possibilities.

Prices for **scheduled return flights** (excluding taxes – about £30, or more if you're routed through the USA) from London to México range from £390 low season to £500 or more in the high season. **Charter flights** to Mexico are fairly common now, usually flying out of Gatwick or Manchester to Cancún, Acapulco or Puerto Vallarta. Charter fares, sometimes under £350 in

SPECIALIST FLIGHT AGENTS IN BRITAIN

Campus Travel, 52 Grosvenor Gardens, London SW1W 0AG (☎0171/730 2101); 53 Forrest Road, Edinburgh EH1 2QP (☎0131/668 3303); 166 Deansgate, Manchester M3 3FE (☎0161/833 2046); *www.campustravel.co.uk. Student/youth travel specialists, with 45 branches on university campuses, in YHA shops and in cities all over Britain. Good Web site.*

Journey Latin America, 12–13 Heathfield Terrace, London W4 4JE (☎0181/747 3108, fax 742 1312; *sales@journeylatinamerica.co.uk*); Barton Arcade, 51–63 Deansgate, Manchester M3 2BH (☎0161/832 1441, fax 832 1551; *man@journeylatinamerica.co.uk*). *The leaders in the field on airfares and tours to Latin America; some of the best prices on high-season flights.*

South American Experience, 47 Causton St, London SW1P 4AT (☎0171/976 5511; *sax@mcmail.com*). *Flight and tailor-made itinerary specialists; very good airfare prices.*

STA Travel, 86 Old Brompton Rd, London SW7 3LH; 117 Euston Rd, London NW1 2SX (☎0171/361 6262; *enquiries@sta.travel.co.uk, www.statravel.co.uk*). *Student/youth travel specialists with an international help desk if you have problems while abroad; dozens of branches throughout UK and worldwide.*

Trailfinders, 42–50 Earls Court Rd, London W8 6FT (☎0171/938 3366); 58 Deansgate, Manchester M3 2FF (☎0161/839 6969); 254–285 Sauchiehall Street, Glasgow G2 3EH (☎0141/353 2224). *Airfare specialists; also tailor-made packages for independent travellers. Other offices in London, Bristol and Dublin.*

Travel CUTS, 295a Regent Street, London W1R 7YA (☎0171/255 2082, fax 528 7732; *sales@ travelcuts.co.uk, www.travel-cuts.co.uk*).*Airfare and independent travel specialists.*

the low season, can also be very good value for high season flights at around £550, though your stay will probably be limited to two or four weeks. The best way to find out about charters is simply to call your local branch of Thomas Cook (☎ 0990/666222 nationally), who deal in huge numbers of charter flights, or try Thomson, who publish a brochure of their charter flights and prices, or simply ask your travel agent.

FLIGHTS FROM BRITAIN

BA's direct flights often work out very good value, especially in the high season, when you might be able to get one for around £450 if you book early. Several **European airlines** also fly from Britain to Mexico, and often work out surprisingly good

value. Iberia flies daily via Madrid (£399 low season/£460 high) from London Heathrow to México and Cancún; they also fly daily from Manchester to the same destinations, though this service requires an overnight stay in Madrid. KLM, from Heathrow via Amsterdam (£405/£570), with five flights a week to México, offers excellent connections throughout the UK on KLM-UK. Air France, from Heathrow via Paris (£399/£455), has five morning flights per week and a daily afternoon flight to México, and Lufthansa, also from Heathrow, via Frankfurt (£395/£450) has a daily afternoon flight.

It's simple enough to **fly to the States** on one of the main European or US carriers and continue from there – most of the airlines we've listed will

AIRLINE TELEPHONE NUMBERS IN BRITAIN

For Web site addresses, see the box "Airlines in North America" on p.4.

Aeroflot	☎0171/355 2233	Iberia	☎0171/830 0011
Aeroméxico	☎0171/734 9354	Lufthansa	☎0345/737747
Air France	☎0181/742 6600	KLM	☎0990/074074
American Airlines	☎0345/789789	Méxicana	☎0171/284 2550
British Airways	☎0345/222111	Taca Group	☎01293/553330
Continental	☎0800/776464	United	☎0845/844 4777
Delta	☎0800/414767	Virgin Atlantic	☎01293/747747

get you to México (and often other destinations in the Republic) the same day. New York is usually the cheapest destination in the States, but it's a long way from Mexico; for speediest connections, it's usually best to fly to Miami (on BA, American or Virgin), Houston (Continental) or Atlanta (Delta). The cheapest high season fares are usually on Continental or Virgin (connection at Miami with Aeroméxico), starting at around £480 (£400 low season) – you're unlikely to get lower than that. If you want a stopover on a budget flight, you'll generally pay upwards of £100 more,

SPECIALIST TOUR OPERATORS IN BRITAIN

Animal Watch, Granville House, London Rd, Sevenoaks, Kent TN13 1DL (☎01732/741612, fax 455441; *mail@animalwatch.co.uk, www. animalwatch.co.uk). Winter trips to Baja California to watch blue and grey whales and their calves, led by expert naturalist and photography guides. Around £2100 for ten days.*

Cathy Matos Mexican Tours, 215 Chalk Farm Rd, London NW1 8AF (☎0171/284 2550, fax 267 2004; *sales@mextours.demon.co.uk). Wide variety of tailor-made tours, including colonial cities, beaches, sightseeing and archeology tours, whale-watching and weddings. UK office for Mexicana.*

Dragoman, Camp Green, Kenton Rd, Debenham, Suffolk IP14 6LA (☎01728/861133, fax 861127; *100344.1342@compuserve.com, www. dragoman.co.uk). Eight-week "Central American Explorer" overland camping expeditions through Mexico to Panamá; around £1400, plus food kitty. Other trips also available.*

Encounter Overland, 267 Old Brompton Rd, London, SW5 9JA (☎0171/370 6845, fax 244 9737; *adventure@encounter-overland.co.uk). Very good-value three- to six-week overland camping and hotel-based trips through Mexico and Central America; for example, 42 days from México via Yucatán to Guatemala for £1800.*

Exodus, 9 Weir Rd, London, SW12 0LT (☎ & fax 0181/673 0859; *sales@exodustravels.co.uk, www.exodustravels.co.uk). Fifteen-day escorted tours, staying at hotels, through the Maya region, for around £1400, inclusive of airfare.*

Explore Worldwide, 1 Frederick St, Aldershot GU11 1LQ (☎01252/344161, fax 343170; *info@explore.co.uk, www.explore.co.uk). Wide range of two- to three-week hotel-based tours to Mexico and Central America. Some tours run year-round. Around £1100 for fifteen days in Mexico, Guatemala and Belize.*

Global Travel Club, 1 Kiln Shaw, Langdon Hills, Basildon, Essex SS16 6LE (☎01268/541732, fax 542275; *global@online.rednet.co.uk, www. global-travel.co.uk). Small company specializing in individually arranged diving and cultural tours to Mexico and Central America.*

Journey Latin America, 12–13 Heathfield Terrace London W4 2JE (☎ & fax 0181/747 8315; *tours@journeylatinamerica.co.uk). Wide range of high-standard economy tours and individual itineraries.*

Mountain Travel Sobek, 67 Verney Avenue, High Wycombe, Bucks HP12 3ND (☎01494/44890; *sales@mtsobekeu.com, www.mtsobek.com). Authentic environmentally responsible adventure: kayaking and whale-watching in the Sea of Cortés, and an amazing expedition up Mexico's highest volcanic peaks.*

Travelbag Adventures, 15 Turk St, Alton, Hants GU34 1AG (☎01420/541007, fax 541022; *mail@travelbag-adventures.co.uk, www. travelbag-adventures.co.uk). Small-group hotel-based tours through Yucatán and Central America, among them an eighteen-day "Realm of the Maya" tour from Cancún for around £950 (land cost only).*

Trek America, 4 Waterperry Court, Middleton Road, Banbury OX16 8QG (☎01295/256777, fax 257399; *postmaster@trekam.demon.co.uk. Small-group adventure trips, featuring two to three weeks' camping or staying at budget hotels across Mexico, including the Copper Canyon at around £590 for nineteen days – flights, food kitty and hotels (where used) are extra.*

Trips Worldwide, 9 Byron Place, Clifton, Bristol BS8 1JT (☎0117/987 2626, fax 987 2627; *trips@trips.demon.co.uk, www.trips. demon.co. uk). Friendly, experienced company with an inspired range of tailor-made itineraries to all Mexican and Central American destinations. Also agents for many other recommended tour operators.*

Wild Oceans, International House, Bank Road, Bristol BS15 2LX (☎0117/984 8040, fax 961 0200; *www.wildwings.co.uk). Naturalist-led tours to observe whales (including blue whale research project), sea-lions and other wildlife in the Sea of Cortés; accommodation on board a comfortable 28-metre boat. Around £1500 for ten days.*

though it may be worthwhile if you also want to spend some time in the States.

It's worth checking if your transatlantic carrier has an **airpass deal** for non-US residents – most major US airlines do – by which you purchase coupons in Britain at a flat rate for a certain number of flights (with a usual minimum of three) in North America. Depending on the airline, the pass will usually also include one or more destinations in Mexico and Canada. For example, a three-flight pass, valid for thirty days, on American costs £259/£309 in the low/high seasons and covers Mexico and Canada; Continental's three-flight pass, also valid on Air Canada, costs £220/£269 in the low/high seasons, but does not include Mexico – useful if you've already booked a separate Continental flight into Mexico. For more on getting to Mexico from North America (including overland routes) see pp.3–9.

For Mexican destinations other than the capital, Continental and Delta have the widest choice, with each airline serving at least ten cities, closely followed by American.

PACKAGES AND INCLUSIVE TOURS

Many companies offer **package tours** to Mexico, and there's an enormous choice to suit all budgets. Trips range from two weeks in a luxury beach hotel to trekking in the Sierra Madre; visits to native markets in Oaxaca or a camping tour of Maya sites in Yucatán. **Wildlife trips** are becoming very popular – you can watch whales off the Baja coast or seek rare birds in the cloud forests of Chiapas. Group tours save the hassle of making your own arrangements and can be good value. The tours are generally relaxed and friendly, usually led by someone from the UK who knows the area, and in many cases there's also a local guide. Several firms offer **tailor-made itineraries**, whereby you decide what you'd like and they arrange it for you. The list opposite (see box) covers the best and most experienced UK operators; all can provide detailed information on each trip. Prices (where given) are a guide only. Most tours operate through the winter period only, though several run year-round.

FLIGHTS FROM IRELAND

Ireland's only direct connection to México is a weekly Aeroflot flight from Shannon (via Miami), costing around IR£650. The cheapest way to get there, however, will almost certainly be to take one of the numerous daily flights from Dublin or Belfast to London and then connect with one of the transatlantic flights detailed in the previous section. BA also fly from Dublin to meet their connections in London to México and Cancún. However, you can also fly from Ireland to the States: Delta has the widest range of **direct flights from Dublin** (and several from Shannon) to New York (JFK) and Atlanta, with daily connections to México. Some flights can be very good deals: with American, you can get a low-

---

USEFUL ADDRESSES IN IRELAND

AIRLINES

Aer Lingus ☎01/705 3333.
Aeroflot ☎01/679 1453.
British Airways ☎0345/222111 (Belfast); ☎1800/626747 (Dublin).
British Midland ☎0345/554554 (Belfast); ☎01/283 8833 (Dublin).

Delta ☎1800/768080 (Dublin).
Iberia ☎01/677 9846 (Dublin).
Lufthansa ☎01/844 5544 (Dublin Airport).
KLM ☎0990/074074 (Belfast).
Ryanair ☎01/609 7800 (Dublin).

FLIGHT AND TOUR SPECIALISTS

Maxwell's Travel, D'Olier Chambers, 1 Hawkins St, Dublin 2 (☎01/677 9479, fax 679 3948). *Latin America specialists; representatives for many of the UK tour operators listed opposite.*

Trailfinders, 4–5 Dawson St, Dublin 2 (☎01/677 7888). *Irish branch of the air-fare and independent travel experts.*

USIT, 19–21 Aston Quay, O'Connell Bridge, Dublin 2 (☎01/602 1700); Fountain Centre, College St, Belfast BT1 6ET (☎01232/324073); *www.usit.ie. All-Ireland student travel agents, with seventeen offices (mainly on campuses) in the Republic and the North.*

season fare to México that includes two flights in the US for IR£515, rising to IR£750 in the high season. With Aer Lingus from Dublin (and in some cases from Shannon) you can get same-day connections to México by flying to New York (JFK); you can also fly with them from Dublin to Amsterdam and pick up a KLM flight to México

from there. KLM's flights from Belfast connect with their services from Amsterdam to México. Iberia's flights from Dublin to México and Cancún – often a good deal at around IR£422–467 – require an overnight stop in Madrid or London. Lufthansa's flights from Dublin also mean you have an overnight stop.

GETTING THERE FROM AUSTRALIA & NEW ZEALAND

The high season for flights to Mexico from Australia and New Zealand is mid-June to mid-July, together with mid-December to mid-January. You can count on paying between A$200 and A$400 more at peak season than the fares quoted below.

From **Australia** the cheapest flights – fares quoted are from major cities, including Brisbane, Cairns, Sydney and Melbourne – are with Japanese

Airlines (JAL) to México via LA or Vancouver with an overnight stop in Tokyo or Osaka (A$1389). Qantas–Continental have more direct, but also more expensive, flights to México via LA (A$1700–1900), as do Aerolineas Argentinas, flying via Auckland and Buenos Aires to México (A$2060). United fly to México via the US or Canada (A$2340), including two stops of your choice from a fixed list of cities in North America.

The best deal, mile for mile, on **RTW fares from Australia** is the "Star Alliance" fare offered by the airlines sponsoring the Sydney 2000 Olympics. For A$2500 you get fifteen stops using any combination of United, Air Canada, Thai, Varig Brazilian, Scandinavian and Lufthansa airlines. Your best bet to get to Mexico using this alliance is with United and then onwards from Mexico with Lufthansa to Frankfurt and Europe, before returning to Australia via Asia.

From New Zealand it's very much the same situation as outlined above: United Airlines (with Mexicana), Air New Zealand (with Aeroméxico) and Qantas (with Continental) all fly from Auckland via LA at prices that start around NZ$2500. If you want more exotic stopovers, Aerolineas Argentinas will take you via Buenos Aires for clos-

---

AIRLINES IN AUSTRALIA AND NEW ZEALAND

Australia		New Zealand	
Aerolineas Argentinas	☎1800/222215	Air New Zealand	☎09/366 2424
Air New Zealand (Australia)	☎02/9223 4666	Delta	☎09/379 3370
Delta	☎02/9251 3211	Qantas	☎09/357 8700
Japanese Airlines	☎02/9272 1111	United	☎09/379 3800
Qantas	☎13/1211		
United	☎13/1777		

DISCOUNT TRAVEL AGENTS IN AUSTRALIA

Accent on Travel, 545 Queen St, Brisbane (☎07/3832 1777).

Anywhere Travel, 345 Anzac Parade, Kingsford, Sydney (☎02/9663 0411).

Brisbane Flight Centre, 260 & 360 Queen St, Brisbane (☎07/3229 9211).

Perth Flight Centre, Shop 53, Forrest Chase, Perth (☎08/9221 1400).

STA Travel, 855 George St, Sydney (☎1300/360 960); 256 Flinders St, Melbourne (☎03/9654 7266); plus other branches nationwide; *www.statravelaus.com.au.*

Student Flights, 125 King St, Newtown, Sydney (☎02/9565 2488; national reservations ☎1800/069 063)

Thomas Cook, 175 Pitt St, Sydney (☎13/1771); plus branches nationwide.

travel.com.au (The Flight Specialists), 80 Clarence Street, Sydney (☎02/9290 1500).

Tymtro Travel, 314 Victoria Ave, Chatswood, Sydney (☎02/9413 1219).

Trailfinders, 8 Spring St, Sydney (☎02/9247 7666); also offices in Brisbane and Cairns.

DISCOUNT TRAVEL AGENTS IN NEW ZEALAND

Flight Centres, National Bank Towers, 205–225 Queen St, Auckland (☎09/309 6171); 203 Papanui Rd, Christchurch (☎03/355 3000); 50–52 Willis St, Wellington (☎04/472 8101); other branches countrywide.

STA Travel, 10 High St, Auckland (☎09/309 0458); 90 Cashel St, Christchurch (☎03/379 9098); 233 Cuba St, Wellington (☎04/385 0561); other offices in Dunedin, Palmerston North and Hamilton.

SPECIALIST AGENTS IN AUSTRALIA AND NEW ZEALAND

Adventure World, 73 Walker St, North Sydney (☎02/9956 7766); 8 Victoria Ave, Perth (☎08/9221 2300); 101 Great Sth Rd, Remuera, Auckland (☎09/524 5118). *Agents for four- to fourteen-day bus and plane sightseeing packages around Mexico with various operators.*

Affordable South America, 118 Queen St, Melbourne (☎03/9600 1733). *Tailor-made packages from the sights of México to trekking in the Yucatán.*

Contours, 84 William St, Melbourne (☎03/9670 6900). *Wide range of packages from overland camping to deluxe travel and conventional touring; also handles scuba, train rides and personal itineraries.*

Destinations Adventure, Premier Building, cnr Queen St and Durham St East, PO Box

6232, Auckland (☎09/309 0464). *Overland expeditions.*

Mexico Reservations Centre, 6 Razorback Plaza, Jindabyne (☎1800/020700). *Accommodation, tours and transfers.*

Peregrine, 258 Lonsdale St, Melbourne (☎03/9663 8611); c/o The Adventure Travel Co., 164 Parnell Rd, Parnell, Auckland (☎09/379 9755). *Two-week to six-month Dragoman overland truck adventures, taking in Mexico en route to Tierra del Fuego.*

South American Adventures, 169 Unley Rd, Unley, Adelaide (☎08/9272 2010). *Experienced in handling travel to Mexico, and acts as booking agent for other tour operators.*

South America Travel Centre, 104 Hardware Lane, Melbourne (☎1800/655051). *Individual, tailor-made itineraries.*

---

er to NZ$3000, while United combines with a variety of Asian carriers for trips via LA, Europe and Asia for around NZ$2700–3400. For **RTW fares** from NZ, the "Star Alliance" fare outlined above also applies to departures originating in Auckland, with prices starting at NZ$2750.

VISAS AND RED TAPE

Citizens of the USA, Canada, the UK, Ireland, Australia, New Zealand and much of Western Europe need no visa to enter Mexico as tourists for less than 180 days. Other Western Europeans can stay for 90 days. Non-US citizens travelling via the USA, however, may need a US visa.

What every visitor does need is a valid passport and a **tourist card** (or *FMT – folleto de migración turística*). Tourist cards are free, and if you're flying direct, you should get one on the plane, or from the airline before leaving. A good travel agent should be able to arrange one for you, too. Otherwise they're issued by Mexican consulates, in person or by post. Every major US city and most border towns have a Mexican consulate; tourist cards and vehicle import forms are also available from all AAA offices in California, Arizona, New Mexico and Texas. Finally, failing all these, you *should* be able to get tourist cards at airports or border crossings on arrival. However, if they've run out, you'll have to twiddle your thumbs until the next batch comes in, and if your passport is not issued by a rich Western country, you may encounter difficulty in persuading border officials to give you a card at all; it's therefore preferable to get one in advance.

Most people officially need a passport to pick up their tourist card, but for **US and Canadian citizens** all that's required is proof of citizenship (an original birth certificate or notarized copy, for instance, or naturalization papers), along with some form of photo ID (such as a driver's license).

US and Canadian citizens can even enter Mexico without a passport if they carry such documents plus their tourist card with them, but it's not advisable, since officials checking your ID may not be aware of this right.

A tourist card is valid for a single entry only: if you intend to enter and leave Mexico more than once, you should pick up two or three. On the card, you are asked how long you intend to stay: always apply for longer than you need, since getting an extension is a frustrating and time-consuming business. You don't always get the time you've asked for in any case: in particular, at Mexico's borders with Belize and Guatemala to the south, you will probably only get thirty days (though they may give you more if you specifically ask), and entering via Chiapas state means you're likely only to get fifteen days (extensions unlikely). Especially if you are not from a rich country, you may also be asked to show sufficient funds for your stay.

A tourist card isn't strictly necessary for anyone who only intends to visit the northern **border towns** and stay less than three days (though you still need a passport or photo ID). In fact, the entire US frontier strip is a duty-free area into which you can come and go more or less as you please; heading further south beyond this zone, however, there are checkpoints on every road after about 30km, and you'll be sent back if you haven't brought the necessary documents and been through customs and immigration.

Don't lose the **blue copy** of your tourist card, which is given back to you after immigration inspection. You are legally required to carry it at all times, and if you have to show your papers, it's more important than your passport. Also, the blue copy must be handed in on leaving the country – without it, you may encounter hassle and delay.

Should you **lose** your tourist card, or need to have it renewed, head for the nearest immigration department office (Departmento de Migracíon); there are downtown branches in the biggest cities. In the case of **renewal**, it's far simpler to cross the border for a day and get a new one on re-entry than to apply for an extension; if you do apply to the immigration department, it's wise to do so a couple of weeks in advance, though you may be told to come back

MEXICAN CONSULATES AND EMBASSIES ABROAD

The following all issue visas and tourist cards.

USA
2827 16th St NW, Washington, DC 20036
(☎202/736-1000); and in 50 other US towns and cities, among them those in the border states listed below.

ARIZONA
541 10th St, Douglas, AZ 85607 (☎520/364-3107); 486 Grand Ave, Nogales, AZ 85621 (☎602/287-2521).

CALIFORNIA
331 W 2nd St, Calexico, CA 92231 (☎619/357-3863); 1549 India St, San Diego, CA 92101 (☎619/231-9741).

TEXAS
724 E Elizabeth St, Brownsville, TX 78520 (☎512/542-2051); 300 E Loyosa St, Del Rio, TX 78840 (☎210/775-2352); 140 Adams St, Eagle Pass, TX 78852 (☎210/773-9255 or 773-9256); 910 E San Antonio St, El Paso, TX 79901 (☎915/533-3644 or 533-3645); 1612 Farragut St, Laredo, TX 78040 (☎210/723-6369); 600 S Broadway Ave, McAllen, TX 78501 (☎210/686-0243 or 686-0244); 127 Navarro St, San Antonio, TX 78205 (☎210/227-1085).

AUSTRALIA
14 Perth Ave, Yarralumla, Canberra, ACT 2600 (☎02/6273 3963); 135 New South Head Rd, Edgecliff, Sydney, NSW 2027 (☎02/9326 1292).

BELIZE
20 N Park St, Belize City (☎02/30193 or 30194).

CANADA
45 O'Connor St, Suite 1500, Ottawa, ON K1P 1A4 (☎613/233-8988); 2000 Mansfield, Montreal, PQ H3A 2Z7 (☎514/288-2502); 199 Bay St, Suite 4440, Commerce Ct W, Toronto, ON M5L 1E9 (☎416/368-2875); 810–1130 W Pender St, Vancouver, BC V6E 4A4 (☎604/684-3547).

CUBA
C 12, #518, Miramar, Playa, Havana 6 (☎07/242383).

GUATEMALA
13 C 7–30, Zona 9, Guatemala City (☎02/334 2981); 9a Av 6–19, Zona 1, Quetzaltenango (☎09/763 1312).

IRELAND
43 Ailesbury Rd, Ballsbridge, Dublin 4 (☎01/260-0699).

NEW ZEALAND
111–115 Customhouse Quay, 8th floor, Wellington (☎04/472-5555).

SOUTH AFRICA
Southern Life Plaza, 1st floor, Hatfield, Pretoria 0083 (☎012/342-5190).

UK
8 Halkin St, London SW1X 8QR (☎0171/235 6393).

---

nearer the actual expiry date. Whatever else you may be told, branches of SECTUR (the tourist office) cannot renew expired tourist cards or replace lost ones – they will only make sympathetic noises and direct you to the nearest immigration office.

Visas, obtainable only through a consulate (in person or by mail), are required by nationals of South Africa and most non-industrialized countries, as well as by anyone entering Mexico to work or to study for more than 180 days. **Business visitors** need a Business Authorization Card available from consulates, and usually a visa too. Anyone **under 18** travelling without both parents needs their written consent (see p.5).

US VISAS

Non-US citizens **travelling through the States** on the way to or from Mexico, or stopping over there, may need a **US visa**. If there's even a possibility you might stop in the States, unless you are Canadian or from a country on the US visa waiver scheme (see below), obtaining a visa in advance is a sensible precaution. You can expect a certain amount of queuing wherever you apply in person, but you can always apply by post instead, provided you allow enough time (usually four weeks). A number of countries, including Britain, the Netherlands, Denmark and Germany, but not Australia, New Zealand, Ireland or South Africa, are on a **visa waiver scheme**, designed to speed up lengthy

EMBASSIES AND CONSULATES IN MEXICO

AUSTRALIA Rubén Darío 55, Colonia Polanco, 11580 México DF (☎5/531-52-25).

CANADA Schiller 529, Colonia Polanco, 11560 México DF (☎5/724-79-00); and in Acapulco, Cancún, Guadalajara, Mazatlán, Monterrey, Oaxaca, Puerto Vallarta, San Miguel de Allende and Tijuana.

IRELAND Av San Jeronimo 790-A, Colonia San Jeronimo Lidice, 10200 México DF (☎5/595-33-33).

NEW ZEALAND José Luis Lagrange 103, 10th floor, Colonia Los Morales, Polanco, 11510 México DF (☎5/250-59-44).

UK Aptdo 96 bis, Río Lerma 71, Colonia Cuauhtémoc, México 06500 (☎5/207-20-89); and in Acapulco, Cancún, Ciudad Juárez, Guadalajara, Mérida, Monterrey, Oaxaca, Tampico, Tijuana and Veracruz.

USA Paseo de la Reforma 305, Colonia Cuauhtémoc, 06500 México DF (☎5/211-00-42); and in Ciudad Juárez, Guadalajara, Hermosillo, Matamoros, Mérida, Monterrey, Nuevo Laredo and Tijuana; addresses for these and for consular agents in other Mexican cities are listed on the following Web site: *www.usembassy.org.mx/-edirector.html*

immigration procedures. Visa waiver forms are available from travel agencies, the airline during check-in, or on the plane, and must be presented to immigration on arrival. Be sure to return the part stapled into your passport when you leave the US: if it isn't returned within the visa expiry time, computer records automatically log you as an illegal alien. If re-entering the US by land from Mexico, you will need to have a form with you in order to be exempt from visa requirements, so make sure you get one in advance. Getting a US visa in Mexico will be a nightmare of queuing and frustration.

Many US airports do not have transit lounges, so even if you are on a through flight you may have to go through US immigration and customs. This can easily take two hours, so bear the delay in mind if you have an onward flight to catch.

CUSTOMS

Duty-free allowances into Mexico are three bottles of liquor (including wine), plus four hundred cigarettes or fifty cigars or 250g of tobacco, plus twelve rolls of camera film or camcorder tape. The monetary limit for duty-free goods is US$150. Returning home, note that it is **illegal to take antiquities** out of the country, and penalties are serious.

COSTS AND MONEY

Mexico is not as cheap as it once was, despite the instability of its currency. Although, in general, costs are lower than you'll find at home, compared with the rest of Central or South America, prices here can come as something of a shock.

In the long term, the **NAFTA** free trade treaty with the US and Canada can probably be expected to keep costs (and, one hopes, wages) rising, though prices will fluctuate somewhat as the peso goes down against the dollar, and inflation moves in to fill the gap. As the peso is so unstable, all prices in the text of the guide section of this book are quoted in **US dollars**; be aware, however, that these will be affected by unpredictable factors such as inflation and exchange rates. Latest developments and your own common sense will determine how you apply them.

COSTS

The developed tourist resorts and big cities are invariably more expensive than more remote towns, and certain other areas, too, have noticeably higher prices – among them the industrialized north, especially along the border, Baja, and all the newly wealthy oil regions. Prices can also be affected by **season**: hotel rooms in the peak tourist season – summer, Christmas and Easter where the tourists are mainly Mexican, but November to May in places like Acapulco, which attract overseas visitors – are far higher than at other times; and special events will also probably be marked by price hikes. Nonetheless, wherever

you go you can probably get by on US$160/£100 a week (you *could* reduce that if you hardly travel around, stay only on campsites or in hostels, live on the most basic food and don't buy any souvenirs, but it hardly makes for an enjoyable trip), while on US$500/£320 you'd really be living very well.

Accommodation prices range from only a couple of dollars for a beach cabaña, through US$6–12/£4–8 for a room in a cheap hotel and US$18–40/£12–26 in the mid-range, to five-star luxury for anything from US$60/£40 upwards. **Food** prices can also vary wildly, but you should always be able to get a substantial meal in a plain Mexican restaurant for around US$4/£3. Most restaurant bills come with fifteen percent *IVA* (*Impuesto de Valor Añadido*, or VAT sales tax) added; this may not always be included in prices quoted on the menu. One major expense, if you intend to travel around a lot, may prove to be **transport**, since distances can be so great. On a per kilometre basis, however, prices are very reasonable: México to Acapulco, for example, a journey of over 400km, costs less than US$20/£14 by first-class bus, while a 24-hour journey such as México to Cancún (1800km) works out at around US$40/£25.

As always, if you're **travelling alone** you'll end up spending more – sharing rooms and food saves a substantial amount. In the larger resorts, you can get apartments for up to six people for even greater savings. If you have an international **Student or Youth Card**, you might also take it along for an occasional reduction on a museum admission price, but don't go out of your way to obtain one, since most concessions are, at least in theory, only for Mexican students. Cards available include the ISIC card for full-time students and the Go-25 youth card for under-25s, both of which carry health and emergency insurance benefits for Americans, and are available from youth travel firms such as STA, who also sell their own card. Even a college photo ID card might work in some places.

Service is hardly ever added to bills, and the amount you **tip** is entirely up to you – in cheap places, it's just the loose change, while expensive joints tend to expect a full fifteen percent. It's not standard practice to tip taxi drivers.

CURRENCY

The "new Mexican Peso", or **Nuevo Peso**, usually written $ (sometimes N$), was introduced in 1993 and is made up of 100 centavos (¢, like a US cent) – it's the equivalent of 1000 old pesos. Bills come in denominations of $10, $20, $50, $100, $200 and $500, with coins of 5¢, 10¢, 20¢, 50¢, $1, $2, $5 and $10. The use of the dollar symbol for the peso is occasionally confusing; the initials MN (*moneda nacional*) are occasionally used to indicate that it's Mexican, not American money that is being used. In any case, the sign is not *exactly* the same: at least in theory, the Mexican peso symbol has only one vertical bar through it, while that of the gringo dollar has two. You may occasionally still come across postage stamps and one or two other things priced in the old currency, but it should then be obvious from the amount.

CURRENCY EXCHANGE

The easiest kind of **foreign currency** to change in Mexico is US dollars cash. US dollar travellers' cheques come second; Canadian dollars and other major international currencies such as pounds sterling, yen and deutschmarks are a poor third, and you'll find it hard to change travellers' cheques in those currencies. Quetzales and Belize dollars are best got rid of before entering Mexico (otherwise, your best bet for changing them is with tourists heading the other way).

Correspondingly, you'll get the best rates for cash dollars, slightly lower rates for dollar travellers' cheques, and rates lower still for other currencies: indeed, it is a good idea to change other currencies into US dollars at home before coming to Mexico, since the difference in the exchange rate more than outweighs the amount you lose in changing your money twice.

Although the **banks** have all been nationalized, each is run differently. The Banco Nacional de Mexico (known as Banamex) is probably the most efficient; Bancomer, almost as widespread, is also a possibility, as is the smaller Banco del Atlantico. Banks are generally open Monday to Friday from 9.30am until 1.30pm, though sometimes with shorter hours for exchange. The commission charged varies from bank to bank, while the exchange rate, in theory, is the same – fixed daily by the government. Only larger branches of the big banks, plus some in tourist resorts, are usually prepared to change currencies other than dollars – and even then often at worse rates than you would get for the dollar equivalent. **ATM cash dispenser machines** are now ubiquitous in Mexico, and make a useful alternative (see opposite).

Casas de cambio (exchange offices) are open longer hours and at weekends, and have varying exchange rates and commission charges; they also tend to have shorter queues and less bureaucratic procedures. They usually give better rates than banks, too, but it's always worth checking, especially if you're changing travellers' cheques. Occasionally, casas de cambio give rates for Canadian dollars, sterling and other currencies that are as good as those they give for US dollars, so again it's worth shopping around, especially if you intend to change a large sum.

If you're desperate, many hotels, shops and restaurants that are used to tourists are prepared to change dollars or accept them as payment, but rates will be very low. There isn't much of a **black market** in Mexico since exchange regulations are relatively loose, and it's not really worth bothering with unless it comes about through personal contacts or you want to do someone a favour.

CASH AND TRAVELLERS' CHEQUES

In touristy places, such as Acapulco and Tijuana, **US dollar bills** are almost as easy to spend as pesos. The big disadvantage with cash, of course, is that, once stolen or lost, it's gone forever. For that reason, most travellers prefer to bring plastic and/or travellers' cheques (personal cheques are virtually worthless in Mexico). But do bring some dollars cash – sometimes you won't be able to change anything else. It's also a good idea to have a mixture of denominations, including a wad of single dollar bills, and to try to bring some pesos (US$50/£30-worth, say), just in case you can't for some reason change money on arrival, or would rather not wait in a long line to do so. Although few US banks keep foreign currency on hand, and banks in Britain, Australia and New Zealand are unlikely to stock Mexican pesos, you should be able to order them from your bank's foreign desk if you give them a few days' notice; or you may find them at specialist exchange desks at the airport.

Travellers' cheques have the obvious advantage over cash that, if you lose them or they're stolen, the issuing company will refund them on production of the purchase receipt, which should for that reason be kept safe and separate from the cheques themselves, along with a record of the serial numbers and a note of those ones you have already cashed. If your cheques do get lost or stolen, the issuing company will expect you to report the loss forthwith to their local office. You pay one to two percent commission to buy the cheques, and usually get a lower rate of exchange for them, but it's worth it for the extra peace of mind.

When **buying travellers' cheques**, get a sensible mix of denominations, and stick to the established names – Thomas Cook, American Express, Visa or one of the major American banks – not only because these will be more recognized, but also because there will be better customer service should they be lost or stolen.

CREDIT AND CASH CARDS

Major **credit cards** are widely accepted and handy for emergencies. Visa and Mastercard are the best; American Express and other charge cards are usually only accepted by expensive places, but an Amex card is worth it for the other services it offers, such as mail pick-up points and dollar travellers' cheque purchase. Unfortunately credit cards are not accepted in the cheapest hotels or restaurants, nor for most bus tickets, but you can use them to get cash advances from banks. Usually there's a minimum withdrawal of around US$75–100.

In addition, you can get cash 24 hours a day from ATMs in most towns of any size in Mexico, using credit cards or **ATM cash cards** from home. Bancomer machines accept Visa and Mastercard; Banamex accept these plus debit cards from the Cirrus and PLUS systems, which allow account holders to withdraw money directly from their current/checking accounts back

---

TOLL-FREE OR COLLECT NUMBERS FOR LOST CARDS OR CHEQUES	
American Express	☎1-800/221-2728
Thomas Cook and.	
Mastercard	☎1-800/223-7373
Visa dial ☎96 and ask for 415/574-7700	

home. In some border towns, some cash machines pay out in US dollars.

Make sure before you leave home that you have a **personal identification number** (PIN) designed to work overseas. Remember, too, that all cash advances on credit cards are treated as loans, with interest accruing daily from the date of withdrawal; there may be a transaction fee on top of this. Finally, be aware that technical hitches are not uncommon – though rare, it has been known for machines not to dispense cash, but to debit your account anyway.

WIRING MONEY

Having **money wired** from home is never convenient or cheap, and should be considered a last resort. Funds can be sent via **MoneyGram** or **Western Union** (see box below). Both companies' fees depend on the amount being transferred, but as an example, wiring US$1000/£700 to Mexico will cost around US$60/£40. The funds should be available for collection at the local Amex or Western Union office within minutes of being sent.

It's also possible to have money wired directly from a bank in your home country to a bank in Mexico, although this is somewhat less reliable because it involves two separate institutions. If you take this route, the person wiring the funds to you will need to know the telex number of the receiving bank.

WESTERN UNION AND MONEYGRAM PHONE NUMBERS

Call the following numbers to find out the location of your nearest agent:

WESTERN UNION		MONEYGRAM	
Australia	☎07/3229 8610 (Brisbane);	Australia	☎02/9886 0666 (Sydney);
	☎1800/649565 (elsewhere).		☎1800/230100 (elsewhere).
Ireland	☎1800/395395.	Ireland	☎1800/559372.
New Zealand	☎09/302 0143.	New Zealand	☎09/379 8243 (Auckland);
UK	☎0800/833833.		☎04/473 7766 (Wellington).
USA and Canada	☎1-800/325-6000.	UK	☎0800/894887.
		USA and Canada	☎1-800/543-4080.

HEALTH

It's always easier to become ill in a foreign country with a different climate, different food and different germs, still more so in a poor country with lower standards of sanitation than you might be used to. Most travellers, however, get through Mexico without catching anything more serious than a dose of Montezuma's Revenge. You will still want the security of health insurance (see "Insurance" on p.27), but the important thing is to keep your resistance high and to be aware of the health risks linked to poor hygiene, untreated water, mosquito bites, undressed open cuts and unprotected sex.

What you eat or drink is crucial: a poor **diet** lowers your resistance. Be sure to eat enough of the right things, including a good balance of protein (meat, fish, eggs or beans, for example), carbohydrates, vitamins and minerals. Eating plenty of peeled fresh fruit helps keep up your vitamin and mineral intake, but it might be worth taking daily multi-vitamin and mineral tablets with you. It's also important to eat enough – an unfamiliar diet may reduce the amount you eat – and get enough sleep and rest, as it's easy to become run-down if you're on the move a lot, especially in a hot climate.

The lack of **sanitation** in Mexico is often exaggerated, and it's not worth being obsessive about it or you'll never enjoy anything. Even so, a degree of caution is wise – don't try anything too exotic in the first few days, before your body has had a chance to adjust to local microbes, and avoid food that has been on display for a while or not freshly cooked. You should also steer clear of salads, and peel fruit before eating it. Avoid raw shellfish, and don't eat anywhere that is obviously dirty (easily spotted, since most Mexican restaurants are scrupulously clean) – street stalls in particular are suspect. For advice on **water**, see p.24.

VACCINATIONS

There are no required **inoculations** for Mexico, but it's worth visiting your doctor at least four weeks before you leave to check that you are up to date with polio, tetanus, typhoid and hepatitis A jabs. Those travelling from the USA or Canada will have to pay for inoculations, available at any immunization centre or at most local clinics. Most

GPs in the UK have a travel surgery where you can get advice and certain vaccines on prescription, though they may not administer some of the less common immunizations. Travel clinics can be more expensive, but you won't need to make an appointment. In Australia and New Zealand, vaccination centres are less expensive than doctors' surgeries. Most clinics will also sell travel-associated accessories, including mosquito nets and first-aid kits.

INTESTINAL TROUBLES

Despite all the dire warnings below, a bout of **diarrhoea** ("Montezuma's Revenge", or simply *turista* as it's invariably known in Mexico) is the only medical problem you're at all likely to encounter. No one, however cautious they are, seems to avoid it altogether, largely because there are no reliable preventative measures. It's caused by the bacteria in Mexican food, which are different from (as well as more numerous than) those found in other Western diets, and is compounded by the change in diet and routine.

If you go down with a mild dose of the runs unaccompanied by other symptoms, this will probably be the cause. If your diarrhoea is accompanied by cramps and vomiting, it could be food poisoning of some sort. Either way, it will probably pass of its own accord in 24–48 hours without treatment. In the meantime, it's essential to replace the fluid and salts you're losing, so drink lots of water with oral rehydration salts – *suero oral* (brand names: *Dioralyte, Electrosol, Rehidrat*). If you can't get these, dissolve half a teaspoon of salt and three of sugar in a litre of water. Avoid greasy food, heavy spices, caffeine and most fruit and dairy products; some say bananas, papayas and prickly pears (*tunas*) are a help, while plain yoghurt or a broth made from yeast extract (such as *Marmite* or *Vegemite*, if you happen to have some with you) can be easily absorbed by your body when you have diarrhoea. Drugs like *Lomotil* or *Imodium* plug you up – and thus undermine the body's efforts to rid itself of infection – but they can be a temporary stop-gap if you have to travel. If symptoms persist for a few days, a course of **antibiotics** may be necessary, but this should be a last resort, following medical advice (see "Getting medical help" on p.26).

MEDICAL RESOURCES

IN THE USA AND CANADA

Canadian Society for International Health, 170 Laurier Ave W, Suite 902, Ottawa, ON K1P 5V5 (☎613/230-2654). *Distributes a free pamphlet, "Health Information for Canadian Travellers", containing an extensive list of travel health centres in Canada.*

Centers for Disease Control, 1600 Clifton Rd NE, Atlanta, GA 30333 (☎404/639-3311; *www.cdc.gov/travel/travel.html*). *Publishes outbreak warnings, suggested inoculations, precautions and other background information for travellers. Web site is outstanding.*

IAMAT (International Association for Medical Assistance to Travelers), 417 Center St, Lewiston, NY 14092 (☎716/754-4883; *www.sentex.net/~iamat*) and 40 Regal Rd, Guelph, ON N1K 1B5 (☎519/836-0102). *A non-profit organization supported by donations, it can provide a list of English-speaking doctors in Mexico, climate charts and leaflets on various diseases and inoculations.*

International SOS Assistance, PO Box 11568, Philadelphia, PA 19116 (☎1-800/523-8930). *Members receive pre-trip medical referral information, as well as overseas emergency services designed to complement travel insurance coverage.*

Travel Medicine, 351 Pleasant St, Suite 312, Northampton, MA 01060 (☎1-800/872-8633). *Sells first-aid kits, mosquito netting, water filters and other health-related travel products.*

Travelers Medical Center, 31 Washington Square, New York, NY 10011 (☎212/982-1600). *Consultation service on immunizations and treatment.*

IN THE UK AND IRELAND

British Airways Travel Clinic, 156 Regent St, London W1 7RA (Mon–Fri 9.30am–5.15pm, Sat 10am–4pm; ☎0171/439 9584). *No appointment necessary. BA also run several other clinics in London as well as nationwide (call*

☎01276/685040 for the one nearest to you), plus airport locations at Gatwick and Heathrow.

Hospital for Tropical Diseases, St Pancras Hospital, 4 St Pancras Way, London NW1 0PE (☎0171/388 9600). *Travel clinic, with recorded message service (☎0839/337733; 49p per min) that gives hints on hygiene and illness prevention as well as listing appropriate immunizations.*

MASTA (Medical Advisory Service for Travellers Abroad), London School of Hygiene and Tropical Medicine. *Operate a pre-recorded 24-hour Travellers' Health Line (☎0891/224100; 50p per min), sending latest specific health advice for your journey by return of post.*

Travel Medicine Services, PO Box 254, 16 College St, Belfast 1 (☎01232/315220).

Tropical Medical Bureau, Grafton St Medical Centre, 34 Grafton St, Dublin 2 (☎01/671 9200).

Tropical Medical Bureau, Dun Laoghaire Medical Centre, 5 Northumberland Ave, Dun Laoghaire, Co. Dublin (☎01/280 4996, fax 280 5603; *tropical@iol.ie, www.tmb.ie*).

IN AUSTRALIA AND NEW ZEALAND

Auckland Hospital, Park Rd, Grafton, Auckland (☎09/379 7440).

Travel Bug Medical and Vaccination Centre, 182 Ward St, N Adelaide (☎08/8267 3544).

Travel Health and Vaccination Clinic, 114 William St, Melbourne (☎03/9670 3871).

Travel Medical & Vaccination Centre, 6 Washington Way, Christchurch 5 (☎03/379 4000).

travel.com.au, 80 Clarence St, Sydney (☎02/9290 1500).

Travellers' Medical and Vaccination Centre, 7/428 George St, Sydney (☎02/9221 7133); plus offices in other mayor cities across the country; *www.tmvc.com.au*.

Travellers' Immunisation Service, 303 Pacific Highway, Lindfield, Sydney (☎02/9416 1348).

MALARIA AND DENGUE FEVER

Malaria, caused by a parasite that lives in the saliva of *Anopheles* mosquitoes, is endemic in many parts of Mexico. Areas above 1000m (such as the capital) are malaria-free, as are Cancún, Cozumel, Isla Mujeres, and all the beach resorts

of the Baja and the Pacific coasts. Daytime visits to archeological sites are risk-free, too, but low-lying inland areas are risky, especially in **Chiapas**, where the presence of strains resistant to the main preventative drug, chloroquine, is suspected. Nonetheless, it's a good idea to take chloroquine (brand names: *Nivaquin, Resochin,*

WHAT ABOUT THE WATER?

In a hot climate and at high altitudes, it's essential to **increase water intake** to prevent dehydration. Most travellers, and most Mexicans if they can, stay off the **tap water**, although a lot of the time it is in fact drinkable, and in practice impossible to avoid completely: ice made with it, unasked for, may appear in drinks, utensils are washed in it, and so on.

Most restaurants and licuaderías use **purified water** (agua purificada), but always check; most hotels have a supply and will often provide bottles of water in your room. **Bottled water** (generally purified with ozone or ultra-violet) is widely available, but stick with known brands, and always check that the seal on the bottle is intact since refilling empties with tap water for resale is not unknown (carbonated water is generally a safer bet in that respect).

There are various methods of **treating water** while you are travelling, whether your source is from a tap or a river or stream. **Boiling** it for a minimum of five minutes is the time-honoured method, but it is not always practical, will not remove unpleasant tastes, and is a lot less effective at higher altitudes — including much of central Mexico, where you have to boil it for much longer.

Chemical sterilization, using either chlorine or iodine tablets or a tincture of iodine liquid, is more convenient, but chlorine leaves a nasty aftertaste (though it can be masked with lemon or lime juice), and is not effective in preventing such diseases as amoebic dysentery and giardiasis. **Pregnant** women or people with **thyroid** problems should consult their doctor before using iodine sterilizing tablets or iodine-based purifiers. Inexpensive iodine removal filters are available and are recommended if treated water is being used continuously for more than a month or is being given to babies.

Purification, involving both filtration and sterilization, gives the most complete treatment. Portable water purifiers range in size from units weighing as little as 60g, which can be slipped into a pocket, up to 800g for carrying in a backpack. Some of the best water purifiers on the market are made in Britain by **Pre-Mac**. For suppliers worldwide contact:

Pre-Mac International Ltd, Unit 5, Morewood Close, Sevenoaks, Kent TN13 2HU (☎01732/ 460333, fax 460222; office@pre-mac.com, www. pre-mac.com).

Avloclor, Aralen), starting about two weeks before you arrive and continuing for a month afterwards.

If you go down with malaria, you'll probably know. The fever, shivering and headaches are like severe flu and come in waves, usually beginning in the early evening. Malaria is not infectious, but can be dangerous and sometimes even fatal if not treated quickly. If no doctor is available, take 600mg of quinine sulphate three times daily for at least three days, followed by three Fansidar (available from a local pharmacy) taken together.

The most important thing, obviously, is to avoid **mosquito bites**. Though active from dusk till dawn, female Anopheles mosquitoes prefer to bite in the evening. Wear long sleeves, skirts or trousers, avoid dark colours, which attract mosquitoes, and put repellent on all exposed skin, especially feet and ankles, which are their favourite targets. Plenty of good brands are sold locally, though health departments recommend carrying high-DEET brands available from travel clinics at home (and some travellers swear by Avon Skin So Soft bath oil). An alternative is to burn coils of pyrethium incense such as Raidolitos (these are readily available and burn all night if whole, but are easy to break in transit). Sleep under a net if you can — one that hangs from a single point is best (you can usually find a way to tie a string across your room to hang it from). Special mosquito nets for hammocks are available in Mexico.

Another illness spread by mosquito bites is **dengue fever**, whose symptoms are similar to those of malaria, plus a headache and aching bones. The only treatment is complete rest, with drugs to assuage the fever.

OTHER BITES AND STINGS

Other biting insects can be a nuisance. These include **bed bugs**, sometimes found in cheap hotels — look for squashed ones around the bed. **Sandflies**, often present on beaches, are only small, but their bites, usually on feet and ankles, itch like hell and last for days. **Head or body lice** can be picked up from people or bedding, and are best treated with medicated soap or shampoo; very occasionally, they may spread typhus, characterized by fever, muscle aches, headaches and eventually red eyes and a measles-like rash. If you think you have it, seek treatment.

Scorpions are mostly nocturnal and hide during the heat of the day under rocks and in crevices, so poking around in such places when in the countryside is generally ill-advised. If sleeping in a place where they might enter (such as a beach cabaña), shake your shoes out before putting them on in the morning, and try not to wander round barefoot. The sting of some scorpions is dangerous and medical treatment should always be sought – cold-pack the sting in the meantime. **Snakes** are unlikely to bite unless accidentally disturbed, and most are harmless in any case. To see one at all, you need to search stealthily – walk heavily and they will usually slither away. If you do get bitten or stung, remember what the snake or scorpion looked like (kill it if you can), try not to move the affected part, and seek medical help: antivenins are available in most hospitals.

HEAT AND ALTITUDE PROBLEMS

Two other common causes of health problems are **altitude** and the **sun**. The solution in both cases is to take it easy. Especially if you arrive in México, you may find any activity strenuous, and the thin air is made worse by the number of pollutants it contains. Allow yourself time to acclimatize. If going to higher altitudes (climbing Popocatépetl, for example), you may develop symptoms of **Acute Mountain Sickness** (AMS), such as breathlessness, headaches, dizziness, nausea and appetite loss. More extreme cases may cause vomiting, disorientation, loss of balance and coughing up of pink frothy phlegm. The simple cure – a slow descent – almost always brings immediate recovery.

Tolerance to the **sun**, too, takes a while to build up: use a strong sunscreen and, if you're walking during the day, wear a hat or keep to the shade. Be sure to avoid dehydration by drinking enough (water or fruit juice rather than beer or coffee), and don't exert yourself for long periods in the hot sun. Be aware that overheating can cause **heatstroke**, which is potentially fatal. Signs are a very high body temperature without a feeling of fever, accompanied by headaches, disorientation and even irrational behaviour. Lowering body temperature (a tepid shower, for example) is the first step in treatment.

Less serious is prickly heat, an itchy rash that is in fact an infection of the sweat ducts caused by excessive perspiration that doesn't dry off. A cool shower, zinc oxide powder and loose cotton clothes should help.

HIV AND AIDS

Over 32,000 cases of **AIDS (SIDA)** have been reported in Mexico, mostly in the centre of the country, and especially in the capital. While the problem in Mexico is no worse than in many other countries, it is still a risk and you should take all the usual precautions to avoid contracting it. In particular, to contemplate casual sex without a condom would be madness – carry some with you (preferably from home; if buying them in Mexico, check the date and remember that heat affects their durability) and insist on using them. They will also protect you from other sexually transmitted diseases.

Should you need an injection or transfusion, make sure that the equipment is sterile (it might be worth bringing a sterile kit from home); any blood you receive should be screened, and from voluntary rather than commercial donor banks. If you have a shave from a barber, make sure a clean blade is used, and don't submit to processes such as ear-piercing, acupuncture or tattooing unless you can be sure that the equipment is sterile.

HEPATITIS AND OTHER DISEASES

Hepatitis A is transmitted through contaminated food and water, or through saliva. It can lay a victim low for several months with exhaustion, fever and diarrhoea, and can even cause liver damage. The new **Havrix** vaccine has been shown to be extremely effective; though expensive (around US$100/£70 for a course of two shots), if you have a second shot within a year, protection lasts for ten years. The protection given by gamma-globulin, the traditional serum of hepatitis antibodies, wears off quickly, and the injection should therefore be as late as possible before departure: the longer your planned stay, the larger the dose.

Symptoms by which you can recognize hepatitis include a yellowing of the whites of the eyes, general malaise, orange urine (though dehydration can also cause this) and light-coloured stools. If you think you have it, avoid alcohol, try to avoid passing it on, and get lots of rest. It's a good idea to go to a **pathology lab** (most towns have them) to get blood tests before seeing a doctor, who should then be consulted in order to monitor your recovery. More serious is **hepatitis B**, passed on like AIDS through blood or sexual contact. There is a vaccine, but it is only recommended for those planning to work in a medical environment. Otherwise, although it is more contagious than HIV, your chances of getting it are low if you take the same precautions against it.

Typhoid and cholera are spread in the same way as hepatitis A. **Typhoid** produces a persistent high fever with malaise, headaches and abdominal pains, followed by diarrhoea. Vaccination can be by injection or orally, but the oral alternative is more expensive and only lasts a year, as opposed to three for a shot in the arm. **Cholera** appears in epidemics rather than isolated cases – if it's about, you should know. It is characterized by sudden attacks of watery diarrhoea with severe cramps and debilitation. The vaccination offers little protection and is not now given for Mexico.

Assuming you were vaccinated against **polio** in childhood, only one (oral) booster is needed during your adult life. Immunizations against mumps, measles, TB and rubella are a good idea for anyone who wasn't vaccinated as a child and hasn't had the diseases. You don't need a shot for **yellow fever** unless you're coming from a country where it's endemic (in which case you need to carry your vaccination certificate).

Rabies exists in Mexico, and the best advice is simply to give dogs a wide berth, and not to play with animals at all, no matter how cuddly they may look. A bite, a scratch or even a lick from an infected animal could spread the disease; wash any such wound immediately but gently with soap or detergent and apply alcohol or iodine if possible. Ideally you should find out what you can about the animal and swap addresses with the owner (if there is one), just in case. If the animal might be infected, act immediately to get treatment – rabies is invariably fatal once symptoms appear. A rabies vaccine is now recommended for trips of more than thirty days. It involves two or three jabs; a booster after one year will protect you for a further three years.

GETTING MEDICAL HELP

For minor **medical problems**, head for the **farmacia** – look for a green cross and the *Farmacia* sign. Pharmacists are knowledgeable and helpful, and many also speak some English. They can also sell drugs over the counter (if necessary) that are only available by prescription at home. One word of **warning** however: in many Mexican pharmacies you can still buy drugs such as *Entero-Vioform* and *Mexaform*, which can cause optic nerve damage and have been banned elsewhere; it is not a good idea, therefore, to use local brands unless you know what they are.

For more serious complaints you can get a list of English-speaking **doctors** from your government's nearest consulate (see p.18); big hotels and tourist offices may also be able to recommend someone. Every Mexican border town has hundreds of doctors experienced in treating gringos (dentists, too), since they charge less than their colleagues across the border. Every reasonably sized town should also have a state- or Red Cross-run health centre (*centro de salud*), where treatment is free.

INSURANCE

There are no reciprocal health arrangements between Mexico and any other country, so travel insurance is essential.

First of all, check to see if you are already covered. **Credit and charge cards** (particularly American Express) often have certain levels of medical or other insurance included, and travel insurance may also be included if you use a major credit or charge card to pay for your trip. Some **package tours**, too, may include insurance.

Whatever cover you are going for, always check the **fine print** of a policy. A 24-hour medical emergency contact number is a must, and one of the rare policies that pays medical bills directly is better than one that reimburses you on your return home. The per-article limit for loss or theft should cover your most valuable possession (a camcorder for example) but, conversely, don't pay for cover you don't need – such as too much baggage or a huge sum for personal liability. Make sure, too, that you are covered for all the things you intend to do. Activities such as climbing, scuba diving and potholing are usually specifically excluded, but can be added for a supplement, usually twenty to fifty percent.

NORTH AMERICAN COVER

Before buying an insurance policy, check that you're not already covered. **Canadian provincial health plans** typically provide some overseas medical coverage, although they are unlikely to pick up the full tab in the event of a mishap. Holders of official **student/teacher/youth cards** are entitled to accident coverage and hospital in-patient benefits – the annual membership is far less than the cost of comparable insurance. **Students** may also find that their student health coverage extends during the vacations and for one term beyond the date of last enrolment. Bank and credit cards (particularly American Express) often provide certain levels of medical or other insurance, and travel insurance may also be included if you use a major credit or charge card to pay for your trip. **Homeowners' or renters'** insurance often covers theft or loss of documents, money and valuables while overseas.

After exhausting the possibilities above, you might want to contact a specialist **travel insurance** company; your travel agent can usually recommend one, or see the box on p.28.

Travel insurance **policies** vary: some are comprehensive while others cover only certain risks (accidents, illnesses, delayed or lost luggage, cancelled flights, etc). In particular, ask whether the policy pays medical costs up front or reimburses you later, and whether it provides for medical evacuation to your home country. For policies that include lost or stolen luggage, check exactly what is and isn't covered (some policies don't insure against **theft** of anything while overseas, and apply only to items *lost* from, or *damaged* in, the custody of an identifiable, responsible third party – hotel porter, airline, guardería, etc), and make sure the per-article limit will cover your most valuable possession.

The best **premiums** are usually to be had through student/youth travel agencies – STA policies, for example, cost US$48–69 for fifteen days (depending on level of coverage), US$80–105 for a month, US$149–207 for two months, US$510–700 for a year. If you're planning to do any "dangerous sports" (potholing, scuba diving, etc), be sure to ask whether these activities are covered: some companies levy a surcharge.

For advice on **auto insurance**, see the "Getting there by car" section (p.9).

INSURANCE COMPANIES AND AGENTS

NORTH AMERICA

Access America, PO Box 90310, Richmond, VA 23230 (☎1-800/284-8300).

Carefree Travel Insurance, PO Box 310, 120 Mineola Blvd, Mineola, NY 11501 (☎1-800/323-3149).

Desjardins Travel Insurance 200 Ave des Commandeurs, Lévis, PQ G6V 6R2 (☎1-800/463-7830).

STA Travel Insurance (☎1-800/777-0112; www.sta-travel.com). Sold by discount agents STA Travel.

Travel Guard, 1145 Clark St, Stevens Point, WI 54481 (☎1-800/826-1300; www.noelgroup.com).

Travel Insurance Services, 2930 Camino Diablo, Suite 300, Walnut Creek, CA 94596 (☎1-800/937-1387; www.travelinsure.com).

Travel Safe, PO Box 7050, Wyomissing, PA 19610 (☎1-800/523-8020, fax 610/678-1238; www.travelsafe.com).

BRITAIN AND IRELAND

Columbus Travel Insurance, 17 Devonshire Square, London EC2M 4SQ (☎0171/375 0011).

Endsleigh Insurance, 97–107 Southampton Row, London WC1B 4AG (☎0171/436 4451).

Marcus Hearn & Co, 65–66 Shoreditch High St, London E1 6JL (☎0171/739 3444).

Worldcover, PO Box 555, Cardiff CF5 6XH (☎0800/365121).

USIT ☎01/679 8333 (Dublin); ☎01232/324073 (Belfast); see p.13 for addresses.

AUSTRALIA AND NEW ZEALAND

UTAG (United Travel Agents Group), 347 Kent Street Sydney, NSW 2000 (☎1800/809462);

AFTA (Australian Federation of Travel Agents), 144 Pacific Highway, North Sydney, NSW 2060 (☎02/9264 3299).

Ready Plan, 141–147 Walker Street, Dandenong, VIC 3175 (☎1800/337462); 10th Floor, 63 Albert Street, Auckland (☎09/379 3208).

Cover More, Level 3, 60 Miller St, North Sydney, NSW (☎02/9202 8000, toll-free ☎1800/251881).

BRITISH, IRISH, AUSTRALIAN & NEW ZEALAND COVER

Travellers from the UK can obtain travel insurance from any bank or travel agent. Most travel agents and tour operators will offer you insurance when you book your flight or holiday, and some will insist you take it – their policies are usually reasonable value, though as ever, you should check the small print. You might choose instead to buy a policy issued by a specialist travel firm like Campus Travel or STA, or by the low-cost **insurers** Endsleigh Insurance and Columbus Travel Insurance (see above for addresses and phone numbers). Two weeks' cover starts at around £27; a month costs from £34. For trips of up to four months, or if this is one of many short trips in one year, good-value policies for long-term travellers can be had from Marcus Hearn & Co: a year's cover (with no single journey exceeding 120 days) will cost around £100, plus £30.50 to include your partner, and £16 for each dependent child under 18. Some insurance companies refuse to cover travellers over 65, or stop at 69 or 74 years of age,

and most that do charge hefty premiums. The best policies for **older travellers**, with no upper age limit, are offered by Age Concern (☎01883/346964). If you have a good "all risks" home insurance policy, it may cover your possessions against loss or theft even when overseas, or you can extend cover through your household contents insurer. Many **private medical schemes** also cover you when abroad – make sure you know the procedure and the helpline number. If you pay for air tickets with **Barclaycard**, Travel Accident Insurance of up to £50,000 is included but this isn't meant to take the place of normal travel insurance; similarly, its well-advertised International Rescue service can provide emergency cash, arrange hospital treatment and help with lost or stolen travel documents, but you still need a good travel insurance policy to cover the eventual costs.

In **Ireland**, travel insurance is best obtained through a travel specialist such as USIT (see p.13 for address and phone). Their policies cost £21 for 6–10 days, £31 for one month. Discounts are offered to students of any age and anyone under 35.

In **Australia and New Zealand**, travel insurance is put together by the airlines and travel agent groups such as UTAG, AFTA, Cover-More and Ready Plan in conjuction with insurance companies. They are all similar in premium and coverage, however Ready Plan give the best value-for-money coverage. Adventure sports are usually covered, but not unassisted diving without an Open Water licence, so check your policy if that's in your itinerary. A typical policy will cost A$190/NZ$220 for one month, A$270/NZ$320 for two months and A$330/NZ$400 for three months.

MAPS AND INFORMATION

The first place to head for information, and for free maps of the country and many **towns, is the Mexican Government Ministry of Tourism (Secretaría de Turismo, abbreviated to SECTUR), which has offices throughout Mexico and abroad. It's always worth stocking up in advance with as many relevant brochures and plans as they'll let you have, since offices in Mexico are frequently closed or have run out.**

Once you're in Mexico, you'll find **tourist offices** (sometimes called *turismos*) run by SECTUR, in addition to some run by state and municipal authorities; quite often there'll be two or three rival ones in the same town. It's quite impossible to generalize about the services offered: some are extremely friendly and helpful, with free information and leaflets by the cart-load; others are barely capable of answering the simplest enquiry. You can call SECTUR in México from anywhere in the rest of the country at local rates on ☎1-800/9-03-92.

MEXICAN GOVERNMENT TOURIST OFFICES OVERSEAS

You can phone the Mexican Government Tourism Office toll-free from anywhere in Canada or the USA on ☎1-800/44-MEXICO.

USA
1911 Pennsylvania Ave NW, Washington, DC 20006 (☎202/728-1750, fax 728-1758). 70 E Lake St, Suite 1413, Chicago, IL 60601 (☎312/606-9252, fax 606-9012). 2707 North Loop West, Suite 450, Houston, TX 77008 (☎713/880-5153, fax 880-1833). 10100 Santa Monica Blvd, Suite 224, LA, CA 90067 (☎310/203-8191, fax 203-8316). 405 Park Ave, Suite 1401, New York, NY 10022 (☎212/755 7261, fax 755-2874). 2333 Ponce de Leon Blvd, Suite 710, Coral Gables, FL 33134 (☎305/443-9160, fax 443-1186). Epcot Center, Ave of the Stars, Lake Buenavista, FL 32830 (☎407/827 5315).

CANADA
1 Place Ville Marie, Suite 1526, Montréal, PQ H3B 2B5 (☎514/871-1052, fax 871-3825). 2 Bloor St West, Suite 1801, Toronto, ON M4W 3E2 (☎416/925-0704, fax 925-6061). 999 W Hastings St, Suite 1610, Vancouver, BC V6C 1M3 (☎604/669-2845, fax 669-3498).

UK
60–61 Trafalgar Square, London WC2N 5DS (☎0171/734 1058).

TRAVEL BOOK AND MAP OUTLETS

NORTH AMERICA

Rand McNally have stores across the USA; call ☎1-800/333-0136 (ext 2111) for the address of your nearest store, or for direct mail maps.

Travel Books & Language Center, 4931 Cordell Ave, Bethesda, MD 20814 (☎1-800/220-2665).

Ulysses Travel Bookshop, 4176 St-Denis, Montréal, PQ H2W 2M5 (☎514/843-9447).

The Complete Traveler Bookstore, 199 Madison Ave, NY 10016 (☎212/685-9007); 3207 Fillmore St, San Francisco, CA 92123 (☎415/923-1511).

Traveler's Bookstore, 22 W 52nd St, NY 10019 (☎212/664-0995).

Sierra Club Bookstore, 6014 College Ave, Oakland, CA 94618 (☎510/658-7470).

Phileas Fogg's Books & Maps, #87 Stanford Shopping Center, Palo Alto, CA 94304 (☎1-800/533-FOGG).

Open Air Books and Maps, 25 Toronto St, Toronto, ON M5R 2C1 (☎416/363-0719).

World Wide Books and Maps, 552 Seymour St, Vancouver, BC V6B 3J5 (☎604/687-3320).

Adventurous Traveler Bookstore, PO Box 1468, Williston, VT 05495 (☎1-800/282-3963; *www.AdventurousTraveler.com*).

The Map Store, 1636 1st St, Washington DC 20006 (☎202/628-2608).

UK AND IRELAND

Maps by **mail or phone order** are available from Stanfords (☎0171/836 1321) and several of the other listed suppliers.

Daunt Books, 83 Marylebone High St, London W1M 3DE (☎0171/224 2295); 193 Haverstock Hill, London NW3 4QL (☎0171/794 4006).

National Map Centre, 22–24 Caxton St, London SW1H 0QU (☎0171/222 2466).

Stanfords, 12–14 Long Acre, London WC2E 9LP (☎0171/836 1321); within Campus Travel at 52 Grosvenor Gardens, London SW1W 0AG (☎0171/730 1314); and within the British Airways shop at 156 Regent St, London W1R 5TA (☎0171/434 4744); 29 Corn Street, Bristol BS1 1HT (☎0117/929 9966)

The Travel Bookshop, 13–15 Blenheim Crescent, London W11 2EE (☎0171/229 5260).

Eason's, 40 O'Connell St, Dublin 1 (☎01/873 3811).

Waterstone's, 7 Dawson St, Dublin 2 (☎01/679 1415); Queens Bldg, 8 Royal Ave, Belfast BT1 1DA (☎01232/247355).

Aberdeen Map Shop, 74 Skene St, Aberdeen AB10 1QE (☎01224/637999).

Heffers Map Shop, 3rd Floor, 19 Sidney St, Cambridge CB2 3HL (☎01223/568467).

Blackwell's, 53 Broad Street, Oxford 0X1 3BQ (☎01865/792792); 13–17 Royal Arcade, Cardiff CF1 2PR (☎01222/395036).

Newcastle Map Centre, 55 Grey St, Newcastle-upon-Tyne NE1 6EF (☎0191/261-5622).

AUSTRALIA AND NEW ZEALAND

The Map Shop, 16a Peel St, Adelaide, SA 5000 (☎08/8231 2033).

Specialty Maps, 58 Albert St, Auckland (☎09/307 2217).

Hema, 187 George St, Brisbane, QLD 4000 (☎07/3290 0322).

Mapland, 372 Little Bourke St, Melbourne, VIC 3000 (☎03/9670 4383).

Perth Map Centre, 884 Hay St, Perth, WA 6000 (☎08/9322 5733).

Travel Bookshop, Shop 3, 175 Liverpool St, Sydney, NSW 2000 (☎02/9261 8200).

MAPS

Good **maps** of Mexico are rare. Road maps on a larger scale than the free handouts (though still not exactly detailed) can be bought at any large bookshop: the Hallwag 1:2,600,000 is one of the clearest, the Nelles 1:2,500,000 better still. Bartholomew's and HFET's 1:3,000,000 maps, and Geocenter's 1:2,500,000, have coloured contours for altitude, and show other physical features, but are weaker on road details. Kevin Healey's 1:3,300,000 shows relief, and also has a map of mileage and driving times, in addition to one showing where indigenous peoples live. **In the USA**, route maps can be bought at gas stations (Mobil and the AAA both produce reasonable ones).

In Mexico, the best maps are those published by Patria, which cover each state individually, and by Guía Roji, who also publish a Mexican Road Atlas and a México street guide. Both makes of map are widely available — try branches of Sanborn's or large Pemex stations.

More detailed, **large-scale maps** – for hiking or climbing – are harder to come by. The most detailed, easily available area maps are produced by International Travel Map Productions, whose 1:1,000,000 Travellers' Reference Map series includes the peninsulas of Baja California and the Yucatán. INEGI, the Mexican government map-makers, also produce very good topographic maps on various scales. They have an office in every state capital and an outlet at México's airport. Unfortunately, stocks can run rather low, so don't count on being able to buy the ones that you want.

GETTING AROUND

Distances in Mexico can be huge, and if you're intending to travel on public transport, you should quickly get used to the idea of long, long journeys. Getting from Tijuana to México, for example, could take nearly two days non-stop. Although public transport at ground level is frequent and reasonably efficient everywhere, taking an internal flight at least once may be worthwhile for the time it saves.

BUSES

Within Mexico, **buses** (long-distance buses are called *camiones*, rather than *autobuses*, in Mexican Spanish) are by far the most common and efficient form of public transport. There are an unbelievable number of them, run by a multitude of companies, and connecting even the smallest of villages. Long-distance services generally rely on very comfortable and dependable vehicles; remote villages are more commonly connected by what look like (and often are) recycled school buses from north of the border.

There are basically two classes of bus, first (*primera*) and second (*segunda*), though on major long-distance routes there's often little to differentiate the two. **First-class** vehicles have numbered, reserved seats, videos and air conditioning, though increasingly many **second-class** lines have all these, too. The main difference will be in the number of stops – second-class buses call at more places, and consequently take longer to get where they're going – and the fare, which is about ten percent higher on first-class services, and sometimes a lot more. You may be able to get a discount with a student card, though it's not, it must be said, especially likely. Most people choose first-class for any appreciably long distance, and second for short trips or if the destination is too small for first-class buses to stop, but you should certainly not be put off second-class if it seems more convenient – it may even prove less crowded. Air conditioning is not necessarily a boon – there's nothing more uncomfortable than a bus with sealed windows and a broken air-conditioner. The videos, by the way, are often in English, and aren't necessarily tasteful family viewing.

On important routes there are also **de luxe or pullman buses**, with names like Primera Plus or Turistar Plus and fares around thirty percent higher than those of first-class buses. They have few if any stops, and waitress service and free snacks and drinks over longer distances, extra-comfortable airline seating, and air conditioning that works – be sure to keep a sweater handy, as it can get very cold. They may also be emptier, which could mean more space to stretch out and sleep. Pullman services almost all have **computerized reservation** services and may accept credit cards in payment: these facilities are increasingly common with the larger regular bus lines, too.

Most towns of any size have a modern, centralized bus station, known as the **Central Camionera** or **Central de Autobuses**, often a long way from the town centre. Where there is no unified terminus you may find separate first- and second-class terminals, or individual ones for each company, sometimes little more than bus stops at the side of the road. In almost every bus station, there is some form of **baggage deposit** (left luggage) office – usually known as a *guardería*, *consigna* or simply *equipaje*, and costing about US$1–2.50/£0.60–1.70 per item per day. Before leaving anything, make sure that the place will be open when you come to collect. If there's no formal facility, staff at the bus companies' baggage dispatching offices can often be persuaded to look after things for a short while.

Always check your route and arrival time, and whenever possible buy tickets from the bus station in advance to get the best (or any) seats; count on paying about US$3–4/£2–3 for every 100km covered. There is very rarely any problem **getting a place** on a bus from its point of origin or from really big towns. In smaller, mid-route places, however, you may have to wait for the bus to arrive (or at least to leave its last stop) before discovering if there are any seats – the increased prevalence of computerized ticketing is easing the problem. Often there are too few seats, and without fluent and loud Spanish you may lose out in the fight for the ticket clerk's attention. Alternatively, there's almost always a bus described as **local**, which means it originates from where you are (as opposed to a **de paso** bus, which started somewhere else), and tickets for these can be bought well in advance.

Weekends, holiday season, school holidays and fiestas can also overload services to certain destinations: again the only real answer is to buy tickets in advance, though you could also try the cheaper second-class lines, where they'll pack you in standing, or take whatever's going to the next town along the way and try for a *local* from there. A word with the driver and a small tip can also sometimes work wonders.

Terms to look out for on the timetable, besides *local* and *de paso*, include *vía corta* (by the short route) and *directo* or *expresso* (direct/non-stop – in theory at least). *Salida* is departure, *llegada* arrival. A decent **road map** will be extremely helpful in working out which buses are going to pass through your destination.

The legendary craziness of Mexican **bus drivers** is nowadays a thing of the past, and many bus companies have installed warning lights and buzzers to indicate when the driver is exceeding the speed limit (though these are often ignored by the driver). **Mechanical breakdown**, in fact, is a far more common cause of delay than accidents. In recent years the government has been trying to improve the safety record through regular mechanical checks and also by keeping tabs on the drivers.

TRAINS

Rail travel is generally less than half the price of the bus in Mexico, but also much slower and rarely on time – that's hours late, not minutes. Nor are trains frequent, with only one a day or three a week on most lines. Many services have been cut since privatization in 1995. In general, train travel is only recommended in northern and central Mexico. The most popular journeys include those from the border to México (where sleeper services represent great value), México to Oaxaca, and the amazing Copper Canyon Railway (see p.125).

There is now only **one class** of travel on Mexican trains (equivalent to the old first class), and there are no sleepers, though seats are comfortable and do recline. **Tickets** are sold only on the day of departure (in places with only one train a day, the *taquilla* may open for ticket sales just an hour or so before the scheduled departure time, which can of course be several hours before the train actually turns up). During holiday periods you may have to queue for the best part of a day in order to get your ticket. To be sure of a seat, it's an idea to turn up fairly early, since overbooking is normal.

Train schedules are hard to come by in Mexico, but are published each month internationally in Thomas Cook's Overseas Timetable (the blue volume), which can be consulted in most public reference libraries in North America, the British Isles, Australia and New Zealand.

PLANES

There are more than fifty **airports** in Mexico with regular passenger flights run by local airlines, plus several smaller airports with feeder services. The two big companies, both formerly state-owned and with international as well as domestic flights, are **Aeroméxico** and **Mexicana**, which between them connect most places to México, usually several times a day. More recently, a handful of smaller, regional airlines have sprung up. Of these, **Aviacsa** serves the Yucatán, Chiapas, Oaxaca and Monterrey, **Aeromar** operates in the Bajío, and **Aero California** mainly in the northwest of the country, especially Baja California. **Taesa** has services mostly in the north, but also operates flights to the Yucatán. **Aerolineas Internacionales**, despite its name, runs internal flights only, from its hub at Cuernavaca. Information about the smaller airlines is not usually available in cities not served by them, nor from Aeroméxico and Mexicana offices, though a good travel agent should be able to help track down details.

Internal **air fares** reflect the popularity of the route: the more popular the trip, the lower the price. Thus the flight from Tijuana to México costs little more than the first-class bus, while the journey from Tijuana to La Paz is three times the bus fare, or twice as much as the rather longer Tijuana–México route. Obviously, fares like the first are a real bargain, but even on more expensive routes they can be well worth it for the time they save. While the smaller airlines are usually cheaper, the price of a ticket on a particular flight doesn't normally vary from agent to agent. There are few discounts, and it's usually twice as much for a round-trip as a one-way ticket.

Mexicana and Aeroméxico offer **multi-flight airpasses**, available only outside Mexico, valid for 2 to 45 days, and with different prices for 2- to 5-flight passes, depending on which region of the country is covered. They save you time spent buying air tickets in Mexico, but they're not a great bargain otherwise. In the US contact the airlines direct; in the UK, call a specialist agent or Mexicana.

FERRIES

Ferries connect Baja California with a trio of ports on the Pacific mainland: Santa Rosalía to Guaymas, and La Paz to Mazatlán and Topolobampo (for Los Mochis). There are also smaller boats to islands off the Caribbean coast: from Playa del Carmen and Puerto Morelos to Cozumel, from Chetumal to Xcalak, and from Cancún to Isla Mujeres. Though not as cheap as they once were, all these services are still pretty reasonable: see the relevant chapters for current fares.

DRIVING

Getting your car into Mexico **properly documented** (see "Getting there" on p.9) is just the start of your problems. Although most people who venture in by car enjoy it and get out again with no more than minor incidents, driving in Mexico does require a good deal of care and concentration, and almost inevitably involves at least one brush with bureaucracy or the law, although the police have eased up of late in response to pressure from above to stop putting the bite on tourists.

Renting a car in Mexico – especially if done with a specific itinerary in mind, just for a day or two – avoids many of the problems and is often an extremely good way of seeing quickly a small area that would take days to explore using public transport. In all the tourist resorts and major cities there are any number of competing agencies, with local operations usually charging less than the well-known chains. You should check rates carefully, though – the basic cost of renting a VW Beetle for the day may be as little as US$15/£10, but by the time you have added insurance, tax and mileage it can easily end up being three or four times that. Daily rates that include unlimited mileage start at around US$55/£35; weekly rates can be better, from about US$250/£160. For shorter distances, mopeds and motorbikes are also available in most resorts.

Drivers from the US, Canada, Britain, Ireland Australia and New Zealand will find that their **licences** are valid in Mexico, though an interna-

---

USEFUL AIRLINE NUMBERS

Aero California ☎1-800/237-6225 (US); ☎5/207-13-92 (Mexico).
Aerolineas Internacionales ☎73/11-22-63 (Mexico).
Aerolitoral ☎1-800/3-62-02 (Mexico).
Aeromar ☎5/627-02-09 (Mexico).
Aeroméxico ☎1-800/237-6639 or ☎713/939-7535 (US); ☎1-800/9-09-99 (toll-free in Mexico); *www.wotw.com/aeromexico*.
Aviacsa ☎1-800/0-06-22 (toll-free in Mexico).
Mexicana ☎1-800/531-7921 (US); ☎1-800/5-02-20 (toll-free in Mexico); *www.mexicana.com*
Taesa ☎1-800/328-2372 (US); ☎1-800/904-63-00 (Mexico).

CAR RENTAL RESERVATION NUMBERS

Avis
USA ☎1-800/331-1084
Canada ☎1-800/331-1084
UK ☎0181/848 8733
Ireland ☎021/281111
Australia ☎1800/225533
New Zealand ☎0800/655111
Web site www.avis.com

Budget
USA ☎1-800/527-0700
Canada ☎1-800/527-0700
UK ☎0800/181181
Ireland ☎0903/24668
Australia ☎13/2727
New Zealand ☎09/375 2222
Web site www.budgetsales.com

Dollar (Europcar/InterRent)
USA ☎1-800/800-4000
Canada ☎1-800/800-4000
UK ☎0345/222525
Ireland ☎01/668 1777
Web site www.europcar.com

Hertz
USA ☎1-800/654-3001
Canada ☎1-800/263-0600
UK ☎0990/996699

Ireland ☎01/676 7476
Australia ☎1800/550067
New Zealand ☎0800/655955
Web site www.hertz.com

Holiday Autos
USA ☎1-800/422-7737
Canada ☎1-800/422-7737
UK ☎0990/300400
Ireland ☎01/454 9090

National
USA ☎1-800/CAR-RENT
Canada ☎1-800/CAR-RENT
UK ☎0990/365365
Ireland ☎021/320755
Australia ☎03/9329 5000
New Zealand ☎0800/800115
Web site www.nationalcar.com

Thrifty
USA ☎1-800/367-2277
Canada ☎1-800/367-2277
UK ☎01494/442110
Ireland ☎01/679 9420
Australia ☎02/9360 4055
New Zealand ☎09/275 6666
Web site www.thrifty.com

tional one is still advisable, especially if yours has no photo on it. It's important to remember you are required to **have all your documents with you** when driving. Insurance is not compulsory, but you'd be foolhardy not to take some out.

The government oil company, Pemex, has a monopoly and sells two types of **fuel**: Nova (leaded) and Magna Sin (unleaded), both of which cost slightly more than regular unleaded north of the border, at about US$1.50 per US gallon. Magna Sin is increasingly available, in response to howls of outrage from US motorists who have ruined their engines using Nova.

Mexican **roads and traffic**, however, are your chief worry. Traffic circulates on the right, and the normal **speed limit** is 40km/hr (25mph) in built-up areas, 70km/hr (43mph) in open country, and 110km/hr (68mph) on the freeway. Some of the new highways are excellent, and the toll (*cuota*) super-highways are better still, though extremely expensive to drive on. Away from the major population

centres, however, roads are often narrow, winding and potholed, with livestock wandering across at unexpected moments. Get out of the way of Mexican bus and truck drivers (and remember that if you signal left to them on a stretch of open road, it means it's clear to overtake). Every town and village on the road, however tiny, limits the speed of through-traffic with a series of **topes** (concrete or metal speed bumps) across the road. Look out for the warning signs and take them seriously; the bumps are often huge. Most people suggest, too, that you should never drive at night (and not just for road safety reasons: see the box) – sound advice even if not always practical. Any good road map should provide details of the more common symbols used on Mexican **road signs**, and SECTUR have a pamphlet on driving in Mexico in which they're also featured. One convention to be aware of is that the first driver to flash their lights at a junction, or where only one vehicle can pass, has right of way: they're *not* inviting you to go first.

BANDITRY: A WARNING

You should be aware when driving in Mexico, especially in a foreign vehicle, of the danger of bandits. **Robberies and even more serious assaults** of motorists do occur, above all in the northwest and especially in the state of Sinaloa. Sometimes robbers pose as police, sometimes as hitchhikers or motorists in distress, so think twice about offering a lift or a helping hand. They may also try to make you stop by indicating there's something wrong with your vehicle. On the other hand, remember that there are plenty of legitimate police checkpoints along the main roads, where you must stop. Roads where there have been regular reports of problems, and where you should certainly try to avoid driving at night, include Hwy-15 (Los Mochis–Mazatlán) and express Hwy-1 in Sinaloa, Hwy-5 (México–Acapulco) in Guerrero, Hwy-75 (Oaxaca–Tuxtepec), Hwy-57 (San Luis Potosí–Matahuela), and near the border, in particular on Hwy-2 (Mexicali–Agua Prieta) and Hwy-40 (Matamoros–Monterrey). The US embassy in Mexico advises **never driving after dark**.

In most large towns you'll find extensive **one-way systems**. Traffic direction is often poorly marked (look for small arrows affixed to lamp-posts), though this is less of a problem than it sounds: simply note the directions in which the parked cars are facing.

Parking in cities is always going to be a hassle, too – the restrictions are complicated and for-eigners are easy pickings for traffic police, who usually remove one or both plates in lieu of a ticket (retrieving them can be an expensive and time-consuming business). Since theft is also a real threat, you'll usually have to pay extra for a hotel with secure parking. You may well also have to fork over on-the-spot "fines" for traffic offences (real or imaginary). In the **capital**, cars are banned from driving on one day of every week, determined by their licence number (see p.275).

Unless your car is a basic model VW, Ford or Dodge (all of which are manufactured in Mexico), **parts** are expensive and hard to come by – bring a basic spares kit. **Tires** suffer particularly badly on burning-hot Mexican roads, and you should carry at least one good spare. Roadside *vulcan-izadoras* and *llanteros* can do temporary repairs; new tires are expensive, but remoulds aren't a good idea on hot roads at high speed. If you have a **breakdown**, there is a free highway mechanic service known as the **Ángeles Verdes** (Green Angels). As well as patrolling all major routes looking for beleaguered motorists, they can be reached by phone via México on ☎5/250-01-23 or 250-82-21 (although they don't actually operate inside the capital, where you should call the AAM – equivalent of the AA or the AAA – on ☎578-75-31). The Ángeles Verdes speak English.

Should you have a minor **accident**, try to come to some arrangement with the other party – involving the police will only make matters worse, and Mexican drivers will be as anxious to avoid doing so as you will. Also, if you witness an accident, don't get involved – witnesses can be locked up along with those directly implicated to prevent them from leaving before the case comes up. In any more serious incident, contact your consulate and your Mexican insurance company as soon as possible.

HITCHING

It's possible to **hitch** your way around Mexico, but it can't be recommended – certainly not in the north. Lifts are relatively scarce, distances vast, risks high, and the roadside often a harsh environment if you get dropped at some obscure turnoff. You may also be harassed by the police. Many drivers – especially truck drivers – expect you to contribute to their expenses, which you may think rather defeats the object of hitching. In short, hitching is **not safe**: robbery is not uncommon, and women in particular (but also men) are advised not to hitch alone. You should wait to know where the driver is going before getting in, rather than stating your own destination first, sit by a door and keep your baggage to hand in case you need to leave in a hurry (feigned carsickness is one way to get a driver to stop). Particularly avoid areas frequented by *bandidos*, such as those listed in the box above.

That said, however, over short stretches, to get to villages where there's no bus or simply to while away the time spent waiting for one, you may find yourself hitching and you'll probably come across genuine friendliness and certainly meet people you wouldn't otherwise. It does help if your Spanish will stretch to a conversation.

LOCAL TRANSPORTATION

Public transport within Mexican towns and cities is always plentiful and inexpensive, though also crowded and not very user-friendly. México has an extensive, excellent **metro** system, and there are smaller metros in Guadalajara and Monterrey, but elsewhere you'll be reliant on **buses**, which pour out clouds of choking diesel fumes; often there's a flat-fare system, but this varies from place to place. Wherever possible we've indicated which bus to take and where to catch it, but often only a local will fully understand the intricacies of the system and you may well have to ask: the main destinations of the bus are usually marked on the windscreen, which helps.

In bigger places **combis** or **colectivos** offer a faster and perhaps less crowded alternative for only a little more money. These are minibuses, vans or large saloons that run along a fixed route to set destinations; they'll pick you up and drop you off wherever you like along the way, and you simply pay the driver for the distance travelled. In México, combis are known as *peseros*.

Regular **taxis** can also be good value, but be aware of rip-offs – unless you're confident that the meter is working, fix a price before you get in. In the big cities, there may be tables of fixed prices posted at prominent spots. At almost every **airport** and at some of the biggest bus stations you'll find a booth selling vouchers for taxis into town at a fixed price depending on the part of town you want to go to – sometimes there's a choice of paying more for a private car or less to share. This will invariably cost less than just hailing a cab outside the terminal, and will certainly offer extra security. In every case you should know the name of a hotel to head for, or they'll take you to the one that pays the biggest commission (they may try to do this anyway, saying that yours is full). Never accept a ride in any kind of unofficial or unmarked taxi.

ACCOMMODATION

Mexican hotels may describe themselves as anything from *paradores, posadas* and *casas de huéspedes* to plain *hoteles*, all terms that are used more or less interchangeably. A *parador* is totally unrelated to its upmarket Spanish namesake, for example, and although in theory *casa de huéspedes* means a small cheap place like a guest house, you won't find this necessarily to be the case.

Finding a room is rarely difficult – in most old and not overly touristy places the cheap hotels are concentrated around the main plaza (the zócalo), with others near the market, train station or bus station (or where the bus station *used* to be, before it moved out of town). In bigger cities, there's usually a relatively small area in which you'll find the bulk of the less expensive possibilities. The more modern and expensive places often lie on the outskirts of towns, accessible only by car or taxi. The only times you're likely to have big problems finding somewhere to stay are in coastal resorts over the peak Christmas season, at Easter, on Mexican holidays, and almost anywhere during a local fiesta, when it's well worth trying to reserve ahead.

All rooms should have an official **price** displayed, though this is not always a guide to quality – a filthy fleapit and a beautifully run converted mansion may charge exactly the same, even if they're right next door to each other. To guarantee quality, the only recourse is never to take a room without seeing it first – you soon learn to spot which establishments have promise. You should

ACCOMMODATION PRICE CODES

All the accommodation listed in *The Rough Guide to Mexico* has been categorized into one of nine **price bands**, as set out below. The prices quoted are in US dollars and normally refer to the cheapest available rates for two people sharing in high season.

① less than US$5	④ US$15–25	⑦ US$60–80
② US$5–10	⑤ US$25–40	⑧ US$80–100
③ US$10–15	⑥ US$40–60	⑨ more than US$100

never pay more than the official rate (though just occasionally the sign may not have kept up with inflation) and in the low season you can often pay less. The charging system varies: sometimes it's per person, but usually the price quoted will be for the room regardless of how many people occupy it, so **sharing** can mean big savings. A room with one double bed (*cama matrimonial*) is invariably cheaper than a room with two singles (*doble* or *con dos camas*), and most hotels have large "family" rooms with several beds, which are tremendous value for groups. In the big resorts, there are lots of **apartments** that sleep six or more and include cooking facilities, for yet more savings. A little gentle haggling rarely goes amiss, and many places will have some rooms that cost less, so just ask (*¿Tiene un cuarto mas barato?*).

Air conditioning (*aire acondicionado*) is a feature that inflates prices – often you are offered a choice. Unless it's quite unbearably hot and humid, a room with a simple ceiling fan (*ventilador*) is generally better; except in the most expensive places, the air-conditioning units are almost always noisy and inefficient, whereas a fan can be left running silently all night and the draught helps to keep insects away. It might seem too obvious to mention, but be careful of the ceiling fans, which are often quite low. Don't stand on the bed, and keep well clear of them when removing any clothes from the upper body. In winter, especially at altitude or in the desert, it will of course be **heating** rather than cooling that you want – if there isn't any, make sure there's enough bedding and ask for extra blankets if necessary.

When looking at a room, you should always check its **insect proofing**. Cockroaches are common, and there's not much anyone can do about them, but decent netting will keep mosquitoes and worse out and allow you to sleep. If the mosquitoes are really bad you'll probably see where previous occupants have splattered them on the walls. Ditto for bedbugs around the bed.

CAMPSITES, HAMMOCKS AND CABAÑAS

There is not usually much alternative to staying in hotels. **Camping** is easy enough if you are hiking in the back country, or happy simply to crash on a beach – beaches cannot be privately owned in Mexico, but robberies are common, especially in places with a lot of tourists. There are very few organized campsites, and those that do exist are first and foremost **trailer parks**, not particularly pleasant to pitch tents in. Of course, if you have a van or RV you can use these or park just about anywhere else – there are a good number of facilities in the well-travelled areas, especially down the Pacific coast and Baja.

If you're planning to do a lot of camping, an **international camping carnet** is a good investment, serving as useful ID and getting you discounts at member sites. It is available from home motoring organizations.

In a lot of less official campsites, you will be able to **rent a hammock** and a place to sling it for the same price as pitching a tent (around US$3/£2), maybe less, and certainly less if you're packing your own hammock (Mexico is a good place to buy these, especially in and around Mérida).

Beach huts, or **cabañas**, are found at the more rustic, backpacker-oriented beach resorts, and sometimes inland. Usually just a wooden or palm-frond shack with a hammock slung up inside (or a place to sling your own), they often do not even have electricity, though as a resort gets more popular, they tend to transform into sturdier beach bungalows with mod cons and higher prices. At backwaters and beaches too untouristed for even cabañas, you should still be able to sling a hammock somewhere (probably the local bar or restaurant, where the palapa serves as shelter and shade).

YOUTH HOSTELS

There are 26 **youth hostels** in Mexico, charging around US$3–5 per person for basic, single-sex dorm facilities. A YH card is not usually neces-

YOUTH HOSTEL ASSOCIATIONS

MEXICO
Dirección General de Causa Joven, SEP,
Serapio Rendón 76, Col San Rafael, Deleg
Cuauhtémoc, CP 06470, México DF (☎5/705-60-72).

USA
**Hostelling International-American Youth
Hostels (HI-AYH)**, 733 15th St NW, Suite 840,
Washington DC 20005 (☎202/783-6161;
www.hiayh.org).

CANADA
Canadian Hostelling Association, Suite 400,
205 Catherine St, Ottawa, ON K2P 1C3
(☎1-800/663-5777 or 613/237-7884).

UK AND IRELAND
Youth Hostel Association (YHA), Trevelyan
House, 8 St Stephen's Hill, St Albans, Herts AL1

2DY (☎01727/845047; *www.yha-england-
wales.org.uk*).
Scottish Youth Hostel Association, 7 Glebe
Crescent, Stirling, FK8 2JA (☎01786/451181;
www.syha.org.uk).
**Youth Hostel Association of Northern
Ireland**, 22 Donegal Rd, Belfast, BT12 5JN
(☎01232/315435).
An Óige, 61 Mountjoy St, Dublin 7 (☎01/830
4555; *www.irelandyha.org*).

AUSTRALIA
Australian Youth Hostel Association, Level 3,
10 Mallett St, Camperdown, NSW 2050
(☎02/9565 1699; *www.yha.org.au*).

NEW ZEALAND
Youth Hostel Association of New Zealand,
PO Box 436, Christchurch 1 (☎03/379 9970;
www.yha.org.nz).

sary, but you may pay more without one. **Rules**,
in most places, are strict (no booze, 11pm curfew,
up and out by 9am) and at holiday periods they're
often taken over completely by Mexican groups.

EATING AND DRINKING

**Whatever your preconceptions about
Mexican food, if you've never eaten in
Mexico they will almost certainly be wrong.
It bears very little resemblance to the con-**
coctions served in "Mexican" restaurants
or fast-food joints in other parts of the world
– certainly you won't find chile con carne
outside the tourist spots of Acapulco. Nor, as
a rule, is it especially spicy; indeed, a more
common complaint from visitors is that after
a while it all seems rather bland.

WHERE TO EAT

Basic meals are served at **restaurantes**, but you
can get breakfast, snacks and often full meals at
cafés too; there are **take-out** and **fast-food**
places serving sandwiches, *tortas* (filled rolls) and
tacos (*tortillas* folded over with a filling), as well
as more international-style food; there are establishments called **jugerías** (look for signs saying
Jugos y Licuados) serving nothing but wonderful
juices (*jugos*), **licuados** (fruit blended with
water or milk) and **fruit salads**; and there are
street stalls dishing out everything from tacos to

orange juice to ready-made crisp vegetable salads sprinkled with chile-salt and lime. Just about every **market** in the country has a cooked food section, too, and these are invariably the cheapest places to eat, if not always in the most enticing surroundings. In the big cities and resorts, of course, there are international restaurants too – **pizza** and **Chinese food** are ubiquitous.

When you're **travelling**, as often as not the food will come to you; at every stop people clamber onto buses and trains (especially second-class ones) with baskets of home-made foods, local specialities, cold drinks, or jugs of coffee. You'll find wonderful things this way that you won't come across in restaurants, but they should be treated with caution, and with an eye to hygiene.

WHAT TO EAT

The basic Mexican **diet** is essentially one of corn (*maíz*) and its products, supplemented by beans and chiles. These three things appear in an almost infinite variety of guises. Some dishes are hot (ask *¿es picante?*), but on the whole you add your own seasoning from the bowls of home-made chile sauce on the table – these are often surprisingly mild, but they can be fiery and should always be approached with caution.

There are at least a hundred different types of **chile**, fresh or dried, in colours ranging from pale green to almost black, and all sorts of different sizes (large, mild ones are often stuffed with meat or cheese and rice to make *chiles rellenos*). Each has a distinct flavour and by no means all are hot (which is why we don't use the English term "chilli" for them), although the most common, *chiles jalapeños*, small and either green or red, certainly are. You'll always find a chile sauce (salsa) on the table when you eat, and in any

decent restaurant it will be home-made; no two are quite alike. Chile is also the basic ingredient of more complex cooked sauces, notably **mole**, an extraordinary mixture of chocolate, chile, and fifty or so other ingredients traditionally served with turkey or chicken (the classic *mole poblano*), but also sometimes with *enchiladas* (rolled, filled tortillas baked in sauce). Another speciality to look out for is *chiles en nogada*, a bizarre combination of stuffed green peppers covered in a white sauce made of walnuts and cream cheese or sour cream, topped with red pomegranate: the colours reflect the national flag and it's served especially in September around Independence Day, which is also when the walnuts are fresh.

Beans (*frijoles*), an invariable accompaniment to egg dishes – and with almost everything else too – are of the pinto or kidney variety and are almost always served *refritos*, ie boiled up, mashed, and "refried" (though actually this is the first time they're fried). They're even better if you can get them whole in some kind of country-style soup or stew, often with pork or bacon, for example *frijoles charros*.

Corn, in some form or another, features in virtually everything. In its natural state it is known as *elote* and you can find it roasted on the cob at street stalls or in soups and stews such as *pozole* (with meat). Far more often, though, it is ground into flour for **tortillas**, flat maize pancakes of which you will get a stack to accompany your meal in any cheap Mexican restaurant (in more expensive or touristy places you'll get bread rolls, *bolillos*). Tortillas can also be made of wheatflour (*de harina*), which may be preferable to outsiders' tastes, but these are rare except in the north.

Tortillas form the basis of many specifically Mexican dishes, often described as *antojitos* (appetizers, light courses) on menus. Simplest of

VEGETARIAN FOOD IN MEXICO

Vegetarians can eat well in Mexico, although it does take caution to avoid meat altogether. Many Mexican dishes are naturally meat-free and there are always fabulous fruits and vegetables available. Most restaurants serve vegetable soups and rice, and items like quesadillas, *chiles rellenos*, and even tacos and enchiladas often come with non-meat fillings. Another possibility is *queso fundido*, simply (and literally) melted cheese, served with tortillas and salsa. Eggs, too, are served anywhere at any time, and many *jugerías* (see p.38) serve huge mixed salads to which grains and nuts can be added.

However, do bear in mind that vegetarianism, though growing, is not particularly common, and a simple cheese and chile dish may have some meat added to "improve" it. Worse, most of the fat used for frying is animal fat (usually lard), so that even something as unadorned as refried beans may not be strictly vegetarian (especially as a bone or some stock may have been added to the water the beans were originally boiled in). Even so-called **vegetarian restaurants**, which are increasingly common and can be found in all the big cities, often include chicken on the menu. You may well have better luck in **pizza** places and Chinese or other ethnic restaurants.

these are **tacos**, tortillas filled with almost anything, from beef and chicken to green vegetables, and then fried (they're usually still soft, not at all like the baked taco shells you may have had at home). With cheese, either or alone or in addition to other fillings, they are called **quesadillas**. **Enchiladas** are rolled, filled tortillas covered in chile sauce and baked; *enchiladas suizas* are filled with chicken and have sour cream over them. **Tostadas** are flat tortillas toasted crisp and piled with ingredients – usually meat, salad vegetables and cheese (smaller bite-size versions are known as *sopes*). Tortillas torn up and cooked together with meat and (usually hot) sauce are called **chilaquiles**: this is a traditional way of using up leftovers. Especially in the north, you'll also come across **burritos** (large wheatflour tortillas, stuffed with anything, but usually beef and potatoes or beans) and **gorditas** (delicious small, fat, corn tortillas, sliced open, stuffed and baked or fried). Also short and fat are **tlacoyos**, tortillas made with a stuffing of mashed beans, often using blue cornflour, which gives them a rather bizarre colour.

Cornflour, too, is the basis of **tamales** – found predominantly in central and southern Mexico – which are a sort of cornmeal pudding, stuffed, flavoured, and steamed in corn or banana leaves. They can be either savoury, with additions like prawn or *elote*, or sweet when made with something like coconut.

Except in the north, **meat** is not especially good – beef in particular is usually thin and tough; pork, kid and occasionally lamb are better. If the menu doesn't specify what kind of meat it is, it's

usually pork – even *bistec* can be pork unless it specifies *bistec de res*. For thick American-style steaks, look for a sign saying *Carnes Hereford* or for a "New York Cut" description (only in expensive places or in the north). **Seafood** is almost always fresh and delicious, especially the spicy prawn or octopus cocktails which you find in most coastal areas (*coctel* or *campechana de camaron/pulpo*), but beware of eating uncooked shellfish. **Eggs** – in country areas genuinely free-range and flavoursome – feature on every menu as the most basic of meals, and at some time you must try the uniquely Mexican combinations of *huevos rancheros* or *huevos a la mexicana*.

MEALS

Traditionally, Mexicans eat a light **breakfast** very early, a **snack** of tacos or eggs in mid-morning, **lunch** (the main meal of the day) around two o'clock or later – in theory followed by a siesta, but decreasingly so, it seems – and a late, light **supper**. Eating a large meal at lunchtime can be a great moneysaver – almost every restaurant serves a cut-price **comida corrida**.

Breakfast (*desayuno*) in Mexico can consist simply of coffee (see "Drinking", opposite) and *pan dulce* – sweet rolls and pastries that usually come in a basket; you pay for as many as you eat. More substantial breakfasts consist of eggs in any number of forms (many set breakfasts include *huevos al gusto*: eggs any way you like them), and at fruit juice places you can have a simple *licuado* (see "Drinking") fortified with raw egg (*blanquillo*). Freshly squeezed **orange juice** (*jugo de* *naranja*) is always available from street stalls in the early morning.

Snack meals mostly consist of some variation on the taco/enchilada theme (stalls selling them are called *taquerías*), but **tortas** – rolls heavily filled with meat or cheese or both, garnished with avocado and chile and toasted on request – are also wonderful, and you'll see takeout *torta* stands everywhere. Failing that, you can of course always make your own snacks with bread or tortillas, along with fillings such as avocado or cheese, from shops or markets. **Sandwiches** – on soft, tasteless bread, and meanly filled – and *hamburguesas* are almost always awful.

You can of course eat a full meal in a restaurant at any time of day, but you'd do well to adopt the local habit of taking your main meal at lunchtime, since this is when **comidas corridas** (set meals, varied daily) are served, from around 1 to 5pm: in more expensive places the same thing may be known as the *menu del día* or *menu turístico*. Price is one good reason: often you'll get four courses for US$5/£3 or less, which can't be bad. More importantly, though, the comida will include food that doesn't normally appear on menus – home-made soups and stews, local specialities, puddings, and above all vegetables that are otherwise a rarity – a welcome chance to escape from the budget traveller's staples of eggs, tacos and beans.

A **typical comida** will consist of "wet" soup, probably vegetable, followed by "dry" soup – most commonly *sopa de arroz* (simply rice seasoned with tomato or chile), or perhaps a plate of vegetables, pasta, beans or guacamole (avocado mashed with onion, and maybe tomato, lime juice and chile). Then comes the main course, followed by pudding, usually fruit, *flan* or *pudin* (crème caramel-like concoctions), or rice pudding. The courses are brought at great speed, sometimes all at once, and in the cheaper places you may have no idea what you're going to get until it arrives, since there'll simply be a sign saying *comida corrida* and the price.

Some places also offer set meals in the **evening**, but this is rare, and on the whole going out to eat at night is much more expensive.

DRINKING

The basic **drinks** to accompany food are water or beer. If you're drinking **water**, stick to bottled stuff (*agua mineral* or *agua de Tehuacán*) – it comes either plain (*sin gas*) or carbonated (*con gas*).

JUGOS AND LICUADOS

Soft drinks (*refrescos*), including Coke, Pepsi, Squirt (fun to pronounce in Spanish), and Mexican brands such as apple-flavoured *Sidral* (which are usually extremely sweet), are on sale everywhere. Far more tempting are the **real fruit juices** and *licuados* sold at shops and stalls displaying the *Jugos y Licuados* sign and known as *jugerías* or *licuaderías*. **Juices** (*jugos*) can be squeezed from anything that will go through the extractor. Orange (*naranja*) and carrot (*zanahoria*) are the staples, but you should also experiment with some of the more obscure tropical fruits, most of which are much better than they sound. **Licuados** are made of fruit mixed with water (*licuado de agua* or simply *agua de . . .*) or milk (*licuado de leche*) in a blender, usually with sugar added. They are always fantastic. *Limonada* (fresh lemonade) is also sold in many of these places, as are *aguas frescas* – flavoured cold drinks, of which the most common are *horchata* (a white and milky extract of tiger nuts), *agua de arroz* (like an iced rice pudding drink – delicious), *agua de jamaica* (hibiscus) or *de tamarindo* (tamarind). These are also often served in restaurants or sold in the streets from great glass jars. Make sure that any water and ice used is purified – street stalls are especially suspect in this regard. Juices and licuados are also sold at many ice-cream parlours – *neverías* or *paleterías*. The **ice cream**, also in a huge range of flavours and more like Italian *gelato* than the heavy-cream US varieties, can also be fabulous.

COFFEE AND TEA

A great deal of **coffee** is produced in Mexico and in the growing areas, especially the state of Veracruz, as well as in the traditional coffeehouses in the capital, you will be served superb coffee. In its basic form, *café solo* or *negro*, it is strong, black, often sweet (ask for it *sin azúcar* for no sugar), and comes in small cups. For weaker black coffee ask for *café americano*, though this may mean instant (if you want instant, ask for "*Nescafé*"). White is *café cortado* or *con un pocito de leche*; *café con leche* can be delicious, made with all milk and no water (ask if it's "hecho de leche"). Espresso and cappuccino are often available too, or you may be offered **café de olla**

A GLOSSARY OF MEXICAN FOOD AND DRINK TERMS

Basics

Azúcar	Sugar	Mantequilla	Butter	Queso	Cheese
Carne	Meat	Pan	Bread	Sal	Salt
Ensalada	Salad	Pescado	Fish	Salsa	Sauce
Huevos	Eggs	Pimienta	Pepper	Verduras/	
				Legumbres	Vegetables

Soups (*Sopas*) and starters

Caldo	Broth (with bits in)	Sopa	Soup
Ceviche	Raw fish salad, marinated in lime juice	De Arroz	Plain rice
		De Fideos	With noodles
Consome	Consommé	De Lentejas	Lentil
Entremeses	Hors d'oeuvres	De Verduras	Vegetable

Eggs (*Huevos*)

a la Mexicana	Scrambled with mild tomato, onion and chile sauce	Rancheros	Fried and smothered in a hot chile sauce
con Jamón	With ham	Revueltos	Scrambled
Motuleños	Fried, served on a tortilla with ham, cheese and salsa	Tibios	Lightly boiled
		con Tocino	With bacon

Antojitos

Burritos	Wheat flour tortillas, rolled and filled		often with ham and avocado too
Chilaquiles	Torn-up tortillas cooked with meat and sauce	Quesadillas	Toasted or fried tortillas with cheese
Chiles rellenos	Stuffed peppers	Queso fundido	Melted cheese, served with tortillas and salsa
Enchiladas	Rolled-up tacos, covered in chile sauce and baked	Sopes	Smaller bite-size versions of tostadas
Enchiladas suizas	As above, with sour cream		
Flautas	Small rolled tortillas filled with red meat or chicken and then fried	Tacos	Fried tortillas with filling
		Tacos al Pastor	Tacos filled with pork
		Tamales	Corn meal pudding, usually stuffed and steamed in banana leaves
Gorditas	Small, fat, stuffed corn tortillas		
Machaca	Shredded dried meat scrambled with eggs	Tlacoyo	Fat tortilla stuffed with beans
		Torta	Filled bread roll
Molletes	Split *torta* covered in beans and melted cheese,	Tostadas	Flat crisp tortillas piled with meat and salad

Fish and seafood (*Pescados y mariscos*)

Anchoas	Anchovies	Jurel	Yellowtail
Atún	Tuna	Langosta	Crawfish (rock lobster)
Cabrilla	Sea Bass	Lenguado	Sole
Calamares	Squid	Merluza	Hake
Camarones	Prawns	Ostión	Oyster
Cangrejo	Crab	Pezespada	Swordfish
Corvina Blanca	White sea bass	Pulpo	Octopus
Dorado	Dolphin Fish (Mahi Mahi)	Robalo	Bass
Filete entero	Whole, filleted fish	Sardinas	Sardines
Huachinango	Red Snapper	Trucha	Trout

Meat (*Carne*) and Poultry (*Aves*)

Alambre	Kebab	*Cerdo*	Pork	*Milanesa*	Breaded
Albóndigas	Meatballs	*Chivo*	Goat		escalope
Barbacoa	Barbecued	*Chorizo*	Spicy sausage	*Pata*	Feet
	meat	*Chuleta*	Chop	*Pato*	Duck
Bistec	Steak (not	*Codorniz*	Quail	*Pavo/Guajolote*	Turkey
	always beef)	*Conejo*	Rabbit	*Pechuga*	Breast
Cabeza	Head	*Cordero*	Lamb	*Pierna*	Leg
Cabrito	Kid	*Costilla*	Rib	*Pollo*	Chicken
Carne (deres)	Beef	*Filete*	Tenderloin/fillet	*Salchicha*	Hot dog or
Carne	Barbecued/	*Guisado*	Stew		salami
ado bado	spicily	*Higado*	Liver	*Ternera*	Veal
	stewed meat	*Lengua*	Tongue	*Tripa/Callos*	Tripe
Carnitas	Spicy pork	*Lomo*	Loin (of pork)	*Venado*	Venison

Vegetables (*Legumbres, verduras*)

Aguacate	Avocado	*Hongos*	Mushrooms
Betabel	Beetroot (often as a *jugo*)	*Jitomate*	Red tomato
Calabacita	Zucchini (courgette)	*Lechuga*	Lettuce
Calabaza	Squash	*Lentejas*	Lentils
Cebolla	Onion	*Nopales*	Prickly pear fronds,
Champiñones	Mushrooms		something like squash
Chícharos	Peas	*Papas*	Potatoes
Col	Cabbage	*Pepino*	Cucumber
Coliflor	Cauliflower	*Rajas*	Strips of green pepper
Elote	Corn on the cob	*Tomate*	Green tomato
Espáragos	Asparagus	*Zanahoria*	Carrot
Frijoles	Beans		

Fruits (*Fruta*) and juice

Chabacano	Apricot	*Mamey*	like a large *zapote*, with sweet
Cherimoya	Custard apple (sweet sop)		pink flesh and a big pip
Ciruelas	Tiny yellow plums	*Mango*	Mango
Coco	Coconut	*Melón*	Melon
Durazno	Peach	*Naranja*	Orange
Frambuesas	Raspberries	*Papaya*	Papaya
Fresas	Strawberries	*Piña*	Pineapple
Granada	Yellow passion fruit	*Plátano*	Banana
Guanabana	Soursop, like a large	*Sandía*	Watermelon
	custard apple	*Toronja*	Grapefruit
Guayaba	Guava	*Tuna*	Prickly pear (cactus fruit)
Higos	Figs	*Uvas*	Grapes
Limón	Lime	*Zapote*	Sapodilla (chicu), fruit of the
			chicle tree

Sweets

Ate	Quince paste	*Ensalada de Frutas*	Fruit salad
Cajeta	Caramel confection often	*Flan*	Crème caramel
	served with...	*Helado*	Ice cream
Crepas	...Pancakes	*Nieve*	Sorbet

Continues over...

Common terms

Asado/a	Roast	Con Mole	The most famous of
Al Horno	Baked		Mexican sauces – it
A la Tampiqueña	Meat in thin strips served with guacamole and enchiladas		contains chile, chocolate and spices – served with chicken or turkey
A la Veracruzana	Usually fish, cooked with tomatoes and onions	A la Parilla	Grilled
		Empanado/a	Breaded
Al Mojo de Ajo	Fried in garlic and butter		
Barbacoaor Pibil	Wrapped in leaves and herbs and steamed/ cooked in a pit		

– stewed in the pot for hours with cinnamon and sugar, it's thick, sweet and tasty. Outside traditional coffee areas, however, the coffee is often terrible, with only instant available (if you look like a tourist they may automatically assume you want instant anyway).

Tea (*té*) is often available too, and you may well be offered a cup at the end of a *comida*. Usually it's some kind of herb tea like *manzanillo* (camomile) or *yerbabuena* (mint). If you get the chance to try traditional **hot chocolate** ("the drink of the Aztecs"), then do so – it's an extraordinary, spicy, semi-bitter concoction, quite unlike the milky bedtime drink of your childhood.

ALCOHOL

Mexican **beer**, *cerveza*, is excellent. Most is light, lager-style *cerveza clara*, fine examples being Bohémia, Superior, Dos Equis and Tecate (the last normally served with lemon and salt); but you can also get dark (*oscura*) beers, of which the best are Negra Modelo, Indio and Tres Equis. Locally bottled beers, such as Sol on the east coast or Pacífico on the west, are often even better than the national labels. You'll normally be drinking in bars, but if you don't feel comfortable – this applies to women, in particular (for more on which, see later) – you can also get takeouts from most shops, supermarkets, and, cheapest of all, **agencias**, which are normally agents for just one brand.

When buying from any of these places, it is normal to pay a deposit of about 30–40 percent of the purchase price: keep your receipt and return your bottles to the same store. Beer is cheapest of all if, instead of buying 330ml bottles, you go for the 940ml vessels known as "*caguamas*" (turkeys), or in the case of Pacífico, "*ballenas*" (whales).

Wine (*vino* – *tinto* for red, *blanco* white) is not seen a great deal, although Mexico does produce a fair number of perfectly good ones. You're safest sticking to the brand names like Hidalgo or Domecq, although it may also be worth experimenting with some of the new labels, especially those from Baja California, which are attempting to emulate the success of their neighbours across the border and in many cases have borrowed techniques and wine-makers from the US.

Tequila, distilled from the maguey cactus in and around the town of Tequila in Jalisco, is of course the most famous of Mexican spirits, usually served straight with lime and salt on the side. Lick the salt and bite into the lime, then take a swig of tequila (or the other way round – there's no correct etiquette). The best stuff is aged (*añejo* or *reposado*) for smoothness; try Sauza Hornitos, which is powerful, or Commemorativo, which is unexpectedly gentle on the throat.

Mescal (often spelt *mezcal*) is basically the same drink, but made from a slightly different type of maguey, younger and less refined. In fact, tequila was originally just a variety of mescal. The worm in the bottom of the mescal bottle, a grub which lives only on the maguey, is there to prove its authenticity – the spurious belief that the worm is hallucinogenic is based on a confusion between the drink and the peyote cactus, which is also called *mescal*; by the time you've got down as far as the worm, you won't be in any state to tell anyway.

Pulque, a mildly alcoholic milky beer made from the same cactus, is the traditional drink of the poor and sold in special bars called *pulquerías*. The best comes from the state of México, and is thick and viscous – it's a little like palm wine, and definitely an acquired taste.

Unfermented *pulque*, called *aguamiel*, is sweet and non-alcoholic.

Drinking other **spirits**, you should always ask for *nacional*, as anything imported is fabulously expensive. Rum (*ron*), gin (*ginebra*) and vodka are made in Mexico, as are some very palatable brandies (*brandy* or *coñac* – try San Marcos or Presidente). Most of the **cocktails** for which Mexico is known – margaritas, piñas coladas and so on – are available only in tourist areas or hotel bars, and are generally pretty strong. *Sangrita* is a mixture of tomato and fruit juices with chile, often drunk as a mixer with tequila.

For drinking any of these, the least heavy atmosphere is in hotel **bars**, tourist areas, or anything that describes itself as a "ladies' bar". Traditional *cantinas* are for serious and excessive drinking, have a thoroughly threatening, macho atmosphere, and are barred to women most of the time; more often than not, there's a sign above the door prohibiting entry to "women, members of the armed forces, and anyone in uniform". Big-city *cantinas* are to some extent more liberal, but in small and traditional places they remain exclusively male preserves, full of drunken bonhomie that can suddenly sour into threats and fighting.

MAIL, PHONES AND THE MEDIA

Although on the face of it Mexico has reasonably efficient postal and telephone systems, phoning home can be a hazardous business, while packages have a tendency to go astray in both directions. One thing to watch is the outrageous cost of international phone calls, faxes and telegrams – call collect or use a calling card wherever possible.

MAIL

Mexican **postal services** (*correos*) are reasonably efficient. Airmail to the capital should arrive within a few days, but it may take a couple of weeks to get anywhere at all remote. **Post offices** (generally open Mon–Fri 9am–6pm, Sat 9am–noon) generally offer a **poste restante/general delivery** service: letters should be addressed to **Lista de Correos** at the *Correo Central* (main post office) of any town; all mail that arrives for the *Lista* is put on a list updated daily and displayed in the post office, but held for two weeks only. You *may* get around that by sending it to "Poste Restante" instead of "*Lista de Correos*" and having letter-writers put "*Favor de retener hasta la llegada*" (please hold until arrival) on the envelope; letters addressed thus will not appear on the *Lista*. Letters are often filed incorrectly, so you should have staff check under all your initials, preferably use only two names on the envelope (in Hispanic countries, the second of people's three names, or the third if they've four names, is the paternal surname and the most important, so if three names are used, your mail will probably be filed under the middle one) and capitalize and underline your surname. To collect, you need your passport or some other official ID with a photograph. There is no fee.

American Express also operates an efficient mail collection service, and has a number of offices all over Mexico – most useful in México, where the address for the most central branch is: c/o American Express, Reforma 234, Col. Juarez, México D.F. They keep letters for a month, and also hold faxes. If you don't carry their card or cheques, you have to pay a fee to collect your mail, although they don't always ask.

Sending letters and cards is also easy enough, if slow. Anything sent abroad by air should have an airmail (*por avión*) stamp on it or it is liable to go surface. Letters *should* take around a week to North America, two to Europe or Australasia, but can take much longer (postcards in particular are likely to be slow). Anything at all important should be taken to the post office and preferably registered rather than dropped in a mail box, although the new special airmail boxes in resorts and big cities are supposed to be more reliable than ordinary ones.

Sending **packages** out of the country is drowned in bureaucracy. Regulations about the thickness of brown paper wrapping and the amount of string used vary from state to state, but most importantly, any package must be checked by customs and have its paperwork stamped by at least three other departments, which may take a while. Take your package (unsealed) to any post office and they'll set you on your way. Many stores will send your purchases home for you, which is a great deal easier. Within the country, you can send a package by bus if there is someone to collect it at the other end.

Telegram offices (*Telegrafos*) are frequently in the same building as the post office. The service is super-efficient, but international ones are very expensive, even if you use the cheaper overnight service. In most cases, you can get across a short message for less by phone or fax.

PHONES

Local **phone calls** in Mexico are cheap, and most hotels will let you call locally for free. Coin-operated public phones, rapidly disappearing, also charge very little for local calls. **Internal long-distance** calls are best made with a **phonecard**. These are available from telephone offices and stores near phones that use them (especially in bus and train stations, airports and major resorts). Many newer public phones say they accept **credit cards**; in practice, however, they often don't.

Slightly more expensive are **casetas de teléfono**, phone offices where someone will make the connection for you. There are lots of them, as many Mexicans don't have phones of their own: they can be simply shops or bars with public phones, indicated by a phone sign outside, in which case you may only be allowed to make local calls, but many are specialist phone and fax places displaying a blue-and-white *Larga Distancia* (long-distance) sign. You're connected by an operator who presents you with a bill afterwards – once connected, the cost can usually be seen clicking up on a meter. There are scores of competing companies, and the new ones, like *Computel*, tend to be better; many take credit cards. Prices vary, so if you're making lots of calls it may be worth checking a few out. There are *casetas* at just about every bus station and airport.

Wherever you make them from, **international calls** are fabulously expensive – using a

---

DIALLING CODES

Calling from long-distance public phones, dial:

Mexico interstate:	☎91 + area code + number
US and Canada:	☎95 + area code + number
UK:	☎98 44 + area code (minus initial zero) + number
Ireland:	☎98 353 + area code (minus initial zero) + number
Australia:	☎98 61 + area code (minus initial zero) + number
New Zealand:	☎98 64 + area code (minus initial zero) + number

To **call collect** or **person-to-person**, dial ☎92 for interstate calls within Mexico, ☎96 for the US and Canada, ☎99 for the rest of the world.

To **call Mexico from abroad**, dial:

From US and Canada:	☎011 52
From UK, Ireland and New Zealand:	☎00 52
From Australia:	☎0011 52

CALLING CARD NUMBERS

US and UK calling card numbers for **English-speaking operator and home billing**:

AT&T	☎95-800/462-4240	**MCI**	☎95-800/674-7000
BT	☎98-800/04400	**Sprint**	☎95-800/877-8000
Canada Direct	☎95-800/010-1990		

phonecard is probably the cheapest option, though even the highest denomination ones won't last long; next best rates are from a *caseta* (though costs vary more than you'd expect, so shop around); calling from a hotel is very extravagant indeed. Charges vary a great deal, but typical *caseta* prices are US$3 a minute to call the US, £4 a minute to the UK. If you plan to make international calls, by far the best plan is to arm yourself in advance with a **charge card** or **calling card** that can be used in Mexico (see the list above); you'll be connected to an English-speaking operator and will be billed at home at a rate that is predictable (if still high). You should be able to get through to the toll-free numbers from any working public phone.

Next best is to **call collect** (*por cobrar*). In theory you should be able to make an international collect call from any public phone, by dialling the international operator (☎09) or getting in touch with the person-to-person direct dial numbers listed opposite, though it can be hard to get through. At a *caseta* there may be a charge for making the connection, even if you don't get through, and a hotel is liable to make an even bigger charge.

Faxes can be sent from (and received at) many long-distance telephone *casetas*: again the cost is likely to be astronomical.

THE MEDIA

Pretty much anywhere with a significant English-speaking presence, you'll be able to seek out copies of México's English-language daily *The News*, a frumpy US-oriented organ that's far inferior to the less widely distributed broadsheet *The Mexico City Times*. As well as the usual wire stories, the latter runs incisive pieces from the *New York Times*, Britain's *Economist* weekly and *Independent* newspaper, and the Saturday issue even includes the Latin American edition of the *Guardian Weekly*. There are also free bulletins in English that can be picked up in México and any-

where with a sizeable tourist population – either in large hotels or from the tourist office – and *Time* and *Newsweek* are widely available, too. Few domestic newspapers carry much foreign news, and what there is is mainly Latin American; they are often lurid scandal sheets, full of violent crime depicted in full colour. Each state has its own press, however, and they do vary: while most are little more than PRI propaganda, others can be surprisingly independent. The best **national paper**, if you read Spanish, is *La Jornada*, which is quite daringly critical of government policy, especially in Chiapas, and whose journalists regularly face death threats as a result. As the press has gradually been asserting its independence since 1995, subjects such as human rights, corruption and drug trafficking are increasingly being tackled, but journalists face great danger if they speak out, not only from shady pro-government groups, but also from the drug traffickers. In 1997 for example, three journalists were murdered and five abducted; many more were victims of lawsuits under Mexico's punitive defamation laws.

On Mexican **TV** you can watch any number of US shows dubbed into Spanish – it's most bizarre to be walking through some shantytown as the strains of the *Dynasty* theme tune come floating across the air. Cable and satellite are now widespread, and even quite downmarket hotels offer numerous channels, many of them American.

Radio stations in the capital and Guadalajara (among others) have programmes in English for a couple of hours each day, and in many places US broadcasts can also be picked up. The BBC World Service in English can be picked up by radios with short wave on 5975kHz in the 49m band, especially in the evening; on 15,220kHz in the 25m band, especially in the morning; and on 17,840kHz, especially in the afternoon. Other possible frequencies include: 6175kHz, 6195kHz, 9590kHz and 9895kHz. The *Voice of America* broadcasts on 15,210kHz, 11,740kHz, 9815kHz and 6030kHz.

TRAVELLERS WITH DISABILITIES

Mexico is not well equipped for people with disabilities, but it is improving all the time and, especially at the top end of the market, it shouldn't be too difficult to find accommodation and tour operators who can cater for your particular needs. The important thing is to check beforehand with tour companies, hotels and airlines that they can accommodate you specifically. The box below details organizations that can advise you as to

which tour operators and airlines are the most reliable.

If you stick to beach resorts – Cancún and Acapulco in particular – and upmarket tourist **hotels**, you should certainly be able to find places that are wheelchair-friendly and used to having disabled guests. US chains are very good for this, with *Choice, Days Inn, Holiday Inn, Leading Hotels of the World, Marriott, Radisson, Ramada, Sheraton* and *Westin* claiming to have the neces-

---

CONTACTS FOR TRAVELLERS WITH DISABILITIES

NORTH AMERICA

Directions Unlimited, 720 N Bedford Rd, Bedford Hills, NY 10507 (☎914/241-1700). *Travel agency specializing in custom tours for people with disabilities.*

Jewish Rehabilitation Hospital, 3205 Place Alton Goldbloom, Chomedy Laval, Montréal, PQ H7V 1R2 (☎514/688-9550, ext 226). *Guidebooks and travel information.*

Mobility International USA, PO Box 10767, Eugene, OR 97440 (Voice and TDD: ☎541/343-1284). *Information and referral services, access guides, tours and exchange programs. Annual membership $25 (includes quarterly newsletter).*

Society for the Advancement of Travel for the Handicapped (SATH), 347 5th Ave, Suite 610, New York, NY 10016 (☎212/447-7284; www.sit-travel.com). *Non-profit travel-industry referral service that passes queries on to its members as appropriate; allow plenty of time for a response.*

Travel Information Service ☎215/456-9600. *Telephone information and referral service.*

Travelin' Talk, Box 3534, Clarksville, TN 37043 (☎615/552-6670). *Publishes a rather pricey directory ($35) of useful organizations.*

Twin Peaks Press, Box 129, Vancouver, WA 98666 (☎360/694-2462 or 800/637-2256). *Publisher of the* Directory of Travel Agencies for the Disabled *($19.95), listing more than 370 agencies worldwide;* Travel for the Disabled *($19.95); the* Directory of Accessible Van Rentals *($9.95); and* Wheelchair Vagabond *($14.95), loaded with personal tips.*

UK AND IRELAND

Holiday Care Service, 2nd floor, Imperial Building, Victoria Rd, Horley, Surrey RH6 7PZ

(☎01293/774535; Minicom ☎01293/776943). *Provides free lists of accessible accommodation. Information on financial help for holidays available.*

Tripscope, The Courtyard, Evelyn Rd, London W4 5JL (☎0181/994 9294). *A national telephone information service offering free transport and travel advice for those with mobility problems.*

RADAR, 12 City Forum, 250 City Rd, London EC1V 8AF (☎0171/250 3222; Minicom ☎0171/250 4119). *A good source of advice on holidays and travel abroad; they also publish their own guides for travellers with disabilities (Mexico is in their Long Haul book, priced £5).*

Disability Action Group, 2 Annadale Ave, Belfast BT7 3JH (☎01232/491011).

Irish Wheelchair Association, Blackheath Drive, Clontarf, Dublin 3 (☎01/833 8241; iwa@iol.ie). *National voluntary organization for people with disabilities, including services for holidaymakers.*

AUSTRALIA AND NEW ZEALAND

ACROD, PO Box 60, Curtin, Canberra, ACT 2605 (☎02/6282 4333). *Can offer advice and keeps a list of travel specialists.*

Barrier-Free Travel, 36 Wheatley St, North Bellingen, NSW 2454 (☎066/551733). *Consultancy service for disabled travellers, with a flat $75 fee for any number of consultations regarding access.*

Disabled Persons Assembly, PO Box 10–138, The Terrace, Wellington (☎04/472 2626). *Umbrella group for all organizations dealing with disability in New Zealand.*

sary facilities for at least some disabilities in some of their hotels. Always check in advance, however, that the hotel of your choice can cater for your particular needs.

You'll find that, unless you have your own transport, the best way to **travel** inside the country may prove to be by air, since trains and buses rarely cater for disabled people, and certainly not for wheelchairs. Travelling on a lower budget, or get- ting off the beaten track, you'll find few facilities. Ramps are few and far between, streets and pavements not in a very good state, and people no more likely than at home to volunteer help. Depending on your disability, you may want to find an able- bodied helper to accompany you. If you cannot find anyone suitable among your own friends or family, the organizations listed opposite may be able to help you get in touch with someone.

WOMEN TRAVELLERS

So many oppressive limitations are imposed on women's freedom to travel that any advice or warning seems merely to rein- force the situation. That said, machismo is engrained in the Mexican mentality and although it's softened to some extent by the gentler mores of indigenous culture, a degree of harassment is inevitable.

On the whole, any **hassle** will be limited to comments (*piropos*, supposedly compliments) in the street, but even situations that might be quite routine at home can seem threatening without a clear understanding of the nuances of Mexican Spanish. It's a good idea to avoid eye contact – wearing sunglasses helps. To avoid matters esca- lating, any provocation is best ignored totally. Mexican women are rarely slow with a stream of abuse, but it's a dangerous strategy unless you're very sure of your ground – coming from a foreign- er, it may also be taken as racism.

Public transport can be one of the worst places for harassment, especially groping in crowded situations. On the México metro, there are separate women's carriages and passages during rush hours. Otherwise, if you get a seat, you can hide behind a newspaper.

Any problems are aggravated in the big tourist spots, where legendarily "easy" tourists attract droves of would-be gigolos. México can feel heavy, though if you're from a big city your- self, it may not seem that different, and requires the same common sense. Away from the cities, though, and especially in indigenous areas, there is rarely any problem – you may as an out- sider be treated as an object of curiosity (or even resentment), but not necessarily with any implied or intended sexual threat. And wherever you come across it, such curiosity can also extend to great friendliness and hospitality. On the whole, the further from the US border you get, the easier things will become – though some women find other Latin American coun- tries further south, which are less used to tourists, infinitely worse.

The restrictions imposed on **drinking** are without a doubt irksome: women are simply and absolutely barred from the vast majority of *canti- nas*, and even in so-called Ladies' Bars "unescort- ed" women may be looked at askance or even refused service. Carrying a bottle is the only answer, since in small towns the *cantina* may be the only place that sells alcoholic drinks.

GAY AND LESBIAN TRAVELLERS

There are no federal laws governing homo-sexuality in Mexico, and hence it's legal. There are, however, laws enforcing "public morality", which although they are sup-posed only to apply to prostitution, are often used against gays out cruising. While July 1997 saw the election of Mexico's first "out" congresswoman, the left-wing PRD's Patria Jimémez, the right-wing party, PAN, has been running anti-gay campaigns in towns and states that it controls, closing gay bars in Monterrey and passing an ordinance against "abnormal sexual behaviour" in Guadalajara.

There are in fact a large number of **gay groups and publications** in Mexico – we've supplied two contact addresses below. The les-bian scene is nothing like as visible or as large as the gay scene for men, but it's there and growing. There are gay **bars and clubs** in the major resorts and US border towns, and in large cities such as the capital, and also Monterrey, Guadalajara, Veracruz and Oaxaca; elsewhere, private parties are where it all happens, and you'll need a contact to find them.

As far as popular attitudes are concerned, reli-gion and machismo are the order of the day, and prejudice is rife. Even so, soft porn magazines for gay men are sold openly on street stalls and, while you should be careful to avoid upsetting macho sensibilities, you should have few prob-lems if you are discreet (camp gay men and butch women, incidentally, are known in Mexico as *obvios*). Many Mexicans of both sexes are bisex-ual, though they do not see themselves as such ("The difference between a straight and a gay," says one gay activist, "is about two beers."). In Juchitán, Oaxaca, on the other hand, gay male transvestites, known as *muxes*, are accepted as a kind of third sex, and the town even has a trans-vestite basketball team.

HIV and **AIDS** (SIDA) are as much a threat in Mexico as anywhere else in the world, and the usual precautions are in order. As for **contacts** within Mexico: lesbians can get in touch with Grupo Lesbico Patlatonalli, Aptdo Postal 1–4045, Guadalajara, Jalisco; while for gay men, CIDHOM (Colectivo de Información de las Homosexualidades en Mexico), Aptdo Postal 13–424, México D.F. 03500, can offer information.

TRAVELLING WITH CHILDREN

A minor aged under 18 needs the permission of *both* parents in order to enter Mexico; if travelling alone, they need written permission on a form signed by both parents at the consulate or on officially notarized affidavits; if travelling with one parent, they need official written permission from the other.

This **law** was introduced in order to prevent parents absconding from the US with their children for the purpose of avoiding court judgements in favour of the other parent. If you are taking your child with you and are not in touch with the other parent, this may cause difficulties, which should be sorted out with the Mexican authorities before leaving home (you'll need proof of sole custody, for example).

Once in the country, you will find that most Mexicans dote on children and they can often help to break the ice with strangers. The main problem, especially with small children, is their extra vulnerability. Even more than their parents, they need **protecting** from the sun, unsafe drinking water, heat, and unfamiliar food. All that chile in particular may be a problem for kids who are not used to it. Remember too that diarrhoea can

> ### US CONTACTS FOR TRAVELLERS WITH CHILDREN
> **Rascals in Paradise**, 650 5th St, Suite 505, San Francisco, CA 94107 (☎1-800/872-7225). *Scheduled and customized itineraries built around activities for kids.*
> **Travel With Your Children**, 40 5th Ave, New York, NY 10011 (☎888/822-4388). *Publisher of* Family Travel Times, *a newsletter that comes out ten times a year. Also publishes a series of books on travel with children, including* Great Adventure Vacations With Your Kids.

be dangerous for a child: rehydration salts (see p.22) are vital if your child goes down with it. Make sure too, if possible, that your child is aware of the dangers of rabies; keep children away from animals and consider a rabies jab.

For touring, hiking or walking, **child-carrier backpacks** are ideal: they can weigh less than 2kg and start at around $75/£50. If the child is small enough, a fold-up buggy is also well worth packing – especially if they will sleep in it, while you have a meal or a drink.

WORK AND STUDY

There's virtually no chance of finding temporary work in Mexico unless you have some very specialized skill and have arranged the position beforehand. Work permits are almost impossible to get hold of. The few foreigners who do manage to find work do so mostly in language schools. It might be possible, though not legal, to earn some money as an English instructor by simply advertising in a local newspaper or on notice boards at a university.

The best way to extend your time in Mexico is on a **study programme** or **volunteer** project. A US organization called **Amerispan** selects **language schools** throughout Latin America, including Mexico, to match the needs and requirements of students, and provides advice and support. For

US STUDY PROGRAMS

AFS Intercultural Programs, 220 E 42nd St, New York, NY 10017 (☎1-800/876-2377; website *www.afs.org/usa*). *Runs summer experiential programs aimed at fostering international understanding for teenagers and adults. Programs in many countries, including Mexico.*

American Institute for Foreign Study,102 Greenwich Ave, Greenwich, CT 06830 (☎1-800/727-2437; *www.aifs.com*). *Language study and cultural immersion for the summer or school year.*

Bernan Associates, 4611-F Assembly Dr, Lanham, MD 20706 (☎1-800/274 4888). *Distributes UNESCO's encyclopedic* Study Abroad.

Elderhostel, 75 Federal St, Boston, MA 02110 (☎617/426 8056; *www.elderhostel.org*). *Runs an extensive worldwide network of educational and activity programs, cruises and homestays for people over sixty (companions may be younger). Programs generally last a week or more and costs are in line with those of commercial tours.*

School for Field Studies, 16 Broadway, Box SA, Beverly, MA 01915-4499 (☎1-800/989-4435; *www.fieldstudies.org*). *Study abroad program focused on environmental problem solving.*

Studyabroad.com *www.studyabroad.com. Web site with listings and links to programs worldwide.*

World Learning, Kipling Road, PO Box 676, Brattleboro, VT 05302 (☎802/257-7751; *www.worldlearning.org*). *Its* School for International Training *(☎1-800/336-1616) runs accredited college semesters abroad, comprising language and cultural studies, homestay and other academic work.* Experiment in International Living *(☎1-800/345-2929) is a summer program for high-school students.*

WORK/VOLUNTEER PROGRAMS

Alliances Abroad, 2220 Rio Grande, Austin, TX 78705 (☎1-888/6-ABROAD or 512/457-8062; *www.studyabroad.com/alliances*). *Immerse yourself in Mexican culture and language by participating in a service project or internship.*

American Friends Service Committee, 1501 Cherry St, Philadelphia, PA 19102 (☎215/241-7295; *www.afsc.org*). *Summer volunteer work camps in Mexican villages for 18–26-year-olds. Spanish fluency required.*

Association for International Practical Training, 10400 Little Patuxent Pkwy, Suite 250, Columbia, MD 21044 (☎410/997-3068; *www.aipt.org*). *Summer internships for students who have completed at least two years of college in science, agriculture, engineering or architecture.*

Council on International Educational Exchange (CIEE), 205 E 42nd St, New York, NY 10017 (☎888/COUNCIL or ☎212/822-2695 for volunteer projects; ☎1-800/349-2433 for book orders; *www.ciee.org*). *Publishes* Work, Study, Travel Abroad *and* Volunteer! The Comprehensive Guide to Voluntary Service in the US and Abroad.

Volunteers for Peace, 43 Tiffany Rd, Belmont, VT 05730 (☎802/259-2759; *www.vfp.org*). *Nonprofit organization with links to a huge international network of "workcamps", two- to four-week programs that bring volunteers together from many countries to carry out needed community projects. Most workcamps are in summer, with registration in April–May. Annual directory costs US$12.*

further information, call (from the US or Canada) ☎1-800/879-6640 (fax 215/751-1986); or write to PO Box 40513, Philadelphia, PA 19106-0513. Their Web site is at *www.amerispan.com*.

In Australia, you can contact the **Australian Volunteers Abroad Service Bureau**, Suite 46, Level 4, 8 Kippax St, Surry Hills, Sydney, NSW 2010 (☎02/9211 1277). **CIEE** (see box above) also now have an Australian branch, at Level 8, 210 Clarence St, Sydney, NSW 2000 (☎02/9373 2730).

EARTHWATCH

Earthwatch matches volunteers with scientists working on a particular project. Recent expeditions in Mexico have included excavations of megafauna in San Miguel de Allende, investigations into pre- and post-Conquest religious architecture in the Yucatán, and a survey of carnivores in the tropical dry forests of Jalisco. Fascinating though this work is, it's not a cheap way to see the country: volunteers must raise $700–2500 (average about $1500) for each one- to two-week stint as a contribution to the cost of research. For more information, access their Web site (*www.earthwatch.org*), or contact one of the following.

Earthwatch HQ, 680 Mt Auburn St, PO Box 9104, Watertown, MA 02272-9104 (☎617/926-8200).
Earthwatch California, Altos Center, Suite F2, 360 S San Antonio Rd, Los Altos, CA 94022 (☎650/917-8186).

Earthwatch Europe, Belsyre Court, 57 Woodstock Rd, Oxford OX2 6HU, UK (☎01865/311600).
Earthwatch Australia, 126 Bank St, S Melbourne, VIC 3205 (☎03/9600 9100).

OPENING HOURS AND HOLIDAYS

It's almost impossible to generalize about opening hours in Mexico; even when times are posted at museums, tourist offices and shops, they're not always strictly adhered to.

The **siesta**, though, is still around, and many places will close for a couple of hours in the early afternoon, usually from 1 to 3pm. The strictness of this is very much dependent on the climate; where it's hot – especially on the Gulf Coast and in the Yucatán – everything may close for up to four hours in the middle of the day, and then reopen until 8 or 9pm. In the industrial north and highland areas, hours may be the standard nine-to-five.

More specifically, **shops** tend to keep fairly long hours, say from 9am to 8pm, though many will close for a couple of hours in the middle of the day. Main **post offices** are open Mon–Fri 9am–6pm, Sat 9am–noon. **Banks** generally open Mon–Fri 9am–1.30pm.

Museums and galleries tend to open from about 9am to 1pm and again from 3 to 6pm. Many have reduced entry fees – or are free – on Sunday, but may open only in the morning, and most are closed on Monday. **Archeological sites** are usually open right through the day.

PUBLIC HOLIDAYS

The main **public holidays**, when virtually everything will be closed, are:

Jan 1	New Year's Day	**Sept 1**	Presidential address to the nation
Feb 5	Anniversary of the Constitution	**Sept 16**	Independence Day
Feb 24	Flag Day	**Oct 12**	Dia de la Raza/Columbus Day
March 21	Benito Juárez Day	**Nov 1/2**	All Saints/Day of the Dead
Good Friday and Easter Saturday		**Nov 20**	Anniversary of the Revolution
May 1	Labor Day	**Dec 12**	Virgin of Guadalupe
May 5	Battle of Puebla	**Dec 24–26**	Christmas

In addition, many places close on **Jan 6** (Twelfth Night/*Reyes*).

FIESTAS AND ENTERTAINMENT

Stumbling, perhaps accidentally, onto some Mexican village fiesta may prove to be the highlight of your travels. Everywhere, from the remotest Indian village to the most sophisticated city suburb, will take at least one day off annually to devote to partying. Usually it's the local saint's day, but many fiestas have pre-Christian origins and any excuse — from harvest celebrations to the coming of the rains — will do.

Traditional dances and music form an essential part of almost every fiesta, and most include a procession behind some revered holy image or a more celebratory secular parade with fireworks. But the only rule is that no two will be quite the same. The most famous, spectacular or curious are listed at the end of each chapter of this guide, but there are many others and certain times of year are fiesta time almost everywhere.

Carnival, the week before Lent, is celebrated throughout the Roman Catholic world, and is at its most exuberant in Latin America. It is the last week of taking one's pleasures before the forty-day abstinence of Lent, which lasts until Easter. Like Easter, its date is not fixed, but it generally falls in February or early March. Carnival is celebrated with costumes, parades, eating and dancing, most spectacularly in Veracruz and Mazatlán, and works its way up to a climax on the last day, Mardi Gras or Shrove Tuesday, when the only thing the inhabitants of certain other countries can manage is to toss the odd pancake.

The country's biggest holiday, however, is **Semana Santa** — Holy Week — beginning on Palm Sunday and continuing until the following Sunday, Easter Day. Still a deeply religious festival in Mexico, it celebrates the resurrection of Christ, and has also become an occasion to venerate the Virgin Mary, with processions bearing her image a hallmark of the celebrations. During Semana Santa, expect transport communications to be totally disrupted as virtually the whole country is on the move, visiting family and returning from the big city to their village of origin: you will need to plan ahead if travelling then. Many places close for the whole of Holy Week, and certainly from Thursday to Sunday.

Secular **Independence Day** (Sept 16) is in some ways more solemn than the religious festivals with their exuberant fervour. While Easter and Carnival are popular festivals, this one is more official, marking the historic day in 1810 when Manuel Hidalgo y Costilla issued the *Grito* (Cry of Independence) from his parish church in Dolores, now Dolores Hidalgo, Guanajuato, which is still the centre of commemoration today. You'll also find the day marked in the capital with mass recitation of the *Grito* in the zócalo, followed by fireworks, music and dancing.

The **Day of the Dead** is All Saints or All Souls' Day and its eve (Nov 1–2), when offerings are made to ancestors' souls, frequently with picnics and all-night vigils at their graves. People build shrines in their homes to honour their departed relatives, but it's the cemeteries to head for if you want to see the really spectacular stuff. Sweetmeats and papier-mâché statues of dressed up skeletons give the whole proceedings rather a gothic air.

Christmas is a major holiday, and again a time when people are on the move and transport booked solid for weeks ahead. Gringo influence nowadays is heavy, with Santa Claus and Christmas trees, but the Mexican festival remains distinct in many ways, with a much stronger religious element (virtually every home has a nativity crib). **New Year** is still largely an occasion to spend with family, the actual hour being celebrated with the eating of grapes. Presents are traditionally given on **Twelfth Night** or Epiphany (Jan 6), which is when the three Magi of the bible arrived bearing gifts — though things are shifting into line with Yankee custom, and more and more people are exchanging gifts on December 25. One of the more bizarre Christmas events takes place at Oaxaca, where there is a public display of nativity cribs and other sculptures made of **radishes**.

DANCE

The **dances**, complicated and full of ancient symbolism, are often a fiesta's most extraordinary feature. Many of the most famous — including the Yaqui stag dance and the dance of *Los Viejitos* (the little old men) — can be seen in sanitized form at **Ballet Folklórico** performances in México or on tour in the provinces. Many states, too, have regular shows put on by regional *folklórico* companies, and many *indígenas* help make ends meet by putting on their people's traditional dances for tourists. The spectacular *Voladores* flying dance of the Totonacs of Veracruz state, for example, is performed regularly at Papantla and the nearby archeological sites.

But you should try at least once to see dance in its authentic state, performed by enthusiastic amateurs at a village celebration. Some of the most impressive are the plant and animal **Las Varitas** and **Zacamson** dances of the Huastecs in the southeastern corner of San Luis Potosí state, performed for the festivals of San Miguel Arcángel (Sept 28–29) and Virgen de Guadalupe (Dec 12). Information is available from tourist offices. Less indigenous are the **Moros y Cristianos** dances celebrating the victories of the Christian *reconquista* over the Muslim Moors in thirteenth- to fifteenth-century Spain, and widely performed in Mexico to this day. Of more recent origin, the masked dance held on **Mardi Gras** in Huejotzingo, northwest of Puebla, re-enacts nineteenth-century battles between Mexicans and the French troops of Emperor Maximilian.

SPORT

You'll find facilities for golf, tennis, sailing, surfing, scuba diving and deep-sea fishing — even riding and hunting — provided at all the big resorts. Sport **fishing**, especially, is enormously popular in Baja California and the big Pacific coast resorts, while freshwater bass fishing is growing in popularity too, especially behind the large dams in the north of the country. The gentler arts of **diving** and snorkelling are big around the

Caribbean, with world-famous dive sites at Cozumel and on the reefs further south. The Pacific coast is becoming something of a centre for **surfing**, with few facilities as yet (though you can rent surfboards in major tourist centres such as Acapulco and Mazatlán) but plenty of Californian surfies who follow the weather south over the winter. The most popular places are in Baja California and on the Oaxaca coast, but the biggest waves are to be found around Lázaro Cárdenas in Michoacán (where, however, local people are not known for their enthusiasm for surfers). A more minority-interest sport for which Mexico has become a major centre is **caving**. With a third of the country built on limestone, there are caverns in most states that can be explored by experienced cavers, potholers or spelunkers.

The Ministry of Tourism publishes a leaflet on participatory sport in Mexico, and can also advise on such things as licences and seasons.

SPECTATOR SPORTS

Mexico's chief spectator sport is **soccer** (*futbol*). Mexican teams have not been notably successful on the international stage, but going to a game can still be a thrilling experience, with vast crowds for the big ones. The capital and Guadalajara are the best places to see a match, with the derby between the two cities a major event in the footballing year. **Baseball** (*beisbol*) is also popular, as is American football (especially on TV). **Jai-alai** (better known as *frontón*, or *pelota*) is Basque handball, common in big cities and played at very high speed with a curved scoop attached to the hand. Points are scored by whacking the ball hard and fast against the end wall, as in squash, but the real scores are made in odds and pesos, since this, for spectators at least, is largely a gambler's sport.

Mexican **rodeos** (*charreadas*), mainly seen in the north of the country, are as spectacular for their style and costume as they are for the events, while **bullfights** remain an obsession: every city has a bullring — México's Plaza México is the world's largest — and the country's *toreros* are said to be the world's most reckless, much in demand in Spain. Another popular bloodsport, usually at village level, is **cockfighting**, still legal in Mexico and mainly attended for the opportunity to bet on the outcome.

Masked wrestling is very popular in Mexico, too, with the participants, Batman-like, out of the game for good should their mask be removed and their secret identity revealed. Nor does the resemblance to comic-book superheroes end with the cape and mask: certain wrestlers, most famously the capital's **Superbarrio**, have become popular social campaigners out of the ring, always ready to turn up just in the nick of time to rescue the beleaguered poor from eviction by avaricious landlords, or persecution by corrupt politicians. For more on wrestling, see p.319a.

CRAFTS AND MARKETS

The craft tradition of Mexico, much of it descended directly from arts practised long before the Spanish arrived, is still extremely strong. Regional and highly localized specialities survive, with villages throughout the republic jealously guarding their reputations – especially in the state of Michoacán and throughout Oaxaca, Chiapas and the Yucatán. There's a considerable amount of Guatemalan stuff about too.

CRAFTS

To buy **crafts**, there is no need these days to visit the place of origin – craft shops in México and all the big resorts gather the best and most popular items from around the country. On the other hand, it's a great deal more enjoyable to see where the articles come from, and certainly the only way to get any real bargains. The good stuff is rarely cheap wherever you buy it, however, and there is an enormous amount of dross produced specifically for tourists.

FONART shops, which you'll come across in major centres throughout Mexico, are run by a government agency devoted to the promotion and preservation of crafts – their wares are always excellent, if expensive, and the shops should always be visited to get an idea of what is potentially available. Where no such store exists, you can get a similar idea by looking at the best of the tourist shops.

Among the most popular items are: **silver**, the best of which is wrought in Taxco, although rarely mined there; **pottery**, almost everywhere, with different techniques, designs and patterns in each region; **woollen goods**, especially blankets and *sarapes* from Oaxaca, which are again made everywhere – always check the fibres and go for more expensive natural dyes; **leather**, especially tire-tread-soled *huaraches* (sandals), sold cheaply wherever you go; **glass** from Jalisco; **lacquerware**, particularly from Uruapán; and **hammocks**, the best of which are sold in Mérida.

Antiquities for sale should be looked at carefully: invariably they prove to be worthless fakes, but should you stumble on anything authentic it is illegal to buy or sell it, and even more illegal to try taking it out of the country.

MARKETS

For bargain hunters, the **mercado** (market) is the place to head. There's one in every Mexican town, which on one day of the week, the traditional market day, will be at its busiest with villagers from the surrounding area bringing their produce for sale or barter. By and large, of course, mercados are mainly dedicated to food and everyday necessities, but most have a section devoted to crafts, and in larger towns you may find a separate crafts bazaar.

Unless you're completely hopeless at bargaining, prices will always be lower in the market than in shops, but **shops** do have a couple of advantages. Firstly, they exercise a degree of quality control, whereas any old junk can be sold in the market; and secondly, many established shops will be able to ship purchases home for you, which saves an enormous amount of the frustrating bureaucracy you'll encounter if you attempt to do it yourself.

Bargaining and haggling are very much a matter of personal style, highly dependent on your command of Spanish and to some extent on experience. The old chestnuts (never show the least sign of interest, let alone enthusiasm; walking away will always cut the price dramatically) do still hold true; but most important is to know what you want, its approximate value, and how much you are prepared to pay. Never start to haggle for something you definitely don't intend to buy — it'll end in bad feelings on both sides. In shops there's little chance of significantly altering the official price unless you're buying in bulk, and even in markets most food and simple household goods have a set price (though it may be doubled at the sight of an approaching gringo).

CRIME AND SAFETY

Despite soaring crime rates and dismal-sounding statistics, you are unlikely to run into trouble in Mexico as long as you stick to the trodden paths. Even in México, which has an appalling reputation, there is little more threat than there would be in an average North American or European city.

Obviously there are areas of the cities where you wander alone, or at night, at your peril; but the precautions to be taken are mostly common sense and would be second nature at home. Travelling in the Zapatista-controlled areas of the state of Chiapas you will undoubtedly come across guerrillas and the army, but tourists are a target of neither and you shouldn't encounter any trouble.

AVOIDING THEFT

Petty **theft** and **pickpockets** are your biggest worry, so don't wave money around, try not to look too obviously affluent, don't leave cash or cameras in hotel rooms, and do deposit your valuables in your hotel's safe if it has one (make a note of what you've deposited and ask the hotelier to sign it if you're worried). Crowds, especially on public city transport, are obvious hotspots: thieves tend to work in groups and tar-

get tourists. Distracting your attention, especially by pretending to look for something (always be suspicious of anyone who appears to be searching for something near you), or having one or two people pin you while another goes through your pockets, are common ploys, and can be done faster and more easily than you might imagine. Razoring of bags and pockets is another gambit, as is grabbing of handbags, or anything left unattended even for a split second. When carrying your valuables, keep them out of sight under your clothes. If you are held up, however, don't try any heroics: hand over your money and rely on travellers' cheque refund schemes and credit card hotlines if appropriate. **Mugging** is less common, but you should steer clear of obvious danger spots, such as deserted pedestrian underpasses in big cities — indeed, steer clear of *anywhere* deserted in big cities. Robbery and **sexual assault** on tourists by cab drivers are not unknown, and the US State Department advises its citizens against hailing a cab in the street in the capital, México. At night the beaches in tourist areas are also potentially dangerous.

When **travelling**, keep an eye on your bags (which are safe enough in the luggage compartments underneath most buses). Trains are a frequent scene of theft. The most dangerous time is when the train stops at a station, since thieves will board and, with luck, have your gear away unnoticed until the train is again on the move. Beware of deliberate distractions. If all the lights suddenly go off at night for no apparent reason, that is also a danger signal.

Drivers are likely to encounter problems if they leave anything in their car. The vehicle itself is less likely to be stolen than broken into for the things inside. To avoid the worst, always park legally (and preferably off the street) and never leave anything visible inside the car. Driving itself can be hazardous, too, especially at night (see p.34).

In the event of trouble, dial ☎06 for the **police emergency** operator. Most phone booths give the number for the local **Red Cross** (*Cruz Roja*).

POLICE

Mexican **police** are, in the ordinary run of events, no better or worse than any other; but they are very badly paid, and graft has become an accepted part of the job. This is often difficult for foreign visitors to accept, but it is a system, and in its own way it works well enough. If a policeman accuses you of some violation (and this is almost bound to happen to drivers at some stage), explain that you're a tourist, not used to the ways of the country – you may get off scot-free, but more likely the subject of a "fine" will come up. Such on-the-spot fines are open to negotiation, but only if you're confident you've done nothing seriously wrong and have a reasonable command of Spanish. Otherwise pay up and get out.

These small **bribes** are known as *mordidas* ("bites"), and they may also be extracted by border officials or bureaucrats (in which case, you *could* get out of paying by asking for a receipt, but it won't make life easier). In general, it is always wise to back off from any sort of confrontation with the police and to be extremely polite to them at all times.

Far more common than the *mordida* is the **propina**, or tip, a payment that is made entirely on your initiative. There's no need to do this, but it's remarkable how often a few pesos can oil the wheels, complete paperwork that would otherwise take weeks, open doors that were firmly locked before, or even find a seat on a previously full bus. All such transactions are quite open, and it's up to you to literally put your money on the table.

Should a crime be committed against you – in particular **if you're robbed** – your relationship with the police will obviously be different, although even in this eventuality it's worth considering whether the lengthy hassles you'll go through make it worth reporting. Some insurance companies will insist on a police report if you're to get any refund (see p.27) – in which case you may practically have to dictate it to the officer and can expect little action – but others will understand the situation. American Express in México, for example, may accept without a murmur the fact that your cheques have been stolen but the theft was not reported to the police. The department you need in order to *presentar una denuncia* (report the theft officially) is the Procuraduría General de Justicia.

The Mexican **legal system** is based on the Napoleonic code, which assumes your guilt until you can prove otherwise. Your one phone call should you be jailed should be to your consulate – if nothing else, they'll arrange an English-speaking lawyer. You can be held for up to 72 hours on suspicion before charges have to be brought. Mexican **jails** are grim, although lots of money and friends on the outside can ameliorate matters slightly.

DRUGS

Drug offences are the most common cause of serious trouble between tourists and the authorities. Under heavy pressure from the US to stamp out the trade, Mexican authorities are particularly happy to throw the book at foreign offenders.

A good deal of **marijuana** (known as *mota*) – that famous Acapulco Gold, as well as weed from the Yucatán, Oaxaca and Michoacán – continues to be cultivated in Mexico, despite US-backed government attempts to stamp it out (at one time, imports of Mexican marijuana were having such a deleterious effect on the US trade balance that the DEA had crops sprayed with paraquat). Cannabis is **illegal**, and foreigners caught in possession are dealt with harshly; for quantities reckoned to be dealable you can wave goodbye to daylight for a long time. For possession of small quantities, you can expect a hefty fine, no sympathy and little help from your consulate.

Other naturally occurring drugs – Mexico has more species of psychoactive plants than anywhere else in the world – still form an important part of many indigenous rituals. Hallucinogenic **mushrooms** can be found in many parts of the country, especially in the states of Oaxaca and in Chiapas, while the **peyote** cactus from the northern deserts is used primarily by the Huichols, but also by other indigenous peoples. It is theoretically illegal, but the authorities turn a blind eye to native use, and even tourists are unlikely to get into much difficulty over personal use (though raids on guesthouses in peyote country have been known).

Heroin has never been a serious problem inside Mexico (though it is produced in the north for export to the US), but **cocaine** is a different story, with the country a major staging post on the smuggling route from Colombia to the United States, and well-connected gangs involved in the trade, especially in Guadalajara and Ciudad Juárez. Use of cocaine, even crack, is becoming as serious a problem in certain northern cities as it is in the US. Best advice as far as this unpleasant trade goes is to steer well clear.

DIRECTORY

ADDRESSES In Mexico addresses are frequently written with just the street name and number (thus: Madero 125), which can lead to confusion as many streets are known only as numbers (C 17). *Calle* (C) means Street; *Avenida*, *Calzada* and *Paseo* are other common terms – most are named after historical figures or dates. An address such as Hidalgo 39 8° 120, means Hidalgo no. 39, 8th floor, room 120 (a ground-floor address would be denoted PB for *Planta Baja*). Many towns have all their streets laid out in a numbered grid fanning out from a central point – often with odd numbered streets running east–west, even ones north–south. In such places a suffix – Ote (for *Oriente*, East), Pte (for *Poniente*, West), Nte (for *Norte*, North), or Sur (South) – may be added to the street number to tell you which side of the two central dividing streets it is.

AIRPORT TAX A departure tax is payable when flying out of Mexico (the equivalent of US$13). This is included in the price of most air tickets, but be sure to check when buying.

BEGGARS When you consider that there's no social security worth mentioning and that most Mexicans are very generous towards them, beggars are surprisingly rare in Mexico. What you will see, though, are people selling worthless trinkets, or climbing onto buses or trains, singing a song, and passing the hat.

ELECTRICITY Theoretically 110 volts AC, with simple two-flat-pin rectangular plugs, so most North American appliances can be used as they are. Travellers from the UK, Ireland, Australasia and Europe should bring along a transformer and a plug adapter. Cuts in service and fluctuations in the current do occur, and in cheap hotels any sort of appliance that draws a lot of current may blow all the fuses as soon as it's turned on.

FILM AND CAMERA EQUIPMENT Film is manufactured in Mexico and, if you buy it from a chain store like Woolworth's or Sanborn's rather than at a tourist store, costs no more than at home (if you buy it elsewhere, be sure to check the date on the box, and be suspicious if you can't see it). Up to twelve rolls of film can be brought into Mexico, and spare batteries are also a wise precaution. Any sort of camera hardware, though, will be prohibitively expensive. Slide film is hard to come by, too.

TIME ZONES Three time zones exist in Mexico. Most of the country is on GMT–6 year-round. In winter, this is the same as US Central Standard Time, but an hour behind when the US and Canada are on Daylight Saving. Baja California Sur and the northwest coastal states of Sonora, Sinaloa and Nayarit are on GMT–7, the same as Mountain Standard Time in the winter, an hour behind it in summer. Confusingly, Baja California Norte *does* observe Daylight Saving Time, making it GMT–7 in summer and GMT–8 in winter, so you won't need to change your watch if crossing the border from California at any time of year. In 1997 a further time zone was created in the state of Yucatán, though at the time of writing this had been scrapped and the state due to revert to GMT–6.

TOILETS Public toilets in Mexico can be quite filthy, and there's often no paper (though someone may sell it outside). They're known usually as *baños* (literally bathrooms) or as *excusados* or *sanitarios*. The most common signs are *Damas* (Ladies) and *Caballeros* (Gentlemen), though you may find the more confusing *Señoras* (Women) and *Señores* (Men). Always carry some toilet paper with you: it's easy enough to buy in Mexico, but it's never there when you need it.

CHAPTER ONE

BAJA CALIFORNIA AND THE PACIFIC NORTHWEST

Mexico's northwest is something of a bizarre – and initially uninviting – introduction to the country. Aspects of what you see here will be echoed constantly as you travel further south, yet in many ways it's resolutely atypical: at once desert and the country's most fertile agricultural area, wealthy and heavily Americanized, yet in parts impoverished, drab and seemingly barren. Nor is the climate exactly welcoming – although the ocean and local conditions help produce one or two milder spots, summer temperatures can hit 50°C, while winter nights in the desert are often really chilly.

Travelling overland from west coast USA you're clearly going to come this way, but on the whole the best advice is to hurry through the northern part at least: once you've crossed the invisible line of the Tropic of Cancer there's a tangible change – the country is softer and greener, the climate less harsh. Here you begin to find places that could be regarded as destinations in their own right, where you might be tempted to stay some time, rather than as a night or two's relief from the rigours of constant travel: the enormous all-out resort of **Mazatlán**, or the quieter Pacific beaches around **San Blas**, for example.

There's a straightforward **choice of routes**: down from Tijuana through the **Baja peninsula** and onwards by ferry from La Paz; or around by the **mainland road**, sticking to the coast all the way or possibly cutting up into central Mexico, either by railway from Los Mochis to Chihuahua, or by road from Mazatlán to Durango. The mainland route is quicker if your only aim is to get to México, but the Baja route is slightly less monotonous and, surprisingly, cheaper – the ferries are good value if you travel as a

---

BORDER CHECKS

Crossing the border, do not forget to go through **immigration and customs** checks. As everywhere, there's a free zone south of the frontier, and you can cross at will. Try to continue south, though, and you'll be stopped after some 20km and sent back to get your tourist card stamped. You can drive throughout Baja without special papers, but if you're planning to continue on the ferries across to the mainland you need to do the necessary paperwork at the border: attempting to rectify your error in La Paz or Santa Rosalía is fraught with difficulties.

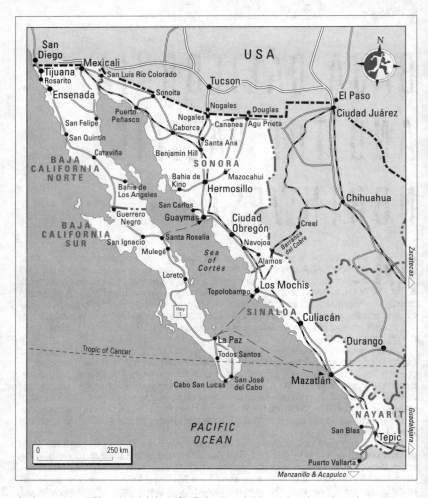

deck passenger. If you're **driving**, the Baja route is also safer: there have been numerous reports of assaults on motorists, especially around Culiacán in Sinaloa.

Baja California has plenty of fanatical devotees, most of whom arrive in light planes or in vehicles capable of heading off across the punishing desert tracks, laden down with fishing and scuba gear. Without such means of transport, it's impossible to get to most of the peninsula's undeniable attractions – completely isolated beaches, prehistoric cave paintings in the hilly interior, excellent fishing and snorkelling, and some great spots for surfing and windsurfing. On the bus all you do is pound down Hwy-1, still a relatively new road and low on facilities. Still, there are beautiful beaches which you can get to in the south by public transport, more crowded ones around Tijuana in the north, and if you're heading straight for the big Pacific resorts – Mazatlán, Puerto Vallarta and on towards Acapulco – it makes a lot of sense to come this way. Early in

---

ACCOMMODATION PRICE CODES

All the accommodation listed in this book has been categorized into one of nine price bands, as set out below. The prices quoted are in US dollars and normally refer to the cheapest available room for two people sharing in high season. For more details see p.36.

① less than US$5	④ US$15–25	⑦ US$60–80
② US$5–10	⑤ US$25–40	⑧ US$80–100
③ US$10–15	⑥ US$40–60	⑨ more than US$100

the year you can witness extraordinary scenes at Scammon's Lagoon, near Guerrero Negro, when hordes of **whales** congregate just offshore to calve.

On the **mainland route**, too, most people stick rigidly to the highway – over 2000km of it from Tijuana to Tepic, where the main road finally leaves the coast to cut through the mountains to Guadalajara. But here at least there's the option to stray from the highway; it's a relatively populous area, and from towns all along the route local buses run to villages in the foothills of the Sierra Madre or down to beaches along the Sea of Cortés and, later, the Pacific. Then again you can leave the coast entirely, heading inland by road or rail over the mountains. On the whole though, the equation is simple: the further south you travel, the more enticing the land becomes. For the first stages it's a question of getting as far in one go as you can stand: try to make it as far as Guaymas, or even Alamos. By the time you reach Mazatlán the pace becomes more relaxed, and you'll increasingly come across things to detain you: village fiestas, tropical beaches, mountain excursions. **Beyond Tepic** you're faced with the choice of following the mainstream and heading inland towards the central highlands, or sticking to the coast, where there's a good road all the way to Acapulco and beyond.

As everywhere, **buses** are the most efficient and fastest form of transport: they run the entire length of the coast road, and from Nogales or Tijuana to México, frequently down through Baja. The **train**, from Nogales or Mexicali to Guadalajara, is more comfortable if you're making the journey non-stop. There are also a number of **flights** taking advantage of deregulated airspace to link the major towns all the way down the coast. Flights **to México** can be especially competitive. Even on less used and therefore more expensive routes, an hour-long flight can be a tempting alternative to a ride of ten hours or more.

If you're **driving**, it's very much quicker to go via Nogales. Even if you're coming from Mexico's west coast, you'll save considerable time by taking US highways via Tucson. Heading down through Baja you could be delayed for a day or two trying to get your car onto a ferry – book ahead if at all possible. **Hitching** should be regarded here only as a last resort: long-distance traffic moves fast and is reluctant to stop, and it's exceedingly hot if you get stranded by the roadside. The north is also the area where most of the "disappearing gringo" horror stories originate.

TIJUANA AND THE BAJA PENINSULA

The early Spanish colonists believed Baja California to be an island and, after failing to find any great riches or to make much impact in converting the Indians, they left it pretty much alone. There's little of historic interest beyond a few old mission centres, and almost all you see dates from the latter half of this century, in particular since Hwy-1 was opened in 1973. Development has continued apace: in the south new resorts are springing up all the time, while what in the early nineteenth century was simply Aunt Joanna's ranch (*El Rancho de Tia Juana*) became a border crossing in 1848 and has not looked back since: **Tijuana** now ranks as Mexico's fourth city. Prohibition in the US was the biggest individual spur, but the city has never been slow to exploit its neighbour's desires, whether they be for sex, gambling or cheap labour.

Tijuana

TIJUANA is *the* Mexican border town – with every virtue and vice that this implies. More than 36 million people cross the border every year – the vast majority of them staying only a few hours – so it can boast with some justification of being the "World's Most Visited City". Which is not to say it's somewhere you should plan to hang around; but if you want to stop off before starting the long trek south, Tijuana is certainly your most practical choice. There's no shortage of reasonable hotels although, as you'd expect, most things are far more expensive than they are further south.

Above all the town is geared towards dealing with hordes of day-trippers, which means hundreds of tacky souvenir stands, cheap doctors, dentists and auto-repair shops, and countless bars and restaurants, pricey by Mexican standards but cheaper than anything you'll find in San Diego. One thing you won't find much of any more – at least not anywhere near the centre of town – is the prostitution and the sex shows for which the border towns used to be notorious. This is partly the result of a conscious attempt to clean the city up, due in part to the changing climate in the US: indeed in many places, though not visibly here, the traffic now runs in the other direction with vast billboards on the American side of the border offering lurid invitations to "Total nudity – 24 hours a day". Tijuana does still thrive on **gambling** though, with greyhound racing every evening; jai alai from 8pm every night except Wednesday in the huge downtown *Frontón Palacio*; and **bullfights** throughout the summer (May–Sept) at two rings, one right on the coast, the other a couple of kilometres southeast of the centre. At the off-track betting lounges all around Tijuana, you can place money on just about anything that moves and monitor progress on the banks of closed-circuit TVs.

The parts of the city most tourists don't see fit less easily into expectations. **Modern Tijuana** is among the wealthiest cities in the Mexican republic, buoyed up by the region's duty-free status and by *maquiladora* assembly plants (raw or semi-assembled materials are brought across the border duty-free, assembled by cheap Mexican labour, and re-exported with duty levied only on the added value). How the NAFTA treaty affects this remains to be seen, but chances are it means further boom times for Tijuana's industrial zone. Downtown, beyond the areas where most tourists venture, the modern concrete and glass wouldn't look amiss in southern California. The flip side of the boom lies along the border, where shantytowns sprawl for miles: housing for the labourers and also, more traditionally, the final staging post for the bid to disappear north.

Arrival

As in so many places in Mexico, Tijuana's **long-distance bus station** is miles from the centre – almost thirty minutes on the local bus. These blue-and-white buses (look for "Central Camionera") run through the centre on C 2-A and pass the border on the way to the terminal; take them in preference to taxis, which, quite legally, charge extortionate fares. **Taxis** to other points in Tijuana are not so bad, provided the meter is working, but you'll still save a lot by finding out which bus to take. The **airport** is slightly closer in than the bus station, and frequent buses run from there into town.

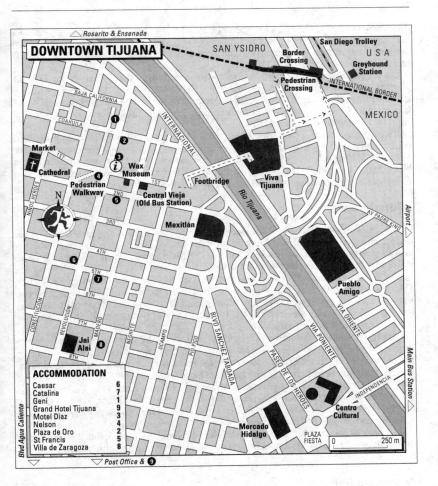

The border

If you have the right documentation, crossing the border (known as *la linea*, the Line) is normally a breeze, though you may have to wait in line, and US immigration can be pretty intimidating if you're entering the States. Heading into Mexico, the main worry is to remember to have your tourist card stamped at migración – people only visiting Tijuana, Ensenada and San Felipe don't need to do this. The border is open 24 hours a day.

On the US side, **San Ysidro**, there's excellent local transport into downtown **San Diego** – buses (US$1.50) and trams (the "San Diego Trolley"; 5am–1am & hourly through Sat night; US$1.75) run every few minutes – and there are plenty of alternatives if you're heading further north. Vans and minibuses, as well as Greyhound and other services, run almost constantly to **Los Angeles**; the Greyhound terminal is right by the border. San Ysidro itself, at least around the border, has little to offer: you'll find

McDonalds and *Burger King*, a few second-hand clothes stores, money exchange places and motor insurance offices, and a number of car parks charging US$3–7 a day. There are also a few motels – closest to the border are the *Gateway Inn* (☎619/428-2251; ⑤) and *Holiday Lodge* (☎619/428-1105; ⑤).

On the **Mexican side** it's only a short walk downtown – through the *Viva Tijuana* shopping mall, over the footbridge, and along C 1 to Revolución. Alternatively you can get downtown (look for "Centro" or "Revolución") or to the bus station (blue-and-white bus marked "Buena Vista/Central Camionera") from the public bus and taxi terminal right by the entrance to *Viva Tijuana*.

It's also possible to **cross the border by bus**, though it usually costs more and sometimes takes longer than walking over and picking up transport the other side. For example, Mexicoach (Revolución and 7th) and Transportes Diamante (Revolución, a block and a half below 1st) both run shuttles to San Ysidro (US$1); Mexicoach also operates a shuttle service between the border and Revolución.

Information

Of Tijuana's three very helpful **tourist offices**, two are right at the frontier – one for pedestrians, another for drivers (insurance available) – either of which is well worth a visit to pick up a free map and some leaflets. The main tourist office is right in the centre of downtown at Revolución and 1st (daily 9am–7pm; ☎66/88-16-85), while on the opposite corner you'll find the often more helpful **Tourism Protection Office** (Mon–Sat 9am–7pm, Sun 10am–5pm; ☎66/88-05-55). This is the office to head for if you become a victim of crime, a rip-off, or simply want to make a complaint (with so many tourists, Tijuana feels safe enough, but there's plenty of petty crime). They also have some maps and general information.

Changing money should be no problem, with casas de cambio on virtually every corner. Most offer good rates – almost identical to those north of the border – though few of them accept travellers' cheques, and if they do, they charge a heavy commission. For cheques you're better off with a **bank**, most of which are on Constitución, a block over from Revolución. There's also an **American Express** office in *Viajes Carrusel* (Mon–Fri 9am–6pm, Sat 9am–noon) way out on Sanchez Taboada at Clemente Orozco, but their rates are poor. US dollars are accepted almost everywhere anyway – again the rates are usually fair, but always check.

The **post office** is at Negrete and 11th (Mon–Fri 8am–7pm, Sat & Sun 9.30am–1pm), though to send international mail or make long-distance **phone** calls, you're better off crossing the border.

Accommodation

By comparison with the rest of Mexico, you pay more for **accommodation** in Tijuana and get less for your money, but at least there's plenty of choice. Watch out for noise and security if you're staying in the centre. None of the budget places along 1st heading west from Revolución is recommended – particularly not for lone women – as most of your fellow guests will only be staying for an hour or less. The more expensive hotels, mostly further out, are better value, but there's little point staying at these unless you're here on business.

Caesar, Revolución 1079 at 5th (☎66/88-05-50). Classy old place with uniformed staff. The restaurant claims to have invented the Caesar salad. Has seen better days, but surprisingly good value. ⑤.

Catalina, 5th 2059 at Madero (☎66/85-97-48). Old but modernized hotel with clean, spacious en-suite rooms. ④.

Geni, Revolución 417, below 1st. Basic, but acceptable and relatively cheap. ③.

Grand Hotel Tijuana, Agua Caliente 4500 (☎66/81-70-00). Twin 23-storey towers mark Tijuana's fanciest hotel. ⑨.

Motel Diaz, Revolución 650, below 1st (☎66/85-71-48). Unit-style motel, worth the money if you need parking. ⑤.

Nelson, Revolución 721 at 1st (☎66/85-43-02). Pleasant, old-fashioned, respectable hotel in ideal, though noisy, location. Colour cable TV. ⑤.

Plaza de Oro, Revolución 588, below 1st (☎66/38-41-12). Comfortable, modern place with cable TV but little character. ④.

St Francis, 2nd between Revolución and Madero (☎66/85-49-03). Clean and old-fashioned. ③.

Villa de Zaragoza, Madero 1480 at 7th (☎66/85-18-32). Modern, upmarket, US-style motel. ⑤.

Downtown Tijuana

If you're here to shop, drink and shake your stuff, you won't need to wander far off the few blocks of Avenida Revolución between 1st and about 8th streets. Here there's an uninterrupted stream of bars, dance clubs, malls, markets and souvenir stalls, and more or less permanent crowds. If you're after anything else, you're in the wrong town, though there are a few purpose-built attractions to occupy some time. Buses between the centre and the border pass the **Centro Cultural** (☎66/84-11-11, ext 301), a spectacularly threatening globe of a complex. Designed by Pedro Ramírez Vázquez – the architect responsible for México's Aztec stadium and Anthropological Museum – it's said to represent the earth breaking out of its shell. Inside, the **Cine Planetario** (Mon–Fri 3–9pm; Sat & Sun 11am–9pm; US$3) hosts a multimedia spectacular on its giant Cinemax screen; the programme changes every four months or so, sometimes featuring English-language films. There are also regular exhibitions and shows, a restaurant, and the inevitable shopping arcade, along with a **museum** (daily 11am–8pm; US$1), which is not at all bad as an introduction to Mexican culture and art, despite the fact that almost everything you see is a reproduction. **El Lugar del Nopal**, C 6 and Av. G, also hosts a variety of artistic events, including exhibitions and live music.

Lesser attractions include the now run-down **Mexitlán** (mid-May to mid-Sept daily 10am–10pm; mid-Sept to mid-May Wed–Fri 10am–6pm, Sat & Sun 9am–9pm; US$1), a miniature Mexican theme park with models of famous Mexican buildings, folklore performances, and more restaurants and shops, which is hard to miss as you approach town from the border; a new and very tacky **wax museum** at Madero and 1st (don't waste your money); and various modern **shopping malls**. Most of these are given over to a mix of duty-free goods and stalls selling souvenirs, fake designer clothing and jewellery – two of the biggest are Viva Tijuana, which you'll walk through on the way to the centre if you cross the border on foot, and Pueblo Amigo.

Eating

With all the crowds passing through Tijuana you might expect some great restaurants, but you'd be disappointed. On the main drag everything is aimed at tourists: Mexican restaurants US-style, almost all of them with loud music and "party" atmosphere. Plaza Fiesta, diagonally opposite the Centro Cultural, has a wide variety of restaurants and fast-food places; you'll find a similar, though smaller, range in any of the shopping plazas.

Plainer Mexican food can be found in the surrounding streets, especially on Madero and Constitución, but despite the fact that migrants from all over Mexico bring their cuisine with them – naming their lonchería or taquería after their home state – there's nothing very exciting even here.

Antojitos Bíbi's, in the Mercado Hidalgo. Clean and inexpensive place for simple meals all day. Handy for the Centro Cultural.

Hotel Nelson, Revolución and 1st. Decent value and very popular Mexican place, serving good food in large portions.

Pipirin, Constitución between 2nd and 3rd. Bargain sit-down taco joint.

Punto Café, Plaza Fiesta. Trendy, low-key place with outside seating, magazines to flick through and an incredible range of coffees.

Tía Juana Tilly's, Revolución 1420 at 7th. Slick, predictably Tex-Mex restaurant with terrace, linked to the jai alai hall. Bow-tied waiters serve up main courses (steaks, chicken, seafood) for around US$7–12.

Tortas Ricardo's, Madero at 7th. A massive range of Mexican dishes served in American diner surroundings. Open late.

Vittorio's, Revolución 1687 at 9th. Full range of well-prepared Italian dishes as well as Mexican staples. Good pizza and great espresso.

Drinking and nightlife

Nearly all the action in Tijuana happens close to Revolución, where numerous **nightclubs** pump out soft rock or dance-oriented rap. English is the lingua franca, dollars are the currency of choice, and the playlist is solidly North American. Most places are open until at least 2am. With competition fierce, cover charges are rare and drinks are often offered two for the price of one: walk along Revolución and pick the most appealing joint on the night. More traditional **Mexican bars**, as well as those featuring "exotic dancers", cluster around 1st and Constitución and on Revolución at 6th.

The pedestrianized Plaza Fiesta (see "Eating") offers the most obvious alternative to the hard-sell party atmosphere of the main drag. Though smaller and slightly calmer, this area, crammed with bars and clubs, offers more real variety and certainly feels more "Mexican".

The Cave, Revolución 1137 between 5th and 6th. Much the same as all the other tourist-oriented places, but at ground level so you can see what you are letting yourself in for.

Diamante Disco, Revolución and 1st. The least intimidating of the seedy Latin bars but still not recommended for unaccompanied women.

People's Sports and Rock, Revolución 786 at 2nd. Consistently one of the better "fun" bars, with a slightly harder edge to the music. Be prepared for the bar staff moving to pour tequila down your throat in an effort to loosen the purse strings.

El Perro Azul, Plaza Fiesta. Arty, bohemian place with live acoustic music, art exhibitions and a mixed, friendly clientele. Open till 2am.

Las Pulgas, Revolución 1127 opposite jai alai. Modern Latin disco with a huge dance floor.

Salón de Baile, 6th between Revolución and Madero. Don't be put off by the lurid wall paintings, this is the real thing: a traditional dancehall with an almost Caribbean feel playing salsa, cumbia and norteño. Look for the big red star.

Listings

Airlines Aeroméxico, Revolución 1236 (☎66/85-44-05); Aero California, Paseo de los Heroes 95, Plaza Río Local C-20 (☎66/84-21-00); Mexicana at the airport (☎66/82-41-84); and TAESA, Paseo de los Heroes 9288-B1 (☎66/84-84-84).

Consulates Australia/Canada, German Gedovius 5-202, Zona Río (☎66/84-04-61); UK, Salinas 1500 (☎66/81-73-23); USA, Tapachula 96 (☎66/81-74-00).

Left luggage Bags can be left at the Central Camionera (daily 6am–10.30pm), in lockers over the border in the Greyhound station (24hr), or next door at Pro-Pack (Mon–Sat 9am–6pm).

MOVING ON FROM TIJUANA

Heading for **the US**, you can pick up Greyhound **buses** (roughly hourly 6am–6pm) as you arrive at the Central Camionera (☎66/26-17-01 for all bus companies) and avoid stopping in Tijuana altogether. The Greyhound goes on to pick up in central Tijuana from the old bus station, Central Vieja (see below), then crosses the border, stopping for passengers at San Ysidro. Slightly more expensive, Transportes Intercalifornias run nine times daily from the airport, Camionera Central, the centre of town, and either side of the border to LA.

The Central Camionera handles departures for almost all **Mexican destinations**, with numerous departures to the west coast and, to a lesser extent, down Baja. Catch the blue-and-white buses marked "Buena Vista" or "Central Camionera". The **Central Vieja** bus station, at Madero and 1st, handles buses to Rosarito (hourly 8am–8pm).

Though they vary greatly depending on demand, **flights** to the rest of Mexico, and particularly to the capital (16 daily; 3hr), can be surprisingly cheap from Tijuana, sometimes dropping to around US$100 or much the same price as a first-class bus. Flights to other destinations are less competitive: typically US$125 to Guadalajara, US$210 to Acapulco, and US$180 to La Paz. Viajes La Mesa, at Madero and 1st (☎66/88-15-11), can help with bookings, but it pays to shop around for the best prices. The **airport** (☎66/83-24-18) can be reached on buses marked "Aeropuerto" from Madero and 2nd.

Rosarito

If you want to escape the pace and noise of Tijuana, head for **ROSARITO**, about 45 minutes' bus ride on the old road to Ensenada. **Beaches** in Tijuana itself are invariably crowded and dirty: Rosarito, while scarcely less popular, has a far longer, sandier strand and a much more restful atmosphere. It's not particularly attractive – the beach is grey, windswept, and none too clean, lined with condo developments and hotels – but it does make for a worthwhile afternoon. You could even stay out here; the motels lining the road are better value than those in town.

To **get to** Rosarito from Tijuana, take one of the colectivo taxis that leave from Madero between 4th and 5th, or head for the old bus station at Madero and 1st, from where buses leave every hour or so; to **get back**, just flag down a bus or colectivo on Rosarito's main street. Rosarito's **tourist office** (daily 9am–7pm; ☎661/2-38-87) is inconveniently situated a twenty-minute walk to the north on the road to Tijuana, and not really worth the effort. There are no budget **hotels**, and probably the cheapest in town is the *Hotel California* (☎661/2-25-50; ⑤). Right on the beach with ocean views is the *Hotel Los Pelicanos* (☎661/2-04-45; ⑤), by the large terracotta-coloured hotel block. The style and charm that made the *Rosarito Beach Hotel* (☎661/2-01-44; ⑦) a Hollywood favourite during the prohibition years has now largely been obliterated by modern refurbishment, but the older rooms still have some character. Along the single street behind the beach is a row of restaurants, cafés and bars, some of them pretty good, in particular the **fish restaurants** and a couple of cafés that serve decent cappuccino and cakes. The party-time focus is *Papas and Beer*, where beach volleyball and knocking back as much Corona as possible is the order of the day.

If you're **continuing south** to Ensenada and beyond, you can pick up long-distance buses (at least hourly) at the autopista toll booth 1km south of the tourist office, past the *Rosarito Beach Hotel*. The coast road down through Rosarito – now supplanted by the motorway to Ensenada – is an attractive drive, lined with seaside villas and condos.

Ensenada, San Felipe and the road south

ENSENADA, just a couple of hours on from Tijuana by the toll road, is favoured by Californians "in the know" – at weekends it's packed with partying groups of southern Californians. It's cheaper, smaller, less exclusively geared to visitors, but still with a pretty clear idea of the value of the US dollar. No more attractive than Tijuana, it does at least have some life of its own as a major port and fish processing centre.

Almost all the action is squeezed into a few streets around the harbour: seafront Boulevard Costero (aka Lázaro Cárdenas), Avenida Mateos (or C 1), which runs parallel, and as far inland as Avenida Juárez (C 5). Here you'll find scores of souvenir shops and outfits offering sport fishing trips, as well as the bulk of the bars, hotels and restaurants. Most visitors come here to eat, drink, shop and little else. If you do want to explore further, you could check out the view from the Chapultepec Hills, overlooking town from the west, or visit the *Bodegas de Santo Tomás* **winery**, one of Baja's largest, which offers tours and regular tastings at Miramar 666 between C 6-A and 7-A (tours daily 11am, 1pm & 3pm; US$2; ☎617/8-33-33). Most of the wines are only passable; if it isn't offered, ask to try the white sherry.

Ensenada also attracts its share of surfers, of course, though as you'll find throughout Baja it really pays to have your own transport. The best **beaches** are at **Estero**, some 10km to the south, 2km off the main road. Occasional local buses run past these to perhaps the most startling attraction in the area, **La Bufadora**, a natural blow-hole or geyser, where the combined action of wind, waves and an incoming tide periodically forces a huge jet of sea water up through a small vent in the roof of an undersea cavern, in ideal conditions attaining 25–30m. Even though it's more than 20km off the main road, it's worth a visit, despite the annoying number of souvenir stands that rather spoil the atmosphere. To get there take a micro from the Tres Cabezas park on Costero at the bottom of Riveroll to Maneadero and another from there.

Ensenada practicalities

The **bus station** (plus guardería) is at C 11 and Av Riveroll: turn right and head down Riveroll to reach the bay – head left when you reach Mateos for the centre of town. There's a second, smaller station a couple of blocks down Riveroll between C 8 and C 9, which handles frequent services to Tijuana. The very helpful COTUCO **tourist office** (Mon–Fri 9am–7pm, Sat & Sun 10am–2pm; ☎61/78-24-11) is on Costero at the corner of Gastelum, where the main road enters town. The SECTUR **tourism protection office** is at Costero 1477 and Rocas (same hours). The **post office** (Mon–Fri 8am–7pm, Sat 9am–1pm) is at Club Rotario 93 and Mateos.

Accommodation

If you're hoping for somewhere to **stay** at the weekend – the best time to be here, if only for the nightlife – you'd be well advised to book, or arrive early; during the week there should be no problem. Most of the hotels are on Mateos and Costero between Riveroll and Espinoza; though **rates** in general are high, the cheaper places tend to be on Mateos.
Bahía, Mateos between Riveroll and Alvarado (☎61/78-21-01). Huge, popular place with big range of rooms. ⑤.
Misión Santa Isabel, Castillo 1100 at Costero (☎61/78-36-16). Modern colonial-style motel, with pool and restaurant *El Campanario*. ⑥.
Motel America, Mateos at Espinoza (☎61/76-13-33). No frills, but OK. Some kitchenettes. ④.
Motel Pancho, Alvarado 211 at C 2a (☎61/78-23-44). Basic but clean. ④.
Hotel Río, Miramar 231 at C 2a (☎61/78-37-33). The best budget deal in town, with surprisingly nice rooms and very friendly owners. ②.

Travelodge, Blancarte 130 at Mateos (☎61/78-16-01). Another good, central motel with pool, and a pricey French-Mexican restaurant, *El Rey Sol*. ⑦.

Eating and drinking

There's plenty of choice of places to **eat and drink** near the hotels. For good, inexpensive food, particularly breakfasts, try the *Plaza Café*, at Mateos between Gastelum and Miramar. One unavoidable attraction is *Hussongs Cantina*, Ruiz 113, whose bumper stickers and T-shirts are seen throughout California; one of a cluster of places around the corner of Ruiz and Mateos, it manages to remain pretty sleazy for all its fame and popularity. Most of the other venues in the vicinity seem to be owned by the Hussong empire, too, but few are as popular as the original. Exceptions include *El Charro*, Mateos 486, with roast chicken and plain Mexican food at reasonable prices served till late, and *Las Brasas*, nearby, which is similar. The bohemian *Café Café*, Mateos and Gastelum, is considerably more low-key, with backgammon and, at weekends, live folk, jazz or blues from both Californias. *Pueblo Café-Deli*, Mateos and Ruiz, is a stylish and popular bar also serving good food.

The stalls at the fish market, by the harbour, sell fish tacos and other **seafood** at a fraction of the price of the fancy restaurants that line Costero. If you do want to sit down and don't mind missing out on the views, for excellent, plain seafood, try *Mariscos Playa Azul*, Riveroll 113, or *El Palmar* at Mateos and Obregón. Among the numerous **Chinese restaurants** is the upmarket *China Land*, at Riveroll 1149, by the bus station.

San Felipe

With so few places in northern Baja boasting a decent beach and reasonable public transport, the prospect of **SAN FELIPE**, a growing Sea of Cortés resort on a dead-end road 200km south of Mexicali, might seem attractive. But its appeal is limited: the entire bay is strung with RV parks, and the dunes between here and the encircling folded ridges of the San Pedro Martin mountains reverberate to the screaming engines of dune buggies and balloon-tired trikes. If you are planning to continue south down Baja, then do just that. But San Felipe does have good swimming – at least at high tide – and if you are confined to the north, it's the best place to rent a catamaran or just relax for a day or so.

San Felipe first came to the attention of fishermen who, in the early 1950s, took advantage of the new tarmac road – built to serve the American radar station to the south on what is now called Punta Radar – to exploit the vast schools of tortuava, a species now fished onto the endangered list. Since the 1980s, the fishing village has grown to accommodate the November-to-April influx of vacationers from north of the border and college students on Spring Break. Apart from lying on the beach, you can rent **dirt bikes** and trikes from a couple of places along the malecón (around US$20 an hour), **catamarans** (similar price; just ask along the beach wherever you see one), or indulge in a little **sport fishing** on tours from a couple of places at the northern end of the malecón.

If the road through the cactus desert south of here to Hwy-1 ever gets improved to the point that it can be negotiated by low-clearance vehicles, this could become an interesting alternative route to southern Baja, but for the moment the hamlet of **Puertecitos**, 85km south (no public transport), is as far as ordinary cars can get – and even then with difficulty.

Practicalities

Buses from Mexicali (4 daily; 3hr) and Ensenada (2 daily; 3hr 30min) arrive 1km inland: turn left out of the bus station and right down Manzanillo to get to Av Mar de

---

DIVING AND FISHING AROUND BAJA CALIFORNIA

Nowhere in Baja California is more than 90km from either the Pacific Ocean or the Sea of Cortés, both bodies of water that support an abundance of **sea life**. The unmatched variety of marine environments makes the Sea of Cortés in particular one of the richest seas in the world, with over 800 species of fish and more than twice as many shellfish. Throughout the peninsula you'll see RVs and off-road vehicles laden with fishing tackle, dinghies and scuba gear, headed for remote fish camps or sheltered bays to launch the dive boat. Opportunities for less well-prepared visitors are limited, but the bigger towns, particularly around **Cabo San Lucas** and **San José del Cabo**, are seething with operators eager to take you out.

The most popular **diving** areas in the north are **Islas Los Coronados**, off Tijuana, but only served by organized trips from San Diego north of the border; and **Punta Banda** and **Islas de Todos Santos**, off Ensenada. In the south, where the waters are a good deal warmer and the fish dramatically colourful, the best spots are the coast off **Santa Rosalía, Bahía de Concepción** south of Mulegé, **La Paz** and **Los Cabos**. From August to November you'll find the ideal combination of water clarity and warmth.

There are a number of regulations governing sport fishing in Mexico; check with a tourist office for a rundown.

Cortez, which runs parallel to the sea. At the junction, the **tourist office** (Mon–Fri 8am–7pm, Sat 9am–3pm, Sun 10am–1pm; ☎65/77-11-55) gives out a map of the town but little else. North from here along Cortez there's a farmacia where you can change money (Mon–Fri 9am–6pm) and, beyond, a Bancomer but no ATM. The **post office** is on Mar Blanco just off Chetumal, five blocks inland. **Hotels** in San Felipe are not particularly cheap, though there are a couple of decent reasonably priced choices: *La Hacienda*, Chetumal 125 (☎65/77-15-70; ⑥), is marginally better than *Chapala Motel*, Mar de Cortez 142 (☎65/77-12-40; ⑤), but the best of all is *El Capitan Motel*, Mar de Cortez 298 (☎65/77-13-03; ⑥), with pool, TVs and a/c. **Camping** is best at the RV parks to the north of town, notably *Ruben's RV Trailer Park*, Golfo de California (☎65/77-10-91; ③), or you can just sleep on the beach around the bottom of Chetumal, where there are showers and toilets.

Not surprisingly, **seafood** is the staple diet here, with several restaurants and numerous stands selling shellfish cocktails along the front. Head for *The Bearded Clam* at the northern end of the beachfront malecón, or *The Red Lobster* at *La Hacienda* hotel.

On to the 28th parallel

Beyond Ensenada you head into Baja California proper – barren and god-forsaken. At times the road runs along the coast, but for the most part the scenery is dry brown desert, with the peninsula's low mountain spine to the left and nothing but sand and the occasional scrubby cactus around the road. The towns are generally drab, dusty and windswept collections of single-storey shacks which belie their supposed wealth. At **SANTO TOMÁS**, 45km from Ensenada, the *El Palomar* motel (☎61/68-23-55; ⑥), with pool, trailer park and restaurant, makes a good place to break the journey; the town itself is known for its wine and a deserted Dominican mission. If you can get off the highway, the attractions of the desert and its extraordinary vegetation become clearer.

Sixty-five kilometres past Santo Tomás, just beyond Colonet, a road turns inland towards the **Parque Nacional San Pedro Martír**. The side road, unsurfaced but in good condition, winds almost 100km up into the Sierra, which includes Baja's highest peaks at over 3000m – snowy in winter. As you climb, the land becomes increasingly green and wooded, and at the end of the road astronomical observatories take advantage of the piercingly clear air. There are breathtaking views in every direction. Numerous ill-defined trails wind through the park, but again, there's no public transport and you need to be fully equipped for wilderness camping if you want to linger.

San Quintín

SAN QUINTÍN is the first town of any size south of Ensenada, and even here, though there are a couple of big hotels, most of the buildings look temporary. There's no reason to stop here unless you intend to head to **Bahía San Quintín**, which is undeniably attractive, with five cinder-cone volcanoes as a backdrop to a series of small sandy beaches, and endless fishing (though not without a permit) and superb clamming that draw campers and RV drivers. The closest of the beaches are some 20km from town, 5km from the highway, and there's no transport to reach them.

Buses from Ensenada stop at **Lázaro Cárdenas**, 5km south of town. If you want to **stay**, the *Hotel La Pinta* (☎61/65-90-08; ⑦) is the luxury option, right on the beach 3km off the highway, some 8km south of Lázaro Cárdenas. More realistic alternatives include *Cielito Lindo* (⑥), close to *La Pinta*, and *Molino Viejo* (⑤) – from where fishing trips can be organized – on the bay; or one of the motels in town: *Las Hadas* (☎61/65-25-70; ③) or *Romo* (☎61/65-23-96; ③), which also has a decent **restaurant**. There are also plenty of camping spots around the bay if you come equipped, and RV sites at the *Molino Viejo*.

El Rosario and Cataviña

Some 60km beyond San Quintín, the highway passes through **EL ROSARIO**, the original site of a Dominican mission. Founded in 1774, the mission was forced by a shortage of water in 1802 to move 3km downstream to **El Rosario de Abajo**, where you can see the ruins: nowadays, however, it's little more than a BMX track for local kids, and definitely not worth getting off the bus for. These days, El Rosario is just another staging point, and modern El Rosario de Arriba consists of just a couple of filling stations and a few restaurants and **motels**. *El Rosario* (③), as you come into town, is good value, if noisy, with trucks roaring down the hill throughout the night, while the *Motel Sinai* (☎61/65-88-18; ④), at the town's southern edge, is quieter and more expensive. There's a rather rocky beach 12km south at Punta Baja.

Beyond El Rosario, the road turns sharply inland, to run down the centre of the peninsula for some 350km to Guerrero Negro. It's a bizarre landscape of cactus – particularly yucca, *cirios*, unique to this area, and *cardones*, which can grow over 15m tall – and rock, with plenty of strange giant formations; much of it is protected within the **Parque Natural del Desierto Central de Baja California**. In the heart of this area is **CATAVIÑA**, comprising a dozen or so buildings strung along the highway, complete with luxury hotel *La Pinta* (⑨), restaurants and trailer park. There's cheaper accommodation at *Rancho Santa Ines*, a couple of kilometres south (④), whose rooms double as dorms when necessary. You can eat here, but the restaurant opposite *La Pinta* is cheaper. If you do stop, take time to look at some of the giant boulders; not far off the highway at Km 171, just before Cataviña, is **La Cueva Pintada**, a tiny cave beneath a huge rock decorated with ancient paintings – circles, dots, sunbursts and stick figures.

Bahía de Los Angeles

The turn-off for **BAHÍA DE LOS ANGELES**, a growing resort on the Sea of Cortés, is about 100km further on from Cataviña. Still a small place, some 70km off Hwy-1, Bahía has a sheltered bay full of marine life hemmed in by contorted mountains. There's little else but a few hotels, cafés and fishing boats. Most visitors are an older generation of North Americans who arrive by light plane or in RVs. If you're passing through here, visit the small bilingual **museum** (daily 9am–noon & 3–5pm; free) marked by a narrow-gauge locomotive, a relic of the gold and copper mines that first attracted Europeans to the area. Mining history and that of the local ranchero life is well covered, along with details of sea life in the bay. The **Isla Angel de la Guarda**, out in the bay, is the biggest island in the Sea of Cortés and the focus of numerous diving and fishing trips. There are no official rental places for **scuba**, **snorkelling** or **fishing gear**, but the hotels can organize equipment rental and you should be able to strike a deal by asking around.

There's a frontier feeling in Bahía. The town has just one communal phone (☎665/0-32-06) and no bus service at all. Hitching from the main highway is a possibility, but be prepared for a long wait. Like everything else in Bahía, **hotels** are expensive. The fanciest are the new *Costa Del Sol* (from USA: ☎562/803-8873; ⑤) and *Villa Vitta* (from USA: ☎619/741-9583; ⑤), both of which have pools, restaurants and all the creature comforts; *Casa Díaz* (from USA: ☎619/278-9676; ⑤) and *Las Hamacas* (⑤) are slightly less luxurious. *Guillermo's Trailer Park* (also with rooms at ⑥) and *La Playa RV Park* both have **camping**, and are seldom packed; for free camping, walk to the beaches to the south. You can eat at any of these places, but for location the restaurant at *Guillermo's* has the edge.

Guerrero Negro

Continuing on the main highway, there's little between Cataviña and the 28th parallel, where an enormous metal monument, and a hotel, mark the border of Baja California Norte and **Baja California Sur**; you'll have to put your watch forward an hour when you cross, unless Baja California Norte is on Daylight Saving Time (April–Oct), in which case there's no change. **GUERRERO NEGRO**, just across the border, offers little in the way of respite from the heat and aridity that has gone before. Flat and fly-blown, it's an important centre for salt production, surrounded by vast salt pans and stark storage warehouses. At most times of year you'll want to do little more than grab a drink and pass straight through. In January and February (and, peripherally, Dec & March–May), however, Guerrero Negro is home to one of Mexico's most extraordinary natural phenomena, when scores of **California gray whales** congregate to calve just off the coast.

The whales, which spend most of their lives in the icy Bering Sea around Alaska, can be watched (at remarkably close quarters; the young are sometimes left stranded on the beaches) from an area within the **Parque Natural de la Ballena Gris**, which surrounds the Laguna Ojo de Liebre. The laguna is also known as **Scammon's Lagoon** after the whaling captain Charles Melville Scammon, who first brought the huge potential of the bay to the attention of rapacious whalers in 1857 – the town gets its name from the *Black Warrior*, an overladen whaling barque that sank here a year later.

At the right times of year there are **organized whale-watching trips**, and an observation tower that guarantees at least a distant sighting. Although talk turns every year to restricting numbers or banning boats altogether, there are currently more tours and **boat trips** than ever. If you can take one, then do so – it's an exceptional experience, and many visitors actually get to touch the whales, which often come right up to bobbing vessels, engines switched off. Whale-watching trips are mainly run from *Don Miguelito's* and *Mario's* (see below): both charge around US$30 per person for a four-hour trip, including a complimentary drink or two.

To get to the shore **with your own vehicle** (it needs to be sturdy), head south from town until you see the park sign; from here a poor sand track leads 24km down to the lagoon. Midway there's a **checkpoint** where you must register your vehicle and its occupants, and at the park entrance a **fee** of around US$3 is charged. To see the whales **from the shore** you'll need to get up early or stay late, as they move out to the deeper water in the middle of the day.

Practicalities

To **stay** in Guerrero Negro, you can choose from numerous hotels and motels strung out along the main drag. Perhaps the best is the *Motel Cabañas Don Miguelito* (☎685/7-02-50; ⑤), to the right as you enter town, with clean rooms with TV, RV spaces, and a good seafood restaurant. Further into town, the *Motel Las Dunas* (☎685/7-00-55; ④) is simple and friendly, as is *Las Ballenas* (☎685/7-01-16; ④), up a side road next to *Mario's* (see below). Slightly better is the *Hotel San Ignacio* (☎685/7-02-70; ④). You can also **camp** on nearby beaches for free – it's usually allowed even inside the park, though you need your own transport to get there.

There are plenty of **restaurants** along the main street, though only a few ever seem to be open at any one time. *Malarrimo*, next to *Don Miguelito*'s, has good seafood and is another place to check about whale-watching trips; *El Asadero Norteño* serves meaty northern specialities; *Mario's*, next to the *Motel El Morro*, is good for breakfast and the basics; for good seafood try *La Palapa*. You can also buy your own fresh produce from the small **market**.

Buses from Guerrero Negro's bus station, near the hotels, are irregular. The three services (one local) which head **north** to Tijuana, and the one to Mexicali, leave at night or early morning; the four **southbound** services – one local, running all the way to La Paz – depart either early in the morning or in the late afternoon and evening.

San Ignacio

Leaving Guerrero Negro, the highway heads inland again for the hottest, driest stage of the journey, across the Desierto Vizcaíno. In the midst of this landscape, **SAN IGNACIO** comes as an extraordinary relief. At the very centre of the peninsula, this is an oasis in every sense of the word; not only green and shaded but, with some of the few colonial buildings in Baja, a genuinely attractive little town. The settlement was founded by the Jesuits (and named after their founder) in 1728, but the area had long been populated by the indigenous **Guaicura**, attracted by the tiny stream, the only fresh water for hundreds of miles. San Ignacio's **church**, built by the first settlers and probably the best example of colonial architecture in the whole of Baja California, dominates the attractive, shaded plaza. Early missionaries were responsible, too, for the palms which give the town its special character, and as well as dates the town produces limes, grapes and olives.

In the bleak Sierras to the north and south are any number of **caves**, many of them decorated with **ancient paintings**. Not much is known about the provenance of these amazing designs, beyond the fact that they were painted at different periods and bear little resemblance to any other known art in this part of the world. Native legend, as related to the earliest colonists, has it that they are the product of a race of giants from the north. Certainly many of the human figures – most paintings depict hunters and their prey – are well over 2m tall. They are, however, extremely hard to visit, reached only by tracks or mule paths and almost impossible to find without a guide. If you're determined, join one of the **tours** arranged from the hotels in town, though these can be pricey. At the beginning of the year, the same guides also offer **whale-watching** trips to the nearby **Laguna San Ignacio**, which some say is a better location even than Guerrero Negro.

Practicalities

The centre of San Ignacio lies almost 3km off the main highway where all the **buses** stop. Upon arrival you may be lucky enough to pick up a taxi, otherwise it's a thirty-minute walk through the palms. Along the way you pass a number of places you could **pitch a tent**, worth considering since there are no budget **hotels**: *La Posada Motel*, at Carranza 22 (☎115/4-03-13; ④), southeast of the zócalo, is the cheapest, and *La Pinta*

(☎115/4-03-00; ⑦) the luxury alternative. Some of the **trailer parks** along the highway and on the road into town have camping space; the most useful, *El Padrino*, almost opposite *La Pinta*, charges US$3–4 per person. Of the many **places to eat** around the central plaza, *Restaurant Chalita* is a traditional Mexican choice (and has a few rooms, if poor value at US$10 per person); *Tota's* is better if somewhat more Americanized. Other facilities in town don't stretch beyond the lone **bank** (Mon–Fri 8.30–11am).

Santa Rosalía

The highway emerges on the east coast at **SANTA ROSALÍA**, which is also the terminal for the ferry to Guaymas (see p.98). An odd little town, wedged in the narrow valley of the Arroyo de Santa Rosalía, it was built as a port to ship copper from the nearby French-run mines of the El Boleo company (see box). Nowadays, the mines are virtually played out and the smelters stand idle, though much of the paraphernalia still lies around town, including parts of a rusting narrow-gauge railway. Currently there is a plan to employ modern techniques to extract the last of the ore from the five million tonnes of tailings, which will provide a much needed financial boost to a community that struggles by on revenue from fishing and the plaster mines on the Isla de San Marcos to the south.

The town itself has something of a temporary look, many of its buildings strikingly un-Mexican in aspect. The workers' houses in the valley resemble those in the Caribbean, with low angled roofs over hibiscus-flanked porches, while grander colonial residences for the managers rim the hill to the north. Look out especially for the **church** on Obregón, a prefabricated iron structure designed by Eiffel and exhibited in Paris before it was shipped here.

SANTA ROSALÍA'S COPPER MINES

While walking in the hills in 1868, one José Villavicencio chanced upon a **boleo**, a blue-green globule of rock that proved to be just a taster of a mineral vein containing more than 20 percent copper. By 1880 the wealth of the small-scale mining concessions came to the notice of the **Rothschilds**, who provided finance for the French El Boleo company to buy the rights and found a massive extraction and smelting operation. Six hundred kilometres of tunnels were dug, a foundry was shipped out from Europe, and a new wharf built to transport the smelted ore north to Washington state for refining. Ships returned with lumber for the construction of a **new town**, laid out with houses built to a standard commensurate with their occupier's status within the company. Water was piped from the Santa Agueda oasis 15km away, and labour was brought in: Yaqui from Sonora as well as two thousand Chinese and Japanese who, finding that Baja was too arid to grow rice, soon headed off to the Mexican mainland. By 1954, falling profits from the nearly spent mines forced the French to sell the pits and smelter to the Mexican government who, though the mines were left idle, continued to smelt ore from the mainland. By the early 1990s this too had stopped.

If you fancy a **short desert walk**, pick a cool part of the day and make a circuit of what remains of the mining equipment and the tunnels that riddle the hills to the north. None of the mines is fenced, so take a torch and explore cautiously. Following C Altamirano from Eiffel's church, you reach the massive kilometre-long above-ground duct, built of furnace slag, which once conveyed fumes from the smelter to the hilltop stack. You can walk along the top of it to the chimney for a superb view of the town and surrounding desert. From here, choose one of the numerous paths that head away inland to a series of gaping maws in the hillside. Either return the same way, pick your way straight down to the town or, with enough time, continue among the low cacti on the mesa, working your way down to the top end of Santa Rosalía.

Practicalities

Hwy-1 runs along the coast, passing between Santa Rosalía's harbour and Parque Morelos. Five streets – avenidas Obregón, Constitución, Carranza, Sarabia and Montoya – run perpendicular to the coast, crossing the numbered calles.

Santa Rosalía's **bus station** lies ten minutes' walk south of Parque Morelos, beyond the ferry terminal. All buses are *de paso*: northbound call in very early in the morning, while those heading south stop mostly in the late morning and late evening. **Ferries** leave twice a week (Wed & Sun at 8am) for the seven-hour trip to Guaymas. Tickets (which cost US$14 for a reclining seat, twice that for a four-berth cabin, nothing for a bike and US$157 for a small car) go on sale at the terminal from 6am, but check times and reserve in advance (☎685/2-00-13), or buy your ticket from a travel agent, as the timetable may change. Car drivers should ensure that their papers are in order for the mainland (see "Border Checks" on p.63).

After the resorts to the north, it comes as some relief to find that Santa Rosalía has a few good-value **hotels**. The budget options include the faded but friendly *Playa* on C 1 (☎115/2-23-50; ③), and the popular *Blanco y Negro* (☎115/2-00-80; ②), just off the southwest corner of Plaza Juárez, four blocks in from the waterfront. The *Olvera* (☎115/2-00-57; ④) and the *Hotel del Real* (☎115/2-00-68; ④) are both on Parque Morelos; the latter is really just as good as the new, upmarket *Minas de Santa Rosalía* (☎115/2-10-60; ④) on Constitución at 10th. The *Hotel Francés* (☎115/2-20-52; ⑤) is a beautiful colonial building on the hill to the north of town, and is good value for a place this luxurious. The *El Morro* (☎115/2-04-14; ⑤), on the highway a short way south of town, offers even more comfort, with sea views, pool and restaurant, and a good beach nearby.

Sadly, no French **restaurants** remain as a reminder of the town's beginnings, but the *Panadería El Boleo* produces some of the best baked goods in these parts, even if the baguettes aren't as crisp as the real thing. Restaurants in general aren't up to very much, though you can eat well enough at *Terco's Pollito*, Obregón on Plaza Morelos. Several cheaper places are scattered along Obregón, many selling great fish and seafood tacos.

Both **banks** are on Constitución: Bancomer changes cheques until noon, Banamex accepts only bills until 1pm, but has an ATM. The **post office** is on Constitución at C 2, and there's a **phone** outside the *Hotel del Real*.

Mulegé and around

Some 60km to the south of Santa Rosalía lies **MULEGÉ** ("Moo-leh-HAY"), a small village on the site of an ancient mission. Like San Ignacio, it's a real oasis, and there's a definite feel of the tropics, too: its laid-back atmosphere is helped by some superb beaches strung out along the coast to the south. Yet again you'll miss out on the best of them without some means of getting about, but here hitching is at least a realistic possibility – many visitors commute to the beaches daily, particularly during the high season from mid-October to April.

Other than as a springboard for the beaches to the south, the main reason to stop here is to take one of the **tours to the cave paintings** out in the Sierra de Guadalupe. This range boasts the most dense collection of rock art in Baja, as well as some of the most accessible, requiring as little as five hours. Getting a group together to cut costs shouldn't prove a problem in high season, but you still need to shop around as the tours differ considerably. Salvador Castro at the *Las Casitas* hotel usually runs trips on Wednesday and Saturday, requiring a minimum of eight people, whereas Kerry Otterstrom, usually found at *El Candil*, runs more adventurous trips to order for as few as four people. Expect to pay US$35 per person. Kerry is also an excellent source of information.

Snorkelling and diving trips (see below) are also available at Mulegé Divers, on Martinez (Mon–Sat; ☎115/3-00-59). A beginner's resort course costs US$70, a snorkelling trip US$30 (including equipment).

Bahía Concepción

There is good diving and fishing immediately around Mulegé, but the best beaches are laid out along the shore of **Bahía Concepción**, between 10km and 50km south. The better stretches of sand include **Playa Punta Arena**, some 16km down the highway followed by 2km on a dirt road, where there are some basic palapa shelters to rent. **Playa Santispac**, some 5km further on, is right on the highway and easy to get to – despite the early stages of development and occasional crowds of RVs, it still has plenty of room to camp (for a fee) and enough life to make staying here longer-term a realistic option. Baja Tropicales at palapa 17 organizes good-value kayaking and snorkelling trips. Further south there are fewer facilities for anything other than self-sufficient camping: **Playa El Requesón** is one of the last and has the best opportunities for this, though with no fresh water.

Mulegé practicalities

From the **bus stop** it's a ten-minute walk into Mulegé: follow the side road, take the right fork onto Martinez then second right onto Zaragoza and the plaza. Bus travellers may have difficulty getting out of the place – for details of timetables, ask at the small café with the "ABC" sign near the bus stop. You have to hope there's room on one of the *de paso* services on the highway, as no buses originate here. Heading south, all services currently pass through between 9am and noon; northbound buses mostly pass in the afternoon or very early morning.

If you want to **stay** in Mulegé, you've a choice of cheap and very basic casas de huéspedes or relatively upmarket hotels. The *Hacienda* (☎115/3-00-21; ⑤), on Madero just off the plaza, is the pick of the latter, with a small pool, though *Las Casitas*, Madero 50 (☎115/3-00-19; ⑤), the former home of Mexican poet José Gorosave, is almost as good. There's also the bright new *Motel Siesta* (no phone; ④), on the road in from the bus stop. Budget alternatives include the *Casa de Huéspedes Nachita* (☎115/3-01-40; ②) and the slightly more comfortable *Manuelita* (☎115/3-01-75; ②), both on Moctezuma, the left fork as you head into Mulegé from the highway, and, slightly better, *Canett* (no phone; ②), on Madero beyond the church. **Campers** should head 1km south of the bus stop (or along the dirt road on the south side of the river from Mulegé) to *Huerta Saucedo RV Park* – also called *The Orchard* (☎115/3-03-00) – where two can pitch a tent for US$6 and guests can rent canoes on the Río Mulegé.

Eating and drinking options are as polarized as the accommodation. The majority of the North American long-stayers and a good many Mexicans gravitate towards the decent and reasonably priced restaurant and bar at *Las Casitas* or the less formal and slightly cheaper *El Candil* on the plaza. To eat less expensively you are limited to taco stands and *El Pollo Salvaje*, just south of the plaza, or a slice of pizza at *Donna Moe's* next to *El Candil*. *Las Casitas* also acts as an informal tourist office for information on other local attractions.

Mulegé has no banks, only a **casa de cambio** with poor rates (daily 9am–1pm & 3–7pm) on the road in, and a small **post office** with a long-distance phone outside on Martinez.

Loreto

LORETO, the next town down the coast, is a far bigger place than Mulegé, on the site of the earliest permanent settlement in the Californias. Founded in 1697 as the head of the Jesuit missions to California, and later taken over by the Franciscans, it was in practice the administrative capital of the entire territory for some 150 years until a devastating earthquake struck in 1829. More recently it has been a popular escape for fishing and diving enthusiasts, and nowadays it's enjoying something of a renaissance, boosted by the development of southern Baja California as a whole. A super-resort along the lines of Cancún was planned some 10km south of town – an airport laid out, roads and electricity put in – but for a long time things went no further as priorities were switched elsewhere. As of now there's the *Stouffer Presidente* hotel, a tennis centre and the beginnings of further construction, but mostly **Nopoló** (as the result will be known) seems deserted. The main upshot seems to be that downtown Loreto itself has been spruced up in expectation, and that prices have risen accordingly. There is, however, the tidy, if impersonal malecón, Boulevard Lopez Mateos, backing the tolerable **town beach**, and, with transport, you can reach some more great stretches of sand a few miles to the south – and good camping territory, too.

The original **mission church** is still standing and, though heavily restored after centuries of earthquake damage, its basic structure – solid, squat and simple – is little changed. The inscription over the door, which translates as "The head and mother church of the missions of upper and lower California" attests to its former importance, as does the Baroque altarpiece originally transported here from México. Next door a small **museum** (daily except Tues 9am–6pm; US$1.25) chronicles the early conversion and colonization of California.

Practicalities

From Loreto's **bus station** it's a fifteen-minute walk east along Salvatierra to the mission church and central plaza, and a further five minutes in the same direction to the beach. Along the way you pass the best of the town's budget **hotels**, *Motel Salvatierra* (☎113/5-00-21; ④), better value than *Casa de Huéspedes San Martín* (☎113/5-04-42; ③) on Juárez, two blocks north of the plaza. The other hotels are relatively expensive, but not bad value for what you get, catering as they do mainly for diving buffs and people who know the area well. If you can afford it, make for the beachfront *Oasis* (☎113/5-02-11; ⑦), three blocks south of the plaza, which has a pool and all the trappings. Otherwise, the most pleasant place to stay is the colonial-style *Misión de Loreto* (☎113/5-00-48; ⑦), Lopez Mateos 1, on the waterfront east of the plaza. **Campers** should head towards the beaches north of town for a free spot, or walk 1km south along Madero to *Loreto Shores RV Park*. On the way is *Villas de Loreto* (☎113/5-05-86; ⑥ including breakfast and bikes), which has a pool, caters for RVs and rents out kayaks.

Finding simple Mexican **food** is no problem at taco stands along Hidalgo or at fancier places around the plaza, notably *Café Olé*, which does good-value breakfasts and antojitos; or try the cinnamon rolls and excellent, if pricey, pizza at *Tiffany's Pisa Parlour* on Hidalgo south of the plaza. **Bancomer** on the plaza changes travellers' cheques until 2.30pm. The **post office** is on Deportiva, just off Salvatierra on the way into town, behind the Cruz Roja building.

From Loreto five buses head north daily (all in the afternoon and early evening) and another handful run south (8am–midnight) to La Paz, five long hours away. If you're confined to the main road there's really nothing to detain you. **El Juncalito**, about 15km south of Loreto, is a nice spot with an RV park. **Ciudad Constitución**, about halfway to La Paz, is a large, modern town with plenty of facilities but nothing else to stop for.

La Paz

Everyone ends up in **LA PAZ** eventually, if only to get the ferry out, and it seems that most of the population of Baja California Sur is gravitating here, too. The outskirts are an ugly sprawl, their development outpacing the spread of paved roads and facilities. But the town centre, modernized as it is, has managed to preserve something of its quiet colonial atmosphere. You can stroll along the waterfront malecón, and for once the beach in town looks inviting enough to swim from – though there are no guarantees on the cleanliness of the water.

The Bay of La Paz was explored by **Cortés** himself in the first years after the Conquest – drawn, as always, by tales of great wealth – but he found little to interest him and, despite successive expeditions, at first merely rapacious, later missionary, La Paz wasn't permanently settled until the end of the eighteenth century. It grew rapidly, however, thanks to the riches of the surrounding sea, and above all as a pearl fishing centre. American troops occupied the town during the Texan war, and six years later it was again invaded, by William Walker in one of his many attempts to carve himself out a Central American kingdom; by this time it was already capital of the territory of California. The pearl trade has pretty much dried up – a mystery disease wiped out most of the oysters – but since the 1960s La Paz has continued to boom, buoyed up by tourists at first flown in, then boosted by the growing ferry service, and now supplemented by the hordes pouring down Hwy-1.

Arrival and information

If you arrive in La Paz by bus you'll be stuck at a **bus station** about 5km out in the suburbs at Jalisco and Independencia. Long-distance services often arrive in the middle of the night and you may have no choice but to walk into town, though this is not recommended. During the day you might be lucky enough to pick up one of the irregular buses ("Centro/Camionera"); a taxi should cost around US$3. **Ferry** passengers arriving at Pichilingue (see below) are better off – there should be buses to town, and also colectivo taxis. From the airport, 12km south, there's a fixed-rate taxi service.

The most useful **tourist office** (daily 8am–10pm; ☎112/2-59-39) is in the centre, on the waterfront at 16 de Septiembre, though there is another with the same hours and information on the highway 5.5km north of town. Apart from the **post office** at the corner of Revolución and Constitución, all the facilities lie between the zócalo and the waterfront, including numerous **banks** and the **American Express** office (Mon–Fri 9am–2pm & 4–6pm, Sat 9am–2pm; ☎112/2-83-00) at Esquerro 1679, behind *Hotel Perla*.

Accommodation

Most of the inexpensive **hotels**, where rooms are good value by Baja standards, are within a few blocks of the zócalo; some of the older fancier places are downtown too, but the newer ones tend to be out along the coast. The **youth hostel**, on Forjadores (☎112/2-46-15; ②), has inexpensive, impersonal dorms, inconvenient for town but fairly close to the bus station; turn right up Jalisco, left along Isabel La Católica, following the one-way traffic to the right, then take the next right and right again, perhaps 1km in all. The nearest **campsite** is *El Cardón Trailer Park* (☎112/2-12-61), about 2km out on the road north.

Cabañas Los Arcos, Paseo Obregón 498 (☎112/2-27-44). Popular fishing centre on the bay. Older cabañas have more character, and are more expensive, than newer hotel rooms – both have a/c. Plus a pool and all other facilities. ⑦.

Hostería del Convento, Madero Sur 85 (☎112/2-35-08). Uncannily similar to *Pensión California*, but smaller and quieter. On the site of a former convent. ③.

Miramar, 5 de Mayo and Domínguez (☎112/2-88-85). Good deal if you get a sea view: comfortable a/c rooms with TV. ④.

Pensión California, Degollado between Madero and Revolución (☎112/2-28-96). Wonderful old building with courtyard and assorted artworks. The plain rooms all have bath and fan. Communal kitchen and laundry. ③.

Perla, Paseo Obregón 1570 at La Paz (☎112/2-07-77). Once *the* place to stay and still a good deal, with a/c, pool and restaurant. ⑦.

Posada San Miguel, Belisario Domínguez, off 16 de Septiembre (☎112/2-18-02). Simple, court-yard rooms in a colonial-style villa. Good value. ③.

Yeneka, Madero, near the zócalo (☎112/5-46-88). Eccentric decor but comfortable; also has a café. ④.

The Town and around

There's not a great deal to see in La Paz itself and if you're staying for any length of time you should head for the beaches. If you're just hanging around waiting for a ferry, how-ever, you can happily fill a day window-shopping in the centre – hundreds of stores take advantage of the duty-free zone – and browsing around the market. The small **Museo Antropológico** (Mon–Fri 8am–6pm, Sat 9am–2pm; free), at 5 de Mayo and Altamirano, is also worth a passing look: exhibits include photos of cave paintings and an ethno-logical history of the peninsula. This is as good as Baja museums get, but has no English labelling. More information on all aspects of Baja, some of it in English, is avail-able in the *Biblioteca de las Californias*, opposite the cathedral on the zócalo.

Beaches ring the bay all around La Paz, but the easiest to get to are undoubtedly those to the south, served by the local bus that runs along Obregón to the ferry ter-minal at Pichilingue. Perhaps the best of the beaches are **Playa del Tesoro**, shortly before Pichilingue, and **Playa Pichilingue**, a walk of fifteen minutes or so beyond the end of the bus route. Both have simple facilities, including a restaurant. There are plen-ty of opportunities for fishing and diving, and for boat trips into the bay; just stroll along the malecón to find people offering the latter – the **Isla Espíritu Santo** is a popular destination. Baja Diving and Service, 1665 Obregón (☎112/2-18-26), offers good **diving and snorkelling** tours and courses. For kayak rental and tours, try Baja Outdoor Activities, Obregón, opposite the tourist office (☎112/5-56-36).

Eating and drinking

Wandering round La Paz you'll find dozens of places to **eat** – the seafood, above all, is excellent. There are numerous inexpensive local restaurants near the market, especially on Serdán and 16 de Septiembre, and around the zócalo.

Bismark II, Altamirano and Degollado. Excellent seafood without having to pay inflated seafront prices.

El Camaron Feliz, opposite *Los Arcos* on the waterfront (☎112/2-90-11). An attractive place to dine on seafood, the location justifying the price.

Pizza La Fabula, Obregón at Independencia and other locations in town. Popular local pizza chain.

El Quinto Sol, Independencia and Belisario Domínguez. Vegetarian and wholefood shop and café; juices and tortas too.

Super Tacos De Baja California, outside *Pensión California*. Seafood tacos with a superb help-yourself salad-bar.

Tequilas Bar and Grill, Mutualisimo and Ocampo. Equally enjoyed by tourists and locals, a bar whose friendly atmosphere centres around the pool table.

La Terraza, Obregón 1570 at La Paz. Cafe-restaurant under the *Hotel Perla*. Popular but pricey spot to watch the world go by. Excellent breakfasts at surprisingly reasonable prices.

Moving on from La Paz

La Paz **bus station** (☎112/2-64-76) is also the southern terminus for the peninsula **buses**. Ten regular daily services head north, one going as far as Tijuana, 22 hours

---

THE FERRY FROM LA PAZ

If you're planning to take the **ferry** across the Sea of Cortés to **Mazatlán** or **Topolobampo** (the port for Los Mochis), you should buy tickets as soon as possible: cabins – either turista (4 bunks), cabina (2 bunks) or especial (suite) – and space for cars are often oversubscribed. There's rarely any problem going salón class (entitling you to a reclining seat), for which tickets are only available a day in advance. On balance, for most people, salón is the best option, as the cabins can be freezing if the a/c works and stiflingly hot if not. Sleeping out on deck is best of all.

Departures for the 18hr run to Mazatlán leave daily at 3pm, except Saturday during the off season (the Wed sailing has salón class only); those for the 9–10hr sail to Topolobampo leave daily except Tues at 8pm.

You can make **reservations** at the downtown ticket office of the operating company, SEMATUR, 5 de Mayo and Prieto (Mon–Fri 7am–1pm & 4–6pm, Sat & Sun 8am–1pm; ☎112/5-38-33), where you'll need to arrive early and be prepared to wait in line; direct at the terminal (☎112/2-51-17); or through local travel agents. The **cost** of tickets, which can be paid for with Visa and Mastercard, ranges from US$21 to US$82, and US$223 for cars (to Mazatlán); from US$14 to US$55, and US$136 for cars (to Topolobampo).

Before buying tickets, car drivers should ensure they have a **permit to drive** on the mainland. This should have been obtained when crossing the border into Mexico, but if not you may have some joy by taking your vehicle and all relevant papers along to the customs office at the ferry terminal a couple of days before you sail. If for some reason you've managed to get this far without having your **tourist card** stamped, you should also attend to that before sailing – there's an immigration office at Obregón 2140, between Juárez and Allende.

To **get to the ferry** itself, which sails from the terminal at Pichilingue, some 14km away, go to the old bus station on the malecón – straight down Independencia from the zócalo – and, again, get there early. There is only one bus an hour, on the hour (8am–5pm; US$0.75). Arrive at the ferry by 1.30pm. According to signs at the terminal, it is illegal to take your own food on board, but since the catering is so poor everyone does and nobody seems to mind.

away (at 10pm), another to Mexicali (4pm). Buses leave roughly hourly (6.30am–6.30pm) for Cabo San Lucas and San José del Cabo; some are routed via Todos Santos, others take the eastern route direct to San José.

Flights leave from the airport, 8km southwest from town (accessible by an expensive taxi ride only). For flight details contact Viajes Perla travel agency, on the corner of 5 de Mayo and Domingues (Mon–Sat 8.30am–7.30pm, Sun 9am–2pm; ☎112/2-86-66).

Los Cabos

Beyond La Paz, the coastline becomes increasingly developed – modern, commercialized, resort-weary. **Los Cabos**, the series of capes and beaches around the southern tip of the Baja peninsula, is one of the fastest developing tourist areas in Mexico – heavily promoted by the authorities and a boom area for the big hotel chains and resort builders. Undeniably beautiful, it's not a place for the penniless traveller to venture unprepared. Not far south of La Paz the highway splits: the fast new road cuts across to the Pacific to run straight down the west coast to **Cabo San Lucas**; the old route trails through the mountains, emerging only briefly above the Sea of Cortés on its long journey to **San José del Cabo**. Neither route offers much to stop for, although there are isolated hotels and developments on beaches all the way around.

Cabo San Lucas

Fifteen years ago **CABO SAN LUCAS**, at the southernmost tip of Baja, was little more than a fishing village occasionally visited by sport fishermen with the means to sail in or fly down. In recent years, however, it has rapidly become the focal point of Los Cabos: condos have sprung up, palms have been transplanted, water has been piped in from San José and everywhere is kept pristine. More like an enclave of the US than part of Mexico, preserving almost nothing that is not geared to tourism, it can be fun for a day or two; though prices are higher than in neighbouring San José (see p.87), there's more of a party atmosphere, with a younger crowd.

Arrival and information
Buses from La Paz (roughly hourly 6am–7pm; 2–3hr) and San José del Cabo (roughly hourly 7am–10pm; 30min) arrive at the junction of Zaragoza and 16 de Septiembre, close to the centre. From the **airport** (see p.87), catch a taxi to San José and a bus from there. There is a direct shuttle to the airport (☎114/3-12-20; US$10). Surprisingly, Cabo has no official **tourist office**, just dozens of places dishing out maps and information, and usually throwing in some timeshare patter while they're at it. There's an ATM, and the best **exchange rates**, at Bancomer (cheques 8.30am–noon) on Lázaro Cárdenas at Hidalgo; after hours several casas de cambio (one by *Giggling Marlin*; see p.87) offer halfway decent rates until 11pm. The **post office** is on Lázaro Cárdenas east of the marina (Mon–Fri 9am–6pm), and there's a **US consul** at Blvd Marina and Camino del Cerro (☎114/3-35-66).

Accommodation
Possibly the best way to enjoy the sands and waters around Cabo San Lucas is to stay in San José (see p.87) and visit for the day on one of the frequent buses. If you do decide to **stay** here for any reason, however, you have the choice of a few good-value places (though none is cheap): the basic *Casa Blanca*, at Revolución between Morelos and Vicario (☎114/3-53-60; ④), has comfortable a/c rooms with bathrooms, while the pricier *Dos Mares*, Zapata east of Hidalgo (☎114/3-03-30; ⑤), has a good location, TVs and

a tiny pool, as well as some studios with kitchens. *Mar de Cortés*, Lázaro Cárdenas between Guerrero and Matamoros (☎114/3-00-32; ⑤), offers decent-sized a/c rooms around a pool, and has a good restaurant, too. If you're here out of season (May–Oct) you may find dramatically reduced rates at one of the swanky beachfront hotels, among them *Solmar Suites*, Playa Solmar, 1km west towards Finisterra (☎114/3-35-35, in US ☎1-800/344-3349; ⑨) – check out their three-nights-plus-meals deal, which can be as little as US$160 off season.

Camping on the local Playa Médano is not encouraged by the beachfront restaurateurs, nor is it particularly safe, but you could toss down a sleeping bag on one of the relatively secluded beaches nearby. Local **RV parks** include *Vagabondos del Mar* (☎114/3-02-90), 3km east; *Club Cabo* (☎114/3-33-48), 4km east; and *Faro Viejo* at Abasolo and Mijares in town. For campers, all cost US$10–12.

The Town

With its great sands and fascinating marine life, Cabo San Lucas should be one of the most attractive spots in Baja. Above all there's the huge **rock arch** at Finisterra – Land's End, where the Sea of Cortés meets the Pacific – an extraordinary place, with a clear division between the shallower turquoise waters on the left and the profound blue of the ocean on the right. A colony of sea-lions lives on the rocks roundabout. You can't walk to the arch, but there are plenty of trips out here from the **marina**, most of which take in one of the small surrounding beaches, more often than not Playa del Amor, which boasts strands on both seas.

Around the marina, down the nearby streets and along the **Playa Médano**, the town's closest safe beach, hawkers constantly tout trips in glass-bottomed boats, fishing, water skiing, paragliding or bungee jumping, and will rent anything from off-road

---

THE CAPE BEACHES

The highway between Cabo San Lucas and San José del Cabo gives access to a welter of superb beaches, many of them visible from the road. Unfortunately, as development continues, access, especially for those on foot, is becoming increasingly difficult. You could just ride along until you see one you fancy, but if you have a preference and are using the bus between the two towns, make sure the driver is prepared to let you off at your desired stop.

Apart from Solmar and Del Amor, all distances are measured east from Cabo San Lucas towards San José del Cabo, 33km away.

Solmar, 1km west. Pacific-side beach with strong undertow. Whale-watching Jan–April.

Del Amor, in centre. Boat access beach spanning the two seas out by El Arco.

Médano, 1km. Cabo's beach. Sand, restaurants, bars and abundant aquatic paraphernalia to rent. Usually uncomfortably crowded.

Cemeterío, 4km. Beautiful swimming beach. Access on foot from Médano.

Barco Varada, 9km. Shipwreck beach. The remains of a Japanese trawler that sank in 1966 are the main diving focus. Rock reefs, too. Access very difficult.

Santa María, 12km. Scuba and snorkelling on rock reefs at both ends. Excellent swimming. Easy access, not far from road.

Punta Chileno, 14km. Underwater sports on rock and sand bottom. Excellent swimming. Easiest access of all.

Canta Mar, 16km. Appropriately dubbed "surfing beach". Occasional point breaks.

Punta Palmilla, 27km. Good safe beach used by San José hotel residents needing escape from the strong rip closer to home. Point and reef breaks when surf's up.

Costa Azul, 29km. Consistently the region's best surf beach. Shore break but rocks at low tide.

quad bikes to jet skis and underwater gear. Competition is fierce, prices change and places come and go, so shop around. **Scuba diving** and **snorkelling** are perhaps the most rewarding of these activities, though the best sites (out towards Finisterra) can only be reached by boat. For gear rental, snorkelling trips and scuba courses, check out the many companies along Blvd Marina, especially in the plazas. Experienced divers shouldn't miss the rim of a marine canyon off Playa del Amor, where unusual conditions at 30m create a "sandfall" with streams of sand starting their 2000m fall to the canyon bottom.

Eating, drinking and nightlife

For reasonably inexpensive **food**, head for Morelos and the streets away from the waterfront. The more touristy places – some of them the most expensive in Baja – cluster around the marina and along Hidalgo. At night, such places compete for the custom of partying visitors by offering **happy hours** (often 6–8pm) and novel cocktails. There's little to choose between them; stroll along and take your pick.

The Barn (El Establo), Zaragoza and Niños Héroes. Friendly little bar.

Cabo Wabo, Guerrero between Lázaro Cárdenas and Madero. Van Halen-owned club fashioned in their image. Loud and lively but often with a hefty cover charge.

Francisco's Café del Mundo, marina waterfront. The best coffee in town. Delicious cakes, US papers, magazines and a harbour view.

Giggling Marlin, Blvd Marina at Matamoros. A Cabo institution, drawing an older set than other choices on the strip. Mostly a place to drink and dance to Latin standards: chances of getting out without hearing *La Bamba* are slim.

Restaurant Latitude 22+, Lázaro Cárdenas, east of Morelos. One of the nicer, less noisy US-style restaurants, done out in nautical theme.

Mariscos Mocambo, Morelos at Revolución. Unpretentious seafood restaurant popular with Mexicans.

The Office, Playa Médano. Restaurant and bar which, along with its neighbours, *Billygan's Island* and *Pirata Cavendish*, pumps out rock classics and offers happy hours. Expensive food and not to everyone's taste.

Restaurant Orale, Zaragoza and 16 de Septiembre. A down-to-earth, cheap, Mexican place. Great food, friendly staff.

La Perla, Lázaro Cárdenas between Matamoros and Abasolo. Very inexpensive and thoroughly Mexican place right in the tourist zone. Good Mexican staples and licuados.

San José del Cabo

SAN JOSÉ DEL CABO, 33km east of Cabo San Lucas, is the older and altogether more traditional of the two resorts, with at least some trace of a town that once existed as a mission, agricultural centre and small port. Though fast being swamped, the old plaza and the Paseo Mijares (which now leads to a modern hotel zone about 1km seaward) are still more or less intact, and there's a small local museum in the Casa de la Cultura. To get to the **beaches** it's a considerable walk down Mijares to the hotel zone, and on from there to find empty sand: they stretch for miles so keep walking until you find a quiet spot.

Practicalities

Alaska, Mexicana, Aero California and Aeromexico all fly to **San José airport**, 11km north of town, with services from several Mexican and US west coast cities. Expensive shuttle-vans run into town. Buses to La Paz pass 1km away. The **bus station** is about fifteen minutes' walk from the centre: turn left out of the station along Gonzales then, after 1km, left onto Mijares and to the zócalo – easily spotted by the church towers. Zaragoza crosses Mijares at this point; Obregón and Doblado run parallel to and either side of Zaragoza. The **tourist office**, which hands out free maps, is right at this junction (Mon–Fri 8am–3pm; ☎114/2-29-60), and the **banks** and other facilities are all nearby. The **post office** is on Mijares on the way to the hotel zone.

San José has a couple of decent budget **hotels**: *Posada San Rafael*, Obregón, north of the zócalo (☎114/2-38-78; ③), is a lot better than it looks, while *Casa de Consuelo*, Morelos and Juárez (☎114/2-06-43; ③), is a little basic, but safe and friendly, and *Hotel Ceci*, Zaragoza 22 (☎114/2-00-51; ③), is very close to the centre, though noise is the chief problem here. Slightly more expensive alternatives include the *San José Inn*, on Obregón (☎114/2-24-64; ④), *Hotel Diana*, Zaragoza 30 (☎114/2-04-90; ④), with a/c and TV, or the comfortable *Hotel Colli* (☎114/2-07-25; ④), on Hidalgo between Zaragoza and Doblado. Down in the hotel zone along the beach you may find bargains out of season, but on the whole most places are expensive and pre-booked. If you're **camping**, head for the (pricey) *Brisa del Mar RV Resort*, on the beachfront southwest of town (at Km 29.5), or to Pueblo La Playa.

There's a huge variety of upmarket **restaurants** along Mijares downtown, but it's less easy to find places with local prices – look around Zaragoza and Obregón. The best-value traditional Mexican food is served at *La Bombilla*, next to *Hotel Colli*; *Jazmin* on Morelos one block west of the zócalo is better, if pricier, and excellent for breakfasts. *El Café Fiesta*, at Mijares 14, serves vegetarian and Mexican food. Amongst the more expensive options, *Tequila*, on Doblado, stands out. Down at the beach in Pueblo La Playa, *La Playita* serves wonderful seafood in a breezy palapa.

Los Barriles and Todos Santos

On the western side of the peninsula, the land is rapidly being bought up and converted into residential developments. Neither of the two big attractions here, game fishing and windsurfing, is easily arranged on the spot, and there's almost nowhere you can turn up and find an inexpensive room. The largest resort is **LOS BARRILES**, 40km north of Cabo San Lucas, a major **windsurfing** centre taking advantage of the near constant strong breeze in the bay. The wind, best in winter, is brilliant for experienced windsurfers (less so for beginners) and makes this a regular venue for international competitions. Hotels are expensive, and you almost certainly need to have booked in advance; but you should be able to camp, either at one of the nearby trailer parks, or on the beach.

Todos Santos

On the new road, just north of the Tropic of Cancer, the farming town of **TODOS SANTOS** marks almost exactly the halfway point between Cabo San Lucas and La Paz. It's also the closest thing to an exception to all the rules about the cape region, with some great beaches in easy reach, affordable hotels, and a bus service. The town's charm has already lured a few-score gringos to the area, and less benign mega-development has been on the cards for some time, so catch it while you can. The best **beaches** – Punta Lobos and San Pedrito, for example – are half an hour or so's walk away; check that they haven't been buried under a new hotel before setting out.

The highway runs through the middle of Todos Santos as C Colegio Militar. Here, and on parallel Juárez, are the **bank**, shops, **post office** and telephones. *El Tecolote* on Hidalgo at Juárez has a great selection of new and used **books**. The **bus** will drop you at the corner of Colegio Militar and Zaragoza. The best **place to stay**, if you can afford it, is the colonial-style *Hotel California* (☎682/5-00-02; ⑤), a block and a half north of Zaragoza on Juárez. Cheaper options are the *Motel Guluarte* (☎682/5-00-06; ③), around the corner on Morelos, and the better value but less convenient *Hotel Miramar* (☎682/5-03-21; ④), Mutualismo and Pedrajo, three blocks off Degollado on the way out of town. There should be no problem camping on the above beaches; the nearest official **campsite**, the *San Pedrito RV Park*, is some 7km south.

Places to eat are mainly on Colegio Militar: you'll find street stalls around the bus stop area and a couple of decent restaurants at the traffic lights a block away. *Caffé Todos Santos*, at Centenario 33 and Tapete, three blocks north and two west from the bus stop, serves first-class cakes, coffee and licuados, as well as more substantial meals. Two very good and correspondingly pricey restaurants serve some of the best food on the peninsula: *Santa Fe*, on the zócalo at Centenario (closed Tues), and *Caravella*, at the end of Juárez (closed Sun).

THE MAINLAND ROUTE

On the mainland route through the northwest, it's the extraordinary **desert scenery** that first grabs your attention. Between Tijuana and Mexicali, especially, stretches a region of awesome barrenness. As you continue south through the states of Sonora and Sinaloa, the desert becomes rockier, which, along with the huge cacti, makes for some archetypal Mexican landscapes. Only as you approach Mazatlán does the harshness finally start to relent, and some colour creep back into the land.

Historically, this part of the country was little more favoured than Baja California. The first Spanish explorers met fierce resistance from a number of indigenous tribes – the Pima, Seri and Yaqui are still among the least integrated of Mexico's peoples – and it wasn't until the late seventeenth century that the Jesuit missionary **Padre Kino** established a significant number of permanent settlements. During the dictatorship of Porfirio Díaz, new road and rail links were established, and after the **Revolution** (many of whose most able leaders came from the northwest) these communications began to be exploited through irrigation and development programmes that brought considerable agricultural wealth. Today the big **ranches** of Sonora and Sinaloa are among the richest in Mexico.

El Gran Desierto

If the peninsula of Baja California is desolate, the northern part of the state – to Mexicali and beyond into northern Sonora – is infinitely, spectacularly, more so. The **drive from Tijuana to Mexicali** is worthwhile for the extraordinary views alone, as the mountains suddenly drop away to reveal a huge salt lake and hundreds of miles of desert below. This is **El Gran Desierto**, and it's a startlingly sudden change to the landscape that precedes it: the western escarpment up from Tijuana through **Tecate** (the small border town where the beer comes from) and beyond is relatively fertile and climbs deceptively gently, but the rains from the Pacific never get as far as the eastern edge, where the land falls away dizzily to the burnt plain and the road teeters between crags seemingly scraped bare by the ferocity of the sun. The heat at the bottom is incredible, the road down terrifying – its constant precipices made worse by the piles of twisted metal at the bottom of each one of them. The new fast toll road has tamed the route somewhat, but it's still a fantastic trip.

Mexicali

MEXICALI, too, is hot – unbearably so in summer, though winter nights can drop below freezing – but despite its natural disadvantages it's a large, wealthy city, the capital of Baja California Norte and an important road and rail junction for the crossing into the States. It's also an increasingly important destination for Mexican migrants looking for work in the *maquiladoras* and, as in Tijuana 160km to the west, the city's hinterland is rapidly being covered by shantytown sprawl. While there may be an exotic ring to the name, there's nothing exotic about the place, and if you come looking for a movieland border town, swing-door saloons and dusty dirt streets, you'll be disappointed. There's more chance of choking to death on exhaust fumes or getting run over trying to cross the street. Even the name, it turns out, is a fake – a sweet-sounding hybrid of Mexico and California with an appalling sibling across the border, **CALEXICO**.

Though it's less commercial than many of the border towns, it's not a place in which you'd choose to spend time, except possibly to prepare for the next stage south, a daunting trip of at least nine hours on the bus to Hermosillo, the first place you might remotely choose to take a break, and a further hour and a half to the much more appealing Guaymas.

During October you'll find a few cultural activities in town – live music, dance, cockfights and the like – taking place as part of the **Fiesta del Sol**; at any other time of year you can fill an hour browsing the local history exhibits at the free **Museo Regional de la Universidad de Baja California**, on Reforma at Calle L.

Arrival and information

The Mexicali **border crossing** is open 24 hours and, except at morning and evening rush hours, is usually relatively quiet, with procedures straightforward. Remember to visit migración if you're travelling further on into Mexico. In **Calexico**, Imperial Avenue leads straight to the border, lined with handily placed auto-insurance offices, banks and exchange places that offer almost identical rates to those in Mexicali; the **Greyhound** station is one block from the frontier on 1st St.

It's possible to get a Golden State bus from LA to the **Central Camionera** in Mexicali: the bus only comes as far as the border, where they bundle you into a taxi for the rest of the journey. The **airport** lies some 20km to the east. Fixed-price **taxis** and minibuses shuttle passengers into town.

Broad avenues lead away from the **frontier**: straight ahead is López Mateos, which will eventually take you straight out of town, passing close by the **train and bus terminals** on the way. To the left, off López Mateos and following the covered walkway from the border, stretches Madero, which, along with parallel Reforma, is the main commercial street downtown. The **local bus stand** is at the back of the small market just up from the border – a couple of blocks up López Mateos to the right. **Taxis** wait at ranks around the junction of López Mateos and Madero.

The **tourist information** booth (nominally daily 8am–8pm) right by the border seldom seems to be open; the **main office** (Mon–Fri 9am–4pm; ☎65/56-10-72) is a very long way down López Mateos at Calafia in the Centro Cívico, a journey not worth making unless you have a special reason. There are several **banks** and casas de cambio very close to the border – Bancomer, on Madero, is closest, and Banamex a couple of blocks up Madero near the **post office**.

Accommodation

Most of Mexicali's cheaper **hotels** can be found in the older streets around the border. Not that there are any great bargains here – indeed, if you're looking for somewhere to stay **Calexico** is arguably better value, with several motels charging under US$40 per night. Try for example the *Don Juan Motel*, 344 4th St East, between Hefferman and Heber (☎760/357-3231; ⑤), or the *El Rancho* (☎760/357-2458; ⑤) opposite.

In **Mexicali**, one of the more acceptable budget places is *16 de Septiembre*, Altamirano 353 (☎65/52-60-70; ③), just south of Mateos. The *Hotel del Norte*, Madero 203 just off López Mateos (☎65/52-81-01; ⑤), is one of the first things you see as you cross the border; it looks better than it is. The *Imperial*, Madero 222 (☎65/53-63-33; ⑤), just beyond, and *Plaza*, Madero 366 (☎65/52-97-57; ⑤), in the next block, are simpler places, but better value. For less than the *Del Norte*, the *Hotel San Juan Capistrano*

(☎65/52-41-04; ④), Reforma 646, a few blocks further from the border, is a far better deal – a rather bland business hotel with a decent restaurant. The *Motel Azteca de Oro*, C de la Industria 600 (☎65/57-21-85; ④), right by the train station, is comfortable and handy for transport: the Camionera is only about ten minutes' walk away up López Mateos. More **expensive hotels** are mainly on the outskirts, particularly along Juárez – the modern, international-style *Lucerna*, for example, at Juárez 2151 (☎65/64-70-00; ⑦). One exception is the new *Crowne Plaza*, near the Centro Civico on López Mateos at Av de los Héroes (☎65/57-36-00; ⑨).

Eating

There are plenty of places to **eat** in the border area, too, with lots of stalls and small restaurants around the market and on Madero and Reforma. The restaurant in the *Del Norte* is convenient, and better than the hotel itself, while on Reforma at Calle D, about six blocks down, *La Parroquia*, though a bit touristy, serves good Mexican food. Entirely off the tourist track are the many restaurants and cafés in and around the Centro Cívico, on Independencia a couple of blocks from the Central Camionera. The Centro itself has a branch of *Sanborn's*, reliable as ever; *Café Petunias*, at Plaza Cholula 1091 off Calafia, is one of many in this area serving sandwiches, juices, and lunch to office workers and shoppers.

Beyond Mexicali

Beyond Mexicali the road towards central Mexico trails the border eastwards, while the rail line cuts south around the northern edge of the Sea of Cortés – between them rises the Sierra del Pinacate, an area so desolate that it was used by American astronauts to simulate lunar conditions. Not far out of Mexicali you cross the border from Baja California into the state of **Sonora**: you'll have to put your watch forward an hour when you cross, unless Baja California Norte is on Daylight Saving Time (April–Oct), in which case there's no change.

There's little to stop for on the road. You'll pass through **San Luis Río Colorado**, something of an oasis with a large cultivated valley watered by the Colorado River, and **Sonoita** (or Sonoyta), a minor border crossing on the river of the same name. Both are pretty dull, though they have plenty of facilities for travellers passing through. Past Sonoita the road cuts inland and turns to the south, hitting the first foothills of the Sierra Madre Occidental, whose western slopes it follows, hugging the coast, all the

---

MOVING ON FROM MEXICALI

Mexicali's **Central Camionera** (☎65/57-24-10; with guardería) is 4km from the border on Independencia at Anahuac, close to the new **Centro Cívico** development and not far off López Mateos. To get there, take a "Calle 6" bus from the local bus stand off Mateos. Altogether well over fifty buses a day head **south** (twenty to México), and there's at least one local service an hour to **Tijuana**. Golden State has an office at the station: three buses leave daily for LA via Palm Springs. On the other hand, you'll have far more choice, and save a few dollars, if you walk across the border to Calexico's Greyhound station.

The **train station** is just off López Mateos, not quite as far out as the Camionera; buses and colectivo taxis heading up Mateos will take you there. One train leaves for **Guadalajara** at 8.50pm daily, containing both first- and second-class carriages, and arrives some 34 hours later. Tickets are sold at the station an hour or so before departure. You can reserve – advisable for first-class during holidays – by calling ☎65/57-21-01, ext 221.

Flights to México and Acapulco leave daily from the airport 20km east of town.

way to Tepic. At **Santa Ana** it meets the Nogales road, and near the tiny village of **Benjamin Hill** rejoins the rail tracks. If you're travelling north you may well have to change buses at Santa Ana (especially en route to Nogales – there are far more buses to Mexicali), though there's little reason there to venture outside the bus terminal.

Puerto Peñasco

On the rail route there's just one place of any size, **PUERTO PEÑASCO**, a shrimping port that, while not particularly attractive, does have good beaches that attract large weekend crowds from across the border (Tucson is only about three hours away). There's a good road down here from Sonoita, and a new one east to Caborca, not far from Santa Ana. If you're on the train it's not really worth breaking the journey – you may well have difficulty getting back on – and the buses are fairly infrequent, with a couple of daily services each to Hermosillo, Mexicali and Nogales. But if you have your own vehicle you may fancy the detour, especially as it's possible to cut east to Caborca and rejoin the main road there. There are plenty of places to stay and to eat, though **rooms** can be a problem at busy weekends. For plain motel rooms try the *Señorial* (☎638/3-20-65; ⑤) or *El Faro* (☎638/3-32-01; ⑤), both just a block or so from the beach; or spend a bit more for the luxury of the *Hotel Viña del Mar* complex (☎638/3-36-01; ⑥). **Seafood** stalls are gathered at the end of Eusebio Kino, while for more substantial Mexican food you can head for *Los Arcos* on Eusebio Kino at Tamarindos.

Nogales to Hermosillo

Compared to most of the frontier, **NOGALES** (its name means walnut trees, few of which are in evidence) is remarkably pleasant. Despite the fact that the Mexican streets are jammed with curio shops and those on the US side with hardware, clothes and electrical stores, and that there's the usual contrast between the neatly planned streets on the US side and the houses straggling haphazardly up the hillside in Mexico, this doesn't *feel* much like a border town. Indeed, the slackening of trade barriers in recent years has seen a marked reduction in small-time cross-border traffic, a process that's likely to continue under NAFTA. There's none of the oppressive hustling and little of the frenetic nightlife that mark Ciudad Juárez, say, or Tijuana.

The **Nogales pass** has been a significant staging post since explorers first passed this way, with evidence of settlements in existence several thousand years BC. After the Conquest it was used by Spanish explorers and surveyors, followed in rapid succession by evangelizing Jesuits (especially the celebrated Padre Kino) and Franciscans on their way to establish missions in California. Nogales itself remained no more than a large ranch, often existing in a state of virtual siege under harassment from the Apaches, until the war with the USA and the ceding of Arizona, New Mexico, Texas and northern California to the Americans in 1848. Thereafter, with the border passing straight through, the town was deliberately developed by both sides to prevent the periodic raids of the other. Yankee troops marched through a few years later, protecting Union supplies shipped in through Guaymas during the Civil War, and there was a constant traffic of rustling and raids from both sides – culminating in the activities of Pancho Villa in the years leading up to the Mexican Revolution. The railway to the coast brought the final economic spur, and the town's chief business remains that of shipping Sonora's rich agricultural produce to the States. Just over the border on the US side an excellent little **museum** of local history (Tues–Fri 10am–noon & 1.30–5pm, Sat 10am–4pm; free), run by the Pimeria Alta Historical Society, records all this, and some of the traditions of the Pima, who this land originally belonged to.

There's little to see between Nogales and Santa Ana, and still less on the long stretch of desert highway from Santa Ana to Hermosillo. Shortly before Santa Ana, however, you pass through the small town of **Magdalena**, where most buses stop briefly. Here there's a mausoleum containing, under glass, the recently discovered remains of **Padre Kino**. Kino, "Conquistador of the Desert", was a Spanish Jesuit priest who came to Mexico in 1687 and is credited with having founded twenty-five missions and converted at least seven local indigenous tribes – among them the Apaches of Arizona and the Pima, Yuma and Seri of Sonora.

Nogales practicalities

Mexican Nogales is a sleepy, provincial town, not a bad place in which to rest up and acclimatize for a while, though accommodation is a little pricey. Crossing the border (24hr) is straightforward; remember to have your tourist card stamped by migración if you're heading further south – there's also an office at the bus station where they can do this. Immediately by the border, the small **tourist office** (Mon–Fri 8am–5pm; ☎631/2-64-46) has a limited amount of local information and maps, while just beyond this you're in an area teeming with blanket stalls and cafés, and a few hotels. These last are concentrated on two streets leading away from the border: Obregón, which eventually becomes the highway south, and Juárez. There are several **banks**, most with ATMs (some giving US dollars), and casas de cambio along López Mateos and Obregón, but if you want to phone or send mail you're better off doing so across the border.

If you're looking for a cheap **place to stay**, there's no need to go any further: possibilities include the *Imperial*, Internaciónal 79 (☎631/2-14-58; ④), right by the border fence west of the checkpoint and probably as basic as you'd want on your first night in Mexico; the *San Carlos*, Juárez 22 (☎631/2-13-46; ④), with more frills, including TV and a/c; and the *Olivia*, Obregón 125 (☎631/2-22-00; ④), another step up in class. There are plenty of cafés and **restaurants** in the same area; *Café Olga*, on Juárez just across the border, is a Nogales institution, and claims to be open 24 hours. Many of the alternatives are far more touristy, with live *mariachi* in the evenings: *Coco Loco*, Obregón 64, is a good example.

The **bus and train stations** are opposite each other on the highway about 5km south of town – local buses (signed "Central Camionera") run from the border, or you can take a taxi, which will cost around US$10. Southbound departures from the Camionera – which has all the usual facilities including long-distance phones and guardería – are frequent, going as far south as Guadalajara (26hr) and México (34hr). One **train** a day heads towards Guadalajara, at 7am, containing both first- and second-class carriages. On the other side of the border, the **Greyhound** station is right by the customs office; buses leave every one or two hours (6.45am–6.45pm) for Tucson and Phoenix.

Agua Prieta

To the east lies another border crossing, **AGUA PRIETA**, just across from Douglas, Arizona. Still a quiet town that sees few tourists, it's gradually growing thanks to the *maquiladora* assembly plants on both sides of the border, and to new roads linking the town to **Janos** (for Ciudad Juárez and Nuevo Casas Grandes) and direct to Hermosillo. Despite the fact that these are barely marked on many maps, they're perfectly good paved highways, and Agua Prieta is thus on the only route from central Mexico to the Pacific between the border and Mazatlán. Several buses a day run in each direction. If you're **staying** over, try the *Hotel Plaza* (no phone; ⑤) on the central plaza – though you may find better value in Douglas, where there's a *Motel 6* among other inexpensive motels.

Hermosillo

From a distance **HERMOSILLO**, the state capital of Sonora, is an odd-looking place, surrounded by strange rock formations and overlooked, right in the centre, by a tall outcrop crowned by radio masts, lit up at night like a helter-skelter. Close up, though, it's less interesting – the boom of the last half-century has wiped out almost everything that might have survived of the old town. Some of the earliest organized **revolutionaries**, including General Alvaro Obregón, were locals, as were many of the early presidents of revolutionary Mexico: Obregón himself, Huerta, whom he overthrew, Plutarco Elías Calles and Abelardo Rodríguez. Their many monuments and the streets named after them reflect the local debt. Today this is a thriving city and big ranching supply centre. The market overflows with meat and the shops are full of tack gear, cowboy hats and boots.

While it's interesting enough to experience such an archetypal Mexican town, there's no reason to stay here long: in any case, Hermosillo, spread-out and car-oriented, is not geared to welcoming visitors, especially those without their own vehicle. If you do have to or want to spend time here, head down to the **beaches** at Bahía de Kino. Short stays can be enlivened by strolling down Serdán past the market, and taking a look at the attractive plaza around the cathedral, across Rosales from the bottom of Serdán. Or check out the Centro Ecológico de Sonora, about 5km south on Blvd Rosales (closed Mon & Tues): take the "Luis Orcí" bus.

Arrival and information

Although the city sprawls, **downtown** Hermosillo is relatively compact. The highway comes into town as Blvd Eusebio Kino, known as Blvd Rosales as it runs north–south through the centre of town: crossing it, Blvd Luis Encinas passes the **bus station**, 3km east of the centre, leaving town to the west, past the airport towards Bahía de Kino (see opposite). Virtually everything you might want to see lies in an area bounded by these two, as well as Juárez and Serdán, the main commercial street downtown, which runs past the bottom of the distinctive hill known as the Cerro de la Campaña.

From the rather isolated **Central Camionera** (with guardería), take a "Ruta 1" microbus, a van (marked "Ranchito") or a "Multirutas" town bus to get downtown. Taxis are expensive and the drivers unwilling to bargain. Almost all the buses passing through Hermosillo are *de paso*, and at times it can be very hard to get on. However, TBC (depot outside the Central Camionera and left a few paces) run a local service to Guaymas, Navojoa and, four times daily, to Alamos.

The **train station** is still further out, by the highway; again there should be colectivos or buses into town. From the **airport**, a short way out on the road towards Bahía de Kino, you can pick up one of the usual fixed-fare taxis. The **tourist office** (generally Mon–Fri 8am–3pm & 5–7pm, Sat 10am–1pm; ☎62/17-00-60) is in the Edificio Sonora Norte, at Comonfort and Paseo Canal; they generally prove helpful, though they have little printed information and seem to come across few visitors.

Other facilities and shops are mostly on Serdán, including numerous **banks** and casas de cambio (there's also a handy Bancomer, with ATM, at Matamoros and Sonora, on the plaza a block from the *Monte Carlo* hotel). The **post office** is at the corner of Serdán and Rosales. Should you want to book a flight out, head for Travesias de Anza, a helpful **travel agency** at Serdán 122-B (☎62/12-26-70).

Accommodation

All the cheaper **hotels** in Hermosillo are strikingly poor value, but some very pleasant mid-range places cater to businesspeople and the wealthy rancheros who come here for the markets. The long-standing budget favourite is the *Monte Carlo*, Juárez at Sonora

(☎62/12-08-53; ④) – about six blocks north of Serdán, and just off Encina by a large plaza. Even here the rooms are little more than acceptable (though they do have good a/c, essential in the summer) and the red-light district starts immediately behind. Of the many very basic casas de huéspedes and hotels there, none is recommended, though *Hotel Royal*, on Sonora near the *Monte Carlo* (☎62/12-01-68; ③), is cheap and safe. For not much more, however, you could stay in the considerably better *Hotel Washington* at Noriega 68, near Guerrero (☎62/13-11-83; ③). The *Hotel Niza*, Plutarco Elias Calles 66, just off Serdán near the market (☎62/17-20-28; ④), has a good location and cable TV, but is still poor value. Much nicer, if you can afford them, are a couple of businesslike places down on Rosales: the solidly comfortable *Hotel San Alberto*, Serdán and Rosales (☎62/13-18-40; ⑤), and the colonial-style *Hotel Kino*, Pino Suárez 151, just off Rosales near the cathedral plaza (☎62/13-31-31; ⑤), which is really a motel, but with all facilities including a pool. The more expensive hotels, and a number of motels, are almost all in the hotel zone, a long way from the centre on Kino.

Eating

Downtown Hermosillo is surprisingly short of decent **places to eat**: Serdán and the surrounding streets are lined with plenty of juice bars and places selling tortas and other snacks, but local people in search of fancier food tend to get in their cars and head for the restaurants situated on the main boulevards or in the hotel zone. All the hotels mentioned above have restaurants that are at least passable, and there are several places on and around the plaza by the *Hotel Monte Carlo*: try *Napy's*, Matamoros 109 between Noriega and Morelia; *La Fabula Pizza*, a branch of a chain at Morelia 34 between Matamoros and Juárez; or the vegetarian restaurant and wholefood shop *Jung* (closed Sun), Niños Héroes 75, between Matamoros and Guerrero.

Bahía de Kino

Offering the nearest beaches to Hermosillo, **BAHÍA DE KINO**, 117km west, is a popular weekend escape for locals and increasingly a winter resort for Americans, many of whom have second or retirement homes down here. There are two settlements around the bay: the old fishing village of **Kino Viejo**, a dusty collection of corrugated-iron huts, passed over by the fruits of development, and the newer **Kino Nuevo** – basically a single road strung with one-storey seafront houses, trailer parks, and a couple of hotels and restaurants. There's really not a lot to it, but the beach is good, with miles of sand – and the offshore islets and strange rock formations make the spectacular sunsets still more worth watching.

Buses leave Hermosillo from a small bus station on Sonora, a block and a half east of the *Monte Carlo*. There are about nine a day – currently hourly from 5.30am to 9.30am, then every two hours up to 5.30pm – with more at busy weekends; they take around two hours. Probably the best-value **place to stay** is the *Motel Kino Bay* (☎624/2-02-16; ⑥), where you'll get a unit with kitchen and all facilities; it's one of the last places on the road, by the *Trailer Park Bahía Kino* (☎624/2-02-16). During the off season you may be able to pitch a tent here and, if you are reasonably discreet and careful with your stuff, camping on the Kino Nuevo beach is a possibility. Opposite the trailer park, the *Restaurant Kino Bay* is a good place to make enquiries about the local area, to sample the local seafood, or simply to enjoy a beer and watch the sun go down. The *Hotel Saro* (☎624/2-00-07; ⑤), soon after you enter Kino Nuevo, has similar facilities, and another decent restaurant.

This whole area used to be inhabited by the **Seri** peoples, and there are still a few communities living round about: one such, on the offshore **Isla Tiburón** (Shark Island), was relocated when the island was made into a wildlife refuge. You may come across Seri hawking traditional, and not so traditional, ironwood carvings along the beach in Kino Nuevo. The tiny **Museo de los Seris** (Wed–Sun 9am–1pm & 3–6pm; free) on the "plaza" in the middle of Kino Nuevo gives a little more information on Seri history.

Guaymas

Back on the route south the next major stop is **GUAYMAS**, an important port with a magnificent, almost landlocked natural harbour, where the mountains come right down to the sea. Although Guaymas claims a proud history – seemingly every adventurer whose eyes ever turned greedily to Mexico sent a gunship into the bay – there's really nothing to see beyond a couple of grandiose Porfiriano bank buildings on the main street. Nonetheless, if you have to choose somewhere to stop, this is definitely a more attractive option than Hermosillo, ninety minutes away, or Los Mochis, six hours on.

The Americans, the French and the British have all at one time or another attempted to take Guaymas (only the Americans had any real success, occupying the town in 1847–8), but the most extraordinary invader was a Frenchman, **Comte Gaston Raousset de Bourbon**. Attempting, with the tacit support of the then president, General Santa Ana, to carve out an empire in Sonora, Raousset invaded twice, holding Guaymas for several months in 1852. His second attempt, in 1854, was less successful and ended with most of the pirates, the count included, captured and shot. There are monuments to the hero of that battle – one General Yañez – all over town.

Today, Guaymas is still a thriving fishing and naval centre and makes few concessions to tourism. At the waterfront there's an attractive plaza where you can sit and look out over the deep bay, alive with the comings and goings of ships, and the scores of fishing boats at anchor. In the south of France this would no doubt be surrounded by outdoor waterfront cafés; this being Mexico, the dockside looks more like a building site. Still, it's a pleasant spot, and there are also some good beaches a short bus ride away.

Arrival and information

Virtually everything that happens in Guaymas happens on Serdán, the main drag which brings southbound traffic from the highway into town from the west, and leaves to the east for Ciudad Obregón via the docks and railway station. This is not a good place to arrive by **train**, since the station is 10km away in the neighbouring town of Empalme; buses run between the two (look for "Empalme" buses on Serdán to get out

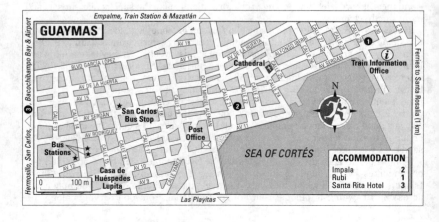

there), but you have to change for a local station bus in Empalme. Check train times at the railway information office, Serdán and C 30.

The **airport**, off the highway west of town, is closer, though here you'll have to rely on taxis for transport. Most people arrive by **bus**, however: the three terminals serving Tres Estrellas, Norte de Sonora, Baldamero Corral (TBC) and Pacifico are right opposite each other on C 14 at Rodríguez, a couple of blocks off Serdán and within walking distance of all the action. **Ferries** from Santa Rosalía arrive at the docks 2km east of the centre, easily reached on local buses along Serdán. For departures, see "Moving on from Guaymas" on p.98.

You'll find several **banks** on Serdán: Bancomer at C 18, and Banamex at C 20 (both with 24hr ATMs); and long-distance **telephones** in Farmacía Bell, Serdán at C 22, as well as in the Tres Estrellas terminal. The **post office** is on Av 10 just off C 20 (C Miguel Aleman), which runs south from Serdán and round the side of the bay. The **Mercado Municipal**, a block off Serdán on C 20, sells fresh food good for picnics.

Accommodation

From the bus stations, Rodríguez leads towards the centre, the street numbers rising as you go. In the first block you pass what looks like a Venetian castle, but is in fact the town jail. The best of the budget **places to stay** in Guaymas is the *Casa de Huéspedes Lupita*, C 15 no. 125 (☎622/2-84-09; ②), right by the prison and just a block from the bus stations. Some rooms have private bath. For a little more comfort, carry on into town and try the *Hotel Impala*, C 21 at Av 12, one block off Serdán (☎622/4-09-22; ④), an oldish place whose price is inflated because it has a lift, or the *Hotel Rubi*, Serdán and C 29 at the far end of the waterfront (☎622/4-01-69; ④), better value for simple, quiet courtyard rooms with private bath, TV and a/c. In the other direction, at Serdán and Mesa (C 9), the *Santa Rita Hotel* (☎622/2-81-00; ④) is also worth a try (not to be confused with the more expensive motel of the same name). One of the prettiest places to stay is the comfortable hotel–trailer park complex, *Las Playitas* (☎622/1-51-96; ③), with a pool, a pleasant restaurant, and rooms in bougainvillea-covered, traditionally furnished cottages. It's out of town on the coast at nearby Las Playitas (see below; take a taxi, or even the local bus). In San Carlos (see below) the *Creston* (☎622/6-00-20; ⑤) is a good option, also with a pool: rates can be reduced by up to fifty percent out of season (it's on the main road and the bus goes past the door).

Eating

Guaymas has plenty of inexpensive, no-nonsense **places to eat**: *Asadero Colibritercos*, between C 14 and C 15, though little more than a glorified taco stand, has a great Mexican-style help-yourself salad bar; and in the next block the ordinary-looking *Todos Comen* serves good antojitos and main meals. Further up, between C 17 and C 18, and also at C 10, *Las 1000 Tortas* dishes out tasty tortas, tacos, quesadillas and comidas. Off to the right you'll find *Restaurant Mandarin*, a Mex-Chinese place in the *Hotel Impala*. Opposite Banamex, *SE Pizzas* also offer a great buffet deal. To sample some of the town's best **seafood** head for *Los Barcos* on the seafront, Av 11 at C 20, with its huge palapa dining area, or the nautically decorated restaurant in the *Las Playitas* complex, where you can dine on huge fishy stews accompanied by live guitar music.

Beaches around Guaymas

The **beach** the locals use is at **MIRAMAR**, an upmarket suburb on Bacochibampo Bay, a few kilometres north of Guaymas. On balance, this is your best bet for swimming, though there is more happening 16km further north at **SAN CARLOS** (somewhat hopefully dubbed "Nuevo Guaymas"), which may be on its way to becoming a big resort. So far it has a couple of big resort hotels, a *Club Med*, a yacht marina, a

---

MOVING ON FROM GUAYMAS

The **ferry to Santa Rosalía** in Baja California leaves from the docks about 2km beyond Guaymas centre – just about any bus heading east on Serdán will take you there. There are currently two sailings a week (Tues & Fri 11am) and you buy tickets from the **terminal** (sales and reservations Mon–Sat 8am–3pm; ☎622/2-23-24); check the timetable and reserve in advance if possible – you'll need to if you plan to take a car across. Single **fares** for the 7hr crossing are currently US$14 for a reclining seat, US$27.50 sharing a simple four-berth cabin and US$157 for a small car.

Many first-class buses on the Mazatlán–Hermosillo run stick to the main highway, skipping Guaymas. There are, however, second-class buses every thirty minutes or so in both directions and a direct TBC service from Hermosillo to Alamos six times daily.

---

country club with a golf course, and scores of villas and half-completed developments all linked to the main highway north by a long avenue of transplanted palms. There are some lovely places here – bays set about with tall crags weirdly sculpted by the wind – and wonderful sunsets, but access to the shore is difficult, and most of the beaches you can reach are stony. As compensation you can rent all manner of **aquatic gear** or go diving, fishing and sightseeing with Gary's (☎622/6-00-49), about 1km south of the marina.

There's a more impressive stretch of sand at **Algodones**, over the hill beyond San Carlos, though there's no public transport out there and it's not exactly walking country. Algodones is where *Catch-22* was filmed, and you can still see parts of the set and the runway built for the production.

You may also be told that there are beaches at **LAS PLAYITAS**, on the other side of Guaymas' bay. Don't believe it: the *Las Playitas* motel–trailer park has a pool and a good restaurant, but the beach is entirely wishful thinking. If you've a couple of hours to kill, though, it is interesting to take the bus out this way for the ride – you can stay on all the way and eventually it will turn round and head back home. You get to see the shipbuilding industry, the fish-freezing and processing centres, and some fine views of the outer stretches of the wreck-strewn bay.

Buses for Miramar and San Carlos leave every thirty minutes or so from C 19 by the post office, but it's easier to catch them as they head up Serdán, for example at the corner of C 18. It can take up to an hour to reach San Carlos. To get to Las Playitas, hop on the bus marked "Parajes" from C Miguel Aleman.

Ciudad Obregón to Alamos

On the main highway, there's little to tempt you to stop between Guaymas and the Sonora state border. **CIUDAD OBREGÓN**, founded in 1928 and named after the president, has thrived on the agricultural development that accompanied the plans to utilize the Río Yaqui. Thanks to the irrigation schemes and huge dams upriver it's now a very large and uncompromisingly ugly town. About the only draw is for fans of cowboy clothing: locally produced **straw stetsons** are among the best and least expensive you'll find anywhere.

NAVOJOA, too, is a rather dull farming town. Where it scores over Ciudad Obregón is in having a reasonably priced hotel, a good market, and above all in being the jumping-off point for Alamos (see below). If you have some time to pass here, it's well worth checking out the **Museo Yaqui** on C Allende and 5 de Febrero. Most **buses** (usually *de paso*) pull in to either the TBC or Transportes de Pacifico stations, near each other around the junction of Guerrero and C de Ferrocarril, a couple of hundred metres away from the train station. Local buses to Alamos (hourly 6.30am–6.30pm) leave from a sep-

---

THE YAQUI

Between Guaymas and Ciudad Obregón lies the valley of the Río Yaqui, traditional home of the **Yaqui**. The Yaqui were perhaps the fiercest and most independent of the Mexican peoples, maintaining virtual autonomy until the beginning of this century. Rebellions, and at times outright war, against the government of the day were frequent – the most significant coming in 1710 and again, after independence, in 1852. The last major uprising was in 1928 during the brief presidency of General Alvaro Obregón. Obregón, himself a Sonoran, was assassinated in México but his plans for the development of the northwest laid the basis for peace with the Yaqui: aided, no doubt, by the fact that earlier regimes had shipped rebels out wholesale to work on the tobacco plantations of Oaxaca. Today the Yaqui enjoy a degree of self-rule, with eight governors, one for each of their chief towns, but their cultural and political assimilation is rapid. One surviving element of Yaqui culture is the celebrated **Danza del Venado**, or Stag Dance, not only performed frequently at local festivals in the villages of this area but also at folklore festivals throughout the republic – and it forms one of the centrepieces of the Ballet Folklórico in México. The chief dancer wears a deer's head, a symbol of good (the stag being the sacred animal of the Yaqui), and is hounded by one or more coyote dancers, falling eventually, after a gallant struggle, to these forces of evil.

---

arate station, some eight blocks west along Guerrero. It takes about fifteen minutes to walk, so in the heat of the day a taxi is well worth the expense. The Transportes de Pacifico bus station is handy for one of the town's cheaper **hotels**, the *Aduana* (②) on Ignacio Allende, which has a/c rooms. Unless time is against you, however, you're better off heading straight through to Alamos.

Alamos

The existence of **ALAMOS**, a Spanish colonial town just five hours' drive from the US border and 50km southeast of Navojoa, hasn't escaped the notice of scores of Americans – predominantly "artists" and retirees – who have chosen to settle here over the last forty years or so, often renovating the otherwise doomed-to-decay colonial architecture. The ex-pat community lives in near-complete social isolation from the local Mexicans, but the necessary economic interaction at least stops Alamos going the way of so many other ex-mining villages in the region. A ride out here to this patch of green makes a very pleasant respite from the monotony of the coastal road. And it's a great place to do nothing for a while: a tour of the town takes no longer than a couple of hours, and there's little else to do but walk in the mountains (an exceedingly hot exercise in summer). The meeting here of the Sonoran and Sinaloan deserts at the foot of the Sierra Madre Occidental has created a fairly unique ecosystem, home to a broad range of flora and fauna. In particular, this is a **birdwatching** mecca, boasting more than 410 different species. The town fills up at the end of January for the annual "Ortiz Tirado" **opera festival**.

Coronado was the first European to pass through this area in 1540, spending most of his time trying to subjugate the Mayo and Yaqui, unaware that below his feet lay some of the richest **silver ore** in Mexico. Silver was discovered late in the seventeenth century and Alamos became Mexico's northernmost silver mining town, within a century a substantial city with its own mint on the coastal branch of the Camino Real. With Mexican independence, control fell into the hands of the Alamada family who, despite initially productive mines, spent the rest of the nineteenth century protecting their piece from political wranglings and petty feuds, and watching over the region's decline. The mint closed in 1896, and even the brief existence of a railway only served to help depopulate a dying town. Alamos languished until the 1940s, when an American, **William Alcorn**, bought numerous houses here and set about selling the property to his countryfolk.

The town's focal point is the beautiful old arcaded **plaza** and the elegant eighteenth-century **cathedral**. Opposite the arcade on the Plaza de Armas, the mildly diverting **Museo Costumbrista de Sonora** (Mon–Fri 9am–1pm & 3–6pm; US$1) illustrates the town's heyday through a mock-up of the mine, and grainy photos of moustachioed workers. More interesting are the town's magnificent old Andalucian-style **mansions**, brooding and shuttered from the outside, but enclosing beautiful flower-filled patios. If poking your head through gaping doorways and visiting the restaurants or bars of houses converted into swanky hotels doesn't satisfy your curiosity, you can take an hour-long **house tour** (Sat 10am; US$3), which leaves from by the bank on the Alameda and visits some of the finest, predominantly American-owned, homes.

Arrival and information

From Navojoa hourly **buses** run to Alamos (6.30am–6.30pm; 1hr), arriving at the bus station on Morelos by the Alameda. There is a Bancomer across the park on Rosales. Follow Rosales east, then Juárez south to reach the Plaza de Armas, the cathedral and the enthusiastic **tourist office** (Mon–Fri 9am–1pm & 3–6pm, Sat & Sun 9am–1pm; ☎642/8-04-50). For reliable information also talk to Celsa in *Las Palmeras*, or ask around for David and Jennifer MacKay. The **post office** is on the approach into town, opposite the *Dolisa Motel and Trailer Park*.

Moving on from Alamos, there are six daily TBC buses (☎642/8-01-75) leaving for Navojoa, Guaymas and Hermosillo in the morning, returning in the late afternoon and evening.

Accommodation

Low-cost accommodation in Alamos is hard to come by, but there are some beautiful moderately priced hacienda-style places, with cool rooms ranged around bougainvillea-draped courtyards. You'll pay 10 to 20 percent less outside the high season of November to April. The town also boasts two **trailer parks**: *Dolisa Motel and Trailer Park* (☎642/8-01-31; also with some rooms ④), a convenient though often crowded site at the entrance to town (open all year), and *Acosta Trailer Rancho*, about 1km east of town (Oct–April; ☎642/8-02-64), a secluded park with camping spots and a pool. To get there, follow Morelos east across the usually dry Arroyo La Aduana then turn left at the cemetery.

Casa Encantada, Obregón 2 (☎642/8-57-60). Beautiful 300-year-old mansion, with fully refitted rooms, some with a/c. The same people also run *Hotel La Mansion* across the road, which has a pool, and breakfast included. ⑤.

Casa de los Tesoros, Obregón 10 (☎642/8-00-10). Just along from the *Casa Encantada*, up behind the cathedral, this eighteenth-century former convent now has a pool and beautifully decorated rooms. Ceiling fans for summer, fireplace for winter. Rates includes breakfast. ⑦.

Enríquez, Juárez on the Plaza de Armas (no phone). Alamos's only cheap hotel and not that pleasant, though serviceable. Just one room has a private bath. ③.

Hotel La Posada, follow signs from *Casa de los Tesoros*. Luxuriously furnished apartments with kitchen and all mod cons for up to six. ⑥ for two sharing, then US$9 per extra person.

Motel Somar, on approach into town, near the *Dolisa* (see above). Big and soulless, but cheap and clean. Rooms with bath and fan. Cheaper for four sharing (US$16.25 between you). ③.

Los Portales, Juárez on the Plaza de Armas (☎642/8-02-11). Beautiful restored hacienda, formerly owned by the Alamada family, with pleasant rooms around a broad stone courtyard but no a/c or pool. ⑤.

Eating and drinking

The best **restaurants** in Alamos are at the fancier hotels, in particular the *Casa Encantada*, *La Posada* and *Casa de los Tesoros*. Opposite *Hotel La Mansion* is *La Casa* *de Café*, a great breakfast place for scrumptious coffee and cake in the courtyard. *Las Palmeras* on the plaza also serves excellent food at very reasonable prices, and *Los Sabinos* (signs from *los Teseros*) is also recommended. There are a number of run-of-the-mill cheaper places around the **market** that fronts onto the Alameda.

Into Sinaloa: Los Mochis

Continuing down the coast and crossing into the state of Sinaloa, the next place of any size is **LOS MOCHIS**, another modern agricultural centre, broad-streeted and rather dull, but a major crossing point for road, rail and ferry, and above all the western terminus of the incomparable **rail trip** between here and Chihuahua through the Barranca del Cobre (see p.125).

The various modes of transport into and out of this area are infuriating in their failure to connect in any way – even the bus stations are on opposite sides of town. The two **rail lines**, the Los Mochis–Chihuahua and the Nogales–Guadalajara, have at least

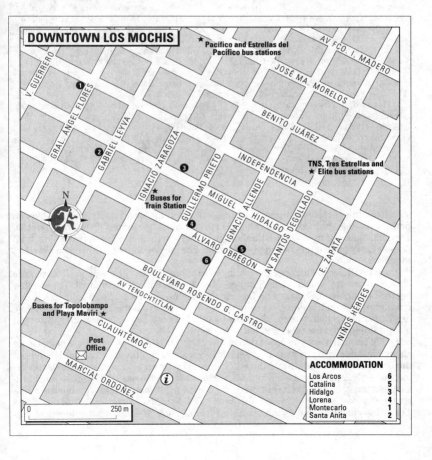

DOWNTOWN LOS MOCHIS

★ Pacifico and Estrellas del Pacifico bus stations

AV FCO. I. MADERO

V GUERRERO

GRAL. ANGEL FLORES

GABRIEL LEYVA

IGNACIO ZARAGOZA

GUILLERMO PRIETO

JOSE MA. MORELOS

BENITO JUAREZ

INDEPENDENCIA

MIGUEL

IGNACIO ALLENDE

HIDALGO

AV SANTOS DEGOLLADO

TNS, Tres Estrellas and ★ Elite bus stations

E. ZAPATA

★ Buses for Train Station

ALVARO OBREGÓN

BOULEVARD ROSENDO G. CASTRO

AV TENOCHTITLAN

NIÑOS HEROES

Buses for Topolobampo and Playa Maviri ★

CUAUHTÉMOC

Post Office ✉

MARCIAL ORDONEZ

i

0   250 m

ACCOMMODATION

Los Arcos	6
Catalina	5
Hidalgo	3
Lorena	4
Montecarlo	1
Santa Anita	2

MOVING ON FROM LOS MOCHIS

Tres Estrellas and Elite **buses** (leaving from Santos Degollado) have more first-class departures than the other services (see opposite); finding a seat on mostly *de paso* buses can be a problem, but with departures north and south every thirty minutes or so you shouldn't have too long to wait. **Trains** are much less convenient: two currently leave for **Chihuahua** each day, the first-class Vista Tren at 6am (arrives Creel 2.30pm, Chihuahua 8pm) and the second-class train at 7am (arrives Creel 5pm, Chihuahua 11pm), though remember that this line works on **Chihuahua time** – an hour later than local time in Los Mochis – so printed timetables will be one hour ahead of the times quoted here. Make sure you know which you are talking about when you find out your train's departure time. Fares on the Vista Tren are currently US$27 to Creel, US$50 to Chihuahua; on the second-class train US$6 to Creel and US$10 to Chihuahua. The **ticket office** at the station opens at 5am for same-day sales for both trains; tickets for the Vista Tren can also be bought the previous day at *Viajes Flamingo,* under the *Hotel Santa Anita* in town.

The **Nogales–Guadalajara** line doesn't in fact come to Los Mochis at all – its junction with the Chihuahua line is actually near **San Blas**, Sinaloa (not to be confused with the better-known San Blas in Nayarit), some 40km inland, at a station known as **Sufragio**. If you're **coming down from Chihuahua**, you should be able to make a direct connection with the slow train to Guadalajara, but you're probably better off waiting for the first-class train, which passes through in the early hours (6.25am heading north, 2.15am coming south). It's better still if you are on the first-class northbound, which, if on schedule, will reach Sufragio just before the Chihuahua-bound Vista Tren comes through, though if you miss it there's nothing to do while you wait for the next train. A bus operates every thirty minutes during the day between Sufragio, San Blas and Los Mochis' Norte de Sinaloa terminal, at the corner of Zaragoza and Ordoñez.

Buses for the forty-minute journey to Topolobampo, and the **ferries**, operate every fifteen minutes from Cuauhtémoc, between Zaragoza and Prieta. Departures for the 9–10hr **crossing to La Paz** are daily except Saturday at 10pm; you can buy tickets as you board, but as ever it's safest to get them, and check the timetable, in advance. The downtown SEMATUR office is in the Viajes Paotam travel agency at Rendón 517 (Mon–Fri 8am–1pm & 3–7pm, Sat 8.30am–2pm; ☎681/5-82-62), about six blocks north of Hidalgo – take Flores, then turn left at Rendón.

attempted to synchronize their schedules, but given the unreliability of timetables on both, this has helped little. The **ferry**, meanwhile, leaves from the port at Topolobampo, 24km away, and although the Chihuahua line goes there, the train doesn't carry passengers beyond Los Mochis. For full details, see "Moving on from Los Mochis".

No matter how you arrange things, if you're taking the ferry or train you'll have little choice but to **stay** at least one night here. Don't expect much excitement. The sweltering grid of streets that makes up Los Mochis has no real focus, but what there is of a **town centre** is on Hidalgo, between Prieto and Leyva. From the Tres Estrellas station, head right along Juárez then, after four blocks, left onto Leyva; from Pacifico turn left along Morelos and take the next left onto Leyva.

To kill an afternoon you could pop out to **TOPOLOBAMPO**, a strange place on an almost Scandinavian coastline of green, deeply inset bays – there's water all around but the ocean itself is invisible and the ferry steams in through a narrow channel, appearing suddenly from behind a hill into what seems a landlocked lake. There are no beaches, unfortunately, but you might persuade a local fisherman to take you out for a ride round the bay and a swim off the boat. The Sociedad Cooperativa de Servicios Turisticos runs trips out to the offshore islands, some of which host colonies of sea-lions. The beach favoured by locals is **Playa Maviri**, ten minutes by bus, from Cuauhtémoc between Zaragoza and Prieta.

Practicalities

The Pacifico and Estrellas del Pacifico **bus stations** are next to each other on Morelos between Zaragoza and Leyva. Norte de Sonora, Tres Estrellas and Elite are based on Santos Degollado, between Juárez and Morelos, within easy walking distance of most downtown hotels and restaurants. The **train station** is 3km from the centre and although there are frequent buses (marked "Colonia Ferrocarril") from Zaragoza, between Hidalgo and Obregón, you can't rely on them to get you there in time for the 6am departure or the late-evening arrival of trains from Chihuahua. **Taxi** fares in Los Mochis are a long-established rip-off, so grin and bear it: if you're aiming to catch an early morning train (see box opposite), try to gather a group of people and arrange in advance for a driver to pick you up. Normally, though, taxis are easy enough to find, especially around the bus stations and *Hotel Santa Anita* – the hotel also lays on a bus for guests only, connecting with the tourist trains (US$3.75).

There are few concessions to tourism in Los Mochis, though you'll find a **tourist office** (Mon–Fri 9am–3pm; ☎681/2-66-40) in the Unidad Administrativa building, Allende and Cuauhtémoc. You can **exchange currency** at Banamex (Mon–Fri until 2pm), at the corner of Prieto and Hidalgo, which also has an ATM. The **post office** is on Ordoñez, between Zaragoza and Prieto (Mon–Fri 9am–2pm & 4–6pm, Sat 9am–1pm).

Since they don't have to try too hard to attract customers, most of whom are simply stuck here, many of the **hotels** in Los Mochis are poor value. The situation for **eating** is equally grim: there are plenty of places around the hotels and the bus terminals, but nowhere really exciting, and hardly anywhere will be open if you arrive late.

Accommodation

Hotel Los Arcos, Allende 534 Sur at Castro (☎681/2-32-53; ②), is the cheapest option, and you can see why. The *Hotel Hidalgo*, on Hidalgo Pte 260 between Prieto and Zaragoza (☎681/2-34-56; ③, or ④ for a room sleeping up to four people), is worth the extra, especially for two or more sharing. Moving up a notch, the *Hotel Catalina*, on Obregón 186 between Allende and Degollado (☎681/2-12-40; ④), is not as good as it looks; you'll get better value for a similar price at the *Lorena*, Obregón at the corner of Prieto (☎681/2-02-39; ④), or especially the *Montecarlo*, Flores at Independencia (☎681/2-18-18; ④), where spacious rooms are set around a colonial-style courtyard. The luxury option is the modernish and rather bland *Hotel Santa Anita*, Leyva and Hidalgo (☎681/8-70-46; ⑨), owned by the same people who operate many of the fancier lodges along the Copper Canyon line. It's often full with tour groups, but is also good for information.

Eating

You're not going to do much gourmet dining in Los Mochis. *Mi Cabaña*, on the corner of Obregón and Allende, serves excellent tacos and burritos; *El Gordo*, a very plain place with good-value comidas, is at Zaragoza and Morelos – handy for the Norte de Sonora and Pacifico bus stations. *La Chispa*, Leyva 115 Sur by Morelos, does particularly good breakfasts and light meals in clean surroundings, as does the a/c *Restaurant Patelería Leon*, Obregón 419 between Leyva and Flores, which also serves decent coffee. The reliable Mexican-Spanish *Restaurant España*, Obregón 525 (☎681/2-23-35), has international pretensions and prices to match. *El Taquito*, just over a block up Leyva from here, near the *Hotel Santa Anita*, is also on the expensive and bland side, but it's clean and reassuring – it claims to be open 24 hours.

DRIVING IN SINALOA

If you have your own vehicle, you should take particular care in Sinaloa. The usual hazards of Mexican **driving** seem amplified (for more on which see p.35), especially around Culiacán, where there are some particularly hazardous stretches of Hwy-15 and there have been reports of robberies and attacks; the smooth new toll road that avoids this is extremely expensive and is also said to be prey to bandits. More importantly, remote areas of the state are notorious **drug-growing** centres, and inquisitive strangers are not welcome, so stick to the main roads. For the same reason, there's a specially high concentration of checkpoints along the highways.

Culiacán

Some 200km south of Los Mochis, **CULIACÁN**, the capital of Sinaloa, is a prosperous city with a population of more than a million, surrounded by some of the richest arable land in Mexico. It appears horribly ugly where it sprawls along the highway, but at its heart it's not too bad – mostly modern, but not unattractive. There's a lot more life in the streets, too, than in any of its near neighbours – probably thanks to the State University in the centre of town. Buses on the main road directly opposite the Camionera will take you to the **Cathedral**, from where you can head three blocks downhill to the **market**. You could pass an hour or so inspecting the artworks in the local **Centro Cultural**, or get to local **beaches** at Atlata or El Tambor, about an hour away by bus. None of this, however, adds up to a very compelling reason to stop, especially as Mazatlán is only another 200km further south. In any case, it's often extremely hard to get back on a bus, all too many of which are *de paso*.

The several **hotels** right by the Central Camionera all seem to charge the same. Given this, the best choice is the *Salvador*, Leyva Solano 297 (☎67/13-44-62; ④), directly opposite. There's better value, and more interesting surroundings, downtown. The *Hotel San Francisco* (☎67/13-58-63; ④), Hidalgo Pte 227, just by the market, is the best choice; you could also try the *Hotel Santa Fe* (☎67/15-17-00; ④), at Hidalgo Pte 243, or the slightly more upmarket, modern and airy *Santa Fe II* (☎67/16-01-40; ④), Hidalgo Pte 321. There's **street food** aplenty round here, and several pizza places, but otherwise not too many restaurants in the centre – the *Restaurant Santa Fe*, Hidalgo Pte 317, isn't bad, or stick with the bus station's restaurant.

Mazatlán

About 20km from **MAZATLÁN** you cross the Tropic of Cancer. The transformation seems sudden: Mazatlán is a tropical town where Culiacán was not, and there's that damp airlessness about it which at first makes breathing seem an effort.

Primarily, of course, Mazatlán is a resort, and a burgeoning one at that, with hotels stretching further every year along the coast road to the north, flanking a series of excellent sandy beaches. The new avenues of hotels may be entirely devoted to tourism, but that said, on the whole Mazatlán seems far less dominated by its visitors than its direct rivals Acapulco or Puerto Vallarta. Most holidaymakers stay in the Zona Dorada, the "Golden Zone", and penetrate the town itself only on brief forays.

Though heavily dependent on tourism, Mazatlán is also Mexico's largest Pacific port and a thrusting town in its own right, and thanks to its situation on a relatively narrow peninsula, the centre of town has preserved much of its old, cramped and thoroughly Mexican atmosphere. There's not a great deal actually to *do* in Mazatlán – you certainly wouldn't come here for the architecture – but it is a pleasant enough place and the

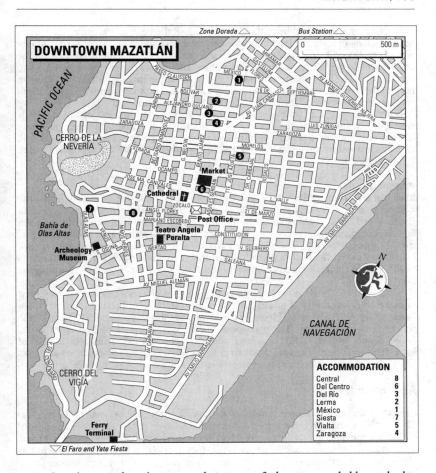

Zona Dorada △   Bus Station △

DOWNTOWN MAZATLÁN

0   500 m

PACIFIC OCEAN

PASEO CLAUSSEN

S. BOLIVAR

ALEJANDRO QUIJANO

ZARAGOZA

CERRO DE LA
NEVERÍA

OCAMPO

JOSE MA.
CANIZALES

Market

Cathedral †

ZOCALO

ANGEL FLORES

MARIANO ESCOBEDO   **Post Office**

**Teatro Angela
Peralta**

Bahía de
Olas Altas

**Archeology
Museum**

LIBERTAD

AV. MIGUEL ALEMÁN

CERRO DEL
VIGÍA

**Ferry
Terminal**

▽ El Faro and Yate Fiesta

MÉXICO

16 DE
SEPTIEMBRE

AV. JUAN CARRASCO

AV. MANUEL GUTIERREZ NÁJERA

ZARAGOZA

LUIS ZÚÑIGA

MORELOS

ROSALES

DR. CARBAJAL

VALLE

21 DE MARZO

CONSTITUCIÓN

V. GUERRERO

GALEANA

CANAL DE
NAVEGACIÓN

N

ACCOMMODATION

Central	8
Del Centro	6
Del Río	3
Lerma	2
México	1
Siesta	7
Vialta	5
Zaragoza	4

separation of town and tourism means that you can find some remarkably good-value hotels on the streets just a few blocks inland. Mexican families mostly stay here, making the beachfront developments almost exclusively foreign preserves. There's an excellent bus service out along the coast road, so staying in town doesn't mean sacrificing the beach-bum lifestyle: with discretion, non-residents can use the hotel pools and the beaches in front of them. Remember to book accommodation well ahead if you are planning to be here around **Semana Santa**, when Mexicans descend on the city for carnival celebrations.

Arrival and information

From the **bus station**, head up the hill to the main road and get on just about any bus heading to the right – they'll get you, by a variety of routes, to the **market**, very central and effectively the terminus for local buses. For the Zona Dorada, walk downhill from the bus station and catch a "Sábalo" bus heading to the right along the coast road.

Arriving by **ferry** you'll be at the docks, south of the centre: there are buses here, but getting an entire ferry-load of people and their baggage on to two or three of them always creates problems. Taxis are in demand, too, so try to be among the first off the boat. If you do get stranded, don't despair: the 1km walk to the centre of the old town isn't too bad. The **train station** is east of town in the Esperanza district; buses run from here to the market, and taxis also meet most arrivals. Mazatlán **airport** is some 20km south of town, served by the usual system of fixed-price vans (US$22) and taxis.

Downtown, you can walk just about everywhere, and the rest of the resort is stretched out 15km along the coast road northwards – all linked by a single bus route and patrolled by scores of taxis and little open *pulmonías* (they look like overgrown golf carts but are usually cut-down VW Beetles; cheaper than taxis as long as you fix the fare before getting in).

Information

Mazatlán's **tourist office** (Mon–Fri 9am–2pm & 4–7pm; ☎69/85-12-20) is in the Edificio Banrural, Av Cámaron Sábalo, opposite *Hotel Quijote*; they're helpful, speak English, and have reasonable maps. In the Zona Dorada, commercial information booths pop up on almost every corner – selling tours and condos, mostly, but some give friendly free advice, too. If you have any trouble – theft, accident and so forth – seek help from what is effectively a **district attorney for tourists** (☎69/14-32-22) at Rodolfo Loaiza 100, in the mall complex opposite the *Hotel Los Sábalos* on the main seafront avenue.

Most places in the Zona accept **dollars** though often at a poor rate, so you may want to make use of Mazatlán's numerous **casas de cambio**. In the old town the main Banamex, on Juárez at Ángel Flores by the zócalo, has the longest hours (8.30am–1pm) and good exchange rates. The main **post office**, Juárez and 21 de Marzo (Mon–Fri 8am–5.45pm, Sat 9am–1pm), is nearby, and you can make calls from any number of **long-distance phones** around the town or in the *larga distancia* places at Serdán 1512 (24hr), in the bus station or at several sites in the Zona.

Accommodation

Almost all Mazatlán's cheaper **hotels** are downtown, within a short walk of the market. There's also a small group around the bus station, convenient for transport and beaches, but not the most appealing part of town. Many have two classes of rooms, with and without a/c. The fancier hotels are all in the Zona Dorada, but even here some of the older places, and those on the fringes, can be real bargains out of high season or for longer stays.

If you're in a group, it's worth looking round for an **apartment**, which are usually great value. **Trailer parks** tend not to last very long, occupying vacant lots and then moving north to keep ahead of development, so perhaps the best course for campers is to drive or take the bus along the beach until you spot a promising location. Two of the most permanent sites are *Trailer Park Playa Escondida*, Playa Escondida (☎69/88-00-77), in a quiet location almost at the end of the bus route, so probably safe from development for a few seasons (it also rents bungalows with kitchenettes; ④), and *Trailer Park Rosa Mar*, Cámaron Sábalo 702 (☎69/83-61-87), which is closer to the action.

The old town

Hotel del Centro, Canizales 705 Pte (☎69/81-26-73). Large clean rooms all with private bath and some with a/c, close to centre. ③.

Hotel Del Río, Juárez and Quijano (no phone). Attractive and clean, though some rooms are very small. ③.

Hotel Lerma, Bolivar, between Serdán and Juárez (☎69/81-24-36). The best deal in town. Big, clean rooms around a very spacious courtyard. ②.

Hotel México, México 201 and Serdán (☎69/81-38-06). Friendly, clean and close to the sea. Rooms can be a bit small. ②.

La Siesta, Olas Altas 11 between Ángel Flores and Escobedo (☎69/81-26-40). Lovely old hotel with great sea views (worth the extra money); drawbacks are small rooms and noise till late from *El Shrimp Bucket* restaurant next door. Off-season rooms for as little as half-price. ④.

Vialta, Jose Azueta 2006, about three blocks north of the market (☎69/81-60-27). Plain but acceptable rooms round a lovely courtyard; some with a/c. ②.

Zaragoza, Zaragoza 217 between Serdán and Juárez (☎69/81-36-66). What you'd expect from almost the cheapest in town, but the bare rooms are clean, with fan and bath, and the whole place feels spacious and cool. ②.

Near the bus station

Emperador, Río Panuco, right opposite the bus station (☎69/82-67-24). Convenience is the main attraction, though rooms are clean and comfortable, with TV and a/c. ③.

La Fiesta, Esperanza (☎69/81-78-88). Big, clean rooms, but fairly basic. ②.

Motel Acuario, Av del Mar near the Aquarium (☎69/82-67-24). A short way down towards the Zona, the *Acuario*'s rooms are spartan, though there is a pool. ④.

Sands Hotel, Av del Mar 1910 (☎69/82-00-00). Facing the beach, straight down from the bus station. Comfortable, US-style motel with pool and sea views; very good value, especially off-season, when prices drop considerably. ⑤ for up to 4 people sharing.

Santa Maria, Ejercito Mexicano (☎69/82-23-04). Uphill from the station. Big and functional, but with good rooms, all with TV. ②.

Zona Dorada

Apartamentos Fiesta, Ibis 502 (☎69/13-53-55). Well into the Zona off Playa Gaviotas, three blocks inland from the *Hotel Balboa Towers*. Basic, good-value apartments and studios in garden setting for four or six people. Normally rented by the week, but in the off season can be rented per night. ③.

Del Real Suites, Av del Mar 1020 (☎69/83-19-55). Well-appointed hotel with parking, a/c, cable TV and a pool. Accommodation (considerably cheaper by the week) is either in large suites with kitchenette (sleeping up to 7), smaller suites or kitchen-less rooms. ④.

Inn at Mazatlán, Camarón Sábalo 6291 (☎69/13-55-00). The place to do it in style; a classy hotel–time share complex that oozes chic (at least by Mazatlán standards). Larger apartment units are excellent value for families or small groups. ⑧.

Las Jacarandas, Av del Mar 2500, at entrance to the Zona (☎69/84-11-77). Like the nearby *San Diego*, an older hotel with a pool that's been left behind by development and can no longer draw the crowds. Fading, but good value; some rooms with a/c and sea views. ③.

Motel Marley, Rodolfo Loaiza 226 (☎69/13-55-33). Comfortable units in small-scale place with great position right on the sand, and a pool. ④.

The Town

As befits a proper Mexican town, Mazatlán's **zócalo** is very much the commercial heart of the city, harbouring the cathedral (modern and not at all attractive), government offices, the post office, main bank branches and travel agencies. Always animated, it's especially lively on Sunday evening (5–7pm), when there's a free *folklórico* show with singing and dancing. Take time to stroll through the **market**, and in the other direction have a look round the newly restored **Plaza Machado**, surrounded by fine nineteenth-century buildings, including the **Teatro Ángela Peralta**, which often hosts interesting events or exhibitions. As far as sights go, that's about it, though you could also check out the small **Museo de Arqueología**, Sixto Osuna 76 (Tues–Sun 10am–1pm & 4–7pm; US$1), just a couple of blocks towards Olas Altas, or the **Aquarium** (daily 9.30am–6.30pm; US$4), just off Av del Mar halfway between town and the Zona Dorada.

There are also some great **views** of town from the top of the Cerro Vigia or Cerro La Nevería; unless you're feeling very energetic, take a *pulmonía* or taxi up. Likewise, the top of the **Faro de Creston** (unrestricted access) at the southern edge of town is a good vantage point, though you'll have to walk up.

The beaches: Olas Altas, the Zona Dorada and Isla de la Piedra

Right in town, **Playa Olas Altas** is a great place to watch the sun go down or the local kids playing, but not the best place to swim – it's rather rocky and the waves tend to be big. Following the seafront drive from here around the rocky coast under the Cerro La Nevería brings you to the **Mirador** – an outcrop of rock from which local daredevil youths plunge into the sea. At little over 10m, it's nowhere near as spectacular as the high-diving in Acapulco (see p.381), but dangerous nonetheless. You'll see them performing whenever there are enough tourists to raise a collection, but generally from 10 or 11am – especially in summer and during *Semana Santa* – and again in the late afternoon (around 5pm) when the tour buses come past.

To get to the **northern beaches** from here, you have to go back into the centre of town or continue all the way round to **Playa Norte**, as the buses don't follow the coast round the Cerro la Nevería. Perfectly adequate though the Playa Norte may be, it's worth heading even further north to the **Zona Dorada**. The sands improve greatly around **Sábalo**, a short way into the Zona, where the first of the big hotels went up, many of which still remain. It really depends from here on what you want – the beaches right in front of the hotels are clean and sheltered by little offshore islands (boats sail out to these from various points along the beach), while further on they're wilder but emptier. The more populous area has its advantages – the beach never gets too crowded (most people stay by their pools and bars) and there's always a lot going on: waterskiing, sailing, parascending behind speedboats, you name it. And if you get bored, there are the hotel pools and bars and any number of tourist watering-holes and shops to pass the time. Among the dozens of artesanía markets and shopping malls, **Sea Shell City**, on Rodolfo Loaiza in the heart of the Zona, stands out as the kitschest of all – a two-storey emporium of sea shells that describes itself as a museum and is definitely worth a look. Stay on the bus past all this, though, and you eventually get to an area where there's far less development. Along the way you can see just how quickly Mazatlán is spreading, and assess progress on the new marina development by the *Hotel Camino Real*. Towards the end of the bus line, make sure you get off somewhere you can reach the beach – often the only access is through villa or condo developments with gates and security. **Buses** (marked "Sábalo") leave from the market on the Juárez side, and run up Av del Mar and right through the Zona to the last hotel, where they turn around. Those marked "Cerritos" can be picked up along Insurgentes and run past Cerritos, eventually turning around twenty minutes or so out of the Zona at Playa Escondida.

Alternatively, south of the town centre, you can take a short and inexpensive boat trip (every 10min; 5am–7pm) from the beach next to the ferry docks to the **Isla de la Piedra**, actually a long peninsula. There is a much more Caribbean feel here, with a very good palm-fringed beach that stretches for miles, excellent for swimming (but watch out for the strong undertow). You could possibly sleep out or sling a hammock on the terrace of one of the small restaurants. Once a very basic community, the Isla is increasingly included in tour itineraries and can, at times, become crowded. On Sundays there is live music and dancing. Also from the ferry docks, the *Yate Fiesta* three-hour **harbour cruise** leaves daily (except Mon) at 11am (☎69/85-22-37 or 85-22-38; US$10).

Eating and drinking

As a rule, Mazatlán's more authentic and lower-priced **restaurants** are in the old town. For rock-bottom prices, seek out the noisy and hectic restaurants on the upper floor of the **market** on the Juárez side. All along the Playa Norte are shacks selling fish at good prices. You can come across bargains in the Zona, too, as long as you don't mind the menu being in English and the prices in dollars. The sheer number of tourists there means lots of competition and **special offers**; breakfast deals are often the best of all.

The old town

Café Pacifico, Constitución 509 at Heriberto Frías. "European pub" that also serves snacks, sandwiches and coffee. A relaxing place to drink (until 2am) without the macho overtones of many Mexican bars.

Restaurant Doney's, Escobedo 610 at 5 de Mayo. Classy and slightly touristy place that's not as pricey as you might think – well worth it for good local food, including a fine comida corrida.

Jade, Morelos and 5 de Mayo. About the only Chinese restaurant in the centre; not at all bad.

El Jardin, right under the bandstand in the zócalo. Cafe with good coffee and breakfasts. Tables outside for watching the world go by.

Karica Papaya, Nelson and Valle, and another at Flores and Frias. Vegetarian food, juices and licuados. Good-value comidas corridas from 12.30 to 4pm.

Hostería Machado, Constitución 519. Fancy restaurant on the Plaza Machado with a piano player in the evening.

Marismeña, Olas Altas. Probably the best seafood restaurant in this part of town, but no outdoor seating.

Pastelería Panamá, Juárez and Canizales, between the zócalo and the market. Fast-food style restaurant/caféteria, good for breakfast but not cheap.

Royal Dutch, Juárez, between Escobedo and Constitución. Great coffee, cakes, snacks and meals (until 10pm), in a relaxing atmosphere around an arcaded patio, marked by a windmill sign.

El Shrimp Bucket, next to the *Hotel La Siesta*, Olas Altas 11, between Ángel Flores and Escobedo. One of the oldest and best-known restaurants in Mazatlán and apparently the original of the Carlos Anderson chain. Now in bigger, plusher premises, it still has plenty of atmosphere and decent, if increasingly pricey food.

Zona Dorada

Carlito's Bar and Grill, next to *Motel Marley*. A great spot to sip a beer and watch the sunset. Also serving good food.

Casa Loma, Gaviotas 104 (☎69/83-53-98). For that perfect romantic, and expensive, evening, this secluded restaurant in a colonial setting has far more atmosphere than the big hotels. Tends only to be open in peak season, however, and reservations are recommended.

No Name Café, Rodolfo Loaiza next to the arts and crafts centre. Food and breakfast specials, but mainly a place for cool beer, party atmosphere, and big-screen TV sports. Typical among many.

El Tío Juan, Rodolfo Loaiza at Bugambilias. Again, just one of many similar places; friendly, English-speaking and not bad value if you choose with care or look for special offers. Cheap breakfasts.

Listings

Car rental Dozens of outlets, including Budget, Camarón Sábalo 402 (☎69/13-20-00), and National, Camarón Sábalo 7000 (☎69/13-60-00).

American Express Camarón Sábalo, Plaza Balboa in the Zona (Mon–Fri 9am–1pm & 4–6pm; ☎69/13-06-00). Poor rates for cheques, but cardholders can receive mail.

Consulates Canada, *Hotel Playa Mazatlán*, Zona Dorada (☎69/13-73-20); USA (representative only), *Hotel Playa Mazatlán* (☎69/13-44-55 and ask for rep).

Language courses Centro de Idiomas, Belisario Domínguez 1908 (☎69/82-20-53), offers courses from a week to a month, starting at around US$100; they can also arrange accommodation with Mexican families.

Laundry Lavafacil opposite the bus station by the *Hotel Fiesta*, and others at regular intervals throughout the Zona – in the Puebla Bonita complex, for example. Also several downtown.

Medical emergencies Cruz Verde, Gutiérrez Nájera and Obregón (☎69/81-22-25).

Police ☎69/83-45-10.

MOVING ON FROM MAZATLÁN

Mazatlán's large **bus station** lies on the main west coast route linking Tijuana and Mexicali in the north with Guadalajara and México in the south. The station has all facilities, including guardería and long-distance phones, and there are constant departures north and south. The region's major **bus companies** – Transportes Norte de Sonora, Tres Estrellas de Oro and Elite (all ☎69/81-38-11), and Transportes del Pacifico (☎69/82-05-77) – all have *de paso* services roughly hourly in both directions and frequent local buses to **Culiacán** (4hr), **Los Mochis** (7hr), **Tepic** (4hr) and **Guadalajara** (4hr). In addition, two buses daily run direct to **San Blas** (currently 11am & 5pm; 4hr). Estrella Blanca (☎69/81-53-81) and Transportes Frontera between them cover the route to **Durango** (13 daily; 6hr). To get to the bus station, take a "Sábalo" bus along the beachfront from Juárez near the market, then walk the 300m along Espinoza.

The **train station** (☎69/84-67-10) – on the west Mexico main line between Guadalajara and Mexicali/Nogales – lies 3km inland from the centre of Mazatlán and is served by one first-class and one second-class train in each direction. **Timetables** change frequently and trains are often late so check locally, but the northbound first-class train, which is comfortable enough to sleep on, is scheduled to reach **Sufragio** (near Los Mochis) in time to meet the tourist train up to the Copper Canyon and Chihuahua. **Tickets** can only be bought at the station and go on sale an hour before the train departs. **Getting to the station** from town, catch the "Insurgentes" bus on Juárez, or a bus heading down Av del Mar in the Zona.

The **ferry to La Paz** (daily except Sat at 3pm; 18hr) leaves the port at Playa Sur, 1km southeast of the centre: catch the "Playa Sur" bus from Juárez. **Information** and tickets are available from SEMATUR (☎69/81-70-20) at the port: a salón class ticket (available on all boats) qualifies you for a reclining seat (US$21), a turista class ticket (daily except Wed) gets you a space in a four-berth cabin (US$41), cabina (US$62) in a two-berth cabin; a small car will cost US$223, and bicycles go free. Food on board isn't great and, though there are signs prohibiting bringing your own, no one checks or seems to care.

Direct **flights** leave Mazatlán airport (☎69/82-23-99), which is 20km south of the city and only reachable by expensive taxi. These are run by Aeroméxico (☎69/14-11-11), Alaska (☎69/85-27-30), Mexicana (☎69/82-72-22), Delta (☎69/82-13-49), Noroeste (☎69/14-38-55) and Saro (☎69/84-97-68), but you'd do better booking through a **travel agent** such as Turismo Coral, 5 de Mayo 1705 (Mon–Fri 8am–7pm, Sat 8am–noon; ☎69/81-32-90), northwest of the zócalo.

Mazatlán to Durango

Leaving Mazatlán, you have the choice of continuing **down the coast** to Tepic and from there along the main road to Guadalajara, or to more Pacific beaches at San Blas and Puerto Vallarta; or cutting **inland to Durango**, (see p.137) and the colonial cities of the Mexican heartland. This road, the first to penetrate the Sierra Madre south of the border, is as wildly spectacular as any in the country, twisting and clawing its way up to the Continental Divide at over 2500m. New vistas open at every curve as you climb from tropical vegetation, through temperate forests of oak, to the peaks with their stands of fir and pine. It can get extremely cold towards the top, so keep plenty of warm clothing on hand to cover the T-shirt and shorts you'll need for the first sweaty hour. Little more than 300km, it's a very slow road, so reckon on six hours to Durango at the least.

Popular with tours from Mazatlán, but quiet otherwise, **CONCORDIA**, 42km inland, is an attractive colonial town with a reputation for making robust wooden furniture, examples of which crop up all over the region. The eighteenth-century Baroque **Church of San Sebastián**, overlooking the shady square, is unique in these parts but otherwise unexceptional, so you might as well press on towards the far grander edifices in the central highlands. For almost four hundred years, **COPALA**, a further thirty minutes on the bus towards Durango and a 1km walk down a side road, was Sinaloa's most important silver mining town. But in 1933 Charles Butters' processing plant closed, putting six hundred people out of work; though the locals picked over the remains until the 1970s, the town's decline was already well advanced. The **jungle**, which has already engulfed the crushing mills and separation tanks, is nibbling at the edges of the village, which today largely relies on tourists from Mazatlán for its survival. Once the day-trippers leave, however, the place takes on a languorous air, making it a relaxing, and cool, place to **spend a night** or two. The *Copala Butter Company*, Plaza Juárez (☎69/85-42-25; ③), has beautiful rooms with bath, and a balcony with views of the eighteenth-century church across the central plaza. It also offers **self-catering** bungalows (⑤), sleeping up to four people. The restaurant here and the only other one in town, *Daniel's*, are both excellent and reasonably priced. Try the local speciality, banana-cream pie.

South of Mazatlán: Tepic

Below Mazatlán the main road steers a little way inland, away from the marshy coastal flatlands. There are a few small beach communities along here, and deserted sands, but on the whole they're impossible to reach without transport of your own, and fly-blown, exposed and totally lacking in facilities once you get there. The first town of any size, capital of the state of Nayarit and transport hub for the area, is **TEPIC**.

Despite its antiquity – the city was founded by Cortés' brother, Francisco, in 1544 – there's not a great deal to see in Tepic. Appealing enough in a quietly provincial way, for most it's no more than a convenient **stopover** before continuing across the mountains to Guadalajara, or a place to switch buses for the coast. And this is probably the best way to treat it, for while the surrounding country is beautiful in parts, it's largely inaccessible and visited only by anthropologists for whom the mountains of Nayarit, homelands of the Huichol and Cora, are rich in interest.

The eighteenth-century **Cathedral**, on the zócalo, is worth a look, as is the small **Museo Regional** (Mon–Fri 9am–7pm, Sat, 9am–3pm; free), at the corner of México and Zapata, south from the zócalo, with a lovely collection of local pre-Columbian and Huichol artefacts. A couple of kilometres south on México, the **Ex-Convento de la Cruz de Zacate**, built in the sixteenth century to house a miraculous cross, has been restored for visitors. Plenty of places sell **Huichol "paintings"**: one of the best is upstairs at *Casa Arguet*, Amado Nervo 132, west of the zócalo.

Tepic's **bus station** lies a couple of kilometres southeast of the centre, but local buses shuttle in and out from the main road outside; similarly, the **train station**, on the main Guadalajara to Nogales line, is 2km east of the centre on Zapata and linked by buses to the centre. The main **tourist office** (Mon–Fri 9am–2pm & 4–7pm, Sat & Sun 10am–1pm) is at México Norte 178 (☎32/12-05-89); there's a smaller branch in the Ex-Convento de la Cruz de Zacate.

For just one night it's easiest to put up with the noise and stay by the bus station. Two cheap **hotels** with little to choose between them – the *Nayar* (☎32/13-23-22; ②) and the *Tepic* (☎32/13-13-77; ②) – stand immediately behind the terminal on Martínez. In the centre, try the *Hotel Serita*, Bravo Pte 112 (☎32/12-13-33; ②), north of the zócalo, or the *Cibrian*, Amado Nervo Pte 163 (☎32/12-86-98; ③), slightly closer. For more comfort, the *Sierra de Alicia*, México Nte 180 (☎32/12-03-25; ③), or the luxurious *Fray Junípero Serra*, Lerdo Pte 23 (☎32/12-22-11; ⑤), right on the zócalo, are good choices. For **food**, there's plenty of choice around the zócalo and on México: *Pat Pac's*, upstairs at México Norte and Morelos, is good, popular and reasonably priced, offering an excellent

---

THE HUICHOL

The **Huichol**, some 10,000 of whom live in the isolated mountain regions around the borders of Nayarit, Jalisco, Zacatecas and Durango, are the indigenous people perhaps least affected by developments in the four and a half centuries since the Spanish invasion of Mexico. New roads are bringing apparently inevitable pressure for "development" of their lands, but for now much of their territory remains accessible only by the occasional mule track or via one of many simple landing strips for light aircraft. In these fastnesses they have preserved their ancient beliefs, government and social forms.

Religion and ritual play such an intimate and constant part in Huichol lives that it's almost impossible for an outsider to comprehend. Even the simplest action or object or item of dress has ritual significance in a religion based on daily life: Mother Earth and Father Sun; the goddess of rain and the god of corn; the deer for hunters, and peyote for food gatherers. Peyote in particular, for which a group of Huichol have to make an annual cross-country pilgrimage to Real de Catorce (p.212), plays an important part in their ceremonials. Huichol brightly coloured wool **"paintings"** are rich in stylized symbols based in nature – animals, suns, moons – and traditional themes of fertility and birth. You can buy these pictures in Tepic and elsewhere. You may see traditionally dressed Huichol at the market or paying homage in the Church of Santa Cruz in Tepic (the missionaries did have some effect, and two Christs have been absorbed into the Huichol pantheon). There's more chance of seeing Huichol life at **religious festivals** in nearby villages, though you should consider whether you want to add your possibly unwelcome intrusion to that of many others.

Getting to Huichol territory is not easy, despite daily light planes from the airport in Tepic; you need permission from the authorities, and of course there are no regular facilities to feed or house visitors, little to see in the collections of mud-floored shacks that make up the villages, and no guarantee that you'll be welcome.

---

breakfast buffet; *Café Diligencias*, México Sur 29, is a good place to linger over a coffee; while *Acuarios*, Morelos Pte 139, serves simple vegetarian dishes. Fancier restaurants, other than those in the hotels, are west of here, near the open spaces of the Parque La Loma: try for example *Roberto's*, 472 Paseo La Loma at Insurgentes, on the far side of the park.

San Blas

West of Tepic lies the coastal plain: sultry, marshy and flat, dotted with palm trees and half-submerged under little lagoons teeming with wildlife. Through this you reach **SAN BLAS**, as godforsaken a little town as you could hope to see – at least on first impression. It was an important port in the days of the Spanish trade with the Orient, wealthy enough to need a fortress to ward off the depredations of English piracy, but though there's still an enviable natural harbour and a sizeable deep-sea fishing fleet, almost no physical relic of the town's glory days remains.

Life in San Blas is very, very slow. The positive side of this is an enjoyably laid-back travellers' scene, with plenty of people who seem to have turned up years ago and never quite summoned the energy to leave. For such a small town, though, San Blas manages to absorb its many visitors – who descend mainly in winter – without feeling overrun, submissive or resentful. In summer it's virtually deserted save for legions of ferocious mosquitoes.

Arrival and information

The majority of the **buses** serving San Blas arrive from Tepic, 65km east, though if you're coming from neighbouring coastal resorts you can save time and hassle by catching either the direct bus from Mazatlán (twice daily) or the service from Puerto Vallarta (twice daily) via Las Varas along the coast. Transportes Norte de Sonora run these and a daily bus to Guadalajara via Tepic.

The **bus station** is on Sonora at the northeastern corner of the zócalo, right in the centre of town. Here Juárez crosses Heroico Batallón de San Blas, which runs 1km south to the town beach, Playa de Barrego. The very helpful **tourist office** (no phone), presently on C Canaliso, is moving to the new Casa de Gobierno on the zócalo as soon as it's completed. Though the Banamex branch, on Juárez just east of the zócalo, cashes cheques (Mon–Fri 8am–noon) and has an ATM, it is plagued by long queues, poor rates and an occasional lack of funds. Change money before you get here or, if pushed, see if the Pato Loco store next to the tourist office will change cheques. The **post office** is a block northeast of the bus station at Sonora and Echevarría, and long-distance **phones** can be found in the bus station.

Accommodation

Part of the appeal of San Blas is that there's plenty of choice of budget **hotels**. Most places are on Juárez or Heroico Batallón. The town is especially well geared to small, **self-catering** groups: "bungalows" and "suites" are apartments with up to six beds, a small kitchen and usually (though you should check) some cooking equipment. Wherever you stay, make sure that the screens are intact and the doors fit or you'll be plagued by biting insects.

The *Coco Loco* trailer park (☎328/5-00-55) is a shady and grassed camping area close to the beach, a kilometre down Batallón from the zócalo. There's also free camping on Playa de Barrego, but the bugs and the availability of good, cheap accommodation make this less than appealing.

Casa María, Batallón at Michoacán (☎328/5-06-32). Friendly in the extreme; rooms with or without bath include use of kitchen; beds in communal rooms at peak times. Having become a popular budget choice, it's often full in winter. ③.

Garza Canela, Paredes 106, follow signs from Batallón (☎328/5-01-12). The best and priciest in town – comfortable a/c rooms, pool, garden, and some kitchenettes. Rates include breakfast. ⑦.

Hotel Morelos, opposite *Casa María* (no phone). Same family and set-up as the *Casa María* (without the kitchen). ③.

Portolá, Paredes 118, two blocks northeast of the zócalo (☎328/5-03-86). Exceptional value. Immaculate rooms with good kitchenettes. Resident or not, you can also rent bikes. ④.

Posada Azul, Batallón, two blocks beyond *Casa María* (no phone). The cheapest in town. Basic, but safe and friendly. ②.

Posada del Rey, Campeche 10, not far from the water (☎328/5-01-23). Possibly the most together hotel in San Blas, with tiny pool and bar, and plain but comfortable rooms with a/c and fans. ⑤.

La Quinta California, Batallón (no phone). Amazingly good-value apartments with well-equipped kitchens, close to the beach behind *El Herradero Cantina*, amongst the trees. ④ for five sharing; ③ for two.

Suites San Blas, down by the beach (☎328/5-05-05). Especially good value for groups or families – units for up to six people with (ill-equipped) kitchen in quiet spot with a pool. ④; ⑥ for six people sharing.

The Town

When not lying on the pristine **beaches** to the south of San Blas or taking the excellent "jungle boat trip" to **La Tovara springs** (see below, for both), most people seem content just to relax or amble about town. A more focused hour can be spent at **La Contadora**, the ruins of a late eighteenth-century fort which, with the vaulted remains of a chapel, crown the Cerro de San Basilio near the river, a kilometre along Juárez towards Tepic (US$0.60). From here you get great views over the town to the ocean, where the small white island on the horizon is said, by the Huichol, to represent peyote. It marks the symbolic starting point of their annual pilgrimage to the central highlands (see box on p.112), the actual start being on the **Isla del Rey**, the lighthouse-topped peninsula across the Estero del Pozo channel from San Blas. The pilgrimage begins a couple of weeks before Easter, with feasts and elaborate ceremonies centred around a sacred **cave** below the lighthouse. Remains of the cave can still be seen, though most of it was criminally destroyed by the government in the 1970s to provide rock for a jetty. You can catch a **boat** across to the Isla del Rey from the landing stage at the end of Héroes 21 de Abril.

La Tovara and the jungle boat trip

The **lagoons and creeks** behind San Blas are almost unbelievably rich in bird and animal life – the ubiquitous white herons, or egrets, above all, but hundreds of other species too, which no one seems able to name (any bird here is described as a *garza* – a heron). The best way to catch a glimpse is to get on one of the three-hour boat trips "into the jungle", the *lancha* negotiating channels tunnelled through dense mangrove, past sunbaking turtles and flighty herons. Best time to go is at dawn, before other trips have disturbed the animals, when you might even glimpse a cayman along the way. Most trips head for **La Tovara**, a cool freshwater spring that fills a beautiful clear pool perfect for swimming and pirouetting off the rope swing – if you're not put off by the presence of alligators, that is. Eat at the fairly pricey palapa restaurant or bring your own picnic.

    Trips leave from the river bridge 1km inland from the zócalo along Juárez: get a group together for the best prices. Rates are fair: around US$16.25 for four and US$3.75 per extra person for two hours; US$25 for four and US$5 per extra for three hours, including a trip to a crocodile farm. You may also want to consider negotiating something longer, giving more time for swimming and wildlife-spotting en route. Shorter jungle boat trips leave from Matanchén (see below) but the longer boat ride from San Blas justifies the marginally higher cost.

The beaches

As well as the fine beaches right in town, there are others some 4km away around the **Bahía de Matanchén**, a vast, sweeping crescent of a bay entirely surrounded by fine soft sands. At the near end, the tiny community of **Las Islitas** on the Playa Miramar has numerous palapa restaurants on the beach, serving up grilled fish and cold beers and, on the point, a group of beautifully situated but expensive cabins for rent. At the far end lie **Aticama** (with more basic shops and places to eat) and the disappointing **Playa los Cocos**. In between, acres of sand are fragmented only by flocks of pelicans and the occasional crab. There are plenty of spots where you can camp if you have the gear and lots of repellent, as well as a trailer park at Los Cocos. The waves here, which rise offshore beyond Miramar and run in, past the point, to the depths of the bay, are in the *Guinness Book of Records* as the longest in the world: it's very rare that they get up enough for surfers to be able to ride them all the way in, but there's plenty of lesser **surfing** potential – surf- and boogie-boards can be rented in Las Islitas or San Blas.

    You can walk from San Blas to Matanchén, just about, on the roads through the lagoons – it's impossible to penetrate along the coast, which would be much shorter – but in the heat of the day it's far easier to get one of the buses ("El Llano"), that leave several times a day from the bus station, or a taxi (bargain fiercely).

Eating and drinking

Seafood is big business in San Blas; as well as at the **restaurants** in town, you can buy it at beachfront palapas and from stands that spring up daily on the streets. There's also plenty of fruit and healthy offerings to cater for the tourists. Down at the beach most places close around sunset, and if you want to eat later you'll have to walk into town – a flashlight to guide your way is a worthwhile investment.

La Isla, C Mercado at Paredes. A must, if only to admire the astonishingly kitsch decor: draped fishing nets festooned with shell pictures, shell mobiles and shell lampshades. Moderately priced meat and seafood dishes of average quality.

McDonald's, Juárez 36. No relation to Ronald, this unpretentious restaurant just off the zócalo is a prime meeting place, particularly among ex-pats who gather here for breakfast. Broad menu and reasonable prices.

Mike's Place, Juárez 36 above *McDonald's*. Quiet drinking midweek but livens up on Friday and Saturday with dancing to anything from Latin to classic rock.

La Terraza, C Batallón, right on the zócalo. Reasonably priced Mexican food and beer. A great place to sit and watch the world go by.

La Tumba de Yako, C Batallón at Querétaro. Kiosk run by the local surf team, popular for its banana bread and natural yoghurt.

Around San Blas: Santiago Ixcuintla and Mexcaltitlán

North of San Blas, from Hwy-15 you could take the turn-off for **SANTIAGO IXCUINTLA**, a market town where the only real interest lies in the **Huichol Centre for Cultural Survival and Traditional Arts** (some way from the centre of town at 20 de Noviembre and Constitución). This co-operative venture, aimed at supporting Huichol people and preserving their traditions, raises money by selling quality Huichol art and offering various classes. From Santiago a road leads straight down to the coast and the **Playa Los Corchos**, a perfect stretch of sand lined with palm trees, by the mouth of the Río Grande de Santiago. Santiago has a few cheap hotels, but no other formal facilities – you might, however, find someone prepared to rent you a room, or else space to sling a hammock under the verandah of one of the beach bars.

To the right beyond Santiago, another road leads across the lagoon to the extraordinary islet of **MEXCALTITLÁN**. The little town here must look something like a smaller version of Aztec Tenochtitlán before the Spanish arrived, laid out in radiating spokes from the centre of the round island. Local transport is by canoe along a series of tiny canals crossed by causeways, and indeed the place is one candidate for the site from which the Aztecs set out on their long trek to the Valley of Mexico. Mexcaltitlán sees very little tourism, but you should be able to find a guide to paddle you around the island, a room at the single **hotel** (④) near the church, and somewhere to eat. If you're in the area around the end of June you should definitely try to visit the island fiesta, on June 29, when there are canoe races on the lagoons and rivers.

Tepic to Guadalajara: Ixtlán

Between Tepic and Guadalajara it's a long climb over the Sierra Madre, with an excellent new toll road much of the way. **IXTLÁN DEL RÍO** is the first place you might be tempted to stop – the only other is Tequila (see p.185). Ixtlán was made famous by Carlos Castaneda's *Journey to Ixtlán*, attraction enough for a few – it's hard to believe that many find what they're after, though, for this is an exceptionally ugly little strip of ribbon development along the highway, beset by constant traffic noise from huge trucks and permanent jams. What it does offer is plenty of hotels and restaurants: if you do want to **stay**, try the *Hidalgo* (④) or the *Santa Rita* (④), two of the more central places on the highway. The *Río Viego*, very near the plaza, is a decent **restaurant**.

Disappointing as it may be in spiritual matters, Ixtlán does have one worthwhile attraction in its **archeological site**, a couple of kilometres east. The site is right by the highway and rail line: there are local buses, and second-class services on the main road should stop. Though not very impressive in comparison with the great sites in central and southern Mexico, this is one of the largest and most important in the west, with numerous heavily restored buildings of plain, unadorned stone. Perhaps most striking is the sheer size of the place. What you can see is extensive, but the site in total is said to cover an area five times larger – and this is an "insignificant" culture of which relatively little is known. The site itself (dawn–dusk) has a series of rectangular buildings forming plazas, each centring on an altar. The finest structure, and the most thoroughly restored, is an unusual circular temple surrounded by a circular wall. The sides, which now slope out slightly, were originally vertical, so that the cylindrical building looked like a brazier. Circular temples like this are usually associated with **Quetzalcoatl** in his guise of Ehecatl, God of Wind, but here the brazier shape may also refer to **Huehueteotl**, the Old God or God of Fire. Outside the site it's easy to spot piles of stones in the farm at the back and odd humps in the surrounding fields; at one point the site fence cuts through an obvious mound.

FIESTAS

FEBRUARY

3 DÍA DE SAN BLAS. The feria in **San Blas** (Nayarit) starts on January 30, with parades, dancing, fireworks and ceremonial.

CARNIVAL (the week before Lent, variable Feb–March) is celebrated with particular gusto in **La Paz** (Baja California Sur), **Ensenada** (Baja California Norte) and **Culiacán** (Sinaloa). The best carnival in the north, though, is at **Mazatlán** (Sin).

MARCH

19 DÍA DEL SEÑOR SAN JOSÉ. Saint's day celebrations in **San José del Cabo** (BCS) with horse races, cockfights and fireworks, and in the hamlet of San José near **Guaymas** (Sonora), where the religious fervour is followed by a fair.

PALM SUNDAY (week before Easter) sees dramatizations of biblical episodes in **Jala** (Nay), an ancient little town between Tepic and Guadalajara.

HOLY WEEK is widely honoured. High points include passion plays in **Jala** (Nay), processions and native dances in **Rosamorada** (Nay), north of Tepic on the main road, and, in the Yaqui town of **Cocorit** (Son) near Ciudad Obregón, pilgrimages and Yaqui dances including the renowned *Danza del Venado*. This can also be seen in **Potam** (Son), on the coast near here, along with curious ancient religious rites and the burning of effigies of Judas.

MAY

3 DÍA DE LA SANTA CRUZ celebrated in **Santiago Ixcuintla** (Nay), north of Tepic, a fiesta rich in traditional dances.

JUNE

1 Maritime celebrations in the port of **Topolobampo** (Sin) with parades and a fair.

24 DÍA DE SAN JUAN. Guaymas (Son), **Navojoa** (Son) and **Mochicahui** (Sin), a tiny village near Los Mochis, all celebrate the saint's day with processions and, later, with native dancing. In **Navojoa** there's a feria that carries on to the beginning of July.

29 In **Mexcaltitlán** (Nay) a religious fiesta in honour of St Peter, with processions in boats round the islet.

JULY

First Sunday *Romería* in **Tecate** (BCN), extremely colourful, with cowboys, carnival floats and music.

25 DÍA DE SANTIAGO. Bizarrely celebrated in **Compostela** (Nay), south of Tepic, where the men ride around on horses all day – the women take over their mounts the following morning and then do the same. Also boasts a fair with fireworks.

SEPTEMBER

8 Formal religious processions in **Jala** (Nay) with traditional dress and regional dances.

16 INDEPENDENCE DAY is a holiday everywhere in the country, and especially lively along the border. **Tijuana** (BCN) has horse and motor races, *mariachi*, dancing, gambling and fireworks, while the much smaller crossing of **Agua Prieta** (Son) has a more traditional version of the same, with parades and civic ceremonies.

28 DÍA DE SAN MIGUEL. A pilgrimage to Boca, a community located very close to **Choix** (Sin), on the railway from Los Mochis. There's dancing and a number of parades in Choix, with a procession to Boca.

OCTOBER

4 DÍA DE SAN FRANCISCO is the culmination of two weeks' fiesta in **Magdalena** (Son), attended by many Indians (Yaqui and Sioux among them) who venerate this missionary saint. Traditional dances.

First Sunday In **Guasave** (Sin), between Los Mochis and Culiacán, a pilgrimage to the Virgen del Rosario, with many dance groups.

Last Sunday Repetition of events in **Guasave** and, in **Ixtlán del Río** (Nay), hundreds of pilgrims arrive to observe the DÍA DE CRISTO REY – more dancing.

NOVEMBER

2 DAY OF THE DEAD celebrations everywhere – **Navojoa** (Son) is one of the more impressive.

DECEMBER

First Sunday Lively festival honouring El Señor de la Misericordia in **Compostela** (Nay).

8 DÍA DE LA INMACULADA CONCEPCIÓN celebrated by the pilgrims who converge on **Alamos** (Son), and in **Mazatlán** (Sin), with parades, music and dancing. **La Yesca**, in a virtually inaccessible corner of Nayarit east of Tepic, has religious ceremonies and a *feria* attended by many Huichol people, which lasts till the 12th.

12 DÍA DE LA VIRGEN DE GUADALUPE. In **Navojoa** (Son), the climax of ten days of activities comes with a procession. **Tecate** (BCN) and **Acaponeta**, on the main road in northern Nayarit, both have lively and varied fiestas.

travel details

BUSES

Services on the main highways south from Tijuana or Nogales are excellent, with constant fast traffic and regular express services, if you want them, from the border all the way to México. Be warned, though, that *de paso* buses can be hard to pick up along the way, especially in Hermosillo, Culiacán and Los Mochis. Baja California has far fewer services. Chief operators are Tres Estrellas de Oro – arguably the most reliable company – Transportes del Pacifico and Transportes Norte de Sonora (TNS), with dozens of second-class companies serving lesser destinations. For long distances and on the busiest routes you might consider one of the pullman services run by companies like Elite, with airline-style seats, drinks, video and icily effective air conditioning. The following frequencies and times are for **first-class services**. Second-class buses usually cover the same routes, running ten to twenty percent slower.

Cabo San Lucas to: La Paz via San José del Cabo (6 daily; 3–4hr); La Paz via Todos Santos (8 daily; 2hr); San José del Cabo (roughly hourly; 30min); Todos Santos (8 daily; 1hr).

Ensenada to: Guerrero Negro (7 daily; 8hr); La Paz (2 daily; 20hr); Loreto (6 daily; 15hr); Mexicali (4 daily; 4hr); San Felipe (2 daily; 3hr 30min); Tijuana (hourly; 1hr 30min).

Guaymas to: Hermosillo (every 30min; 1hr 30min); Los Mochis (every 30min; 5hr); Mexicali (every 30min; 11hr); Navojoa (every 30min; 3hr); Nogales (hourly; 5hr 30min); Tijuana (every 30min; 14hr).

Guerrero Negro to: Ensenada (7 daily; 8hr); La Paz (3 daily; 12hr); San Ignacio (7 daily; 3hr); Santa Rosalía (7 daily; 4hr); Tijuana (7 daily; 10hr).

Hermosillo to: Bahía de Kino (9 daily; 2hr); Guaymas (every 30min; 1hr 30min); Mexicali (every 30min; 9–10hr); Nogales (hourly; 4hr); Tijuana (every 30min; 12–13hr).

La Paz to: Cabo San Lucas via Todos Santos (8 daily; 2hr); El Rosario (2 daily; 16hr); Ensenada (2 daily; 20hr); Guerrero Negro (3 daily; 12hr); Loreto (7 daily; 5hr); Mulegé (5 daily; 7hr); San Ignacio (3 daily; 9hr); San José del Cabo via eastern route (6 daily; 3–4hr); Santa Rosalía (5 daily; 8hr); Tijuana (1 daily; 22hr); Todos Santos (8 daily; 1hr).

Los Mochis to: Guaymas (every 30min; 17hr); Mazatlán (every 30min; 7hr); Navojoa (every 30min; 2–3hr); Tijuana (every 30min; 19hr); Topolobampo (every 15min; 40min).

Mazatlán to: Culiacán (every 30min; 4hr); Durango (13 daily; 6hr); Guadalajara (every 30min; 9hr); Los Mochis (every 30min; 7hr); San Blas (2 daily; 4hr); Tepic (every 30min; 4hr); Tijuana (every 30min; 26hr).

Mexicali to: Ensenada (4 daily; 4hr); Guaymas (every 30min; 11hr); Hermosillo (every 30min; 9–10hr); San Felipe (4 daily; 3hr); Tijuana (every 30min; 3hr).

Navojoa to: Ciudad Obregón (every 30min; 1hr 30min); Guaymas (every 30min; 3hr); Los Mochis (every 30min; 2–3hr); Tijuana (every 30min; 17hr).

Nogales to: Agua Prieta (2 daily; 3–4hr); Guaymas (hourly; 5hr 30min); Hermosillo (hourly; 4hr).

San Blas to: Mazatlán (2 daily; 4hr); Puerto Vallarta (2 daily; 3–4hr); Santiago Ixcuintla (3 daily; 1hr); Tepic (hourly; 1hr 30min).

Santa Rosalía to: Guerrero Negro (7 daily; 4hr); La Paz (5 daily; 8hr); Loreto (8 daily; 3hr); Mulegé (8 daily; 1hr); San Ignacio (7 daily; 1hr); Tijuana (4 daily; 14hr).

Tepic to: Guadalajara (every 30min; 5hr); Mazatlán (every 30min; 4hr); Puerto Vallarta (hourly; 3–4hr); San Blas (hourly; 1hr 30min); Tijuana (every 30min; 30hr).

Tijuana to: Culiacán (every 30min; 22hr); El Rosario (4 daily; 6hr); Ensenada (hourly; 1hr 30min); Guadalajara (every 30min; 35hr); Guaymas (every 30min; 14hr); Guerrero Negro (7 daily; 10hr); Hermosillo (every 30min; 12–13hr); La Paz (1 daily; 22hr); Loreto (4 daily; 17hr); LA (12 daily; 4hr); Los Mochis (every 30min; 19hr); Mazatlán (every 30min; 26hr); Mexicali (every 30min; 3hr); Mulegé (4 daily; 15hr); Navojoa (every 30min; 17hr); San Ignacio (4 daily; 13hr); Santa Rosalía (4 daily; 14hr); Tepic (every 30min; 30hr).

TRAINS

The main line through northwestern Mexico runs from Nogales to Guadalajara, connecting with the Sonora–Baja California line to Mexicali at Benjamín Hill (Son.), and with the amazing Chihuahua–Los Mochis Copper Canyon railway at Sufragio (Sin.). One train – with first- and second-class carriages – runs in each direction each day. Remember that on both lines timetables are confused by the hour's difference between the region covered in this chapter and the rest of Mexico. The Los Mochis–Chihuahua Vista Tren departs Los Mochis daily at 6am, regular train at 7am local time.

PLANES

Almost every town of any size has an airport, with flights, not necessarily direct, to México. Busiest are Tijuana – with half a dozen flights a day to the capital by a variety of routings and a couple direct to Guadalajara – and La Paz, with flights to México and many towns along the mainland coast. Mazatlán is the busiest of all. Aero California is the biggest of the new local operators, though Mexicana and Aeroméxico operate flights to major Mexican cities, often at prices little higher than the equivalent cost of the bus.

La Paz to: Guadalajara (1 daily); Los Angeles via Loreto (1 daily); México (1 daily); Tijuana (2 daily); Tucson (1 daily).

Mazatlán to: Denver (3 weekly); La Paz (1 daily); Los Angeles (3 daily); México (4 daily); Tijuana (2 daily).

FERRIES

All ferries linking Baja to the mainland were, until recently, state-run and subsidized, their primary function being to help the development of the peninsula. As part of the government's privatization programme, they were sold off to a Japanese concern which runs them on a commercial basis. Accordingly, prices have risen for all users. Private vehicles do not have a high priority, and at times may have to wait days for space. Even foot passengers face extremely long queues: best arrive at the office well before it opens on the morning of departure (morning before for early ferries) – most offices are open 8.30am–1pm.

La Paz to: Mazatlán (daily except Sat/daily during holiday periods; 18hr); Topolobampo (daily except Tues; 9–10hr).

Santa Rosalía to: Guaymas (2 weekly; 7hr).

CHAPTER TWO

BETWEEN THE SIERRAS: NORTHEAST ROUTES

Thehe central and eastern routes into Mexico are considerably shorter than the west coast road, and, though they don't have the beaches, they do offer direct access to the country's colonial heart and much to see along the way. The high plain between the flanks of the Sierra Madre is also cool – even uncomfortably so in winter – and the highways crossing it are fast.

You'll find most interest heading down from **Ciudad Juárez**: highlights include the important archeological site of **Paquimé** at Casas Grandes, and in **Chihuahua** and **Durango** a foretaste of the majestic colonial cities to come in the country's heartland. If you happen to be passing through in March or April, you may be lucky enough to catch the desert in bloom – it's a riot of colour after a little rain.

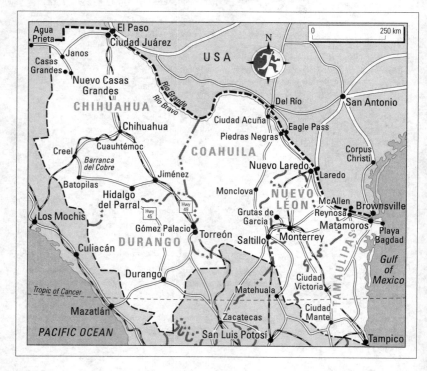

ACCOMMODATION PRICE CODES

All the accommodation listed in this book has been categorized into one of nine price bands, as set out below. The prices quoted are in US dollars and normally refer to the cheapest available room for two people sharing in high season. For more details see p.36.

① less than US$5	④ US$15–25	⑦ US$60–80
② US$5–10	⑤ US$25–40	⑧ US$80–100
③ US$10–15	⑥ US$40–60	⑨ more than US$100

There's a historic appeal, too: this was the country most fiercely fought for in the Revolution, and the breeding ground for Pancho Villa's *División del Norte*. The supreme attraction, though, must be the train journey through the **Copper Canyon** from Chihuahua to the Pacific coast: a thirteen-hour ride over soaring peaks and around the walls of vast canyons down to the steamy coastal plain. To the east, along the fastest route to the capital, **Monterrey** is a heavily industrialized city that has nevertheless managed to retain its finest sights; nearby **Saltillo** offers an escape into tranquil mountains.

Following the **Gulf Coast** is less recommended – it's steaming hot in summer and not particularly interesting at the best of times. It is, though, the shortest way south, and if you stick it out past the refineries you'll reach the state of Veracruz (see p.390), with its fine beaches and wealth of archeological remains.

THE CENTRAL CORRIDOR

Rapid and efficient bus services run throughout the central area, the best of the main lines probably being Transportes Chihuahuenses and Omnibus de México, with Estrella Blanca mounting a strong challenge as you head south. The journey non-stop to the capital can take as little as 25 hours. If your plan is simply to get to the capital, you might also consider the train, which leaves Ciudad Juárez daily at 10pm, reaching México some 36 hours later.

Ciudad Juárez

CIUDAD JUÁREZ, some two hundred miles south of Albuquerque, New Mexico, is perhaps the least attractive of all the border towns – modern, sprawling and ugly, as well as extremely confusing to find your way around and, at times, positively intimidating. There's little doubt that the best thing to do on arrival is to leave. In less than five hours you can reach Chihuahua or, rather closer, Nuevo Casas Grandes, the base for excursions to the archeological site at Casas Grandes.

Originally a small settlement on the Santa Fe trail, known as Paso del Norte, Ciudad Juárez did have a brief moment of glory when Benito Juárez established his government here after he'd been driven out of the south by Maximilian – you can visit the

BORDER CHECKS

Crossing the border, do not forget to go through **immigration and customs** checks. As everywhere, there's a free zone south of the frontier, and you can cross at will. Try to continue south, though, and you'll be stopped after some 30km and sent back to get your tourist card stamped.

house from which he governed, on 16 de Septiembre. The town changed hands frequently during the Revolution, most notably in 1913, when Pancho Villa, having stolen a train, managed to fool the local commander into expecting reinforcements and steamed into the middle of town with 2000 troops completely unopposed. Gaining access to the border and to arms from the north, this was one of the exploits that forged Benito's reputation.

In the last couple of years, the town's own reputation has been shaped by its role as the seat of the Juárez cartel, who, along with the Arellano Felix brothers in Tijuana, control much of Mexico's massive **drug-running** empire, masterminding cross-border trafficking of Colombian heroin and Andean cocaine. The Juárez cartel's boss, Amado Carillo Fuentes, died during a botched plastic surgery operation in late 1997, and the subsequent power struggle has intensified the level of violence such that there are sometimes several drug-related homicides in a week. Your chances of getting caught in the crossfire are minuscule, but with so little to detain you, you might as well avoid taking chances.

Arrival and information

The two downtown **bridges over the Río Bravo** from El Paso to Ciudad Juárez are one-way for vehicles, those southbound taking Santa Fe St, which crosses the border and becomes Av Juárez in El Paso. Though you can enter by foot on either bridge, your best bet is to walk with the traffic, though visitors planning to push deeper into Mexico will need to visit immigration close to the Mexican side of the northbound crossing. An alternative is to take a short hop on the frequent El Paso–Juárez Trolley (US$1), which leaves from the bus stops in downtown El Paso and deposits you over the border on Av Juárez, the main drag.

As soon as you cross the border the sordid nature of the place is immediately apparent: the blood banks and second-hand clothes emporia on the US side give way to cut-rate doctors and dentists and cheap bars on the Mexican side. However, if you're staying, this is the place to be, in what's left of the old town. The **market** is a few blocks from the border straight up Lerdo, and the streets around it are home to most of the cheaper places to stay and eat.

If you **drive** across the border, you can avoid downtown Ciudad Juárez altogether by taking the Cordova bridge, a couple of kilometres east of the centre, or the new Zaragoza toll bridge, still further east, which directly connects the US and Mexican highway systems.

Information

The Ciudad Juárez **tourist office**, Juárez 807 (Mon–Fri 8am–2.30pm & 4–7pm, Sat & Sun 8am–2pm), is just fifty metres from the Santa Fe/Juárez border. Published opening hours are unreliable, but if you find them open, they can fill you in on details of bullfights, *charreadas* and other local entertainments, as well as supply maps and information about things you'll be seeing further south. It's easy enough to change money at **casas de cambio** and tourist shops along Juárez and 16 de Septiembre; most banks are on 16 de Septiembre, too. Many places accept dollars, but make sure you know the current exchange rate before you do any such deals. The **post office** lies at the corner of Lerdo and Peña, one block south of 16 de Septiembre.

Accommodation

None of the hotels in Ciudad Juárez is particularly good value by Mexican standards, so you might be tempted to stay across the border in El Paso, where the best budget choice is the atmospheric *Gardner Hotel*, 311 E Franklin St (☎915/532-3661, fax 532-

0302; ③ per person for HI members, ④ for non-members) – where John Dillinger stayed in the 1920s – a very nice HI hostel with all the usual self-catering facilities but no private rooms.

Del Prado, in Pronaf centre (☎16/16-88-00). The most luxurious option. ⑥.

Impala, Lerdo Nte 670 (☎16/15-04-31, fax 12-41-97). The pick of the pricier places: comfortable, clean and modern, right by the border, with a/c and cable TV. ④.

Juárez, Lerdo Nte 143 (☎16/15-03-58). A battered and basic budget choice, marginally better than some of the others. ③.

Koper, Juárez Nte 124 (☎16/15-03-24). Another basic, scruffy hotel, but cheap and central. ③.

San Carlos, Juárez Nte 131 (☎16/15-04-19). A small cut above the local norm. For the few extra pesos you get cleaner rooms, en-suite bathrooms with constant hot water, and a pleasant TV lounge overlooking the street. ③.

Santa Fe, Lerdo Nte 675 (☎16/15-15-22, fax 15-15-60). Opposite the *Impala* and similar, though cheaper. Quite nice, airy rooms, with a/c and TV with HBO, and a 24hr restaurant. Comfortable and convenient for late arrivals. ④.

The Town

If you decide to kill an hour strolling around the modest sights of downtown Juárez, be careful not to wander far off the main thoroughfares. Where 16 de Septiembre crosses Juárez, in the old customs building, the *Aduana*, there's a small, and mostly missable, **Museo Histórico** (Tues–Sun 10am–6pm; free), which traces the development of the town. A couple of blocks west of here on 16 de Septiembre you'll find a partly colonnaded square flanked by the cathedral and the seventeenth-century **Misión de Guadalupe**, around which the town grew up.

If you have more time, however, it's worth making for the **Museo de Arqueología del Chamizal** (Mon–Sat 9am–2pm, Sun 1–8pm; free) in the Parque Chamizal, east of the centre near the river, and the **Museo de Arte y Historia** (Tues–Sun 10am–7pm; US$0.30) in the **Pronaf tourist centre** – which also houses a huge, touristy craft market – not far from the bus station (local bus #8 runs there from the centre). Both museums offer limited introductions to Mexico; the former also has displays of some remarkable pottery from Casas Grandes (see below).

Eating

Places to eat are plentiful around the centre and border area, although new arrivals should probably take it easy on the street food. The fancier options line Juárez near the border. **El Paso** offers better value, however, and if you've been in Mexico some time, you may well want to rush across the border to somewhere like the *San Francisco Grill*, opposite the posh *Paso del Norte* hotel on Pioneer Plaza, which serves not too expensive New American brunches and dinners in an upmarket setting.

El Coyote Inválido, Juárez Nte 625 at Av Colon. Bright and breezy budget taco house that stays open late and serves up hearty chile relleno burritos and filling breakfasts.

La Nueva Central de Ciudad Juárez, 16 de Septiembre 322 Pte. Cavernous, cream-tiled and brightly lit place serving Mexican favourites and basic Chinese specialities.

Nuevo Restaurante Martino, Juárez Nte 643. Classy restaurant with high prices and varied cuisine.

Restaurant El Palenquinto, on Juárez Nte, just before 16 de Septiembre (opposite the *Hotel Koper*). Good, inexpensive option for plain Mexican food.

Santa Fe, Lerdo Nte 675. Hotel restaurant open 24hr, serving enchiladas and sandwiches.

MOVING ON FROM CIUDAD JUÁREZ

Ciudad Juárez enjoys excellent **bus connections** with the whole of north and central Mexico from its modern **Central de Autobuses** (24hr guardería). To get there take a local bus (#1A, #1B, or look for "C Camionera" on the windscreen) from the corner of Guerrero and Villa by the market. You could also squeeze into one of the horribly cramped **shuttle vans** running to and from the border. There are constant departures with one company or another down the main highway to Chihuahua and points beyond, and every couple of hours for Nuevo Casas Grandes (via Janos). One particularly useful service if you're in a mad rush is the single overnight bus to Creel (near the Copper Canyon, see p.129), currently leaving at around 8pm.

If you plan to head straight through, you should be able to get the hourly bus (US$5) direct to the Camionera Central from the El Paso Greyhound terminal at 1007 S Santa Fe St (and vice versa).

The **train station**, with one México-bound departure daily at 7pm, is reached by going straight up Lerdo from the border – a bus plies the route, but at twelve blocks it's just about walkable. The booking office is open 10am–noon and 4.30–7pm.

Paquimé and Nuevo Casas Grandes

The only reason to stop in **NUEVO CASAS GRANDES** is to visit the nearby village of Casas Grandes and the adjacent archeological site of **Paquimé** (Tues–Sun 10am–5pm; US$1.30, free on Sun), much the most important, and certainly the most striking, in northern Mexico. Originally home to an agricultural community and comprising simple adobe houses (similar to those found in Arizona and New Mexico), it became heavily influenced by Mesoamerican, probably Toltec, culture. Whether this was the result of conquest or, more likely, trade is uncertain, but from around 1000 to 1200 AD, Paquimé flourished. **Pyramids** and **ball-courts** were constructed and the surrounding land irrigated by an advanced system of **canals**. At the same time local craftsmen were trading with points both south and north, producing a wide variety of elaborate ornaments and pottery. Among the finds on the site (almost all of them now in the National Museum of Anthropology in México) were cages that held exotic imported birds, whose feathers were used in making ornaments; necklaces made from turquoise, semi-precious stones, and shells obtained from the Sea of Cortés; and other objects of copper, bone, jade and mother-of-pearl.

Much must have been destroyed when the site was attacked, burned and abandoned around 1340 – either by a marauding nomadic tribe such as the Apache or in the course of a more local rebellion. Either way, Paquimé was not inhabited again, its people abandoning their already depleted trade for the greater safety of the Sierras. When excavation began in the late 1950s, there were only a few low hills and banks where walls had been, but by piecing together the evidence archeologists have partly reconstructed the adobe houses – the largest of which have as many as fifty interconnecting rooms – which surround the open courtyard of the **ceremonial centre**. Originally two or three storeys high, the foundations have been resconstructed to waist-height, with an occasional standing wall giving some idea of scale.

To fully appreciate the sophistication of this civilization, it pays first to pop into the spanking new **Centro Cultural Paquimé** (Tues–Sun 10am–5pm; free), a beautifully laid out, if thinly stocked museum, architecturally designed to mimic the ruins of the defence towers that once stood. A large model of how Paquimé must have looked, interactive touch-screen consoles with commentary in Spanish and English, plus intelligent displays of artefacts aid interpretation. Modern examples of finds from the surrounding area – drums, dolls in native costume, ceramics and ceremonial masks – compete with the Paquimé artefacts, notably the beautiful pottery, its often anthropomorphic vessels decorated in geometric patterns of red, black and brown on a white or cream background. The cultural parallels are strongly evident though the jury is still out on whether descendants of Paquimé citizens number among the Tarahumara or other local indigenous people.

Practicalities

To **reach the site** you have first to travel 260km south of Ciudad Juárez through dusty chaparral and cotton country to Nuevo Casas Grandes. You then take one of the frequent yellow buses ("Casas Grandes/Col Juárez") from the corner of Constitución and 16 de Septiembre to the plaza in Casas Grandes (about 15min), from where the site is signposted – it's a bare ten-minute walk.

Nuevo Casas Grandes itself is small and not especially interesting; if you leave Ciudad Juárez very early you can visit the site and continue to Chihuahua in the same day – a route that is longer but certainly more interesting than the main highway (though rains can take out the road south of Nuevo Casas Grandes). **Buses** arrive outside the adjoining Estrella Blanca and Omnibus de Mexico offices on Obregón, just steps from the basic hotel *Juárez*, Obregón 110 (☎169/4-02-33; ②), the cheapest place to **spend the night**, with small simple rooms and hot water on request. On the main street, a couple of blocks away, you'll find the hotel *California*, Constitución 209 (☎169/4-11-10; ④), but best of all is the *Motel Piñon*, Juárez Nte 605 (☎169/4-06-55; ④), a couple of blocks beyond the *California*, which boasts TV, reliable hot water and a swimming pool, and occasionally gives tours of the ruins – it even has a small museum of Paquimé clay pots.

Eating is a fairly basic affair, with a number of simple taquerías dotted around town, and slightly more upscale places such as *Dinno's Pizza* at the corner of Constitución and Minerva, which does small but tasty pizzas for US$4 as well as reliable burrito and enchilada staples.

Los Mochis to Chihuahua: The Copper Canyon Railway

The thirteen-hour **rail journey** that starts on the sweaty Pacific coast at Los Mochis, fights its way up to cross the Continental Divide amid the peaks of the Sierra Madre, then drifts down across the high plains of Chihuahua must rate as one of the world's most extraordinary. Breathtaking views come thick and fast as the line hangs over the vast canyons of the **Río Urique**. Chief of these is the awesome rift of the **Barranca del Cobre**, with a depth, from mountain top to valley floor, of more than 2000m, and breadth to match – by comparison, the Grand Canyon is a midget. Scenically, however, there's no comparison with the great canyons of the southwestern USA, and if you've visited them you may find the canyons here a little disappointing. Part of the difficulty is in getting a true sense of their enormity and beauty: there are none of the well-marked hiking tracks and official campgrounds that might tempt casual exploration north of the border, and serious hikers really need to devote the best part of a week to their endeavours.

The dream of the original builders, the *Kansas City, Mexico and Orient Railway Company*, was to carve a new route from the American Midwest to the Pacific, and in the early part of the twentieth century they had made it right across the plains, but were defeated by the sheer technical complexity of crossing the mountains. And it's easy to see why. Only in 1953 did the Mexicans start work on the final link, an engineering feat demanding the construction of 73 tunnels and 28 major bridges, which took a further eight years to complete.

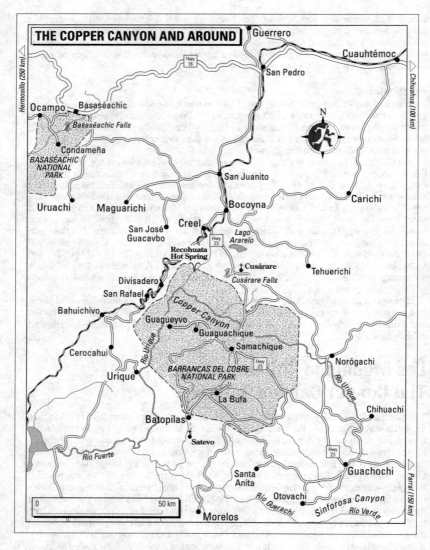

Even when the bare mountain peaks here are snow-covered, the climate on the canyon floors is semitropical – a fact that the indigenous **Tarahumara**, who were driven into these mountain fastnesses after the Spanish Conquest, depend on, migrating in winter to the warmth of the deep canyons. The **Tarahumara**, whose population totals some 50,000, live in isolated communities along the rail line and in the stretch of mountains known as the Sierra Tarahumara, eking out an existence from the sparse patches of cultivable land. Although as everywhere their isolation is increasingly encroached upon by commercial forestry interests, ranchers and growing numbers of travellers, they remain an independent people, close to their traditions. Their religious life, despite centuries of missionary work, embraces only token aspects of Catholicism and otherwise remains true to its agrarian roots – their chief deities being the gods of the sun, moon and rain. Above all, the tribe are renowned as runners: a common feature of local festivals are the foot races between villages that last at least a day, sometimes several on end, the runners having to kick a wooden ball ahead of them as they go.

The route

The train timetable (see box on p.128) more or less dictates that you tackle the journey eastbound from the coast to the mountains, otherwise you may well find yourself travelling along the most dramatic stretch of the line in the dark. The start of the journey is an inauspicious grind across the humid coastal plain, with passengers in the air-conditioned carriages settling back in their reclining seats while the rest just sweat. The first-class cosseting becomes less of a benefit as the line breaks into the mountains and you start climbing into ever cooler air. It was this section that finally defeated the original builders and from the train fanatic's point of view, this is the bit you've been waiting for. For six hours, the train zigzags upwards dizzily, clinging to the canyon wall, rocking across bridges, plunging into tunnels blasted through the rock, only to find itself constantly just a few metres above the track it covered twenty minutes earlier. Eventually, you arrive at **Divisadero**, where there's a halt of about fifteen minutes to marvel at the view. At first it seems a perverse choice for a stop, with nothing around but the mountain tops and crowds of Tarahumara hawking their crafts and food, including delicious *gorditas*. But walk a little way down the path and you're suddenly standing on the edge of space, on the lip of a vast chasm. Below you are the depths of the **Barranca del Cobre** and, adjoining it, the Barranca de Balojaque and the Barranca de Tararecua. There are a couple of expensive places to stay here (see below), but for most people it's all too rapidly back on the train, which clanks on for an hour to **CREEL**, just past the halfway stage and, at 2300m, close to the highest point of the line. This is the place to stop if you want seriously to explore the Sierra Tarahumara and the canyons; it gives easy access into some remarkable landscapes, and boasts the only reasonably priced hotel options en route. (See p.130 for details on staying in Creel and exploring the Sierra Tarahumara.)

From Creel, the train takes a further six hours to reach Chihuahua – though beautiful, it's not a truly spectacular run. In fact, if the train timetable doesn't suit, there's really no reason why you shouldn't take the **bus** from Creel to Chihuahua: it's priced between the first- and second-class train fares but is quicker than both and covers much the same ground. East of Creel both bus and train begin to leave the Sierra Tarahumara behind as the route runs through gentle, verdant grazing land that wouldn't look out of place in some romantic Western. In many ways, this is pioneer ranching country, centred on the town of **CUAUHTÉMOC**, 70km from Creel and 130km from Chihuahua. This is also a chief centre for **Mennonites**, people you'll come across throughout northern Mexico – the men in their bib-and-tucker overalls and straw stetsons, as often as not trying to sell the excellent cheese that is their main produce; the women, mostly silent, wrapped in long, black nineteenth-century dresses with maybe a dash of colour from a headscarf. The sect, founded in the sixteenth century by a Dutchman, Menno Simonis, believe only in the Bible and their personal conscience: their refusal to do military service or take national oaths of loyalty has led to a long history of persecution.

The Mennonites arrived in Mexico early this century, having been driven from Frisia to Prussia, thence into Russia and finally to Mexico by way of Canada – each time forced to move on by the state's demand for military tribute or secular education. These days many are returning to Canada as impoverished emigrants, forced out of Mexico by limited land and a growing population. Among themselves the Mennonites still speak a form of German, although so corrupted as to be virtually unintelligible to a modern German-speaker.

Rail practicalities

The Copper Canyon line is operated by the Ferrocarril de Chihuahua al Pacifico (CHP, pronounced *Shé Pé*). There are two **trains**: the first-class **Estrella**, which is primarily a tourist service; and the second-class **Mixto**, less than a quarter of the price but considerably slower and less comfortable. You're better off taking the Estrella service, not only because it has air conditioning and reserved, reclining seats, but also because the Mixto (US$10), though a more rustic experience, tends to run late, so that particularly if you're travelling from Chihuahua out to the coast, you may pass many of the best sections in the dark.

Tickets for the Mixto can only be bought from the station on the morning of departure, but Estrella tickets can be pre-booked either at the station or with any travel agency in México – to be sure of a first-class seat reserve early, especially from May to September and during Semana Santa. **Prices** for the full journey from Los Mochis to Chihuahua are around US$10 on the Mixto, closer to US$50 on the Estrella.

It's advisable to break up the journey, not only to get the most out of it, but also because the trip, even travelling first-class, is very exhausting. Section costs are based on a per kilometre rate, so you'll pay hardly any more no matter how often you break the journey; if you're travelling in the Estrella and want to maintain your reservation throughout the entire journey, however, you'll have to front up at either Los Mochis or Chihuahua and ask for an escala, which, for a fifteen percent surcharge, allows you to make up to two overnight stops along the way.

The Mixto is subject to seemingly random **cancellation** at any time, but both services may be cancelled due to derailed freight trains, or landslides, which plague the track during the rainy season.

THE CHP TIMETABLE

Currently the Estrella runs daily in both directions, whereas the Mixto runs three times weekly each way – from Chihuahua on Monday, Wednesday and Friday, from Los Mochis on Tuesday, Thursday and Saturday – but always check to see if the service is running. Second-class carriages have been spotted tagged onto the first-class train, and it seems only a matter of time before there is only one train a day in each direction. The official times below are not entirely reliable, and trains (particularly the Mixto) frequently run late.

	Estrella		Mixto	
Los Mochis*	7am	8.50pm	8am	11.25pm
Sufragio*	7.45am	8pm	9.10am	10.25pm
Bahuichivo	12.15pm	3.30pm	2pm	5.30pm
Divisadero	1.35pm	1.45pm	4.45pm	3.30pm
Creel	3.15pm	12.25pm	6.20pm	2pm
Cuauhtémoc	6.30pm	9.15am	10.15pm	10.40am
Chihuahua	8.50pm	7am	1.05am	8am

*The train operates, and the timetable is given, in Chihuahua time (Central Standard Time), but Los Mochis and Sufragio are actually an hour ahead of this (Mountain Standard Time). So by local time, the trains leave Los Mochis an hour earlier, at 6am and 7am. If you're changing trains at Sufragio, there's an hour's difference between the timetables of the CHP and the FCP.

You'll save money by taking along your own **food and drink**, but it's not essential; both are available on the train (though not cheaply), and throughout the journey people climb on board or stand on the platforms selling tacos, chiles rellenos, fresh fruit, hot coffee and whatever local produce comes to hand.

Creel and the Sierra Tarahumara

CREEL is a dusty little place with echoes of the Old West in its log cabins and its street scenes: you'll see Tarahumara arriving on foot for supplies, ranchers on horseback, forest managers cruising in shiny new pick-ups. The town was named after the state governor, Enrique Creel, son of the US ambassador to Mexico in the 1930s, who founded timberworks in the area. Now just one saw mill remains, but with the town's ideal location as a base for exploring the Sierra Tarahumara, tourism is fast becoming the main source of income. The main street, Lopez Mateos, is increasingly being taken over by hotels, and even American franchises – *Best Western* and the like – are moving in, but it remains an attractive escape nonetheless, friendly and still relatively quiet. Remember that this is a mountain town at an altitude of 2300m, making the evenings cool year-round with the occasional snowfall in midwinter.

There isn't a great deal to do in the town itself; pretty much everything of interest is either on Francisco Villa, along the north side of the train lines, or Lopez Mateos, which runs west from the zócalo, also parallel to the tracks. You can pass half an hour in the **Museo de la Casa de las Artesanías**, on the zócalo (Tues–Sat 9am–1pm & 3–7pm, Sun 9am–1pm; US$1), which displays some fine examples of local handicrafts – including Tarahumara baskets woven from the long needles of the Apache pine – and panels on Enrique Creel and the construction of the railway.

There's an easy **hike** up the shrine-topped cliff face in town, which offers splendid bird's-eye views. Walk through the car park of the *Motel Parador de la Montaña* towards the rear field, and carry on towards the barbed-wire fence by the large boulder. Simply follow the steps carved into the rock face and you quickly reach the top of the cliff. To your right you'll see the train station, to your left the beginnings of the Copper Canyon and the Tarahumara lands, scattered with **rock formations** that locals insist include frogs, mushrooms, a nativity scene and even the eagle on the cactus of the Mexican flag.

Arrival and information

The train is obviously the way to **arrive** but, wonderful though it is, the vagaries of the timetable may induce you to catch one of the frequent buses that run between Creel and Chihuahua – no great loss as the road pretty much follows the rail line. If you're in a real hurry, there's even a single daily direct bus from Ciudad Juárez to Creel, leaving there at around 8pm and arriving in Creel at 5am. Both train station and bus stop are by the zócalo in the centre of town, where there's a **tourist office** of sorts in the Jesuit mission shop, Artesanías Misión (Mon–Sat 9.30am–1pm & 3–6pm, Sun 9.30am–1pm), with limited information and local topographical maps. They also sell Tarahumara **crafts** – blankets, wooden dolls and drums – and photos of the Tarahumara, who on the whole dislike being photographed by tourists. Outside there is a plan of the town showing pretty much everything you're likely to need: a **bank** (dollar and travellers' cheque exchange and cash advances Mon–Fri 9am–1.30pm) and **post office** on the zócalo, long-distance **telephones** all over town, and a **laundry** (Mon–Fri 9am–2pm & 3–6pm, Sat 9am–2pm) in the two-storey house on C Villa, opposite the zócalo.

Accommodation

The number of good **places to stay** in Creel grows every year, and most either meet the train with courtesy buses or dispatch small children to drum up business.

Alternatively, take advantage of the courtesy buses that run to one of the luxury **lodges** out in the nearby countryside. RV-drivers might fancy the new KOA campground on the edge of town, but **campers** are better off beside Lago Arareco, 7km south of Creel.

Casa Margarita, Mateos 11 on the zócalo (☎ & fax 145/6-00-45). It seems like most people stay at one of the two *Margarita* establishments. The budget choice is here at the original, typically bursting at the seams with backpackers and a few better-heeled travellers making the best of a set-up that includes hearty and simple, but often delicious, breakfast, and dinner. The dorm (just US$4) is cramped but the rooms are comfortable and come with private facilities. Dorms ①; rooms ④.

Casa Valenzuela, Lopez Mateos 68 (☎145/6-01-04). Frankly unappealing but cheap and central, usually with vacant rooms even in peak season. ④.

Nuevo Barrancas del Cobre, Francisco Villa 121, right across from the station (☎145/16-00-22, fax 16-00-43). Slightly upmarket hotel with pleasant enough old rooms (some considerably better than others) and much nicer, newer a/c suites (⑥) in log-cabin style, with TV and rooms sleeping up to four. Basic ④; a/c ⑥.

The Lodge at Creel, Lopez Mateos 61 (☎145/6-00-71, fax 6-00-82, in US ☎1-800/879-4071). Creel's most luxurious lodging now run by *Best Western*. ⑦.

Margarita's Plaza Mexicana, on Elfida Batista Caro off Mateos (☎ & fax 145/60–02-45). The fancier of the two *Margarita* places with new and spacious a/c rooms ranged around a courtyard, and a popular bar on site; again the price includes breakfast and dinner. ⑤.

Motel Parador de la Montaña, Mateos 44 (☎145/6-00-75, fax 6-00-85). Television, tastefully decorated rooms and plenty of hot water make this the pick of the more luxurious places. ⑥.

Pension Creel, 1km out of town along Lopez Mateos (no phone). The town's cheapest rooms; pleasant, clean and mostly with two single beds costing US$7 per person. There are full self-catering facilities and a spacious lounge. ③.

Eating and drinking

Almost all Creel's **restaurants and bars** are along Lopez Mateos. The tiny *Mi Café*, at no. 21, serves bargain tortas, burritos and licuados, as well as hotcake and cornflake breakfasts; *Restaurant Lupita* serves reliable Mexican staples at modest prices, and *The Lodge at Creel*, at no. 61, serves quality meals with a more American flavour, which won't break the bank. There are also several bars lining Lopez Mateos: many foreigners gravitate to *Laylo's Lounge*, at no. 25, to keep up with the latest US sports via satellite. Backpackers are usually drawn to the drink specials in the bar at *Margarita's Plaza Mexicana* (see above).

The Sierra Tarahumara

Just about every hotel in Creel runs **organized trips** into the surrounding country or further afield to the canyons – enquire at *Margarita's*, the *Nuevo*, the *Motel Parador*, or try one of the specialist operators like Tara Adventures on Cristo Rey, north of the tracks (☎145/6-02-24). All companies run much the same set of tours with little to choose between them: for the lengthier tours, remember to take your own lunch along. Most only give the faintest impression of what the canyons are like, but if you've only got a day or two and want to get out of town, then you've little choice but to take one. With more time you should definitely arm yourself with a map and set out to explore independently. Public transport is highly irregular at best, but hitching is surprisingly easy to the places that are accessible by road. Don't venture off the beaten track alone, however, as this can be harsh and unforgiving country, and you don't want to stumble across illicit marijuana plantations. *Margarita's* is a good place to meet up with fellow explorers, or Margarita herself can fix up inexpensive local guides. Rather more expensive, but definitely worth it if you can afford it, is **horseback riding** in the vicinity (US$4 an hour from *Margarita's Plaza Mexicana*). Again, you can do this on an organized trip or simply take a ride out into the country. Another possibility is to rent a **mountain bike** either from Tara Adventures on Cristo Rey, north of the tracks

(☎145/6-02-24), or from Expeditiones Umárike, on C Ferrocarril, 500m west of the station, for around US$10 a day. The latter also offer rock-climbing instruction and have a tiny café with one of the few espresso machines in town.

Perhaps the most popular of the tours is the four-hour spin around a few minor local sights along the road south towards Guachochi. The usual itinerary includes a less-than-thrilling weathered boulder known as **Elephant Rock**; the pretty mountain **Lago Arareco**, 7km from Creel; and **Cusárare**, about 10km further on, where there's an attractive 35-metre fall and an almost entirely original seventeenth-century Jesuit mission church with Tarahumara wall-paintings. The tour generally costs US$8.

A full-day tour in the same direction heads to the organ-pipe formations of **La Bufa** (US$18), the canyon of the Río Batopilas on the road to Batopilas. The trip claims to visit four of the region's canyons, though it turns out to be just a long drive through some admittedly impressive scenery – much of it not unlike the stratified towers and buttes of Arizona – turning back well short of Batopilas. Some of the best of the views can also be seen on the bus from Creel to Guachochi (see below).

There's also a full-day tour (US$18) away from the canyonlands, to the famous 254-metre **Basaséachic Falls**, protected in the Parque Nacional de Basaséachic. Said to be the highest single cascade in North America, this makes a long, but spectacularly rewarding, day's excursion – about four hours' driving followed by almost two hours on foot. Unfortunately the falls are virtually impossible to reach except as part of an organized excursion, and these only set off when there are enough takers to justify them. Tours also run to the **Recohuata hot spring** (8hr; US$18), where you can bathe in steamy sulphurous waters, and the Jesuit Mission shop in Creel run trips to San Ignacio **Arereco Mission**, a Tarahumara reserve run by the Jesuits, just ten minutes' drive from Creel. There are plenty of crafts on sale here: if you insist on taking photos, make sure you give your subjects a small tip or gift. Around the mission are superb pine forests, Indian cave dwellings and a set of weird rock formations known as the "valley of the mushrooms".

Batopilas, Guachochi and the lodges

Though Creel is the longest established and best-known place to stay in the Sierra, there are a number of alternative bases, which some feel offer better opportunities for exploring the deep canyons. One of the best is the former mining town of **BATOPILAS**, some 150km southwest of Creel, tucked right into the bottom of the canyon and stretching for a mile along the side of the river of the same name – it's larger than you might expect for a place only connected by dirt road pushed through at the end of the 1970s. The Spanish found silver here in 1632 and mined it for centuries, the industry continuing until shortly after the revolution. Today, it's a peaceful, subtropical place – resplendent with bougainvillea, palms and citrus trees – that can be hard to tear yourself away from. Mostly the pleasure is in just being in the canyons and lazing around, but there are couple of specific **hikes** you can make. The best of these is to the "**Lost Cathedral**", a huge mission church 7km south at Satevo, standing in splendid isolation in a canyon bottom. The Tarahumara congregation just about prevent it from crumbling away completely, and the dry climate has kept the eighteenth-century murals in surprisingly good condition. Another track follows the Camino Real for three or four hours to the village of Cerro Colorado. Locals will point you to other trails, often best tackled with a guide; ask locally.

Buses leave Creel three times a week (Tues, Thurs & Sat at 7.15am) for the six-hour journey to Batopilas (returning Wed, Fri & Mon at 5am). Tickets are available from Artesanía Raramuri on Lopez Mateos, opposite *Restaurant Lupita*. On even the swiftest visit you'll have to **stay** here at least one night, which is best done on a budget at *Hotel Palmera* (☎145/6-06-33; ③), about a kilometre out of town along the river, or at the considerably more basic *Hotel Batopilas* (②), on the plaza. The luxury option is *Copper Canyon Riverside Lodge* (see below), an elegant restored nineteenth-century hacienda where you're likely to want to stay for weeks.

An alternative is to head directly south towards Parral and Durango via the cowboy town of **GUACHOCHI**, 130km south of Creel, a disappointing destination, but reached along a dramatic and newly tarmacked mountain highway skirting the top edge of the great canyons and passing much of the best of the scenery seen on tour to "La Bufa". If current schedules hold, the 11.30am Estrella Blanca **bus** from Creel will get you to Guachochi in time to briefly tour the dusty streets, grab a bite to eat and catch the 4.45pm bus onwards for 190km to Parral – another dramatic ride, this time through magnificent cactus-strewn mountain scenery. The Estrella Blanca bus station is at the northern end of town, almost a kilometre from the Transportes Ballezanos station, which also has buses on to Parral. If you get stuck, you'll find the very basic *Hotel Orpimel* (②), immediately above the Transportes Ballezanos station, and, around 300m north, the superior *Hotel Melina* (☎154/3-03-40; ⑤), which has a/c rooms with TV, and a decent restaurant. Committed hikers can even use Guachochi as a base for exploring the remote **Sinforosa Canyon**.

For a chance to experience the canyons that's both more accessible than Batopilas and more appealing than Guachochi, consider the **lodges** overlooking the canyons near stations along the rail line, all of which offer a variety of organized excursions. At DIVISADERO, the *Cabañas Divisadero Barrancas* (☎14/15-11-99; ⑨) are perched right on the canyon lip, and the *Posada Barranca del Cobre* (reservations in Los Mochis ☎681/8-70-46, fax 2-00-46; from USA ☎1-800/896-8196; ⑨ with all meals). The best hotel in the area, though, comes just before the Divisadero stop, at BARRANCA DIVISADERO, where a bus takes you to the *Hotel Mansión Tarahumara* (in Chihuahua ☎14/15-47-21, fax 16-54-44; ⑨), a medieval castle in the middle of the canyon. Rates include all meals.

At BAHUICHIVO, on the rail line 50km west of Divisadero, buses will pick you up to take you to the extremely attractive *Hotel Misión* (reservations in Los Mochis: ☎681/8-70-46, fax 2-00-46; from USA ☎1-800/896-8196; ⑧ with all meals), in the mountain village of CEROCAHUI.

Two other possibilities, best organized before you arrive in Mexico, are the *Copper Canyon Lodges* (in US ☎248/340-7230 & ☎1-800/776-3942, fax 340-7212, *www.coppercanyonlodges.com*), with both a lovely small hotel at Cusárare and another at Batopilas (see above). They normally offer all-inclusive multiday packages combining both hotels and starting from Chihuahua. Summer rates work out around US$1400 a week for two, but booking in advance and accepting certain conditions can halve this.

Chihuahua

You're unlikely to see any of those revolting little short-haired, bug-eyed dogs in **CHIHUAHUA**, the capital of the largest state in the republic. They do come from here originally, but their absence is presumably because the vicissitudes of a dog's life in Mexico are too great for so pathetic a creature. Perhaps, too, because few could stand the fumes of this transport hub and industrial centre, which marshals the state's mineral and agricultural wealth.

Though the gloom in poor weather is depressing — and a stay of a night or two is ample for most — Chihuahua can be really attractive, with an ancient centre surrounded by suburbs of magnificent nineteenth-century mansions in the best Gothic-horror tradition. This is also *vaquero* heartland and one of the best places in the country to look for **cowboy boots**: you're spoilt for choice in the centre, especially in the blocks bounded by C 4, Juárez, Victoria and Ocampo.

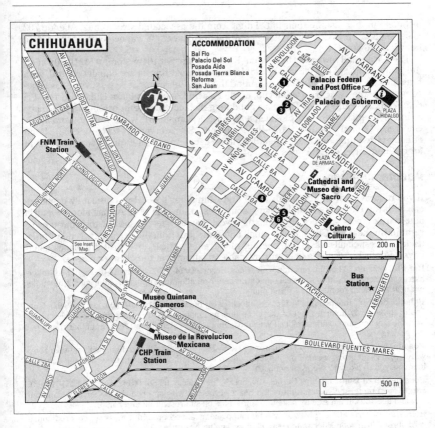

Arrival and information

Transport in and out of Chihuahua is not well co-ordinated, frustrating the many travellers who come here only to take the Copper Canyon rail line. The **Central Camionera** (with 24hr guardería and long-distance phone offices) is miles out, near the airport on Av Aeropuerto; local buses from the main road outside run to and from Av Juárez in the centre, and there are plenty of taxis. From the airport, the usual system of official transport operates – buy your voucher as you leave the terminal.

The Ferrocarriles Nacionales de Mexico (Ciudad Juárez–México) **train station** is closer in, but still a long walk north of the centre; go straight up División del Norte for 100m then left along Av Technologico, picking up any bus marked "Centro". Arriving from the Copper Canyon (see p.128) at the **CHP station**, a similar distance southeast of the centre, you can take a bus into the centre, but you'll probably want to take a taxi; indeed you may have little choice, since you and your luggage will be grabbed by eager drivers the minute you step out.

Central Chihuahua is compact enough for you to **get around** everywhere on foot, but bear in mind that addresses can initially be confusing. Even-numbered cross streets lie to the north of the central Plaza de Armas and odd numbers to the south, with shop or hotel numbers taking their initial digit from the associated street; thus, Allende 702 is between C 7 and C 9 north of the centre, but Allende 607 will be south of the centre between C 6 and C 8.

There's a small **tourist office** (Mon–Fri 9am–7pm; Sat 10am–2pm; ☎14/10-10-77) on the ground floor of the Palacio de Gobierno, and most **banks** are equally central, with branches on Victoria and Libertad around the Plaza de Armas. The **post office** is located opposite the Palacio de Gobierno, in the Palacio Federal on Plaza Hidalgo (Mon–Fri 8am–7pm, Sat 9am–1pm). There's a good long-distance **phone booth** in the pharmacy at Independencia 808, east of Aldama (Mon–Sat 8am–8pm), while *Rojo y Casavantes*, Guerrero 1207 at Allende (Mon–Fri 9am–6pm, Sat 9am–noon; ☎14/15-58-58), is an effective **travel agency**, which handles all the usual American Express services except for cashing travellers' cheques.

Accommodation

If you're arriving from the north you'll find Chihuahua's **hotels** wonderfully economical, with the cheaper examples lying southwest of the Plaza de Armas along Victoria and Juárez. Those a street or two further west may be a few pesos cheaper, but they're right in the heart of Chihuahua's small and tame, but nonetheless seedy, red-light district: C 10 especially has a fair number of extremely cheap dives. All the places listed have 24-hour hot water; a/c is only available in summer at the cheaper places.

Bal Flo, C 5a no.702 at the junction with Niños Heroes (☎14/16-03-00, fax 16-03-35). The bunker-like exterior softens within to reveal one of the better middle-range choices, featuring slightly poky but neat and clean rooms with TV and phone. ④.

Palacio del Sol, Independencia 116, five blocks west of centre (☎14/16-60-00, fax 15-49-97). Top-notch, multistorey luxury; most of the large international standard rooms offer expansive views over the city and come with satellite TV. Gymnasium, pricey cafeteria and restaurant/bar round out the package. ⑦.

Posada Aida, C 10 no.105, west of Juárez (☎14/15-38-30). Spick-and-span hotel with simple rooms with showers all facing a small plant-filled modern courtyard, with orange trees and the only chihuahuas you're likely to see. A bargain. ②.

Posada Tierra Blanca, Niños Heroes 100, beside the Palacio del Sol (☎14/15-00-00, fax 16-00-63). Large, open motel-style place right in the heart of the city with an open-air pool, gymnasium and tidy and spacious, if not exactly tasteful, rooms, plus on-site restaurant and bar. ⑤.

Reforma, Victoria 809 (☎14/12-58-08). Simple place arranged around a massive, covered courtyard, its smallish rooms decorated with chunky, ageing furniture. ②.

San Juan, Victoria 823 (☎14/10-00-35, fax 10-26-83). Simple, old-fashioned hotel that's well cared for and friendly, with some rooms off a courtyard and newer wooden-floored ones in a block behind, some with TV. About the best for the price. ②.

The Town

Chihuahua centres on the teeming **Plaza de Armas**, where the city's fine **Cathedral** stands opposite a wonderfully camp statue of the city's founder in the very act of pointing to the ground, as if to say "Right lads, we'll build it here". The Baroque, twin-towered temple was begun in 1717 but took more than seven years to complete: work well worth it, though, since for once the interior detail is the equal of the facade. In a modernized crypt beneath the cathedral the small **Museo de Arte Sacro** (Mon–Fri 10am–2pm & 4–6pm; US$1) displays some fine examples of Mexican religious art from the eighteenth century, notably a selection of sombre saints by Francisco Martinez, and a collection of dark and forbidding images in which Christ is pushed, pulled, stabbed and punched.

Also on the Plaza de Armas is the imposing, but relatively modern, **Palacio Municipal** – follow Victoria down past this and you'll come to the Plaza Hidalgo, dominated by the **Palacio de Gobierno**. Now lined with bold murals of scenes from Mexico's colonial past painted by Aarón Piña Mora, this was originally a Jesuit College, and later converted to a military hospital after the expulsion of the Jesuits – here Padre Miguel Hidalgo y Costilla and Ignacio Allende, the inspiration and early leaders of the Mexican War of Independence, were executed in 1811, their severed heads sent for public display in Guanajuato (see p.241). The site of the deed is marked (despite the fact that the building has been reconstructed several times since) and, by crossing the road to the adjacent Palacio Federal, you can visit the **Calabozo de Hidalgo**, at the corner of Juárez and Guerrero (daily 9am–7pm; US$0.20), "Hidalgo's dungeon", where they were held beforehand. Along with numerous incomprehensible letters, there are various relics of Hidalgo and the revolution, including his pistol, chest and crucifix. A golden eagle marks the entrance.

More recent history is commemorated in Chihuahua's premier sight, the **Museo de la Revolución Mexicana**, C 10 no.3010 (Tues–Sat 9am–1pm & 3–7pm, Sun 9am–5pm; US$1.30), which occupies Pancho Villa's former home. This enormous mansion was inhabited, until her death in the early 1980s, by Villa's "official" widow (there were allegedly many others), who used to conduct personal tours: it has now been taken over by the Mexican army and put on a more official footing. The collection is a fascinating mix of arms, war plans and personal mementoes, including the bullet-riddled 1922 Dodge in which Villa was assassinated in 1923 and a funerary mask clearly showing the bullet wound in his forehead. Quite apart from the campaign memories, the superbly preserved old bedrooms and bathrooms give an interesting insight into Mexican daily life in the early twentieth century.

The museum is some 2km east of the centre. To get there, walk along Ocampo, or take a bus (marked "Ocampo"), and continue two blocks past the huge church and two blocks to the left along Mendez. You may well want to break the journey at the extraordinarily elaborate **Museo Quinta Gameros** (Tues–Sun 10am–7pm; US$1.30, US$1 on Sun), at the junction of C 4 and Paseo Bolivar. Just the sort of thing that Villa and his associates were hoping to stamp out, the building was designed by a successful mine owner as an exact replica of a Parisian home. The interior is sumptuously decorated, with magnificent Art-Nouveau stained glass and ornate woodwork, and, curiously, scenes from Little Red Riding Hood are painted on the children's bedroom wall.

On the way back, call in at the **Centro Cultural de Chihuahua**, Aldama 430 at Ocampo (Tues–Sun 10am–2pm & 4–7pm; free), which puts on concerts and exhibitions from time to time and has a small but briefly diverting permanent display on the ruins at Paquimé (see p.124) with some nice pots.

MOVING ON FROM CHIHUAHUA

To get to the **Ferrocarriles Nacionales** train station take a "Villa Colón" or "Granjas Colón" bus from the centre. You'll have to ask someone to tell you where to get off (by the *Motel El Capitan*) because the station is invisible from the road. As both trains pass through at inconvenient hours – southbound at 12.20am, and 6.25am northbound – you're unlikely to find the ticket office open during the day, so it's hardly worth trying to obtain a ticket in advance. In fact the train authorities seem intent on forcing you to use the bus; pick up local buses to the **Central Camionera** at the corner of Ocampo and Juárez or along Niños Heroes.

For the Copper Canyon (see p.125), the **CHP train station**, 2km south of the centre, is reached by buses marked "Sta Rosa" or "Col Rosalia", which run along Ocampo. Get out a couple of blocks past the big church (impossible to miss) and walk a couple of blocks to the right down Mendez to the station. There are occasional cancellations so it's a good idea to visit the station ticket office a day ahead (officially Mon–Sat 6am–2pm, Sun 6–10am).

Eating, drinking and entertainment

There's no shortage of good **places to eat** in Chihuahua, from basic cafés around the **market** (west of Juárez between C 4 and C 6), through taco stalls nearer the centre, to fancier steak houses and American burger restaurants around the main plazas. The southern end of C Victoria has some of the best options, and tends to stay open late.

For traditional, back-slapping cantina **drinking**, pick one of the swing-door places at the southern end of Juárez, though take care. If you're after something a little more upmarket, rub shoulders with Chihuahua's more monied set at the bars and clubs along Juárez's northern reaches, close to its junction with Colon. Alternatively, you can always see a subtitled American **movie** (around US$2) at Sala 2001, Guerrero at Escorza, and Cinema Revolución, where Doblado meets C Neri Santos.

Café Merino, Juárez 616 at Ocampo. Reliable antojitos and tortas in clean surroundings at reasonable prices. Open 24hr but closed Tues.

La Calesa, 3300 Juárez at Colon (☎14/16-02-22). One of Chihuahua's fanciest restaurants, all dark wood panels, crisp linen tablecloths, sparkling wine glasses and waistcoated waiters. Northern-style meat cuts are the house speciality. Expect to pay US$8 for chiles rellenos *de camaron* and up to US$13 for a massive plate of succulent *mariscos*. Bookings recommended at weekends.

Casa de los Milagros, Victoria 810, opposite *Hotel Reforma*. Casual restaurant and bar comprising a beautiful colonial courtyard with tinkling fountain, surrounded by numerous small rooms. Here, Chihuahua's well-groomed meet for margaritas (US$2), one of forty brands of tequila (US$1–5 a shot), real coffee and light snacks such as *quesadilla de flor de calabaza* (squash flower; US$4), burgers and salads. Open at 8am daily for breakfast and nightly from 5pm to midnight or later.

Dino's Pizza, Doblado 301. Delicious pizzas made with a strangely sweet dough (US$7 buys one big enough for two) and with an excellent range of toppings. Also sandwiches and spaghetti dishes. Stays open late.

Mi Café, Victoria 1000, almost opposite the *Hotel San Juan*. Safe American-style diner with prices and quality both a little above average. The US$4 breakfast menu is in English and Spanish and extends from norteño and ranchero dishes to hotcakes and syrup. Come here later for burgers, sandwiches and steak and seafood mains.

El Vegetariano, Libertad 1703. Chihuahua's only vegetarian restaurant, which is light on atmosphere but serves a US$3 daily buffet of soup, salad and soya-based dishes (1–4pm), and also sells vegeburgers, yoghurt and granola, wholemeal bread and hearty cakes. Closed evenings and all Sun.

South to Durango

Below Chihuahua sprawls a vast plain, mostly agricultural, largely uninteresting, broken only occasionally by an outstretched leg of the Sierra Madre Occidental. The train crosses at night, buses hammer through relentlessly and you'd be wise to follow their lead. At **Jiménez** the road divides, with Hwy-49 heading straight down through Gómez Palacio and Torreón, while Hwy-45 curves westwards to Durango. The non-stop route for Zacatecas and México is quicker, but if time is not your only consideration the Durango route offers far more of interest.

Torreón and **Gómez Palacio**, on the faster of the two routes, are virtually contiguous – there would be only one city were it not for the fact that the state border runs through the middle: Torreón is in Coahuila, Gómez Palacio in Durango. They're as dull as each other – modern towns anyway, both were devastated by heavy fighting in the revolution. There's no need whatsoever to stop, though one consolation if you do is that they mark the start of wine-growing country, and you can sample the local produce (not the country's best) at various *bodegas*. On the longer route, **Durango** is the first of the Spanish-colonial towns that distinguish Mexico's heartland, and while it's not a patch on some of those further south, it will certainly be the most attractive place you've come to yet. That said, it's a good eight to ten hours on the bus from Chihuahua, so you might consider breaking the journey in **Hidalgo del Parral**.

Parral

PARRAL, or "Hidalgo del Parral" as it's officially known, is fixed in the Mexican consciousness as the town in which General Francisco "Pancho" Villa was assassinated, but the town's history goes back much further. Much of it is linked with the metal-rich stubby hills all around, where, in the early years after the Conquest, the Spanish set up a mine in the little town of **Santa Barbara**, 25km away, to extract silver above all, but also lead, copper and some gold. Santa Barbara soon became the capital of the province of Nueva Viscaya, a territory that stretched as far north as Texas and southern California; the capital was transferred to Parral after its foundation in 1638.

Mining is still Parral's chief activity and its outskirts are grubbily industrial – at the centre, though, the tranquil colonial plaza features a couple of remarkable buildings put up by prospectors who struck it rich. Chief of these are the **Palacio Pedro Alvarado**, an exuberantly decorated folly of a mansion built in the eighteenth century by a successful silver miner, and, across the river, the **Iglesia de la Virgen del Rayo**. Legend has it this was constructed by an Indian on the proceeds of a gold mine he had discovered and worked in secret; the authorities tortured him to death in an attempt to find the mine, but its location died with him. There's also a small museum in the house from which Villa and his retinue of bodyguards were ambushed, but it is seldom open.

Practicalities

Parral's compact colonial heart is around twenty minutes' walk from the main **bus terminal** (daytime luggage storage) – turn left, then left again onto Independencia – or take a bus or taxi from just outside. The cheapest acceptable **hotel** in town is the clean and simple *Hotel Fuentes*, Maclovio Herrera 79 (☎152/2-00-16; ②). For a few more pesos the best bet is *Hotel Acosta*, near the main plaza on Agustin Barbachano 3 (☎152/2-02-21; ③), a pleasant old establishment with wooden floors, a rooftop terrace and 1950s atmosphere. For a touch more luxury, only a stone's throw from the bus station, stroll to the restaurant-equipped *Hotel Los Arcos*, Dr Pedro de Lille 5 (☎152/3-05-97, fax 3-05-37; ⑤), where rooms front onto a modern courtyard and come with satellite TV and a VCR with choice of English-language videos. In the centre just off the plaza, the bright and cheery 24-hour *Restaurant Morales*, Coronado 18, serves *pozole de puerco* for US$3 and excellent enchiladas suizas, made with chicken, guacamole and green chile. If you've a taste for a torta or burger, stop off at the *OK Parral*, Independencia 215, on your walk from the bus station into town.

Durango

Although the Sierra Madre still looms on the western horizon, the country around **DURANGO** itself is flat – with just two low hills marking out the city from the plain. The **Cerro del Mercado**, a giant lump of iron ore that testifies to the area's mineral wealth, rises squat and black to the north, while to the west, a climb up the **Cerro de los Remedios** provides a wonderful panorama over the whole city. The old town shelters between these two, with newer development straggling eastwards and southwards. Durango's **fiesta**, on July 8, celebrates the city's foundation on that day in 1563. Festivities commence several days before and run right through till the fiesta of the Virgen del Refugio on July 22 – well worth going out of your way for, though rooms are booked solid.

Arrival and information

Since passenger trains no longer run here, you'll be arriving at the **Central de Autobuses** (24hr guardería) over 4km out of town; to get to the centre, turn right out of the station and wait just beyond the pedestrian overbridge for buses marked "Centro/Camionera".

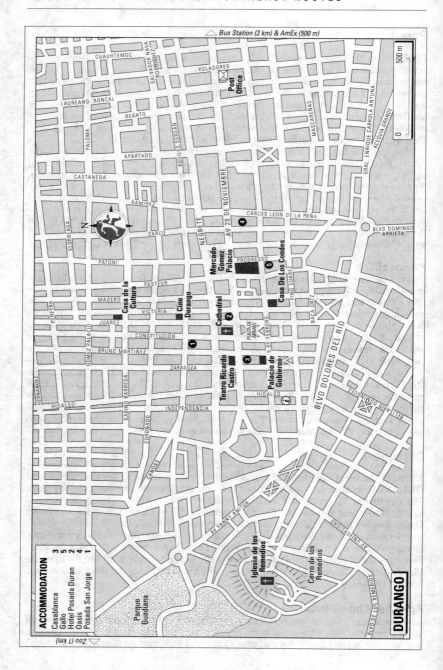

△ Bus Station (2 km) & AmEx (500 m)

DURANGO

ACCOMMODATION

Casablanca	3
Gallo	5
Hotel Posada Duran	2
Oasis	4
Posada San Jorge	1

△ Zoo (1 km)

These will drop you right at the Plaza de Armas near the cathedral. Facing the cathedral, turn left along 20 de Noviembre for three blocks then left down Hidalgo for two blocks to reach the **tourist office**, at Hidalgo 408 Sur (Mon–Fri 9am–3pm & 4–7pm, Sat & Sun 11am–2pm; ☎18/11-21-39). Despite its compact, grid-plan centre, getting your bearings in Durango can initially be a little tricky, so it's as well to know that addresses south of Aquiles Serdán (two blocks north of the cathedral) are appended "Sur", and those west of Zarco (six blocks east of the cathedral) are tagged "Pte".

For **currency exchange**, there's a convenient branch of Bancomer right by the plaza at the corner of 20 de Noviembre and Constitución, in addition to several other banks nearby. The **post office** is at 20 de Noviembre 500b Ote, some twelve blocks east of the cathedral, and **American Express** operates from 20 de Noviembre 810 Ote (Mon–Fri 9am–7pm, Sat 10am–5pm; ☎18/17-00-83), a further three blocks east of the post office; catch "Tecno" buses along 20 de Noviembre. The handiest booth for **long-distance calls** is at Bruno Martinez 206 Sur at Negrete (Mon–Sat 8am–9.30pm, Sun 8am–3pm). For **laundry**, there's the *Lavandería Automática Ale*, at 232 Lázaro Cárdenas Nte (Mon–Sat 9am–7pm), reached by catching an eastbound bus fifteen blocks along 20 de Noviembre to Lázaro Cárdenas, then walking two blocks north.

Accommodation

There's no shortage of **rooms** in Durango, though you should book ahead if you want to visit during the fiesta. Cheaper places are mostly pretty grim: if price is your only concern, try around the market, though even here the better places charge heavily. If you're willing to spend a little more, Durango has a couple of very fine places worth splashing out on.

Casablanca, 20 de Noviembre 811 Pte at Zaragoza (☎18/11-35-99). Big, old-fashioned colonial hotel. Spacious and comfortable if unexciting. ⑤.

Gallo, 5 de Febrero 117 at Progresso (☎18/11-52-90). About the best of the real budget places, with large bright rooms and constant hot water. ②.

Hotel Posada Duran, 20 de Noviembre beside the cathedral (☎18/11-24-12). The best place to stay in town. An old, slightly faded colonial mansion with large wooden-floored rooms set around the first floor of an inner courtyard – many of them with windows opening out over the plaza and the better ones with TV. There's a bar downstairs, and credit cards are accepted. Booking highly recommended. ③.

Oasis, Zarco 317 at 5 de Febrero (☎18/11-45-61). Small, clean rooms with shower, near the market. ①.

Posada San Jorge, Constitución 102 Sur at Serdán (☎18/13-32-57, fax 11-60-40). Far and away the best of the pricier places, a gorgeous and recently remodelled hotel in a colonial house, with a two-storey courtyard alive with caged birds and chatter from the restaurant. Rooms, all with cable TV, are individually decorated in rustic fashion, with tiled floors, wood beams, bold paintwork and potted cacti. ⑤.

The Town

Almost all the monuments in downtown Durango cluster in a few streets around the Plaza Principal and the huge covered market nearby. On the plaza itself is the **cathedral**, its two robust domed towers dwarfing the narrow facade. It's a typical Mexican church in every way: externally imposing, weighty and Baroque, with a magnificent setting overlooking the plaza, and yet ultimately disappointing, the interior dim and by comparison uninspired. Facing it from the centre of the plaza is a bizarre little two-storey bandstand from the top of which the town band plays on Sundays; underneath, a small shop sells expensive local crafts.

Following Av 20 de Noviembre down from the cathedral (it stretches away to the left as you face it) brings you to the grandiose Porfiriano **Teatro Ricardo Castro**. Turn south here onto Bruno Martinez, past the Teatro Victoria, and you come out in another plaza, its north side dominated by the porticoed facade of the **Palacio de Gobierno**. Originally the private house of a Spanish mining magnate, this was taken over by the local government after the War of Independence. The stairwells and walls of the two-storey, arcaded patio inside are decorated with murals by local artists depicting the state's history. On the west side of the square, an ancient **Jesuit monastery** now houses the offices of the University of Durango.

From here Av 5 de Febrero leads back to the **Casa de los Condes**, the most elaborate of the Spanish-style mansions. Built in the eighteenth century by the Conde de Suchil, sometime Spanish governor of Durango, its exuberantly carved columns and wealth of extravagant detail are quite undamaged by time. History has given the mansion some strange functions, though: it was the seat of the local Inquisition for some time – and a more inappropriate setting for their stern deliberations would be hard to imagine – while nowadays it operates as a bank, having had a brief spell as sort of upmarket shopping mall. A little further along 5 de Febrero, you reach the back of the **market**: covering a whole block on two storeys, there's just about everything anybody could want here, from medicinal herbs to farm equipment, as well as a series of little food stalls upstairs.

Back at the plaza, you can stroll up Constitución, a lively shopping street with several small restaurants, to the little church and garden of Santa Ana, much more peaceful than the plaza for an evening *paseo*. On the east side lies the **Casa de la Cultura** (Tues–Fri 9am–6pm, Sat & Sun 10am–6pm; US$0.20), an old converted mansion with separate rooms dedicated to local, native styles of weaving, ceramics, basketware and mask-making. Enthusiastic guides explain all, and there are often interesting temporary exhibitions.

Parque Guadiana and Cerro de los Remedios

If you've got kids in tow, or just fancy a break from bus diesel fumes, make for the prominent Cerro de los Remedios, 2km west of the city centre, or more particularly, **Parque Guadiana** on its northern flanks – take a bus marked "Remedios/Parque Guadiana" from outside the cathedral – a vast area of fragrant eucalyptus and shady willows, dotted with fountains and kids' playgrounds, and with a **miniature train** (Fri 3–7pm, Sat & Sun 11am–7pm; US$0.20). On the western side of the park, on Anillo de Circunvalacion, is the **Zoológico Sahuatoba** (Tues–Sat 10am–6pm; free), a collection of lions, tigers, hippos, monkeys and the like that's surprisingly well presented considering the free entry. Buses marked "Tierra Y Libertad" come directly here from the corner of Serdán and Victoria.

The **Cerro de los Remedios**, rising immediately above the park and the zoo, is home to Durango's monied classes, and expensive modern homes are climbing inexorably towards the hilltop **Iglesia de los Remedios**, which commands a wonderful view over the entire city. The most direct way to walk up here from the city is to take the steps at the western end of Juan García.

Eating and entertainment

It isn't difficult to find decent **places to eat** in Durango, among them – and for no apparent reason – a proliferation of reputable Italian places. Your cheapest eating options are the stalls upstairs in the **market**, some of which serve excellent food. Adjacent streets, and those off the main plaza, are also good hunting grounds, but the greatest concentration is along the first half-dozen blocks of Constitución going north from the plaza, where both fashionable and more modest eating and drinking places fill the gaps between the boutiques. Apart from Sunday evening, when the streets around the plaza are blocked off for the weekly free **entertainment** – mainly Norteño and Ranchera bands – nightlife revolves around the restaurants. If you want to see a **film**, check what's on at Cine Durango, at the corner of Victoria and Serdán.

Café Opera, Negrete 1005 Pte at Independencia. Relaxed restaurant serving delicious, predominantly Italian dishes at modest prices. Closed Mon.

Corleone Pizza, Constitución 110 Nte at Serdán. Straightforward and dimly lit place serving good, and slightly sweet, pizzas and an admirable range of cocktails.

Fuente de Sodas, 5 de Febrero 517 at Juárez, right by the plaza. Hangout popular with Durango's youth, who tuck in to huge ice-cream waffle-cones or great hunks of melt-in-the-mouth apple pie and sip flavoured coffees.

Restaurante Paese Mio Italiano, Constitución 454 at Pereyra. Superb and fairly formal Italian restaurant serving antipasti for around US$5, a wonderful rice, shrimp and mushroom risotto for US$6, Sicilian salad for US$4 and crispy pizzas for US$7. Closed Mon.

Samadhi Vegetarian, Negrete 403 Pte between Madero and Victoria. Small and fairly characterless place, which nevertheless serves a bargain veggie comida for US$2, yoghurt, salads and vegetable-filled enchiladas. Daily 8am–10pm.

La Terraza, 5 de Febrero 603, on the first floor overlooking the plaza opposite the cathedral. Only worthwhile for drinks or a pizza if you can get a window seat to watch the world go by.

Las Tres Carabelas, Juárez 102 Sur at Serdán. You'd expect this place, neatly tucked into a peaceful colonial atrium, to charge three times the price; it's actually a bargain, serving US$2 breakfasts, tortas, hamburgers and excellent comidas on white tablecloths.

Around Durango

The full title of Durango's tourist office is the *Dirección de Turismo y Cinematografía del Estado de Durango*. Not so long ago they spent much of their time organizing the vast number of **film** units that came to take advantage of the surrounding area's remarkably constant, clear, high-altitude light, the desert and mountain scenery (Westerns were the speciality), and the relatively cheap Mexican technicians and extras. Although only half a dozen movies have been shot here over the last decade, you can still see the paltry remains of the permanent sets at **Chupaderos** and **Villa del Oeste**. The main road from Parral runs within a few hundred metres of the movie towns, so it's easy enough to get there by bus, and to flag one down when you leave – alternatively you get a pretty good, if fleeting, view as you pass by.

Parral-bound buses departing from Durango's main bus station will drop you 8km north at **Villa del Oeste** (Tues–Sun noon–midnight; US$3), a kind of small theme park comprising the hundred-metre-long street of Bandido, which looks straight out of the Wild West until you realize the saloons and shops have been re-fashioned into a themed restaurant, music hall and a bar & grill. You can show off your horseback skills (US$8 an hour), and there's even a disco on Friday nights.

If all this sounds too cheesy, stay on the bus to the dusty village of **CHUPADEROS**, 2km further north, where the villagers have pretty much taken over the set: the church and "Prairie Lands Hotel" are lived in, one house is a grocery store, and the livestock exchange has been commandeered by Alcoholics Anonymous. A good way to link the two towns is to catch the bus out to Chupaderos, then follow the track past the lived-in church, across the train tracks and through scrubby, cactus-strewn desert 2km to a kind of back entrance to Bandido in Villa del Oeste, where you may or may not be charged entry. It is a particularly nice walk in the late afternoon, past the heat of the day.

An alternative day out is to head 35km south to **El Saltito**, a waterfall surrounded by bizarre rock formations, which has itself been a recurrent film location: the bus can drop you on the road 4km away. On any of these trips, watch out for **scorpions**: there's a genus of white scorpion unique to this area, which, though rare – the only place most people see one is encased in the glass paperweights on sale all over the place – has a sting that is frequently fatal.

On **leaving Durango** you face a simple choice: **west** to the Pacific at Mazatlán, over an incredible road through the Sierra Madre (see p.110), which is itself a worthwhile journey; or **south** to Zacatecas (p.220), among the finest of Mexico's colonial cities.

MONTERREY AND THE NORTHEAST ROUTES

The **eastern border crossings**, from Ciudad Acuña to Matamoros, are uniformly dull – dedicated solely to the task of getting people and goods from one country to the other. In this they are at least reasonably efficient, with immigration officials on both sides well used to coping with mass cross-border traffic. In most, Mexican tourist cards are routinely issued at the border, while Mexican consulates in the Texan towns across the Río Grande can handle any problems. If you're walking over the bridges, there's a small toll to pay: keep a selection of US coins for the turnstiles.

Once across the border, you're faced with the choice of pressing on south (invariably the best option) or choosing a suitable hotel from the dozens on offer. If you're eager to head on from the border towns of **Nuevo Laredo**, **Reynosa** or **Matamoros** there are frequent city bus services to the main bus stations, though you have to walk a few blocks to catch them. The bus stations in **Ciudad Acuña** and **Piedras Negras** are in town, within walking distance of the border crossing.

Once through the border towns, you could be forgiven for hot-footing straight to The Bajío (Chapter 4) or even Veracruz (Chapter 7), but you're talking at least twelve hours on the bus and a lot longer by train; besides it would be a pity to miss **Monterrey**, Mexico's industrial dynamo and home to a few essential sights. Neighbouring **Saltillo** is also worthwhile, if only as a pleasant place to break a long journey. Direct buses from the border to Monterrey, México and most of the major northern cities are frequent and efficient. Although there are trains from Nuevo Laredo to the capital, the service is slow, uncomfortable and seldom reliable, if cheap.

The Lower Río Grande Valley: Ciudad Acuña to Matamoros

The Río Grande, known to Mexicans as the *Río Bravo del Norte*, forms the border between Texas and Mexico, a distance of more than 1500km. The country through which it flows is arid semi-desert, and the towns along the lower section of the river are heavily industrialized and suffer from appalling environmental pollution. This is the *maquiladora* zone, where foreign-owned assembly plants produce consumer goods, most of them for export to the States. There are few particular attractions for tourists, and most visitors are here for the cheap shopping or simply passing through on their way south.

Ciudad Acuña and around

The smallest of the border towns, **CIUDAD ACUÑA** (setting of the low-budget Mexican thriller *El Mariachi* and its sequel *El Regreso del Mariachi*) is quiet, relaxed and intensely hot. The zócalo has a small **museum** on one side, with a tiny collection of fossils and

---

BORDER CHECKS

Crossing the border, do not forget to go through **immigration and customs** checks. As everywhere, there's a free zone south of the frontier, and you can cross at will. Try to continue south, though, and you'll be stopped after some 30km and sent back to get your tourist card stamped.

MOVING ON FROM ACUÑA

Onward transport is more frequent from the towns further south, and it may be easier to head to Piedras Negras, ninety minutes away, and change **buses** there: however, there are a few daily services to **Saltillo** (7hr) and **Monterrey** (8hr) via Monclova, and a couple to México and Torreón. In addition El Aguila buses go to **Guadalajara** (1 daily), **Zacatecas** (2 daily) and **Chihuahua** (1 daily). The airline-style Expresso Futura buses (a/c, reclining seats, toilets and videos) have one daily service each to México, Querétaro and San Luis Potosí.

---

artefacts, in addition to rows and rows of deathly dull photographs of local dignitaries. Given there's little to do in the town itself, the best idea is to press on south, unless you're drawn by the offerings around Acuña: watersports enthusiasts are amply catered for at the **Presa Amistad**, a huge artificial lake straddling the border, while to the west the starkly beautiful mountains, canyons and desert of the interior of Coahuila State invite cautious exploration. The huge and scarcely visited **Parque Internacional del Río Bravo**, opposite Big Bend National Park in Texas, offers superb wilderness, but you'll need a well-equipped vehicle to cope with the rugged terrain; there's no public transport.

Arriving over the bridge from Del Rio, Texas, the bus drops you at the **border** post, where there's a map of the town in the modern customs building, together with some limited tourist information. The **bus station**, at the corner of Matamoros and Ocampo, is just five blocks from the border and one from the plaza. Most shops and restaurants are glad to change your dollars, at a fairly good rate for small amounts, but for proper exchange there's a choice of banks and **casas de cambio**. Of the **banks**, Bancomer, Madero 360, off Juárez, has a 24-hour ATM, as does Banamex, at the corner of Matamoros and Hidalgo. The **post office** is on Hidalgo 320, past Juárez. You'll pass several **hotels** as you walk down Hidalgo from the border: none is especially good value, but if you have to stay try the *San Jorge*, Hidalgo 165 (☎877/2-50-70; ④), which has pleasant, a/c rooms, or the spacious *San Antonio*, corner of Hidalgo and Lerdo (☎877/2-51-08; ⑤). Also good for one night, especially if you're very tired, is the *Coahuila*, Lerdo 160, one block off Hidalgo (☎877/2-10-40; ②); if you're desperately poor, the *Alfaro*, Madero 240, between Juárez and Lerdo (no phone; ①), will do. You may prefer not to stay in town at all: 30km south of Acuña the road to Piedras Negras (see below) passes through **JIMÉNEZ**, where there are plenty of tranquil spots for **camping**, and the new *Hotel Río San Diego* (④) occupies a relaxing position overlooking the river. Back in Acuña, good-value **cafés** and loncherías line Matamoros – the *Café Garcia* has an unusual no-smoking policy – and there's the decent *Pappa's Pizza* at the corner of Madero and Matamoros.

Piedras Negras and Monclova

Friendly and hassle-free, with the most laid-back immigration officers you're likely to encounter anywhere in Mexico, **PIEDRAS NEGRAS** is the ideal border town. The unpretentious main square is directly opposite the international bridge, and hotels and restaurants aren't far away. Nonetheless, there's no reason to stay longer than it takes to catch the first bus south, which traverses a parched plain with some wildly eroded land, then cuts through gaps in the mountains past **Monclova**, some four hours from Piedras Negras. Now little more than the site of a vast steelworks, Monclova can make a useful staging point, but you wouldn't go out of your way to visit.

Piedras Negras' extremely helpful **tourist office** (daily 9am–2pm & 4–7pm), by the main square as you enter Mexico from the US, has free maps of the town and Eagle Pass on the other side, as well as of other cities in Coahuila. From the customs post Allende runs straight ahead towards the bus station, while Hidalgo heads left past one

MOVING ON FROM PIEDRAS NEGRAS

The bus station is a fifteen-minute walk from the main plaza along Allende. The main companies, Blancos and Aguila, operate a decent second-class service, with frequent departures to all the major points south. Expresso Futura buses run to **México**, **Aguascalientes** and **Monterrey**, while Turistar Ejecutivo luxury buses serve **México**, **Monclova** and **Querétaro**. Frontera second-class buses have frequent departures to **Nuevo Laredo**, three hours away. The Coahuilense service to **Saltillo** takes around seven hours.

If you're headed **Stateside**, cross the border to Eagle Pass, Texas, and walk 200m north to the Greyhound station, which has four direct departures to San Antonio daily, and one a day to Dallas.

of the better value **hotels**, *Hotel Santos*, Hidalgo 314 at the corner of Matamoros (☎878/2-30-28; ④), though like almost all the others in town it seems to be suffering from years of neglect and border-town overpricing. Alternatively, continue a couple of blocks along Hidalgo to the market square, where *Hotel del Centro*, Allende 510 (☎878/2-50-30; ③), and the similarly priced *Muzquiz* next door, are best left in favour of *Hotel Coahuila*, Zaragoza 117 Sur (②), where equally bad rooms are half the price. Better still, stretch for the nearby and comfortable *Hotel Santa Rosa*, Guerrero 401 Ote, on the corner of Morelos (☎878/2-04-00; ④), set around a plant-filled courtyard, or the luxurious *Autel Rio*, Padre de las Casas 121 Nte, at Teran (☎878/2-70-64, fax 2-73-04; ⑤), with a TV in every room, a swimming pool and plenty of parking space. For a decent **meal**, make for *Café Gitanos*, part of the market at the corner of Allende and Zaragoza. For **currency exchange**, head for Cambios Coahuila (Mon–Fri 8.30am–5.30pm), in Sangar's Shopping Center, Allende and Xicotencatl, close to the bus station, or in the market at Zaragoza 107. Bancomer (Mon–Sat 9am–5pm), one block from the main plaza on Morelos and Abasolo, has a 24-hour ATM.

Nuevo Laredo

The giant of the eastern border towns, **NUEVO LAREDO** is alive with the imagery and commercialism of the frontier. It doubles as the transport hub for the whole area, with dozens of departures to México and all major towns in the north. Cross-border traffic, legal and illegal, is king here, and both bridges from the Texan town of Laredo are crowded with pedestrians and vehicles 24 hours a day. Mexican insurance offices and sleazy cantinas greet you, while tired horses hitched to buggies wait dispiritedly for their next load of pasty, overweight tourists.

You'll do best to head straight out: the road **south from Nuevo Laredo** – towards the vibrant northern capital, Monterrey – at first crosses a flat, scrub-covered, featureless plain, but after an hour the scenery begins to improve. Far to the west the peaks of the **Sierra Madre** rise abruptly. Easily the most noticeable plants are the giant yuccas known as **Joshua Trees**; to the early settlers their upraised, spiky branches brought to mind Joshua praying in supplication.

Arrival and information

As a tourist, entering or leaving Mexico, you'll take Puente Internacional #1: there's a small toll, payable in dollars or pesos if you're heading north, but in US currency only (35¢) when Mexico-bound. Despite the crush, immigration usually proceeds smoothly, though expect long queues crossing to the US in the mornings and on Sunday evenings. The small **tourist office** (daily 8am–8pm; ☎87/12-01-04) at the border post is occasionally deserted, but you may be able to pick up leaflets as you pass, including a useful map of the town – these maps are also available from lobbies of the larger hotels, theoretically for guests only.

Coming from Laredo, head up Guerrero, past the curio shops and dozens of casas de cambio, and you'll find everything you're likely to need within seven or eight blocks of the border. Walk past the first square, **Plaza Juárez**, home to the cathedral and Nuevo Mercado de la Reforma craft market, and head for the main square, the palm-shaded **Plaza Hidalgo**, easily the most pleasant spot in Nuevo Laredo. It's a pity there are no pavement cafés on the plaza, but pretty much everything else you'd want is nearby. Buses to the **Central Camionera** (marked "Carretera"; see box below) leave from outside the Palacio Municipal – which houses the **post office** – tucked around the back on Camargo. Bancomer and Serfin **banks**, both with ATMs, are around the corner at the junction of Reforma and Canales, which is is also a good area to begin looking for a **hotel** if you need one.

There are plenty of decent **places to eat** around town: try the air-conditioned, reasonably priced and friendly *Café Almanza*, Gonzalez 272, on the south side of Plaza Hidalgo, and the slightly upmarket restaurant in the *Hotel Reforma*, around the corner at Guerrero 806.

Accommodation
Although there's no shortage of inexpensive **hotels** in the city centre – especially along Hidalgo – many of them are extremely run-down, and frequented by prostitutes and their clients, so check what you're getting very carefully before parting with any money. Nonetheless, against the admittedly low standard of hotels in Mexican border towns in general, Nuevo Laredo's are pretty good value and in reasonable condition.

Los Dos Laredos, Matamoros 108 (☎87/12-24-19). Simple, plain rooms with bathrooms and fairly plentiful hot water, and evening accompaniment from the local clubs. Only one block from the border; turn right along C 15 de Julio. ②.

Fiesta, Ocampo 559 (☎87/12-47-37). Relatively modern place with unrealized pretentions to grandeur but comfortable a/c rooms all with telephone, some larger and with TV (US$21.4). ④.

La Finca, Reynosa 811 (☎87/12-88-83). Modern motel-style place with a/c, TV-equipped rooms that are always clean and in good condition. Excellent value. ④.

Nuevo Romano, Doctor Mier 800, one block east from Plaza Hidalgo (☎87/12-23-91). Recently remodelled and refurbished, this is particularly good value, all rooms being spacious and with TV. ③.

Sam's, Hidalgo 2903 (☎87/12-59-32). One of the cheapest decent places in the centre: good value and reliable. ②.

MOVING ON FROM NUEVO LAREDO

Nuevo Laredo's huge **Central Camionera** (guardería Mon–Sat 7am–10pm, Sun 7am–5pm) is some distance south of town, but battered city buses (marked "Puente"/"Centro") run frequently between here, the border crossings and Plaza Hidalgo; it's about a 25-minute journey. The **main bus companies** are Omnibus de México, Elite, Tamaulipas and Turistar, along with Transportes Frontera, Transportes del Norte and Tres Estrellas de Oro, and many more; you'll have no trouble getting a bus to Monterrey (3hr) or México (15hr), day or night. Other destinations include Saltillo, Ciudad Victoria, Guadalajara and Zacatecas; there are even a couple of services to Acapulco.

If you're **heading into the States** by bus, four companies – Greyhound, Turismos Rapidos, El Esresso and Azabache – all offer identically priced direct services from the Central Camionera to San Antonio (US$15), Austin (US$25), Houston (US$25) and Dallas (US$30).

There are currently only three **train** departures each week, leaving for Monterrey (4–5hr), Saltillo (7–8hr), San Luis Potosí (15hr) and México (25hr) at 6.55pm on Tuesday, Thursday and Saturday. To **get to the train station** on foot, you face a walk of about twenty minutes; from the border, head up Guerrero nine or ten blocks, then turn right along Mina or Gutiérrez for another ten blocks. Ticket sales commence two hours before departure.

The **Nuevo Laredo International Airport** is a long taxi ride (about US$10) out of town. There's actually nothing international about it, as the only two (very expensive) flights are to Guadalajara and México (on Mexicana).

Reynosa

A very easy border crossing and excellent transport connections combine to make **REYNOSA** a favourite point to enter Mexico. A sprawling industrial city, filled with car repair shops and Pemex plants, it in fact holds little to detain you, but the centre is compact, people are generally friendly – and coming and going is simple. Crossing the international bridge over the Río Bravo from McAllen, Texas (25¢ coin-op pedestrian toll), don't forget to call in at the migración office (assuming you're headed south) and perhaps the small **tourist office** (Mon–Fri 8am–8pm), though don't expect too much enlightening information. The **bus station** is probably your first priority, and though buses do run into the centre and out again to the Central Camionera, it's probably easier simply to tackle the twenty-minute walk. Immediately off the bridge, head straight on along Lerdo de Tejada, which soon becomes Zaragoza, to the Plaza Principal, where you'll find a couple of **banks** with ATMs (it's about five blocks in all). From here the bus station can be reached by following Hidalgo, the pedestrianized main street, for a few blocks then turning left into Colón.

Hotels here aren't great value for money, but *Hotel Avenida*, Zaragoza 885 Ote, (☎87/22-05-92; ④), and *Hotel Internacional*, Zaragoza 1050 (☎ & fax 87/22-33-18; ④), both on the walk to the centre from the border, are certainly comfortable enough, the latter having the edge, just. *Hotel Confort*, Hidalgo 325 Nte (☎87/22-27-01; ③), has reasonable, if ageing rooms and some newer, pricier ones (④); and *Hotel Estación*, Hidalgo 305 Sur, some six blocks south of the plaza (☎89/22-73-02; ②), is a less than appealing, and not wonderfully clean, introduction to Mexican hotels, but it's at least cheap. Opposite the bus station there's the luxurious *Grand Premier Hotel*, Colón 1304 (☎89/22-48-50, fax 22-11-50; ⑥).

There are a number of inexpensive **food stalls** and a Gigante supermarket by the bus station, and a well-stocked **market** on Hidalgo, midway between the train station and the plaza. For a proper meal, you can't fault *Café Paris*, Hidalgo 873 Nte, which serves very good breakfasts and comidas in comfortable surroundings – occasionally someone wheels past a trolley full of cakes for your delectation.

MOVING ON FROM REYNOSA

The Valley Transit Co. operates **buses** between Reynosa and **McAllen, Texas**, roughly every fifteen minutes until 11.30pm. The 9km journey takes about forty minutes, including immigration. Autobuses Americana run two services daily to **Houston**.

Buses **to the rest of Mexico** include services to Matamoros and Ciudad Victoria; Tampico, Tuxpan and Veracruz on the Gulf coast; and even an overnight bus to Villahermosa (24hr). There is no longer a passenger **train** service from Reynosa.

Matamoros

MATAMOROS, across the Río Grande from the southernmost point of Texas, at Brownsville, is a buzzing, atmospheric town. The busy but compact centre, focused on **plazas** Hidalgo and Allende and the **Mercado Juárez**, on C 9 and C 10, is an accurate introduction to Mexican cities further south. It's also a surprisingly youthful place, with an enlivened entertainment scene: the plazas and shopping streets seem to be almost entirely filled with teenagers, their numbers swollen by Americans beating the Texan age limit on drinking.

If you've got an hour to kill, pop along to the **Museo Casamata**, Santos Degollado at Guatemala (Tues–Sat 8am–5pm, Sun 10.30am–1.30pm; free), a collection of memorabilia from the revolution, in addition to a selection of Huastec ceramics, housed in a fort begun in 1845 to repel invaders from north of the border. When Zachary Taylor stormed in the following year, however, the building was still unfinished.

Playa Bagdad (formerly "Playa Lauro Villar"), Matamoros' pleasant beach, 35km east of town was renamed after the US port of Bagdad, which stood at the mouth of the Río Grande and was at one stage the only port supplying the Confederates during the Civil War. Clean (though watch out for broken glass), and pounded by invigorating surf, it offers the chance for a first (or last) dip in the surf off Mexico's Gulf coast, and is very popular at weekends with Mexican families, who gather in the shade of the palapas that stretch for miles along the sand. There are lots of **seafood restaurants**, but few actually seem to offer much worth eating, so most locals bring picnics or cook on the public barbecues. You'll need half a day to make a worthwhile trip out to the beach, though you can **camp** for free in the sandhills. To get there, take a combi marked "Playa" from the Plaza Allende, which drops you off in the car park by the Administracion. It takes about an hour, and the office has showers (small charge) and lockers where you can safely store your clothes while you swim.

Arrival and information

Stateside, Brownsville **Chamber of Commerce**, 1600 E Elizabeth St (Mon–Fri 8am–5pm; ☎956/542-4341; fax 504-3348), has leaflets on the valley of the Río Grande and sells a map (US$1) of both Brownsville and Matamoros, though with luck you should be able to get a free Matamoros map from the Matamoros **tourist office** (Mon–Fri 9am–7pm; ☎88/12-36-30) right at the Mexican border post, or at the reception areas of the bigger, more expensive hotels. Having paid your quarter toll, walked across the bridge and dealt with immigration, you'll be wanting the casa de cambio at the border before boarding the fixed-price peseros, known here as "maxi taxis", which run frequently along Obregón to the centre and the **bus station**, a long way south (look for "Centro" for Plaza Allende, "Puente Internacional" for the border, or "Central" for the bus station).

Better **currency exchange** facilities exist in the centre: head for Banorte, on Morelos between C 6 and C 7. There are also branches of Bancomer, corner of Matamoros and C 5, and on the plaza itself, and Serfin (all operate Mon–Fri 9am–3pm).

Accommodation

Staying in Matamoros is no problem, with hotels in all price categories, including several good budget choices on Abasolo, the pedestrianized street between C 6 and C 11, a block north of Plaza Hidalgo. There has been a recent upsurge in **more expensive** accommodation: if you're in a large group, it can be worthwhile asking for a suite.

Alameda, Victoria 91 at C 10 (no phone). Lovely, clean and well-furnished rooms with TV, either in the main hotel (US$11) or across the road where they are larger and newer, a/c affairs (US$17). A great deal for Matamoros. ③.

Autel Nieto, C 10 no.1508, between Bravo and Bustamante (☎88/13-08-57). Well-kept, carpeted rooms all with cable TV and telephone. There's a two-bedroom master suite that sleeps nine. Parking space. ④.

Fiesta Gallo, very near the bus station. If you're only interested in a comfortable bed for the night, then this fits the bill. Has a decent restaurant, too. ③.

México, Abasolo 807 between C 8 and C 9 (☎88/12-08-56). Simple, comfortable and the price is right. ②.

Minerva Paula, Matamoros 125 and C 11 (☎88/16-39-66, fax 16-39-71). Luxury option, with wall-to-wall carpeting, a/c and heating, colour TV with cable, restaurant, phones and parking. ④.

Plaza Riviera, corner of Morelos and C 10 (☎88/16-39-98, fax 16-42-99). Very comfortable refurbished hotel split into two buildings, one with parking. About the best in this price range: rooms are light, spacious and feature cable TV. ⑤.

MOVING ON FROM MATAMOROS

The Central Camionera (☎88/12-27-77), equipped with a post office, 24-hour guardería and round-the-clock restaurant – as well as a Gigante supermarket across the road – is well served by buses to the US and to the interior of México.

El Expresso, cheaper than Greyhound, runs to Houston (6hr 30min). Reynosa, Monterrey, Ciudad Victoria and México have frequent departures, and there is also a bus to Puebla. Heading **west**, Transportes Estrella de Oro serves Mexicali, Guadalajara and Mazatlan, while Autotransportes de Oriente covers the **coast route**, with buses to Tampico (7hr), Tuxpan (11hr), Veracruz (16hr) and Villahermosa (24hr).

Ritz, Matamoros 612 and C 5 (☎88/12-11-90). Comfortable a/c hotel; rates include buffet breakfast. There's a suite available for six people. Plus plenty of safe parking. ⑤.

San Francisco, C 10, between Abasolo and Gonzalez (☎88/13-02-79). By far the best central budget hotel; basic and clean rooms with shared showers. ②.

Eating

Although most **restaurants** in Matamoros are fairly expensive – lots cater for cross-border trade – there are plenty of places for cheap filling meals lining C 10, just off Plaza Allende, and C 9 between Matamoros and Bravo. Great coffee and *pan dulce* breakfasts are available from *Los Panchos*, on the Plaza Allende, a café popular with locals. To order simply sit down and the waiter will bring coffee and a basket of *pan dulce*; just pay at the counter for what you've eaten. For lunch, head for *El Chinchonal*, C 9 and Matamoros; for an early dinner try *Las Dos Repúblicas*, nearby on C 9, which dishes up huge plates of tortillas, tacos, quesadillas and the like until 8pm.

The coast route

The eastern seaboard has so little to recommend it that even if you've crossed the border at Matamoros, you'd be well advised to follow the border road west to **Reynosa** and then cut down to Monterrey (see p.151). Unless you're determined to go straight down through Veracruz to the Yucatán by the shortest route, avoiding México altogether, there seems little point in coming this way. Even the time factor is less of an advantage than it might appear on the map – the roads are in noticeably worse repair than those through the heartland, and progress is considerably slower. Beyond Tampico, it's true, you get into an area of great archeological interest, with some good beaches around Veracruz, but this is probably best approached from the capital. Here in the northeast there's plenty of sandy beachfront, but access is difficult, beaches tend to be windswept and scrubby, and the whole area is marred by the consequences of its enormous oil wealth: there are refineries all along the coast, tankers passing close offshore, and a shoreline littered with their discards and spillages. It's also very, very hot.

At the time of the Spanish Conquest this area of the Gulf coast was inhabited by the **Huastecs**, who have given their name to the region around Tampico and the eastern flanks of the Sierra Madre Oriental. Huastec settlement can be dated back some three thousand years: their language differs substantially from the surrounding native tongues, but has close links with the Maya of Yucatán. **Quetzalcoatl**, the feathered serpent god of Mexico, was probably of Huastec origin.

The Huastecs were at their most powerful between 800 and 1200 AD – just before the Aztecs rose to dominance – and were still at war with the Aztecs when the Spanish arrived and found willing allies here. After the successful campaign against Tenochtitlán, the Aztec capital, the Spanish, first under Cortés and later the notorious Nuño de Guzmán, turned on the independent-minded Huastecs, decimating and enslaving their former allies.

Ciudad Victoria

CIUDAD VICTORIA, capital of the state of Tamaulipas, is little more than a place to stop over for a night. It's not unattractive but neither is it interesting, and while the surrounding hill country is a paradise for hunters and fishing enthusiasts, with a huge artificial lake called the **Presa Vicente Guerrero**, others will find little to detain them. The **bus station** (guardería daily 7am–10pm) is a couple of kilometres out and if you arrive late the *Hotel Colonial* (②), left out of the station and then first left, is a good bet as long as you avoid the noisy front rooms. Local buses run into the centre, where most of the town's facilities are concentrated around the zócalo, Plaza Hidalgo. Here there are several **hotels**, including the excellent *Los Monteros*, Hidalgo 962 (☎131/2-03-00; ②), a lovely old colonial building with large rooms that are much cheaper than you might think. Almost equally high standards and similar prices are maintained by a couple of places a block or so away: *Hotel Posada Don Diego*, Juárez 814 Nte (☎131/2-12-79; ②), has some nicer, larger rooms (③).

Tampico

Between Ciudad Victoria and **TAMPICO**, very much the country's busiest port, the vegetation along the road becomes increasingly lush, green and tropical – the Tropic of Cancer passes just south of Ciudad Victoria, and the Río Pánuco forms the border with the steamy Gulf state of Veracruz. As a treasure port in the Spanish empire, Tampico suffered numerous pirate raids and was destroyed in 1684. The rebuilding finally began in 1823, the date of the cathedral's foundation, and in 1828 Spain landed troops in Tampico in a vain and shortlived attempt to reconquer its New World empire. The discovery of oil in 1901 set the seal on Tampico's rise to prominence as the world's biggest oil port in the early years of this century.

The older parts of town, by the docks and former train station, have a distinct Caribbean feel, with peeling, ramshackle clapboard houses and swing-door bars: vivacious and occasionally heavy. Yet Tampico is also a newly wealthy boom town, riding the oil surge with a welter of grand new buildings founded on the income from a huge refinery at the mouth of the Río Pánuco. Downtown, this dual nature is instantly apparent. Within a hundred metres of each other are two plazas: the **Plaza de Armas**, rich and formal, ringed by government buildings, the cathedral (built in the 1930s with money donated by American oil tycoon Edward Doheny) and the smart hotels; and the **Plaza de la Libertad**, raucous, rowdy – there's usually some form of music played from the bandstand each evening – and peopled by wandering salesmen. Ringed by triple-decker wrought-iron verandahs, it has been spruced up in recent years to form an attractive square, almost New Orleans in flavour.

Sadly, the docks pretty much cut off the centre of town from the water, leaving little actually to do but head away from the waterfront – and the seamier sides of the downtown – north to **Ciudad Madero**, Tampico's growing twin town, or onwards to **Playa Miramar**. The journey out is best made by bus or one of the lumbering 1970s Chevy colectivos (marked "Playa"; find them on Lopez de Lara, three blocks east of the Plaza de Armas), which will take you past the graceful arc of the new harbourmouth bridge some 7km to the affluent, new and neatly planned suburbs of Ciudad Madero. Here it's worth calling in to see the Huastec artefacts in the small but excellent **Museo de la Cultura Huasteca** (Mon–Fri 10am–5pm, Sat 10am–3pm; free) in the Tecnológico Madero; get out at the Madero's central plaza, turn left along 1 de Mayo, and the museum is about 1km along, two blocks past the telecom tower. Playa Miramar, Tampico's town beach, lies a further 8km out (same buses and colectivos). Be warned that the water, so close to the refinery and the mouth of the river, is **heavily polluted**, and swimming is not recommended. That said, during the summer months, Semana Santa and weekends year-round, it seems that all Tampico is out here; at other times it's a little dispiriting with only a few run-down hotels, though there are a couple of little restaurants serving good fresh fish and offering showers for a small fee. This is also good **camping** territory, with a stand of small trees immediately behind the beach, and if you have your own transport you can drive miles up the sand to seek out isolation. In fact that's one other disadvantage out here – everyone insists on driving their cars around the beach, most local learners seem to take their first lessons here, and even the bus drives on to the sand to turn round.

Practicalities

Tampico's **bus station** (24hr guardería) is in an unattractive area some 10km north of the city. From here, take a bus or rattling colectivo downtown. Buses back to the camionera leave from the Plaza de la Libertad, at the corner of Olmos and Carranza. The grid-plan downtown area centres on the Plaza de Armas, where the junction of Carranza and Colón marks the point where the cardinal suffixes on street names change. Currently there is no tourist office, and nowhere seems to have maps, but the **post office** is easy to find, upstairs in the "Correos" building in the north side of the Plaza de la Libertad, and there are **banks** on the Plaza de Armas and all through the central area.

One thing you can say for Tampico is that there's no shortage of **hotels**, though most are either expensive or very sleazy. If you don't want the hassle of carrying your bags downtown and searching for a room, then try either of the hotels opposite the bus station: *Hotel La Central,* Rosalio Bustamante 224 (☎12/17-09-18; ②), offers very good value, and *Hotel Santa Elena*, Rosalio Bustamante 303 (☎ & fax 12/13-35-07; ④), less so, though you do get a/c rooms with TV and there's a good, if pricey, restaurant. Downtown, many of the cheaper hotels around the docks, train station and market area operate partly as brothels. Your best option here is the clean and simple *Nuevo Mundo*, at the corner of Olmes and Mendez (no phone; ②), where small, clean rooms are especially good value for lone travellers. For more spacious and brighter rooms, opt for the *Capri*, Juárez Nte 202 (☎ & fax 12/12-26-80; ②), about four blocks north of the plaza; or the slightly less central *Regis*, Madero 605 Ote (☎12/12-02-90; ②), where rooms are carpeted and come with a/c. Better still, head for the Plaza de la Libertad and the more comfortable *Posada del Rey*, Madero Ote 218 (☎12/14-10-24, fax 12-10-77; ④).

There are more than enough good **places to eat** to keep you happy for the day or so you might spend here. The market, a block south of the Plaza de la Libertad, has numerous excellent food stalls: *Cafeteria Kamilo*, on Olmos, is a particular favourite and always clean. In town, there are good breakfasts and comidas at both *Cafeteria Emir*, Olmos 207 Sur, and *Cafe y Neveria Elite*, Diaz Miron 211 Ote, the latter a quiet haven in this noisy town. There's also a *Restaurant Vegetariano*, Altamira 412 Ote, serving bargain veggie comidas from noon to 6pm. But the best dining, if only for the location, is at *La Troya*, in the *Hotel Posada de Rey*, which has a great verandah overlooking the Plaza de la Libertad, a strong seafood menu and two-for-one drinks from 6pm to 8pm.

The road to San Luis Potosí

It is a seven-hour run from Tampico to San Luis Potosí (see p.213) – ideal for a sleep-over on a night bus you might think, but there are a couple of places you could consider breaking the journey. The town of **Río Verde**, surrounded by lush fields of maize, coffee and citrus fruit, is ringed by thermal springs and has the benefit of a small lake, the **Laguna de la Media Luna**, which is popular with snorkellers and divers. Further east still, the highway comes to **Ciudad Valles**, a busy commercial town some 140km from Tampico and the coast.

Monterrey and around

Third city of Mexico, capital of Nuevo León and the nation's industrial stronghold, **MONTERREY** is a contradictory place. The vast network of factories, the traffic, urban sprawl, pollution and ostentatious wealth that characterize the modern city are relatively recent developments; the older parts retain an air of colonial elegance and the setting remains one of great beauty. Ringed by jagged mountain peaks – which sadly serve also to keep in the noxious industrial fumes – Monterrey is dominated above all by one, the Cerro de la Silla or "Saddle Mountain". But what makes Monterrey really outstanding are its most recent developments: the modern architecture and the bold statuary sprouting everywhere, an expression of Mexico at its most confident. Even if it is not to your taste, there is nowhere better to set yourself up for the dramatic contrast of the colonial heartland to come.

In addition to the national and religious holidays, Monterrey celebrates its foundation on September 20, followed by a four-week festival known as the **Feria de**

DOWNTOWN MONTERREY

ACCOMMODATION

Capri	2
Colonial	8
Don Diego	7
Estación	1
Fastos	4
Gran Hotel Ancira	10
Nuevo León	6
Royalty	9
Victoria	3
Youth Hostel	5

Monterrey. The **Festival Alfonso Reyes**, with plenty of music and theatre, is held in the last week of October and the first week in November.

Arrival and information

Monterrey is the transport hub of the northeast, with excellent national and international connections. Flights from the rest of Mexico and from Dallas land at Mariano Escobedo **international airport** (☎8/345-44-32), 6km or so northeast of the city, only accessible by taxi for around US$6–8. On arrival you'll find pricey luggage storage and somewhere to change money.

Scores of **buses** pull into the enormous Central Camionera, northwest of the centre on Av Colón, complete with its own shopping centre, 24-hour guardería and post office. To get from the **bus station** to the central Macroplaza, turn left towards the Cuauhtémoc metro station (see below) and take Line 2, or pick up a #1, #7, #17 or #18 bus heading down Pino Suárez and get off at a suitable intersection: Ocampo, Zaragoza or Juárez, for example. **Trains** from México and Nuevo Laredo arrive some six blocks northwest of the Central Camionera, at the end of Victoria. For transport downtown the best bet is to walk five minutes towards the bus station and pick up the metro at the Central station: turn right out of the train station, left into Victoria then right along Bernardo Reyes.

There's usually someone who can speak English at the helpful **tourist office**, Hidalgo Ote 477 (Tues–Sun 10am–5pm; ☎83/345-08-70 or 345-09-02), right among the fancy hotels, just west of *Hotel Colonial*. They offer a wide variety of maps and leaflets – including the handy quarterly "What's On Monterrey" – and information on hotel prices and local travel agencies. For **tourist information** when dialling from outside Nuevo León, call ☎91/800-83-222; from the US, ☎1-800/235-2438.

You can **change money** at any of the several casas de cambio on Ocampo, between Zaragoza and Juárez (Mon–Fri 9am–1pm & 3–6pm, Sat 9am–12.30pm), and change **travellers' cheques** at banks (almost all with ATMs), most of which are on Padre Mier, right downtown – Banamex, Pino Suárez 933 Nte, which changes money until 1pm, is one example. The main **post office** (Mon–Fri 8am–7pm, Sat 9am–1pm) is in the Palacio Federal at the north end of the Macroplaza.

City transport

Though limited in scope, the best way to get around Monterrey – and certainly between downtown and the bus and train stations – is to take the clean and efficient **metro**, which runs on two lines: Line 1 is elevated and runs east–west above Colón (you see it as soon as you emerge from the bus station); and Line 2 runs underground from the north of the city to the Macroplaza (at the station General I. Zaragoza), connecting with Line 1 at Cuauhtémoc metro stop, right by the bus station. It's simple to use: tickets cost about US$0.30 per journey and are available singly or as a multi-journey card (at a small saving) from the coin-operated ticket machines. The system runs from around 5am until midnight.

The streets of Monterrey are almost solid with **buses**, following routes that appear incomprehensible at first sight. The city authorities have taken steps to resolve the confusion by numbering all the stops (*paradas*), having the fares written on the windscreen and occasionally providing the tourist office with **route plans**, but it still takes a fair amount of confidence to plunge into the system. The old clangers are slowly being replaced by more modern versions known as *panoramicos*, found on useful routes like #1, #17 and #18, which run north–south through town and out to the northern sights.

Accommodation

Accommodation in Monterrey is not especially good value. The majority of the **budget hotels** are near the bus station, mainly on the other side of Av Colón, safest crossed on the footbridge. It's not the most pleasant part of town, permanently noisy and crowded, a touch seedy and some way from the centre, but it's reasonably safe and the metro will whisk you into town in ten minutes. Amado Nervo, heading south off Colón immediately opposite the bus station, holds several possibilities, but it's best to penetrate a little further if you want to avoid the worst of the noise. Even so, you're unlikely to find anything half-decent under US$12.

Further **downtown** rooms are of a different class altogether, in modern and "international" hotels, all with a/c and many with a pool. Geared up for business travellers, they lower their prices slightly at weekends. There's a good concentration in the so-called "zona hotelera" around Plaza Hidalgo.

Gran Hotel Ancira, Hidalgo and Escobedo, on Plaza Hidalgo (☎8/343-20-60 or 800/9-00-90, fax 342-48-06; from USA reserve on ☎1-800/333-3333). Outstanding among the upmarket options, built as a grand hotel before the revolution and full of period elegance. ⑨.

Capri, Victoria 1402 Pte (☎8/375-00-52, fax 372-91-64). Best of the middle-market places in this area. Modern and well kept with a small restaurant and bar, off-street parking, and light, spacious rooms with TV and a/c. ④.

Colonial, Hidalgo Ote 475 (☎8/343-67-91, fax 342-11-69). The small, ageing TV- and a/c-equipped rooms are much less expensive than anything else in the area, but still fairly poor value for money. ⑤.

Don Diego, Montemayor 802 at Matamoros (☎8/342-01-21). About the best value for money of all the hotels, nicely placed on the edge of the Barrio Antiguo, with comfortable and clean a/c rooms, all with TV. ④.

Estación, Victoria 1450 Pte (☎8/375-07-55). One of the nicest in the area with simple, comfortable and clean rooms arranged around a central courtyard. From the train station, turn right then left at *Restaurant Hernandez*; from the bus station turn right, then right up Bernardo Reyes for two blocks, then left into Victoria. ③.

Fastos, Colón 956 Pte, right opposite the bus station (☎8/372-32-50 or 800/718-39-24, fax 372-61-00). Comfortable, modern hotel with large rooms all featuring a/c and satellite TV. Not bad value for Monterrey if you don't mind being so far from downtown. ⑤.

Nuevo León, Amado Nervo 1007 Nte (☎8/374-19-00). About the best value of several places on this street (but only just), and the cheapest rooms for lone travellers. ③.

Royalty, Hidalgo Ote 402 (☎8/340-98-00). Straightforward, middle-of-the-road business-style hotel with a/c rooms, cable TV, gym, jacuzzi and a tiny pool. ⑦.

Victoria, Bernardo Reyes 1205 Nte (☎8/375-48-33). Slightly faded hotel that's about the cheapest decent place around. Could do with a lick of paint, but is friendly, safe and only a block from the bus station with some central rooms that aren't too noisy. From the bus station, turn right along Colón then right onto Bernardo Reyes. ③.

Youth Hostel, Madero 3500 Ote, at the Parque Fundidora (☎8/355-73-80, fax 355-73-70). Huge and soulless but well-maintained place with dorms of differing sizes, all with the mixed blessing of a TV. Excellent value comidas are served and there is even the possibility of camping in the central garden. Midnight curfew. Take Line 1 east to Y Griega metro station, walk 300m west along Colón then left into Prisciliano Elizondo, and the *Villa Deportiva Juvenil* is the white building straight ahead. ①.

The City

First impressions of Monterrey are unprepossessing – the highway roars through the shabby shantytown suburbs and grimy manufacturing outskirts – but the **city centre** is quite a different thing. Here colonial relics are overshadowed by the office blocks and expensive shopping streets of the "zona commercial", and by some extraordinary modern architecture – the local penchant for planting buildings in the ground at bizarre angles is exemplified above all by the **Centro Cultural Alfa** (see below) and the **Instituto Tecnológico**. The city in general rewards a day of wandering, but there are certainly three places worth going out of your way to visit – the old **Obispado**, on a hill overlooking the centre, the giant **Cerveceria Cuauhtémoc** to the north, and the magnificent **Museo de Arte Contemporaneo** (MARCO).

At the heart of Monterrey, if not the physical centre, is the **Macroplaza** (officially the Plaza Zaragoza, and sometimes known as the "Gran Plaza"), which was created by demolishing some six complete blocks of the city centre, opening up a new vista straight through from the intensely modern City Hall to the beautiful red stone Palacio de Gobierno on what used to be Plaza 5 de Mayo. This is Mexican planning at its most extreme: when the political decision comes from the top, no amount of conservationist or social considerations are going to stand in the way, especially as the constitution's "no re-election" decree makes every administrator determined to leave some permanent memorial. The result is undeniably stunning, with numerous lovely fountains, an abundance of striking statuary, quiet parks and shady patios edged by the cathedral, museums and state administration buildings. There are frequent concerts, dances and other entertainments laid on; in the evenings people gravitate here for no better reason than a stroll, and to admire the laser beam that flashes out across the city from the top of the tall, graceful slab of orange concrete known as the **Faro del Comercio**.

West of the Macroplaza are smart shops, multinational offices and swanky hotels, centred on the little **Plaza Hidalgo** – a much more traditional, shady place, with old colonial buildings set around a statue of Miguel Hidalgo. The original Palacio Municipal, now superseded by the modern building, is here, acting today as an occasional cultural centre. Otherwise, the pavement cafés make a pleasant stop-off – though food is expensive. Pedestrianized shopping streets fan out behind, crowded with window-gazing locals.

Another part of the old centre survives to the east and has even grabbed the "**Barrio Antiguo**" tag, which seems appropriate for this increasingly gentrified district populated by chi-chi little galleries, appealingly laid-back cafés and, once the sun has gone down, the city's best nightlife opportunities. The city authorities are even playing ball, installing old-fashioned street lamps and taking measures to calm the traffic.

To the south is the dry bed of the Río Santa Catarina, now largely given over to playing fields, overlooked by the first slopes of the Cerro de la Silla, which rise almost immediately from its far bank.

Of Monterrey's two main **markets** – Juárez and Colón – the latter, on Av de la Constitución, south of the Macroplaza, is more tourist-oriented, specializing in local *artesanía*. Incidentally, the best of Monterrey's **flea markets** (*pulgas*; literally fleas) is also held on Constitución: market days are irregular, but ask any local for details.

Around the Macroplaza: MARCO and the history museum

The **cathedral**, with its one unbalanced tower, is a surprisingly modest edifice, easily dominated by the concrete bulk of the new **City Hall**, squatting on stilts at the southern end of the square. Inside there's a small archeological collection, while in the **Palacio de Gobierno** at the other end of the square is a room devoted to local history. Between the two lie the city's newest and most celebrated museums.

The real star here is the wonderful **Museo de Arte Contemporaneo**, or **MARCO**, at the junction of Zuazua and Ocampo by the cathedral (Tues, Thurs, Fri & Sat 11am–7pm, Wed & Sun 11am–9pm; multiple entry on any one day US$2, free on Wed). You're greeted by Juan Soriano's *La Paloma*, an immense, fat, black dove whose curvaceous lines stand in dramatic contrast to the angular terracotta lines of the museum building. It was built in 1991 to a design by Mexico's leading architect, **Ricardo Legorreta**, whose buildings are all highly individual but share common themes: visitors from the southwest of the USA may recognize the style from various buildings dotted around Texas, Arizona and New Mexico. Inside, none of the floors and walls seem to intersect at the same angle. The vast, at times whimsical, open plan centres on an atrium with a serene pool into which a pipe periodically gushes water: at the sound of the pump gurgling to life, you find yourself drawn to watch the ripple patterns subside. You might imagine that such a courageous building would overwhelms its contents, but if anything the opposite is true.

Apart from a couple of monumental sculptures tucked away in courtyards, there is no permanent collection, but the standards maintained by the temporary exhibits are phenomenally high. A key factor in this is undoubtedly the bias towards Latin American, and particularly Mexican artists, who are currently producing some of the world's most innovative and inspiring work. The quality art bookshop and fancy café are both worth visiting, but don't fail to stop by the lovely bar, right by the central pool.

Just north of MARCO lies the city's newest museum, the **Museo de Historia Mexicana**, Dr Coss 445 Sur (Tues–Thurs 11am–7pm, Fri–Sun 11am–8pm; Tues free, Wed–Fri US$1.30, Sat & Sun, US$0.65), another bold architectural statement, though save for the double-helix staircase, a less successful one. The contents, too, seem oddly uninspired. All the ingredients appear to be there – displays on Mexico's ancient civilizations, an extensive array of traditional costumes, interactive computer consoles and the story of the revolution, along with associated paraphernalia – but it is strangely unaffecting.

El Obispado

The elegant and recently renovated **Obispado**, the old Bishop's Palace, tops Chepe Vera hill to the west of the centre, but well within the bounds of the city. Its commanding position – affording great views when haze and smog allow – has made it an essential target for Monterrey's many invaders. Built in the eighteenth century, it became in turn a barracks, a military hospital and a fortress: among its more dramatic exploits, the Obispado managed to hold out for two days after the rest of the city had fallen to the Texan general Zachary Taylor in 1846. The excellent **museum** inside (Tues–Sun 10am–5pm; US$2) records its long history with a little of everything: religious and secular art, arms from the War of Independence, revolutionary pamphlets and old carriages.

You get to the Obispado along Padre Mier, passing on the way the monumental modern church of **La Purisima**. Take the R4 bus, alighting where it turns off Padre Mier, then continue to the top of the steps at the end of Padre Mier and turn left; it's a ten-minute walk in all. Return to the centre using any bus heading east on Hidalgo.

North of the centre: Cerveceria Cuauhtémoc, Parque Niños Héroes and the glass museum

If you're thirsty after all this, a visit to Monterrey's massive **Cerveceria Cuauhtémoc** is (Cuauhtémoc Brewery) all but compulsory. This is where they make the wonderful Bohemia and Tecate beers you'll find throughout Mexico (as well as the rather bland Carta Blanca), and somehow it seems much more representative of Monterrey than any of the city's prouder buildings. Free guided tours of the brewery run almost constantly throughout the day, and of course you are rewarded afterwards with free beer amidst strutting peacocks in the pleasant gardens outside – where the blackened tree trunks bear witness to the city's industrial pollution. Tours start across the road from the brewery at the **Museo de Monterrey**, Alfonso Reyes 2202 Nte, 1km north of the bus station (Mon–Fri 9am–5pm, Sat 9am–3pm; free), and this is the sign to look for if you want to find the place. Inside there's a museum of brewing, a rather incongruous art gallery and a much more congruous Sporting Hall of Fame, commemorating the heroes of Mexican baseball. The *Café Museo*, in the museum, serves an excellent (though meaty) set lunch, with more beer included. To get there take Line 2 to its northern terminus (General Anaya station) and walk 300m south.

Some 3km north of the brewery lies the vast **Parque Niños Héroes** (Tues–Sun 10am–3pm; US$0.50), chiefly a gentle retreat from the city best visited at weekends when the throng of Mexican families enjoying themselves goes some way towards masking the slightly run-down nature of the place. Among the semi-formal gardens and boating lake are minor sights (all free with park entry) such as the spherical aviary, a transport museum with fifty-odd vintage and classic cars and trucks, and the **Pinacoteca**, a small art gallery featuring mostly missable oils and sculpture by Nuevo León artists. The main attraction here are some fine pieces by Fidias Elizondo, notably the arching female nude "La Ola".

Architecturally more compelling is the **Biblioteca Magna Universitaria**, Alfonso Reyes 4000 (Mon–Fri 8am–5pm, Sat 9am–1pm; free), in the northern end of the park but only accessible from the street. This is another fine example of the work of Ricardo Ligorreta (see p.154), and though the design is completely different, the parallels to the MARCO building are strong: in fact it sometimes feels more like an art gallery than a library. Again, it is a constantly surprising building, with squares within circles and sudden courtyards, but with an overall sense of space and fun.

The park and library entrances can be reached on **buses** #17 and #18 from Padre Mier or on Cuauhtémoc outside the Cuauhtémoc metro station. To get back, take the same bus from Barragan on the western side of the park: the exits on this side are only sporadically open and you may have to make a long detour right round the park.

For decades, glass production has been one of Monterrey's industrial strengths (for one thing, it has to provide all the beer bottles), and to tap into the long history of Mexican glassware, pop along to the **Museo del Vidrio**, at the corner of Zaragoza and Magallanes (daily except Thurs 9am–6pm; free). A small but select display of pieces over the centuries and a mock up of a nineteenth-century apothecary only act as a prelude to the attic, where modern, mostly cold-worked glass sculpture is shown to advantage: Raquel Stolarski's *Homage to Marilyn* is particularly fine. To get there take Line 1 to "Del Golfo" station, walk two blocks west then two blocks north up Zaragoza.

South of the centre: Centro Cultural Alfa

Like some vision from H.G. Wells' *The War of the Worlds*, the cylindrical form of the **Centro Cultural Alfa**, Roberto Gaza Sada 1000, 8km south of the city centre (Tues–Fri 3–9pm, Sat 2–9pm, Sun noon–9pm; US$4), rises out of the ground at a rakish angle providing an unusual venue for Omnimax films. If you've never seen one of these superwide-vision movies before, or have kids to entertain, it may be worth the trip out here. Otherwise, the few science demonstrations and hands-on experiments aren't really worth the bother. If you do come, don't miss Rufino Tamayo's stained glass opus, outside the main complex, in the Universe Pavilion. The only way to get here is on the **free shuttle bus**, which leaves from a dedicated stop at the western end of the Alameda on Washington. Times vary, but it runs roughly on the hour from 3pm to 7pm and also on the half-hour at weekends.

Eating, drinking and nightlife

Monterrey's **restaurants** cater to hearty, meat-eating norteños, with *cabrito al pastor* or the regional speciality *cabrito asado* (whole roasted baby goat) given pride of place in window displays. You'll find scores of tiny bars and rather sleazy places to eat near the bus station – especially at the little market just south of Colón – but up here your best bet is to stick to one of the safer-looking fast-food joints. For fresh produce you could do worse than join the locals at the **Mercado Juárez**, north of the Gran Plaza on Aramberri. In the **centre** you can do a lot better, but you also pay more, especially at the dozens of places around the Gran Plaza.

After dark, the place to head is the Barrio Antiguo, five square blocks of cobbled streets bounded by Dr Coss, Matamoros and Constitución. On Friday and Saturday evenings (9pm–2am), the police block off the junctions leaving the cobbled streets – especially Padre Mier and Madero – to hordes of bright young things surging back and forth in search of the best vibe. You're best off taking their lead, but among specific recommendations try *Constanza*, Morelos 859 Ote, *Las Cantatas*, Morelos 1006 Ote, and *Reloj*, Padre Mier 860 Ote, all very popular and charging US$2–5 entry (less or nothing at all on Wed and Thurs). In the Barrio, too, are a few late-closing cafés (see below), which make the best destinations for a quieter evening.

Restaurants, cafés and bars

La Casa del Maiz, Abasolo 870b Ote at Dr Coss, Barrio Antiguo. Airy, modern place taking its decorative cues from MARCO down the street, and serving unusual Mexican dishes, either with or without meat. Try the *memelas la maica*, a kind of thick tortilla topped with a richly seasoned spinach and cheese salsa. Closed Sunday evenings and all day Monday.

Café Paraiso, Morelos 958 Ote, Barrio Antiguo. Late-closing multi-roomed café and bar with local artworks on the walls, serving a fabulous range of coffees, delicious and huge tortas with fries (US$4) and fairly pricey drinks, though there is a two-for-one happy-afternoon from 1pm to 4pm daily.

Coliseo Cafetería, Colón 235. Clean and cheerful 24-hour place near the bus station, serving regular Mexican staples at low prices.

El Infinito, Raymondo Jardón 904 Ote, Barrio Antiguo. A surprising little find, with sofas and a small library (some English books), serving some of Monterrey's best espressos and lattes. Cakes and sandwiches, too, and at weekends there is often live acoustic music.

Las Monjitas, Morelos 240 Ote at Galeana. Waitresses dressed as nuns dish up Mexican steaks and a catholic selection of quality antojitos, including house specialities such as *platillo Juan Pablo II*, an artery-hardening concoction combining salami, pork, bacon, peppers, grilled cheese and guacamole. Beautiful azulejos on the walls make the slightly elevated prices worthwhile. There's a second branch a couple of blocks along at Escobedo 913 Sur.

Restaurante Vegetariano Superbom, upstairs at Padre Mier 300, near Galeana, Zona Centro. Excellent vegetarian comidas (US$4), and an all-you-can-eat buffet (US$6) from noon until 5pm. Closed Sat.

Sanborn's, Morelos near the Plaza Hidalgo, Zona Centro. As safe a bet as ever for sandwiches and snacks: great if your stomach's feeling homesick.

La Tumba, Padre Mier 827 Ote, Barrio Antiguo (☎8/345-68-60). Trendy cybercafé with live acoustic music on Thursday, Friday and Saturday nights (US$2–5 cover) and Internet access at US$3 per hour.

Listings

American Express American Express Travel Service, San Pedro 215 Nte, Colonia del Valle (Mon–Fri 9am–6pm, Sat 9am–noon; ☎8/318-33-85) holds clients' mail, and replaces and cashes travellers' cheques.

Bookstores Sanborn's, on Morelos near the Macroplaza (daily 9am–10pm), holds a good selection of English-language books, magazines and guides, as does the American Bookstore, Garza Sada 2404a (Mon–Fri 9am–7pm, Sat 10am–7pm, Sun 10am–3pm).

Car rental If you fancy renting wheels to get out to the sights immediately around Monterrey, or to explore the mountains, head for Plaza Hidalgo where all the main agencies have offices. Flash, Ocampo 325 Pte (☎8/344-70-02), are currently about the cheapest, charging about US$50 a day plus US$13 per 100km. If you're planning to cover some distance, Budget, Hidalgo 433 Ote (☎8/340-41-00), who charge US$70–75 a day all-inclusive, might be a better bet.

Cinema There are handy mainstream showings at Cuauhtémoc 4, corner of Cuauhtémoc and Washington, close to the Alameda; and Voladero Espoch Cultural, Padre Mier 1099 Ote at Naranja (☎8/343-35-01), shows arthouse films every Sunday at 6pm. The schedule is usually posted in *Café Paraiso*.

Consulates Canada, Ground Floor, Zaragoza 1300, Zona Centro (Mon–Fri 9am–1pm & 2.30–5.30pm; ☎8/344-32-00); USA, Constitución 411 Pte. (Mon–Fri 8am–2pm; ☎8/345-21-20).

Emergencies Angeles Verdes (☎8/340-21-13); Cruz Roja (☎8/375-12-12); Cruz Verde (☎8/311-00-33); police (☎8/342-45-46).

Internet access See *La Tumba* under "Restaurants, cafés and bars", p.157.

Laundry Lavandería Automática, Padre Mier 1102 Ote at Antillón (Mon–Sat 8am–7pm).

Photographic supplies There are photo developing places selling print film all over the place, but for specialist needs head for Photos de Llano, Padre Mier 565 (Mon–Sat 9am–8pm).

Travel agencies Several local agencies offer tours of the city and to surrounding attractions: try Cantera Travel (☎492/2-90-65) in the Mercado Gonzales Ortega mall.

Around Monterrey

After a day or two the bustle of Monterrey can get to you, but you can escape to the surprisingly wild and beautiful country that surrounds it. Without your own vehicle, however, getting around the sights in the vicinity can be awkward. An exception is getting out to the subterranean caverns of **Grutas de Garcia**, which despite some impressive stalactites and stalagmites and an underground lake, have lost some of their appeal through overdevelopment. Only 40km west of Monterrey near the village of **VILLA GARCIA**, they are a popular outing from Monterrey, especially at weekends, when hundreds cram onto the funicular tram (US$5) from the village; you can walk there in about thirty minutes. Buses run several times daily to Villa Garcia from outside the camionera, about a block and a half towards the train station; buy your ticket either from the Transportes Monterrey–Saltillo office or on the bus.

There's wilder country to the south in the **Parque Nacional Cumbres de Monterrey**, centred on the **Cañon de la Huasteca**, about 20km east of Monterrey, an impressive mountain ravine some 300m deep with vertical cliffs that have become a playground for committed rock climbers. Within it is the **La Huasteca** "Ecological Park" (daily 9am–6pm; cars US$1, pedestrians US$0.15) with barbecue pits, picnic areas and a pool for children, all designed to cope with the weekend influx from the city.

The trip to the 25-metre **Cascada Cola de Caballo** (Horsetail Falls), 35km south of Monterrey, is only really worthwhile after the rains – you can hire horses and burros to ride in the hilly Parque Nacional Cumbres de Monterrey, where there are views from the top of the falls and plenty of opportunity for hiking and camping. To get here by bus, take a Lineas Amarillas service to **El Cercado**, where colectivos wait to take you to the falls: once there, horse-buggy rides are available, and there are lovely swimming spots. With permission from the Administracion you can camp for free.

Another alternative is to head up to the **Mesa Chipinque**, a mountain plateau just 18km from Monterrey with famous views back over the city. Here again you can hire horses (from the enormously flash *Motel Chipinque*) to explore the hinterland. If you want an **organized trip** to the caves or falls, try OSETUR (☎8/347-15-99), whose very

---

MOVING ON FROM MONTERREY

You'll have no trouble getting an onward bus from the **Central Camionera** at almost any time of day or night; as well as the border destinations (including Ciudad Juárez) and México, there are buses to points all around the country, including Guadalajara and Mazatlán. The bus station is divided into six "salas", or halls, each broadly serving different points of the compass; just ask at the first one you come to and someone will direct you to the right sala. Monterrey is also a good place to pick up transport into Texas: Transportes del Norte has direct connections with the Greyhound system with transfers in Nuevo Laredo; and Americanos run direct to San Antonio (7hr; US$25), Houston (10hr; US$35) and Dallas (12hr; US$40).

As for **trains**, a joint first- and second-class train leaves for Saltillo, San Luis Potosí and México just after midnight on Wednesday, Friday and Sunday mornings and another runs in the opposite direction to Nuevo Laredo at 2.50am on Tuesday, Thursday and Saturday. The ticket office opens two hours before departures.

reasonably priced day-excursions depart from Ocampo behind the *Gran Hotel Ancira* in Monterrey.

Saltillo

SALTILLO, capital of the state of Coahuila, is the place to head for if you can't take the hustle of Monterrey. Lying just 85km to the southwest, down a fast road that cuts through the Sierra Madre Oriental and a high desert of yucca and Joshua trees, it's infinitely quieter and, at 1600m above sea level, feels refreshingly cool and airy.

There's not a great deal to do in Saltillo, but it's a great place to stroll around admiring the smattering of beautiful buildings and soaking up some atmosphere. Two contrasting, and almost adjoining, squares grace the centre of town: the **Plaza Acuña** marks the rowdy heart of the modern city, surrounded by crowded shopping streets, while the old **Plaza de Armas** is formal, tranquil, illuminated at night and sometimes hosts music performances. Facing the Palacio de Gobierno across a flagged square, the magnificent eighteenth-century **cathedral** is one of the most beautiful in northern Mexico, with an elaborately carved Churrigueresque facade and doorways, an enormous bell tower and a smaller clock tower. On the south side of the square the **Instituto Coahuilense de Cultura** (Tues–Sun 9am–7pm; free) hosts often diverting temporary exhibits by Coahuila artists.

The town's oldest streets fan out from the square, with some fine old houses still in private hands. One historic building worth seeking out is the carefully preserved old **Ayuntamiento** (town hall) on the corner of Aldama and Hidalgo. The walls of the courtyard and the staircase are adorned with murals depicting the history of Saltillo from prehistoric times to the 1950s. Calle Victoria spurs west off the square, passing a few hundred metres of the city's major shops and cinemas, on the way to the **Alameda**, a shaded, tree-lined park, peopled with students looking for a peaceful spot to work: there are several language schools in Saltillo as well as a university and technical institute, and, in summer especially, numbers of American students come here to study Spanish.

Saltillo is famous, too, for its **sarapes**, and there are several small shops where (at least on weekdays) you can watch the manufacturing process – the best is tucked at the back of the *artesanía* shop El Sarape de Saltillo, Hidalgo 305 Sur (Mon–Sat 9am–1pm & 3–7pm). Sadly the old ways are vanishing fast, and most now use artificial fibres and chemical dyes: all too many of those on sale in the market are mass-produced in virulent clashing colours.

Practicalities

City buses (marked "Centro/Camionera") run from Saltillo's main **bus station** (no guardería), 3km southwest of the centre, to the cathedral on the Plaza de Armas, and onwards a couple more stops to the Plaza Acuña, right at the heart of things. The **train station** is closer in, just a few blocks southwest of the Alameda, but still a twenty-minute walk. Strategically positioned **maps of the city** – at the bus and train stations and on both squares – help orientation. The **post office** is at Victoria 453 and there are long-distance phones and banks with ATMs all over the centre of town.

Most of the better-value **hotels** are in the side streets immediately around Plaza Acuña: both *Hotel Jardín* (or *de Avila*), Padre Flores 211 (☎84/12-59-16; ②), and *Hotel Bristol*, Aldama 405 Pte (☎84/10-43-37; ②), are good-value budget places, the latter having the edge with cable TV. If you can afford a little more and want to savour some olonial atmosphere, have a look at the *Urdiñola*, Victoria Pte 207 (☎84/14-09-40; ④), with its tiled open lobby dominated by a wide staircase flanked by suits of armour, and fountains playing amidst the greenery of the courtyard.

Restaurants in Saltillo tend to close early, and the ones in the centre mainly cater for office workers and students. There are, as always, plenty of cheap places to eat around the **Mercado Juárez**, beside the Plaza Acuña, which is a decent market in its own right – as a tourist you are treated fairly and not constantly pressed to buy. The *Café Victoria*, on Padre Flores just south of Plaza Acuña, is good for breakfasts, bulging tortillas and comidas corridas. At the western end of Victoria by the Alameda, *Terazza Romana* serves up toothsome pasta dishes for around US$6 and fine pizzas for a dollar or two more. If you're stocking up for a journey, pick up wholemeal bread, great carrot cake and the like from *Natura*, Victoria 668.

From Saltillo you can head **southeast to Zacatecas** or follow the direct route **to México** via San Luis, passing through Matehuala (with the possibility of branching off to the mountain ghost town of Real De Catorce) and Querétaro. Going through Zacatecas, though slower, gives you the chance to visit more of the beautiful colonial cities north of the capital. For San Luis Potosí and points south to México, you'll need to be at the train station at 2.45am on Wednesday, Friday and Sunday. The **northbound** train from Saltillo to Monterrey and Nuevo Laredo passes at around 11.30pm on Monday, Wednesday and Friday.

FIESTAS

Carnival (the week before Lent, variable Feb–March) is at its best in the Caribbean atmosphere of **Tampico** (Tamaulipas) – also in **Ciudad Victoria** (Tam) and **Monterrey** (Nuevo León).

MARCH
19 FESTIVAL DE SAN JOSÉ. Celebrated in **Ciudad Victoria** (Tam).
21 Ceremonies to commemorate the birth of Benito Juárez in **Matamoros** (Coahuila), near Torreón.

APRIL
12 Processions and civic festival in honour of the nineteenth-century resettlement of **Tampico** (Tam), with dress of that era. Celebrations continue for two weeks.
27 FERIA DEL AZUCAR. In **Ciudad Mante** (Tam), south of Ciudad Victoria; very lively with bands, dancing and fireworks.

MAY
FERIA COMERCIAL. In **Monterrey** (NL), a trade fair leavened with sporting events, bullfights, dances and public spectacles.
3 DÍA DE LA SANTA CRUZ. **Tula** (Tam), between Ciudad Victoria and San Luis Potosí, stages a fiesta with traditional dance. In **Gómez Palacio** (Durango), the start of an agricultural and industrial fair that lasts two weeks.

15 DÍA DE SAN ISIDRO. Observed in **Guadalupe de Bravos** (Chihuahua), on the border near Ciudad Juárez, with dances all day and parades all night. Similar celebrations in **Matamoros** (Coah) and **Arteaga** (Coah), near Saltillo.

JUNE
13 DÍA DE SAN ANTONIO DE PADUA. Marked in **Tula** (Tam) by religious services followed by pastoral plays and traditional dances. Colourful native dancing, too, in **Vicente Guerrero** (Dgo), between Durango and Zacatecas.
25 DÍA DE SANTIAGO. The start of a week-long fiesta in **Altamira** (Tam), near Tampico.

JULY
4 DÍA DE NUESTRA SEÑORA DEL REFUGIO. Marked by dancing and pilgrimages in **Matamoros** (Coah).
8 Durango (Dgo) celebrates its founders' day, coinciding with the feria and crafts exhibitions.
23 FERIA DE LA UVA. In **Cuatro Cienegas** (Coah), a spa town near Monclova.

AUGUST
6 Fiesta in **Jiménez** (Chih) with traditional dances, religious processions and a fair. Regional dancing, too, in **Saltillo** (Coah).

9 Exuberant FERIA DE LA UVA in **Parras** (Coah), between Saltillo and Torreón.

13 Saltillo (Coah) begins its annual feria, lively and varied.

SEPTEMBER

8 DÍA DE LA VIRGEN DE LOS REMEDIOS Celebrated with parades and traditional dances in **Santa Barbara** (Chih), near Hidalgo del Parral, and **San Juan del Río** (Dgo), between here and Durango.

10 Dancing from before dawn and a parade in the evening mark the fiesta in **Ramos Arizpe** (Coah), near Saltillo.

11 Major feria on the border at **Nuevo Laredo** (Tam).

15–16 INDEPENDENCE. Festivities everywhere, but the biggest in **Monterrey** (NL).

OCTOBER

25 Joint celebrations between the border

town of **Ciudad Acuña** (Coah) and its Texan neighbour Del Rio. Bullfights and parades.

NOVEMBER

3 DÍA DE SAN MARTIN DE PORRES is the excuse for a fiesta, with native dances, in **Tampico** (Tam) and nearby **Altamira** (Tam).

DECEMBER

4 Santa Barbara (Chih) celebrates its saint's day.

8–12 Fiesta with dancing virtually non-stop in **Matamoros** (Coah).

12 DÍA DE NUESTRA SEÑORA DE GUADALUPE. A big one everywhere, especially in **Guadalupe de Bravos** (Chih), **El Palmito** (Dgo), between Durango and Parral, **Ciudad Anahuac** (NL) in the north of the state, and **Abasolo** (NL), near Monterrey. **Monterrey** itself attracts many pilgrims at this time.

travel details

BUSES

Services on the chief routes to and from the frontier (Ciudad Juárez–Chihuahua–Torreón/Durango and from the border to Monterrey–Saltillo–San Luis Potosí/Zacatecas) are excellent, with departures day and night. There are also direct services to México from just about everywhere. The best lines are generally, on the central route, Omnibus de Mexico and Transportes Chihuahuenses, in the east Frontera, Transportes del Norte and Autobuses del Oriente (ADO). Estrella Blanca, ostensibly a second-class company, often beats them all for frequency of services and efficiency. What follows should be taken as a minimum.

Chihuahua to: Ciudad Juárez (at least hourly; 5hr); Creel (every 2hr; 4hr); Jiménez (roughly hourly; 3hr); México (every 2hr; 18hr); Nuevo Casas Grandes (5 daily; 4hr 30min); Zacatecas (every 2hr; 12hr).

Ciudad Acuña to: Monterrey (4 daily; 8hr); Piedras Negras (hourly; 1hr 30min); Saltillo (8 daily; 7hr).

Ciudad Juárez to: Chihuahua (at least hourly; 5hr); Durango (at least hourly; 16hr); Jiménez (at least hourly; 8hr); México (10 daily; 24hr); Nuevo Casas Grandes (hourly; 4hr); Parral (at least hourly; 10hr); Torreón (at least hourly; 12hr); Zacatecas (every 2hr; 16hr).

Ciudad Victoria to: Matamoros (hourly; 4-5hr); Monterrey (hourly; 4hr); Tampico (hourly or better; 3hr); Reynosa (9 daily; 4-5hr).

Creel to: Chihuahua (7 daily; 4-5hr); Ciudad Juárez direct (1 daily; 9hr); Guachochi (3 daily; 3hr).

Durango to: Aguascalientes (20 daily; 6hr); Ciudad Juárez (at least hourly; 12-14hr); Fresnillo (11 daily; 3hr); Mazatlán (9 daily; 7hr); México (14 daily; 12-13hr); Monterrey (20 daily; 9hr); Parral (9 daily; 6hr); Torreón (6 daily; 4hr 30min); Zacatecas (roughly hourly; 4hr 30min).

Guachochi to: Chihuahua (6 daily; 7–9hr); Creel (1 daily; 3hr); Parral (6 daily; 3hr 30min).

Matamoros to: Ciudad Victoria (hourly; 4–5hr); Monterrey (hourly; 4hr); Reynosa (every 45min; 2hr); Tampico (hourly; 7–8hr).

Monterrey to: Ciudad Victoria (hourly; 4hr); Dallas, TX (3 daily; 12hr); Guadalajara (15 daily; 12hr); Houston, TX (3 daily; 10hr); Matamoros (hourly; 4hr); Matehuala (12 daily; 4–5hr); México (hourly; 12hr); Nuevo Laredo (every 30min; 3hr); Piedras Negras (7 daily; 5–7 hr); Reynosa (every 30min; 3hr); Saltillo (constantly; 1hr 30min); San Antonio, TX (4 daily; 7hr); San Luis Potosí (12 daily; 7hr); Tampico (12 daily; 7–8hr); Zacatecas (hourly; 6hr).

Nuevo Casa Grandes to: Chihuahua (hourly; 4hr 30min); Ciudad Juárez (hourly; 4hr).

Nuevo Laredo to: Acapulco (2 daily; 20hr); Austin, TX (14 daily; 7hr); Dallas, TX (14 daily; 9hr); Guadalajara (5 daily; 14hr); Houston, TX (9 daily; 7hr); México (5 daily; 15hr); Monterrey (every 30min; 3hr); Piedras Negras (5 daily; 3hr); Reynosa (8 daily; 4hr); Saltillo (8 daily; 4–5hr); San Antonio (hourly; 4hr); San Luis Potosí (8 daily; 12hr); Tampico (2 daily; 10hr); Zacatecas (5 daily; 8hr).

Parral to: Chihuahua (roughly hourly; 4hr); Durango (9 daily; 6hr); Guachochi (6 daily; 3hr 30min).

Piedras Negras to: Ciudad Acuña (hourly; 1hr 30min); México (3 daily; 18hr); Monterrey (7 daily; 5–7hr); Nuevo Laredo (5 daily; 3hr); Saltillo (12 daily; 7hr).

Reynosa to: Ciudad Victoria (9 daily; 4–5hr); Matamoros (every 45min; 2hr); México (6 daily; 14–16hr); Monterrey (every 30min; 3hr); Nuevo Laredo (8 daily; 4hr); San Luis Potosí (9 daily; 9–10hr); Tampico (hourly; 7hr); Zacatecas (10 daily; 9hr).

Saltillo to: Ciudad Acuña (8 daily; 7hr); Guadalajara (13 daily; 10hr); Matehuala (8 daily; 2hr 30min); Mazatlán (4 daily; 12hr); México (8 daily; 12hr); Monterrey (constantly; 1hr 30min); Nuevo Laredo (8 daily; 4–5hr); Piedras Negras (12 daily; 7hr).

Tampico to: Ciudad Victoria (hourly or better; 3hr); México (every 1–2hr; 8hr); Matamoros (hourly; 7–8hr); Monterrey (12 daily; 7–8hr); Nuevo Laredo (2 daily; 10hr); San Luis Potosí (11 daily; 7hr); Veracruz (8 daily; 9hr).

Torreón to: Ciudad Juárez (at least hourly; 12hr); Zacatecas (10 daily; 6hr).

TRAINS

The Copper Canyon railway (see p.125) is the big attraction in this region – one of the few train journeys in Mexico that you might want to take simply for the experience.

There are also two main lines heading south from the border to México. From Ciudad Juárez (see p.124) a daily service sets off for the capital, via Chihuahua, Zacatecas and Querétaro, while from Nuevo Laredo there are three trains a week to Monterrey, Saltillo, San Luis Potosí and México. Trains are excruciatingly slow and unreliable, often taking far longer than the scheduled 24 hours or so from the border to the capital. As usual with Mexican trains, it's always best to check timetables.

PLANES

There are frequent flights from most of the major cities to the capital – Chihuahua, Monterrey and Tampico all have several a day. From Monterrey you can also fly to Guadalajara and Acapulco, and there are international services to Dallas, Houston, San Antonio and Chicago. From Nuevo Laredo you can get to the capital and Guadalajara.

CHAPTER THREE

GUADALAJARA TO MÉXICO

Separated from the country's colonial heartland by the craggy peaks of the Sierra Madre, the land that stretches from Guadalajara to México, through the semitropical states of **Jalisco** and **Michoacán**, has an unhurried ease that marks it out from the rest of the country. Cursed by a complex landscape – now lofty plain, now rugged sierra – the area is, nevertheless, blessed with supreme fertility and is as beautiful and varied as any Mexico has to offer, from fresh pine woods and cool pastures to lush tropical forest. Both states stretch all the way to the coast, with resorts and beaches that range from the sophistication of Puerto Vallarta to the simplicity of Playa Azúl: this coastal strip is covered elsewhere in this book, starting on p.352.

Something of a backwater until well into the eighteenth century, the high valleys of Michoacán and Jalisco were left to develop their own strong regional traditions and solid agricultural economy: there's a wealth of local produce, both agricultural and traditionally manufactured, from avocados to tequila, glassware to guitars. Relative isolation has also made the region a bastion of conservatism – in the years following the Revolution, the Catholic *Cristero* counter-revolutionary guerrilla movement enjoyed its strongest support here.

Easy-going **Guadalajara** – Mexico's second city – is the area's best-known destination, packed with elegant buildings and surrounded by scenic country. Further afield the land spreads, spectacularly green and mountainous, studded with volcanoes and lakes, including **Lago de Chapala**, where D.H. Lawrence wrote *The Plumed Serpent*. There are also some superb colonial relics, especially in the towns of **Morelia** and **Pátzcuaro**, although in the latter it's the majestic setting and the richness of Indian traditions that first call your attention. This powerful indigenous culture still in evidence more than compensates for the paucity of physical remains from the pre-Hispanic era, though the ruins of **Tzintzuntzán** on Lago Pátzcuaro are certainly impressive. **Fiestas** around here – and there are many – are among the most vital in Mexico, and there's a legacy of village handicrafts that survives from the earliest days of the Conquest.

Jalisco and Michoacán are among the most serene states in the country – relaxing, easy to get about, and free of urban hassle. Add to this the fact that Jalisco is the home of **mariachi** and of **tequila** and you've got a region where you could easily spend a couple of weeks exploring without even beginning to see it all.

GUADALAJARA AND JALISCO

Guadalajara dominates the state of **Jalisco** in every way – not just the capital, it is quite simply the main attraction. If you spend any time in the region, you're inevitably

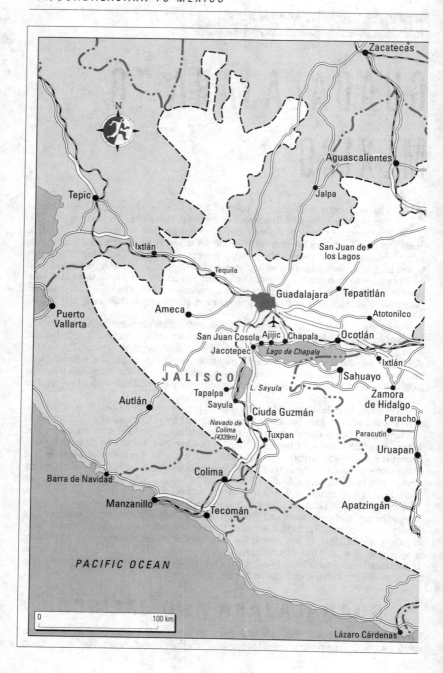

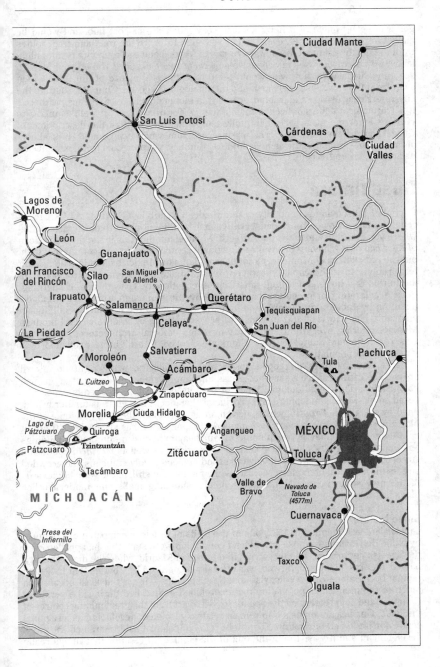

going to spend much of it here: it's also very much a transport hub, and would be almost impossible to avoid, even should you wish to. Here the road and train routes from the northwest meet the onward routes to México and the country's central highlands, with a growing web of expensive new *cuota* roads to speed you on your way. To see only Guadalajara, however, would be to miss the real nature of the state, which away from the capital is green, lush and mountainous. **Lago de Chapala**, south of the city, offers easy escape and tranquil scenery; in mountain villages like Tapalpa, there's fresh air and rural life still lived at the old tempo. **Tequila** offers . . . well, tequila. The **climate** is for the most part delightfully temperate, too. Though the descriptions of Guadalajara as the "city of eternal spring" are somewhat exaggerated, it is almost always warm – on much the same latitude as Bombay, yet protected from extremes by its altitude, around 1600m.

Guadalajara

Capital of Jalisco and second city of the Mexican Republic, **GUADALAJARA** has a reputation as a slower, more conservative and traditional place than México, somewhere you can stop and catch your breath. Many claim that this is the most Mexican of Mexican cities, having evolved as a regional centre of trade and commerce, without the imbalances of Monterrey's industrial giants or México's chaotic scale. Being less frenetic than the capital, however, doesn't make it peaceful, and by any standards this is a huge, sprawling, noisy and energetic city. Growth has, if anything, been accelerating in recent years, boosted by the campaign to reduce México's pollution by encouraging people and industry to move to the provinces. Still, it's an enjoyable place to visit and in which to see something of traditional and modern Mexico, offering everything from museums and colonial architecture, to magnificent revolutionary murals by José Clemente Orozco, to a nightlife enlivened by a large student population.

Parks, little squares and open spaces dot Guadalajara, while right downtown around the cathedral are a series of plazas unchanged since the days of the Spanish colonization. This small colonial heart of the city can still, at weekends especially, recall an old-world atmosphere and provincial elegance. The centre is further brightened by the **Plaza Tapatía**, which, driven straight through the heart of some of the oldest parts less than ten years ago, manages to look as if it has always been there. It creates new sight-lines between some of Guadalajara's most monumental buildings and opens out the city's historical core to pedestrians, as well as *mariachi* bands and street theatre. Around this relatively unruffled nucleus revolve raucous and crowded streets more typical of modern Mexico, while further out still, in the wide boulevards of the new suburbs, you'll find smart hotels, shopping malls and modern office blocks.

Some history

Guadalajara was founded in 1532, one of the fruits of a vicious campaign of Conquest by Nuño de Guzmán – whose cruelty and corruption were such that he appalled even the Spanish authorities, who threw him into prison in Madrid, where he died. The city, named after his birthplace, thrived, was officially recognized by Charles V in 1542, and rapidly became one of the colony's most Spanish cities – in part at least because so much of the indigenous population had been killed or had fled during the period of Conquest and suppression by the Spaniards. Set apart from the great mining centres of the Bajío, Guadalajara managed to remain relatively isolated, developing as a regional centre for trade and agriculture. The tight reins of colonial rule restrained the city's development, and it wasn't until the end of the eighteenth century that things really took off, as the colonial monopolies began to crumble. Between 1760 and 1803 the city's population tripled to reach some 35,000, and a new university was established, as the city became famous for the export of wheat, hides, cotton and wool.

When the empire finally fell apart, Guadalajara supported Hidalgo's Independence movement and briefly served as his capital, becoming capital of the state when the break with Spain finally came. By the beginning of the twentieth century it was already the second largest city in the republic, and in the 1920s the completion of the rail link with California provided a further spur for development. More recently, the exodus from México and attempts at decentralization have swollen numbers here still more.

Arrival

Guadalajara's **airport** is some 17km southeast of the city on the road to Chapala. Facilities include money exchange and car rental, and there's also the usual system of fixed-price taxis and vans to get you downtown (around US$8.50 – vouchers are sold inside the terminal). A much cheaper bus service (every 15min; 6am–9pm; US$1) also runs to and from the old bus station – the Camionera Vieja (see below) – from where you can hop on another bus, or walk, to the centre.

Right out in the city's southeastern suburbs, Guadalajara's **Central Camionera** is one of Mexico's newest and largest bus stations, with seven terminals strung out in a wide arc, as well as its own shopping centre (Nueva Central Plaza) and hotel (see "Accommodation", p.170). Each of the terminals has an extremely helpful information desk – they'll advise exactly which **bus into town** to take to get where you're going, and can also book accommodation. Local buses #102, #616 and #644 ("Centro"), and the slightly dearer turquoise TUR bus, stop outside each terminal, most of them taking you to Av 16 de Septiembre, within walking distance of the cathedral if not right past it. The last city bus out is at around 11pm. Bus #275 from behind Terminal 1 also runs to the centre until around 10.30pm.

Some second-class buses from local destinations, including Tequila, Tapalpa, Ciudad Guzmán and the villages on the shores of Lake Chapala, as well as the airport service, use the **Camionera Vieja**, the old downtown terminal, surrounded by cheap hotels and only a short bus ride (#176, #616 and others) up Calzada Independencia from the centre. If you're coming from somewhere only an hour or two away, it can be worth the slightly less comfortable second-class journey for the convenience of this much more central point of arrival.

The **train station** is a couple of kilometres south of the centre at the bottom of Calzada Independencia. To get into town, pick up one of the taxis waiting outside or one of the buses – #142 and #621, for example – that head up Independencia towards the centre.

Orientation

The centre of the old city is a relatively compact grid around the junction of **Morelos** and **16 de Septiembre**, by the huge bulk of the **Cathedral**; east of here Morelos leads to the **Plaza Tapatía** and the **Mercado Libertad**, while to the west are busy shopping streets. **Juárez**, a couple of blocks south, is actually the main east–west thoroughfare in the centre, heading out to the west past the **University** (where it becomes Vallarta), and crossing avenidas **Chapultepec** and **Américas** in an upmarket residential area. Further west still, it crosses **López Mateos**, a main through-route, which heads south past the **Plaza del Sol**, a shopping centre surrounded by big hotels, restaurants and much of Guadalajara's best, but quite expensive, nightlife, and eventually heading out of the city as the main road towards Colima and the coast.

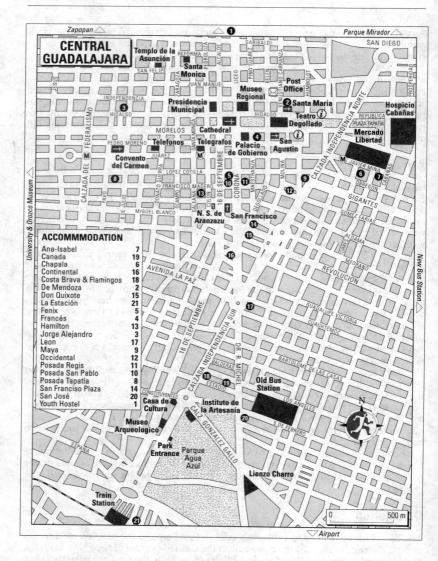

The main north–south arteries in the centre are the **Calzada del Federalismo**, along which the *tren ligero*, the city's metro, runs, and **Calzada Independencia**, which runs from the train station, up past the **Parque Agua Azul**, the old bus station, the market and Plaza Tapatía, and eventually out of the city to the **Parque Mirador**. Finally, **Revolución** leads off Independencia towards the southeast – to Tlaquepaque, the new bus station and Tonalá. If you fancy taking a **city tour** to get your bearings, try Panoramex, Federalismo Sur 944 (☎3/647-09-72; US$15).

Information

The helpful state **tourist office** is at Morelos 102 (Mon–Fri 9am–8pm, Sat & Sun 9am–1pm; ☎3/658-00-49), off Plaza Tapatía, where there is also a tourist information booth run by the city council. In addition, there are information booths at the Camionera and the airport, as well as a free tourist information phone line from elsewhere in the country (☎91-800/36-3-22).

Although any of the banks throughout the centre – the cluster including Banamex and Bancomer around Corona and Juárez, for example – offer **currency exchange**, casas de cambio, many of them around the corner of Maestranza and López Cotilla, are quicker, open longer and offer almost identical rates. After hours, the bigger hotels will usually change money at a considerably worse rate.

Guadalajara's main **post office** (Mon–Fri 8am–7pm, Sat 9am–2pm) is at Venustiano Carranza 16, the junction with Independencia. Casetas for long-distance phone calls include Computel, in the Edificio Mulbar at Corona 181 and Madero, and also in the Camionera Vieja (Sala B and outside), and the Camionera Nueva (Terminal 2), Telefónica Digital, at Sanchez 375 between Ocampo and Galeana, and one in Bonetería Norma, at Morelos 51 on Plaza Tapatía. There are also plenty of **public phones**, including some relatively quiet ones around Plaza Tapatía.

Car rental agencies can be found at the airport, as well as downtown where they're concentrated on Av Niños Héroes near the *Sheraton* (not far from the Parque Agua Azul); those here include Alamiz, Niños Héroes 961-B (☎3/614-63-93); Argus, Niños Héroes 968 (☎3/614-95-54); Budget, Niños Héroes 934 (☎3/614-10-53); National, Niños Héroes 961-C (☎3/614-45-95, or at the airport ☎3/688-56-45); and Quick Rent a Car, Niños Héroes 954 (☎3/614-60-52).

City transport

Guadalajara is a very big city, but getting around is not too difficult once you've got the hang of the comprehensive system of public transport. In the centre, most of the main attractions are within walking distance of each other, and elsewhere using public transport is relatively straightforward as almost all **buses** are funnelled through the centre on a few main roads and have their destinations written on the windscreen. The sheer number of buses and the speed at which they move can make things slightly more difficult, however, especially at peak hours when you may have to fight to get on: if possi-

---

SOME USEFUL BUS ROUTES

All of these also run in the opposite direction: the #600 numbers are minibuses.

#55 Plaza del Sol–Parque Agua Azul–Camionera Vieja–Tonalá
#60 Calzada Independencia–Soccer stadium and bullring–Barranca de Oblatos
#142 Centro–FFCC (train station)
#190 Centro–Zapopan
#275 Nueva Camionera–Tonalá–Tlaquepaque–Centro–Zapopan
#616 Nueva Camionera–Camionera Vieja–Centro
#621 Centro–FFCC (train station)
#629 Centro–Morelos (westbound)/Pedro Moreno (eastbound)–Minerva Circle
#639 Centro–Barranca de Oblatos
TUR turquoise bus Nueva Camionera–Tonalá–Tlaquepaque–Centro–Zapopan
Trolley bus Independencia Centro–Soccer stadium and bullring–Zoo

ble, get a local to show you exactly where your bus stops. The new **tren electrico urbano**, or metro system, with one north–south and one east–west line, is designed for local commuters, and you're not likely to use it.

Taxis are also reliable if you're in a hurry, and for a group they don't work out too expensive as long as you establish a price at the outset; many downtown taxi-ranks post a list of fixed prices. From the centre to the Plaza del Sol, Nueva Camionera or Zapopan should cost around US$4.50; slightly less to Tlaquepaque, twice as much to the airport (US$9).

Accommodation

Most of Guadalajara's **cheap hotels** are around the old bus station or in the streets south of the Mercado Libertad, areas that are noisy and none too appealing. The more **expensive** establishments, meanwhile, tend to be a long way out to the west of the city. In either case there are alternatives in the centre, within walking distance of the historical heart of the city, and if you can find space this is definitely the place to be.

Guadalajara's **youth hostel** is at Alcalde 1360 (☎3/824-65-15; ①), a short ride (bus #54) north of the city centre along Alcalde. It's a big place with sparse, single-sex dorms – call ahead to reserve. If you arrive late at night at the **Camionera Central** and all you want to do is sleep, there's a hotel right by the entrance: *El Parador* (☎3/600-09-10, fax 600-00-15; ④) is modern and soulless, but has a pool and reasonably soundproof rooms with TV.

In the centre

Continental, Corona 450 (☎3/614-11-17). Modern but smaller and cheaper than many of the business hotels, just down the road from the fancy, high-rise *Aranzazú*. ④.

Don Quixote, Héroes 91 at Degollado (☎3/658-12-99, fax 614-28-45). Friendly, small hotel with rooms around a colonial-style courtyard. ⑤.

Fenix, Corona 160 (☎3/614-57-14, fax 613-40-05). Large, modern building in the centre of things: it's a *Best Western*, which probably explains its popularity. Though it's somewhat overpriced, there are sometimes promotional deals. ⑦.

Francés, Maestranza 35 (☎3/613-11-90, fax 658-28-31). Just off the plaza behind the cathedral, this beautiful colonial building is much the most atmospheric and appealing of Guadalajara's more expensive hotels. ⑤.

Hamilton, Madero 381, between Galeana and Ocampo (☎3/614-67-26). Clean and friendly, a popular spot with backpackers and young Mexican couples. ②.

Jorge Alejandro, Hidalgo 656 (☎3/658-10-51, fax 616-41-36). Spotless and comfortable, central hotel in a recently renovated colonial building. ④.

De Mendoza, Carranza 16, at Hidalgo (☎3/613-46-46, fax 613-73-10). Plush establishment in a refurbished colonial convent; all amenities including pool. ⑧.

Posada Regis, Corona 171, near López Cotilla (☎ & fax 3/613-30-26). Bizarre, ramshackle old building with high-ceilinged rooms around a peaceful, covered courtyard (cheapest rooms are on the roof). Nylon sheets are the big minus here. ③.

Posada San Pablo, Madero 218 at Corona (☎3/613-33-12). Hard to spot; clean rooms around a dark, covered courtyard replete with flowers and birds. ②.

<table>
<tr><td colspan="3">**ACCOMMODATION PRICE CODES**</td></tr>
</table>

All the accommodation listed in this book has been categorized into one of nine price bands, as set out below. The prices quoted are in US dollars and normally refer to the cheapest available room for two people sharing in high season. For more details see p.36.

① less than US$5	④ US$15–25	⑦ US$60–80
② US$5–10	⑤ US$25–40	⑧ US$80–100
③ US$10–15	⑥ US$40–60	⑨ more than US$100

Posada Tapatía, López Cotilla 619 (☎3/614-91-46). A pleasant, friendly little place in a prettily decorated old house. Some rooms are cleaner and brighter than others. ③.

San Francisco Plaza, Degollado 267 at Héroes (☎3/613-89-54, fax 613-32-57). Nice old place around a series of courtyards. ⑤.

Around the Mercado Libertad

Ana-Isabel, Javier Mina 164 (☎3/617-79-20). Next door to the *Imperio* (☎3/617-50-42; ③) and the better of the two, with clean rooms, TV and parking. Worth bargaining if they're not full, though bear in mind this is a very noisy area. ③.

Chapala, José María Mercado 84 (☎3/617-71-59). Around the corner from the *Ana-Isabel*, clean and simple, but a touch dark. ②.

Maya, López Cotilla 39 at Huerto (☎3/614-54-54). Bare but decent rooms in a rough, noisy area, but better than on Javier Mina, with parking facilities. ④.

Occidental, Villa Gómez 17 at Huerto, just off Independencia behind the *Avenida* (☎3/613-84-06 or 613-84-08). Simple, good-value rooms with showers; there's a garage and a restaurant for cheap comidas. ②.

South of centre: Calzada Independencia and the Camionera Vieja

Canada, Estadio 77 (☎3/619-40-14, fax 619-31-10). One of dozens surrounding the Camionera Vieja, this large place is pretty good value with the bonus of the excellent *Restaurante Ottawa*. Some better, pricier rooms available. ②.

Costa Brava, Independencia Sur 739, near Los Angeles (☎3/619-23-24 or 619-23-27). New, friendly hotel. The slightly more expensive rooms have TV. ②.

Flamingos, Independencia Sur 725 (☎3/619-87-64). Next door to the *Costa Brava*: bigger, rougher, and cheaper. ②.

Leon, Independencia Sur 557 (☎3/619-61-41). Basic, bare and the least expensive of all. ②.

San José, 5 de Febrero 116 at Dr Michel (☎3/619-11-53). The smartest of the places round the Camionera, though inevitably noisy. ②.

The City

Any tour of Guadalajara starts almost inevitably at the **Cathedral**. With the Sagrario, or sacristy, next door, it takes up an entire block at the very heart of the **colonial centre**, which is bordered by four plazas. At weekends and on warm evenings the plazas are packed, the crowds entertained by an array of street performers and wandering musicians; there are frequently bands playing during the day, too. All around is the traffic, noise and bustle of the busiest commercial areas of downtown Guadalajara: to the east the crowds spill over into Plaza Tapatía and its upmarket shops, beyond which is the complete contrast of the old market; unmodernized shopping streets to the west are no less busy.

Venture a little further and the atmosphere changes again. Guadalajara's rapid expansion has swallowed up numerous communities that were once distinct villages but are now barely distinguishable from the suburbs around them. Heading **west** the university area blends into chic suburbia and some of the city's most expensive real estate. **East**, Tlaquepaque and Tonalá are the source of some of the area's finest handicrafts. And finally to the **north**, Zapopan has a huge, much revered church and a museum of indigenous traditions, while the Barranca de Oblatos offers stunning canyon views and weekend picnic spots.

The Cathedral

With its pointed, tiled twin towers, Guadalajara's **Cathedral** is a bizarre but effective mixture of styles. Building work began in 1561 and wasn't finished until more than a century later – since then, extensive modifications, which effectively disguise the fact that there was ever a plan behind the design, have included a Neoclassical facade and new towers (the originals collapsed in an 1818 earthquake). The interior is best seen in the evening, when the light from huge chandeliers makes the most of its rich decoration; the picture of the Virgin in the sacristy is attributed to the Spanish Renaissance artist **Murillo**.

Flanking the cathedral is a series of bustling plazas, often the scene of demonstrations and impromptu street performances. The **Plaza de los Laureles**, planted with laurel trees and with a fountain in the centre, faces the main west entrance, while to the north, by the porticoed **Presidencia Municipal** (less than fifty years old, though you wouldn't know it), lies the **Rotonda de los Jaliscienses Ilustres** in the centre of another plaza. This Neoclassical circle of seventeen Doric columns is the latest architectural expression of Jaliscan pride and commemorates the state's martyred heroes.

The Museo Regional

Across the plaza north of the cathedral, the **Museo Regional** (Tues–Sat 9am–6.30pm, Sun 9am–2.30pm; US$1.75, free on Sun) is housed in an eighteenth-century colonial mansion – originally a religious seminary, later a barracks and then a school. It's a supremely elegant setting for an extensive and diverse collection. Downstairs, the collection starts with a section devoted to regional **archeology** – from stone tools and the skeleton of a mammoth through to the finest achievements of western Mexican cultures in pottery and metal-working. The peoples of the west developed quite separately from those in southern and central Mexico, and there is considerable evidence that they had more contact with South and Central American cultures than with those who would now be regarded as their compatriots. The deep **shaft tombs** displayed here are unique in Mexico, but were common down the west coast in Peru and Ecuador. Later the Tarascan kingdom, based around Pátzcuaro (see p.192), came almost to rival the strength of the Aztecs – partly due to their more extensive knowledge and use of metals. Certainly the Aztecs tried, and failed, to extend their influence over Tarascan territory, though following Cortés' destruction of Tenochtitlán the Tarascans submitted relatively peacefully to the Conquistadors.

Upstairs, along with rooms devoted to the state's **modern history** and ethnography, is a sizeable gallery of colonial and modern art. Most remarkable here is the large

---

JOSÉ CLEMENTE OROZCO

José Clemente Orozco (1883–1949) was a member, along with Diego Rivera and David Siqueiros, of the triumvirate of brilliant Mexican artists who emerged from the Revolution and who transformed painting here into an enormously powerful and populist political statement, especially through the medium of the giant mural. Their chief patron was the state – hence the predominance of their work in official buildings and educational establishments – and their aim was to create a national art that drew on native traditions. Almost all their work is consciously educative, rewriting – or, perhaps better, rediscovering – Mexican history in the light of the Revolution, casting the Imperialists as villains and drawing heavily on pre-Hispanic themes. Orozco, a native of Jalisco (he was born in Zapotlán, now Ciudad Guzmán), was perhaps the least overtly political of the three: certainly his later work, the greatest of which is here in Guadalajara, often seems ambiguous. As a child he moved to Guadalajara and then México, where he was influenced by the renowned engraver Posada, and most of his early work is found in the capital, where he painted murals from 1922 to 1927. There followed seven years in the USA, but it was on his return that his powers as an artist reached their peak, in the late 1930s and 1940s, above all in his works at the Hospicio Cabañas and the University of Guadalajara.

collection of **nineteenth-century portraiture**, a local tradition that captures relatively ordinary Mexicans in a charmingly naive style – nowadays they'd be snapshots for the family album, and indeed many have the imposed formality familiar from early photography.

The Palacio de Gobierno and the Orozco murals

On the other side of the cathedral, south of the Sagrario, the **Plaza de Armas** centres on an elaborate kiosk – a present from the people of France – where the state band plays every Thursday and Sunday evening. Dominating the eastern side of the square is the Baroque frontage of the **Palacio de Gobierno** (daily 9am–8.30pm; free). Here Padre Miguel Hidalgo y Costilla (the "father of Mexican Independence") proclaimed the abolition of slavery in 1810 and here, in 1858, Benito Juárez was saved from the firing squad by the cry of *"Los Valientes no asesinan"* – the brave don't murder. Both these events are commemorated inside, but the overwhelming reason to penetrate into the arcaded courtyard is to see the first of the great **Orozco murals** on the stairway.

The mural here is typical of Orozco's work (see box) – Hidalgo blasts through the middle triumphant, brandishing his sword against a background of red flags and the fires of battle. Curving around the sides of the staircase, scenes depict the Mexican people's oppression and struggle for liberty, from a pre-Conquest Eden to post-revolutionary emancipation. Upstairs in the domed Congress hall a smaller Orozco mural also depicts Hidalgo, this time as *El Cura de Dolores* (the priest from Dolores), legislator and liberator of slaves.

Plaza de la Liberación

The largest of the four squares is the **Plaza de la Liberación**, where the back of the cathedral looks across at the **Teatro Degollado**. Built in the mid-nineteenth century and inaugurated during the brief reign of Maximilian, the theatre is an imposing, domed Neoclassical building, with a Corinthian portico on whose pediment is a frieze depicting the Greek Muses. It still stages a full programme of drama and concerts, as well as the Sunday morning *folklórico* dances – details are posted up around the entrance. The impressively restored interior alone justifies the price of a show ticket, most notably the frescoed ceiling illustrating scenes from Dante's works.

On either side of the theatre are two small churches, **Santa María** and **San Agustín**, each all that remains of a former monastery. San Agustín has a fine Baroque facade; relatively plain Santa María is one of the oldest churches in the city, built in the seventeenth century on the site of the city's first cathedral. Next door, one of the old monastic buildings is now the **Palacio de Justicia**.

East along the Plaza Tapatía: the Hospicio Cabañas

At the back of the theatre you're at the beginning of the new **Plaza Tapatía**, with a view all the way down to the Hospicio Cabañas. The plaza is almost entirely lined with swish department stores and glossy office buildings, but for all that the pedestrianized area, dotted with modern statuary and fountains, is an undeniably attractive place to wander and window-shop. It takes its name from *tapatío* – an adjective used to describe anything typical of Guadalajara, supposedly derived from the capes worn by Spanish grandees. Guadalajarans themselves are often referred to as *Tapatíos*.

At the far end of the plaza, the **Hospicio Cabañas** (Tues–Sat 10.15am–5.45pm, Sun 10.15am–2.45pm; US$1 plus US$1.25 for a camera, free on Sun) was founded as an orphanage by the bishop Juan Cabañas y Crespo in 1801 and took nearly fifty years to complete, during much of which time it operated as a barracks. It was an orphanage again, however, when **Orozco** came to decorate the chapel in 1939. The Hospicio is a huge and beautiful building, with no fewer than twenty-three separate patios surrounded by schools of art, music and dance; an art cinema/theatre; various government offices; and a small cafeteria. The chapel, the **Capilla Tolsa**, is a plain and ancient-looking structure in the form of a cross, situated in the central patio right at the heart of the building. The **murals**, in keeping with their setting, are more spiritual than those in the government palace, but you certainly couldn't call them Christian – the Conquistadors are depicted as the Horsemen of the Apocalypse, trampling the native population beneath them. The Man of Fire – who leads the people from their dehu-manizing, mechanized oppression – has a symbolic role as liberator, which is clearly the same as that of Hidalgo in the palace murals: in this case he is a strange synthesis of Christian and Mexican deities, a Christ–Quetzalcoatl figure. There are benches on which you can lie back to appreciate the murals, and also a small museum dedicated to José Clemente Orozco, with sketches, cartoons and details of the artist's life.

Almost alongside the Hospicio is the vast **Mercado Libertad**, which Guadalajarans claim is the world's largest market under one roof. It's an entirely modern building, but not in the least a modern market – as well as the touristy souvenir stalls you'll find *curanderas* offering herbal remedies, little stalls selling basic foods and vast piles of colourful fruit, vegetables, chocolate and spices, and traditional leather goods, from saddles to clumpy working boots. It's huge, chaotic and engrossing, but before you buy crafts here, it's worth paying a visit to the **Instituto de la Artesanía** in the Parque Agua Azul, or to the expensive boutiques in Tlaquepaque, to get some idea of the poten-tial quality and value of the goods (for both, see below).

South of the Plaza de Armas
South of the Plaza de Armas, the churches of **San Francisco** and **Nuestra Señora de Aranzazu** face each other across Av 16 de Septiembre. San Francisco lies on the site of what was probably Guadalajara's first religious foundation – a Franciscan monastery established in the years just after the Conquest. The present church was begun in 1684 and has a beautiful Baroque facade. Aranzazu, by contrast, is entirely plain on the out-side, but conceals a fabulously elaborate interior, with three wildly exuberant, heavily carved and gilded churrigueresque retablos. The **Jardín de San Francisco**, which would be pleasantly peaceful were it not for the number of local buses rattling by, lies across from these two.

Parque Agua Azul
Several different buses ("Parque Agua Azul") run down from here to the **Parque Agua Azul** (Tues–Sun 10am–6pm; US$0.50). Again, you couldn't really describe the park as peaceful: there's always some kind of activity going on and the green areas are permanently packed with kids enjoying the zoo, miniature train rides and playgrounds. An outdoor concert bowl (the *concha*) hosts popular free performances on Sundays, and weekends see football games, too, and constant crowds. Nonetheless, by Guadalajara stan-dards, it's a haven of peace, especially during the week, and the entrance fee includes attractions such as a dome full of butterflies; exotic caged birds, including magnificent tou-cans; a palm house also full of tropical birds; and a strange, glass-pyramid orchid house.

Perhaps the greatest attraction of the park, however, is the **Instituto de la Artesanía Jalisciense** (Mon–Fri 10am–6pm, Sat 10am–5pm, Sun 11am–3pm; free; entered from Calzado González Gallo). A showcase for regional crafts that is as much a museum as a shop, this is just plain fabulous, with examples of all sorts of local arte-sanía – furniture, ceramics, toys, glassware, clothing – all of the highest quality. Not surprisingly it's expensive, but for what you get the prices are not unreasonable. Across the road, the **Casa de la Cultura** (Mon–Sat 9am–9pm; free) is by contrast a disappointment: extensively covered in ultra-modern murals and frescoes, it houses a permanent exhibition of modern art, the State Library, and an information service for cultural events in the city. Equally a let-down is the **Museo Arqueológico** (daily 10am–2pm; free), a low, modern building opposite the park entrance. It rarely seems to be open even when it's meant to be, and the small collection of relics of western cultures inside is really only of specialist interest.

West of the Plaza de Armas

The area to the west of the cathedral is a great part of the city for aimless meandering. There has been far less modernization in this direction, and the busy shopping streets, many of them closed to traffic, turn up fascinating glimpses of traditional Mexican life and plenty of odd moments of interest. There's a small general **market** at Santa Monica and Hidalgo. A little further out, the university area is quieter than the centre, the streets broader, and there's also a younger atmosphere, with plenty of good restaurants and cafés, while further out still are expensive residential areas, interesting in their own way for the contrast to crowded downtown.

The old **Telegrafos** building – also known as the "Ex-Templo de la Compañia" and now a university library (Mon–Fri 9am–9pm, Sat 9am–5pm; free) – lies just west of the Plaza de Armas at the junction of Pedro Moreno with Colón. Originally a church, the building later became a university lecture hall, during which time the nineteenth-century Neoclassical façade was added and it was decorated with **murals** by **David Siqueiros** and **Amado de la Cueva**. Later still it housed the telegraph offices. The murals here, depicting workers, peasants and miners in a heroic-socialist style, provide an interesting contrast to Orozco's work. Outside there's an attractive little plaza, and the pedestrianized streets make a pleasant escape from the traffic, if not the crowds.

Immediately to the north are several examples of the beautiful, little-known Baroque churches that stud Guadalajara. The closest is the **Templo de Santa Monica**, on Santa Monica between San Felipe and Reforma, with fabulously rich doorways and an elegant, stone interior. The nearby **Templo de San Felipe Neri**, San Felipe at Contreras Medellin, is a few years younger – dating from the second half of the eighteenth century – and more sumptuously decorated, with a superb facade and lovely, dilapidated tower overgrown with a tangle of plants. Both of these churches have extravagantly decorated rain spouts – in the form of dragons on San Felipe. A block along Contreras Medellin, at the corner of Juan Manuel, the **Templo de las Capuchinas** is by contrast a completely plain, fortress-like structure; inside, though, it's more interesting, with paintings and a lovely vaulted brick roof. Between these two, Contreras Medellin is lined with old printing shops, *imprentas*, where you can see the clanking, ancient presses at work. Back on the main route west, at Juárez and 8 de Julio, the ex-**Convento del Carmen** was one of the city's richest monasteries, but its wealth has largely been stripped, leaving an austere, white building of elegant simplicity. Modern art exhibitions, dance events and concerts are regularly staged here.

The University to the Plaza del Sol

If you're heading any further west, you may want to take a bus or taxi (anything heading for the Plaza del Sol should pass all the areas below, or look for "Par Vial"), although the **University** is still within easy walking distance (15min) of the centre. Here you can see more of **Orozco**'s major murals, among the first he painted in Guadalajara, in the **Museo de los Artes**, at Juárez 975 (Tues–Sat 10am–8pm, Sun noon–6pm; US$0.65, free on Sun), opposite the modern main university building at Juárez and Díaz de León (aka Av Tolsa). Head for the main hall (the *Paraninfo*) to see the frescoed dome and front wall. Again, the theme fits the setting: in this case the dome shows the glories and benefits of education, while the wall shows the oppressed masses crying out for books and education, which are being denied them by fat capitalists and the army. Behind the university buildings, across López Cotilla, the **Templo Expiatorio**, a modern neo-

Gothic church, features some innovative stained-glass and an attractive altar. Across Díaz de León a block south at no. 300, you'll find the **Instituto Cultural Norteamericano**. Basically a language school, the Institute has English-language magazines lying around and a café at the back. You may not be supposed to wander in off the streets, but no one seems to mind.

Beyond the university, Juárez changes its name to Vallarta, and the character of the street changes rapidly, too. Within ten blocks, around the major junction of **Vallarta and Chapultepec**, you find yourself in a very different city, a far quieter place of broad avenues, expensive shops and pleasant restaurants, with drive-in burger joints and big houses in the back streets. Many of the airlines have their offices out here, along with American Express and several consulates; there's a large branch of Sanborn's at Vallarta and General Martín. Further out, Vallarta crosses the major artery of López Mateos at the Minerva Circle, an intersection marked by a triumphal arch.

Most buses turn left at the Minerva Circle down López Mateos Sur towards the **Plaza del Sol**, a vast commercial development said to be one of the largest in Latin America. There's an enormous shopping centre, as well as new administrative offices, and inside a couple of good cafés, an ice-cream parlour and, in the evenings, several disco-clubs. Also on López Mateos are numerous big hotels and themed restaurants – all very much the modern face of suburban Mexico.

San Pedro Tlaquepaque and Tonalá

The most celebrated of Guadalajara's suburbs, **SAN PEDRO TLAQUEPAQUE** is famous for its artesanías and for its **mariachi** bands. Once a separate town, some 5km southeast of the centre, it has long since been absorbed by urban sprawl, and its traditional crafts taken over almost entirely by tourism; the streets are lined with shops selling, for the most part, pretty tacky goods at thoroughly inflated prices. Nevertheless, it's worth seeing, and there are still quality pieces among the dross – notably some of the ceramics and glassware on which the area's reputation was founded.

Tlaquepaque centres around a pleasantly laid-back main square complete with bandstand, on whose northern side is the tangerine-roofed church of San Pedro. To its west, the three-domed Sanctuario de la Virgen de la Soledad is an almost equally distinctive landmark. Along the square's southern side runs Independéncia, Tlaquepaque's main street. The #275 or TUR bus from the centre will drop you three blocks south on Porvenir, and can be picked up for the return journey two blocks north of Independencia on Constitución. You can also get on or off on General Marelino García Barragán at the western end of Independencia and Constitución, by a brick pedestrian overbridge and traffic circle.

To see some of the best artesanías, visit the small **Museo Regional de la Ceramica** (Tues–Sat 10am–4pm, Sun 10am–1pm; free), at Independencia 237, which has displays of pottery not only from Tlaquepaque but from all over the state, and especially Tonalá (see below). Most of what's on show is for sale – the place is more store than museum – but there's also a traditional kitchen to see, complete with all its plates, pots and pans, and displays of the individual works of some of the finest craftsmen, and the building is a fine old mansion in its own right. Almost all of the fancier **shops** are nearby on **Independencia**, many of them again occupying colonial-era houses that are interesting in themselves. Closed to traffic, it's a pleasant street along which to window-shop. Among the more worthwhile stores are Sergio Bustamante, at no. 236, opposite the museum, where there are flamingos and peacocks in the patio to go with Sergio's famous fantastical figures in papier mâché and bronze – lovely to look at, even if the price and size are such that you won't be buying. Opposite each other a block west of the museum are La Casa Canela (no. 258; Mon–Fri 10am–2pm & 3–7pm, Sat 10am–6pm, Sun 11am–3pm) and Antigua de Mexico (no. 255), two more lovely houses that sell upmarket fabrics, furniture and antiques to a mainly Mexican clientèle. Juárez, one block south of Independencia, has fewer – but slightly less touristy – stores and, at no. 317, a workshop where you can see glass being blown.

A more compelling reason to make the trip out to Tlaquepaque, though, is to stop off at **El Parian**, an enclosed plaza that is in effect the biggest bar you've ever seen. Since the shops all close down for a siesta anyway, you have every excuse to hang out here for a couple of hours. There are actually a dozen or so separate establishments around this giant courtyard, but since everyone sits outside, the tables tend to overlap and strolling serenaders wander around at random, it all feels like one enormous place. They all charge much the same, too, and offer the same limited range of food – basically birria, quesadillas and queso fundido – plus lots to drink: prices seem reasonable on the menu, but watch out for the cost of the drinks and for added service charges. At the weekend, particularly Sunday afternoons, you'll see *mariachi* at its best here, when the locals come along and offer their own vocal renditions to the musicians' backing. On weekdays it can be disappointingly quiet.

You'll find El Parian on Independencia, just east of the main square. There are a couple of fine colonial churches here, too, and several **banks** in case you've been carried away by the shopping experience. And if you've had too good a time to struggle home, or you really take the purchasing seriously, you can **stay** right here at the *Posada en el Parian*, Independencia 74 (☎65/635-21-89; ②). There's a small local **Mercado Municipal** behind Independencia opposite El Parian (entrance by the hotel); and numerous fancy **restaurants** on Independencia if El Parian is not for you.

Pottery is slightly cheaper at **TONALÁ**, a ceramics manufacturing centre some 8km beyond Tlaquepaque, but the trip is really only worthwhile if you are seriously planning to shop. Market days are Thursday and Sunday, when things are considerably more animated and the village is crammed with salespeople and shoppers – but be warned that ceramics sold on stalls tend to be rejects from the shops.

To get to San Pedro Tlaquepaque from the centre of town, take a #275 or TUR bus heading south on 16 de Septiembre, or a trolley-bus south on Federalisimo. Some of these buses continue to Tonalá, and both Tlaquepaque and Tonalá are on the route taken by many of the buses that run between the new bus station and the centre.

Zapopan

ZAPOPAN, some 6km northwest of the city centre, is served by the #275 and TUR buses at the opposite end of their routes from Tlaquepaque. The **Basilica de la Virgen de Zapopan** here is one of the most important churches in the city, much revered by the Huichols. Pope John Paul II gave a mass in the giant plaza in front of the church during a visit to Mexico in 1979; a statue commemorates the event. The Baroque temple houses a miraculous image of the Virgin that was dedicated to the local Indians by a Franciscan missionary, Antonio de Segovia, after he had intervened in a battle between them and the Conquistadors. Since then, it has been constantly venerated and is still the object of pilgrimages, especially on October 12, when it returns from the cathedral to the church in a massive procession – some 200,000 people march it back – having toured, and been displayed in, all the churches in Guadalajara. This is one of the highlights of the city's *Fiestas de Octubre*.

Beside the church, a small **museum** (daily 9.30am–1pm & 3.30–6pm; free) exhibits clothes and objects relating to Huichol traditions, as well as a photographic display of their modern way of life. They also sell Huichol crafts, including psychedelic yarn paintings (*cuadros de estambre*) and beadwork.

Zapopan has its own **tourist office**, at Vincente Guerrero 233, two blocks behind the church (Mon–Fri 9am–9pm, Sat 9am–1pm; ☎3/636-67-27), with further information about what to see and do in Zapopan and the surrounding area.

Barranca de Oblatos

Also to the north of the city, out at the end of Calzada Independencia, the **Barranca de Oblatos** is a magnificent 600-metre-deep canyon, along the edge of which a series of parks offer superb views and a welcome break from the confines of the city. The **Parque Mirador** ("Parque Mirador" bus north along Independencia) is a popular family spot with picnic areas and excellent views, while the **Parque Barranca de Oblatos** (bus #639 from Vicente Guerrero at the southwest corner of the Hospicio Cabañas) is more of a student haunt, with swimming pools, picnic areas and plenty of young lovers. Also on the edge of the canyon, the city **zoo** (Tues–Fri 10am–5pm, Sat & Sun 10am–6pm; US$0.25; bus #60, #62A, #62D or trolley-bus north on Independencia) has superb views from its northern end, along with a relatively well-kept selection of Mexican and international wildlife.

Eating and drinking

They take their food seriously in Jalisco as a rule, and Guadalajara boasts literally hundreds of **places to eat**. Among the local specialities dished up at street stalls, bars and the markets are *birria*, consisting of beef or lamb in a spicy but not particularly hot sauce, served with tortillas or in tacos; roast goat; and *pozole*, a stew of pork and hominy (ground maize). In the centre, there seems to be more choice west of the cathedral, where traditional cafés and restaurants line **Juárez**; the **University** area also offers good food, especially during semester. For cheap, basic meals, the area around the old bus station is crowded with possibilities, none wildly exciting, while upstairs in the **Mercado Libertad** seemingly hundreds of little stands each displays their own specialities. Though there are plenty of more **expensive** places round the centre, they tend to be rather dull: in the evenings, locals are far more likely to be found out in the suburbs, or enjoying a raucous night at one of many themed restaurants on López Mateos Sur, a US$4 taxi-ride from the centre.

A couple of good **panaderías**, for bread and cakes for a picnic, are Pan Estilo Mexico, Santa Monica 96 at Independencia, and Pasteleria Luvier, Colón 183 at Madero. Then there's always McDonald's, at Juárez and Colón.

Downtown cafés and licuados

Café Madoka, Gonzalez Martínez 78, at Juárez. Big, traditional café, serving medium-priced good breakfasts, soups and antojitos. You can also just sip a coffee and play a game of dominoes.

Café Madrid, Juárez 264. A smaller coffee-bar, again good for moderately priced breakfasts, comidas corridas at lunchtime, and sandwiches.

Café Oasis, Morelos 435, between Colón and Galeana. Bustling place handy for the centre – tacos, sandwiches and egg dishes.

Cafeteria Aroma de Café, Galeana 154 at López Cotilla. Small café with various kinds of coffee and good-value, low-priced set breakfasts.

Cafeteria Restaurant Malaga, 16 de Septiembre 220. Large café-restaurant with a moderately priced comida corrida, breakfasts, snacks, coffee, and even tarot readings.

Nectar, Hidalgo 426. Juice, ice-cream and yoghurt bar offering instant refreshment, including tortas, tacos and fruit salads, close to the cathedral.

La Terraza, Juárez 442 at Ocampo, upstairs. Balconied bar with beer, tacos, and tables overlooking the street.

Villa Madrid, López Cotilla 533, at Gonzalez Martínez. Great licuados, fruit salads and yoghurt, as well as more substantial dishes.

Downtown restaurants

Alta Fibra, Sanchez 370 between Ocampo and Galeana. Reasonably priced vegetarian restaurant with a wholemeal bakery next door.

Cebollas, Colón 176 at López Cotilla. Low-priced antojitos, snacks and meals, and good-value set breakfasts.

Chong Wah, Juárez 558 at Gonzalez Martinez. Moderately priced Cantonese food to eat in or take away.

La Chata, Corona 126 between López Cotilla and Juárez. Excellent medium-priced Mexican meat dishes, including *mole* and *platillo jalisciense* (chicken with side snacks).

Devechan, López Cotilla 570. Vegetarian restaurant with good-value buffet and breakfasts.

El Farol, Moreno 466 at Galeana, upstairs. Pleasant, reasonably priced old restaurant with good tamales and tacos – try for a table by the window.

La Gran China, Juárez 590 near the *Chong Wah*. Chop-suey house with good-value lunchtime set menu.

Lido, Colón 294 at Miguel Blanco. Spanish-style bar and restaurant, serving good, moderately priced Mexican *moles*, sandwiches, snacks and a reasonably priced set menu.

Nuevo Faro, López Cotilla 24. Simple restaurant with great-value, cheap comidas corridas.

La Rinconada, Morelos 86 Plaza Tapatía (☎3/613-99-14). Boasting a Colonial setting and serving seafood, US-style steaks and a range of Mexican specialities, including *birria* and ox tongue in a spicy Veracruz sauce. Expensive.

Sanborn's, 16 de Septiembre and Juárez. Plush restaurant with a wide selection of international and Mexican food, and a more informal café on the opposite corner across 16 de Septiembre.

Sandy's, Colón 39, at Moreno. Mezzanine-floor tables overlook the crowds of shoppers; simple Mexican food served.

Tacos El Pastor, Juárez 424, between Galeana and Ocampo. Fast, flavoursome tacos; popular and cheap though some choices (like *oreja* – pig's ear – or *cabeza* – head) are probably best avoided.

Taquería Los Faroles, Corona 250 at Sanchez. Popular taco and torta joint with a wide range of tacos served till midnight daily.

University and further out

La China Poblana, Juárez 887, by the university. Reasonably priced, traditional Puebla dishes, including *mole* and *chiles en nogada*.

La Choza Grill, Calzada Federalismo 176 at López Cotilla. Smaller version of the big places out on López Mateos, and not so far from the city-centre. Pricey meat and seafood dishes.

Guadalajara Grill, López Mateos Sur 3771 (☎3/631-56-22). Part of the *Carlos'n'Charlie* chain: Tex-Mex food, loud music, party atmosphere and dancing. It's a good idea to reserve in advance.

Los Itacates, Chapultepec Nte 110 at Justo Siera, four blocks north of Vallarta (☎3/825-11-06). Traditional Mexican food with live-music evenings. Best booked in advance.

Mesón de Sancho Panza, Castellanos 112, on the west side of the Parque de la Revolución. Classy but not outrageously expensive Spanish restaurant, with a good-value, moderately priced Sunday menu (US$6). Photos on the wall commemorate a visit by Pope John Paul II.

Entertainment and nightlife

Though it has perked up in recent years, Guadalajara's nightlife is still less than hot. Most of the fashionable, younger-crowd places tend to be a long way out – the Plaza del Sol complex, for example, houses a couple of clubs, as do many of the big hotels out this way. Any of them will knock a severe hole in your wallet.

On the other hand, you needn't spend anything at all in the **Plaza de Mariachis**, a little area hard by the Mercado Libertad and the church of San Juan de Dios, where *mariachi* bands stroll between bars, playing to anyone prepared to cough up for a song. If they play for you personally, you'll have to pay (check how much before they start), but there are usually several on the go nearby. You'll also find *mariachi* bands out in Tlaquepaque, and theatre and dance performances in town at the Teatro Degollado.

Lively downtown **bars** tend to be a tad sleazy, though those listed below are worth a try.

Bars and clubs

Baron, first floor above ground, Edificio Mulbar, Corona 181. Bar-restaurant with Latin music, including live acts. Daily 7pm–5am. No cover.

Coco & Coco, Corona 172. Popular downtown nightclub, playing mixed music but mainly Latin. Mon–Sat 8pm–3am, Sun 5pm–midnight. Cover US$2.

Copenhagen 77, López Cotilla and Marcos Castellanos, on the west side of the Parque de la Revolución. Restaurant and bar with live jazz 8.30pm–12.30am. No cover.

Duran, Duran, Madero 289. Dark disco-bar that fills up at weekends which is dead other nights, though it does a good-value set menu. No cover.

Panchos, Galeana 186 between Madero and López Cotilla. Small, mainly gay club with mixed music. Daily 8pm–3am. No cover.

Las Yardas, Juárez 37. Very 1970s, with coloured lights and dark corners. Live music 5–10pm. No cover.

Performing arts

There is a regular programme of **theatre and dance** in the beautiful Teatro Degollado and a series of events put on by the state Fine Arts department in the former Convento del Carmen and other sites around the city. You can pick up details from the tourist office.

Guadalajara's **ballet folklórico** – two hours of impressive traditional dance performed by the university dance troupe – is staged in the Teatro Degollado every

---

MOVING ON FROM GUADALAJARA

For transport to the **airport** from the centre of town take a taxi for around US$9, or a bus from the Camionera Vieja (Autobuses Guadalajara–Chapala in Sala A, every 15min 6am–9.30pm). There are constant **flights** to México, as well as departures to most other Mexican cities, and direct connections to many US, Canadian and Central American destinations.

Long-distance buses all leave from the new Central Camionera, way out in suburbia. To get there from the centre, take a #275, #275A, or #644 from 16 de Septiembre, or one of the buses marked "Nueva Central" heading south along Independencia or 16 de Septiembre. The station is huge and can be confusing, though each of the seven terminals has an information booth that can help with advice on where to catch your bus. Very broadly, each terminal serves a different area, but since they're organized by bus company rather than route, it's not quite that simple – there are buses to México from just about every terminal, for example. In general, make for **Terminals 1 and 2** for destinations in Jalisco, Colima and Michoacán, plus many of the pullman services to México, México via Morelia and many towns in the Bajío; **3 and 4** serve the north and northwest, with buses to the US border and up the Pacific coast, plus points en route; **5** for eastbound services towards San Luis Potosí and Tampico, as well as some more local services; **6** for the Bajío, the northeast and many local second-class buses; **7** for the north and northeast again, as well as México. If you're heading for somewhere just an hour or so away – Chapala or Tequila, say – it's usually quicker and easier to take a second-class bus from the **Camionera Vieja**, downtown. The two camioneras are connected by unnumbered "Maletero" microbus and #616 minibus.

Daily **trains** run to México (9pm, arriving 12hr later) and north to Nogales and Mexicali (at noon). Bus #621 runs to the station from Corona and Sanchez by San Francisco church.

There are plenty of **travel agencies** around the centre, including in the lobbies of all the big hotels, or head for American Express or Thomas Cook/Wagons Lits (see "Listings" opposite).

Sunday at 10am (except when the company's on tour) and is definitely worth getting up for: tickets are sold at the theatre ticket office (daily 10am–1pm & 4–7pm; ☎3/613-11-15). The state dance company performs a similar ballet, though its reputation isn't as good, in the Cine-Teatro Cabañas in the Hospicio Cabañas every Wednesday at 8.30pm and Sunday at 10am. Tickets go for around US$3 from the Hospicio (details ☎3/617-43-22, ext 122).

Less formally, you'll find **bands** playing and crowds gathered somewhere round the central plaza complex every weekend and often during the week, too (most Tuesdays and Thursdays), and there's always entertainment of some kind laid on in the Parque Agua Azul.

The entire month of October in Guadalajara is dominated by the famous **Fiestas de Octubre**, with daily events including *charreadas* (rodeos) and processions (the biggest on the 12th) and fireworks each night. In **Tlaquepaque** the big day is June 29: endless *mariachis*, dances and a mass procession.

Sport

Jaliscans pride themselves on their equestrian skills, and other entertainments include regular *charreadas* every Sunday in the Lienzo Charro, out on the road to the airport near the Parque Agua Azul (for details call ☎3/619-32-32), and in winter **bullfights** in the Plaza Nuevo Progreso a long way north on Calzada Independencia (☎3/637-99-82). Right opposite this is the mighty Estadio Jalisco (☎3/637-05-63), the enormous **football** stadium where FC Guadalajara (Las Chivas) play their home soccer matches, familiar to many from the 1970 and 1986 World Cups. Buses #52C, #60, #62 and the Independencia trolley run up Calzada Independencia past the bullring and football stadium.

Listings

Airlines Aerocalifornia, López Cotilla 1423 (☎3/826-19-01); Aeroméxico, Corona 196 (☎3/669-02-02); American, Vallarta 2440, Plaza los Arcos local 9-106 (☎3/615-79-44); Continental, Galería Hotel Presidente, López Mateos and Moctezuma, Local 8 & 9, first level (☎3/647-42-51); Delta, López Cotilla 1701 (☎3/630-31-30); Mexicana, Mariano Otero 2353 (☎3/112-00-11); Taesa, López Cotilla 1531-B (☎3/616-89-89); United, Vallarta 2440, Local A13 (☎3/616-94-89).

Books In English, from Sanborn's, Juárez between 16 de Septiembre and Corona, and at Vallarta 1600, or Sandi Bookstore, Tepeyac 718 in Colonia Chapalita; many of the larger bookstores around the centre also have a small selection of English-language books.

Consulates Canada, *Hotel Fiesta Americana*, Local 30, Aurelio Aceves 225 (☎3/615-56-42); Denmark, Circunvalación Agustín Yañez 2343, fourth floor (☎3/669-55-15); El Salvador, Guadalupe 4385 (☎3/121-87-12); Germany, Corona 202 (☎3/613-96-23); Guatemala, Mango 1440, Col Fresno (☎3/811-15-03); Honduras, Ottawa 1147, Col Providencia (☎3/817-49-98); Netherlands, Calzada Lázaro Cárdenas 601, sixth floor (☎3/811-26-41); Norway, Km5, Antigua Carretera a Chapala 2801 (☎3/812-14-11); Sweden, Guadalupe Montenegro 1691 (☎3/825-16-16); UK, Miguel Angelo de Quevado 601 (☎3/615-01-97); US, Progreso 175 (☎3/625-27-00).

Exchange American Express, Vallarta 2440 (Mon–Fri 9am–7pm, Sat 9am–1pm; ☎3/630-02-00); Thomas Cook, Circunvalación Agustín Yañez 2343-D (☎3/669-55-07).

Laundry Aldama 125, off Independencia a few blocks south of the Mercado Libertad (Mon–Sat 9am–8pm).

Markets The giant Mercado Libertad is just one – every city barrio has its own. They include the very touristy Mercado Corona near the cathedral, and craft markets in Tlaquepaque and Tonalá. The Sunday flea market El Baratillo is vast, sometimes stretching a mile or more along Javier Mina, starting a dozen blocks east of the Mercado Libertad.

Pharmacy Farmacía de Descuento, in the centre at Pedro Moreno 518 (Mon–Sat 8am–10pm, Sun 9am–9pm).

Lago de Chapala and around

The largest lake in Mexico, **Lago de Chapala** lies just over 50km south of the city. Some 30,000 North Americans are said to live in and around Guadalajara, and a sizeable proportion of them have settled on the lakeside – particularly in **Chapala** and in the smaller village of **Ajijic**. English is spoken widely, and there's even an English newspaper produced there. This mass presence has rendered the area rather expensive and in many respects somewhat sanitized, but it cannot detract from the beauty of the lake itself, and at weekends and holidays day-trippers from the city help to create an enjoyable party atmosphere. Panoramex (see p.168) run a day-trip to Chapala and Ajijic from Guadalajara (US$12.50).

Chapala

CHAPALA, on the shore of the lake, is a sleepy, even dull community most of the time, but can become positively festive on sunny weekends, when thousands come to eat, swim (though the water is none too clean) or take a boat ride, visiting one of the lake's islands. Shoreline restaurants all offer the local speciality, *pescado blanco*, famous despite its almost total lack of flavour, and street vendors sell cardboard plates of tiny fried fish from the lake, very like whitebait. Head to the left along the promenade, past streets of shuttered nineteenth-century villas, and you'll find a small crafts market.

Buses leave the old bus station in Guadalajara for Chapala throughout the day (Sala A, half-hourly; 50min). From Chapala, regular services run on to Ajijic and Jocotepec (and from there back to Guadalajara by a more direct route along the highway to the coast). From the bus station, the main street, Madero, heads six blocks down to the lakeside. The main square is halfway along it, with Hidalgo, the road to Ajijic, branching off right after five blocks. The *Nido*, Madero 202 (☎376/5-21-16; ④), is the town's oldest **hotel**, still rich with turn-of-the-century resort atmosphere. It's also a good spot for a meal, the walls of the restaurant decorated with old black-and-white photographs of Chapala. A little less expensive is the *Hotel Candileras*, López Cotilla 363 (☎376/5-22-79; ④), a friendly little place just off the main square. If you plan to stay for a while, ask about the special monthly rates at the hotels; houses and **apartments** are advertised on the noticeboard in the Farmacía Morelos, at Madero 423 on the main square. There are **casa de cambio** and a **caseta telefónica** on the corner of Madero and Hidalgo, and a bookshop stocking books and magazines in English at Madero 447. The **post office** is a couple of blocks along Hidalgo.

Ajijic

Though just 6km west of Chapala, **AJIJIC** has a completely different atmosphere. Undeniably picturesque, it's a smaller, quieter and more self-consciously arty place, with numerous little crafts shops – you get the distinct feeling that the ex-pats here resent the intrusion of outsiders, regarding themselves as writers or artists *manqués*, hoping to pick up some of the inspiration left behind by **D.H. Lawrence** and more recent residents like Ken Kesey. In truth, there's little evidence that Lawrence liked the place at all (though he may have disliked it less than he did the rest of the country), but then he can't have had much time to appreciate it, since in just eight weeks here he turned out an almost complete 100,000-word first draft of *The Plumed Serpent* (or *Quetzalcoatl* as it was then titled). Sybille Bedford, too, passed through with barely more than a glance:

After another hour we came to a much larger village with proper mud houses and a market place.
For three hundred yards, potholes were agreeably replaced by cobble-stones.
"Now what about this place?"
"Ajijic," said the driver.
"I dare say," said E.

Bedford, though, was on her way to the idyllic colonial backwater of her *Visit to Don Otavio* further round the lake – an experience so exquisite that anything else would pall beside it. Still, she probably had the right idea about Ajijic: it may be a wonderful place to retire, with a thriving ex-pat social and cultural life, but as a visitor you're likely to have exhausted its charms in a couple of hours, which is quite long enough to have wandered by the lake, seen the little art galleries, read the noticeboards and been shocked by the price of everything.

The **bus** drops you where the Carretera Chapala meets Colón, which runs six blocks southward to the lake, with the main square (where you'll find a map of the village) halfway along it. There are a number of luxurious but rather expensive **hotels** in Ajijic, as well as **apartments** and houses to rent for longer stays; check out the noticeboards in shops, galleries and the **post office**, which is at Colón 4. The *Nueva Possada*, at Donato Guerra 9 (☎376/6-14-44; ⑤), by the lake three blocks east of Colón, is a comfortable, welcoming place with lovely gardens and waterside views. For anyone on a budget, the *Hotel Mariana*, off the main square at Guadalupe Victoria 10 (☎376/6-22-21; ④), is probably the best bet, although it does look a little weary these days.

There's also good **food**: the *Nueva Posada* offers pricey but excellent dining in a wonderful lakeside setting, as does the original *Posada Ajijic*, two blocks westwards, while numerous places in the village cater to ex-pat appetites with healthy sandwiches and juices.

San Juan Cosola and Jocotepec

Five kilometres or so along the lakeshore to the west, **SAN JUAN COSOLA** is a resort of a different kind, where a small cluster of hotels offers visitors the chance to bask in natural thermal waters said to have healing properties. The *Motel Balneario* (☎376/1-03-02; ⑥), right beside the lake, is the cheapest, most popular, and the only one open to day-trippers (who can pay US$4 to use the pools). Opposite, *Condominias Cosala* (☎376/1-03-21 to 23; up to four people sharing ⑨) has rooms with TV, around a pool, while on the main road the *Villas Buenaventura* (☎376/1-03-03, fax 1-03-02; ⑥) offer upmarket suites with two bedrooms and a kitchen, and some with a naturally heated jacuzzi.

The last major community along the north shore of the lake, **JOCOTEPEC** is the largest but with fewer tourists and foreign residents than the others. Its chief claim to fame is the manufacture of *sarapes* with elaborately embroidered motifs. You can buy them all around the main square, or at the Sunday market.

Buses between Jocotepec and Guadalajara run on two routes, either along the lakeshore via Chapala, or more directly via the highway from the coast (every 30min).

South towards the coast: Tapalpa

Some of the most delightful alpine scenery in the country lies southwest of Lago Chapala, on the road to Colima. You'll miss much of it if you stick to the super-efficient new toll road, though even that has its exciting moments in the mountains: the following places are all reached from the far slower, far more attractive old road. For a couple of days' relaxation amid upland pastures and pine forests – perfect rambling country – the town of **TAPALPA** makes an ideal base. With its ancient, wooden-balconied houses and magnificent surroundings of ranch country and tree-clad hills, it's beginning to be discovered as a weekend escape from the city, and can get quite crowded, but for the moment its charm is little affected. It's a place to appreciate the cool, fresh air, to walk and to wind down.

Though there's a village feel around the plaza, with its eighteenth-century wooden *portales* and two impressive churches, this is actually a fair-sized place, and messy development on the outskirts reflects rapid growth. The best **walks** are out on the road towards Chiquilistlán (signed as you enter Tapalpa). Here you rapidly escape into fresh-scented pine forest, passing the romantic ruins of a *fabrica* – an old water-driven paper mill – and climb towards a gorgeous valley of upland pasture, studded with wild flowers and with huge boulders that look as if they've been dropped from the sky. About an hour from Tapalpa, this would be a fantastic place to camp, and you probably could with permission, though there are private property signs all along the road. There's good walking in almost any direction from Tapalpa, in fact, and plenty of wildlife, especially birds, to spot; you can also hire **horses** (look for the signs) – a popular ride is to the local waterfall. Be warned that it's very cold in winter, and even the summer nights can get decidedly chilly. Locals brew their own mescal in the village, which may help keep out the draughts; it's sold from the barrel in some of the older shops and is extremely rough (but also very cheap).

Practicalities

Second-class **buses** run from Guadalajara's old bus station to Tapalpa (Sala B, 6.30am–5.30pm; hourly; 3hr 15min); it's advisable to book your return as soon as you arrive, as the late buses are the most popular. In Tapalpa they stop near the ticket office, which is at Matamoros 135, just southwest of the plaza below the red church. Four daily services go direct to Ciudad Guzmán (2hr), but many more pass by the junction of the main road (El Crucero, some 20km away); it's easy enough to catch a bus, or even hitch, down there.

For most things, head for Tapalpa's main plaza, where several of the old buildings have been refurbished as restaurants and hotels, and there's even an efficient branch of Ban Crecer (**exchange** Mon–Fri 9am–1pm). The municipal **tourist office**, on the north side of the plaza, does not seem to have fixed hours, but you may be lucky and arrive when it's open. The cheapest **place to stay** by some way is the *Hotel Tapalpa* (no phone; ③), above the *Restaurante Tapalpa* on the southern (lower) side of the plaza, with simple rooms and warm showers – expensive for what you get, but there's little competition. The *Posada la Hacienda*, a few doors to its left at Matamoros 7 (☎343/2-01-93; ④), offers little more for a rather higher price, though the rooms are a bit airier. Far nicer – indeed another world altogether – is the *Casa de Maty*, a few doors the other way at Matamoros 69 (☎ & fax 343/2-01-89; ⑤), a beautiful place whose rooms are comforatably rustic. Also offering luxury with country-style charm is the *Villa de San José*, just two blocks southeast of the plaza at Ignacio Lopez 91 (☎343/2-04-51; ⑤). At some weekends all the rooms can be taken, but during the week you'll often be the only outsider.

Numerous **restaurants** serve plain country food – you get good steaks and dairy products up here – though many are open weekends only. One of the best is *Paulinos*, with balcony seats over the plaza and simple but excellent food; cheap food can be found below the plaza's red church opposite the bus ticket office.

On to Colima: Ciudad Guzmán

Beyond the turn-off for Tapalpa, the old main road starts to climb in earnest into the Sierra Madre, passing though **Sayula** (the name chosen by Lawrence for his town on Lago Chapala) and the sizeable city of **CIUDAD GUZMÁN**. Birthplace of José Clemente Orozco, this is a busy, thoroughly Mexican little city, with attractive colonnaded streets in the centre, though there seems little reason to stop except to break a journey. If you do visit, don't miss the lovely little **Museo de las Culturas de Occidente** (Tue–Sun 10am–4.45pm; US$1) on Dr Angel González, just off Reforma one block from the plaza – Reforma is the street that leads from the highway and bus station eastwards into town. It's just one room, but there are some lovely figures and animals in the collection of local archeology, and often an interesting temporary display that may include early works by **Orozco**. As ever, almost everything else is on or around the plaza, where you'll find banks, money changers, phones and **places to stay**. The *Hotel Zapotlan*, at Portal Morelos 61 (☎343/2-00-40, fax 2-47-83; ②), on the west side of the square, has a beautiful old wrought-iron courtyard, which sadly the rooms don't live up to (there's a variety of rooms at a variety of prices, so take a look around); a block to the south, the *Hotel Flamingos*, at Federico del Toro 133 (☎343/2-01-03; ②), has less character but is clean and quiet. The cheapest place to stay is the *Hotel Morelos*, off the southwest corner of the square at Refugio Barragán del Toscano 20 (no phone; ③), whose rooms are basic, but clean.

Back on the plaza are a few taquerías and a couple of **restaurants**: the *Juanito*, at Portal Morelos 65, a few doors from the *Hotel Zapotlan*, and the *Hacienda*, in the northeast corner at Portal de Sandovar 38. There's also the *Romances*, a bar-restaurant in the arcade at Portal Morelos 85. Cheap food and drink can also be found at the bus station.

Buses to Ciudad Guzmán stop at a station ten minutes' walk from the plaza (local bus #6 will drop you very nearby), though most people will find it quicker to walk into town than to wait for a bus. There are buses roughly hourly to Guadalajara's Camionera Nueva (2hr), and cheaper but slower buses every hour to the Camionera Vieja (3hr 30min). There are also hourly buses the other way to Colima (1hr) and Manzanillo (3hr), and three daily services direct to México (9hr).

Between Ciudad Guzmán and Colima, the drive becomes truly spectacular, through country dominated by the **Nevado de Colima** – at 4335m the loftiest and most impressive peak in the west, which is snowcapped in winter. The new road slashes straight through the mountains via deep cuts and soaring concrete bridges, while the old one twists and turns above and beneath it as it switchbacks its way through the hills. Both have great views of the Nevado, at least when it's not covered in cloud. If you're on the old road, close your windows as you pass through **Atenquique**, a lovely if odorous hidden valley some 25km from Ciudad Guzmán, which is enveloped in a pall of fumes from a vast paperworks plant. Not far from here, off the road but on the main train line to the coast, and served by two buses an hour from Ciudad Guzmán, **Tuxpan** is a beautiful and ancient little town, with a few hotels – it's especially fun during its frequent, colourful fiestas.

Tequila

The approach to **TEQUILA**, some 50km northwest of Guadalajara, is through great fields of spiky blue agave, a species of maguey cactus. It's from these ugly plants that they make the quintessentially Mexican liquor to which the town lends its name, producing it in vast quantities at a series of local distilleries (pulque and mescal are made from a different species of maguey). More than 100 million litres of tequila are manufactured annually, and this simple product alone accounts for some three percent of Mexico's export earnings. The town itself is a rather dusty, but pretty, little place, whose scattering of bourgeois mansions and fine church are somewhat overwhelmed by the trappings of thriving modern business. But no matter: you don't come here to sightsee, you come to drink. Or at least to visit the distilleries.

They've made tequila here since the seventeenth century and probably earlier, but the oldest and most important surviving **distillery** is La Perseverancia, the Sauza operation founded in 1875, where tours are available in English or Spanish (US$2.50). To get there, follow Ramon Corona from the plaza down beside the Banco Promex. If you'd like to learn more, Sauza also operate an experimental cactus farm, again open to the public (same ticket as the distillery), on the edge of town at Rancho El Indio, where they have planted some 197 different varieties of maguey. The other main distillery, José Cuervos, also offer tours (US$1.25), which can be arranged through the tourist desk in front of the town hall in the main square. There are plenty of cafés around the plaza in Tequila for less potent drinks.

It's easy enough **to get to Tequila** on regular buses from Guadalajara's old bus station (Sala B, every 20min; 1hr 45min); there are also tours from Guadalajara run by Panoramex (see p.168) for US$20 (less if you pay in pesos), among others.

San Juan de los Lagos and Lagos de Moreno

Heading east from Guadalajara towards León, Aguascalientes and the Bajío, the old highway runs through **SAN JUAN DE LOS LAGOS**. From its outskirts, about 150km from Guadalajara, San Juan seems like just another dusty little town, but in the centre you'll find an enormous bus station surrounded by scores of hotels. This is thanks to the vast parish church and the miraculous **image of the Virgin** that it contains, making it one of the most important pilgrimage centres in Mexico. The site's busiest dates – when the place is crammed with penitents, pilgrims seeking miraculous cures, and others who are just there to enjoy the atmosphere – are February 2 (**Día de la Candelaria**) and December 8 (**Fiesta de la Inmaculada Concepción**), but celebration spills over, and there are several lesser events throughout the year, notably the first fortnight of August and the entire Christmas period. There's little chance of finding a room at these times and little point in staying at any other, so it's best to treat San Juan de los Lagos as a day-trip from – or stopover between – Lagos de Moreno and Guadalajara (less than an hour from the former, around three hours from Guadalajara).

Lagos de Moreno

Just 45km east of San Juan, **LAGOS DE MORENO** lies on the intersection where the road from México to Ciudad Juárez crosses the route from Guadalajara to San Luis Potosí and the northeast. Though the town has always been a major staging post, surprisingly few people stop here now and, despite the heavy traffic rumbling around its fringes, it's a quiet and rather beautiful little town, with colonial streets climbing steeply from a small river to a hilltop monastery.

Cross the bridge by the bus station and head to your left along the stream, away from the choking fumes of the main road, and it's hard to believe you're in the same place. The **zócalo** is the place to head, whether you plan to stay a couple of hours or a few days: in the streets around are a massive Baroque church and a scattering of colonial mansions and official buildings, including an unfeasibly forbidding-looking jail that's still in use. Once you've seen the centre, you might want to embark on the long climb up to the **hillside church** – the monastery is inhabited by monks, so you can't visit, and the church itself is tumbling down, but it's worth the trek, especially towards sunset, for the views alone.

There are several run-down but comfortable **hotels** near the zócalo. The delightful and friendly *Hotel Plaza* (③), right on the square at Juárez 426, has clean rooms around an open courtyard. Also on the square itself, the *Hotel Paris* (☎474/2-02-00; ③) is a bizarre, stark building and a little overpriced for what you get; the slightly posher *Hotel Colonial* (☎474/2-01-42; ④), Hidalgo 279, has its own restaurant and a very friendly and helpful manager. The zócalo also boasts a few good **bars** and **places to eat**.

Getting **to and from Lagos de Moreno** could hardly be easier: there are buses at least every thirty minutes from Guadalajara, León, Aguascalientes, Zacatecas and México.

INTO MICHOACÁN

To the southeast of Jalisco and Guadalajara, **Michoacán** state is one of the most beautiful and diverse in all Mexico – spreading as it does from a very narrow coastal plain, with several tiny beach villages (see Chapter 6), up to where the Sierra Madre Occidental reaches out eastwards into range after range of wooded volcanic heights. Several of the towns, including the delightfully urbane capital, **Morelia**, are utterly colonial in appearance, but on the whole Michoacán's attractions are simpler ones. The land is green and thriving everywhere – in **Uruapan** the lush countryside seems to press in on the town, and is certainly the main attraction – while throughout the state there is a very active native tradition and a strength of indigenous culture matched only in the state of Oaxaca. This is largely thanks to Michoacán's first bishop, **Vasco de Quiroga**, one of the very few early Spanish colonists to see the Indian population as anything more than a slave-labour force. The fruits of Quiroga's efforts are most clear in and around **Pátzcuaro**, the beautiful lakeside town that was his base. Here and in the surrounding villages, traditional and introduced crafts from weaving to guitar-manufacture have flourished for centuries, and today this region is one of the most important sources of Mexican *artesanías*. Native traditions also draw large crowds to the lake for the **Day of the Dead** at the beginning of November, one of the most striking of Mexican celebrations.

On the whole, Michoacán is a region that people travel through rather than to, however. Morelia, Pátzcuaro, Uruapan and other towns lie conveniently on a direct route from Guadalajara to México. You could easily spend several days in each, or weeks trying to explore the state fully, but even in a couple of days passing through you can get a strong flavour of the area.

Some history
When the Spanish first arrived here in 1519, they found the region dominated by the **Tarascan (Purépecha)** kingdom, whose chief town, Tzintzuntzán, lay on the shores of Lago Pátzcuaro. Their civilization, a serious rival to the Aztecs before the Conquest, had a widespread reputation for excellence in art, metal-working and feathered ornaments. The Tarascans submitted peaceably to the Spanish in 1522, and their leader was converted to Christianity, but this didn't prevent the massacres and mass torture that Nuño de Guzmán meted out in his attempts to pacify the region and make himself a fortune in the course of the next few years. **Quiroga** was appointed bishop in an attempt to restore harmony – Guzmán's methods going too far even for the Spanish – and succeeded beyond all expectation. Setting himself up as the champion of the native peoples, his name is still revered today. He encouraged the population down from the mountains whence they had fled, established settlements self-sufficient in agriculture and set up missions to teach practical skills as well as religion. The effects have survived in a very visible way for, despite some blurring in objects produced for the tourist trade, each village still has its own craft speciality: lacquerware in Pátzcuaro and Uruapan, pottery in Tzintzuntzán, wooden furniture in Quiroga, guitars in Paracho.

Vasco de Quiroga also left behind him a deeply religious state. Michoacán was a stronghold of the reactionary *Cristero* movement, which fought a bitter war in defence of the Church after the Revolution. Perhaps, too, the ideals of Zapata and Villa had less appeal here; Quiroga's early championing of native peoples' rights against their new overlords meant that the hacienda system never entirely took over Michoacán and, unlike most of the country, the state boasted a substantial peasantry with land it could call its own.

Guadalajara to Uruapan

From Guadalajara, the direct route to México heads east through the major junction of La Piedad to join the super-highway outside Irapuato. If you can afford to dawdle a little, though, it's infinitely more rewarding to follow the slower, southern road through Zamora and Morelia, taking a couple of days to cut off through Uruapan and Pátzcuaro. From Uruapan, a reasonably good road slices south through the mountains to the Pacific coast at Lázaro Cárdenas (see p.371).

Leaving Guadalajara, you skirt the northeastern edge of Lake Chapala before cutting south, heading into Michoacán and reaching **ZAMORA DE HIDALGO**, some 200km away. Founded in 1540, Zamora today has little intrinsic interest. However, if you're planning to head straight down to Uruapan you may want to change buses here: it's possible to go direct from Guadalajara, but there are far more buses to Morelia, and if you get as far as Zamora there's a much more frequent service to Uruapan. The town boasts several small restaurants and a market very close to the bus station, but little to go out of your way for. The old cathedral, unusually Gothic in style, is ruined and often closed, but you can while away some time on the pleasant grassy plaza in front.

The turn-off for Uruapan actually comes in the village of **Carapán**, some 40km further on; as an alternative to changing in Zamora, you could get off here and flag down a bus going south. The route, on a road winding through pine-draped hills, is a beautiful one. About halfway along you pass through the village of **PARACHO**, which has been famous for the manufacture of stringed instruments since Quiroga's time. Every house seems to be either a workshop, a guitar shop or both. The instruments vary enormously in price and quality – many are not meant to be anything more than ornamental, hung on the wall rather than played, but others are serious and beautifully handcrafted. Though you'll find them on display and for sale in the markets and artesanías museums in Uruapan or Pátzcuaro, if you want to buy, stop off here. Paracho also hosts a couple of fascinating **fiestas**. On Corpus Christi (the Thursday after Trinity, usually late May/early June) you can witness the dance of *Los Viejitos*. This, the most famous of Michoacán's dances, is also one of its most picturesque, with the dancers, dressed in baggy white cotton and masked as old men, alternating between parodying the tottering steps of the *viejitos* they represent and breaking into complex routines. Naturally enough, there's a lot of music, too. August 8 sees an even more ancient ceremony, whose roots go back to well before the Spanish era: an ox is sacrificed and its meat used to make a complicated ritual dish – *shuripe* – which is then shared out among the celebrants.

Uruapan

URUAPAN, they say, means "the place where flowers bloom" in the Tarascan language, though *Appleton's Guide* for 1884 tells a different story: "The word Uruapan comes from *Urani*, which means in the Tarasc language "a chocolate cup", because the Indians in this region devote themselves to manufacture and painting of these objects." Demand for chocolate cups, presumably, has fallen since then. Whatever the truth, the modern version is certainly appropriate: Uruapan, lower (at just over 1500m) and warmer than most of its neighbours, enjoys a steamy subtropical climate and is surrounded by thick forests and lush parks.

It's a prosperous and growing town, too, with a thriving commerce based on the richness of its agriculture (particularly a vast export market in **avocados**) and on new light industry. To some extent this has come to overshadow the old attractions, creating ugly new development and displacing traditional crafts. But it remains a lively place with a fine market, an abiding reputation for **lacquerware**, and fascinating surroundings – especially the giant waterfall and "new" volcano of Paricutín.

Arrival and information

Most visitors arrive at Uruapan's modern **bus station**, 3km from the centre; a local bus (marked "Centro") from right outside will take you down to the Jardín Morelos, the plaza in the heart of town, or back again from there. There are also three **trains** a week from Pátzcuaro, Morelia and México, and the other way from Lázaro Cárdenas, but it's a painfully slow way to travel. Again, there's a bus into town from the station.

Uruapan's **tourist office** (daily 9am–2pm & 4–7pm; ☎452/3-61-72) is at Ocampo 64, in the arcade under the *Hotel Plaza* on the west side of Jardín Morelos; both the tourist office and the hotel give away a good map of town. There are numerous **banks** in the streets around the plaza if you need to change money, and **casas de cambio** at Portal Matamoros 18 on the south side of the plaza, Portal Degollado 15 in the northeast corner, Carranza 14D, just west of the plaza, and Obregón 1D to its east. The **post office** (Mon–Fri 9am–8pm, Sat 9am–1pm) is at Reforma 11, three blocks south of the plaza. Long-distance **casetas** include Computel at Ocampo 3 on the west side of the plaza and at the bus station, and Telmex at 5 de Febrero 12A, just south of the plaza.

Accommodation

Uruapan seems to have more than its fair share of **hotels**, most of them conveniently sited around – or at least within walking distance of – Jardín Morelos.

Capri, 10 Portal Degollado 10 at the eastern end of the plaza (no phone). Basic and busy, right in the heart of town, with the action of the plaza often spilling over into the lobby. A much better bet than the *Oseguera* and the *Modetno* on the same block. ②.

Concordia, Portal Carillo 8 (☎452/3-04-00). On the plaza, modern, clean and efficent: all rooms with TV and phone. Parking facilities. ⑤.

Gran Hotel Acosta, Filomena Mata 325 (☎452/3-45-64). Opposite the bus station, this is hardly an ideal spot, but if you're passing through it does offer clean, simple, reasonably priced rooms. ②.

Mansion del Cupatitzio, at the north end of the Parque Eduardo Ruiz (☎452/3-20-70 or 3-20-90, fax 4-67-72). Uruapan's finest hotel, with pool, restaurant and beautiful grounds. ⑥.

Mi Solar, Juan Delgado 10, a block north of the plaza (☎452/4-09-12). Large, clean rooms with sporadic hot water, set around two large courtyards. ②.

Hotel del Parque, Independencia 124, near the Parque Nacional (☎452/4-38-45). Best deal of the cheapies: clean and friendly, with large rooms (those at the front are nicest but a bit noisy), en-suite bathrooms and parking facilities. ③.

Plaza Uruapan, Ocampo 64 (☎452/3-35-99, fax 3-39-80). Big, modern hotel at the western end of the plaza, with good views from the rooms and the second-floor restaurant. ⑥.

Regis, Portal Carillo 12 (☎452/3-58-44). Friendly place in a central location with its own parking lot; rooms have TV and some overlook the plaza. ④.

Victoria, Cupatitzio 11 (☎452/3-67-00; fax 3-96-62). Another fine, modern hotel with a garage and good restaurant. ④.

Villa de Flores, E Carranza 15 (☎452/4-28-00). Clean, simple rooms around a beautiful little courtyard filled, as the name suggests, with flowers, though it does have a rather lurid colour scheme. ④.

The Town

The **Jardín Morelos**, a long strip of tree-shaded open space, is in every sense the heart of Uruapan. Always animated, it's surrounded by everything of importance: shops, market, banks, post office, principal churches and most of the hotels. This is the place to head first, either to find a hotel or simply to get a feel for the place. On the plaza, too, is the town's one overt tourist attraction, *La Huatapera*. One of the oldest surviving buildings in Uruapan, it has been restored to house the **Museo Regional de Arte Popular** (Tues–Sun 9.30am–1.30pm & 3.30–6pm; free), an impressive display of crafts from the region, especially Uruapan's own lacquerwork. The small courtyard with its adjoining chapel was built by Juan de San Miguel, the Franciscan friar who founded the town itself. Later it became one of Bishop Quiroga's hospitals and training centres, so its present function seems appropriate. The carving around the windows bears a marked Arab influence, as they were crafted by Christianized Moorish artesans from Spain (*Mudéjares*). The wares shown are of the highest quality, and are worth close inspection if you plan to go out hunting for bargains in the market or in the shops around the park. The art of making lacquer is complex and time-consuming, involving the application of layer upon layer of different colours, with the design cut into the background: all too many of the goods produced for tourists are simply given a couple of coats – one for the black background with a design then painted on top – far quicker and cheaper, but not the same thing at all.

The **market** begins right behind the museum. Walk round to the back and you come first to the **Mercado de Antojitos**, a large open section just half a block south of the plaza, where women serve up meals for stallholders and visitors alike at a series of long, open-air tables. This is where you'll find the cheapest, and very often the freshest and best, food in town. The rest of the market sprawls around here, along Corregidora and up Constitución – replete with herbs, fruit, trinkets, shoe stalls and hot-dog stands. It's not a particularly good place to buy **native crafts**, though – the market that sells those is altogether more commercialized, and concentrated in a series of shops along **Independencia**, which leads up from the plaza to the Parque Nacional. At the top of this street are several small places where you can watch the artisans at work – some are no more than a single room with a display of finished goods on one side and a worktable on the other, while others are more sophisticated operations. Opposite the entrance to the park is a little "craft market", mostly selling very poor souvenirs.

The Río Cupatitzio and the Parque Nacional Eduardo Ruíz

The **Parque Nacional Eduardo Ruíz** (daily 8am–6pm; US$0.50) is perhaps Uruapan's proudest asset, a luxuriant tropical park in which the Río Cupatitzio rises and through which it flows in a little gorge via a series of man-made cascades and fountains. The river springs from a rock known as *La Rodilla del Diablo* ("the Devil's knee"), so called, runs the legend, because water gushed forth after the Devil knelt here in submission before the unswerving Christian faith of the drought-ridden population. Alternatively, Beelzebub met the Virgin Mary while out strolling in the park, and dropped to his knees in respect. *Cupatitzio* means "where the waters meet", though it's invariably translated as "the river that sings" – another appropriate, if not entirely accurate, tag. If you don't feel like walking to get here, take a bus up Independencia.

Some 12km out of Uruapan, the Cupatitzio crashes over the **waterfall of La Tzaráracua**, an impressive 25-metre plunge amid beautiful forest scenery. This is a popular outing with locals, especially at weekends, and hence easy enough to get to – take one of the buses (marked "Tzaráracua") from Madero at Cupatitzio, a block south of the plaza, or share a taxi. If it seems too crowded here, make for the smaller fall, **Tzararacuita**, about 1km further downstream.

Eating and drinking

The best place to sample local delights at low prices has to be the **Mercado de Antojitos**; otherwise there are several good cheap cafés on Independencia, just off the plaza, all serving a selection of hamburgers, tacos, pizzas, sandwiches and superb licuados.

Café Tradicional de Uruapan, Emiliano Carranza 5. Great breakfasts, superb local coffee, ice cream, cakes and antojitos.

Comida Economica Mary, Independencia 59. Wholesome home-style cooking at low-prices; great for breakfast and lunch.

La Lucha, Portal Matamoros 15, on the south side of the plaza. A small bar basically serving only coffee, but it's good.

La Pergola, south side of the plaza at Portal Carrillo 4. Reasonably priced, popular restaurant serving a good comida corrida, local coffee and a selection of regional and national dishes.

Rincon del Burrito Real, Portal Matamoros 8, on the south side of the plaza. A reasonable place for breakfasts, burgers, enchiladas and burritos.

Super Soya, Portal Matamoros 18, on the south side of the plaza. Juices, ice creams and good-value vegetarian meals.

Paricutín

An ideal day-trip from Uruapan, which gives you an unusual taste of the surrounding countryside, is to the "new" **Volcano of Paricutín**, about 20km northwest of town. On February 20, 1943, a peasant working in his fields noticed the earth begin to move and then to smoke. The ground soon cracked and lava began to flow – eventually, over a period of several years, engulfing the village of Paricutín and several other hamlets, and forcing the evacuation of some seven thousand inhabitants. The volcano was active for eight years, producing a cone some 300m high and devastating an area of around twenty square kilometres. Now there are vast fields of cooled lava, black and powdery, cracked into harsh jags, along with the dead cone and crater. Most bizarrely, a church tower – all that remains of the buried hamlet of San Juan Parangaricutiro – pokes its head through the surface. During its active life, the volcano drew tourists from around the world, and indeed it's partly responsible for the area's current development; less exciting now, it continues to get a fair number of visitors, though as the years pass the landscape is sure to soften. Such events are not altogether unprecedented – Von Humboldt devoted more than ten pages of his book on New Spain to the volcano of Jorullo, south of Pátzcuaro, which appeared equally suddenly in September 1759 – this was still hot enough, he reported, that "in the year 1780, cigars might still be lighted, when they were fastened to a stick and pushed in". Jorullo is no longer the subject of any interest – indeed no one seems to know quite where it is.

To get to the volcano, start early. Take a bus (headed toward Los Reyes or Zicuicho) from the Central Camionera in Uruapan to the village of **ANGAHUAN** (half-hourly 5am–7.45pm; about 40min). The bus drops you on the highway outside the village, from where you should walk to the plaza and turn right down Juárez for about 200m until you pass a superbly carved wooden building on the left; there take a left turn (signposted) and head straight on for about a kilometre. You eventually arrive at the Centro Turistico de Angahuan (☎452/5-03-85; entry US$1), which offers superb views of the volcano from its *mirador*, and has a small **museum** (daily 6am–8pm) with diagrams (explained in Spanish only) of the volcano and local plate tectonics. The Centro also has dorms with full facilities (US$16), and six-bunk cabins, each with an open fire (US$10 for two people); alternatively, you can pitch a tent in the grounds.

Though the trip to the Centro Turistico and the half-buried church can be done in a morning, the journey to the crater is more complicated. In Angahuan you should have no problem finding a guide, whether you want one or not. It's not really necessary if you're just going up the hill for a look, but it seems harsh not to allow the locals some profit from their misfortune (although the volcano was not all bad news, its dust proving a fine fertilizer on the fields that escaped the full flow). For the longer journey to the centre you do need a guide, and probably a horse, too; it's not an outrageous expense, and certainly well worth it. A short ride out to the buried church takes just thirty minutes; a full ascent of the volcano is a day-trip: take some provisions.

Angahuan's own church, in the main plaza, is worth a second glance as you pass through the village. Built in the sixteenth century, its doorway is carved in the largely Arab *Mudéjar* style by Andalusian artesans (Andalusia was the centre of fine arts in the Arab empire until the fall of Granada in 1492). The cross in the courtyard, on the other hand, is most definitely Mexican, complete with serpents, a skull and other pre-Hispanic motifs. In the street to the right of the church (as you look at it), across from the side gate of the courtyard, a door carved in more modern style recounts the history of the volcano from its first appearance to the arrival of tourists seeking it out.

Pátzcuaro

PÁTZCUARO is almost exactly halfway between Uruapan and Morelia, some 60km from both, yet strikingly different from either. Much smaller – little more than a village, really, swollen somewhat by the tourist trade – it manages to be at one and the same time a far more colonial town than Uruapan, and infinitely more Indian than Morelia. For this reason, Pátzcuaro could rightly be called the most classic of Mexican towns: dotted with Spanish-style mansions and sumptuous churches, yet owing little or nothing in its lifestyle to the colonists. Add to this the fact that it sits by the shore of probably the most beautiful **lake** in Mexico – certainly the most photogenic, especially during Pátzcuaro's famed **Day of the Dead** celebrations (see p.196) – and it's hardly surprising that it acts as a magnet for tourists, Mexicans and foreigners alike. In the vicinity, you can take trips around the lake, visit other, less developed villages, and see the site of **Tzintzuntzán**, one-time capital of the Tarascan kingdom.

Arrival and information

The new **bus station** in the south of town is about fifteen minutes' walk, or a brief bus ride ("Centro" or "Col Popular"), from the centre. If you arrive by **train** you'll be further out still, but again a "Centro" bus will take you in. Buses back to both train and bus stations can be picked up in Plaza Bocanegra. Although the outskirts of Pátzcuaro straggle a kilometre or so down to the lakeshore, and some of the more expensive hotels are strung out along this drive, the centre of town is very small indeed, focusing on the two main squares, **Plaza Vasco de Quiroga** (or Plaza Grande) and **Plaza Bocanegra** (Plaza Chica).

The **tourist office** (Mon–Sat 9am–2pm & 4–7pm, Sun 9am–2pm; ☎434/2-12-14) is at Plaza Quiroga 50A, on the north side of the plaza. For **currency exchange** there are banks on both plazas and casas de cambio at Plaza Quiroga 67 on the north side of the plaza, at Ibarra 2 just off the plaza, and at the corner of Padre Lloreda and Ahumada near the *Hotel Valmen*.

The **post office** is on Obregón 13 (Mon–Fri 8am–4pm, Sat 9am–1pm). You can **phone and fax** from Computel on the north side of Plaza Bocanegra, or casetas at Portal Hidalgo 67 on the west side of Plaza Quiroga, Dr Mendoza 21 between the plazas, or in the entrance to the *Posada de la Rosa* on Plaza Bocanegra; card-phones seem to be virtually non-existent.

Accommodation

Few of Pátzcuaro's many **hotels** are very cheap, but it does have some of the best mid-range places you'll find anywhere, and if you're prepared to pay a little extra for a lot more elegance you should get excellent value. Most are on one or other of the plazas, with the ritzier establishments surrounding Vasco de Quiroga and a more basic selection around the Plaza Bocanegra. Wherever you stay, check that there will be an adequate **water supply** – Pátzcuaro suffers regular shortages.

During the first two days of November, when the town celebrates the **Day of the Dead** on the lake, there is little chance of getting a room anywhere near Pátzcuaro without prior booking.

Concordia, Portal Juaréz 31, Plaza Bocanegra (☎434/2-00-03). Large, chilly place but probably the best bargain in town. Simple clean rooms, some without bathrooms. ③.

Los Escudos, Portal Hidalgo 73, west side of Plaza Vasco de Quiroga (☎434/2-01-38). Beautiful colonial building with rooms around two flower-filled courtyards; all have carpet and TV, some their own fireplaces. There's also a superb restaurant. ④.

Fiesta Plaza, Plaza Bocanegra 24 (☎ & fax 434/2-25-15). Big, simple hotel with three floors of rooms set around an open courtyard. ⑤.

Gran Hotel, Plaza Bocanegra 6 (☎434/2-04-43). Clean, friendly hotel with small rooms and a good restaurant. ④.

Hotel Posada de la Basilica, Arciga 6 (☎434/2-11-08, fax 2-06-59). Up the hill opposite the basilica. Simple rooms in an old colonial building with superb views across the town's rooftops. ⑥.

Mansion Iturbe, Portal Morelos 59, north side of Plaza Vasco de Quiroga (☎434/2-03-68, fax 43/13-45-93; *pazcuaro@mail.giga.com*). Another colonial mansion retaining plenty of grandeur. Rates are lower out of season, and every fourth night is free. ⑨.

Misión San Manuel, Portal Aldama 12 (☎434/2-13-13). The great colonial front hides a modern interior, nevertheless this ex-convent offers comfortable rooms with fireplaces. ⑤.

Hotel Meson del Gallo, on Lerin near the basilica. One of the best hotels in town, complete with pool and excellent restaurant (see p.195). ⑤.

Posada de la Rosa, Portal Juaréz 29, Plaza Bocanegra (☎434/2-08-11). Next door to the *Concordia*; smaller, with rooms around an upstairs courtyard, and the lowest prices in town. ②.

Posada de la Salud, Serrato 9 (☎434/2-00-58). Beside the basilica, a short walk from the centre. Beautiful little hotel, peaceful and spotless; some rooms have fireplaces. Good value. ③.

Posada San Rafael, Plaza Vasco de Quiroga 16 (☎434/2-07-70). One of the largest and fanciest hotels, with a long modern extension in colonial style behind the genuinely colonial front. ④.

Valmen, Lloreda 34 (☎434/2-11-61). Large clean rooms with bathrooms and low prices, but a 10pm curfew. ②.

The Town

More than anywhere in the state, Pátzcuaro owes its position to Bishop Vasco de Quiroga's affection for the indigenous peoples (you'll find his statue in the centre of the plaza that bears his name). It was he who decided, in the face of considerable opposition from the Spanish in Morelia (then known as Valladolid), to build the cathedral here. And although subsequent bishops moved back to Morelia, a basis had been laid: indeed it's the fact that Pátzcuaro enjoyed a building boom in the sixteenth century and has been something of a backwater ever since that creates much of its charm. Throughout the centre are old mansions with balconies and coats-of-arms, barely touched since those early years.

The plazas

Nothing much worth seeing in Pátzcuaro lies more than a few minutes' walk from **Plaza Bocanegra**, named for Gertrudis Bocanegra, a local Independence heroine, and **Plaza Vasco de Quiroga**. The finest of Pátzcuaro's mansions are on the latter – especially the seventeenth-century **Casa del Gigante**, with its hefty pillars and crudely carved figures, and another nearby said to have been inhabited by Prince Huitzimengari, son of the last Tarascan king. Both are privately owned, however, and not open to visitors. There are more on the Plaza Bocanegra, but the most striking thing here is the **Biblioteca** (Mon–Fri 9am–2pm & 4–7pm). The former sixteenth-century church of San Agustín, it has been converted into a library and decorated with

murals by Juan O'Gorman depicting the history of Michoacán, and of the Tarascans in particular. O'Gorman (1905–82) possessed a prodigious talent, and is one of the muralists who inherited the mantle of Rivera and Orozco: his best-known work is the decoration of the interior of Chapultepec Castle in México. The paintings here couldn't be described as subtle, and he certainly ensures that the anti-imperialist point is taken – and even O'Gorman manages to find praise for Vasco de Quiroga.

The Basilica

East of the Plaza Bocanegra, Quiroga's cathedral – the **Basilica**, or Colegiata – though never completed, is massive for such a small town. Even so, it is often full, for the Indians continue to revere Don Vasco's name and the church possesses a miraculous healing image of the Virgin, crafted in the traditional Tarascan method out of *pasta de caña*, a gum-like modelling paste made principally from maize. Services here, especially on saints' days, during fiestas – when the scrubby little **park** around the church becomes a fairground – or on the 8th of each month, when pilgrims gather to seek the Virgin's intercession, are extraordinary: you'll witness the worshippers in an intense, almost hypnotic fervour.

Museo de Artes Populares

The **Museo de Artes Populares**, at the corner of Quiroga and Lerin, south of the basilica (Tues–Sat 9am–7pm, Sun 9am–3pm; US$1.75, free on Sun), occupies the ancient Colegio de San Nicolas. Founded by Quiroga in 1540, the college is now devoted to a superb collection of regional handicrafts: local lacquerware and pottery; copperware from Santa Clara del Cobre; and traditional masks and religious objects made from *pasta de caña*, which, apart from being easy to work with, is also very light, and hence easily carried in processions. Some of the objects on display are ancient, others the best examples of modern work, and all set in a very beautiful building. Almost opposite, the church of **La Compañía** was built by Quiroga in 1546 and later taken over by the Jesuits. Quiroga's remains and various relics associated with him are preserved here.

Casa de los Once Patios

A short walk south of the art museum, on Lerin, the **Casa de los Once Patios** (daily 10am–7pm, though individual stores may keep their own hours) is an eighteenth-century convent converted into a crafts showhouse, full of workshops and expensive boutiques. As its name suggests, the complex is set around a series of tiny courtyards, and it's a fascinating place to stroll through even if you can't afford the goods. You can watch restored treadle looms at work, admire the intricacy with which the best lacquerware is applied, and wander at liberty through the warren of rooms and corridors.

El Humilladero and Cerro del Estribo

In the other direction, a thirty-minute walk from the basilica up Serrato, lies the church known as "**El Humilladero**" (frequent buses, marked "El Panteon", also run here). Probably the oldest in Pátzcuaro, this stands on the site where the last Tarascan king, Tanganxoan II, accepted Spanish authority. "The place of humiliation", then, may seem an appropriate tag with hindsight, though a more charitable view suggests that Tanganxoan was simply hoping to save his people from the slaughter that had accompanied resistance to the Spanish elsewhere. The chapel itself offers little to see, so you might be better saving your hiking energies for a climb up the **Cerro del Calvario**, the tiny hill just west of town. A few minutes' walk will reward you with a great view of the lake, which is invisible as long as you stay in town. Leave the Plaza Grande on Ponce de León, pass the old customs house and a little plaza in front of the church of San

Francisco, and keep straight on until you start climbing the hill. At the top is the little **chapel of El Calvario**, and if you take the road to the right here you can carry on to the much higher **Cerro del Estribo** (Stirrup Hill), about an hour's walk. For the better view with less effort, you could take a taxi, which leaves you at the bottom of 417 steps that climb to the summit.

Eating and drinking

Most of Pátzcuaro's hotels have their own **restaurants**, with fairly standard menus throughout – lots of good-value, if unexciting, comidas corridas. One feature of virtually all menus is *pescado blanco*, the rather flabby white fish from the lake, and *sopa tarasca* – a tomato-based soup with chile and bits of tortilla in it that's usually very good. Cheap eats are hard to come by, but there are a few basic food stalls in the **market**. This used to operate just one day a week in the streets leading up from the Plaza Bocanegra, but nowadays there is some activity every day, though Monday and Wednesday tend to be slow – it's at its most colourful and animated on Friday, when the *indígenas* come in from the country to trade and barter their surplus. Most evenings you can also get basic food from the stalls set up in the Plaza Bocanegra. For the best **fish**, you'll want to go down to the lake, where a line of restaurants faces the landing jetty (see below). Stalls outside the *Hotel los Escudos* in Plaza Quiroga sell good **ice cream**, including tamarind, tequila and corn flavours.

Restaurants and cafés

Dany's, Zaragoza 32, between the plazas. Charming little restaurant serving a selection of moderately priced international and Mexican food in a very civilized atmosphere, complete with crisp tablecloths and wine list.

Misión del Arriero, in the *Hotel Meson del Gallo* on Lerin near the basilica. Considerably more expensive restaurant than most, but with a very successfully contrived colonial atmosphere and interesting Mexican food.

El Monje, Plaza Quiroga 14. Good restaurant with reasonably priced breakfasts and lunchtime menu, but no credit cards accepted.

El Patio, Plaza Quiroga 19. Quite a chic little restaurant offering good coffee, reasonably priced breakfasts, Mexican antojitos, steaks, sandwiches and, of course, fish.

Lago de Pátzcuaro

Pátzcuaro's other great attraction is, of course, **the lake**. It's less than an hour's walk down to the jetty (follow the "embarcadero" signs), while buses and minibuses leave from the Plaza Bocanegra – those marked "Lago" will drop you right by the boats, while "Santa Ana" buses pass close by.

With the completion of several new roads, the lake itself is no longer the major thoroughfare it once was – most locals now take the bus rather than paddle around the water in canoes – but there is still a fair amount of traffic and regular trips out to the closest island, **Janitzio**. Fares are fixed (get your ticket before you board) but there are almost always sundry "extras". Chief of these is a chance to photograph the famous butterfly nets wielded by indigenous fishermen from tiny dug-out canoes. It's hard to believe that anyone actually uses these nets for fishing any more – they look highly impractical – but there's almost always a group of islanders lurking in readiness on the far side of the island, only to paddle into camera range when a sufficiently large collection of money has been taken.

Longer **trips around the lake** and visits to the other islands, or private rental of a boat and guide, can be arranged at the embarcadero, either through the office there or by private negotiation with one of the boatmen. Prices are high, but not prohibitive if there are a few of you.

The **Day of the Dead** (November 1, and through the night into the next day) is celebrated in spectacular fashion throughout Mexico, but nowhere more so than on Lago Pátzcuaro. Although many tourists come to watch, this is essentially a private meditation, when the locals carry offerings of fruit and flowers to the cemetery and hold vigil over the graves of their ancestors all night, chanting by candlelight. It's a spectacular and moving sight, especially earlier in the evening as *indígenas* from the surrounding area converge on the island in their canoes, each with a single candle burning in the bows.

Janitzio

From the moment you step ashore on the island of **Janitzio**, you're besieged by souvenir hawkers. Don't be put off, though, for the views from the top of the island, which rises steeply from the water to a massive statue of Morelos at the summit, are truly spectacular. If the hawkers seem persistent, that's because tourism is the only possible source of a meagre income apart from fishing on this impoverished island. Up the single steep street, between the stalls selling pottery and crude wood-carvings, a series of little restaurants display their wares out front – most have good fish, and often great bubbling vats of *caldo de pescado*.

Tzintzuntzán

The remains of **TZINTZUNTZÁN** (daily 9am–6pm; US$1.75, free on Sun), ancient capital of the Tarascans, lie 15km north of Pátzcuaro on the lakeshore. The site was established around the end of the fourteenth century, when the capital was moved from Pátzcuaro, and by the time of the Conquest the Spanish estimated that there were as many as 40,000 people living here, with dominion over all of what is now Michoacán and large parts of the modern states of Jalisco and Colima. Homes and markets, as well as the palaces of the rulers, lay around the raised **ceremonial centre**, but all that can be seen today is the artificial terrace that supported the great religious buildings (*yacatas*), and the ruins, partly restored, of these temples.

Even if you do no more than pass by on the road, you can't fail to be struck by the scale of these buildings and by their elliptical design, a startling contrast to the rigid, right-angled formality adhered to by almost every other major pre-Hispanic culture in Mexico. Climb up to the terrace and you'll find five *yacatas*, of which two have been partly rebuilt. Each was originally some 15m high, tapering in steps from a broad base to a walkway along the top less than two metres wide. Devoid of ornamentation, the *yacatas* are in fact piles of flat rocks, held in by retaining walls and then faced in smooth, close-fitting volcanic stone. The terrace, which was originally approached up a broad ceremonial ramp or stairway on the side furthest from the water, affords magnificent views across the lake and the present-day village of Tzintzuntzán. Tzintzuntzán means "place of the hummingbirds"; you're unlikely to see one nowadays, but the theory is that there were plenty of them around until the Tarascans – who used the feathers to make ornaments – hunted them to the point of extinction.

Down in the **village**, which has a reputation for producing and selling some of the region's best ceramics, you'll find what's left of the enormous **Franciscan Monastery** founded around 1530 to convert the Tarascans. Much of this has been demolished, and the rest substantially rebuilt, but there remains a fine Baroque church and a huge atrium where the indigenous people would gather to be preached at. Vasco de Quiroga originally intended to base his diocese here, but eventually decided that Pátzcuaro had the better location and a more constant supply of water. He did leave one unusual legacy, though: the olive trees planted around the monastery are probably the oldest in Mexico, since settlers were banned from cultivating olives in order to protect the farmers back in Spain.

To get to Tzintzuntzán, take a Quiroga-bound bus from Pátzcuaro's Central Camionera.

Tinganio

If Tzintzuntzán has piqued your interest, then you might also want to check out the older, pre-Tarascan ruin of **TINGANIO** (daily 10am–5pm; US$1.25, free on Sun), on the outskirts of the village of **Tingambato**, roughly halfway between Pátzcuaro and Uruapan. This was first inhabited around 450–600 AD and greatly expanded between 600 and 900 AD. The site is small but pretty and well restored, with a combination of influences: that of Teotihuacán is prevalent and evident in the pyramid that dominates the religious area, overlooking a plaza with a cruciform altar, beyond which is a ball-court, suggesting Toltec influence. Beyond the ball-court, another, unexcavated, pyramid lies under a grove of avocado trees. In the residential area just to the north, a sunken plaza with two altars and five stairways, each to a separate residence is very much in the style of Teotihuacán, but the tomb under the largest residence (which the caretaker will open on request) has a false dome suggestive of Maya influence. Surrounded by beautiful countryside, the site is best appreciated from atop the pyramid. Except on Sundays, you'd be unlucky to see another tourist here.

Second-class buses between Pátzcuaro and Uruapan (every 15min each way) stop in Tingambato, where you follow the main street (signposted "Zona Arqueologica" or with a pyramid symbol) south through town, under a bridge, and then turn right by a school after a few hundred metres to reach the site. A new road from Pátzcuaro to Uruapan, still due to open at the time of writing, will bypass the village and probably reduce the number of buses.

Quiroga

Thanks to its position at the junction of the roads from Pátzcuaro and Morelia to Guadalajara, **QUIROGA**, 10km beyond Tzintzuntzán, is another village packed with craft markets, but the only genuinely local products seem to be painted wooden objects and furniture. Really it's no more than a stopover, but if you find yourself waiting here, do take time to wander down to the market. There's a regular bus service between Quiroga and Pátzcuaro, and if you're coming **direct from Guadalajara** to Pátzcuaro, this is the most straightforward route (don't miss the views over the lake from the north, shortly before you reach Quiroga). Logically, this would also be the quickest way of doing the journey in reverse, **from Pátzcuaro to Guadalajara**, but things aren't always that simple: there's no guarantee that you're going to be able to get onto one of the fast buses along the main road – most pass though Quiroga full, without stopping. So you may be forced to go from Quiroga to Morelia or back to Pátzcuaro, and take a bus to Guadalajara from there – that way you're guaranteed a seat.

Morelia

The state capital, **MORELIA** is in many ways unrepresentative of Michoacán. It looks Spanish and, despite a large indigenous population, it feels Spanish – with its broad streets lined with seventeenth-century mansions and outdoor cafés sheltered by arcaded plazas, you might easily be in Salamanca or Valladolid. Indeed, Valladolid was the city's name until 1828, when it was changed to honour local-born Independence hero José María Morelos.

And Morelia has always been a city of Spaniards – one of the first they founded after the Conquest. That honour fell on two Franciscan friars, Juan de San Miguel and Antonio de Lisboa, who settled here among the native inhabitants in 1530. Ten years later, they were visited by the first Viceroy of New Spain, Antonio de Mendóza, who was so taken by the site that he ordered a town to be built, naming it after his birthplace and sending fifty Spanish families to settle it. From the beginning, there was fierce rivalry between the colonists and the older culture's town of Pátzcuaro. During the lifetime of

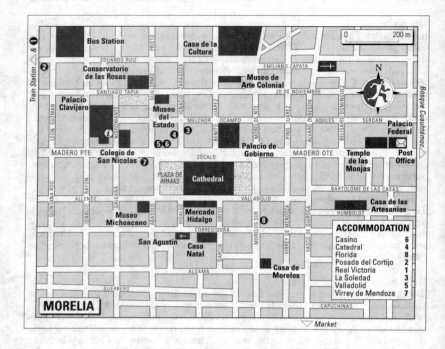

Vasco de Quiroga, Pátzcuaro had the upper hand, but later the bishopric was moved here, a university founded, and by the end of the sixteenth century there was no doubt that Valladolid was predominant.

There are specific things to look for and to visit in present-day Morelia, but the city as a whole outweighs them: it's been declared a "national monument", which allows no new construction that doesn't match perfectly with the old, such that it preserves a remarkable unity of style. Nearly everything is built of the same faintly pinkish-grey stone (*trachyte*), which, being soft, is not only easily carved and embellished but weathers quickly, giving even relatively recent constructions a battered, ancient look.

Arrival and information

Morelia's **Central Camionera** is one of the few bus stations in Mexico to remain within walking distance of the city centre; the Plaza de Armas lies just four or five blocks southeast. If you arrive by **train**, you'll have to take a bus to the centre, as the station is 2km west of town on the city's outskirts, on Av Periodismo; buses stop right opposite the station.

Between the bus station and the centre, the **tourist office**, in the Palacio Clavijero, at Nigromante 79, just off Madero Pte (Mon–Fri 9am–8pm, Sat & Sun 9am–7pm; ☎43/17-23-71, or toll-free from out-of-state ☎91-800/4-50-23), has a few maps and leaflets, and the staff are friendly and very helpful. There are plenty of very grand **banks** along Madero Ote, open for exchange on weekday mornings. **Casas de cambio** can be found at Nigromante 132, Valladolid 22, 137-A and 150, Morelos Nte 50-B and 328-A, Aquiles Serdán 30, and 20 de Noviembre 110. The **post office** is at Madero Ote 369 (Mon–Fri 8am–8pm, Sat & Sun 9am–1pm), where Telmex has **phone and fax** offices (Mon–Fri 9am–8pm, Sat 9am–noon). Computel also offers long-distance phone and fax from its offices inside and opposite the bus station, and at Madero Pte 157 (daily 7am–10pm); other casetas are at Madero Pte 398 opposite the post office, and Zaragoza 101 at Ocampo. For Internet access, check out the *Shareweb Cybercafé*, Madero Ote 573 (see "Eating and drinking" below).

Plenty of **local buses** ply up and down Madero, though getting around town is easy enough without them.

Accommodation

Though there are plenty of inexpensive hotels scattered around the **bus station**, it's worth splashing out a little more to stay closer to the centre, where you have the choice of some wonderful fading, colonial hotels.

Casino, Madero Pte 229, Portal Hidalgo on the Plaza de Armas (☎43/13-13-28, fax 12-12-52; *casino@infosel.net.mx*). All rooms with carpet, TV and hot water, set around a covered courtyard. ⑥.

Catedral, Ignacio Zaragoza 37 (☎43/13-07-83, fax 13-04-06). Rooms around a restaurant in another covered colonial courtyard, although here you certainly pay for the atmosphere. ⑥.

Colonial, 20 de Noviembre 15 (☎43/12-18-97). The best-value budget hotel, friendly and clean; most rooms have bathroom, and some (at slightly higher prices) have TV. ②.

Florida, Morelos Sur 161, southeast of the Plaza de Armas (☎43/12-10-38). Comfortable and clean, all rooms with TV and phone. ④.

Posada del Cortijo, Eduardo Ruiz 673 (☎43/12-96-42, fax 13-12-81). Virtually opposite the bus station, basic but convenient and fairly cheap. ④.

Real Victoria, Guadalupe Victoria 245, a block west of the bus terminal (☎43/13-23-00, fax 17-01-71). The broad colonial front conceals a modernized interior: all rooms have phone and TV. Popular with Mexican businesspeople. ⑤.

La Soledad, Ignacio Zaragoza 90, just off the Plaza de Armas (☎43/12-18-88, 12-18-89 or 12-18-90, fax 12-21-11; *www.hsoledad.com*). Spectacular colonial building that used to be a convent, with rooms set around a beautiful open courtyard (⑥), or lower-priced ones in the less attractive back courtyard (⑤).

Valladolid, Madero Pte 241, Portal Hidalgo on the Plaza de Armas (☎43/12-46-63). Great position under the colonial arches, though rooms are a little dark and run-down. ④.

Virrey de Mendoza, Madero Pte 310 (☎43/12-06-33, fax 12-67-19). Fantastic colonial grandeur: even if you can't afford to stay it's worth dropping by to take a look. The rooms are just as impressive as the lobby, with no expense spared. ⑦.

The Town

Avenida Francisco Madero, which runs along the north side of Plaza de Armas and the cathedral, is very much the main street of Morelia, with most of the important public buildings and major shops strung out along it. Everything you're likely to want to see is within easy walking distance of the Plaza de Armas.

Around the Plaza de Armas

At the heart of the city, Morelia's massive **Cathedral** boasts two soaring towers that are said to be the tallest in Mexico. Begun in 1640 in the relatively plain Herrerian style, the towers and dome were not completed for some hundred years, by which time the Baroque had arrived with a vengeance: nevertheless, component parts harmonize remarkably, and for all the cathedral's size and richness of decoration, perfect proportions prevent it from becoming overpowering. The interior, refitted towards the end of the last century, after most of its silver ornamentation had been removed to pay for the wars, is simple and preserves, in the choir and sacristy, a few early colonial religious paintings.

Flanking the cathedral, the Plaza de Armas (or de los Martíres) is the place to sit around in the cafés under its elegant arcaded *portales*, with a coffee and a morning paper (you can buy the *Mexico City News* from the stands here), revelling in the city's leisurely pace. On the southwestern edge of the plaza, at the corner of Allende and Abasolo, the **Museo Michoacáno** (Tues–Sat 9am–7pm, Sun 9am–2pm; US$1.75, free on Sun) occupies a palatial eighteenth-century mansion. Emperor Maximilian lodged here on his visits to Morelia, and it now houses a collection reflecting the state's diversity and rich history: the rooms devoted to archeology are, of course, dominated by the **Tarascan culture**, including pottery and small sculptures from Tzintzuntzán, but also display much earlier objects, notably some obsidian figurines. Out in the patio are two magnificent old carriages, while upstairs the colonial epoch is represented in a large group of religious paintings and sculptures and a collection of old books and manuscripts.

A smaller square, the **Plaza Melchor Ocampo**, flanks the cathedral on the other side. Facing it, the **Palacio de Gobierno** was formerly a seminary – Independence hero Morelos and anti-hero Agustín Iturbide studied here, as did Ocampo, a nineteenth-century liberal supporter of Benito Juárez. It's of interest now for the **murals** adorning the stairway and upper level of the patio: practically the whole of Mexican history, and each of its heroes, is depicted. A little further down Madero are several **banks** that are among the most remarkable examples of active conservation you'll see anywhere: all Mexican banks are sumptuous, but they usually go in for steel and glass, marble floors and modern statuary – these are old mansions that have been refurbished in traditional style, and somehow manage to combine reasonably efficient operation with an ambience that is wholly in keeping with the setting.

West and north of the plaza

One block west of the Plaza de Armas, the **Colegio de San Nicolas** is part of the University of Morelia. Founded at Pátzcuaro in 1540 by Vasco de Quiroga, and moved here in 1580, the college is the second oldest in Mexico and hence in all the Americas – it now houses administrative offices and various technical faculties. To the side, across Nigromante, is the public library in what was originally the Jesuit church of **La Compañía**, while next to this is the beautiful **Palacio Clavijero**, converted into government offices. At the bottom of Nigromante, on another charming little plaza, you'll come across the Baroque church of Santa Rosa and, beside it, the **Conservatorio de las Rosas** – a music academy founded in the eighteenth century. From time to time it hosts concerts of classical music – the tourist office should have details.

Also here, at the corner of Santiago Tapia and Guillermo Prieto, is the new **Museo del Estado** (Mon–Fri 9am–2pm & 4–8pm, Sat & Sun 9am–2pm & 4–7pm; free). Inside, the complete furniture and fittings of a traditional farmacía have been reconstructed, after which you move, somewhat incongruously, to the prehistory and archeology collections. This is mostly minor stuff, though there's some fine, unusual Tarascan jewellery, including gold and turquoise pieces, and necklaces strung with tiny crystal skulls. Upstairs, there's one room of colonial history and various ethnological exhibits illustrating traditional local dress and lifestyles.

Heading east from here, or north from the Plaza de Armas on Juárez, the **Museo de Arte Colonial** (Tues–Fri 10am–2pm & 5–8pm, Sat & Sun 10am–2pm & 4.30–7pm; free) lies opposite the Plaza de Carmen. Its collection of colonial art is almost entirely regional, and not of great interest. Of greater interest on the north side of the plaza, entered from Morelos, the beautiful old Convento del Carmen now houses the **Casa de la Cultura** (open all day, but museum and most exhibits Mon–Fri 10am–8pm, Sat 10am–6pm, Sun 10am–5pm). It's an enormous complex, worth exploring in its own right, with a theatre, café, space for temporary exhibitions and classes, and the fascinating little **Museo de la Mascara** (mask museum) scattered around the former monastic buildings. On Sunday evenings at 6pm, there's usually a performance of music, dance or theatre in the front patio.

South and east of the plaza

Six blocks south of the Casa de la Cultura, or two blocks south of Plaza Melchor Ocampo, on Morelos Sur, the **Casa Museo de Morelos** (daily 9am–7pm; US$1.25, free on Sun) is the relatively modest eighteenth-century house in which Independence hero José María Morelos y Pavon lived from 1801. It's now a museum devoted to his life and the War of Independence. Nearby, at the corner of Corregidora (the continuation of Alzate) and Garcia Obeso, you can see the house where the hero was born, the **Casa Natal de Morelos** (daily 10am–2pm & 4–7pm; free), which now houses a library and a few desultory domestic objects. This in turn is virtually next door to the church of **San Agustín**, from where pedestrianized Hidalgo runs up one block to the Plaza de Armas and opposite whose attractive facade is a tiny market area, the **Mercado Hidalgo**.

Walk a couple of blocks in the other direction – or take Valladolid directly from the Plaza Ocampo – to find the **Casa de las Artesanías** (Mon–Sat 10am–3pm & 5–8pm, Sun 10am–4.30pm; free), possibly the most comprehensive collection of Michoacán's crafts anywhere, almost all of them for sale. The best and most obviously commercial items are downstairs, while on the upper floor are a series of rooms devoted to the products of particular villages, often with craftspeople demonstrating their techniques (these are staffed by villagers and hence not always open), and a collection of historic items that you can't buy. It's all housed in what used to be the monastery of **San Francisco**, whose church, facing onto the little plaza next door, can also be visited.

JOSÉ MARÍA MORELOS Y PAVON

A student of Hidalgo, **José María Morelos** took over the leadership of the Independence movement after its instigators had been executed in 1811. While the cry of Independence had initially been taken up by the Mexican (Creole) bourgeoisie, smarting under the trading restrictions imposed on them by Spain, it quickly became a mass popular movement. Unlike the original leaders, Morelos (a *mestizo* priest born into relative poverty) was a populist and genuine reformer; even more unlike them, he was also a political and military tactician of considerable skill, invoking the spirit of the French Revolution and calling for universal suffrage, racial equality and the break-up of the hacienda system, under which workers were tied to an agricultural system. Defeat and execution by Royalist armies under Agustín de Iturbide came in 1815 only after years of guerrilla warfare, during which Morelos had come within an ace of taking the capital and controlling the entire country. When Independence was finally gained – by Iturbide, now changed sides and later briefly to be emperor – it was no longer a force for change, rather a reaction to the fact that by 1820 liberal reforms were sweeping Spain itself. The causes espoused by Morelos were, however, taken up to some extent by Benito Juárez and later, with a vengeance, in the Revolution – almost a hundred years after his death.

Finally, in the far east of the city, about fifteen minutes' walk along Madero from the Plaza de Armas, past the Baroque facade of the **Templo de las Monjas**, is an area of tree-lined walks and little parks on the edge of town, through the middle of which runs the old **aqueduct**. Built between 1785 and 1789, these serried arches brought water into the city from springs in the nearby hills. On the right is the largest of the parks, the **Bosque Cuauhtémoc**, in which there are some beautifully laid-out flower displays and, 300m along Av Acueducto, a small **Museum of Contemporary Art** (Tues–Sun 10am–2pm & 4–8pm; free), featuring a variety of Latin American work. To the left, Fray Antonio de San Miguel (named for the bishop who built the aqueduct) runs down to the vastly overdecorated **Santuario de Guadalupe**, where market stalls, selling above all the sticky local *dulces*, set up at weekends and during fiestas.

Eating and drinking

For a reasonably priced sit-down meal, the area around the bus station is the best bet – most of the hotels there also have **restaurants** that serve a fairly standard comida corrida. Eating a full meal in any of the cafés on the Plaza de Armas will prove expensive, but they're good for snacks or for a breakfast of coffee and *pan dulce*. In the evening you can eat outdoors at places set up along traffic-free Hidalgo (between the plaza and San Agustín) and around the Mercado Hidalgo.

Chief of Morelia's specialities are its **dulces**, sweets made of candied fruit or evaporated milk – cloyingly sweet to most non-Mexican tastes, they're very popular here. You can see a wide selection at the **Mercado de Dulces y Artesanías**, up Gomez Farias from the bus station and on the left-hand side, around the back of the Palacio Clavijero. As its name suggests, they also sell handicrafts here, but on the whole nothing of any class. Morelians also get through a lot of *rompope* (a drink that you'll find to a lesser extent all over Mexico) – again, it's very sweet, an egg-flip concoction based on rum, milk and egg with vanilla, cinnamon or almond flavouring. Finally, as always, there are food stalls and plenty of raw ingredients in the **market**, but Morelia's big Mercado Independencia is on the whole a disappointment, certainly not as large or varied as you'd expect. On Sunday – market day – it perks up a little. Get there by going towards the Plaza San Francisco and then a long six or seven blocks south on Vasco de Quiroga.

Acuarius, Hidalgo 75. Vegetarian restaurant – pleasant setting in a courtyard off the street, but unadventurous food.

Cafe del Teatro, in the Teatro Ocampo, on Ocampo and Prieto. Its lush interior makes this one of the most popular spots in town for good coffee and people-watching – try and get a table overlooking the street.

MOVING ON FROM MORELIA

Moving on from Morelia should present no problem at all. Three weekly **trains** run to México, and the other way to Pátzcuaro, Uruapan and Lázaro Cárdenas. There are also **buses** to just about anywhere in the state and to most other conceivable destinations elsewhere in the country: very frequently to Guadalajara, Pátzcuaro, Uruapan and México; regularly north to Salamanca, for Guanajuato and Querétaro.

The **shortest route to México**, via Zitácuaro and Toluca, is very beautiful – passing through the Mil Cumbres (Thousand Peaks) – but mountainous and slow. Some buses go round by the faster roads to the north. If only for the scenery, you should try to take the former route – these mountains are the playground of México's middle classes, and there are a couple of places of interest along the way.

Los Comensales, Zaragoza 148. Pretty courtyard setting complete with caged birds. The comida corrida is good value; splash out a bit more for Mexican specialities, including a tasty chicken in rich, dark *mole*.

Copa de Oro, Juárez 194B at Santiago Tapia. Simple place for fresh jugos and tortas.

Paco, Eduardo Ruíz 539, opposite the bus station. Good-value, cheap, but tasty and filling breakfasts, comidas corridas and standard Mexican dishes.

El Rey Tacamba, Madero Pte 157, Portal Galeana, opposite the cathedral. Small, bustling restaurant favoured by townspeople for its good, solid, local food.

Shareweb Cybercafé, Madero Ote 573. The coffee's good, but that's not why you come here: this is one of very few internet cafés in the republic, and so popular that you may need to book a time-slot in advance. Prices are very reasonable (net or e-mail US$2.50 per hour), and the staff friendly and helpful. Open Mon–Sat 10am–10pm, Sun 2–10pm; *shareweb@morelia.teesa.mx*.

Super Cocina las Rosas, Santiago Tapia 270A. Simple, home-style food at low prices. A good place for breakfast (from 8.30am).

Vegetariano Hindú, Madero Ote 549. Good, inexpensive (but not very Indian) vegetarian salads, soups, veggie-burgers and breakfasts – opens at around 9.30am.

Woolworth, Mendoza 60. Excellent selection of celestial hamburgers in the superb setting of a former church.

Towards México: the Monarch Butterfly Sanctuary

From November to mid-April, more than 100 million Monarch butterflies migrate from the USA and Canada to the lush mountains of Michoacán to reproduce. It's an amazing sight: in the cool of the morning, they coat the trees, turning the entire landscape a rich, velvety orange, while later in the day the increased humidity forces them to the ground, where they form a thick carpet of blazing colour. Although the butterflies sometimes come as far down as the highway, the best place to see them is in the **butterfly sanctuary**, where a guide will show you around and give you a short explanation (some guides speak English) of their life-cycle and breeding habits (Nov 16–Mar 31 daily 8am–5.30pm; US$1.50; further information from the tourist office in Morelia or the information booth on the highway outside Zitácuaro, towards Toluca; ☎715/3-06-75).

The sanctuary lies in the mountains above the small village of **El Rosario**, about 150km east of Morelia. **To get there** by public transport, take a bus from Morelia (20 daily; 2hr 30min), Toluca (5–6 per hour; 1hr 40min) or México (5–6 per hour; 3hr) to Zitácuaro, and from there another bus to the village of **Ocampo** (every 15min; 30min; coming from Morelia, you could change buses at San Felipe where the road turns off for Ocampo). From Ocampo, there are buses to the sanctuary itself; alternatively there are tours from Zitácuaro, and one direct bus a day (currently leaving Zitácuaro at 12.15pm).

Accommodation in El Rosario is fairly limited; by far the best place to stay is the mining town of **Angangueo**, jammed into the narrow valley just below El Rosario, 10km beyond Ocampo (buses from Zitácuaro continue to Angangueo). Here you'll find the comfortable and very friendly *Hotel Don Bruno*, at Morelos 92 on the way into the village (☎ & fax 715/6-00-26; ⑤), which has its own restaurant, and the more basic *Casa de Huéspedes El Paso de la Monarca*, at Nacional 20 near the centre of the village (☎715/8-01-86 or 8-01-87; ②). The road up to the sanctuary, C Matamoros, branches off from C Morelos where it becomes C Nacional. There are no buses up from Angingueo, but regular trucks do the run; alternatively, you could walk – it's a scenic hike of one or two hours, but uphill all the way and so a better bet for the return journey. From Ocampo (where there are also hotels), four buses a day do the run up to El Rosario, as well as regular colectivos until about 5pm.

FIESTAS

Both Jalisco and Michoacán preserve strong native traditions and are particularly rich in fiestas: the list below is by no means exhaustive, and local tourist offices will have further details.

JANUARY

6 DÍA DE LOS SANTOS REYES (Twelfth Night). Many small ceremonies – **Los Reyes** (Michoacán), south of Zamora and west of Uruapan, has dancing and a procession of the Magi. **Cajititlán** (Jalisco), on a tiny lake near Guadalajara, also has traditional dances.

8 San Juan de las Colchas (Mich) commemorates the eruption of Paricutín with a dance contest and traditional dress. Many of the homeless villagers moved to this village near Uruapan.

15 In **La Piedad** (Mich), traditional dances and a major procession for local saint's day.

20 DÍA DE SAN SEBASTIAN. Tuxpan (Jal), a beautiful village between Ciudad Guzmán and Colima, has traditional dances including the unique *Danza de los Chayacates*. Start of the mass pilgrimages to **San Juan de Los Lagos** (Jal), which culminate on Feb 2.

FEBRUARY

1 In **Tzintzuntzán** (Mich), the start of a week-long fiesta founded in the sixteenth century by Vasco de Quiroga.

2 DÍA DE LA CANDELARIA (Candlemas). Celebrated in **Lagos de Moreno** (Jal) with pilgrimages, but much more so in nearby **San Juan de Los Lagos** (Jal), where it's one of the largest such celebrations in Mexico.

CARNIVAL (the week before Lent, variable Feb–March) is particularly good in **Zinapecuaro** (Mich), near Morelia, with pretend bulls chasing people through the streets; **Copandaro** (Mich), also near Morelia on the shores of Lago Cuitzeo, has similar fake bullfights, rodeos and marathon dances; and in **Charapán** (Mich), near Uruapan, you can see the dance of *Los Viejitos*. All these are best on Carnival Tuesday.

MARCH

PALM SUNDAY is the culmination of a week's celebration in **Uruapan** (Mich) – the Indians collect palms from the hills and make ornaments from the leaves, sold here in a big *tianguis*.

HOLY WEEK is observed everywhere. In **Copandaro** (Mich), they celebrate the whole of the week, especially on the Thursday with the ceremony of Washing the Apostle's Feet, and Good Friday when they act out more scenes from Christ's passion. These passion plays are quite common, for example at **Tzintzuntzán** (Mich) and the hamlet of Maya near **Lagos de Moreno** (Jal). In **Ciudad Hidalgo** (Mich), there's a huge procession.

MAY

CORPUS CHRISTI (variable: the Thursday after Trinity) is celebrated in the neighbouring villages of **Cheran** and **Paracho**, in Michoacán.

3 DÍA DE LA SANTA CRUZ. Native dances in **Ciudad Hidalgo** (Mich), *mariachi* – and tequila – in **Tequila** (Jal).

Last Sunday DÍA DEL SEÑOR DE LA MISERICORDIA. A fiesta in honour of this highly venerated image in **Tuxpan** (Jal) – includes native dances.

JUNE

24 DÍA DE SAN JUAN. Purepero (Mich), between Uruapan and La Piedad, starts a week-long fiesta.

29 DÍA DE SAN PEDRO. In **Tlaquepaque** (Jal) a highly animated festival with *mariachi*, dancing and processions.

JULY

First Sunday Torchlit religious processions in **Quiroga** (Mich).

22 DÍA DE MARIA MAGDALENA. Fiesta in **Uruapan** (Mich), featuring processions of animals.

26 Culmination of a week-long feria in **Acatlán de Juárez** (Jal), south of Guadalajara: regional dress, dances and fireworks.

28 FIESTAS DEL SEÑOR DEL CALVARIO in **Lagos de Moreno** (Jal) until August 6th.

AUGUST

8 Very ancient "pagan" fiesta in **Paracho** (Mich).

15 DÍA DE LA ASUNCION (Assumption) sees a large fair in **Santa Clara del Cobre** (Mich), near Pátzcuaro, coinciding with markets of the renowned hand-made copperware.

SEPTEMBER

8–12 A festival in **San Juan de las Colchas** (Mich), with its climax on the 14th.

30 In **Morelia** (Mich), celebrations for the birthday of Morelos.

OCTOBER

Guadalajara's FIESTAS DE OCTUBRE run throughout the month.

4 DÍA DE SAN FRANCISCO. Saint's day celebrations culminate in a week of pilgrimages to **Talpa** (Jal), near Guadalajara, where the faithful come bearing flowers and candles. Celebrated, too, in **Jiquilpa** (Mich), between Zamora and Lake Chapala, and in **Uruapan** (Mich), where it's one of the year's biggest.

12 DÍA DE LA RAZA commemorates Columbus's discovery of America. Feria in **Uruapan** (Mich) and, in **Guadalajara**, the highlight of the fiestas is an enormous pilgrimage to the Virgin of Zapopan.

16 Native dances and an all-night procession honour a much-revered image of Christ in **Cuitzeo** (Mich), on Lago Cuitzeo north of Morelia.

21 DÍA DE SAN JOSÉ. In **Ciudad Guzmán** (Jal), the climax of a lively feria that lasts from the 12th to the 23rd.

22 Apatzingan (Mich), in beautiful mountain country south of Uruapan, has a fiesta that includes dance competitions and rodeos, on the rather flimsy excuse of the anniversary of the 1814 Constitution.

24–26 The FESTIVAL DE COROS Y DANZAS in **Uruapan** (Mich) sees a competition between Tarascan Indian choirs and dance groups. Great.

DÍA DE CRISTO REY. On the last Sunday in October, an ancient series of dances in honour of Christ the King in **Contepec** (Mich), south of Querétaro, east of Morelia. Also processions and regional costume.

NOVEMBER

2 DÍA DE LOS MUERTOS (All Souls'). The famous Day of the Dead is celebrated everywhere, but the rites in **Pátzcuaro** (Mich) and on the island of **Janitzio** are the best known in Mexico. Highly picturesque, too, in **Zitácuaro** (Mich).

DECEMBER

8 DÍA DE LA INMACULADA CONCEPCIÓN. In **San Juan de Los Lagos** (Jal), the high point of a massive feria that attracts thousands of pilgrims and boasts an enormous crafts market. **Sayula** (Jal), between Guadalajara and Ciudad Guzmán, also has impressive displays of native dance. In **Tequila** (Jal), not surprisingly, the celebrations are more earthy, with rodeos, cockfights and fireworks. On the same day **Pátzcuaro** (Mich) celebrates La Señora de la Salud, an event attended by many Tarascan pilgrims and the scene of Tarascan dances including *Los Viejitos*.

Continues over

Continued from over

12 DÍA DE LA VIRGEN DE GUADALUPE. Large fiesta in **Jiquilpan** (Mich) with fireworks and a torchlit procession in which locals dress in the Mexican colours, green, white and red. **Tapalpa** (Jal) attracts pilgrims from a wide area, with regional dances in front of the church.

23 In **Aranza** (Mich), a tiny village near Paracho, they perform pastoral plays on Christmas Eve. In **Tuxpan** (Jal), there are very ancient dances and a large religious procession.

travel details

BUSES

Relatively densely populated, this area is crisscrossed by thousands of services, local ones between towns and villages, and long-distance runs that call in at all major towns on their routes. It can occasionally be difficult to pick up a *de paso* seat on the latter: they're not normally sold until the bus has arrived. What follows is a minimum, covering the major stops only – it should be assumed that these buses also call at the towns en route.

In general the fastest and most efficient operators are Omnibus de Mexico and Tres Estrellas de Oro, though there's little to choose between the first-class companies. Flecha Amarilla cover many of the local runs and are fairly reliable – Estrella Blanca is better but less frequent.

Guadalajara (Camionera Nueva) to: Aguascalientes (terminals 2, 3, 6 & 7; 2–3 hourly; 4hr); Colima (terminal 2; 2–3 hourly; 5hr); Guanajuato (terminals 1, 2 & 6; 11 daily; 6hr); Lagos de Moreno (terminal 5; half-hourly); Manzanillo (terminal 2; 2 hourly; 6hr); Mazatlán (terminals 3 & 4; 2 hourly; 7hr); México (terminals 1, 2 & 3; 4 hourly; 7–9hr); Morelia (terminal 2; 2–3 hourly; 6hr); Pátzcuaro (terminal 2; 2 daily; 6hr); Puerto Vallarta (terminals 2, 3 & 4; 27 daily; 8hr); Querétaro (terminal 5; half-hourly; 5hr); San Luis Potosí (terminal 5; 25 daily; 5hr); Tepic (terminals 1, 2, 3, 4 & 6; 10 hourly; 5hr); Tijuana (terminal 4; 11 daily; 32hr); Uruapan (terminal 2; 18 daily; 5hr).

Guadalajara (Camionera Vieja) to: Ajijic (hourly; 1hr); Chapala (half-hourly; 50min); Jocotepec (half-hourly; 1hr); Tapalpa (hourly; 3hr 15min); Tequila (every 20 mins; 1hr 45min).

Morelia to: Aguascalientes (4 daily; 7hr); Guadalajara (hourly; 6hr); Guanajuato (hourly; 3hr 30min); León (every 20min; 4hr); México (at least half-hourly; 6hr); Pátzcuaro (every 10min; 1hr); Querétaro (every 40min; 4hr); Toluca (hourly; 4hr); Zitácuaro (20 daily; 2hr 30min).

Pátzcuaro to: Guadalajara (2 daily; 6hr); México (hourly; 7hr); Morelia (every 10min; 1hr); Quiroga (every 15min; 30min); Uruapan (every 10min; 1hr).

Uruapan to: Guadalajara (18 daily; 5hr); Lázaro Cárdenas (hourly; 6hr); Los Reyes (hourly; 1hr); México (half hourly; 6hr); Morelia (every 15min; 2hr); Paracho (every 30min; 40min); Pátzcuaro (every 10min; 1hr).

TRAINS

Guadalajara is the region's train hub, with trains daily to México via Querétaro; to Nogales and Mexicali via Tequila; also to Ixtlán, Tepic, Mazatlán, Culiacán, Ciudad Obregón and Hermosillo. Trains run **from Morelia** three times weekly to México via Acambaro and Toluca; and to Lázaro Cardenas via Pátzcuaro and Uruapan.

PLANES

Guadalajara to: Acapulco, Boston, Cancún, Chicago, Chihuahua, Ciudad Juárez, Ciudad Obregón, Cuernavaca, Culiacán, Dallas/Fort Worth, Durango, El Paso, Greensboro, Hermosillo, Houston, Ixtapa, Kansas City, La Paz, León/Guanajuato, Los Angeles, Los Mochis, Manzanillo, Mazatlán, Mexicali, Miami, Monclova, Monterrey, Morelia, New York City, Nuevo Laredo, Oakland (CA), Oaxaca, Phoenix,

Piedras Negras, Puebla, Puerto Vallarta, Querétero, Saltillo, San Diego, San Francisco, San José (CA), San José del Cabo, San Luis Potosí, Tepic, Tijuana, Torreón, Uruapan, Zacatecas.

Morelia to: Chicago, Guadalajara, León/Guanajuato, Los Angeles, México, Oakland (CA), Querétero, San Francisco, San José (CA), Tijuana, Uruapan, Zacatecas.

Uruapan to: Culiacán, Guadalajara, México, Morelia, Tijuana.

CHAPTER FOUR

THE BAJÍO

R ichly fertile, wild and rugged, and scattered with superb ancient towns, the twisting hills and beautiful valleys of the **Bajío** spread across the central highlands almost from coast to coast and as far south as the capital. This has long been the most heavily populated part of the country, providing much of the silver and grain that supported Mexico throughout the years of Spanish rule. As the colonial heartland, the legacy of Spanish architecture remains at its most impressive here, in meticulously crafted towns that – at their cores at least – have changed little over the centuries, while the surrounding country has been much the most consistently developed, both agriculturally and industrially.

Mexico's broad central plateau narrows and becomes hillier as it approaches the Valley of México. Here in the Bajío proper – the states of **Guanajuato and Querétaro** – are its finest colonial cities, founded amid barren land and grown rich on just one thing: **silver**. Before the arrival of the Spanish, this was a relatively unexploited area, a buffer zone between the "civilized" peoples of the heartland and the barbarian **Chichimec** tribes from the north. Though the Aztecs may have tapped some of its mineral wealth, they never began to exploit the area with the greed, tenacity and ruthlessness of the new colonists. After the Conquest, the mining cities grew rich, but in time they also grew restive under the heavy hand of control from Spain. The wealthy **Creole** (Spanish-blooded but Mexican-born) bourgeoisie were free to exploit the land and its people, but didn't control their own destinies and were forced to pay punitive taxes; lucrative government posts and high positions in the Church were reserved exclusively for **Gachupines**, those actually born in Spain, while the *Indigenos* and poor mestizos were condemned either to landless poverty or to near fatal labour in the mines. Unsurprisingly, then, the Bajío was fertile ground for **revolutionary ideas**. This land is *La Cuna de la Independencia* (the Cradle of Independence), where every town seems to claim a role in the break with Spain. In **Querétaro** the plotters held many of their early meetings, and from here they were warned that their plans had been discovered; in **Dolores Hidalgo** the famous *grito* was first voiced by Father Hidalgo, proclaiming an independent Mexico; and from here he marched on **San Miguel de Allende**, picking up more volunteers for his armed rabble as he continued towards a bloody confrontation in **Guanajuato**.

Approaching the Bajío from the north you cross several hundred miles of semi-desert landscape punctuated only by the occasional ranch, where fighting bulls are bred, or defunct mining town, such as the wonderfully strange semi-ghost-town of **Real de Catorce**, its mines and mansions now totally deserted. Only then do you reach the colonial cities of **Zacatecas** and **San Luis Potosí** – both eponymous state capitals – that mark a radical change in landscape and architecture. Though they're outside the Bajío proper, both are showcase examples of the region's architectural and historical heritage, sharing all the attributes of the towns further south. San Luis, a large modern metropolis, has its share of monuments, but Zacatecas is far more exciting, an oasis of culture and sophistication built in mountainous isolation on the bounty of the silver mines that riddle the landscape hereabouts.

Some 300km south, beyond the modern town of **Aguascalientes**, you enter the green belt of the Bajío proper, which, despite the total abandonment of its silver mines,

ACCOMMODATION PRICE CODES

All the accommodation listed in this book has been categorized into one of nine price
bands, as set out below. The prices quoted are in US dollars and normally refer to the
cheapest available room for two people sharing in high season. For more details see p.36.

① less than US$5	④ US$15–25	⑦ US$60–80
② US$5–10	⑤ US$25–40	⑧ US$80–100
③ US$10–15	⑥ US$40–60	⑨ more than US$100

continues to thrive with centres of study, culture and tourism, and thrusting modern
cities benefiting from their proximity to the capital and the main transport routes.

If you're heading straight for México, you'll bypass almost everywhere of interest,
cutting through the industrial cities of **León** – famous for its leather – and **Irapuato**
before joining the highway past Celaya and Querétaro. This would be a mistake: crazily ranged up the sides of a ravine, **Guanajuato** is quite simply one of the country's richest and most scenic colonial towns, with one of its finest Baroque churches, a thriving
student life, and, for good measure, the ghoulish Museum of Mummies. The gorgeous
hillside town of **San Miguel de Allende** also has its advocates, as much for its wonderful setting as for the comforts of home, ensured by a large population of foreign
artists and language students. **Dolores Hidalgo** in particular, is a point of pilgrimage
for anyone with the least interest in Mexico's Independence movement, as is, to a lesser extent, **Querétaro**, a large and industrial city that preserves a fine colonial quarter
at its heart.

It's easy enough to **get around** the Bajío – all the towns of interest lie close together, bus services are excellent, and the **hotels** are some of the best you'll find in the
entire country.

Matehuala and Real de Catorce

Matehuala is the only place of any size along the highway that links Saltillo, around
260km to the north, and San Luis, around 200km south. With the gradual improvement
in Mexican roads to speed you on your way – Hwy-57 is now a relatively smooth and
fast divided highway south of Matehuala – there's little need to stop here, though the
town is pleasant enough, with a pretty church on a leafy plaza, several small hotels and
reasonable restaurants. In truth, it serves best as a staging-post for the ancient and now
all-but-deserted mining town of **Real de Catorce**.

Matehuala

A typically bustling, northern commercial town, **MATEHUALA** is not a place you're
likely to be tempted to stay more than one night. In fact you probably won't even need
to do that, as the main **bus station**, just off the highway on 5 de Mayo, 2km south of
the centre, also serves **buses to Catorce**. Currently these leave at 5.45am, 7.45am,
9.45am, 11.45am, 1.45pm and 5.45pm and call at the local bus station in Matehuala, cnr
Guerrero and Mendez, before the steep two-hour run into the mountains.

If you do stay over, you can pick up "Centro" buses and taxis outside the main bus
station, though if you don't have much luggage it's an easy enough walk, straight up
5 de Mayo and then left on Insurgentes when you've reached the centre – you can't
miss the grey concrete bulk of the barrel-shaped church a couple of blocks off the
main plaza. The three main **hotels** are all within a block of the main plaza: *Hotel*

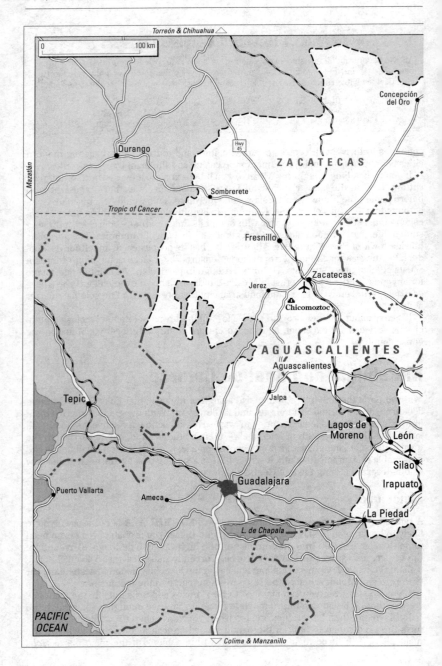

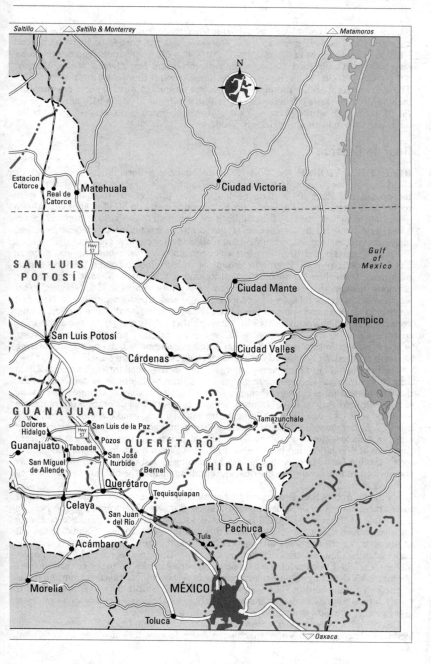

Alamo, Guerrero 116 (☎488/2-00-17; ②) is the cheapest and quite acceptable though an extra US$2 is well spent at *Hotel Matehuala*, at the corner of Bustamante and Hidalgo, a block north of the plaza (☎488/2-06-80; ②), where rooms surround a massive columned courtyard. Between the two, the brand new *Hotel de Valle*, Morelos 621 (☎488/2-37-70; ④), offers spacious, clean rooms if astonishingly ugly decor. There are several pricier motel-style places out on the main road. Local **restaurants** include the *Fontinella*, close to the *Hotel Matehuala*, at Morelos 618, and the *Santa Fe*, Morelos 709, on the plaza, the latter of which is strong on seafood. Food at the main bus station is also surprisingly good.

Real de Catorce

REAL DE CATORCE (or "Villa Real de Nuestra Señora de la Concepción de Guadalupe de los Alamos de los Catorce", its full title) is quite an extraordinary place. Its population of some 40,000 at the peak of its silver production – the hills around were reckoned to be the second-richest source of precious metals in Mexico, after Guanajuato – declined to virtually zero by the middle of the twentieth century. A few hundred inhabitants now hang on in an enclave at the centre, surrounded by derelict, roofless mansions and, further out, crumbling foundations and the odd segment of wall.

Probably even before they were known to contain silver, the mountains around were a rich source of **peyote**. Even now groups of Huichol Indians make the long annual pilgrimage from their homelands in and around northeastern Nayarit to gather the precious hallucinogenic cactus, which they regard as essential food for the soul. This journey, on foot, can take up to a month. Peyote also attracts a number of New-Age tourists to Catorce, and some of them live here semi-permanently. The foreign contingent coexists amiably with locals who survive either prospecting for silver and hoping that the old veins can be reopened, or hoping for brighter prospects from tourism, which is now gathering pace. Every year a new restaurant or hotel opens up, catering as much to Mexican tourists as curious backpackers from further afield.

The town is built in a high canyon that you approach by road through a tunnel 2.3km long. It's only broad enough for one vehicle at a time, with a place to pass in the middle. The bigger buses can't get through, so you'll probably have to change buses at the tunnel entrance. As you drive through, the odd mine-shaft leads off into the mountain to either side – by one there's a little shrine where a lone candle seems always to be burning. In the town, the austere, shuttered stone buildings blend with the bare rocky crags that enclose them – at 2700m the air is cool and clean, but you can't get away from the spirit of desolation that hangs over it all. There's not much in the way of sights to visit – the big Baroque church, the Museo Parroquial and the Pantheón – but simply wandering around, kicking up the dust and climbing up into the hills are big and worthwhile pastimes here.

It's the church of **San Francisco** that attracts most Mexicans to Catorce, or rather the miraculous figure of Saint Francis of Assisi (known as *Panchito*, Pancho being a diminutive of Francisco) housed here. You'll soon spot the shrine by the penitents kneeling before it, but take time to head through the door labelled "Salida" to the left of the altar, where the walls are covered with handmade retablos giving thanks for cures or miraculous escapes effected by the saint. They're a wonderful form of naive folk art, the older ones painted on tin plate, newer examples on paper or card or even photographs, depicting the most amazing events – last-minute rescues from the paths of oncoming trains and the like – all signed and dated with thanks to *Panchito* for his timely intervention. October 4, the saint's day, sees thousands of pilgrims crammed into Catorce, and almost no chance of finding anywhere to stay.

The church's **Museo Parroquial** (Sat & Sun 10am–4pm; US$0.20) has a small collection of old coins, rusting mine machinery, dusty documents – anything, in fact, found lying among the ruins that looks interesting. Across the square, the **Casa de Moneda** is a magnificent old mansion whose sloping site means that it has two storeys on one side, three on the other. This is where Catorce's silver was minted into coin. Enquire at the Presidencia Municipal on the highest side of the plaza to obtain keys to see the lovely old **Palenque de Gallos** (where cock-fights were once held) or head out along Zaragoza to the ruinous Plaza de Toros, opposite the **Pantheón** (daily except Tues 8am–4pm; free) where Catorce's dead lie covered by rough piles of dirt all around the mouldering church.

Practicalities

On arrival, as likely as not, you'll be accosted by a knot of small boys eager to carry your bags and guide you to their favoured casa de huéspedes in return for a small *propina*. Ensure you've a peso or two handy and follow their lead. You're not obliged to accept what they show you but chances are you'll get a plain and small but clean room, which at least claims 24hr hot water, for around US$5, perhaps substantially less.

The single main street, Lanzagorta, runs down through the town past the church square and the shaded plaza. On the way down you'll pass the first of the **hotels**, *La Providencia* (②), which offers poor value and serves mediocre food. Better **budget** possibilities are *Hospedaje Familiar* (②), at the top end of the church square, with comfortable enough cells; and *Casa de Huéspedes San Francisco* (②), on up from the plaza, where a dollar more affords slightly more comfortable rooms. For even simpler and cheaper rooms try the last shop on the left on Zaragoza, the road to the Plaza de Toros and cemetery. At the other end of the scale, Catorce has some wonderful hotels, if you can afford them. The best of the lot is the friendly *Meson de la Abundancia* (④), on Lanzagorta just past the church, recently remodelled from the ruins and full of huge stone-built rooms with beamed ceilings, rug-covered brick floors and ancient doors with their original hefty keys. A close contender is *Hotel Corral del Conde* (④), on Constitución, where you get a whole suite of beautifully furnished rooms and electric blankets to ward off the winter nights. The *Hotel El Real* (④), Morelos 20, behind the Casa de Moneda, is another attractive option, a tastefully converted old house with clean, airy rooms and native decoration; the modern *Quinta la Puesta del Sol* (④), on Zaragoza, on the way to the Plaza de Toros, offers less atmosphere; it does, however, have satellite TV and great views down the valley to the plains. All these places tend to be much busier at weekends, and you should consider reserving in advance for the Saint's day, over Christmas and New Year, Semana Santa and through July and August: there's just **one phone in town**, ☎488/2-37-33, or you can fax 2-47-33.

All of the fancier places except for *Corral del Conde* serve **food**; again *Meson de la Abundancia* is the pick of the bunch serving moderately priced Mexican dishes and some lovely Italian tortes. Catorce also has two Italian-oriented restaurants: *El Real* is the more expensive but does good pizza and hearty breakfasts, while *El Cactus*, by the plaza does a fine cannelloni, great tortas and a huge range of fancy teas. Cheaper food can be found at the fairly basic stalls along the main street.

San Luis Potosí

Situated to the north of the fertile heartland, the sprawling industrial centre of **SAN LUIS POTOSÍ** owes its existence and architectural splendour to a wealth of mineral deposits. Though it can by no means equal the beauty of Zacatecas or Guanajuato, it does have a fine colonial centre and makes a good stop-off if you're heading south from Monterrey towards the Bajío proper.

San Luis was founded as a Franciscan mission in 1592, but it wasn't long before the Spanish discovered rich deposits of gold and silver in the country round about and

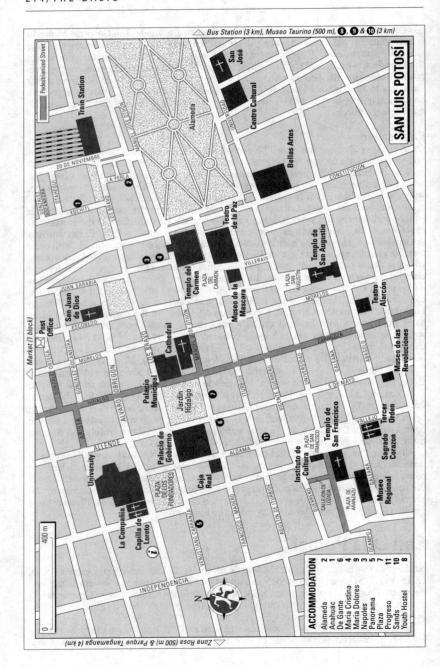

△ Bus Station (3 km), Museo Taurino (500 m), ❽, ❾ & ❿ (3 km)

SAN LUIS POTOSÍ

■ Pedestrianized Street

Train Station

△ Market (1 block)

✉ Post Office

San José

Centro Cultural

Bellas Artes

Teatro de la Paz

Templo del Carmen

PLAZA DEL CARMEN

Museo de la Máscara

Templo de San Augustín

PLAZA SAN AGUSTÍN

Teatro Alarcón

Museo de las Revoluciones

San Juan de Dios

Cathedral

Palacio Municipal

Jardín Hidalgo

University

La Compañía

Capilla de Loreto

Palacio de Gobierno

PLAZA DE LOS FUNDADORES

Caja Real

Instituto de Cultura

PLAZA DE SAN FRANCISCO

Templo de San Francisco

Tercer Orden

Sagrado Corazón

Museo Regional

PLAZA DE ARANZAZÚ

△ Zona Rosa (500 m) & Parque Tangamanga (4 km)

0   400 m

N

INDEPENDENCIA

ACCOMMODATION

Alameda	2
Anahuac	1
De Gante	6
Maria Cristina	4
Maria Dolores	9
Napoles	3
Panorama	5
Plaza	7
Progreso	11
Sands	10
Youth Hostel	8

began to develop the area in earnest. They added the name Potosí (after the fabulously rich mines in Bolivia) in the expectation of rivalling the original, but though this was a thoroughly wealthy colonial town, that hope was never fully realized. Unlike its erstwhile rivals, however, San Luis still is prosperous – most of the silver may have gone but working mines churn out zinc and lead – with a considerable modern industrial base. As a result, San Luis, while preserving a little-changed colonial heart, is also a large and lively modern city.

Arrival and information

Almost all long-distance buses arrive at the main suburban **bus station** (officially Terminal Terrestre Potosina; pricey 24hr guardería), around 3km east of the centre on Hwy-57: for downtown and the Alameda you'll want to head left as you exit, so cross the footbridge and pick up a bus for "Centro". San Luis' immediate hinterland is served by what used to be the main bus station, now a near-abandoned shell some 400m east – and an easy walk should you have the need. The old bus station looks lively in comparison to the **train station**, which is more centrally located on the north side of the Alameda within easy walking distance of the centre and most of the accommodation, but is now only served by two trains (see "Moving On", p.220).

For general information, head for the helpful **tourist office** (Mon–Fri 8am–8pm, Sat 9am–1pm; ☎48/12-99-06, fax 12-67-69), Alvaro Obregón 520, a block west of the Plaza Fundadores. They hand out a detailed **map** of the town and "San Luis Sensational", a fairly comprehensive guide to the city.

There are **banks** all around the main plazas, including Banamex and the Banco del Atlántico at Allende and Obregón, and several casas de cambio in the same area. The **post office** is a little way north of the centre at Morelos 235 near where it crosses Gonzales Ortega. Larga distancia **telephones** are easy to find: among many others there are Computel offices in the bus station, at Universidad 700 on the Alameda, and at Carranza 360, opposite the *Hotel Panorama*.

Accommodation

The cheapest **rooms** are to be found in the run-down area near the train station close to the **Alameda**. Places on the back streets can be quieter than the generally more atmospheric places closer to the main plazas, where the **Jardín Hidalgo** is the focus. Even here, though prices are good, there are few truly outstanding options, and for a little luxury you may prefer some of the more modern places around the bus station.

Alameda, La Perla 3, behind the *Pemex* station on the north side of the Alameda (☎48/18-65-58). Very basic and rather noisy, but clean, safe and inexpensive. The best of a number of similar places in this area. ②.

Anahuac, Xochitl 140 at Los Bravo (☎48/12-65-05, fax 14-49-04). Bright, clean and cheery rooms make this friendly and comfortable hotel about the best in the train-station area, provided you can stomach the sappy photos emblazoned with scripture extracts. Some rooms with TV, for two dollars more. ③.

De Gante, 5 de Mayo 140, corner of Jardín Hidalgo (☎48/12-14-92, fax 12-20-58). Central and comfortable but with little atmosphere; chiefly of interest if you can get a room overlooking the Jardín Hidalgo. ④.

Maria Cristina, Juan Sarabia 110 between Othón and Los Bravo (☎48/12-94-08, fax12-88-23). Rooms decked out with heavy wooden furniture distinguish this large, modern and smart hotel, which is popular with hurried Mexican business people. ⑤.

Maria Dolores, Hwy-57, opposite the Central Camionera (☎48/22-18-82, fax 22-06-02). One of the swankiest of San Luis' hotels, all low-rise and set around attractive gardens studded with palms and swimming pools. Restaurants, bars and nightclubs fill ancillary buildings, and rooms, all with cable

TV and mini-bars mostly have direct access to lawns. There are almost always sizeable reductions from the rack rate if you ask. ⑥.

Napoles, Juan Sarabía 120 (☎48/12-84-18, fax 12-22-60). Modern and well-maintained business hotel with parking, cable TV and phone in all rooms. One of the best in this price range. ④.

Panorama, Venustiano Carranza 315, west of Plaza Fundadores (☎48/12-17-77 or 1-800/4-80-01, fax 12-45-91). Slick, upmarket business hotel – the plushest in the centre of town. ⑤.

Plaza, Jardín Hidalgo 22, on Madero (☎48/12-46-31). Friendly hotel in a beautiful old building in the heart of the city with a fine, dark lobby and basic but comfortable rooms, some more expensive ones with TV. Great value for the location. ③.

Progreso, Aldama 415, at Iturbide (☎48/12-03-66). One of the best deals among the downtown hotels; a musty old hotel with stacks of character, fairly basic rooms, many off a great well of a lobby, and all the hot water you could hope for. Better rooms come with TV. ②.

Sands, Hwy-57, 100m east (right) of the Central Camionera (☎48/18-24-36, fax 18-24-73). Excellent-value hacienda-style motel set around a pool and shaded lawns. High-standard rooms all have cable TV, fans and adjacent parking. ④.

Youth Hostel, 300m east of the bus terminal, at Diagonal Sur (☎48/18-16-17). A rather desperate option, far from the centre with single-sex dorms, an 11pm curfew and a sporadic water supply: to get there walk left along the main highway outside the bus station entrance to the truck dealership and cross the (busy) road to the *Villa Deportiva Juvenil* inside the sports grounds. ①.

The City

Despite its uninviting industrial outskirts, the centre of San Luis Potosí is calm and beautiful, set on a tidy grid of largely pedestrianized streets around a series of little colonial plazas, chief among which is the **Jardín Hidalgo**, the old Plaza de Armas, surrounded by state and city government offices and overlooked by the cathedral. North of the plaza, pedestrianized Hidalgo, and the streets around it, comprise the city's main shopping area: the department stores near the plaza give way to smaller, simpler shops as you approach the **Mercado Hidalgo**, a good place for souvenirs and fresh produce. Further up, continuing along Alhóndiga, the street stalls and stores become increasingly basic until you reach another, much larger produce and clothing market, beyond the main road that delineates the edge of the centre. Hidalgo's southern continuation, Zaragoza, is also traffic-free and heads through a more up-and-coming area, while to the west lies swanky Av Carranza, which, five blocks from Jardín Hidalgo, becomes a fully fledged *zona rosa*, the fancy restaurants and designer boutiques running for perhaps a kilometre to the leafy square of Jardín Tequis.

Jardín Hidalgo and around

Certainly not the most elegant of the city's churches, the **Cathedral** dominates the east side of the **Jardín Hidalgo**. Built in the early eighteenth century, successive generations have ensured that little remains of the original. Facing the cathedral across the square is the long facade of the **Palacio de Gobierno** (Mon–Fri 8am–9pm, Sat & Sun 8am–2pm; free), with its balustraded roof. This, too, has been substantially refurbished over the years, but at least any alterations have preserved the harmony of its clean Neoclassical lines. Inside, you can visit the suite of rooms occupied by Benito Juárez when San Luis became his temporary capital in 1863: head up the stairs and turn left. French troops supporting Emperor Maximilian soon drove him out, but Juárez returned in 1866, and in this building confirmed the death sentence passed on Maximilian. There's an absurd waxwork model of Juárez with the Princess Salm Salm, one of Maximilian's daughters, kneeling before him pleading for the emperor's pardon. He refused, "thus ending the short-lived empire," according to the state government's leaflet, "and strengthening, before all peoples and the entire world, Mexico's prestige as a liberty loving nation". Just behind the cathedral lies **Casa Othón**, Othón 225 (Tues–Fri 10am–2pm & 4–6pm, Sat 10am–2pm; free), a rather lifeless tribute to San Luis' most famous poet mainly comprising some of his furniture.

Plaza de San Francisco and Plaza de los Fundadores

Immediately behind the Palacio de Gobierno you can admire the ornate Baroque facade of the **Caja Real** – the old mint – one of the finest colonial mansions in San Luis. It is now owned by the university, which plans to hold temporary exhibitions here, but in the meantime you can usually walk in and take a look during the day: notice the gentle gradient of the stairway, supposedly to make it easier to lug boxes full of gold and silver up and down. Take a left turn from here, along Aldama, and you come to the quiet **Plaza de San Francisco**, a shaded area redolent of the city's colonial history. It's named for the Franciscan monastery whose church, the **Templo de San Francisco**, towers over the west side. The monastery itself now houses the **Museo Regional** (Tues–Sat 10am–7pm, Sun 10am–5pm; US$1.30, free on Sun), an excellent collection of pre-Hispanic sculpture and other archeological finds, displays of local Indian culture and traditions, and articles relating to the history of the state of San Luis Potosí. In addition to a fine cloister, there's access, upstairs, to the lavish Baroque chapel, **Capilla de Aranzazu** – said to be the only chapel in Latin America located on an upper floor – with exceedingly rich and enthusiastically restored churrigueresque decoration. Inside and through the side chapels lies a miscellaneous collection of religious paintings and artefacts, including massive iron-plated offering boxes into which newly converted Indians were encouraged to place their gold and silver, and a couple of gruesome crucifixes, one of wax, the other fashioned from sugar cane and employing human ribs and toenails. At the back of the museum, the **Plaza de Aranzazu** is another pleasant open space.

At the far end of the Plaza de San Francisco, two more tiny and elaborate churches, **Sagrado Corazon** and the **Templo del Tercer Orden**, stand side by side, with a small, plain presbyterian chapel, seeming terribly incongruous amid all this Baroque grandeur, facing them across Galeana. On the plaza to the right of San Francisco, the **Instituto de Cultura** (Mon–Sat 10am–2pm & 4–7pm; free) is worth a quick look as much for its attractive architecture as the high-class artesanía shops and galleries that surround the courtyard. Also in the area is the small **Museo de las Revoluciones**, 5 de Mayo 610 (Tues–Fri 10am–2pm & 4–6pm, Sat 10am–4pm, Sun 10am–2pm; free), with changing exhibits displayed in the house where Independence hero Jose Mariano Jiménez was born.

Aldama runs four blocks north from the Plaza de San Francisco to the paved **Plaza de los Fundadores**, a much larger and more formal open space than the Jardín Hidalgo. Nothing much seems to happen here, though, despite the fact that it's dominated by the enormous Neoclassical **State University**. Alongside are two more small churches, **Capilla de Loreto** and **La Compañia**, while the fine arcaded portals of the square continue around the corner into Av Venustiano Carranza.

Plaza del Carmen, San Agustín and the Alameda

The **Templo del Carmen**, on the little **Plaza del Carmen** up towards the Alameda, is the most beautiful and harmonious of all San Luis' churches. Exuberantly decorated with a multicoloured tiled dome and elaborate Baroque facade, it has an equally flashy interior: in particular, a fantastically intricate retablo attributed to eighteenth-century eccentric and polymath Francisco Tresguerras. Beside it, where once stood the monastery, is the bulky **Teatro de la Paz**, built in the nineteenth century under Porfirio Diaz and typical of the grandiose public buildings of that era, though its modern interior fails to live up to the extravagance of the exterior. Directly opposite the theatre, you'll find the **Museo de la Mascara** (Tues–Fri 10am–2pm & 4–6pm, Sat & Sun 10am–2pm; US$0.20), a compulsive and fascinating place, exhibiting everything from pre-Hispanic masks to costumes that are still worn for fiestas and traditional dances. Included are the so-called "giants of San Luis", eight enormous models representing four royal couples (from Africa, Europe, Asia and America), which are flaunted in the streets during the festival of Corpus Christi in May. Look out, too, for the funerary mask made from a skull inlaid with a mosaic of turquoise and black stone. Displays instruct (in Spanish) as to the meaning and continued significance of many of the dances.

South of the museum, another magnificent Baroque exterior, that of the **Templo de San Agustín**, faces out onto the tiny Plaza San Agustín – there's little to offer if you venture inside, however. East on Universidad from here, you reach the southern side of the Alameda, where the **Centro de Difusion Cultural** (Tues–Sat 10am–2pm & 5–8pm, Sun 10am–2pm & 6–8pm; free) occupies a concrete building that looks like a modern church. It holds temporary exhibitions, usually of modern art. The **Alameda** itself, ringed by heavy traffic, is crowded with strolling families, photographers, candy-sellers, and people waiting for local buses.

Beyond the Centro Cultural lies the Plaza de Toros. If you're fascinated by "La Corrida" but would never attend, do so vicariously at the adjacent **Museo Taurino**, at the corner of Universidad and Triana (Tues–Sat 11am–2pm & 5.30–8pm; free), where, if you can rouse the custodian (buzz the second door on the left), you'll be shown ranks of dramatic promotional posters dating back to the glory days, elaborate blood-encrusted suits of lights and an array of stuffed heads all missing at least one ear.

Parque Tangamanga

If urban life is getting you down, the green expanse of the **Parque Tangamanga** in the south of the city beckons: the entire vast acreage is piped for muzak and offers picnic spots, fitness circuits and a couple of small lakes. In addition to the joggers, soccer players and cyclists – you can rent bikes for US$2 an hour, daily except Mon – who come here, inevitably, since this is Mexico, there are also lots of people driving their cars right through the middle of it all. Founded in the early 1980s, the park still lacks maturity, but it makes a pleasant weekend outing nonetheless, with the added attraction of the **Museo de Arte Popular** (Tues–Fri 10am–2pm & 4–6pm, Sat 10am–2pm; free), a showcase museum–shop of local crafts, at the bottom of Tatanacho opposite the main park entrance. You can walk to the park in an hour through the *zona rosa* then south, or catch buses marked "Ruta 32" or "Parques del Sur" from the Alameda.

Eating, drinking and nightlife

The centre of San Luis seems to have a surfeit of **places to eat**, with lots of cafes and simple restaurants offering good-value *menús del día*, though little that's more exciting. Local specialities to look out for include enchiladas and *Tacos Potosinas* (or *Huastecas*), dripping with salsa and cheese. There are also lots of panaderías (try *La Americana*, Galeana 433, opposite the regional museum) and cake shops (*GloMar*, Plaza Hidalgo 21, by the *Hotel Plaza* is very fancy), especially on Hidalgo and Morelos as they head north from the centre towards the market. The **Mercado Hidalgo** includes a host of food stalls, but the place is too packed and noisy for anything other than a hurried snack. *Costanzo* is a wonderful local confectioner, with branches on Carranza at Plaza Fundadores, and at Galeana 420 by the Museo Regional.

For anything more than good filling food in humdrum surroundings you're going to have to wander along Carranza (affectionately known as "La Avenida") into what is effectively San Luis' *zona rosa*, starting half a kilometre west of Plaza Fundadores. Within half a dozen long blocks are located some of the best the city has to offer, usually quite expensive. This is also the place to head for **nightlife**, which, at weekends anyway, is pretty lively with many places staying open until the wee hours. Most of the nightclubs play a mix of the latest US and European club grooves and Latin beats, and generally charge little or no money to get in midweek and only a minimal entry at weekends: US$5 max. Places to check out include the popular *Staff*, Carranza 423, the basement *Opus*, Carranza 763 and *Huff!* (see below).

Cafés, restaurants and bars: Downtown

Café la Parroquia, Carranza at Plaza Fundadores. Comfortable middle of the range café, where crusty rolls replace the traditional stack of tortillas. Excellent breakfasts and comida corrida – a firm favourite with local office workers.

Café Pacifico, Los Bravo and Constitución. A bustle of gossip, action and moderately priced food. Open 24hr, this very popular café-restaurant even has a non-smoking section.

El Callejón de San Francisco, Callejón de Lozada 1, just west of the Plaza de San Francisco (☎48/12-45-08). Delightful beam-and-stone restaurant, with a gorgeous rooftop terrace for sipping an afternoon beer while taking in the assorted spires and domes of the San Francisco church. Antojitos such as chicken fajitas and *Enchiladas Potosinos* are served at surprisingly modest prices. Booking advised for dinner, especially at weekends. Closed Mon.

Los Frailes Café, Universidad 165 by Plaza de San Francisco. Youthful evening café with occasional live acoustic music at weekends.

Mariscos El Sardinero, Othón 355A, on Plaza del Carmen. Good seafood restaurant with comida corrida for around US$5.

Restaurant Posada del Virrey, Jardín Hidalgo 3, on the north side. Fine food in fine surroundings – the former home of the Spanish viceroy – with a mildly Mexican menu that includes great seafood.

San Carlos, Othón at Constitución, right by the Alameda. The best breakfast deal in town: an all-you-can-eat US$4 buffet comprising juice, coffee, half a dozen cereals, yoghurt, burritos, egg dishes and bread rolls. The antojito and mainstream Mexican mains – served all day – are comparable good value.

Tortas del Progreso, Aldama 415, under the *Hotel Progreso*. Simple torta and taco place behind one of two original doors facing each other under the hotel: this is the one marked "Cantina"; the *Comedor*, opposite, is a slightly fancier restaurant, with good seafood.

Tropicana, Othón 355B, on Plaza del Carmen. Juices, yoghurt, tortas and healthfood, with plenty of choice for vegetarians.

Cafés, restaurants and bars: La Avenida

Huff!, Carranza 1137. Small, dim and amiable bar with a trendy following and big-screen MTV. Most punters eventually gravitate next door to what ranks as one of San Luis' best nightclubs, which goes by the same name.

La Cava del Gallego, Carranza 1040. Spanish-style bar that's fine for a quiet drink or as a place to practise your Spanish by discussing the football or the bulls on TV.

La Corriente, Carranza 700, right at the start of the Avenue. Lovely restaurant centred on a shaded courtyard and specializing in Mexican steak dishes (US$5–7) but also offering a wide range of enchiladas, chaquiles and a good comida corrida at prices that are modest for this part of town.

Osaka Sushi Bar, Carranza 1405, beyond Jardín Tequis. Reasonably priced sushi, teppanyaki and Mexican *botanas* (bar snacks), along with fairly pricey sashimi, served in numerous small rooms off a fern-filled courtyard.

Listings

American Express Grandes Viajes, Carranza 1077, a fifteen-minute walk west of downtown (☎48/17-60-04, fax 11-11-66). Major travel agency (Mon–Fri 9am–7pm, Sat 10am–1pm) offering the full range of AmEx services (Mon–Fri 9am–2pm & 4–6pm, Sat 10am–1pm).

Books and newspapers The newsstands on Los Bravo, just off the Jardín Hidalgo, often have the México-based English-language daily *The News*, and you may get a recent copy of *Newsweek* or *Time*. Sanborn's, in the Plaza Tangamanga shopping centre, close to the Parque Tangamanga, has a slightly wider selection.

MOVING ON FROM SAN LUIS POTOSÍ

Most traffic from San Luis is heading south on **Hwy-57** towards México, along fast divided highway all the way. Unless you're in a crazy hurry, though, you should definitely turn off into the Bajío proper, to Guanajuato, San Miguel or Dolores Hidalgo, some of the most fascinating towns in the whole of the republic. **Hwy-70**, the route east to Tampico and the Gulf of Mexico, can hardly compete for interest, but it does run though a few towns of minor interest along the way.

Buses cover every conceivable route, with departures for México and Monterrey every few minutes, for Guadalajara, Tampico and the border at least hourly. Flecha Amarilla has excellent second-class services to the Bajío: Dolores Hidalgo fourteen times daily, San Miguel every couple of hours, Guanajuato slightly less frequently. Local buses marked "Central" will take you to the bus station from Av Universidad on the south side of the Alameda.

San Luis is also on the main México–Monterrey **train** line, though "main" is a substantial overstatement these days: one train runs north to Saltillo, Monterrey and Nuevo Laredo leaving at 5.30pm on Monday, Wednesday and Friday; the other is México-bound, departing at 10.30am on Wednesday, Friday and Sunday, and passing through León, Guanajuato and Querétaro.

Car rental Budget (☎48/12-14-11) have an office inside the *Hotel Maria Dolores*, opposite the Central Camionera.

Cinemas Cinema Alfa, Carranza 307, just off the Plaza de Fundadores, has just one screen; Avenida Cinemas, Carranza 780, ten minutes' walk west of the centre, has eight; and Multicinemas (☎48/17-55-56), out in the Plaza Tangamanga shopping centre, has another three.

Emergencies For general emergencies, call ☎06; for medical emergencies, the handiest clinic is Beneficencia Española, Carranza (☎48/11-56-94), or just call Cruz Roja (☎48/15-36-35); for the judicial police (☎48/14-84-93); the highway police (☎48/18-29-06).

Laundry Lavandería la Burbuja, at Carranza 1093, fifteen minutes' walk west of downtown (Mon–Sat 8am–8pm, Sun 9am–2pm), washes and dries at reasonable rates.

Pharmacy Farmacía Perla, Escobedo at Los Bravos (☎48/12-59-22), is always open, while Farmacia Avenida, Carranza 783 (☎48/12-32-28), operates long hours.

Zacatecas

ZACATECAS, 2500m up and crammed into a narrow gully between two hills, packs more of interest into a small space than almost anywhere in Mexico and must rank, alongside Guanajuato, as one of the Bajío's finest colonial cities. Its beauty enhanced by the harshness of the semi-desert landscape all around, it remains much as the British Admiralty's *Handbook of Mexico* described it in 1905: "irregular", its streets "very narrow, steep, and frequently interrupted by stone steps" and "much exposed to winds blowing through the gorge". Those same winds gust bitterly cold in winter, and even though many of the once-cobbled streets are now paved and choked with traffic, the town is otherwise little changed.

All views are dominated by the **Cerro de la Bufa**, with its extraordinary rock cockscomb crowning the ridge some 150m above the city; at night it's illuminated, with a giant cross lit up on top. A modern Swiss cable car connects the summit with the Cerro del Bosque (or del Grillo) – a superb ride straight over the heart of the old town. From the Cerro de la Bufa itself, commanding views take in the entire city, its drab new suburbs and the bare hills all around, pockmarked with old mine-workings. From this height, the city's sprawl isn't particularly inviting, but it's when you get down there, among the narrow streets, twisting alleys, colonial fountains, carved doorways and ornate churches, that the city's real splendour is revealed.

Some history

It didn't take the Spanish Conquistadors long to discover the enormous lodes of **silver** in the hills of Mexico's central highlands, and, after some initial skirmishes with the Zacateco Indians, the city of Zacatecas was founded in 1546. For the next three centuries its mines disgorged fabulous wealth to enrich both the city and the Spanish crown; in 1728 the mines here were producing one-fifth of all Mexico's silver. Though bandits and local indigenous groups continuously preyed on the town, nothing could

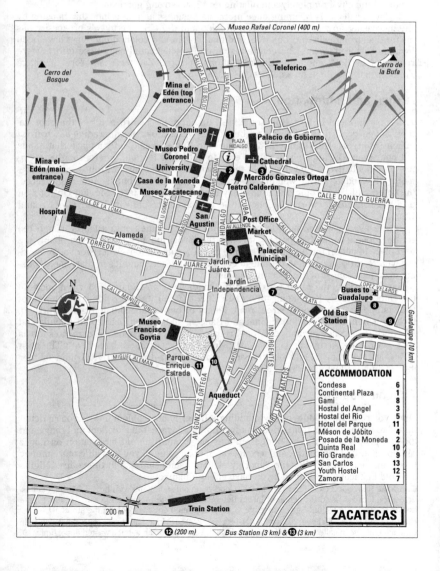

Museo Rafael Coronel (400 m)

Cerro del Bosque

Cerro de la Bufa

Teleferico

Mina el Edén (top entrance)

Santo Domingo

Palacio de Gobierno

Museo Pedro Coronel

Mina el Edén (main entrance)

University

Cathedral

Casa de la Moneda

Mercado Gonzales Ortega

Museo Zacatecano

Teatro Calderón

CALLE DONATO GUERRA

Hospital

CALLE DE LA LOMA

San Agustin

Post Office

Market

Alameda

AV TORREÓN

Palacio Municipal

AV JUÁREZ

Jardin Juárez

Jardin Independencia

Buses to Guadalupe

CALLE MANUEL PONCE

Guadalupe (10 km)

Old Bus Station

Museo Francisco Goytia

MIGUEL ALEMÁN

Parque Enrique Estrada

Aqueduct

Train Station

ACCOMMODATION

Condesa	6
Continental Plaza	1
Gami	8
Hostal del Angel	3
Hostal del Rio	5
Hotel del Parque	11
Méson de Jóbito	4
Posada de la Moneda	2
Quinta Real	10
Rio Grande	9
San Carlos	13
Youth Hostel	12
Zamora	7

ZACATECAS

0   200 m

(200 m)   Bus Station (3 km) & (3 km)

deter the fortune-hunters and labourers from around the world – Spanish nobles, African slaves, German engineers, British bankers – drawn by the prospect of all that wealth. The end of the boom, when it came, was brought about more by the political uncertainties of the nineteenth century than by the exhaustion of the mines, some of which still operate today. Throughout nearly a century of war, Zacatecas itself became an important prize: there were major battles here in 1871, when Benito Juárez successfully put down local rebels, and in 1914 when Pancho Villa's **Division del Norte** captured the city, completely annihilating its 12,000-strong garrison.

Today Zacatecas is booming once more, its business and light industry boosted by the increasing flow of traffic between Mexico and the US. The town's prosperity has ensured a strong vein of civic pride, and many of the old colonial buildings have been lovingly restored, giving the centre a rich and sophisticated air. These efforts were rewarded in 1994 when the United Nations declared Zacatecas a "World Heritage Zone", which put them on a level with Guanajuato.

Arrival and information

Zacatecas' modern **bus station** lies some 4km out of the centre, south of the train station, and currently has no guardería, but comes with a kiosk masquerading as a **tourist office** (Mon–Sat 9am–1pm & 2–8pm, Sun 9am–1pm) – really only a place that hands out poor maps. Fortunately, it's dead easy to get a bus (#8 and others; roughly every few minutes between 7am–10pm) or taxi downtown. The **train station** is more conveniently located – within walking distance of the centre – but is now a sad place, unstaffed and seeing only one train a day in each direction (see "Moving On" box on p.229). From the **airport** take one of the official *combis* into the centre, for around US$12.

Zacatecas' one-way system forces most **local bus** routes onto a loop through the centre, most at some time passing through the Jardín Independencia. It's probably the best place to get off the bus if you've come from the bus station – wherever you're heading, you're almost certain to be able to get there from here, and it's in reasonable walking distance of most of the accommodation.

Barely marked, the **main tourist office** hides away on Hidalgo 693, right opposite the cathedral (daily 8am–8pm; ☎492/4-15-52 & 4-03-93); they provide a smattering of leaflets and that same poor street map. Plenty of **banks** are situated along Hidalgo, including Banamex, Bancomer, Bital and Bancen, all between Juárez and Allende and all offering currency exchange (Mon–Fri 9am–1pm), as do **casas de cambio** such as Divisa San Luis, Arroyo de la Plata 201 (Mon–Fri 9am–6pm, Sat 9am–3pm). The **post office** is at Allende 111 (Mon–Fri 8am–7pm, Sat 9am–1pm), and you'll find further information in "Listings" on p.228.

Accommodation

Once you're in the middle of town, finding a **hotel** is no problem unless you're determined to go for rock-bottom prices; budget hotels are rare, but excellent mid-range and top-line places abound. The budget options are around the old bus station on López Mateos, south of the centre, and a couple aren't bad value. If you've a little more money to spend, head straight for the superbly elegant establishments in the centre. Nights are cold in Zacatecas, so check you have enough blankets.

Condesa, Juárez 102 (☎ & fax 492/2-11-60). Good-value old-style hotel with huge lobby in a fantastic central location amid the action of Jardín Independencia. The rooms, some with TV, don't quite live up to expectations, unless you manage to get a balconied one overlooking the street. ④.

Continental Plaza, Hidalgo 703 (☎492/2-61-83, fax 2-90-54). In a palace opposite the Palacio de Gobierno they've installed a bland international hotel. Very comfortable, but a wasted opportunity. ⑧.

Gami, López Mateos 309 (☎ & fax 492/2-80-05). For US$3 more than the *Río Grande* or *Zamora* you get larger and better decorated rooms with TV. A large modern establishment that's clean and comfortable, if a little noisy and inconveniently situated. ②.

Hostal del Angel, 1 de Mayo 211 (☎492/2-50-26). A great little find, hidden among the colonial streets right in the centre, east of the Mercado Gonzales Ortega. This friendly, cosy hotel occupies a simple, colonial building, has simple rooms with en-suite baths, great views from the rooftop, in-house laundry and use of the owner's kitchen. It may be worth paying extra (④) for the larger rooms. ②.

Hostal del Río, Hidalgo 116 (☎492/4-00-35, fax 2-78-33). Rambling but characterful colonial place right in the heart of things. All rooms are whitewashed and come with simple decor and TV, but the large ones (US$24, sleeping up to five) are simply huge. ④.

Hotel del Parque, Av Gonzalez Ortega 302a (☎492/2-04-79). Modern, clean and fairly central place that's a cut above the real budget places. Rooms come with TV, and some have views of the adjacent park and aqueduct. ②.

Mesón de Jóbito, Jardín Juárez 143 (☎ & fax 492/4-17-22, reservations ☎800/4-40-00). An entire colonial street has been converted into a superb luxury hotel, very pretty and very plush, with all rooms a/c, some with jacuzzis. Bar, restaurant and just about everything else. ⑧.

Posada de la Moneda, Hidalgo 413, opposite the Mercado Gonzales Ortega (☎ & fax 492/2-08-81). Brilliant location for a pleasant but unspectacular hotel popular with Mexican businesspeople. ⑤.

Quinta Real, Av Gonzalez Ortega, by the aqueduct (☎492/2-91-04, fax 2-84-40). Gorgeous and outrageously luxurious hotel in the shadow of the colonial aqueduct, which beautifully incorporates what was once Zacatecas' bullring. Every comfort is taken to the nth degree; at US$124, a place worth saving up for. ⑨.

Río Grande, Calzada de la Paz 513 (☎492/2-53-49). Best budget deal in town, big but friendly, clean and well-kept; all rooms with endlessly hot showers, and fresh towels daily. It's not easy to find – from the old bus station cross López Mateos on the footbridge and walk up the narrow street behind *Refacciones Valadez*. ②.

San Carlos, beside the new bus station (☎492/2-00-32). Comfortable, big and modern, but only a good option if you're passing through or leaving very early. ④.

Zamora, Plaza Zamora, top of C Ventura Salazar, by Jardín Independencia (☎492/2-12-00). Central and cheap, but these are its only virtues. ②.

Youth Hostel, C Celaya (☎492/2-02-23). A bargain US$2 (no membership needed) gets you basic, single-sex dorms, and an 11pm curfew, ten minutes' walk into the centre and proximity to the #8 bus route. Coming from the Camionera Central, get off the bus by the first footbridge and follow C Celaya for 100m. Enter the *Instituto de la Juventud y de Deportes* and turn right towards the terracotta-coloured tower, which stands in front of the hostel. ①.

The Town

Although it can be tiring if you're not used to the altitude, by far the most rewarding way to enjoy Zacatecas is by aimless wandering, particularly in the cool of the evening, when the streets are filled to bursting. This is a city of constant surprises, with narrow alleys crowding in on each other as they scramble about the steep-sided ravine, revealing a series of little plazas and glimpses of tiny hidden courtyards. In the beautifully preserved town centre the highlight is undoubtedly the ornate **Cathedral**, from where all other main sights are within walking distance.

Though the cathedral is the formal heart of the city, and the adjacent **Plaza Hidalgo**, in front of the Palacio de Gobierno, is where formal events take place, life for locals revolves more around the **Jardín Independencia**. Just a few paces from the market and from the important junction of Juárez and Hidalgo, this is in effect the city's main plaza, where people gather in the evenings, hang out between appointments and wait for buses. The only place to really challenge the Jardín Independencia is the **Alameda**, a thin strip of stone benches, splashing fountains and a bandstand. Always full of students from the nearby university, it makes both a cool retreat from the heat of the day and a popular spot for the evening *paseo*.

Around the cathedral

Zacatecas' flamboyant **Cathedral** is the outstanding relic of the city's years of colonial glory: built in the pink stone typical of the region, it represents one of the latest, and arguably the finest, examples of Mexican Baroque architecture. It was completed in 1750, its facades carved with a wild exuberance unequalled anywhere in the country. The interior, they say, was once at least its equal – furnished in gold and silver, with rich wall hangings and a great collection of paintings – but as everywhere, it was despoiled or the riches removed for "safekeeping", first at the time of Juárez's reforms and later during the Revolution; only the structure itself, with its bulky Doric columns and airy vaulting, remains to be admired. On each side of the cathedral there's a small plaza: to the north the formal Plaza Hidalgo, to the south a tiny paved *plazuela*, **Plaza Huizar**, which often hosts lively street theatre and impromptu musical performances.

The **Plaza Hidalgo** is surrounded by more colonial buildings. On the east side, the eighteenth-century **Palacio de Gobierno** was built as a home by the Conde Santiago de la Laguna and subsequently bought by the state government. In keeping with local fashion, a modern mural depicting the city's history embellishes the interior courtyard. Opposite, along with what is now the *Hotel Continental Plaza*, lies the Palacio de Justicia, locally known as the **Casa de la Mala Noche**. According to legend, its builder, Manuel de Rétegui, was a mine-owner down to his last peso, which he gave away to a starving widow to feed her family. He then spent a long night of despair in the house ("la mala noche"), contemplating bankruptcy and suicide, until at dawn his foreman hammered on the door with the miraculous news that a huge vein of silver had been struck, and they were all to be rich.

On the other side of the cathedral, the **Mercado Gonzales Ortega** is a strikingly attractive market building, built at the end of the last century. It takes advantage of its sloping position to have two fronts: the upper level opening onto Hidalgo, the lower floor with entrances on Tacuba. Converted into a fancy shopping mall, it's now filled with tourist shops and smart boutiques, as well as some excellent cafés. On Hidalgo opposite the Mercado, the **Teatro Calderón** is a grandiose nineteenth-century theatre. Below the Mercado, head to the right down Tacuba past another delightful square, **Plazuela Goyita**, and you'll come to the real **market**, tucked in behind the Palacio Municipal.

Santo Domingo and the Museo Pedro Coronel

Climbing up from the west side of Plaza Hidalgo towards the Cerro del Bosque are streets lined with more mansions – some restored, some badly in need of it, but all deserted now by the mining moguls who built them. The church of **Santo Domingo** stands raised on a platform above the plaza of the same name, just up from the Plaza Hidalgo – its hefty, buttressed bulk a stern contrast to the lightness of the cathedral, though it was built at much the same time. In the gloom of the interior you can just make out the gilded churrigueresque retablos in the chapels.

Next door, the **Museo Pedro Coronel** (Mon–Wed, Fri & Sat 10am–2pm & 4–7pm, Sun 10am–5pm; US$1.50) occupies what was originally a Jesuit monastery attached to the church. Pedro Coronel Rivera was a local artist, brother of Rafael Coronel (see below) and a son-in-law of Diego Rivera, which perhaps explains how he managed to gather an art collection that reads like a Who's Who of modern art: you'll find paintings here by Picasso, Kandinsky, Chagall, Dalí and Miró among others, as well as sketches by Goya, architectural drawings by Piranesi, Hogarth engravings and a few of Pedro's own works. It's undeniably an amazing collection – astonishing that one person could create it – but it's nothing like as good as the list of names makes it sound. With the exception of a few of the Mirós, these are all very minor works, not particularly well lit or displayed. Some of the peripheral collections are more interesting, those of West African and Oriental art, and some pre-Columbian antiquities in particular. The building itself was converted into a hospital, a barracks and a prison before its recent restoration, and one of the grimmer dungeons is also preserved as an exhibit.

On the same street, in another converted mansion, is the main building of the Universidad Autonoma de Zacatecas, the **University Rectory** – a good place to check the noticeboards for details of local events – and below this, on C Dr Hierro, is the **Casa de la Moneda**, Zacatecas' mint in the days when every silver-producing town in Mexico struck its own coins. Further along you come to the **Museo Zacatecano**, Dr Hierro 301 (daily except Tues 10am–5pm; US$1.50), where some superb and wonderfully natural 1940s' photos of Huicholes lead to a room chock-full of some two hundred Huichol embroideries, incorporating an amazing range of geometric designs, as well as maize symbols, deer and butterflies, all executed in black, red and green (for death, life and prosperity respectively). It should come as no surprise that peyote features in a big way, usually depicted by eight diamonds, a logo strangely adopted by the *Vips* chain of pharmacies and restaurants. Nothing is labelled but one of the attendants may well give you an unbidden guided tour. Most of the rest of the museum is given to a display of religious iconography; a couple of hundred wonderfully naïve hand-painted retablos, including a couple of sixteenth-century examples) and depicting just about every saint, martyr and apostle going.

Across the street lies the church of **San Agustín** (Mon–Fri 10am–2pm & 4–5pm, Sat 10am–2pm), an early eighteenth-century temple which, after the Reform Laws, was converted into a casino, while the adjoining monastery became a hotel. It has been under restoration for nearly twenty years now, and though it's essentially complete, there are still chunks of statuary scattered around with apparently nowhere to go. It must have been very beautiful once, and there's still a very un-Mexican simplicity and charm to the place, and a magnificent relief telling the story of St Augustine. A series of before-and-after photographs in the nave chronicle the restoration work.

Museo Rafael Coronel

Pedro Coronel may have amassed a spectacular art collection, but his brother Rafael has a far more beautiful museum, the centrepiece of which is a huge collection of traditional masks, possibly the finest in Mexico. The wonderful **Museo Rafael Coronel** (Mon, Tues & Thurs–Sat 10am–2pm & 4–7pm, Sun 10am–5pm; US$1.50) occupies the **ex-Convento de San Francisco**, on the north side of town. Founded in 1593 as a Franciscan mission (the facade is said to be the oldest in the city), it was rebuilt in the seventeenth century and started to deteriorate after the Franciscans were expelled in 1857, the damage completed by bombardment during Villa's assault. The building and gardens have now been partially but beautifully restored, and the museum brilliantly integrated with the ruins. There are over three thousand masks on show, with another two thousand in storage; work is underway on more gallery space. The masks trace the art's development in what is now Mexico, from some very ancient, pre-Columbian examples to some contemporary masks: often there are twenty or more variations on the same theme, and one little room is entirely full of the visages of Moors and Christians from the *Danza de los Moros y Cristianos*. As well as the masks, you can see Coronel's impressive collections of ceramics and puppets, the town's original charter granted by Philippe II in 1593 and sketches and drawings connected with his wife Ruth Rivera, architect and daughter of Diego. If you don't fancy the walk here to or from town, several bus routes, including #5, #8 and #9, pass close by.

The aqueduct and Museo Francisco Goytia

In quite the other direction you can follow the line of the **aqueduct** that used to carry water to the south of the city. Not much of it remains, but what there is can be inspected at closer quarters from the little **Parque Enrique Estrada** on Gonzales Ortega – the continuation of Hidalgo up the hill from the centre. At the back of the park, in what was once the governor's residence, stands a third local artist's museum, the **Museo Francisco Goytia** (Tues–Sat 10am–1.30pm & 5–7.30pm, Sun 10am–3pm; US$1.50). Goytia was one of Mexico's leading painters early in this century, and this enjoyable little museum houses a permanent exhibition of his work and that of more modern local artists (including Pedro Coronel), as well as temporary displays and travelling art shows.

Mina El Edén

The **Mina El Edén** (daily 11am–6.30pm; US$2) is perhaps the most fascinating and unusual of all Zacatecas' attractions. The entrance to this old mine is right in the city, up a road behind the modern hospital, from where a small train takes you to the beginning of the sixteenth-century shafts in the heart of the Cerro del Bosque, some 300m below the summit. The half-hour guided tour – which takes in only a fraction of the workings and is only available in full-speed-ahead Spanish – is a very Mexican experience, which involves being herded into two separate underground shops selling rocks from the mine, viewing a pathetic artificial waterfall and fed all sorts of stupefying statistics, but all done with boundless charm. Some of the numbers are terrifying: if the guide is to be believed, fatalities among the workers ran to eight every day at the height of production. It seems perfectly possible when you're down there – level upon level of old galleries fall away for some 320m beneath you, inaccessible since the mine flooded when production stopped in the mid-1960s. Inside now are diverting subterranean pools, chasms crossed on rickety wooden bridges and, of course, a ghost. The entire hill is honeycombed with tunnels, and in one of them a lift has been installed that takes you up to the slopes of the Cerro del Bosque, about 200m from the lower station of the cable car (you can also enter the mine from this end, though you may have a longer wait for a guide). It's a remarkable round-trip from the depths of the mine to the top of La Bufa.

To reach the mine, take a bus from the Jardín Independencia up Juárez to the hospital (buses marked "IMSS"), or walk, taking in a pleasant stroll along the Alameda followed by a brief climb.

The cable car

The lower station of the **cable car** (daily 10am–6pm, US$1 each way; services can be disrupted by strong winds) is on the slopes of the Cerro del Bosque, near the back entrance to El Edén. Once you're used to the altitude, it's an easy climb up from San Agustín, or bus #7 will bring you right to the door. Most people take a return trip to the top of the Cerro de la Bufa, but walking back down is no great strain. The views down on the houses as you pass right over the city-centre are extraordinary.

At the summit of the Cerro de la Bufa, after you've taken in the superb panorama of Zacatecas and its surroundings, visit the little **Capilla del Patrocinio**, an eighteenth-century chapel with an image of the Virgin said to perform healing miracles, and stroll around the observatory, on the very edge of the crags. Also up here, the **Museo de la Toma de Zacatecas** (Tues–Sun 10am–4.30pm; US$1), full of revolutionary arms and memorabilia, honours Pancho Villa's spectacular victory in the town, also commemorated with a dramatic equestrian statue outside.

Behind, hunkered below that great crest of rock, the **Mausoleo de los Hombres Illustres** is where *Zacatecanos* who have made their mark on history are buried, or at least have their memorials. There are still a few empty places, and it would be a magnificent place to end up – as close to heaven as you could wish, with great views while you're waiting.

Eating, drinking and entertainment

Zacatecas always seems busy, especially in the evenings, and it has a flourishing little **café** society centred on Hidalgo around the Mercado Gonzales Ortega: *La Terraza* and the *Café Acropolis* (see below) in particular. There are also plenty of **restaurants** around central Zacatecas – just about all the hotels have one, for example. For inexpensive tacos, tostadas and sandwiches, head back down towards the old bus station: Ventura Salazar is lined with places serving quick snacks. While in Zacatecas, you should sample *tunas*, the succulent green or purple fruit of the prickly pear cactus. In season, they're sold everywhere, ready-peeled, by the bucket-load, or if you go out into the country you can pick your own, though a pair of heavy gloves is a distinct advantage here.

Nightlife, especially at weekends during term-time, is livelier than you might expect, though less seems to happen in the bars than on the streets where there always seems to be some procession on or a band playing, usually in the small plaza at either end of the Mercado Gonzales Ortega. The **bars** are mostly in the same area, but you'll be hard pressed to find any live music other than sappy combo in some of the fancier restaurants.

Zacatecas has one important **fiesta** – at the end of August and straying into the first two weeks in September – which you should definitely try to get to if you're around. The highlight is the battle between Moors and Christians (an import from Spain, where these stylized struggles are common) on the Cerro de la Bufa. August 27 is the main day, but festivities spill over several days before and after, with **bullfights** – the fiercest fighting bulls in all Mexico are bred around Zacatecas – and plenty of traditional carousing.

Restaurants and cafés

@rroba Cyber Café, C Felix U Gómez 520b, up behind Museo Pedro Coronel. (daily 9am–10pm; *chmnet@gauss.logicnet.com.mx*). More cyber than café, but with fairly up-to-date equipment and full Internet access for a bargain US$2 per hour.

Acropolis, beside the cathedral in the corner of the Mercado Gonzales Ortega. Very popular cafe serving excellent but quite pricey breakfasts, ice cream, fruit juices, good coffee and main meals. English menus are available. Daily 8.30am–10pm.

Café Anis, Hidalgo 306. Low-key place that's good for breakfast, and coffee and cakes all day.

Café La Terraza, Mercado Gonzales Ortega. Overlooking Tacuba, with great views of the passing action (and sun until mid-afternoon), this is a favourite spot for watching the world go by while drinking beer, supping on licuados or snacking on sandwiches and ice cream, though it isn't as pricey as you'd expect, nor is the food as good as you might hope.

Chacatecas, Ignacio Hierro 401. Fairly pricey and trendy restaurant with steaks cooked in all manner of ways and *Camarones Tequila*, shrimps flame-grilled at your table in butter and Sauza, all for US$12. Upstairs is a lively bar (see below).

Chucho El Roto, Juárez 413b. Bohemian hole-in-the-wall that stays open until midnight serving low-cost and tasty plates of tacos, including their steak, veal, bacon, onion and cheese special (US$3), all nicely presented on artesanía ceramics.

El Mesón del Obispo, Allende 117. Lovely upstairs restaurant, bar and art gallery in the colonial surroundings of the bishop's former residence. *Enchiladas Zacatecanas* and *Mole Poblano* prop up a menu mostly oriented towards grilled chicken dishes (US$6) and succulent steaks (US$5–8).

Garufa, Jardín Juárez 135. Argentinian restaurant specializing in gargantuan and super-succulent steaks imported from the pampas (US$14–20), along with much cheaper salads and pasta dishes, served in attractive rustic surroundings.

Gorditas Doña Julia, Hidalgo 409. A one-trick pony, only serving gorditas (50¢ each) stuffed with either various cuts of meat, refried beans, shredded nopal cactus in a hot salsa, or mole and rice, either to go or eat in this cheerfully bright, open-fronted restaurant.

La Tramoya, Ignacio Hierro 506a. Basic, youthful café and fascinating contemporary art gallery, which links to the *Pinacoteca Universitaria* gallery, two doors up, by means of the third tier-of-the-gods of *Teatro Calderón* (see p.224), where there's a permanent exhibition of eighteenth-century religious painting and displays on the history of the theatre.

Quinta Real, Gonzalez Ortega, in the hotel (see under "Accommodation"). Pick of the bunch for an expensive, formal meal, if only for the setting overlooking the former bullring. Expect to spend around US$30 a head for a full meal of nopal stuffed with shrimp, chicken in a tamarind sauce, dessert, coffee and something from the wine list (which includes a good Mexican selection).

Restaurante la Bodeguilla, Callejon de San Agustín 103. Small, sophisticated, Spanish-style tapas bar with a smartish, student atmosphere, freshly baked empanadas on the counter every afternoon and surprisingly modest prices. A popular evening hangout, too.

Restaurante el Tragadero, Juárez 132, by the Alameda. Inexpensive and reliable traditional Mexican restaurant with delicious and piquant *Enchiladas Zacatecas* for under US$3.

Rusch, Alameda 430, at the top end. The closest thing Zacatecas has to a vegetarian restaurant, with economical, nutritious and wholesome variations on Mexican staples (roughly half of them veggie) on a daily rota, along with wholegrain bread baked on the premises. Very popular with students from the university. Weekdays only, 8am–4pm.

Taqueria la Unica Cabaña, Jardín Independencia. Always alive with activity, this is one of the town's cheapest and most popular taco restaurants. Good, basic food served with wonderful salsas and beer at bargain prices in clean surroundings. Wonderfully fruity and thirst-quenching aguas are also sold to go.

Uno Colibri, Rayón 311 at Quisano. Bright and breezy, daytime and early evening café, which doesn't open until 10.30am but still serves bargain breakfasts (including cornflakes, muesli and hot-cakes), equally economical comidas corridas and delicious natural fruit juices. Closed Sat.

Viva Pizza, Jardin de la Madre 112, at the bottom-end of the Alameda. Moderately priced US-style pizzas served in several small rooms decorated with Americana. For delivery call ☎2-79-65.

Bars and clubs

Chacatecas, Ignacio Hierro 401. Through the restaurant (see above) and upstairs is one of Zacatecas' finer bars, especially if you can get a seat out on one of the balconies. Modern US and Latin grooves accompany the smart, young set over beers, cocktails and US$4 Irish coffees produced at your table by what must be the most elaborate and protracted process ever devised.

Discoteca el Mina, main entrance to El Mina. Zacatecas' major club, right in the heart of the Cerro del Bosque, with a lively atmosphere from around 11pm and plenty of Latin numbers, US and European dance tunes. Thurs–Sat 9pm–3am; US$6 entry.

El Elephante Blanco, by the lower cable-car station. The main competition for *Discoteca El Mina* and with great views over town. While cheaper, it has less atmosphere and a 2am closing, but it's not bad once it hots up after around 11.30pm. US$4 entry.

La Cantera, Tacuba, beneath the Mercado Gonzales Ortega. Touristy "fonda musical"; friendly and lively, serving up good traditional food, local wine and live music.

La Nueva Galicia, Plaza Goytia. Restaurant and glossy bar that's fine for a quiet drink to get the evening going.

La Otra España, Tacuba 208, opposite Mercado Gonzales Ortega. Lively, dark bar with happy hour from 6pm to 9pm when Mexican spirits go two for the price of one.

El Paraíso, in the Mercado Gonzales Ortega. Very popular mid-price bar that's usually seething at weekends.

Listings

American Express Viajes Mazzocco, C Sierra de Alica 115, opposite Basilica Fatima, behind Parque Enrique Estrada (Mon–Fri 9am–7pm, Sat & Sun 9am–2pm; ☎492/2-08-59, fax 2-55-59), hold mail, cash and replace travellers' cheques, and organize city tours (see below).

Books and newspapers About all you'll find is the odd (often old) copy of *Newsweek* at places such as Multicosas on the Jardín Independencia.

Cinema Salas 2000, López Mateos 430, just uphill from the old bus station, and Futura, in the shopping centre beside the train station, both show mostly first-run Hollywood movies for around US$2. The Cine Club Universitario, Alameda 414, currently shows more arthouse movies every second Thursday for next to nothing; check the monthly *Agenda Cultural* leaflet available from the tourist office.

MOVING ON FROM ZACATECAS

Situated at one of northern Mexico's crucial crossroads, the Zacatecas **bus terminal** is a hive of activity both day and night. There are frequent long-distance bus services to all parts of **northern Mexico**, including hourly buses to Durango and Chihuahua, some of which push on through to the border at **Ciudad Juárez**. There are also direct buses running to Torreón and Monterrey hourly and one daily to Mazatlán (currently at 12.30pm; 12hr); you could also catch the first bus to Durango and get a connection to Mazatlán from there. Heading **south**, the highway **to México** splits, with hourly buses along either route – the faster, western route runs via Aguascalientes and Léon, while the eastern route runs via San Luis Potosí – the two roads meet again at Querétaro. There are also hourly buses to Guadalajara. To **get to the bus terminal**, take one of the buses marked "Camionera" (mostly Ruta 7 & Ruta 8), which run regularly from the Jardín Independencia.

A **train** service runs to Aguascalientes and overnight to México leaving at 4.55pm, in addition to one daily northbound train for Chihuahua and Ciudad Juárez, departing at 12.50pm. You could also **fly** to México on a daily service: the local airport (some 20km to the north of centre, reached by taxi) has regular connections to Tijuana and Morelia, too, as well as international services to Chicago and Los Angeles.

Internet access See *@rroba Cyber Café* under "Restaurants and cafés" on p.227.

Laundry Lavandería El Indio Triste, Tolosa 826 at C Genaro Codina (Mon–Sat 9am–9pm): wash and dry for US$1 a kilo. Also Lavanderías Cristy, Insurgentes 139 (Mon–Sat 9am–6pm).

Photographic supplies There are photo developing places selling print film all over the place, but for modest specialist needs head for Super Foto, Gonzalez Ortega 140 at Juárez, who stock a reasonable range of slide film at good prices.

Travel agencies and tours Several local agencies handle general travel requirements and offer tours of the city and to surrounding attractions: try Viajes Mazzacco (see above under "American Express") and Operadora Zacatecas, Hidalgo 630, opposite the *Hotel Crown Plaza* (Mon–Sat 9am–8pm, Sun 9am–4pm; ☎492/4-00-50). All the bigger hotels stock leaflets detailing tours to Guadalupe (US$12) and to Chicomoztoc (US$15), among other destinations.

Around Zacatecas: Guadalupe and Chicomoztoc

It's well worth the trip out to Guadalupe – virtually a suburb of Zacatecas, and within easy striking distance – to see the **Convento de Guadalupe**, a rich, sumptuously decorated monastery, rare in that it has survived the centuries more or less unscathed, and for that reason is one of the most important such buildings in Mexico. Further out (you'll need to allow the best part of a day), the ruins of **Chicomoztoc**, a great fortress town in the desert, are in contrast quite unadorned, but enormously impressive nonetheless. You can venture out to either place independently, though several travel agents in Zacatecas offer tours to the sites (see above).

Guadalupe

Local buses run out to **GUADALUPE**, 10km southeast of Zacatecas' centre, every few minutes from a little bus station on Callejón de Barra, just east of the old bus terminal. Once there, you can't miss the enormous bulk of the church, with its dome and asymmetric twin towers. You enter through a flagged, tree-studded courtyard; the entry to the church is through the elaborate Baroque facade straight ahead, while the entrance to the museum and **monastery** (daily 10am–4.30pm; US$2, free on Sun) is to the right. The monastery, founded in 1704, is a vast and confusing warren of a place, with seemingly endless rows of cells opening off courtyards, stairways leading nowhere and mile-long corridors lined with portraits of monks and vast tableaux from the life of Saint Francis. There are guided tours in Spanish, but it's more enjoyable to wander alone, viewing the paintings – which cover every wall – at your own pace, and possibly tagging on to a group for a few minutes when your paths cross. You'll have to time your visit to arrive after 2pm on Sunday to gain access to the monastery's two highlights: the **Coro Alto**, the raised choir at the back of the church, with its beautifully carved and painted wooden choirstalls, and the **Capilla de Napoles**, whose Neoclassical domed roof is coated in elaborately filigreed gold leaf. Presumably, 150 years ago, such sights were not altogether unusual in Mexican churches – today it's the richest you'll see anywhere. You can look into the chapel from the *Coro Alto* and anytime from an entrance at the side of the main church, but the gates are officially only opened on special occasions.

Next door to the monastery, the **Regional History Museum** (Tues–Sun 10am–4.30pm; free) houses a collection of indigenous art and a marginally interesting transport exhibition with a reconstructed pre-Hispanic stone-wheeled cart, sumptuous horse-drawn carriages and nice bits of antique railway rolling stock.

Chicomoztoc

The **ruins of CHICOMOZTOC** (daily 10am–4pm; US$2, free on Sun), also known as **La Quemada**, lie some 40km south from Zacatecas on the road to Villanueva and Guadalajara. The scale of the complex isn't apparent until you're inside – from the road you can vaguely see signs of construction, but the whole thing, even the huge restored pyramid, blends so totally into the mountain behind as to be almost invisible. No two archeologists seem to agree on the nature of the site – its functions or inhabitants – even to the extent that many doubt it was a fortress, despite its superb natural defensive position and hefty surrounding walls. Most likely it was a frontier post on the outskirts of some pre-Aztec sphere of domination – probably the Toltecs – charged with keeping at bay the southward depredations of the Chichimeca. Alternatively, it could simply be the work of a local ruling class, having exacted enough tribute to build themselves these palaces, and needing the defences to keep their own subjects out. Huichol legends seem to support the second theory: there was an evil priest, the story runs, who lived on a rock surrounded by walls and covered with buildings, with eagles and jaguars under his command to oppress the population. The people appealed to their gods, who destroyed the priest and his followers with "great heat", warning the people not to go near the rock again. Chicomoztoc was in fact destroyed by fire around 1300 AD and was never reoccupied; even today, the Huichols, in their annual pilgrimage from the Sierra Madre in the west to collect peyote around Real de Catorce to the east, take a long detour to bypass this area.

In addition to the reconstructed temple, you'll see here a large hall with eleven pillars still standing, a ball-court, an extensive (if barely visible from the ground) system of roads heading out into the valley, and many lesser, ruinous structures all listed for eventual reconstruction. Much of the restoration work is based on drawings produced over the course of ten years from 1825 by a German mining engineer, Carlos de Burghes. Copies are on show in the superb **museum** at the site (daily 10am–3.30pm; admission included in site entrance fee), which makes a masterful job of bringing the place alive with a select display of artefacts, a detailed model of the area and several explanatory videos (in Spanish only).

Most visitors arrive by car or on a tour, but **getting to Chicomoztoc** is easy enough by public transport with Villanueva-bound Perzona buses leaving every half-hour or so from the old bus station in Zacatecas. They're usually happy to drop you at the start of the 2km access road (ask for "las ruinas"); the journey to this point takes about an hour, from where you've got a 25-minute walk to the entrance. To get back, hike to the highway and either flag down the first bus you see, or stick your thumb out while you're waiting.

Aguascalientes

The lively industrial town of **AGUASCALIENTES**, 100km south of Zacatecas, is an important and booming provincial capital. In among its newer buildings are some fine colonial monuments. A couple of excellent **museums**, in addition, make this a good place to stop over for a day or two, especially when you take into account the town's reputation for some of the finest **fiestas** in Mexico – rarely a week goes by without celebration, or at least a band playing in one of the plazas at the weekend – and for the manufacture of excellent wines and brandy.

Arrival, information and orientation

Both the **train station** and the **Central Camionera** are some way from the centre on the city's ring road (Av Circunvalación): from both there's a frequent bus service into the Plaza de Armas, at the heart of town. Here, and on the adjoining Plaza de la Republica, known also as the **Plaza de la Patría**, are all the important public buildings, the cathedral, government offices, the fancier hotels and a handful of **banks** – both Banamex and Bancomer are on 5 de Mayo on the north side of the plaza. The **tourist office** is also in the plaza, on the ground floor of the Palacio de Gobierno (Mon–Sat 9am–3pm & 5–7pm; ☎491/15-11-55); if they've run out of maps, neighbouring Turisste, at the corner of Nieto and the plaza, sell an excellent one. **Casetas de larga distancia** and **casas de cambio** are mostly clustered around the post office on Hospitalidad, a block north of the plaza and reached by following Morelos then turning right.

Many of the streets around the central plaza are pedestrianized, and most things you'll want to see are in easy walking distance. **North of the plaza**, Juárez and 5 de Mayo both run to the market, with Morelos parallel to the east. **East** of the plaza, the major shopping and commercial thoroughfare of Madero heads toward the train station. **West**, Moctezuma soon becomes Venustiano Carranza, which runs past the side of the cathedral and the Casa de la Cultura to the Jardín San Marcos, while to the **south**, José María Chavez runs a couple of blocks to López Mateos, a major through route.

Accommodation

Budget accommodation in Aguascalientes is located mostly around the **market area** (those picked out below are a couple of blocks north of the market, five blocks from the centre), while some of the hotels on and around the **Plaza de la Patría** offer real luxury. During the feria, rooms are almost impossible to obtain at short notice and are likely to **cost** at least fifty percent more.

Colonial, 5 de Mayo 552 (☎ & fax 491/15-35-77). Comfortable hotel with parking lot. All rooms with TV, phone and large windows letting in plenty of light. ③.

Don Jesús, Juárez 429 (☎491/15-55-98). Basic, big and bare, very near the market, but fairly quiet and OK for the price, though you might prefer to pay the extra US$2 for a newer, carpeted room. ②.

Gomez, Av Circunvalación, beside the bus station (☎491/78-21-20). Not bad if you arrive late or plan to push on early. ③.

Hotel Posada San Rafael, Hidalgo 205, one block east of the plaza along Morelos then left (☎491/15-77-61). Plain, good-value rooms with fans, TV and plenty of parking. ②.

Imperial, Plaza Principal (☎491/15-16-50). Very faded elegance in a fine colonial building, but the best value on the plaza; particularly if you can get a room with a balcony. ④.

Praga, Zaragoza 214, three blocks east of the plaza along Morelos then left (no phone). About the cheapest rooms you'll find in town: perfectly decent though nothing flash. ①.

Río Grande, Plaza Principal (☎491/16-16-66). Modern, luxury hotel, offering bags of comfort if no soul. ⑥.

Roble, 5 de Mayo 540 (☎ & fax 491/15-39-94). Big, clean and relaxed, with friendly, committed management and plenty of parking space. ④.

Rosales, Guadalupe Victoria (☎491/15-21-65). A bargain for the location, right by the north side of the plaza, with pleasantly furnished rooms around a central courtyard. Hot water gives out by around 6pm. ②.

Señorial, Colón 104, south side of the Plaza Principal (☎491/15-16-30). Simple, carpeted rooms, but decent value for the location, particularly the corner rooms overlooking the plaza. ③.

Youth Hostel, in a sports complex at Av de la Convención and Jaime Nuño, in the suburb of Colonia Héroes (☎491/18-08-63). Single-sex dorms and an 11pm curfew; to get there, take bus #20 from outside the bus station. ①.

The City

The entire centre of Aguascalientes is undermined by a series of tunnels and catacombs carved out by an unknown tribe; unfortunately these are all closed to the public, and the most ancient constructions you'll see here are the colonial buildings around the centre. If you want to visit one of the **hot springs** from which the city takes its name, head for the *Balneario Ojocaliente*, which has a series of not-so-hot pools and bathing chambers, just outside town on the road to San Luis Potosí. To get there, take a blue ("Ruta Madero") bus from the centre.

Around the Plaza de la Patría

The **Plaza de la Patría** is the place to start any exploration of Aguascalientes. In the centre of this enormous area is the **Exedra**, an amphitheatre-shaped space for performances, overlooked by a column topped with a Mexican eagle. Chief of the buildings around it is the **Palacio de Gobierno**, a remarkably beautiful Neoclassical structure, built in reddish volcanic rock around an arcaded courtyard with a grand central staircase, and decorated with four marvellous **murals** by the Chilean Oswaldo Barra Cunningham, who learnt his trade from the greatest muralist of them all, Diego Rivera. The first of these, at the back on the ground floor, were painted in 1962, and others span the years hence: the most recent (from 1992) are at the front of the building.

Next door, the modern **Palacio Municipal** is bland in comparison, while down the other side of the plaza, the eighteenth-century **Cathedral** has recently been refurbished to reveal its full glory, in an over-the-top welter of gold and polished marble. The **Pinacoteca Religiosa**, in an annexe, has a collection of eighteenth-century religious paintings that is well worth a look.

Venustiano Carranza leads down beside the cathedral to the **Casa de la Cultura** (daily 7am–9pm; free), a beautiful old mansion given over to music and dance classes and the occasional exhibition. The noticeboard here is an excellent place to find out what's on around town, and in the patio there's a small café (see below under "Eating") – a tranquil spot to have a drink and a rest. A little further down Carranza, on the opposite side, the **Museo Regional de Historia** (Tues–Sun 10am–2pm & 5–8.30pm; US$1.50, free on Sun) chronicles local history, from a fossilized mammoth tusk and traditional crafts to the Revolution. Further west on Carranza, the **Jardín San Marcos** is a long enclosed park offering some shady places, flanked by the **Templo del San Marcos** at one side and, nearby, the modern **Casino de la Feria**, with its giant *palenque*, where cock-fights are staged – this is the site of the city's famous fiestas (see below). The new **Paseo de la Feria** cuts through to López Mateos, its modern buildings in complete contrast to what went before. Few maps yet show accurate detail of this area, much of which is pedestrianized with the main roads passing underneath in tunnels, but it's worth taking a walk this way just to see

POSADA – THE MOST MEXICAN ARTIST

José Guadalupe Posada was perhaps the most Mexican of all artists, his often macabre work familiar even when his name is not: Diego Rivera was not far wrong when he described the prolific Posada as "so outstanding that one day even his name will be forgotten". He was born in Aguascalientes in 1852, a baker's son later apprenticed to a lithographer. In 1888 he moved to the capital (having meanwhile lived in León for some time), and started to create in earnest the thousands of prints for which he soon became known. He mainly worked for the editor and printer Vanegas Arroyo, and his images appeared on posters and, mostly, in the satirical broadsheets that flourished despite – or more likely because of – the censorship of the Porfiriano era. Some of Posada's work was political, attacking corrupt politicians, complacent clergy or foreign intervention, but much was simply recording the news (especially disasters, which so obsess the Mexican press to this day), lampooning popular figures, or observing everyday life with a gleefully macabre eye. Later, the events and figures of the Revolution, grotesquely caricatured, came to dominate his work.

Although the *calaveras*, the often elegantly clad skeletons that people much of his work, are best known, the museum devoted to him in Aguascalientes covers the full range of his work. It all bears a peculiar mix of Catholicism, pre-Columbian tradition, preoccupation with death and black humour that can only be Mexican – and that profoundly affected all later Mexican art. Rivera and Orozco are just two of the greats who publicly acknowledged their debt to Posada. Technically, Posada moved on from lithography to engraving in type metal (producing the characteristic hatched effect seen in much of his work) and finally to zinc etching, an extremely rapid method involving drawing directly onto a zinc printing plate with acid-resistant ink, and then dipping it until the untouched areas corroded.

what wealthy, modern Mexico can look like: here there are numerous upmarket restaurants and clubs, the *Hotel Fiesta Americana*, *Canal 6* TV headquarters and the *Expo Plaza* by the bullring, with plenty of greenery and post-modern neo-colonial architecture to boot.

The Museo Posada and the Museo de Aguascaleientes

Though it only occupies a couple of rooms in a small building some way south of the centre, the **Museo José Guadalupe Posada** (Tues–Sun 10am–6pm; US$1) is one of the main reasons to visit Aguascalientes, almost a place of pilgrimage for his devotees. Two rooms, plus another for temporary exhibitions, contain scores of prints, along with the original plates, contemporary photos and biographical information in Spanish; there is also work here by Manuel Manilla, a predecessor of Posada. A few poorly pressed prints are for sale. The museum occupies the former priest's house of the **Templo del Señor del Encino**, an elegant colonial church of pinkish stone with a pretty tiled dome; inside is the miraculous and much venerated "black Christ" of Encino. To get there, head east from the plaza and take the first right, Díaz de León, south for about seven blocks. In front of the church and museum there's a pleasant, quiet square, at the heart of a peaceful old neighbourhood.

The **Museo de Aguascalientes** (Tues–Sun 11am–6pm; US$1) lies in the opposite direction, east from the plaza then north on Zaragoza. Its art collection, mostly modern, is none too exciting, though there are lots of works by Saturnino Hernán, a local who was a contemporary and friend of Diego Rivera's but who died young and never really achieved much recognition. Opposite the museum, the over-the-top **Templo de San Antonio**, built around the turn of the century, has a muddled facade with some vaguely discernible Neoclassical elements. Inside, murals provide a blaze of colour.

Eating, drinking and entertainment

Ordinary **restaurants** are surprisingly thin on the ground in Aguascalientes, though all the large hotels on the plaza have their own. In addition, plenty of simple places along Juárez serve good, tasty barbecued chicken, and there are taco and seafood places in the **market** itself, between Juárez and 5 de Mayo at Alvaro Obregón; the smaller **Mercado de Artesanías**, on Obregón off Juárez, doesn't have much in the way of decent crafts, but it does have more eating places without the crush and smells of the market itself. Fancier places to eat line López Mateos, especially just west of the centre toward the Paseo de la Feria. While you're in town you should try some of the local **wine** (not always easy except in the more expensive restaurants) or at least the brandy: *San Marco* is the best known, made here and sold all over the republic. The **Patio Domecq**, where, supposedly, you can taste local wines and watch some of the processes involved in making them, is on López Mateos near the Paseo de la Feria; opening days – not to mention hours – appear to be utterly random, however.

The most important **fiesta** in the city – famous throughout Mexico – is the ancient **Feria de San Marcos**, celebrated in the Jardín San Marcos during the last couple of weeks of April and the beginning of May. The **Feria de la Uva**, in mid-August, celebrating the grape harvest, is almost as popular, with a giant procession (the *Romería de la Asuncion*) on the 15th.

Restaurants

Café La Parroquia, Hidalgo 222. Cool, student café offering mainly sandwiches and burgers, along with the obligatory cappuccino.

Cafetería Centro Cultural, Madero 311. Quiet, slightly formal spot for coffee and cakes with operatic accompaniment. Open until 10pm.

Chirri's, Carranza 301. Plenty of traditional, well-presented Mexican dishes at mid-range prices, but more a place to stop in for a beer and top up on all manner of *botanas*. Always thick with roving minstrels eager to serenade you.

Jugos Acapulco, Allende 106, between 5 de Mayo and Juárez. Juice bar that also serves *hamburguesas* and more substantial meals; good for breakfast.

Kiko's Merendero, Paseo de la Feria 132 (aka Arturo Pani), at Jardín San Marcos. More bar than restaurant, but food is on offer to soak up the drinks.

La Cava del Gaucho, Paseo de la Feria 114, near Nieto. One of many fancier restaurants along here, this one Argentine-style, open till 2am with live music.

La Musa Café Bistro, inside Casa de la Cultura on Carranza. Serene spot for top-quality quiche, salads and that Mexican rarity, a strong espresso; not exactly cheap.

Restaurante Mitla, Madero 218. Very popular, old-fashioned Mexican restaurant, with white-jacketed waiters serving a good selection of national and local dishes, including seafood and very reasonable comidas corridas.

Restaurante Vegetariano, Madero 409. Small, inexpensive place serving tasty wholefood breakfast from the menu and US$3 buffet lunches (daily noon–5pm). Also à la carte dinner on Sat at 7pm.

MOVING ON FROM AGUASCALIENTES

Aguascalientes is situated on the Hwy-45 between Zacatecas and León, and there are hourly **buses** in either direction, many continuing as far as Chihuahua to the north and México to the south (via Irapuato and Querétaro). There are also slower services to Guadalajara and San Luis Potosí. For Guanajuato, you'll probably be quicker taking a bus first to León and getting a connection from there. **To get to the station** from the centre, catch a bus marked "Camionera" from beside the cathedral in Venustiano Carranza .

Aguascalientes is also on the main **train line** between México and Ciudad Juárez. The daily northbound train leaves Aguascalientes at 10.05am, southbound at 7.50pm. Buses #19 and #31 run along Madero to the train station.

León

Heading south from Aguascalientes, the highway and near-constant buses pass through the town of Lagos de Moreno (see p.186) to **LEÓN**, a teeming, industrial city 60km away. There's a long tradition of leatherwork here – reflected today in the scores of shoe factories and, in the centre, hundreds of shoe shops: it's a good place to buy hand-tooled cowboy boots. The bus station is some way out, and most people take one look and get no further, but if you're changing buses here anyway, it's well worth taking a couple of hours to wander round the centre – even if you just spend ten minutes in the bus station you'll see stacks of shoeboxes being loaded into just about every waiting bus.

In town, the **Plaza de los Fundadores** is not at all what the rest of the city would lead you to expect – very spacious, tranquil and elegant, with a fine eighteenth-century cathedral built by the Jesuits and a typically colonial Palacio Municipal. Little else survived a disastrous flood in 1883, but the plaza is surrounded by broad boulevards lined with shops, and there are a couple of other churches that deserve a look: the Baroque **Templo de los Angeles** and the extraordinary marble **Templo Expiatorio** on Madero, where you can visit a series of underground chambers.

León also has the region's main **airport**, the nearest to both Guanajuato and San Miguel de Allende, with flights from all over Mexico and Houston, Dallas, LA, Chicago and more. On arrival, many just grab a cab direct to their destination, but there are also very infrequent buses and colectivos (around US$12) to León, and second-class buses ply the highway outside between León and Guanajuato: wave madly at any you see.

Guanajuato

Shoe-horned into a narrow ravine, **GUANAJUATO** was for centuries the wealthiest city in Mexico, its mines pouring out silver and gold in prodigious quantities. Today it presents a remarkable sight: emerging from the surrounding hills you come upon the town quite suddenly, a riot of colonial architecture dominated by the bluff (and rather ugly) bulk of the university, tumbling down hills so steep that at times it seems the roof of one building is suspended from the floor of the last. Declared a UNESCO World Heritage Zone in 1988, Guanajuato is protective of its image: there are no traffic lights or neon signs here, and the topography ensures that there's no room for new buildings.

This is an extremely enjoyable place to visit, peaceful, yet with plenty of life in its narrow streets (especially during term-time), lots of good places to eat and drink, and plenty to see – it's never dull and always surprising. There's an old-fashioned, backwater feel to the place, reinforced by the students' habit of going serenading in their black capes, the brass bands playing in the plazas, and the general refusal to make any special effort to accommodate the flood of tourists – who thankfully never really manage to disturb the daily ebb and flow.

Orientation

Maps of Guanajuato don't always help, but in practice it's not in the least difficult to find your way around. The streets run in close parallel along the steep sides of the valley, while almost directly beneath the town's main thoroughfare, Av Juárez, passes an underground roadway. This, the **Subterraneo Miguel Hidalgo**, was built as a tunnel to take the river under the city and prevent the periodic flooding to which it was liable – and in the process to provide a covered sewer. The river now runs deeper below ground, and its former course, with the addition of a few exits and entrances, has

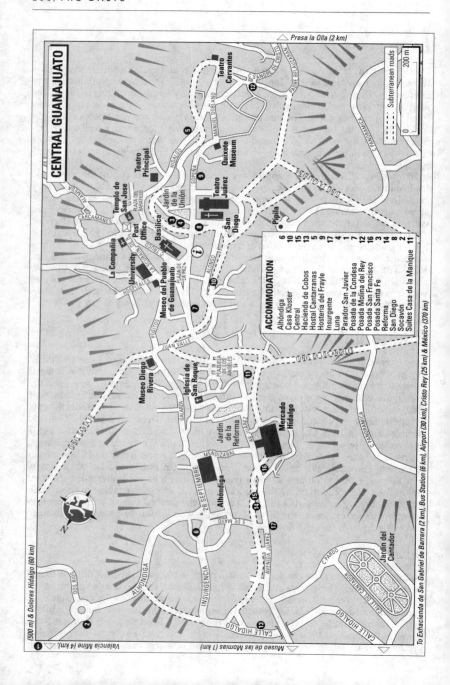

CENTRAL GUANAJUATO

△ Presa la Olla (2 km)

─── Subterranean roads

0   200 m

ACCOMMODATION

Alhóndiga	6
Casa Kloster	10
Central	15
Hacienda de Cobos	13
Hostal Cantarranas	5
Hostería del Frayle	9
Insurgente	17
Luna	4
Parador San Javier	1
Posada de la Condesa	7
Posada Molina del Rey	12
Posada San Francisco	16
Posada Santa Fe	3
Reforma	14
San Diego	8
Socavón	2
Suites Casa de la Manique	11

Teatro Cervantes

Quixote Museum

Teatro Principal

Teatro Juárez

Templo de San José

La Compañia

University

Post Office

Basilica

Jardín de la Unión

San Diego

Museo del Pueblo de Guanajuato

Pipila

Museo Diego Rivera

Iglesia de San Roque

Jardín de la Reforma

Mercado Hidalgo

Alhóndiga

Jardín del Cantador

(500 m) & Dolores Hidalgo (60 km)

Valencia Mine (4 km)

Museo de las Momias (1 km)

To Exhacienda de San Gabriel de Barrera (2 km), Bus Station (6 km), Airport (30 km), Cristo Rey (25 km) & México (370 km) proved very handy in preventing traffic from clogging up the centre entirely; more tunnels have since been added to keep the traffic flowing. If you're interested, some bus routes go through the tunnels, or you could take a drive through in a taxi.

When walking – the only way to get around the city – it's enough to know that **Av Juárez** runs straight through the heart of town along the ravine floor and that everything of interest is either on it, or just off it on the lower slopes. Should you get lost, simply head downhill and you'll get back to Juárez. The town has two alternative centres: the western end is somewhat rougher, focused on the plaza outside the **Mercado Hidalgo**, where there is always plenty of action in the bars and cheap cafés; while to the east, where Juárez becomes Sopeña, the city is calmer, focusing on the **Jardín de la Unión**, with its shaded restaurants, happy tourists and neatly clipped trees.

Arrival and information

The **bus station**, with a small tourist information booth, guardería and long-distance phones, lies 6km west of the city. Regular local buses ("Centro–Central") shuttle into town in about fifteen minutes, usually terminating outside the Mercado Hidalgo, leaving a ten-minute walk if you're staying close the Jardín de la Unión. The nearest **airport** is some 30km west of Guanajuato and closer to León; taxis direct to Guanajuato should cost around US$20, and if you're prepared to schlep a few hundred metres from the airport out to the highway you can flag down second-class buses north to León or south to Silao and Guanajuato.

It's worth checking out the **tourist office** at Plaza de la Paz 14 (Mon–Fri 9am–7.30pm, Sat & Sun 10am–2pm; ☎473/2-03-97), at least for the **free map**; there are also lots of private information booths throughout town, including at the bus station, offering tours and hotel reservations. The **post office** (Mon–Fri 8am–8pm, Sat 8am–1pm) is at the eastern end of Positos, behind the Jardín de la Union, where there's a Telmex office (Mon–Fri 9am–8pm, Sat 8am–1pm) with **phone**, fax and telegram services; there are plenty of other *larga distancia* places, including one at Juárez 110. **Banks** can be found along Juárez: Bancomer at #9, Bital on the Plaza de la Paz, and a convenient branch of Banorte between the Plaza de la Paz and the Jardín Unión. Outside bank hours, try Divisas, Juárez 33 (daily 9am–3pm & 4–7pm).

Accommodation

Rooms in Guanajuato can at times be hard to come by, especially on Mexican public holidays, at Christmas, *Semana Santa* and during the **International Cervantes Festival** (two or three weeks in October) – at these times it's worth trying to book several weeks ahead. If you can get a room on such occasions, you'll pay around a fifty percent premium on the rates quoted here, which are already fairly high by Mexican standards. Budget options are ranged at the western end of Juárez (those just off the main drag are quieter), but by far the best place to stay is around the **Jardín de la Unión**, even if plaza-view rooms come with a sizeable premium and, at weekends, *mariachi* accompaniment until well gone midnight.

Near the Mercado Hidalgo

Alhóndiga, Insurgencia 49 (☎473/2-05-25). Small and plain but very friendly place a short walk north of the centre, with TV and parking. ④.

Central, Juárez 111-A (☎473/2-00-80). The best of the cheap hotels around the Jardín Reforma, comprising simple rooms, all with TV. ③.

Hacienda de Cobos, Padre Hidalgo 3 (☎ & fax 473/2-01-43). Comfortable and attractive motel-style rooms around a large central plaza; it has a pool, too. Good if you have a car. ⑤.

Insurgente, Juárez 226 (☎473/2-31-92, fax 2-69-97). Central hotel with 85 clean, carpeted, comfortable rooms, but overpriced unless you get one with a seventh-floor view. ⑤.

Posada San Francisco, Juárez and Gavira, beside the market (☎473/2-24-67, fax 2-28-04). Central and large; the simple, spotless rooms all have private bathrooms. ④.

Reforma, Juárez 113 (☎473/2-04-69). About the cheapest option in town: dark and basic but fairly clean. TV-equipped front rooms (④) are considerably lighter and more spacious but also noisy. ②.

Socavón, Alhóndiga 41-A (☎ & fax 473/2-48-85). A dark tunnel opens into the sunny courtyard of this small, friendly place, with attractive brick-ceilinged rooms, all with TV. A short walk from the centre but worth it, and there's a restaurant on site. ④.

Suites Casa de la Manique, Juárez 116 (☎473/2-76-78, fax 2-83-06). Eight large suites, very nicely decorated and all with TV and mini-bar. No premium for those fronting the street, but reserve early. ⑤.

The Jardín de la Unión and around

Cantarranas, Cantarranas 50 (☎473/2-52-41, fax 2-17-08). A great, friendly and clean little place tucked away in the backstreets, which looks nothing from the outside and features a wonderful rooftop terrace with views of the Pípila. Rooms come with king-size beds, and the suites (⑤) all come with a kitchen stocked with utensils. There's even a three-room suite sleeping six (⑥). Great for a night or two and wonderful for longer stays. ④.

Casa Kloster, C de Alonso 32, reached from Juárez down the Callejon de la Estrella at its entry to Plaza de la Paz (☎473/2-00-88). Best budget deal in town, hugely popular with backpackers. Clean, simple rooms – avoid those by the street – around a flower-filled courtyard alive with caged birds. There are communal bathrooms with good hot showers, and rates are per person, making this a steal for singles. Management prefers couples to be married. ③.

Hosteria del Frayle, Sopeña 3 (☎ & fax 473/2-11-79). Lovely colonial-style building with comfortable, if uninspired rooms. ⑤.

Luna, Jardín de la Unión (☎473/2-97-20, fax 2-97-25). Slightly faded hotel right in the heart of things with comfortable rooms, including the cheapest you'll find with plaza views (⑥). ⑤.

Posada de la Condesa, Plaza de la Paz 60 (☎473/2-14-62). Cheap and central, but rooms, all with showers, are small and scruffy, and the opening of a loud nightclub next door doesn't help matters. ②.

Posada Santa Fé, Jardín de la Unión (☎473/2-00-84, fax 2-46-53). Very comfortable old hotel right in the heart of the city, with a good rooftop terrace, but leaning heavily on its location. ⑦.

San Diego, Jardín de la Unión (☎ & fax 473/2-56-26). Fine colonial warren of a place in the very centre with spacious international-style rooms, all with satellite TV. There are great views from its front rooms (⑦). ⑤.

The outskirts

Parador San Javier, Plaza Aldama 92, 1km from centre on the road to Valenciana (☎473/2-06-26, fax 2-31-14). Beautiful hotel set in the magnificent manicured grounds of a former colonial hacienda, complete with lovely pool, posh bar and flash restaurant. Everything to the highest standard and wall-to-wall with flunkies. Suites (⑧) and rooms (⑦) available.

Posada Molino del Rey, Padre Belaunzavan and Sancho Panza (☎473/2-22-23, fax 2-10-40). At the east end of town, very reasonably priced but some distance from buses. ⑤.

The City

There must be more things to see in Guanajuato than in virtually any town of its size anywhere – churches, theatres, museums, battlefields, mines and mummified corpses. To get to some of these, you'll need to take the bus, but most places are laid out along **Juárez**: if you start your explorations from the **Mercado Hidalgo** and walk east, you'll be able to see much of what Guanajuato has to offer in a day. Wandering through the maze of narrow alleys that snakes up the side of the ravine is a pleasure in itself, if only to spot their quirky names – Salto del Mono (Monkey's Leap), for example, or C de las Canterranas (Street of the Singing Frogs). Incidentally, frogs crop up everywhere around town – in sculpture, artesanías and T-shirts – a reference to the native source of the town's name, Quanax-huato, meaning "Place of Frogs".

Mercado Hidalgo to the Plaza de la Paz

The first building of note as you head east up Juárez from the bus station is the **Mercado Hidalgo**, a huge iron-framed construction reminiscent of British Victorian railway-station architecture, crammed with goods of every description. Beyond the market, to the left and through the **Jardín de la Reforma**, with its fountain and arch, you get to the lovely, quiet **Plaza San Roque**. A small, irregular, flagged space, the plaza has a distinctly medieval feel, heightened by the raised facade of the crumbling church of **San Roque** that towers above. It's a perfect setting for the city's lively annual **International Cervantes Festival** (see p.244). The Callejon de los Olleros leads back down to Juárez, or you can cut straight through to the livelier **Plazuela San Fernando**, with its stalls and restaurants. Return to Juárez from here and you emerge more or less opposite the **Plazuela de los Angeles**. In itself this is little more than a slight broadening of the street, but from here steps lead up to some of Guanajuato's steepest, narrowest alleys. Just off the plazuela is the **Callejon del Beso**, so called because it is so slim that residents can lean out of the upper-storey windows to exchange kisses across the street – naturally enough there are any number of *Canterbury Tales*-style legends of cuckolded husbands and star-crossed lovers associated with it. To learn more, join one of the *callejoneadas* (see p.244), which pass this way, or engage the services of one of the small children who hang around eager to tell a tale.

The **Plaza de la Paz** lies east of the Jardín de la Reforma, beyond a number of banks on Juárez. For a distance here, Juárez is not the lowest road – Alonso cuts down to the right, to rejoin Juárez a little further along. Plaza de la Paz itself boasts some of the town's finest **colonial buildings**, among which the late eighteenth-century mansion of the Condes de Rul y Valenciana (then owners of the richest mine in the country) stands out as the grandest. It was designed by Eduardo Tresguerras, undoubtedly the finest Mexican architect of his time, and played host briefly to Baron Alexander Von Humboldt, the German naturalist and writer on Mexico, an event commemorated by a plaque. The **Casa de Gobierno**, a short way down towards the Jardín de la Unión, is another fine mansion, this time with a plaque recording the fact that Benito Juárez lived there in 1858, when Guanajuato was briefly his provisional capital. On the far side of the plaza stands the honey-coloured **Basilica de Nuestra Señora de Guanajuato**, the Baroque parish church that houses an ancient image of the Virgin, patroness of the city. This wooden statue, which now sits amidst silver and jewels, was given to Guanajuato in 1557 by Philip II, in gratitude for the wealth that was pouring from here into Spanish royal coffers. At the time it was already old and miraculous, having survived more than eight centuries of Moorish occupation hidden in a cave near Granada in Spain.

Around the Jardín de la Unión

From the Plaza de la Paz, you can cut up to the university, but just a short distance further east on Juárez is the **Jardín de la Unión**, Guanajuato's zócalo. It's a delightful little square – or rather triangle – set back from the street, shaded with trees, surrounded by cafés, tables spilling outside, and with a bandstand in the centre from which the town band regularly adds to the early evening atmosphere. This is the best time to sit and linger over a drink, enjoying the passing spectacle of the evening *paseo*.

Facing the Jardín across Juárez stands the Baroque church of **San Diego**, inside which are several old paintings and interesting chapels – one altar in particular is dedicated to the infant Jesus and mawkishly filled with toys and children's tiny shoes left as offerings. Next door is the imposing Neoclassical frontage of the **Teatro Juárez** (Tues–Sun 9am–1.45pm & 5–7.45pm; US$1), all Doric columns and allegorical statuary. The interior of the theatre is fabulously plush – decked out in red velvet and gilt, with chandeliers and a Moorish proscenium – as befits its period: built at the end of the last century, it was opened in 1903 by the dictator Porfirio Diaz himself.

Beyond the Jardín, Juárez becomes Sopeña, lined by fancy boutiques, restaurants and bars as far as the pretty pink church of San Francisco, which marks the Plazuela San Francisco. Here, too, is the **Museo Iconográfico del Quijote** (Tues–Sat 10am–6.30pm, Sun 10am–3pm; free), an extraordinary little collection devoted entirely to Don Quijote: mainly paintings of him – including some by Pedro and Rafael Coronel – but also a couple of Dalí prints, a copy of a Picasso drawing, murals, tapestries, sculptures, busts, miniatures, medals, plates, glassware, chess sets, playing cards, pipes, cutlery, you name it. Beyond here, Sopeña becomes Manuel Doblano and begins to climb the hill behind, eventually becoming the Paseo de la Presa. A walk of thirty minutes or so takes you through some of Guanajuato's fancier residential districts before ending up at the Presa de la Olla and the Presa San Renovato, two small green and rather unimpressive **reservoirs**. This is a popular picnic spot, and you can rent rowing boats or sit out at a restaurant by the Presa de la Olla. A number of buses run out here (look for "La Olla" or "Presa"), heading through town on the underground street – steps near the church of San Diego will take you down to a subterranean bus stop.

Pípila

The **Monumento al Pípila**, on the hillside almost directly above the Jardín de la Unión, affords fantastic views of Guanajuato. You seem to be standing directly on top of the church of San Diego, and if there is a band playing in the plaza it can be clearly heard up here. It's an especially wonderful spot in the 45 minutes or so between the sun going behind the hills and the light disappearing altogether, as the lights start to come on in town. The steep climb takes about twenty minutes going up, ten minutes coming down: the bottom half is lit but the top isn't, so don't wait for total darkness before you descend. There are several possible routes up through the alleys – look for signs saying "al Pípila" – including up the Callejon del Calvario, to the right off Sopeña just beyond the Teatro Juárez, from the Plazuela San Francisco, or climbing to the left from the Callejon del Beso; the signs run out, but if you keep climbing as steeply as possible you're unlikely to get lost. Along the way there are various viewpoints and romantic nooks. There's also a bus ("Pípila") that takes you round the scenic Carretera Panoramica. Pípila was Guanajuato's own Independence hero (see opposite): for a few coins you can climb up inside his statue (daily 7.30am–8pm; US$0.20) to a point immediately behind his shoulder – from where you can't really see very much at all.

Around the university

At the back of the Jardín de la Unión and on the left, the **Plaza del Baratillo** is a small space with a quiet café and a clutch of crafts shops. From here the **Teatro Principal** is down to the right, while curving on round to the left there's the church of **La Compañia**. The highly decorated monumental Baroque church is just about all that's left of a Jesuit seminary founded in 1732, an educational establishment that eventually metamorphosed into the **State University**, now one of the most prestigious in Mexico. The university building is in fact quite modern – only forty-odd years old – but designed to blend in with the town, which, for all its size, it does surprisingly effectively. There's not a great deal of interest inside to the casual observer, but wander in anyway: noticeboards detail local cultural events, and there's often a temporary exhibition of some kind. High on the fourth floor you'll find the **Museo de Historia Natural** (Mon–Fri 10am–6pm; free), a small collection of beetles, butterflies and assorted beasts, including a small two-headed goat. Next door to the university building, the **Museo del Pueblo de Guanajuato** (Tues–Sun 10am–6.30pm; US$1) is a collection of local art and sundry oddities, housed in the seventeenth-century home of the Marqués de San Juan de Rayas. It's an attractive building with a nice little Baroque chapel, where much of the decoration has been replaced by modern murals painted by one of the current standard-bearers of the Mexican muralist tradition, José Chávez Morado.

Positos leads west from the front of the university to the fascinating **Museo Diego Rivera** (Tues–Sat 10am–6.30pm, Sun 10am–2.30pm; US$1), which occupies the birthplace of Guanajuato's most famous son. For most of his life Rivera, the ardent Revolutionary and Marxist, went unrecognized by his conservative home town, but with international recognition of his work came this museum, in the house where he was raised until he was six. The place is far bigger than it looks from the outside: downstairs it's furnished in nineteenth-century style, with some pieces said to be the Rivera family's, and upstairs are many of Rivera's works, especially early ones, in a huge variety of styles, and a large temporary exhibition space. Although there are no major works on show, the many sketches and small paintings are well worth a look.

The Alhóndiga

The **Alhóndiga de Granaditas**, the most important of all Guanajuato's monuments, lies west of the Museo Diego Rivera, more or less above the market. Originally a granary, later a prison, now a very good regional museum, this was the scene of the first real battle and some of the bloodiest butchery in the long War of Independence. Just thirteen days after the cry of Independence went up in Dolores Hidalgo, Father Hidalgo approached Guanajuato at the head of his insurgent force – mostly peons armed with nothing more than staves and sickles. The Spanish, outnumbered but well supplied with firearms, shut themselves up in the Alhóndiga, a redoubtable fortress. The almost certainly apocryphal story goes that Hidalgo's troops could make no impact until a young miner, nicknamed **El Pípila** ("the Turkeycock"), volunteered to set fire to the wooden doors – with a slab of stone tied to his back as a shield, he managed to crawl to the gates and start them burning, dying in the effort. The rebels, their path cleared, broke in and massacred the defenders wholesale. It was a short-lived victory – Hidalgo was forced to abandon Guanajuato, leaving its inhabitants to face Spanish reprisals, and was eventually tracked down by the royalists and executed in Chihuahua. His head and the heads of his three chief co-conspirators, Allende, Aldama and Jiménez, were suspended from the four corners of the Alhóndiga as a warning to anyone tempted to follow their example, and there they stayed for over ten years, until Mexico finally did become independent. The hooks from which they hung are still there on the outside walls.

Inside, there's a memorial hall devoted to the Martyrs of Independence and a **museum** (Tues–Sat 10am–2pm & 4–6pm, Sun 10am–3pm; US$2, free on Sun; entry ceases 30min before closing). On the staircases are **murals** by local artist Chavez Morado, depicting scenes from the War of Independence and the Revolution, as well as native folklore and traditions. The collection, mostly labelled in Spanish only, spans local history from pre-Hispanic times to this century: the most interesting sections cover the Independence battle and everyday life in colonial times. There are the iron cages in which the rebels' heads were displayed and lots of weapons and flags, as well as a study of Guanajuato's mining industry. There's also plenty of art, especially a wonderful series of portraits by Hermengildo Bustos; and don't miss the small artesanías section by the side door, which displays a bit of everything from fabrics and clothes to saddles and metalwork.

La Valenciana

From close by the Alhóndiga on C Alhóndiga, buses ("Valenciana"; infrequent enough to make a short taxi-ride a worthwhile investment) wind their way 5km uphill to the mine and church of **La Valenciana**. Near the top of the pass here, overlooking Guanajuato where the road to Dolores Hidalgo and San Miguel heads off north, you'll see the elaborate facade of the church of an extraordinarily sumptuous **church** with its one completed tower. Built between 1765 and 1788, it's the ultimate expression of

Mexico's churrigueresque style, with a profusion of intricate adornment covering every surface – even the mortar, they say, is mixed with silver ore. Inside, notice especially the enormous gilded retablos around the main altar and in each arm of the cross, and the delicate filigree of the roof vaulting, especially around the dome above the crossing.

The church was constructed for its owner, the Conde de Rul y Valenciana, who also owned La Valenciana **silver mine** – for hundreds of years the richest in Mexico, tapping Guanajuato's celebrated Veta Madre (Mother Lode). The mine just about operates still, on a vastly reduced level, but exploitation continues apace with a clutch of ways to lure tourists to the associated silver shops, rock sellers and restaurants. A road running west from beside the church leads 400m to the **Mina La Valenciana** (daily 8am–7pm; US$0.40), where you're guided around the surface workings – essentially winding gear and a few decaying buildings. Outside the gates the **Leyendas de la Mina Encantada** (daily 8am–7pm; US$0.70) offers a mock-up mine and assorted stories, while the original mine entrance now operates as the **Bocamina San Cayetano** (daily 10am–6pm; US$1), the name commemorating the saint who gets credit for the Mother Lode's discovery. Donning a hard hat fails to lend credibility to a brief tour of the upper 50m of tunnels, which end in a shrine to the mine's patron. A visit to the excellent and expensive *Casa de la Conde de la Valenciana* restaurant, opposite the church, however, makes the journey up here all the more worthwhile. If you're a real rock enthusiast, then on your way back to town you might call in at the **Mineralogy Museum** (Mon–Fri 9am–1pm & 4.30–7pm; free), which houses some 25,000 rock samples. The museum is in the mining department of the university, in a building on your left as you head out of town towards Valenciana, about 3km from central Guanajuato – ask for the "Escuela de Minas y Metalurgia".

Museo de las Momias

Halfway up the hill following Juárez west of town, the ghoulish *Panteón*, or **Museo de las Momias** (daily 9am–7pm; US$2), holds a very different sort of attraction. Here, lined up against the wall in a series of glass cases, are more than a hundred mummified human corpses exhumed from the local public cemetery. All the bodies were originally laid out in crypts in the usual way, but if after five years the relatives were unable or unwilling to make the perpetuity payment, the remains were removed. Many are found to have been naturally preserved, and the "interesting" ones are put on display – others, not properly mummified or too dull for public titillation, are burned or transferred to a common grave. The wasted, leathery bodies vary from some more than a century old (including a smartly dressed mummy said to have been a French mining engineer) to relatively recent fatalities, who presumably have surviving relatives. The burial clothes hang off the corpses almost indecently – others are completely naked – and the guides delight in pointing out their most horrendous features: one twisted mummy, its mouth opened in a silent scream, is the "woman who was buried alive"; another, a woman who died in childbirth, is displayed beside "the smallest mummy in the world". It's all absolutely gross, but nevertheless with a macabre fascination. For an extra dollar you'll be admitted to the **Salon del Culto a la Muerte** (same hours), a recent house-of-horrors-style extension, with an array of holographic images, jangly motorized skeletons and yet more mummies. The hawkers outside selling mummy models and sticks of rock in the shape of mummies are equally easy to resist. To get to the museum, either walk from the centre of town, following the signs out along Juárez, or take the bus ("Panteón" or "Momias") that runs up the hill past the main entrance.

The Ex-Hacienda de San Gabriel de Barrera

If the crush of Guanajuato gets too much for you, head 2km west (either by foot or take any bus going to the Camionera Central) to the **Ex-Hacienda de San Gabriel de Barrera** (daily 9am–6pm; US$0.70), a colonial home now transformed into a lovely –

Rancher, Nuevo León

Prickly pear cactus, Durango

Bahía Concepción

Scrapyard and giant cactus near the US border

Whale watching, Laguna San Ignacio, Baja California

Copper Canyon Railway, Chihuahua

Landscape near Creel, Chihuahua

Truck and horse, the Bajío

Real de Catorce

Day-of-the-Dead skeletons

Icon stall, Real de Catorce

Templo de San Francisco, San Luis Potosí

little museum. The beautifully restored **gardens** of the hacienda range through a bizarre selection of international styles – including English, Italian, Roman, Arabic and Mexican – and make a wonderful setting for the house, which has been restored in colonial style. Cool rooms evoke daily life among the wealthy silver barons of nineteenth-century Guanajuato, but include numerous fine pieces of furniture dating back several centuries: grand and opulent on the ground floor, rich in domestic detail upstairs. It's a great place to wander at ease and brings home the sheer wealth of colonial Guanajuato.

Cerro de Cubilete and the statue of Cristo Rey

If you approached Guanajuato from León, you'll already have seen the huge statue of **Cristo Rey** crowning the 2661-metre **Cerro de Cubilete**. Variously claimed to occupy the geographical centre of the republic (or just the state of Guanajuato), it seems a wonderful coincidence that it should be on the highest hill for miles. Nevertheless, the complex of chapels and pilgrims' dormitories is without question magnificently sited with long, long views across the plains. At its heart is the twenty-metre bronze statue – erected in 1950 and ranking as the world's second largest image of Christ, just behind the one above Río de Janeiro – standing on a golden globe flanked by cherubs, one holding a crown of thorns, the other the golden crown of the "King of Kings".

The easiest way to get up here is on one of the tours advertised all around Guanajuato, though you can save a bit of money by nipping out to the Central Camionera and picking up one of seven daily Autobuses Vasallo de Cristo, which run up there in around thirty minutes.

Eating

Finding something **to eat** in Guanajuato is easy – it's impossible to walk more than a few yards down Juárez without passing some kind of café or restaurant. At the eastern end of **Juárez**, a whole series of very plain little places serve the standard Mexican staples, many of them also offering inexpensive comidas corridas; the **university area**, too, has plenty of choice. Rather more adventurous, and cheaper still, are the stalls in the modern annexe of the **Mercado Hidalgo**: two floors of delights (and horrors), where you'd be advised to take a careful look at what's on offer before succumbing to the frantic beckoning of the stallholders – some stalls are distinctly cleaner and more appetizing than others. Up around the **Jardín de la Unión**, the pricey outdoor restaurants are well worth visiting; in fact many people seldom stray from the excellent range of places all within five minutes walk of each other along Sopeña and the surrounding streets. For bread and cakes, try *Panadería la Purísima*, Juárez 138, or the *Panificadora Guanajuato*, by the church on the Plaza de la Paz.

Los Alpes Cafeteria y Nevería, in courtyard off Positos near the university. Student hang-out, for ice cream, coffee and snacks.

Arnadi, Plazuela de San Francisco 12. Eat-in pastelería with window seats that catch the afternoon sun.

Café Cervantino, Positos 109, just east of the Alhóndiga. Quiet little café in the back streets, serving tasty breakfasts at low, low prices.

Café Dada, Plaza del Baratillo. Guanajuato's coolest café, serving probably the best coffee. Sparsely furnished and with plenty of magazines (some in English) and chess and backgammon sets.

El Café Galeria, Sopeña 10, right by the Teatro Juárez. Fashionable hang-out with eating inside and a very popular outdoor terrace across the road where prices are high and the service slow.

El Limón, Sangre de Cristo 4, east of Jardín de la Unión. Tiny vegetarian restaurant with just three tables, serving veggieburgers, tortas and soya licuados. Open daily until 9pm.

Las Piñatas, Alonso 34. Brightly coloured, moderately priced restaurant decorated with piñatas, serving excellent gazpacho, curried chicken, brie quesedillas and Thai iced coffee.

Pinguis, northeast corner of Jardín de la Unión. The best bargain in the Jardín: a buzzing, friendly place for excellent breakfasts, comidas corridas and a good choice of Mexican and international main meals.

Pizza Piazza, branches throughout town, including Plazuela San Fernando, Juárez 67 and Hidalgo 11. Spaghetti, hamburgers and, as you might expect, pizza.

Tasca de los Santos, Plaza de la Paz. Smart Spanish restaurant with outdoor tables, serving European delights such as paella, chicken in white wine and *Jamon Serrano*. Moderate to expensive.

Tortas la Pulga, Plaza de la Paz 36. Tiny sandwich bar, very popular with students. Either take away or eat in chairs along the corridor and outside. Tasty and cheap.

Truco 7, Truco 7. Beautiful little café with a relaxed, student atmosphere. Great moderately priced breakfasts, comidas, salads, steaks, and wonderful garlic soup with an egg poached in it. To avoid a dollop of corn syrup in your cappuccino, ask for it *sin miel.*

Nightlife and entertainment

Guanajuato is a great spot for sitting around knocking back bottles of beer, with a host of superb bars in which to do just that. Things are especially jumping at weekends, when refugees from the bigger cities, including México and León, come here to enjoy themselves. The rougher bars are down on Juárez around Mercado Hidalgo, where the cantinas are generally reserved for men and prostitutes.

An excellent way to pass an hour or so is to follow one of the organized **Callejoneadas** – walking tours that wind through the side streets and back alleys following a student minstrel group known as *Estudiantinas*. They're aimed at Mexicans, so without fluent Spanish and some local knowledge you'll miss most of the jokes and risqué tales, but they're great fun all the same. You can get details of these from any of the information booths, and at Juárez 210 where they'll sell you tickets entitling you to some wine as you promenade, but it's easier just to tag along. In high season, there's something happening most nights of the week, but at any time of the year Friday and Saturday nights are your best bet. Hang around the Jardín de la Union around 9pm and just follow the crowd.

During the **International Cervantes Festival** in October you can see, among other things, the famous *entremeses*, swashbuckling one-act plays from classical Spanish theatre performed outdoors in Plaza San Roque. You don't need good Spanish to work out what's going on – they're highly visual and very entertaining, even if you can't understand a word. There's a grandstand for which you have to book seats, but it's easy enough to join the crowds watching from the edges of the plaza for free. Groups of students (who perform the *entremeses*) will quite often put on impromptu performances outside festival times, so it's worth wandering up here in the early evening just to see if anything is happening, especially on Saturday nights. For details of the festival, check with the tourist office. Other events are held in the Teatro Juárez and the Teatro Principal.

For a quieter evening, Guanajuato also has three **cinemas**.

Bars and clubs

Bar Ocho, Constancia 8. Youthful bar set up with sofas for intimate conversation, and a pool table upstairs. Bargain beer and tequila deals nightly.

Capitolios, Plaza de la Paz 62. The newest of the town's discos, thumping the night away from Thursday to Saturday.

La Dama de las Camelias . . . es el, Sopeña 34, opposite Museo Iconografico. Great, atmospheric bar, which stays open until dawn and comes with imaginative decor, incorporating evening dresses, high-heeled shoes and smashed mirror fragments. Closed Sun.

Guanajuato Grill, Alonso 4. The town's main disco, fairly tacky and usually packed with local teenagers doing very little but sweating and listening to the music.

Los Lobos, Juárez 27. Dim and often crowded bar that resounds nightly to thumping rock classics. Low-cost two-for-one beers all night.

MOVING ON FROM GUANAJUATO

Heading for Dolores Hidalgo couldn't be simpler, with half-hourly departures from C Alhóndiga, right in town just below the Alhóndiga. For other destinations, make for Guanajuato's **Central de Autobuses** (via local buses marked "Centro–Central" from Juárez), where there are regular services to Guadalajara, México, San Luis Potosí and Aguascalientes and almost constant departures for León and San Luis de la Paz. There are few buses direct to San Miguel de Allende, for which it's often easier to change in Dolores: if you have any problem getting anywhere else, head for León, which is on the main north–south highway and has much more frequent services. Viajes Frausto, Juárez 10, close to the Jardín de la Unión (☎473/2-35-80), have the timetables, fares and booking facilities for all first-class companies operating from the bus station.

Guanajuato state **airport**, 30km west, between Silao and León, has daily flights to major Mexican cities and the USA. To get there, catch a second-class bus to León and get off as you pass the airport (or fork out US$20 or so for a taxi).

Rincón del Beso, Alonso 21. Trendiest bar in town, with loud live music, particularly at weekends, and lots of small, secretive rooms for people to sin in. Attracts an older, sophisticated crowd, and doesn't really hot up until 11pm.

Listings

American Express Viajes Georama, Plaza de la Paz 34 (Mon–Fri 9am–8pm, Sat 10am–2pm; ☎473/2-51-01, fax 2-19-54), run a good travel agency and have all the usual AmEx services.

Books and newspapers Nowhere specializes in English-language books, so the best you can hope for is a copy of *The News* or international magazines from newspaper vendors in the Jardín de la Unión: try after 11am for that day's edition.

Cinemas The Cine Club de la Universidada de Guanajuato frequently show films in English in the Teatro Principal, while Cine Años have occasional showing at Teatro Cervantes. Check fly-posters around town.

Emergencies Police ☎473/2-02-66 Cruz Roja (☎473/2-04-87). and Hospital Regional de Guanajuato, Carretera Guanajuato–Silao (☎473/3-15-73) deals with medical emergencies.

Internet access Redes Internet, Alonso 70 (☎473/2-06-11), south of Juárez just west of the Plaza de la Paz. Sluggish machines in a cramped space at a pricey US$5 an hour.

Laundry Lavandería del Centro, Sopeña 26 (Mon–Sat 9am–8pm; ☎473/2-06-80).

Language schools The main language school is the Centro de Idiomas at the University of Guanajuato (☎473/2-00-06, fax 2-72-53; *montesa@quijote.ugto.mx*), which runs exchange programmes with universities around the world and accepts other students for their summer courses, run through June. They're aimed more at improvers than beginners, concentrating on Mexican and Latin American culture and costing US$550 for a four-week full-time programme. Students are encouraged to live with Mexican families; board is an additional US$16 or so per day with all meals.

Taxis Radio Taxis ☎473/2-65-34.

Tours Kiosks all over town offer a fairly standard package of bus tours, all for around the same price and usually with at least a couple of departures daily. You're unlikely to get much from the City Tour (3hr; US$5), or those to Dolores Hidalgo and San Miguel de Allende (8hr; US$10), or León and around (8hr; US$10), but might be interested in one to the Cristo del Rey statue (3hr; US$5).

Dolores Hidalgo and around

Fifty kilometres or so from both Guanajuato and San Miguel de Allende, **DOLORES HIDALGO** is as ancient and as historically rich as either of its southern neighbours. This was Father Hidalgo's parish, and it was from the church in the main plaza here that the historic **Grito de la Independencia** ("Cry of Independence") was first issued.

Perhaps because of its less spectacular situation, though, or perhaps because there is no university or language school, Dolores hasn't seen a fraction of the tourist development that has overtaken elsewhere. It's a good bet, though, for a one-night stopover, and certainly if you can't find accommodation in Guanajuato or San Miguel, this is the place to head; you'll get a better room here for half the cost. True, there is less to see, but it's an elegant little town and thoroughly Mexican; busy, too, as it sits on a traditionally important crossroads on the silver route from Zacatecas.

Just a block or two from the bus station as you walk towards the central plaza, the **Casa Hidalgo** (Tues–Sat 10am–6pm, Sun 10am-5pm; US$2, free on Sun), Hidalgo's home, has been converted into a museum devoted to his life, very much a point of pilgrimage for Mexicans on day-trips. It's a bit heavy on written tributes from various groups to the "Father of Independence" and on copies of other correspondence he either sent or received – including his letter of excommunication from the Inquisition less than a month after the Grito – but it's interesting nonetheless.

Continuing in the same direction, you come to a beautifully laid-out plaza, overlooked by the exuberant facade of the famous church, where a left turn takes you to the **Museo de la Independencia Nacional**, Zacatecas 6 (daily except Thurs 9am–5pm; US$0.70, free on Sun). Inside, vibrant, graphic murals depict significant scenes from Mexican history from the Aztec perception of the world through to the life of Hidalgo. Don't miss the glass cabinets filled with record sleeves and cowboys boots which pay homage to the greatest Ranchera singer of all time, José Alfredo Jimenez, another of Dolores' sons.

Besides a couple of other graceful churches, there's little else but the attraction of the dilapidated old streets themselves. As you wander around, look out for the locally made **ceramics**. They're on sale everywhere and are a very ancient tradition here. The bigger shops are near the Casa Hidalgo.

Practicalities

Dolores is connected to both San Miguel and Guanajuato by regular, rapid **buses** to and from the Flecha Amarilla terminal, on Hidalgo beside the river. Herradura de Plata also has a terminal at the corner of Chiapas and Yucatán, from where buses run every thirty minutes south to San Miguel de Allende and México, and north to San Felipe.

There's little need to visit Dolores' small **tourist office** (Mon–Fri 9am–3pm & 5.30–8pm, Sat & Sun 9am–3pm), on the main plaza by the church, but they can give advice on where to buy ceramics. Local **hotels** are all reasonable: *Posada Cocomacán*, Plaza Principal (☎418/2-00-18; ④); *Hotel Caudillo*, Querétaro 8, beside the church (☎ & fax 418/2-01-98; ④); and the simple *Posada Dolores*, Yucatán 8, past the Independence Museum then left (☎418/2-06-42; ②), easily missed behind a small doorway and espe-

---

THE GRITO DE LA INDEPENDENCIA

On the night of September 15, 1810, **Padre Miguel Hidalgo y Costilla** and some of his fellow plotters, warned by messengers from Querétaro that their intention to raise a rebellion had been discovered, decided to bring their plans forward. At dawn on the 16th, Hidalgo, tolling the church bell, called his parishioners together and addressed them from the balcony of the church with an impassioned speech ending in the **Grito de la Independencia** – "¡Mexicanos, Viva Mexico!" That cry is repeated every year by the president in México and by politicians all over the country at midnight on September 15, as the starting point for Independence Day celebrations. September 16 remains the one day of the year when the bell in Dolores Hidalgo's parish church is rung – though the bell in place today is a copy of an original that was either melted down for munitions or hangs in the Palacio Nacional in México, depending on which story you believe.

cially good value for lone travellers. There's no need to stray far from the plaza to eat well – *Hotel Caudillo* has a good **restaurant**, or you could try *El Patio Bar & Grill*.

East of Dolores: San Luis de la Paz, Pozos and San José Iturbide

If you carry straight on through Dolores, after 40km you hit the road between San Luis Potosí and Querétaro at **San Luis de la Paz**. From here a minor road runs south, parallel to the main Hwy-57, through **Pozos**, 50km to **San José Iturbide**, which is 35km from San Miguel de Allende.

SAN LUIS is the largest of this string of three towns, a typically Mexican provincial settlement with one main street, a colonial plaza, and horses tied up alongside farmers' pick-up trucks outside the market. It's a good place to buy rugs and *sarapes* at reasonable prices, though most of what is made here is sent off to the markets in larger towns. If you need to stay, there are a couple of small, cheap hotels on the main street just up from the bus terminal.

Twenty minutes south, the road to San José passes through what was once a rich and flourishing mining community called Real de Pozos. Now just known as **POZOS** (or, officially, Mineral de Pozos), it describes itself as a ghost town, but is far from dead, with several hundred people living clustered around the gaping maw of half a church. Don't expect swing doors flapping in the breeze and tumbleweed gusting through the streets, but you will find vast areas of crumbling masonry inhabited only by the odd burro. In fact, the place seems to be in the throes of a small revival in its fortunes with low rents attracting a number of groups producing high-quality pre-Colombian instruments for sale – mostly drums, flutes, stone xylophones and slit gongs, and not cheap. Start at the **Sala de Cultura** (daily 10am–4pm) on Ocampo, and check for prominent signs in the surrounding streets.

If the prospect of moody walks through mine ruins scattered across the harsh agave desert isn't enough to entice you **to stay**, you might just be tempted by *Casa Mexicana*, Plaza Principal (☎468/8-25-98 ext 116, fax 8-30-30; in USA ☎212/751-6958; ⑨), a gorgeous four-bedroom B&B with exquisite and highly individual rooms going for US$110 set around an attractive garden, and with an on-site art gallery. Nicely prepared meals (which are included in the room rate) are also served to non-guests, or you could just drop in for a margarita. It's the only place to stay in town, though they do have a considerably cheaper annexe which may be available, especially if you book in advance.

Further south, **SAN JOSÉ** is an immaculate town centred on its tidy plaza, chiefly distinguished by the behemoth of a Neoclassical church, dedicated to Agustín de Iturbide, a local opportunist who started the War of Independence as a general loyal to Spain – inflicting major defeats on Morelos – only to change sides later. Having helped secure Mexico's Independence without any concomitant reform, he briefly declared himself emperor in 1822. The plaque reads, accurately enough, "from one of the few towns which have not forgotten you". There are frequent **bus services** between San José and San Luis de la Paz and on to Querétaro, but if you get stuck – not such a bad thing – there's the *Hotel Los Arcos* (☎419/8-03-30; ④), right by the church and a couple of cheaper places on the streets nearby.

San Miguel de Allende

Set on a steep hillside overlooking the Río Laja, **SAN MIGUEL DE ALLENDE** seems at first sight little different from any other small colonial town, dominated by red rooftops and domed churches. Its distinct character, though, is soon apparent: it's home to a very high-profile colony of artists and writers, fleshed out with less ambitious retirees from the USA and by flocks of students drawn to the town's several language

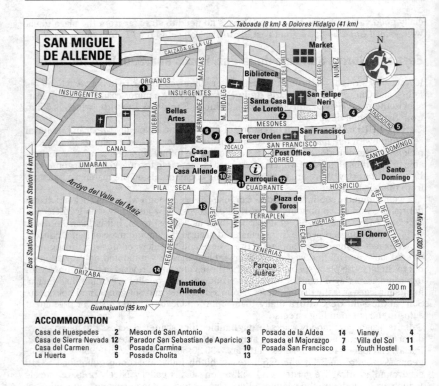

Taboada (8 km) & Dolores Hidalgo (41 km)

SAN MIGUEL DE ALLENDE

ACCOMMODATION

Casa de Huespedes	2	Meson de San Antonio	6	Posada de la Aldea	14	Vianey	4
Casa de Sierra Nevada	12	Parador San Sebastian de Aparicio	3	Posada el Majorazgo	7	Villa del Sol	11
Casa del Carmen	9	Posada Carmina	10	Posada San Francisco	8	Youth Hostel	1
La Huerta	5	Posada Cholita	13				

and arts schools. Like such a community anywhere it's inward-looking, bitchy and gossip-ridden, but it's also extremely hospitable and much given to taking newcomers under its wing.

There are good reasons why this should have happened in San Miguel – chiefly that it's a very picturesque town with a perfect climate and, for the artists, good light throughout the year. What got it started, though, was the foundation in 1938 of the **Instituto Allende**, an arts institute that enjoyed an enormous boost after World War II when returning GIs found that their education grants could be stretched much further in Mexico. Its fame established, San Miguel has never looked back, and for all its popularity remains one of the most pleasant places you could pick to rest up for a while in comfort.

There are few sights as such, but the whole town (which has been a national monument since 1926, hence no new building, no flashing signs, no traffic lights) is crowded with old seigneurial mansions and curious churches. It was founded in 1542 by a Franciscan friar, Juan de San Miguel, and as "San Miguel El Grande" became an important supply centre for the big mining towns, and a stopover on the main silver route from Zacatecas. The name was later changed to honour Ignacio Allende, a native who became Hidalgo's chief lieutenant. The country hereabouts is still ranching territory, though increasingly being taken over by the tourists and foreigners: attractions include a traditional spa at Taboada, a golf course nearby, water-skiing on the new reservoir and horse-riding at a couple of dude ranches.

Arrival and information

Although San Miguel has a surprisingly poor **bus service**, this is still the easiest way to arrive, perhaps expedited by a change at Guanajuato or Querétaro if you're coming from some distance. The **bus station** (no guardería) is about 2km south of the centre, from where there are taxis and regular local buses (marked "Central/Estación") that run in along C Canal. **Trains** arrive around two kilometres further out in the same direction (take the same buses to get to centre): there's a daily service to Querétaro, Tula and the capital at 1.10pm and in the other direction to San Luis Potosí, Monterrey and Nuevo Laredo at 2.35pm. The closest airport is near León (see p.235).

San Miguel's extremely helpful **tourist office** (Mon–Fri 10am–2.30pm & 5–7pm, Sat 10am–1pm, Sun 10am–noon; ☎ & fax 415/2-65-65) is in the southeast corner of the zócalo (known variously as "Plaza Principal" or "Jardín de Allende"), more or less next door to the Parroquia, tucked in beside *La Terrazza* restaurant. As well as the usual ranks of leaflets and maps, they can provide details of local art classes and language courses. Most other facilities are nearby: the **post office** (Mon–Fri 8am–7pm, Sat 9am–1pm) is a few paces east at Correo 16; and you can **change money** at Banamex, at the corner of Canal, Banorte half a block east along San Francisco, or at a **casa de cambio** – try Deal at Correo 15 and at Juárez 27 (both Mon–Fri 9am–6pm, Sat 9am–2pm).

For more information, pick up one of the free ad-driven booklets scattered around town or, for really detailed coverage, consult *The Insider's Guide to San Miguel* by Archie Dean (US$10) – there's a copy at the library. Also check our "Listings" below (p.254).

Accommodation

Most of San Miguel's hotels are near the zócalo, and, like pretty much everything in San Miguel, the large ex-pat influence makes them more expensive here than in other towns in the Bajío. With the exception of an excellent youth hostel, budget places are thin on the ground, but if you're prepared to pay a little more you can stay in one of dozens of places with gorgeous rooms set around delightful courtyards or gardens. The pricier places specifically catering to snowbirds from north of the border tend to charge more during the popular December to March high season; more budget places adjust their prices upwards during Semana Santa and over the September fiesta season.

The city also offers **long-stay apartments**, which can work out to be economical; ask at the tourist office for details, or check noticeboards around town.

Casa del Carmen, Correo 31 (☎ & fax 415/2-08-44). Beautiful and intimate hotel run by a US–Mexican couple. Comfortable and totally secure, with spacious and well-appointed rooms, each different. Rates includes breakfast and lunch. ⑦.

Casa de Huéspedes, Mesones 27 at Reloj (☎415/2-13-78). Beautiful little second-floor hotel: friendly and calm, with clean, well-kept rooms – some with balconies – fluffy towels and fresh flowers. An especially good deal for singles who don't fancy the youth hostel. ③.

Casa de Sierra Nevada, Hospicio 35 between Sollano & Recreo (☎415/2-04-15, fax 2-23-37; from US ☎1-800/341-5995). Fabulously luxurious hotel with rooms around a beautiful colonial courtyard, built in 1580 and lush with greenery – this must rank in the international big league. They've now taken over several houses across the street and have even opened an equally sumptuous outpost at Santa Elena 2, at the north end of the Benito Juárez park. Suites from US$270, rooms from US$187. ⑨.

La Huerta, Cerrada de Beccera (☎415/2-18-81). A little inconveniently sited and not especially attractive, but the cheapest private rooms in town. ②.

Hotel Posada Carmina, Cuna de Allende 7, a few metres south of the zócalo (☎415/2-04-58, fax 2-01-35). The pick of the not-so-outrageously expensive places. Large, plainly furnished rooms with brick floors, high ceilings and white walls (⑥) are set amid yet more colonial splendour around a beautiful courtyard; and there are cheaper but still very nice rooms in an adjacent wing. No credit cards. ⑤.

Hotel Posada de San Francisco, Plaza Principal 2 (☎ & fax 415/2-72-13). Ageing but comfortable rooms in a lovely and sedate colonial building at surprisingly reasonable prices for its location right on the zócalo. ⑥.

Mesón de San Antonio, Mesones 80, at Hernández Macías (☎415/2-05-80, fax 2-28-97). Slightly drab but spacious, carpeted rooms around a small garden with a swimming pool. The extra US$5 for a two-level suite (⑤) is money well spent. ④.

Parador San Sebastian de Aparicio, Mesones 7 at Nuñez (☎415/2-70-84). Cool and calm, with simple rooms around a colonial courtyard. ③.

Posada Cholita, Hernández Macías 114, south of Cuadrante (☎415/2-28-98). A cheery paint job enlivens spacious rooms in this small hotel. Not at all bad for the price. ④.

Posada de la Aldea, Ancha de San Antonio 11 (☎ & fax 415/2-10-22). Clean and comfortable but dull rooms all have modern amenities in this enormous hotel – with pool, tennis courts and parking – whose main virtue is being opposite the Instituto Allende. ⑥.

Posada El Mayorazgo, Hidalgo 8, just north of the zócalo (☎415/2-13-09, fax 2-38-38). A small, modern and slightly run-down building with "suites" around a compact courtyard. All come with kitchen, washing machine, cable TV and cooker, making them ideal for long-stayers at around US$400 a month. ③.

Vianey, Aparicio 18 (☎415/2-45-59). Modern, spotless and somewhat faceless, but a decent fall-back if others are full. ③.

Villa del Sol, Cuadrante 3 at Sollano (☎415/2-07-42, fax 2-32-85). Another fine colonial establishment with a pool and gardens overlooking the back of the Parroquia, though rooms don't match up to those around the corner at *Hotel Posada Carmina*. ⑥.

Youth Hostel, Organos 34 at Quebrada (☎415/2-06-74). Cheapest place to stay in town, very clean, very friendly and always full of backpackers swapping travel information or making use of the kitchen facilities and washing machine. The single-sex dorms (②; less twenty percent discount with youth hostel or student card) are fairly basic but spacious, and there are a few private rooms too (③); free breakfast for all. Everyone gets a short morning chore. There's also an excellent deal on Spanish lessons with one of the schools (see "Listings").

The Town

Head first to San Miguel's **zócalo**, within walking distance of almost everything you'll want to see and the main focus of activity in the town's compact centre. The **Instituto Allende**, south of the centre and just about in walking distance from there (though it's a steep climb back up), is an alternative hub, and an especially useful source of information for anyone who wants to stay longer than the couple of days that suffices for sightseeing.

Wherever you go in town, it seems that any place that's not a café or restaurant is operating as some kind of gallery or **artesanía** shop. There's an absolutely bewildering array of goodies from all over Mexico for sale, and what's here is often some of the best available, though naturally the prices are correspondingly high, sometimes bordering on extortionate.

The zócalo

The most famous of the city's landmarks, **La Parroquia** – the parish church – takes up one side of the **zócalo**. This gloriously over-the-top structure, with a towering pseudo-Gothic facade bristling with turrets and spires, was rebuilt towards the end of the last century by a self-taught Indian stonemason, Zeferino Gutiérrez, who supposedly learned about architecture by studying postcards of the great French cathedrals and then drew diagrams in the dust to explain to his workers what he wanted. Inside, the patterned tilework of the floor and ceiling, the azulejos along the walls and the pure semicircular vaulting along the nave exhibit distinct Moorish influences.

Opposite the church is a block containing the **Palacio Municipal** and the **Galería San Miguel**, one of the most prestigious of the many galleries showing local artists' work. The remaining two sides of the square are lined with covered *portales*, under whose arches vendors of drinks and trinkets shelter from the sun, with a row of shops behind them. On the zócalo, too, are some of San Miguel's most distinguished mansions, all of them – like almost every home in San Miguel – built in the Spanish style. The **Casa de Don Ignacio de Allende**, on the corner of Allende and Umaran, was the birthplace of the Independence hero: a plaque notes *Hic natus ubique notus* – "here was born he who is famous everywhere." The house now operates as the **Museo Historico de San Miguel de Allende** (Tues–Sun 10am–4pm; free), with two floors of pots and diagrams exploring Mexico's pre-Hispanic and colonial past, naturally concentrating on the San Miguel area.

On the next corner, Hidalgo and Canal, you can see the **Casa de los Condes de Canal**, with an elaborately carved doorway and elegant wrought-iron grilles over the windows. Near here, too, just half a block down Umaran, is the **Casa de los Perros**, its central balcony supported by little stone dogs. Forbidding, even grim, from the outside, these mansions mostly conceal patios decked with flowers or courtyards with fountains playing. If you want to see inside some, and if you think you could take it, the English-speaking community organizes a **House and Gardens Tour** every Sunday, leaving at noon from the Biblioteca Publica (see below). You'll see details on posters around the town.

North of the zócalo

Leave the zócalo uphill on San Francisco, and the streets seem less affected by outsiders – Spanish or *norteamericano*. The architecture, it's true, is still colonial, but the life that continues around the battered buildings seems cast in a more ancient mould. A block along San Francisco, the elaborate churrigueresque facade of the church of **San Francisco** contrasts sharply with its Neoclassical towers, tiled dome and plain interior, and quite overshadows the modest simplicity of its smaller neighbour, **Tercer Orden**. Behind, San Miguel's old market area has been refurbished to create a new plaza, where you'll find the **Oratorio de San Felipe Neri** sitting in the centre of a little group of churches and chapels. Its Baroque facade shows signs of native influence – presumably the legacy of indigenous labourers – but the main interest lies within a series of paintings, among them a group depicting the life of San Felipe, attributed to Miguel Cabrera. One of its chapels, the **Santa Casa de Loreto** (entered from next door), is a copy of the Holy House at Loreto in Italy, and was put up by the Conde Manuel de la Canal; he and his wife appear as statues above their tombs in its gilded octagonal interior.

The town's **market** has been re-sited north of here, off C Colegio, and has managed to remain almost entirely traditional, with fruit, vegetables, medicinal herbs, pots and pans all on display, and little specifically for the tourist among the cramped tables with their low canvas awnings. Official market day is Sunday, but no one seems to have told the locals, and it's pretty busy all week. Behind the regular market (with an entrance on the Callejon de Loreto) is a new **Mercado de Artesanías**, though nothing here seems especially good value. You'll find much more exciting goods in the many crafts shops around town.

From the Oratorio you can head down Insurgentes to the **Biblioteca Publica** (Mon–Sat 10am–2pm & 4–7pm), which lends a substantial collection of **books in English** (see "Listings" below). They also sell a number of cheap second-hand books – either duplicates or those deemed too lightweight for preservation in the library. Inside the library, the *Café Santa Ana* offers a quiet space to sit down and read.

Bellas Artes

The Centro Cultural "El Nigromante" – also known as **Bellas Artes** – is on Hernandez Macías, just one block downhill from the zócalo. Housed in the beautiful cloistered courtyard of the old **Convento de la Concepción**, it's an arts institute run by the state Fine Arts organization, concentrating on music and dance, but to a lesser extent teaching visual arts, too. Mexicans can take courses here for virtually nothing; foreigners pay rather more. Around the courtyard there are various exhibitions, and several murals, including an entire room covered in one by David Siqueiros, devoted to the life and works of Allende. There's also the lovely *Las Musas* café (see opposite). The church of **La Concepción**, part of the complex, is lovely, too, and noted mainly for its tall dome raised on a drum, again said to be the work of the untrained Zeferino Gutiérrez.

Instituto Allende and around

The famous **Instituto Allende** lies down at the bottom of the hill following Hernandez Macías south from La Concepción. On the way, at the corner of Cuadrante, you pass the **Casa del Inquisidor**, an eighteenth-century mansion with a particularly fine facade, now operating as an antiques and artesanías shop, so you can take a look inside. Opposite is the old building that served as a jail for the Inquisition. The Instituto itself, on the edges of the old town, occupies a former hacienda of the Condes de la Canal – it was moved here in 1951 when the government recognized its success and it was accredited by the University of Guanajuato. It offers courses in all kinds of arts from painting to sculpture to photography, in crafts like silverwork and weaving, and Spanish-language instruction at every level (see box), all within beautiful, park-like grounds. There's a café down here, too, and the noticeboards are covered with offers of long-term accommodation, requests for and offers of rides through Mexico and up to the States, and information about what's going on in San Miguel.

At the back of the Institute, along Tenerias, the refreshing, shaded **Parque Benito Juárez** was created out of the fruit orchards that belonged to many of the city's old families. The homes roundabout are still some of the fanciest in town. From here it's an uphill walk to **El Chorro**, the little hill whose springs supply the city with water, and site of the town originally founded by Juan de San Miguel. There are good views of the

---

LANGUAGE SCHOOLS IN SAN MIGUEL DE ALLENDE

For many, the reason to be in San Miguel is to learn Spanish. Noticeboards around town advertise private lessons, but most people end up taking one of the courses run by the four main **language schools**, each of which offers a range of courses taught by professional Mexican teachers. Instruction is almost entirely in Spanish, with the focus on practical usage rather than academic theory, and students usually stay with a local family (count on US$15–20 a day for full board) to consolidate the instruction.

The most prestigious of the schools is the Instituto Allende, Ancha de San Antonio 20 (☎415/2-01-90, fax 2-45-38; *ferr@abasolo.ugto.mx, www.instituto-allende.edu.mx*), which conducts university-credited four-week courses (US$445) throughout the year at all levels. There are also less demanding monthly courses, intensive programmes, and classes for you to apply your new-found skills to studying Mexican history and art.

With the institute's long-standing reputation, the other schools have to compete on both price and quality, and do both admirably. The Academia Hispano Americana, Mesones 4 (☎415/2-03-49, fax 2-23-33), also operates four-week sessions (US$400), with discounts for enrolling in more than one course, as well as more intensive courses and extension courses in Mexican folklore among other subjects. A third contender is the Centro Mexicano de Lengua y Cultura, Orizaba 15 (☎415/2-07-63), with the option of taking as little as an hour's instruction a day (US$100 for four weeks), or a week only of their four-week courses. Finally, the Instituto Habla Hispana, Calzada de la Luz 25 (☎ & fax 415/2-07-13; *hhispana@iname.com*), runs month-long courses for US$360 and offers a huge fifty-percent discount to youth-hostel residents.

town from here (and some old-fashioned tubs where locals come to do their washing), but if you've the energy, climb on higher still to **El Mirador**, the viewing point on the road to Querétaro, where you'll find more spectacular panoramas: San Miguel below, the broad plain and the ridge of mountains before Guanajuato in the distance.

Eating, drinking and entertainment

Eating in San Miguel can be an expensive business; even local staples such as cappuccinos and margaritas are likely to cost half as much again as they would in, say, Querétaro, or even touristy Guanajuato. Though there are restaurants where you can get a standard comida or a plate of tacos for little more than you would pay elsewhere – the daytime *menú del día* is usually a good bet – in the main you'll find yourself giving in to temptation and gravitating to places serving anything from sushi to fondue and more besides. It can be a tremendous relief for long-term travellers, with loads of stuff you may not have tasted for weeks: vegetarians, especially, should take full advantage. Cafés, too, are plentiful, usually lively with students and ex-pats who often seem to do little but hang out in such places all day – not such a bad idea. Quality is excellent, and with delicate gringo tums in mind, many places prominently advertise their assiduous use of sanitized water.

Nightlife here can come expensive, too, but again there's lots of it to choose from, a refreshing change in itself. Your best bet is to gather with everyone else in the zócalo – to take the air, stroll around and check out what's going on.

Restaurants

Café de la Parroquia, Jesús 11, at Cuadrante. A great little place with seats inside or in the courtyard, justly popular with ex-pats for breakfasts of hotcakes or yoghurt and fruit. Good Mexican food served as well – tamales, chilaquiles and the like – and coffee all day long. Closed Mon.

La Finestra Caffe, Plaza Colonial, opposite Belles Artes. Another popular and relaxed breakfast café with sun streaming in through the windows, delicious *Huevos a la Cazuela* (baked in a pot with hot sauce and cheese), and top-class coffee and pastries all day. Closed Tues.

La Grotta, Cuadrante 5, at Allende. The best of San Miguel's pasta and pizza joints, tucked away in a cosy basement and serving crispy pizza, calzone, tasty plates of pasta, fresh salads and a small selection of *secundi piatti*.

El Harem, Ancha de San Antonio 12, on the road out to the Instituto Allende. Arabic restaurant serving houmous with pitta bread, lamb brochettes and stuffed vine leaves at low prices.

Meson de San José, Mesones 38, at Chiquitos. Lovely patio-restaurant serving quality Mexican mains for US$7 and several cheaper vegetarian choices.

Las Musas, in the Bellas Artes complex. Beautifully sited café away from the traffic noise, where students take a break over coffee, sandwiches, ice cream and croissants.

Las Palomas, Correo 9, just east of the zócalo. Hole-in-the-wall serving gorditas, tacos and quesedillas filled with a choice of mushrooms, nopales, chiles, mole and more for about US$0.50 each.

Pato Café, Correo 24, at Recreo. A cluster of tables in a shady courtyard for eating baguettes (US$3–4) stuffed with smoked salmon and capers or triple salami, or for washing down delicious pastries with fine coffee or tea from a selection of exotic blends. Closed Mon.

El Pegaso, Corregidora 6. Where *norteamericanos* and well-off San Miguel youth come for gazpacho, chicken burgers and pastrami sandwiches. Closed Sun.

Restaurant El Infierno, Mesones 25, at Chiquitos. Very pleasant little Mexican seafood place, serving a good-value comida corrida at around US$5. Two-for-one "happy hour" from 2pm to 5pm.

Restaurant La Terrazza, next door to the Parroquia. Basic pizzas at quite high prices, but you're paying for the location: this is a superb spot from which to watch the world go by.

Restaurant La Vendimia, Hidalgo 12, a block north of the zócalo. Sophisticated little place in lush colonial courtyard, where you can dine on trout, steaks, sea bass and the like (US$8–10) to the strains of live guitar music in the background.

Tatsu Sushi, Correo 24. Tiny place to sit at the bar or small tables and nibble on sushi and sashimi at US$1–1.50 a piece. Closed Tues.

El Ten-ten Pie, Cuna de Allende 21, one block south of the zócalo. Graffiti-covered café serving good Mexican staples and always popular for coffee or a game of chess.

El Tomate, Mesones 60, east of Hidalgo. Spartan vegetarian place with soya- and spinach-based burgers, exotic salad concoctions and a US$5 three-course *menú*.

Bars and clubs

Bar Coco, Hernandez Macías 85, at Umarán. Popular unpretentious bar in the centre of town with a mixed local and gringo crowd and live music every night with no cover. Two-for-one *hora de amigos*, 6–8.30pm.

Char Rock, Correo 7. Mostly cheesy cover bands, but can be fun if the 7–9pm happy hours manage to pack people in.

El Gato Negro, Mesones 10, at Nuñez. Tiny and hip swing-door cantina (women welcome) absolutely plastered in photos of Marilyn – plus a couple of Jim Morrison and John Lennon – with nightly live music from funk to flamenco. The booze is cheap by San Miguel standards, and there's no cover.

El Ring, Hidalgo 25, two blocks north of the zócalo. Glitzy club playing an eclectic selection of salsa, banda, cumbia, and European and American dance tunes from Wednesday to Sunday (roughly 10pm–4am). Weekend cover charge US$4–6.

Mama Mia, Urumán 8, just west of the zócalo. Probably the most happening nightspot in town, with a restaurant, video bar, live music nightly – salsa and jazz mainly – and a weekend rooftop terrace with live acoustic artists.

Listings

American Express Viajes Vertiz, Hidalgo 1, just north of the zócalo (Mon–Fri 9am–2pm & 4–6.30pm, Sat 10am–2pm; ☎415/2-18-56), hold mail and re-issue stolen or lost cheques but don't cash them.

Books and newspapers Sit at breakfast cafés popular with the ex-pats and small boys will deliver *The News* and the *Mexico City Times* to your table; alternatively purchase these, and international weeklies, from newspaper vendors around town. Airport novels and weightier fiction along with hardbacks, magazines and art supplies are all stocked by El Colibri, Diez de Sollano 30, a block or so south of the zócalo (Mon–Sat 10am–3pm & 4–7pm).

Cinemas *Hotel Villa Jacaranda*, Aldama 53, at Terraplén (☎415/2-10-15), hosts English-language movies every night at 7.30pm (US$4 including a drink and popcorn): a new film starts each Tuesday.

Consulates Canada, Mesones 38, at Chiquitos (Mon–Fri 10am–2pm; ☎415/2-30-25, after-hours' emergencies ☎1-800/7-06-29); USA, Hernández Marcías 72, opposite Belles Artes (Mon & Wed 9am–1pm & 4–7pm, Tues & Thurs 4–7pm; ☎415/2-23-57, for emergencies ☎2-00-68).

Emergencies Cruz Roja ☎415/2-16-16; Police ☎415/2-00-22.

Internet access Estación Internet, Recreo 11, south off Correo (Mon–Fri 9am–2pm & 4–8pm, Sat 9am–2pm; ☎415/2-73-12; *estacion@mpsnet.com.mx*), have a few reasonably up-to-date machines rented at a whopping US$4 per half-hour.

Laundry Lavandería Correo, Correo 42 (Mon–Sat 8am–8pm, Sun 9am–3pm; ☎415/2-26-95), offers a same-day service at low prices.

Library The Biblioteca Publica, Hernández Macías 75, allows visitors to borrow books after obtaining a library card (two passport photos and US$3; valid one year) and leaving a US$12 deposit.

Mail Apart from the post office at Correo 16, there are numerous express postal services. DHL are opposite the post office at Correo 21, and FedEx and UPS have agencies next door.

Pharmacy Farmacia Hidalgo, Hidalgo 40, is open daily 8am–10pm.

Photographic supplies For specialist equipment, professional and black-and-white film, make for La Fotographia, Aldama 1, at Cuadrante (Mon–Fri 10am–6pm, Sat 10am–2pm; ☎415/2-23-12).

Phones Collect calls all around the globe can be made from the cardphone inside Helados Bing at the northeastern corner of the zócalo (it only uses one peso), plus there are Lada phones all over town, and a *larga distancia* place at the bus station (Mon–Sat 8am–8pm, Sun 7am–10pm).

Around San Miguel: Taboada and Atotonilco

Although, as ever, there are buses to every village in the vicinity, San Miguel also has dozens of travel agencies and tour operators which, as well as tours of the city, offer many local excursions: try, for example, the Travel Institute of San Miguel, Cuna de Allende 11 (☎415/2-00-78), half a block from the plaza. One of the simplest and most enjoyable outings is to **TABOADA**, 8km northwest of San Miguel off the road to Dolores, where the warm thermal waters are ideal for soaking your bones. Easiest to reach are the mineral pools (all different temperatures) at **La Gruta Balneario** (roughly 10am–midnight; US$4), right by the highway and accessed by Dolores-bound buses from the San Miguel bus station. Alternatively, enquire at San Miguel's youth hostel, which frequently books the whole place for the evening and charges US$5, including transport. Opposite the Gruta, a side road leads 2km (no public transport) to the luxurious surroundings of the *Hotel Hacienda Taboada*, which also offers fine, hot bathing and puts on a magnificent outdoor buffet at weekends costing around US$20.

Another worthwhile outing is to **SATURNARIO DE ATOTONILCO** (easily confused with the larger Atotonilco el Grande in Jalisco state), 5km further in the same direction, then 3km down a side road (again no public transport). This is a rural indigenous community, whose church has come to be a centre of pilgrimage for two reasons – it was founded by Padre Felipe Neri, later canonized, and it was from here that Padre Hidalgo, marching from Dolores to San Miguel, took the banner of the Virgin of Guadalupe that became the flag of the Mexicans in the War of Independence. Allende was married here, too. The six chapels of the church, liberally plastered with murals and freely interspersed with poems, biblical passages and painted statues, demonstrate every kind of Mexican popular art, from the naive to the highly sophisticated. There are more warm pools here, too.

Querétaro and around

Most people seem to hammer straight past **QUERÉTARO** on the highway to México, catching sight of only the expanding industrial outskirts and the huge modern bus station. Yet of all the colonial cities in the Bajío, this is perhaps the most surprising, preserving a tranquil colonial core that boasts magnificent mansions and some of the country's finest ecclesiastical architecture. Little more than two hours from México, and at the junction of every major road and rail route from the north, it's also a wealthy and booming city, one of the fastest-growing in the republic thanks to state encouragement for investment outside the capital.

Some history

There's a history as rich and deep here as anywhere in the republic, starting before the Conquest when Querétaro ("rocky place") was an Otomí town subject to the **Aztecs**; many Otomí still live in the surrounding area. In 1531 the Spanish took control relatively peacefully, and under them it grew steadily into a major city and provincial capital before becoming, in the nineteenth century, the setting for some of the most traumatic events of Mexican history. It was here, meeting under the guise of Literary Associations, that the **Independence** conspirators laid their earliest plans. In 1810 one of their number, Josefa Ortiz de Dominguez, wife of the town's Corregidor (or governor – she is known always as "La Corregidora"), found that her husband had learned of the movement's intentions. Although locked in her room, La Corregidora managed to get a message out warning the revolutionaries, thus precipitating an unexpectedly early start to the struggle for Independence.

ACCOMMODATION

La Casa de la Marquesa	5
Hidalgo	4
Impala	9
Mesón de Santa Rosa	2
Plaza	1
Posada Academia	6
Posada Acueducto	8
Posada Colonial	7
Youth Hostel	3

QUERÉTARO

Bus Station (5 km)

Later in the century, less exalted events took place. The **Treaty of Guadalupe Hidalgo**, which ended the Mexican–American War by handing over almost half of Mexico's territory – Texas, New Mexico, California and more – to the USA, was signed in Querétaro in 1848. And in 1867, Emperor Maximilian made his last stand here: defeated, he was tried by a court meeting in the theatre and finally faced a firing squad on the hill just to the north of town – the Cerro de las Campañas. The same theatre hosted an important assembly of Revolutionary politicians in 1916, leading eventually to the signing here of the 1917 Constitution, still in force today.

Arrival, orientation and information

Querétaro's **Central Camionera**, at a massive new site some 6km south of town, is one of the busiest there is, with two separate but adjacent buildings: Sala A for long-distance and first-class companies; Sala B for shorter runs and second-class companies. Fixed-price taxis (buy a ticket from the kiosk) run from outside both terminals, and an endless shuttle of local buses ("Ruta 8" is the most convenient) runs to the centre from the end of Sala B. To get back to the bus station, pick up eastbound routes #36, #44 and others on Zaragoza by the Alameda. The **train station** is 1km north of the centre; again there are buses ("Ruta 8" runs up Ocampo to within 100m of the station), but it's as easy to walk straight up Juárez, or grab a cab. Trains pass southbound to México at 4.10am and 4.35am (daily), and at 3pm (Wed, Fri & Sun only); northbound services go to Guadalajara daily at 12.30am, to León, Zacatecas, Chihuahua and Ciudad Juárez daily at 1.15am, and to San Luis Potosí, Monterrey and Nuevo Laredo at 1pm (Mon, Wed & Fri only).

For all its sprawl, Querétaro is easy enough to find your way around once you get to the centre, since the core remains confined to the grid laid down by the Spanish: all tiny plazas interconnected by pedestrian walkways known as *andadores*. Local buses run anywhere you might want to visit, and taxis are extremely cheap – on the whole, however, walking proves simpler.

Main focus is the zócalo, the **Jardín Zenéa**, with its typical triumvirate of bandstand, clipped trees and bootshines. To the west lies the commercial centre with the bulk of the shops, but you'll find much of your time spent to the west among the giftshops, restaurants and bars leading to the Plaza de la Independencia. One very good way of getting to grips with the layout of the old town, and at least a brief glimpse of most of the important buildings, is to join the ninety-minute **walking tour** (daily 10.30am & 5pm; US$1.30), which sets out from the **tourist office**, at Pasteur 4 Nte (Mon–Sat 8am–8pm, Sun 9am–8pm; ☎42/12-14-12, fax 12-10-94), and is conducted mostly in Spanish, though many guides will moonlight in English. The tourist office also sells excellent city maps for US$0.20. There are several **banks** (currency exchange Mon–Fri 9am–3pm) around the Jardín Zenéa, and the **post office** is at Arteaga 5, three blocks to the south, with the Mercantil Divisas **casa de cambio**, Corregidora 108 (Mon–Fri 9am–5pm, Sat 9am–2pm), not far away. As well as **phones** all around the centre, there are *larga distancia* places at the bus station and inside Libros y Revistas, at the corner of Madero and Juárez.

Accommodation

For **hotels**, head straight for the zócalo and the streets in the immediate vicinity. Though streetside rooms may be noisy, there's a fair selection of places in this area, two of them particularly gorgeous (and expensive), in addition to several at the budget end of the range, some very basic. Where Querétaro trips up is in the mid-range, with few decent choices: if you can't stretch to the pricier places, go for the better rooms at say the *Hidalgo* or *Acueducto*.

La Casa de la Marquesa, Madero 41 (☎42/12-00-92, fax 12-00-98). One of Mexico's finest hotels, very central and housed in a wonderful mansion with a gorgeous Moorish courtyard. The antique-furnished rooms (US$135) are also magnificent, though for something truly special you'll want a suite (US$170–200). Breakfast included. ⑨.

Hidalgo, Madero 11 Pte, just off Jardín Zenéa (☎42/12-00-81). Simple but clean rooms set around an open courtyard, all with bath and cable TV, and some of the larger rooms with balconies for just over a dollar more. Good budget option. ③.

Impala, Colón 1 (☎42/12-25-70, fax 12-45-15). Big, modern, overbearing place at the south end of the Alameda; businesslike and soulless. ④.

Mesón de Santa Rosa, Pasteur 17 (☎42/24-26-23, fax 12-55-22). Superb luxury hotel, very quiet, calm, beautiful and sophisticated, in an old colonial mansion on the Jardín Independencia, with a great restaurant. Rooms for US$115. ⑨.

Plaza, Juárez Nte 23, on the Jardín Zenéa (☎42/12-11-38). On the zócalo: clean, but a touch faded and impersonal. All rooms with bath, TV and phone. ③.

Posada Academia, Pino Suárez 3 (no phone). Clean and basic rooms are nothing special but cheap and have TV (US$1 more for colour). ②.

Posada Acueducto, Juárez 64 Sur, at Arteaga (☎42/24-12-89). Attractively decorated and well-cared-for hotel, right in the centre, with modern rooms around a central parking area. The large suites (④) are particularly nice. ③.

Posada Colonial, Juárez 19 Sur (☎42/12-02-39). Low standards with bathless rooms at rock bottom prices, and better rooms (②) with shower and TV. Only if you are desperately poor. ①.

Youth Hostel, Av Ejercito Republicano, behind the ex-Convento de la Cruz, about a fifteen-minute walk from the centre (☎42/23-43-50). This *Villa Juvenil* is one of Mexico's better, relatively handy and with clean, if cramped, single-sex dorms and 24hr hot water, but an inconvenient 10.30pm curfew. ①.

The City

Dominating the **Jardín Zenéa**, Querétaro's main square, the church of **San Francisco** was one of the earliest founded in the city. Its beautiful facade incorporates a dome covered in azulejos – coloured tiles imported from Spain around 1540 – but for the most part San Francisco was rebuilt in the seventeenth and eighteenth centuries. Adjoining, in what used to be its monastery, is the **Museo Regional** (Tues–Sun 10am–7pm; US$2, free on Sun). The building alone is reason enough to visit – built around a large cloister and going through in the back to a lovely chapel, it's far bigger than you imagine from the outside. Inside the displays are eclectic: the keyhole through which La Corregidora passed on her news; early copies of the Constitution; the table on which the Treaty of Guadalupe Hidalgo was signed; and quantities of ephemera connected with Emperor Maximilian, whose headquarters were here for a while. There are also the more usual collections relating to local archeology, and a sizeable gallery of colonial art – altogether well worth an hour or two.

South of the museum lies the **Plaza de la Constitución**, a square that used to hold the market and at the time of writing was being undermined by a subterranean car park. Better to head a block north to the junction of Juárez and Peralta and the **Teatro de la Republica** (Mon–Fri 10am–2pm & 5–8pm, Sat 9am–noon; free), a grand nineteenth-century structure, which has played a vital role in Mexican history: here a court met to decide the fate of Emperor Maximilian, and the 1917 Constitution was agreed. A small exhibition celebrates these events, though the main reason to go in is to take a look at the theatre itself.

Around the Plaza de la Independencia

The little pedestrianized alleys that lead up to the east of the Jardín are some of the city's most interesting: crammed with ancient houses, little restaurants, art galleries and shops selling junky antiques and the opals and other semiprecious stones for which the area is famous. If you buy, make sure you know what you're getting. The first of several little plazas, almost part of the Jardín Zenéa, is the **Jardín Corregidora**, another beautiful square, with an imposing statue of La Corregidora and several restaurants and bars where you can sit outside. The pedestrianized Andador Libertad runs past art galleries and boutiques from the Plaza de la Constitución to the **Plaza de la Independencia**, or Plaza de Armas, a very pretty, arcaded open space. In the middle of the plaza stands a statue of Don Juan Antonio Urrutia y Arana, Marques de la Villa del Villar del Aguila, the man who built Querétaro's elegant aqueduct, providing the city with drinking water. Around the square is the **Casa de la Corregidora**, now the Palacio Municipal (Mon–Fri 8am–9pm, Sat 9am–2pm; free). It was here, on September 14, 1810, that La Corregidora was locked up while her husband made plans to arrest the conspirators, and here that she managed to get a message to Ignacio Perez, who carried it to San Miguel and Dolores, to Allende and Hidalgo. It's an elegant building, but there's not a great deal to see inside.

The commercial centre

The more interesting restaurants and bars remain around the eastern plazas, but the commercial centre of Querétaro lies west of the zócalo, on and around **Avenida Madero**. This is where you'll find most of the shops, on formal streets lined with stately mansions. At the corner of Madero and Allende, the little Jardín de Santa Clara features a famous **Fountain of Neptune**, designed by Tresguerras in 1797. **Francisco Eduardo Tresguerras** (1765–1833) is rightly regarded as one of Mexico's greatest architects – he was also a sculptor, painter and poet – and was almost single-handedly responsible for developing a native Mexican style diverging from (though still close to) its Spanish roots. His work, seen throughout central Mexico, is particularly evident here and in nearby Celaya, his birthplace. Beside the fountain rises the deceptively simple church of **Santa Clara**, once attached to one of the country's richest convents. Inside it's a riot of Baroque excess, with gilded cherubs and angels swarming all over the profusely decorated altarpieces.

Carry on west down Madero and you get to the **Palacio de Gobierno** and the **Cathedral**, eighteenth-century buildings, neither of which, by Querétaro's standards, is particularly distinguished. Cut south down Allende, however, and you'll find the **Museo de Arte de Querétaro**, Allende 14 Sur (Tues–Sun 11am–7pm; US$1.30, free on Tues) occupying the former **Palacio Federal** on Allende, by the church of San Agustín. Originally an Augustinian monastery (it has also been a prison and a post office in its time), this is one of the most exuberant buildings in a town full of them: at its most extreme, in the cloister, every surface of the two storeys of portals is carved with grotesque figures, no two quite alike, and with abstract designs. The sculptures, often attributed to Tresguerras though almost certainly not by him, are full of religious symbolism, which, if you can, you should try to get someone to explain to you. The large figures supporting the arches, for example, all hold their fingers in different positions – three held up to represent the Trinity, four for the Evangelists and so on. The contents of the museum are good, too: upstairs a brief history of the building and artworks up to the eighteenth century; downstairs there are nineteenth- and twentieth-century art and temporary exhibition spaces. There's some good modern Mexican painting here, too. Around the corner lies the **Casa de los Perros**, at Allende 16 at Pino Suárez, a mansion named for the ugly canine gargoyles that line its facade.

The church of **Santa Rosa de Viterbo** sits further out in this direction, at the junction of Arteaga and Montes. Its interior rivals Santa Clara for richness of decoration, but here there is no false modesty on the outside either. Two enormous flying buttresses support the octagonal cupola – remodelled by Tresguerras – and a blue- and white-tiled dome. The needling tower, too, is Tresguerras' work, holding what is said to be the first four-sided public clock erected on the American continent.

Convento de la Cruz

Slightly further afield, but still in easy walking distance, the **Convento de la Cruz** (Tues–Fri 9am–2pm & 4–6pm, Sat & Sun 9am–4.30pm; small donation requested) is built on the site of the battle between the Spanish and the Otomí in which the Conquistadors gained control of Querétaro. According to legend, the fighting was cut short by the miraculous appearance of Saint James (*Santiago* – the city's full name is Santiago de Querétaro) and a dazzling cross in the sky, which persuaded the Indians to concede defeat and become Christians. The **Capilla del Calvarito**, opposite the monastery entrance, marks the spot where the first mass was celebrated after the battle. The monastery itself was founded in 1683 by the Franciscans as a college for the propagation of the faith (*Colegio Apostolico de Propaganda Fide*) and grew over the years into an important centre for the training of missionaries, with a massive library and rich collection of relics.

Because of its hilltop position and hefty construction, the monastery was also frequently used as a fortress: one of the last redoubts of the Spanish in the War of Independence, it was Maximilian's headquarters for the last few weeks of his reign – he was subsequently imprisoned here to await execution. Nowadays you can take guided tours: greatest source of pride is the **Arbol de la Cruz**, a tree whose thorns grow in the shape of little crosses. The tree grew, so the story goes, from a walking stick left behind by a mysterious saintly traveller who slept here one night – certainly it does produce thorns in the form of crosses, but that may not be so rare. The monks, however, appear very excited by the phenomenon and point out that an additional five percent of the thorns grow with extra spikes to mark the spots where nails were driven through Christ's hands and feet.

Come up to the monastery in the late afternoon then wander 200m beyond along Av Ejército Republicano to the **Mausoleo de la Corregidora** (daily 6am–6pm; free), where the heroine's remains, along with those of her husband, are surrounded by statues of illustrious Queretanos. Across the road a *mirador* provides a superb sunset-view of the city's **Aqueduct**, a beautiful 1.3-kilometre-long series of arches up to 23m high, which once brought water into the city from springs nearly 6km away. Spotlit at night, it looks magnificent, especially as you drive into town. *Café Tulipe* and *Café Amadeus* are both a short stroll down the hill from here.

Cerro de las Campañas

Northwest of the centre, the gentle eminence of the **Cerro de las Campañas** ("Hill of Bells") commands wider, if rather less scenic, views over Querétaro and its industrial outskirts. Maximilian and his two generals, Miguel Miramón and Tomás Mejía, faced the firing squad here. The hill is dominated by a vast stone statue of the victor of that particular war, Benito Juárez, glaring down over the town from its summit. In order to reach the summit, avoid the parts of the new university-campus sprawl up one slope and instead make for the entrance to the neatly tended **Parque Municipal del Cerro de las Campañas**, Av Justo Sierra (daily dawn–dusk; US$0.20).

Eating, drinking and nightlife

There's plenty of good food in Querétaro, and some delightful places to sit outside amid the alleys and plazas east of the **Jardín Zenéa**. The zócalo itself has plenty of rather cheaper places. If you want to get together something of your own, head for the **market**, sprawled across several blocks just off Calzada Zaragoza, not far from the Alameda. While in Querétaro look out for a couple of **local specialities**, particularly a hearty lentil soup laced with chunks of dried fruit: it sounds weird but is delicious, though hard-line vegetarians won't appreciate the pork-broth base. Also try *Enchiladas Queretanas*, tortillas fried in a chile sauce and stuffed with onions and cheese. In better places they may come topped with potatoes and carrots.

Evening entertainment tends to involve a couple of beers in one of the restaurants or an hour or two lingering in one of the cafés. More lively **nightlife** is harder to find, with the key bars and clubs scattered around the suburbs – a taxi-ride or two apart. Most places have some sort of live music on Thursday, Friday and Saturday nights, when you can expect to pay US$2–5 to get in. Perhaps the best starting point is Bernardo Quintana (go to the eastern end of the aqueduct then south) where *J.B.J. O'Briens* fun bar, at no.109, and an outpost of the *Carlos 'N Charlie's* chain, at no.160, prove popular with the richer local youth. Across from the latter, at no.177, *Los Infiernos* is open primarily for hot salsa from Wednesday to Sunday. Elsewhere there are full-blown weekend discos at *Qui*, Monte Sinaí 103, and *La Iguana*, inside the *Hotel Santa María* on Universidad.

1810, Jardín Independencia. Moderately-priced sidewalk restaurant which does both the regional specialities (mentioned above) to perfection and seems less afflicted by cheesy crooners than other places on the Jardín.

Barra Expres Café, Andador 16 de Septiembre 40. A relaxed stop for the best coffee in town.

Café Amadeus, corner Calzada de los Arcos and Puente de Alvarado, halfway along the aqueduct. Good place for coffee and cake, but also serving fine breakfasts and antojitos, all to the strains of Mozart.

Café del Fondo, Pino Suárez 9, west of Juárez. Airy multi-roomed café serving bargain breakfasts from 7.30am, mushroom and asparagus soup and the like through the day, and good coffee and cakes at all times until around 10.30pm.

Café Los Alcatraces, Andador V. Carranza at Río de la Loza. Excellent spot for standard low-cost Mexican fare, especially the US$3 buffet breakfasts – complete with cereals, yoghurt, eggs, frijoles, chilaquiles, tamales, atole, toast, coffee and more – and a similar buffet lunch. Closed Sun.

Café Regio, Pino Suárez 24a, between Allende and Guerrero. The smell of roasting beans advertises this ideal spot for a coffee-and-cake break in the commercial centre, just along from the Museo de Arte and the Casa de los Peros.

Café Tulipe, Calzada de los Arcos 3, near the west end of the aqueduct. A definite favourite with everyone from students to Querétaro's wealthier residents for its French-tinged menu, coffee and delectable cakes, all at surprisingly modest prices. The deliciously gloopy fondue and *caldo conde* (a black bean, cream and herb soup) are especially delicious.

Fonda del Refugio, Jardín Corregidora. Not-too-expensive, very elegant place to sit outside, drink, and watch the world go by.

Mesón de Santa Rosa, Jardín Corregidora. Superb restaurant serving Mexican specialities and Spanish food in a beautiful setting, with correspondingly high prices.

Ostionería Tampico, Jardín Corregidora. Top-notch seafood at moderate prices, best selected from one of three daily comidas.

Quadros, 5 de Mayo 16. Light snacks are available, but this is primarily a café and bar with several intimate rooms off the central well of a colonial mansion. There's some form of live entertainment (usually folk or jazz) most nights of the week, especially Thursday to Saturday when there is a cover charge of a couple of dollars. Local artists provide the decor.

Teotlamatilztli, Independencia 5 Ote. Reliable vegetarian cafe serving healthy salads, burger, enchiladas, hotcakes and a wide selection of flavoured yoghurts. The comida is a bargain.

Listings

American Express Turismo Beverly Querétaro, Tecnologico 118 (Mon–Fri 9am–2pm & 4–6pm, Sat 9am–noon; ☎42/16-15-00), has all the usual services. It's around 2km southwest of the centre, reached by buses running west along Zaragoza to Tecnologico then 200m south.

Books and newspapers *The News* and international weeklies can usually be found at the newspaper stands around the Jardín Zenéa. Beyond that, Unidad Cultural del Centro, on the east side of the Jardín Zenéa, stock a handful of English-language books, and Sanborn's, on Constituyentes, 2km southeast of the centre, have a wide range of magazines.

Cinemas There's nothing central. The ten-screen Cinepolis is behind the bullring on Constituyentes, almost 3km southeast of the centre. Buses run along Constituyentes but a taxi is a lot easier. Local daily papers list what's playing.

Emergencies Police ☎42/12-02-06.

Laundry Lavandería Verónica, Hidalgo 153, at Ignacio Pérez (Mon–Fri 9am–2.30pm & 4.30–8pm, Sat 9am–3pm), lies less than 1km west of the centre.

Around Querétaro

From Querétaro you can race straight into the capital on Hwy-57, one of the fastest roads in the country, but before you do, there are three worthwhile local destinations – **Bernal**, **San Juan del Río** and **Tequisquiapan** – where you could easily spend a pleasant day or two. If you are México-bound and not reliant on public transport, then there are also a couple of places that might be visited en route: the ancient Toltec capital of Tula, and Tepotzotlán, with its magnificent Baroque architecture, both of which are covered in Chapter 5.

Bernal

The pretty village of **BERNAL**, 45km east of Querétaro, hunkers under the skirts of the monolithic Peña de Bernal, a 450-metre-high chunk of volcanic rock which dominates the plains all around. Here you can follow the rough but clearly marked path up about two-thirds of the way to the top (up to an hour to ascend, half that to get down), where there's a small shrine and long views stretching out below. Only appropriately equipped rock climbers should continue up the metal rungs to the summit, passing a memorial plaque to an earlier adventurer along the way.

Avoid coming out here at weekends, when half of Querétaro has the same idea, but mid-week it can be delightfully peaceful: the mountain is likely to be deserted and you'll be about the only thing disturbing the lovely village plaza with its attractive church and terracotta-washed buildings, sumptuous in the afternoon light. The centre is ringed by narrow streets full of shops selling handicrafts, and there's even a small and sporadically open **tourist office** on Hidalgo, which runs west from the plaza. Also on Hidalgo is the nicest place **to eat**, in the shaded courtyard of *Meson de la Roca*, at no. 5, serving moderately priced and well-presented Mexican dishes.

Buses from Querétaro's main Camionera (Sala B) drop you on the highway five minutes' walk from Bernal centre; it's worth remembering that the last bus back passes at around 5pm. If you get stuck, or just fancy a night here (no bad thing), there are plain but clean and comfortable **rooms** at *Posada Peña*, Turbidé 3, behind the church (☎427/7-12-77; ②), and the slightly more distant *Hotel Villa San Carlos*, Ezequiel Montes 110, 600m west (no local phone, but in Querétaro call ☎42/13-04-61; ④), with carpeted rooms, and some larger suites with great views of the rock.

San Juan del Río

Though **SAN JUAN DEL RÍO**, 50km or so south of Querétaro, looks like nothing at all from the highway, it is in fact a major market centre, and a popular weekend outing from Querétero and the capital. Among the goods sold here are gemstones – mostly local opals, but also imported jewels, which are polished and set in town – as well as baskets, wine and cheese. If you're going to buy gems, be very careful: it's easy to get ripped off without expert advice. Other purchases are safer, though not particularly cheap on the whole. The best-known wine is *Hidalgo*, a brand name sold all over the country and usually reliable. You can visit their cellars, **Cavas de San Juan**, a short distance out of town on the road to Tequisquiapan.

Most México-bound buses no longer call here, but direct buses from Querétaro (Clase Premiere from Sala A) take some forty minutes to get to San Juan del Río's **bus station**, a couple of kilometres south or town. A local bus will drop you at the arcaded Plaza de los Fundadores, where you'll find a small **tourist office**, at Juárez 30. The Mercado Reforma and the central Jardín Independencia are a couple of long blocks north of here up Hidalgo. If you decide that you'd like to stay a while to enjoy San Juan's unhurried atmosphere, take your choice of three good **hotels**, all near the Plaza de los Fundadores where Juárez crosses Hidalgo: the friendly, pleasant and comfortable *Estancia*, Juárez 20 (☎467/2-00-38, fax 2-27-46; ③); the simple and inexpensive *San Juan*, Hidalgo 4 Sur (☎467/2-00-13; ②); or, best of all, *Layseca*, around the corner from the latter at Juárez 9 (☎467/2-01-10; ③), an old colonial house with rooms set around a beautiful open courtyard.

Tequisquiapan

Some 20km north of San Juan, along a road lined with factories and workshops, **TEQUISQUIAPAN** is a former Otomí village now overrun by villas catering for wealthy Mexicans, who come here partly to enjoy the springs, but mostly to gorge themselves at the pavement restaurants and shop in the boutiques; some cheap, many expensive and almost all of the highest standard. The village remains very picturesque, if somewhat exclusive, and like San Juan del Río has a big crafts market – especially active on Sundays – one block from the main plaza. At the end of May running into June, Tequisquiapan hosts a major wine and cheese festival, the **Feria Nacional de Queso y Vino**, which is well worth going a bit out of your way for – there's plenty of free food and drink, and no shortage of other entertainments. When the attraction of artesanía-shopping begins to pale, you'll probably want to press on, but if you're prepared to part with at least US\$20 for **accommodation**, you can choose from the thirty-odd hotels packed into this tiny place, most ranged around bougainvillaea-draped courtyards, many with pools fed by springs. On the plaza itself, try *La Plaza*, Juárez 10 (☎427/3-00-05; ⑤), a perfect luxury hotel, very relaxed, with its own pool; *Casablanca*, 5 de Mayo (☎427/3-00-78; ④), slightly cheaper but still smart; or *Posada Los Arcos*, Moctezuma 12 (☎427/3-05-66; ④). A couple of inconveniently timed direct **buses** run from Querétaro to Tequisquiapan (extra ones during the feria), but for the most part you'll need to change onto a local service from San Juan, then walk the ten minutes into the plaza from the bus station.

FIESTAS

The Bajío is one of the most active regions in Mexico when it comes to celebrations. The state of Guanajuato, especially, is rich in fiestas: the list below is by no means exhaustive; local tourist offices will have further details.

JANUARY

1 NEW YEAR'S DAY widely celebrated. Feria in **Dolores Hidalgo** (Guanajuato).

6 Feria begins in **Matehuala** (San Luis Potosí), lasting till the 15th.

20 DÍA DE SAN SEBASTIAN. In **San Luis Potosí** (SLP) the climax of ten days of pilgrimages; in **León** (Gto) the religious festival coincides with the agricultural and industrial fair.

21 San Miguel de Allende (Gto) honours Ignacio Allende with a parade, dances and bullfights.

FEBRUARY

1 Cadereyta (Que), northeast of Querétaro, holds a festival famous for its cockfights – also religious processions, dancing and *mariachi*.

CARNIVAL, the week before Lent (variable Feb–March). On the Sunday **Yuriria** (Gto), between Celaya and Morelia, has real bullfights, processions and dances.

MARCH

First Friday. FIESTA DEL SEÑOR DE LA CONQUISTA held in **San Miguel de Allende** (Gto).

PALM SUNDAY (week before Easter) is the culmination of a week's celebration in **San Miguel de Allende** (Gto), with a pilgrimage to Atotonilco.

HOLY WEEK is observed everywhere. There's a huge procession, while in **San Miguel de Allende** every family constructs an elaborate altar, proudly displayed in their homes. *Semana Santa* is a big deal in **San Luis Potosí** (SLP), particularly Good Friday's "Procession of Silence", when an effigy of Christ's dead body is paraded through the streets.

APRIL

In early April (variable) **Irapuato** (Gto) holds its FERIA DE LA FRESA (Strawberry Fair) in honour of the region's principal cash crop.

25 FERIA DE SAN MARCOS in **Aguascalientes** (Ags) runs for around a week either side of this date. One of the largest and most famous in Mexico, there's dancing, bullfights, music and great wine.

MAY

24 Empalme Escobeda (Gto), near San Miguel de Allende, has a fiesta lasting until the next Sunday, with traditional dances including that of *Los Apaches*, one of the few in which women take part.

CORPUS CHRISTI (variable – the Thursday after Trinity) is celebrated in **San Miguel de Allende** (Gto). The following Wednesday sees a very ancient fiesta in **Juchipila** (Zac), between Zacatecas and Guadalajara, with flowers and dances including the famous *Jarabe Tapatío*, the Mexican Hat Dance. In **San Luis Potosí** (SLP), *Corpus Cristi* sees the *gigantes* (see p.218) out on show.

Continues over

The FERIA NACIONAL DE QUESO Y VINO in **Tequisquiapan** (Que) runs from late May through early June.

JUNE

23 FESTIVAL DE LA PRESA DE OLLA in **Guanajuato** (Gto).

29 DÍA DE SAN PEDRO. **Chalchihuites** (Zac), between Zacatecas and Durango, stages a "Battle of the Flowers" in which local kids take part.

JULY

4 Acambaro (Gto), a very ancient town between Celaya and Morelia, has a fiesta with religious processions, music and many traditional dances.

13 San Miguel de Allende (Gto) holds a fiesta for one of its patron saints, San Antonio de Padua, involving a procession of crazily dressed revellers known as "Los Locos".

16 DÍA DE LA VIRGEN DEL CARMEN celebrated in **Celaya** (Gto).

25 DÍA DE SANTIAGO widely observed. Mass pilgrimages to **San Luis Potosí** (SLP); saint's day celebrations in **Santiago Maravatio** (Gto), near Irapuato; stylized battles between Moors and Christians in **Jesús María** (Ags), near Aguascalientes.

AUGUST

15 DÍA DE LA ASUNCION (Assumption) coincides with the FERIA DE LA UVA in **Aguascalientes** (Ags) and the FERIA DE LA CAJETA in **Celaya** (Gto), celebrating the syrupy confection made here.

25 DÍA DE SAN LUIS hugely enjoyed in **San Luis Potosí** (SLP) – giant procession and fireworks.

27 In **Zacatecas** (Zac), battles between Moors and Christians on the Cerro de la Bufa are the highlight of several days' celebrations.

SEPTEMBER

On weekends throughout September and into early October, **San Miguel de Allende** (Gto) has bull-running in its main streets, known as the "Sanmiguelada" or "Pamplonada".

1 DÍA DE LA VIRGEN DE REMEDIOS justifies a fiesta in **Comonfort** (Gto), near San Miguel de Allende. Traditional dances.

8 In **Jerez** (Zac), the start of a festival lasting till the 15th.

14 Ten days of pilgrimages to the Señora del Patrocinio start in **Zacatecas** (Zac), coinciding with the FERIA NACIONAL and all sorts of secular entertainments, especially bullfights.

15–16 INDEPENDENCE CELEBRATIONS everywhere, above all in **Dolores Hidalgo** (Gto) and **Querétaro** (Que), where they start several days early. In **San Miguel de Allende** (Gto), the re-enactment of the "The Grito" on the night of the 15th is followed by fireworks and parades.

28 Start of the three-day festival of San Miguel in **San Felipe** (Gto), north of Dolores Hidalgo, with Otomí dances and battles between Moors and Christians.

DÍA DE SAN MIGUEL (variable, a Friday around the end of Sept) is the most important of **San Miguel de Allende's** (Gto) many fiestas: two days of processions, concerts, dancing, bullfights and ceremonies.

OCTOBER

3 DÍA DE SAN FRANCISCO DE ASIS. Major pilgrimage to **Real de Catorce** (SLP) and festivities in the town.

4 DÍA DE SAN FRANCISCO. **Nochistlán** (Zac), between Aguascalientes and Guadalajara, holds a feria lasting to the end of the month. In **San Miguel de Allende** (Gto), a huge firework display at 4am commemorates San Miguel's fight with the devil, a battle known as the "Alborada".

23 Coroneo (Gto), south of Querétaro, begins a three-day feria.

NOVEMBER

2 DÍA DE LOS MUERTOS (All Souls). The famous Day of the Dead is celebrated everywhere.

7–14 FIESTA DE LAS ILUMINA-CIONES in **Guanajuato** (Gto).

Last Sunday. Fiesta and crafts markets in **Comonfort** (Gto).

DECEMBER

8 DÍA DE LA INMACULADA CONCEP-CIÓN. **Dolores Hidalgo** (Gto) combines a religious festival with a feria and traditional dancing.

16–25 The traditional Christmas Posadas are widely performed. Particularly good in **Celaya** (Gto). In **Querétaro** (Que), on the 23rd, there's a giant procession with bands and carnival floats.

travel details

BUSES

Relatively densely populated, the Bajío is crisscrossed by thousands of services, locally between towns and villages, and long-distance runs that call in at all major towns en route. It can occasionally be difficult to pick up a *de paso* seat on the latter: they're not normally sold until the bus has arrived. As the roads converge on major destinations, so the number of buses increases – there's a constant stream calling in at Querétaro, for example, before the last 2hr 30min stretch to México. In general the fastest and most efficient operators are Omnibus de Mexico and Tres Estrellas de Oro, though there's little to choose between the first-class companies. Flecha Amarilla covers many of the local runs and is fairly reliable – Estrella Blanca is better but less frequent. What follows is a minimum, covering the major stops only – it should be assumed that these buses also call at the towns en route.

Aguascalientes to: Guadalajara (9 daily; 6hr); Guanajuato (5 daily; 4hr); León (hourly; 2hr); México (hourly; 7hr); Querétaro (hourly; 6hr); San Luis Potosí (14 daily; 2hr 30min); San Miguel de Allende (11 daily; 4hr); Zacatecas (every 30min; 2hr).

Dolores Hidalgo to: Guanajuato (every 20min; 1hr); México (every 40min; 5hr); Querétaro (every 40min; 2hr); San Luis Potosí (14 daily; 2hr 30min); San Luis de la Paz (every 20min; 1hr); San Miguel de Allende (every 15min; 50min).

Guanajuato to: Aguascalientes (4 daily; 4hr); Dolores Hidalgo (every 20min; 1hr); Guadalajara (5 daily; 6hr); León (constantly; 40min); México (7 daily; 4hr); Querétaro (8 daily; 3hr); San Luis de la Paz (5 daily; 2hr 30min); San Luis Potosí (10 daily; 3hr); San Miguel de Allende (9 daily; 1hr 30min).

León to: Aguascalientes (hourly; 1hr); Guadalajara (hourly; 4hr); Guanajuato (constantly; 40min) México (hourly; 5hr); Querétaro (hourly; 2hr); Zacatecas (hourly; 4hr).

Matehuala to: Real de Catorce (6 daily; 2hr); Saltillo (8 daily; 2hr); San Luis Potosí (hourly; 2hr 30min).

Pozos to: San José Iturbide (every 30min; 40min); San Luis de la Paz (every 30min; 20min).

Querétaro to: Aguascalientes (hourly; 6hr); Dolores Hidalgo (every 40min; 2hr); Guadalajara (hourly; 6hr); Guanajuato (8 daily; 3hr); León (hourly; 2hr); México (every 10min; 3hr); San Luis Potosí (hourly; 2hr 30min); San Juan del Río (every 15min; 35min); San Miguel de Allende (every 30min; 1hr); Zacatecas (hourly; 5hr).

San Juan del Río to: México (every 15min; 2hr); Querétaro (every 15min; 35min); Tequisquiapan (every 10min; 25min).

San José Iturbide to: Querétaro (constantly; 1hr 10min); Pozos (every 30min; 40min); San Luis de la Paz (every 30min; 1hr).

San Luis de la Paz to: Dolores Hidalgo (every 20min; 1hr); Pozos (every 30min; 20min); San José Iturbide (every 30min; 1hr).

San Luis Potosí to: Aguascalientes (14 daily; 2hr 30min); Dolores Hidalgo (14 daily; 2hr 30min); Guadalajara (13 daily; 4–5hr); Guanajuato (10 daily; 3hr); Matehuala (hourly; 2hr 30min); México (hourly or better; 5hr); Monterrey (12 daily; 7hr); Nuevo Laredo (8 daily; 12hr); Querétaro (hourly; 2hr 30min); San Miguel de Allende (8 daily; 3hr); Tampico (11 daily; 7hr); Zacatecas (10 daily; 3hr).

San Miguel de Allende to: Aguascalientes (11 daily; 4hr); Dolores Hidalgo (every 15min; 50min); Guanajuato (9 daily; 1hr 30min); México (every

40min; 4hr); San Luis Potosí (8 daily; 3hr);
Querétaro (every 30min; 1hr).

Tequisquiapan to: México (every 30min; 2hr);
San Juan del Río (every 10min; 25min).

Zacatecas to: Aguascalientes (every 30min;
2hr); Chihuahua (hourly; 12hr); Ciudad Juárez
(hourly; 15–18hr); Durango (hourly; 5hr);
Guadalajara (hourly; 5hr); León (hourly; 4hr);
México (at least 15 daily; 8hr upwards);
Monterrey (hourly; 6hr); Nuevo Laredo (5 daily;
8hr); Puerto Vallarta (3 daily; 14hr); Querétaro
(hourly; 6hr); San Luis Potosí (10 daily; 3hr);
Tijuana (3 daily; 36hr); Torreón (hourly; 6hr).

TRAINS

Zacatecas, Aguascalientes and Querétaro are all
on the main rail line from México to the border at
Ciudad Juárez, which sees a departure each
morning from México. There are also morning
departures on Monday, Wednesday and Friday on
the route from the capital to San Luis Potosí and
Monterrey. In addition there is a daily service
from México to Querétaro, San Luis Potosí, San
Miguel de Allende and Guadalajara, leaving the
capital early in the morning and returning in the
afternoon. Train stopping times are listed in each
town account.

CHAPTER FIVE

MÉXICO AND AROUND

The **Valley of México** has been the the the country's centre of gravity since earliest pre-history – long before the concept of a Mexican nation existed. Based in this mountain-ringed basin – 100km long, 60km wide, 2500m high, dotted with great salt- and fresh-water lagoons and dominated by the vast snowcapped peaks of Popocatépetl and Ixtaccíhuatl – were the most powerful civilizations the country has seen. Today the lakes have all but disappeared, and the mountains are shrouded in smog, but it continues to be the heart of the country – its physical centre, the generator of every political, cultural and economic pulse.

At the crossroads of everything sprawls the vibrant, elegant, choking, crime-ridden fascination of **México**. In population the largest city in the world, with more than twen-

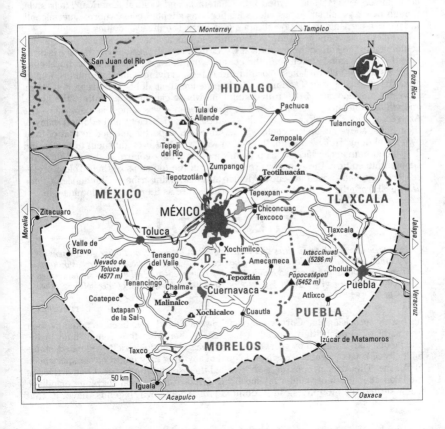

ty million inhabitants, its lure is irresistible. Colonial mansions and excavated pyramids vie for attention with the city's fabulous museums and galleries, while above them tower the concrete and glass of thrusting development. But above all, the city is alive – exciting, sometimes frightening, always bewildering, but boldly alive. You can't avoid it, and if you genuinely want to know anything of Mexico you shouldn't try – even if the attraction does sometimes seem to be the same ghoulish fascination that draws onlookers to the site of a particularly nasty accident.

Round about there's escape and interest in every direction: to the north **Tula** and **Teotihuacán** and the magnificent Baroque treasures of **Tepotzotlán**; to the west the market town of **Toluca** and the rural retreats of the mountainous national parks; to the south **Cuernavaca** with its ancient palaces and the silver town of **Taxco**; in the east the volcanoes, **Cholula**, and ultra-colonial, thriving **Puebla**.

It is above all the **Aztecs**, whose warrior state was crushed by Cortés, who are associated with the area. But they were relative newcomers, forging their empire by force of arms in less than two centuries and borrowing their culture, their science, their arts, even their language from Valley societies that had gone before. **Teotihuacán**, whose mighty pyramids still stand some 50km northeast of the modern city, was the predominant culture of the Classic period and the true forebear of the Aztecs – a city of some 200,000 people whose influence spread throughout the country, south to the Maya lands in the Yucatán and beyond into Guatemala and Central America. Their style, though never as militaristic as later societies, was adopted everywhere: Quetzalcoatl, the plumed serpent, and Tlaloc, the rain god, were Teotihuacán deities.

For all its pre-eminence, though, Teotihuacán was neither the earliest, nor the only settlement in the Valley: the pyramid at **Cuicuilco**, now in the south of the city, is probably the oldest stone structure in the country, and there were small agricultural communities all around the lakes. Nor did the Aztecs, arriving some five hundred years after the destruction of Teotihuacán, acknowledge their debt. They regarded themselves as descendants of the **Toltec** kingdom, whose capital lay at **Tula** to the north, and whose influence – as successors to Teotihuacán – was almost as pervasive. The Aztecs consciously took over the Toltec, military-based, society, and adopted many of their gods: above all Quetzalcoatl, who assumed an importance equal to that of their own tribal deity, Huitzilopochtli, the god of war, who had brought them to power and demanded human sacrifice to keep them there. In taking control of the society while adopting its culture, the Aztecs were following in the footsteps of their Toltec predecessors, who had arrived in central Mexico as a marauding tribe of Chichimeca ("Sons of Dogs") from the north, absorbing the local culture as they came to dominate it.

THE CAPITAL

And when we saw all those cities and villages built in the water, and other great towns on dry land, and that straight and level causeway leading to Mexico, we were astounded. These great towns and cues and buildings rising from the water, all made of stone, seemed like an enchanted vision from the tales of Amadis. Indeed, some of our soldiers asked whether it was not all a dream.

Bernal Díaz

It's hardly surprising that Cortés and his followers should have been so taken by their first sight of **Tenochtitlán**, capital of the Aztecs. For what they found, built in the middle of a lake traversed by great causeways, was a beautiful, strictly regulated, stone-built city of 300,000 people – easily the equal of anything they might have experienced in Europe. The Aztec people (or as they called themselves, the Mexica) had arrived at the lake, after years of wandering and living off what they could scavenge or pillage from settled communities, in around 1345. Their own legends have it that

Huitzilopochtli had ordered them to build a city where they found an eagle perched on a cactus devouring a snake, and this they duly saw on an island in the middle of the lake; this is the basis of the nopal, eagle and snake motif that forms the centrepiece of the modern Mexican flag and appears everywhere, from coins and official seals to woven designs on rugs. The reality was probably more desperate – driven from place to place, the lake seemed a last resort – but for whatever reasons it proved an ideal site. Well stocked with fish, it was also fertile, once they had constructed their *chinampas*, or floating gardens of reeds, and virtually impregnable, too: the causeways, when they were completed, could be flooded and the bridges raised to thwart attacks (or to escape, as the Spanish found to their cost on the *Noche Triste*; see p.293).

The **island city** eventually grew to cover an area of some thirteen square kilometres, much of it reclaimed from the lake, and from this base the Aztecs were able to begin their programme of expansion: first, dominating the Valley by a series of strategic alliances, war and treachery, and finally, in a period of less than a hundred years before the Conquest, establishing an empire that demanded tribute from and traded with the most distant parts of the country. This was the situation when **Cortés** landed on the east coast in 1519, bringing with him an army of only a few hundred men, and began his long march on Tenochtitlán. Several key factors assured his survival: superior weaponry, which included firearms; the shock effect of horses (never having seen such animals, the Indians at first believed them to be extensions of their riders); the support of tribes who were either enemies or suppressed subjects of the Aztecs; and the unwillingness of the Aztec emperor to resist openly.

Moctezuma II (Montezuma), who had suffered heavy defeats in campaigns against the Tarascans in the west, was a broodingly religious man who, it is said, believed Cortés to be the pale-skinned, bearded god Quetzalcoatl, returned to fulfil ancient prophecies. Accordingly he admitted him to the city – fearfully, but with a show of ceremonious welcome. By way of repaying this hospitality the Spanish took Moctezuma prisoner, and later attacked the great Aztec temples, killing many priests and placing Christian chapels alongside their altars. Meanwhile, there was growing unrest in the city at the emperor's passivity and at the rapacious behaviour of his guests. Moctezuma was eventually killed – according to the Spanish stoned to death by his own people while trying to quell a riot – and the Spaniards driven from the city with heavy losses. Cortés, and a few of his followers, however, escaped to the security of Tlaxcala, most loyal of his native allies, there to regroup and plan a new assault. Finally, re-armed and reinforced – their numbers swelled by indigenous allies – and with ships built in secret, they laid a three-month siege, finally taking the city in the face of suicidal opposition in August 1521.

The city's defeat is still a harsh memory – Cortés himself is hardly revered, but the natives who assisted him, and in particular Moctezuma and Malinche, the woman who acted as Cortés's interpreter, are non-people. You won't find a monument to Moctezuma in the country, though Cuauhtémoc, his successor who led the fierce resistance, is commemorated everywhere; Malinche is represented, acidly, in some of Diego Rivera's more outspoken murals. More telling, perhaps, of the bitterness of the struggle, is that so little physical evidence remains: "All that I saw then," wrote Bernal Díaz, "is overthrown and destroyed; nothing is left standing." The victorious Spanish systematically smashed every visible aspect of the old culture, as often as not using the very stones of the old city to construct the new, and building a new palace for Cortés on the site of the Aztec emperor's palace. A few decades ago it was thought that everything was lost; slowly, however, particularly during construction of the Metro and in the remarkable discovery of remains of the **Templo Mayor** beneath the colonial Zócalo, remains of Tenochtitlán have been brought to light.

The **new city** developed slowly in its early years, only attaining the level of population that the old had enjoyed at the beginning of the twentieth century. It spread far wider, however, as the lake was drained, filled and built over – only tiny vestiges remain today – and grew with considerable grace. In many ways it's a singularly unfortunate place to site a modern city. Pestilent from the earliest days, the inadequately drained waters harboured fevers, and the Indian population was constantly swept by epidemics of European diseases. Many of the buildings, too, simply began to sink into the soft lake bed – a process not helped by regular earthquakes. You'll see old churches and mansions leaning at crazy angles throughout the centre, and repairs to damage caused by the disastrous **earthquake** of September 1985 are still not complete.

Visiting the city, though, the horrors that recent growth and industrialization have brought are of more immediate concern. The city's **population**, estimated at around 25.6 million (from fewer than five million in 1960), is the world's largest by far, while **pollution**, churned out by industry but even more by the chaotic traffic, is trapped in the bowl of mountains, hanging permanently in a pall of smog over the city. As you fly in, and often, even, as you arrive by bus over the mountains, you descend from clear blue skies into a thick greyish-yellow cloud: Popocatépetl and Ixtaccíhuatl, the volcanoes on which every visitor used to comment ("Japanese-contoured shapes of pastel blue and porcelain snow, and thin formal curls of smoke afloat in a limpid sky", wrote Sybille Bedford in the 1950s), are now rarely visible from the centre. Many find that their eyes smart from the atmospheric contamination within hours of arriving – just breathing is said to be the equivalent of smoking forty cigarettes a day, and chronic bronchitis is endemic among residents. At 2240m, there wasn't much oxygen to begin with. Not surprisingly, México is also the city with the most petty crime in the country, and where you feel least secure walking the streets at night: the centre is safe enough, as are the luxurious suburbs, but you should avoid walking elsewhere at night.

None of this should deter you from coming here, however – a certain seaminess amid the elegance of the new quarters and the genteel decay of the old is all part of the city's undeniable charm. Get to know it slowly, and exercise the sort of caution you would in any major city, and you'll enjoy it a lot more. You'll find the city much easier to take if you acclimatize to the country first – if at all possible try not to spend too long here when you first arrive.

Orientation

For all its size and the horrors of its traffic, México, once you're used to it, is surprisingly easy to find your way around. Certainly there is more logic in its plan than in any European city, and given an efficient and very cheap, if horrendously crowded, public transport system, and reasonably priced taxis, you should have no trouble getting about. Remember the **altitude** – walking gets tiring quickly, especially for the first day or two.

Traditional centre of the city is the **Zócalo**, or Plaza Mayor; the heart of ancient Tenochtitlán and of Cortés' city, it's surrounded by the oldest streets, largely colonial and unmodernized. To the east, the ancient structures degenerate rapidly, blending into

MÉXICO OR MEXICO CITY?

First, forget that you're in Mexico City. As far as a Mexican is concerned you're not, you're in **México**, or El DF (El "day effé"). It's a source of infinite confusion to visitors, but the fact is that the country took its name from the city and México, in conversation, almost always means the latter (in the country it's written "México DF" – the Distrito Federal being the administrative zone that contains most of the urban areas). The nation is La República, or in speeches La Patria: very rarely Mexico.

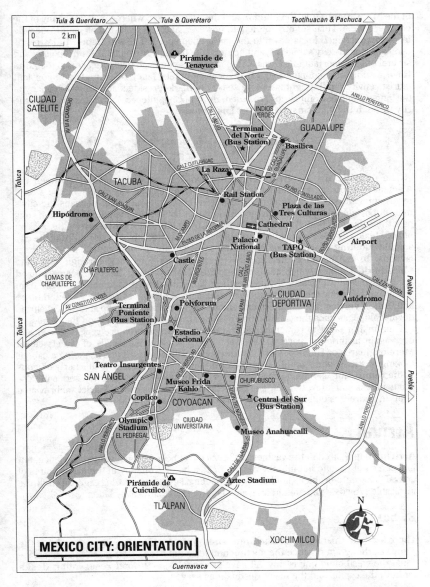

Tula & Querétaro △   △ Tula & Querétaro   Teotihuacan & Pachuca △

0   2 km

CIUDAD
SATELITE

♦ Pirámide de
Tenayuca

INDIOS
VERDES

GUADALUPE

Terminal
del Norte
(Bus Station)   ★   ● Basilica

TACUBA

La Raza

● Rail Station

Plaza de las
Tres Culturas

● Hipódromo

Cathedral

Palacio
National

Plaza de las
Tres Culturas ●

Airport

LOMAS DE
CHAPULTEPEC

CHAPULTEPEC

● Castle

TAPO
(Bus Station)

Polyforum ●

CIUDAD
DEPORTIVA

● Autódromo

★ Terminal
Poniente
(Bus Station)

● Estadio
Nacional

Teatro Insurgentes ●

SAN ÁNGEL

Museo Frida
Kahlo

● CHURUBUSCO

Copilco ●

COYOACAN

★ Central del Sur
(Bus Station)

Olympic
Stadium ●

CIUDAD
UNIVERSITARIA

EL PEDREGAL

● Museo Anahuacalli

Pirámide de
Cuicuilco ♦

● Aztec Stadium

TLALPAN

N

Toluca △   △ Toluca

Puebla △   Puebla △

MEXICO CITY: ORIENTATION

XOCHIMILCO

Cuernavaca ▽

the slums that surround the airport. Westwards, avenidas **Madero** and **Juárez** lead to
the **Alameda**, the small park that marks the extent of the old city centre. Here is the
Palacio de las Bellas Artes, the main post office and the landmark Torre Latino-
Americano. Carry straight on past here and you get into an area, between the ugly bulk

of the **Monumento a la Revolución** and the train station, where you'll find many of the cheaper hotels. Turn slightly to the left, however, and you're on the elegant **Paseo de la Reforma**, which leads down to the great open space of **Chapultepec Park**, recreation area for the city's millions, and home of the national Museum of Anthropology and several other important museums. Off to the left as you head down Reforma is the **Zona Rosa** with its chic shopping streets, expensive hotels, fancy restaurants and constant tourist activity. On the right is a more sedate, upmarket residential area, where many of the long-established embassies are based. Beyond Chapultepec, Reforma runs out of the city through the ultra-smart suburb of **Las Lomas**.

The **telephone area code** for México is ☎5.

The **Avenida de los Insurgentes** crosses Reforma about halfway between the Alameda and the park. Said to be the longest continuous city street in the world, Insurgentes bisects México more or less from north to south. It is perhaps the city's most important artery, lined with modern commercial development. In the south it runs past the suburb of **San Ángel** and close by **Coyoacán** to the **University City**, and on out of México by the **Pyramid of Cuicuilco**. Also in the southern extremities of the city are the **Floating Gardens of Xochimilco** – virtually the last remains of the great lagoons. In the outskirts Insurgentes meets another important through-route, the **Calzada de Tlalpan**, which heads back to the Zócalo, passing the Rivera Museum and the other side of Coyoacán. To the north, Insurgentes leaves the centre past the train station, and close by the northbound bus station, to sweep out of the city via **Guadalupe** and **Indios Verdes**. The northern extension of Reforma, too, ends up at the great shrine of Guadalupe, as does the continuation of the Calzada de Tlalpan beyond the Zócalo.

One further point to remember is that many **street names** are repeated over and over again in different parts of the city – there must be hundreds of streets called Morelos, Juárez or Hidalgo, and a good score of 5 de Mayos. If you're taking a cab, or looking at a map, you should always be clear which area you mean – it's fairly obvious in the centre, but searching out an address in the suburbs can lead to a series of false starts unless you know the name of the official **colonia**, or urban district (abbreviated "Col" in addresses outside the centre), that you're looking for.

Arrival

Arriving unprepared in the vastness of México can be a disconcerting experience, but in fact it's not hard to get into the centre, or to a hotel, from any of the major points of arrival. The only problem is likely to be hauling large items of luggage through the invariable crowds – you should take a taxi if you are at all heavily laden.

By bus

There are four chief **long-distance bus stations** in México, one for each point of the compass, though in practice the northbound terminal handles far more than its share, while the westbound one is tiny. All have **guarderías**, and **hotel reservation desks** for both the capital and the major destinations served.

Terminal del Norte
With all the direct routes to and from the US border, and services to every major city **north** of México (including the fastest services from and to Guadalajara and Morelia),

CHECKLIST OF DESTINATIONS FROM MÉXICO'S BUS TERMINALS

TERMINAL DEL NORTE	San Miguel de Allende	Tuxpan
Aguascalientes	Teotihuacán	Tuxtla Gutiérrez
Chihuahua	Tepic	Veracruz
Ciudad Juárez	Tijuana	Villahermosa
Ciudad Obregón	Torreon	Zempoala
Colima	Tula	
Dolores Hidalgo	Uruapa	
Durango	Zacatecas	*SUR*
Guadalajara		Acapulco
Guanajuato		Chilpancingo
Guaymas	*TAPO*	Cuautla
Hermosillo	Amecameca	Cuernavaca
León	Cancún	Iguala
Los Mochis	Campeche	Ixtapa
Manzanillo	Chetumal	Oaxtepec
Matamoros	Cordoba	Puebla
Matahuela	Cozumel	Puerta Vallarta
Mazatlán	Fortín de las Flores	Taxco
Mexicali	Ixtaccíhuatl	Tepoztlán
Monterrey	Jalapa	Zihuatanejo
Morelia	Mérida	
Pachuca	Oaxaca	*PONIENTE*
Patzcuar	Orizaba	Guadalajara
Puerto Vallarta	Palenque	Morelia
Querétaro	Popocatepétl	Pátzcuaro
Saltillo	Puebla	Querétaro
San Luis Potosí	San Cristóbal de las Casas	Toluca
	Tehuacan	Uruapán

the **Terminal del Norte**, Av de los Cien Metros 4907, is by far the largest of the city's four stations. There's a **Metro** station (Terminal de Autobuses del Norte; line 5), and city buses head south from here on Insurgentes, about four blocks away – anything that says "Metro Insurgentes" will take you down Insurgentes, past the train station, across Reforma, and on to the edge of the *Zona Rosa*.

In the vast lobby, government-run booths sell **tickets for colectivos**. It's the same procedure in all the bus stations – there's a large map of the city marked out in zones, with a standard, set fare for each; you pick where you're going (almost certainly "Centro") and buy a ticket, then walk outside and you'll be hustled into a cab going your way. Once it's full you leave and supposedly get dropped at any address you choose within the stated zone. There are just two problems: first, the driver may drop you a block or two from your hotel rather than take a major detour through the one-way systems (best to accept this unless it's very late at night), and second, he may demand a large tip, which you're in no way obliged to pay.

TAPO
Eastbound services use the most modern of the termini, the **Terminal de Autobuses de Pasajeros de Oriente**, always known as **TAPO**. Buses for Puebla, for Veracruz, and for places that you might think of as south – Oaxaca, Chiapas and the Yucatán, even Guatemala – leave from here. It's located on Av Ignacio Zaragoza, out towards the airport; there's a **Metro** station inside the same modern complex (San Lazaro; line 1), and regular buses and colectivos ply Zaragoza towards the Zócalo and the Alameda.

Central de Autobuses del Sur

Buses **to the Pacific Coast** – Cuernavaca, Taxco, Acapulco and Zihuatanejo in particular – leave from the **Central de Autobuses del Sur**, Av Tasqueña 1320. It's at the end of Metro line 2 (Tasqueña), which is also a big terminus for local buses from the centre. If you arrive here by Metro, ignore the signs that point to the "Central de Autobuses", which lead to the city bus stands; the long-distance terminal is immediately obvious when you go out to the front of the Metro station.

Terminal Poniente

Finally, for the **west**, there's the **Terminal Poniente**, at the junction of Calles Sur and Tacubaya. The smallest of the termini, it basically handles traffic to Toluca, but it's also the place to go for the slower, more scenic routes to Morelia, Guadalajara and other destinations in Jalisco and Michoacán, via Toluca. Reached by Metro line 1 to Observatorio, there are also buses heading south on Reforma (Metro Observatorio) or from the stands by the entrance to Chapultepec Park.

By air

The **airport** is some way from the centre but is still very much within the city limits – you get amazing views as you come in to land, low over the buildings. There are **tourist information** and hotel reservation desks here, and several **banks**, which change money 24 hours a day. As you emerge from Customs and Immigration, or off an internal flight, you'll be besieged by offers of a taxi into town. Ignore them; by the main exit doors you'll find a booth selling tickets for the SETTA airport transit, a system of **official taxis**, with a scale of fares posted according to where you want to go. You simply buy a ticket, then take it outside and present it to the driver of one of the waiting white-and-yellow taxis. The system has been set up to avoid rip-offs, and you won't do any better. If you go with an unofficial driver – as often as not it turns out to be a private car – you're very unlikely to pay less, whatever extravagant claims they may make, and there's always the remote possibility that you could find yourself relieved of your money and luggage and dumped by the roadside somewhere. If you're travelling extremely light you could also go in on the Metro (Terminal Aerea; line 5, up to the left from the main terminal building) or walk out to the main road and catch a bus.

By train

All mainline **trains** arrive at the **Estación Central de Buenavista**, just off Av Insurgentes Nte, about nine blocks from its junction with Reforma. Until the completion of Metro line B, which will reach Buenavista, there's no Metro station particularly near, but you'll find a large taxi rank right outside, and buses and taxis heading south on Insurgentes towards Reforma and the *Zona Rosa*, or west on Mosqueta towards the Zócalo. Many of the cheaper hotels are within easy walking distance.

City transport

You'll want to **walk** around the cramped streets of the centre. Heading for Chapultepec, though, or the *Zona Rosa*, you're better off taking the **bus** or **Metro** – it's an interesting walk all the way down Reforma, but a very long one. And for the outer suburbs you've clearly got no choice but to rely on taxis or public transport. You'll save a lot of hassle if you avoid travelling during **rush hour** (about 7–9am & 5–7pm).

Tours that take in the city and often include the surrounding area are available from most of the more expensive hotels, and from specialist operators such as Grey Line,

Londres 166 (☎208-11-63); Maxi Tours, Amberes 69 (☎525-68-12); and American Express, with various locations around the city (☎326-28-77).

Driving

If you have a car, it's best to choose a hotel with secure parking and leave it there for the duration of your stay, except possibly to do a tour of the south of the city. Driving in the city is a **nightmare**, compounded by confusing one-way and through-route systems, by the impossibility of finding anywhere to park and by traffic police who can spot foreign plates a mile off and know a potential "fine" when they see one. What is more, as an anti-pollution measure all cars are banned from driving between 5am and 10pm on one weekday depending on the last digit of their **number plate**: you cannot drive on Monday if your plate ends with 5 or 6, Tuesday 7 or 8, Wednesday 3 or 4, Thursday 1 or 2, or Friday 9 or 0; between 10pm and 5am and at weekends, no ban applies. If you do insist on driving, note that the "Green Angels" that operate throughout the rest of the country (see p.35) do not operate within México: for **breakdown help** call the AAM (equivalent of the AA or the AAA) on ☎578-75-31.

The Metro

México's **Metro** (enquiries ☎709-11-33) has a **flat fare** of roughly US$0.20. The last train leaves from each end of the line at midnight (1am Sat night), with the first train at 5am Mon–Fri, 6am Sat, and 7am Sun. Tickets are sold individually or, slightly cheaper, in blocks of 25; buying several at a time saves a lot of queueing and messing about with tiny quantities of change every time you get on.

It's a superb modern system, French-built, fast, silent and expanding all the time, but there are problems. Worst of these are the crowds – unbelievable during rush hours, when the busiest stations in the centre designate separate entries for women and children only, patrolled by armed guards to protect them from the crush. At such times it can also get unbearably hot, and don't even think of trying to carry anything larger than a briefcase. In theory you're never allowed **luggage** of any size on the Metro, but in practice you can if you board at a quiet station at a quiet time.

Once you've got into the system, there are no maps, just pictographic representations of the line you are on. So before you set off you need to work out which way you'll be travelling on each line, and where to change: direction is indicated by the last station at either end of the line (thus on line 2 you'll want either "Direccion Cuatro Caminos" or "Direccion Tasqueña"); interchanges are indicated by the word *Correspondencia* and the name of the new line. You may be able to pick up a complete map of the system from the ticket office; more often than not they've run out, but there's one on p.276.

City buses

At one time **buses** in México were beaten-up old bone-shakers trailing plumes of black smoke behind them, but nowadays they have smartened up their act and are generally comfortable and also very efficient, if you know where you're going. There's a **flat fare** of roughly US$0.20 per journey, as for the Metro.

The two most **useful routes** are #55 along Reforma, and #17 along Insurgentes from Indios Verdes in the north, past the Terminal del Norte, the train station, Metro Insurgentes and eventually on to San Ángel and the university in the south. Colectivos and other buses cover large sections of these routes. There are also **trolleybuses** running in both directions along Lázaro Cárdenas (the "Eje Central"). Like colectivos, buses display their destinations in the front window, which is somewhat more helpful than looking for route numbers, since the latter are usually not posted up.

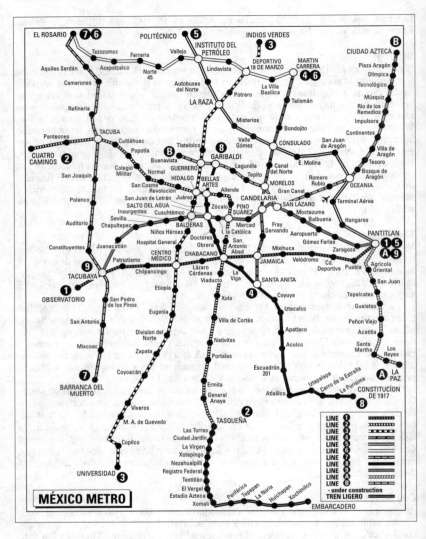

MÉXICO METRO

The area just by **Chapultepec Metro station** and the entrance to the park is also a major downtown bus terminus, from where you can get to almost any part of the city. Note that during **rush hour** it can be almost impossible to get a bus: once they're full, they simply don't stop to let passengers on.

Colectivos and taxis

Running down the major through-routes, especially on Reforma and Insurgentes, you'll find **peseros** (colectivos), which are faster but charge more than the bus (far less than a regular taxi, however) and will let you on and off anywhere along their set route. They're mostly VW vans or large American saloons, usually pale green with a white roof, and have their destination displayed on the windscreen – the driver may sometimes hold up a number of fingers to indicate how many free seats he has. Like buses, peseros have route numbers, but routes often have branches, and a vehicle may start or finish in the middle of a route rather than at the end, so again it's more helpful to check the destination in the window. One of the most **useful routes** is #2, which runs Monday to Friday from Chapultepec Park via the Alameda to the Zócalo.

Ordinary **taxis** come in a variety of forms. Cheapest and best are the green-and-white (indicating use of unleaded gasoline) or yellow-and-white cabs, often Beetles, that cruise the streets looking for custom. These should have a meter (make sure it's switched on) and are extremely good value compared to anywhere in Europe or North America – the smaller taxis seem to charge less and can negotiate the traffic much more easily. Be warned that they can't always adjust taxi meters fast enough to keep up with inflation – if the fare at the end of your journey isn't what's shown on the meter, there should be a conversion chart handy. The orange cabs that wait at *sitios* (taxi ranks) charge slightly more, but in general work the same way. Watch out, though, for *turismo* taxis, with their notorious hooded meters; they lie in wait outside hotels and charge rates at least treble those of ordinary taxis. In the normal course of events you should avoid them, but they do have a couple of advantages, namely that they're almost always around and that many of the drivers speak some English. They can be worth it if, for example, you need to get to the airport in a hurry (for which they charge no more than a SETTA cab would) or if you want to go on a tour for a few hours. In the latter case, with some ferocious haggling, you might even get a bargain. If you need to **phone a taxi**, try Servitaxis (☎516-60-20), Taximex (☎519-76-90), or Transportación Terrestre al Aeropuerto (☎571-49-13). Again, it's virtually impossible to get a taxi in the rush hour.

Information

You can pick up information in the booths at the airport and the bus stations; in town there's a **tourist office** at Amberes 54 in the *Zona Rosa* (daily 9am–9pm; ☎525-93-80). The SECTUR office at Presidente Mazaryk 172, Colonia Polanco (Mon–Fri 8am–8pm, Sat 10am–3pm; in México ☎250-0123, elsewhere in the country call at local rates on ☎91-800/90-392, from the US or Canada ☎1-800/482-9832), is perfectly helpful but a long way from the centre. There is also an information booth on Genova between Londres and Hamburgo in the *Zona Rosa*.

Useful local **guides**, city **maps** (the best produced by Guia Roji), English-language magazines and pulp paperbacks are sold at Sanborn's and in many big hotels. Free publications, such as *The Gazer* and *Concierge*, listing restaurants, bars and nightclubs, are available at larger hotels and some restaurants. See also under "Listings" on p.319.

Banks throughout the city are open normal hours, and there are 24-hour branches at the airport. Many will only change money in the morning, however. Best bet for currencies other than US dollars are branches of **Banamex**. Most large hotels and shops will change travellers' cheques and cash dollars, but the quickest and easiest places to change money are **casas de cambio**: you'll find several in the *Zona Rosa*, especially on Ambares and Londres, and a couple on Reforma by the *Hotel Crowne Plaza*, just south of the Monumento a la Revolución; also downtown, at Madero 3 and 27, La Palma 40, 16 de Septiembre and Bolivar, and Juárez 34; and at the Terminal de Autobuses del Norte. They don't all give the same rate (so shop around if changing a large amount), and many of them only change US dollars. Most will take travellers' cheques, but often for substantially less than cash – even more than with cash, it's worth shopping around if these are what you're carrying.

The main **post office** is at the corner of Lázaro Cárdenas and Tacuba, behind Bellas Artes (Mon–Sat 8am–9pm, Sun 8am–7pm). Local, domestic long-distance and international **phone calls** can be made from any public phone with a phonecard. Otherwise, a number of shops have public phones (for **international services** look for the blue Larga Distancia signs). You can dial direct from most big hotels, but it will cost much more. Useful **casetas de larga distancia** include: Madero 53 in the city centre (Mon–Fri 8am–8pm, Sat 8am–7pm); Izazaga 10, near the Salto de Agua Metro (Mon–Fri 10am–8pm); Terminal del Norte (the one at the southern end of the terminal is open 24hr); TAPO at Local #20 in the tunnel to the Metro (daily 7am–11pm); Terminal del Poniente (one open 24hr); and two at the airport (daily 7am–11pm).

Opening hours for most businesses in México are from 10am until 7pm. Some, but increasingly few, close for a siesta from around 2pm to 4pm.

Accommodation

On any street, in any unlikely corner of the city, there seems to be at least one of the **thousands of hotels** in México. The vast majority of tourists stay in the expensive modern places of the *Zona Rosa*, or in the even more costly, still flashier hotels overlooking Chapultepec Park.

The avenues around the **Zócalo** are awash with accommodation. Avenida 5 de Mayo is as good a place as any to begin, with a dozen or so fairly good options in close proximity. The hotels in this area are generally older and more established than elsewhere; high ceilings, internal courtyards and some rather dark rooms are common. Most are comfortable, and considering the location – right in the heart of things near many of the sights – excellent value. The area's main drawback is its distance from any good nightlife. Though not the place to head on a tight budget, if you look hard enough you can find luxury accommodation at moderate prices in the **Zona Rosa**, where you'll be spoilt for choice for cafés, posh restaurants, bars and clubs. Between the *Zona Rosa* and the Alameda, in the area centring on the **Revolución monument**, most hotels, like the area itself, are rather humdrum – though you'll find some luxury places at lower rates than in the rest of the city. Those along **Reforma** are expensive.

There's another group of hotels **north of the Alameda**, very convenient if you're arriving or leaving the city by train, but this is a rather less attractive area to stay on the whole, and can be a little intimidating at night. The hotels around **the Alameda** itself are very good value, though the further south you go, the less salubrious the area becomes (and the cheaper the hotels).

Around the Zócalo

Azores, Brasil 25 (☎521-52-20 or 521-52-22, fax 512-00-70). Clean, comfy rooms with TV and bathroom. ③.

Buenos Aires, Motolinia 21 (☎518-21-37). A friendly place, with rooms arranged around a central patio. Be warned that the cantina next door is overpriced. ③.

Catedral, Donceles 95 (☎518-52-32; fax 512-43-44). All rooms with TV, FM stereo and telephone, and some with jacuzzi. Also a good restaurant, and a terrace overlooking the cathedral. Very popular. ⑤.

Concordia, Rep de Uruguay 13 (☎510-41-00). Quite a walk from the Zócalo, so it should have vacancies at busy times. Rooms with bath, TV and phone. ③.

Congreso, Allende 18 (☎510-44-46). Near the Museo Nacional de Arte. All rooms are en-suite and have TV. Secure parking. ③.

Gillow, Isabel La Católica 17 (☎518-14-40 to 46, fax 512-20-78). Highly recommended luxury hotel with large rooms, in-house travel agency, and a great restaurant. ⑤.

Gran Hotel Ciudad de México, 16 de Septiembre 82 (☎510-40-40 to 47, fax 512-67-72). An attraction in itself, this hotel on the Zócalo has infinitely more style than the skyscrapers of the *Zona Rosa*. Even if not staying, wander into the lobby and look at its opulent interior complete with Tiffany stained-glass dome, wrought-iron lift-cages and exotic stuffed birds. Rooms are drab by comparison, though the modernized suites are better. ⑧.

Isabel, Isabel La Católica 63 (☎518-12-13, fax 521-12-33). Good-value hotel with services, such as taxis and laundry, normally offered at much larger hotels. Restaurant and cantina. ③.

Juárez, 1ª Cerrada de 5 de Mayo 17 (☎512-69-29). Good-value, quiet hotel in a side street away from the bustle. Comfortable rooms with TV and bathroom. ③.

Lafayette, Motolinia 40 (☎521-96-40). Popular, very comfortable place; all rooms with TV and bathroom. Laundry service available. ③.

Majestic, Madero 73 (☎521-86-00, fax 512-62-62). Luxury hotel on the Zócalo. Try the restaurant on the seventh floor for fantastic breakfasts, or just a coffee to admire the view. It has more character (and is quite a bit cheaper and more conveniently located) than the plush *Zona Rosa* establishments. ⑧.

Marina, Allende 30 (☎518-24-45 to 48). On the same street, and very similar to the Congreso above. ⑧.

Montecarlo, Uruguay 69 (☎521-25-59, fax 510-00-81). Originally an Augustinian monastery, and later lived in briefly by D.H. Lawrence. Quiet, comfortable and with a beautiful inner courtyard. ③.

París, Rep del Salvador 91 (☎709-50-00). A massive place, friendly and cheap but with rooms arranged prison-style on concentric landings. All have phones, some TV; not all have windows. ②.

Rioja, 5 de Mayo 45 (☎521-83-33). A bit ramshackle with rather dingy rooms, but cheap, safe and central. ②.

San Antonio, 2° Callejón de 5 de Mayo 29 (☎512-99-06). Quiet, friendly place hidden away in a side street between 5 de Mayo and La Palma. ③.

Washington, 5 de Mayo 54 (☎512-35-02). Clean hotel with cable TV and a shrine in the lobby. Recommended. ③.

Zamora, 5 de Mayo 50 (☎512-82-45). Friendly hotel just two blocks from the Zócalo; low-priced and very popular so you may have to book ahead at busy times. ②.

The Zona Rosa

Casa Gonzalez, Rio Sena 69 (☎ & fax 514-33-02). Good, friendly, comfortable and clean lodgings, with home-cooked food. It's usually full, so book in advance. ⑤.

Century, Liverpool 152 (☎726-99-11, fax 525-74-75). Five-star hotel with all the mod cons you would expect. Rooms go for about US$140. ⑨.

El Ejecutivo, Viena 8 (☎566-64-22, fax 705-54-76). Friendly hotel with reasonable prices. ⑥.

Hotel del Principado, Londres 42 (☎ & fax 533-29-44 to 48). Comfortable hotel, all rooms with TV and phone. Laundry service and parking available. ⑤.

Marco Polo, Amberes 27 (☎511-18-39, fax 533-37-27). Beautiful and stylish, this small luxury hotel caters for an artistic Mexican clientele. Standard double rooms around US$160, plus some stunning penthouse suites, should you fancy a honeymoon or something. ⑨.

Royal, Amberes 78 (☎228-99-18, fax 514-33-30). Friendly, modern hotel with excellent Spanish restaurant. Rooms around US$130. ⑨.

Segovia Regency, Chapultepec 328 (☎511-30-41, fax 525-03-91). Reliable place, often fully booked with regulars, so it's best to reserve ahead, especially during the week. ⑥.

Vasco de Quiroga, Londres 15 (☎566-19-70, fax 535-60-20). Small, intimate hotel with piano-bar and travel agency. ⑥.

From the Alameda north to Buenavista Station

Buenavista, Bernal Díaz 34 (☎535-57-04). Bottom-of-the-barrel option. Watch your luggage and bring earplugs. ①.

Hotel de Cortés, Hidalgo 85 (☎518-21-84, fax 512-18-63). Just north of the Alameda, the present building dates from the 1780s, although originally it was a sixteenth-century Augustinian way-house. The cool, central patio houses a restaurant and a coffee house seemingly a million miles from the bustle of the Alameda. Facilities are generally very good, although perhaps a little over-priced. ⑧.

Londres, Plaza Buenavista 5 (☎705-09-10, fax 566-20-26). Beautifully decorated interior and a warm family atmosphere. On a quiet square, and with a good restaurant, it's the very best in the area for the price. TV in each room. ⑦.

Managua, Plaza de San Fernando 11 (☎512-13-12, fax 521-30-62). Clean, quiet place, in a restful location facing the Jardín de San Fernando, just north of the Alameda. ③.

Marconi, Héroes 8 (☎521-28-33). Clean rooms, though small and a bit dark, but good. ②.

Polly, Orozco y Berra 25 (☎512-88-81) All rooms with bathroom and TV. ②.

South of the Alameda

Bamer, Juárez 52 (☎521-90-60, fax 510-17-93). Faded grandeur, but big, comfortable old rooms and great position overlooking the Alameda. ⑥.

Monte Real, Revillagigedo 23 (☎518-11-49 to 56, fax 512-64-19). Quiet family hotel with comfortable rooms, though the muzak in the lobby and corridors is a bit irritating. ⑥.

Panuco, Ayuntamiento 148 (☎521-29-16, fax 510-88-31). Good-value hotel, if in uninspiring surroundings. ③.

San Francisco, Luis Moya 11 (☎521-89-60, fax 510-88-31). Airy rooms with pleasant, Art-Decoish decor and friendly staff. ⑥.

Around the Revolución monument

Casa de los Amigos, Ignacio Mariscal 132 (☎705-05-21, fax 705-07-71). Clean and comfortable Quaker-run hostel in a huge house built for José Clemente Orozco, very popular with travellers. Comfortable rooms, or dorms (US$6.25 per person), with communal kitchen and good-value breakfasts. Minimum stay of two nights, maximum two weeks. House regulations include a no-alcohol rule. ③.

De Gante, Sullivan 9 (☎592-21-21, fax 592-27-62). Just on the edge of the *Zona Rosa*. Pleasant airy rooms, though with slightly gaudy decor. Services include a solarium. ⑤.

Fontán, Colón 27 and Reforma (☎518-54-60, fax 521-92-40). Close to the Alameda, with reasonable luxury at a moderate price. ⑧.

Mayaland, Antonio Caso 23 (☎566-60-66, fax 535-12-73). Squat, ugly building with very pleasant rooms. Bar, restaurant and travel agency. ④.

Royalty, Jesus Terán 21 (☎566-92-55). Very reasonable rates, but rather dark rooms. ②.

Further out

Hotel Brasilia, Av de los Cien Metros 4823 (☎587-85-77, fax 368-27-14). If you arrive by bus at the Terminal del Norte and are concerned only with getting some sleep in silence, head for this good-value hotel, about 100m south of the terminus (to your left as you exit). All rooms have TV, tiled bathrooms, and there's even a decent restaurant. ④.

San Lorenzo, Lorenzo Boturini 176 (☎588-45-40). Slightly dingy but the best of a small group of really cheap hotels near San Antonio Abad Metro station, a couple of stops south of the Zócalo; this one located 200m north of the station. ②.

Central México

Quite apart from the extraordinary **Aztec remains** in México – chief of which is the **Templo Mayor** on the Zócalo – there's a wealth of great colonial buildings, among them the **Cathedral** and **National Palace** around the Zócalo and **Maximilian's castle** in Chapultepec. There are also superb museums – the **Museo de Antropología** ranks with the world's best, Diego Rivera's **Museo Anahuacalli** with its most bizarre – and art not only in the galleries but in **murals** adorning public buildings everywhere, particularly the startling **University City**. As a backdrop to all México's quite remarkable sightseeing is a diverse, dynamic **street life** unequalled in Latin America.

The Zócalo and around

The vast paved open space of the **Zócalo** – properly known as the Plaza de la Constitución and said to be the second-largest such city square in the world after Moscow's Red Square – is the city's political and religious centre. It – and by extension every other town square in Mexico – gets its name from a monument to Independence that was planned for the centre of the square by General Santa Ana. Like most of his other plans this went astray, and only the statue's base was ever erected: *el Zócalo* literally means the plinth. Here stand the great **Cathedral**, the **Palacio Nacional** with the offices of the President, and the city administration – all of them magnificent colonial buildings. But the area also reflects other periods of the country's history. This was the heart of **Aztec Tenochtitlán**, too, and in the recently excavated **Templo Mayor** you can see remarkable remains from the magnificent temples on this site. It is a place constantly animated, and for most of the year spectacularly illuminated at night. Among the more certain entertainments is the ceremonious lowering of the national flag from its giant pole in the centre of the plaza each evening at sundown. A troop of presidential guards march out from the palace, strike the enormous flag and perform a complex routine at the end of which the flag is left, neatly folded, in the hands of one of their number. You get a great view of this, and of everything else happening in the Zócalo, from the rooftop bar in the *Hotel Majestic* at the corner of Madero.

The Zócalo, does of course, have its seamier side. México's economic plight is most tellingly reflected in the lines of unemployed who queue up around the cathedral looking for work, each holding a little sign with his trade – plumber, electrician or mechanic – and a box with a few scavenged tools.

The Cathedral

It's the **Cathedral** (Mon–Sat 11am–5pm, except during services; free), flanked by the parish church of El Sagrario, which first draws the eye, with its heavy, grey Baroque facade and squat, bell-topped towers. Like so many of the city's older, weightier structures, the cathedral has settled over the years into the soft wet ground beneath – the tilt is quite plain, despite extensive work to stabilize the building in recent years. The first church on this site was constructed only a couple of years after the Conquest, using stones torn from the Temple of Huitzilopochtli, but the present structure was begun in 1573 to provide México with a cathedral more suited to its wealth and status. The towers weren't completed until 1813, though, and the building incorporates a plethora of architectural styles throughout. Even the frontage demonstrates this: relatively austere at the bottom, where work began in the years soon after the Conquest, flowering into full Baroque as you look up, and topped by Neoclassical cornices and clock tower. Inside, it was seriously damaged by fire in 1967, and the earthquake in 1985, and is still under repair – the chief impression, when the scaffolding is removed, is of a vast and rather gloomy space. By contrast, **El Sagrario** seems on the surface much richer, with its liberal use of gold paint and exuberant churrigueresque carving.

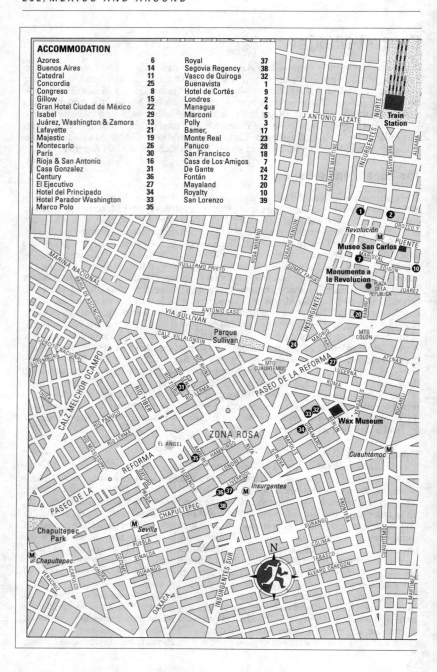

ACCOMMODATION

Azores	6	Royal	37
Buenos Aires	14	Segovia Regency	38
Catedral	11	Vasco de Quiroga	32
Concordia	25	Buenavista	1
Congreso	8	Hotel de Cortés	9
Gillow	15	Londres	2
Gran Hotel Ciudad de México	22	Managua	4
Isabel	29	Marconi	5
Juárez, Washington & Zamora	13	Polly	3
Lafayette	21	Bamer,	17
Majestic	19	Monte Real	23
Montecarlo	26	Panuco	28
París	30	San Francisco	18
Rioja & San Antonio	16	Casa de Los Amigos	7
Casa Gonzalez	31	De Gante	24
Century	36	Fontán	12
El Ejecutivo	27	Mayaland	20
Hotel del Principado	34	Royalty	10
Hotel Parador Washington	33	San Lorenzo	39
Marco Polo	35		

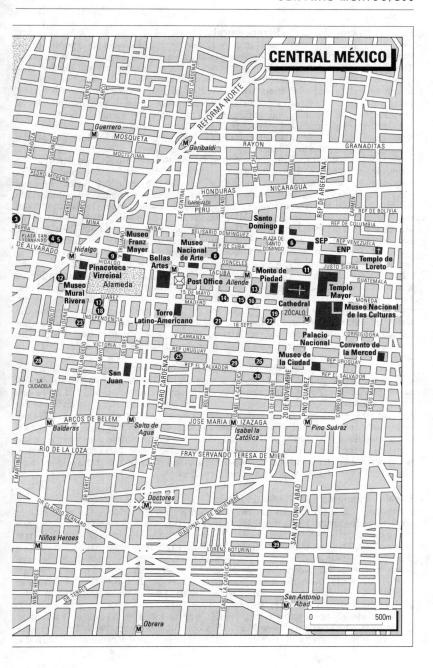

Palacio Nacional and the Rivera murals

The other dominant structure on the Zócalo is the **Palacio Nacional** (daily
9am–5.30pm; free but bring ID), its facade taking up a full side – more than 200 metres.
The so-called New Palace of Moctezuma stood here, and Cortés made it his first residence too, but the present building, for all its apparent unity, is the result of centuries
of agglomeration and rebuilding. Most recently – in 1927 – a third storey was added.
From 1562 the building was the official residence of the Spanish Viceroy, and later of
presidents of the Republic, and it still contains the office of the President, who makes
his most important pronouncements from the balcony – especially on September 15,
when the *Grito de Dolores* signals the start of Independence celebrations around the
country. Benito Juárez lived here until his death in 1872.

The overriding attraction is the series of **Diego Rivera murals** that decorate the
stairwell and middle storey of the main courtyard (there are fourteen courts in all).
Begun in 1929, these are classic Rivera: they rank with the best of his works. The great
panorama of Mexican history around the **main staircase** combines an unbelievable
wealth of detail with savage imagery and a masterly use of space. On the right-hand
wall Quetzalcoatl sits in majesty amid the golden age of the Valley of Mexico, with an
idealized vision of life in Teotihuacán, Tula and Tenochtitlán around him. The main section depicts the Conquest, oppression, war, inquisition, invasion, Independence and
eventually Revolution. Almost every major personage and event of Mexican history is
here, from the grotesquely twisted features of the Conquistadors, to the heroes: bald-
ing white-haired Hidalgo with the banner of Independence; squat, dark Benito Juárez
with his Constitution and laws for the reform of the Church; Zapata, with a placard proclaiming his cry of "Tierra y Libertad"; Pancho Villa, moustachioed and swaggering.
On the left is post-revolutionary Mexico and the future, with Karl Marx pointing the
way to adoring workers, and businessmen clustered over their tickertape: a somewhat
ironic depiction of the metropolis with its skyscrapers and grim industrial wastes. The
surrealist artist Frida Kahlo, Rivera's wife, is depicted, too, behind her sister Cristina in
a red blouse with an open book.

A series of smaller panels was intended to go all the way round the upper (now middle) storey, a project that was probably always over-optimistic. Those that were completed reach halfway round and mostly depict the idyll of various aspects of life before
the Conquest – market day, hunting scenes and so on. The last show the arrival of the
Spanish. The uncoloured first panel lists the products that the world owes to Mexico,
including maize, beans (frijoles), chocolate, tobacco, cotton, tomatoes, peanuts, prickly
pears and chicle (the source of chewing gum). Also on the middle storey is the chamber used by the Mexican Legislature from 1845 to 1872, when it was destroyed by fire.
It was restored in 1972 and you can pop in for a look at it, as well as at the original copy
of the 1857 Constitution, which was drawn up there.

The Ayuntamiento and Monte de Piedad

Continuing round the Zócalo clockwise from the Palacio Nacional, the third side is
taken up by the city and Federal District administration, the **Ayuntamiento**, while shel-
tering under the arcades of the fourth is a series of shops, almost all of which sell hats
or jewellery. This practice of giving over a whole street to one particular trade is one
that you'll still find to some extent throughout the city: even very near here there are
places where you can buy nothing but stationery, other blocks packed exclusively with
shoe shops. It's probably the most concrete hangover of Aztec life – their well-regulat-
ed markets were divided up according to the nature of the goods on sale, and the practice was continued by colonial planners.

For strange shopping experiences, though, you can't beat the **Monte de Piedad**, at
the corner of the Zócalo with 5 de Mayo. This huge building, supposedly the site of the
palace in which Cortés and his followers stayed as guests of Moctezuma, is now the

National Pawn Shop. The most unbelievable variety of stuff put up for hock is displayed here – a better selection than you'd find in the average mail order catalogue and including office machinery, beds, jewellery, artworks, dentists' chairs – anything, in fact, that will go through the doors. From time to time they hold major auctions to clear the place out, but it's worth coming here just to take in the atmosphere and watch the milling crowds.

The Templo Mayor

Just off the Zócalo, down beside the cathedral, lies the entrance to the site where the **Templo Mayor** (Tues–Sun 9am–5pm; US$2, free on Sun) has been excavated. What you see are the bare ruins of the foundations of the great temple and one or two buildings immediately around it, all highly confusing since, as was normal practice, a new temple was built over the old at the end of every 52-year calendar cycle (and apparently even more frequently here) so that there were a whole series of temples stacked inside each other like Russian dolls. Arm yourself with a cutaway diagram (free from the ticket office) or look at the models and maps in the museum first (see below) and it all makes more sense.

Although it's been known since the beginning of this century that Tenochtitlán's ceremonial area lay under this part of the city, it was generally believed that the chief temple, or Teocalli, lay directly beneath the cathedral. Archeological work only began in earnest in 1978 after workmen uncovered a vast stone disc weighing about eight tons and depicting **Coyolxauhqui**, goddess of the moon. Logic demanded that this must lie at the foot of the temple of Huitzilopochtli, and so the colonial buildings were cleared away and excavation began. Coyolxauhqui was the daughter of Coatlicue, the mother goddess who controlled life and death; on discovering that her mother was miraculously pregnant, Coyolxauhqui vowed to wipe out the dishonour by killing her. Huitzilopochtli, however, sprung fully armed from the womb (like Athena in Greek mythology), decapitated and dismembered his sister and threw her body down a mountain. He then proceeded to drive off the four hundred other brothers who had gathered to help her: they scattered to become the stars. Coyolxauhqui is thus always portrayed with her head and limbs cut off, and was found here at the foot of the Temple of Huitzilopochtli symbolizing her fall from the mountain. The human sacrifices carried out in the temple were in part a re-enactment of this – the victims being thrown down the steps afterwards – and in part meant to feed Huitzilopochtli with the blood he needed as sun god to win his nightly battle against darkness. The Great Temple was also dedicated to Tlaloc, the infinitely more peaceful god of rain, and at its summit were two separate sanctuaries, reached by a monumental double stairway.

Of the seven reconstructions of the temple, layers as far down as the second have been uncovered: of this you see only the top – the bottom is now well below the water table. Confusing as it is trying to work out what's what, it's a fascinating site, scattered with odd sculptures, including some great serpents, and traces of its original bright paintwork. Seeing it here, at the heart of the modern city, brings the ceremonies and sacrifices that took place all too close to home. The **museum**, entered through the site on the same ticket, helps set it all in context, with some welcome reconstructions and models of how Tenochtitlán would have looked at its height. There are some wonderful pieces retrieved from the site, especially the wall of skulls as you enter, the eagle in Room 1 with a cavity in its back for the hearts of sacrificial victims, and of course the huge **Coyolxauhqui stone**, displayed so as to be visible from points throughout the museum. The design is meant to simulate the temple, so you climb through it to reach two rooms at the top, one devoted to Huitzilopochtli, the other to Tlaloc. The only problem is that the whole place is extremely dimly lit; so much so that many of the labels (which are in Spanish only) are illegible. Nonetheless you shouldn't miss it – the best items are towards the top, including some superb stone masks such as the one from Teotihuacán, black with inset eyes and a huge earring, typical of the objects paid in tribute by subject peoples from all over the country. On the highest level are two magnificent, full-size terracotta eagle warriors and numerous large stone pieces from the site. The descent back to ground level concentrates on everyday life in Aztec times – with some rather mangy stuffed animals to demonstrate the species known to the Mexica – along with a jumble of later items found while the site was being excavated.

Calle Moneda

Behind the Palacio Nacional, at C Moneda 13, is the **Museo Nacional de las Culturas** (Tues–Sun 9.30am–6pm; free), a collection devoted to the archeology and anthropology of other countries. The museum occupies the sixteenth-century Casa de la Moneda, originally the official mint and now immaculately restored, with rooms of exhibits set around a quiet patio. It's more interesting than you might imagine: reflecting Mexico's historical alignment it has a substantial Eastern European section. **Calle Moneda** itself is one of the oldest streets in the city, and it's fascinating to wander up here and see the rapid change as you leave the immediate environs of the Zócalo. The buildings remain almost wholly colonial, but from the prim refurbishment of the museum they gradually become shabbier and shabbier, interspersed with buildings abandoned after earthquake or subsidence damage, blending within four or five blocks into a very depressed residential area. Here you'll find street stalls spreading up from the giant market of La Merced, to the south.

Just a block beyond the museum, the orange dome of the church of **Santa Inés** stands out a mile off. This, though, is its most striking feature, and there's little else to admire apart from the delicately carved wooden doors. Opposite, its entrance in C Academia, is the **Academia de San Carlos**. This still operates as an art school, though on a very reduced scale from its nineteenth-century heyday: inside are galleries for temporary exhibitions and, in the patio, copies of classical sculptures. Above them invariably twitter scores of birds, trapped inside the glassed-over courtyard. Further up Moneda, which by this time has changed its name to Emiliano Zapata, the **Templo de la Santísima** boasts one of the city's finest Baroque facades.

North of the Zócalo

Calle Seminario (which later becomes Argentina) leads past the Templo Mayor to the Ministry of Education, or **SEP** (Mon–Fri 9am–6pm, Sat 9am–4pm; free), where Rivera painted his first **murals** on returning from Paris. The inspiration behind them was **José Vasconcelos**, revolutionary Minister of Public Education but better known as a poet and philosopher, who promoted educational art as a means of instilling a sense of history and cultural pride in a widely illiterate population. As such, he is the man most directly responsible for the murals in public buildings throughout the country. Here, three floors of an enormous double patio are entirely covered with frescoes, as are many of the stairwells and almost any other flat surface. Rivera's work is very simple compared with what he later achieved, but the style is already recognizable: panels crowded with figures, drawing inspiration mainly from rural Mexico, though also from an idealized view of science and industry. The most famous panel on the ground floor is the relatively apolitical *Día de los Muertos*, which is rather hidden away in a dark corner at the back, but there are equally striking images on the far wall (*Quema de las Judas* and *La Asamblea*, for example) and the lovely *El Canal de Santa Anita* opposite. On the first floor the work is very plain, mostly in tones of grey – here you'll find the shields of the states of Mexico and such general educational themes as *Chemistry* or *Physics*, mostly the work of Rivera's assistants. On the second floor are heroes and heroic themes from the Revolution. At the back, clockwise from the left-hand side, the triumphant progress of the Revolution is traced, culminating in the happy scenes of a Mexico ruled by its workers and peasants.

More **murals**, for which Vasconcelos was also responsible, adorn the eighteenth-century **Colegio de San Idelfonso** (also called the "Escuela Nacional Preparatoria", or "ENP"; Tues–Sun 11am–5.30pm; US$2.50), nearby at San Idelfonso 33, with an imposing facade that fills almost a whole block. Many artists are represented, including Rivera and Siqueiros, but the most famous works here are those of **José Clemente Orozco**, which you'll find on the main staircase and around the first floor of the main patio. As everywhere, Orozco, for all his enthusiasm for the Revolution, is less sanguine about its prospects, and modern Mexico is caricatured almost as savagely as the pre-revolutionary nation.

Continue to the west (the street changes its name from San Idelfonso to República de Cuba), and you reach the little colonial plaza of **Santo Domingo**. There's a fountain playing in the middle and eighteenth-century mansions lining the sides, with the fine Baroque church of Santo Domingo on the site of the country's first Dominican monastery. Under the arcades you'll find clerks sitting at little desks with portable typewriters, carrying on the ancient tradition of public scribes. It's a sight you'll find somewhere in most large Mexican cities – their main function is to translate simple messages into the flowery, sycophantic language essential for any business letter in Spanish, but they'll type anything from student theses to love letters. Alongside them are street printers, who'll churn out business cards or invitations on the spot, on anti-quated hand presses.

On the east side of the plaza, on Av Brasil, the **Museo de la Medicina** (daily 10am–6pm; free) was once the headquarters of the Inquisition in New Spain, and you can explore the cells and dungeons where heretics were punished. Although the cruelty of the Inquisition is often exaggerated, their facilities appear gruesome indeed. The museum itself has interesting displays on indigenous medicine, religion and herbalism as well as the progress of western medicine from colonial times to the present. A "wax room" shows full-colour casts of various skin diseases, injuries and infections.

Avenida Brasil leads from here back to the Zócalo, or if you retrace your steps past the ENP you'll arrive at the **Plaza de Loreto**. This, too, is a truly elegant old square, crowded with pigeons, but unlike Santo Domingo it's entirely unmodernized. On one side the **Templo de Loreto** with its huge dome leans at a crazy angle: inside, where some restoration work is going on, you'll find yourself staggering across the tilted floor. **Santa Teresa**, across the plaza, has a bizarre cave-like chapel at the back, entirely artificial. Behind the Templo Loreto is a large and rather tame covered market, the **Mercado Presidente Rodriguez**, inside which are a series of large murals dating from the 1930s by an assortment of artists including Antonio Pujol and Pablo O'Higgins.

Nearby, the **Museo de la Caricatura**, Donceles 99 (Tues–Sun 10am–6pm; US$0.65), exhibits a limited selection of work from Mexico's most famous caricaturists. The most bizarre are nineteenth-century prints of skeletal *mariachis* by José Guadalupe Posada, a great influence on the later **Muralist Movement**. The museum coffee house is a pleasant place to break your journey, its walls decorated with cartoons. From here you can either turn left and go back to Av Brasil or right to Av Argentina and back to the Zócalo.

South of the Zócalo

Leaving the Zócalo to the south, Pino Suárez heads off from the corner between the Palacio Nacional and the Ayuntamiento towards the Museo de la Ciudad. First though, right on the corner of the square, is the colonial-style modern building housing the **Suprema Corte de Justicia** (Mon–Fri 9am–5.30pm; free but must show ID). Inside are three superb, bitter murals by Orozco – *Proletarian Battles*, *The National Wealth* and *Justice*. The last, depicting justice slumped asleep on her pedestal while bandits rob the people of their rights, was not surprisingly unpopular with the judges and powers that be, and Orozco never completed his commission here.

The **Museo de la Ciudad de México** (Tues–Sun 10am–6pm; free but bring ID) is a couple of blocks further down, housed in the colonial palace of the Condes de Santiago de Calimaya. This is a fabulous building, with carved stone cannons thrusting out from the cornice, magnificent heavy wooden doors and, on the far side, a hefty plumed serpent obviously dragged from the ruins of some Aztec temple to be employed as a cornerstone. The contents of the museum trace the history and development of the city from prehistoric to modern times, through everything from fossil remains to photographs of Villa and Zapata entering in triumph to architectural blueprints for the future. Perhaps most interesting, though, are the models of Tenochtitlán at its peak, and the old maps and paintings that show the city and the lake as they once were, with the gradual spread of development and disappearance of the water. There are also plans superimposing the map of ancient Tenochtitlán onto the modern streets – giving some idea of its location and extent. On the top storey is preserved the studio of the landscape artist Joaquin Clausell, its walls plastered in portraits and little sketches that he scribbled between working on his paintings. The museum also presents a multimedia show (in Spanish) describing the city's evolution – supposedly daily at 11am, but only if there are enough customers (usually the case at weekends).

More or less opposite is a small open space and an entrance to **Pino Suárez Metro station**, where an Aztec shrine uncovered during construction has been preserved as an integral part of the concourse. Dating from around the end of the fourteenth century, it was dedicated to Quetzalcoatl in his guise of Ehecatl, god of the wind. From here a **subterranean walkway** lined with bookstores runs back to the Zócalo Metro station.

Before this, though, you should cross the road from the museum for a look at the church and hospital of **Jesus Nazareno**. The **hospital**, still in use, was founded by Cortés himself in 1528 on the site where, according to tradition, he first met Moctezuma. As such it's one of the oldest buildings in the city, and exemplifies the severe, fortress-like construction of the immediate post-Conquest years. The **church**, which contains the remains of Cortés, hidden away in an insignificant looking tomb, has been substantially remodelled over the years. Its vaulting was decorated by Orozco with a fresco of the Apocalypse – it's currently under restoration, but you can still have a look at it.

Heading east from here along Salvador or Uruguay takes you to the giant **market** area of La Merced, passing, on Uruguay, the beautiful cloister that is all that remains of the seventeenth-century **Convento de la Merced**. Westwards you can stroll down some fairly tatty old streets heading towards the *Zona Rosa*, passing several smaller markets. It's much more interesting, however, to return to the Zócalo and strike down towards the Alameda from there.

A worthwhile detour at this point would be a visit to the **Museo de la Indumentaria Mexicana**, José Maria Izázaga 108 (though closed for refurbishment at the time of writing), displaying indigenous costumes from all over Mexico. Across the road, in a handsome colonial building, the **Museo de la Federación de Charros** (Mon–Fri 10am–6pm; free), at Izázaga 77, by Isabel la Catolica Metro station, is dedicated to all things cowboy, with lots of boots, hats, spurs and saddles, wagons and paintings on the same theme.

West to the Alameda

The streets that lead down from the Zócalo towards the Alameda – Tacuba, 5 de Mayo, Madero, 16 de Septiembre and the lanes that cross them – are the most elegant in the city: least affected by any modern developments and lined with ancient buildings and traditional cafés and shops, and with mansions converted to offices, banks or restaurants. Few of these merit any particular special attention, but it's a pleasant place simply to stroll around.

Along Madero

On **Madero** you'll pass several former aristocratic palaces given over to a variety of uses. At no. 27 on the corner of Bolivar stands the mansion built in 1775 by mining magnate José de la Borda (see p.339) for his wife, with a magnificent balcony. Just south at Bolivar 31, the **Spanish-Mexican Club** is a fine example of how the wealthy used to amuse themselves, and how some apparently still do. If you can talk your way in, the interior is superb. Fitted out with Moorish-style dining rooms, vast ballrooms, enormous chandeliers and endless works of art, it's hard to believe it was only built at the beginning of this century – witness the sort of extremes that led to the downfall of the Díaz regime. Still further down Madero, you'll find the **Palacio de Iturbide**, now occupied by Banamex, thoroughly restored – the banks seem able to afford the best restoration work. Originally the home of the Condes de Valparaiso in the eighteenth century, it was from 1821 to 1823 the residence of the ill-fated "emperor" Augustín de Iturbide. Nowadays it houses free art exhibitions laid on by the bank.

In the next block, the last before you emerge at Bellas Artes and the Alameda, the churrigueresque church of **San Francisco** stands on the site of the first Franciscan mission to Mexico. Fragments of the original large complex can be seen behind it. Opposite is the renowned **Casa de los Azulejos** – now a branch of Sanborn's – its exterior swathed entirely in blue and white tiles from Puebla. The building survived a gas explosion in 1994, which did quite a bit of structural damage; luckily no one was hurt, and one of the most famous parts of the building, the giant Orozco mural on the staircase, suffered few ill effects. Inside you'll find a restaurant in the glassed-over patio, as well as all the usual shopping.

At the end of Madero, you're at the extent of the colonial city centre, and standing between two of the most striking buildings in modern México: the Torre Latino-Americano and the Palacio de las Bellas Artes. Both, though it seems incredible to draw any comparison, are products of this century.

The Torre Latino-Americano

The steel-and-glass skyscraper of the **Torre Latino-Americano** was until recently the tallest building in Mexico and, indeed, the whole of Latin America. It's now been outdone by the *Hotel de Mexico* (on Insurgentes Sur) and doubtless by others in South America, but it remains the city's outstanding landmark and a point of reference no matter where you are. In the unlikely event of a clear day, the views from the top are outstanding; if it's averagely murky you're better off going up after dark when the lights delineate the city far more clearly. There's a charge to go up to the top two floors (daily 9.30am–11pm; US$3), where there's a caged-in observation deck, a café, permanent crowds and, for some bizarre reason, an aquarium – or you can go up to the *Muralto* restaurant and bar on the 41st floor for nothing. If you're really mean you could do this, catch the view, study the menu and decide not to eat after all, but if you have a drink you'll be able to sit in luxury and take it all in at your leisure for little more than it costs to get to the *mirador*. On the ride up, plans explain how the tower is built, proudly boasting that it is the tallest building in the world to have withstood a major earthquake (which it did in 1985, though others may now rival the claim). The general principle appears to be similar to that of an angler's float, with enormously heavy foundations bobbing around in the mushy soil under the capital, keeping the whole thing upright.

Bellas Artes

The tower is certainly a more successful engineering achievement than the **Palacio de las Bellas Artes** (Tues–Sun 10am–6pm; US$2 , free on Sun), which has very obviously subsided. On the other hand, Bellas Artes is extremely beautiful, which you certainly couldn't say of the Tower. It was designed in 1901, at the height of the Díaz dictatorship, by the Italian architect Adamo Boari and constructed, in a grandiose Art-Nouveau style, of white marble imported from Italy. Building wasn't actually completed, however, until 1934, with the Revolution and several new planners come and gone. Now it's the headquarters of the National Institute of Fine Arts; venue for all the most important performances of classical music, opera or dance; home of the **Ballet Folklórico**; and a major art museum. It's worth getting to a performance in the theatre (preferably by the Ballet Folklórico – see "Entertainment and nightlife" on p.316) if only to see the amazing Tiffany glass curtain depicting the Valley of México and the volcanoes. The whole interior, in fact, is magnificent – an Art-Deco extravaganza incorporating spectacular lighting and stylized masks of the rain god, Chac.

The **art collections** are on the upper floors. In the galleries you'll find a series of exhibitions, permanent displays of Mexican art and temporary shows of anything from local art-school graduates' work to that of major international names. Of constant and abiding interest, however, are the great **murals** surrounding the central space. On the first floor are *Birth of Our Nationality* and *Mexico Today* – dreamy, almost abstract works by **Rufino Tamayo**. Going up a level you're confronted by the unique sight of murals by **Rivera, Orozco** and **Siqueiros** gathered in the same place. Rivera's *Man in Control of the Universe* (or *Man at the Crossroads*), celebrating the liberating power of technology, was originally painted for the Rockefeller Center in New York, but destroyed for being too leftist – this is Rivera's own copy. It's worth studying the explanatory panels on either side, which reveal some of the theory behind this complex work. Several smaller panels by Rivera are also displayed; these, too, were intended to be seen elsewhere (in this case on the walls of the *Hotel Reforma*, downtown) but for years were covered up, presumably because of their unflattering depiction of tourists. Themes include *Mexican Folklore and Tourism, Dictatorship*, the *Dance of the Huichilobos* and, perhaps the best of them, *Agustín Lorenzo*, a portrayal of a guerrilla fighter against the French. You get the impression, though, that none of these were designed to be seen so close up. *Catharsis*, a huge, vicious work by Orozco, occupies almost an entire wall, and there are also some particularly fine examples of Siqueiros's work: three powerful and original panels on the theme of *Democracy* and a bloody depiction of *The Torture of Cuauhtémoc* and his resurrection.

The Correo Central and Palacio de Minería

Around the back of Bellas Artes, at the corner of Tacuba and Lázaro Cárdenas, you'll find the **Correo Central**, the city's main post office. Completed in 1908, this too was designed by Adamo Boari, but in a style much more consistent with the buildings around it. Look closely and you'll find a wealth of intricate detail, while inside it's full of richly carved wood. On the first floor is a small museum of old documents and objects relating to the postal service, though the only item of interest to most is a giant picture made of postage stamps. Directly behind the Correo on Tacuba is the **Palacio de Minería**, a Neoclassical building completed right at the end of the eighteenth century, which makes an interesting contrast with the Post Office and with the Museo Nacional de Arte (formerly the Palacio de Comunicaciones) directly opposite, the work of another Italian architect, Silvio Contri, in the first years of this century. Behind the mining school on Filomeno Mata is the small **Convento de las Betlemitas**, a seventeenth-century convent that now houses an army museum (Tues–Sat 10am–6pm, Sun 10am–4pm; free), with a small exhibition of antique arms, and explanations mostly in Spanish – strictly for weaponry enthusiasts.

The Museo Nacional de Arte

The **Museo Nacional de Arte**, Tacuba 8 (Tues–Sun 10am–5.30pm; US$2, free on Sun), is set back from the street on a tiny plaza in which stands one of the city's most famous sculptures, **El Caballito**, portraying Carlos IV of Spain. This enormous bronze, the work of Manuel Tolsa, was originally erected in the Zócalo in 1803. In the intervening years it has graced a variety of sites and, despite the unpopularity of the Spanish monarchy (and of the effete Carlos IV in particular), is still regarded affectionately. The latest setting is appropriate, since Tolsa also designed the Palacio de Minería (see above). As for the museum itself, which occupies the second and third floors, it's something of a disappointment. The interest is mainly historical, for although there are more than a thousand works covering Mexican art from pre-Hispanic times to the present, they are on the whole mediocre examples, spiced only occasionally with a more striking work. Come here to see something of the dress and landscape of old Mexico, and also some of the curiosities. The prodigious painting of the *Family Tree of San Basilio*, for example, is wonderful – incorporating parents, grandparents and great-grandparents, along with a good scattering of uncles, aunts, sisters and brothers, each of whom were saints in their own right. The naive *Esta es la Vida* is also a typically Mexican painting; as depicted here, life consists almost exclusively of drunkenness and death.

The Alameda

From behind Bellas Artes, Lázaro Cárdenas runs north towards the **Plaza Garibaldi** (see "Entertainment and nightlife" on p.315) through an area crowded with seedy cantinas and eating places, theatres and burlesque shows. West of the Palacio de Bellas Artes, Av Hidalgo takes you to the **Alameda**. First laid out as a park at the end of the sixteenth century, and taking its name from the *alamos* (poplars) then planted, the Alameda had originally been an Aztec market and later became the site where the Inquisition burned its victims at the stake. Most of what you see now – formally laid-out paths and flowerbeds, ornamental statuary and fountains – recalls the last century, when it was the fashionable place to stroll. It's still popular, always full of people, the haunt of ice-cream and sweet vendors, illuminated at night, and particularly crowded at weekends, but it's mostly a transient population – office workers taking lunch, shoppers resting their feet, messengers taking a short cut. The Alameda was one of the areas worst hit by the 1985 earthquake, and a number of buildings are still shored up and under repair, while others (on the south side) have been cleared but not yet replaced.

The Museo Franz Mayer and Museo de la Estampa

On the north side of the Alameda, Hidalgo traces the line of an ancient thoroughfare. Some of the old buildings on its north side, including the churches of **Santa Veracruz** and **San Juan de Dios**, were severely damaged in the earthquake and have been refurbished as museums. The **Museo Franz Mayer** here (Tues–Sun 10am–5pm; US$1.50, US$1 on Tues, free on Sun) is dedicated to the applied arts, and occupies the sixteenth-century hospital attached to San Juan de Dios. It's packed with the personal collection of Franz Mayer, a keen horder of Mexican arts and crafts who settled here from Germany: colonial furniture, textiles and carpets, watches, Spanish silverwork, religious art and artefacts, a valuable collection of sculpture and paintings, and some fine colonial pottery from Puebla. There is also much furniture and pottery from Asia, reflecting Mexico's position on the trade routes, as well as a library with rare antique editions of Spanish and Mexican authors and a reference section on applied arts. Even if this doesn't sound like your thing, it's well worth seeing: it's a lovely building, beautifully furnished, and offering a tranquil escape from the crowds outside. The coffee bar, too, is a delight, facing a courtyard filled with flowers and a fountain – there's a charge of US$0.50 for those not visiting the museum.

The **Museo de la Estampa**, virtually next door in the former church of Santa Veracruz (Tues–Sun 10am–6pm; US$1.25, free on Sun), has engravings and printing plates from pre-Columbian times to the modern age, specializing in the nineteenth century. It's an art form that is taken seriously in Mexico, where the legacy of José Guadalupe Posada (see p.233) is still revered; his works are predictably the highlight.

Museo de Artes y Industrias Populares

On Juárez, across from the park's semicircular monument to Benito Juárez, is the **Museo de Artes y Industrias Populares** (Mon–Sat 10am–6pm; free), housed in the chapel of the former convent of Santa Clara. It has displays of craftworks, native art and traditional techniques, some ancient, most contemporary, much of which is also on sale. West along Juárez, on the opposite side of the road just beyond the park, is a small **crafts shop** run by FONART, the government agency that promotes quality arts and crafts and helps the artisans with marketing and materials.

The Museo Mural Rivera and Pinacoteca Virreinal

One of the buildings worst hit by the earthquake was the *Hotel del Prado*, whose Rivera mural *Dream of a Sunday Afternoon in the Alameda* was one of the area's chief attractions. The mural survived and can now be seen in the **Museo Mural Diego Rivera** (Tues–Sun 10am–6pm; US$1.25; son et lumière Tues–Fri 11am & 4pm, Sat & Sun 11am, 1pm, 4pm & 5pm), at the western end of the Alameda, at the corner of Balderas and Colón. It's an impressive work – comprising almost every famous Mexican character from Cortés, his hands stained red with blood, to Rivera himself, portrayed as a child between his mother and daughter, out for a stroll in the park – but one suspects that its popularity with tour groups is as much to do with its relatively apolitical nature as for any superiority to Rivera's other works. A table explains every character in the scene (look out also for José Guadalupe Posada, appearing as one of his trademark skeletons), and there are also displays on the history of the mural – the original included a placard with the words "God does not exist", which caused a huge furore and Rivera was eventually forced to paint it out before the mural was displayed to the public – and on the move, which involved picking up the entire wall and transporting it around the Alameda.

Almost next door to the museum, you'll find the **Pinacoteca Virreinal**, at Dr Mora 7 (Tues–Sun 9am–5pm; US$1.25, free on Sun), a collection of colonial painting (*Virrey* being the Spanish for Viceroy) in the glorious seventeenth-century monastery of San Diego. The galleries are mostly filled with florid religious works of the seventeenth and eighteenth centuries, but some are exquisitely executed while others are fascinating for their depiction of early missionary work, and all are superbly displayed around the church, chapel and cloister of the old monastery. There are occasional concerts here in the evening – mostly chamber music or piano recitals.

Around the Monumento a la Revolución

Beyond the Alameda, avenidas Juárez and Hidalgo lead towards the Paseo de la Reforma. Across Reforma, Hidalgo becomes the **Puente de Alvarado**, following one of the main causeways that led into Tenochtitlán. This was the route by which the Spanish attempted to flee the city on the *Noche Triste* (Sad Night), July 10, 1520. Following the death of Moctezuma, and with his men virtually under siege in their quarters, Cortés decided to escape the city under cover of darkness. It was a disaster: the Aztecs cut the bridges and, attacking the bogged-down invaders from their canoes, killed all but 440 of the 1300 Spanish soldiers who set out, and more than half their native allies. Greed, as much as anything, cost the Spanish troops their lives, for in trying to take their gold booty with them they were, in the words of Bernal Díaz, "so weighed down by the stuff that they could neither run nor swim". The street takes its name from Pedro de Alvarado, one of the last Conquistadors to escape, crossing the broken bridge "in great peril after their horses had been killed, treading on the dead men, horses and boxes". Recently a hefty gold bar – exactly like those made by Cortés from melted-down Aztec treasures – was dug up here.

Puente de Alvarado: San Fernando and the Museo San Carlos

The church of **San Hipolito**, at the corner of Reforma and Puente de Alvarado, was founded by the Spanish soon after their eventual victory, both as a celebration and to commemorate the events of the *Noche Triste*. The present building dates from 1602, though over the years it's been damaged by earthquakes and rebuilt, and it now lists to one side. West along Puente de Alvarado is the Baroque, eighteenth-century church of **San Fernando**, by the plaza of the same name. Once one of the richest churches in the city, San Fernando has been stripped over the years like so many others. Evidence of its former glory survives, however, in the highly decorative facade and in the *panteon*, or graveyard, crowded with the tombstones of nineteenth-century high society.

Continuing along Puente de Alvarado you'll find the **Museo de San Carlos** (daily except Tues 10am–6pm; US$1.25, free on Sun), at no. 50 on the left-hand side, which houses the country's oldest art collection, begun in 1785 by Carlos III of Spain, and comprising largely European works of the seventeenth and eighteenth centuries. Travelling exhibitions are also frequently based here. The building itself is a very beautiful Neoclassical design of Manuel Tolsa's, with something of a bizarre history. Its inhabitants have included the French Marshal Bazaine, sent by Napoleon III to advise the Emperor Maximilian – who presented the house to him as a wedding present on his marriage to a Mexican woman – and the hapless Mexican general and sometime dictator Santa Ana. Later it served for a time as a cigarette factory.

Along Juárez to the monument

Leaving the Alameda on Juárez, you can see the massive, ugly bulk of the **Monumento a la Revolución** ahead of you. The first couple of blocks, though, are dull, commercial streets, heavy with banks, offices, travel agents, expensive shops. The junction with

Reforma is a major crossing of the ways, and is surrounded by modern skyscrapers and one older one – the marvellous Art Deco **National Lottery building**. In here, you can watch the winning tickets being drawn each week, although the Lottery offices themselves have been moved to an ordinary-looking steel-and-glass building opposite. Beyond Reforma, Juárez continues in one long block to the **Plaza de la República** and the vast monument. Originally intended to be a new home for the *Cortes* (or parliament) its construction was interrupted by the Revolution and never resumed – in the end they buried a few heroes of the Revolution under the mighty columns (including presidents Madero and Carranza) and turned the whole thing into a memorial. More recently the **Museo Nacional de la Revolución** (Tues–Sat 9am–5pm, Sun 9am–3pm; US$0.65, free on Wed) was installed beneath the monument, with a history of the Revolution told through archive pictures, old newspapers, films and life-size tableaux. Among the offices and large hotels around the plaza you'll find the **Frontón México**, where frontón matches are held most evenings (see "Sport" on p.318).

Paseo de la Reforma and the Zona Rosa

The **Paseo de la Reforma** is the most impressive street in México. Laid out by Emperor Maximilian to provide the city with a boulevard to rival the great European capitals – and doubling as a ceremonial drive from his palace in Chapultepec to the centre – it also provided a new impetus, and direction, for the growing metropolis. The original length of the broad avenue ran simply from the park to the junction of Juárez, and although it has been extended in both directions, this stretch is still what everyone thinks of as Reforma. "Reforma Norte", as the extension towards Guadalupe is known, is almost a term of disparagement – and while the street is just as wide (and the traffic just as dense), you won't find people strolling here for pleasure. Real Reforma, though, remains *the* smart thoroughfare – ten lanes of traffic, lines of trees, imposing statues at every intersection. There are perhaps three or four of the original French-style, nineteenth-century houses surviving along its entire extent. Elsewhere, even relatively new blocks are constantly torn down to make way for yet newer, taller, more prestigious towers of steel and glass.

It's a long walk – some 5km – from the Zócalo to the gates of Chapultepec, made more tiring by the altitude and the constant crush, noise and fumes of the traffic. You'd be well advised to take the bus – they're frequent enough to hop on and off at will. The *glorietas*, roundabouts at the major intersections, each with a distinctive statue, provide easy landmarks along the way. First is the **Glorieta Colón**, with a statue of Christopher Columbus. Around the base of the plinth are carved various friars and monks who assisted Columbus in his enterprise or brought the Catholic faith to the Mexicans. The Plaza de la República is just off to the north. Next comes the crossing of Insurgentes, nodal point of all the city's traffic, with **Cuauhtémoc**, last emperor of the Aztecs and leader of their resistance, poised aloof above it all in a plumed robe, clutching his spear, surrounded by warriors. Bas-relief engravings on the pedestal depict his torture and execution at the hands of the Spanish, desperate to discover where the Aztec treasures lay hidden. **El Ángel**, a golden winged victory atop a column nearly 50m high, is the third to look out for – the place to get off the bus for the heart of the *Zona Rosa*.

Zona Rosa

Parallel to Reforma to the south lies the **Zona Rosa** – an area bordered by Reforma and Av Chapultepec, the park to the west and spilling across Insurgentes in the east. You'll know you're there by the street names, famous cities all: Hamburgo, Londres, Genova, Liverpool. Packed into a tiny area here are hundreds of bars, restaurants, hotels and above all shops, teeming with the city's wealthy and would-be elegant, and vast numbers of tourists. You'll also find the highest concentration of beggars and rip-offs anywhere in the city – there are official multilingual policemen wandering around specifically to help tourists (they wear little flag emblems to denote which languages they speak), but there are also impressively uniformed unofficial guides whose only task is to persuade you to go to whichever shop or market employs them. You should come and look – for the constant activity, **street entertainers**, especially around the corner of Hamburgo and Florencia, and incredible diversity of shops and places to eat and drink – but remember that everything is very expensive. It's also worth noting that this is no longer where the very best hotels and classiest shops are located. They've generally moved out to **Colonia Polanco**, on the northern edge of Chapultepec.

On the fringes of the *Zona*, at Londres 6, there's the **Museo de Cera**, or Wax Museum (Mon–Fri 11am–7pm, Sat & Sun 10am–7pm; US$3), thoroughly and typically tacky, with a basement chamber of horrors that includes Aztec human sacrifices. Also here is the **Museo de lo Increíble** (same hours and prices; joint ticket for the two museums US$4.50), which displays such marvels as flea costumes and hair sculpture.

On the other side of Reforma, where the streets are named after rivers (Tiber, Danubio and the like) is a much quieter, posh residential area, where many of the older embassies are based. You can spot the US embassy (which is actually on Reforma) by the vast queues snaking around it throughout the day. Near the British embassy is the **Museo Venustiano Carranza**, Rio Lerma 35 (Tues–Sat 9am–7pm, Sun 11am–3pm; US$1). Housed in the mansion that was the México home of the revolutionary leader and president who was shot in 1920, it contains exhibits relating to his life and to the Revolution. Not far away, just north of the junction of Reforma and Insurgentes, the **Parque Sullivan** hosts open-air exhibitions and sales of paintings, ceramics and other works of art every Sunday: some of them are very good, and a pleasant holiday atmosphere prevails.

Chapultepec and the Museo Nacional de Antropología

Chapultepec Park, or the Bosque de Chapultepec, is a vast green area, some 1000 acres in all, dotted with trees, scattered with fine museums – among them the marvellous **Museo de Antropología** – boating lakes, gardens, playing fields and a zoo. Ultimately, it provides an escape from the pressures of the city for seemingly millions of Mexicans: on Sundays, when at least a brief visit is all but compulsory and many of the museums are free, you can barely move for the throng. They call it, too, the lungs of the city, and like the lungs of most of the inhabitants, its health leaves a lot to be desired. Large areas, towards the back where it's less frequented, have been fenced off to give them a chance to recover from the pounding they take from the crowds. There has even been talk of sealing the whole place off for three years to give the grass a chance to grow back and allow the plants to recover their equilibrium. Whatever the hopes or fears of the authorities, though, this is never likely to happen – public outrage at the very suggestion has seen to that. Meanwhile it still manages to look pretty good and remains one of Mexico's most enduring attractions.

Chapultepec Hill

The rocky outcrop of **Chapultepec** (the Hill of the Locust), which lends its name to the entire area, is mentioned in Toltec mythology, but first gained historical significance in the thirteenth century when it was no more than another island among the lakes and salt marshes of the valley. Here the Mexica, still a wandering, savage tribe, made their first home – a very temporary one before they were defeated and driven off by neighbouring cities, provoked beyond endurance. And here they returned once Tenochtitlán's power was established, channelling water from the springs into the city, and turning Chapultepec into a summer resort for the emperor, with plentiful hunting and fishing around a fortified palace. Several Aztec rulers had their portraits carved

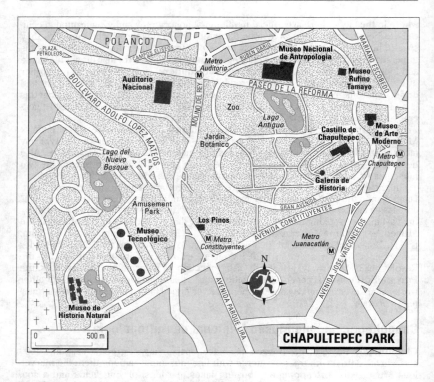

into the rock of the hill, though most were destroyed by the Spanish soon after the Conquest.

The hill, crowned by Maximilian's very peaceful looking "castle", confronts you as soon as you enter. In front of it stands the strange, six-columned monument dedicated to the **Niños Héroes**, commemorating the cadets who attempted to defend the castle (then a military academy) against American invaders in 1847. According to the story, probably apocryphal, the last six flung themselves off the cliff wrapped in Mexican flags rather than surrender. The **Castillo** itself was built only in 1785 as a summer retreat for the Spanish viceroy – until then it had been the site of a hermitage established on the departure of the Aztec rulers. Its role as a military school followed Independence, but the present shape was dictated by Maximilian who remodelled it in the image of his Italian villa. Today it houses the National History Museum.

First, though, as you climb the hill, you pass the modern **Gallery of History** (daily 9am–5.30pm; US$1.75, free on Sun) devoted to "the Mexican people's struggle for Liberty". It's known in full as the "Museo Galeria de la Lucha del Pueblo Mexicano por su Libertad", or colloquially as the "Museo del Caracol" for the snail-like spiral through which you follow the displays. These, with the use of models, maps and dioramas, trace the history of the constant wars that have beset the country – from Independence, through the American and French interventions to the Revolution. There are also murals by Siqueiros and Juan O'Gorman.

Spread over two floors of the castle, the **Museo Nacional de Historia** (Tues–Sun 9am–5pm; US$1.75, free on Sun) is a more traditional collection. The setting is very much part of the attraction, with many rooms retaining the opulent furnishings left behind by Maximilian and Carlota, or by later inhabitants with equally expensive tastes – notably Porfirio Díaz. Rivalling the decor is a small collection of carriages, including the fabulously pompous state coaches favoured by Maximilian. The bulk of the exhibits downstairs, though, follow a straight historical progression, starting with a small collection of pre-Hispanic objects and reproductions of Aztec codices, moving through weapons and paintings of the Conquest and on to documents, pictures, memorabilia and patriotic relics from every era of Mexican development. There are several murals here as well, including a number of works by Orozco and Siqueiros, but the ones by **Juan O'Gorman** most directly attract attention for their single-minded political message. Upstairs is a more miscellaneous collection of objets d'art, jewellery, period costume, furniture, clocks and a host of other bric-a-brac. There should really be wonderful views from here, across the city to Popocatépetl and Ixtaccíhuatl, but of course there never are.

Museo Nacional de Antropología

The park's outstanding attraction – for many people the main justification for visiting the city at all – is the **Museo Nacional de Antropología** (Tues–Sat 9am–7pm, Sun 10am–6pm; US$2, free on Sun; ☎553-62-66), beyond doubt one of the world's great museums, not only for its collection, which is vast, rich and diverse, but for the origi-

---

FINDING YOUR WAY AROUND THE ANTHROPOLOGY MUSEUM

The museum merits more than a single visit, though if you're rushed you can follow the logical progression round from one room to the next, with each gallery devoted to a separate period or culture. All open separately onto the central space, however, so if you've the luxury of time it's easy enough, and far more satisfactory, to pick one or two rooms to take in on each of several separate visits.

As you come into the **entrance hall** there's a shop selling postcards, souvenirs, books in several languages on Mexican culture, archeology and history, and detailed guides to the museum, which provide full descriptions of most of the important pieces. Straight ahead is a small circular space with temporary exhibitions, usually devoted to the latest developments in archeology and often very interesting. More of these lie to the right, beyond Rufino Tamayo's mural of a battling jaguar and serpent, where you'll also find the library and museum offices as well as the small **Sala de Orientación**, which presents an audiovisual overview of the major ancient cultures. The ticket office, and the entrance to the museum proper, is by the huge glass doors to the right. You can buy tickets here, too, for the regular guided tours – free in Spanish, or for a fee in English, French or German. They're very rushed, but do get you round the whole thing with some form of explanation: labelling inside is rather hit-and-miss, and often in Spanish only. Instead of a real guide, you can also rent a taped commentary to carry around with you.

The full **tour of the museum** starts on the right-hand side with three **introductory rooms** explaining what anthropology is, the nature of and relationship between the chief Mesoamerican cultures, and the region's pre-history. Skip or skim them if you're in a hurry. They're followed on the right-hand side by halls devoted to the **pre-Classic**, **Teotihuacán** and **Toltec** cultures. At the far end is the vast **Mexica** (Aztec) room, followed around the left wing by **Oaxaca** (Mixtec and Zapotec), **Gulf of Mexico** (Olmec), **Maya** and the cultures of the north and west. Every hall has at least one outstanding feature, but if you have limited time, the Aztec and the Maya rooms are the **highlights**: what else you see should depend on what area of the country you plan to head on to. The first floor is given over to the **ethnography collections** devoted to the life and culture of the various indigenous groups today: stairs lead up from each side. Downstairs, behind the hall devoted to the cultures of the north and west, is a very welcome restaurant.

nality and practicality of its design. Opened in 1964, the exhibition halls surround a patio with a small pond and a vast square concrete umbrella supported by a single slender pillar around which splashes an artificial cascade. The halls are ringed by gardens, many of which contain outdoor exhibits.

The museum is located about half a mile into the park beside the Paseo de la Reforma; you can take the **bus** virtually to the entrance, or walk easily from Chapultepec Metro station or any of the other museums at this end of the park. The entrance from Reforma is marked by a colossal statue of the rain god Tlaloc – the story goes that its move here from its original home in the east of the city was accompanied by furious downpours in the midst of a drought.

PRE-CLASSIC

The **Pre-Classic** room covers the development of the first cultures in the Valley of México and surrounding highlands – pottery and clay figurines from these early agricultural communities predominate. Notice especially the **small female figures** dated 1700–1300 BC from Tlatilco (a site in the suburbs), probably related to some form of fertility or harvest rites. Later the influence of the growing Olmec culture begins to be seen in art, including the amazing **acrobat**, also from Tlatilco. With the development of more formal religion, recognizable images of gods appear: several of these, from Cuicuilco in the south of the city, depict **Huehueteotl**, the old god or god of fire, as an old man with a brazier on his back.

TEOTIHUACÁN

The next hall is devoted to **Teotihuacán** (see p.321), the first great city in the Valley of México. Growing sophistication is immediately apparent in the more elaborate nature of the pottery vessels and the use of new materials, shells, stone and jewels. There's a full-scale reproduction of part of the **Temple of Quetzalcoatl** at Teotihuacán, brightly polychromed as it would originally have been, and copies of some of the frescoes that adorned the city, including *The Paradise of Tlaloc*, a depiction of the heaven reserved for warriors and ball-players who died in action. Many **new gods** appear, too – as well as more elaborate versions of Huehueteotl, there are representations of Tlaloc, of his companion Chalchiutlicue, goddess of rivers and lakes, of Mictlantecuhtli, god of death (a stone skull, originally inlaid with gems), and of Xipe Totec, a god of spring, clothed in the skin of a man flayed alive as a symbol of regeneration.

TOLTEC

The **Toltec** room actually begins with objects from Xochicalco, a city near modern Cuernavaca (see p.338), which flourished between the fall of Teotihuacán and the heyday of Tula. The large stone carvings and pottery show distinct Maya influence: particularly lovely is the stylized stone **head of a macaw**, similar to ones found on Maya ball-courts in Honduras. Highlights of the section devoted to Tula are the weighty stone carvings, including one of the Atlantean columns from the main temple there, representing a warrior. Also of note are the **Chac-mool**, a reclining figure with a receptacle on his stomach in which sacrificial offerings were placed, symbolizing the divine messenger who delivered them to the gods; the **standard bearer**, a small human figure that acted as a flag pole when a standard was inserted into the hole between its clasped hands; next to it the stone relief of a **dancing jaguar**; and the exquisite sculpture of a **coyote's head** with a bearded man emerging from its mouth – possibly a warrior in a headdress – inlaid with mother-of-pearl, and teeth made of bone.

MEXICA

Next comes the biggest and richest of them all, the **Mexica Gallery**, characterized above all by massive yet intricate stone sculpture, but also displaying pottery, small stone objects, even wooden musical instruments. Two of the finest pieces stand at the entrance: the **Ocelocuauhxicalli**, a jaguar with a hollow in its back in which the hearts of human sacrifices were placed (it may have been the companion of the eagle in the Templo Mayor museum; the two were found very close to each other, though over eighty years apart); and the **Teocalli de la Guerra Sagrada** (Temple of the Sacred War), a model of an Aztec pyramid decorated with many of the chief gods and with symbols relating to the calendar. There are hundreds of other powerful pieces – most of the vast Aztec pantheon is represented – and everywhere snakes, eagles, and human hearts and skulls are prominent. Among them is a vast statue of **Coatlicue**, goddess of the earth, life and death, and mother of the gods. She is shown beheaded, with two serpents above her shoulders representing the flow of blood; her necklace of hands and hearts and pendant of a skull represent life and death respectively; her dress is made of snakes; her feet are eagles' claws. As a counterpoint to the viciousness of most of this, be sure to notice **Xochipilli**, the god of love and flowers, dance and poetry. You'll come across him wearing a mask and sitting cross-legged on a throne strewn with flowers, to the left of the entrance as you come in. Also impressive is a reconstructed version of **Moctezuma's headdress**, resplendent in bright blue Quetzal feathers.

The undoubted highlight, though, is the enormous (24-tonne) **Piedra del Sol**, the Stone of the Sun or Aztec Calendar Stone. The latter, popular name is not strictly accurate, for this is much more a vision of the Aztec cosmos, completed under Moctezuma only a few years before the Spanish arrived. The stone was found by early colonists, and deliberately reburied for fear that it would spread unrest among the population. After being dug up again in the Zócalo in 1790 it spent years propped up against the walls of the cathedral. You'll pick up the most detailed description on a guided tour, but briefly: in the centre is the sun god and personification of the fifth sun, Tonatiuh, with a tongue in the form of a sacrificial knife and claws holding human hearts on each side, representing the need for human sacrifice to nourish the sun. Around him are symbols for the four previous incarnations of the sun – a jaguar, wind, water and fiery rain; this whole central conglomeration forming the sign for the date on which the fifth world would end (as indeed, with defeat by the Spanish, it fairly accurately did). Encircling all this are hieroglyphs representing the twenty days of the Aztec month and other symbols of cosmic importance, and the whole thing is surrounded by two serpents.

OAXACA

Moving round to the third side of the museum you reach the halls devoted to cultures based away from the highlands of the centre, starting, in the corner of the museum, with the **Zapotec** and **Mixtec** people of Oaxaca. Although the two cultures evolved side by side, the Zapotecs flourished earliest (from around 900 BC to 800 AD) as accomplished architects with an advanced scientific knowledge, and also as makers of magnificent pottery with a pronounced Olmec influence. From around 800 AD many of their sites were taken over by the Mixtecs whose overriding talents were as craftsmen and artists, working in metal, precious stone and clay. The great site for both is Monte Albán (see p.428).

Of the Zapotec collection notice above all the fine sense of movement in the human figures: the reproduction of part of the carved facade of the Temple of the Dancers at Monte Albán; a model of a temple with a parrot sitting in it (in the "Monte Albán II" case); vases and urns in the form of various gods; and the superb jade mask representing the bat god. Among the Mixtec objects are many beautifully polychromed clay vessels including a cup with a hummingbird perched on its rim, and sculptures in jade and quartz crystal. Reproductions of Zapotec and Mixtec tombs show how many of the finer small objects were discovered.

GULF OF MEXICO

Next is the **Gulf of Mexico** room, in which are displayed some of the treasures of **Olmec** art as well as objects produced in this region during the Classic period. The Olmec civilization is considered the mother culture of Mexico for its advanced development as early as 1500 BC, which provided much of the basis for later Teotihuacán and Maya cultures. Olmec figures are delightful, but have many puzzling aspects, in particular their strikingly African features, nowhere better displayed than in some of the famed **colossal heads** dating from 1200–200 BC, long before Africa is supposed to have had any connection with the Americas. Many of the smaller pieces show evidence of deliberate deformation of the skull and teeth. Outstanding are the statue known as "the wrestler" – arms akimbo as if on the point of starting a bout – and the many tiny objects in jade and other polished stones. The later cultures are substantially represented, with fine figures and excellent pottery above all. The two most celebrated pieces are a statue of **Huehueteotl**, looking thoroughly grouchy with a brazier perched on his head, and the so-called **Huastec Adolescent**, a young Huastec Indian priest of Quetzalcoatl (perhaps the god himself) with an elaborately decorated naked body and a child on his back.

MAYA

The hall devoted to the **Maya** is perhaps the most varied of all, reflecting the longest-lived and widest-spread of the Mesoamerican cultures. In some ways it's a disappointment, since their greatest achievements were in architecture and in the decoration of their temples – many of which, unlike those of the Aztecs, are still standing – so that the found objects seem relatively unimpressive. Nevertheless, there are reproductions of several buildings, or parts of them, friezes and columns taken from them, and extensive collections of jewellery, pottery and minor sculpture. Steps lead down into a section devoted to burial practices, including a reproduction of the Royal Tomb at **Palenque** (see p.488) with many of the objects found there – notably the prince's jade death mask. Outside, several small temples from relatively obscure sites are reproduced, the Temple of Paintings from **Bonampak** among them. The three rooms of the temple are entirely covered in frescoes representing the coronation of a new prince, a great battle, and the subsequent punishments and celebrations: very much easier to visit than the originals, and in far better condition.

NORTHERN AND WESTERN SOCIETIES

As a finale to the archeological collections on the ground floor, there's a large room devoted to the north and the west of the country. **Northern** societies on the whole developed few large centres, remaining isolated nomadic or agricultural communities. The small quantities of pottery, weapons and jewellery that have survived show a close affinity with native tribes of the American Southwest. The **west** was far more developed, but it, too, has left relatively few traces, and many of the best examples of **Tarascan culture** (see p.172) remain in Guadalajara. Among the highlights here are some delightful small human and animal figurines in stone and clay, a Tarascan Chacmool, and a copper mask of Xipe Totec representing a flayed human face.

THE ETHNOGRAPHY SECTION

To get to the **Ethnography section**, cross the courtyard back towards the beginning of the museum before climbing the stairs – otherwise you'll go round in reverse order. The rooms relate as far as possible to those below them, showing through photographs, models, maps and examples of local crafts the lifestyle of surviving indigenous groups in the areas today. Regional dress and reproductions of various types of hut and cabin form a major part of this inevitably rather sanitized look at the poorest (and most oppressed) people in Mexico, and there are also objects relating to their more important cults and ceremonies.

The rest of the park

The enormous success of the Museo de Antropología has led to a spate of other auda-cious modern exhibition halls being set up in the park. Two are very close by. The **Museo de Arte Moderno** (Tues–Sun 10am–5.30pm; US$1.50, free on Sun) is not far from the entrance to the park between Reforma and the Niños Heroes monument. Two low circular buildings, linked by a corridor, house a substantial permanent collection of twentieth-century Mexican and Latin American art, including works by Rivera, Orozco and Siqueiros, as well as landscapes of the Valley of México by José Velasco (one of Rivera's teachers) and hauntingly surreal canvases by Frida Kahlo. Often though, it's the temporary exhibitions that prove more arresting. Outside the building, fenced off from the rest of the park, is a sculpture garden.

Nearby, on the other side of Reforma and up towards the Museo de Antropología, another collection of modern art graces the **Museo Rufino Tamayo** (Tues–Sun 10am–5.45pm; US$2, free on Sun) – this time an internationally based show. It was built by, and stocked with, the collection of the artist **Rufino Tamayo**, whose work in murals and on smaller projects is far more abstract and less political than the Big Three, but who was nevertheless their approximate contemporary and enjoys an international reputation almost as high. There is much of his own work here, and exhibits of his tech-niques and theories, but also an impressive collection of European and American twen-tieth-century art – most of it from Tamayo's private collection. Artists represented may include Picasso, Miró, Magritte, Francis Bacon and Henry Moore – not all of these are on permanent display.

More modern art can be found north of the Anthropology Museum in the rather classy district known as the **Colonia Polanco**. Here, at Tres Picos 29, just up the road from the Canadian Embassy, is the **Sala de Arte Público David Siqueiros** (Tues–Sun 10am–6pm; US$1.25, free on Sun), a small but interesting collection of the great muralist's later work and photographs.

The **Zoo**, on Reforma beyond the Anthropology Museum, retains the distinction of being the only place outside China to have successfully bred Giant Pandas (at least naturally – several others now have test-tube pandas). Indeed there seems to be a veritable production line of the beasts; every time you visit the city there are posters advertising a new baby bear (*Osito Panda*). The zoo has recently undergone a long-awaited landscaping, and the enclosures are now as modern as anywhere in the world. Near here, too, is a small Children's Zoo, and, a little further up Reforma, the **Botanical Gardens**.

On the far side of the gardens, Reforma crosses Molino del Rey, a street named for the major battle here during the Mexican–American War, continues past the **Auditorio Nacional** – a major venue for dance, theatre and music events, with a couple of small theatres and the enormous Auditorium – and leaves the park via the Fuente de Petróleos, a complex of modern skyscrapers surrounding a monument to the national-ization of the oil industry. Beyond, it heads into Las Lomas, an expensive suburb whose luxury villas are mostly hidden behind high walls and heavy security gates.

Nuevo Bosques de Chapultepec

If you head south on Molino del Rey, you approach the new section of the park (Nuevo Bosques de Chapultepec, or "Chapultepec, Segunda seccion"), which, while consider-ably less attractive, offers two more museums, an amusement park and a restaurant that occupies one of the city's more daring pieces of modern architecture. On Molino del Rey itself, though, you first pass the **Presidential Palace**, "Los Pinos", surround-ed by presidential guards' barracks. This, plus the fact that much of the surrounding park is fenced off to recuperate, makes it extremely difficult to walk from one side to the other, especially when you add the impossibility of crossing the *periférico*. It's much easier to either take the Reforma bus out to the Plaza Petroleos and walk down from there, or to get a bus (#30) from Chapultepec Metro station along Av Constituyentes, which skirts the southern edge of the park.

This bus drops you right by the **Museo de Historia Natural** (Tues–Sun 10am–5pm; free), ten interconnecting domes filled with displays on nature and conservation, biology and geology, including rundowns on Mexico's mineral wealth, flora and fauna. Modern and well presented, it's particularly popular with kids. From here there's a miniature "railway" that will take you round the new part of the park, or it's not far to walk: head away from the road and you'll pass the artificial lake; beneath the fountain (the Fuente Lerma) is an underwater painting by Rivera. Beyond the lake you can see the rollercoaster and giant wheel of the **Amusement Park**, and beside this the **Museo Tecnológico** (Tues–Sun 9am–5pm; free).

If you're travelling with kids, head for the new **Museo del Papalote**, or Kite Museum, at Constituentes 268 (Mon–Fri 9am–1pm & 2–6pm, Sat & Sun 10am–2pm & 3–7pm; US$2), essentially a museum to childhood, with hands-on exhibits and, on most days, the atmosphere of a psychopathic kindergarten.

South to the suburbs

México spreads itself furthest to the south, where a series of old villages swallowed up by the urban sprawl harbour some of the most enticing destinations outside the centre. The colonial suburbs of **Coyoacán** and **San Ángel**, each with a couple of worthwhile museums, make a tranquil respite from the city centre's hustle, and a startling contrast to the ultra-modern bravado of the architecture of the university and the residential area of the **Pedregal**. There are echoes of ancient Mexico, too, in the archeological sites of **Copilco** and **Cuicuilco**, in the "floating gardens" of **Xochimilco** – what remain of the great valley lakes – and in Diego Rivera's remarkable collection of antiquities in the **Museo Anahuacalli**.

Insurgentes

Insurgentes, the most direct approach to the suburbs, is interesting in its own right: leaving behind the Glorieta de Insurgentes (the roundabout at Insurgentes Metro sta-

---

GETTING TO THE SOUTHERN SUBURBS

It's not at all difficult to get out to any of these sites on **public transport**, but getting from one to the other can be tricky if you're cutting across the main north–south routes. None of the connections is impossible, but it's worth taking a few short taxi rides – from San Ángel to Coyoacán, for example, or from Coyoacán to the Rivera Museum. If you're really pushed, and want to see as much as possible in a day or even an afternoon, you might consider getting a **tourist taxi** to take you round the lot. If you bargain furiously, this may not be as expensive as it sounds; indeed it sometimes seems that you can barely be paying for the fuel used. Since both the Rivera Museum and the Convento de Churubusco are open late, it can be stretched to a long day's trip. Alternatively, of course, there are **coach tours** run by several of the bigger travel agencies in the *Zona Rosa*.

The main approach is along **Insurgentes Sur**, where you'll find a constant stream of buses and peseros heading for San Ángel and the University City. Their main destinations should be chalked up, or displayed on a card, on the windscreen – look for "San Ángel ", "Ciudad Universitaria", "CU", or "UNAM" for Universidad Nacional Autónoma de México. Other **main terminals** for heading south are the bus stands by Metro Chapultepec or at Metro Tasqueña for services along the Calzada de Tlalpan and to the southwest of the city, above all to Xochimilco.

tion), it runs almost perfectly straight all the way out to the university, lined the whole way with huge department stores and malls, cinemas, restaurants and office buildings. A little under halfway to San Ángel, you pass on the right the enormous **Hotel de México**, the tallest building in the city. The complex taken as a whole is also surely the ugliest, already looking distinctly tatty, despite its modernity.

Also on your right is the garish **Polyforum Cultural Siqueiros**, designed and decorated by **David Siqueiros**, its exterior plastered in brash paintings designed by Siqueiros and executed by some thirty young artists. Inside, it contains what is allegedly the world's largest mural (about 4500 square metres), painted by Siqueiros alone (daily 10am–7pm; US$0.65), entitled *The March of Humanity on Earth and Towards the Cosmos*. In theory the floor revolves to let you take it all in, though in practice they only turn it on if there is a large enough gathering of people. For the full impact of the changing perspectives and use of sculptural techniques, large groups can arrange to see a *son et lumière* in English or Spanish (☎536-45-22). Elsewhere, the building houses visiting art exhibitions and a sizeable display of expensive crafts for sale.

Beyond this monster you shortly pass, on the same side, a huge sports centre with the **Estadio Nacional**, a 65,000-seat soccer stadium, and the **Plaza México**, the largest bullring in the world, with a capacity of 50,000. Finally, just before San Ángel comes the **Teatro de los Insurgentes**, its facade covered in a huge mosaic designed by Diego Rivera depicting the history of Mexican theatre, and assorted historical figures. At the top are *Los Insurgentes* of Mexico's War of Independence: Hidalgo, Morelos and Benito Juárez on the left, and Zapata on the right.

San Ángel

From the choked traffic of Insurgentes at its junction with Avenida La Paz, a short walk will take you up to the colonial suburb of **SAN ÁNGEL**, with its markets and ancient mansions around flower-draped patios. A very exclusive place to live, it's also a popular spot to visit (especially on Saturdays for the market), and is packed with little restaurants and cafés where you can sit outside and watch the crowds go by.

Climb La Paz up to Av Revolución and you'll find, on the left, the old Carmelite Convent, now the **Museo del Carmen** (Tues–Sun 10am–4.45pm; US$1.75, free on Sun). There's a collection of colonial religious paintings and sculpture here, and mummies in the crypt, but the convent itself is the chief attraction, a lovely example of early seventeenth-century architecture with domes covered in multicoloured (predominantly yellow) tiles and an almost tropical garden in the cloister. Heading up Av Revolución to the right, past a small flower market, you reach the **Museo de Arte Carrillo Gil** (Tues–Sun 10am–6pm; US$1.25, free on Sun), a somewhat incongruous but surprisingly good museum of modern art. There are works by Mexicans including Rivera, Orozco and Siqueiros, and an international collection that takes in Rodin, Picasso, Kandinsky and Klee.

If you cross straight over Revolución from the convent and continue up the hill, the centre of San Ángel and the oldest mansions lie ahead. **Plaza San Jacinto** is the target, a delightful square that is the centrepiece of the **Bazar Sábado** and animated throughout the week. Initially, the Saturday market was based in one of the mansions on the square, which still opens every weekend selling upmarket crafts and artworks, but nowadays there are stalls in all the surrounding streets with fairground rides and freak shows that feature assorted tattooed and bearded ladies. Also on the plaza is the **Casa del Risco**, sometimes known as the "Centro Cultural Isidro Fabela" (Tues–Sun 10am–5pm; free), an eighteenth-century mansion housing the said Isidro Fabela's collection of antique furniture and paintings, with an extraordinary fountain in the patio made from old porcelain plates and cups, broken and unbroken.

Half a kilometre up Av Altavista from the Museo Gil is the famous *San Ángel Inn*, a luxurious restaurant in the restored **Hacienda de San Ángel**. Expensive (the food is very good) and packed with tourists since it's included on many day-trip itineraries, it's nevertheless worth visiting for the lovely gardens and courtyards. Also on Altavista, on the corner with Diego Rivera, is the **Museo-Estudio Diego Rivera** (Tues–Sun 10am–6pm; US$1.25, free on Sun), where you can see Rivera's studio and his personal, rather wonderful, collection of popular and pre-Hispanic art.

El Pedregal

Beyond San Ángel, it's possible to head south through the **Jardines del Pedregal de San Ángel**, more often known simply as "El Pedregal". The Pedregal is actually the name of a vast lava flow that spreads across from here through the University City and on to the south of Coyoacán, but the section south of San Ángel is the thickest, the most craggy and dramatic. It was regarded as a completely useless stretch of land, the haunt of bandits and brigands, until in the early 1950s an architect named Luis Barragan began to build extraordinarily imaginative houses here, using the uneven lava as a feature. Now it's filled with the most amazing collection of luxury homes – you're not allowed to build here unless you can afford a sufficiently large piece of land and an architect to design your house – which have become a tourist attraction in themselves. Bus parties ride through in much the same way as they do in Beverly Hills or Hollywood, spotting the homes of the famous. Public transport up here is sparse, though there are buses from San Ángel – if you're mad about modern architecture, you might try getting a taxi to drive you round for thirty minutes or so.

Coyoacán

On the other side of Insurgentes from San Ángel, some distance away, lies **COYOACÁN**, another colonial township that has been absorbed by the city. Even before the Conquest it was a sizeable place, the capital of a small kingdom on the shores of the lake subjugated by the Aztecs in the mid-fifteenth century. Cortés based himself in Coyoacán during the siege of Tenochtitlán, and continued to live here while the old city was torn down and construction began on the capital of Nueva España. It remains very peaceful, far less visited than San Ángel, and with a couple of lovely, lively plazas. The focus of the area is the spacious **Plaza Central**, which is actually made up of two adjoining plazas – **Plaza Hidalgo** and the **Jardín del Centenario**. Here stand the ancient church of San Juan and a small **Palacio Municipal** (also known as the **Casa de Cortés**) said to have been built by Cortés himself. Inside are two Rivera murals depicting the Conquest and the torture of Cuauhtémoc: the latter is particularly apposite since it was in Coyoacán that the Aztec leader was tortured and finally killed. Nearby, in the small **Plaza de la Conchita**, the **Capilla de la Concepción** has a wonderful Baroque facade. Overlooking the square, the **Casa de la Malinche** is the house in which Cortés installed his native mistress – and where he allegedly later murdered his wife shortly after her arrival from Spain.

Coyoacán is one of the city's main stomping grounds for artists, artisans and musicians. Activity centres around the *Café el Parnaso*, attached to a bookshop on the corner of the square, and the *Hijo del Cuervo* bar at the opposite side – both are good places to check out the latest trends, as well as to relax and watch the world go by. On Sunday, there's a **market** in the Plaza Central – the whole area is taken up by stalls and various rock, folk and reggae bands. It's far and away the most fun place to buy your souvenirs, though most of the stuff can be found cheaper elsewhere. Reflecting all this joyous cultural activity, the **Museo de Culturas Populares**, close to the Plaza Hidalgo at Hidalgo 289 (Tues–Thurs 10am–6pm, Fri–Sun 10am–8pm; free), has colourful displays on popular cultural forms, including the circus, popular religion, wrestling (for more on which, see p.319) and revue.

FRIDA KAHLO

Frida Kahlo (1907–1954) is perhaps Mexico's most internationally famous artist. Her paintings, deeply personal, centre on herself, her insecurities and her relations with family, her country and her politics. "I paint myself," she said, "because I am so often alone, and because I am the subject I know best."

Kahlo started painting in 1925, following a bus accident that left her with spine and leg injuries that were to dog her throughout her life, eventually rendering her virtually unable to walk – towards the end of her life, she did most of her painting from her bed. In 1928, she joined the **Communist Party**, and the following year **married** Diego Rivera (see p.285), divorcing him in 1939 and remarrying him a year later. Their circle of friends included Trotsky (with whom she had an affair), Cuban Communist Julio Antonio Mella and muralist David Siqueiros (who was later implicated in an attempt to kill Trotsky, see p.306). In 1932, Kahlo went with Rivera to the United States for two years, and in 1939 to Paris, but her roots were firmly fixed in Mexico, and in particular **Coyoacán**, where she lived in her family's house until her death.

Her **works** incorporate a number of surrealist elements and much dreamlike symbolism. They include some rather gruesome depictions of death, including a portrait commissioned by *Vanity Fair* publisher Claire Boothe Luce of her friend Dorothy Hale, who had committed suicide by jumping from a building. Kahlo depicted Hale's death, and a shocked Luce endeavoured to destroy the painting (though she was dissuaded, and it's now in the Phoenix Art Museum). Kahlo's most famous paintings, however, are her **self-portraits**, which all too often depict her inner pain at her injuries and her series of miscarriages and aborted pregnancies.

Despite her pain and increasing disability (her right leg was amputated in 1953), Kahlo continued her political activism and philanthropy, and died after defying medical advice and taking part in a demonstration against American intervention in Guatemala, while she was convalescing from pneumonia in July 1954.

The Museo Frida Kahlo

The **Museo Frida Kahlo** (Tues–Sun 10am–5.45pm; US$1.25) is just a few minutes' walk from the centre of Coyoacán, six blocks along Centenario and then down C Londres to the right – it's painted bright blue and hard to miss. Kahlo's morbid, dream-like art reflected the pain of her own life – a polio victim as a child who then suffered severe injuries in a drastic bus accident, she spent much of her later life confined to a wheelchair, to her bed or in a hospital. Her canvases almost always feature herself: a fixed expression on her face, above a body sliced open, mutilated or crippled.

The museum occupies Kahlo's family home (she was born here in 1910), where she later returned to live with Diego Rivera from 1929 to 1954. As well as her own paintings – the best of which are frequently off in touring exhibitions – the collection includes drawings by Rivera, and mementoes of their life together and their joint interest in Mexico's artistic heritage. The museum reflects, too, in its extraordinary decoration, littered with pre-Hispanic artefacts and more modern folk items (in particular, bizarre papier-maché animals and figures), the coterie of artists and intellectuals of which they were the centre in the 1930s and 40s. Trotsky stayed here for a while and later settled nearby, and D.H. Lawrence too was a frequent visitor to friends in Coyoacán, though he had little political or artistic sympathy with Kahlo – or with Trotsky for that matter.

Trotsky's House

The Museo y Casa de Trotsky, **Trotsky's House** (Tues–Sun 10am–5pm; US$1.25), is not far away at Viena 45, near the corner of Morelos – about three blocks down and a

THE ASSASSINATION OF TROTSKY

The **first attempt on Trotsky's life** in his house at Coyoacán, which left more than seventy scars in the plaster of the bedroom walls, came at 4am on May 24, 1940. A heavily armed group (led by the painter David Siqueiros, who had been a commander in the Spanish Civil War) overcame the guards and pumped more than two hundred shots into the house, an attack that Trotsky, his wife and son survived by the simple expedient of hiding under their beds. After this, the house, already heavily guarded, was fortified still further. But the assassin was already a regular visitor who had been carefully building up contacts for nearly two years: posing as the businessman boyfriend of a trusted Trotskyist who was being slowly converted to the cause, bringing presents for the wife and kids. Although never wholly trusted, it seemed natural enough when he turned up on the afternoon of August 20 with an article that he wanted Trotsky to look over, and Trotsky invited him into the study. About thirty seconds later, the notorious **ice-pick** (the blunt end), which had been concealed under the killer's coat, smashed into Trotsky's skull. He died some 24 hours later, in hospital after an operation failed to save his life – his brain, they say, was vast. The killer, who called himself Frank Jackson and claimed to be Belgian, served twenty years in jail, though he never explained his actions or even confessed to his true identity, **Jaime Ramon Mercader del Río**.

couple to the left. This house is virtually the only memorial to Trotsky anywhere in the world – his small tomb stands in the gardens. Here the genius of the Russian Revolution and organizer of the Red Army lived and worked in exile, and here Stalin's long arm finally caught up with him (see box). The house, with steel gates and shutters, high walls and watchtowers, seems at first a little incongruous surrounded by the bourgeois homes of a prosperous suburb, but inside it's a human place, set up as he left it, if rather dustier: books on the shelves, his glasses smashed on the desk, and all the trappings of a fairly comfortable ordinary life (except for the bullet holes).

Practicalities

You can **get to Coyoacán** from San Ángel on buses heading down Altavista by the *San Ángel Inn* (or more easily by taxi), or from the centre on buses from Metros Chapultepec, Insurgentes, or Cuauhtémoc. In each case look for "Coyoacán" or "Colonia del Valle/Coyoacán". There's also a trolley bus that runs down Lázaro Cárdenas (against the flow of traffic) from a stop close by Bellas Artes. Metro line 3, too, passes close by, though note that Viveros station is considerably closer to the action than Coyoacán: from here walk south on Av Universidad, then turn left (east) to reach the centre. If you're coming straight from the centre of town down Av Cuauhtémoc or Av Lázaro Cárdenas, it makes sense to visit the Kahlo and Trotsky museums first, in which case you'll want to get off the bus immediately after passing under Av Río Churubusco.

The University City and Cuicuilco

Beyond Coyoacán and San Ángel, Insurgentes enters the great lava field of the Pedregal. To the left of the road is the **UNIVERSITY CITY** (Ciudad Universitaria), dominated by the astonishing, twelve-storey **Library**. Each face of this rectangular tower is covered in a mosaic designed by **Juan O'Gorman** – mostly natural stone with a few tiles or glass to supply colours that would otherwise have been unavailable. Representing the artist's vision of the country's progression through history, the focus of the larger north and south faces is on pre-Hispanic and colonial Mexico; on the west wall, the present and the university coat-of-arms; on the east, the future ranged around a giant atom. It's remarkable how this has been incorporated as an essential feature of the building – at first it appears that there are no windows at all, but look closely and you'll see that in fact they're an integral part of the design, appearing as eyes, mouths or as windows of the buildings in the mosaic.

More or less beside this are the long, low **administration buildings** (*rectoría*) with a giant mural in high relief (or a "sculptural painting") by Siqueiros, intended to provide a changing perspective as you walk past or drive by on Insurgentes. At the front here, too, are the University Theatre and the **Museo Universitario de Ciencias y Artes** (Mon–Fri 9am–5pm, Sat & Sun 10am–5pm; free), the latter a wide-ranging general collection, with interactive scientific exhibits, plus exhibitions on contemporary art and culture. Behind them spread out the enormous grounds of the main campus, starting with a large esplanade known as the "Plaza Mayor", with sculptural groups dotted around a shallow artificial pond. Towards the back are more murals, adorning the Faculties of **Science** and **Medicine**; continue past these to reach another grassy area with the **Botanical Gardens** and several large walls against which the students play frontón.

After some forty years of use, parts of the campus are beginning to show their age: certainly it's no longer the avant-garde sensation it was when it opened – but it remains a remarkable architectural achievement. The whole thing was built in just five years (1950–55) under the presidency of Miguel Alemán, and is now one of the largest universities in the world. It's also the oldest on the American continent: granted a charter by Philip II in 1551, the University of Mexico occupied a succession of sites in the city centre (including the Hospital de Jesus Nazareno and what is now the Escuela Nacional Preparatoria), was closed down several times in the nineteenth century and was finally awarded its status as the Universidad Nacional Autonoma de México in 1929.

Directly across Insurgentes from the main buildings is the sculptured oval of the 100,000-seater Estadio Olímpico, its main facade decorated with a mosaic relief by Diego Rivera representing the development of human potential through sport. Any taxi driver will tell you that the **Olympic Stadium**'s curious shape was deliberately designed to look like a giant sombrero, but this, sadly, is not the case; it's undeniably odd, though, half sunk into the ground as if dropped here from a great height and slightly warped in the process.

"Ciudad Universitaria" **buses** stop at a terminus right in front of the main complex. You can also get here by the Metro (Copilco is closer than Universidad), in which case you'll be right at the back of the campus and have to walk all the way through, past the frontón courts and medical faculty, to reach the library.

Cuicuilco

To get to the pyramid of **CUICUILCO**, carry on down Insurgentes (buses marked "Tlalpan") to where it crosses the great ring road, the *periférico* – the site is just beyond the junction (there are also buses round the *periférico*: look for "Perisur" or "Villa Olimpica"). If you follow the *periférico* round, you'll see pieces of sculpture at regular intervals by the roadside – each was a gift from a different country at the time of the 1968 Olympics – and pass the former Olympic Village, now a high-rise residential area. The site itself, however, is dominated by the circular temple clearly visible from the road. This is much the oldest construction of such scale known in central Mexico, abandoned at the time of the eruption of Xitle (the small volcano that created the Pedregal, which took place around 100–300 AD) just as Teotihuacán was beginning to develop. Not a great deal is known about the site, much of which has been buried by modern housing (completing the work of the lava), though other structures have been uncovered, notably at the Olympic Village. The pyramid is composed of three sloping tiers (of a probable original five) about 17m high by 100m in diameter, approached by a ramp and a stairway. A small **museum** (daily 9am–5pm; free) displays objects found here and at contemporary settlements.

Xochimilco

For all that the canals are heavily polluted, their level dropping alarmingly year by year, the "floating gardens" adjoining the suburb of **XOCHIMILCO** offer the most intense carnival atmosphere every weekend – and are likely to be one of your most memorable experiences of the city. Xochimilco remains the most popular Sunday outing for thousands of Mexicans, and it's also the one place where you get some feel for the ancient city (or at least an idealized view of it) with its waterborne commerce, thriving markets and dazzling colour. **Rent a boat**, its superstructure decorated with an arch of paper flowers, and you'll be punted around miles of canals, continually assaulted by women in tiny canoes selling flowers or fruit, or with a precarious charcoal brazier burning under a pile of tortillas, chicken and chile, or by larger vessels bearing entire *mariachi* bands in their full finery who, for a small fee, will grapple alongside you and blast out a couple of numbers.

The floating gardens themselves are no more floating than the Titanic: following the old Aztec methods of making the lake fertile, these *chinampas* are formed by a raft of mud and reeds, firmly rooted to the bottom by the plants. As well as amusing the hordes of visitors, the area is still a very important market-gardening and flower-producing centre for the city – if you wander the streets of Xochimilco town you'll find garden centres everywhere, and wonderful flowers and fruit in the market (though whether it's healthy to eat food raised on these filthy waters is open to question). Off the huge central plaza is the lovely sixteenth-century church of **San Bernardino**, full on Sundays with a succession of people paying homage and leaving offerings at one of its many chapels; in the plaza itself there are usually bands playing, or mime artists entertaining the crowds.

For the easiest **approach to Xochimilco**, take the Metro to Tasqueña station (line 2) and from there the tren ligero to Embarcadero (the end of the line); there are also buses and peseros from Tasqueña, as well as buses direct from the centre, down Insurgentes and around the *periférico* or straight down the Calzada de Tlalpan. On Sundays many extra services are laid on.

To get a boat follow the "Embarcadero" signs. What you **pay** depends on the size of the punt, how long you want to go for, and most importantly your skill at bargaining (it'll be harder on a weekday, when there are few people about). Since you pay by the boatload, it's much better value to get a group together, and probably more enjoyable, too – remember that there are likely to be sundry extras including the cold beers thoughtfully provided by the boatman, and any flowers, food or music you find yourself accepting on your way. While Sunday is by far the most crowded and animated day, Saturdays are lively, too, and you can rent a boat any day of the week for a little solitary cruising.

Down the Calzada de Tlalpan

The **Calzada de Tlalpan** is the other main approach to the south, running down more or less from the Zócalo to cross the *periférico* not far from Xochimilco. If you want to do the full circuit of the south, head back towards the centre this way: you'll pass the giant **Estadio Azteca** beside the Calzada very close to its junction with the *periférico*. Along the way, there are two superb museums – both of them also quite close to Coyoacán.

Museo Anahuacalli

Heading back from Xochimilco towards the centre, you'll pass the bizarre **Museo Anahuacalli**, Museo 15 (Tues–Sun 10am–6pm; US$1.25), designed and built by **Diego Rivera** to house his own huge collection of pre-Hispanic artefacts. It's an extraordinary structure, inspired by Maya and Aztec architecture, a sombre mass of black volcanic stone atop a hill with magical views, especially from the roof terrace: Popocatépetl and

Ixtaccíhuatl seem really close here, their snowy peaks glistening on even the smoggi-est days. The exquisite objects in the collection often form part of a thoroughly imagi-native display: one small chamber contains nothing but a series of **Huehueteotls**, all squatting grumpily under the weight of their braziers. In the studio, there's a lively ball-game group and a series of wonderfully familiar animals.

As a brief guide to what you'll see, the ground floor is devoted to objects from the main cultures of the Valley of Mexico – Teotihuacán, Toltec and Aztec – which provid-ed Rivera with an important part of his inspiration. On the first floor, rooms devoted to the west of Mexico (arguably the best such collection in the country) surround the huge airy room that Rivera, had he lived, would have used as a studio. It's been fitted out as if he had anyway, with portraits and sketches including preliminary studies for *Man in Control of the Universe*, his massive mural in the Palacio de las Bellas Artes. On the top floor are more Aztec objects, along with pottery and small figures from Oaxaca and the Gulf coast. Up here you can also get out onto the roof, for the entrancing views.

The museum is on C Museo, just off Av División del Norte: *peseros* to the junction include Ruta #90 or Ruta #79 from Salto del Agua Metro (look for "Estadio Azteca" on the windscreen), or Ruta #2 from Chapultepec Metro ("Alberca Olimpica"), but the eas-iest way to get there is by tren ligero from Tasqueña Metro station to Xotepingo, fol-lowing the sign "Salida a museo" (to the right) on leaving, and 100m up Xotepingo to División del Norte.

Museo Nacional de las Intervenciones

The **Museo Nacional de las Intervenciones**, 20 de Agosto and General Anaya (Tues–Sun 10am–6pm; US$1.75, free on Sun), occupies the old Franciscan **Convento de Churubusco**, some 3km to the north. It owes its present role to the 1847 battle in which the invading Americans, led by General Winfield Scott, defeated a Mexican force under General Anaya – another heroic Mexican effort whereby the outnumbered defenders fought to their last bullet. The exhibits are devoted to the history of foreign military adventures in Mexico and to nationalist expansionism in general. Skeletons in the cupboards of Britain, Spain, France and the USA are all loudly rattled.

You'll notice the building, though, first of all – a stunner, especially if you arrive at the darkening of day as the lights are coming on in the gardens. The exhibits themselves may not mean a great deal unless you have a reasonable grasp of Mexican history; they're labelled only in Spanish and not very fully at that. You start with an introduction to Imperialism and an exhibition – changed monthly – on some aspect of it. The muse-um proper, on the upper floors, is devoted largely to the Mexican–American wars and the loss of 2,500,000 square kilometres of Mexican territory. It's a very different per-spective from that of the Alamo. Spanish and French interventions are covered, too, as is the role of western finance generally in upholding the Díaz regime.

The museum is on General Anaya between the Calzada de Tlalpan and Av Division del Norte, very close to General Anaya Metro station: turn right as you leave the muse-um and you'll see the trains passing at the end of the road. From the Rivera Museum, take the tren ligero and then go one stop on the Metro, or take a pesero up Division del Norte and get off at the large Pemex station just before the underpass which carries Av Río Churubusco. From Coyoacán, it's just about in walking distance (east on Hidalgo from the plaza and fork left on General Anaya), or you can take a pesero (Ruta #1).

North of the centre

There's less to see north of the centre of México, but two sites of compelling interest – the great **Basilica of Guadalupe** and the emotive **Plaza de las Tres Culturas** – well deserve the afternoon it takes to cover both. Further out, and harder to get to, you'll find the pyramids of **Tenayuca** and **Santa Cecilia**, the two most dramatically preserved remains of Aztec architecture in the city.

Plaza de las Tres Culturas

Site of the ancient city of **Tlatelolco**, the **Plaza de las Tres Culturas** will be your first stop. Today, a lovely **colonial church** rises in the midst of the excavated ruins, which are in turn surrounded by a **high-rise housing complex**: all three great cultures of Mexico side by side.

You can **get to the Plaza** de las Tres Culturas either on Metro line 3 (Tlatelolco), or by bus. It lies between Insurgentes Nte and Reforma Nte: on the former take any bus north ("Indios Verdes") and get off shortly before the black, A-shaped skyscraper that marks the Monumento a la Raza; on the latter, "La Villa" buses pass within about three blocks on their way to Guadalupe.

The ruins

Tlatelolco was a considerably more ancient city than Tenochtitlán, based on a separate but nearby island in the lake. For a long time, under independent rule, its people existed in close alliance with the Mexica of Tenochtitlán, and the city was by far the most important commercial and market centre in the Valley – even after its annexation into the Aztec empire in 1473 Tlatelolco retained this role. By the time the Spanish arrived, much of the swampy lake between the two had been filled in and built over: it was to Tlatelolco that Cortés and his troops came to marvel at the size and order of the market. Cortés estimated that 60,000 people, buyers and sellers, came and went each day, and Bernal Díaz wrote (after several pages of detailed description):

> *We were astounded at the great number of people and the quantities of merchandise, and at the orderliness and good arrangements that prevailed . . . every kind of goods was kept separate and had its fixed place marked for it . . . Some of the soldiers among us who had been in many parts of the world, in Constantinople, in Rome, and all over Italy, said that they had never seen a market so well laid out, so large, so orderly, and so full of people.*

In 1521 the besieged Aztecs made their final stand here, and a plaque in the middle of the plaza recalls that struggle: "On the 13th of August 1521," it reads, "defended by the heroic Cuauhtémoc, Tlatelolco fell under the power of Hernan Cortés. It was neither a triumph nor a defeat, but the painful birth of the mixed race that is the Mexico of today". The ruins are a pale reflection of the original, whose temples rivalled those of Tenochtitlán itself: some idea of their scale can be gained from the size of the bases. The chief temple, for example, had by the time of the Conquest reached its eleventh rebuilding – what you see now corresponds to the second stage, and by the time nine more were superimposed it would certainly have risen much higher than the church that was built from its stones. On top, probably, was a double sanctuary like that on the Great Temple of Tenochtitlán. The smaller structures include a square **tzompantli**, or Wall of Skulls, near which nearly two hundred human skulls were discovered, each with holes through its temples – presumably the result of having been displayed side by side on long poles around the sides of the building.

The church and later buildings

The **church** on the site was erected in 1609, replacing an earlier Franciscan monastery. Parts of this survive, arranged about the cloister. Here, in the early years after the Conquest, the friars established a college at which they instructed the sons of the Aztec nobility in European ways, teaching them Spanish, Latin and Christianity: Bernardino de Sahagun was one of the teachers, and it was here that he wrote down many of the customs and traditions of the natives, compiling the most important existing record of daily Aztec life in the process.

The **modern buildings** that surround the plaza – mostly a rather ugly 1960s housing project but including the Ministry of Foreign Affairs – represent the third culture. The contemporary state of Mexico was rather more brutally represented on October 2, 1968, when troops and tanks were ordered to fire on almost a quarter of a million students demonstrating here. It was the culmination of several months of student protests over the government of the day's social and educational policies, which the authorities were determined to subdue with only ten days left before the ceremonial opening of the Olympic Games in the city. Estimates of deaths vary from an official figure at the time of thirty to student estimates of more than five hundred, but it seems clear that hundreds is more accurate than tens. The Mexican philosopher Octavio Paz saw it all as part of the cycle of history – a ritual slaughter to recall the Aztec sacrifices here – but it's perhaps better seen as an example of at least one thread of continuity between all Mexico's civilizations: the cheapness of life and the harsh brutality of their rulers.

Basilica de Nuestra Señora de Guadalupe

The **Basilica de Nuestra Señora de Guadalupe** is in fact a whole series of churches, chapels and shrines, set around an enormous stone-flagged plaza and climbing up the rocky hillock where the miracles that led to its foundation occurred. It can be reached by **Metro** lines 3 and 6 (La Villa Basilica), by **buses** and peseros north along Reforma ("Metro La Villa"), or by trolleybus from Metro Hidalgo ("Indios Verdes"). The Virgin of Guadalupe, Mexico's first indigenous saint, is still the nation's most popular – the image recurs in churches throughout the country, and the Virgin's banner has been fought under by both sides in almost every conflict the nation has ever seen, most famously when Hidalgo seized on it as the flag of Mexican Independence. According to the legend, a christianized native, **Juan Diego**, was walking over the hill (formerly dedicated to the Aztec earth goddess, Tonantzin) on his way to the monastery at Tlatelolco one morning in December 1531. He was stopped by a brilliant vision of the Virgin, who ordered him, in Nahuatl, to go to the bishop and tell him to build a church on the hill. Bishop Juan de Zumarraga was unimpressed until, on December 12, the Virgin reappeared, ordering Diego to gather roses from the top of the hill (yes, in December) and take them to the bishop. Doing so, he bundled the flowers in his cape, and when he opened it before the bishop he found the image of the dark-skinned Virgin imprinted into the cloth. The cloak today hangs above the altar in the gigantic modern basilica: it takes its name from the celebrated (and equally swarthy) Virgin in the Monastery of Guadalupe in Spain.

The **first church** was built in 1533, but the large Baroque basilica you see now was completely reconstructed in the eighteenth century and again remodelled in the nineteenth and twentieth. Impressive mostly for its size, it is anyway closed to the public while being shored up – around the back you can go into a **museum** (Tues–Sun 10am–6pm; US$0.25), which contains some of the church's many treasures of religious art and a large collection of ex-votos. To the left of the great plaza is the modern **home of the image** – a huge church with space inside for 10,000 worshippers and for perhaps four times that when the great doors all round are thrown open to the crowds. It's always crowded, and there seems to be a service permanently in progress. The famous cloak hangs above the main altar, and to avoid constant disruption there's a passageway round behind the altar which takes the devout to a spot right underneath – strips of moving walkway are designed to prevent anyone lingering too long here, but they never seem to be working.

From the plaza you can walk round to the right and up the hill past a series of little chapels associated with the Virgin's appearance. Loveliest is the **Capilla del Pocito**, in which is a well, said to have sprung forth during one of the apparitions. Built in the eighteenth century, it consists of two linked elliptical chapels, a smaller and a larger, with colourful tiled domes and magnificently decorative interiors. On the very top of the hill, the **Capilla de las Rosas** marks the spot where the miraculous roses grew.

Around all this, there swirls a stream of humanity – pilgrims, sightseers, priests and salesmen offering candles, souvenirs, pictures of the Virgin, snacks, any number of mementoes. On December 12, the anniversary of the second apparition, their numbers swell to hundreds of thousands. Many cover the last miles on their knees in an act of penance or devotion, but for others it is more of a vast fiesta, with dancing, singing and drinking throughout the day.

Tenayuca and Santa Cecilia

In the extreme north of the city, just outside the boundaries of the Distrito Federal, lie the two most wholly preserved examples of **Aztec**-style architecture. They're hard to reach by public transport, but can thoroughly repay the effort involved if you've an interest in the Aztecs. **Tenayuca** is just off the Av de los Cien Metros, some 6km north of the Terminal del Norte. Take the Metro to 18 de Marzo (five blocks west of the Basilica de Nuestra Señora de Guadalupe) or La Raza and catch a pesero to Tenayuca. From there walk up the hill past the bridge over the river (roads are very busy) and past the square to the museum site. There are also peseros on Lázaro Cárdenas northwards from Bellas Artes. To **Santa Cecilia** there are peseros from Tenayuca, and from Metro stations 18 de Marzo and Rosario, but it's also just about within walking distance of, or a short taxi-ride to, Tenayuca. Some bus tours take both in on their way to Tula and Tepotzotlán.

Tenayuca

Tenayuca (daily 9am–5.45pm; US$1.25, free on Sun) is another site that predates Tenochtitlán by a long chalk – indeed there are those who claim it was the capital of the tribe that destroyed Tula. In this, its history closely mirrors almost all other Valley settlements: a barbarian tribe from the north invades, conquers all before it, settles in a city and becomes civilized, borrowing much of its culture from its predecessors, before being overcome by the next wave of migrants. There's little evidence that Tenayuca ever controlled a large empire, but it was a powerful city and provides one of the most concrete links between the Toltecs and the Aztecs. The pyramid that survives dates from the period of Aztec dominance and is an almost perfect replica – in miniature – of the great temples of Tlatelolco and Tenochtitlán. Here the structure and the monumental double stairway are intact – only the twin sanctuaries at the top and the brightly painted decorations would be needed for it to open for sacrifices again tomorrow. This is the sixth superimposition; five earlier pyramids (the first dating from the early thirteenth century) are contained within it (and revealed in places by excavations), while originally there was a seventh layer built on top, of which some traces remain.

The most unusual and striking feature of Tenayuca's pyramid is the border of interlocking stone **snakes** that must originally have surrounded the entire building – well over a hundred of them survive. Notice also the two coiled snakes (one a little way up the north face, the other at the foot of the south face) known as the "turquoise serpents": their crests are crowned with stars and aligned with the sun's position at the solstice.

Santa Cecilia Acatitlán

A poor road leads north from Tenayuca to **Santa Cecilia Acatitlán** (Tues–Sun 10am–5pm; US$1.25), where there's another pyramid – much smaller and simpler but wholly restored and remarkably beautiful with its clean lines. Originally this was a temple with a double staircase very similar to the others, but it was discovered during excavation that one of the earlier structures inside was almost perfectly preserved. The ruined layers were stripped away to reveal what, after some reconstruction, is the only example of a sanctuary more or less as it would have been seen by Cortés. It's a very plain building, rising in four steps to a single roofed shrine approached by a broad ramped stairway. The studded decorations around the roof represent either skulls or stars. You approach the pyramid through a small museum in a colonial house, whose displays and grounds are both well worth a look.

Eating

Eating out seems to be the main pastime in the capital, with restaurants, cafés, taquerías and juice stands on every block, many of them very reasonably priced, even in the heart of the *Zona Rosa*, along Reforma, or just off the Zócalo. As throughout the country, you should make your main meal a late lunchtime comida if you want to eat cheaply and well.

The choice of **where to eat** is almost limitless in México, ranging from traditional coffee houses to fast-food lunch counters, and taking in Japanese, French, Spanish, expensive international and rock-bottom Mexican cooking along the way. There's even a small Chinatown of sorts, south of the Alameda, where a cluster of **Chinese** restaurants line C Dolores. There are also the traditional food stalls in **markets** throughout the city. Merced is the biggest, but not a terribly pleasant place to eat: at the back of the Plaza Garibaldi, there's a market hall given over to nothing but food stands, each vociferously competing with its neighbours.

México also abounds in **rosticerías**, roast chicken shops, serving tasty set meals and crispy chicken with beer, in a jolly atmosphere. There are a couple on 5 de Febrero. For licuados, sodas, ice cream, fruit salads and tortas, try a **jugería**: *Jugos Canada* at 5 de Mayo 49 is very good if a little pricey. **Pasterías**, or cake shops, sell cheap pastries and bread rolls for economical breakfasts: *Pastería Madrid*, 5 de Febrero 25, is good and also has its own restaurant. If you've got a sweet tooth, make for the *Dulcería de Celaya*, 5 de Mayo 39 – a wonderful **sweet shop**, with candied fruit *comates* and *dulce de membrillo*.

There are also several **chains** with branches throughout the city – dull on the whole but reliable. **Sanborn's** is the best known, not particularly cheap but good for a breakfast of coffee and *pan dulce* or for reasonably authentic Mexican food tailored to foreign tastes: chief outlets are in the *Zona Rosa* on Ambares at Londres and Niza at Hamburgo; just off Reforma next to the Sheraton; and on the street leading up to the Plaza de la República; the House of Tiles by Bellas Artes; 16 de Septiembre just down from the Zócalo; and in San Ángel . **VIPs** is cheaper and serves filling Mexican and American dishes – there are branches at Uruguay 51, Insurgentes Norte and Magnolia near the train station, on C Ramirez just off the Plaza de la República, and in the *Zona Rosa*. For palatable, authentic tacos, try *Tacos Beatriz* (at Motolinia 32 in the city centre, and Londres 104 in the *Zona Rosa*, among others). Burger places are on the whole to be avoided.

Asian and Pacific

Chez Wok, Tennyson 117, Col Polanco (☎281-34-10). A high-class establishment, specializing in Peking and north Chinese cuisine. Reservations advised.

Comida Chen, Allende 26. A low-priced Mexican diner that also does chop suey, available alone or as part of a comida corrida.

Kam Ling, 1ª Cerrada de 5 de Mayo 14 (☎521-56-61). Chinese food to eat in or take away. Chinese set menus from around US$3; the Mexican menu is even cheaper.

Mauna Loa, San Jerónimo 240, Pedregal de San Ángel (☎616-27-77). A rather pricey Polynesian restaurant.

Pabellon Coreano, Estocolmo 16 (☎525-25-09). Expensive, sophisticated Korean restaurant.

Sushi Coy, Mexico 180. Small, moderately priced Japanese restaurant near Coyoacán Metro.

Kam Ling, Londres 114, *Zona Rosa*. Café-restaurant with low-priced Cantonese and Mexican cuisine, including Chinese set meals and a lunchtime comida corrida.

European and American

Angus, Copenhague 31, *Zona Rosa* (☎511-86-33), and Desierto de los Leones 43, San Ángel (☎550-83-45). The best steaks in town, with a choice of cuts and side dishes. Reserve in advance.

Champs Elysées, Reforma 326, *Zona Rosa* (☎525-72-59). The city's top French restaurant: truly excellent food, but you don't want to know how much it costs. Reserve.

Shirley's, Reforma 108, and Londres 102-B. Set breakfasts and lunches, and a range of salads, sandwiches and meat dishes.

Via Appia, Hamburgo 28, *Zona Rosa* (☎207-08-75). Classy Italian restaurant.

Mexican

Café el Popular, 5 de Mayo 52. Cheap place serving simple food 24hr a day. A little cramped with a fast turnover, but great for breakfast, coffee and snacks. There is now a second branch at 5 de Mayo 10.

Café de Tacuba, Tacuba 28. Good coffee and excellent food come at a price, though this doesn't deter the folk who've been packing it out since 1912. One of the country's top bands is sponsored by the café and thus bears its name.

Flash Taco, Monte de Piedad 13. Video bar on the Zócalo, serving good if somewhat expensive tacos, as well as set breakfasts and, on weekdays, executive lunches.

Majestic Hotel, Madero 73. A high-class restaurant with a terrace overlooking the Zócalo. Even if you can't stretch to a meal, it's well worth popping up for a coffee or a beer just to take in the view.

Panchos, Uruguay 84. A small restaurant offering set meals only, but at very low prices. Breakfasts are generous and huge.

Parrilla Leonesa, Bolivar 29-A and Insurgentes Sur 86. Smart, clean restaurant offering good, moderately priced steaks and grills.

San Ángel Inn, Diego Rivera 50, San Ángel (☎616-05-37). Very popular, upmarket restaurant in a beautiful old hacienda; book in advance.

El Tajín, in the Centro Veracruzano, Miguel Ángel de Quevedo 687, Coyoacán (☎659-44-47). Veracruz specialities; the fish dishes, such as *Huachinango à la Veracruz* and *Mojarra al Mojo del Ajo*, are exquisite.

Seafood

Bolivar 12, Bolivar 12 (☎521-20-16). Upmarket downtown fish eatery, whose specialities include seafood mole, and fish and seafood tacos.

Danubio, Uruguay 3 (☎512-09-12). Established restaurant that has specialized in seafood in all its guises for the last fifty years. Set menu US$9.

El Faro de Belgrado, Belgrado 9, *Zona Rosa* (☎207-60-77). Posh fish restaurant offering such delights as *Arroz a la Marinera* (seafood paella), or squid braised in its own ink.

El Marisquito, Donceles 12-B, opposite the Senate House. Join the politicos in eating high-class fish and seafood dishes.

Spanish and South American

Camino Real Hotel, Mariano Escobedo 700, near Chapultepec Metro (☎203-21-21). Excellent tapas bar and more formal restaurant.

La Guardía del Gaucho, Mina 214. Rather a posh Argentinian restaurant, serving up large hunks of juicy grilled meat.

Meson del Perro Andaluz, Copenhague 26, *Zona Rosa* (☎514-74-80). Very popular Spanish restaurant with a lively atmosphere.

Restaurante Centro Castellano, Uruguay 16 (☎510-14-16). Huge restaurant occupying three floors, dishing up great, hearty meals with lots of seafood, and with an US$8 set menu.

Restaurante Centro Catalán, Bolivar 31. Good barbecued meats, plus lamb and rabbit paella, all served to live music. The set menu costs around US$7.50.

Vegetarian

Centro Naturista, Dolores 10, south of the Alameda. Macrobiotic canteen with soups and juices, tortas and quesadillas, and a US$1.50 set menu.

Comedor Vegetariano, Motolinia 31. A friendly place with an amazingly good-value set menu, including a help-yourself salad plate, three courses, dessert, juice, and coffee or tea. Unfortunately, only open 1–6pm daily.

Restaurante Vegetariano Yug, Varsovia 3, *Zona Rosa*. Worthy bookshop and contact point for vegetarians and vegans, with set breakfasts, salads, antojitos, and a US$4.50 buffet daily except Sat from 1pm.

El Vegetariano, Filomeno Mata 13, between Madero and 5 de Mayo. Very tasty vegetarian food in the centre of town, serving salads, breads and a range of egg dishes.

Vegetariano Lindavista, Insurgentes Nte 1892 (☎577-05-62). Way out near Metro 18 de Marzo, this renowned veggie eatery has occasional set-menu offers, and gives classes on vegetarian food preparation.

Entertainment and nightlife

There's a vast amount going on in México, which is the nation's cultural and social centre as much as its political capital. A lot of the obvious **nightlife**, though, is rather tame in its attempt to be sophisticated – Mexicans themselves favour discos with a diet of American music, while for the tourists they lay on piano bars or "typical" Mexican bands, Herb Alpert-style. Two attractions, however – the *mariachi* music in the **Plaza Garibaldi** and, to a lesser extent, the **Ballet Folklórico** – transcend this, and although both are unashamedly aimed at tourists, they have an enduring appeal, too, for Mexicans. Finding other forms of **live music** in the capital is an unpredictable business, full of disappointments but with occasional delights. Many of the best venues are to be found in the south, towards Coyoacán and San Ángel. Most places play rock and Latin; good jazz is virtually non-existent. **Nightclubs**, concentrated in the *Zona Rosa*, tend to play a mixture of styles every night: try *Mekano*, at Génova 44, or *Urano*, at Hamburgo 123. Some music venues have a relatively high cover charge, which includes free drinks.

Listings for current cinema, theatre and other **cultural events** can be found in the English-language *Mexico City Times*; local newspapers in Spanish will have more detail (certainly for films), or you could try the weekly magazine *Tiempo Libre*. While Mexican theatre tends to be rather turgid, there are often excellent classical music **concerts** and performances of **opera** or **ballet** by touring companies. Bellas Artes and the Auditorio Nacional are again the main venues, but other downtown theatres as well as the Polyforum and the Teatro de los Insurgentes may also have interesting shows. On most Sundays, there's a free concert in Chapultepec Park near the lake.

There are at least ten **cinemas** along Reforma, which show all the latest releases. English-language movies, at least in the city centre, are almost always shown in English with subtitles, though occasionally they are dubbed; major films open here up to a year before they reach Europe and are sometimes released even before they've been seen in the USA. If you go to the cinema arrive early, as popular screenings frequently sell out.

Plaza Garibaldi

Entertainment in the **Plaza Garibaldi** is not for those of nervous disposition. Here in the evenings gather hundreds of competing **mariachi** bands, all in their tight, silver-spangled *charro* finery and vast sombreros, to play for anyone who'll pay them among the crowds wandering the square and spilling out of the surrounding bars. A typical group consists of two or four violins, a brass section of three trumpeters standing some way back so as not to drown out the others, three or four men on guitars of varying sizes, and a vocalist – though the truly macho serenader will rent the band and do the singing himself. They take their name, supposedly, from the French *mariage* – it being traditional during the nineteenth-century French intervention to rent a group to play at weddings. You may also come across **norteño** bands from the border areas with their Tex-Mex brand of country music, or the softer sounds of **marimba** musicians from the south. Simply wander round the square and you'll get your fill – should you want to be individually serenaded, pick out a likely looking group and negotiate your price. At the back of the square is a huge market hall in which a whole series of stalls serve simple food and vie furiously for custom. Alternatively, there are a number of fairly pricey restaurant-bars around the square.

The Plaza Garibaldi is on Lázaro Cárdenas about five blocks north of Bellas Artes. Take line 8 to Metro Garibaldi, or you could walk through a thoroughly sleazy area of cheap bars and cafés, streetwalkers, grimy hotels and several brightly lit theatres offering burlesque and strip shows. As the night wears on and the drinking continues, it can get pretty rowdy around the square and pickpockets are always a threat: despite a high-profile police presence, you'd be better off not coming laden down with expensive camera equipment or an obviously bulging wallet. The last Metro leaves at midnight, and you'd be advised to be on it.

Ballet Folklórico

The **Ballet Folklórico** is a total contrast: a long-running, internationally famed compilation of traditional dances from all over the country, elaborately choreographed and designed, and interspersed with Mexican music and singing. That said – and despite the billing – there's nothing very traditional about the Ballet. Although it does include several of the more famous native dances, they are very jazzed up and incorporated into what is, in effect, a regular musical that wouldn't be out of place on Broadway.

The best place to see the Ballet Folklórico is in the original setting of the Palacio de Bellas Artes, where the theatre is an attraction in itself. There are performances (usually) on Sunday at 9.30am and 8.30pm, and Wednesday at 8.30pm. Tickets, however, can be hard to come by, and pressure of other events occasionally forces a move to the Auditorio Nacional in Chapultepec Park. You should try to book at least a couple of days in advance – either contact the Bellas Artes box office direct (☎512-36-33), book through Ticketmaster (☎525-90-00) or arrange to go with an organized tour, for which you'll pay a considerable premium. Rival troupes, often every bit as good, perform at the Teatro de la Danza, behind the Auditorio Nacional (Metro Auditorio; ☎280-87-71).

Drinking and live music venues

Cantinas in México, as in the rest of the country, are very much a male preserve, but here at least things are beginning to change. Even so, it's safer for women to stick to **hotel bars** (most of which are in the centre) or to the established night spots and tourist enclaves. **Pulquerías** are to be found on Plaza Garibaldi, though these can get rather rough and raucous as the night wears on (see under "Mariachi" below).

Antillanos, Francisco Pimentel 78, Col San Rafael, near Metro San Cosme (☎592-04-39). Salsa and other Hispano-Caribbean rhythms. Thurs–Sat 9pm–3am; cover US$6.50.

Apolos Golden Club, Insurgentes Sur 1236 (☎575-81-77). Women-only club. Wed–Sat from 8pm, floor show 10.30pm–12.30am; cover US$15 with free drinks.

Babel, Tacuba 47 (☎510-08-05). A theatre-bar with occasional live music. Thurs–Sat 10pm–2am; cover US$12.50.

Bar Léon, Brasil 5 (☎510-30-93). Lively salsa bar. Tues–Sat 8pm–3am; cover US$3.

Bar L'Opera, 5 de Mayo near Bellas Artes. A traditional watering hole, quite tame though still predominantly male, and worth a visit just to see the magnificent fin-de-siècle decor – ornate mahogany panelling, a brass-railed bar and gilt-framed mirrors in the booths.

Bull Dog, Insurgentes 149 and Sullivan (☎566-81-77). Rock venue with live bands. Thurs–Sat 10pm–4am; cover US$15.

La Casa del Canto, Local 4, Glorieta Insurgentes, near Insurgentes Metro. A rock venue with live bands most nights. Unusually for Mexico, it has wheelchair access. Daily 6pm onwards; cover varies.

Casa Rasta, Florencia 44, *Zona Rosa* (☎511-38-51). Reggae club with live Jamaican band. Wed–Sun from 10pm; cover US$12.50 for men, free for women Wed & Thurs; US$17.50 for men, $4 for women Fri & Sat, with free drinks.

Clandestine Disco Bar, Colón 1, near Alameda (☎518-19-91). Gay men's bar with shows; daily from 8pm. Cover Sun–Thurs US$3, Fri & Sat US$11 with free drinks.

La Guadalupana, Higuera 14, Coyoacán. Bar serving good food, as well as imported beer and spirits. Daily noon–11pm.

El Hábito, Madrid 13, Coyoacán (☎659-63-05). Small and quirky theatre and music club. Tues–Sat 10.30pm–midnight.

Harry's Bar, Amberes 45, in the *Zona Rosa*. A popular tourist hang-out with a good atmosphere.

El Hijo del Cuervo, Jardin Centario 17, Coyoacán (☎659-89-59). Recommended, hip and arty venue with occasional theatre improvs and poetry readings. Right on the Jardín, next to Sanborn's.

La Mariposa, Izázaga 7, near Salto del Agua Metro (☎761-13-51). Gay disco. Cover US$10.

Osiris, Niza 22, *Zona Rosa* (☎525-66-84). Sweaty rock venue, cramped but atmospheric. Tues–Sun 8pm–3.30am; weekend cover US$3.

Rock Stock, Reforma 260 at Niza (☎525-60-23). Rock venue with occasional live bands. Thurs–Sat 10pm–4am; cover aound US$8.

Salon Colonia, Manuel M Flores 33, Obrera (☎578-06-19). Live *danzón* music. Sun 4–10pm, Wed 6–11.30pm; cover around US$3.

Zig-Zag Factory, Pasaje Gante 15 at Venustiano Carranza (☎512-18-08). Gay bar for both sexes. Wed from 9pm, Thurs–Sat from 10pm; cover US$5, but free before 11pm Wed.

Markets and shopping

The big advantage of **shopping** in the capital is that you can get goods from all over the country; the disadvantage is that they will be considerably more expensive here. By far the greatest concentration of tourist shops can be found in the **Zona Rosa** – pricey leather goods, jewellery, clothes, handicrafts and souvenirs abound, and there's a roaring trade in fake designer labels, especially Gucci and Lacoste, which are sold everywhere and very rarely genuine. Places here are worth a look, but certainly don't offer good value by Mexican standards.

For anything you really need – clothes and so on – you're better off going to one of the big **department stores**. Liverpool has a branch at Venustiano Carranza 92, and there's a branch of El Palacio de Hierro at 20 de Noviembre 3, just off the Zócalo. **Sanborn's**, good for books, sells quantities of tacky souvenirs, too, and every branch has a sizable pharmacy. Much the best **crafts** outside the markets are sold at the various government-run **FONART** shops – there's a branch at Juárez 89 near the Alameda, and one at Venustiano Carranza 115 in Coyoacán. You should go to one anyway to get an idea of price and quality before venturing into any serious bargaining in the markets.

Every area of the city has its own **market** selling food and essentials, and many others set up stalls for just one day a week along a suburban street.

Markets
Central Artesanal Buenavista, Aldama 187, just east of the train station. Handicrafts from around the country, but rather pricey compared to the Ciudadela (see below). Daily 9am–6pm.

Centro Artesanal de San Juan (Mercadote de Curiosidades Mexicanas), about five blocks south of the Alameda along Dolores. Modern tourist-oriented complex: one of the best places for crafts (silver in particular) and for haggling. Near Salto de Agua Metro (west on Arcos de Belen and second right). Mon–Sat 9am–7pm, Sun 9am–4pm.

Ciudadela, on Balderas near Balderas Metro. The best place in the capital to buy regional crafts and souvenirs from every part of the country. If you forgot to pick up a hammock in the Yucatán or some Olinalá laquerwork in Guerrero, fear not: you can buy them here for not much more. Mon–Sat 11am–7pm, Sun 11am–5pm.

Coyoacán markets. There are two interesting markets in Coyoacán: the daily markets three blocks up from Plaza Hidalgo are typically given over to food, while on Sunday a craft market converges on the plaza itself. There you can buy any manner of *típico* clothing and that essential souvenir, the Marcos doll, made in Chiapas by the Maya.

Flower markets. Very close to San Juan, at the corner of Luis Moya and E. Pugibet, there's a small market selling nothing but flowers – loose, in vast arrangements and wreaths, growing in pots, even paper and plastic. Similar markets can be found in San Ángel and Xochimilco.

La Lagunilla, Rayon, a couple of blocks north of the Plaza Garibaldi. Comes closest to rivalling La Merced (see below) in size and variety, but is best visited on a Sunday when the *tianguis* expands into the surrounding streets, with more stalls selling stones, used books, crafts and bric-a-brac. Get there on buses ("La Villa") heading north on Reforma, or walk from Metro Garibaldi.

Mercado de Sonora, three blocks from La Merced on Av Fray Servando Teresa de Mier. This market is famous for its sale of herbal medicines, medicinal and magical plants and the various *curanderos* (indigenous herbalists) who go there. Metro La Merced.

La Merced, La Merced Metro. The city's largest market, a collection of huge modern buildings, which for all their size can't contain the vast number of traders who want to set up here. Sells almost anything you could conceive of finding in a Mexican market, though fruit, vegetables and other foods take up most space. Daily 6am–6pm.

Sport

Sport is probably the city's biggest obsession, and **football** (soccer), throughout its winter season, the most popular. The big games are held at the Estadio Azteca (capacity 108,500, shared between three teams: América, the nation's most consistently successful club side, Cruz Azul and Necaxa), the Estadio Mexico (seating 65,000, and home of the university side, UNAM) and the Ciudad de los Deportes (45,000, home team Atlante) – check local papers for fixture details. The **biggest games** of the season are generally those between México sides and those from Guadalajara. Having adopted the American Football system of mini-leagues leading to play-offs, the league competitions can be rather dull until the fight for play-off positions begins. América, which is owned by Emilio Azcáarraga, who also owns the Televisa TV monopoly, is viewed by opponents and most neutrals as the government's "official" team, which gives their fixtures a certain edge. Estadio Azteca can be reached by *tren ligero* or Ruta #26 ("Xochimilco") colectivo, both from Metro Tasqueña; Estadio México is reached by "Tlalpán" bus from Metro Chilpancingo; Ciudad de los Deportes is reached by colectivo Ruta #27 ("Apatlaco") from Metro San Antonio.

Throughout the year you can watch **frontón** (pelota, or jai alai) right in the city centre: it's a pretty dull game unless you're betting – it's losing popularity even among locals – but you can wander in and out freely throughout the evening sessions (Mon–Sat). Games are held at the Frontón México on the Plaza de la República. There's **horse racing**, too, throughout the year (Tues, Thurs & Sat & Sun afternoons) at the Hipodromo de las Americas: buses and peseros heading west on Reforma will take you there – look for "Hipodromo". More exciting horsey action is involved in the *charreadas*, or **rodeos**, put on by amateur but highly skilled aficionados most weekends; venues and times vary, so check the press to find out what's going on. Finally, there are **bullfights** every Sunday afternoon in the winter season at the giant Plaza

WRESTLING

After football, *lucha libre*, or **wrestling**, is Mexico's most popular spectator sport. Over a dozen venues in the capital alone host fights six nights a week for a fanatical public. Widely available magazines, comics, photonovels and films recount the real and imagined lives of the rings' heroes and villains. The main bouts are shown daily on TV, which can be a good way to absorb the finer points of the Mexican version of the sport.

Mexican wrestling is generally faster, with more complex moves, and more combatants in the ring at any one time than you would normally see in an American or British bout. This can make the action hard to follow for the uninitiated. More important even than the moves is the maintenance of stage personas, most of whom, heroes or villains, wear masks. The *rudos* (baddies) indulge in sneaky, underhand tactics to foil the opposition, while the *técnicos* (goodies) try and win fair and square. This cod battle between good and evil requires a massive suspension of disbelief: crucial if you want to join in the fun.

One of the most bizarre features of wrestling in recent years has been the emergence of wrestlers as political figures. Perhaps the most famous of all, **Superbarrio** ("Superneighbourhood") arose from the struggle of México's tenant associations for fair rents and decent housing after the 1985 earthquake. He has since become part of mainstream political opposition, regularly challenging government officials to step into the ring with him, and acting as a sort of unofficial cheerleader at opposition rallies. Other wrestlers have espoused political causes, such as Jalapa's Superecologista Verde ("Green Superecologist") who campaigns on environmental issues, including the demanded closure of Laguna Verde nuclear power station.

The most famous wrestler of all time, however, was without doubt **El Santo** ("the Saint"). Immortalized in more than twenty movies, with titles such as *El Santo vs the Vampire Women*, he would fight, eat, drink and play the romantic lead without ever removing his mask, and until after his retirement, he never revealed his identity. His reputation as a gentleman in and out of the ring was legendary, and his death in 1984 widely mourned. His funeral was allegedly the second-best attended in Mexican history after that of President Obregón. His son fights under the name of Hijo del Santo ("Son of Santo") at the legendary Coliseo venue, at Peru 77, Col Centro.

Mexico, the largest bullring in the world. Any bus heading south on Insurgentes will pass close by, or take colectivo Ruta #27 ("Apatlaco") from Metro San Antonio.

Listings

Airlines The main ones are Aerocalifornia, Reforma 332 (☎207-13-92); Aerocaribe, Zola 535, 23rd floor (☎227-02-60 ext 3826); Aeroméxico, Reforma 445 (☎228-99-10, or toll-free ☎91-800-90-999); Aeromar, Dante 14-806, Col Nueva Anzures (☎629-03-88); Air Canada, c/o Continental (see below); American, Reforma 300 (☎209-14-00); America West Airlines, Reforma 322 (☎235-92-92); Aviacsa, Insurgentes Sur 1292 (☎448-8900); British Airways, Reforma 10, 14th floor (☎628-05-50); Canadian, Reforma 390 (☎208-18-83); Continental, Andrés Bello 45, 18th floor (☎280-34-34); Delta, Horacio 1855 (☎202-16-08); Iberia, Reforma 24 (☎130-30-30); Mexicana, handiest office at Juárez 82 and Balderas (☎325-09-90); Northwest, Reforma 381 (☎202-44-44); Noroeste, Nayarit 60 (☎564-42-71); United, Hamburgo 213 (☎627-02-22); US Air, Reforma 10 (☎628-05-00); Virgin, Río Nilo 80-501 (☎208-15-17).

Airport enquiries ☎571-36-00.

American Express Central office and clients' mail service at Reforma 234 in the *Zona Rosa* (☎207-71-37). Six offices throughout the city.

Books and newspapers English-language books and magazines are available from the American Book Store, Madero 25 downtown, Insurgentes Sur 1636 opposite the Teatro de los Insurgentes, and Revolución 1570 in San Ángel; or at the Librería Britanica, Madero 40-B; or Gandhi at Juarez 4.

You can also get news in English, and extensive listings, from the *Mexico City Times* or *The News*, sold on newsstands throughout the centre.

Car rental Thousands of agencies throughout the city – small local operations are often cheaper than the big chains. Try Budget (☎533-04-51 or 533-04-52; airport ☎784-30-11); Coyoacán Rent (☎536-50-14); Hertz (☎592-28-67 or 69); or Limousines Tolteca (☎531-97-51).

Cultural institutes US, Instituto Mexicano Norteamericano de Relaciones Culturales, Hamburgo 115 in the *Zona Rosa*; UK, Instituto Anglo-Mexicano de Cultura, Antonio Caso 127. Both organize film shows, lectures and concerts, run language courses in Spanish and English, and have library facilities. They can be useful places for contacts, and if you're looking for work, long-term accommodation or travelling companions their noticeboards are good places to start.

Embassies and consulates Australia, Ruben Dario 55, Col Polanco (☎531-52-25); Belize, Bernardo de Galves 215, Lomas de Chapultepec (☎520-13-46); Canada, Schiller 529, Col Polanco (☎724-79-00); Cuba, Presidente Masaryk 554, Col Polanco (☎280-80-39); Ireland (honorary consul), Av San Jerónimo 790-A, Col San Jerónimo (☎595-33-33); Guatemala, Explanada 1025 in Lomas de Chapultepec (daily 9am–2pm; visas issued on the spot for a fee; ☎550-75-20); Honduras, A Reyes 220 (☎515-66-89); New Zealand, J.L. LeGrange 103, Col Polanco (☎281-54-86); UK, Rio Lerma 71, *Zona Rosa* (☎207-20-99); USA, Reforma 305 (☎211-00-42).

Emergencies All services ☎080; police enquiries ☎588-51-00; Cruz Roja ☎557-57-57; Medica Movil (mobile paramedic unit), Querétaro 58, Col Roma (☎598-62-22); Locatel gives information on missing persons and vehicles, medical emergencies, emotional crises and public services (☎658-11-11).

Hospital The American-British Cowdray Hospital (ABC) is at C Sur 136 (☎230-80-00). Embassies should be able to provide a list of multi-lingual doctors if necessary.

Language schools Many places run Spanish courses: the Casa de los Amigos, Av Ignacio Mariscal 132, keeps lists and details of language schools in Mexico and Central America.

Laundry Self-service launderettes are surprisingly rare in México, but most hotels should be able to point one out for you. Options include Lavandería Automatica, Edison 91; La Eficaz, Antonio Caso 100; and Lavanet, Chapultepec 463.

Pharmacies Sanborn's offers a wide range of products at most branches, as well as dispensing some prescription drugs. Other options include El Fenix, at Isabel la Católica and 5 de Mayo, and Paris, at Isabel la Católica and 5 de Febrero. There's a homeopathic pharmacy at Mesones 111-B.

MOVING ON FROM THE CITY

By far the most comfortable way to get out of México is **to fly** – it's especially worth it if you have limited time in the country and wish to visit the Yucatán. The two main Mexican carriers, Mexicana and Aeroméxico, cover more than fifty destinations between them. To get **to the airport**, it's easiest to take a regular taxi, but you can also phone SETTA the day before (☎571-93-44) to arrange to be picked up from your hotel.

All México's **bus stations** are used by hordes of competing companies, and the only way to get a full idea of the **timetable** for any given destination is to check each one individually – different companies may take different routes and you can sometimes waste hours by choosing wrongly. We've given a checklist of destinations from each one on p.273. Though it's rare not to be able to get on any bus at very short notice, it can be worth booking in advance for long-distance journeys or for express services to popular destinations – that way you'll have a choice of seat and be sure of getting the fastest service. If you're uncertain which bus station you should be leaving from, simply get into a taxi and tell the driver what your ultimate destination is – he'll know where to take you. You'll find places to eat, and stalls selling food and drink for the journey, in all the termini.

If you're planning to leave by **train** you should get your tickets as far in advance as possible. Certainly don't leave it to the last minute, as you often have to queue for hours. The **ticket offices** are theoretically open from 6am to 10pm daily, but they have a tendency to close for siestas or whenever else they feel the urge.

For details of **destinations, frequencies and journey times** of public transport from México, see the "Travel details" on p.350.

Tourist cards Should you lose yours, or want an extension, officially you apply to the Secretaria de Gobernacion at Chapultepec 284 (Mon–Fri 9am–1.30pm; ☎626-72-00). Extensions are only issued when your original length of stay is almost finished, and will require proof that you have sufficient funds to support yourself.

Travel agencies American Express, see above; Tourismo Flammel, Alvaro Obregón 143, Col Roma (☎525-07-36); Viajes Bojorquez, Juárez 97 (☎518-22-00); Wagonslits Viajes, Juárez 88 (☎512-54-03), Balderas 33 (☎518-11-80), and Hamburgo 195, *Zona Rosa* (☎208-03-53). Amparo, Río Sena 82, Col Cuauhtémoc (☎207-21-88), usually have the best prices for international flights.

Women's groups La Casa de los Amigos (see under "Language schools" above) have details of women's groups and support women's development projects.

Work Very hard to come by – there's some chance of finding a job teaching English, or maybe au pair-type work. Look in the *México News* classifieds, or advertise your services to give private lessons in one of the Spanish papers.

AROUND THE CITY

Breaking out of the capital in any direction, you'll find targets of interest within a couple of hours' drive. First, and the one day-trip that everyone seems to take, are the massive pyramids and ancient city of **Teotihuacán**, about 50km northeast. Directly north, on the road to Querétaro, lies **Tula**, the centre that succeeded Teotihuacán as the Valley's great power. Its site is perhaps slightly less impressive, but imposing nonetheless, and on the way you can stop in **Tepotzotlán**, which holds some of the finest Baroque and colonial art in the country.

To the west, **Toluca**, on the old road to Morelia, hosts a colossal market every Friday, and the surrounding country is full of mountain retreats where Mexicans go to escape the pressures of the city. **Cuernavaca** has long been a sought-after refuge – packed with colonial mansions and gardens, it's also close to several important archeological sites – while beyond it lies the road to Acapulco and the tourist mecca of **Taxco**, renowned for its silver jewellery. East towards the Gulf Coast, on the plain behind the great **volcanoes** stands **Puebla**, one of the most colonial towns in the country, but also one of its most crowded as well as a major industrial centre. Nearby, **Tlaxcala** and **Cholula** were important allies of the Aztecs when Cortés marched this way from the coast. Tlaxcala is now a wonderfully quiet colonial town, while at Cholula is the rubble of the largest pyramid in Mexico. Here the Conquistadors claimed to have erected a church on the site of each pagan temple, and there's said to be a chapel for every day of the year.

San Juan Teotihuacán and around

It seems that every visitor to México heads out to **Teotihuacán** at some stage: there's a constant stream of tours, buses and cars heading this way, and the site itself is crawling with people, increasingly so as the day wears on. On the way you pass a couple of places that, if you're driving, are certainly worth a look, but barely merit the hassle involved in stopping over on the bus. First, at the village of **TEPEXPAN**, is a **museum** (Tues–Sun 10am–5pm; free) housing the fossil of a mammoth dug up in the surrounding plain (then marshland). There's also a skeleton known as the "Tepexpan Man", once claimed to be the oldest in Mexico but recently revealed as less than two thousand years old. This whole area is a rich source of such remains – the Aztecs knew of their existence, which is one of the reasons they believed that the huge structures of Teotihuacán had been built by a race of giants. The museum is a fifteen-minute walk from the village, near the motorway toll booths, where any second-class bus will drop you: the village itself is attractive, with a good café on C de los Reyes, just off the main square.

THE RISE AND FALL OF TEOTIHUACÁN

The **rise and fall** of Teotihuacán is almost exactly contemporary with Imperial Rome. From around 600 BC, there was evidence of small agricultural communities in the vicinity and by 200 BC a township had been established on the present site. From then until 1 AD (the period known as **Teotihuacán I**) the population began to soar, and the city assumed its most important characteristics: the great Pyramids of the Sun and Moon were built, and the Calle de los Muertos laid out. Development continued through **Teotihuacán II** (1–350 AD) with more construction, but most importantly with evidence of the city's influence (in architecture, sculpture and pottery) occurring at sites throughout modern Mexico and into Guatemala and Honduras. From 350 to around 650 (**Teotihuacán III**) it reached the peak of population and power, with much new building and addition to earlier structures. Already by the end of this period, however, there were signs of decline, and the final period (**Teotihuacán IV**) lasted at most a century before the city was sacked, burnt and virtually abandoned. This presumably, was the result of attack by northern tribes, probably the Toltecs, but the disaster may in the end have been as much ecological as military. Vast forests were cut down to build the city (for use in columns, roof supports, door lintels) and huge quantities of wood burnt to make the lime plaster that coated the buildings: the result was severe soil erosion that left the hillsides as barren as they appear today. In addition, the agricultural effort needed to feed so many people (with no form of artificial fertilizer or knowledge of crop rotation) gradually sapped what land remained of its ability to grow more.

Whatever the precise causes, the city was left, eventually, to a ruination that was advanced even by the time of the Aztecs. To them it represented a holy place from a previous age, and they gave it its present name, which translates as "The Place Where Men Became Gods". Although Teotihuacán features frequently in Aztec mythology, there are no written records – what we know of the city is derived entirely from archeological and artistic evidence so that even the original name remains unknown.

A little further on lies the beautiful sixteenth-century monastery of **San Agustin Acolman** (daily 9am–6pm; US$2.50). Built on a raised, man-made terrace (probably on the site of an earlier, Aztec temple), it's a stern-looking building, lightened by the intricacy of its sculpted facade. In the nave and around the cloister are preserved portions of early murals depicting the monks, while several of the halls off the cloister display colonial religious painting and pre-Hispanic artefacts found here. **CHICONCUAC** to the south is rather more of a detour, but on Tuesdays, when there's a large market that specializes in woollen goods, sweaters and blankets, it's included in the itinerary of many of the tours to the pyramids. Again, this is hard to get to on a regular bus, and if you want to visit the market it's easier to do so as an entirely separate trip – buses, again, from the Terminal del Norte.

The site

Teotihuacán is not, on first impression, the most impressive site in Mexico – it lacks the dramatic hilltop setting or lush jungle vegetation of those in the south – but it reveals a city planned and built on a massive scale, the great pyramids so huge that before their refurbishment one would have passed them by as hills, without a second glance. At its height this must have been the most imposing city ever seen in pre-Hispanic America, with a population approaching 200,000 spread over an area of some 156 square kilometres (as opposed to the four square kilometres of the ceremonial centre). Then, every building – grey hulks now – would have been covered in bright polychrome murals.

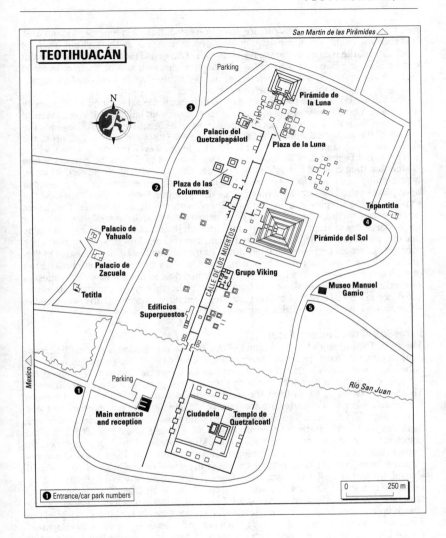

Street of the Dead

From the main entrance, you emerge at the bottom of the restored Calle de los Muertos (which originally extended 1.5km further south) opposite **La Ciudadela**, the Citadel. This enormous sunken square, surrounded by stepped platforms and with a low square altar in the centre, was the city's administrative heart, with the houses of its chief priests and nobles arranged around a vast meeting place. Across the open space stands a tall pyramid construction inside which, during excavation, was found the **Templo de Quetzalcoatl**. With the back of the newer pyramid demolished, the elaborate (Teotihuacán II) temple structure stands revealed. It rises in four steps (of an original six), each sculpted in relief and punctuated at intervals by the stylized heads of Quetzalcoatl, the plumed serpent, and **Tlaloc**, the rain god. Traces of the original paint can be seen in places. This theme – with the goggle-eyed, almost abstract mask of Tlaloc and the fanged snake Quetzalcoatl, its neck ringed with a collar of feathers – recurs in later sites throughout the country.

The **Calle de los Muertos** (Street of the Dead) forms the axis around which the city developed. A broad causeway linking all the most significant buildings, it was conceived to impress, with the low buildings that flank most of its length serving to heighten the impact of the two great temples at the northern end. Other streets, leading off to the rest of the city, originally intersected it at right angles, and even the Río San Juan, which you cross just beyond the Citadel, was canalized so as not to disturb the symmetry (the bridge that then crossed it would have extended the full width of the street). Its name is something of a misconception, since it is neither a simple street – rather a series of open plazas linked by staircases rising some thirty metres between the Citadel and the Pyramid of the Moon – nor in any way linked with the dead. However, the Aztecs believed the buildings that lined it, then little more than earth-covered mounds, to be the burial places of kings. They're not, and although the exact function of most remains unclear, all obviously had some sacred significance. The design, seen in the many reconstructions, is fairly uniform: low three- or four-storey platforms consisting of vertical panels (*tableros*) supported by sloping walls. In many cases several are built on top of each other – nowhere more clearly demonstrated than in the Edificios Superpuestos (**superimposed buildings**) on the left-hand side shortly beyond the river. Here you can descend a metal staircase to find excavated structures underneath the present level – these may have been the living quarters of Teotihuacán's priests.

Pyramids of the Sun and Moon

The great **Pirámide del Sol** (Pyramid of the Sun) is Teotihuacán's outstanding landmark, a massive structure second in size only to Cholula of Mexico's ancient buildings (Cholula is a total ruin). Its base is almost exactly the same size as that of the great Pyramid of Cheops in Egypt, but since this is not a true pyramid it is very much lower. There are wonderful views from the top nonetheless, and the bulk is all the more remarkable when you consider the accuracy of its alignment: on two days a year (May 19 and July 25), the sun is directly over the pyramid at noon, and the main west facade faces the point at which the sun sets on these days. This alignment just off the cardinal points determined the line of the Calle de los Muertos and of the entire city. Equally remarkable is the fact that the 2.5 million tonnes of stone and earth used in its construction were brought here without benefit of the wheel or any beast of burden, and shaped without use of any metal tool. The pyramid you see was reconstructed by Leopoldo Batres in 1908, in a thoroughly cavalier fashion. He blasted, with dynamite, a structure that originally abutted the south face, and stripped much of the surface in a search for a more complete building under the present one. In fact, the Pyramid of the Sun, almost uniquely, was built in one go at a very early stage of the city's development (about 100 AD), and there is only a very small older temple right at its heart. As a result of Batres's stripping the stone surface, the temple has eroded considerably more than it might otherwise have done. He also added an extra terrace to the original four.

You approach by a short staircase leading to the right off the Calle de los Muertos onto a broad esplanade, where stand the ruins of several small temples and priests' dwellings. The main structure consists of five sloping layers of wall divided by terraces – the large flat area at the top would originally have been surmounted by a sanctuary, long disappeared. Evidence of why this massive structure came to be raised here emerged in 1971 when archeologists stumbled on a tunnel (closed to the public) leading to a clover-leaf-shaped **cave** directly under the centre of the pyramid. This, clearly, had been some kind of inner sanctuary, a holy of holies, and may even have been the reason for Teotihuacán's foundation and the basis of its influence. Theories abound as to its exact nature, and many fit remarkably with legends handed down through the Aztecs. It's perhaps most likely that the cave was formed by a subterranean spring, and came to be associated with Tlaloc, god of rain but also a bringer of fertility, as a sort of fountain of life. Alternatively, it could be associated with the legendary "seven grottoes", a symbol of creation from which all later Mexican peoples claimed to have emerged, or to have been the site of an oracle, or associated with a cult of sacrifice – in Aztec times the flayed skins of victims of Xipe Totec were stored in a cave under a pyramid.

At the end of the Street of the Dead rises the **Pirámide de la Luna** (Pyramid of the Moon), a smaller structure built slightly later (but still during Teotihuacán I and one of the oldest you see), whose top, thanks to the higher ground on which it's built, is virtually on a level with that of the Pyramid of the Sun. The structure is very similar, with four sloping levels approached by a monumental stairway, but for some reason this seems a very much more elegant building: perhaps because of the smaller scale, or perhaps as a result of the approach, through the formally laid-out **Plaza de la Luna**. The top of this pyramid offers the best overview of the site's layout, looking straight back down the length of the central thoroughfare.

Lesser structures

The **Palacio de Quetzalpapálotl** (Palace of the Quetzal-butterfly) lies to the left of the Plaza de la Luna, behind the low temples that surround it. Wholly restored, it's virtually the only example of a pre-Hispanic roofed building in central Mexico and preserves a unique view of how the elite lived at Teotihuacán. The rooms are arranged around a patio whose elaborately carved pillars give the Palace its name – their stylized designs represent birds (the brightly coloured Quetzals, though some may be owls) and butterflies. In the galleries around the patio several frescoes survive, all very formalized and symbolic, with the themes reduced almost to geometric patterns. **Mural art** was clearly very important in Teotihuacán, and almost every building has some trace of decoration, though much has been removed for restoration. Two earlier buildings, half buried under the palace, still have substantial remains: in the **Palacio de los Jaguares**, jaguars in feathered headdresses blow conch shells from which emerge curls of music, or perhaps speech or prayers to Tlaloc (who appears along the top of the mural); in the **Temple of the Plumed Shells**, you see a motif of feathers and sea shells along with bright green parrots. Other murals, of which only traces remain, were found in the temples along the Street of the Dead between the two pyramids.

Such art was not reserved for the priests' quarters – indeed some of the finest frescoes have been found in outlying "apartment" buildings. At **Tepantitla**, a residential quarter of the old city across the road from the back of the Pyramid of the Sun, the famous *Paradise of Tlaloc* mural (reproduced in the National Museum of Anthropology, see p.298) was discovered. Only a part of it survives here, but there are others in the complex depicting a procession of priests and a ball-game. All have great vitality and an almost comic-strip quality, with the speech bubbles emerging from the figures' mouths, but their themes always have a religious rather than a purely decorative intent. More can be seen at **Tetitla**, to the west of the main site, and **Atetelco**, a little further west, just off the plan.

There are two **museums** near the Pyramid of the Sun, of which the more interesting is the **Museo del Sitio**, to the south of the pyramid, with artefacts and sculptures from the site, many of them extremely fine. There is also a reconstruction of Teotihuacán in its heydey, partly under a glass floor, and graves complete with exhumed skeletons. The **Museo de Manuel Camio**, in a colonial-style building just outside entrance no. 5, is less interesting, dealing mainly with the excavations of the city. Both museums are covered by the site ticket.

Practicalities

Buses head out to **Teotihuacán** every thirty minutes or so (6am–8pm; 1hr) from the Terminal del Norte. Go to the second-class (left-hand) side of the bus station and look for the Autobuses Teotihuacán stand in Sala 8. (Be aware that these buses have recently been targeted by bandits, so make sure you're not carrying a lot of cash.) It's worth getting an early start to arrive before the worst of the crowds. A road, the Carretera de Circunvalacion, surrounds the main structures at **the site** (8am–5pm; US$2, free on Sun), with parking spaces at intervals and several restaurants. At the principal entrance – said to be the site of the original market, and from where the Calle de los Muertos leads north through the ceremonial centre to the great pyramids – there's a restaurant, several shops and market-type stalls. Alternatively, there's an interesting if slightly pricey **place to eat** near the site called *La Gruta*, a restaurant in a massive cavern behind the Museo de Manuel Cameo, near entrance no. 5. To see the whole site and its outlying buildings could take a full day, but the most important structures can be viewed in a few hours; this involves a lot of climbing and walking, and can be exhausting at such an altitude. You can pick up buses back **to México** from behind the Pyramid of the Sun.

Tula

In legend at least, the mantle of Teotihuacán fell on Tollan, or **TULA**, as the next great power to dominate Mexico. History, legend and archeological evidence, however, are here almost impossible to disentangle, and often flatly contradictory. The Aztecs regarded their city as the descendant of Tula and hence embellished its reputation – the streets, they said, had been paved with gold and the buildings constructed from precious metals and stones; the Toltecs, who founded Tula, were the inventors of every science and art. In reality it seems unlikely that this was ever as large or as powerful a city as Teotihuacán had been – or as Tenochtitlán was to become – and its period of dominance (about 950 to 1150 AD) was relatively short. Yet all sorts of puzzles remain about the Toltec era, and in particular the extent of their influence in the Yucatán – at Chichén Itzá much of the architecture appears to have been influenced by the Toltecs (see p.544). Few people believe that the Toltecs could actually have had an empire, or an infuence, that stretched so far: however warlike (and the artistic evidence is that Tula was a grimly militaristic society, heavily into human sacrifice), they would have lacked the manpower, resources, or any logical justification for such expansion. Nevertheless, they were there.

The answer lies, perhaps, in the legends of **Quetzalcoatl** that surround the city. Adopted from Teotihuacán, the plumed serpent attained far more importance here in Tula, where he is depicted everywhere. Again the facts and legends are almost impossible to extricate, but at some stage Tula certainly had a ruler regarded as Quetzalcoatl who was driven from the city by the machinations of the evil god Texcatlipoca. In legend, Quetzalcoatl fled to the east where he either burnt himself to become the morning star or sailed across the ocean on a raft of snakes, promising one day to return (a prophecy that Cortés turned skilfully to his advantage). What may actually have happened is that the ruler was defeated in factional struggles within Tula and, in exile with his followers, eventually reached Maya territory where they established a new Toltec regime.

The site

Only a small part of **the site** itself (daily 10am–5pm; US$1.75, free on Sun) is of interest: though the city spreads over some considerable area only some of it has been excavated, and the outlying digs are holes in the ground, meaningful only to the archeologists who created them. The ceremonial centre, however, has been partly restored. Centrepiece is the low five-stepped pyramid of the **Templo de Tlahuizcalpantecuhtli** (Temple of the Morning Star), atop which stand the famous **Atlantes**. These giant, five metre-tall figures originally supported the roof of the sanctuary: they represent Quetzalcoatl in his guise as the morning star, dressed as a Toltec warrior. They wear elaborately embroidered loincloths, sandals, and feathered helmets, with ornaments around their necks and legs – for protection, each bears a sun-shaped shield on his back and a chest piece in the form of a stylized butterfly. Each carries an *atlatl*, or spear-thrower, in his right hand and a clutch of arrows or javelins in his left.

Other pillars are carved with more warriors and gods, and these reliefs are a recurrent theme in Tula: the entire temple was originally faced in sculpted stone, and although this was pillaged long ago you can see some remnants from an earlier incarnation of the temple – prowling jaguars and eagles, symbols of the two great warrior groups, devouring human hearts. In front of the temple is a great L-shaped colonnade, where the partly reconstructed pillars originally supported a huge roof under which, perhaps, the priests and nobles would review their troops or take part in ceremonies in the shade. Part of a long bench survives, with its relief decoration of a procession of warriors and priests. More such benches survive in the **Palacio Quemado** (Burnt Palace – it was destroyed by fire), next to the temple on the western side. In the middle of its three rooms, each a square, roofed area with a small central patio to let light in, is the best preserved of them, still with much of its original paint, and two Chacmools.

The main square of the city stood in front (south) of the temple and palace, with a low altar platform in the centre and the now ruinous pyramid of the Templo Mayor on the eastern side. The larger of two **ball-courts** in the central area is on the western side of the square: although ruinous, this is one of the closest links between Tula and Chichén Itzá – of identical shape and orientation to the great ball-court there, and displaying many of the same features. To the north of the temple stands the **Coatepantli** (Serpent Wall), elaborately carved in relief with images of human skeletons being eaten by giant rattlesnakes; beyond this, across an open space, there's a second ball-court, smaller but in better order.

Practicalities

Buses run from México's Terminal del Norte (Autobuses del Valle de Mezquital; every 40min, less than 1hr 30min; slower services via a refinery – "via Refinario" – run every 20min), and from Querétaro (9 daily; 2hr) to the modern town of **Tula de Allende** in the Valley just below the ruins. The **entrance to the site** is on the far side of the town, a considerable walk (about 30min) all the way round the perimeter fence: turn right out of the bus station to the main road (Ocampo), where you turn right again, over the river and left before the train tracks (signposted "Zona Arqueologica") and left after a kilometre, just before the railway bridge over the road. If you don't fancy the walk, either get off the bus just as it enters the town by the bridge, where the road (signed "Zona Arqueologica") branches off to the right towards the entrance, or take a taxi from the zócalo. There's a small modern **museum** (daily 10am–5pm), with assorted statues, artefacts and displays on the Toltecs, just inside the gate.

In Tula itself it's worth taking a few minutes to look over the impressive, fortress-like **Franciscan monastery and church** (built around 1550). There are several good cafés and **restaurants** around the main square.

Tepotzotlán

Logically, **TEPOTZOTLÁN** lies en route from Tula to the capital, but if you're relying on public transport it's not easy getting from one to the other. It may be easiest to visit the two separately – Tepotzotlán is easily close enough to the city to be a morning's excursion, though once you're there you may find the place seduces you into staying longer. The town is small and thoroughly Mexican-colonial, and the clear air, trees, hills and views make a wonderful antidote to the big city blues. Though it's somewhat touristy, commercialization is still low-key, and the majority of visitors are Mexican: on Saturdays it's particularly enjoyable, with a holiday atmosphere but no crowds.

The Town

Atmosphere apart, the reason people come to Tepotzotlán is to see the magnificent Baroque **Colegio de San Francisco Javier** and the **Museo Nacional de Arte Virreinal** that it houses. These, though, are attraction enough. The church was founded by the Jesuits, who arrived in 1580 with a mission to convert the Otomí locals. Most of the huge complex you see today was established during the following century, but constantly embellished right up to the expulsion of the Jesuits in 1767. The facade of the church – considered one of the finest examples of churrigueresque architecture in the country – was completed barely five years before this. The wealth and scale of all this gives some idea of the power of the Jesuits prior to their ouster; after they left, it became a seminary for the training of regular priests until the late nineteenth century, when the Jesuits were briefly readmitted. The Revolution led to its final abandonment in 1914.

Colegio de San Francisco Javier

The main entrance to the **Colegio de San Francisco Javier** (Tues–Fri 10am–5pm, Sat & Sun 10am–6pm; US$1.75, free on Sun) leads into the **Claustro de los Aljibes**, with a well at the centre and pictures of the life of Ignacio Loyola (founder of the Jesuits) around the walls. The entrance to the church is off the cloister, but the main flow will take you round the museum first before leading back here. Directly off the cloister are the **Orfebrería** (the store of precious metals), packed with a treasure of beautiful silver reliquaries and crucifixes, censers, custodia, vestments and even a pair of silver sandals; and the **Botica**, or pharmacy, with bottles, jars, pestles and mortars, and all the other equipment of an eighteenth-century healer. The **Capilla Doméstica** also opens off the cloister, a whirl of painted and gilded Rococo excess, with a magnificent gilded retablo full of mirrors and little figures.

Descending a level, you come to the **Claustro de los Naranjos**, planted with orange and lemon trees and with a fountain in the middle. Around it are displays of wooden religious statuary – Balthazar and Caspar, two of the three kings, are particularly fine. Other rooms contain more colonial miscellany – lacquer work, furniture (notably an inlaid wooden desk) and clothes. Outside extends the walled **Huerta**, or garden, some three hectares of it still beautifully maintained, with lawns, shady trees and floral displays, as well as vegetables and medicinal herbs cultivated as they would have been by the monks. Dotted around are various architectural pieces and large sculptures, including the original eighteenth-century **Salto del Agua** that stood at the end of the aqueduct carrying water from Chapultepec into México (a replica of the fountain stands in the capital now, near Metro Salto del Agua).

Back inside, as you continue round the cloister, there's a room devoted to arms and armour, a substantial collection including an amazing giant penknife that opens into a sword. The **upper storey** around the cloister is mainly devoted to the Spanish trade with Asia, which was conducted via Mexico: included here are fine pieces of Chinese porcelain; statuary; intricate *taracea* (marquetry or inlaid work) in various materials, especially mother-of-pearl; and various furnished rooms.

Heading towards the exit, you'll pass the way down to the interior of the **church**. If the facade is spectacular, it's still barely preparation for the dazzling interior. Dripping with gold, and profusely carved with a bewilderment of saints and cherubim, it strikes you at first as some mystical cave of treasures. The main body of the church and its chapels house five huge gilded retablos, stretching from ceiling to floor, each more gloriously curlicued than the last, their golden richness intensified by the soft yellow light penetrating through the alabaster that covers the windows. This, though, is only the start, for hidden to one side is arguably the greatest achievement of Mexican Baroque, the octagonal **Camarín de la Virgen**. It's not a large room, but every inch is elaborately decorated, and the hand of the native craftsmen is clearly evident in the exuberant carving – fruit and flowers, shells and abstract patterns crammed in between the angels. There are mirrors angled to allow visitors to appreciate the detail of the ceiling without straining their necks. The Camarín is reached through the **Capilla de la Virgen de Loreto**, inside which is a "house" faced in azulejos – supposedly a replica of Mary's house, in which Jesus grew up.

Practicalities

To **get to Tepotzotlán** from México take a bus from Metro Cuatro Caminos (aka Toreo) or Rosario. The buses are slow, rattling their way round the suburbs for what feels like hours (though the total journey is actually little over an hour) before finally leaving the city. Alternatively, you can take the Tula bus, or a second-class service to Querétaro, either of which departs from the Terminal del Norte, and get off at the first motorway tollbooths (Caseta de Tepoxotlán). From here it's about a twenty-minute walk to Tepotzotlán, west on a minor road, and there's a good chance of being able to hitch or catch a local bus. You can also get off at the tollbooths if you want to visit Tepotzotlán on the way back from Tula. Alternatively, you can visit Tepotzotlán first, then walk down to the tollbooths to get a bus to Tula or back to México, though it can prove hard to flag one down, since not all buses stop here.

You'll find plenty of places to **eat and drink** around the plaza, and at weekends there'll probably be *mariachi* musicians playing. The *Hostería del Convento*, in the seminary's grounds, is fairly pricey but has excellent Mexican food. Of the places overlooking the zócalo, *Pepe* and the *Carta Blanca* on the west side are slightly better value than the *Restaurant Virreyes* on the north side.

In the week before Christmas, the *pastorelas*, or **nativity plays**, staged here are renowned – and booked up long in advance; at other times, you may well catch a concert in the church or cloisters.

Toluca

TOLUCA DE LERDO, capital of the state of México, and at nearly 2800m the highest city in the country, is today a large and modern industrial centre, with only a few minor attractions. It is, however, surrounded by beautiful mountain scenery – dominated by the white-capped Nevado de Toluca – and the site of what is allegedly the largest single **market** in the country, despite being halved in size by the city's government. Held a couple of kilometres southeast of the centre, just east of the bus station, every Friday (and to a lesser extent throughout the week), the market constitutes the overriding reason to visit, attracting hordes of visitors from the capital. It is so vast that there can be no question of its being overwhelmed by tourists; quite the opposite, many outsiders find themselves overwhelmed by the scale of the place, lost among the thousands of stalls and crowds from the state's outlying villages. There's a substantial selection of local crafts – woven goods and pottery above all – but also vast areas selling more humble everyday domestic items. For an idea of what quality and prices to expect, head first for the Casa de Artesanías, Paseo Tollocan 700 Ote, a few blocks east of the market.

In the centre of town stands the nineteenth-century **Cathedral** and, to its east, the mustard yellow church of **Santa Cruz**. These are surrounded on three sides by *portales* lined with shops, restaurants and cafés: Portal Madero runs to the south on Hidalgo, Portal 20 de Noviembre to the east on Allende, and Portal Reforma to the west on Bravo. To the north lies the massive open Plaza de los Mártires, in the northwest corner of which, the **Museo José Maria Velasco** (Tues–Sun 10am–6pm; free) displays a goodly collection of nineteenth-century paintings. Northeast of Plaza de los Mártires, on the other side of the Palacio del Gobierno dominating the plaza's north side, is Plaza Garibay, rather prettier with shrubbery and fountains. In its northwest corner, the **Museo de Bellas Artes** (Tues–Sun 10am–6pm; US$0.25, free on Sun) shows off some of the best fine arts in the state, while at its eastern end, Toluca's **Botanical Gardens** (Tues–Sun 9am–5pm; US$0.70) are housed in an enormous Art-Nouveau greenhouse with amazing stained-glass windows in the Mexican muralist style.

Some 10km west of Toluca, the **Centro Cultural Mexiquense** harbours several museums (all Tues–Sun 10am–6pm; US$0.70, free on Sun) scattered in park-like grounds. Among them are the **Museo Regional**, devoted to the archeology and history of the state, a small **Museo de Arte Moderno** and, perhaps the most interesting, the **Museo de Artes Populares**, a collection of local crafts, ancient and modern, in a restored hacienda. Attached to this last is the **Museo de la Charrería**, full of cowboy equipment, papier-mâché figures from the Day of the Dead, clothes and textiles, "Tree of Life" sculptures and the like. Although local buses run out there, you really need your own transport to explore the place fully.

Practicalities

An almost uninterrupted stream of **buses** leaves México's Terminal Poniente for Toluca throughout the day; the journey takes about an hour. Toluca's modern **Central Camionera** is right by the market. If you arrive during the day, you can get a bus to the city centre from the station or on the highway (Paseo Tollocán) to the left of the station; after 8.30pm, you'll be reliant on taxis, but disregard those at the bus station entrance – they charge roughly double the price of the ones that run along the main road (5 de Mayo) at the side of the station building. Banamex and Serfin on the Portal Maderro **change dollars**.

There are plenty of places to eat and some grotty hotels around the market, but there's little point in staying in Toluca unless you plan to stop over Thursday night, get to the market early, and continue west – though be warned that it can be hard to **find a room** on Thursdays. At the terminal itself, *Terminal* (☎72/17-45-88; ③) is good, despite its grotty surroundings; there's a restaurant at the station as well. Best option in the city centre is the *Colonial*, Hidalgo Ote 103 (☎72/15-97-00, fax 14-70-66; ④), a quiet, cosy place with a good restaurant, bar and live music. For something cheaper, the *Hotel San Carlos*, at Portal Madero 210 (☎72/14-43-43; ③), has definitely seen better days, with sporadic hot water, but is under renovation and OK for a night. *San Francisco*, Rayon Sur 104 (☎72/13-44-15, fax 13-29-82; ⑤), is a more luxurious option, with its own pool, bar and restaurant.

As usual, the markets and outlying areas are the places to go for budget **food**, while around the Portales there are some good, pricier choices. The *Hostería de las Ramblas*, at Portal 20 de Noviembre 107, is an excellent place for lunch or dinner, while the *Restaurante Impala*, at Portal Madero 218, does good food at moderate prices. The

unnamed restaurant opposite the *Impala* at Hidalgo Pte 231 has low-priced set menus –
a little bland, but good and filling – while *Las Ramblitas*, Portal Reforma 108, does good
and very reasonable set breakfasts. The *Coffee Station*, Portal Madero 212, is one of several places serving great if slightly pricey coffee, and a range of simple, set breakfasts.

Moving on from Toluca, there are frequent **buses** from the terminal to México,
Chalma, Cuernavaca, Morelia, Ixtapan, Malinalco, Querétaro and Taxco during the day
(at night the terminal appears to close and services are much less frequent). Buy the
ticket direct from the driver at the appropriate rank. Elite runs daily services to destinations as far afield as Mazatlán, Tijuana and Mexicali. *De paso* services from México
to Zitácuaro usually stop on the bypass 500m south of the bus station.

Around Toluca

Although most villages around Toluca do have a bus service – if only once or twice a day
– this region is easiest explored by car. One trip you will definitely miss out on unless
you drive is a visit to the volcano, the **Nevado de Toluca**, or Xinantécatl (4690m). A
rough dirt road – not practicable during the rainy season or midwinter – leads all the way
to two small lakes (the **Lagos del Sol** and **de la Luna**) in the heart of the crater. From
its jagged lip the views are breathtaking: below you the lakes; eastwards a fabulous vista
across the Valleys of Toluca and Mexico; and to the west a series of lower, greener hills
ranging towards the peaks of the Sierra Madre Occidental. You need a tough vehicle to
get up here, and healthy lungs to undertake even a short climb at 3000m.

Easier is a visit to the archeological site of **Calixtlahuaca** (Tues–Sun 10am–5pm;
US$1.25, free on Sun), just north of the city (a US$3 taxi-ride away) and accessible by local
bus (from Juárez, two blocks east of the *portales*). This was the township of the Matlazinca
people, inhabited from prehistoric times and later subjugated by the Aztecs, who established a garrison here in the fifteenth century. Calixtlahuaca was not a willing subject, and
there were constant rebellions; after one, in 1475, the Aztecs allegedly sacrificed over
11,000 Matlazinca prisoners on the **Temple of Quetzalcoatl**. This, several times built
over, is the most important structure on the site. Dedicated to the god in his role as
Ehecatl, god of wind, its circular design is typical, allowing the breezes to blow freely
around the shrine. See also the remains of the pyramid devoted to Tlaloc, and the nearby
tzompantli (skull rack), both constructed of the local pink and black volcanic stone.

West from Toluca, the road towards Morelia and the state of Michoacán is truly
spectacular. Much of this wooded, mountainous area – as far as Zitácuaro – is given
over to villas inhabited at weekends by wealthy refugees from the capital, and nowhere
more so than **VALLE DE BRAVO**, reached by turning off to the left about halfway. Set
in a deep, pine-clad valley, the town sits on the eastern shore of an artificial lake, the
Presa Miguel Alemán. There's everything here for upmarket relaxation: boat trips,
sailing, swimming, water-skiing, riding, hiking and golf. It's an expensive place, but
does make for a very relaxing break – especially if you come during the week, when
fewer people are about and hotels drop their prices. Among the more reasonably priced
places to stay is the *Posada Casa Vieja* (☎726/2-03-38; Fri & Sat ④, rest of the week ②),
Juárez 101, with clean, bright rooms and ample hot water. There's a reasonable bus service that makes the two-and-a-half-hour journey from México via Toluca.

South towards Taxco

A strange thing about the route west is that as you descend from Toluca, so the country becomes more mountainous: where Toluca is on a very high plateau, broken only
by the occasional soaring peak, the lower country to the west is constantly, ruggedly
hilly. It's also warmer, and far more verdant. Much the same happens as you head

south, although here you head across the plateau for some way until you start to go down into the mountains. There are frequent buses along these roads, and several places of interest on the way. The first village, less than 10km out of Toluca, is **METEPEC**, famed as a pottery-making centre. Brightly coloured local wares can be found at craft shops throughout the country; supposedly the figures that characterize these pots were originally inspired by the saints on the facade of Metepec's sixteenth-century Franciscan monastery, and in this century Diego Rivera taught the villagers new techniques of colouring and design. There's a market here on Mondays. After some 25km you pass **TENANGO DEL VALLE**, from where you can visit the excavated remains nearby of the large fortified Malatzinca township of **Teotenango** (Tues–Sun 9am–2pm & 3–5pm; US$0.75, free on Sun). To get there from the centre of the village, head north along Porfirio Díaz Nte, then take a left up Roman Piña Chan. There's a small museum on site.

TENANCINGO, the next village of any size along Hwy-55, is perhaps more interesting, and here there are a couple of small **hotels** – try the *Hotel Jardín* in an old mansion on the zócalo (☎740/2-01-08; ②) – which make this a quiet alternative to Toluca or Taxco. Liqueurs made from the fruit that grows in abundance on the surrounding plain, and finely woven traditional *rebozos* (shawls) are sold here, many of them produced at the lovely monastery of **El Santo Desierto**. The chief reason to stop, however, is the proximity of the amazing Aztec ruins at **Malinalco** (see opposite), which can be reached by regular buses (every 15min; 30min), most of which continue on to Chalma.

Continuing on the main road, the next possible stop is **IXTAPAN DE LA SAL**, a long-established spa whose mineral-rich waters are supposed to cure a plethora of muscular and circulatory ills. From the **bus station**, walk up Benito Juárez, the town's main road, to reach the centre. You can swim in Ixtapan's pools – this is cheaper in the old town, where Balneario Municipal on Allende, two blocks east of the bus station (daily 7am–6pm) charges US$1.25, but more elegant at the Balneario Ixtapan, at the very top of Juárez (daily 7am–7pm; US$6.25). The price includes entry to the massive **aqua park**, with slides and fairground-style rides. The town gets pretty packed out at weekends, when it may be hard to find a room, but there are some very pleasant **hotels** to choose from, among them the *Guadalajara*, a block north of the Balneario Municipal at Allende 3 (☎714/3-03-57; ②), a friendly, basic place where all rooms have hot water, in theory at least. At the excellent-value *Casa Sarita*, three blocks east and one north, at Obregón 542 (☎714/3-01-72; ③), you can take full board and tuck into the hotel's good wholesome food. For more luxury, try the *Avenida*, towards the top of Juárez at no. 614, near the *Balneario Ixtapan*. (☎714/3-02-41, fax 3-10-39; ⑤), a three-star hotel with swimming pool, whose rooms all have TV, phone and FM radio. Alternatively, on Aldama, four blocks north of the bus station, and nearby on Juárez, you'll find various casas de huéspedes with prices in the ③ bracket. Some of these lock you in after 11pm (or out, if you stay out too late).

Further south, just before Taxco, you pass close to the vast complex of caves known as the **Grutas de Cacahuamilpa** (daily 9am–5pm, guided tours hourly; US$2). This network of caverns, hollowed out by two rivers, extends for some 70km – although the one-and-a-half-hour obligatory guided tour obviously takes in only a fraction, passing evocative rock formations with names like "the hunchback" and "the bottle of champagne". Among the graffiti you're shown a rather prim note from the wife of Maximilian – "Maria Carlota reached this point". Alongside, Lerdo de Tejada, who became president in 1872, five years after Maximilian's execution, has scrawled "Sebastian Lerdo de Tejada went further". There's a swimming pool by the entrance to the caves, as well as a restaurant and several food stalls; buses continue on to Taxco or Cuernavaca. **Buses and combis** to the caves each leave hourly from opposite the Flecha Roja bus terminal on Av Kennedy in Taxco: *combis* on the hour, buses on the half hour.

Malinalco and Chalma

Though the Aztec site of **MALINALCO** is small – still incomplete at the time of the Conquest – and relatively little visited, it is undeniably one of the most evocative of its kind to survive. Carved in part from the raw rock of a steep mountainside, this was the setting for the sacred **initiation ceremonies** by which Aztec youth became members of the warrior elite. The village itself is a lovely little place surrounded by rich villas – many of them, complete with swimming pools, the weekend retreat of the capital's privileged few – and centred on the huge Augustinian church of Santa Monica. You'll be dropped by bus in the plaza in front of the church, from where **the site** (Tues–Sun 9am–6pm; US$1.75, free on Sun) is some twenty minutes' walk up a very steep, stepped path.

Looking back over the village and valley, the **ruins** may be small, but they are undeniably impressive, the main structures and the stairways up to them partly cut out of the rock, partly constructed from great stone blocks. The most remarkable aspect is the circular inner sanctuary of the **Templo Principal** (House of the Eagle), hewn entirely from the face of the mountain. You approach up a broad staircase on either side of which sit stone jaguars – in the centre an all but worn-away human statue would have held a flag. To one side of the entrance, a broken eagle warrior sits atop Quetzalcoatl, the feathered serpent; guarding the other side are the remains of a Jaguar warrior, representative of the second Aztec warrior class. The doorway of the sanctuary itself, cut through a natural rock wall, represents the giant mouth of a serpent – entrance was over its tongue, and around it traces of teeth are still visible. Right in the centre of the floor lies the figure of an eagle, and on the raised horseshoe-shaped bench behind are two more eagles and the pelt of a jaguar, all carved in a single piece from the bedrock. Behind the first eagle is a hole in the ground where the hearts of human sacrificial victims would be placed, supposedly to be eaten while still beating as the final part of the initiation into warriorhood.

Other structures at the site include a small circular platform by the entrance, unfinished at the time of the Conquest, and a low pyramid directly in front of the main temple. Beyond this lie two larger temples. The first, Edificio III, again has a circular chamber at the centre, and it is believed that here Aztec warriors killed in battle were cremated, their souls rising to the heavens to become stars. Edificio IV was originally a temple of the sun; much of it was used to construct the church in the village. Outside the site, visible from about halfway up the steps to the ruins, you can see another prehistoric building nestling among the mountains. It's still used by local residents as a place of pilgrimage: formerly a shrine to an Aztec altar-goddess, it is now dedicated to San Miguel.

Minalco has a very helpful **tourist office** on the main plaza (Mon–Fri 9am–3pm, Sat 9am–1pm; ☎714/7-01-11), and several **places to stay**, handiest of which is the *Hotel Santa Mónica*, Av Hidalgo 109 (☎714/7-01-21; ②), just below the plaza on the way to the site; if you find no one in attendance, the owner runs a shop on the plaza. At the northern end of the village, on the way in from Tenancingo, is the homely and spotless *Hotel Marmil*, at Progreso 606 (☎714/7-09-16; ③), with very pleasant country-style rooms and some four-person self-catering bungalows (⑤). There are also a couple of good RV park/campsites nearby.

Getting to the site: Chalma

Malinalco may seem on the face of it to be somewhat isolated, but in practice it's not difficult to reach by public transport. Though Tenancingo offers one possible approach, the easiest way in is via the tiny village of **CHALMA**, on good roads all the way. There are **direct buses** to Chalma from México's Terminal Poniente, and also from Toluca and from Cuernavaca via Santa Marta (this is a slightly rougher ride: if you're driving, avoid the direct road signed from Chalma back to Cuernavaca, which rapidly deteriorates to a frightening, mountainous single track). From Chalma, colectivos leave for Malinalco every few minutes. They set off from the main street by the taxi sign, downhill from where most buses stop.

Chalma is so well served by bus because it's an important centre of **pilgrimage**, attracting vast crowds every Sunday, and at times of special religious significance (especially the first Friday in Lent, *Semana Santa* and September 29) so many people converge here that it's impossible to get anywhere near the church. At such times pilgrims camp out for miles around to take part in the rituals, a fascinating blend of Christian and more ancient pagan rites: the deity Oztocteotl, god of caves, was at one time venerated in a natural cave here, but he was "miraculously" replaced by a statue of Christ on arrival of the first missionaries. In the seventeenth century, this crucifix was moved to a new church, the **Santuario de Chalma**, now the place of pilgrimage and of miraculous appearances of a Christ-like figure. As well as paying their devotions to Christ, the pilgrims bathe in the healing waters that flow from the cave. Despite all this, and the fact that the town is surrounded by impressive craggy peaks, it has to be added that Chalma is a complete dump, its filthy, muddy streets lined with stalls offering tacky souvenirs. Nearby **AHUE-HUETE** also has a shrine visited by many pilgrims, at a spot where a miraculous spring issues from the roots of a huge old tree. Many people stop here first (it's before Chalma on the way from México), and some proceed the last few kilometres to Chalma on foot.

Cuernavaca and around

The old road to Acapulco ran out from the capital via Cuernavaca and Taxco, and although the modern route (Hwy-95D) skirts the former and gives Taxco a wide berth, both remain firmly established on the tourist treadmill. The journey starts well: a steep, winding climb out of the Valley of México into refreshing pine forests, and then gently down, leaving the city pollution behind. It's a fast road, too, and, smog permitting, offers lovely views back over the DF.

CUERNAVACA has always been a place of escape from the city – the Aztecs called it *Cuauhnahuac* (Place by the Woods), and it became a favourite resort and hunting ground for their rulers. Cortés seized and destroyed the city during the siege of Tenochtitlán, but he, too, ended up building himself a palace here, the Spanish corrupting the name to Cuernavaca (Cow Horn) for no better reason than their inability to cope with the original. The fashion then established has been followed ever since – among others by the Emperor Maximilian and the deposed Shah of Iran – but for the casual visitor the modern city is in many ways a disappointment. Its spring-like climate remains, but as capital of the state of Morelos, Cuernavaca is rapidly becoming industrialized and the streets in the centre permanently clogged with traffic and fumes. The gardens and villas that shelter wealthy Mexicans and ex-pats are almost all hidden behind high walls, or so far out in the suburbs that you won't see them. It seems an ill-planned and widely spread city, certainly not easy to get about on foot. Food and lodging, too, come relatively expensive, in part thanks to the large foreign contingent, swelled by tourists and by students from the many language schools. On the other hand, the town is attractive enough and makes a good base for heading north to the village of **Tepoztlán**, with its raucous fiesta, or south to the ruins of **Xochicalco**. It may also be worthwhile taking a trip to **Cuautla** if you are at all interested in Mexican history: Emiliano Zapata is buried here in the Jardín Revolución del Sur.

Arrival and information

Buses run every few minutes to Cuernavaca from México's Central del Sur: of the three lines you can take **from the capital**, Flecha Roja is probably the best since its

Cuernavaca terminal, on Morelos, is central and easy to find. Pullman de Morelos also stops quite close to the centre, at the corner of Abasolo and Netzahualcoyotl; simply walk up the latter and you find yourself at the heart of things. The first-class Estrella de Oro terminus is a long way south of the centre on Morelos – worth getting to, though, if you're continuing on the long ride south to Acapulco and the coast. Estrella Roja services **to and from Puebla** pull in at a station three blocks south of the zócalo at Cuauhtémotzin and Galeana. Buses **to México** leave most frequently (every 15min) from Pullman de Morelos, with fewer from Flecha Roja and Estrella de Oro. Buses to Tepoztlán and Cuautla leave from the local bus stand just south of the market (head east on Degollado to find it), with other buses to Cuautla from Estrella Roja, along with buses to Miacatlán (for the Crucero de Xochicalco).

The very helpful and well-informed state **tourist office** is well south of the centre, near the Estrella de Oro terminus, at Morelos Sur 802 (Mon–Fri 8am–9pm, Sat & Sun 10am–4pm; ☎73/14-38-72); it's a good idea to come here to pick up a map, since Cuernavaca can be very confusing. They also have information on buses and excursions, and leaflets on several other destinations around the country.

The **post office** (Mon–Fri 8am–7pm, Sat 9am–1pm) is on the southwest corner of the zócalo, with a public **phone and fax** office next door (Mon–Fri 8am–6pm, Sat 9am–4.30pm, Sun 9am–12.30pm). Downtown **casas de cambio** include Divinter, at Hidalgo 7-C by Galeana, and Gesta on the corner of Galeana and Lerdo de Tejada, with two more on Morrow at nos. 8 and 11.

Accommodation

Cuernavaca's tourist office has a long list of **hotels** and contact addresses for families offering **private rooms**, the latter a service aimed at students attending local language schools – the schools themselves and their noticeboards are also good sources for such accommodation. Many of the cheaper options are just north of the centre, on Matamoros and the streets that connect it with Morelos: you'll pass several if you walk in from the Flecha Roja bus station.

América, Aragón y León 111 (☎73/18-61-27). Basic but respectable place in a street mostly full of dives; rooms with bath are more expensive. ⑤.

Colonial, Aragón y León 104 (☎73/18-64-14). Across the street from the *América* and a bit less basic; the most comfortable hotel in Aragón y León. ④.

Iberia, Rayon 7 (☎73/12-60-40). Large rooms and friendly staff. Parking available. ④.

Las Mañanitas, Ricardo Linares 108 (☎73/14-14-66, fax 18-36-72; *reyl@infosel.net.mx*). One of the best luxury hotels in Cuernavaca, with popular restaurant and bars. ④.

Royal, Matamoros 11 (☎73/18-64-80, fax 14-40-18). One of a number of similar places along Matamoros; comfortable rooms with bath, and space for parking. ③.

Papagayo, Motolina 13 (☎73/14-17-11). With its swimming pool and children's area this place can get raucous, but the rooms are good value and the price includes breakfast. ⑤.

Roma, Matamoros 405 (☎73/18-87-78). Simple but clean; all rooms have bathroom and overhead fan. ③.

The Town

The zócalo – as ever, the heart of the city – comprises the Plaza de Armas and the smaller Jardín Juárez, with its bandstand, to the northwest. Right on the plaza, the **Palacio de Cortés** (Tues–Sun 10am–5pm; US$1.75, free on Sun) houses the **Museo Regional Cuauhnahuac**. Building work began as early as 1522, when, although Tenochtitlán had fallen, much of the country had yet to fall under Spanish control, and the fortress-like aspect of the palace's earlier parts reflects this period. Over the centuries, though, it's been added to and modified substantially – first by Cortés himself and his descendants, later by the state authorities to whom it passed – so that what you see today is every bit a palace. The museum is a good one, covering local archeology and history, with a substantial collection of colonial art, weaponry and everyday arte-facts, including a reproduction of a modern Tlahuica Indian hut. The highlight, though, is the series of Diego Rivera **murals** around the gallery. Depicting Mexican history from the Conquest to the Revolution, they concentrate in particular on the atrocities committed by Cortés, and on the revolutionary Emiliano Zapata, who was born in nearby Cuautla, raised most of his army from the peasants of Morelos, and remains something of a folk hero to the locals. From the balcony here, if you're lucky, there are wonderful views to the east, with Popocatépetl in the far distance. Around the main entrance, you can see excavated traces of the Aztec pyramid that originally occupied the site.

Around the twin plazas of the zócalo, you'll find a series of **cafés** where you can sit outdoors. Head out from here along Hidalgo, and you'll reach the **Cathedral**, founded by Cortés in 1529. Bulky and threatening from the outside (at one stage there were actually cannons mounted along the battlemented roof line), it has been remarkably tastefully refurbished within: stripped almost bare and painted in plain gold and white. Traces of murals, discovered during the redecoration, have been uncovered in places – they have a remarkably East Asian look and are believed to have been painted by a Christian Chinese or Filipino artist in the days when the cathedral was the centre for missions to the Far East. The main Spanish trade route then came through here, with goods brought across the Pacific to Acapulco, overland through central Mexico, and on from Veracruz to Spain. The present bishop of Cuernavaca is one of the country's most liberal and, apart from doing up his cathedral, is renowned for his outspoken sermons and for the "Mariachi Mass" that he instituted here. Every Sunday, this service is con-ducted to the accompaniment of traditional Mexican music and usually attracts large crowds.

South of the cathedral, at the corner of Nezahualcoyotl and 20 de Noviembre, the **Museo Robert Brady** (Tues–Sun 10am–6pm; US$2.50) occupies a former convent built in the sixteenth century and houses the the private collection of the Iowa-born artist, who moved to Cuernavaca in the 1960s and died in 1986. Including paintings by Frida Kahlo, Rufino Tamayo and Graham Sutherland, as well as objets d'art from around the world, both old and new, and with two outside patios complete with sculp-tures, the collection is arranged aesthetically, without regard to history, geography or classification of artists' style. As a result, what you see is a beautiful home rather than a typical museum, and is well worth a visit.

A block to the west, at Morelos 103, is the entrance to the **Jardín Borda** (Tues–Sun 10am–5.30pm; US$1.25, free on Sun), a large formal garden laid out by the Taxco min-ing magnate José de la Borda (see p.339) in the eighteenth century. Both the gardens and Borda's mansion are in a rather sorry state, but they remain a delightfully tranquil reminder of the haven Cuernavaca once was – and no doubt still is behind the walls of its exclusive residences. Maximilian and Carlota adopted Borda's legacy as their week-end home, but Maximilian also had a retreat in Cuernavaca that he shared with his native mistress, "La India Bonita". Officially named "La Casa del Olindo", this second house was popularly known as "La Casa del Olvido" since the builder "forgot" to include quarters for Carlota. Rather more distant – 2km southeast of the centre, at Matamoros 200 in the Colonoa Acapantzingo – is the **Museo de la Herbolaria** (daily 9am–5pm; free), whose grounds and collection of medicinal plants are worth taking a taxi (or a long walk) to see.

Other sites scattered further out in the fringes of the city include the sole significant reminder of the pre-colonial period, the **Pyramid of Teopanzolco** (daily 10am–5pm; US$1.25, free on Sun). Even this was so effectively buried that it took an artillery bom-bardment during the Revolution to uncover it. To the northeast of the centre beyond the train station (which is what the gunners were aiming at), it's a small temple in which two pyramids can be seen, one built over the other. The pyramid can be reached by city bus #10 from Degollado and Reelección.

Eating and drinking

You don't need to wander far from the centre to find good **places to eat**: there's a particulary fine group around the zócalo.

Café Parroquia, Guerrero, in the northwest corner of the zócalo. Perhaps the best café in the city, with the cheapest beer in the centre, and also a couple of Lebanese dishes on the menu.

La India Bonita, Morrow 6, just off Morelos. Lovely restaurant with a pleasant outdoor patio, excellent but moderately priced food (including set breakfasts) and impeccable service.

Pollo y Más, Galeana 4. Opposite the zócalo, serving tasty roast chicken, enchiladas and antojitos.

Taxco, Galeana 12. Popular address for tasty and filling low-priced meals, with efficient service. A good place for breakfast.

Vienes, Lerdo de Tejada 302. Sophisticated restaurant for continental-style coffee, cakes and entrées.

Tepoztlán

One of the most interesting side-trips from Cuernavaca is to **TEPOZTLÁN**, just 20km away but, until recently at least, an entirely different world. In a narrow valley spectacularly ringed by volcanic mountains, the village was an isolated agrarian community, inhabited by Nahuatl-speaking people whose life can have changed little between the time of the Conquest and the beginning of this century. It was on Tepoztlán that Oscar Lewis based his classic study of *Life in a Mexican Village*, and traced the effects of the Revolution on it: the village was an important stronghold of the original Zapatista movement. New roads and a couple of luxury hotels have changed things, but the stunning setting survives, as does a reputation for joyously boisterous fiestas (especially the drunken revelry of the night of September 7).

On the zócalo, where a **market** is held on Sundays and Wednesdays, stands the massive, fortress-like **Dominican Monastery**. It was indeed a fortress for a while during the Revolution, but is now in a rather beautiful state of disrepair. Around the back, part of the church has been given over to a museum (Tues–Sun 10am–6pm; US$0.50) with a remarkably good archeological collection. Several pre-Hispanic temples have been found on the hilltops roundabout and you can reach one, atop the artificially flattened **Cerro del Tepozteco** (daily 10am–5pm; US$1.25, free on Sun), after an exhausting climb of an hour or so along a well-signposted path from the village. The pyramid here was dedicated to Tepoztecatl, a god of *pulque* and of fertility, represented by carvings of rabbits. There were so many *pulque* gods that they were known as the four-hundred rabbits: the drink was supposedly discovered by rabbits nibbling at the agave plants from which it is made. This one gained particular kudos when the Spanish flung the idol off the cliffs only for his adherents to find that it had landed unharmed – the big September fiesta is in his honour.

Frequent **buses** leave Cuernavaca's local bus stand for Tepoztlán, which many people visit as a day-trip. There's all of three **hotels** in town: cheapest is *La Cabaña,* on the main road near where the bus stops (no phone; ③). The *Posada del Tepoxteco*, at Paraiso 3 (☎739/5-00-10, fax 5-03-23; ⑥), and *Hotel Tepoztlán*, at Industrias 6 (☎739/5-05-22 or 5-05-23, fax 5-05-03; ⑥), both offer more comfort for higher prices, with breakfast included. There's a Bancomer for **currency exchange** near the bus stop and plenty of **restaurants**, the best of which is the *Luna de Mextli* on the road heading down to the monastery.

Xochicalco

Some 38km from Cuernavaca, this time to the south, lie the ruins of **Xochicalco** (daily 10am–5pm; US$1.75, free on Sun). While not much is known of the history of this site or the peoples who inhabited it, it is regarded by archeologists as one of the most significant in central Mexico, forming as it does a link between the Classic culture of Teotihuacán and the later Toltec peoples. Xochicalco flourished from around the seventh century AD to the tenth – thus overlapping with both Teotihuacán and Tula – and also shows clear parallels with Maya and Zapotec sites of the era.

The setting, high on a bare mountain top, is reminiscent of Monte Albán (see p.428), the great Zapotec site near Oaxaca and, like Monte Albán and the great Maya sites (but unlike Tula or Teotihuacán), Xochicalco was an exclusively religious and ceremonial centre rather than a true city. The style of many of the carvings, too, recalls Zapotec and Maya art. Their subjects, however, and the architecture of the temples, seem to form a transition between Teotihuacán and Tula: in particular, Quetzalcoatl first appears here in human guise, as he was to appear at Tula and almost every subsequent site, rather than simply as the feathered serpent of Teotihuacán. The ball-court is almost identical to earlier Maya examples, and similar to those that later appeared in Tula. For all these influences, however, or perhaps because there are so many of them, it's almost impossible to say which was dominant: some claim that Xochicalco was a northern outpost of the Maya, others that it was a subject city of Teotihuacán that survived (or perhaps precipitated through revolt) the fall of that empire.

Much the most important surviving monument here is the **Pirámide de Quetzalcoatl**, on the highest part of the site. Around its base are carved wonderfully elaborate plumed serpents, coiling around various seated figures and symbols with astronomical significance – all clearly Maya in inspiration. On top, part of the wall of the sanctuary remains standing. Not far from here, to the left and slightly down the hill, you'll find the entrance to the **Subterranean Passages**, a couple of natural caves that have had steps and tunnels added. You may have to persuade the guard to unlock the passages for you. In one, a shaft in the roof is so oriented as to allow the sun to shine directly in at times of equinox – any other time you'll need a flashlight to make out remains of frescoes on the walls. There's a site museum on the next hilltop.

Half-hourly **buses** from Cuernavaca's Pullman de Morelos terminal, headed to Miacatlán, will take you to the Crucero de Xochicalco, 4km from the site, from where you'll have to walk. If you're driving, or if you go with a tour, you can continue down the road beyond Xochicalco to the caves of Cacahuamilpa (see p.332), from where Taxco (see below) is only a short distance. Alternatively it's about an hour's walk from the site back to the main road, where you should be able to flag down a passing bus in either direction.

Taxco

Silver has been mined in **TAXCO** since before the Conquest, and although its sources have long been depleted, it still forms the basis of the town's fame and its livelihood. Nowadays, though, it's in the shape of jewellery, made in hundreds of workshops to be sold throughout the country and in a bewildering array of shops (*platerías*) catering to the tourists in Taxco itself. It's an attractive place, a mass of narrow cobbled alleys lined with red-roofed, whitewashed houses straggling steeply over the hills. At intervals the pattern is broken by some larger mansion, by a courtyard filled with flowers, or by the twin spires of a church rearing up – above all the famous Baroque wedding cake of **Santa Prisca**.

Taxco's development, though it might seem a prosperous place now, has not been a simple progression – indeed on more than one occasion the town has been all but abandoned. Although the Spaniards came running at the rumours of mineral wealth here (Cortés himself sent an expedition in 1522), their initial success was short-lived, and it wasn't until the eighteenth century that **José de la Borda** struck it fabulously rich by discovering the San Ignacio vein. It is from the short period of Borda's life that most of what you see dates – he spent one large fortune on building the church of Santa Prisca, others on more buildings and a royal lifestyle here and in Cuernavaca – but by his death in 1778 the boom was already over. In 1929 a final revival started with the arrival of the American William Spratling, who set up a jewellery workshop in Taxco, drawing on the local traditional skills and designs. With the completion of a new road around the same time, the massive influx of tourists was inevitable, but the town has handled it fairly well, becoming rich at the expense of just a little charm.

Arrival and information

Both **bus stations** are on Av J.F. Kennedy, the main road that winds around the side of the valley below the town. To get in from the Flecha Roja terminal (near which are a couple of hotels handy for late arrivals), turn left up the hill and then left again to climb even more steeply past the church of Veracruz to the zócalo, **Plaza Borda**. Arriving at Estrella de Oro, head straight up the steep alley directly across from you until you come, on your right, to the Plazuela San Juan, and from there down Cuauhtémoc to the zócalo.

There's a small **tourist office** on Av Kennedy at the very northern end of town (daily 9am–8pm; ☎762/2-07-98), in addition to a tourist information desk at the Flecha Roja terminal, which also has a guardería. You can **change money** at the casa de cambio on the Plazuela de San Juan, which offers good rates and civilized opening hours (Mon–Fri 9am–3pm & 5–7pm, Sat 10am–2pm).

Accommodation

Taxco has some excellent **hotels**, and when most of the day-trippers have left, the place settles into a calmer mode. There are plenty of inexpensive places near the zócalo; at the higher end of the scale you're swamped with choices, in particular some lovely, restored colonial buildings that now serve as comfortable, popular hotels.

Agua Esondida, Plaza Borda 4, on the zócalo (☎762/2-07-26, fax 2-13-06). Quite a classy establishment, though it can be noisy due to the night-time revelries on the square. ⑤.

Los Arcos, Juan Ruiz de Alarcón 2 (☎762/2-18-36, fax 2-79-82). Good-value rooms, one with a little attic, in a pretty colonial building a couple of blocks east of the zócalo. ④.

Casa Grande, Plazuela de San Juan 7 (☎762/2-09-69, fax 2-11-08). Friendly place with a pleasantly run-down kind of charm. ③.

Melendez, Cuauhtémoc 6 (☎762/2-00-06). Large hotel with formal atmosphere – its restaurant is reasonable, and especially good for breakfast. ⑤.

Posada de los Castillo, Juan Ruiz de Alarcón 7 (☎ & fax 762/2-13-96). Lovely colonial hotel, near the zócalo, with rooms decorated in bright tiles and old wood. ④.

Santa Prisca, Cena Oscuras 1 (☎762/2-00-80, fax 2-29-38). Attractive converted colonial building just off the zócalo, with a pleasant patio and a variety of rooms, some of which have their own terrace. ⑤.

The Town

Just south of **Plaza Borda** you'll find Taxco's one outstanding sight: the church of **Santa Prisca**, a building so florid and expensive that it not surprisingly provokes extreme reactions. Aldous Huxley, in his journey *Beyond the Mexique Bay*, regarded the town, and the church in particular, with less than affection:

> *In the eighteenth century, Borda, the mining millionaire, built for Taxco one of the most sumptuous churches in Mexico – one of the most sumptuous and one of the most ugly. I have never seen a building in which every part, down to the smallest decorative detail, was so constantly ill proportioned. Borda's church is an inverted work of genius.*

But that is the minority view – most would follow Sacheverell Sitwell (who loved anything frilly) in his view that:

> *its obvious beauties in the way of elegance and dignity, and its suitability to both purpose and environment are enough to convert those who would never have thought to find themselves admiring a building of this kind.*

Its hyper-elaborate facade towers over the zócalo, and inside there's a riot of gilded churriguresque altarpieces and other treasures including paintings by Miguel Cabrera, a Zapotec native who became one of Mexico's greatest colonial religious artists. Through a courtyard off the zócalo, at Plaza Borda 1 (left and down the stairs), the **Museo de Platería** (daily 10am–6pm; US$1) has temporary exhibitions in a variety of media, in addition to a permanent collection of silver. Almost next door, the **Centro Cultural de Taxco** (Mon–Sat 10am–3pm & 5–8pm, Sun 10am–4pm; free) houses exhibitions of Mexican art, some of them very interesting.

To reach the **Museo Guillermo Spratling** (Tues–Sun 9am–6pm; US$1.75, free on Sun), William Spratling's personal collection of antiquities, go round to the back of the church on C Veracruz. It's an interesting miscellany, impressively displayed over three floors, and includes a small display devoted to the history of the town. Not far from here on Juan Ruíz de Alarcon, the street parallel to Veracruz, is the **Casa Humboldt**, an old staging inn named for the German explorer-baron who spent one night here in 1803. A beautiful colonial building, it now contains a small **art museum** (Tues–Sat 10am–5pm, Sun 9am–3pm; US$1.25).

Beyond these few sights, the way to enjoy Taxco is simply to wander the streets, nosing about in the *platerías*, stopping occasionally for a drink. If you're **buying silver** you can be fairly sure it's the real thing here (check for the hallmark: .925 or "sterling"), but prices are much the same as they would be anywhere and quality and workmanship can vary enormously: there's everything from mass-produced belt buckles and cheap rings to designer jewellery that will set you back thousands of dollars. Whatever you buy, the shops off the main streets will be cheaper and more open to bargaining. A section in the **market**, down the steps beside the zócalo, is given over to the silver hawkers and makes a good place to start. The bulk of the market, however, seems to specialize in rather tacky tourist goods.

Eating and drinking

Finding somewhere to **eat** in Taxco is no problem at all, though the enticing places around the zócalo tend to be expensive. For rock-bottom prices, the **market** has a section given over to food stalls, which are better than they look, or you can carry on through to emerge on the street below, where you'll find a couple of reasonable local restaurants. All except the cheapest of the hotels, too, have their own dining rooms.

In the evening everyone gathers around the zócalo to see and be seen, to stroll or to sit outdoors with a coffee or a drink. You can join in from one of the famous bars – *Berta's*, the traditional place to meet, almost next to the church at no. 2, or *Paco's*, more fashionable nowadays, just across the way at no. 4.

Puebla

East of the capital, a fast new road climbs steeply, with glorious views of the snowy heights of Popocatépetl and Ixtaccíhuatl, to **PUEBLA**. Little more than an hour on the bus from México, this is the Republic's fourth-largest city, and one of its hardest to pin down. On the whole it's a disappointment, with the initial impression of industrial modernity imparted by the huge Volkswagen works on the outskirts compounded by the permanently clogged, raucous and rushed streets of the centre. To top it off, there are few good places to stay, with rooms expensive and often booked up. Yet this is as historic a city as any in Mexico, and certainly in the centre there's a remarkable concentration of interest – a fabulous **cathedral**, **"hidden" convent**, museums and colonial **mansions** – while the mountainous country round about is in places startlingly beautiful. Nevertheless, Puebla is unlikely to tempt you into staying particularly long, and in a packed day you can see both the city and nearby Cholula, either returning to México or continuing westwards overnight.

The city was founded by the Spanish in 1531 and, rare for this area, was an entirely new foundation – preferred to the ancient sites of Cholula and Tlaxcala because there, presumably, the memories of indigenous power remained too strong. It rapidly assumed great importance as a staging point on the journey from the capital to the port at Veracruz, and for the trans-shipment of goods from Spain's Far Eastern

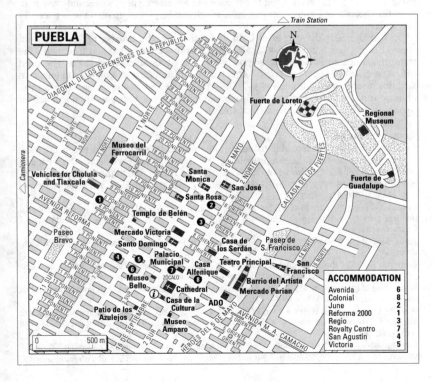

colonies, which were delivered to Acapulco and transported across Mexico from there. Wealth was brought, too, by the reputation of its ceramic and tile manufacture (still very much in evidence), which was in part due to the abundance of good clays, in part to its settlement by Spaniards from Talavera who brought traditional skills with them. The city did well out of colonial rule, and perhaps not surprisingly it took the wrong side in the War of Independence. As a result, it preserves a reputation for conservatism and traditional values, not dispelled even by the fact that the start of the Revolution is generally dated from the assassination of Aquiles Serdán in his Puebla home.

Military defeat, too, seems to play an even larger part in Puebla's history than it does in most of Mexico – the city fell to the Americans in 1847 and to the French in 1863 – but what's remembered is the greatest victory in the country's history, when a force of some two thousand Mexicans defeated a French army three times its size in 1872. To this day, May 5 (**Cinco de Mayo**) is commemorated with a massive fiesta here, and with a public holiday throughout the country.

Arrival and information

Puebla's **Central Camionera**, known by the acronym CAPU (Central de Autobuses de Puebla), lies far out in the northwest of the city. There are frequent local buses and colectivos to and from the centre. Back to CAPU from town, they can be picked up along 9 Nte or 9 Sur: you'll need to get back out for all except local second-class journeys (to Tlaxcala or Cholula, for example, which can be picked up on 6 Pte between 11 and 13 Nte).

On C 5 Ote near the corner of C 16 de Septiembre, the **tourist office** (Mon–Sat 9am–11.30pm, Sun 9am–2pm; ☎22/46-12-85) provides information and free maps; the same maps are available at many hotels and tourist sights around town. The **post office**, at calles 16 Septiembre and 5 Ote, has an efficient *Lista de Correos* and telegram facilities; there's also a branch at C 2 Ote 411. Serfin and Banamex on Reforma will **change money**, and there's a casa de cambio in the arcade between the north side of the zócalo and C 2 Ote, and another at CAPU.

Accommodation

Finding somewhere reasonable **to stay** in Puebla can be difficult, but hotels are easy to spot as they nearly all have a protruding "H" sign, and most are just to the west and north of the zócalo. On the whole, the closer to the zócalo, the higher the price.

Avenida, 5 Pte 336 (☎22/32-21-04). Basic but friendly and relatively clean and quiet. Hot water 6.30–11am & 7.30–11pm only. ①.

Colonial, 4 Sur 105 (☎22/46-42-92, fax 46-08-18, *colonial@giga.com*). Luxury in a beautiful colonial building next to the Autonomous University of Puebla. All rooms have TV and phone, and there's a fine restaurant to boot. ⑤.

June, 5 de Mayo 1402 (☎22/42-05-86). Simple rooms but clean enough and all with private bathroom. ②.

Reforma 2000, 4 Pte at the corner of 11 Nte (☎22/42-33-63). Homely and comfortable with carpeted, spacious rooms, TV and phone. Nice bar and restaurant, plus parking facilities. ④.

Regio, 5 de Mayo 1004 (☎22/32-47-74). Some rooms with private bath; the communal bathroom has hot water only 6–10am. ①.

Royalty Centro, Portal Hidalgo 8 (☎22/42-02-02 or 42-02-04, fax 42-47-43). Luxury on the zócalo; satellite TV, room service, parking and telephone and fax facilities. The restaurant overlooking the zócalo is good, too. ⑤.

San Agustín, 3 Pte 531 (☎ & fax 22/32-50-89). Parking, two good restaurants and cable TV. ③.

Victoria, 3 Pte 306 (☎22/32-89-92). Next to Bello Museum. Basic rooms but all with bathroom. ②.

The Town

Any tour of the city must start in the **zócalo**, centre of the numbering system for the ancient grid of streets, and where looms the great **Cathedral**, second-largest in the republic. Under construction from 1562 until the middle of the following century, its ornamentation is amazing – especially the interior, decked out in onyx, marble and gilt. There are frequent free guided tours and, if the tower is open, you can take in exceptional panoramas from the top. Behind the cathedral, near the tourist office, lies the old Archbishop's Palace, converted to a library in the seventeenth century (the Biblioteca Palafoxiana, reputed to be the oldest library in the Americas), and now housing the original collection of ancient books and manuscripts on the upper floor. Downstairs, the **Casa de la Cultura** hosts regular exhibitions of local arts and crafts (Tues–Sun 10am–5pm; free, US$1.25 for the library).

The best museum in Pueblo, the modern **Museo Amparo**, at the corner of C 2 Sur and C 9 Ote (daily except Tues 10am–6pm; US$2, free on Mon), features art from pre-Hispanic, colonial and modern Mexico. The pre-Columbian era is particularly well represented, detailed on computer screens and in English and Spanish audio-cassette tours.

North of the zócalo

Head north from the zócalo along 5 de Mayo and you reach the church of **Santo Domingo** at the corner of 4 Pte. Its Capilla del Rosario is, even in comparison to the cathedral, a quite unbelievably lavish orgy of gold leaf and Baroque excess; a constant hushed, shuffling stream of devotees lights candles and prays for miraculous cures to its revered image of the Virgin. Next door, at 5 de Mayo 409, is the **Pinacoteca Bello y Zetina** (Tues–Sun 10am–4pm; free), which displays the paintings and furniture of the wealthy Bello household during the nineteenth century. Just north of here on 5 de Mayo and 6 Ote, the **Mercado Victoria** was Puebla's main market, but is now a rather sanitized shopping centre. East of the market, the **Casa de los Serdán** (Tues–Sun 10am–4.30pm; US$1.25, free on Tues) records the liberal struggles of the Serdán family against the dictatorship of Porfirio Díaz. The assassination of Aquiles Serdán in this house was one of the most important steps in the fall of Díaz: the date of Serdán's death, November 18, 1910, is in the absence of any firmer indicators generally recognized as marking the start of the Revolution. In the house the bullet holes have been lovingly preserved, and a huge smashed mirror still hangs on the wall where it appears in contemporary photos of the carnage.

Nine blocks north of the zócalo, at 18 Pte 103, you'll find the remarkable "hidden" convent of **Santa Monica** (Tues–Sun: summer 10am–7pm, winter 9am–5pm; US$1, free on Sun). Here, from the suppression of the church in 1857 until their discovery in 1934, several generations of nuns lived hidden from the public gaze behind a smoke-screen of secret doors and concealed passages. Just how secret they were is a matter of some debate – many claim that the authorities simply turned a blind eye – and certainly several lay families were actively supportive, providing supplies and new recruits. But it makes a good story, embellished by the conversion of the building into a museum that preserves the secret entrances along with many religious artworks and a beautiful cloister. In the same general direction, at 14 Pte 305 on the corner of 3 Nte, lies the convent of **Santa Rosa** (Tue–Sun 10am–4pm; US$1.25, free on Sat), whose main claim to fame is that the great *Mole Poblano* was invented in its kitchens. You can sample this extraordinary sauce – made of chocolate, numerous varieties of chile, and any number of herbs and spices – with chicken, turkey or enchiladas at any restaurant in Puebla.

East of the zócalo and further afield

The rest of the interest is concentrated mostly to the east and northeast of the zócalo. At the end of 4 Ote lie the **Mercado Parian** – mostly given over to rather tawdry tourist souvenirs – and the **Barrio del Artista**, traditionally the artists' quarter, now selling work aimed squarely at the tourist market. The **Teatro Principal**, nearby, is a fine eighteenth-century theatre, said to be the oldest on the continent, which still hosts occasional performances. Walking back to the zócalo, you can stop in at the **Casa del Alfeñique**, an elaborate old mansion covered in Puebla tiles, which now houses the regional museum (Tues–Sun 10am–4.30pm; US$1.25, free on Tues). Within, you can see period furnishings, Puebla ceramics, a small archeological section and an excellent display of colonial art.

Further afield, the historic forts of **Guadalupe** and **Loreto** (both Tues–Sun 10am–4.30pm; US$1.25, free on Sun) and the modern **Regional Museum** (Tues–Sun same times; US$1.25, free on Tues), crown a hill to the northwest, marking the site of the constant battles and sieges of the nineteenth century. Fuerte Loreto contains a small military museum, while the Regional Museum is largely devoted to the area's archeology and ethnology. You'll also find the **Natural History Museum** (Tues–Sun 10am–4.30pm; US$1.25, free on Tues) and a **Planetarium**. To get there take a Ruta #72 colectivo (marked "Fuertes" or "Laredo") from Bvd de los Heroes del 5 de Mayo, three blocks east of the zócalo.

Eating, drinking and nightlife

You really should try a *Pollo con Mole Poblano* while you're here, either at one of the **restaurants** on the zócalo or at any of the many *fondas típicas* around the central area. For cheaper food, head for the area around the Mercado Victoria, or if you crave the familiar there's a *Sanborn's* at C 2 Ote 6, just off 5 de Mayo, and a *VIPs* nearby at C 2 Ote and C 2 Nte. The best-known – and most touristy – restaurant in town is *Fonda de Santa Clara*, a couple of blocks west of the zócalo at C 3 Pte 307, which serves local food with an upmarket twist in a pretty room decorated with Mexican art.

Nightlife in Puebla centres round the *Zona Esmeralda*, ten blocks east of the zócalo, where there's a string of bars and clubs to keep you going. Closer to the centre, *Cafe-Bookshop Teorema*, C 7 Nte, has live music from 9.30pm until midnight, and serves good food, beer and spirits and excellent cappuccino; cover is usually around US$1.50. Otherwise, many people head out to **Cholula** to join the lively, studenty atmosphere there; buses back to Puebla run until 4am.

Cholula and around

The ruins of **CHOLULA**, and the largest pyramid in Mexico, lie just 15km west of Puebla. A rival of Teotihuacán at its height, and the most powerful city in the country between the fall of Teotihuacán and the rise of Tula, Cholula was at the time of the Conquest a vast city of some four hundred temples, famed as a shrine to Quetzalcoatl and for the excellence of its pottery (a trade dominated by immigrant Mixtecs). But it paid dearly for an attempt, inspired by its Aztec allies, to ambush Cortés on his march to Tenochtitlán: the chieftains were slaughtered, their temples destroyed and churches built in their place. The Spanish claimed to have constructed 365 churches here, one for each day of the year, but although there are a lot, the figure certainly doesn't approach that. There may well be 365 chapels within the churches, though, which is already a few hundred more than the village population could reasonably need. The great multidomed **Capilla Real**, on the Plaza Principal (Mon–Sat 9am–1pm & 4–7pm, Sun 9am–7pm), is the most interesting and least crumbling, along with the Convento de San Gabriel next door. Most of the rest, like the colonial glories of Cholula itself, seem to have been left quietly to crumble away. It's a pleasantly tranquil place to decay at least, and there are a couple of basic cafés on the zócalo where you can sit and join the endless inactivity.

If you want to explore some of the churches round about, **ACATEPEC**, easily reached by local bus, is the place to head. The spectacular village church here, San Francisco, has a superb Baroque facade entirely covered in glazed bricks and azulejos of local manufacture. It's not particularly large, but is beautifully proportioned, and quite unexpected in this setting.

Just a kilometre's walk away in the village of **TONATZINTLA**, the plain facade of the church of Santa María conceals a remarkably elaborate Baroque treasury. Here local craftsmen covered every available inch in ornament, interspersing bird, plant and native life with the more usual Christian elements. Acatepec lies on the road from Puebla to Izúcar de Matamoros, so you should be able to pick up a bus heading directly back.

The site

To get an impression of the city as it once looked, head first for Cholula's site **museum**, not far from the entrance (Tues–Sun 10am–5pm; US$1.75, free on Sun; ticket includes both the museum and the site). Even the **Great Pyramid** is not much to look at these days – at least as a building. Still covered in earth, it makes a not inconsiderable hill; a stiff climb up it brings you to the church of **Nuestra Señora de los Remedios** and a viewing position from which you can attempt to count the churches. Within the hill, a series of tunnels dug during excavations can be explored: more than eight kilometres of them in all wind through the various stages of construction, but only a small proportion is open to the public – poorly lit but fascinating. Emerging at the end of one tunnel, you'll find a small area of open-air excavations, where part of the great pyramid has been exposed alongside various lesser shrines.

Practicalities

Buses leave CAPU in Puebla for Cholula every thirty minutes or so, and there's a constant stream of second-class buses and colectivos from 6 Pte, between 11 and 13 Nte. In Cholula they drop you at 12 Pte and 5 de Mayo (where they can also be picked up for the return journey); from there, head down 5 de Mayo to get to the centre of town. From the zócalo, follow Morelos past the railway track to reach the pyramid.

There are a couple of **hotels** in Cholula, the most economical being the *Reforma,* Morelos and 4 Nte (☎22/47-01-49; ②). At the *Trailer Park las Americas*, on the outskirts at 6 Nte and 30 Ote (☎22/47-01-34), you can pitch a tent or park a trailer for US$4 per person. As the site of the Universidad de las Americas campus, Cholula has become the **nightlife capital** of the Puebla region: discos and bars cluster around 14 Pte and 5 de Mayo. *Paradise* (open from 10pm; no cover) is probably the most lively.

Heading onwards you can get an Estrella Dorada bus straight to México from their Cholula office, 12 Pte between 3 Nte and 5 de Mayo (half-hourly; 2hr 30min), though it might actually save time to go via Puebla.

Tlaxcala and around

TLAXCALA, capital of the tiny state of the same name, is about 30km north of Puebla. As Cortés's closest ally in the struggle against the Aztecs, the town suffered a very different fate from that of Cholula, and one that in the long run has led to an even more total disappearance of its ancient culture. For although the Spanish founded a town here – now restored and very beautiful in much of its original colonial glory – to the

Mexicans Tlaxcala was a symbol of treachery, and to some extent still is. Siding with Spain in the War of Independence didn't help greatly either, and whether for this reason, or for its genuine isolation, development has largely passed Tlaxcala by.

The town sits in the middle of a fertile, prosperous-looking upland plain surrounded by rather bare mountains and dominated, as you approach, by the **Santuario de Ocotitlán**, on a height to the east. At the centre you'll discover an exceptionally pretty and very much rehabilitated colonial town, comfortable but in the final analysis fairly dull. Most of the interest lies very close to the zócalo, laid out with fountains and an ancient bandstand, populated by pigeons and squirrels. One entire side is taken up by the **Palacio de Gobierno** (daily 8am–8pm; free), whose patterned brick facade is broken by ornate windows and doorways. The building incorporates parts of a much earlier structure, erected soon after the Conquest, and inside boasts a series of brilliantly coloured murals by Desiderio Hernandez Xochitiotzin (a contemporary of Rivera's) dating from the early 1960s. Recently restored, the panels depict the history of the Tlaxcalan people from their migration from the north to their alliance with Cortés; the most spectacular are one on the stairs depicting the Spanish Conquest, and another at the bottom showing the Great Market. Also on the zócalo the **Palacio de Justicia** has a giant clock, illuminated at night, which actually keeps time.

From a second, smaller plaza south of the zócalo, a broad flagged path leads up to the ex-Convento de San Francisco. Here, wrapped around the cloister, the **Museo Regional de Tlaxcala** (Tues–Sun 10am–5pm; US$1, free on Sun) covers local life from prehistoric times to the present day – an unexceptional collection but well displayed in a series of bare, whitewashed rooms. The church next door is also relatively plain, though it has a beautiful vaulted wooden ceiling and choir, decorated in *artesonado* style. The colourful azulejos inlaid in the floor echo a popular local fashion. One large chapel, more richly decorated than the rest, contains the font in which Xicohténcatl and the three other Tlaxcalan leaders were baptized in the presence of Cortés. Opposite, another small chapel bears traces of ancient frescoes. Tlaxcala's second museum is the **Museo de Artes y Tradiciones Populares**, at Bulevar Mariano and 1 de Mayo (Tues–Sun 10am–6pm; US$0.75), a pleasant little display of traditional crafts and customs, notably the manufacture and consumption of *pulque*.

Some 17km from Tlaxcala lies the ancient site of **Cacaxtla** (daily 10am–5pm; US$2, free on Sun), where a series of murals depicting battle scenes, which are clearly Maya in style, continue to baffle archeologists. Two kilometres west of Cacaxtla, the ruins of **Xochitecatl** (same hours and ticket) have three impressive pyramids and monolithic stones. These can be reached by colectivo ("San Miguel del Milagro") from Bulevar Mariano and Lardizábal, or by bus to the nearby village of Natavitas from either Tlaxcala or Puebla. Alternatively, every Sunday the tourist office runs **guided tours** to both sites for US$2; you're picked up outside the *Hotel Posada San Francisco* at 10am and dropped off at 1pm. They run a Sunday tour of the town itself, too, for the same price, also visiting the rather less impressive archeological site of **Tizatlán** (daily 10am–5pm, free), 4km north of town; this can be reached independently by colectivo from 1 de Mayo and 20 de Noviembre.

Practicalities

There is an almost constant stream of **buses** between Tlaxcala and Puebla or México, in addition to the many local services serving nearby villages (both the *camionetas* roaming round town, and the real thing from the Camionera). Arriving, you can walk from the bus station to the zócalo in about ten minutes: exit and turn right downhill to the next main junction, then take a right down Av Guerrero for five blocks and left down Independéncia. At the back of the Palacio de Gobierno there's a helpful **tourist office** (daily 10am–6pm; ☎246/2-00-27), where you can pick up useful free maps and book guided tours. There's a good **casa de cambio** almost opposite, on Lardizábal.

Just beyond the zócalo on Juárez, the *Mansión Xicohténcatl*, Juárez 15 (☎246/2-19-00; ②), is a reasonable **place to stay**; at the other end of the scale is the Club Med-run *Hotel Posada San Fransisco*, occupying a lovely old mansion on the zócalo at no. 17 (☎246/2-60-22, fax 2-68-18; ⑦). Most other facilities – banks, post office and the like – cluster round the zócalo. **Places to eat** (there's something of a shortage of restaurants in Tlaxcala) are found under the portales on the east side of the zócalo, or along Juárez. To return to the bus station, take the camioneta that stops on the corner by the church just off the zócalo.

Popocatépetl and Ixtaccíhuatl

Although you get excellent views of the snow-clad volcanic peaks of **Popocatépetl** and **Ixtaccíhuatl** from almost anywhere west of the capital, spending some time in the **Parque Nacional de Volcanes** that encompasses their lower slopes, is an exceptional experience. "Popo", at 5452m the taller of the two, hasn't had a full-throated eruption since 1802, but has been rumbling and fuming away since September 1994: at time of writing the whole area is on "Yellow Alert", with evacuation procedures posted throughout surrounding towns. Obviously, you should check the latest situation before going anywhere near. "Ixta", 5285m, ranks third in height in the republic, after the Pico de Orizaba and Popo, and is a challenging climb for serious mountaineers (see box below).

The names stem from an Aztec Romeo-and-Juliet-style legend. Popocatépetl (Smoking Mountain) was a warrior, Ixtaccíhuatl (White Lady) his lover, the beautiful daughter of the emperor. Believing Popocatépetl killed in battle, she died from grief, and when he returned alive he laid her body down on the mountain, where he eternally stands sentinel, holding a burning torch. From the west, Ixta does somewhat resemble a reclining female form and the various parts of the mountain are named accordingly – the feet, the knees, the belly, the breast, the neck, the head, the hair.

CLIMBING IXTACCÍHUATL

Until recently you could ascend **Popo**, up to the crater rim from where Cortés' men were repeatedly lowered to gather sulphur for gunpowder, and onwards to the summit. At present, however, climbing the mountain has been suspended due to the suspected imminence of its eruption.

Ixta can still be climbed, but it's a serious proposition for experienced climbers only, chiefly because it involves a night or two with all your gear at very high altitude, and a technical three-kilometre-long ridge traverse (often requiring ropes) to reach the highest point. The trailhead is at La Joya some 12km from Tlamacas, beyond the microwave station visible on the side of Ixta. To arrange a **guide** for the climb, and to obtain further information, you should contact the Mountaineering Association, at Tlaxcala 47, in the Colonia Roma in México (☎5/584-46-95). You will also require the right **equipment**: a hat, scarf, thick gloves, warm sweater, wind-proof jacket and dark sunglasses are the minimum. In addition you'll want to rent strong boots, crampons and an ice-axe. More specialist information can be found in Hilary Bradt's *Backpacking in Mexico and Central America*, or more fully in R.J. Secor's *Mexico's Volcanoes* (see "Books" in Contexts, p.633).

What **season** you choose to climb counts for a lot. The best time is usually from October to January, when the snow is firm, and the storms common in February and March haven't yet set in. During the rainy season, from April to September, the mountain is covered in soft snow, making it even heavier work than normal.

To get to the national park, take a "Servicio Volcánes" bus from TAPO (every 10min; 5am–10pm) to **Amecameca** (usually just Ameca), a lovely little town an hour south of México. Dramatic views of the mountain peaks are bizarrely framed by the palms of the zócalo, around which you'll find a couple of good, inexpensive hotels.

FIESTAS

JANUARY

6 DÍA DE LOS SANTOS REYES (Twelfth Night). The Magi traditionally leave presents for children on this date: many small ceremonies include a fiesta with dancing at **Nativitas** (Distrito Federal), a suburb near Xochimilco, and at **Malinalco** (México state).

17 BENDICION DE LOS ANIMALES. Children's pets and peasants' farm animals are taken to church to be blessed. A particularly bizarre sight at the Cathedral in **México** and in **Taxco** (Guerrero), where it coincides with a fiesta running over into the following day.

FEBRUARY

2 DÍA DE LA CANDELARIA is widely celebrated, especially in **Cuernavaca** (Morelos).

CARNIVAL (the week before Lent, variable Feb–March) is especially lively in **Cuernavaca** (Mor) and nearby **Tepoztlán** (Mor); also in **Chiconcuac** (Méx) on the way to Teotihuacán. In **Xochimilco** (DF), for some reason, they celebrate Carnival two weeks after everyone else.

MARCH

On the Sunday following March 9, a large feria with traditional dances is held at **San Gregorio Atlapulco**, near Xochimilco (DF).

PALM SUNDAY (the week before Easter) sees a procession with palms in **Taxco** (Gro), where representations of the Passion continue through Holy Week.

HOLY WEEK itself is observed everywhere. There are very famous passion plays in the suburb of **Itzapalapa** (DF), culminating on the Friday with a mock-crucifixion on the Cerro de la Estrella,

and similar celebrations at **Chalma** (Méx) and nearby **Malinalco**. In **Cholula** (Puebla), with its host of churches, the processions pass over vast carpets of flowers.

APRIL

Cuernavaca's (Mor) flower festival, the FERIA DE LA FLOR, usually falls in early April.

MAY

1 May Day, a public holiday, is usually marked by large marches and demonstrations in the capital. In **Cuautla** (Mor), the same day sees a fiesta commemorating an Independence battle.

3 DÍA DE LA SANTA CRUZ is celebrated with fiestas, and traditional dancing, in **Xochimilco** (DF), in **Tepotzotlán** (Méx) and in **Valle de Bravo** (Méx).

5 Public holiday for the battle of Puebla – celebrated in **Puebla** (Pue) itself with a grand procession and re-enactment of the fighting.

15 DÍA DE SAN ISIDRO. Religious processions and fireworks in **Tenancingo** (Méx), and a procession of farm animals through **Cuernavaca** (Mor) on their way to be blessed at the church.

On the third Monday of May, there's a large religious festival in **Tlaxcala** (Tlax) as an image of the Virgin is processed around the town followed by hundreds of pilgrims.

CORPUS CHRISTI (variable – the Thursday after Trinity). Thousands of children, rigged out in their Sunday best, gather in **México's** Zócalo to be blessed.

JUNE

29 DÍA DE SAN PEDRO observed with processions and dances in **Tepotzotlán**

(Méx) and traditional dancing in **San Pedro Actopan** (DF), on the southern outskirts of México.

JULY

16 DÍA DE LA VIRGEN DEL CARMEN. Dancers, and a procession with flowers to the convent of Carmen, in **San Ángel** (DF).

25 DÍA DE SANTIAGO particularly celebrated in **Chalco** (Méx), on the way to Amecameca. The following Sunday sees a market and regional dances at the **Plaza de las Tres Culturas** (DF) and dances, too, in **Xochimilco** (DF).

29 DÍA DE SANTA MARTA in **Milpa Alta** (DF), near Xochimilco, celebrated with Aztec dances and mock fights between Moors and Christians.

AUGUST

13 Ceremonies in **México** commemorate the defence of Tenochtitlán, with events in the Plaza de las Tres Culturas, around the statue of Cuauhtémoc on Reforma and in the Zócalo.

15 DÍA DE LA ASUNCION (Assumption) honoured with pilgrimages from **Cholula** (Pue) to a nearby village, and ancient dances in **Milpa Alta** (DF).

SEPTEMBER

8 A very ancient ceremony in **Tepoztlán** (Mor), a Christianized version of homage to the Pyramid of Tepozteco, and more usual candle-lit religious processions in **Cuernavaca** (Mor).

15–16 INDEPENDENCE CELEBRATIONS everywhere, above all in the Zócalo in **México**, where the President proclaims the famous *Grito* at 11pm on the 15th.

21 DÍA DE SAN MATEO celebrated in **Milpa Alta** (DF).

29 DÍA DE SAN MIGUEL provokes huge pilgrimages to both **Taxco** (Gro) and **Chalma** (Méx).

OCTOBER

4 DÍA DE SAN FRANCISCO sees a feria in **Tenancingo** (Méx), with much traditional music-making, and is also celebrated in **San Francisco Tecoxpa** (DF), a village on the southern fringes of the capital.

12 In **Tlaxcala** (Tlax), a fiesta centring around one of the ancient churches.

NOVEMBER

1–2 DÍA DE LOS MUERTOS (All Souls) is observed by almost everyone, and the shops are full of chocolate skulls and other ghoulish foods. Tradition is particularly strong in **San Lucas Xochimanca** (DF) and **Natívitas** (DF), both to the south of the city.

22 DÍA DE SANTA CECILIA. Santa Cecilia is the patron saint of musicians, and her fiesta attracts orchestras and *mariachi* bands from all over to **Santa Cecilia Tepetlapa** (DF), not far from Xochimilco.

DECEMBER

1 FERIA DE LA PLATA. The great silver fair in **Taxco** (Gro) lasts about ten days from this date.

12 DÍA DE NUESTRA SEÑORA DE GUADALUPE – a massive pilgrimage to the **Basílica of Guadalupe** (DF) runs for several days round about, combined with a constant secular celebration of music and dancing.

CHRISTMAS. In the week leading up to Christmas, *posadas* – nativity plays – can be seen in many places. Among the most famous are those at **Taxco** (Gro) and **Tepotzotlán** (Méx).

travel details

The capital is the centre of the nation to such an extent that any attempt at a comprehensive list of the comings and goings would be doomed to failure. What follows is no more than a survey of the major services on the main routes: it must be assumed that intermediate points are linked at least as frequently as those mentioned.

BUSES

Literally thousands of buses leave México every day, and you can get to just about any town in the country, however small, whenever you want. The Terminal del Norte in particular serves as a base for a bewildering number of companies. Those below are a bare minimum of the main road routes. Journey times given are for the fastest services.

Terminal del Norte

Aguascalientes (hourly; 7hr); Ciudad Juárez (20 daily; 26hr); Dolores Hidalgo (every 40min; 5hr); Guadalajara (every 30min; 7hr); Guanajuato (16 daily; 4hr); Hermosillo (hourly; 30hr); León (hourly; 5hr); Los Mochis (hourly; 24hr); Matamoros (5 daily; 16hr); Morelia (hourly; 6hr); Nuevo Laredo (hourly; 15hr); Querétaro (every 10min; 1hr 30min–3hr); Saltillo (10 daily; 10hr); San Luis Potosí (half-hourly; 5hr 30min); San Miguel Allende (every 40min; 4hr); Tepic (2–3 hourly; 6hr); Tuxpan (5 daily; 15hr); Uruapan (hourly; 6hr); Zacatecas (6 daily; 8hr).

Terminal de Autobuses de Pasajeros de Oriente (TAPO)

Campeche (4 daily; 12+hr); Cancún (3 daily; 30+hr); Jalapa (1–2 hourly; 6hr 30min); Mérida (4 daily; 28hr); Oaxaca (at least hourly; 6hr); Orizaba (20 daily; 4hr); Palenque (3 daily; 16hr); Playa del Carmen (3 daily; 30+hr); Puebla (every 5min; 2hr); Puerto Escondido (1 daily; 12hr); San Cristóbal de las Casas (6 daily; 24hr); Tehuacan (hourly; 4hr); Tehuantepec (7 daily; 12hr); Tuxtla Gutiérrez (9 daily; 18hr); Veracruz (hourly; 8hr); Villahermosa (roughly hourly; 14hr).

Terminal de Autobuses del Sur

Acapulco (at least hourly; 6–9hr); Chilpancingo (hourly; 3hr 30min); Colima (12 daily; 11hr);

Cuautla (every 15min; 1hr 30min); Cuernavaca (every 10min; 1hr 30min); Ixtapa (16 daily; 10hr); Puerto Vallarta (9 daily; 14hr); Puerto Escondido (3 daily; 15hr); Taxco (7 daily; 3hr 30min); Topoztlan (hourly; 1hr); Zihuatanejo (6 daily; 9hr).

Terminal Poniente

Morelia (every 20min; 7hr); Pátzcuaro (10 daily; 7hr); Toluca (every 5min; 1hr 30min).

Cuernavaca to: Acapulco (Estrella de Oro and Flecha Roja terminals, 12 daily; 5hr); Puebla (Estrella Roja terminal, hourly; 4hr), Taxco (Flecha Roja terminal, 11 daily; 1hr 30min); Toluca (hourly; 3hr).

Puebla to: Oaxaca (12 daily; 7hr); Veracruz (hourly; 6hr 30min); Cuernavaca (hourly: 4hr).

Taxco to: Acapulco (10 daily; 5hr); Cuernavaca (11 daily; 1hr 30min); Toluca (hourly; 2hr).

Toluca to: México (every 5min; 1hr 30min); Cuernavaca (hourly; 3hr); Morelia (every 20min; 4hr 30min); Ixtapan (half-hourly; 1hr); Querétaro (12 daily; 3hr 30min).

TRAINS

México to: Oaxaca (daily); Lázaro Cárdenas (3 weekly) via Morelia, Pátzcuaro and Uruapan; Ciudad Juárez (daily) via León, Aguascalientes, Torreón and Chihuahua; Guadalajara (daily); Veracruz (2 daily plus 3 weekly); Nuevo Laredo (3 weekly) via San Luis Potosí and Monterrey; Puebla; Querétaro.

PLANES

México to most airports in the country, and many destinations worldwide. Major destinations within Mexico include Acapulco (served by Aeroméxico, Mexicana and Taesa); Cancún (Aeroméxico, Mexicana, Taesa); Ciudad Juárez (Aeroméxico, Aerocalifornia, Taesa); Chihuahua (Aeroméxico, Taesa); Guadalajara (Aeroméxico, Mexicana, Aerocalifornia, Taesa); Matamoros (Aeroméxico, Aerocalifornia); Mazatlán (Aeroméxico, Mexicana, Aerocalifornia); Merida (Aeroméxico, Mexicana, Taesa, Aviacsa); Monterrey (Aeroméxico, Mexicana,

Aerocalifornia, Taesa, Aviacsa); Nuevo Laredo (Mexicana); Oaxaca (Aeroméxico, Mexicana, Aviacsa); Puerto Escondido (Mexicana); Puerto Vallarta (Aeroméxico, Mexicana); Tijuana (Aeroméxico, Mexicana, Aerocalifornia, Taesa); Tuxtla Gutierrez (Aeroméxico, Mexicana, Aviacsa); Villahermosa (Aeroméxico, Mexicana, Taesa).

Puebla to Chicago: Dallas/Fort Worth; Guadalajara; México; Monterrey; Tijuana.

CHAPTER SIX

ACAPULCO AND THE PACIFIC BEACHES

T he 800km stretch of coast between Puerto Vallarta and Punta Maldonada, where the Sierra Madre reaches out to the ocean to form a string of coves, bays and narrow stretches of sand, is lined with some of Mexico's most popular resorts. **Acapulco** – the original, the biggest, and still for many the best – is a steep-sided, tightly curving bay that for all its excesses of high-rise development remains breathtakingly beautiful, from a distance at least. This is still the stamping ground of

the wealthy, whose villas, high around the wooded sides of the bay, offer isolation from the packaged enclaves below. It's pricey, but not ridiculously so, and despite the tourists, the city itself remains very Mexican, at times run-down and often rather tawdry, as befits its status as a working port.

Puerto Vallarta, second in size and reputation, feels altogether smaller, more like the tropical village it claims to be, while in fact spreading for miles along a series of tiny beaches. More chic, younger, more overtly glamorous and certainly far more single-mindedly a resort, it lacks Acapulco's great sweep of sand but makes up for it with cove after isolated cove. Heading south from here, **Barra de Navidad** is a lovely crescent of sand, backed for once by flatlands and lagoons, with a village at either end. By contrast **Manzanillo**, also well connected with Guadalajara, is first and foremost a port and naval base – its pitch for resort status seems something of an afterthought. **Zihuatanejo** and its purpose-built neighbour **Ixtapa** are the most recently developed, the latter so much so that there's nothing there but brand new hotels. Zihuatanejo is more attractive: almost, to look at, a mini-Acapulco, with magnificent villas mushrooming on the slopes overlooking the bay.

All along this coast, between the major centres, you'll find **beaches**: some completely undeveloped; others linked to a village with a few rooms to rent and a makeshift bar on the sand; and the odd few with an isolated, maybe even luxurious, hotel. The ocean breakers can be wild, positively dangerous at times, and there are minor discomforts – unreliable or nonexistent water and electricity supplies, vicious mosquitoes – but the space and the simplicity, often just an hour's drive from a packed international resort, are well worth seeking out.

Most people arrive on the new, fast – and expensive – *Autopista del Sol* from México to Acapulco, but the **coast road**, whatever some old maps may say, is perfectly feasible (if a little rough in the final stretches) all the way from the US border to Guatemala. Between Puerto Vallarta and Acapulco, it's a good modern highway; unrelentingly spectacular as it forces its way south, sometimes over the narrow coastal plain, more often clinging precariously to the fringes of the Sierra where it falls away into the ocean.

Most **buses** heading down from **Mazatlán** turn inland to Guadalajara, but many also continue to **Puerto Vallarta**, and from there on down Hwy-200 towards Acapulco. Guadalajara itself has very frequent bus connections with Puerto Vallarta, **Barra de Navidad** and **Manzanillo**, while from central Michoacán you can head down to the coast at **Lázaro Cárdenas**. **Zihuatanejo** has direct bus services from México. Plentiful buses also run between these resorts, though you may have to change if you're travelling long-distance. It's easy to get from Puerto Vallarta to Barra de Navidad, and from there to Manzanillo and from Manzanillo to Lázaro Cárdenas, but there are few direct services from Puerto Vallarta all the way down. In the state of Guerrero there are occasional **military checkpoints** on the roads, where all traffic is stopped and searched. Tourists usually assume that this is for drugs, which may be at least partly true, though the check rarely amounts to more than a peremptory prod at the outside of your case; more importantly the wild and relatively undeveloped hills retain a reputation for banditry and guerrilla activity. This is not something you need expect to come across, but travelling these roads you should keep your passport and papers handy and not carry anything you wouldn't want discovered.

Prices in the resorts, particularly for accommodation, are dictated largely by **season**, which, in the bigger places, stretches from early or mid-December to after Easter or the end of April. In high season the swankier hotels on the Pacific coast charge about double the off-season rates and need to be booked in advance. Budget hotels vary their rates less, but costs are still twenty to thirty percent down outside the peak season. Smaller beach towns catering exclusively to Mexicans have a shorter season, usually just December and *Semana Santa*, but the same rules apply.

Puerto Vallarta

By reputation the second of Mexico's beach resorts, **PUERTO VALLARTA** is smaller, quieter and younger than Acapulco. In its own way, it is actually every bit as commercial – perhaps more so, since here tourism is virtually the only source of income – but appearances count for much, and Puerto Vallarta, while doing all it can to catch up with Acapulco, appears far less developed. Its hotels are scattered along several miles of coast, the greatest concentration in **Nuevo Vallarta**, north of the town and sliced through by an eight-lane strip of asphalt, but there are no tall or obviously modern buildings in the centre; and the tropical village atmosphere, an asset assiduously exploited by the local tourist authorities, does survive to a remarkable degree.

The town's relative youth is undoubtedly a contributing factor. Until 1954 Puerto Vallarta was a small fishing village where the Río Cuale spills out into the Bahía de Banderas; then Mexicana airlines, their hand forced by Aeroméxico's monopoly on flights into Acapulco, started promoting the town as a resort. Their efforts received a shot in the arm in 1964, when John Huston chose Mismaloya, 10km south, as the setting for his film of Tennessee Williams' play **The Night of the Iguana**, starring Richard Burton. The scandalmongering that surrounded Burton's romance with Elizabeth Taylor – who was not part of the cast but came along – is often attributed to putting Puerto Vallarta firmly in the international spotlight: "a mixed blessing" according to Huston, who stayed on here until his death in 1987, and whose bronze image stands on the Isla Río Cuale in town.

The package tourists stay, on the whole, in the beachfront hotels around the bay, but are increasingly penetrating the town centre to shop in the pricey boutiques and malls that line the streets leading back from the beach, and to eat in some of the very good restaurants both on the malecón and downtown. Nevertheless, what could be a depressingly expensive place to visit turns out to be liberally peppered with good-value hotels and budget restaurants, especially during the low season (Aug–Nov).

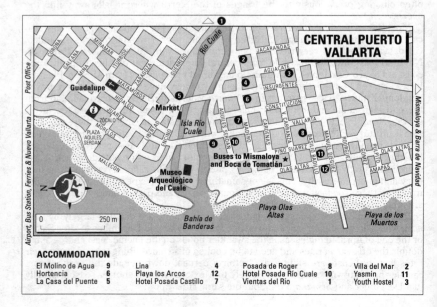

ACCOMMODATION

El Molino de Agua	9	Lina	4	Posada de Roger	8	Villa del Mar	2
Hortencia	6	Playa los Arcos	12	Hotel Posada Río Cuale	10	Yasmin	11
La Casa del Puente	5	Hotel Posada Castillo	7	Vientas del Rio	1	Youth Hostel	3

TIME ZONES

Remember that **if you've come south** from Tepic, San Blas, Mazatlán or points north along the coast, you need to advance your watch an hour: the time zone changes at the state border, just north of Puerto Vallarta's airport.

Puerto Vallarta today is one of the **gay** centres of Mexico, with a great deal more tolerance for – and entertainment geared towards – the gay scene than almost any other Mexican town.

Arrival and information

The **Río Cuale**, spanned by two small bridges, divides Puerto Vallarta in two. Most of the town – the main square, official buildings, market, and the bulk of the shops and restaurants – lies on the north side. South you'll find the town beach and the cheaper hotels. It's a very small place, hemmed in by the ocean and by the steep slopes behind – downtown, you can walk just about anywhere. Frequent local **buses** run around the edge of the Bahía de Banderas to the north, towards the hotel zone (buses marked "Hoteles"), and, rather less frequently, south to the smaller beaches.

The **airport** lies 7km north of the centre on the coastal highway, and is linked to the city by local buses that stop a few steps outside the perimeter fence. Airport taxis go right to the door but are, as ever, expensive: if you can find a colectivo it should be around a third of the price. About 1.5km further north lies the brand new, long-awaited **Central Camionera**, served by frequent local buses into town.

The tolerably helpful **tourist office** (Mon–Fri 9am–7pm, Sat 9am–1pm; ☎322/2-02-42) is in the municipal palace just across the zócalo from the main **Banamex** (which will change cheques 9am–2pm). Numerous **casas de cambio** line the nearby streets: some offer criminal exchange rates but those at Su Casa, around the corner on Morelos, aren't bad, and it stays open until 9pm (6pm on Sun). The main **post office** is at Juarez 628 and Abasolo (Mon–Fri 8am–7.30pm, Sat 9am–1pm), and there is a **long-distance phone** booth on Cárdenas near Pino Suarez. For up-to-date, if promotional, information on what's going on in town, pick up the daily *Vallarta Today* (free, in gringo hangouts). If you find yourself in any sort of trouble or just need advice, approach one of the people dressed in white uniforms and pith helmets – these are the **tourist police**.

Accommodation

With the exception of the long string of big package hotels along the beach, Puerto Vallarta's **places to stay** are within easy walking distance of each other. Most of the more affordable options lie south of the Río Cuale, though there are a couple of places worth considering north of the river. The **budget accommodation** is concentrated along Madero – slightly seedy at night – but remember, too, that the pricier places can transform into bargains during the low season, when prices can be as much as halved. For groups of up to six, fully equipped **apartments** can be very good value.

The town's only formal **campsite** is the grassy *Puerto Vallarta Trailer Park* (☎322/2-28-28), several kilometres north of the hotel zone. Free camping on any of the more popular beaches around the middle of the bay is out, but if you're reasonably well equipped and protected against mosquitoes you could try **Punta de Mita**, at the northern end of the bay or **Boca de Tomatlán** to the south (where the main road turns inland), each of which from time to time sees small communities establishing themselves on the sand. At **Yelapa**, a southern beach to which there are boat trips from town (see below), there's a small but rather pricey hotel, or you might be able to rent a hut or find somewhere to sling a hammock.

ACCOMMODATION PRICE CODES

All the accommodation listed in this book has been categorized into one of nine price bands, as set out below. The prices quoted are in US dollars and normally refer to the cheapest available room for two people sharing in high season. For more details, see p.36.

① up to US$5   ④ US$15–25   ⑦ US$60–80
② US$5–10   ⑤ US$25–40   ⑧ US$80–100
③ US$10–15   ⑥ US$40–60   ⑨ US$100 and over

South of the Río Cuale

Hotel Posada Castillo, Madero 272 at Constitución (☎322/3-14-38). Very basic, but clean, rooms. Good rooftop views from top floor. Seems to have space when everywhere else is full. ③.

Hotel Posada Río Cuale, Serdán 242 at Vallarta (☎ & fax 322/2-09-14). One of the best designed of the central hotels, with rooms staggered around gardens to give an open feel. Comfortable a/c rooms with balconies and a decent bar-restaurant beside the pool. ⑥.

Hortencia, Madero 336 at Insurgentes (☎322/2-24-84). Spacious, light quarters that justify the extra cash over the real cheapies. ④.

Lina, Madero 376, east of Insurgentes (☎322/2-16-61). Simple, clean, but slightly gloomy rooms around a courtyard. ②.

El Molino de Agua, Vallarta 130 (☎322/2-19-57, fax 2-60-56). Fully in keeping with Puerto Vallarta's tropical village image, with cabins dotted around a pool in big, tranquil gardens where the Río Cuale meets the sea. ⑧.

Playa Los Arcos, Olas Altas 380 at Diéguez (☎322/2-15-83). The best of the beachfront hotels, with well-appointed a/c rooms around a large pool. ⑧.

Posada de Roger, Basilio Badillo 237 at Vallarta (☎322/2-06-39, fax 3-04-82). Fairly modern, spacious, colonial-style hotel. Attractive rooms set around a shady courtyard, where excellent breakfasts are served. Only a couple of blocks from the beach, and with a small pool. ⑤.

Villa del Mar, Madero 440 at Jacarandas (☎322/2-07-85). Relaxed, long-time favourite of budget travellers. All rooms have bathrooms; the larger (slightly more expensive) ones also have small balconies. Some two-person apartments available. ③.

Yasmin, Basilio Badillo 168 (☎322/2-00-87). Clean rooms with fans, around a verdant courtyard one block from the beach. ④.

Youth Hostel, Aguacate 302-A and Badillo (☎322/2-21-08). Single-sex dorms in pleasant surroundings. ②.

North of the Río Cuale

Casa Kimberley, Zaragoza 445 (☎322/2-13-36). Time-warped small hotel in the house Richard Burton bought for Liz Taylor's birthday in 1964. Except for the Liz memorabilia, the decor is little changed from when she sold it ten years later. Rooms are comfortable enough, with access to kitchenette and free breakfasts, but this is really a place for Liz freaks. Prices drop by fifty percent in low season. ⑤.

La Casa del Puente, Insurgentes just north of the river behind *Restaurant La Fuente del Puente* (☎322/2-07-49). A real home from home: spacious, elegantly furnished apartments (overlooking the river), and an extremely friendly owner. Only two "suites" (with fully equipped kitchens), and one double room, so book early. ⑥.

Vientos del Río, Cuahtemoc 460, at the end of Guerrero (☎322/2-17-58). Three beautiful, fully furnished suites with wonderful views over the river. ⑥.

The Town

Apart from the **beaches**, and the tourist shops that pack the centre of town, there's not a great deal to do in Puerto Vallarta; certainly nothing in the way of sights or architecture. You could fill an hour or two, though, wandering around the area between the two plazas and on the island in the river. The **zócalo**, where everyone gathers in the evenings and at weekends, is backed by the **Church of Guadalupe**, its tower a city landmark, topped with a huge crown modelled on that of Maximilian's wife, Carlota, in the 1860s. Just down from here on the malecón, the old seafront, is the **Plaza Aquiles Serdán**, with a strange little amphitheatre looking out over the sea, and 100m off to the north another Puerto Vallarta icon, the seahorse statue. In between the plaza and the statue are many new, fantastical sculptures.

On the **Isla Río Cuale** a small park surrounds a clutch of shops and restaurants. At the seaward end there's a tiny, irregularly open, local **archeology museum** (daily except Mon 10am–2pm & 4–6pm), with half a dozen cases of local discoveries. Further inland, expensive restaurants and **galleries** line the middle of the island towards the Insurgentes Bridge. Beyond, past **John Huston's statue**, there's a park and a patch of river where women come to do the family washing, overlooked from the hillsides by the fancy villas of "Gringo's Gulch".

Beaches in and around Puerto Vallarta

Puerto Vallarta's **beaches** vary in nature as you move round the bay: those to the north, out near Nuevo Vallarta and the airport, are long, flat stretches of sand often pounded by surprisingly heavy surf; south, a series of steep-sided coves shelter tiny, calm strands. The town beach, **Playa de los Muertos** (Beach of the Dead), or "Playa del Sol" as the local tourist office would like it known, falls somewhere between the two extremes: not very large and reasonably calm, yet facing apparently open water. This is the most crowded of all, with locals, Mexican holidaymakers and foreign tourists, and in many ways it's the most enjoyable – plenty of people and activities on offer, food and drink close at hand. But don't leave anything of value lying about. The **gay** section of this beach centres around the *Looney Tunes* bar – look out for the blue chairs.

To the **north**, the best beaches tend to front the big hotels, which, since they all have pools and poolside bars, leaves the sand virtually deserted. However, it only really makes sense to make a special journey out here if you plan to sneak in and use the pool – easily enough done – since on all but the calmest days there's sand blowing around and waves that are great for surfers but not so good for swimming. The beaches can be rather dirty, too, except right in front of the fancier hotels, where staff keep a patch cleared.

The smaller stretches of sand to the **south** are far more popular, and though the bus service in this direction is less regular, there's no real problem in getting out to them. Buses leave regularly from Carranza, between Pino Suárez and Olas Altas. There are small beaches every few hundred metres, difficult to get to unless you're staying at one of the hotels or condos that back them, but the best-known and most convenient is **Mismaloya**, some 10km out of Puerto Vallarta. Here John Huston filmed *The Night of the Iguana*, building his film set on the southern side of a gorgeous bay at the mouth of what was once a pristine, jungle-choked gorge. Plans to turn the set and crew's accommodation into tourist cabins never came to anything, and now the huge and expensive *La Jolla de Mismaloya* hotel (⑨) completely dominates the valley. For a small fee you can still wander out to the point and the ruins of the film set. A string of identical palapa restaurants sell beer and seafood cocktails, and boats are on hand to take you snorkelling at **Los Arcos**, a federal underwater park and "eco-preserve" around a group of offshore islands, some formed into the eponymous arches. A superb array of brightly coloured fish – parrot, angel, pencil, croaker and scores of others – negotiate the rock walls and the boulder-strewn ocean floor 5m below. In addition to the scheduled ninety-minute trips from the beach, boats are rented to groups for unlimited periods: if you're feeling adventurous, you could even rent snorkelling gear in Puerto Vallarta beforehand, get off the bus almost as soon as you see Los Arcos, and swim out to the islands; they're less than 300m offshore.

TRIPS FROM PUERTO VALLARTA

There are **boat trips** out to Mismaloya from Puerto Vallarta; and for the beaches further round in this direction – Playa Los Animas, Quimixto and Yelapa are the most common destinations – a boat is the only means of access. Travel agents all over town tout a variety of excursions, most of which leave from the new marina. Compare prices and what's on offer in the way of food and drink – if meals are not included it's worth taking your own food along. At **Yelapa** there's a small "typical" village not far from the white sand beach, and a waterfall a short distance into the jungle. It's no longer really deserted – there's a hotel and several tourist cabins – nor is it cheap, but with luck you might be able to rent a hut for very little, or at least you can always find somewhere to sleep out. To get there more cheaply, try going down to Puerto Vallarta dock early in the morning, when supply boats might give you a ride.

The others – Quimixto, Las Animas and so on – are beaches pure and simple. If you want to go **snorkelling** or **scuba diving** at either of them, tours are led by Chico's Dive Shop, Díaz Ordaz 770-2 (daily 8am–10pm; ☎322/2-18-95). You can rent gear here, too (US$9 a day for the mask, snorkel and fins; US$40 for the full scuba rig, including tank). It is usually too stiflingly humid to consider anything as energetic as **mountain biking**, but Mountain Bike Adventures, Guerrero at Miramar, just north of the upper river bridge (☎322/3-16-80), rents out bikes (US$25 a day), but prefers you to take one of their organized tours into the jungly slopes behind the town and beyond (from US$44).

The stream running across Mismaloya beach flows down from **El Edén** – where the movie *Predator* was filmed – which you can reach either by foot or horseback. En-route you'll pass an open-air **restaurant** in a beautiful setting by a waterfall with a natural pool in which you can swim. There's another idyllically set, if expensive, restaurant a further 10km beyond Mismaloya on the main highway south, just after it turns inland. Below the restaurant, the Río Tuito tumbles over a jumble of smoothed rocks or, in drier times, forms cool, clear pools perfect for whiling away an afternoon. There's no formal **accommodation**, but there are sites for fully equipped campers. Immediately upstream in the small village of Las Juntas y Los Veranos, are *Gringo Jerry's* and the very upmarket *Orquedia's*, more of the same, but if anything even more spectacular, with wooden walkways out to the huge rocks midstream.

Eating

Finding somewhere to eat in Puerto Vallarta is no problem – tourist restaurants offering cocktails by candlelight abound – but eating cheaply is rather less easy. As usual, the market – on the north bank of the river by the upper bridge – has a few cheap *comedors* tucked away upstairs, overlooking the river, well away from the souvenir stalls that fill the rest of the building. Taco and hot-dog stands line the streets, while vendors on the beach offer freshly caught fish, roasted on sticks. For a **fast-food** fix, head for the glut of burger chains and pizza places on the malecón and north into the hotel zone. Gutiérrez Rizo Supermarket, at Serdán and Constitución, sells **picnic** supplies. South of the Río Cuale along Av Olas Altas, and particularly on Basilio Bodillo between Suárez and Insurgentes, several **restaurants** bridge the gap between out-and-out tourist traps and plainer eating houses. Of **more expensive places** you can really take your pick: most offer some form of music or entertainment, or at least a good view while you eat, and almost all display their menus outside, so you know what you're letting yourself in for.

South of the Río Cuale

Las Brisas, Serdán 438 (☎322/2-12-15). Away from most of the crowds, this excellent, upmarket seafood restaurant lies on a quiet street opposite the top end of Isla Río Cuale.

Casa de los Hotcakes, Basilio Badillo 289. Ridiculously named tent-like affair serving good pancakes, waffles and blintzes to a tourist crowd.

Page in the Sun, Olas Altas and Diéguez. A nice little café, with tables in the sun, great coffee, licuados, chess and magazines, which doubles as a used-book shop and is situated in one of the town's most popular spots.

El Palomar de los Gonzáles, Aguacate 425 (☎322/2-07-95). Elegant, mainly Mexican and seafood restaurant, high on the hill to the south of the centre with fine views over the city. The place to take your credit card for that romantic candlelit dinner. Evenings only, from 6pm.

Señor Book, Olas Altas and Gomez. Another café-bookshop with all the virtues, if not quite as good a location as *A Page in the Sun*.

El Torito, Vallarta 290 at Carranza. Bar and restaurant for sports jocks, with satellite coverage of everything from *Serie A* to the Superbowl. Ribs a speciality.

El Tucán, Vallarta 332 at Basilio Badillo. Very good-value Mexican and continental breakfasts, omelettes and pancakes until 2pm, served in the cool courtyard of the *Posada de Roger* hotel.

Karpathos Taverna, Gómez 116 at Playa de los Muertos (☎332/3-15-62). Airy dinner-only restaurant delivering a fairly standard Greek menu. The prices aren't too bad though, and the food's great, though the service is reported to be slow.

Los Tres Huastecas, Olas Altas 444 at Francisco Rodrígues. Bargain Mexican and seafood restaurant, right near Playa de los Muertos, with top-value comidas corridas.

Vallarta Paradise, Lázaro Cárdenas 341, west of Insurgentes. Nothing but straightforward good Mexican food. About the cheapest decent breakfasts and comidas corridas around.

North of the Río Cuale

Chef Roger, Rodríguez 267 (☎322/2-59-00). Pricey but serving consistently excellent Swiss food.

La Chata, Malecón 708 at Dominguez (☎322/3-16-84). Typically tasty Jaliscan food, lightly spiced. Enliven it with whatever you fancy from the stuff on the table. Live music in the evenings and happy hour all afternoon. Not cheap.

La Dolce Vita, Malecón 680 at Dominguez. Pizzas and pasta at reasonable prices. Extremely popular.

Le Bistro Jazz Café, Isla Río Cuale, just east of Insurgentes (☎322/2-02-83). Sophisticated, predominantly seafood dining in classical surroundings or al fresco, soothed by cool jazz. On the expensive side but a great place to wind down. Open from 9am for breakfast, too. Closed Sun.

Mi Casa Buffet, Av México 1121, in *Hotel Marlyn*. Follow the malecón north. All-you-can-eat buffet, with mainly meat dishes and salads. Open daily 1–9pm.

Nightlife and entertainment

The malecón is the obvious centre of night-time activity, lined with places that specialize in creating a high energy party-time atmosphere. Old favourites like the *Hard Rock Café* and *Carlos O'Brian's* are here, along with local contenders *Zoo* and *No Name Café*. None has a cover charge and most are at ground level, making it easy to wander along and take your pick of the **happy hours**. South of the river also has its share of clubs, more down-to-earth and maybe more varied. Worth a visit is *Club Roxy*, Vallarta 217 at Madero, a popular bar/club with an excellent resident band and a great atmosphere that attracts locals and tourists alike (no cover). *The Jazz House*, Rodríguez at Olas Altas, hosts first-class jazz in a tastefully decorated venue that should be more popular; it also serves good if slightly pricey food. **Gay** clubs include *Paco Ranch* and *Paco Paco*, also on Vallarta.

More formal **nightclubs** charge up to US$15 for entry, though by asking around you'll come across free nights early in the week, should find half-price coupons (try the timeshare touts), and can always try talking your way in. *Christine's*, at the *Hotel Krystal* way up in the hotel zone, is lively, expensive and pretentious.

Sunday tends to be quiet – some places close – except on the zócalo where, from around 6pm, huge crowds gather around the dozens of taco and cake stands and listen to the brass band. And there's always the **pool hall** at Madero 279.

MOVING ON FROM PUERTO VALLARTA

All buses now leave from the new **Central Camionera**, which has a guardería and *larga distancia* telephones. Most of the big companies have retained their former offices in town, south of the river, for reservations. **Elite** and **Tres Estrellas de Oro** (☎322/2-66-66, or 1-08-48 at the station), run first-class services to destinations including Acapulco, Guadalajara, Mazatlán and México. **ETN** (☎322/3-29-99) run super-deluxe services to Guadalajara and México, while **Primera Plus** (☎322/2-69-86) first-class buses go to Barra de Navidad, Colima, Guadalajara and Manzanillo. **Second-class** services, run by Autocamiones del Pacífico and Transportes Cihuatlán (both ☎322/2-10-15, or 1-08-69 in the station), go to Guadalajara (2 daily; 9hr), Manzanillo (9 daily; 5–7hr) and Tepic (every 30min; 2hr 30min).

Puerto Vallarta is well served by **flights** to other Mexican cities, the USA and Canada. Prices vary dramatically with season and availability but, organized from this end, tend not to be cheap. You can contact the airport for further details or call the airlines direct (see below under "Listings"). Travel agents or any of the many agencies north of the river can also provide up-to-date information and advice.

Listings

Airlines Aero California (☎322/4-27-77); Aeroméxico (☎322/1-10-97); Alaska (☎322/3-03-50); American (☎322/1-17-99); Continental (☎322/1-10-25); Delta (☎322/1-10-32); Mexicana (☎322/4-89-00); Taesa (☎322/1-15-21).

Airport information ☎322/1-12-98.

American Express, Morelos 660 at Abasolo (☎322/3-29-55), holds mail and changes cheques though at poor rates.

Consulates Canada, Zaragoza 160 (Mon–Fri 9am–noon, until 1pm in winter; ☎322/2-53-98); USA, same address (Mon–Fri 9am–1pm; ☎322/2-00-69).

Emergencies English-speaking medics at CMQ Clinic, Basilio Badillo 365, between Insurgentes and Aguacate (☎322/3-19-19); Cruz Roja ☎322/2-15-33.

Laundry Lavandería Blanquita, Madero 407, east of Aguacate (Mon–Sat 8am–8pm). There's also a full-service place just up from here at Madero 430 (8am–8pm).

Pharmacy CMQ, Basilio Badillo 367 (☎322/2-29-41), next to CMQ Clinic, is open 24hr; or try Lux, Insurgentes 51 (☎322/2-19-09).

Travel agents SAET Travel Service, in the Centro Commercial, corner of Morelos and Rodríguez (Mon–Fri 9am–2pm & 4–7pm, Sat 9am–2pm; ☎322/2-18-86).

North of Puerto Vallarta: Punta de Mita

North of Puerto Vallarta, over the state line in Nayarit, the **Bahía de Banderas** arcs out to **Punta de Mita**, some 30km away. A summer preserve for Mexicans from Guadalajara and a winter retreat for RVers from the north, these gorgeous beaches offer facilities in just a couple of spots – **Nuevo Vallarta** and **Bucerías** – leaving miles of secluded strand for camping. To get out there from Puerto Vallarta, the best bet is to catch any northbound local bus to the *Sheraton Hotel*, then flag down an Autotransportes Medina "Punta de Mita" bus.

The embryonic development of **NUEVO VALLARTA**, 9km north of Puerto Vallarta's airport, is a planned mega-resort that has yet to fruit. As you might expect, the beach is great and there's the *Club-Med*-style Jack Tar Village, where US$40-odd will buy you a day frolicking with all the watersports gear. Here, too, is the arty-crafty **Museo Regional Bahía de Banderas** (daily 9am–2pm; free). **Bahía Azul**, a couple of kilometres further along the same fine sand beach, is a mainly Mexican strand with facilities limited to one shop on the main road.

It's better to push on to another great beach at **BUCERÍAS**, the last of the bay resorts on Hwy-200, with views across the water to Puerto Vallarta from the seafront **restaurants**. *Adriano's* in particular is superb, if pricey. There's a smallish town here, several apartment-type places, *Motel Marlyn* (⑤) and the *Bucerías Trailer Park*.

Keeping to the coast, you leave the main highway for Punta de Mita, passing the beach-free fishing village of **Cruz De Huanacaxtle** and **Playa Manzanillo**. Just over the headland, the coral sand **Piedra Blanca** has a nice relaxed atmosphere, apartments (☎361/7-60-31; ⑦) and an adjacent trailer park. The Punta de Mita road continues through jungly terrain, with small roads dipping down to secluded beaches, the two *enramadas* (restaurants under palapas) at **Destiladeras** being the only facilities. Camping on the beach is great, but you need to bring everything. If you're lucky, though, you may find the freshwater seepage on the beach that gives the place its name.

PUNTA DE MITA is more developed. You have to camp if you want to stay, but at least there's a grocery store, and you can spend the day snorkelling or boogie boarding with gear rented from the same people who run sport fishing trips and cruises out to the offshore wildlife sanctuary of **Islas Las Marietas**.

Bahía de Navidad

There's not a great deal to delay you in the 200-odd kilometres south from Puerto Vallarta to Barra de Navidad. For much of the way the road runs away from the coast, and where it finally does come in striking distance of the ocean it's either for a fabulously expensive resort development, as at **Costa Careyes**, or a beach, such as **Tenacatitla**, which is easily outshone by those on the **Bahía de Navidad**. The most tempting-looking beaches are approximately halfway at **Chamela**, a small resort stretched around the wide Bahía de Chamela, with a couple of trailer parks and simple facilities.

Better to press on to the twin towns of **Barra de Navidad** and **San Patricio-Melaque**, among the most enticing destinations on this entire stretch of coastline. They're not undeveloped or totally isolated – indeed, families from Guadalajara come here by their hundreds, especially at weekends – neither are they at all heavily commercialized: just small, simple, very Mexican resorts. The entire bay, the Bahía de Navidad, is edged by fine sands and, if you're prepared to walk, you can easily leave the crowds behind. Regular buses and colectivos connect the two communities, or you can walk it along the beach in around half an hour.

Barra de Navidad

Lying towards the southern end of the bay, where the beach runs out and curves back round to form a lagoon behind the town, **BARRA DE NAVIDAD** is easily the more appealing of the Bahía de Navidad communities. A couple of kilometres north, San Patricio-Melaque, at the other end of the same beach, is less attractive and more commercial, but if you can't find a room in Barra, it makes a good second choice, with a considerably wider range of hotels.

The much anticipated opening of the *Gran Bahía* hotel, golf course and marina complex across the channel from Barra de Navidad has, as yet, changed surprisingly little, not even spoiling the view from the beach. If you have time, it's worth taking a boat over to check it out. Catch one outside the *Restaurant Manglito* near the jetty. They run across the channel every half-hour from 6.30am to 7.30pm (US$0.25) and, less frequently, to the beaches on the other side. Beach-restaurant-backed **Colimilla** (US$1.50 return), across the Laguna de Navidad, is the most popular destination, chiefly for the seafood and as a base for the two- or three-kilometre walk over to the rough Pacific beach of Playa de Cocos. The *cooperativo* also offers fishing trips, lagoon tours and water skiing.

Practicalities

Buses arrive in Barra at either of two terminals almost opposite each other on Av Veracruz, the town's main drag. The services you are likely to need – post office, *larga distancia* phones and hotels – are all close by: in any case, it only takes twenty minutes to walk around the whole town. The one shortcoming is that there is **no bank** or casa de cambio, and the few places that will change money (such as at Legazpi 264, or next to the bus station) offer criminal rates. Cihuatlán, fifteen minutes' bus ride away, has the nearest bank with an ATM and other facilities, or there's a casa de cambio in San Patricio. The **tourist office** (Mon–Fri 9am–7pm, Sat 9am–1pm; ☎335/5-51-00) is tucked away in some outbuildings of a private club just back from the beach at the north end of town. They can advise on anything happening locally – usually not much – though you can probably obtain more useful information from Bob, who runs Bob's Bookswap, at Mazatlán 61, two rooms absolutely packed with English-language paper-backs: bring one and take one, no charge.

Barra has a couple of small cheap **hotels** and some classier options. Free camping is also a possibility along the beach to the north of town. It's easiest to follow the beach, rather than the road, up to a point where you feel comfortable, as beach access is limited. The best budget option in town is *Posada Pacifico*, inland at Mazatlán 136 (☎335/5-53-59; ③), a simple, friendly place with clean airy rooms, some with bal-conies. Slightly run-down, *Bungalows Karelia*, on López de Legazpi by the central plaza (☎335/5-53-84;⑤), has a nice seafront verandah and apartments with simple kitchens. *El Delfín*, Morelos 23 (☎335/5-50-68; ⑤), is a multistorey hotel with spacious clean rooms, a small pool, and sea views from the upper floors. The slightly worn but good-value *Hotel Sand's*, Morelos 24 (☎335/5-50-18; ⑤), includes breakfast in the price, has a large garden over-looking the lagoon and a decent swimming-pool that non-residents can use if they buy a drink from the bar (two-for-one cocktails 2–6pm).

Of the many good **restaurants** in Barra most are on Legazpi, or else at the junction of Veracruz and Jalisco, where *Restaurant Patty* is the best of a number of similar bud-get places serving excellent *ceviche*, fresh fish and meaty Mexican staples. Next door, *Ivette* dishes up good pizza, while diagonally opposite, *Café Ambar* is renowned for its crêpes, salads and vegetarian dishes. *Café El Sol*, on Legazpi at Sinaloa, is an airy, bohemian place with a good choice of vegetarian dishes. Slightly pricier than most, *Banana's*, on Legazpi opposite Jalisco, offers very good breakfasts. Exclusively **seafood restaurants** crowd Legazpi and Morelos down towards the point: *El Manglito* is one of the best. **Nightlife** is limited to playing pool, drinking and listening to live music at *Piper Lover's Bar and Grill* on Legazpi, and dancing at *El Galeón* disco (Morelos) or *Sunset's* (Legazpi).

San Patricio-Melaque

SAN PATRICIO-MELAQUE seems much more of a real Mexican town, with its zóca-lo, church, largish market, and substantial **bus station** at the junction of Carranza and Gómez Farías. Opposite, in the Pasaje Commercial, you'll find the town's only **casa de cambio**, with a *larga distancia* phone (Mon–Sat 9am–2pm & 4–7pm, Sun 9am–2pm); rates are poor. The **post office** is hidden on Orozco, round the corner from *Hotel San Patricio*.

There's no **tourist office**, and **eating** options are limited to the identikit restaurants along the northern end of the beachfront, the cheaper comidas on the streets beach-side of the zócalo and around the market on C Corona.

Very cheap **camping** is an option on the patch of wasteland at the northern end of the beach beyond the restaurants, and there's a full facility campsite right by the beach, *Trailer Park Playa*, Gómez Farías 250 at López Mateos (☎333/5-50-65), but if you want a roof over your head, walk along Gómez Farías, parallel to the beach. *San Patricio,*

Gómez Farías 413 (☎333/5-52-44; ④), is the best of the budget places, with outside kitchens and a communal dining area; some apartments (sleeping up to eight) have kitchenettes. There's safe parking, too. In the same vein, *El Marquez*, Gómez Farías 407 (☎333/5-52-13; ⑤), is more luxurious and considerably more expensive. *Posada Pablo de Tarso*, Gómez Farías 408 (☎333/5-51-17; ④), has comfortable and nicely furnished rooms, with TV and phone, around a verdant courtyard, and a good pool; apartments (⑤–⑥) sleep between three and six people. Note that during **Semana Santa**, even the high-season rates quoted here can double.

Manzanillo

Two roads head **inland to Guadalajara** from this part of the coast. The direct-looking route from Barra de Navidad is indeed reasonably fast (although any route has to tangle spectacularly with the Sierra Madre), but it's also very dull, with just one town of any size, the dusty, provincial and untempting community of Autlán. The journey along the coast to **Manzanillo** and inland via **Colima** is considerably more interesting, not only for the towns themselves but also for the spectacular snowcapped volcanoes that come beyond.

Just an hour down the road from the Bahía de Navidad, **MANZANILLO** is a very different sort of place: a working port where tourism – although highly developed – very definitely takes second place to trade. Downtown, it has to be said, is not at all attractive: crisscrossed by railway tracks, rumbling with heavy traffic and surrounded by a bewildering array of inner harbours and shallow lagoons that seem to cut the place off from the land. You can easily imagine that a couple of hundred years ago plague and pestilence made sailors fear to land here, and it's not surprising to read in an 1884 guide to Mexico that "the climate of Manzanillo is unhealthy for Europeans, and the tourist is advised not to linger long in the vicinity". Few tourists do stay even now – most are concentrated in the hotels and club resorts around the bay to the west – but although the streets are still narrow and none too clean, the town is healthy enough and there's a certain shabby romance in staying in the centre. Certainly it's a lot more interesting than the sanitized resort area, and cheaper, too. Buses out to the beach are frequent and efficient, but if you are kicking your heels in the centre, you could climb one of Manzanillo's **hills** for a better view of the bay.

Arrival, information and accommodation

Manzanillo's **bus station** is inconveniently sited more than 1km east of town, and though there are buses (marked "Centro") these are slow and avoid the zócalo, where you really want to be. Better to walk or take a taxi. Manzanillo's commercial core centres on its zócalo, the **Jardín Alvaro Obregón**, right on the harbourfront opposite the main outer dock. All the hotels, restaurants, banks and offices are a very short walk away. Banamex and Bancomer **banks** (both with ATMs) are next to each other on Av México at C 10 de Mayo, there's a *larga distancia* booth (daily 8am–10pm; collect calls) on the Jardín Obregón at Dávalos 27, and the **post office** is a block east at Juárez and 5 de Mayo.

Finding a **place to stay** is no problem in Manzanillo; there's a range of budget to moderately priced hotels, though nothing special, close to the centre. Prices at all but the cheapest drop by about 25 percent outside the July, August, Christmas and *Semana Santa* **high season**. Close to the bus station, *Casa de Huéspedes del Puerto*, Manuel Alvarez 3 (☎333/2-36-95; ②), is basic and inexpensive: to get there turn left beside the bus station and take a second right. In town the cheapest bet is *Casa de Huéspedes Petrito*, Allende 20 (☎333/2-01-87; ③), with small, clean rooms and shared showers. Just off the zócalo, the *Emperador*, Dávalos 69 (☎333/2-23-74; ③), has decent rooms

MOVING ON FROM MANZANILLO

Half a dozen **bus** companies provide services from the **Central Camionera** along the coast and inland to **Colima** and **Guadalajara**. Both Transportes Sur de Jalisco and Soc. Coop de Transportes run to Colima (6 an hour between them; 2hr), the former also serving Tecomán (every 20min; 1hr), Guadalajara (8 daily; 5–6hr) and Lázaro Cárdenas (6 daily; 6–7hr). Autobuses de Occidente runs first-class buses to Colima (every hour; 1hr 30min) and Guadalajara (every hour; 6hr). Pacifico/Cihuatlán serve Barra de Navidad (1hr 30min) and **Puerto Vallarta** (6hr) with hourly second-class and two first-class buses a day, and Elite runs first-class to **Acapulco** (12hr) and all points to Tijuana (38hr).

with hot showers and fans, and a cheap *comedor*, too – far better value than some of the pricier places nearby. If you have the money, though, head straight for *Colonial*, Av México 100 (☎333/2-10-80; ④), where attractive rooms with TV are set around a Moorish-style courtyard with Andalucian azulejos and a cooling fountain. If you want to be by the sea, try *Motel Playa San Pedrito*, José Azueta 3 (☎333/2-05-35; ④), a rambling place around a pool and tennis court, backing onto **Playa San Pedrito**, about 1km east of the centre (twenty minutes' walk from the zócalo along the waterfront); spacious and well-equipped apartments sleeping six (⑤) are available. This beach is probably your best bet for camping, too: Manzanillo has no trailer park and all the other beaches are pretty built up.

Eating and drinking

Places to eat are concentrated around the zócalo, with several good cafés overlooking the Jardín Obregón itself. *Chantilly* on Juárez (closed Sat) and *Roca del Mar*, diagonally opposite, both serve a huge range of decent meals, top-value comidas corridas and good espresso and cappuccino. Between the two, *Portofino*, Juárez 116 (☎333/2-42-93), is mainly a pizza delivery place but you can eat in, too. Heading east along Morelos, parallel to the waterfront, you come to *La Perlita*, which dishes up antojitos and seafood on shaded tables close to the water and, a little further along, *Lychee*, Niños Héroes 397 (closed Sun), which serves not bad, moderately priced Chinese food. If you head down México, Manzanillo's main commercial and shopping street, you'll find a whole series of other possibilities, from take-away taquerías and the tiny vegetarian *Yacatecuhtli*, at no. 249, to the fancy restaurant in the *Hotel Colonial*. At the other end of the scale, there are several very cheap places – grimy and raucous on the whole – in the market area three blocks down México and on the left, and at the bottom end of Juárez by the train tracks.

The coast around Manzanillo

While locals might go **swimming** from the tiny harbour beach of San Pedrito and in the Laguna de Cuyutlán behind the town, both are thoroughly polluted. Far better to head for beaches around the bay proper, where the tourist hotels congregate. The nearest of these, at **LAS BRISAS**, are in fact very close to town, just across the entrance to the inner harbour, but to get there by road you have to go all the way round the Laguna de San Pedrito, before turning back towards Manzanillo along the narrow strip of land that forms Las Brisas. Frequent buses from the centre (marked "Las Brisas") run all the way along the single seafront drive; it's a rather strange area, as much suburb as resort, and the beach, steeply shelving and often rough, is perhaps not as good as those round the bay in the other direction. As the original seaside strip, Las Brisas offers a number of older, and consequently cheaper, hotels and restaurants, but – except when it's flooded by holidaymakers from Guadalajara – the whole place has a depressing, run-down feel. If you want to stay by the beach, take the bus out here and have a look around – *Las Brisas*, Lázaro Cárdenas 1243 (☎333/3-27-16; ③), and the marginally better equipped *Star*, Lázaro Cárdenas 1313 (☎333/3-25-60; ④), are among the cheapest. Several places offer **cabins or apartments** for larger groups, but none is particularly good value: *Bungalows Angelica*, Lázaro Cárdenas 1578 (☎333/3-29-82), with a pool and apartments for up to six people for US$80, is about the best but not by much. If you can afford it, continue to *La Posada*, Lázaro Cárdenas 201 (☎333/3-18-99; ⑧), a delightful small hotel with huge breakfasts included.

Better and more sheltered swimming can be found along the coast further round, where the bay is divided by the rocky Peninsula de Santiago. "Miramar" buses run all the way round to the far side of the bay, past the settlements of **Salahua** and **SANTIA-GO** and a string of beaches. The best are around the far edge of the peninsula (get off the bus at Santiago). Here you'll find the excellent-value **hotel** *Maria Cristina*, 28 de Augusto 36 (☎333/3-24-70; ④), two blocks inland from Santiago's zócalo, with a pool, a pleasant garden and some rooms that can take four people (⑤). There are several restaurants here, too, both in the village and down on the beach: *Juanito's*, on the highway, is a long-standing favourite with gringos and locals alike.

If you're prepared to walk a little way out onto the peninsula, you can reach the beautiful cove of **La Audiencia**, with calm water and tranquil sand. From here, if you're feeling reasonably energetic and looking smart enough to get past the guards, you can climb over the hill to **Las Hadas** (☎333/3-00-00; ⑨) – the amazingly flashy, glistening white hotel–villa complex where Dudley Moore and Bo Derek frolicked in the film *10*. It's worth seeing even if you can't afford a drink at any of the many bars. There's more flash and glitz at the *Club Maeva* (☎333/3-01-41; ⑧), further round the bay on the **Playa Miramar**, but on the whole the hotels in the vicinity are thoroughly average, and **nightlife**, such as it is, is confined to a few discos strung out along the coast road.

South from Manzanillo

If all you need is a heaving ocean and a strip of beach backed by a few *enramadas*, then you're better off skipping Manzanillo altogether in favour of a series of infinitely preferable, though tiny, resorts that adorn the shoreline 50–80km beyond. Easily accessible by bus, **Cuyutlán**, **Paraíso** and **Boca de Pascuales** boast great beaches that draw Mexican holidaymakers, but none is in any way elaborate, each equipped with very few facilities. To **get to Cuyutlán and Paraíso** from Manzanillo, catch a bus (every 15min) 50km to the inland market town of **Armería**. The town has a bank, post office, a long-distance bus stop on the main street, and, should you need to stay, a good-value hotel, *México* (no phone; ②), right on the main drag. Buses onward to Cuyutlán (every 30min; 20min) leave from outside *Ruly's Sol Deposito* three blocks to the north. Head round the corner to the market for buses to Paraíso (every 45min; 15min), a few kilometres further south. For **buses to Boca de Pascuales** (every 30min until 6pm; 25min), you'll need to take a direct bus from Manzanillo and change at the market town of **Tecomán**, 20km south of Armería. Buses also run from here to Colima and Lázaro Cárdenas, and there are banking facilities on hand.

Cuyutlán

CUYUTLÁN, the largest of the three coastal resorts some 12km southwest of Armería, is perhaps the most appealing, backed by an immense coconut grove that stretches along a narrow peninsula from here almost to Manzanillo. The old town around the zócalo is sleepy, its inhabitants idling away the day on wooden verandahs under terracotta roofs. Life in the hotels by the beachfront malecón isn't much faster, except during the Christmas, *Semana Santa* and August high season, when things liven up considerably and you should book ahead if you want to stay.

In spring, the coast both here and further south is subject to the **Ola Verde**: vast, dark green waves up to 10m high that crash down on the fine grey sand. Theories to explain their green hue vary widely – from the angle of the sun refracting off the wave to algal bloom – but whatever the reason, the Ola Verde has entered Cuyutlán mythology. At other times of the year the surf is impressive but easier to handle.

Outside the high season, **hotels** are affordable (rates usually per person in low season) and all clustered within a block or two of the junction of Hidalgo and Veracruz. The ones to go for are *Morelos*, Hidalgo 185 (☎332/6-40-13; ④), with good clean rooms, fans and hot water; and the fifty-year-old *Fenix*, Hidalgo 201 (☎332/6-40-82; ④), which has some great old-fashioned rooms opening onto spacious communal verandahs. *San Rafael*, Veracruz 46 (☎332/6-40-15; ④), is only marginally better and probably not worth the extra cost. Rates quoted are all high season. All three hotels boast good seafood restaurants.

To get to **Cuyutlán**, you can take the bus from Armería, or drive on either Hwy-200 (signed turn-off 5km before Armería) or the new and little-used Manzanillo–Colima autopista that runs along the coast.

Paraíso and Boca de Pascuales

With your own vehicle you can reach **PARAÍSO** directly from Cuyutlán, but by bus you'll have to return to Armería. From there it is 8km to this tiny place, which gives the impression that it is only just hanging on, with a few neglected buildings either side of the dust and cobble street. The beach is fun, though, with banks of crashing surf, and a few *enramadas* behind. Only at *Hotel Paraíso*, right on the seafront (mobile ☎331/7-18-25; ⑤), is the feeling of dilapidation dispelled; the older rooms have character, but the new wing is more comfortable, and everyone uses the pool and watches the sunset from the bar. If you **camp** on the beach they'll let you use a shower, especially if you buy a drink. About the only other place to stay is the plain *Posada Valencia* (☎331/2-14-80 and ask for *Posada Valencia*; ④).

Smaller still, **BOCA DE PASCUALES**, 13km from Tecomán, is little more than a bunch of palapa restaurants and a beach renowned for huge waves. Swimming can be dangerous, but otherwise it's a fine place to hang out for a few days. Beach **camping** is your best option; the *Estrella de Sur* (③), on the way in, is poor value. The best **restaurant**, the expensive *Hamacas del Mayor*, serves top-notch seafood.

Colima

Inland **COLIMA**, capital of the state of the same name, 100km from Manzanillo, is a distinctly colonial city, and a very beautiful one too, famed for its parks and overlooked by the perfectly conical **Volcán de Colima** and, in the distance, the Nevado de Colima. It doesn't offer a whole lot in the way of excitement, but it's a pleasant place to stop over for a night or two: cooler than the coast, but never as cold as it can get in the high mountains, and with some good-value hotels and restaurants to boot.

Archeological evidence – much of it explained in the city's museums – points to three millennia of rich cultural heritage around Colima, almost all of it wiped out with the arrival of Cortés' lieutenant Gonzalo de Sandoval who, in 1522, founded the city on its present site. Four years later Cortés decreed that Colima – named after Cilimán, a former ruler of the local Nahua people – should be the third city of New Spain after Veracruz and México. However, Acapulco's designation as the chief Pacific port at the end of the sixteenth century deprived Colima of any strategic importance and, com-

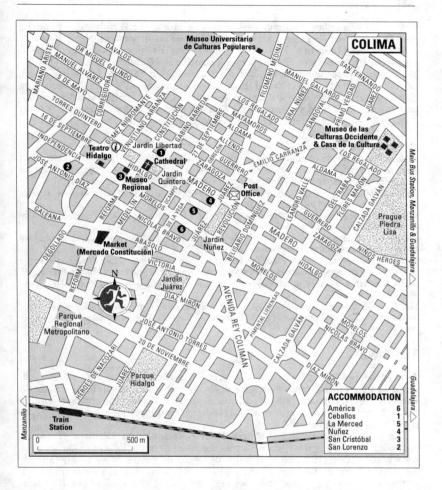

bined with a series of devastating earthquakes, left it with few grand buildings to show for its former glory. The town makes up for this with a chain of shady formal **plazas** and a number of attractive **courtyards**, many of them now used as restaurants and cafés, wonderfully cool places to catch up on writing postcards – though the selection of these is uniformly awful.

Arrival and information

Some 2km east of the centre, Colima's **main bus station**, the Central de Autobuses (often referred to as Central Nuevo), handles frequent first- and second-class buses from Guadalajara, Lázaro Cárdenas, Manzanillo, México and further afield. Taxis and city buses marked "Centro" run towards the central plaza. Most second-class Manzanillo buses and all local services operate from the **Terminal Suburbana** (confusingly known as "Central Camionera"), 2km out on the opposite, western, periphery and also served by city buses.

Colima's willing but practically useless **tourist office**, Portal Hidalgo 20 (Mon–Fri 9am–3pm & 6–9pm, Sat 9am–1pm; ☎331/2-43-60), lies on the western side of the zócalo – the **Jardín Libertad**. The most useful **bank**, Banamex (exchange Mon–Fri 9am–1.30pm), is nearby on Hidalgo between Medellín and Ocampo, and has an ATM, but the Majapara **casa de cambio**, Juárez and Morelos (Mon–Sat 9am–2pm & 4.30–7pm), offers better rates for both cash and cheques. Su Casa, Madero 150 (Mon–Sat 9am–7pm, Sun 9am–2pm), has reasonable rates and longer hours. The **post office** is at Madero 247, and you can keep in touch through the Computel *larga distancia*, Morelos 234 (daily 7am–10pm; collect calls), at the opposite end of the Jardín Núñez.

Accommodation

Colima boasts plenty of reasonable hotels within a few blocks of the centre. Rates don't vary much year round, but places do fill up rapidly during the *San Felipe* and *Todos los Santos* fiestas in early to mid-February and late October to early November.

América, Morelos 162 (☎331/2-03-66). Colima's swankiest hotel, a pretty characterless, international-style place with all the facilities – but no pool. ⑤.

Ceballos, Portal Medellín 12 (☎331/2-44-44). Colonial hotel right on the Jardín Libertad, with wonderfully spacious halls and not bad, but less impressive, rooms. ⑤.

La Merced, Hidalgo 188 (☎331/2-69-69). Lovely old hotel with fan-ventilated rooms around a central patio, and some less attractive, newer a/c rooms. TV and parking. ③.

Núñez, Juárez 88 (☎331/2-70-30). Reliable budget place on Jardín Núñez, ranged around a central courtyard. Large rooms with showers are almost twice the price of small ones without. Parking. ②.

San Cristóbal, Reforma 98 at Independencia (no phone). Central with clean basic rooms, some with private bathroom. ③.

San Lorenzo, Cuauhtémoc 149, two blocks west then two south from the southwest corner of the zócalo (☎331/2-20-00). Best value of the budget places. Excellent clean rooms with soap and towels provided. ②.

The Town

As in all these old cities, life in Colima centres on the **zócalo**, where you'll find the government offices (take a quick look at the distinctly second-rate murals in the Palacio de Gobierno) and the unimpressive Neoclassical cathedral. Quite out of character for this part of Mexico, however, the town actually boasts a few things to see, too: chiefly a couple of really good **museums**.

The most central of these, Colima's **Museo Regional de Historia** (Tues–Sat 9am–6pm, Sun 5–8pm; free), stands across the street from the Palacio de Gobierno in a lovely old building that also houses the university art gallery. Move swiftly through the stuff on **local crafts** – though the animal and diabolical masks used in traditional dances are interesting – and make for the later rooms, chock-full of **pre-Hispanic ceramics**: gorgeous figurines with superbly expressive faces, fat Izcuintli dogs and people working on mundane, everyday tasks. Though characteristic of western Mexican culture, these examples are specific to Colima, many of them found in *tumbas de tiro* – well-like tombs up to 16m deep, more commonly found in South America and the Pacific Islands. The cultural parallel isn't well understood, but explanatory panels (all in Spanish) show the different styles.

More widely trumpeted than the regional museum, the **Museo de Las Culturas del Occidente** (Tues–Sun 9am–7pm; free), 1km northeast of the Jardín Núñez, holds another substantial collection of local archeology. You'll see the same kind of thing here as in the former, but more figurines: dogs with litters fighting, people blowing conch shells, playing musical instruments and dancing, even a man in a caiman mask whose dances were said to avert hurricanes. There's also a more detailed explanation of the rural agricultural society that produced such well-preserved tombs; again, all in

CLIMBING THE NEVADO DE COLIMA

The **Parque Nacional Nevado de Colima** comprises two beautiful volcanoes, snow-capped in winter, rising north of Colima. The Volcán de Colima (3900m), also known as "Volcán de Fuego", is officially still active and smokes from time to time, though there seems little imminent danger. It is far less frequently climbed than its larger and less active brother, the **Nevado de Colima** (4335m), which is popular with local mountaineers during the clear, dry winter months. Unless there's a lot of snow – in December and January crampons and an ice-axe are essential – and provided you are fit and can get transport high enough, it's less of a climb than a relatively easy **hike** up to the summit. The problem is getting someone to take you up to the cabin at **La Joya** (3500m) – from where it is also possible to make an assault on Volcán de Colima – or on to the microwave station a little way beyond, from where it is a stiff but non-technical walk. Hitching isn't an option; the logging roads up here are rough, requiring high clearance or four-wheel drive vehicles, and see very little traffic. Your best bet is to set three days aside, take a sleeping bag and waterproofs, pack enough food and water for the trip, and plan to walk from the highway.

   To get there, take a bus to **Tonaya** from the Central de Autobuses in Colima, or one of the more frequent buses to Ciudad Guzmán and change for Tonaya. Ask the driver to drop you off on the highway, where an unpaved side road leads 3km to **Fresnito**. About 300m along the main highway past this junction, a vehicle track leads off on the left towards a house, then veers to the left. Follow this – it soon becomes a path – and keep going on the most obvious path heading up and you should arrive (in about 6–8hr) at the La Joya hut, just below the tree line. An alternative is to follow the dirt road into Fresnito, where there are very limited supplies, and ask for the road to La Joya. Take this and keep right until the route becomes obvious. This rough service road for the microwave station leads up through cow pastures and goes right past the hut, again about six to eight hours walking. Following this you do at least have a chance of hitching. You can tank up from the supply of running water here, but don't expect to stay in the hut, which is often locked, and even if open may be full as it only sleeps six. You should plan on a day from La Joya to the summit and back, then another to get back to Colima, though a very fit walker starting before dawn could make the trip back to Colima, or at least Ciudad Guzmán, in a day.

Spanish. In the same park as the museum, an auditorium hosts occasional concerts and films. Look for posters advertising what's on.

   With more time to spare, wander eight blocks north of the zócalo to the **Instituto Universitario de Culturas Populares** (Mon–Fri 9am–2pm & 4–7pm, Sat 9am–2pm; free), which has a good but poorly explained collection of masks, a few old photos of some spectacular dances, and a small musical instrument collection including a violin made from scrap wood and a Modelo beer can. Reproductions of some of the ceramic pieces shown at the other two museums are made outside under the banyan tree.

   On a hot day, you can cool off in one of two parks, the **Parque Piedra Lisa** to the east – the "sliding stone" in the name referring to a rock that is said to ensure your return if you slide on it – and the **Parque Regional Metropolitano** (dawn–dusk) to the southwest. The latter has a small, depressing zoo, a boating lake with boats for rent, and a swimming pool (daily 10am–4.30pm).

Eating and drinking

For a town of its size, Colima has a great range of places to eat, from restaurants serving **Oaxacan** and local specialities to the region's best **vegetarian** food.

Ah que Nanishe, 5 de Mayo 267, west of Mariano Arista (☎331/4-21-97). Surprisingly inexpensive courtyard restaurant specializing in dishes from the owner's native Oaxaca. Well worth the walk out from the centre.

MOVING ON FROM COLIMA

To get to the **Terminal Suburbana**, catch bus #2 on Morelos; for the **Central de Autobuses** take either #4 on Zaragoza, #6 on Revolución or Jardín Núñez, or #18 on Medina at Zaragoza. Dozens of buses head **inland to Guadalajara** or down to **Manzanillo**, but heading south you may find it quicker to leap on the first bus to Tecomán (every 15min; 45min) and change there for Lázaro Cárdenas.

Café la Arábica, 162 Guerrero, west of Juárez. The smell of roasting Colimense beans heralds this tiny coffee shop. "Americano", espresso or cappuccino made from excellent locally grown, roasted and ground coffee – but little else – is served.

Lakshmi del Centro, Madero at Revolución. Mainly a wholefood shop and bakery producing great banana and carrot bread, but with a restaurant area for veggieburgers and nutritious drinks.

Los Naranjos, Gabino Barreda 34, north of Madero (☎331/2-00-29). Slightly upmarket restaurant. *Machaca norteña* is a speciality, and you can get a substantial comida corrida for around US$5.

Los Portales, Hidalgo on the Jardín Libertad. Nice place on the zócalo, great for sitting outside and watching the world go by. Reasonably priced antojitos and seafood dishes.

El Trebol, 16 de Septiembre and Degollado. Comfortable and very cheap place, just off the zócalo, for egg dishes, tortas and light meals.

Restaurant Vegetariano Samadhi, Filomeno Medina 125. Sit at tables around the palm-shaded colonnade and feast on something inexpensive and delicious from the varied (almost entirely veggie) menu, including veggieburgers, crêpes, delicious licuados and wonderful-value comidas corridas served from 1 to 4pm. Daily 8am–10pm, Thurs until 5pm.

Around Colima: Comala

The best time to be in Colima is on a clear winter day when the volcanoes in the **Parque Nacional Nevado de Colima** dominate the views to the north. Climbing them, while not that difficult, needs some planning (see box, p.369). You can get a closer look, however, by spending an afternoon at **COMALA**, 10km north of Colima. Not only do you get a fantastic view of the mountains from the town's colonial plaza but you can sip a beer or margarita while competing *mariachi* bands pitch for your business. Four **restaurants**, huddled together under the zócalo's southern portal, each try to outdo the other by producing better *botanas* – plates of snacks, dips and tacos – free with drinks until about 6pm. Of course drinks are expensive, but stay for an hour or so and you won't need a meal. There's little to choose between them, so, if you can face the roving *mariachis*, a restaurant crawl might be an idea. Find a place where one band dominates, otherwise you find yourself trying to disentangle the sound of three. Friday and Saturday are the liveliest times, when you can mingle with day-tripping, predominantly middle-class Mexicans; on Sundays and Mondays there are craft markets in the square. **Buses** come out here from Colima's Terminal Suburbana (every 15min; 20min).

South to Lázaro Cárdenas

Beyond the state of Colima you run into a virtually uninhabited area: there are occasional beaches, but for the most part the mountains drop straight into the ocean – spectacular, but offering no reason to stop. Moving into Michoacán, **CALETA DE CAMPOS**, some 70km short of Lázaro Cárdenas, is the first and in many ways the best place to stop. It's a small village, barely electrified and with distinctly dodgy plumbing, but with two lovely beaches and an impressive ocean view. The streets are unpaved, and horses stand tied to hitching posts alongside the campers of dedicated American surfers and the fancy new cars belonging to visitors from the city. There are two **hotels** – *Yuritzi* (☎753/6-01-92; ③), recommended, with its own generator and water supply, and *Los Arcos* (no phone; ③) – and a string of makeshift bar-restaurants down at the beach. For much of the year it's virtually deserted, but in winter, when the Californian beach boys come down in pursuit of sun and surf, and at weekends, when families pile in from Lázaro Cárdenas, it enjoys a brief season. If both hotels are full, which at such times they can be, beg a hammock under the thatch of one of the beach bars: most are happy enough to have you as long as you eat there, too, though you may be bitten by voracious mosquitoes.

In any case the beach should definitely be seen at night, when, if the conditions are right, the ocean glows a bright, luminous green. This is not a product of the excellent local beer, or of the Acapulco Gold that allegedly grows in the surrounding mountains, but a naturally illuminated, emerald-green plankton: go swimming in it and you'll come out covered in sparkling pinpoints. The phenomenon is common to much of this coast, and also seen in Baja California – but is nowhere as impressive as here. One word of warning: the second beach, cut off by a narrow, rocky point, looks like an unspoilt paradise (which it is), but you can only get there by boat or a stiff climb over the rocks – try to swim round and you'll be swept out to sea by a powerful current. Locals are well used to picking up tourists who suddenly find themselves several hundred metres offshore.

In addition to the occasional long-distance services, local buses make the trip from Caleta de Campos to **LÁZARO CÁRDENAS** several times a day. But there's little reason to go there except to get somewhere else – it's strictly industrial, dominated by a huge, British-funded steelworks. You'll find several small **hotels** around the bus terminals, which are next to each other in the centre. From the station served by Galeana, Sur de Jalisco and Parhikuni, walk out the front, turn right, right again and second right to get to the station served by Tres Estrellas, Estrella Blanca and others. The **train station** is on the outskirts, the sole daily train leaving at noon for Morelia twelve hours away. On the whole, it is better to press on or catch a local bus from the Galeana station to Playa Azul.

Playa Azul

Once a small-time, slow-moving beach not far removed from Caleta de Campos, **PLAYA AZUL** has been rather overrun by the growth of the city, but there are still numerous reasonably priced hotels and not a bad beach, backed by scores of palapa restaurants. Aside from lying on the sand, all there is to do is walk 2km north to see the rusting hulk of the *Betula*, a Norwegian sulphuric acid carrier that foundered in 1993 (all the acid has now gone).

The road in crosses four streets, parallel to the beach and running down to the vast plaza at the southern end. The bus will pass the recommended *Hotel Playa Azul* (☎753/6-00-24; ④), where the best rooms have a/c and a pool view. You can also camp here, though the campground is little more than a patch of dirt behind the hotel. The pool, though, is a better prospect: US$1.25 for non-guests, it is free if you eat in the decent hotel restaurant. For somewhere a little cheaper, try the rather run-down *Maria Isabela* (☎753/6-00-30; ③), on the far side of the plaza, which has a pool; or *Bungalows de la Curva* (☎753/6-00-58; ③), which isn't spotless but does have rooms with cooking equipment. The budget option is the clean but basic *Del Pacífico* (☎753/6-01-06; ②), at the northwestern corner of the plaza. Most people, though, sleep on the beach or, better still, in hammocks strung out at a beachfront bar. The **beachfront restaurants** satisfy most cravings, and *Coco's*, one street back, is good for breakfasts, burgers and pizza.

Zihuatanejo and on to Acapulco

Although it's only about 7km from Ixtapa to Zihuatanejo, the two places could hardly be more different. **IXTAPA**, a purpose-built, computer-planned "paradise" resort, is quite simply one of the most soulless towns imaginable – to say nothing of being one of the most expensive. Twentysome years down the line, it still hasn't begun to mellow or wear itself in, and its single coastal drive still runs past a series of concrete boxes of varying heights. These completely cordon off Ixtapa's sole attraction from the road, forcing those who can't afford the hotels' inflated prices to trespass, or even use the hotels' facilities. You might want to visit one of the clubs in the evening, but you will definitely not want to stay.

ZIHUATANEJO, on the other hand, for all its growth and popularity in recent years, has at least retained something of the look and feel of the village it once was – what building there has been is small-scale and low-key. Nevertheless, as soon as you arrive you know you are in a resort: taxi drivers are forever touting for custom, trinket and tacky T-shirt shops are abundant, and as likely as not there'll be a cruise ship moored out in the bay. But at least here there are a fair number of small, reasonably priced hotels (though noticeably more expensive than the lowest rates in Acapulco) and some inexpensive restaurants. For some it's the ideal compromise – quiet, almost dead by night, yet with the more commercial excitements of Ixtapa in easy reach. The one real

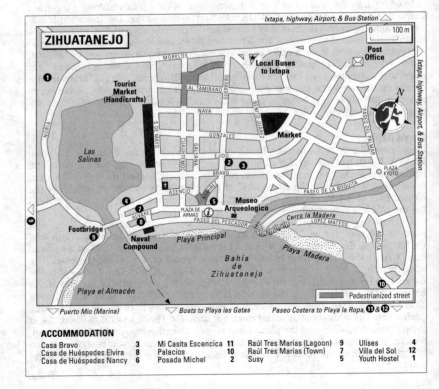

ACCOMMODATION

Casa Bravo	3	Mi Casita Escencica	11	Raúl Tres Marias (Lagoon)	9	Ulises	4
Casa de Huéspedes Elvira	8	Palacios	10	Raúl Tres Marias (Town)	7	Villa del Sol	12
Casa de Huéspedes Nancy	6	Posada Michel	2	Susy	5	Youth Hostel	1

problem is its popularity – with strictly controlled development, rooms can be hard to find in the centre of Zihuatanejo, a region of barely ten small blocks hemmed in by the main roads into town, the yacht marina and the beach.

Arrival and information

Buses arrive at Zihuatanejo's new station (with guardería), about twenty minutes' walk from the centre of town. There are plenty of taxis outside and if you walk a couple of hundred metres to the left you can pick up passing "Zihuatanejo" buses, which will generally drop you off at the top of Juárez, the place where the Ixtapa minibuses leave (6am–10pm; every 10min). Buses marked "Noria" go straight past the youth hostel and *Casa de Huéspedes Nancy*. *Combis* making the thirty-minute run between Zihuatanejo and the **airport**, 20km south (and only 2km off the highway to Acapulco), also pass by the bus station, before dropping off (and picking up) just outside the mercado, at Gonzales and Juárez.

Zihuatanejo's facilities are widely scattered. The moderately helpful **tourist office** (Mon–Fri 9am–3pm & 6–8pm, Sat 9am–2pm, Sun 9am–5pm; ☎ & fax 755/4-83-01) is right by the Plaza de Armas on Alvarez; the **post office** (Mon–Fri 8am–8pm, Sat 9am–1pm) is on a street with no name at the northeastern corner (look for signs); and the most useful **bank**, Bancomer (foreign exchange 9am–1.30pm), lies at the corner of Juárez and Bravo. The **casas de cambio** don't generally offer good rates, but Central de Cambios Guiball, on Galeana west of Bravo, is open until 8.30pm daily and has a *larga distancia* phone for inexpensive collect calls.

Accommodation

Zihuatanejo's high **season** is fairly long, from mid-November or earlier to the end of April. Outside those times some of the slightly more expensive hotels drop their rates to those of the budget places – which tend to vary their prices less. Rates are generally charged per person, not per room, so there's little advantage for groups. Just ten minutes' walk from the centre, the **youth hostel**, Paseo de las Salinas (☎755/4-46-62; US$5 per person), is one of the better examples of its kind, with four-bed single-sex rooms.

Playa la Madera, while part of Zihuatanejo, has a different feel, slightly removed and a touch exclusive – though not necessarily more expensive. **Playa la Ropa**, more than a kilometre from the centre, feels a world apart; at its southern edge, *Los Cabañas Trailer Park* (☎755/4-47-18) is a small, clean campsite and trailer park that is more like someone's back garden. You can also camp officially at the north end of Playa Linda, north of Ixtapa.

Central Zihuatanejo

Casa Bravo, Nicolás Bravo 11 (☎755/4-25-48). Good little hotel; most rooms with fans, TV and private bath. All-day hot water and towels provided. ⑤.

Casa de Huéspedes Elvira, Alvarez 8 (☎755/4-20-61). Small rooms with basic bathrooms around a verdant courtyard and right by the beach. ③.

Casa de Huéspedes Nancy, Paseo del Cantil 6 (☎755/4-21-23). Clean and tidy guesthouse with hammocks on the roof and a peaceful location, but still only ten minutes' walk from the waterfront over the lagoon footbridge. Buses marked "Noria" pass the door. ③.

Posada Michel, Ejido 14 (☎755/4-74-23). Bright hotel right in the centre. Particularly good value off-season. ⑤.

Raúl Tres Marias (Town), Alvarez 52 (☎755/4-67-06). The classier of the two branches of this hotel, though without a lot of character. Shiny and spotless, with some sea views, a/c and bathrooms with hot water all day. ⑤.

Raúl Tres Marias (Lagoon), Noria 4 (☎755/4-21-91). Just across the wonderfully rickety lagoon footbridge from its sister hotel and close to the centre. This is the budget option, with clean basic rooms opening onto flower-filled terraces. ③.

Susy, Alvarez 3 (☎743/4-23-39). Well-run hotel with pleasant, modern rooms with small balconies, fans and shower. Some more expensive ones with TV and a/c. ⑤.

Ulises, Armada de México (☎755/4-37-51). Very good-value, budget option. Clean, spacious rooms with bath and fans. Close to the sea. ③.

Playa la Madera and Playa la Ropa

Brisas del Mar, Playa la Madera (☎755/4-21-42). Spacious rooms and a pool. Charges US$65 for apartments that sleep up to six. ⑥.

Bungalows Allec, Playa la Madera (☎755/4-20-02). Well-appointed apartments with rooms for two (④) and apartments for four (⑤).

Bungalows Sotelo, López Mateos, Playa la Madera (☎755/4-63-07). In a league all its own, with deluxe apartments with a/c, jacuzzi, satellite TV and great sea views. Prices start at US$100 for four people sharing. ⑨.

Mi Casita, Escencica, on the headland between Playa la Madera and Playa la Ropa (☎743/4-45-10). Front rooms have a great view of the bay from the hammocks swinging on the balcony outside. The rooms are all well furnished and excellent value, but a long way from the beach. ⑦.

Palacios, Adelita, Playa la Madera (☎743/4-20-55). Good, spacious and clean rooms, with tiled bathrooms and sea views from the balconies. Small pool, too. Rooms with a/c cost twenty percent more. ⑤.

Villa del Sol, Playa la Ropa (☎755/4-22-39). Claims to be the best small beach-hotel in Mexico. Lush gardens of hibiscus and bougainvillea hide spacious luxury suites all with terraces and some with small private pools. Of course there's a big pool, too, a private patch of beach and flunkies everywhere. Expensive even off-season, but great if you can stretch to it: Rooms are US$210, and there's a US$100 minimum to be spent on food per day. ⑨.

Villas Miramar, Adelita, Playa la Madera (☎755/4-21-06). Beautiful hotel with rooms on both sides of the road. Those with sea views and access to a small pool cost more than others set in luxuriant gardens around a large pool. Also a penthouse suite with kitchen for four people (US$110). ⑦.

The Town and beaches

Zihuatanejo has a few things to distract you from lying on the beach. Quite apart from jetskiing, parascending and getting dragged around on a huge inflatable banana, you could arrange to go **fishing** for dorado, yellowtail, bonito or big game. Trips, run by Lanchas de Pesca (☎755/4-37-58), leave from the pier in Zihuatanejo. Prices vary according to the size of your group: seven hours' fishing costs US$120 for four people, US$250 for six. **Scuba diving** courses are organized by Zihuatanejo Scuba Centre, Cuauhtémoc 3 (☎755/4-21-47). A full-day resort course with one dive costs US$70, and reef dives for certified divers will set you back US$45 for one, US$70 for two. Full certification takes six days and costs US$450.

Just behind the beach you'll find the **Museo Arqueologico de la Costa Grande** (Tues–Sun 9am–7pm; US$0.50), a small and simple affair, and not deserving more than twenty minutes, though it does its best to tackle the history of what has always been a fairly insignificant region.

The beaches

Four beaches surround Bahía de Zihuatanejo. **Playa Principal**, in front of Zihuatanejo, is unspectacular, but interesting to watch when the fishermen haul in their catch early in the morning and sell much of it there and then. A narrow footpath heads east from the end of the beach across the normally dry outlet of a drainage canal, then winds around a rocky point to the calm waters of **Playa la Madera**, a broad golden strand with a couple of restaurants, and hotels and condos rising up the hill behind. Climb the steps between the condos to get to the road if you want to continue a kilometre or so over the headland, past the mirador with great views across the bay, to **Playa la Ropa**, which takes its name – "Clothes Beach" – from the silks washed up here when one of the *Nao de China* (see p.376) was wrecked here. This is Zihuatanejo's finest road-accessible beach, palm fringed for more than a mile, with a variety of beachfront restaurants and hotels. You can walk a further fifteen minutes beyond the end of Playa la Ropa to **Playa las Gatas**, the last of the bay's golden beaches, its crystalline blue water surrounded by a reef, giving it the enclosed feel of an ocean swimming pool. This makes it safe for kids, though the sea bottom is mostly rocky and tough on tender feet. Nonetheless, the clear waters are great for **snorkelling** – you can rent gear from vendors among the rather pricey palapa restaurants. Las Gatas is directly opposite the town and accessible by launches (daily 8am–4pm, last return 5pm; 15min; US$2.50 return), run by Lanchas de Pesca (see above). Buy tickets at the entrance to the pier.

The long sweep of **Ixtapa's** hotel-backed **Playa de Palmar** is fine for volleyball or just relaxing, but often too rough for easy swimming, and plagued by the inevitable jet-skis. Powered watersports are also in evidence at the inappropriately named **Playa Quieta**, some 5km north of Ixtapa. The water here is wonderfully clear and the surrounding vegetation magnificent, but you won't get anything to eat or drink unless you pay handsomely to enter the confines of Ixtapa's *Club Med*. Boats leave Playa Quieta for **Isla Ixtapa** (9am–5pm; US$2.50 return), a small island a couple of kilometres offshore with two swimming beaches, a spot reserved for diving, watersports gear rental, and a few restaurants – but nowhere to stay. You can also get there on a daily launch from Zihuatanejo, which leaves at 11.30am (1hr; US$6.25). The boat returns at 4.30pm.

The names of Playa Quieta and the next beach on, **Playa Linda**, should be swapped; the latter is by far the more relaxed, with generally safe swimming, though under the right conditions it receives good surf.

Eating, drinking and nightlife

You can barely move for **restaurants** in Zihuatanejo: the waterfront Paseo del Pescador is the place for fresh fish, expensive drinks and atmosphere; the cheapest place, as ever, is the **market** on Juárez. There isn't much **nightlife** in town, however: for that people head over the hill to Ixtapa and the clubs in the big hotels. A typical Ixtapa night out starts at *Carlos 'n' Charlie's* and progresses to the trendy and expensive *Christine's* at the *Hotel Krystal*. Buses to Ixtapa run until about 10pm; after that you'll need to get a taxi.

Las Brasas, at Cuauhtémoc and Bravo. Simple but very cheap breakfasts and comidas corridas served in this cavernous restaurant that runs through to Galeana.

Café Marina, Paseo del Pescador. Cosy little place on the waterfront serving pizza, tortas and home-made yoghurt through the high season, and great spaghetti dishes on Wednesday nights. English-language book swap, too.

Cafetería Nueva Zelanda, at Cuauhtémoc and Ejido. You pay slightly over the odds for the good licuados, tortas, breakfasts and cappuccinos in this often busy café.

Cenaduria Artelia, down a small alley off Nicolás Bravo. A great little spot to sit outdoors and eat tacos, enchiladas and the like until gone 11pm.

Mariscos El Acacio, Ejido at Galeana. Simple seafood restaurant, much cheaper – though considerably less atmospheric – than those on Paseo del Pescador.

Panadería Francesa, at Galeana and Gonzales. The name might be wishful thinking, but they do produce good sesame-topped wholemeal bread, croissants and pastries.

La Sirena Gorda, Paseo del Pescador. Fairly expensive but well-sited, right where evening strollers can watch you dine on succulent tuna steaks and seafood cocktails in the balmy night air.

Splash Bar, Guerrero at Ejido. Coloured bulbs illuminate this dim bar, where people lurk in corners playing chess or backgammon to the accompaniment of constant surf and ski videos. Open 5pm–1am, with two-for-one drinks 7–8pm.

On to Acapulco

From Zihuatanejo to Acapulco – along Hwy-200, a fast road with regular buses – the aspect of the coast changes again: becoming flatter, more heavily populated and regularly cultivated. At **PAPANOA**, 50km on, there's a beautiful beach, some 15km long, overlooked from the point at its far end by the *Hotel Club Papanoa* (☎742/7-04-50; ⑥). Obviously someone's plan for a luxurious, *Club Med*-style development, it never quite panned out – there's still considerable comfort, a pool, and a stairway down to the beach through manicured gardens, but the place has a distinctly run-down air. It's not exactly cheap, but nor is it in the high luxury bracket, and a double room is easily large enough for four. You could, too, camp out quite easily on this stretch of sand, getting supplies from the nearby village of **El Morro De Papanoa**. The hotel restaurant is also good value, and the staff friendly.

Beyond Punta Papanoa the road again leaves the coast for a while – although with sturdy transport of your own, there are several places where you could find your way down to a surf-pounded beach – not to rejoin it until shortly before Acapulco itself. Of little interest otherwise, **Coyuca de benitez**, the last village of any size, has some pleasant restaurants overlooking the Río Coyuca, and you can arrange boat-trips down-river into the Laguna de Coyucán. Nearby you could certainly find somewhere to camp or sling a hammock at **Playas de San Jeronimo**, but again it's an exposed, windswept and wavy stretch of sand. You could also get a minibus from Coyuca to the beach at **El Carrizol**, where it's possible to rent a reasonably priced bungalow.

Acapulco

Everyone – even if they've not the remotest idea where it is – has heard of **ACAPULCO**, but few people know what to expect. Truth is that, as long as you don't yearn to get away from it all, you'll find almost anything you want here, from magnificent beaches by day to clubs and discos by night. That said, however, the manicured and sanitized hotel zone, where everything is geared towards North American package tourists, can be thoroughly off-putting, as can some of the restaurants and clubs, which exhibit a snobbery seldom seen elsewhere in Mexico. In the old town, the grime, congestion and exhaust fumes are the most apparent aspects of the city's **pollution problem**, which peaks in the rainy season when everything from plastic bags to dead dogs gets washed off the streets and back alleys into the bay.

What Acapulco undoubtedly has going for it, however, is its stunning **bay**: a sweeping scythe-stroke of yellow sand backed by the white towers of the high-rise hotels and, behind them, the jungly green foothills of the Sierra. And, even though there are hundreds of thousands of people here throughout the year – the town itself has a population approaching one and a half million and even out of season (busiest months are Dec–Feb) most of the big hotels remain nearly full – it rarely seems oppressively crowded. Certainly there's always space to lie somewhere along the beach, partly because of its sheer size, partly because of the number of rival attractions from hotel pools to para-sailing and "romantic" cruises. **Hawkers**, too, are everywhere – there's no need to go shopping in Acapulco, simply lie on the beach and a string of goods will be paraded in front of you. Most of the hawkers are easy enough to handle, but they can become irritating and at times heavy. For women, and women alone in particular, the constant pestering of would-be gigolos can become maddening, and for anyone the derelict downtown backstreets can be dangerous at night – remember that this is still a working **port** of considerable size and in the midst of all the tourist glitz real poverty remains: don't leave things lying about on the beach or temptingly displayed in hotel rooms.

Though there's little to show for it now beyond the star-shaped Fuerte de San Diego and a few rusty freighters tied up along the quayside, Acapulco was from the sixteenth century one of Mexico's most important ports, the destination of the famous *Nao de China*, which brought silks and spices from Manila and returned laden with payment

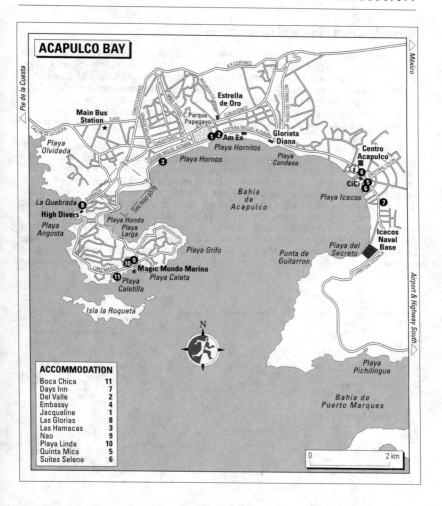

ACAPULCO BAY

ACCOMMODATION

Boca Chica	11
Days Inn	7
Del Valle	2
Embassy	4
Jacqueline	1
Las Glorias	8
Las Hamacas	3
Nao	9
Playa Linda	10
Quinta Mica	5
Suites Selene	6

0   2 km

in Mexican silver. Most of the goods were lugged overland to Veracruz and from there shipped onwards to Spain. Mexican independence, Spain's decline and the direct route around southern Africa combined to kill the trade off, but for nearly three hundred years the shipping route between Acapulco and the Far East was among the most prized and preyed upon in the world, attracting at some time or other (if you believe all the stories) every pirate worth the name. In one such raid, in 1743, Lord Anson (the "Father of the British Navy") picked up silver worth as much as £400,000 sterling from a single galleon and altogether, with the captured ship and the rest of its cargo and crew, collected booty worth over a million even then. With the death of its major trade, however, Acapulco went into a long, slow decline, only reversed with the completion of a road to the capital in 1928. Even so, but for tourism it would today be no more than a minor port.

Arrival, orientation and information

Most **buses** arrive at the Central de Autobuses on Ejido, 3km northwest of the zócalo, from where you can pick up buses marked "Centro" or "Caleta" to get to the area where the cheaper hotels are located. Estrella de Oro buses from México and Zihuatanejo arrive at their own terminal, 3km west of the zócalo, again connected by "Caleta" city buses. Both stations have a guardería. The **airport**, 30km east of the city, is linked only by expensive taxis and the Transportaciones Aeropuerto shuttle service. If you intend to leave by plane (see p.385), you save money by buying a return ticket for the shuttle on your arrival.

Acapulco divides fairly simply into two halves: the **old town**, which sits at the western end of the bay, with the rocky promontory of **La Quebrada** rising above it and curving round to protect the most sheltered anchorage; and the new **resort area**, a clump of hotels and tourist services following the curve of the bay east. A single seafront drive, the **Costera Miguel Aleman** – usually just "Costera" – stretches from the heart of the old town right around the bay, linking almost everything of interest. You can reach everywhere near the zócalo on foot, but to get further afield, frequent **buses** (look for "Cine Río/La Base", "Zócalo" or "Caleta directo") run all the way along Costera. From the east these travel past all the big hotels, then turn inland onto Cuauhtémoc, where they pass the Estrella de Oro **bus station** and the **market** before rejoining the Costera just before the zócalo. "Caleta" buses continue round the coast to Playa Caleta.

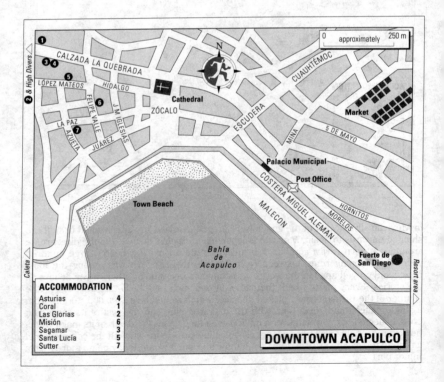

ACCOMMODATION

Asturias	4
Coral	1
Las Glorias	2
Misión	6
Sagamar	3
Santa Lucía	5
Sutter	7

DOWNTOWN ACAPULCO

ADDRESSES ALONG COSTERA

Finding places along Costera can be tricky, as the numbering system is completely mean-ingless: 50 could be followed by 2010, which is next door to 403. The best **landmarks**, apart from the big hotels, are (moving east from the zócalo) **Parque Papagayo**, the roundabout with the **Diana Glorieta statue** and the CiCi **waterpark**. An additional dif-ficulty is the construction of a new ring road, which is disrupting some bus routes. The descriptions given here are as accurate as possible, but check routes locally when trav-elling by bus.

Most of the things you need cluster around the zócalo. The **post office** (Mon–Sat 8am–8pm for most services, Sun 8am–1pm for stamps) is on Costera, two blocks east of the zócalo, before the Banamex **bank** (exchange Mon–Fri 9am–2pm), which has the best rates and hours. Nearby on Costera there's a **casa de cambio**, but rates are poor. If you miss the bank, it's far better to head to the hotel zone along Costera, where sev-eral places offer good rates for US and Canadian dollars and much worse ones for European currencies: try Money Express (Mon–Fri 8am–10pm), opposite the *Fiesta Americana* hotel. Long-distance and collect **phone calls** can be made from Telplus (daily 7am–10pm), just east of the post office. Acapulco's **tourist office** (daily 9am–7pm; ☎74/84-44-16) is at Centro Acapulco, a block west of CiCi. Unless you strike lucky and encounter an enthusiastic staff member, you're likely to come away with lit-tle but an armful of brochures and Acapulco's **free magazines** – *Info Acapulco*, *Adventure in Acapulco*, and the glossy *Acapulco Magazine* – all full of thinly disguised advertising. For more edifying reading, try the **book swaps** at some of the budget hotels, browse through the selection at the bigger hotels and at Sanborn's, just west of the zócalo, or check the second-hand books in the postcard shop on Azueta near the junction with La Quebrada.

Accommodation

As with everything in Acapulco, hotel rooms are far less expensive in the **old town**. Head for the streets immediately to the west and slightly inland of the **zócalo**, in the calles La Paz and Teniente José Azueta, and particularly on Calzada La Quebrada where it leads up the hill. In contrast to most of Mexico, the hotels in this area tend to charge by the person rather than by the room.

You won't find places as cheap out along **Costera** but, if you want to stay out by the tourist beaches and the clubs, there are a few reasonably priced options, especially off-season, when even some of the fancier hotels along Costera become quite competitive-ly priced. For **longer stays**, perhaps a better choice is to make for the smaller beach-es of **Caleta** and **Caletilla**, a ten-minute bus ride from the centre. Hotels here are rather older, mostly patronized by Mexican families, and often booked up in advance. The best plan is to start off in the centre and from there work out where you'd ideally like to be based.

Still further out there's **Pie de la Cuesta** (see p.383), a quiet alternative 15km north of Acapulco. This is the only place with official year-round **camping**, at *Acapulco Trailer Park* (☎748/60-00-10).

Acapulco's **high season** lasts longer than most, from late November or early December through to the end of April.

In the centre

Asturias, La Quebrada 45 (☎74/83-65-48). Reasonable budget option, with a small pool. ④.

Coral, La Quebrada 56 (☎74/82-07-56). Perhaps the best of the many budget places along this road. Clean rooms with wide streetside balconies, a pool and cheap breakfasts downstairs. ④.

Las Glorias, La Quebrada (☎74/83-11-55). Though you pay for the location (US$175) – right above the rocks where the divers plummet – this is still a fine hotel with cottage-like rooms with kitchenettes ranged along the clifftop. Three pools. ⑨.

Misión, Felipe Valle 12 (☎74/82-36-43). The best hotel in the centre. An old colonial-style house, formerly the American consulate and later a Wells Fargo office, with attractive rooms spread out around a mango-shaded patio. Continental or Mexican breakfasts, and book swap. ⑥.

Sagamar, La Quebrada 51 (☎74/83-50-53). From the same mould as *Coral* and *Asturias*, but with the addition of a suite (⑤ for four sharing) with a stove and fridge but no utensils. ④.

Santa Lúcia, Av Adolfo López Mateos 33 (☎74/82-04-41). Fan-ventilated rooms with TV, private bathrooms and towels provided. Good value. ④.

Sutter, José Azueta 10 (☎74/82-02-09). Plain but clean and spacious rooms with fans and bathrooms. Rear rooms are quieter. ③.

Along Costera

Due to the confusing nature of Costera's numbering system (see p.379), the following hotels are listed in order of their **distance along Costero** from the zócalo.

Hamacas, Costera 239, 1km east of the zócalo (☎74/83-77-46). The closest international-standard hotel to the zócalo. Swimming pool, tennis court and comfortable rooms with cable TV. ⑧.

Jacqueline, Gonzalo Gomez Espinoza 6, opposite the eastern entrance to Parque Papagayo on Costero (☎74/85-93-38). Basic but good, clean rooms with a/c and shower with 24hr hot water. ⑤.

Del Valle, Gonzalo Gomez Espinoza 150, next door to *Jacqueline* (☎74/85-83-36). Better value than *Jacqueline*, with more spacious, modern rooms (some with a/c) and a pool. ④.

Embassy, Costera 50, opposite CiCi (☎74/81-08-81). Best value in this part of town, with a small pool and mostly a/c rooms. Some have seen better days, so look at a couple before deciding. ⑤.

Quinta Mica, Cristóbal Colón 115 (☎74/84-01-21). Slightly run-down but good-value hotel with a pool. A/c rooms with equipped kitchenettes. Six-person "bungalow" available: ⑤ off-season, ⑧ peak. ⑥.

Suites Selene, Cristóbal Colón 175 (☎74/84-29-77). Similar though slightly less well kept than *Quinta Mica*. Suites for four people: ⑥ off-season, ⑦ peak. ⑤.

Days Inn, Costera 2310, past CiCi (☎74/84-53-32). A sky-scraping "Inn" with large pool. The a/c rooms with TV and – at least from the upper floors – great views along the bay are surprisingly good value. Rates are identical for one to four people. ⑧.

Caleta and Caletilla

Boca Chica, on the point at the western end of Caletilla (☎74/83-66-01). Beautifully sited hotel with a pool and some great views, especially from the Junior Suites (off-season US$93; peak US$124). The smaller rooms are considerably less good (US$120). ⑨.

Nao, east end of Caleta (☎74/83-87-10). Faded but acceptable hotel with a pool, usually full of Mexican families. Fan-cooled rooms with shower, some much better than others. ④.

Playa Linda, Costera 1, as you reach Caleta (☎74/82-08-14). Recently renovated hotel with nicely decorated rooms, some with balconies. A few rooms (sleeping up to four) have kitchenettes. ⑥.

Pie de la Cuesta

The following hotels are listed in order of **distance from Hwy-200**. All are right by the beach and reduce their prices dramatically out of season.

Villa Nirvana (☎74/60-16-31). Delightful place with spacious rooms around an attractive garden and great pool. ⑤.

Bungalows María Cristina (☎74/60-02-62). Suites for up to five people with fully equipped kitchens and balconies (⑥) are the main attraction here, though the rooms are fine, too. ⑤.

Ukae Kim (☎74/60-21-87). Huge luxurious rooms with separate sitting area, some with balconies and sea views. Beachside pool. ⑦.

Casa de Huéspedes Playa Leonor (☎74/60-03-48). The budget option: simple but clean rooms, breezier on the upper floor. ④.

The Town

No one comes to Acapulco for the sights. By day, if people aren't at the beach or asleep, they're mostly scouring the expensive shops. If you only do one thing in Acapulco, though, make sure you see its most celebrated spectacle, the leap of the daredevil **high divers**.

About the only place in Acapulco that gives even the slightest sense of the historic role the city played in Mexico's past is the **Museo de Acapulco** (Tues–Sun 9.30am–6.30pm; US$1.75, free on Sun), inside the **Fuerte de San Diego**, an impressive, if heavily restored, star-shaped fort built in 1616 to protect the Manila galleons from foreign corsairs. The building's limited success is charted inside the museum, where displays also extend to the spread of Christianity by the proselytizing religious orders and a small anthropological collection. Air-conditioned rooms make this a good place to ride out the midday heat, and you can pop up on the roof for superb views over Acapulco. The **Centro Cultural** (Mon–Sat 10am–8pm; free) has a library, an art gallery and crafts store and also hosts a regular programme of cultural events with a regional bias. Check out the timetable. Surrounded by beautiful gardens (daily 9am–6pm), the ultra-modern **Centro Acapulco convention centre** is packed with upmarket shops, pricey restaurants and a futuristic disco.

Geared up for bored kids, the **Parque Papagayo** offers boating, roller skating, gondola rides and the like, all easily accessible from Playa Hornos, as Costero dives through a tunnel at this point. Further east round the bay near the Centro Acapulco, the **Centro Infantil CiCi** (daily 10am–6pm; US$7.50, children US$5.50) offers dolphin shows (noon, 2.30pm & 5pm) and water-based rides.

Acapulco's divers

Acapulco's famed **clavadistas** plunge some 35m from the cliffs of La Quebrada into a tight, rocky channel, timing their leap to coincide with an incoming wave. Mistimed, there's not enough water to stop them hitting the bottom, though the chief danger these experts seem to face is getting back out of the water without being dashed against the rocks. It could easily be corny, but it's undeniably impressive, especially when floodlit at night. The posted rota of dives is unreliable, but the times – 12.45pm, 7.30pm, 8.30pm, 9.30pm and 10.30pm – are rigidly adhered to. A typical display involves three exponents, one or two taking the lower (25m) platform, the remainder diving from the upper level after first asking for the Virgin's intervention at the cliff-top shrine.

TOURS IN ACAPULCO

Anything from a two-hour trip around the town to a day-trip to México can be made by **guided tour** from one of Acapulco's hundreds of travel agents or any large hotel. Unless you're very short of time, however – or desperately bored – it's not worth dishing out the sums charged for the privilege.

Boat-trips are more appealing. You can rent your own cruiser – inevitably very expensive – along the malecón to go sea-fishing or diving (haggle fiercely), or try one of the assorted bay cruises or outings in glass-bottomed boats. You'll see details and prices posted up all over town; you can book in any big hotel or simply go down to the quayside – either opposite the zócalo or a few hundred metres west – at departure time. Night-time excursions are particularly appealing, illuminated by the lights of the town shining out from all around the bay. After dark, too, most of the boats lay on some kind of entertainment as they cruise: the huge *Yate Hawaiano*, for example, boasts three bars and dance floors. Prices vary with the length of the trip and what is offered, but US$10–20 for a couple of hours with a free bar is typical at night, US$8–12 with no free bar during the day.

The final diver in the last show carries a pair of flaming torches. From the road you can see the spectacle for nothing, but you'll get a much better view if you go down the steps to a **viewing platform** (US$1.25) more or less opposite the divers. Get here early for a good position. Alternatively, you can sit in the bar at the *Playa Las Glorias* hotel (US$12 cover includes two drinks) or watch from their expensive *La Perla* restaurant (US$24 buffet including two drinks). To get there, simply climb the Calzada la Quebrada from the town centre, about fifteen minutes' walk from the zócalo.

The beaches

To get to the best of the sands **around Acapulco Bay** from the centre of town, you're going to have to get on the bus: there is a tiny beach right in front of the town but it's not in the least inviting, with grey sand made greyer by pollutants from the boats moored all around it.

Caleta, Caletilla and La Roqueta
Playas Caleta and **Caletilla** (any "Caleta" bus from Costera) have a quite different atmosphere from those in the main part of the bay. Very small – the two are divided only by a rocky outcrop and breakwater – they tend to be crowded with Mexicans (the foreign tourists who once flocked here have since decamped east), but the water is almost always calm and, by Acapulco's standards, the beach is clean. Most enticingly, you can sit at shaded tables on the sand, surrounded by Mexican matrons whose kids are paddling in the shallows, and be brought drinks from the cafés behind; not particularly cheap, but considerably less than the same service would cost at the other end of the bay. There are showers here too and, on the rock, the **Magic Mundo Marina** (daily 9am–6pm; US$3.75, kids US$2), a watersports complex similar to CiCi, with a predictable aquarium and sea-lion show, decent waterslides and a choice of the pool or the bay to swim in.

From outside the complex, small boats ply the channel to the islet of **La Roqueta**, where there are more and yet cleaner beaches, a small zoo (Mon & Wed–Sun 10am–5pm; US$1) and beer-drinking burros, one of the town's less compelling attractions. Catch one of the glass-bottomed boats (frequent, daily 8am–5.30pm) and keep your ticket for the return journey: US$2.50 for the direct launch or US$3.75 for those that detour past the submerged one-tonne nickel and bronze statue of the Virgin of Guadalupe. Whether you are off to La Roqueta or only going to Caleta, leave early (especially at weekends) for the best of the sun and at least a sporting chance of getting a beach chair or a patch of sand. Behind the beach a group of moderately priced restaurants and cheaper loncherías offer good breakfasts and fish lunches.

Along Costera and on to Revolcadero
The main beaches, despite their various names – Hamacas, Hornos, Hornitos, Morro, Condesa and Icacos – are in effect a single sweep of sand. It's best to go some considerable distance round to **Playa Condesa** or **Playa Icacos**, in front of hotels like the *Hyatt Continental* and the *Holiday Inn*, or opposite the Centro Acapulco, where the beach is far less crowded and considerably cleaner. Here, too, it's easy enough to slip in to use the hotel showers, swimming pools and bars – there's no way they're going to spot an imposter in these thousand-bed monsters. The *Hyatt*, at the very far end, is the swankiest of the bunch. The beaches around here are also the place to come if you want to indulge in such frolics as being towed around the bay on the end of a parachute, water skiing, or sailing. Outfits offering all of these are dotted at regular intervals along the beach; charges are standard though the quality of the equipment and the length of the trips can vary.

Beyond this end of the bay to the south are two more popular beaches: **Puerto Marqués** and **Revolcadero**. On the way you'll pass some of the fanciest hotels in Acapulco. *Las Brisas*, overlooking the eastern end of the bay, is probably the most exclusive of all, its individual villas offering private swimming pools and pink jeeps to every occupant. Puerto Marqués (buses marked "Puerto Marqués") is the first of the playas, a sheltered, deeply indented cove with restaurants and beach chairs right down to the water's edge. It's overlooked by two more deluxe hotels – very calm, very upmarket, though the beach itself isn't. You can continue by road to Revolcadero (though only an occasional bus comes this far) or get there by boat down a narrow inland channel. The beach, a long exposed stretch of sand, is beautiful but frequently lashed by a surf that makes swimming impossible.

Pie de la Cuesta

Pie de la Cuesta, around 15km north of Acapulco, is even more open to the vicissitudes of the ocean. Definitely not for swimming – even if it weren't for the massive backbreaking waves that dump on the beach, there are said to be sharks offshore – but as good a place as you can imagine to come and watch the sun sink into the Pacific or to ride horseback along the shore. The sand extends for miles up the coast, but at the end nearer Acapulco, where the bus drops you, there are several rickety bars and some tranquil **places to stay**, away from the hubbub of the city (see p.380).

Behind, and only separated from the ocean by a hundred-metre-wide sandbar on which Pie de la Cuesta is built, lies the **Laguna de Coyuca**, a vast freshwater lake said to be three times the size of Acapulco Bay, which only connects with the sea after heavy rains. Fringed with palms, and rich in bird and animal life, the lagoon is big enough to accommodate both the ubiquitous noisy jetskiers and the more sedate three-hour **boat-trips** (11.30am, noon & 1.30pm; US$3.75) that visit the three lagoon islands – stopping on one for lunch (not included in price) and swimming. The bus ("Pie de la Cuesta") runs east every ten minutes or so past the zócalo along Costera. The last bus back leaves around 8pm.

Eating and drinking

Though it may not seem possible, there are even more **restaurants** than hotels in Acapulco. To eat cheaply, though, you're confined to the area around the **zócalo**. Places actually on the square tend to be quite expensive but are great for lingering over breakfast at an outdoor table.

Eating by the **beach** – where there's some kind of restaurant at every turn – is of course very much more expensive, and increasingly so as you head east, but, if you have the cash to spare, many of these places, along with the fancy tourist traps between the hotels, are very good. Throughout the tourist zone, especially along Costera, *100% Natural*, a chain of 24-hour "healthy" eating places, serve good salads, fruit shakes, burgers and the like at grossly inflated prices. Alternatively, you can choose from *McDonald's*, *KFC*, the *Hard Rock Café* and the raucous Mexican fun bars *Iguanas Ranas*, *Carlos 'n' Charlie's* and *Señor Frog*.

One thing to look out for wherever you are on Thursday is **pozole**, a hearty pork and vegetable stew, served up almost everywhere. No one seems to be able to explain why, but *Jueves Pozolero* is now an institution.

In the centre

El Amigo Miguel, Juárez 31. Two locations at the junction of Juárez and Azueta, both serving good seafood at reasonable prices in clean, if harsh, surroundings.

Restaurant Astoria, inland end of the zócalo. Quiet café, cheaper and classier than *Las Flores*, tucked just off the plaza. Good coffee and light meals.

Fat Farm, Juárez 10, a block west of the zócalo. Inexpensive tourist-oriented restaurant with a central patio that's good for idling over breakfast, though the food often fails to match expectations. Book swap.

Las Flores de Acapulco, on the zócalo. Good for Mexican dishes, cocktails or just a coffee. Not the cheapest on the square but a pleasant spot to linger, and a popular meeting place for travellers.

Marisol, one block from the zócalo on La Paz. Offers a terrific variety of tasty Mexican dishes at bargain prices.

Restaurant del Puerto, on Juárez a block from the zócalo. Another great budget restaurant in the centre. Good-value comidas corridas all day for US$3.

La Torta, La Paz, opposite the *Marisol*. Very much like its neighbour, offering a great choice of inexpensive Mexican dishes.

Along Costera

Tropicana Copacabana, just west of Parque Papagayo on Costero. One of a series of similar restaurant-bars that tend to play cumbia, merengue and salsa as much as American rock. Try also *Horizonte* and *Amigo Miguel*.

Los Tres Amigos Mexicana, just east of the Diana Glorieta. Just one of many al fresco places in this area, which start out as restaurants in the early evening then turn into raucous bars around happy hour. Try also *Taboo* and *Disco Beach*.

Dino's, on Costera east of Diana Glorieta (☎74/84-00-37). Fancy, expensive and very good Italian restaurant with pretty much the full range of Italian dishes (minus pizza) and a smattering of international meals.

Doña Blanca, opposite Plaza Bahía. Help-yourself, buffet-style place offering basic but filling food.

Cocula, opposite the Centro Cultural. Moderate to expensive restaurant right on Costera, dishing up huge tasty breakfasts and specializing in grilled chicken.

Nightlife

If you were so inclined, and perhaps more importantly, if you were extremely rich, you could spend several weeks in Acapulco doing nothing more than trawling its scores of nightclubs and bars, discos and dinner-dances. There are people who claim never to have seen the town during daylight hours. Anywhere with music or dancing will demand a hefty cover charge before they even consider letting you spend money at the bar.

However, prices can drop if you haggle, especially on weeknights and in the off-season when business is slow. This is particularly effective for larger groups. Look out, too, for **"Ladies Free" nights**, which, when offered at a place that normally has a "free bar", means women get in for about half price.

Virtually all the clubs and discos are out along **Costera** in the hotel district, beyond CiCi – they move in and out of fashion with such bewildering rapidity that recommendations are virtually impossible. Some, like *Baby-O*, try to maintain a spurious exclusivity by turning people away at the door, but most can afford to do this only at the height of the season. Look for queues outside to see what's flavour of the month. Among the more consistently popular discos are *Baby-O*, *Andromeda's* and *Atrium* in the same area, *Bey's Rock* and *News* a little further west and, way up on the hill beyond the naval base, the huge, glitzy and extremely expensive *Extravaganza*, *Fantasy* and *Palladium*. *Relax*, opposite the *El Presidente* hotel, is one of the better **gay hangouts**. If you're not easily intimidated you could also try some of the **downtown bars and cantinas**: you'll find a couple that aren't too heavy around the bottom of Azueta – *La Sirena*, for example – but these aren't recommended for women on their own. More traditional entertainment can be found at the *Hyatt Continental*, just in front of Playa Icacos, which features nightly performances by a troupe of the **Ballet Folklórico**. Although the admission is a bit steep, and the waiters persistent, the large-scale show – around sixty singers/dancers/musicians plus full regalia – is undeniably impressive.

If you prefer a quieter time, walk up behind the cathedral on the zócalo to where a few regulars play **chess** in the evening. You're welcome to have a game (US$1) and can order soft drinks.

Listings

Airlines Aeroméxico (☎74/85-16-00; at the airport ☎66-91-09); American (airport ☎66-92-27); Delta (☎74/66-93-31); Mexicana (☎74/84-25-64; airport ☎66-91-38); Taesa (☎74/86-56-00; airport ☎66-93-93). **Airport information** (☎74/66-94-29 or 66-94-34).

American Express La Gran Plaza, at Costera 1628 between Parque Papagayo and Diana Glorieta (Mon–Sat 10am–7pm; ☎74/69-11-00). Will hold mail, but has awful exchange rates.

Car rental A car is more of a liability than a help in Acapulco, though for heading along the coast or shooting up to Taxco it may be worthwhile. Try Avis (☎74/62-00-75); Budget (☎74/81-05-92); Dollar (☎74/84-30-66); or Hertz (☎74/85-89-47).

Consulates Canada, Centro Commercial Marbella, Glorieta Diana (☎74/85-66-00); France, Costa Grande 235 (☎74/82-33-94); Germany, Antón de Alaminos 46 (☎74/84-74-37); UK, *Las Brisas Hotel* (☎74/84-16-50). Also Austria, Spain, Finland, Netherlands, Norway and Sweden: consult the telephone directory or the tourist office.

Laundry Ghost Cleaners, José María Iglesias 9, near the zócalo (Mon–Fri 8am–2pm & 4–8pm, Sat 8.30am–2pm).

Emergencies Cruz Roja (☎74/85-41-00 or 85-41-01); Emergency IMSS Hospital (☎74/86-36-08 or 87-00-75); Sociedad de Assistencia Medico Turistica (☎74/85-59-59 or 85-58-00) in *Condominium Capri*, on Costera near Acapulco Plaza, and in the *Camino Real* hotel; tourist police (☎74/80-02-10).

Pharmacy Plenty of 24hr places in the hotel zone along Costero; Super Flash, Costera and 5 de Mayo, just east of the fort.

Travel agents About the nearest to the zócalo is Las Hamacas (☎74/84-68-87), about 1km east. A number of other agents are interspersed between the hotels along Costera.

MOVING ON FROM ACAPULCO

Two stations handle Acapulco's intercity **buses**. The first-class **Estrella de Oro** terminal at the corner of Cuauhtémoc and Wilfrido Masseiu (city buses marked "Cine Río" from opposite the zócalo) handles hourly buses to México (4hr 30min) and three services daily to Lázaro Cárdenas (6hr). The much larger **Central de Autobuses** (aka Estrella Blanca; ☎74/69-20-28; city buses marked "Ejido") handles the unified services of several companies; don't be surprised if you find yourself on a bus that doesn't match the company named on your ticket. The "Informes" booth in the middle of the line of ticket-sellers will point you in the right direction for your particular queue.

Buses to México leave continually day and night in five classes: Turistar Plus and Primera are the ones to go for, as the spacious seating and free drinks of the expensive executive-style buses fail to justify the extra expense. Second-class, avoiding the autopista, is very slow. You can also get to **Chilpancingo** and **Taxco**, while first- and second-class buses run to **Zihuatanejo**, half of them continuing on to **Lázaro Cárdenas**. Buses also leave hourly for **Puerto Escondido** until 6pm, after which there are three overnight services, which fill early.

To get to Acapulco's **airport** you can take an expensive taxi or contact the **Transportaciones Aéropuerto shuttle** service, Costera 284 (☎74/85-93-60), though this works out more cheaply if you have bought a return ticket upon arrival at the airport. Cheaper still is to take a town bus to Puerto Marquéz, then another from there to the airport. Frequent flights leave Acapulco for México and numerous other Mexican and US destinations. For up-to-date details, contact any travel agent.

Chilpancingo

Nestled in a bowl in the Sierra Madre Occidental, 130km north of Acapulco, restful **CHILPANCINGO**, Guerrero's modest state capital, makes a cool stop-off – it's higher than 1000m – on the trip inland to the capital. Well off the tourist circuit, it is lent a youthful tenor by the large student population of the state university: activity focuses on the stately zócalo, a pristine traffic-free area.

The modern **Ayuntamiento** and **Palacio de Gobierno** combine a harmonious blend of Neoclassical and colonial influences. The latter is adorned with a huge bronze sculpture, "El Hombre Hacia el Futuro"; there's more monumental metal-work, along with busts of famous Guerrerans, in the Alameda, three blocks east along Juárez.

Directly opposite its replacement, the former Palacio de Gobierno houses frequently changing exhibitions in the **Instituto Guerrerence de Cultura** and the excellent little **Museo Regional de Guerrero** (both Tues–Sun 11am–6pm; free). Well laid-out displays – some labelled in English – record the history of the state's native peoples from their migration from Asia across the Bering land bridge thirty thousand years ago to the Maya and Teotihuacán influences on their pottery and stelae. With the coming of the Spaniards, the region benefited from the Manilla galleons that put into Acapulco and from Chilpancingo's location on the *Camino de China* from the coast to México. But the city's most dramatic chapter – vividly depicted on murals around the internal courtyard – came with the Independence struggle. After Hidalgo's defeat in the central highlands it was left to the southern populist movement, fuelled by the spread of land-grabbing haciendas and led by the skilled tactician **José Maria Morelos**, to continue the campaign. With almost the whole country behind them, they forced the Spanish – who still held México – to attend the Congress of Chilpancingo in 1813, where the Declaration of Independence was issued and the principles of the constitution – chiefly the abolition of slavery and the equality of the races – were worked out. Ultimately the congress failed and within two years the Spanish had retaken Guerrero and executed Morelos.

Practicalities

Buses from México and Acapulco arrive at either the Estrella Blanca terminal, 1km east of the zócalo on 21 de Marzo – turn right then right again along Juárez – or the Estrella de Oro station, Juárez 53, five blocks east of the zócalo. Minibuses run into town along Juárez and back out along the parallel Guerrero. Madero crosses these two streets just before the zócalo, and it is around here you'll find all the essential services.

Easily the best **place to stay** is *Posada Meléndez*, opposite the Estrella de Oro bus station, at Juárez 50 (✆747/2-20-50; ④), its vast corridors immaculately tiled with individually painted inserts and furnished with heavy colonial-style chairs. Rooms with double beds all have balconies, and it's worth paying a little extra for a suite with separate sitting room. There are a couple of less expensive places near the zócalo: the colonial *Hotel Cardeña*, Madero 13 (no phone; ③), with overpriced en-suite rooms and cheaper bathless ones around a courtyard, and *Hotel Chilpancingo*, Alemán 8 (✆747/2-24-46; ②), with primitive but serviceable cells.

You can **eat** light meals or cake with an espresso at *El Portal*, beside the cathedral on Madero, or find more substantial meals at *Marthita*, Guerrero 6B, and *La Parroquía*, off the north side of the zócalo. The café in the *Casino del Estudiantes*, on Guerrero near Madero, is cheap and good, and the best place to ask if there is anything happening in the way of **nightlife**.

South of Acapulco: the Costa Chica

It's hardly surprising that most tourists zoom straight through the stretch of Hwy-200 south of Acapulco: there's little in the way of facilities between here and Puerto Escondido – a good seven hours on the bus. However, if you have your own transport, it's worth taking some time out to explore this occasionally bizarre coastline, not least for the few great **beaches**.

The people who inhabit the area towards the border of Oaxaca are for the most part either indigenous Amuzgo or black – the latter, descendants of African Bantu slaves who escaped and settled here. In fact the look of the land is vaguely reminiscent of Africa – flat grazing country, many of whose villages consist of thatched huts. In **Coajinicuilapa**, the impression is reinforced by the predominance of round constructions, though these are in fact as much a local *indígena* tradition as an African one. From here a road runs some 20km down to the coast at **Punta Maldonada**, which, along with nearby San Nicolas, has some beautiful beaches but virtually no facilities, and only one or two buses a day. It's famed, above all, for glass-clear water and is perfect for skin diving and snorkelling – most people come down in campers to take advantage.

If you want to break your journey in rather more comfort, there are two possibilities. **Ometepec**, an old gold-mining town a few kilometres inland of the main road before it reaches Coajinicuilapa, has several small hotels. Although it's off the highway, there are hourly buses to Acapulco, so it's easy enough to get back to the junction and pick up transport heading south from there. The second option is **Pinotepa Nacional**, across the border in the state of Oaxaca, where again there are a number of basic places to stay. Pinotepa's Sunday market is one of the best in the region, a meeting place for local Amuzgo, Mixtec and Chatino Indians.

FIESTAS

JANUARY

NEW YEAR'S DAY is celebrated everywhere. In **Cruz Grande** (Guerrero), on the coast road about 120km east of Acapulco, the start of a week-long feria.

2nd Tuesday, DÍA DE JESÚS AGONIZANTE is marked in **Colima** (Colima) by a mass pilgrimage to a nearby hacienda.

26 In **Tecomán** (Col), on the coast road, a colourful religious procession.

FEBRUARY

2 DÍA DE LA CANDELARIA (Candlemas) celebrated in **Colima** (Col) and **Tecomán** (Col) with dances, processions and fireworks. Similar events in **Zumpango del Río** (Gro), on the road from Acapulco to México, and particularly good dancing in **Atzacualoya** (Gro), off this road near Chilpancingo.

5 Fiesta Brava – a day of bullfights and horse races – in **Colima** (Col).

CARNIVAL (the week before Lent: variable Feb–March). **Acapulco** (Gro) and **Manzanillo** (Col) are both famous for the exuberance of their celebrations; rooms can be hard to find.

MARCH

6 Local fiesta in **Zumpango del Río** (Gro) lasts through the night and into the following day – traditional dances.

10 Exuberant FIESTA DE SAN PATRICIO in **San Patricio** (Jal) continues for a week.

19 DÍA DE SAN JOSÉ is the excuse for fiestas in **Tierra Colorada** (Gro), between Acapulco and Chilpancingo, and **San Jeronimo** just outside Acapulco.

Continues over

HOLY WEEK is widely observed: the Palm Sunday celebrations in **Petatlán** (Gro), just south of Zihuatanejo, are particularly fervent.

MAY

3 DÍA DE LA SANTA CRUZ. Saint's day festival in **Cruz Grande** (Gro).

5 The victorious battle of Cinco de Mayo commemorated – especially in **Acapulco** (Gro).

8 In **Mochitlán** (Gro), near Chilpancingo, the Festival de las Lluvias has pre-Christian roots: pilgrims, peasants and local dance groups climb a nearby volcano at night, arriving at the summit at dawn to pray for rain. Also a local fiesta in **Azoyu** (Gro), just off the coast road south of Acapulco.

15 DÍA DE SAN ISIDRO provokes a week-long festival in **Acapulco**. Celebrations too in **San Luis Acatlán** (Gro), south along the coast, where you might see the rare *Danza de la Tortuga* (Dance of the Turtle), and in **Tierra Colorada** (Gro).

31 Puerto Vallarta (Jal) celebrates its Founder's Day.

JUNE

1 DÍA DE LA MARINA (Navy Day) in the ports, particularly **Manzanillo** and **Acapulco**.

13 DÍA DE SAN ANTONIO. A feria in **Tierra Colorada** (Gro).

3rd Sunday. Blessing of the Animals at the church of Jesús Agonizante outside **Colima** (Col).

JULY

25 At **Coyuca da Benitez** (Gro), very near Acapulco, festival of the patron saint. A colourful fiesta too in **Mochitlán** (Gro).

AUGUST

6 A fiesta in **Petatlán** (Gro) distinguished by dances and a mock battle between *indígenas* and Spaniards.

23 DÍA DE SAN BARTOLOMÉ. In **Tecpán de Galeana** (Gro), between Acapulco and Zihuatanejo, religious processions the preceding night are followed by dancing, music and fireworks.

SEPTEMBER

15–16 INDEPENDENCE CELEBRATIONS almost everywhere.

28 DÍA DE SANTIAGO celebrated in several villages immediately around **Acapulco** (Gro).

29 DÍA DE SAN MIGUEL exuberantly exploited in **Azoyu** (Gro) and **Mochitlán** (Gro).

NOVEMBER

First week **Colima**'s major feria runs from the last days of October until November 8.

2 DAY OF THE DEAD is widely observed, with picturesque traditions in **Atoyac de Alvarez** (Gro), just off the Acapulco–Zihuatanejo road.

DECEMBER

12 DÍA DE NUESTRA SEÑORA DE GUADALUPE, patroness of Mexico. In **Atoyac de Alvarez** (Gro) and **Ayutla** (Gro), there are religious processions and traditional dances, while **Acapulco** enjoys more secular celebrations. In **Manzanillo** (Col) the celebrations start at the beginning of the month, while in **Puerto Vallarta** (Jal) they continue to the end of it.

travel details

BUSES

Bus services all along the coast are frequent and fast, with the possible exception of the stretch between Manzanillo and Lázaro Cárdenas, and there are almost constant departures on the major routes heading inland. The southern sector – Acapulco and Zihuatanejo – is served largely by Estrella de Oro (first-class) and Flecha Roja (second-class). In the north there's more competition, but since everywhere of size has a unified Central Camionera, this is rarely a problem. Tres Estrellas de Oro, Transportes del Pacifico and Omnibus de Mexico are the first-class standbys, while Autobuses de Occidente, TNS and Flecha Amarilla are the most widely seen second-class outfits. The following list covers **first-class services** and some local second-class services. On most routes there are as many, if not more, second-class buses, which take around twenty percent longer.

Acapulco to: Chilpancingo (hourly; 2hr); Cuernavaca (7 daily; 6hr); Guadalajara (3 daily; 17hr); Lázaro Cárdenas (8 daily; 6–7hr); Manzanillo (5 daily; 12hr); México (frequently; 5–9hr); Puerto Escondido (10 daily; 7hr); Puerto Vallarta (2 daily; 10hr); Salina Cruz (7 daily; 12–13hr); Taxco (4 daily; 4hr); Tijuana (3 daily; 35hr+); Zihuatanejo (every 30min; 4–5hr).

Barra de Navidad to: Cihuatlán (every 30min; 15min); Colima (1 daily; 2hr 30min); Guadalajara (10 daily; 6–7hr); Manzanillo (3 daily; 1hr 30min); Puerto Vallarta (2 daily; 5hr).

Chilpancingo to: Acapulco (hourly; 2hr); México (hourly; 3hr 30min).

Colima to: Barra de Navidad (1 daily, 2hr 30min; 15min); Comala (every 15min; 20min); Guadalajara (hourly; 3hr); Lázaro Cárdenas (6 daily; 6–7hr); Manzanillo (hourly; 1hr 30min); México (12 daily; 11hr); Puerto Vallarta (1 daily; 6hr); Tecomán (every 15min; 45min).

Lázaro Cárdenas to: Acapulco (8 daily; 6–7hr); Colima (6 daily; 6–7hr); Guadalajara (3 daily; 6hr); Manzanillo (9 daily; 6hr); México (5 daily; 11–14hr); Morelia (10 daily; 7–8hr); Pátzcuaro (1 daily; 7hr); Puerto Vallarta (3 daily; 12hr); Uruapán (5 daily; 6hr); Zihuatanejo (hourly; 2hr).

Manzanillo to: Acapulco (5 daily; 12hr); Barra de Navidad (3 daily; 1hr 30min); Colima (hourly; 1hr 30min); Guadalajara (hourly; 5–6hr); Lázaro Cárdenas (9 daily; 6hr); Puerto Vallarta (11 daily; 5–7hr); Tijuana (3 daily; 38hr).

Puerto Vallarta to: Acapulco (2 daily; 10hr); Barra de Navidad (2 daily; 5hr); Colima (1 daily; 6hr); Guadalajara (at least hourly; 6–7hr); Lázaro Cárdenas (3 daily; 12hr); Manzanillo (11 daily; 5–7hr); Mazatlán (2 daily; 8hr); México (6 daily; 14hr); Tepic (every 30min; 2hr 30min).

Zihuatanejo to: Acapulco (every 30min; 4–5hr); Ixtapa (continuously; 15min); Lázaro Cárdenas (hourly; 2hr); Mazatlán (6 daily; 7–8hr); Salina Cruz (2 daily; 17–18hr).

TRAINS

The main rail line in the region linking **Manzanillo** to **Colima** and **Guadalajara** has been indefinitely suspended. A second line links **Lázaro Cárdenas** and **Morelia**, the daily train leaving at noon and arriving in Morelia at midnight.

PLANES

This section of Mexico's coast is well served by **flights**, with international services to Acapulco, Puerto Vallarta and Zihuatanejo and domestic flights to various points in between. Guadalajara and México are accessible from Manzanillo, Ixtapa/Zihuatanejo and Acapulco; Acapulco also has flights to US cities including Chicago, Dallas, Houston and Los Angeles.

Puerto Vallarta is one of the busiest air hubs in Mexico, with flights to: Chicago (1 daily); Dallas (1 daily); Denver (1 daily); Detroit (1 daily); Guadalajara (8 daily); Houston (1 daily); Los Angeles (4 daily); Los Cabos (2 weekly); México (6 daily); San Diego (1 daily); San Francisco (1 daily); and Seattle (1 daily).

CHAPTER SEVEN

VERACRUZ

The central Gulf coast is among the least visited yet most distinct, atmospheric areas of Mexico. From the capital you descend through the southern fringes of the Sierra Madre Oriental, past the country's highest peaks, to a broad, hot and wet coastal plain. In this fertile tropical zone the earliest Mexican civilizations developed, and it remained densely populated throughout the pre-Hispanic era. Cortés himself began his march on the capital from Veracruz, and the city remains, as it was throughout colonial history, the busiest port in the country. Rich in agriculture – coffee, vanilla, tropical fruits and flowers grow everywhere – the Gulf coast is further enriched by oil and natural gas deposits.

The few tourists who find their way here are mostly passing through. In part, at least, this is because the area doesn't especially need them and makes no particular effort to attract them; and in part the **weather** can be blamed – it rains more often and more heavily here than just about anywhere else. Yet even in the rainy season the torrential downpours are short-lived, and within a couple of hours of the rain starting, you can be back on the steaming streets in bright sunshine. Though there are long, windswept beaches all down the Atlantic coast, they are less beautiful than their Pacific or Caribbean counterparts, and many suffer pollution from the busy shipping lanes, the oil industry or even sewage outlets. Most of the coastal towns are commercial centres, with little of interest to detain the visitor.

That said, the eastern slopes of the Sierra Madre hold a number of colonial cities worth a look at least in passing: **Jalapa**, seat of the state government, deserves more, with a balmy climate and a superb archeological museum to repay a stay. And **Veracruz** is among the most welcoming of all Mexican cities – too busy with its own affairs to create a separate life for visitors, you're drawn instead into the atmosphere of a steamy tropical port with strong echoes of the Indies. Within a couple of hours lie **La Antigua**, where Cortés established the first Spanish government in the Americas, and **Zempoala**, ruined site of the first civilization he subdued. **El Tajín**, near the coast in the north of the state, is one of the most important archeological sites in the country, and **Filo Bobos**, only recently excavated, is also well worth a visit. Both sites are in an area where **Totonac** culture retains powerful influence. To the south, **Catemaco** is a beautiful lake set in an extinct volcanic crater, where you can see the last remaining tract of Gulf Coast rainforest. The area is renowned as a meeting place for native *brujos* and *curanderos*, witches and healers.

The **food** here, too, is great – not only local coffee, fruit and vanilla (Mexicans inevitably take home a plastic bottle of vanilla essence as a souvenir), but also seafood.

Huachinango a la Veracruzana (red snapper Veracruz-style) is served across the country, and is of course on every menu here. But there are many more exotic possibilities, from langoustines and prawns to *jaiba*, a large local crab; look out for anything made with *chile chipotle*, a hot, dark brown chile with a very distinctive (and delicious) flavour – *Chilpachole de Jaiba* is a sort of crab chowder that combines the two. Sweet tamales, too, are a speciality, and to wash it all down, the local brewery at Orizaba produces several distinctive beers – cheaper on the whole, and better, than the big national brands.

The route from México

If you take the direct bus **from México to Veracruz** you'll bypass every major town en route on the excellent toll highway; if you're driving yourself, be warned that tolls are extremely high. If time is short, the fast Hwy-150 is a blessing – Veracruz and the coast are very much the outstanding attractions – but there are at least three cities in the mountains that merit a stop if you're in no hurry. This is, however, the rainiest area of all, and while it brings bounties in terms of great coffee and a luxuriance of flowers, downpours can become a problem. Particularly irritating – especially in October and November – is what the locals call *chipichipi*, a persistent fine drizzle caused by warm airstreams from the Gulf hitting cooler air as they reach the eastern face of the Sierra. When it's not raining, though, this is among the most beautiful drives in Mexico. As Ixtaccíhuatl gradually disappears behind you, the snow on the Pico de Orizaba comes into view, and the plains of corn and maguey in the west are supplanted on the eastern slopes by woods of pine and cypress, and by green fields with fat and contented cows out to pasture.

Orizaba

ORIZABA, first major town in the state of Veracruz, some 150km from Puebla, is largely an uninviting industrial city. What Orizaba lacks in charm, though, it makes up for in location, positioned at the foot of the **Pico de Orizaba** (or Citlaltépetl), a perfectly formed volcano and, at 5700m, the highest peak in Mexico.

There's further comfort in that the most important industry here is brewing, with the giant Cerveceria Moctezuma producing some of the best **beer** in the republic – ask at the tourist office for details of tours. Seeing the town need only take a couple of hours even so, and there are more attractive places to spend the night further down the road at Fortín and Córdoba. If, however, you plan to tackle the Pico de Orizaba – and the **climb**, detailed in R.J. Secor's *Mexican Volcanoes*, is only for serious mountaineers – you should change here for the second-class bus to the villages of Serdán or Tlachichuca, from where the main trails start.

Orizaba's **tourist office** (Mon–Fri 10am–1pm & 5–7pm, Sat 10am–1pm; no phone), on Norte 1 between Poniente 2 and 4, right behind the Palacio Municipal, can help with further information. Should you need **to stay**, the *Hotel Trueba*, Oriente 6 at Sur 11, near the ADO bus station (☎272/4-29-30, fax 4-27-18; ④), is comfortable and affordable. Slightly cheaper and on the same street is the colonial *Gran Hotel de France* (☎272/5-23-11 or 5-29-01; ③), Oriente 6 no. 186 at Sur 5.

Fortín de las Flores

FORTÍN DE LAS FLORES ("Fortress of the Flowers"), at a point where a beautiful minor route cuts across country to Jalapa, lies on the old road to Córdoba, 11km northeast of Orizaba. Its name is singularly appropriate: here more than anywhere in the state you'll see flowers all over the place – in the plaza, in the hotels, on the hillsides all around. Rain, which is frequent from May to December, and the constant muggy warmth ensure their growth – in particular, with the coming of the rains in May, wild orchids bloom freely.

Here you can visit the **Hacienda de las Animas**, once a residence of Maximilian and Carlota, now part of the luxurious hotel *Fortín de las Flores* (☎27/13-00-55; ⑦), at Av 2 between Calles 5 and 7. Rooms are reasonable considering the facilities: there's a huge swimming pool, and the gardens are exquisite. You can fully appreciate the luxuriance of the vegetation a few kilometres out of town at the **Barranca de Matalarga**: above the ravine flourish plantations of coffee and fruit trees, while the banks of the torrent itself are thick with a stunning variety of wild plants, which attract hummingbirds and insects of all kinds.

Fortín is a small town, but with a number of inexpensive **places to stay**: try the *Bugambilias* (☎27/13-05-22; ③), not far from the *Fortín de las Flores* (see above), on Av 1 between Calles 7 and 9; several other cheap places to stay and **to eat** are nearby on Av 1, while the *Bugambilias* itself has a decent restaurant.

Córdoba

Second-class buses take the mountain road from Fortín to Jalapa fairly regularly, but it's only a few kilometres further on towards the coast – and a short local bus ride – to **CÓRDOBA**. At the centre of the local coffee trade, this is a busy modern town grown up around a somewhat decaying colonial centre. Founded in 1618 by thirty Spanish families – and so also known as the City of the Thirty Knights – its main claim to fame is that here, in 1821, the last Spanish viceroy, Juan O'Donoju, signed a treaty acknowledging Mexican Independence with General Iturbide, soon to become emperor. This took place in the Palacio de los Condes de Zeballos – known as the **Portal de Zevallos**, on the zócalo.The Portal is now filled with cafés and restaurants, where you can sit and sample Cordoban coffee or the local drink, Julep, a cocktail of wine and mint. There's little else to do, but it's a pleasant enough place to while away an hour or two.

Practicalities

There are two **bus** terminals in Córdoba: the permanently crowded and confused AU terminal, ten minutes' walk from the zócalo at Av 7 and C 9; and the quieter ADO first-class terminal, Av 3 at C 4. **Moving on** from Córdoba, you're more likely to get a seat on the main routes at the latter terminal. Buses to Fortín de las Flores leave every ten minutes or so from the corner of C 3 and Av 5 and take about fifteen minutes. The **post office** (Mon–Fri 8am–8pm, Sat & Sun 9am–1pm) is in the Palacio Municipal on Av 3, half a block from the plaza towards the ADO station.

As well as the more pricey **hotels** around the zócalo, you'll find plenty of cheap places scattered about, especially along Av 2. Closest to the action are the *Virreinal*, by the side of the cathedral at the corner of Av 1 and C 5 (☎27/12-23-77; ④), and the *Mansur*, in the same block of Av 1, which is quiet, though not cheap (☎27/12-60-00; ④). Slightly further out are the pleasant *Iberia*, Av 2 no. 919 (☎27/12-13-01; ③), and the *Marina*, Av 2 at C 11 (☎27/12-26-00; ③), which has a restaurant. Around the zócalo, the **places to eat** are good but pricey: the *Restaurant El Cordobés* has a varied menu, huge comidas and an excellent Sunday buffet. There's also a good restaurant at the *Virreinal*. Cheaper options are along Av 2. For breakfast and heaps of fresh fruit, the ADO bus station café is unbeatable.

Jalapa

Although it's a slower route, a number of buses go from México to Veracruz via **JALAPA** (or Xalapa, as locals and bus companies frequently spell it). The state capital, Jalapa is remarkably attractive despite its relative modernity and traffic-laden streets, and is set in countryside of sometimes breathtaking beauty. The city sprawls across a tumbling hillside below the volcanic peak of the Cofre de Perote (4282m), and enjoys a richness of vegetation almost the equal of Fortín's (with which it also shares a warm, damp climate). In addition to these natural advantages, Jalapa has been promoted by its civic leaders as a cultural centre, and frequent music festivals, or other events, may well add to your stay. Home of the **University of Veracruz**, it's a lively place, enjoyable even if you do nothing more than hang out and watch life pass by.

Arrival and information

Jalapa's modern **bus station**, with every facility including a **tourist information** kiosk where you can book rooms, is a couple of kilometres east of the centre on 20 de Noviembre. You can get to town either by taxi or bus: the journey to the centre by regulated taxi, booked from a booth in the station, will cost about US$1. Buses marked "Centro" run along 20 de Noviembre; back to the bus station, they're marked "CAXA"

(Central de Autobuses de Xalapa). If you're heading on **from Jalapa to Veracruz** you'll pass through Zempoala (see p.401), and if you have a couple of hours it's well worth breaking the journey here to visit the ruins.

To **change money**, try Banco Serfin at Zamora and Mata (Mon–Fri 9–11.30am), or the casa de cambio nearby at Zamora 36-A (Mon–Fri 9am–2pm & 4–6.30pm, Sat 9.30am–1pm). The **post office** (Mon–Fri 7am–6pm) is on the corner of Diego Leño and Zamora.

Accommodation

Though there are some charming hotels in Jalapa, the city also boasts some of the lousiest budget accommodation in the state, but for a couple of exceptions.

Hotel del Bosque, Revolución 163 (☎28/17-69-80). A long way from the zócalo, but cheap and clean. ③.

Limón, Revolución 8 (☎28/17-22-04, fax 17-93-16). The best budget option, close to the centre, with small, very clean rooms around a courtyard, and a laundry. ②.

Maria Victoria, Zaragoza 6 (☎28/18-60-11, fax 18-05-21). Comfortable rooms each with TV and phone. ⑤.

Meson de Alferez, Zaragoza at Sebastian Camacho (☎28/18-63-51 or 18-01-13, fax 12-47-03). Beautiful, converted colonial house, once belonging to Alferez Real de Xalapa, who governed Veracruz when it was part of New Spain. Each room is unique, luxurious and charmingly decorated, and there's an excellent restaurant in the basement with some vegetarian options on the menu. Breakfast included. ⑤.

Principal, Zaragoza 28 (☎28/17-64-00). One of the best budget options, close to the zócalo, with clean comfortable and light rooms. ③.

Posada Santiago, Ursulo Galván 89, near the Parque Juárez (☎28/18-63-33). Clean and friendly, family-owned place. Some rooms with TV. ③.

The Town

Downtown – the small colonial area around the Parque Juárez – is the main attraction. Here, the eighteenth-century **Cathedral** and **Palacio de Gobierno** (with murals by the Chilean artist José Chaves Morado) both deserve to be seen, and, at dusk, the trees around the zócalo are filled with extraordinarily raucous birds. Jalapa's lively arts crowd meets up at the **Agora de la Ciudad**, a cultural centre in the Parque; and just west on Av M Avila Camacho is the **Teatro del Estado**, home to the state orchestra – for more on both of these see "Nightlife", opposite.

If you're feeling energetic, you could also climb **Macuiltepec**. At 1590m, this is the highest of the hills on which the town is built, and from its *mirador* – if you're lucky – you might catch a glimpse of the Gulf. About thirty minutes' walk from the centre (or a ride on the "Tepic" bus), Macuiltepec also boasts an Ecological Park at its base, with a specially designed barbecue and picnic area. Entrance is from C Tepic or Volcán de Colima (Tues–Sun 6am–5pm).

Jalapa's outstanding sight, however, is the **Archeology Museum** (Tues–Sun 9am–5pm; US$2.50) located on the outskirts of town – take any bus marked "Xalapa" along Dr Lucio. They say it's the second-best archeological museum in the country after México, and for good reason. Certainly the collection itself can rival any outside the capital in both extent and quality, and the building that houses it, flowing down the hillside in a series of spacious marble steps, may well be the finest in the country. It's a wonderful introduction to the various pre-Hispanic cultures of the Gulf coast. You start at the top of the hill, where the first halls deal with the **Olmecs**. There are several of the celebrated colossal stone heads, a vast array of other monumental statuary and some beautiful masks. Later cultures are represented mainly through their pottery – lifelike human and animal figurines especially – and there are also displays on the architecture of the major sites: El Tajín, Zempoala and so on. Finally, with the **Huastec** culture come more giant stone statues. Some of the larger, less valuable pieces are displayed in the landscaped gardens outside. There's a café on the first floor, and also a shop selling fantastic, though expensive, masks.

Around Jalapa

With more time on your hands, a number of worthwhile excursions can be made into the jungly country around Jalapa. Just a couple of kilometres south of the city, on the road to Coatepec (local bus), is the **Jardín Botanico Francisco Clavijero** (Tues–Sun 10am–5pm; free), a collection of plants native to the state, from jungle to mountain forest. Further out in the same direction, the villages of **Coatepec** itself and **Teocelo** are also worth a visit, mainly for their beautiful setting. Nearby is the spectacular **Cascada de Texolo**, a triple waterfall that can be admired from an ancient iron bridge. Many of the scenes in the film *Romancing the Stone* were shot around these villages and waterfalls, and there are more sets from the film around the village of **Naolinco**, north of Jalapa. All can be reached by local bus; further details are available from the Jalapa tourist office. To get to the Cascada de Texolo, take a bus from the ADO station to Xico (about 20min), and get off at the outskirts of the village, by a tiny church. Then ask the way – it's forty minutes' hot walk along a paved road through banana and coffee plantations, but worth it. On the road to Veracruz, 10km outside the city, is the **museum of El Lencero** (Tues–Sat 10am–5pm), a colonial hacienda that was once the property of the controversial general and president, Antonio López de Santa Anna. It is preserved in its full nineteenth-century splendour, and the grounds and surrounding countryside are stunning, too. The Chilean poet Gabriela Mistral stayed here in 1949, and wrote about the fine view of the coast.

Eating and drinking

Good **food** is abundant in Jalapa; the city is home to the **jalapeño** pepper, which you'll probably taste in all main meals. Another one of the great pleasures here is local coffee served with *pan dulce* in a traditional café. Several of these, including the very popular *La Parroquia*, can be found on Zaragoza, the street just below the zócalo; they serve good full meals, too. Or head for the *Café Latino*, at the bottom of Zamora, near the post office, which serves good breakfasts and a bewildering variety of delicious, if not always authentic, coffees – their "Turkish" coffee is made with ice cream and coke. Inexpensive full meals can as ever be found around the market, but more appetizing restaurants, and some good jugo and torta places, are concentrated around Av Enriquez (the continuation of Camacho on the other side of the zócalo). Carillo Puerto, an alley leading uphill off Enriquez by the *Hotel Regis*, has several good-value, Mexican family restaurants, popular at lunch, including *La Fonda* and the excellent *El Mayab*, that latter of which serves a huge, fresh comida. For **vegetarians**, *El Champiñón* (Mon–Fri only), at Allende 78, has excellent food and a noticeboard for contacts. *El Bodegon*, Leona Vicario, a few blocks from the zócalo between Allende and Ursulo Galvan, has an excellent menu and will prepare dishes to order; the friendly manager also has a wide range of tequilas, which he enjoys sharing with guests. There's an Internet café in the arcade linking Enriquez with the western end of Zamora.

Nightlife

Jalapa is a city of great creative energy, boosted by a large student community, a number of good theatres and an excellent orchestra. The *Teatro del Estado*, at the corner of M Avila Camacho and C de la Llave, hosts regular performances by the **Orquesta Sinfónica de Jalapa**, including some free off-season concerts (June–Aug), in addition to dance and theatre, while *Agora de la Ciudad*, Parque Juárez, is an arts centre with a cinema, theatre, gallery, bookshop and coffee shop – and variable opening times.

A number of **bars** offer live music and occasionally poetry readings or theatre, and there are numerous **nightclubs** catering for all tastes. *Los Molinos*, Ursulo Galván 57, is a restaurant-bar offering a wide selection of spirits, as well as free live entertainment at weekends (Mon–Sat 8pm–1am). *Plaza Crystal*, C 3a de Melchor Ocampo 75, near CAXA, is a big complex of clubs, shops and cinemas, popular with Jalapeños, and where you can find everything from techno to salsa.

A free fortnightly listings sheet, *La Farándula*, is available from cafés, museums and galleries, and provides useful information on where to go and what to see.

Veracruz

VILLA RICA DE LA VERACRUZ was the first town founded by the Spanish in Mexico, a few days after Cortés' arrival on Good Friday, 1519. The first development – little more than a wooden stockade – was in fact some way to the north, later being moved to La Antigua (see p.400) and subsequently to its present site in 1589. But the modern city is very much the heir of the original; only recently, for the first time since its foundation, has Veracruz begun to lose its position as the most important port in Mexico (to Tampico and Coatzacoalcos), and its history reflects every major event

ACCOMMODATION

Amparo	5
Baluarte	6
Cielo	10
Colonial	4
Emporio	1
Mar y Tierra	7
Marisol de Veracruz	11
Oriente	3
Sevilla	2
Royalty	9
Villa Rica	8

CENTRAL VERACRUZ

0   200 m

from the Conquest onwards. "Veracruz", states Paul Theroux, "is known as the 'heroic city'. It is a poignant description: in Mexico a hero is nearly always a corpse."

Though tranquil enough today, the port's past has been a series of "invasions, punitive missions and local military defeats . . . humiliation as history". This started even before the Conquest was complete, when **Panfilo Narvaez** landed here on his ill-fated mission to bring Cortés back under the control of the governor of Cuba, and continued intermittently for the next four hundred years. Throughout the sixteenth and seventeenth centuries, Veracruz and the Spanish galleons that used the port were preyed on constantly by English, Dutch and French buccaneers. In the **War of Independence** the Spanish made their final stand here, holding the fortress of San Juan Ulúa for four years after the country had been lost. In **1838** the French occupied the city, demanding compensation for French property and citizens who had suffered in the years following Independence; in **1847** US troops took Veracruz, and from here marched on to capture the capital; in **1862** the French, supported by Spanish and English forces that soon withdrew, invaded on the pretext of forcing Mexico to pay her foreign debt, but ended up staying five years and setting up the unfortunate Maximilian as emperor; and finally in **1914** US marines were back, occupying the city to protect American interests during the Revolution. These are the *Cuatro Veces Heroica* of the city's official title, and form the bulk of the history displayed, with a certain bitterness, in the museums.

The first, and the lasting, impression of Veracruz, however, is not of its history or bitterness, but of its life now. The city is one of the most enjoyable places in the republic in which simply to be, to sit back and watch – or join – the daily round. This is especially true in the evening when the tables under the *portales* of the plaza fill up, and the drinking and the *marimba* music begin – to go on through most of the night. **Marimba** – a distinctively Latin-Caribbean sound based around a giant wooden xylophone – is *the* local sound, but at peak times there are *mariachi* bands, too, and individual strolling crooners, all striving to be heard over each other. When the municipal band strikes up from the middle of the square, confusion is total.

Arrival and information

The **bus stations**, both ADO first-class and AU second-class, are a long way from the centre on Av Díaz Mirón (the entrance to second-class is actually on the street behind, La Fragua). Any bus heading to the right as you come out should take you to the centre – most will have "Díaz Mirón" or "Centro" on the windscreen; if not, ask. They head straight to the end of Díaz Mirón, round a confusing junction at the Parque Zamora, and then take a variety of routes that mostly end up on Independencia as it runs past the zócalo. To get back, head for 5 de Mayo, parallel to Independencia, and take any bus marked "Camionera". The **train station** is very central, only about five blocks from the zócalo along the dock-front. If you fly in, the **airport** is 10km or so south of the city; Transportacion Aeropuerto runs the usual system of official colectivos and taxis downtown – for a pick-up to the airport, call them on ☎29/32-35-20.

Although Veracruz is a large and rambling city, the downtown area, once you've got to it, is relatively small and straightforward – anywhere further afield can be reached by local bus from somewhere very near the **zócalo**. This, to an even greater extent than usual, is the epicentre of city life in Veracruz – not only the site of the cathedral and the Palacio Municipal, but the place where everyone gathers, for morning coffee, lunch, afternoon strolls and night-time revelry.

Information

The very helpful **tourist office** (daily 9am–9pm; ☎29/32-19-99), on the ground floor of the Palacio Municipal right on the zócalo, publish an interesting guide to the city's history, arts and culture, written by Don Bernardo Lorenzo Camacho, who's usually on hand to answer any questions. There are two **casas de cambio**, at Morelos no. 241 & no. 486 (daily 8am–noon), though check the rates before you change money; you might also try Bancomer and Banamex on Independencia, both of which change travellers' cheques. The **post office** (Mon–Fri 8am–8pm, Sat & Sun 9am–noon) is on the Plaza de la República, a couple of blocks north of the zócalo. There are Ladatel phones throughout the city, and a fax and copy centre where you can make international calls, at Morelos 255.

Accommodation

There's a **hotel** right next to the first-class bus station, and several very cheap and rather grim places around the back of the second-class bus terminal, but unless you've arrived very late at night, there's no point in staying this far out. The other cheap places are mostly within a couple of blocks of the zócalo, often around the market; they're nothing to write home about, and noise can be a real problem, but at least you should find a clean room with a fan. There are also a few more expensive options on the zócalo itself. Alternatively, you could try staying out by the beach, where there are some reasonable Mexican family-oriented hotels and a number of **campsites** down towards Boca del Río.

Amparo, Serdán 482 (☎29/32-27-38). One of a cluster of cheap places, behind the zócalo near the market. ②.

Baluarte, Canal 265 at Av 16 de Septiembre (☎29/32-60-42). Well-kept hotel with pool, TV, a/c and views of the Baluarte de Santiago, though not the friendliest of places. ④.

Cielo, S Perez Abascal 580 (☎29/37-23-67). Pleasant enough but inconvenient unless you've arrived late at the second-class bus terminal. ③.

Colonial, Lerdo 117 (☎29/32-01-93, fax 32-24-65). Luxury option in the centre with a swimming pool, garage, a/c rooms and ubiquitous muzak. ⑤.

Emporio, Paseo de Malecon 244 at Insurgentes (☎29/32-00-20 or 32-22-22, fax 31-22-61). Big, luxurious US-style hotel with all the associated amenities, including pool and slightly pricier rooms with a sea view. ⑦.

Mar y Tierra, M Avila Camacho at Figueroa (☎29/32-02-60). One of the best mid-priced options on the seafront, and only ten minutes from the zócalo. A/c rooms in the old (at the front) and new buildings are very different, so look first: some have sea views. ④.

Marisol de Veracruz, Díaz Mirón 1242 (☎29/32-53-99). Three blocks from the ADO terminal. Clean rooms with fan or a/c; quieter than the nearby *Central*. ④.

Oriente, Lerdo 20 (☎29/31-26-15 or 31-24-90, fax 31-27-40). Very near the zócalo. Rooms with balconies are best – others are a little musty. Some have a/c. ④.

Royalty, M Avila Camacho and Abasolo (☎29/36-14-90). Clean and friendly, quiet and close to the centre, with a/c rooms plus some cheaper ones with a fan, TV and small balcony. Accepts credit cards. ④.

Sevilla, Morelos 359 (☎29/32-42-48). Basic rooms with TV and fan close to the zócalo. ③.

Villa Rica, M Avila Camacho 7 (☎29/32-07-82). A little way out, just past Doblado, but close to the water. Small, simple rooms with fans. ③.

The City

The outstanding sight in Veracruz is the **Castillo de San Juan de Ulúa**, the great fortress that so signally failed to protect the harbour. In most cases this was hardly the fault of its defenders, since every sensible invader landed somewhere on the coast nearby, captured the town and, having cut off the fort by land and sea, called for its surrender. Prior to closing for refurbishment in 1997, the fortress was the thoroughly rundown and fitting location for the climactic chase scene in *Romancing the Stone*, with its unguarded ten-metre drops and dingy, dripping corridors. The newly renovated fort should be open by the end of 1998. Ask at the tourist office for details of new opening times for both the fort and the site museum.

Back in town, the first of two worthwhile museums occupies an old mansion on Zaragoza, about five blocks from the Palacio Municipal.The **Museo de la Ciudad** (Mon–Sat 9am–4pm; US$0.25) covers local history and folklore from the earliest inhabitants to the 1914 US invasion. Inevitably, it's rather a potted version, and many of the exhibits go completely unexplained, but there's some beautiful Olmec and Totonac sculpture, including one of the giant Olmec heads; thought-provoking information on Mexico's African population, much of which was concentrated in this area after the slave trade; and relics of the city's various "heroic defenders". Just two blocks away from the Museo de la Ciudad, towards the sea, the facades of **Las Atarazanas** are worth a passing look. These colonial warehouses once backed onto the sea and were built for the storage of arms and wares used by the troops that protected the city from pirates. From here it's an easy walk, down past the market, to the malecón at the side of the harbour, where the town's second museum, the **Museo Venustiano Carranza** (Tues–Fri 9am–1pm & 4–6pm, Sat & Sun 9am–noon; free), is in the old *faro* (lighthouse), alongside the huge Banco de México building on Insurgentes. Venustiano Carranza established his Constitutionalist government in Veracruz in 1915 (with the support of US President Woodrow Wilson, whose troops then occupied the town), living in the Castillo de San Juan while running his government – and the war against Villa and Zapata – from this lighthouse building. There's a fine statue of Carranza outside, looking exactly as John Reed describes him in *Insurgent Mexico*: "A towering, khaki-clad figure, seven feet tall it seemed . . . arms hanging loosely by his side, his fine old head thrown back." Inside are gathered assorted memorabilia of his government's term here, and you can view Carranza's bedroom and living room. Offical opening hours seem to be at the whim of the navy, whose local headquarters the building also houses.

Two blocks south and three west from the Carranza museum, you can't miss the **Baluarte de Santiago**, a seventeenth-century fort between Av 16 de Septiembre and Gómez Faria. Originally one of nine forts along a 2650-metre-long wall, the Baluarte is now the only survivor – it's hard to imagine that the sea reached this far when the fort was built in 1635. You can go inside for a wander around the small museum (daily 9am–5pm; US$2, free on Sun), which has a few exhibits of exquisite pre-Columbian gold jewellery discovered in the 1980s by a local octopus fisherman. Most of his find had been melted down and sold before the authorities got wind of it, and though only a fraction remains, it's still a significant contribution to what little remains from colonial times.

The city's newest attraction, and well worth a visit, is the **Acuario de Veracruz** (Mon–Fri 10am–7pm, Sat & Sun 9am–7pm; US$2.50, children half-price), in the shopping centre next to the *Hotel Villa del Mar*, on Blvd M Avila Camacho. Designed by a Japanese architect, this modern and well-run aquarium has some large pelagic fish, including sharks, barracuda and huge tarpon, as well as smaller tanks filled with a variety of salt, brackish and fresh-water fauna. There are also some interesting educational exhibits, in addition to skeletons of various marine mammals and turtles.

To see marine life at closer quarters, head for Tridente, M Avila Camacho 165 (☎ & fax 29/31-79-24), near the *Mar y Tierra* hotel, one of the city's best **dive shops**. They offer guided dive trips to some twenty-two little-visited reefs, including those around Veracruz's offshore islands, along with PADI certification at a better rate than in the Caribbean.

Veracruz beaches

You wouldn't make a special trip to Veracruz for its **beaches** – although for Mexicans from the capital it's a relatively cheap and handy resort, and there are hotels, however ugly, catering to them for miles to the south – but for an afternoon's escape to the sea, they're quite good enough. Avoid **Villa del Mar**, which is the closest, most crowded and least clean, and head instead to **Mocambo** or **Boca del Río**. Buses (marked "Boca del Río") head out to both from the corner of Zaragoza and Serdán; or get a lift in one of the vans marked "Playas", which leave regularly to Mocambo from every corner along the malecón, arriving twenty minutes later at the *Hotel Mocambo* (☎29/22-02-05, fax 22-02-12; ⑥), a grand old hotel freshly renovated. From here, follow the street down to the wide sandy beach, where the water is warm and calm – though from time to time it can be pretty filthy. As its name suggests, the small village of Boca del Río is located at the mouth of a river – watch out for the persistent boat-trip touts. If you're stuck out here and want an inexpensive **place to stay**, try *Playa Del Oro*, Paseo Ejercito 23 (no phone; ④), opposite the *Mocambo*, the cheapest of the few budget options.

Tridente (see above) have an eco-tourism site, with camping and a restaurant, at **Anton Lizardo**, a small village beyond Boca del Rio. From here they run boat-trips to the best beaches and reefs near Veracruz, on the offshore coral islands. These have white sands, clean water and very few visitors. Tridente can help you get permission to stay on one of the islands if you have your own tent.

Eating and drinking

"A la Veracruzana" is a tag you'll find on menus all over the country, denoting a delicious sauce of onions, garlic, tomatoes, olives, chiles and spices, served with meat or fish. And not surprisingly, there are **seafood restaurants** all over Veracruz, although by no means is each one particularly good value. The zócalo itself is ringed by little bars and cafés, but these are really places to drink, and though most do serve food, or at least sandwiches, it's generally overpriced and not up to much.

One place you should definitely try is the *Gran Café del Portal*, just off the zócalo on Independencia, opposite the cathedral, which claims its locally grown coffee is the best in the country – certainly the *lechero* (white coffee) is extremely good. As you sip your coffee here, you'll be confronted by some of Mexico's most unusual touts – from boys selling balsa toucans and fortune tellers, to uniformed nurses offering to take your blood pressure. For good breakfasts and comidas, try the *Cocina Economica*, at Mariano Escobedo and Xicoténcatl, past Blvd M Avila Camacho.

For more substantial meals, there are a whole series of small **fish restaurants** around the market, and the top floor of the market building itself is given over to cooked food stalls. Between here and the zócalo (leave the square through the passageway, Portales Miranda, behind the cathedral) is another small square with a group of restaurants. Here *La Gaviota* serves good comidas and plain meals 24 hours a day, which won't go amiss after an evening in the zócalo bars. For seafood in slightly less frenetic surroundings, head up Zaragoza towards the museum, where you'll find *El Tiburón* and *El Pescador*, good places to sample a *coctel* of real *jaiba* (crab).

If you feel like a change of cuisine, try *Le Gourmet*, on the malecón between the hotels *Villa Rica* and *Royalty*, which serves delicious salads and soups, and apart from *Chicago Pizza*, at Zamora 288, is the only place with anything even vaguely **vegetarian** in central Veracruz – they'll cook you a cheese omelette if you ask.

La Antigua and Zempoala

Heading north from Veracruz, there's a short stretch of highway as far as Cardel, at the junction of the coastal highway and the road up to Jalapa. **LA ANTIGUA**, site of the first real Spanish town in Mexico, lies just off this road. Although it does see an occasional bus, you'll find it much easier and quicker to take one heading for Cardel (about every thirty minutes from the second-class terminal in Veracruz) and get off at the toll-booths. From here it's only about twenty minutes' walk up a signed road.

For all its antiquity, there's not a great deal to see in La Antigua; however, it is a beautiful, broad-streeted tropical village on the banks of the **Río La Antigua** (or Río Huitzilapan), and at weekends makes a popular excursion for Veracruzanos, who come to picnic by the river and to swim or take boat rides. Lots of seafood restaurants cater to this local trade. In the semi-ruinous centre of the village stand a couple of the oldest surviving Spanish buildings in Mexico: the **Edificio del Cabildo**, built in 1523, housed the first *Ayuntamiento* (local government) to be established; the **Casa de Cortés**, a fairly crude construction of local stone, was built for Cortés himself a few years later; and the parish church, too, dates from the mid-sixteenth century, though it's been altered and restored several times since. On the riverbank stands a vast old tree – the *Ceiba de la Noche Feliz* – to which, according to local legend, Cortés moored his ships when he arrived here.

Zempoala

That Cortés came to this spot at all, after first landing near the site of modern Veracruz, was thanks to the invitation of the Totonac of **ZEMPOALA** (or Cempoala), then a city of some 25,000 to 30,000 inhabitants. It was the first native city visited by the Conquistadors ("a great square with courtyards", wrote Bernal Diaz, "which appeared to have been lime coated and burnished during the last few days . . . one of the horse-men took the shining whiteness for silver, and came galloping back to tell Cortés that our quarters had silver walls . . . ") and quickly became their ally against the Aztecs. Zempoala, which had existed in some form for at least eight hundred years, had been brought under the control of the Aztec empire only relatively recently – around 1460 – and its people, who had already rebelled more than once, were only too happy to stop paying their tribute once they believed that the Spanish could protect them from retribution. This they did, although the "Fat Chief" and his people must have begun to have second thoughts when Cortés ordered their idols smashed and replaced with crosses and Christian altars.

Cortés left Zempoala in August 1519 for the march on Tenochtitlán, taking with him two hundred Totonac porters and fifty of the town's best warriors. The following May he was forced to return in a hurry by the news that Panfilo Narvaez had come after him with a large force, on a mission to bring the Conquistadors back under the control of the governor of Cuba. The battle took place in the centre of Zempoala, where, despite the fact that Narvaez's force was far larger and had taken up defensive positions on the great temple, Cortés won a resounding victory: the enemy leaders were captured and most of the men switched sides, joining in the later assaults on the Aztec capital.

The **archeological site** (daily 8am–6pm; US$2, free on Sun) dates mostly from the Aztec period, and although obviously the buildings have lost their decorative facings and thatched sanctuaries, it's one of the most complete examples of an Aztec ceremonial centre surviving – albeit in an untypically tropical setting. The pyramids with their double stairways, grouped around a central plaza, must have resembled those of Tenochtitlán, though on a considerably smaller scale. Apart from the main, cleared site, consisting of the **Templo Mayor** (the largest and most impressive structure, where Narvaez made his stand), the Great Pyramid and the Templo de las Chimeneas, there are lesser ruins scattered throughout and around, the modern village. Most important of these are the Templo de las Caritas, a small temple on which a few carvings and remains of murals can still be seen, in open country just beyond the main site, and the Templo de Ehecatl, on the opposite side of the main road through the village. You need a couple of hours to explore the site.

Practicalities: Cardel

There are **buses** (second-class) to Zempoala from both Veracruz and Jalapa, but it's quicker – certainly if you plan to continue northwards – to go back to **Cardel** and change there for a first-class service. Coming **from La Antigua**, you can go back to the main road, get a bus on to Cardel and go on from there. From Cardel there are plenty of green-and-white taxis to the site, but the minibuses that leave every thirty minutes from the south side of the plaza are cheaper. Cardel itself is not of much interest, but has several seafood restaurants and a couple of small **hotels** around the plaza. They're rather expensive, though the *Plaza*, Independencia 25 Pte (☎2-02-88; ④), just opposite the ADO bus stop, may let you bargain off-season. Best value is the friendly *Maty*, Carretera Nacional, on the outskirts of town opposite the hospital (☎2-02-67; ③), which has a good restaurant. From Cardel you can head down to a good beach at **Chachalacas** (another short bus journey), a small fishing village with a luxury hotel and some excellent seafood.

North to Tuxpán

Continuing north, there's very little in the long coastal stretch (some four hours on the bus) from Cardel to Papantla. The village of **Quiahuitzlán**, about 70km from Veracruz, bears the name of a fortified Totonac town visited by Cortés, with some fairly unimpressive ruins nearby. At **Laguna Verde** there's a nuclear power station (presently closed as a result of much controversy), and at **Nautla** you pass the largest town en route, surrounded by coconut groves. Although there are long, flat stretches of sand much of the way, they are pretty uninviting – desolate, windswept and raked by grey surf. Only in the final stretch does the beach offer much temptation, with several (expensive) motels dotted between Nautla and **Tecolutla**, a low-key resort a few miles off the main road. If you crave the beach you can stay here (try the basic *El Guerro Callejas*, on Murillo Vidal; no phone; ②) and still get to Papantla and El Tajín with relative ease.

Tlapacoyan

Some 50km southwest of Nautla, bounded to the south by the Río Bobos and to the north by the Río Maria de la Torre, **TLAPACOYAN** is surrounded by jungly hills and pre-Columbian ruins. Most important of these are the massive undeveloped sites of **Filo Bobos**, inaugurated in 1994 as part of a plan to turn the area into a major tourist destination. The town itself is still largely unspoiled, a friendly place going about its main business as a centre of citrus fruit production. Captured briefly by the Aztecs on a raid from the port of Nauhtla (Nautla), in 1865 Tlapacoyan was taken by Austrian troops loyal to Emperor Maximilian, and after a long siege it finally fell to imperial troops in November. One of the republican commanders, Colonel Ferrer, distinguished himself in the battle and was elevated to the rank of general. Today his statue stands in the main square.

Regular **buses to Tlapacoyan** run from Jalapa, Papantla, Veracruz, Puebla and México. ADO buses drop off in the centre of town. Turn left at 5 de Mayo and walk up Héroes de Tlapacoyan for the main square. Second-class services to Nautla leave from the terminal opposite ADO. **Hotels** are thin on the ground, but in the centre there are a few quiet, good-value choices. Try the *Melgarejo*, Gutiérrez Zamora 399 (☎231/5-00-57; ③), some of whose rooms come with TV; or, on the square itself, the *Hotel Plaza* (☎231/5-05-20, fax 5-12-51; ③) or the *San Agustín* (☎231/5-00-23; ③), the latter of which also has the best restaurant in town, and organizes river trips to Filo Bobos.

Filo Bobos

Work continues at the **Filo Bobos** archeological project, which opened to the public in 1994. Here you can visit two of the more than five pre-Hispanic sites so far identifed along the Río Bobos valley. Both **El Cuajilote** and **Vega de la Peña** are well worth visiting as much for the beauty of their location, the birdlife and the serenity, as for the ruins themselves.

No one yet knows for certain who occupied the Filo Bobos sites. Signs of a fertility cult suggest a **Huastec** influence, yet the other sculpture found is more Totonac in style, and the earliest buildings at El Cuajilote, which may be as old as 1000 BC, are decidedly Olmec. Archeologists are now speculating that Filo Bobos was the centre of an as yet unknown, syncretistic Mesoamerican civilization, which provided an important trade link between the Gulf coast, its environs and the central valleys.

The **trail** that leads to and links the two sites cuts through ranchland running along the sides of the Río Bobos, with steep rainforested hills rising to either side. There are unexplored mounds of pre-Columbian rubble all along the way, and you're unlikely to see any other tourists.The first and most impressive site you come to is **El Cuajilote**, with platforms and pyramids arranged around a rectangular central plaza measuring 31,500 square metres. The surrounding buildings imitate the shape of the valley, and appear to be a series of temples dedicated to a fertility cult: a monolithic, phallic stela more than two metres tall and orientated to the stars stands in the middle of the plaza, and at Shrine A4 more than 1500 other phallic figurines were found, though none of these remains on site today. You can also make out a ball-court and some sculptures, including one of giant frog – this may also be a fertility symbol.

The trail continues to the site of **Vega de la Peña**, four kilometres away, which covers some eight thousand square metres. There's little doubt that structures buried beneath the lush greenery extend beyond that; some archeologists believe they may have stretched as far as Nautla. If true, this would radically alter the accepted conception of Mexican and Mesoamerican pre-Columbian history, placing this coast in a far more prominent position than previously thought. What you see here today are small buildings, with more palatial dwellings than at El Cuajilote, and a small ball-court.

The complete **walk** takes about six hours and begins at a little village called **Santiago**, reached by bus from the Terminal Regional de Tlapcoyan on the corner of 5 de Mayo and Valdez, two blocks from the zócalo at Tlapacoyan. The bus driver will drop you in the village at the mouth of the road that leads to El Cuajilote. The walk down this

---

EL BAILE DE LOS NEGRITOS

Popular at festivals across the state of Veracruz, the frenetic **Baile de los Negritos** is a Totonac dance dating back to colonial times, when black slaves were imported in numbers to work on local plantations, often living and labouring alongside *indígenas*. Stories abound as to the origin of the dance; the most popular version has it that a female African slave and her child escaped from a plantation near Papantla, and lived in the dense jungle with the local indigenous groups. After her child was poisoned by a snake bite, the mother, using African folk medicine, began to dance herself into a trance. The Totonacs around her found the spectacle highly amusing and, it is said, began to copy her in a spirit of mockery.

The costumes of the dance are influenced by colonial dress, and the dancers wear a snake motif around the waist. The dance is directed by a "Mayordomo", the title given to plantation overseers in the colonial era. If you're in Tlapacoyan for the **Feast of Santiago** (July 24), dedicated to the town's patron saint, or the **Day of the Assumption** (August 16), you'll see the dance at its best and most spectacular; at other times it's held on a smaller scale in other village festivals in the area.

road takes about an hour, though you can cut through fields to make it a little quicker, along a steep, mossy and slippery path known as "aceite vueltos". The path is not always clear, but there are ranches along the road, and locals will point you in the right direction. From El Cuajilote, a path leads out of the back of the site towards Vega de la Peña, and from there another leads to a manned river crossing with a small restaurant. From here it's a straightforward walk up a road lined with banana plantations to the village of **Encanto**, where you can catch local buses to Tlapacoyan. The site wardens at both El Cuajilote and Vega de la Peña are very helpful and will ensure that you are on the right path, as will the locals.

Papantla

PAPANTLA is by far the most attractive town on the route north, flower-filled and straggling over an unexpected outcrop of low, jungly hills. It's also one of the most important centres of the Mexican **vanilla** industry – the sweet, sticky odour frequently hangs over the place, and vanilla products are on sale everywhere – as well as being one of the surviving strongholds of **Totonac** life. You'll see Totonacs wandering around bare-footed in their loose white robes, especially in the market. You can also regularly witness the amazing **dance-spectacle** of the *Voladores de Papantla* here at Papantla and at El Tajín (see below). The best views across the city are from the tower on the Sanctuario de Cristo Rey – the pretty church you pass as you enter the town by bus.

Practicalities

First-class **buses** use the ADO terminal on Juárez, some way out of town; you can just about walk, climbing straight up Juárez until you meet Enriquez, where you turn right for the centre of town, but it's easier to take a taxi. It can be hard to get a bus out, as most are *de paso*: book ahead for a local service, or take second-class, at least as far as Poza Rica, from where there's much more choice. The chaotic second-class Transportes Papantla terminal is more central on 20 de Noviembre – again, walk straight up to the zócalo. Buses **to El Tajín** via Chote (where you change) run from here, or there are direct minibuses from behind the *Hotel Tajín* at fifteen minutes past

---

THE VOLADORES DE PAPANTLA

The dance of the **Voladores** involves five men: a leader who provides music on flute and drum, and four performers. They represent the five earthly directions – the four cardinal points and straight up, from earth to heaven. After a few preliminary ceremonies, the five climb to a small platform atop the pole, where the leader resumes playing and directs prayers for the fertility of the land in every direction. Meanwhile, the four dancers tie ropes, coiled tightly around the top of the pole, to their waists and at a signal fling themselves head first into space. As they spiral down in ever-increasing circles the leader continues to play, and to spin, on his platform, until the four hit the ground (or hopefully land on their feet, having righted themselves at the last minute). In all they make thirteen revolutions each, symbolizing the 52-year cycle of the Aztec calendar. Although the full significance of the dance has been lost – originally the performers would wear bird costumes, for example – it has survived much as the earliest chroniclers reported it, largely because the Spanish thought of it as a sport rather than a pagan rite. In Papantla and El Tajín (where performances take place more frequently) it has become, at least partly, a tourist spectacle – though no less hazardous for that – as the permanent metal poles attest. If you can see it at a local village fiesta, there is still far more ceremony attached, particularly in the selection of a sufficiently tall tree and its erection in the place where the dance is to be performed.

each hour. There's a small **tourist office** in the Palacio Municipal (theoretically open Mon–Fri 9am–3pm, Sat 9am–1pm). Both Banamex and Bancomer, on Juan Enriquez south of the *Hotel Premier*, change **travellers' cheques**, though it can be a very slow process.

There are several reasonably priced **hotels** in Papantla. The *Premier*, on the zócalo (☎784/2-00-80 or 2-27-00, fax 2-10-62; ⑤), has pleasant modern rooms, can change travellers' cheques and organizes horseback rides to El Tajin. The *Tajín* (☎784/2-06-44, fax 2-01-21; ⑤), diagonally opposite and next to the cathedral, is as comfortable and has good views across the city. Cheaper options include the *Totonacapan* (☎784/2-12-24; ③), on Olivio near the second-class bus terminal, and the *Trujillo* (no phone; ②), near the extraordinary, pink Rococo cinema on 5 de Mayo.

Restaurants are cheap and plentiful, though most are fairly ordinary. The *Premier* is the poshest in town, while *Plaza Pardo* overlooks the plaza and is a lively place from which to watch the evening action. The excellent *Enriquez* is just off the zocalo, behind the *Premier*. Vegetarians could try *Idea Pizza*, on Obispo, the street behind the *Tajin* hotel, while anyone on a tight budget should head for the eateries along Olivio, which leads off the zócalo towards the second-class bus station.

El Tajín

However charming and peaceful Papantla may be, the main reason anyone comes here is to visit the ruins of **EL TAJÍN**, by far the most important archeological site on the Gulf coast, and a much more interesting and impressive collection of buildings than the more recent remains of Zempoala. The current opinion is that the principal architecture dates from the Classic period (300–900 AD), declining in the early Post-Classic (900–1100). By the time of the Conquest it had been forgotten, and any knowledge of it now comes from archeological enquiries since the accidental discovery of the site in 1785. El Tajin remains one of the most enigmatic and least understood of all of Mexico's ancient cities. No one even knows who built it. Some claim it was the Huastecs, others the Totonacs, but although "Tajín" means thunderbolt in Totonaca, experts consider it unlikely to have been built by their ancestors. Most archeologists prefer not to speculate too wildly, instead calling the civilization "Classic Veracruz" after its archeological hallmarks. You'll notice many of these at El Tajín, the most obvious of which are the niches and the complex ornamental motifs known as "scrolls", the latter of which are most prevalent on items and bas-reliefs associated with the ball game, with which they were so obsessed (look at some of the stone "yokes" in the site museum). "Classic Veracruz" influence was widespread, and is strongly felt at Teotihuacán, such that some consider it may have been the Veracruzanos who built that city.

Despite many years of effort, only a small part of the huge site has been cleared, and even this limited area is constantly in danger of being once more engulfed by the jungle: stand on top of one of the pyramids and you see green mounds in every direction, each concealing more ruins.

The site

The site (daily 9am–5pm; US$3, free on Sun) divides broadly into two areas: **Tajín Viejo**, the original explored area centring on the amazing Pirámide de los Nichos, and **Tajín Chico**, a group of administrative buildings built on an artificial terrace. From the entrance (where, as well as the museum, there's a café and bar) a track leads through a small group of buildings, and into Tajín Viejo. Before you reach the square in front of the pyramid you pass several **ball-courts**, the most important, on your left, being the South Court, or **Juego de Pelota Sur**. There are seventeen such courts, possibly more, and the game must have assumed an importance here far greater than at any other known site: we know little of the rules, and courts vary widely in size and shape,

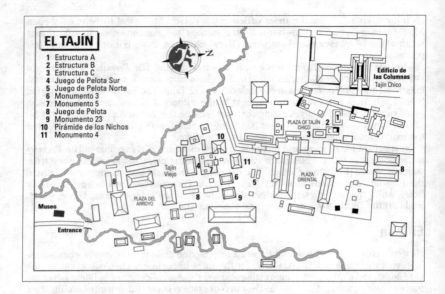

EL TAJÍN

1 Estructura A
2 Estructura B
3 Estructura C
4 Juego de Pelota Sur
5 Juego de Pelota Norte
6 Monumento 3
7 Monumento 5
8 Juego de Pelota
9 Monumento 23
10 Pirámide de los Nichos
11 Monumento 4

but the general idea was to knock a ball through a ring or into a hole without the use of the hands. Clearly, too, there was a religious significance, and at El Tajín the game was closely associated with human sacrifice. The superb bas-relief sculptures that cover the walls of the South Court show aspects of the game, and include portrayals of a decapitated player, and another about to be stabbed with a ritual knife by fellow players, with Death awaiting to his left. These bas-reliefs are constant feature of the site, adorning many of the ball-courts and buildings, with more stacked in the museum, but those in the South Court are the most striking and best preserved.

The unique **Pirámide de los Nichos** is the most famous building at El Tajín, and indeed one of the most remarkable and enigmatic of all Mexican ruins. It rises to a height of about 20m in six receding tiers, each face punctuated with regularly spaced niches; up the front a steep stairway climbs to a platform on which the temple originally stood. If you tally up the niches, including those hidden by the stairs and those, partly destroyed, around the base of the temple, there are 365 in all. Their exact purpose is unknown, but clearly they were more than mere decoration: perhaps each would hold some offering or sacrifice, one for each day of the year, or they may have symbolized caves – the dwellings of the earth god. Originally they were painted deep red, with a blue surround, to enhance the impression of depth. Niches predominate on other buildings at the site, and some bear the attribute of Quetzalcoatl, the plumed serpent, Tajín's most depicted god.

Around the plaza in front of the pyramid stand all the other important buildings of Tajín Viejo. Opposite is Monumento 3, a similar pyramid without the niches, and behind it Monumento 23, a strange steep-sided bulk, one of the last structures to be built here. To the right of the Pirámide de los Nichos, Monumento 2, a low temple, squats at the base of Monumento 5, a beautiful truncated pyramid with a high decorative pediment broken by a broad staircase; on the left, Monumento 4 is one of the oldest in El Tajín, and only partly restored.

From the back of Monumento 4 the path continues, past the **Juego de Pelota Norte** with its worn relief sculptures, up onto the levelled terrace of **Tajín Chico**. Originally this raised area was supported by a retaining wall, part of which has been restored, and reached by a staircase opposite the ball-court. Only parts of the buildings now survive, making a rather confusing whole. **Estructura C**, and the adjoining Estructura B, are the most impressive remains: Estructura C has stone friezes running around its three storeys, giving the impression of niches. In this case, they were purely decorative, an effect that would have been heightened by a brightly coloured stucco finish. It has, too, the remains of a concrete roof – originally a huge single slab of poured cement, unique in ancient Mexico. **Estructura A** also had a covered interior, and you can still get into its central terrace via a narrow staircase, the entrance covered by a false arch of the type common in Maya buildings. On the hill above Tajín Chico stood the **Edificio de las Columnas**, which must have dominated the entire city. Here El Tajín's governor, 13 Rabbit, lived – bas-reliefs on columns recorded his exploits, and some of these are now on show in the museum. The building is little restored, and bits of broken, pre-Columbian pottery litter the area, but you can clamber to the top for a fine view over the site.

Practicalities

The easiest way to **get to El Tajín** from Papantla is to take one of the camionetas that regularly leave from behind the *Hotel Tajín*; alternatively a bus from the second-class terminal will take you to **Chote**, where you can change. There are also buses direct from El Tajín, or from Chote, to **Poza Rica** (marked "El Chote" and "San Andrés"), where you can connect with services to México as well as up or down the coast. In itself, though, Poza Rica is not a place of any delights – a dull, oil-boom city with something of a reputation for violence. If you are continuing northwards, you'd be much better off in Tuxpán, about an hour up the coast.

Tuxpán

Straddling the river of the same name, the town of **TUXPÁN** (or Tuxpam, pronounced "Toosh-pam") offers a far preferable overnight stay to its uglier southern neighbour, Poza Rica, on the journey up the coast to Tampico (see p.149). That said, it's an unattractive place, its oblong concrete houses offering slim shade to barking dogs, in a landscape further marred by half-built oil platforms.

The zócalo and marketplace both spill out onto the north river bank. Small boats shuttle you from here across the river to the town's single most interesting attraction, the **Museo de la Amistad Mexico–Cuba** (Mon–Sat 8am–4.30pm, Sun 8am–3pm; free). Occupying the house where Fidel Castro spent a year planning his revolutionary return to Cuba, the museum focuses on Castro, Che Guevara and Spanish imperialism in the Americas in general. The revolutionaries sailed from Tuxpán in December 1956 in the *Granma*, almost sinking on the way, and arrived in Cuba to find Batista's forces waiting. A replica of the *Granma* stands on the river bank. To get there, walk inland a couple of blocks to Obregón then turn right, heading back to the river at the end of the street.

Tuxpán's only other attraction are some long, if mediocre, beaches at **Barra de Tuxpán**, by the river mouth some 12km east of town. **Buses** (marked "Playa") run all day along riverside Reforma, past fishing boats and tankers, and arrive twenty minutes later at a vast stretch of grey sand. There are restaurants and changing rooms here and some palapas where you can sling a hammock.

Practicalities

The first-class ADO terminal lies at the junction of Reforma and Rodríguez, one block from the river and some 300m east of the zócalo – follow the river along Reforma to get to the centre. Omnibus de México (with both first- and second-class services) is not far away – 300m further east beside the huge bridge across the river.

Moving on, there's at least one ADO **bus** an hour to Tampico, Veracruz and México (via Poza Rica), and there are eight a day to Papantla. Buses for the nearby village of Tamiahua (see below) leave every hour or so from the Omnibus de México terminal.

The helpful **tourist office** (Mon–Fri 9am–5.30pm; ☎783/4-01-77, fax 4-64-07) is on the zócalo, at Juárez 20. There's a **laundry** next door to the *Café Bohemio*, on Ocampo. **Change money** or travellers' cheques at the Bancomer or Banamex, both on Juárez.

The best **places to stay** in town are the cheap *Tuxpán* (☎783/4-41-10; ②), Juárez at Mina, and the more expensive *Reforma*, Juárez 25 (☎783/4-02-10, fax 4-06-25; ⑤), which has a/c rooms with TV, as well as the best restaurant in town. Alternatively, cheap **restaurants** line Juárez, while the *Nuevo 303* on Pipila, leading down from Juárez to the river, is popular with locals. *Café Bohemio*, Ocampo 6, just west of the zócalo, serves good-value breakfasts and tasty cakes.

South of Veracruz

Leaving Veracruz to the south, Hwy-180 traverses a long expanse of plain, a country of broad river deltas and salt lagoons, for nearly 150km, until it hits the hills of the volcanic **Sierra Tuxtla**. This is one of the most beautiful stretches of Veracruz, boasting picturesque **fishing villages**, **volcanoes**, **waterfalls** and the idyllic **Lake Catemaco**, around which the last expanse of Gulf Coast **rainforest** is preserved. The region is most important, however, as the birthplace of Mexico's first civilization, the **Olmecs**. Here lies the sacred mountain – the **Volcán de San Martín** – which the Olmecs believed to be the place where the world was created; they built a replica "creation mountain" at their city, La Venta, on the border with Tabasco (see p.503). Although archeologically important, their second major city at **Tres Zapotes**, near Santiago Tuxtla, is little more than a mound in a maize field – and virtually impossible to get to without your own transport. Beyond the Tuxtla mountains, there's more low, flat, dull country all the way to Villahermosa (see p.496).

Alvarado and Tlacotalpan

ALVARADO is the first stop en route south from Veracruz, an extraordinary town on a narrow strip of land between the sea and the Laguna de Alvarado, some 70km from Veracruz. It's a working fishing port, and as such a real slice of old-fashioned Mexico: as soon as the bus pulls in to the raucous main street, it's invaded by people selling the most extraordinary variety of food, drink and souvenirs. There are plenty of hotels in sight, but it's not somewhere you'd want to stay long. You might, however, be tempted to stop for a meal – the fishing fleet is enormous and there are lots of good fish **restaurants** along the front. Alvarado's Port Authority restaurant, especially, is famed for its excellence and is also cheap, since it is genuinely used by port workers and fishermen.

If you want somewhere small, quiet, and entirely off the tourist circuit to stay, try instead **TLACOTALPAN**, some twenty minutes away on the spectacular road that heads inland towards Tuxtepec and eventually Oaxaca. Still on the edges of the Río Papaloapan, close to the lagoon, it's a very pretty village, and although there's absolutely nothing laid on, you can rent boats on the river, and fish or swim. There are a couple of small hotels on the main street near where the buses stop, but avoid the posada, which doubles as a brothel.

Los dos Tuxtlas

The two townships of **Santiago Tuxtla** and **San Andrés Tuxtla** together form the hub of the attractive, volcanic hill country that emerges beyond Alvarado. Things become much more interesting at this point, and the cooler climate is an infinite relief.

San Andrés Tuxtla

SAN ANDRÉS TUXTLA is the larger of the two Tuxtlas, and the one where most buses will drop you (many long-distance services pull in here for a brief stop). The majority of buses stop at the top of the hill where the highway passes by – the first-class bus terminal is a short way into town from here, at the top of Juárez, which leads straight down to the zócalo. Other, second-class buses will drop you by the market, again within easy walking distance of the centre.

Local buses run from here to Santiago Tuxtla and Catemaco, but there are a couple of more local attractions. **La Laguna Encantada** is a volcanic lake about 2km from the town and a popular local swimming spot. It can be reached in less than an hour on foot: follow Belisario Dominguez to the top where it crosses the highway, turn right (towards Catemaco), and after a couple of hundred metres a signed path leads up to the left. Be sure to go in a group, however, as locals persistently warn of armed robberies. The spectacular **Salto de Eyipantla** is a little further afield, but served by frequent local buses that leave from 5 de Mayo where it meets the market. This series of three waterfalls, reached down 244 worn steps from a car park, is a beautiful spot, but can get packed out in summer.

Most **accommodation** and other facilities are very close to the zócalo or on Juárez: the *Catedral* (☎294/2-02-37; ②), on Pino Suárez (reached via the alley beside the church), is clean and friendly, or you could try the *Colonial* (☎294/2-05-52; ②), or *Figueroa* (☎294/2-02-57; ③), one block away at the corner of Suárez and Belisario Dominguez. All are very basic, but good value for the money. A number of fancier hotels are visible from the square: the *San Andrés* (☎294/2-06-04; ④), at Madero 6, is the most reasonable, with the *Hotel de los Pérez* (☎294/2-07-77, fax 2-36-46; ④), Rascon 2, a little classier and pricier. **Food** options include cafés on the zócalo and a number of reputable fish and seafood restaurants along Madero, past the *San Andrés – Mariscos Chazaro*, at no. 12, is good – and others up by the first-class bus terminal. There's an excellent **market**, too.

Santiago Tuxtla and Tres Zapotes

SANTIAGO TUXTLA is considerably quieter, and demands something more of an effort to visit, since it lies a little distance from the highway and many buses simply ignore the place – though there are very frequent connections with San Andrés. A giant Olmec head stands in the centre of the zócalo, on one side of which is a small museum of local archeology and ethnography (Tues–Sat 9am–6pm, Sun 9am–3pm; US$2). Although Santiago is itself a beautiful spot, the main reason people come here is to visit the important Olmec site of **Tres Zapotes**, a little less than an hour away by local bus. Frankly, the journey is barely worth it, a painfully slow ride by unreliable bus (or taxi) to what is basically just a **museum** (daily 9am–4pm; US$2) containing little that is not duplicated elsewhere. Its main interest lies in a series of stelae inscribed with Olmec glyphs. Of the site itself, nearby, virtually nothing can be seen.

There are a couple of small **hotels** in town, including the remarkably good *Castellanos* (☎294/7-03-00; ④), right on the zócalo with all facilities, as well as some cheaper places – and plenty of **restaurants** and cafés, again around the zócalo.

Catemaco and around

Squatting on the shore of a large, mountain-ringed lake – by tradition a centre of native witchcraft – **CATEMACO** is a much more picturesque spot to break the journey before the long leg south. Veracruzanos arrive in force at weekends and holidays, but it's little spoiled for all that – although hotels can be expensive. Watch out for the touts, though, who'll try and persuade you to attend a native spiritual purification ceremony or to visit the place where Sean Connery's *Medicine Man* was filmed.

There isn't a great deal to do here – haggle at the dock over the price of a boat-trip round the lake or to one of the islands, or visit the local waterfall or one of the lake beaches – but it's no less appealing for that. The only tourist sight is the **Basilica de Nuestra Señora del Carmen**, decorated with multicoloured tiles. The original statue of the Virgen del Carmen can be seen in a narrow grotto in El Tegal, around twenty minutes' walk around the lakeshore. A local bus from the plaza (marked "La Margarita") goes round much of the shore, passing a couple of beaches and the beautiful Río Cuetzalpan.

An appalling road leads from Catemaco, through ranchland only recently chopped out of the rainforest, to **the coast**, where you'll find some of Veracruz's best, tourist-free, beaches. At **Montepio**, there are a couple of posadas (③), the better of which is nearer the sea. There's also a more expensive hotel at **Playa Escondida**, a beautiful beach some 15km from Montepio. Camionetas leave Catemaco from C Lerdo at Revolucion, five blocks from the lakeshore, every fifty minutes and take more than two hours to make the 38km journey (about US$2) to Montepio.

Practicalities

Catemaco is slightly off the main road, and although there are some direct **buses** from Veracruz, there's no need to make a special effort to get one, as local services from San Andrés regularly make the short journey back and forth. **Moving on**, second-class buses depart the AU terminal on 2 de Abril for all the main towns in western Mexico; try to buy tickets a day in advance, since seats are numbered. On the zócalo, Comermex **bank** (Mon–Fri 10am–1pm), changes travellers' cheques, while the **post office** is just round the corner towards the *Hotel Juros*.

On the whole, **hotels** right on the lake are expensive, though out of season prices do drop. Otherwise, there are several places a couple of streets inland, just down from where the buses stop: people may try to accost you as you arrive to take you to a hotel, but rooms are easy enough to find without help. On the lakeside very close to the centre, *Julita* (☎294/3-00-08; ③), Av Playa 10, offers simple, clean rooms with fans and is probably the best value in town; further along, at no. 14, *Juros* (☎294/3-00-84; ④) has a fantastic rooftop swimming pool, but rooms vary in quality. *Los Arcos* (☎294/3-00-03; ⑤), next door to the *Juros*, at Madero 7 and Mantillo, has pleasant rooms with fans and TV, while *Catemaco* (☎294/3-00-45; ⑤), on the zócalo opposite Comermex, offers a/c, TV, a pool and restaurant. The *Hotel del Lago* (☎294/3-01-60; ⑤), Paseo del Malecón, on the lakeside at the edge of the village on the Tuxtla road, is a secure, friendly place with small, clean rooms with a/c, a palm-ringed pool and restaurant. By far the best place to stay if you want to appreciate the area's natural beauty, however, is *Nanciyaga* (☎ & fax 294/3-01-99), an eco-tourist facility on the far shore of the lake, little visited by Westerners and a great place to meet young Veracruzanos; cabañas in the jungle (④) have room for up to four people. The organizers rent canoes, arrange guided walks through the forest and teach traditional Mexican arts and crafts. You can also undergo a cleansing in a **Temazcal**, a traditional Mesoamerican sauna that purifies body and soul. It's only 7km by taxi to *Nanciyaga*; you can also get there by launch.

Seafood **restaurants** abound on the shore and around the zócalo, most offering the local speciality, *mojarra* (small perch from the lake), best sampled when cooked *a la* *tachagobi* – with a delicious hot sauce. One of the best deals is the comida corrida in the *Restaurant Aloha*, on the lakeshore.

Coatzacoalcos and Acayucán

The **northern shore** of the Isthmus of Tehuantepec – the narrowest part of Mexico – is less attractive, with a huge industrial zone stretching from the dirty concrete town of Minatitlán to **COATZACOALCOS** (formerly Puerto México, the Atlantic railway terminus), dominated by a giant oil refinery. If you have to stop here, Coatzacoalcos is definitely the better choice: big enough to have a real centre and with plenty of hotels and restaurants around the Camionera. Coatzacoalcos also boasts a spectacular modern bridge – known as Coatzacoalcos II – by which the main highway bypasses the town. If you're on a bus heading downtown you'll cross the Río Coatzacoalcos by an older, lesser suspension bridge. In legend, Coatzacoalcos is the place from which Quetzalcoatl and his followers sailed east, vowing to return.

Crossing the north of the Isthmus you'll also inevitably pass through **ACAYUCÁN**, where the coastal highway and the trans-Isthmus highway meet. The enormous bus station and equally giant market cater for all the passing travellers; there's little otherwise but mud or dust. Make your visit a short one and, if you have any choice at all, press straight on through to Villahermosa (see p.496). If you do need to **stay**, go for the *Joalicia*, at Zaragoza 4 on the zócalo (☎924/5-08-77; ④), or the more luxurious *Kikadu*, Ocampo Sur 7 (☎924/5-04-10; ⑤), just off the zócalo.

FIESTAS

JANUARY

In the last week of January **Tlacotalpan** has a fiesta with dances, boat races and bulls let loose in the streets.

FEBRUARY

2 DÍA DE LA CANDELARIA. Colourful Indian fiesta in **Jaltipán** on the main road south of Catemaco, which includes the dance of *La Malinche* (Malintzin, Cortés' Indian interpreter, known to the Spanish as Malinche, is said to have been born here), recreating aspects of the Conquest. Also the final day of celebrations in **Tlacotalpan**.

4 Agricultural festival in **Otatitlán**, near the Oaxaca border off the road from Alvarado to Oaxaca, where many Indians attend a midnight mass to bless their crops.

CARNIVAL (the week before Lent, variable Feb–March) is celebrated all over the region, most riotously in **Veracruz**.

MARCH

On the first Friday, the FERIA DEL CAFÉ in **Ixhualtán**, a coffee-growing town near Córdoba – both trade fair and popular fiesta.

18–19 FIESTAS DE SAN JOSÉ. In **Naranjos**, between Tuxpán and Tampico, a fiesta with many traditional dances celebrates the local patron saint. Similar events in **Espinal**, a Totonac village on the Río Tecolutla, not far from Papantla and El Tajín, where with luck you can witness the spectacular *Voladores*.

HOLY WEEK. Recreations of the Passion are widespread in this area. You can witness them in **Papantla** – where you'll also see the *Voladores* – in **Coatzintla**, a Totonac village near Tajín, in **Cotaxtla**, between Veracruz and Córdoba, and in **Otatitlán**. **Naolinco**, a beautiful village near Jalapa, stages a mock crucifixion on Good Friday. Also celebrations in **Catemaco** – and in the port of **Alvarado** – a far more ribald Fish Fiesta following hard on the heels of the Veracruz Carnival.

APRIL

15–17 (approx.) FERIA DE LAS FLO-RES. Flower festival in **Fortín de las Flores**.

MAY

3 Hundreds of pilgrims converge on **Otatitlán** to pay homage to the village's *Cristo Negro*.

27 DÍA DEL SAGRADO CORAZON. The start of four days of festivities in **Naranjos**.

CORPUS CHRISTI (variable, the Thursday after Trinity) sees the start of a major four-day festival in **Papantla** and, in particular, regular performances by the *Voladores*.

JUNE

13 DÍA DE SAN ANTONIO. Fiesta in **Huatusco**, between Córdoba and Veracruz.

24 DÍA DE SAN JUAN celebrated in **Santiago Tuxtla**, with dancing, and in **Martinez de la Torre**, on the road inland from Nautla, where the *Voladores* perform.

JULY

15 DÍA DE LA VIRGEN DEL CARMEN. A massive pilgrimage to **Catemaco**, accompanied by a fiesta which spills over into the following day.

24 DÍA DE SANTIAGO is celebrated with fiestas in **Santiago Tuxtla** and **Coatzintla**; each lasts several days. In **Tlapacoyan** you can see the bizarre *Baile de los Negritos*.

AUGUST

14 Teocelo, a village in beautiful country between Jalapa and Fortín, celebrates an ancient fiesta with dance and music.

15 In **Tuxpán**, a week-long feria begins, and includes dancing and *Voladores*.

16 In **Tlapacoyan**, the *Baile de los Negritos* is held to commemorate the Day of the Assumption.

24 Córdoba celebrates the anniversary of the signing of the Treaty of Independence.

SEPTEMBER

15–16 Independence celebrations take place everywhere.

21 DÍA DE SAN MATEO sees secular as well as religious celebration in **Naolinco**.

30 Coatepec, between Jalapa and Fortín, celebrates its patron's day – processions and dances.

OCTOBER

7 FIESTA DE LA VIRGEN DEL ROSARIO, patroness of fishermen. In **La Antigua** she is honoured with processions of canoes on the river, while **Alvarado** enjoys a more earthy fiesta, filling the first two weeks of the month.

NOVEMBER

2 DAY OF THE DEAD is honoured everywhere – the rites are particularly strictly followed in **Naolinco**.

30 Fiestas in **San Andrés Tuxtla**, carrying on into December 1.

DECEMBER

12 DÍA DE LA VIRGEN DE GUADALUPE widely observed, especially in **Huatusco**, **Cotaxtla**, and **Amatlán de los Reyes**, near Córdoba.

24 Christmas, of course, celebrated in **Santiago Tuxtla** with a very famous festival that lasts until Twelfth Night – January 6.

travel details

BUSES

First-class buses are mostly operated by Autobuses del Oriente (ADO) – remarkably slick and efficient. Second-class is dominated (at least on long hauls) by Autobuses Unidos (AU), more of a mixed bag. The following is a brief rundown of the routes, and should be taken as a minimum.

Jalapa to: México (8 daily; 6hr 30min); Papantla (4 daily; 3hr); Tlapacoyan; Veracruz (frequently; 2hr 30min).

Poza Rica to: México (8 daily; 5hr); Tuxpán (frequently; 1hr); Veracruz (10 daily; 4hr 30min).

Tuxpán to: Jalapa (7 daily; 6hr); México (9 daily; 6hr); Poza Rica (frequently; 1hr); Tampico (10 daily; 3hr); Veracruz (6 daily; 5hr 30min).

Papantla to: México (6 daily; 6hr); Poza Rica (frequently; 30min); Tlapacoyan (4 daily; 3hr); Tuxpán (8 daily; 1hr); Veracruz (6 daily; 5hr).

Veracruz to: Coatzacoalcos (10 daily; 5hr 30min); Córdoba (15 daily; 2hr 30min); Jalapa (frequently; 2hr 30min); México (15 daily; 8hr); Oaxaca (4 daily; at least 8hr); Orizaba (15 daily; 3hr 30min); Papantla (10 daily; 4hr); Poza Rica (10 daily; 4hr 30min); San Andrés Tuxtla (10 daily; 3hr); Villahermosa (10 daily; 7hr)

TRAINS

From Veracruz, two trains daily (departing 10am and 10pm) make the nine-hour journey **to México** via Cordoba, Fortín and Orizaba, while a single, morning train (8.14am) makes the ten-hour journey three days a week (Tues, Thurs & Sat) from Veracruz to México via Jalapa. A daily service also operates from **Veracruz to Tapachula**, on the border with Guatemala – a gruelling 24hr journey.

PLANES

There are regular flights to **México** from Veracruz, and three a week from Poza Rica. There are also flights available from Veracruz to **Oaxaca** and **Cancún**, but the schedules regularly change. The tourist office or travel agents in Veracruz or Jalapa can provide you with the latest information.

CHAPTER EIGHT

OAXACA

The state of **Oaxaca** (pronounced "wa-*ha*-ka") marks the break between North American central Mexico and Central America. Here the two chains of the Sierra Madre converge, to run on as a single range, through the country's narrowest point, the Isthmus of Tehuantepec, right into South America and the Andes. The often barren landscapes of northern Mexico are left behind, replaced by thickly forested hillsides, or in low-lying areas by swamp and jungle. It is all very much closer to a Central American experience than anything that has gone before, a feeling compounded by the relative lack of development – the Mexican economic "miracle" has yet fully to transform the south.

Indigenous traditions remain powerful in this area. The old tongues are still widely spoken, and there are scenes in the villages which seem to deny that the Spanish Conquest ever happened. Oaxaqueño resourcefulness, pride and craft skills are manifest everywhere. For the colour and variety of its markets, and the fascination of its fiestas, there is no rival in Mexico. One of Oaxaca's most rewarding and eye-opening experiences can be a stay in one of the central valleys' **Tourist Yú'ù** facilities, where you'll

be a guest of the local indigenous community. Less enticingly, but arising out of the same traditions, the region has witnessed considerable **political disturbance** in recent years, though protest has never been as manifest as in its more troubled neighbour, Chiapas.

The laid-back city of **Oaxaca** itself is the prime destination, close enough to México and the mainstream to attract large numbers of tourists to its fine crafts stores, markets and seemingly constant fiestas. Here you can see one of the region's – and the whole of Iberian America's – most magnificent **Baroque churches**, others of which proliferate across the state, fusing Spanish and native influences. From the earliest times the valley of Oaxaca was inhabited by the same Zapotec and Mixtec peoples who comprise the bulk of its population now. Their ancient sites – at **Monte Albán**, **Yagul** and **Mitla** – are less well known than their contemporaries in central and eastern Mexico, but every bit as important and impressive.

The growing Pacific resorts of **Puerto Escondido**, **Puerto Ángel** and **Huatulco** are also easily reached from the city. Their reputation for being unspoiled beach paradises is no longer entirely justified – Escondido in particular is a resort of some size, with an international airport, and there's another huge resort under construction at Huatulco. All along this coast you'll discover some of the emptiest and best **Pacific beaches** in Mexico, easily reached from the main centres.

The resorts are all around 250km from Oaxaca, reached via spectacular mountain roads that take a minimum of six hours to traverse. Although there are regular **buses** to **Pochutla**, just inland from Puerto Ángel, and thence on to Puerto Escondido, it's a slow and occasionally heart-stopping journey. Many people prefer to **fly** down, either with Aeromorelos from Oaxaca to Escondido – an experience in itself – or with Mexicana direct from México to Escondido or Huatulco. There are also regular bus connections along the coast, from Acapulco in the north or Salina Cruz in the south, and a direct overnight service between México and Puerto Escondido.

Getting there from México

There are two routes to Oaxaca **from México**. The first, via **Hwy-135**, which links to the México–Puebla–Córdoba autopista, takes only five hours and is the more travelled route. The slower, ten-hour, journey on **Hwy-190** passes through the spa town of **Cuautla**, remarkable only as the birthplace of Emiliano Zapata, and **Huajapan de León**, a town of little interest but marking the beginning of *mescal*-producing territory, with spiny, bluish-green maguey cactuses cultivated all around the road. This also marks the beginning of the **Mixteca**, one of the State's most interesting regions. On the side road that leads from here to the spa town of Tehuacán, you pass through one of the largest and most impressive **cactus forests** in the republic. Both routes take in some interesting mountain scenery (particularly the autopista), with cacti and scrub in the early stages giving way to thicker vegetation as you approach Oaxaca, and both are well served by buses.

To reach Oaxaca **from Acapulco**, it's probably quicker to go through México, but there are relatively frequent buses up from the Pacific coast at **Pinotepa Nacional**; more frequently, and equally uncomfortably, from **Puerto Escondido** or Pochutla, the service town for **Puerto Ángel**. That said, if you are travelling along the Pacific coast, it seems a pity to miss out on the region's excellent beaches just to get to Oaxaca quickly.

Tehuacán

The only place that merits a stop as you speed down the autopista from México to Oaxaca is **TEHUACÁN**, the source of the bulk of the bottled mineral water (*Agua de Tehuacán*) consumed throughout Mexico. A spa town of some antiquity, relaxing, easy-paced, temperate in every sense of the word, its centre is dotted with buildings from the town's early-twentieth-century heyday. The tiled arcade-fronted house on the zócalo, with its Moorish flourishes, was obviously designed with Vichy or Evian in mind and bears a plaque to Señor Don Joaquim Pita, who first put the water in bottles. Take a look, too, at the underside of the colonnade for highly graphic murals depicting the five regions that make up Tehuacán district. A more pedestrian introduction to the region fills the halls of the **Museo del Valle de Tehuacán** (Tues–Sun 10am–5pm; US$1), at Reforma Nte 200 in the elegant ex-Convento de Carmen, featuring a brightly coloured tiled dome that dominates the skyline in this part of town. A tiny collection of prehistoric relics shores up the thinly illustrated story of maize in Mesoamerica and particularly in the Tehuacán valley, which was the first place to truly cultivate (rather than simply harvest) the crop some six or seven thousand years ago – ample evidence that this was one of the earliest inhabited areas in Mexico.

All this can be seen in a couple of hours, but if you decide to stay in town you can fill the time by heading out to the **springs** on the outskirts to sample the clean-tasting water, or take a dip at **Balneario Ejidal San Lorenzo** (daily 6.30am–6pm; US$2), a large complex of sun-warmed pools (including one Olympic-sized affair), most of which use the local springs. Catch a bus from the Autobuses Unidos bus station to San Lorenzo, a suburb 5km west of the centre.

Practicalities

Most **long-distance buses** arrive at the ADO station on Independencia, two blocks west of the zócalo. Second-class buses from México, Oaxaca and elsewhere arrive at the Autobuses Unidos station near the junction of C 5 Ote and C 5 Sur, on the opposite side of the centre. Independencia runs all the way out to the suburb of San Lorenzo, past ADO and the **train station** (☎238/2-11-34), seven blocks from the centre: services to Oaxaca leave at 3am and 10am, to Puebla at 1.30am and 3pm, the former continuing to the capital.

The best-value **place to stay** in Tehuacán is the *Hotel Montecarlo* (☎238/3-19-41; ④), five blocks out at Reforma Nte 400, with a pool, parking and large clean rooms around a huge garden. *Hotel México*, Independencia at Reforma, one block west of the zócalo (☎238/2-25-19; ⑥), is considerably more luxurious, and there's a good budget choice, the *Hotel Madrid*, C 3 Sur 105 (☎238/3-15-24; ③), with gardens, a parrot and somewhat overpriced en-suite rooms – go for those without bathrooms. **Banks** (with ATMs) and other services are mostly on Reforma.

Oaxaca

The state-capital **OAXACA** sprawls across a grand expanse of deep-set valley, 1600m above sea level, some 500km southeast of México. Its colour, its folklore, the huge extent of its native market and its thoroughly colonial centre combine to make this one of the most popular, and most rewarding, destinations for travellers. Even the increase in package tourism and the pedestrianization of Macedonia Alcalá, the main thoroughfare from the zócalo to the cathedral, a street now lined with high-class handicraft and jewellery shops, have done little to destroy the city's gentle appeal.

Increasingly, it's becoming an **industrial** city – the population is well over 200,000, the streets choked and noisy – yet it seems set to remain easy to handle. In the centre, thanks to strict building regulations, the provincial charm is hardly affected, and just about everything can be reached on foot. Provincial it remains, too, in its habits – the big excitements are dawdling in a café, or gathering in the plaza to stroll and listen to the town band; by eleven at night the city is asleep.

Once central to the **Mixtec** and **Zapotec** civilizations, the city later took a lesser role. Cortés, attracted by the area's natural beauties, took the title of *Marques del Valle de Oaxaca*, and until the Revolution his descendants held vast estates hereabouts. But for practical purposes, Oaxaca was of little interest to the Spanish, with no mineral wealth and no great joy for farmers (though coffee was grown). The indigenous population was left to get on with life far more than was generally the case, with only the interference of a proselytizing Church to put up with. The city's most famous son, **Benito Juárez**, is commemorated everywhere in Oaxaca, a privilege not shared by **Porfirio Díaz**, the second most famous Oaxaqueño, whose dictatorship most people choose to forget.

Arrival, information and city transport

Both **bus stations** in Oaxaca are a good way from the centre – at least twenty minutes' walk. First-class (with guardería) is on Calzada Niños Héroes de Chapultepec, north of the centre, from where your best bet is to get a taxi in: if you're absolutely determined

BENITO JUÁREZ

Despite the blunder and poor judgement of his later years, **Benito Juárez** ranks among Mexico's greatest national heroes. He was *the* towering figure of nineteenth-century Mexican politics, and his maxim "El respeto al derecho ajeno es la paz" – the respect of the rights of others is peace – has been a rallying cry for liberals ever since. A **Zapotec**, he strove against nineteenth-century social prejudices and, through four terms as president, successfully reformed many of the worst social remnants of Spanish colonialism, earning a reputation for honesty and fair dealing.

Juárez was born outside the city, at San Pablo Guelatao, in 1806. His parents died when he was three, and he grew up speaking only Zapotec; at the age of twelve he was adopted by priests and moved to Oaxaca, where he was educated. Turning his talents to law, he provided his legal services free to impoverished villagers, and by 1831 had earned a seat on Oaxaca's municipal council, lending voice to a disenfranchised people. Juárez rose through the ranks of the city council to become **state governor** from 1847 to 1852, on a liberal ticket geared towards improving education and releasing the country from the economic and social stranglehold of the Church and aristocracy. In 1853 the election of a conservative government under Santa Ana forced him into eighteen months of exile in the USA.

Liberal victory in 1855 enabled Juárez to return to Mexico as minister of justice and lend his name to a law abolishing special courts for the military and clergy. His support was instrumental in passing the **Ley Lerdo**, which effectively nationalized the Church's huge holdings, and bills legalizing civil marriage and guaranteeing religious freedom. In 1858, President Ignacio Comonfort was ousted by conservatives enraged by these reforms, and Juárez, as the head of the Supreme Court, had a legal claim to the presidency. However, he lacked the military might to hold México and retired to Veracruz, returning three years later, victorious in the War of Reform, as **constitutionally elected president** for further attempts to reduce the power of the Church. Hog-tied by an intractable Congress and empty coffers, Juárez suspended all debt repayments for two years from July 1861. To protect their investments, the British, Spanish and French sent their armies in, but when it became apparent that Napoleon III had designs on control of Mexico, the others pulled out leaving France to install Habsburg Archduke **Maximilian** as puppet emperor. Juárez fled again, this time to Ciudad Juárez on the US border, but by 1867 Napoleon III had buckled under Mexican resistance and US pressure, and Juárez was able to return to the capital and his army to round up and execute the hapless Maximilian.

Juárez was returned as president at the **1867 elections** but alienated much of his support by unconstitutional attempts to use Congress to amend the constitution. Nevertheless, he was able to secure another term in the 1870 elections, spending two more years trying unsuccessfully to maintain peace before dying of a heart attack in 1872.

to walk, turn left along the main road about four blocks to Av Juárez, left again for nine or ten blocks to Independencia or Hidalgo, then right to the zócalo. On Juárez you can start to pick up city buses. The second-class terminal – where you'll find a **casa de cambio** with good rates (daily 9am–7pm) and a guardería (6am–9pm) – is west of the centre by the new market buildings: walk past these, across the train tracks and the *Periferico*, and on up Trujano towards the centre. The **train station** is still further out, but from here there is a good bus service ("Colonia Reforma"/"Santa Rosa"/"Centro") that will take you right into the centre. From the **airport**, 5km south of the city, a colectivo service (Transportacion Terrestre Aeropuerto) will drop you right by the zócalo for under two dollars. On **leaving** (see p.427), you should buy tickets in advance wherever possible – especially for early morning departures on popular routes, to México or to San Cristóbal.

Information

Oaxaca's chief **tourist office** (Mon–Fri 9am–3pm & 6–8pm, Sat 9am–2pm; ☎951/6-09-84, fax 6-15-00) is inside the Palacio Municipal, on Independencia opposite the Alameda, with another branch (daily 9am–8pm; ☎951/6-48-28) at 5 de Mayo 200, on the corner of Morelos. Both are extremely helpful, and well worth visiting if you want to discover little known areas of the state. They have piles of maps, leaflets and other handouts, including two free monthly **English-language newspapers**, the *Oaxaca Times* and *Oaxaca*, both of which have topical features and useful events listings.

Casas de cambio litter the centre of town – the ones on the zócalo, at Hidalgo 820 and at Alcalá 100-A all give near identical rates to the banks and also open longer hours (usually daily 8am–8pm). Some of them change European currencies but at insulting rates. Most **banks** have ATMs and are open for foreign exchange from 9am to 12.30pm. The **American Express** office, on the zócalo at the corner of Hidalgo and Valdivieso (Mon–Fri 9am–2pm & 4–8pm; ☎951/6-27-00), generally offers poor rates.

The **post office** (Mon–Fri 9am–7pm, Sat 9am–1pm), also on Independencia, by the Alameda, shelters a row of Ladatel **phones** for collect calls. There are plenty more all over Oaxaca, and a Computel place at Trujano 204, just west of the zócalo. You can get a reasonable selection of new and second-hand **English-language books** (including some on local history, Mexican architecture and religion) from the Librería Universitaria, Guerrero 108, just off the zócalo (Mon–Sat 9.30am–2pm & 4–8pm), or try the main library, the Biblioteca Circulante de Oaxaca, Alcalá 305 (Mon–Fri 10am–1pm & 4–7pm, Sat 10am–1pm), between Matamoros and Bravo, or the excellent, predominantly arts library at the Graphic Arts Institute, Alcalá 507. There are a number of **Internet cafés**, including the beautifully set *Milenium Cybercafé*, near the church of Santo Domingo at 5 de Mayo 412 (Mon–Sat 10am–2pm & 4–8pm, ☎951/4-80-24, *milenium@infosel.net.mx*). They also have a copy and printing service and rent out computers.

Oaxaca is an excellent place to live as a student. **Spanish classes** can be arranged through Centro de Idiomas at the Benito Juárez University of Oaxaca (☎ & fax 951/6-59-22). Write to them at Centro de Idiomas, Burgoa s/n, Oaxaca, Oaxaca 68000. You can also do courses in Latin American literature and Mexican civilization and culture. You'll find the **best postcards** in town at Distribudora Lumy, at 5 de Mayo 143, near Santo Domingo.

City transport

Walking is by far the best way of getting around compact Oaxaca. The **bus** routes are Byzantine in their complexity and once you've hopped on the right one the traffic is so slow that you could have taken a pleasant stroll to your destination in half the time. **Taxis** are a better bet; they can be found on Independencia near the cathedral, or flagged down anywhere.

Getting out to the sites around the valley is a different matter. Buses from the second-class bus station are frequent . There are also vast numbers of **colectivos** heading for destinations all over the state. These depart, when full, from various points around the city (ask the tourist office), mostly from outside the new market, and are only a little more expensive. **Car rental** is as expensive here as everywhere in the country, but if you are planning extensive exploration of the valley may prove worthwhile, allowing you to take a week of long waits for a couple of days of independence. In town, try Arrendadora Express, 20 Novembre 204A (☎ & fax 951/6-67-76), who are cheap and reliable – they charge US$40 a day for a VW Beetle, have a number of other cars and motorbikes, and also rent mountain bikes (US$6.50 per day).

Accommodation

Although there are hundreds of **hotels** in Oaxaca, there are thousands of visitors, and if you arrive late you may well have difficulty finding a room. Under such circum-

---

ACCOMMODATION PRICE CODES

All the accommodation listed in this book has been categorized into one of nine price bands, as set out below. The prices quoted are in US dollars and normally refer to the cheapest available room for two people sharing in high season. For more details, see p.36.

① up to US$5	④ US$15–25	⑦ US$60–80
② US$5–10	⑤ US$25–40	⑧ US$80–100
③ US$10–15	⑥ US$40–60	⑨ US$100 and over

---

stances, it's best to take anything that's offered and look for something better the next morning. Alternatively, call at the main tourist office and consult their list of **families** who take in guests on a daily basis (usually around US$10 per person), or try the 5 de Mayo branch for a list of **apartments**, many of them fairly central, which also charge around US$10 per person.

The bulk of the **cheaper places** are south of Independencia, especially between the old market and C Trujano: Trujano, Díaz Ordaz, García and Aldama all have a multitude of possibilities. Closer to the **zócalo** and to the north, both prices and quality tend to be rather higher, though there are some surprisingly good-value places. Prices in general drop by ten to twenty percent outside the Christmas, *Semana Santa*, July and August high season.

The only **campsite** anywhere near town is Trailer Park Oaxaca (☎951/5-27-96; US$10), just over 3km north of the centre at the corner of Heroica Escuela Naval Militar and Violetas: follow Niños Héroes east five blocks from the first-class bus station and turn left up Ruíz.

Tourist Yú'ù facilities are dotted around Oaxaca's valleys and are a fascinating and economical alternative to staying in the city (see box), and are also more convenient if you wish to visit some of the artisan communities or the ruins at Mitla or Yagul. You can pitch a tent in their grounds, but there's no real need as they are so cheap and have self-catering facilities.

Around the zócalo

Antonio's, Independencia 601 (☎951/6-72-27, fax 6-36-72). Tastefully decorated hotel with attractive, smallish rooms with TV around two stone-paved courtyards. Very good value considering the quality and location. ④.

Francia, 20 de Noviembre 212 (☎951/6-48-11). Faded, somewhat gloomy and cavernous colonial hotel where D.H. Lawrence spent some time in 1925. ④.

Monte Albán, Alameda de León 1 (☎951/6-27-77, fax 6-32-65). Beautiful colonial-style hotel right opposite the cathedral. Excellent value with some lovely external rooms and less good internal ones. ④.

Pombo, Morelos 601 (☎951/6-26-73). Oddball but central, with plain rooms, some spacious and airy, others little more than cupboards. Some showers have stoves in which you burn rolled up paper and wood shavings when you want hot water. ②.

Las Rosas, Trujano 112 (☎951/4-22-17). Surprisingly peaceful and spacious white rooms all around a colonnaded courtyard where tea and coffee are available and there are magazines to read. ⑤.

Youth Hostel (CREA), Fiallo 305, south of Guerrero (☎951/4-13-51). One of the most popular in the country, though rather cramped. Backpackers get washing and cooking facilities, mixed dorms or private rooms. The hostel also rents bikes and show videos every night. Dorms ①; double rooms ②.

North of Independencia

Calesa Real, García Vigil 306 (☎951/6-55-44). Azulejo-tiled corridors, a small pool and attractive tile-floored rooms with locally made rugs make this one of the best of the central top-end places. ⑤.

Camino Real Oaxaca, 5 de Mayo 300 (☎951/6-06-11; in US ☎1-800/722-6466). Oaxaca's priciest hotel by a long stretch (US$190), in the beautifully converted sixteenth-century ex-convento de Santa Catalina. Not particularly welcoming – money talks here. ⑨.

Las Golondrinas, Tinoco y Palacios 411 at Allende (☎951/4-32-98, fax 4-21-26). Charming rooms each with separate reception area and bathroom in an old colonial house with a flower-filled courtyard. Very tranquil and very Oaxaca. ⑤.

Posada Margarita, Labastida 115 (☎951/6-28-02). Almost in the shadow of Santo Domingo, one of the best of the budget hotels with some spacious high-ceilinged older rooms and smaller modern affairs, all with private bath. Some rooms are a little musty, so check yours out first. ③.

Principal, 5 de Mayo 208 (☎951/6-25-35). Colonial-style place with a central courtyard and good rooms with private bathrooms. A good deal less of a splurge than the *Camino Real* just up the road. ⑤.

Santa Isabela, Morelos 800 (☎951/5-20-49). The best option for budget travellers, in a tastefully decorated, converted colonial house. There are two spacious rooms, five dormitories and a communal area where you can cook, play your own tapes and catch up with other travellers over a beer. ②.

South of Independencia

Cabaña, Mina 203 (☎951/6-59-18). Very basic, no-frills rooms come with or without shower. ②.

Fortín, Díaz Ordaz 312 (☎951/6-27-15). Best cheapy in the area. Clean, light and fairly spacious with a safe box for belongings. Rooms come with or without shower. ②.

Lupita, Díaz Ordaz 314 (☎951/6-57-33). Very cheap, small, bare rooms with or without shower. ②.

Mesón del Angel, Mina 518 (☎951/6-66-66). Soulless hotel with some ugly Sixties rooms and a more tasteful modern wing, huge pool, parking, TVs and phones. ⑥.

Vallarta, Díaz Ordaz 309 (☎951/6-40-67). Clean and pleasant but overpriced place, worth considering if there's nothing else available. ④.

Hotel Posada del Rosario, 20 Noviembre 508 (☎951/6-41-12, fax 4-49-11). The best mid-price option in the area. Rooms come with or without TV and a/c. Those on the ground floor are worst – the best are at the front on the second floor. There's parking, and you can pay with credit cards. ③.

Yagul, Mina 103 (☎951/6-27-50). Pleasant, with a little garden and spacious clean rooms, but a bit overpriced. ④.

STAYING IN LOCAL COMMUNITIES AROUND OAXACA: TOURIST YÚ'Ù

In 1994 SEDETUR and the Secretaria de Turismo opened the first batch of **Tourist-Yú'ù** – Zapotec for "house" – small self-contained houses scattered through the villages of the Oaxaca valleys. These help to bring income to the local villages while minimizing the disruptive effects of mass tourism. Visitors are shown around the village by the locals and are given the opportunity to view community life at close quarters.

Alternatively, SEDETUR can make reservations at a number of other locally built and run **hostels** for tourists. Some of these are equally charming and even more off the beaten track, though facilities tend to be a little more basic.

Either make convenient and economical bases for exploring the communities and archeological sites in the centre of Oaxaca state. Many have their own particular handicraft tradition, such as carpet-weaving, wickerwork or pottery; others often have a community museum devoted to the archeological finds in the area and the life of the villagers. Some are in areas of outstanding natural beauty, where locals will take you horseback riding, trout fishing or caving.

The Tourist Yú'ù are designed to sleep six (the hostels sleep more), with a bedroom, a fully equipped kitchen with stove and refrigerator, and outside shower and toilets which can also be used by people camping in the grounds. Each facility has a custodian who collects US$5 per person (US$3 for students), US$15 for groups of six, and US$2 for campers.

Bookings can be made – preferably a few days in advance, especially for the more accessible sites – through SEDETUR (☎951/6-09-84, fax 6-15-00), Oaxaca's tourist office, inside the Palacio Municipal.

The City

Simply being in Oaxaca, absorbing its life and wandering through its streets, is an experience, especially if you happen to catch the city during a fiesta (they happen all the time – the most important are listed at the end of the chapter), but you should definitely take time out to visit the **State Museum** and the **Museo Tamayo**, the **market** (shopping in Oaxaca is quite simply some of the best in the entire country), the **churches** of Santo Domingo and La Soledad, and to get out to Monte Albán and Mitla. All in all it could be a long stay.

Around the zócalo

The **zócalo**, closed to traffic and constantly animated, sees a steady stream of beggars, hawkers, businesspeople, tourists and locals. On Sundays and many weekday evenings there's a band playing in the centre, or else a performance or exhibition opposite the cathedral. On the south side, the Neoclassical, Porfiriano **Palacio de Gobierno** features historical murals, second-rate by Mexican standards; you reach the rather clumsy **Cathedral** from the northwest corner, opposite. Begun in 1544, its construction was only completed in the eighteenth century, since when it has been repeatedly pillaged and restored: as a result, despite a fine Baroque facade, it's not the most interesting of Oaxaca's churches. It is impressively big, though, with a heavy *coro* blocking the aisle in the heart of the church.

Walk past the cathedral and the Alameda, then right onto Independencia, and you reach the **Teatro Macedonio de Alcalá** in a couple of blocks. Still operating as a theatre and concert hall, it's typical of the grandiose public buildings that sprang up across Mexico around the turn of the century – the interior, if you can see it (try going to a show, or sneaking in before one), is a magnificent swathe of marble and red plush.

North of the zócalo

Heading north from the zócalo, Valdivieso crosses Independencia to become Macedonio Alcalá, the city's pedestrianized shopping street, a showcase for the best Mexican and Oaxacan **crafts**. This is the place to come for exquisitely intricate silver designs, finely executed, imaginative textiles, and the highest prices: check the quality here before venturing out to the villages where they are made. Four blocks up Alcalá stands the church of **Santo Domingo** (daily 7am–1pm & 4–8pm; no sightseeing during mass; free). Considered by Aldous Huxley to be "one of the most extravagantly gorgeous churches in the world", this sixteenth-century extravaganza is elaborately carved and decorated both inside and out, the external walls solid, defensive and earthquake-proof, the interior extraordinarily rich. Parts were damaged during the Reform Wars and the Revolution – especially the chapels, pressed into service as stables – but most have now been restored. Notice especially the great gilded main altarpiece and, on the underside of the raised choir above you as you enter, the family tree of the Dominican order, in the form of a vine with leafy branches and tendrils, busts of leading Dominicans and a figure of the Virgin right at the top. The place drips with gold leaf throughout, beautifully set off in the afternoon by the light flooding through a predominantly yellow window. Looking back from the altar end you can appreciate the relief scenes high on the walls, the biblical events depicted in the barrel roof, and above all the ceiling of the choir, a vision of the heavenly hierarchy with gilded angels swirling in rings around God. The adjoining **Capilla del Rosario** is also richly painted and carved: the Virgin takes pride of place in another stunning altarpiece, all the more startlingly intense in such a relatively small space.

Behind the church, the old Dominican monastery has been restored to house the **Museo Regional de Oaxaca**, closed for refurbishment in 1997 and due to open in late

1998. The damage caused by its use as a barracks during the Revolution is finally due to be repaired and the exhibits re-installed. When it reopens, you should be able to see the magnificent **Mixtec jewellery** discovered in Tomb 7 at Monte Albán (see p.428), which constitutes a substantial proportion of all known prehispanic gold, since anything the early Spanish found they plundered and melted down. Highlights of the collection include a couple of superbly detailed gold masks and breastplates. The museum also owns smaller gold pieces, and objects in a wide variety of precious materials – mother-of-pearl, obsidian, turquoise, amber and jet among them. Contact the tourist office for details of opening times and admission charges.

Across the road, the **Graphic Arts Institute** (Mon & Wed–Sun 10.30am–8pm; free) displays changing exhibits of works by nationally renowned artists. It's worth popping in just to amble around the small rooms of what was once a rather grand colonial house and to spend an hour in the excellent art library.

West of the zócalo

Four blocks back down Alcalá, then three blocks to the right, lies the **Museo Rufino Tamayo** (Mon & Wed–Sat 10am–2pm & 4–7pm, Sun 10am–3pm; US$1.50), a private collection of prehispanic artefacts, gathered by the Oaxaqueño abstract artist who ranks among the greatest Mexican painters of the century. Rather than set out to explain the archeological significance of its contents, this classy collection is deliberately laid out as an art museum, showing objects as aesthetic forms, and includes truly beautiful items from all over Mexico. Aztec, Maya and western indigenous cultures all feature strongly, while there's surprisingly little that is Mixtec or Zapotec. There are also some contemporary works.

Around the corner on J.P. García, the **Iglesia de San Felipe Neri** is mostly Baroque, with a richly decorated proliferation of statues on the plateresque facade and an equally ornate, gilt altarpiece, but what really makes it unusual is its interior decor. The church was used as barracks during the Revolution and, by the 1920s, needed to be repainted: which it was in an unusual Art Nouveau/Art Deco style. This is also where Benito Juárez got married.

The **Basilica de Nuestra Señora de la Soledad**, not far to the west along Independencia, contains an image of the *Virgen de la Soledad* – not only Oaxaca's patron saint, but one of the most revered in the country. The sumptuously decorated church, late seventeenth-century with a more recent facade, is set on a small plaza surrounded by other buildings associated with the Virgin's cult. This is where the best ice cream in town – if not the whole of Mexico – is sold (see p.425), and the adjoining **Plaza de la Danza** is a setting for outdoor concerts, *folklórico* performances, or specialist craft markets. A line of ramshackle stalls behind the ice-cream vendors sells gaily coloured religious icons. Just below the church, there's a small **museum** (Mon–Sat 10am–2pm, Sun 11am–2pm; US$0.15) devoted to the cult. It's a bizarre jumble of junk and treasure – native costumes displayed on permed blonde 1950s dummies; ex-voto paintings giving thanks for miracles and cures – among which the junk is generally far more interesting. The museum also explains how the church came to be built here, after the image miraculously appeared, in 1620, in a box on the back of a mule.

South of the zócalo: shopping in Oaxaca

The only local church to compare with La Soledad, in terms of the crowds of worshippers it attracts, is the ancient **San Juan de Dios**, right in the heart of the old market area. Here villagers who've come to town for the day and market traders drop in constantly to pay their devotions.

Saturday, by tradition, is **market day** in Oaxaca, and although nowadays the markets operate daily, it's still the day to come if you want to see the old-style *tianguis* at its best.

MARKET DAYS IN THE VILLAGES AROUND OAXACA

Despite Oaxaca's many crafts stores, if it's quality you're after, or if you intend to buy in quantity, visiting the **villages** from which the goods originate is a far better bet. Each has a different speciality (**Teotitlán del Valle**, for example, for *sarapes*, or **San Bartolo Coyotepec** for black pottery; see pp.432 and 435), and each has one market a week. Though there's no guarantee that you'll be able to buy better or more cheaply, you will be able to see the craftspeople in action, you may be able to have your own design made up, and quite apart from all that, a village market is an experience in itself.

MONDAY **Miahuatlan**: *mescal*, bread, leather.

TUESDAY **Santa Ana del Valle**: general.

WEDNESDAY **Etla**: meat, cheese, flowers.

THURSDAY **Zaachila**: meat, nuts; **Ejutla**: *mescal*, embroidered blouses.

FRIDAY **Ocotlán**: flowers, meat, pottery, textiles.

SATURDAY **Oaxaca**: everything.

SUNDAY **Tlacolula**: ceramics, rugs, crafts; **Tlaxiaco**: leather jackets, blankets, *aguardiente*.

---

indígenas flood in from the villages in a bewildering variety of costumes, and Mixtec and Zapotec dialects replace Spanish as the lingua franca. The majority of this activity, and of the serious business of buying and selling everyday goods, has moved out to the **new market** by the second-class bus station, but the old **Mercado Benito Juárez**, downtown, still sells the bulk of village **handicrafts**, as well as plenty of fruit and veg. Be warned that it's very touristy – you're harassed far more by the vendors and have to bargain fiercely – and the quality of the goods is also often suspect. **Sarapes**, in particular, are often machine-made from chemically dyed artificial fibres: these look glossy, and you can also tell real wool by plucking out a thread – artificial fibres are long, thin and shiny, woollen threads short, rough and curly; (and if you hold a match to it, a woollen thread will singe and smell awful; an artificial one will melt and burn your fingers). There are numerous shops along the Alkali that will give you a good idea of the potential quality.

Out from the centre

Although it's fairly easy to find your bearings in the centre of town, to get a fix on Oaxaca's relation to the rest of the valley and Monte Albán, take a hike (about 45min from the zócalo) up **Cerro del Fortín**, on the northwestern edge of the city. It is steep, but the views are rewarding and in the evening you can call in on the **Planetario Nundenui** (45min shows in Spanish only: Wed, Fri & Sat at 7pm, Sun 6pm & 7pm; US$1.50). The road up here passes the **Auditorio Guelaguetza**, the venue for the annual festival known as **Lunes del Cerro** ("Monday of the Hill"), primarily because the folk dances take place on the first two Mondays after July 16. Around Christmas, many of Oaxaca's boisterous celebrations also take place here.

Eating and drinking

Food is more than just good in Oaxaca, and it's readily available on almost every street corner. The cheapest places to eat are in the **markets** – either in a section of the main market around 20 de Noviembre and Aldama, or in the new one by the second-class bus station – where you'll find excellent **tamales**. More formal but still basic restaurants are to be found in the same areas as the cheaper hotels, especially along Trujano. The **zócalo** is ringed by cafés and restaurants where you can sit outside – irresistible as ever and not as expensive as their position might lead you to expect – and there are plenty of simple places for everyday meals in the streets round about. Try the excellent, dirt-cheap licuado bar, frequented only by Mexicans, on 20 de Noviembre, oppo-

---

FOOD AND DRINK IN OAXACA

Oaxaca is a wonderful city for gourmands: local specialities worth trying are **tamales** – in just about any form, and often better from street or market vendors than in restaurants – as well as **Mole Oaxaqueño**, which is not significantly different from *mole* anywhere else, but good nonetheless, and very special home-made **ice cream**. *The* place to go for ice cream is the plaza in front of the church of La Soledad, full of rival vendors and tables where you can sit and gorge yourself while watching the world go by. Flavours are innumerable and often bizarre, including *elote* (corn), *queso*, *leche quemada* (burnt milk – even worse than it sounds), *sorbete* (cinnamon-flavoured sherbet) and rose, exotic fruits like *mamey*, *guanabana* and *tuna* (prickly pear, a virulent purple that tastes wonderful), as well as more ordinary and less good varieties such as chocolate, nut and *coco*.

It's something of a leap from here to **mescal** (or *mezcal*), which is *the* local drink, sold everywhere in bottles that usually have a dead worm in the bottom. This creature lives on the maguey cactus and is there to prove it's genuine: you don't have to eat it, though few people are in any state to notice by the time they reach the bottom of the bottle, and no one seems to come to much harm, at least not from the worm. Basically, mescal is a rougher version of tequila, and developed at the same time, when the Spaniards introduced distillation after the Conquest. It's drunk the same way, with a lick of salt and lime. **Specialist shops** all around the market – try *El Fornoso*, J.P. García 405, and *El Flor de Maguey*, 20 de Noviembre 606 – sell mescal in various qualities (including from the barrel), and most also sell it in souvenir pottery bottles, which are amazingly cheap.

At the south side of the market, your nose will lead you to C Mina, which is lined with **spice** vendors, selling plump bags of the chile-and-chocolate powder that makes up Oaxacan *mole*. Cinnamon-flavoured **chocolate** powder is also available, for cooking or making into drinking chocolate.

---

site the bus ticket office, or the gorgeous cakes at *Tartamiel* in front of the cinema on Trujano. Oaxaca also provides welcome relief for **vegetarians**, who have been restricted to endless huevos and quesadillas in other parts of the country.

Around the zócalo

Los Girasoles, 20 de Noviembre 102. Mid-price food in generous portions, including some inexpensive options for vegetarians, especially good breakfasts and excellent mescal.

El Jardín, on the zócalo. One of the best cafés for watching life go by, if little to choose between it and *Mario's Terranova*, *La Primavera* or *El Asador Vasca* – though the last does serve excellent Spanish-style food.

Restaurant Quickly, Alcalá 100, just north of the zócalo. Touristy menu with huge portions and lots of green vegetables. Nothing special but inexpensive.

Del Vitral, Guerrero 201, east of Bustamente (☎951/6-31-24). Oaxaca's finest restaurant – and one of Mexico's best – in an amazing seigneurial hall with chandeliers, fireplaces and a series of French fin-de-siècle glass panels of a Louis Quinze patio and fountain. Oaxaqueño and international cuisine with a hint of nouvelle, and you can still walk away with change from US$30 after three courses. Open 8am–11pm, with live piano music in the afternoon and evening.

North of Independencia

Flor de Loto/La Brujita, Morelos 509 at Díaz. Predominantly vegetarian restaurant catering to Westerners with a menu that includes pasta, pizza and some meat dishes. Good comida corrida. The coffee bar within is run by "La Brujita", alias Susan McGlynn, a larger-than-life American Oaxaqueña, who makes the tastiest coffee in the state – as well as organizing interesting tailor-made trips around the valley.

El Manantial Vegetariano, Tinoco y Palacios at Matamoros. Vegetarian Mexican breakfasts, inexpensive veggieburgers and fruit shakes are the order of the day at this small but excellent wholefood restaurant. Closes 8pm.

Madre Tierra, 5 de Mayo 411. A beautiful place for breakfast, set in a little colonial courtyard in the shadow of Santo Domingo, serving good food and great coffee.

Morgan, Morelos 601, by *Hotel Pombo*. Small Italian-run restaurant with a limited range of very good, cheap pasta, Mexican breakfasts, some of the best coffee in town and what must be one of the world's most out-of-date noticeboards. Daily except Sun 7.30am–1pm & 5.30–10pm.

La Sol y La Luna, Bravo 109, west of Alcalá (☎951/4-81-05). An appealing cluster of small, dimly lit rooms and an open courtyard make up this well-priced restaurant. The soups, salads, pasta, steaks and deep-pan pizza are reliable, the choice of background music less so.

El Topil, Plazuela Labastida opposite *Posada Margarita*. Simply decorated restaurant specializing in Oaxacan dishes, including tamales in *mole* and a cheese fondue that bears no relation to the Swiss dish. The service isn't what the white shirts and bow ties would lead you to expect. Moderately priced.

L'Italiano, Díaz 102. Great wine list, and reasonable Italian food for between US$3 and US$5.

South of Independencia

Alex, Díaz Ordaz 218 at Trujano. Pleasant place, orientated to Westerners, where you can sit over good-value food, especially the excellent breakfasts, huge licuados and US$3 comidas corridas. Mon–Sat 7am–9pm, Sun 7am–noon.

Las Chalotes, Fiallo 116 (☎951/6-48-97). French menu that runs from couscous and fondue to terrines and stuffed quail: the surroundings are cosy enough to make you want to linger. Tues–Sun 2–11pm.

Nightlife

If you're not content sitting around the zócalo over a coffee or a beer, whiling away a balmy night to the accompaniment of *mariachi* or brass bands, don't expect too much of evenings in Oaxaca. The **folk dances** at the *Camino Real Oaxaca* and *Monte Albán* hotels are another possibility, but there's nothing much more lively even at weekends. Weeknights are quieter still, though there is frequently some kind of cultural activity outside both the church of Santo Domingo and the cathedral.

Eclipse, Díaz 219. Mainstream American dance music, with expensive drinks and a cover charge Fri and Sat nights. Thurs–Sat until 2am.

Hipotesis, Morelos 519 at Díaz. Tiny, wood-beamed bohemian café-bar, with live music especially at weekends. Light snacks and good coffee. Daily except Sun 1pm–1am.

London, Hidalgo 1002 at Fiallo. A (very loosely) Beatles-themed bar – apparently there's a twin called *Liverpool* somewhere out in the suburbs – with live music daily (10pm–1am). No cover and reasonably priced drinks, but the attempt at a British pub atmosphere fails dismally.

Principal, 20 de Noviembre 110. Club catering to a mid- to late-twenties crowd. Some Latin tunes but mostly American. Free on Thurs; US$5–10 cover at weekends.

La Tentacion, Matamoros 101. Live Latin and rock. Wed–Sat 10pm–2am.

Listings

Airlines Aeroméxico, Hidalgo 513 (☎951/6-10-66); Aeromorelos, Macedonia Alcalá 501B (☎951/6-09-74); Aviacsa, Calzada Díaz 102 (☎951/3-18-01); Mexicana and Aero Caribe, Fiallo 102 at Independencia (☎951/6-73-52 or 6-02-66).

Airport information ☎951/1-53-32.

Consulates Canada ☎951/3-37-77; France ☎951/4-19-00; Italy ☎951/5-31-15; Spain ☎951/3-37-77; UK & Germany ☎951/6-72-80; USA ☎951/4-30-54.

Emergencies English-speaking doctor, Francisco Hernandez ☎951/4-42-76; Cruz Roja ☎951/6-44-55; Police ☎951/2-66-14.

International phone calls/faxes There are Ladatel phones everywhere. MultiTel (☎951/4-76-69, fax 6-65-10; *Multitel@Itonet2.Itox.mx*), Alcala 100A, has fax, phones and Internet access.

Laundry Azteca Laundry, 404B Hidalgo (Mon–Sat 8am–8pm, Sun 10am–2pm).

MOVING ON FROM OAXACA

Unless you need to get to Puerto Escondido in a hurry, the **bus** is, as usual, the best way to travel on from Oaxaca. From the **first-class** station on Chapultepec, bus companies Cristóbal Colón and ADO between them run regular first-class and pullman services to México, Puebla, Puerto Escondido, Pochutla, San Cristóbal, Tehuacán and Villahermosa. Cristóbal Colón has a downtown **ticket office** at 20 de Noviembre 204A (Mon–Sat 9am–2pm & 4–7pm), and ADO has one inside the American Express office, on the zócalo at the corner of Hidalgo and Valdivieso (Mon–Fri 9am–2pm & 4–8pm). Slower, cheaper, more frequent and less comfortable services leave from the **second-class** bus station near the new market, to México (mostly overnight), Puerto Escondido, Pinotepa Nacional, Pochutla, Salina Cruz, Tuxtla Gutiérrez and other destinations.

If you are prepared to take the risk of having stuff stolen while you sleep, the **overnight train to México** is unusually convenient and phenomenally cheap at around US$14 in first-class and US$8 in second-class (the latter about a third of the bus fare). The train (which no longer has sleepers) leaves at 7pm, arriving in México about 10am: an equivalent overnighter follows the same timetable in the opposite direction. A second train (no first-class) runs only as far as **Puebla**, leaving Oaxaca at 7.30am, while another arrives from Puebla at around 6pm. To get to the **train station**, catch buses marked either "Colonia Reforma" or "Santa Rosa", or walk twenty minutes west along Independencia.

Numerous **flights** leave Oaxaca, predominantly for México (5 daily with Mexicana, 2 daily with both Aeroméxico and Aviacsa, and 1 daily with PAL), but also to Puerto Escondido (six-seater Aerovega and Aeromorelos), Huatulco (Aeromorelos), and Cancún via Tuxtla Gutiérrez, Villahermosa and Mérida (Aero Caribe and Aviacsa). Prices increase dramatically during Mexican holiday times, but as a rough guide expect to pay between US$50 and US$100 to México, US$90 to Puerto Escondido and US$160 to Mérida. Oaxaca's **airport** is about 10km south of the city on the road to San Bartolo Coyotepec and Ocotlán. Buses between Oaxaca and these two towns (from the second-class bus station) pass within a kilometre or so of the airport, but it is far easier to contact Transportacion Terrestre Aeropuerto, on the Alameda (☎951/4-43-50), who, if you book with them the day before your flight, will pick you up at your hotel and deliver you for a charge of around US$3.

Photographic supplies Oaxakolor is the best place for film and supplies. It has the best choice of slide film, including Velvia, and is the only place in town that stocks Fuji Reala.

Travel agents Universal Travel Centre, C Fiallo 117, on the first floor (Mon–Sat 9am–9pm, Sun 9am–1pm; ☎951/4-70-39 or 4-69-43), has good deals and English-speaking staff.

Around Oaxaca: the Zapotec and Mixtec heartland

The region around Oaxaca can be divided into two parts: the **Central Valleys**, which radiate from the state capital to the south and east, towards Mitla, Ocotlán and Zaachila; and the **Mixteca**, which extends northwest towards Puebla and arcs down to the Pacific coast via Tlaxiaco and Pinotepa Nacional. The central valleys include the state's most famous and frequented archeological centres, while the Mixteca, rich in ruined Dominican convents and ancient towns and villages, is less visited but well worth exploring.

This area saw the development of some of the most highly advanced civilizations in Mexico, most notably the Zapotecs and Mixtecs. Their craft skills – particularly Mixtec weaving, pottery and metal-working – were unrivalled, and the architecture and planning of their cities, especially at Zapotec-built **Monte Albán**, stand out among ancient

Mexico's most remarkable achievements. Their traditions, the village way of life and prehispanic languages are vigorously preserved by their ancestors today.

Some history

Civilization in the Oaxaca valleys is as old as any in Mexico. The story begins with the **Zapotecs**, who founded their first city, San José Mogoté (now little more than a collection of mounds a few kilometres north of the state capital), some time before 1000 BC. As the city grew in wealth, trading with the Pacific coastal communities, its inhabitants turned their eyes to the stars, and by 500 BC they had invented the first Mexican calendar and were using hieroglyphic writing. At this time, San José, together with other smaller villages in the area, established a new administrative capital at Monte Albán, a vantage point on a mountain spur overlooking the principal Oaxaca valley. By waging war on potential rivals, the new city soon came to dominate an area that extended well beyond the main valley – the peculiar *danzante* figures that you can see at the ruins today are almost certainly depictions of prisoners captured in battle. As the population expanded, the Zapotecs endeavoured to level the Monte Albán spur to create more space – the result was an engineering project that boggles the mind. Without the aid of the wheel or beasts of burden, millions of tons of earth were shifted to create a vast, flat terrace on which the Zapotecs constructed colossal pyramids, astronomical observatories and palaces. By the time of Christ, the city was accommodating some twenty thousand people, and Monte Albán not only controlled the smaller townships in the valley below, but had a sphere of influence as extensive as that of its great imperial trading partner, Teotihuacán, to the north.

Just like Teotihuacán, however, Monte Albán mysteriously began to collapse from about 700 AD, and the Zapotec influence across the central valleys waned. Only Yagul and Mitla, two smaller cities in the principal valley, expanded after this date, though they never reached the imperial glory of Monte Albán. The gap left by the Zapotecs was slowly filled by the **Mixtecs**, prehispanic Mexico's finest craftsmen, who expanded into the southern valleys from the north to occupy the Zapotecs' magnificent cities. Influenced by the Zapotec sculptors' abstract motifs on the walls at Mitla, the Mixtecs concentrated their artistic skills on metalwork and pottery, examples of which can be seen in the state capital's museums. By the fifteenth century, the Mixtecs had become the favoured artisans to Mexico's greatest empire, their conquerors, the Aztecs – Bernal Diaz recounts that Moctezuma only ate from plates fashioned by Mixtec craftsmen.

Monte Albán

Imagine a great isolated hill at the junction of three broad valleys; an island rising nearly a thousand feet from the green sea of fertility beneath it. An astonishing situation. But the Zapotecs were not embarrassed by the artistic responsibilities it imposed on them. They levelled the hill-top; laid out two huge rectangular courts; raised pyramidal altars or shrines at the centre, with other, much larger, pyramids at either end; built great flights of steps alternating with smooth slopes of masonry to wall in the courts; ran monumental staircases up the sides of the pyramids and friezes of sculpture round their base. Even today, when the courts are mere fields of rough grass, and the pyramids are buried under an obscuring layer of turf, even today this high place of the Zapotecs remains extraordinarily impressive . . . Monte Albán is the work of men who knew their architectural business consummately well.

Aldous Huxley, *Beyond the Mexique Bay*

In the sixty years since Aldous Huxley visited, little has changed at **MONTE ALBÁN**. The main structures have perhaps been cleared and restored a little more, but it's still the great flattened mountain-top (750m by 250m), the overall lay-out of the ceremonial precinct and the views over the valley that impress more than any individual aspect. Late afternoon, with the sun sinking in the valley, is the best time to see it.

It seems almost madness to have tried to build a city here, so far from the obvious livelihood of the valleys and without even any natural water supply (in the dry season water was carried up and stored in vast urns). Yet that may have been the point – to demonstrate the Zapotecs' mastery of nature. Certainly, the rulers who lived here must have commanded a huge workforce, first to create the flat site, later to transport materials and keep it supplied. What you see today is just the very centre of the city – the religious and political heart later used by the Mixtecs as a magnificent burial site. On the terraced hillsides below lived a population that, at its peak, reached more than twenty thousand: craftsmen, priests, administrators and warriors, all, presumably, supported by tribute from the valleys. Small wonder that so top-heavy a society was easily destabilized.

Arrival

Monte Albán (daily 8am–5pm; US$1.75, free on Sun) is just 9km from Oaxaca, up a steeply switchbacking road. Autobuses Turisticos operating from the *Hotel Mesón del Angel* (see p.421) hold a monopoly on **buses from Oaxaca** to Monte Albán (US$2 return). In peak season buses depart more frequently, but usually they leave at 8.30am (returning at 11am), 9.30am (back at noon), and hourly until 3.30pm (returning at 5.30pm), giving at best two hours at the site – barely enough to see it even quickly. If there's space, you can return on a later bus, but you may have to pay half the fare again. It's sometimes possible to hitch a ride or find a taxi (which for four or five people is not much more expensive than the bus), and walking back is also a realistic option: more than two hours, but downhill almost all the way – get a guard or one of the kids selling "genuine antiquities" to show you the path. The **bus from Zaachila** (see p.435) passes close to the front of the site, but it's a stiff walk (about 1hr 30min) from there. There's a car park, restaurant and souvenir shop by the entrance, and a small **museum** in the same complex: the collection is tiny, but there are good photographs of the site and its surroundings before and after clearing and restoration.

MONTE ALBÁN

Tumba 104
N
Oaxaca
Tumba 7
Plataforma Norte
Plaza
Juego de Pelota
Sistema IV
Edificio G
Los Danzantes
Edificio H
Edificio I
Monticulo J
Monticulo M
Plataforma Sur

0   100 m

The site

You enter the **Great Plaza** at its northeastern corner, with the ball-court to your left and the bulky north platform to your right. Sombre, grey and formal as it all appears now, in its day, with its roofs and sanctuaries intact, the whole place would have been brilliantly polychromed. The **Plataforma Norte** may well have been the most important of all the temples at Monte Albán, although now the ceremonial buildings that lined its sides are largely ruined. What survives is a broad monumental stairway leading up to a platform enclosing a square patio with an altar at its heart. At the top of the stairs are the remains of a double row of six broad columns, which would originally have supported a roof to form a colonnade, dividing this plaza off from the main one.

The **eastern side** of the Great Plaza consists of an almost continuous line of low buildings, reached by a series of staircases from the plaza. The first of them looks over the **Juego de Pelota** (ball-court), a simple I-shaped space with no apparent goals or target rings, obviously an early example. Otherwise, the platforms on the east side are relatively late constructions dating from around 500 AD onwards. Facing them from the middle of the plaza is a long tripartite building (**Edificios G, H** and **I**) that must have taken an important role in any rites celebrated here. The central section has broad staircases by which it can be approached from east or west – the lower end temples have smaller stairways facing north and south. From here a complex of tunnels runs under the site to several of the other temples, presumably to allow the priests to emerge suddenly and miraculously in any one of them. You can see the remains of several of these tunnels among the buildings on the east side.

South of this central block, **Monticulo J**, known as the Observatory, stands alone in the centre of the plaza. Both its alignment – at 45 degrees to everything else – and its arrow-shaped design mark it out from its surroundings. Although the orientation is almost certainly for astronomical reasons, there's no evidence that this was actually an observatory; more likely it was built (around 250 AD, but on the site of an earlier structure) to celebrate a military victory. Relief carvings and hieroglyphs on the back of the building apparently represent a list of towns captured by the Zapotecs. In the vaulted passage that runs through the heart of the building, several more panels carved in relief show *danzante* figures (see below) – these, often upside down or on their sides and in no particular order, may have been reused from an earlier building.

The southern end of the mountain-top is dominated by its tallest structure, the **Plataforma Sur**. Unrestored as it is, this vast square pyramid still offers the best overview of the site. Heading back from here up the western side of the plaza, you'll pass just three important structures – the almost identical **Monticulo M** and **Sistema IV**, with the great Dancers Group between them. Monticulo M and Sistema IV, which are probably the best preserved buildings on the site, both consist of a rectangular platform reached by a stairway from the plaza. Behind this lies a small sunken square from which rises a much larger pyramid, originally topped by a roofed sanctuary.

The gallery and building of **Los Danzantes** (the Dancers) are the most interesting features of Monte Albán. A low wall extending from Monticulo M to the base of the Danzantes building forms the **gallery**, originally faced all along with blocks carved in relief of Olmec or African-featured "dancers". Among the oldest (dating from around 500 BC) and most puzzling features of the site, only a few of these *danzantes* remain in situ. Quite what the nude male figures represent is in dispute. Many of them seem to have been cut open and may represent sacrificial victims or prisoners; another suggestion is that the entire wall was a sort of medical textbook, or that the figures really are dancers, or ball-players or acrobats. Whatever the truth, they show clear Olmec influence, and many of them have been pressed into use in later buildings throughout the site. The Danzantes **building** itself is one such, built over and obscuring much of the wall. It's a bulky, relatively plain rectangular platform with three temples on top – tunnels cut into the structure by archeologists reveal earlier buildings within, and more of the dancing figures.

Several lesser buildings surround the main plaza, and although they're not particularly interesting, many contained tombs in which rich treasures were discovered (as indeed did some of the main structures themselves). **Tumba 104**, reached by a small path behind the Plataforma Norte or from the car park area, is the best preserved of them. One of several in the immediate vicinity, this vaulted burial chamber still preserves excellent remains of murals. **Tumba 7**, where the important collection of Mixtec jewellery now in the Oaxaca Museum was found, lies a few hundred metres down the main road from the site entrance. Built underneath a small temple, it was originally constructed by the Zapotecs towards the end of Monte Albán's heyday, but was later emptied by the Mixtecs, who buried one of their own chiefs here along with his magnificent burial trove.

The road to Mitla

Mitla, some 45km from Oaxaca, just off Hwy-190 as it heads towards Guatemala, involves a slightly longer excursion. It's easy enough to do, though: buses leave from the second-class terminal every thirty minutes or so throughout the day. On the way are several of the more easily accessible **native villages**, some of which have community museums. Check with the tourist office which one has a market on the day you're going – there will be more buses and much more of interest once you get there. Also en route are a couple of smaller, lonelier ancient sites. If you rent a car in Oaxaca, you can take in all of this in a single day. If you want to explore the valley further, it's a good idea to stay in one of the villages. some of which have self-catering **Tourist Yú'ù** facilities (see p.421), which are as comfortable as many of Oaxaca's budget hostels.

Santa María del Tule
At **Santa María del Tule**, a first stop on Hwy-190 as you head east out of Oaxaca, you pass the famous *Arbol del Tule* in a churchyard by the road. This mighty tree, said to be at least two thousand years old (some say three thousand), is a good forty metres round, slightly fatter than it is tall. A noticeboard gives all the vital statistics: suffice to say that it must be one of the oldest living (and flourishing) objects on earth, and that it's a species of cypress (*Taxodium mucrunatum*) that has been virtually extinct since the colonial era. An extremely tacky souvenir market takes advantage of the passing trade, and there are various food and drink stalls, but if you're on the bus (on the left-hand side heading for Mitla) you get a good enough view as you pass.

Abasolo and Papalutla
Abasolo and **Papalutla**, two tiny Zapotec adobe villages which receive very few visitors, sit just a few kilometres apart along a road that leaves Hwy-190 about 5km after Santa María del Tule. Much is still traditional here, from the style of cooking to the cultivation of maize. Locals play a variation of the prehispanic Mexican ball-game against other villages on Sundays. Papalutla is a basket-weaving centre – ask for "la casa de Adrian" if you want to see them being made. The pace of life quickens during the village fiestas: August 15–23 in Abasolo, the third Sunday in October in Papalutla. There are a couple of tiny shops where you can buy eggs and vegetables (you can also arrange for a woman to cook for you), and you can rent mules at either village. Both villages also have **Tourist Yú'ù**. Buses head out here from Oaxaca's second-class terminal every hour from 5.30am until 9.30pm.

Dainzú
Seven kilometres further on Hwy-190 from the turn-off for Abasolo, **DAINZÚ**, the first significant archeological site, lies about 1km south of the main road (daily 8.30am–6pm;

US$1.50, free on Sun). A Zapotec centre broadly contemporary with Monte Albán, Dainzú stands only partially excavated in a harsh landscape of cactus-covered hills. The first structure you reach is **Edificio A**, a large and rambling construction, with elements from several epochs, set around a courtyard. The highlight of this building is a tomb with a jaguar doorway. Nearby is the ball-court, only one side of which has been reconstructed, and higher up the hill **Edificio B**, the best preserved part of the site. Along the far side of its base a series of dancer figures can be made out, similar to the Monte Albán dancers except that these clearly represent ball-players.

Teotitlán del Valle

Just before the archeological site of Lambityeco, a road leads 4km to **TEOTITLÁN DEL VALLE**, the most famous weaving town in Oaxaca. All over town you see bold-patterned and brightly coloured **rugs** and **sarapes**, some following traditional designs from Mitla, others imitating twentieth-century designs, among them those of Escher. Most are the product of cottage industry: even if you're not buying, poke your head into the compounds with rugs hanging outside. When dropped off the bus, you'll probably be pointed along a street to the left, which leads to the **mercado de artesanías**. You'll see the widest range here – ask to rummage in the back and you'll find some especially nice pieces – and prices are generally cheaper than in Oaxaca.

The village has an interesting **community museum** with displays on prehispanic artefacts, and information about carpet-weaving and life in the area. Inside the local church, whose walls are studded with bits of Zapotec temple, worship is a strange fusion of Catholic and prehispanic ritual.

Teotitlán has a few small **restaurants**, and about 3.5km outside, back towards Hwy-190, there's a **Tourist Yú'ù**. There are direct buses out here every hour or so from Oaxaca, and frequent micros from Tlacolula, further east along Hwy-190.

Benito Juárez

Perched on a ridge at 3000m overlooking the Oaxaca valleys, the little village of **BENITO JUÁREZ** is prone to spectacular sunsets – in clear weather you can see all the way to Mexico's highest mountain, Pico Orizaba. Locals can cook for you, or take you on horse or donkey rides, and there's a river where you can fish for trout. Facilities are basic, and accommodation is limited to the slightly run-down **Tourist Yú'ù**, but it's nonetheless a charming and relaxing place to spend a few days. Camionetas from Teotilán climb the steep, rough road through the forested hills every hour. Take a sleeping bag as it gets chilly up here – they get some snow in winter.

Tlacolula and Santa Ana del Valle

Back in the valley below Benito Juárez, just a few kilometres beyond Teotitlán del Valle, **TLACOLULA** is a scruffy and dirty village, but worth a stop to see the sixteenth-century **church**, about 1km to the south of the main road, its interior as ornate as Oaxaca's Santo Domingo, though less skilfully crafted. In the adjoining chapel, some gory carvings of martyrs include a decapitated St Paul. There's also a large **market** here on Sunday. Buses leave every ten to fifteen minutes for Tlacolula from Oaxaca's second- class bus station.

A road leading north from the junction at Tlacolula goes to **SANTA ANA DEL VALLE**, smaller than Teotitlán but also specializing in rugs. Lucio Aquino Cruz, at Morelos 2, makes some of the most exquisite rugs in Mexico – it's worth visiting his house just to see them, even if they are beyond your price range. Alternatively place orders with Lucio for your own designs – and you can see the production from beginning to end. One side of the small central square is devoted to the **Shon-Dany Community Museum** (which is open most days – ask at the tourist office if it's closed and you want to visit). Its name is Zapotec, meaning "foot of the hill", and it marks the exact spot where a couple of tombs were discovered in the 1950s and more recently excavated. Probably contemporary with Dainzú and Monte Albán, the Zapotec site here produced some fine glyphs. Excavations have also been carried out beneath what are now basketball courts outside, enough pots and stones being recovered to fill the small but impressive co-operatively run museum. The local weaving industry is also covered and, though panels are all in Spanish, the gist is clear enough.

There's a **Tourist Yú'ù** in Santa Ana if you want to stay. Marciano, the local baker, makes delicious bread, and there's a shop where you can buy basic provisions. Small buses leave every few minutes from Tlacolula, and there are direct buses from Oaxaca's second-class bus station.

Yagul

The site of **YAGUL** lies just to the north of the highway after about 35km – a couple of kilometres uphill from where the bus from Oaxaca stops. It's a much larger area, spread expansively across a superb defensive position, and although occupied by the Zapotecs from a fairly early date, its main features are from later on (around 900–1200 AD, after the fall of Monte Albán) and show **Mixtec** influence. On the lowest level is the **Patio de la Triple Tumba**, where the remains of four temples surround an altar and the entry to the **Triple Tomb**, whose three chambers show characteristically Mixtec decoration. Immediately above the patio, you'll see a large and elegantly simple ball-court, and a level above this, the maze-like **Palacio de los Seis Patios**. Probably a residential complex, this features six small courtyards surrounded by rooms and narrow passages. Climbing still higher towards the crest of the hill and the fortress, you pass several lesser remains and tombs, while from the fortress itself there are stunning views of the valley, and a frightening rock bridge across to a natural watchtower.

Mitla

The town of **MITLA** ("Place of the Dead"), where the bus from Oaxaca finally drops you, is some 4km off the main road and just ten minutes' walk from the site of the famous ruins. It's an unattractive, dusty little place where you'll be harassed by would-be guides and vendors of handicrafts (there's also a distinctly second-rate crafts market by the ruins). By way of some consolation, there's an **archeological museum** (*Museo Frissel de Arte Zapoteca*; daily 9am–5pm; US$1.50) in the village, whose exhibits look remarkably free of wear for their age. Accommodation can be found at the *Hotel Mitla* (☎956/8-01-12; ③), or *La Zapoteca* (☎956/8-00-26; ③), in town on the way to the ruins.

The **history of Mitla** is a complicated one, and still far from agreed among archeologists. The abstract designs on the buildings seem to echo patterns on surviving Mixtec manuscripts, and have long been viewed as pure Mixtec in style. But more recent opinion is that the buildings were built by Zapotecs and that the city was a ceremonial centre occupied by the most important Zapotec high priest. This *Uija-Tao*, or "great seer", was described by Alonso Canesco, a fifteenth-century Spaniard, as being "rather like our Pope", and his presence here would have made Mitla a kind of Vatican City.

The site

The **site** itself (daily 8.30am–6pm; US$1.50, free on Sun) may seem disappointing on first sight: it's relatively small, and in the middle of the day overrun with visitors. But on closer inspection the fame of the place becomes more justifiable. The palace complexes are magnificently decorated with elaborate stone mosaics. You'll see it at its best if you arrive towards closing time, when the low sun throws the patterns into sharp, shadowed relief, and the bulk of the visitors have left.

The **Grupo de las Columnas**, the best-preserved and most impressive of the palace complexes, is the obvious place to head from the entrance. The only other sites that these long, low, fabulously decorated buildings recall in any way are the two post-Classic sites of El Tajín (see p.405) and Uxmal (see p.535), which, along with other evidence, suggests that there may have been some contact between these most influential groups.

The first large courtyard is flanked by constructions on three sides – its central **Templo de las Columnas** is magnificent, precision engineered and quite overpowering in effect. Climbing the broad stairway and through one of three entrances in its great facade, you come to the **Salon de las Columnas**, named after the six monolithic, tapered columns of volcanic stone that supported its roof. A low, narrow passageway leads from here into the small **inner patio** (*Patio de las Grecas*), lined with some of the most intricately assembled of the geometric mosaics. Four dark rooms that open off it continue the patterned mosaic theme. It is here that the *Uija-Tao* would have lived. If the latest theory is correct, the Zapotec architects converted the inner room of the traditional Mesoamerican temple, in which priests usually lived, into a kind of exquisitely decorated "papal flat" arranged around a private courtyard. The second courtyard of the Columns group, adjoining the southwestern corner of the first, is similar in design though perhaps less impressive in execution. Known as the **Patio de las Tumbas**, it does indeed contain two cross-shaped tombs – long since plundered by grave robbers. In one the roof is supported by the **Columna de la Muerte**; embrace this, they say, and the gap left between your outstretched fingers tells you how long you have left to live.

The **Grupo de la Iglesia**, a short distance north, is so called because the Spanish built a church over, and from, much of it. Two of its three original courtyards survive, however, and in the smaller one the mosaic decoration bears traces of the original paint, indicating that the patterns were once picked out in white from a dark red background.

Three other groups of buildings, which have weathered the years less well, complete the site. All of them are now right in the modern town, fenced off from the surrounding houses: the **Grupo de los Adobes** can be found where you see a chapel atop a pyramid; the **Grupo del Arroyo** is very nearby; and the **Grupo del Sur** lies right beside the road to the main site.

Hierve el Agua

Before it's too late, visit **Hierve el Agua**. Some 25km east of Mitla, down a side road that leads to **San Lorenzo Albarradas** (Hierve el Agua lies just beyond), it's the site of the spectacular limestone "waterfalls" that you'll see in photographs all over Oaxaca City. Tourism here threatens to be more destructive than in the rest of the valley, and the people running the little restaurants near the falls are a little less friendly than others in the Oaxaca villages. The area is beautiful, though, and the stars at night awe-inspiring – there's no electricity and the hills shield any glow from Oaxaca's valleys. There are two ill-equipped **Tourist Yú'ù**, and a few **restaurants** which close after sunset. It's a two- to three-hour drive up here from Oaxaca through some beautiful countryside. Three buses are scheduled to make the journey from Oaxaca every day, leaving the second-class bus terminal at 5.10am, 8.10am and 2.10pm, and returning at 8am, 11am and 5pm, but they are erratic, so it's best to check with the tourist office in Oaxaca when you make your reservation.

The valleys south of Oaxaca

The two roads that run almost due south of Oaxaca don't have the same concentration of interesting villages and sites as the Mitla road, but there is plenty to occupy a day or so. Again, you can travel around the area by **public transport** on market days – by far

El Rosario *mariposa* sanctuary

Taxi, México

Rivera mural, Palacio Nacional, México

Rickshaws on the Zócalo, México

Cliff diver, Acapulco

Fray Tormenta, the wrestling bishop

Beach view, Acapulco

Fishing on Lake Catemaco, Veracruz

Ocatlán market, Oaxaca

ALEX ROBINSON

Jalapeño chiles

ALEX ROBINSON

Triqui textiles, Oaxaca

PETER WILSON

San Cristóbal de las Casas, Chiapas

the best time to go – but cycling on rented bikes from Oaxaca isn't as arduous as it might sound, especially if you keep out of the midday heat.

San Bartolo Coyotepec and Ocotlán

Fifteen kilometres south of Oaxaca on the main highway to Puerto Ángel lies **SAN BARTOLO COYOTEPEC**, as unprepossessing a town as you could imagine, famed only for its shiny black, purely ornamental pottery – **barro negro brillante** – found in crafts shops all around Oaxaca, but made only at the small factory here. From the bus stop, a road, one side awash with black pottery vendors, leads to the pottery where, in 1934, Doña Rosa developed the manufacturing technique. Her family still run the sole "factory", now very tourist-oriented, with pieces ranging from beautifully simple amphorae to ghastly clocks and breast-shaped mugs. Prices are supposed to be fixed, and at the factory they probably are, but places down the road will haggle; just remember your piece has to get home and the stuff is fragile. **Buses** to San Bartolo Coyotepec leave Oaxaca's second-class bus station every thirty minutes.

The same buses continue to **OCOTLÁN**, chiefly noted for the **clay ware** – pots, utensils and figures – crafted by the Aguilar sisters. On the approach into town, look out on the right for the adjacent workshops of Guillermina, Josefina and Irene, each producing slightly different items, though the distinctive Aguilar style, originated by their mother, shows through them all. Again, you can find examples in Oaxaca, but a trip out here allows you to see the full range, including figures of animals, men and women at work and play, and even nativity scenes are all considered fair game, often gaudily decorated in polka dots or geometric patterns. Try to make it on a Friday when the weekly **market** takes place not far from the **Parroquia de Santo Domingo de Guzmán**, with its newly restored facade and multiple domes richly painted with saints. Take a peek in at the gilded south transept.

Arrazola, Cuilapan and Zaachila

The other major region of interest in this area is along, or beside, the road to Zaachila that runs southwest from Oaxaca past the foot of Monte Albán. **ARRAZOLA**, an easy cycle-ride 5km off to the right from this road, is the home of the local woodcarvers and painters who produce the delightful boldly patterned animals from copal wood that you'll see for sale in Oaxaca and all over Mexico. Carvers from other villages are catching on to the popularity of these whimsical, spiky figures and producing the polka-dot, hooped or expressionist examples themselves, but few, if any, are better than in Arrazola.

The village of **CUILAPAN**, 14km from Oaxaca (buses from the second-class bus station), seems insignificant beneath the immense sixteenth-century hulk of the Dominican **ex-Convento de Santiago Apóstol**, which, though badly damaged, is still an impressive place to wander around, with a Renaissance twin-aisled nave and largely intact vaulting. One section is still roofed, and mass is said here amid the clangs and echoes of ongoing restoration work. The real interest, however, lies around the back in the **cloister** (daily 10am–6pm; US$1.50), which features a few faded frescoes on the wall. Look out for the sign pointing to the back wall, where Vincente Guerrero was executed by firing squad after spending his captivity here.

Buses from Oaxaca to Cuilapan continue 5km to **ZAACHILA**, which has a colourful Thursday market. Come here on that day and you've got the best chance of being able to get into the **zona arqueologica** (nominally Mon–Fri 9am–6pm, Sat & Sun 9am–4pm; US$1.50, free on Sun), up behind the multi-domed church. There's not a great deal to see, but you can step down into the two opened tombs – of what is probably a much larger site – and, when your eyes become accustomed to the gloom, pick out detailed bas-relief geometric figures on the lintel and owls guarding the entrance.

Two marvellous glyphs show who was interred here: Señor Nine Flower, probably a priest, depicted carrying a bag of copal for producing incense.

The Mixteca

The two areas of Oaxaca's Mixteca region – the barren hills of the **Mixteca Baja** and the mountainous, pine-clad **Mixteca Alta** – are not as obvious tourist destinations as the Central Valleys. Although they hold some interesting colonial architecture, the prehispanic sites here are far less spectacular, and there are no artisan centres to compare with Teotitlán or Arrazola. But fewer tourists mean that you are likely to have vast ruined monasteries and little-visited Mixtec ruins to yourself, and though you'll pick-up fewer trinkets at the colourful Mixtec markets you'll know that you're witnessing a scene that has remained relatively unchanged since before Cortés.

Public transport through the region is straighforward. Hwy-135, one of the country's best roads, cuts through the Baja's deforested hillsides, eventually reaching México. Hwy-125 leads off 135 to the south, traversing the steeper slopes of the Mixteca Alta, eventually arriving at Puerto Escondido via a long and circuitous route. There are frequent buses and camionetas from Oaxaca heading out to the monasteries and the major towns.

The Baja: Yanhuitlan, Teposcolula and Coixtlahuaca

Among the **Mixteca Baja**'s highlights are a trio of **Dominican monasteries** – at Yanhuitlan, Teposcolula and Coixtlahuaca – once centres of mass conversion, but each now eerily deserted and crumbling. These vast and imposing relics of Mexico's imperial past are widely regarded as among the country's most important colonial buildings. All three can easily be visited as a day-trip from Oaxaca if you have your own transport; less easily so by public transport, though it's possible (see below).

Head out on Hwy-190 for about 120km to reach the first monastery, at **Yanhuitlan**, the permanent seat of the vicarage of the Mixteca during the sixteenth century. The church is built on an enormous prehispanic platform, no doubt intended to remind the Mixtecs of the supremacy of the new religion. Inside are many original paintings and sculptures – the principal altarpiece, dating to 1570, is the work of the Spanish artist Andres de la Concha. **Teposcolula**, on Hwy-125 in the village of the same name, has one of the finest *capillae abiertae* in the Americas. These graceful open-air chapels were used for mass preaching and conversion, and are only found in the New World. The exconvent of San Juan Bautista, at **Coixtlahuaca**, a couple of kilometres off Hwy-135, dates from 1576 and has some unusual sculpture on the facade, depicting grand rosettes, symbols of the passion and John the Baptist flanked by saints Peter and James. There's an impressive churrigueresque altarpiece within.

To see all three monasteries in a single, if long, day-trip from Oaxaca, catch a minibus from Transporte Tlaxiaco, a small terminal on J.P. Garcia, between Arista and Nuno del Mercado. The minibuses leave when full, approximately every hour, and take about an hour and a half to reach Yanhuitlan. You can catch the next bus, or a taxi, to Teposcolula, less than 25km away. From Teposcolula, take a cab or catch a second-class bus to El Crucero, at the junction of Hwy-125, Hwy-190 and Hwy-135, only about 10km from the town. Frequent first- and second-class buses heading to México or Oaxaca stop here. Catch one going towards México and get off after about 20km at turn-off to Coixtlahuaca. The monastery is about 1.5km up a side road.

The Alta: Tlaxiaco and around

Hwy-125 climbs into the **Mixteca Alta** after Teposcolula, entering some beautiful pine forest as it gets closer to Tlaxiaco. On the way, about 50km after Teposcolula, lies **Huamelulpan**, two kilometres up a side road. This tiny mountain village has an extensive and mostly unexplored Mixtec archeological site, with two large plazas cut out of a hill, a ball-court, and some temple complexes. Some of the sculptures found here have been embedded in the walls of the colonial church. Other artefacts from the ruins are displayed in the small **museum**, which also has information about indigenous medicines – these are still used by traditional healers in the local community. The surrounding countryside is picturesque, with deer and coyotes in the woodland, and the villagers are very friendly. They administer a small, very basic tourist lodge here (bookings through the tourist office in Oaxaca, or just turn up as you're likely to be the only visitor; ①). A woman in the grocery shop on the main square can prepare food for you.

Tlaxiaco, a fifteen-minute bus ride beyond Huamelulpan, is famed for its *pulche*, a fermented drink made from the cactus. The town has a lively Saturday market, and though it's not a particularly attractive place, could serve as a base for exploring the nearby countryside and the Mixtec and Triqui villages nearby. The *Hotel del Portal* (☎955/2-01-54; ④), in a converted colonial house on the main plaza, is a wonderful **place to stay**, especially if you make sure you get a room in the old building. Cheaper options include the *Colón* (☎955/2-00-13; ②), Colón 11, or the *Hotel Mexico* (no phone; ①), Hidalgo 13. The *Rincon de Gon* **restaurant**, next door to the *Hotel Colón*, has a good menu, including regional dishes as well as some vegetarian options, and puts on live music on Thursdays and Fridays.

Camionetas for Tlaxiaco leave from Oaxaca's Transporte Tlaxiaco, on J.P. Garcia, between Arista and Nuno del Mercado (hourly; 3hr). There are also **second-class buses**. Moving on from Tlaxiaco, buses leave for **Pinotepa Nacional**, where you can change for Puerto Escondido and the Pacific Coast. There are also buses from Tlaxiaco to México and Puebla.

Puerto Escondido

PUERTO ESCONDIDO is no longer the hippy hangout it was thirty-odd years ago. With direct flights from the capital and an already widespread reputation, it has firmly established itself as a mainstream resort, with the strings of souvenir shops and constantly spiralling prices that all this entails. Escondido still has a lot going for it, though, with **beaches** stretched out around the bay for miles in each direction and an atmosphere that remains, against all the odds, small-town. There are no really big hotels, and most of the visitors are young, with surfing high on their agendas.

Indeed, it is along the surf beach, **Zicatela**, less than a kilometre away from the centre, that most of the recent changes have taken place. Where once stood just a few weather-beaten huts, there's now a thriving community with several good hotels – most with pools, since the sea is almost always too rough for swimming – and great restaurants. Everything revolves around surfing and being outdoors: you can get your hair cut while watching the surfers on the boards, or watch a video of the morning's action in one of the hotels. Non-surfers have cottoned on to the relaxed pace, and Zicatela is now as much a destination as Escondido town itself, especially between August and November. At either end of this season, Escondido is packed for the **surf tournaments**: a locally sponsored event in late August and an international one – possibly due for inclusion on the professional tour – in late November. Despite its laid-back atmosphere, however, it is in Zicatela that the rumours of **muggings** in Puerto Escondido originate – mostly they're overstated but everyone advises against walking on the beach at night. The road by the hotels is fine.

Arrival, orientation and information

Puerto Escondido can be loosely divided into three zones; all contiguous but with completely different characters. The **old town** sprawls across the hill behind the bay, with

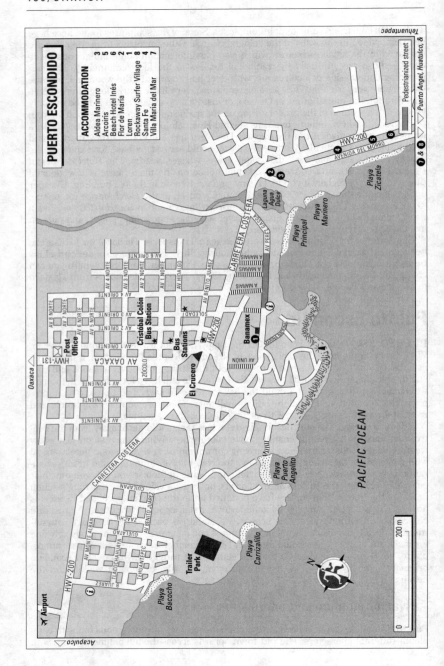

the newer **tourist zone** spilling down towards the water and concentrated along Av Peréz Gasca. **Zicatela** beach runs east then south from here.

The four **bus stations** are all near each other in the old town on the hill near El Crucero, the junction where the main road between the old town and the tourist zone crosses the Carretera Costera (Hwy-200). From here it's ten minutes' walk to the centre and about twenty to Zicatela; taxis to the centre cost about US$2. **Flights** from Oaxaca and México arrive at the airport 3km north of town, from where taxis (around US$7) and a cheaper minibus run into the centre.

The main **tourist office** (Mon–Fri 9am–2pm & 6–8pm, Sat 9am–1pm; ☎958/2-01-75) is out on Hwy-200 to the north of town, and there's a tourist booth (with sporadic opening times) near the western end of the pedestrianized section of Peréz Gasca, the town's main thoroughfare. In the pedestrianized section, where there are several **Ladatel** phones (free collect calls), there's also a *larga distancia* office next door to the **casa de cambio** (daily 9am–2pm & 5–8pm). The rates at the latter aren't great; better to make it just up the hill to the often busy Banamex (exchange Mon–Fri 9am–noon), which also has an ATM. There's a self-service **laundry** (daily 8am–8pm) next door.

The **post office** (Mon–Fri 9am–6pm, Sat 9am–noon) is in the old town at C 7a Nte, though you can get stamps from postcard vendors (at a half-peso premium) and chance your luck with the mail boxes along Peréz Gasca. Out in Zicatela, there are few facilities: the Puerto y Bahías **casa de cambio** is supposed to be open daily from 9am to 2pm and 4pm to 7pm, but seldom is.

Accommodation

Finding **somewhere to stay** in Puerto Escondido shouldn't be a problem, except over Christmas or during the major surfing contests, when prices, seldom very low, are pushed up higher still. Standards are high across the board, from simple cabañas to tasteful rooms. For **campers** the best bet is the *Puerto Escondido Trailer Park* (☎958/2-00-77), a spacious and grassy full-facility site with a pool, out on the west side of town above Carrizalillo beach. *Trailer Park Neptune*, by the eastern end of Playa Principal (☎958/2-03-27), is less good: a tatty but reasonably shady and well-located ground with cabins for the same price as pitching a tent – rates quadruple in December, however.

In town
Aldea Marinero, C del Morro, Playa Marinero (no phone). Slightly grotty rooms and spaces in cabañas. Fans and hammocks cost extra. ①.

Flor de María, C del Morro, Playa Marinero (☎958/2-05-36). One of the best-value places in town, its design and decor showing the hand of the Italian owner. Fan-cooled rooms with beautifully tiled bathrooms, and a rooftop pool with restaurant and great views. ⑤.

Loren, Peréz Gasca 507 (☎958/2-00-57). High-standard hotel away from the sea but with a good pool and impressively low off-season prices, which can be slashed by up to fifty percent. ⑥.

Zicatela beach
The hotels below are listed in order of distance from Puerto Escondido.

Santa Fe (☎958/2-01-70, fax 2-02-60). Puerto Escondido's top hotel, catering to an older crowd, with very comfortable balconied rooms and a villagey feel. ⑧.

Cabo Blanco (no phone). Rustic rooms for rent at this popular seafood restaurant and live music venue. It can be noisy. ②.

Arcoiris (☎958/2-04-22). One of the best and most relaxing places on the beach. Luxuriant gardens and a secluded pool hide behind a block of spacious, comfortable rooms, some with fully equipped kitchen, some without. ⑤.

Beach Hotel Inés (☎958/2-07-92). Hammocks around the palm-shaded pool and the restaurant-bar are the centre of (in)activity here. Rooms range from simple cabañas to cool, white-painted apartments, with kitchens and a/c. ④.

Rockaway Surfer Village (☎958/2-06-68). Aptly named hotel where dedicated surfers hole up for the entire season. Simple but nice cabañas (with hammocks but no showers) around the pool sleep up to four. Surf shop and volleyball court. Prices halved in the low season. ③.

Villa María del Mar (☎958/2-10-91). Cabaña-like rooms with fan, hammock and private bath scattered around a compound with a pool. It's 400m beyond the end of the paved Zicatela road, so out of season, when the restaurant is closed, you'll appreciate being able to cook your own food here. ③.

The beaches

There's absolutely nothing to do in Escondido but swim, surf, laze on the beach and eat and drink. In most places you needn't move all day, as you'll be regularly approached by ice-cream carts, people trying to sell cold drinks or hot snacks, and vendors of T-shirts and trinkets. The choice of beaches even within a couple of kilometres of town is impressive: take your pick from the town strand, with the convenience of shops and bars nearby, pounding surf beaches or secluded coves ideal for snorkelling.

There are three main beach areas: the **town beach**, which stretches round to the east and south from the town centre; the surfing mecca of Zicatela; and the trio of small coves to the west. The sand directly in front of town is perhaps a little overused, and shared, too, with the local fishermen and the activities of the port. A little to the east, beyond where the Laguna Agua Dulce occasionally reaches the sea, **Playa Marinero** is quieter, sometimes graced with gentle surf. But the real big stuff is southeast, beyond the little headland, where **Zicatela** stretches 2km to the point. One of the world's top surf beaches, Zicatela regularly receives perfectly formed beach breaks of 4m for days on end and occasionally a seven- or eight-metre monster stirred up by south Pacific storms between August and November. Surf- and boogie-boards can be rented from a number of places along Zicatela beach. When it is pumping, consider your strength and swimming fitness before venturing into the waves: they're very powerful, there's a significant rip and occasionally even experienced surfers drown.

Everything is much calmer in the coves to the west of the town. **Puerto Angelito** is the closest, divided in two by a rocky outcrop. It's about twenty minutes' walk from town, either by a track that leads to the left off Peréz Gasca, or direct from the highway on a signed road leading down opposite the *El Padrino* restaurant (the two paths meet above the beach). An alternative is the recently completed concrete footpath that sets out from the western end of the town beach, dipping and turning over the coastal rocks and eventually climbing up to a road. Follow this inland, then turn left along another road, which turns into steps onto the beach. Both the little inlets have small beaches and excellent **snorkelling** among the rocks, but you'll have to bring your own gear or rent some at great expense from the handful of makeshift restaurants.

The next bay, **Carrizalillo**, is reached along the same track, following signs to the *Puerto Escondido Trailer Park*. At the end you have to scramble down over the rocks to reach the sand, guaranteeing that there won't be too many other people around. **Bacocho Bay** is further, following the highway out towards the airport and then cutting through the new hotel zone. Small boats will bring you round here from town, which is a great deal easier than walking and usually cheaper than a taxi; you can also arrange boat-rides to beaches further afield. There aren't many hotels here yet, so Bacocho offers good, secluded swimming; though again, caution is needed, as this beach is open to the ocean. *Coco's Bar and Restaurant* serves good, if pricey, **food**; eat, and you can use their pool for free.

Eating, drinking and nightlife

It doesn't cost much to eat well in Escondido: many of the **restaurants** and cafés are laid-back, low-key affairs with plenty of natural light and a cool breeze. The **seafood** is always fresh, and you can vary your diet with **vegetarian** food, excellent **bread and cakes** and **Italian food** from the inordinately large number of Italian restaurants. Most of the restaurants double as bars, and some even host live music. The large Italian contingent can usually be found glued to the Italian film *Puerto Escondido* – which is more about drug running from Real de Catorce than high intrigue in a beach resort – shown nightly at *Spaghetti House*.

There are more **films** on show at *Cine Club Ariel* (nightly Tues–Sun; US$3; ☎958/2-02-44), this time art-house, usually in English or with subtitles. The screen is just by the *Villa María del Mar* hotel, about 400m beyond the rest of the hotels at Zicatela. Shows start at 9pm. Otherwise, nightlife is concentrated in the **bars** along Peréz Gasca.

In town

Barfly, Peréz Gasca. One of a couple of neighbouring places with early evening happy hours and usually live music until late. Unusually for Escondido, the taped music sometimes runs for over thirty minutes without a Bob Marley or U2 track.

La Gota de Vida, Peréz Gasca at the bottom of the hill. Reasonable vegetarian place serving yoghurt, granola, soya burgers and houmus during the day.

La Patisserie, C del Morro, Playa Marinero. Croissants and pastries from *Carmen's* at Zicatela, plus sandwiches, fruit salads and yoghurt served in a quiet palm hut with a book swap.

El Son y La Rumba, Andador Mar y Sol, off Peréz Gasca. Salsa bar with a tiny dance floor where gringos fail to imitate the locals. Some cumbia, merengue and reggae. Opens around 10pm.

Spaghetti House, just off the eastern end of Peréz Gasca. About the best Italian place in town. Not expensive and great food, with a tatty video of *Puerto Escondido* playing in the background.

Zicatela beach

The restaurants below are listed in order of distance from Puerto Escondido.

Cabo Blanco. The best seafood on the beach at reasonable prices. Fish or shrimps dressed with a choice of delicious sauces: Thai curry or lime, wine and cream. Live music most nights draws a lively crowd.

Carmen's. Tiny pavement bakery with great espresso, *pain au chocolat*, *pain aux raisins* and spinach rolls. After 4pm they have that day's *The News*, México's English-language daily.

El Cafecita. Rightly popular, open-fronted palapa restaurant. A great place for breakfasts, burgers and burritos through the day, and seafood in the evening. Check out the daily specials and two-for-one drinks 5.30–7pm.

Art and Harry's Surf Inn. Favourite evening spot where surfers and their acolytes come to watch the sun go down and drink two-for-one beers, staying on to play pool and look over that morning's surf photos on the noticeboard. Tasty, good-value salads, seafood and burgers served all day.

Around Puerto Escondido: the lagoons

Though most people find it almost impossible to drag themselves off the beaches of Puerto Escondido, there are a couple of boat-trips worth making. **LAGUNA MANIAL-TEPEC**, about 15km west of Puerto Escondido, is cut off from the sea most of the year, forming a freshwater lake unfeasibly rich in wildlife. You can easily spot fifty-odd species in a day, among them several types of heron, ibis, egret, duck and cormorant, along with lily walkers and parrots. **Buses** run out here from El Crucero, or you can go with an organized tour through one of the travel agencies in Puerto Escondido.

With more time to spare – preferably a couple of days so you can stay over – the wildlife of the **LAGUNAS DE CHACAHUA** and the beach at the far end make a more

MOVING ON FROM PUERTO ESCONDIDO

Of the four **bus stations**, Estrella Blanca, at Oaxaca and Benito Juárez (☎958/2-00-86), is the most useful, with first- and second-class buses to Acapulco, Huatulco, México and Salina Cruz. The next best is Cristóbal Colón at C 1 Ote at C 1 Nte, which has buses to Oaxaca, including one overnight. Estrella del Valle, Hidalgo at C 3 Ote (☎958/2-00-50), runs **to Oaxaca** in three classes: deluxe (at 10.30pm; 6hr), first-class (2 daily; 6hr) and second-class (6 daily; 8hr). Transportes Oaxaca Istmo, Hidalgo at C 1 Ote, operates second-class to Salina Cruz (5 daily; 5hr), with one a day continuing to Tuxtla Gutiérrez (10hr).

You can get a morning or evening **flight** to Oaxaca with Aerocaribe (Mon, Wed, Fri & Sun). There's also one daily Mexicana flight to México. You can save money on taxis by engaging the services of Transportes Aeropuerto y Turistico (☎958/2-01-23), whose office is in town at the foot of the hill of Peréz Gasca. For more information contact Erikson **travel agents** (☎958/2-03-89) on Peréz Gasca at Andador Libertad.

interesting venture. Catch a bus from El Crucero (every 20min) to **Río Grande**, 50km west of Puerto Escondido on Hwy-200, then change on to one of the frequent minibuses to the one-time cacao and cotton port of **Zapotalito**. The road does continue a short way from here to the beach and palapa restaurants at Cerro Hermosa, but it is better to take a *lancha* to Playa Chacahua – you could also rent one to tour the lagoon, but unless you have a special interest in tangled webs of mangroves you might as well make straight for the beach. There's a restaurant and some scruffy **rooms** (②) by the water, and more just across the lagoon – cabañas (③) and a huge beach, calm enough in parts but with some good surf. There's also space to camp and a row of outdoor seafood **restaurants** where you could hang a hammock.

Puerto Ángel and around

Though it's pretty well-known these days, **PUERTO ÁNGEL** still goes about its business as a small, scruffy fishing port with minimum fuss. Everything remains resolutely small-scale, and you'll find pigs and chickens mingling with the visitors on the streets. Set around a sheltered bay ringed by mountains, it has two, rather dirty beaches: one right in front of town, the other opposite, beyond a rocky promontory and the mouth of a small stream. There's no bank, only one *larga distancia* place, just back from the pier, near the **post office**, no police and very few shops. Small hotels, rooms and simple places to sling a hammock, however, are abundant, some of the most promising on the road between the main village and the second beach, Playa del Panteón.

Locals are always fishing off the huge concrete dock in Puerto Ángel – which never seems to be used for anything else – catching yellowtail tuna and other gamefish with a simple rod and line. Not surprisingly, there's superb **seafood** everywhere.

Of the **beaches**, the Playa del Panteón, reached by road or a path around the base of the cliffs to the west, is the cleaner and quieter, with interesting snorkelling round the rocks. By the afternoon, though, it's in shade, so most people wander round to the town beach. With just a little more effort you can visit one of the far better beaches either side of Puerto Ángel. To the west is the more primitive **Zipolite**, while to the east, about fifteen minutes' walk up the Pochutla road and then down a heavily rutted track to the right, you'll find **Estacahuite**. Here there are three tiny, sandy coves, divided by outcrops of rock. The rocks are close in, so you can't swim far, but there's wonderful snorkelling and rarely more than a couple of other people around. In a pleasantly breezy palapa overlooking the first of the coves, the *Club Playa Estacahuite* (fancy name, simple place) serves amazingly good food.

Practicalities

Puerto Ángel's **hotels** are a bit scattered and, in general, you can't phone to check availability; but the village is small enough that you should be able to find someone to mind your bags while you look around. The places listed below represent only a third of the total, but you'll find little better. **Restaurants** are all the way along the waterfront in town, where *La Villa Florencia* serves Italian food, while *El Tiburón Dormido*, near the naval base, serves high-quality seafood.

Accommodation

Casa de Huéspedes Capy, on the road to Playa del Panteón (☎958/4-30-02). Not as good as the nearby *Puesto del Sol*, it is nevertheless cheaper and the rooms with private bath aren't bad. ③.

Casa de Huéspedes Gundí y Tomas, up some steps opposite the naval base in the centre. Friendly atmosphere, open-sided lounge area with views of the bay, and decent meals. The cheaper rooms leave a bit to be desired. Hammock space for a couple of dollars. ③.

Posada Cañon del Vata, inland from the far end of Playa del Panteón (☎958/7-09-02). Simple but beautifully furnished rooms – seats carved from huge logs and neat tile details – spread through a jungly hillside behind Playa del Panteón, most of them barely visible from the others and reached on winding paths. You'd think you were miles from a beach. There's a palapa with hammocks and a rooftop bar for guests to relax and watch the sunset, meat-free communal meals (US$6) each evening, and even a place to wash clothes. Perfect for recharging batteries. ④.

Puesta del Sol, on the right as you head to Playa del Panteón. The pick of the cheaper hotels. Not much in the way of a view but clean, airy rooms, a laundry and communal space lined with photos taken by the husband of the congenial, knowledgeable owner. Breakfast. ③.

Rincón Sabroso, on the hill, up steps near the *Restaurant Las Espress*. Pleasing rough-tiled rooms with fans, baños and hammocks outside make this hotel a steal. ③.

Zipolite

Though some people rave about Puerto Ángel, others are ecstatic about **ZIPOLITE**, 3km along the road north, whose reputation as the ultimate in relaxed beach resorts has become legendary. The travellers' grapevine is alive with tales of the widely available hallucinogens, low living costs and liberal approach to nudity – rumours that are largely well-founded. Certainly nude bathing – predominantly at the northern end – is sanctioned by the local military, who patrol the area as light-handedly as men in big jackboots can. Keep cover handy for trips to the restaurants, though. As for **drugs**, grass, mushrooms and acid are as illegal as – though more prevalent than – anywhere else in Mexico, and unscrupulous dealers are not above setting people up. Theft, too, is rife, but seems in no way to detract from the lure of a few days of complete abandonment.

The **beach** itself is magnificent, long and gently curving, pounded by heavy surf with a rip that requires some caution: drownings are depressingly common. All the way along, palapa huts cater for simple needs. **Seafood** and egg dishes are everywhere, rentable **hammocks** are strung from every rafter and many places offer simple **rooms**: share, if only to store your gear safely.

Practicalities

The best **place to stay** is in one of *San Cristobal*'s fifty clean and cockroach-free cabañas (②), towards the west end of the beach. If you want something cheaper, most of the other cabañas will allow you to sling up a hammock for US$1.50. You can also try the cheap cabañas at *Palapa Kati*, a little further east, or *Lyoban*, right at the far east end (①). For **food**, the Italian-owned *El Eclipse*, 300 metres east of *San Cristobal*, serves wonderful pizzas. There's a **laundry** service in the street behind, and a **chemist** on the road out of Zipolite towards Puerto Ángel.

For anything other than the simplest needs you'll have to catch the **buses** that run to Puerto Ángel and on to Pochutla (every 20min, until around 8pm). **Taxis** are plentiful, or you can walk in around forty minutes, though this is not advisable after dark.

For something much more luxurious, try *Mario's*, perched on the ridge between Zipolite and San Agustinillo, the next beach along. With one of the most spectacular views on the Mexican Pacific, cabañas go from about US$50. The restaurant here is the best in the area. Catch any Mazunte-bound camioneta to get here, or walk – it's about 3km from Zipolite.

Mazunte

Rounding the headland north of Zipolite you come to **San Agustinillo**, another fine beach backed by a few palapa restaurants with hammock space, followed by the tiny village of **MAZUNTE**, once notorious as the site of a turtle abattoir that at its most gruesome slaughtered three thousand head a day. In 1990 the Mexican government, bowing to international environmental pressure, effectively banned the industry overnight, removing in one fell swoop the livelihood of the village. Ironically, ecotourism has been encouraged in its place. Mazunte is certainly an attractive place, with a beautiful beach and a relaxed atmosphere very different to that in Zipolite. There's now a turtle museum here (though closed at the time of writing because of devastation caused by Hurricane Pauline). You can **stay**, too, either camping on the sand, in cabins rented locally or at expensive cabañas (⑥) at the western end of the beach.

Getting to Mazunte from Puerto Escondido, you can save going through Pochutla and Puerto Ángel by getting dropped off at **San Antonio**, a cluster of just a few houses and a restaurant, from where you can hitch or take a taxi the 5km to Mazunte. Buses from Mazunte go to Zipolite, Puerto Ángel and Pochutla (every 30–40min).

Pochutla

Anyone visiting Puerto Ángel and the beaches either way along the coast comes through **POCHUTLA**, a dull place 2km north of Hwy-200, some 12km from Puerto Ángel. Apart from catching a bus to the coast there's no reason to come here, though long stayers will need to return to change money – there are no banks at the beaches – and perhaps to visit the market for provisions.

The **bus stations** – the new second-class Estrella del Valle and the first-class Garcela and Cristóbal Colón – are close to each other on Cárdenas, which runs from Hwy-200 into the centre of town. Further along Cárdenas, either the Bancomer or the Inverlat, both with ATM, will **change money** (9–11am) at a half-decent rate. Of the **hotels**, *Hotel Pochutla*, Madero 102 (☎958/4-00-33; ②), on the central plaza, is comfortable and spacious, while *Hotel Santa Cruz*, Lázaro Cárdenas 88 (☎958/4-01-16; ②), near the bus stations, is much poorer with noisy front rooms.

Buses frequently head down to Puerto Ángel and Zipolite, along with colectivos or *especial* taxis; *especial* costs well over five times as much, so go colectivo – you should rarely have to wait long for fellow passengers. In Puerto Ángel, the taxis drop off at the rank by the dock. If you want to go further, over to Playa del Panteón for example, make this clear as you set out or you'll be charged an outrageous amount for the last part of the journey (you probably will be anyway, but at least you'll be prepared). There are also regular buses west to Puerto Escondido, east to Huatulco and inland to Oaxaca.

Huatulco and around

Heading **east from Puerto Ángel** towards Salina Cruz, there's 170km of coast that until recently was quite untouched. It's a slow, hot drive – but an enjoyable one – along a jungly coastal strip regularly cut by small rivers and giving frequent tantalizing glimpses of fabulous-looking beaches. All of these are extremely tough to get to, however, and few are as idyllic as they appear: quite apart from the total lack of facilities, they're marred by strong winds, tricky currents, and, as you approach Salina Cruz, increasing oil pollution.

At **HUATULCO**, some 35km from Puerto Ángel, where previously you'd have found only a couple of fly-blown villages and nine stunning sandy bays, the latest of Mexico's purpose-built resorts is well underway. By the late 1980s there was an airport, four large hotels including a *Club Med* and a *Sheraton*, and an expectation of rapid expansion. More recently, however, progress has slowed: probably a blessing as it gives FONATUR – the government tourist development agency whose baby Huatulco is – a chance to carry out its professed intention to preserve **ecological zones** among the hotels and to ensure that the infrastructure (especially sewage treatment plants) is working in time. For the moment, only two of the nine bays have been developed, though new roads mean that there is now access to eight of them. The long-term effects of this remain to be seen, but this is a large area, and it may be years before the outlying bays are spoilt. Until then, they're not far from the paradise that the brochures describe, though the lack of budget accommodation remains a problem.

Huatulco is the all-encompassing name of the resort, with **Santa Cruz Huatulco**, the village on the coast, as its focus. It's been cleaned up in expectation of becoming an "authentic Mexican village", something it patently fails to be, comprising a marina, handicraft stalls, a few relatively inexpensive seafood restaurants and a handful of condos. There's no reason to stay here – and nowhere reasonably priced to do so – but at the *embarcadero* you can organize horseback rides to **Maguey Beach**, fishing and diving trips, or catch boats that (on demand) ply the coast to the more remote bays. All of these have at least some sort of *enramada*, and **San Agustín**, one of the most developed, is lined with seafood restaurants.

Access to the beach at **Tangolunda**, 5km northeast over the headland, is almost completely cut off by the aforementioned international hotels and the swanky homes of the likes of Julio Iglesias and ex-Mexican president Salinas. The only public access is by the road leading to *Club Med* and, of course, you can sneak into the *Sheraton* for a swim in the pool, but there's little else to do and the restaurants are grossly overpriced.

Crucecita

The purpose-built town of **CRUCECITA** (also, confusingly, known as **Santa Cruz**, especially by the bus companies), 2km inland from Santa Cruz Huatulco, serves both bays. Though designed to house the ten thousand Mexicans needed to support the bayside hotels, it is now becoming a tourist centre in its own right, probably helped along by the slow progress elsewhere. Certainly it boasts a zócalo, shops and various businesses, along with pizza joints, costly stores and an outpost of the *Carlos 'n' Charlie's* fun bar chain, a sure sign of resort status. Nevertheless, in its fifteen years of existence, it has matured well to become a thriving and enjoyable place.

Finding a budget **place to stay** in Crucecita, while easier than around the bays, is still a problem, though outside the high season (Dec, *Semana Santa*, July & Aug) prices drop by around thirty percent. The cheapest **hotel** is the basic *Hospedaje Gloriluz* (☎958/7-01-60; ③), on Pochote near the entrance to town, between Gardenia and Bugambilia, which run parallel down to the zócalo. Or you can try the basic but clean *Posada Miguel*, Colorin 303 (no phone; ③). *Alonso Cardenas*, C Acacia 211

(☎958/7-11-56 or 7-03-62; ④), has a variety of cheap furnished rooms and apartments to rent (from US$15 to US$55), and can be bargained down.

The bulk of the **restaurants** surround the zócalo, among them *Oasis*, on the corner of Bugambilia and Flamboyan, which serves up reasonably priced tortas as well as excellent sushi. For something simpler and cheaper, try *Grillos*, on the zócalo. All these places, and everywhere else in Crucecita, lie within easy walking distance of the **bus stations** which line Gardenia. The **post office** is a bit further out on the road to Santa Cruz Huatulco, where you'll also find a number of **banks** (with ATMs). Triton Dive Centre, on the pier at Crucecita's bay, offer dive-trips in the area, along with PADI and NAUI certification. They also speak English.

On to the Isthmus

The **Isthmus of Tehuantepec**, where the Pacific and the Atlantic are just 210km apart and the land never rises to more than 250m above sea level, is the narrowest point of Mexico. For years – until Panama got there first – there were plans to cut a canal through here: as it is, the coast-to-coast railway (still a link in the line to Guatemala) was, in the late nineteenth century, an extremely busy trade route, the chief communication link between the American continent's east and west coasts. It's a hot and steamy region, long run-down and not in any way improved by the trappings of the 1980s oil boom, and one where the only good reason to stop is if there's a **fiesta** going on – they're among the most colourful in the country. Otherwise, you can go straight through – from Oaxaca to **Tuxtla Gutiérrez** and from there on to **San Cristóbal** – in a single, very long, day. Only if you plan to head straight for the Yucatán is there any particular reason to cross the Isthmus: it's considerably quicker to stick to the lowlands, though a lot duller than the route through highland Chiapas.

Historically, the *indígenas* of this region, especially in the south, have always had a **matriarchal society**. But though you'll still find women dominating trade in the markets, this is a tradition that is dying faster than most others in macho Mexico. Nevertheless, at least some elements remain: the women are spectacularly colourfully dressed, and draped with gold jewellery; it's still the mother who gives away her child at a wedding (and occasionally still the eldest daughter who inherits any land); and on feast days the women prove their dominance by climbing to the rooftops and throwing fruit down on the men in the *Tirada de Frutas*.

Salina Cruz

SALINA CRUZ, 130km east of Huatulco on the coast, was the Pacific terminus of the trans-Isthmus railway and the port through which everything was shipped. Nowadays, again exporting oil in large quantities, it's a sprawling, unattractive place, with a reputation for crime and brawling violence. **Buses** all arrive and leave from terminals close to each other 2km from the centre on the northern outskirts, so changing from trans-Isthmus to coastal buses should present no problem, nor any need to head downtown.

If you do get stuck here for the night, head for the plaza and C 5 de Mayo, leading off it, where you'll find the *Hotel Fuentes* (☎971/4-02-93; ③) at Camacho 114, the basic but comfortable *Hotel Magda* (☎971/4-01-07; ③), two doors away, and, best of all, the *Posada del Jardín*, Camacho 108 (☎971/4-01-62; ③).

La Ventosa, the nearby beach village, reached by bus from the side of the plaza, may once have been picturesque, but it's now spoilt by the oil refinery backdrop. As windy as its name implies, and polluted too, it's a run-down place, where most of the seafront restaurants seem in danger of dissolving into the sea. The best **hotel**, conveniently the first one you reach, is the *Posada Rustrian* (③), which has a courtyard and a garden.

Tehuantepec

The modest town of **TEHUANTEPEC**, 14km north of Salina Cruz, preserves the local traditions of the Isthmus most visibly, has some of the best of the fiestas, and is also an extremely pleasant place to stop, with a fine zócalo and several inexpensive hotels around it. In the evening, the zócalo really comes alive, with people strolling and eating food from the many stalls set up by the townswomen, who proudly wear the traditional flower-embroidered *huipil* and floor-length velvet skirt of the Zapotec – a costume adopted by the artist Frida Kahlo in some of her self-portraits. Tehuantepec is a tiny place where a walk of ten blocks in any direction will take you out into the countryside. Despite this – or perhaps because it's so concentrated – the town is extraordinarily noisy, the constant din of passing buses made worse by the motor tricycles (*motos*) that locals use as taxis. There's really no reason to stay long, and the number of second-class buses makes it extremely easy to leave, but if you do stop awhile pop into the **Casa de Cultura** (Mon–Fri 4–9pm, Sat 9am–2pm; free), where dance, music and art workshops are held in the remains of the Dominican ex-convento Rey Cosijoní, started in 1544 at the behest of Cortés and named after the incumbent Zapotec king. You can wander around and take a look at the few remaining frescoes by taking Hidalgo from the north side of the zócalo and following it right as it becomes Guererro.

The ruins of Guiengola

The hill-top fortress of **GUIENGOLA**, 15km north of Tehuantepec, was the Zapotec stronghold on the Isthmus, and in 1496 its defenders successfully fought off an attempt by the Aztecs to gain control of the area, which was never fully incorporated into their empire. It continued to be a centre of resistance during the early years of the Conquest and was a focus of Indian revolt against Spanish rule throughout the sixteenth and seventeenth centuries.

At the site you'll see remains of pyramids and a ball-court, but the most striking feature is the massive **defensive wall**. By definition, Guiengola's superb defensive location makes it somewhat inaccessible and it's probably best to take a taxi, though buses to Oaxaca do pass the turn-off to the site, 8km from Tehuantepec on the main road (look out for the "Ruinas Guiengola" sign). From here it's a hot, seven-kilometre, uphill walk. The site is open daily, and if the caretaker is around you may be asked to pay a small fee, though you'll almost certainly have the place to yourself.

Tehuantepec practicalities

Buses stop at several stations near each other at the northern edge of town on Hwy-190, a twenty-minute walk or a short *moto* ride from the centre. Some local services also pause at the end of 5 de Mayo, 100m west of the zócalo. There's a **post office** and **bank** on the north side of the square; on 5 de Mayo itself you'll find a Bancomer with good rates and an ATM, and a **caseta de larga distancia** (7am–10pm). **Hotels** aren't far away: *Donaji* (☎971/5-00-64; ③), at Juárez 10, a block south of the zócalo, is marginally the best, overlooking the Parque Juárez and with a rooftop view over the town. The simple *Casa de Huéspedes Istmo*, Hidalgo 31 (☎971/5-00-19; ②), is better value for money.

Calle Juana, south from the zócalo, has two of the best **places to eat**: *El Portón* serves extremely cheap sandwiches and regional antojitos; *Café Colonial*, at no. 66, stays open later (until 10pm) and dishes up good local food, including chicken prepared in almost every way imaginable. On the zócalo itself, *Jugos Hawaii* is good for tortas and licuados, and be sure to try some of the cornbread that local women hawk insistently to everyone arriving on the bus.

While Tehuantepec is a major stopping point en route to Oaxaca or the Chiapas coast, few buses originate here, so **moving on**, you may find it easier to take one of the constant stream of buses to **Juchitán**, 26km away (see below), and continue from there. The main long-distance routes, operated by first-class Cristóbal Colón and

Autobuses Unidos, serve Oaxaca, México, Tuxtla Gutiérrez, Coatzacoalcos and Villahermosa, and there are also buses to San Cristóbal and Puerto Escondido; you can buy tickets in advance. Several second-class companies also operate between the main towns on the Isthmus, and there are constant departures for Salina Cruz.

Juchitán

JUCHITÁN, just 26km east of Tehuantepec and the point where the road meets the railway to Guatemala, is not much more attractive than Salina Cruz. It does, however, enjoy native traditions and fiestas similar to those of Tehuantepec, a good market and a rather sleazy tropical port atmosphere. The town is best known in modern Mexico, however, for having somehow managed to elect a reforming socialist government in the early 1980s. The PRI didn't take kindly to their activities, and eventually the state governor found a pretext to remove local officials from power and replace them with party faithfuls. The political trouble – and violence – that followed has largely blown over, but local events still occasionally make the front pages, and Juchitán's fiestas have a tendency to become political demonstrations.

The **bus** stations line the highway and you won't have long to wait, whichever direction you're heading. If you do need to stay the night, Tehuantepec is a much better base. The fanciest **place to stay** is the overpriced *Hotel La Mansión* (☎971/1-20-55; ⑤), Prolongacion 16 de Septiembre 11, a couple of blocks towards town from where most of the buses stop. Better to press on 2km along 16 de Septiembre, past several poor-value hotels, to the adequate *Casa de Huéspedes Echazarreta* (no phone; ②) on the **zócalo**. Here you'll also find the **post office**, a **Banamex** and some good **places to eat**, notably the *Casa Grande*, which serves reasonably priced seafood in an elegant cool atrium.

FIESTAS

JANUARY

1 NEW YEAR'S DAY is celebrated everywhere, but is particularly good in **Oaxaca** (Oaxaca) and **Mitla** (Oax).

14 Fiesta in **Niltepec** (Oax), on the Pacific coast road.

20 DÍA DE SAN SEBASTIAN. Big in **Tehuantepec** (Oax), **Jalapa de Díaz** (Oax), near Tuxtepec, and in **Pinotepa de Don Luis** (Oax), near the coast and Pinotepa Nacional.

FEBRUARY

2 DÍA DE LA CANDELARIA. Colourful Indian celebrations in **Santa María del Tule** (Oax) and in **San Mateo del Mar** (Oax), near Salina Cruz.

21 Gueletao (Oax), near Oaxaca, celebrates the birthday of Benito Juárez, born in the village.

22–25 Feria in **Matias Romero** (Oax), between Juchitán and Coatzacoalcos.

CARNIVAL (the week before Lent – variable Feb–March) is at its most frenzied in the big cities – especially **Oaxaca** (Oax) – but is also celebrated in hundreds of villages throughout the area.

25 Fiesta in **Acatlán** (Puebla), with many traditional dances.

MARCH

HOLY WEEK is widely observed – particularly big ceremonies in **Pinotepa Nacional** (Oax) and nearby **Pinotepa Don Luis** (Oax), as well as in **Jamiltepec** (Oax).

MAY

3 DÍA DE LA SANTA CRUZ celebrated in **Salina Cruz** (Oax), the start of a week-long feria.

8 DÍA DE SAN MIGUEL. In **Soyaltepec** (Oax), between Oaxaca and Huajuapan de León, festivities include horse and dog races, as well as boating events on a nearby lake.

15 DÍA DE SAN ISIDRO sees peasant celebrations everywhere – famous and picturesque fiestas in **Juchitán** (Oax).

19 Feria in **Huajuapan de León** (Oax).

CORPUS CHRISTI (variable – the Thursday after Trinity) sees a particularly good feria in **Izúcar de Matamoros** (Pue).

JUNE

24 DÍA DE SAN JUAN falls in the midst of festivities (22–26) in **Tehuantepec** (Oax).

JULY

On the first Wednesday of July, **Teotitlán del Valle** (Oax), near Oaxaca, holds a fiesta with traditional dances and religious processions.

23 Feria in **Huajuapan de León** (Oax).

25 DÍA DE SANTIAGO provokes widespread celebration – especially in **Izúcar de Matamoros** (Pue), **Niltepec** (Oax) and **Juxtlahuaca** (Oax).

In **Oaxaca** itself, the last two Mondays of July see the famous festival of GUE-LAGUETZA (or the *Lunes del Cerro*), a mixture of traditional dancing and Catholic rites on the Cerro del Fortín. Highly popular; tickets for the good seats are sold at the tourist office.

AUGUST

13–16 Spectacular festivities in **Juchitán** (Oax) and lesser fiestas in **Nochixtlán** (Oax), between Oaxaca and Huajuapan de León, and on the 15th in **Tehuantepec** (Oax).

24 Fiesta in **San Bartolo Coyotepec** (Oax), near Oaxaca.

31 Blessing of the animals in **Oaxaca** – locals bring their beasts to the church of La Merced to be blessed.

SEPTEMBER

3–5 **Juchitán** (Oax) once again hosts a series of picturesque celebrations.

8 Religious ceremonies in **Teotitlán del Valle** (Oax), in **Putla** (Oax), on the road inland from Pinotepa Nacional, and in **Tehuantepec** (Oax).

25 FIESTA DE SAN JERONIMO in **Ixtepec** (Oax) lasts until October 2.

29 DÍA DE SAN MIGUEL is celebrated in **Soyaltepec** (Oax).

OCTOBER

1 Several barrios of **Tehuantepec** (Oax) have their own small fiestas.

On the first Sunday in October, the DÍA DE LA VIRGEN DEL ROSARIO is celebrated in **San Pedro Amuzgos** (Oax). On the second Sunday there's a large feria in **Tlacolula** (Oax), near Oaxaca, and on the second Monday the FERIA DEL ARBOL based around the famous tree in **Santa María del Tule** (Oax).

18 Indian fiesta in **Ojitlán** (Oax), near Tuxtepec, with a formal, candlelit procession.

24 In **Acatlán** (Pue), a fiesta with processions and traditional dances.

NOVEMBER

2 DAY OF THE DEAD is respected everywhere, with particularly strong traditions in **Salina Cruz** (Oax) and in **San Gabriel Chilac** (Pue), near Tehuacán.

25 Patron Saint's day in **Mechoacán** (Oax), on the coast near Pinotepa Nacional.

29 DÍA DE SAN ANDRES celebrated in **San Juan Colorado** (Oax), on the coast road near Pinotepa Nacional.

DECEMBER

8 DÍA DE LA INMACULADA CONCEP-CIÓN is widely observed – especially with traditional dances in **Juquilla** (Oax), not far from Puerto Escondido, and **Zacatepec** (Oax), on the road inland from Pinotepa Nacional.

16–25 The pre-Christmas period is a particularly exciting one in **Oaxaca**, with posadas and nativity plays nightly. The 18th is the FIESTA DE LA VIRGEN DE LA SOLEDAD, patroness of the state, with fireworks, processions and music. The 23rd is the FIESTA DE LOS RABANOS (Radishes), when there's an exhibition of statues and scenes sculpted from radishes. On Christmas Eve there's more music, fireworks and processions before midnight mass. Throughout it all, **buñuelos** – crisp pancakes that you eat before smashing the plate on which they are served – are dished up at street stalls.

travel details

BUSES

The following frequencies and times are for first-class services. Scores of second-class buses usually cover the same routes, taking 10–20 percent longer.

Huatulco to: Puerto Escondido (4 daily; 3–4hr); Pochutla (hourly; 1hr); Oaxaca (3 daily, 7–8hr); Salina Cruz (3 daily; 2hr 30min); San Cristóbal (2 daily).

Oaxaca to: México (at least hourly; 6hr); Pochutla (3 daily; 7hr); Puerto Escondido (3 daily; 8–10hr); San Cristóbal (2 daily; 12hr); Tehuacán (8 daily; 6hr); Tehuantepec (hourly; 4–5hr); Villahermosa (2 daily; 12hr) Veracruz (3 daily; 9hr)

Pochutla to: Huatulco (hourly; 1hr); Oaxaca (3 daily; 8hr); Puerto Escondido (hourly; 1hr); Salina Cruz (hourly; 4hr); San Cristóbal (1 daily; over 12hr).

Puerto Ángel to: Pochutla (every 20min; 20min); Zipolite (every 20min; 10min).

Puerto Escondido to: Acapulco (at least hourly; 7–8hr); Huatulco (hourly; 2hr); México (2 daily; 12hr); Oaxaca (3 daily; 10hr); Pochutla (hourly; 1hr); Salina Cruz (7 daily; 5–6hr); Tehuantepec (1 daily; 5–6hr).

Salina Cruz to: Acapulco (7 daily; 11hr); Huatulco (7 daily; 2hr 30min); Oaxaca (4 daily; 5hr); Pochutla (hourly; 4hr); Puerto Escondido (7 daily; 5–6hr); Tehuantepec (every 30min; 20min).

Tehuacán to: Córdoba (every 30min; 3hr); México (hourly; 4hr); Oaxaca (15 daily; 6hr); Veracruz (every 30min; 4hr).

Tehuantepec to: Coatzacoalcos (10 daily; 6hr); México (7 daily; 12hr); Oaxaca (hourly; 4–5hr); Puerto Escondido (1 daily; 5–6hr); Salina Cruz (every 30min; 20min); San Cristóbal (2 daily; 8hr); Tuxtla Gutiérrez (7 daily; 5hr); Veracruz (3 daily; 9hr).

TRAINS

One train, with first- and second-class carriages, runs daily in each direction between México and Oaxaca; another, second-class only, runs between Puebla and Oaxaca.

PLANES

Oaxaca to: Cancún via Tuxtla, Villahermosa and Merida (daily); Huatulco (daily); México (10 daily); Puerto Escondido (2 daily); Veracruz (3 per week).

Puerto Escondido to: México (1 daily); Oaxaca (2 daily).

CHAPTER NINE

CHIAPAS AND TABASCO

E ndowed with a stunning variety of cultures, landscapes and wildlife, **Chiapas**, Mexico's southernmost state, has much to tempt visitors. Deserted Pacific beaches, rugged mountains and ruined cities buried in steamy jungle offer a bewildering choice, added to which the observation of **indigenous traditions** continues – albeit with a struggle – almost everywhere. Chiapas was actually administered by the Spanish as part of Guatemala until the early nineteenth century, when it seceded to join newly independent Mexico, and today it is second only to Oaxaca in the proportion of Indians in its population.

The villages around **San Cristóbal de las Casas**, in the geographic centre of the state, are the stronghold of indigenous culture. A visit here is an entry to another age and, though tolerated, your presence is barely acknowledged. There is, of course, a darker side to this: picturesque as their life may seem to tourists, the indigenous population has long been bypassed or ignored by the political system, their land and their livelihood under constant threat from modernization, or straightforward seizure.

Long before open revolt broke out on New Year's Day 1994 (see below), a revived **Zapatista** peasant movement had carried out attacks on army patrols, and despite official denials of armed insurrection the army had raided training camps in search of "subversives": news of such happenings was successfully suppressed, however, until the situation burst into the world's consciousness. There is currently a very heavy army presence in what the Mexican authorities refer to as the **"conflict zone"**, a fluid area with uncertain boundaries in the southeastern corner of the state, occupied by the Zapatistas and over which the army is attempting to regain control. At its widest extent this could be anywhere east of the road from San Cristóbal via Ocosingo to Palenque, though in essence it means the **Lacandón region** (often referred to as *el monte* or *la selva*), now almost encircled by the distant reaches of both sections of the **Frontier Highway**. Though you're extremely unlikely to stumble into trouble visiting the main attractions in this region, such as the Lagos or the ruins of Bonampak, and the army will always treat genuine tourists with respect, you should get **up-to-date advice** before visiting (see the box on p.454): in a volatile situation such as this, things can change quickly.

The state of **Tabasco** is less obviously attractive than its neighbour state – steamy and low-lying for the most part, with a major oil industry to mar the landscape. Recently, however, the state has been seeking to encourage tourism, above all pushing the legacy of the **Olmecs**, Mexico's earliest developed civilization. The vibrant, modern capital, **Villahermosa**, has a wealth of parks and museums, the best-known of which, the **Parque La Venta**, displays the original massive Olmec heads. In the extreme southwest, bordered by Veracruz or Chiapas, a section of Tabasco reaches

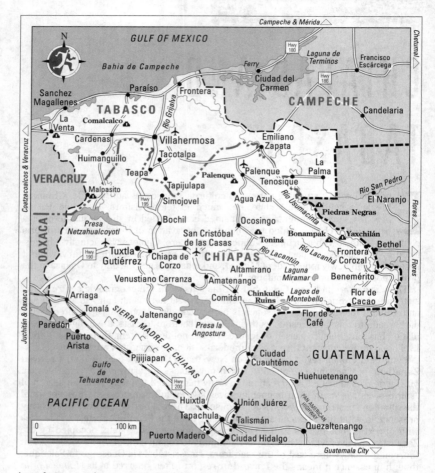

into the mountains up to 1000m high. Here, in a region almost never visited by outsiders, a low-impact tourism initiative allows you to splash in pristine rivers and waterfalls and explore the astonishing ruins of **Malpasito**, a city of the **Zoque** culture, about whom little is known. Tabasco is also the starting point for river trips into **Guatemala**.

CHIAPAS

Despite the rebellion of 1994, tourists continue to come to Chiapas; some, indeed, come specifically to witness the unfolding events. Before visiting, however, you should get **up-to-date advice**: though travel was apparently safe at the time of writing, in a volatile situation such as this things can change quickly.

The terrain of Chiapas ranges from the Pacific coastal plain, backed by the peaks of the Sierra Madre de Chiapas, through the mainly agricultural Central Depression, irrigated by the Río Grijalva, rising again to the highlands, **Los Altos de Chiapas**. Beyond the highlands the land falls away again: in the north to the Gulf coast plain of Tabasco, while to the east a series of great rivers, separated by the jungle-covered ridges of the **Lacandón rainforest**, flow into the Río Usumacinta, which forms the border with Guatemala.

The **climate**, too, can vary enormously. In one theoretical day you could be basking on the beach at Puerto Arista in the morning, and spending a chilly night by a fireside in the old colonial capital of San Cristóbal de las Casas. Generally the lowlands can be almost unbearably hot and humid, with heavy afternoon rainfall in summer, making a dip in the sea or river (or pool) a daily necessity. Days in the highlands can also be hot, and you'll need to carry water if you're hiking, but by evening you may need a sweater.

For its size Chiapas has the greatest **biological diversity** in North America. A visit to the **zoo** in the state capital of **Tuxtla Gutiérrez**, which houses only animals native to the state, will whet your appetite for the region's natural wonders. In the huge **Montes Azules Biosphere Reserve**, reached from Palenque, a section of the largest remaining rainforest in North America has been preserved. This is also the home of the **Lacandón Maya**, who retreated into the forest when the Spanish arrived, and shunned contact until fifty years ago. There's **cloud forest** in the south, protected in the **El Triunfo Biosphere Reserve** and, far easier to visit, the beautiful lakes and hills of the **Lagos de Montebello National Park**.

The Classic-period Maya site of **Palenque**, on the northern edge of the highlands, is one of Mexico's finest ancient sites and has been the focus of much recent restoration work. The limestone hills in this area are pierced by crystal-clear rivers, creating exquisite waterfalls – most spectacularly at **Agua Azul**. Palenque is also the best starting point for a trip down the **Usumacinta valley**, to visit the remote ruins of **Bonampak** and **Yaxchilán**. The Frontier Highway pushes on south beyond these sites to the growing town of Benemérito, where you can get a boat to **Guatemala**, or visit **Las Guacamayas**, on the **Río Lacantún**, where some new tourist accommodation (sponsored by the state government to encourage economic development) enables you to visit the southern edge of the Monte Azules Reserve.

Though travelling independently to **Chajul**, on the south bank of the Lacantún (at the time of writing the end of the of the Frontier Highway) is possible, it's not recommended, due to the military situation in Chiapas. However, the two sections of the highway will meet soon, and you may be able to you head around the border on an arduous circuit to the Lagos de Montebello and back to San Cristóbal – if and when an effective peace agreement is reached between the Mexican government and the Zapatista rebels.

Travelling around Chiapas is not difficult: the main cities are connected by a network of good, all-weather roads and the **Pan-American Highway** passes from west

THE ZAPATISTA REBELLION

THE OPENING SHOTS

On **January 1, 1994**, the day the NAFTA treaty came into effect, several thousand lightly armed rebels, wearing their uniform of green or black army-style tunics and black balaclavas, occupied San Cristóbal de las Casas, the former state capital and Chiapas' major tourist destination. From the balcony of the Municipal Palace, **Subcomandante Marcos**, the Zapatistas' enigmatic leader, or at least main spokesperson, read *La Declaración de la Selva Lacandona*, declaring war on the "seventy-year-old dictatorship . . . of traitors", and demanding the resignation of the Mexican president and the state governor, and an overhaul of the country's archaic political structure. Simultaneously, in a series of bold, carefully executed strikes, the rebels, the Zapatista Army of National Liberation (EZLN), occupied the towns of Las Margaritas, Ocosingo and Altamirano, making the same demands.

After a thirty-hour occupation, during which they destroyed government equipment and municipal records, the EZLN withdrew from San Cristóbal. The next day, the Mexican army began its furious counterattack with ground troops and aircraft. Dozens of civilians and Zapatistas were killed as the army retook **Ocosingo**; a series of isolated attacks by groups claiming to support the rebellion led the army to believe there was a serious possibility of a nationwide revolution, and for several days journalists were kept away from the conflict zone.

Meanwhile, erudite, witty and penetrating communiqués signed by Marcos, sent from a secret destination in the Lacandón rainforest and published in the Mexican and international press, became a major feature of the battle to keep the struggle in the world spotlight. The war was waged by the Zapatistas with the pen and the **Internet** – and they were winning. Reports of widespread human rights abuses committed by the army – including summary execution of suspected rebels and terrorizing civilians – caused an international outcry, and on January 13 a **ceasefire** took effect. In the meantime, dozens of *campesino* and indigenous organizations in Chiapas formed a representative body, **CEOIC** (later, **CONAI**), presided over by **Bishop Samuel Ruiz** of San Cristóbal, calling for an end to human rights abuses and the start of peace negotiations.

PEACE NEGOTIATIONS

At first talks appeared to go well, but on March 23, the **assassination of Luis Donaldo Colosio**, the PRI presidential candidate – effectively the next Mexican president – sparked conspiracy theories and halted the peace process. The EZLN withdrew, believing the army was preparing an attack, but continued to consult with communities in the area, and in June announced a rejection of the proposals.

Mexico's **general election** on August 21, 1994, passed relatively quietly, though when the results were announced the main left-wing opposition party, the **PRD**, accused the PRI of fraud and organized a series of demonstrations and marches in Chiapas. When the PRI candidate took office, the opposition candidate assumed the role of parallel governor, establishing with the support of the Zapatistas a **"Rebel Government in Transition"**. On September 28, the assassination of Ruiz Massieu, General Secretary of the PRI, heightened tension, and the army waited at the ends of the roads leading to Zapatista-controlled areas.

Within days of the new president, Ernesto Zedillo, taking office in **December 1994**, the Zapatistas made their first major foray through the army cordon, briefly occupying several towns. Despite the provocation, Zedillo's response was restrained, and no major offensive was ordered immediately, though reports of rebels on the move sent panic through Mexico's financial markets, leading to a massive **devaluation of the nuevo peso**.

In February 1995, however, President Zedillo asserted his strength of purpose as Mexico's leader by unmasking the mysterious "Subcomandante Marcos" as **Rafael**

Guillén, a former university professor and veteran of 1970s guerrilla movements, and ordered the army to arrest him. This hardened attitude was more to boost his credibility as president than a realistic attempt to subdue the uprising by military force. Nevertheless an **army offensive** temporarily re-occupied some of the Zapatista-controlled territory, spreading fear among the indigenous community and creating thousands of **internal refugees** as peasants fled to the mountains.

Despite these apparent setbacks, or even because of them, the Zapatistas continued to enjoy popular sympathy, and the government was forced to re-open negotiations. After detailed national and international consultations the Zapatistas insisted that any solution to the conflict must include a recognition of indigenous rights. Eventually, in February 1996, amid mutual suspicion and a strengthening of the Mexican army's presence in Chiapas, the **San Andrés Accords on Rights and Indigenous Cultures** were signed. The Accords recognized the right to education in indigenous languages and guaranteed representation in national and state legislatures; in theory a new beginning, which would attempt to remedy centuries of discrimination. Any hopes of a real settlement were premature, however, as the government failed to move on the constitutional and legal changes necessary to implement the Accords. The unspoken policy appeared to marginalize the Zapatistas and contain political unrest within Chiapas, and, by doing so, avoid a protracted (and possibly high-profile) **counter-insurgency war**; costly both in humanitarian terms and in the unfavourable international reaction this would inevitably cause. Each side accused the other of deliberately stalling the peace talks, and of placing contradictory interpretations on what had been agreed so far.

The EZLN had by now lost any chance of regaining the initiative in an armed conflict and the Mexican government steadfastly refused to accept international arbitration. The Zapatistas' support was weakening as the forces ranged against them consolidated their power. The army gradually tightened the cordon around the Zapatista strongholds; roads and bases were built and troop numbers (currently around 25,000) were as high as ever. Right-wing **paramilitary groups**, financed and armed by ranchers and landowners and affiliated to the PRI, long a feature of political oppression in Chiapas, continued to grow in strength and brutality. Known collectively as *guardias blancas* – white guards – and able to act with apparent impunity, they have carried out an escalating campaign of terror against the indigenous population and anyone suspected of being a Zapatista sympathizer. Hundreds of people have been attacked and murdered, and thousands more driven from their homes, but the worst atrocity (which made headlines around the world) was the **massacre** of 45 displaced Tzotzil Indians in a church in the village of **Acteal**, north of San Cristóbal, on December 22, 1997. This provoked such a storm of outrage that the government was forced to act; dozens of paramilitaries and police suspected of taking part in the massacre were arrested and both Mexico's interior minister, Emiliano Chuayffett, and the Chiapas governor, César Ruiz Ferro, resigned.

THE CRISIS CONTINUES

The massacre and its aftermath once again placed Chiapas in the centre of the political agenda, and increased demands for implementation of the peace accord were made. The extra troops sent to Chiapas did nothing to halt the activities of the paramilitaries. Indeed their incursions into EZLN strongholds, retaking and occupying several of the 38 *municipios rebeldes* – autonomous authorities – set up by the Zapatistas caused Bishop Ruiz to resign as mediator in June 1998. CONAI was dissolved, negotiations ceased completely, and it appears that the government's strategy is indeed to overcome the rebels by military means.

At the time of writing the Zapatistas still control much of the land they took at the beginning of the conflict (over ten percent of Chiapas) but a peaceful end to the conflict

Continues over

is more remote than at any time since the uprising began. In México and San Cristóbal demonstrations continue to be held in support of the Zapatistas, and in San Cristóbal Zapatista dolls and Marcos souvenirs, emblazoned with his masked features, sell in their thousands.

A word of **warning**, though, if your sympathies extend beyond giving economic assistance to the indigenous souvenir makers: there is a concerted **anti-foreigner campaign** under way in Chiapas at present. Government officials, citing the "infestation of foreign activists who stir up and manipulate many indigenous groups contrary to constitutional order" claim that the presence of *simpatico* foreigners influences and even controls political opposition in the state. Although there are foreign observers in "civil peace camps" in the Zapatista areas, they are not recognized as such by the Mexican authorities. Being in (or even near) the **conflict zone** invites suspicion of taking part in political activities – illegal for foreigners – and several people have recently been deported.

If you do go be as fully informed as you can: **SIPAZ**, the International Service for Peace (☎ & fax in USA 408/425-1257; *sipaz@igc.org*) does have a volunteer programme in Chiapas and their **Web site** – *www.nonviolence.org/sipaz* – provides the best regular updates and analysis of the situation in Chiapas. The **EZLN supporters' Web site** – *www.ezln.org* – has superb links, including the relevant pages of *La Jornada*, a respected Mexican newspaper, and is also an excellent source of information.

to east through some of the most spectacular scenery in the state. In the south the coastal highway offers a speedy route from **Arriaga**, near the Oaxaca border, right through to **Tapachula**, almost on the frontier with Guatemala. In the out-of-the-way places, particularly in the jungle, travel is by dirt roads, which, though generally well maintained, can cause problems in the rainy season. These more remote places are also fairly well served by public transport, though it's more likely to be *combis* and trucks taking people and produce to and from markets, than the comfortable buses of the main roads.

The Chiapas coast

Hwy-200, much of it recently upgraded, provides a fast route from the Oaxaca border to Tapachula: if you plan on getting **to Guatemala** as quickly as possible, this is the road to take. It traverses the steamy coastal plain of the **Soconusco**, running about 20km inland, with the 2400-metre peaks of the **Sierra Madre de Chiapas** always in view. These little-visited mountains, protected by National and Biosphere Reserve status, are penetrated by roads only at their eastern and western extremities. The plain itself is a fertile agricultural area, mainly given over to coffee and bananas, though there are also many *ranchos*, where cattle grow fat on the lush grass; the excellent local **cheese** is celebrated in the *Esposición de Quesos*, held in Pijijiapan the week before Christmas.

Arriaga

ARRIAGA, the first town on the Chiapas coast road, is a dusty, uninteresting place, but its location at the junction of Hwy-195 (the road over the mountains to Tuxtla) means you may have to change buses here. The **Central de Autobuses**, with plenty of first- and second-class connections, is on the main road, south of the train tracks, six blocks from the zócalo. Microbuses for Tonalá leave constantly from just south of

---

ACCOMMODATION PRICE CODES

All the accommodation listed in this book has been categorized into one of nine price bands, as set out below. The prices quoted are in US dollars and normally refer to the cheapest available room for two people sharing in high season. For more details, see p.36.

① up to US$5	④ US$15–25	⑦ US$60–80
② US$5–10	⑤ US$25–40	⑧ US$80–100
③ US$10–15	⑥ US$40–60	⑨ US$100 and over

the zócalo, passing (though not stopping at) the bus station en route. **Hotels** in Arriaga aren't generally recommended; if you get stuck, try *Hotel Iris* (②), signposted from the bus station, or the *Colonial* (②), across the train tracks from the bus station.

Tonalá

Larger and marginally more inviting than Arriaga, **TONALÁ** is just a thirty-minute *microbus* ride away down Hwy-200, which, as Av Hidalgo, forms the town's main street. All the bus companies terminate along Hidalgo: the main first-class companies pull in about 1km west of the zócalo; second-class to the east.

Everything you need in Tonalá is either on the **zócalo** – Parque Esperanza – or within a couple of blocks of it. The central feature of the park is the **Estela de Tlaloc**, a large, standing stone carved by the Olmecs, depicting the rain god Tlaloc. If you're stuck for something to do, you could always visit the **Museo Arqueológico**, on Hidalgo across from Cristóbal Colón, though the Olmec and Maya exhibits here appear to have been abandoned. Next door is the Centro de Producción Artesanal, where artists and students make ceramics using both traditional and modern methods.

Tonalá's **tourist office**, on the ground floor of the Palacio Municipal (Mon–Fri 9am–3pm & 6–8pm, Sat 9am–2pm), isn't an essential stop, though it does have information about beaches nearby. The heat and constant traffic noise makes **staying** in Tonalá rather uncomfortable; you're better off heading to the beach at Puerto Arista (below). The hotels near the first-class buses are overpriced; head towards the zócalo for the *Tonalá* (☎966/3-04-80; ③), at Hidalgo 172, which has some a/c rooms. The *Farro* (☎966/3-00-33; ②), a block south of the zócalo at the corner of 16 de Septiembre and Matamoros, has reasonable budget rooms and a restaurant. The best hotel in the centre is the *Galilea* (☎966/3-02-39; ④), on the east side of the zócalo, which has clean, quiet rooms with private bathrooms and TV. Several good **restaurants** and food stalls also ring the zócalo. **Leaving Tonalá**, most buses are *de paso*, and you may have to wait until the bus arrives to see if there's a seat; alternatively, you could catch a *microbus* to Arriaga and buy your ticket there. *Combis* and taxis to **Puerto Arista** (US$0.50 per person) and **Boca del Cielo** leave at least every twenty minutes (or when full) from the corner of 5 de Mayo and Matamoros, a couple of blocks south of the zócalo in the **market** area, where the streets are crammed with fruit and vegetable stalls.

Puerto Arista

Although this quiet village may not be everyone's idea of a perfect beach resort, **PUERTO ARISTA**, with its miles of clean sand and invigorating surf, does offer a chance to escape the unrelenting heat of the inland towns. There's little to see, and you have to stay under the shade of a palapa near the shore to benefit from the breezes, but it's a worthwhile stop if you've been doing some hard travelling. While the waves are definitely refreshing, you need to be aware of the potentially dangerous **rip tides** that sweep along the coast – never get out of your depth.

The road from Tonalá joins Puerto Arista's only street at the lighthouse. Here you're in the centre of town: walk a couple of kilometres left or right and you'll be on a deserted shoreline; ahead lies the beach, with hotels and restaurants packed closely together. You won't feel crowded though, unless you arrive in *Semana Santa*, as there seem to be at least as many buildings abandoned or boarded up as there are occupied.

There are many **hotels** in Puerto Arista but few customers: prices are difficult to determine since most places will try to overcharge outrageously. The best bet is to have a *refresco* or a cold beer at a restaurant and ask if you can leave your bags while you have a good look around. The cheaper places are basic and not particularly good value; bargain with the owner and you may be able to knock the price down. The more established hotels, such as *La Puesta del Sol* (②), the nearby *Brisas del Mar* (②) and the *Agua Marina* (turn right at the lighthouse; ②), are all clean and well run, but best here is the *Arista Bugambilias* (☎966/3-07-67 ext. 116; ⑤), with a pool and private garden on the beach. Turn left at the lighthouse, and you'll see signs for more hotels and several vey basic cabaña places. The *Lucerito* (☎966/3-07-67 ext. 152; ④), just back from the beach, is a great bargain, with tiled rooms with a/c, and a pool. There are a couple of dozen beachfront palapa **restaurants**, serving basic seafood, but only five or six ever open at any one time. Most will rent you a hammock or let you sling your own for a couple of dollars. And you can always **camp** on the beach for free.

You can easily get transport 15km along the coast to **Boca del Cielo** (no hotels), a cluster of houses and fishing boats on the landward side of a lagoon, where you can board a *lancha* (US$6.50 return) and speed across to a beautiful, deserted beach.

Tonalá to Tapachula

With your own vehicle, you can explore some of the side roads leading from Hwy-200 in the 220km between Tonalá and Tapachula: either up into the mountains, where the heavy rain gives rise to dozens of rivers and waterfalls, or down to near-deserted beaches. Most coastal villages are actually on the landward side of a narrow lagoon, separated from the ocean by a sandbar. These sandbars block many rivers' access to the sea, causing marshes to form and providing a superb wetland habitat, the highlight of which is an **ecological reserve** protecting 45km of coastline near **Acacoyagua** – the state tourist authorities are building a hotel here. Travelling **by bus**, it's much more difficult (though still possible) to take in destinations off the main road, and you need to be prepared to hitch and camp. At **HUIXTLA**, 42km before Tapachula, Hwy-211 snakes over the mountains via Motozintla to join the Pan-American Highway near Ciudad Cuauhtémoc and the Guatemalan border at La Mesilla. This bone-shaking road offers stupendous mountain views and is covered by buses running between Tapachula and Comitán and San Cristóbal de las Casas.

Tapachula

Though most travellers see it as no more than an overnight stop en route to or from Guatemala, **TAPACHULA** does actually have something to offer, being a gateway to both the coast and the mountains, with a lovely setting at the foot of the 4000-metre Volcán Tacaná. A busy commercial centre, known as the capital of the Soconusco, the southeastern region of the state, it grew in importance in the nineteenth century with the increasing demand for coffee and bananas. As a border city, it has a lively cultural mix, including not only immigrants from Central America, but also small German and Chinese communities. The **Museo Regional de Soconusco** (Tues–Sun 10am–5pm;

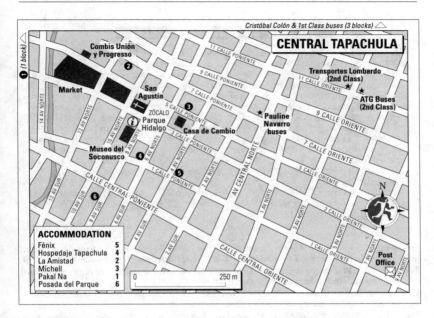

US$0.50), in the same building as the tourist office, tells their story, as well as displaying scraps of excavated finds from local ruins.

Arrival and information

The **tourist office** (daily 9am–3pm & 6–9pm; ☎962/5-54-09) is on the ground floor of the old Palacio Municipal, on the west side of the zócalo. The helpful staff will call a hotel for you and give you a city map. The town's layout is a little confusing, for while the streets are laid out in the regular numbered grid common in Chiapas, the zócalo, **Parque Hidalgo**, is not at its centre. It's not too far away, though: C Central meets Av Central three blocks east and a block south of the zócalo. All the main **bus stations** are north of the centre; the various second-class companies have their terminals within walking distance of the zócalo, while first-class Cristóbal Colón is further out at C 17 Ote between Av 3 Nte and Av 5 Nte.; taxis to the centre are cheap (under US$1); walking takes about twenty minutes. The **post office** (Mon–Fri 8am–6pm, Sat 8am–1pm) is a long way southeast of the zócalo, between 7 and 9 Nte. The main **banks** are one block east of the zócalo, but for changing cash and travellers' cheques you'll get a much quicker service from Cambios Tapa in the Plaza Victoria, a block east of the zócalo along C 5 Pte (Mon–Sat 8am–6pm, Sun 9am–1pm).

If you need a **Guatemalan visa**, the **consulate** is at C 2 Ote 33, between Av 7 and Av 9 Sur (Mon–Fri 8am–4pm; ☎962/6-12-52).

Accommodation

There's at least one **hotel** near any of the bus stations, but the ones around the second-class terminals are often sleazy. Calle 11 also has a few, and there's a clutch on Av 8 Nte, between calles 11 and 13 Pte. Some rather desperate-looking places can be found around the **market**, which straggles down the hill west of the zócalo, although there are also some surprisingly good-value hotels, too.

MOVING ON FROM TAPACHULA

First-class buses for destinations throughout Mexico leave from the Cristóbal Colón terminal; any bus or *combi* from the centre to Talismán passes the entrance. Some of the better second-class services also leave from here. If you're heading directly **to Guatemala** you can take advantage of the twice-daily luxury Galgos service, which takes you right through the border (US$28; 5–6hr). The main **second-class bus** operators are Rapidos del Sur, at 9 Pte and 14 Nte, for the coast as far as Salina Cruz; Autobuses Paulino Navarro, 7 Pte between C 2 and Central Nte, for the coast road, Ciudad Hidalgo and Puerto Madero. The most frequent service to San Cristóbal is with Lombardo (second-class) at 11 Ote and 3 Nte, with hourly services between 4am and 8pm (7hr 30min); Autotransportes Tuxtla Gutiérrez operate long-distance but comfortable second-class services from the same location. Union y Progreso, 5 C Pte between 12 and 14 avenidas Nte, runs frequent *combis* to Unión Juárez and to the Talismán Bridge for the Guatemalan border.

Tapachula's **airport** (☎962/6-22-91), 18km south on the road to Puerto Madero, is served by Aeroméxico (☎962/6-20-50), Aviacsa (☎962/6-14-39), Taesa (☎962/6-37-32) and several smaller commuter airlines.

Hospedaje Chelito, Av 1 Nte at the corner of C 17 Ote (☎962/6-24-28). Handy location just around the corner from the Cristóbal Colón buses (head left out of the terminal), with some a/c rooms. ③.

Fénix, Av 4 Nte 19, near the corner of C 1 Pte (☎962/5-07-55). Good value at the price: rooms have a/c, and there's a cooling fountain in the courtyard. ④.

La Amistad, C 7 Pte 34, between 10 and 12 avenidas Nte (☎962/6-22-93). The best budget hotel in the city; clean, cool rooms around a flower-filled courtyard. ②.

Michell, C 5 Pte 23A (☎962/6-88-74). Modern hotel half a block east of the zócalo; all rooms have a/c and TV and doubles have balconies. Accepts Visa and Mastercard. ⑤.

Pakal-Na, Av 16 Nte 44 (☎962/6-60-46). Almost at the edge of town, though only four blocks west of the zócalo, past the market. Very comfortable rooms with a/c, private bath and TV. Parking. Accepts Visa and Mastercard. ⑤.

Posada del Parque, Av 8 Sur 3, two blocks south of the zócalo (☎962/6-51-18). Clean, quiet and very good value. ②.

Hospedaje Tapachula (formerly **Carballo**), Av 6 Nte 18, off the southwest corner of the zócalo (☎962/6-43-70). One of the cheapest in town; rooms at the back are best. ②.

Eating and drinking

There are more than enough **restaurants** around the zócalo to satisfy all tastes. Most are on the south side, where *Nuevo Doña Leo* has the best-value breakfast and comida corrida, together with tortas and tacos; *Los Comales* is similar, but a bit more expensive. The restaurant at the *Hotel Don Miguel*, C 1 Pte, off the southeast corner of the zócalo, is pretty fancy but does a great-value breakfast. As usual, there are cheap places to eat and some fine *panaderías* to be found around the market area, beginning with the row of juice bars on Av 10 Pte, a block west of the zócalo.

Unión Juárez

The small town of **UNIÓN JUÁREZ**, high on the flank of the Volcán de Tacaná, 43km from Tapachula, offers a chance to escape the heat of the lowlands. The journey from Tapachula follows the valley of the **Río Suchiate**, which forms the border with Guatemala. Unión Juárez is almost on the border and hikers can obtain permission here to cross into Guatemala on foot at Talquián, 10km north. There are also some excellent **day-hikes** to waterfalls and, with a guide, you can even reach the volcano's summit, at 4092m the highest point in Chiapas. This is a two- to three-day trip, with a cabin to sleep in at the top, though you'll need to bring a warm sleeping bag at least.

Buses for Unión Juárez leave every twenty minutes from the Unión y Progreso station in Tapachula. At **CACAHOATÁN**, where the bananas and *cacao* give way to coffee, you change to a *combi* run by Transportes Tacaná – the whole journey takes around one hour twenty minutes. There are just two **places to stay**: the budget but comfortable *Posada Aljoad*, half a block off the west side of the plaza (☎964/7-20-25; ②), which has rooms with private, hot-water bathrooms around a courtyard and a good inexpensive restaurant; and the good-value *Hotel Colonial Campestre*, which you pass as you enter the town from the south (☎964/7-20-00, fax 7-20-15; ⑤), whose rooms are spacious and recently modernized, with TV and en-suite bathrooms. The latter is an especially friendly place with a good **restaurant**, *La Suiza Chiapaneca*, and serves as a great base to explore the volcano – Fernando, the owner's son, can guide you. On the north side of the plaza, the *Carmelita* and *La Montaña* are also good, inexpensive restaurants. *Combis* leave for Cacahoatán (and Tapachula) from the east side of the plaza (every 30min until 8pm).

The ruins of Izapa

Though the road to the border passes right through the archeological site of **IZAPA**, few visitors bother to stop, which is a pity, since as well as being easy to get to, the site is large – with more than eighty temple mounds – and important for its evidence of both the Olmec and early Maya cultures. Izapa culture, in fact, is seen as a transitional stage between the Olmecs and the glories of the Classic Maya period; here you'll see early versions of the rain god Chaac and others in elaborate bas-relief on the stone facings of the temples. Founded as early as 800 BC, Izapa continued to flourish throughout the Maya Pre-classic period, until around 300 AD; most of what remains is from the later period, perhaps around 200 AD, and the site continued to be occupied until the Post-classic.

The **northern side** of the site (left of the road as you head to the border) is more accessible than the southern half. There's a ball-court, and several *stelae*, which, though not Olmec in origin, are carved in a recognizable Olmec style, similar to monuments at other early Maya sites. The **southern side**, down a track about 1km back along the main road, is a good deal more overgrown, but you can spot altars with animal carvings – frogs, snakes and jaguars – and several unexcavated mounds.

There's a caretaker at Izapa, and you'll be charged a small fee. To **get there**, take any bus or *combi* to the Talismán border and ask the driver to drop you at the site, which is signposted from the road.

The Guatemalan border: the Talismán Bridge and Ciudad Hidalgo

Both of these southern crossing points are easy places to enter Guatemala, but the **Talismán Bridge** is closer to Tapachula and better for onward connections. From Tapachula, *combis* (operated by Unión y Progreso) run frequently (taking about 30min), passing the Cristóbal Colón bus station on the way.

In theory, there's a small toll to pay to cross the bridge, but the **immigration procedure** is generally pretty slack and trouble-free. At present US citizens and nationals of EC states (apart from Ireland) don't need visas and must simply get a Guatemalan **tourist card**. This should be free, but officials often illegally ask for money. How you get out of this depends on your attitude (and that of the immigration official). For those who need a visa, there's a **Guatemalan consulate** in Tapachula. Changing money is best done in Tapachula, but there's no shortage of casas de cambio at the border, and you'll get only a slightly less favourable rate.

There are several **hotels** and **restaurants** at the border, some technically in Mexico, some in Guatemala, but almost all of them over the bridge in the no-man's land between the two border posts. None is particularly good value, but the *Buenavista* and the *Handall* hotels (both ②) are the best of the bunch. Heading **onwards**, Guatemala City is about five to six hours away: there's usually a bus waiting, but if not, take a bus or van to **Malacatán** and continue from there. The best way though is to take the Galgos service from Tapachula to Guatemala City (see p.460). Travelling **into Mexico**, there's no shortage of *combis* to Tapachula and plenty of first-class buses from Tapachula onwards. You'll probably have your passport checked many times along Hwy-200, so be prepared.

The border town of **CIUDAD HIDALGO** is a very busy road crossing and the point where the train enters Guatemala, but it's less convenient if you're travelling by bus. There's a **casa de cambio** (and freelance moneychangers) at the corner of Av Central and C Central Sur, and several **hotels**; the *Hospedaje La Favorita*, C Central Ote (②) is best. Plenty of willing locals offer to pedal you across the Puente Rodolfo Robles to **Ciudad Tecún Umán** in Guatemala, but it's an easy walk. Cristóbal Colón runs a **bus** from Ciudad Hidalgo to México daily at 6pm, but it's much easier to take a bus or *combi* to Tapuchula (45min) and change there. There's almost always one waiting by the casa de cambio.

The Chiapas highlands

There is nowhere in Mexico so rich in scenery or indigenous life as inland Chiapas. Forested uplands and jungly valleys are studded with rivers and lakes, waterfalls and unexpected gorges, and flush with the rich flora and fauna of the tropics – wild orchids, brilliantly coloured birds, and monkeys. Even now the network of roads, though growing, is skeletal, and for much of its history the isolation of the state allowed its **indigenous population** to carry on their lives little affected. In the villages, you'll see the trappings of Catholicism and of economic progress, but in most cases these go no deeper than the surface: daily life is still run in accordance with ancient customs and beliefs.

Strong and colourful as the traditions are – away from the big towns, Spanish is still very much a second language – the economic and social lot of the *indígena* population remains greatly inferior to that of *ladinos*. The **Zapatista rebellion**, centred in this area, did not appear from nowhere. The oppressive exploitation of the *encomienda* system remained powerful here far longer than in parts of Mexico more directly in the government eye (there were local rebellions, quickly suppressed, in the early eighteenth and late nineteenth centuries), and despite some post-revolutionary land redistribution, most small villages still operate at the barest subsistence level. Not surprisingly, many of the customs are dying fast, and it's comparatively rare to see men in traditional clothing, though many women still wear it. Conversely, such traditions as do survive are clung to fiercely, and you should be extremely sensitive about **photography** – especially of anything that might have religious significance – and donning **native clothing**, the patterns on which convey subtle social and geographic meaning.

Tuxtla Gutiérrez

TUXTLA GUTIÉRREZ, the capital of the state, does its best to deny most of Chiapas' attraction and tradition – it's a fast-growing, modern and crowded city. Though not actually in the highlands, it's the main gateway from central Mexico and a major transport hub; you may well end up having to stay the night. It's not a bad place – there's a fascinating **zoo** and some excellent **museums** to fill some time – but there's no call to stay longer than necessary, and your best bet may be to carry straight on through to San Cristóbal.

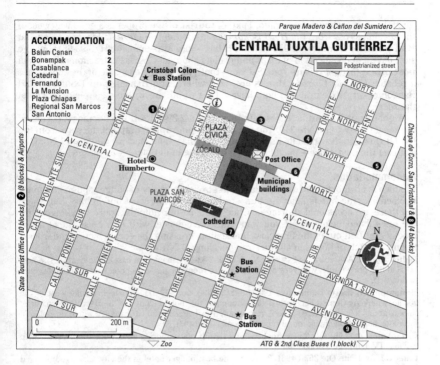

Arrival and orientation

Tuxtla has two **airports**. The **Aeropuerto San Juan**, near Ocozocautla on a hilltop often shrouded in fog, 28km to the west of town, is generally used only in summer; colectivos run from here into the city. **Aeropuerto Francisco Sarabia** is more convenient, 7km west of the city; taxis or colectivos will take you into the centre. First-class **buses** pull in to the ADO/Cristóbal Colón station on Av 2 Nte at C 2 Pte. To reach the centre (you can leave luggage at the juice bar *Miroslava* opposite), turn left from the entrance onto C 2 Pte Nte and left again when you reach Av Central. The main second-class terminal, used by Autotransportes Tuxtla Gutiérrez (ATG) and a couple of smaller companies, takes up half a block of 3 Sur Ote, near 7 Ote, 1km southeast of the centre: for the zócalo, follow C 2 Sur west past the market area until you hit C Central Sur, then turn right.

The centre of town is arranged in the usual Chiapas **grid of numbered streets** fanning out from Av Central, which runs east–west, and C Central, which runs north–south; often you'll see the streets named not just as Av 3 Nte, but as Av 3 Nte Pte, which defines which quarter of the city you're in – it can be extremely confusing if you're looking for the junction of 3 Nte Pte with 3 Pte Nte. **Avenida Central** (also known as Av 14 de Septiembre and Blvd Belisario Domínguez) is the town's focus, with the **zócalo** right at the centre.

Information

The most central place to pick up maps and information is at the **municipal tourist office**, conveniently located in the underpass at C Central Nte and Av 2 Nte Ote; unfortunately opening hours are erratic. Tuxtla's **tourist office** proper is a good way west of the zócalo, across from the *Hotel Bonampak* in the *Edificio Plaza de las Instituciones* at Blvd Belisario Domínguez 950 (Mon–Fri 9am–3pm & 6–9pm; ☎961/3-93-96), but the staff have a good selection of maps and leaflets about all Chiapas' attractions. The main **post office** (Mon–Fri 8am–7pm, Sat 9am–1pm), just off the east side of the zócalo, has a reliable *Lista de Correos*. **Banks** are everywhere, and Banamex on 1 Sur Pte, and Bancomer on Av Central Pte, both have ATMs – both are within a couple of blocks of the zócalo.

A good **travel agent** is Viajes Miramar (☎961/2-39-30), off the northeast corner of the zócalo at Av 1 Ote Nte 310. You can obtain **topographic maps** of the state from the INEGI (Instituto Nacional de Estadística, Geografía y Información) office, on 1 Nte Ote, just past the post office – useful if you're travelling in out-of-the-way places.

Accommodation

Tuxtla has no shortage of decent **places to stay**, with plenty of budget options. Though inexpensive, the hotels near the **bus stations** are noisy. Most hotels have hot water, but there are occasional shortages. Check, too, if your hotel has pure drinking water: the ones listed below do. If you want the convenience, with less noise, head a few blocks east (left out of the first-class bus station, crossing the zócalo by the underpass) to find a clutch of hotels in all price ranges along **2 Nte Ote**.

Balun Canan, Av Central 944 (☎961/2-30-50, fax 2-82-49); about 1km east of the centre. The best hotel in this price range, with very comfortable, a/c rooms, a garden, a good restaurant and secure parking. ④.

Bonampak, Belisario Domínguez 180 (☎961/3-20-50, fax 2-77-37). Fourteen blocks west of the zócalo, where Av Central becomes Blvd Domínguez, this hotel belongs to the Best Western chain. Rooms are all a/c, and there's a pool, restaurant, travel agency and car hire. It's worth dropping in for a look at the Bonampak mural reproductions (see p.493). ⑤.

Casablanca, Av 2 Nte Ote 25 (☎961/1-03-05). Friendly place offering good-value rooms, some with a/c and TV. Luggage storage. ③.

Catedral, Av 1 Nte Ote 367 (☎961/3-08-24). The best budget hotel in the city. Clean rooms, tiled bathrooms, even a bedside light. ②.

Faro, Av 1 Nte Ote 1007 (☎961/2-26-61). Some way east of the centre, but handy for Parque Madero, this very quiet hotel has good-sized rooms. ②.

Fernando, Av 2 Nte Ote 515 (☎961/3-17-40). The best value in this area: large, comfortable rooms and helpful staff. Parking available. ②.

La Mansión, C 1 Pte Nte 221 (☎961/2-21-51). Only a block west of the zócalo and a block from Cristóbal Colón, this comfortable, affordable hotel has a lift and a good-value restaurant. ③.

Plaza Chiapas, Av 2 Nte Ote 299 (☎961/3-83-65). Modern hotel with great prices. All rooms have private bath, some have balcony. ②.

Regional San Marcos, C 2 Ote 176 at Av 1 Sur (☎961/3-19-40). Good-value modern hotel, a block south of the zócalo and a block east of the cathedral. Rooms are clean, with private shower, and some have a/c, plus there's a good restaurant. ④.

San Antonio, Av 2 Sur Ote 540 (☎961/2-27-13). Clean, friendly, inexpensive hotel near the ATG terminal. Rooms are large with private bath. Good budget restaurant next door. ②.

The City

Sights downtown are few: the **zócalo**, known as the "Plaza Cívica", is the chief of them, recently refurbished with much ostentatious marble, fountains, and the very restrained, whitewashed **San Marcos Cathedral**. Its bell tower is one of the leading local entertainments: every hour a mechanical procession of the twelve apostles goes through a complicated routine accompanied by a carillon of 48 bells. At the side of the cathedral, the **Plaza San Marcos** is full of life, its ever-growing **handicraft market** bustling with vendors from all over Chiapas. In the main plaza, across Av Central, there's often free live music, especially at weekends. Also worth seeing is the **Hotel**

Bonampak, whose lobby has copies of the Maya murals from Bonampak (see p.493). On the way, between calles 9 and 10, you pass the clean and very popular **Parque la Marimba**, a favourite evening gathering-spot for strolling and listening to the *marimba* bands.

Slightly further afield, you could also head out to the **Parque Madero**, northeast of the centre, where the small **Museo Regional de Chiapas** (Tues–Sun 9am–4pm; US$1.50) displays artefacts and maps detailing the pre-Columbian groups living in Chiapas. Highlights include intricately carved human fencers from the ruins of Chiapa de Corzo (see p.466). Botanical gardens and an *Orquideario* full of blooms native to the Chiapas jungle are in the same complex, reached along a shaded walkway. To get there, head north from the zócalo and then turn right onto Av 5 Nte Ote for 2km; or take a *combi* marked "Parque Madero" along Av Central.

The zoo

If you do have half a day to spare, however, it's far more worthwhile to spend it at the Zoológico Miguel Alvárez del Toro, or **ZOOMAT** (Tues–Sun 8.30am–5.30pm; free, but donations welcome), on a forested hillside south of the city. There's a **bus** out there, #60, marked "Cerro Hueco" or "Zoológico", which you can catch on C 1 Ote between avenidas 6 and 7 Sur, a bit of a walk from the centre – it's very slow and roundabout, though, and a **taxi** (US$1) is a great deal easier.

The zoo claims to have every species native to Chiapas, from spiders to jaguars, and by any standards, it's excellent, with good-sized cages, complete with natural vegetation, freshwater streams, and a conservationist approach. There is, for example, one dark cage with a label that announces the most destructive and dangerous species of all: peer in and you're confronted with a reflection of yourself. A number of animals, including *guaqueques negros* (agoutis) – rodents about the size of a domestic cat – and some very large birds, are free to roam the zoo grounds. Occasionally you'll witness bizarre meetings, as these creatures confront their caged relatives through the wire. This is particularly true of some of the pheasants – *ocofaisan* and *cojalita* – where the descendants of the caged birds are freed but make no attempt to leave because they naturally live in family groups. People of nervous disposition should avoid the *Vivario*, which contains a vast and stomach-turning collection of all the snakes, insects and spiders you might meet on your travels.

Eating and drinking

The centre of Tuxtla has dozens of **restaurants**, and you need never wander more than a block or so either side of Av Central to find something in every price range. Juice bars are everywhere, and there are also some great bakeries along Av Central. The very **cheapest** places are on Av 2 Sur, while between the second-class bus area and the centre you'll pass several tiny, family-run restaurants, each serving an excellent-value comida corrida. More cheap places to eat can be found in the Mercado Díaz Ordáz, C Central Sur, between avenidas 3 and 4 Sur.

All the larger hotels have a restaurant attached, and these are often good value. *Gringo's Chicken*, on C 2 Ote just south of Av Central, may satisfy a longing for cooking *estilo Americano*, though the combination of southern-fried chicken with chile, tortillas and southern-fried potatoes is uniquely Mexican. Most popular for socializing and people-watching are the swish restaurants on C 2 Ote Sur, behind the cathedral, always packed with smartly dressed locals. Prices for the Mexican food at *La Parroquia*, under the portales behind the cathedral, are not too high, and there's a good breakfast buffet. Next door, the *Trattoria San Marco* serves good portions of pizza, Mexican food, and great gateaux at slightly higher prices. For **vegetarian** food, try *Nah Yaxal*, just off Av Central at C 6 Pte Nte, west of the zócalo. It's clean and modern, though a little pricey.

MOVING ON FROM TUXTLA

Cristóbal Colón, ADO and Maya de Oro buses all depart from the **first-class station** at the corner of Av 2 Nte Ote and C 2 Pte Nte; Rapidos del Sur (RdS), a good second-class line, is adjacent. Main destinations include México (16hr), Veracruz (11hr), and Oaxaca (9hr). RdS serve the Chiapas coast; and Maya de Oro run luxury services to México, Mérida (14hr) and Cancún (18hr). The various **second-class terminals** are dotted around the city. The main one, at the junction of Av 3 Sur Ote. and C 6 Ote Sur, is used by Autotransportes Tuxtla Gutiérrez (ATG), and serves Oaxaca, Villahermosa, Mérida and Palenque. There's even a service to Chetumal, Playa del Carmen and Cancún. Other local buses operate from the street outside. Getting **to San Cristóbal** is extremely easy: ATG have frequent departures, and *combis* leave from outside the terminal whenever they have a full load; from a block away on Av 8 Ote, between 2 and 3 Sur, Omnibus de Chiapas runs a frequent and inexpensive service. A shared taxi to San Cristóbal (four people) will cost only US$4 each.

It's only a short taxi-ride to the **Aeropuerto Franciso Sarabia**; if you're flying from the San Juan airport check with your airline (Aviacsa ☎961/2-80-81; Mexicana/Aerocaribe ☎961/2-00-20)about a *combi* .

Opposite, there's a good bread and cheese shop. The *Café Avenida*, next to the *Hotel Avenida*, at Av Central 224, is an authentic Mexican coffee shop, and there are several **bakeries** in the blocks west of the café.

Tuxtla to San Cristóbal: the Sumidero Canyon

Driving east from Tuxtla towards San Cristóbal, you'll catch occasional glimpses of the lower reaches of the **Cañon del Sumidero**. Through this spectacular cleft the Río Grijalva runs beneath cliffs that in places reach almost 1500m in height. To appreciate it better, take the road that runs north from Tuxtla past a series of *miradores*, in a National Park that includes all the most scenic sections of the canyon. The best views are from the *mirador* known as **La Coyota**, or at the end of the road near the restaurant *La Atalaya*. There's no public transport (other than joining a tour), but to see at least the lower reaches you could take a "Km 4" *combi* from Tuxtla heading north along 11 Ote Nte, past the Parque Madero, and get off at the turnaround point. From here, it's a 25-minute walk to the first *mirador*, **La Ceiba**, for stunning views of the canyon and river. There's usually sufficient traffic to make hitching a possibility, though be sure to take water along.

For better views still, take a **boat-ride** through the canyon. Regular boat-trips run from **Cahuaré**, where the highway crosses the river, or the small colonial town of **Chiapa de Corzo** (see below), for under US$10 per person. The trip lasts a couple of hours, passing several waterfalls (best during the rains) and entering caves in the cliffs, enlivened by commentary that points out such detail as the spot where hundreds of Chiapanec warriors flung themselves off the cliff rather than submit to the Spanish. The river is dead calm since a dam was constructed not far beyond the canyon.

Chiapa de Corzo

CHIAPA DE CORZO is an elegant little town overlooking the river, barely twenty minutes by bus east from Tuxtla. An important centre in Pre-Classic times, this is the place where the oldest **Long Count date**, corresponding to December 7, 36 BC, has been found on a *stela* (the remaining ruins are on private land behind the Nestlé plant, beyond the far end of 21 de Octubre). There are at least a dozen **places to eat** on the riverside here, and plenty to see: the most striking feature is an amazingly elaborate sixteenth-century fountain, which dominates the zócalo. Built of brick in the *mudéjar* style, in the shape of the Spanish crown, the fountain is one of the most spectacular surviving early colonial monuments in Mexico – a tribute to the painstaking restoration. The small **museum of regional handicrafts** next to the cathedral, in a cobbled courtyard surrounded by the ancient brick arches of the Convento de **Santo Domingo** (Tues–Sun 10am–4pm; US$0.50), features the local painted and lacquered gourds.

There are two **hotels** in town: the basic *Los Angeles*, on the southeast corner of the zócalo (③); and the new, more upmarket **Hotel La Ceiba**, Domingo Ruíz 300 (☎961/6-07-73; ⑤), three blocks west from the zócalo, which is very quiet and comfortable, with a/c rooms and a small pool.

To **get to Chiapa**, hop on one of the *microbuses* that leave every five minutes from the Transportes Chiapa–Tuxtla office at 3 Ote Sur and 3 Sur Ote in Tuxtla (there's another company round the corner at 2 Ote Sur and 2 Sur Ote). It's easy enough to get back: *microbuses* leave from the northeast corner of the zócalo.

The ruins of Chiapa de Corzo

Strategically located on an ancient trade route high above the **Río Grijalva**, the ruins of **Chiapa de Corzo** comprise some two hundred structures scattered over a wide area of private property, shared among several different owners and sliced in two by the Pan-American Highway. Mound 32, a small flat-topped pyramid, is clearly visible at the road junction as you head east of town. This is the longest continually occupied site in Chiapas, beginning life as a farming settlement in the early Pre-Classic period (1400–850 BC). By the late Pre-Classic (450 BC–250 AD), it was the largest centre of population in the region, trading with all of Mesoamerica. What you see today are mainly low pyramids, walls and courtyards.

To **get to the site** from town, take any *microbus* heading east, get off at the junction with Hidalgo and follow the signs. After about ten minutes, you'll come to an unmarked gate in a fence on the right; go to the house (officially closed Mon) and pay the US$0.75 **fee** to the family who farm among the ruins. **Walking**, it's about 3km northeast from the zócalo in Chiapa de Corzo, passing the beautifully located sixteenth-century church ruin of San Sebastián on the way.

Bochil and Simojovel

Just beyond Chiapa de Corzo, the **road to Villahermosa** – a spectacular wind down to the Gulf plain – cuts off to the north. Few tourists take this route, since ahead the Pan-American Highway continues to the far more enticing destination of San Cristóbal. The road climbs at first through mountains wreathed in cloud to **BOCHIL**, some 60km from Tuxtla, where some buses pull over for a rest stop. It's a pleasant small town, a centre for the **Tzotzil Maya**, and a good base from which to explore the surrounding hills and villages. Most people still wear the traditional dress, or *traje*: the women in white *huipiles* with red embroidery, pink ribbons in their hair and dark blue skirts, and maybe a few men in the white smock and trousers rolled up to the knee. You'll be stared at, usually covertly, and, as always, should be *very* wary of **taking photographs**, not merely out of simple courtesy but because you may be taken for a government agent – these towns protested very strongly at the election result in August 1994, and in December 1994 were briefly occupied by the Zapatistas, who destroyed public records. There are a couple of simple **places to stay**, including the *Posada San Pedro* (②), whose basic rooms are set out around a courtyard on 1 Pte Nte, a block from the plaza: head for Banamex at the top of the plaza and turn right. Bochil has a frequent second-class bus service to Tuxtla, with Autotransportes Tuxtla–Bochil. Five kilometres beyond Bochil, at **Puerto Cate**, a side road to the right leads down to **San Andrés Larráinzar**, a Tzotzil village 23km along the dirt track. Trucks ply the route, and from

San Andrés you can reach **San Juan Chamula**, 18km away, which is well connected by *combis* to San Cristóbal. This makes for an interesting route to or from San Cristóbal – but you'll need to check the current political situation and set off fairly early.

Combis run regularly up the minor road to **SIMOJOVEL**, 40km away at the head of a spectacular valley, the source of most of the amber you'll find sold in local markets. Should you want **to stay**, the *Casa de Huéspedes Simojovel*, one block south of the plaza, on Independencia (②), has basic rooms round a flower-filled courtyard.

Jaltenango

Completely unused to visitors, the small town of **JALTENANGO**, jumping-off point for the **Reserva Biosfera El Triunfo**, is just a three-hour bus ride south of Tuxtla. Also known as **Angel Albino Corzo**, it lies at the junction of three rivers and is surrounded by coffee *fincas* on the slopes of the Sierra Madre de Chiapas. The highest peaks of the reserve, a refuge for Chiapas' tropical wildlife, are covered in dense **cloud forest**.

Of the three **hotels** here, the *Hotel Esperanza* (②), one block east of the plaza, is by far the best; there are also a couple of basic **restaurants** and a bakery. Apart from the main road, the streets are unpaved. Tracks lead up to the hills, and if you're a wildlife enthusiast you could easily spend a few days exploring the area, though to get the best out of a visit you need to camp and get the help of a local guide. **Buses** leave Tuxtla several times a day from the Cuxtepeques y Anexas station at C 10 Ote and Av 3 Nte, running via Jaltenango to Cuxtepec, high up at the head of a forested valley.

San Cristóbal de las Casas

Just 80km from Tuxtla Gutiérrez, **SAN CRISTÓBAL DE LAS CASAS** is almost 1700m higher – a cool place with an unrivalled provincial colonial charm. Its low, white-washed red-tiled houses seem huddled together on the plain as if to keep out enemies; indeed, the town was designed as a Spanish stronghold among an often hostile indigenous population – the attack by Zapatista rebels in January 1994 was the latest in a long series of uprisings. It took the Spanish four years to pacify the area sufficiently to establish a town here in 1528. Officially named "Ciudad Real" (Royal City), it was more widely known as "Villaviciosa" (Evil City) for the oppressive exploitation exercised by its colonists. In 1544, Bartolomé de las Casas was appointed bishop, and promptly took an energetic stance in defence of the native population, playing a similar role to that of Bishop Vasco de Quiroga in Pátzcuaro (see p.193). His name – added to that of the patron saint of the town – was held in something close to reverence by the *Indígenas*. Throughout the colonial era, San Cristóbal was the capital of Chiapas, then administered as part of Guatemala, and it lost this rank in 1892 only as a result of its reluctance to accept the union with Mexico.

Though it's the local crafts and the indigenous way of life that draw people to San Cristóbal, this romanticization is not always appreciated by the *indígenas* themselves, who not surprisingly resent being treated as tourist attractions or objects of amateur anthropology. Nevertheless, the life of the town depends on the life of the people from surrounding villages, who fill its streets and dominate its trade. Many of the salespeople are **expulsados** – converts to evangelical Protestantism expelled by the village leaders – now living in shanties on the edge of town and unable to make a living from farming. The women making crafts to sell to tourists soon took advantage of the publicity generated by the Zapatistas; the most popular souvenirs are now **Marcos dolls**, complete with ski mask, rifle and bandoliers – there's even a female Zapatista doll of Romana, who is reputed to be in a position of command in the movement.

△ Market

History Museum and
Centro Cultural

Casa Na
Bolom Museum

Sna
Jolobil

Santo
Domingo

Cathedral

Palacio
Municipal

ZÓCALO

Guadalupe

Post
Office

ACCOMMODATION

Casa Blanca	14
Casa Na Bolom	2
Ciudad Real	12
Don Quijote	7
El Paraíso	4
Posada B & B	11
Posada del Barón	9
Posada Casa Real	10
Posada Chilam Balam	16
Posada Diego de Mazariegos	5 & 6
Posada Gladys	1
Posada Margarita	8
Posada Morales Bungalows	15
Rancho Nicolás	17
Rincón del Arco	3
Santa Clara	13

San
Cristóbal

Tienda de
Artesanos

Bellas
Artes

Templo
del Carmen

Transportes
Lacandónia
buses

0   200 m

**SAN CRISTÓBAL
DE LAS CASAS**

Buses
(2nd class)

Buses
(1st class)

Comitán ▽ ▽ Buses for Tuxtla

Despite being the main focus of the Zapatista attack, the town was only occupied for thirty hours, and no tourists were harmed; many, in fact, took advantage of the opportunity to be photographed with the rebels. For the time being, San Cristóbal remains one of the most restful and enjoyable places in the republic to spend a few days doing very little, with an infrastructure set to cater for its young, predominantly European visitors.

Arrival and information

The road from Tuxtla Gutiérrez to San Cristóbal is one of the most spectacular in Mexico, twisting through the mountains and constantly climbing, breaking through the cloud into pine forests. First impressions of San Cristóbal itself, as the modern parts of the city sprawl unattractively along the highway, are not the best. In the centre, though, there is none of this unthinking development.

Whether you arrive by first- or second-class **bus**, you'll almost certainly be just off the Pan-American Highway (Hwy-190) at the southern edge of town. From the Cristóbal Colón **first-class terminal**, at the junction of Insurgentes and the Carretera Panamericana, walk straight along Insurgentes up to the zócalo, about seven blocks. There's no guardería at the bus station, but you can rent **lockers** at the Tienda El Paso, one block up Insurgentes on the left. **Second-class** services stop along the Pan-American Highway either side of Cristóbal Colón. The newly opened **airport** is 18km east of the town; a taxi in to the centre costs US$5.

The helpful **state tourist office**, just off the southwest corner of the zócalo at Hidalgo 2 (Mon–Fri 9am–9pm, Sat 9am–8pm, Sun 9am–2pm; ☎962/8-65-70), is one of the best in the country, with good free city maps, up-to-date lists of hotels in all price ranges, bus times and events. Staff know Chiapas well, and there's usually someone who speaks English (and possibly other European languages). Free **listings** magazines with information on hotels, restaurants and excursions are usually available. There are more bulletin boards in and around the **municipal tourist office** in the Palacio Municipal, on the northeast corner of the zócalo. The excellent *Mapa Turistico de Chiapas* (1:400,000 scale, 1cm:4km) is available at most of the bookstores in town and some hotels, though not at the tourist offices.

Several **bank** branches (with ATMs) surround the zócalo; most will exchange dollars and give cash advances (mornings only). You'll get much quicker exchange, however, at good rates from Casa de Cambio Lacantún, Real de Guadalupe 12 (Mon–Sat 8am–2pm & 4–8pm, Sun 9am–1pm); they change most major currencies and also usually have Guatemalan quetzales. The **post office** is at the corner of Cuauhtémoc and Crescencio Rosas, southwest of the zócalo (Mon–Fri 8am–7pm, Sat 9am–1pm); in addition, most hotels have *Mexipost* boxes, and many of the larger ones sell stamps. There are Ladatel **phones** on the zócalo, under the arches of the Palacio Municipal, and in the Cristóbal Colón terminal; hotels and restaurants have casetas. You can make and receive **phone calls**, and receive **faxes and email** at Librería La Pared, Hidalgo 2, next to the tourist office (☎962/8-72-32, fax 8-63-67; *lapared@sancristobal.podernet.com.mx*), though you must arrange to be there to receive phone calls – messages cannot be taken.

Accommodation

San Cristóbal boasts some of the best-value **budget and mid-price hotels** in Mexico. Walking up Insurgentes from the bus station to the zócalo, you'll pass examples in all price ranges. Press on a little further along Real de Guadalupe, off the northeast corner of the zócalo, and you'll find many more. An ever larger proportion of hotels call themsleves "posadas": apart from the convivial ambience this is presumably meant to convey, being a posada apparently also confers certain tax advantages on the establishment. All but the most basic places now have hot water, though not necessarily all the time. Nights can be pleasantly cool in summer, but cold in winter, so make sure there are enough blankets.

For **longer stays**, check out the many noticeboards in the bus stations and popular cafés, where you'll find rooms and even whole houses for rent. The closest official **campsite** is at *Rancho San Nicolás* (see below).

Budget and mid-price

Posada Bed and Breakfast, two locations on the same street, at Madero 46 and 83 (☎962/8-04-40). The name says it all; good-value, inexpensive lodging including a reasonable breakfast. Use of kitchen for a small fee. Shared bathrooms. Prices charged per person (US$3.25). ②.

Bungalows Posada Los Morales, Ignacio Allende 17 (☎962/8-14-72). Whitewashed stone cabins each with living room with fireplace, bath (generally with hot water) and stove, in a hillside garden four blocks west of the zócalo. Authentic colonial atmosphere, right down to the ancient wooden furniture and flagstones, and wonderful views of the town. ④.

Posada Casa Blanca, Insurgentes, on the right just before the zócalo (no phone). One of the best-value budget hotels, conveniently located. Rooms are basic but clean; private showers with hot water. ②.

Posada Casa Real, Real de Guadalupe 51 (☎962/8-13-03). Lovely, friendly hotel with a flower-filled courtyard. Large rooms all with very comfortable double beds, and a place for washing and drying clothes on the sunny rooftop terrace. No private baths, but there is hot water. Prices are US$4 per person, so very good value for singles. ②.

Posada Chilam Balam, Niños Heroes 9 (☎962/8-43-40). Simple, friendly hotel a few blocks west of the zócalo, with single-storey red-tiled rooms around a courtyard, and a *pila* in the tiny garden to wash clothes in. Hot water but no private bathrooms. ②.

Posada del Barón, Belisario Domínguez 2 (☎ & fax 962/8-08-81). Well-run, new hotel one block east of the zócalo. Each room has a spotless tiled bathroom with plenty of hot water. You can make international calls, and there's usually a member of staff who speaks English. ④.

Posada de Gladys, Real de Mexicanos 16 (☎962/8-57-75) A popular travellers' hangout with both dorms and private rooms and a friendly atmosphere. ①.

Posada Margarita, Real de Guadalupe 34 (☎962/8-09-57). Long-standing budget favourite. Rooms are bare but comfortable (no private showers, but communal ones are clean). Good, inexpensive café in the blue-and-white tiled courtyard, and the restaurant (next door) has live music most nights. Good travel agency and luggage storage, too. ②.

Rancho San Nicolás, 2km east of the centre, on the extension of Francisco León (☎962/8-00-57). Primarily a campsite and trailer park, but also has a few rooms in a pleasant country setting. ③.

More expensive

Casa Na Bolom, Vicente Guerrero 33 (☎962/8-14-18, fax 8-55-86). Staying in this famous museum and research centre was formerly possible only for invited scholars and archeologists (see p.473) – now it's open to anyone. Comfortable rooms with fireplaces, decorated with village artefacts and original photos taken by Gertrude Blom. Non-residents can eat dinner here if they book ahead – or just turn up for breakfast (7.30–10am) or Sunday lunch (1–4pm). ⑤.

Ciudad Real, Plaza 31 de Marzo 10 (☎962/8-04-64). Colonial mansion, superbly located overlooking the zócalo; popular with European tour groups. Most rooms rise above the covered courtyard (now a dining room, adorned with potted palms); quieter ones are at the back. Friendly, helpful staff. ⑥.

Don Quijote, Cristóbal Colón 7; turn left where Colón crosses Real de Guadalupe (☎962/8-09-20, fax 8-03-46). Newish hotel on a quiet street. Comfortable, well-lit, carpeted rooms with shower and constant hot water. The lobby is decorated with original costumes from Chiapas villages collected by the owner. Free morning coffee. English and French spoken. ④.

El Paraíso, 5 de Febrero 19 (☎ & fax 962/8-00-85). A wonderfully restored colonial-style house. Rooms are smallish but very comfortable, and the restaurant is excellent. Great value at this price. German and English spoken. ⑤.

Posada Diego de Mazariegos, 5 de Febrero 1 (☎962/8-18-25). San Cristóbal's top historic hotel, in two colonial buildings, either side of General Utrilla. Many rooms feature a fireplace and antique furniture; bathrooms are beautifully tiled. Often busy with tour groups. ⑥.

Rincón del Arco, Ejercito Nacional 66, corner of Vicente Guerrero (☎962/8-13-13, fax 8-15-68). Lovely, well-priced luxury hotel. The large rooms with antique furniture, fireplaces and beautifully tiled bathrooms are set around a courtyard or in delightful gardens. About 1km northeast from the zócalo, it's just a block from *Casa Na Bolom* and affords gorgeous views of the surrounding hills. Restaurant and parking. ⑤.

Santa Clara, Insurgentes 1, corner of the zócalo (☎962/8-11-40, fax 8-10-41). A former colonial mansion, known locally as *La Casa de la Sirena* for the sixteenth-century carvings of mermaids on the outside walls. The large rooms have antique furniture, and public areas are adorned with colonial weapons and suits of armour. Heated pool and good restaurant. ⑤.

The City

There aren't that many specific things to do in San Cristóbal: the true pleasures lie in simply wandering the streets and in getting out to some of the nearby villages. If you've come here to study or to buy textiles and weavings from the villages, several superb places offer the chance to preview indigenous crafts.

As always the **zócalo**, Plaza 31 de Marzo, is worth seeing, not so much for the relatively ordinary sixteenth-century cathedral (though it does have a nice *artesonado* ceiling and elaborate pulpit) as for some of the colonial mansions that surround it. For a full description of the city's colonial churches and monuments, pick up a copy of

Richard Perry's excellent book *More Maya Missions: Exploring Colonial Chiapas*, available in the bookstores listed on p.475. The finest of the mansions is **La Casa de la Sirena**, now the *Hotel Santa Clara*, which was probably built by the Conquistador Andrés de la Tovilla in the mid-sixteenth century and has a very elaborate doorway around the corner on Insurgentes.

In the middle of the zócalo there's a bandstand, which now incorporates a café, but even when no band is playing the city authorities provide piped music for people strolling here. If you haven't already come across them, this is probably where you'll first encounter some of San Cristóbal's insistent **salespeople**, mostly women and girls from the villages, traditionally dressed and in no mood to take no for an answer. You must either learn to say no as if you really mean it, or else accept that they'll break your resistance eventually. Bear in mind that they really do need the income: many have been expelled from their villages for converting to Protestantism and live in desperate hardship.

Templo del Carmen
From the zócalo, Hidalgo leads south to the **Templo del Carmen**, by the Moorish-style (*mudéjar*) tower and arch across the road, and once served as the gateway to the city. The church is not particularly inspiring architecturally, but you can pop in to see the adjoining cultural complex, with the Casa de la Cultura and **Instituto de Bellas Artes**. Considering the amount of artistic activity in and around San Cristóbal, these are pretty disappointing – especially since a serious fire in 1993 destroyed several eighteenth-century religious paintings – but sometimes there's an interesting temporary exhibition, concert or recital. On the way here, at the corner with Niños Heroes, you pass the **Tienda de los Artesanos de Chiapas** (Tues–Sun 9am–2pm & 5–8pm), a state-run venture that provides an outlet for Chiapas' textiles and crafts at fair prices. The weaving and embroidery exhibited here are as good as in any museum, and if you're planning to visit any of the villages have a look here first to get an idea of the particular *traje* you'll encounter.

The museums and Santo Domingo
In the other direction, General Utrilla leads north from the zócalo towards the market. At no. 10 (Plaza Siván), the small **Museo del Ambar** (daily 10am–6pm; free) displays amber found in the Simojovel Valley; you can buy authentic pieces here, too (La Pared, on Hidalgo, also has a very good selection of genuine amber at reasonable prices).

Santo Domingo, further up, is perhaps the most intrinsically interesting of San Cristóbal's churches, with a lovely pinkish Baroque facade embellished with Habsburg eagles. Inside, it's huge and gilded everywhere, with a wonderfully ornate pulpit – see it in the evening, by the dim light of candles, and you can believe it's all solid gold. Being so close to the market, Santo Domingo is often full of traders and villagers, and the area in front of the church is filled with craft stalls – often the best place to buy souvenirs. Appropriately, then, part of the former *convento* next door has been converted into a craft co-operative (San Jolobil) selling textiles and other village products. The quality here is generally good, and prices correspondingly high. A block behind the church, in another part of the monastery, the **Museo Etnografía y Historia**, or Centro Cultural de los Altos de Chiapas (Tues–Sun 10am–5pm; US$1.50), has gorgeous displays of textiles as well as vivid portrayals of how the Indians fared under colonial rule. For scholars, the **library** at the rear is a fascinating place to study old books and records of Chiapas, and the gardens are a relaxing place to rest.

The market
San Cristóbal's daily **market** lies beyond Santo Domingo along General Utrilla. It's a fascinating place, if only because here you can observe indigenous life and custom

without causing undue offence. What's on sale is mostly local produce and household goods, although there are also good tire-soled leather *huaraches* and rough but warm sweaters, which you might well feel the need of. The market is far bigger than at first you suspect, so make sure you see it all (though beware that the main covered part is full of really gross, bloody butchers' stalls). Wander through the covered parts, including the section selling clothes, then up and down the hill behind. At the top there's a pleasant square and the *Café la Terraza del Cerrillo*, unfortunately open evenings only.

For higher quality **crafts**, you'd actually be better off at one of the stores in town, especially on Real de Guadalupe – those furthest from the zócalo, like *Artesanías Real* at no. 44, and *Artesanías Chiapanecas* at no. 46C, are the best.

Casa Na Bolom

Opposite Santo Domingo, Chiapa de Corzo leads east towards the **Casa Na Bolom** at Vicente Guerrero 33, a private home, museum and library of local anthropology (Tues–Sun 9am–1pm; ☎962/8-14-18; *nabolom@sclc.ecosur.mx*), devoted especially to the isolated Lacandón Maya (see p.492). This was the home of Danish explorer and anthropologist Frans Blom, who died in 1963, and his Swiss wife Gertrude (Duby), an anthropologist and photographer who died in 1993. Today it's renowned as a centre for the study of the region. The **Museo Moxviquil** (tour of house, grounds and museum in English or Spanish Tues–Sun at 4.30pm, US$2.50 including film; guided tours in Spanish only at 11.30am, US$2) exhibits discoveries from the site of Moxviquil (see p.478), as well as an excellent map. After the tour, a film about the life of the Bloms and the destruction of the Lacandón forest is shown, and sometimes a video on Lacandón agriculture. Na Bolom also hosts some volunteer cultural and agricultural projects. Write or call for details.You can also **stay** here (see under "Accommodation").

Guadalupe and San Cristóbal

Further afield, two churches dominate views of the town from their hilltop sites: **Guadalupe** to the east and **San Cristóbal** to the west. Neither offers a great deal architecturally, but the climbs are worth it for the views – San Cristóbal, especially, is at the top of a dauntingly long and steep flight of steps. Be warned, though, that women have been subjected to harassment at both of these relatively isolated spots (especially San Cristóbal): don't climb up here alone or after dark. Just below Guadalupe is the wonderful *Café Dorado*; open in the afternoon for coffee, meals and stunning sunset views of the city.

Eating, drinking and entertainment

There's a huge variety of good **restaurants** along Insurgentes and in the streets immediately around the zócalo, especially on Madero. Where San Cristóbal really scores, however, is in lively places that cater to a disparate, somewhat bohemian crowd, made up of university and language-school students, a permanent population of young American outcasts and a constant stream of travellers. Lots of places to eat are vaguely arty, with a coffeehouse atmosphere and interesting menus that feature plenty of vegetarian options. There are a couple of good **bakeries** on Diego de Mazariegos, two blocks west of the zócalo.

As for **nightlife**, many of these same places host **live music** in the evenings, only rarely imposing a cover charge. There are even a couple of **discos** in the big hotels: one at the *Posada El Cid* on the Pan-American Highway, another at the *Hotel Rincón del Arco*, towards the *Casa Na Bolom*, at Ejercito Nacional and Guerrero.

San Cristóbal also boasts three **cinemas**: the *Cine Las Casas*, Extensión Universitaria, Guadalupe Victoria 21, showing a wide selection of Mexican and international films; the *Cinema Santa Clara*, 16 de Septiembre 30, showing mainly Mexican films; and *El Puente*, Real de Guadalupe, screening other Latin American and foreign films. As always, check current listings in the tourist office on Hidalgo.

Cafés and restaurants

Los Anafres, Flavio de Paniagua 2, near the corner with Utrilla. Friendly little Mexican restaurant where you can eat indoors or in a sunny courtyard. Their speciality are grilled meats brought to your table on the *anafre*, but there are also good vegetarian choices and great soups.

Café Altura, 20 de Noviembre 19. Best of several coffee shops around here, serving organic coffee and natural foods. Gentle music and poetry in the evenings.

Café Dorado, Real de Guadalupe, just below the church. Opens at 4pm to offer a welcome rest to visitors climbing the steps to Guadalupe church. Pasta, pizza and wonderful sunsets.

Café Restaurant Milán, Insurgentes 79C. Opposite the Cristóbal Colón terminal. Very good little restaurant with the best-value breakfasts this side of town.

Café El Puente, Real de Guadalupe 55. Excellent café serving good inexpensive salads, soups, sandwiches and delicious cakes; also acts as a cultural centre, with newspapers and magazines, lectures, film shows and a good noticeboard. Closed Sun.

Café San Cristóbal, Cuahtémoc 2, near the corner with Insurgentes. Tiny old coffeehouse, subtly refurbished, and popular with the regulars who come here to play chess and read the newspapers.

Casa del Pan, Dr Navarro 10 (closed Mon). Superb range of vegetarian food and baked goods, including bagels, made with locally grown organic ingredients and at very reasonable prices. A meeting place for expatriate aid-workers, and owners Kip and Ronald Nigh are active in development projects for indigenous women and organic agriculture. Cookbook available. Live music nightly.

Emiliano's Moustache, Cresencio Rosas 7, near Cuauhtémoc. Vast range of authentic tacos – the *especiál* is big enough for two – with some vegetarian chioces. Music in the evening.

Las Estrellas, Escuadron 201 6, opposite the bandstand outside Santo Domingo church. Inexpensive place for artesanía shoppers to break for lunch; eat indoors or in the shady courtyard. Wide choice of food, including some vegetarian dishes, and good service.

El Faisán, Madero 2, just off the zócalo. Pricey but excellent French food.

La Galería, Hidalgo 3, just south of the zócalo. Increasingly sophisticated restaurant where international food is served in the refined atmosphere of a colonial mansion, surrounded by some fairly expensive art. Faint vestiges of its hippy origins remain. Evening music.

Guelaguetza, Diego Mazariegos, near Allende. Oaxaqueño specialities.

Latinos, C Diego de Mazariegos 19. More of a late night music venue, but with good Mexican, vegetarian and international food. Many types of music: Latin, of course, with salsa, reggae, jazz and rock.

Madre Tierra, Insurgentes 19, corner of Hermanos Domínguez. European-style restaurant in a colonial house, often with live salsa or classical music. Great, healthy food includes home-made soup, salad and pasta. The next-door bakery and deli sells wholewheat bread and carrot cake until 8pm. The upstairs terrace bar has good views of ancient walls and red-tiled roofs.

El Mirador II, Madero 16. The best cheap Mexican restaurant on Madero; good comidas corridas.

La Parilla (closed Mon), corner of Belisario Domínguez and Dr Navarro, on a tiny square. Specializing in grilled meats, including *alambres al queso*, similar to a kebab with melted cheese; they also serve great pizza. Sit on one of the saddles used as bar stools to enjoy the atmosphere and great views.

Paris-Mexico, Madero 20. Superb authentic French and Mexican cuisine, expertly cooked and not overpriced – try the daily lunch special, a three-course meal of soup, crêpe and dessert, always with a vegetarian option.

Plaza Mirador, Plaza 31 de Marzo 2. Surprisingly inexpensive considering the location overlooking the zócalo, and serving tasty filling meals, usually with a vegetarian choice.

Restaurante Normita II, corner of Juárez and José Flores, one block southeast of the plaza. A great little restaurant, serving Jaliscan specialities and inexpensive breakfasts.

Restaurante Tuluc, Insurgentes 5. Justifiably popular, with a good comida corrida and dinner specials, this the first place to open in the morning (6am); ideal if you have to catch an early bus.

El Teatro Café, 1 de Marzo 8 (☎962/8-31-49). Superb, moderately priced French and Italian food. Boasts the only rooftop dining area in San Cristóbal – definitely the best place to enjoy the sunset as you eat. French and English spoken.

Listings

Bike rental An enjoyable way to get out to the surrounding villages. Best rental is at Los Pinguinos, 5 de Mayo 10B (☎962/8-02-02). Well-maintained bikes for about US$2 per hour, US$8 per day, and takes tours to local attractions. German and English spoken.

Bookstores Librería Chilam Balam, on General Utrilla near Dr Navarro, has a wide selection, including academic and educational books; also guides and topographic maps of Chiapas. Librería La Pared, Hidalgo 2, next to the tourist office, has new guidebooks (including *Rough Guides*) and the largest selection of new and second-hand books in English and other languages in southern Mexico; you can rent, trade or buy books. Accepts Visa and Mastercard. Other useful bookshops are Librería Soluna, Real de Guadalupe 13B, with a fair choice of books, including guides, and Librería La Quimera, Real de Guadalupe 24B. Casa Na Bolom, Vicente Guerrero 33, also has an excellent library (Mon–Thurs 9am–3pm, Fri 9–11am) and sells some books and maps of the Lacandón forest.

Internet access and email Get connected to the Web at the excellent *Cyberc@fé*, a new, well-equipped Internet café in the Pasaje Mazariegos mall, in the first block along Real de Guadalupe (Mon–Sat 9am–10pm, Sun 11am–9pm; ☎962/8-74-88; *cybercafe@sancristobal.podernet.com.mx*).

Language courses Centro Bilingüe, in Centro Cultural El Puente, Real de Guadalupe 55 (☎ & fax 962/8-37-23; *spanish@sancristobal.podernet.com.mx*), is the longest-established language school in San Cristóbal. Instituto Jovel, María Adelina Flores 21 (☎ & fax 962/8-40-69; *jovel@sancristobal. podernet.com.mx*), is newer but highly recommended. Both offer courses at various levels, and can arrange accommodation with local families.

Laundry Lava Sec, Crescencio Rosas 12; Lavorama, Guadalupe Victoria 20A; Lavendaría Mixtli, corner of 1 de Marzo and 16 de Septiembre; and several more.

MOVING ON FROM SAN CRISTÓBAL

San Cristóbal is pretty well connected, and you can get directly to most destinations in the state and throughout the Yucatán. The tourist office maintains an accurate and up-to-date list of all **bus times** – check first. Ticket lines are long, so try to buy your onward ticket in advance. Tuxtla Gutiérrez (2hr) is served frequently by most companies, and in addition *combis* tout for customers outside the bus stations on the Pan-American Highway.

Villahermosa (7hr) is not so well served, though there are a few first-class services daily with Cristóbal Colón; it's easier to get any bus to Tuxtla and change there. For **Palenque** (5hr), there are plenty of first- and second-class departures, day or night. All buses going to Palenque call at Ocosingo (2hr 30min), and in addition there's plenty of passenger-van traffic: just go to the highway and someone will call out to you. Several first-class buses head for **Ciudad Cuauhtémoc** (via Comitán; 2hr) on the Guatemalan border: Cristóbal Colón takes 3hr 30min, while Transportes Lombardo, on the Pan-American Highway to the east of the junction with Insurgentes, runs second-class services beginning at 4.30am, most of which continue to **Tapachula** (7hr 30min). On the highway you'll also find any number of *combis* to **Comitán**.

For **Oaxaca** (12hr) there are two overnight services at 5pm and 7pm; other departures are from Tuxtla. The first-class companies all have at least two daily services **to México** (19hr). For and **Campeche** (10hr) and **Mérida** (13hr), Transportes Lacandónia has a second-class bus at 1.15pm; while a first-class service leaves at 9.30pm. For the **Yucatán coast**, Maya de Oro has a luxury service at 9.30pm, calling at Chetumal (10hr; for Belize) Playa del Carmen (14hr) and Cancún (17hr).

Aerocaribe operate **regional flights** five days a week to Palenque, Tuxtla, Villahermosa, Cancún and have connections throughout Mexico; there are also **international flights** to Flores, for Tikal (check with a recommended travel agent).

Travel and tour agencies Santa Ana Tours, 16 de Septiembre 6 (☎962/8-02-98) are best for international tickets. For domestic flights and tours, the best agents are Viajes Lacantún, Madero 16 (☎962/8-25-88); Viajes Chinkultic, Real de Guadalupe 34, in the *Posada Margarita* (☎ & fax 962/8-09-57); or Viajes Pakal, Cuauhtémoc 6B (☎962/8-28-18).

Around San Cristóbal

Excursions to the villages around San Cristóbal should be treated with extreme sensitivity. Quite simply, you are an intruder, and will be made to feel so – be very careful about taking photographs, and certainly never do so inside churches (theoretically you need a permit from the tourist authorities in Tuxtla Gutiérrez for any photography in the villages; in practice you should always get permission locally). There's a well-worn travellers' tale, true in its essentials, of two gringos being severely beaten up for photographing the interior of the church at San Juan Chamula. You should also be careful about what you wear: cover your legs, and don't wear native clothing – it may have some meaning or badge of rank for the people you are visiting.

The best time to make your visit is on a Sunday, when most villages have a market, or during a fiesta. At such times you will be regarded as having a legitimate reason to come, and you'll also find some life – most villages are merely supply points and meeting places for a rural community and have only a very small permanent population. In recent years, some families have been driven out of the villages for abandoning traditional religion for evangelical Protestantism – they live in poverty on the outskirts of the city.

Some kind of trip out of San Cristóbal is definitely worth it, though, if only for the ride into the countryside, even if on finally reaching a village you find doors shut in your face and absolutely nothing to do (or, conversely, are mobbed by begging kids). The indigenous people in the immediate vicinity of San Cristóbal and to the west are generally **Tzotzil** speaking, those a little further to the east **Tzeltal**, but each village has also

developed its own trademarks in terms of costumes, craft specialities and linguistic quirks: as a result, the people are often subdivided by village or groups of villages and referred to as Chamulas, Zinacantecos, Huistecos (from Huistán) and so on.

It's a good idea to find out about village life before you go; San Cristóbal's Tienda de Artesanos, on Hidalgo (see p.472), has a good display on the villages, with pictures of the local dress in each, and the tourist office can supply details of tours and bus timetables where relevant.

Transport and tours

Inexpensive *combis* leave frequently for Chamula and Zinacantán, less often but still several times a day for other villages, from the end of Utrilla, just north of the market in San Cristóbal. If you'd rather take an **organized tour** (around US$8–9 per person), there are several to choose from. Among the best are those led by Mercedes Hernández Gómez, who grew up in Zinacantán – her knowledge is so extensive that she never gives the same tour twice. Meet by the kiosk in the zócalo at 9am; she'll be carrying her distinctive umbrella. Alex and Raul's "Culturally Responsible Excursions" leave from outside the municipal tourist office on the zócalo at 9.30am (☎962/8-37-41). From the tourist office, you can also get details on **horseback tours** into the surrounding area: the *Posada Margarita* is one of several places organizing riding tours. Many of the organized tours go to the **Grutas de San Cristóbal** (also called "Rancho Nuevo" caves; daily 9am–5pm; US$0.50), an enormous cavern extending deep into a mountain about 10km to the southeast. This is quite far enough to get saddle sore if you're not used to riding, though the horses are placid enough even for total beginners. Make sure you agree your itinerary before setting off: some guides expect you to turn round and head home as soon as you reach your destination. The caves can also be reached by bus since they're barely half a kilometre from the main road to Comitán. Look for the "Rancho Nuevo" sign on the right. A track leads for about 1km from the road through a pine-forested park with hiking trails often used by the army. If you want to go by **bike** (rent one from Pinguinos on 5 de Mayo), it's about a fifty-minute ride, uphill most of the way from San Cristóbal.

Another favourite trip is to **El Arcotete**, a large, natural limestone arch that forms a bridge over a river. To get there, follow Real de Guadalupe out of town, past the Guadalupe church, where it then becomes the road to Tenejapa; El Arcotete is down a signed track to the right about 3.5km past the church.

San Juan Chamula

SAN JUAN CHAMULA is the closest of the villages to San Cristóbal and the most frequently visited. It's also the most commercialized – prices in the market are certainly no bargain, and local kids will pester you for "presents", chanting *"regaleme"*, the whole time. The best way to deal with the situation is to select just one or two children and buy a couple of the painted clay animals or braided bracelets they're selling, then tell all the others you've bought all you're going to and hope they'll go to someone else. To get the most out of a visit you really need to go on one of the organized tours (see above); questions are answered honestly and in full.

Chamula is little more than a collection of civic and religious buildings with a few houses – most of its population actually lives on isolated farms or *ejidos* in the countryside. Protestant converts among the villagers were driven out thirty years ago, and only some of the Catholic sacraments are accepted. The rituals practised in the **church** at Chamula – a mixture of Catholic and traditional Maya practice – are extraordinary, and the church itself is a glorious sight, both outside and in, where worshippers and tourists shuffle about in the flickering light of a thousand candles. Before you enter, though, be sure to obtain permission (and buy a ticket; US$0.50) from the "tourist office", to the right-hand side of the plaza as you face the church. Do *not* take **photographs** inside, or even write notes.

A couple of comedores on the plaza provide simple, filling meals and in the cantina you can buy *Pox* (pronounced posh), a wickedly strong cane alcohol used as an offering in the church and also simply to get celebrants blind drunk. There are fairly regular colectivo departures from San Cristóbal's market to Chamula, especially frequent for the Sunday market. If you take a bus up, the 10km back is an easy and delightful walk, almost all downhill.

Zinacantán
ZINACANTÁN is also reasonably close, some 15km, and accessible on public transport. It's an easy walk from Chamula (about 1hr 30min), slightly harder in the other direction: if you reach Zinacantán early enough on Sunday morning you'll have time to look around, visit the market, and still walk to Chamula before the market there has packed up (Chamula's stays open longer than the others, presumably in honour of its foreign visitors). Zinacantán also has a **museum**, called Museo Ik'al Ojov ("Our Great Lord"), with displays of costumes from different hierarchical groups and a tableau of a house interior (daily 8am–6pm; donation).

Tenejapa and Huistán
A number of other villages can be reached by early morning buses from the market area, although you may have difficulty getting back. **TENEJAPA**, about 28km northeast of San Cristóbal through some superb mountain scenery, is the closest easily accessible Tzeltal village, and has a particularly good Sunday market: there's even a *pensión* here, though the only reason to stay would be to **hike** into the surrounding mountains. *Combis* leave for Tenejapa from Bermudas, an unmarked side street running east from the market, near the corner with Yajalon, about hourly or when full (1hr). Last one back to San Cristóbal leaves Tenejapa at 3pm. **HUISTÁN**, some 36km out, just off the road to Ocosingo, is Tzotzil, and with more than the usual amount of villagers in traditional dress..

Moxviquil
MOXVIQUIL, a completely deserted ruined **ancient site**, is a pleasant excursion of a few hours on foot from San Cristóbal; it's best, however, to study the plans at the Casa Na Bolom first (see p.473), as all you can see when you get there are piles of rough limestone. To get there, find Av Yajalon, a few blocks east of Santo Domingo, and follow it north to the end (about 30min) at the foot of tree-covered hills, in a little settlement called Ojo de Agua. Head for the highest buildings you can see, two timber shacks with red roofs. The tracks are at times indistinct as you clamber over the rocks, but after about 300m a lovely side valley opens up on your left – suitable for camping. The main path veers gradually to the right, becoming quite wide and leading up through a high basin ringed by pine forest. After 3km you reach the village of **Pozeula**; the ruins are ahead of you across a valley, built on top of and into the sides of and a hill.

Laguna Miramar
A much more remote excursion is a visit to **Laguna Miramar**, 190km southeast of San Cristóbal, in the heart of the Lacandón forest. Miramar, the largest lake in southeast Mexico, is now a pristine part of the Montes Azules Biosphere Reserve, and staying here enables you to experience the the largest surviving area of rainforest in North America. There are no settlements on the shore, and an island in the lake has traces of a fortress, which was a stronghold of the Maya until it was finally conquered in 1559.The high canopy forest here is home to abundant wildlife, including howler and

spider monkeys, tapirs and jaguars, and there are rivers and caves to explore. A trip here is a unique expedition, costing around US$200, and usually involves flying in from Ocosingo (see p.483), though you can get a *combi* from Ocosingo to the *ejido* of **Emiliano Zapata** (5hr), where you register with the village committee. For details, contact Fernando Ochoa at the *Casa de Pan* in San Cristóbal (☎967/8-04-68).

San Cristóbal to Guatemala: Comitán and Montebello

Beyond San Cristóbal, the Pan-American Highway continues to the border through some of Chiapas' most scintillating scenery. **Amatenango del Valle** is a Tzeltal-speaking village with a reputation for good unglazed pottery, but **Comitán** is the only place of any size – jumping-off point not only for Guatemala and for the **Lagos de Montebello National Park**, but for the Classic period **Maya** sites of Junchavín and Tenam Puente.

Comitán and around

An attractive town in its own right, **COMITÁN** is spectacularly poised on a rocky hillside and surrounded by country in which wild orchids bloom freely. Once a major **Maya centre** of population (Bonampak and Yaxchilán, even Palenque, are not far away as the parrot flies across the jungle), Comitán was originally a Maya town known as Balún Canán (Nine Stars, or Guardians), renamed Comitlán (Place of Potters in Nauhatl) when it came under Aztec control. The final place of any note before the border (the inaptly named Ciudad Cuauhtémoc is no more than a customs and immigration post with a collection of shacks), today Comitán is a market and supply centre for the surrounding agricultural area. There's a **Guatemalan consulate** in addition to a collection of reasonable **hotels**, and it's a good place to rest if you've some hard travelling through the Lacandón forest or into Guatemala ahead of you.

Arrival and information

Buses stop along the Pan-American Highway, a long six or seven blocks from the centre. Only Cristóbal Colón has a terminal (with guardería); all the others just pull in at the roadside.

Comitán's layout can be confusing at first, particularly as many streets are being renamed; pick up a free map from the **tourist office** in the Palacio Municipal on the zócalo (Mon–Sat 9am–8.30pm, Sun 9am–2pm; ☎963/2-40-47). They will also have the latest information on who needs Guatemalan visas. The **consulate** itself is at the corner of C 1 Sur Pte and Av 2 Pte Sur, a couple of blocks southwest of the zócalo (Mon–Fri 8am–4.30pm; ☎ & fax 963/2-26-69; US$10 fee for visa). If you need only a tourist card pick one up at the border. Also on the zócalo is a **Bancomer** for currency exchange, plus dollar cash advances and ATM. The **post office** is one and a half blocks south on Central Sur (Mon–Fri 8am–7pm, Sat 8am–1pm). There's even an **Internet café**, *Internet Comitán*, behind the tourist office in Pasaje Morales 12 (daily 9am–2pm & 4–9pm; *sinco@comitan.podernet.com.mx*). The best **travel agent** is Viajes Balun Canan, Av 1 Nte 31 (☎963/2-03-07), though they can only arrange internal flights.

Moving on from Comitán, there are plenty of buses and *combis* to Ciudad Cuauhtémoc for the border, and San Cristóbal and Tuxtla to the west. Heading for the **Lagos de Montebello**, buses or *combis* leave about every fifteen minutes from the terminal on Av 2 Pte Sur, between Calles 2 and 3 Sur, about three blocks southwest of the zócalo. Otherwise, you can just wait for one to come along on the highway heading south.

Accommodation

Comitán has plenty of hotels, especially good value in the budget range. Nights are much cooler than days, so you'll need at least one blanket.

Hospedaje Colonial, C 1 Nte Ote 13 (☎963/2-50-67). Basic, clean rooms with private bath and secure parking. ②.

Hospedaje Montebello, 1 Pte Nte 10, a block northwest of the zócalo (☎963/2-35-72). Great budget hotel. Large, clean rooms around a courtyard, some with private bath, and the communal shower is really hot. Clothes-washing facilities. ②.

Hospedaje Primavera, C Central Pte 4, just west from the zócalo (no phone). Basic but clean rooms round a courtyard, with several budget places to eat nearby. ②.

Lagos de Montebello, on the Pan-American Highway at the junction with 3 C Nte Pte (☎963/2-10-92, fax 2-39-18). Modern, comfortable rooms round a shady courtyard. Convenient if you're travelling by car. ④.

Pensión Delfín, Av Central 19A, right on the zócalo (☎963/2-00-13). Good value, with modernized rooms and dependable hot water. Not all rooms have windows. ③.

Posada del Virrey, Av Central Nte 13 (☎963/2-18-11). Bright, modern rooms around a courtyard, with private bath and TV. ④.

The Town

Comitán's zócalo, on several levels and with plenty of shady places to rest, is surrounded by the municipal buildings, the Santo Domingo church, shops, restaurants and the theatre. Opposite the tourist office, adjoining the church on the corner of the plaza, the **Casa de Cultura** (daily 9am–8pm; free) features murals on the courtyard walls and has exhibits on local history, while the splendid little **Museum of Archeology** (Tues–Sun 10am–5pm; free), at the far end of the courtyard, presents an easily understandable chronology on local Maya sites. Just half a block away you can also visit the **Museo Belisario Domínguez** (Tues–Sat 10am–6pm, Sun 9am–1pm; free), a collection of mementoes in the former home of the local doctor and politician who was assassinated in 1913 for his outspoken opposition to Huerta's usurpation of the presidency. The town also boasts a wealth of beautiful churches, many of them of historical and architectural interest, though only Santo Domingo and San Sebastián are truly colonial.

Eating and drinking

Apart from in the hotels, most of the best **places to eat** in Comitán are on the **zócalo** – for really good-value Mexican food served in clean surroundings, try *Helen's Enrique*, with tables under the arches, or the the *Restaurant Nevelandia*, and there are a couple of cheaper places. The **market**, two blocks east of the zócalo, is filled with fruit stands and has some very good comedores.

The ruins of Junchavín and Tenam Puente

Junchavín (daily 7am–5pm; free) is about a 45-minute walk northwest from Comitán's zócalo: follow Av Central Nte for about 2km until you reach the church of Santa Teresita on the right, recognizable by its two tall bell towers. The road immediately past the church to the right, signposted **Quija**, will lead you out of town into hilly farming country. The entrance to the site is on the left after 1500m. Hundreds of steps lead up to a small flat-topped pyramid about 5km high, flanked by two smaller structures. The best time to visit is early or late in the day to avoid the heat. Views are superb, and it is said you can see Chinkultic, 45km to the southeast. *Combis* from the zócalo run along the road to Quija; ask at the tourist office for times.

   Tenam Puente is a much larger site, a few kilometres off the Pan-American Highway, 15km to the south of Comitán. A bus leaves for the *ejido* of **Francisco**

Sarabia from 3 Ote Nte in Comitán at 8.30am, but you can take any bus heading south and get off at the junction, 11km on the right, then hitch or walk the 3km to the village. People here are friendly and will direct you to the ruins, which lie a kilometre beyond the school and playground. The path is difficult to find among the bushes and corn-fields, but you'll soon see stone terraces and mounds, and eventually several large structures, including a twenty-metre pyramid. There are pleasant walks in the forested hills around here, but you'll need to take water.

Comitán to Lagos de Montebello

The **Parque Nacional Lagos de Montebello** stretches along the border with Guatemala down to the southeast of Comitán, beautiful wooded country in which there are more than fifty lakes, sixteen of them very large. You could see quite a bit of the park in a long day-trip – buses cover the route all day from 5am, with the last bus leaving the park entrance around 7.30pm – but to really enjoy the beautiful lakes and forest, and to visit the small but spectacular **ruins of Chinkultic**, you're better off stay-ing in or near the park.

If you intend to head off the beaten track, you'll need to get hold of a good **map** before you arrive. The restaurant at the park headquarters displays an excellent topo-graphic map of Chiapas, copies of which are sometimes available at the tourist offices in Comitán or bookshops in San Cristóbal, though by far the best source is INEGI in Tuxtla (see p.464). The road leading to the National Park turns off the Pan-American Highway 16km from Comitán at the village of **La Trinitaria**, with the park entrance 36km further on. In the recent past, there were frequent **army checkpoints** along this road and you may still be asked for your passport at any time. The soldiers are invari-ably polite but make sure your tourist card is valid.

Accommodation on the road to the park

The most comfortable of the several **places to stay** along the road is the *Parador Museo Santa María*, about 18km along on the right (☎967/8-09-88; ⑤). A former hacienda, it's a lovely place furnished with antiques and oil paintings; don't expect too many mod cons, though – the rooms are lit with oil lamps. Another 12km brings you to the best budget accommodation on the road, the *Hospedaje and Restaurant La Orquidea* (②), better known simply as *Doña María's*. Here there are half a dozen sim-ple cabins with electric light, and (possibly) hot showers in a separate building. It's a very *simpatico* place, run by Doña María Domínguez, who has given much help and support to Guatemalan refugees – you may find volunteers staying here. It's certainly very peaceful, set among the pines, just a short walk from the Chinkultic ruins, with a restaurant serving good helpings of simple food; buses stop right outside.

The ruins of Chinkultic

Just before *Doña María's* on the Lagos de Montebello road, a 2km track leads off to the left to the Classic period Maya ruins of **CHINKULTIC** (US$2). So far only a small pro-portion of the site has been cleared and restored, but it's well worth a visit for the set-ting alone. Climb the first large mound, and you're rewarded with a view of a small lake, with fields of maize beyond and forested mountain ridges in the background. Birds, butterflies and dragonflies abound, and small lizards dart at every step. A ball-court and several *stelae* have been uncovered, but the highlight is undoubtedly the view from the top of the tallest structure, **El Mirador**. Set on top of a steep hill, with rugged cliffs dropping straight down to a *cenote*, the temple occupies a commanding position; though peaceful now, this was clearly an important hub in ancient times.

Park practicalities

The park entrance is 4km past *Doña María's*, and the paved road ends a few kilometres beyond the entrance at the **park headquarters**, after passing some of the more accessible and picturesque lakes. This is where the *combis* turn round, and there's a free lakeshore **campsite** and some simple cabañas (②) and a **restaurant**, the *Bosque Azul*, overlooking the lake of the same name. The combination of pine forest and lakes is reminiscent of Scotland or Maine, with miles of hiking potential: for the less energetic, roadside viewpoints provide glimpses of many of the lakes, including the Laguna de Siete Colores, lent different tints by natural mineral deposits and the surroundings. The small river flowing out of the lake (head for the bridge signed "paso de soldaldo") passes through an exquisitely beautiful, jungle-lined gorge and under a massive natural limestone arch before disappearing into a cave beneath a cliff face. Small boys will greet you and offer to guide you to the *grutas*; though you won't really need their help, they are friendly and do have a genuine interest in showing the caves to visitors. **Horses** are available for hire from behind the restaurant.

Tziscao and the Frontier Highway east

Near the entrance to the park, the recently paved **Frontier Highway** turns off to the right. Still inside the park boundaries, it passes the village of **TZISCAO**, a tiny settlement on the shore of Laguna Tziscao. On the lake's edge here is the *Albergue Tziscao*, an unofficial youth **hostel** (no membership needed). While its location is great, and you can rent boats to paddle on the lake, the three-tiered concrete bunks (US$2) give you the impression of being in a cave, and you'll almost certainly need a sleeping bag. Food and cold beer is available. To follow the trail around the lake, go back to the junction beyond the church and turn right. Along the way you pass **Laguna Internacional**, where the border is marked by a white obelisk at either end of the lake. Entering Guatemala here is *not* recommended. Beyond Tziscao, the Frontier Highway (served by buses from Comitán) continues for another 70km through mountains and jungle with some spectacular views and precipitous drops, to the end of the line at Flor de Café. The largest settlement along the road is **Las Maravillas de Tenejapa**, a lovely village with a restaurant but no accommodation, about three and a half hours from Tziscao.

Flor de Café stands at the foot of a steep limestone ridge formed by a finger of the Sierra la Colmena. Though the road goes no further at present, there's a track over the ridge connecting with the village of **Peña Blanca**, two hours away, a neat, clean *ejido* where you can get food, drinking water and, if you want, a guide to **Nuevo San Andrés** on the Río Lacantún, from where there are occasional boats downstream to **Ixcán** and **Chajul**. At Chajul there are buses to **Benemérito** (see p.495), for Bonampak, Yaxchilán, and **Palenque**. To make this journey you'll need camping equipment and should be prepared to wait for connections. Be very aware that this route traverses the "conflict zone" (see p.454), where the Zapatistas, paramilitaries and the Mexican army are engaged in guerrilla warfare: you may well be stopped by any of them and forbidden to proceed.

Ciudad Cuauhtémoc and the Guatemalan border

A visit to the Lagos de Montebello is a good introduction to the landscapes of Guatemala, but if you want to see the real thing, it's only another 60km or so from the La Trinitaria junction (plenty of passing buses) to the **Mexican border post** at **CIUDAD CUAUHTÉMOC**. There's nothing here but a few houses, the immigration post, a restaurant and the Cristóbal Colón bus station; the two **hotels** are not recommended.

The **Guatemalan border post** is at La Mesilla, a three-kilometre taxi-ride away (about US$0.50 per person in a shared taxi). As always, the crossing is best attempted in daylight. The border is open until at least 10pm, but onward transport will be difficult if you leave it this late. If you require a **visa**, you should really have got one before now: chances are you'll be let in if you agree to pay the entry charge, which could be as much as US$10. Officially, if you have a visa or tourist card (or are British, in which case you need neither), there is **no charge** for entering Guatemala. However, the La Mesilla border post is the worst in the country for exacting illegal charges from tourists, with the customs officers sometimes joining in with demands for *inspección aduanal*. If you think you've been charged too much – anything over US$1 – politely but firmly refuse to pay or, failing that, demand a receipt and, if you feel up to it, report the incident.

Buses on to Huehuetenango, Quezaltenango and Guatemala City wait just over the border, leaving at least every hour until about 4pm. The **money changers** will give you reasonable rates for travellers' cheques or dollars, not as good for pesos. There are a couple of adequate **bars** on the Guatemalan side, and several **hotels** up the street from the border: the *Maricruz* is best. **Getting into Mexico** is much easier: the Mexican tourist card will be issued free. Vans or buses will be waiting to take you to **Comitán** (passing La Trinitaria junction). The last **direct bus** to San Cristóbal is the Cristóbal Colón at 6.30pm (3hr 30min).

San Cristóbal to Palenque

Heading from San Cristóbal to the Yucatán, the best route takes you **to Palenque**, via Ocosingo, on a good paved road that's frequently used by buses and colectivos (a journey of around 5hr). It's an impressive and beautiful journey as the road winds around the spectacular mountain valleys, lush with greenery, and it's easier than ever to stop off and visit **Toniná ruins** and the awesome waterfalls at **Agua Azul** – just two of the attractions along the way.

Ocosingo and the surrounding area was the heartland of the **Zapatista** rebellion, so check on security before stopping in any of the villages along here, and be prepared to be searched by the Mexican army on the road. In the largely Tzeltal villages around Ocosingo, all of the women, if none of the men, wear traditional clothing.

Ocosingo

All things being equal (which they may not be), **OCOSINGO** makes a good place to escape the tourist crowds of San Cristóbal or Palenque. It's not as pretty as San Cristóbal, but it's certainly a great deal more attractive than Palenque, its streets lined with single-storey, red-tiled houses and the air thick with the scent of wood smoke. It's a town that has stayed close to its country roots, with plenty of cowboys in from the ranches in their stetsons and pick-ups. It's also the jumping-off point for the stunning Maya site of **Toniná**.

Buses all stop on or near the main road: walk down the hill and you can hardly miss the zócalo. It's surrounded by elegant *portales* and a big old country church, as well as an *Ayuntamiento* with a thoroughly incongruous modern first floor, complete with tinted-glass office windows. The best of the **hotels**, the *Hotel Central* (☎967/3-00-24; ④), sits under a modern section of the *portales* by the *Restaurante La Montura*. Cheaper recommendations include the *Margarita* (☎967/3-02-80; ③), down the side street by the *Restaurante Montura*, which has some a/c rooms; the *Hospedaje San José* (☎967/3-00-39; ②), off to the left at the bottom of the zócalo; and the *Agua Azul*, 1 Ote Sur (head right at the church; ☎967/3-03-02; ②), with comfortable rooms aound a courtyard. Several **places to eat** face the square – *Los Portales* is good but shuts very early – and the *Rahsa*, the best restaurant in town, is on 3 Sur Ote, a side street southwest of the plaza. The **food market**, straight down Av Central from the zócalo, sells locally produced cheeses, including a round waxy variety and delicious cream cheese.

Leaving Ocosingo is easy enough until mid-evening, with frequent buses and *combis* to San Cristóbal and Palenque. The last ATG buses in either direction leave at 7.30pm – though they're *de paso* and so are likely to be later.

Toniná

Considering how little-known it is, the Classic period Maya site of **TONINÁ** (daily 9am–4pm; US$1.50), some 14km east of Ocosingo, is surprisingly big, and restoration work is uncovering many more buildings. It centres on an enormous grassy plaza, once surrounded by buildings, and a series of seven artificial terraces climbing the hillside above it. At the bottom are two restored ball-courts and an overgrown pyramid mound; as you climb the hill, passing corbel-arched entrances to two vaulted rooms on the right, you begin to get an impression of Toniná's vastness. The sixth and seventh terraces each have a number of small temples, while beyond are more huge mounds, currently under excavation. From the top there are fine views of the surrounding country.

There are also tombs on both the fifth and sixth levels, one of which contains an enormous mask of the Earth Monster, a powerful force in Maya cosmology. The most striking feature, however, is the enormous **Mural of the Four Suns**, on the sixth platform. This amazingly well-preserved stucco codex tells the story of Maya cosmology by following the four suns (or eras of the world) as they were created and destroyed. The worlds are depicted as decapitated heads surrounded by flowers. A grinning, skeletal Lord of Death presents a particularly graphic image as he grasps a defleshed human head. At the time of writing another mural (not open to visitors at present) had just been discovered and the new **museum** was about to open.

Practicalities

The **road from Ocosingo** is now paved, and colectivos or trucks leave frequently from the market area, mainly heading for the large new army base by the turn-off to the site. From there, it's only a 2km walk, and easy enough to persuade the driver to take you all the way to the site. A taxi from Ocosingo costs US$5 to the ruins or to the neat wooden **cabins** of the *Rancho Esmeralda*, signed just before the turn-off to the site (fax only 967/3-07-11). The comfortable private cabins (④) have no electricity and no private bath, but the spacious, thatched shared bathroom has hot water, and you'll be made very welome, even if you turn up without booking. American owners Glen and Ellen, who built the cabins to provide income until the macadamia trees they planted produced nuts, now find they have unexpected success: they're just a ten-minute walk from the ruins, and the recent excavations and discoveries mean a regular flow of visitors. It's a wonderful, tranquil setting, and the food is both superb and plentiful. You can also **camp** at the *Rancho* (①).

Agua Azul, Agua Clara and Misol-Há

A series of stunningly beautiful **waterfalls** are the chief attractions along the winding mountain road between Ocosingo and Palenque. And, although the awesome cascades on the Río Shumulhá at **Agua Azul** and the exquisite waterfall at **Misol-Há** are usually visited on a day-trip from Palenque, it's perfectly possible (and more rewarding) to visit and stay nearby en route – they certainly deserve more than the quick glimpses offered on tours. Both places have accommodation, and there's a new hotel at the *ejido* of **Agua Clara**, on the riverbank a few kilometres from Agua Azul.

Agua Azul

AGUA AZUL, in the Parque Nacional Agua Azul, 4km down a track from the road and 54km before Palenque, is now a major tour-bus destination, and there are microlight flights over the falls, or horse-riding tours for the less foolhardy. If you come **by bus**, it will drop you at the crossroads, where there are usually taxis waiting to take you to the base of the falls. Otherwise it's a 45-minute walk down to the bottom (and at least an hour's sweaty hike back up): at the end of the track you pay to enter the park (US$0.60). Here, where the tour buses park, there are several restaurants and a **campsite** with hammock space. You can **stay** and **eat** better at *Comedor & Camping Casa Blanca*, at the top of the main fall, where there are also simple beds and hammock space in a large barn-like building (①), and the owners hire out horses. Of course, you can camp free almost anywhere if you walk upstream a way: the best spot is a tiny beach by the entrance to a magnificent gorge. There's a difficult trail leading up and over the top. Be sure to keep a close eye on your belongings, though, and be warned that muggings have been reported. You should walk upstream anyway, where perilous-looking bridges cross the river at various points, for this really is an area of exceptional beauty, with dozens of lesser falls above the developed area. At the right times of year, the river is alive with butterflies. Higher up, the swimming is safer, too – though watch out for signs warning of dangerous currents as there are several tempting but extremely perilous spots, and people drown here every year.

Agua Clara

A few kilometres beyond the Agua Azul turn, a signed track on the left passes through the *ejido* of **Agua Clara**, leading down to the Río Shumulhá again, here emerging from another gorge. On the riverbank, the *Hotel Agua Clara* (☎934/5-11-30 in Palenque; ④ including continental breakfast) has comfortable, spacious rooms with shared bathrooms. Part of a project to bring economic benefits to the local people, the **hotel and restaurant** are managed by the villagers, who are genuinely keen to welcome you. A rickety (but safe) suspension bridge crosses the swirling river, and there are **canoes and kayaks** for rent.

Misol-Há

At **Misol-Há**, 20km from Palenque, a 30m waterfall provides a stunning backdrop to a pool that's safe for swimming (US$0.60). A fern-lined trail leads along a ledge behind the wide cascade – refreshing from the spray and mist without even swimming – and the air of the lush rainforest is filled with bird calls. It's an easy 1500-metre walk from the road, and there's inexpensive **accommodation** in some of the most beautiful wooden cabañas in Mexico (☎ & fax in Palenque 934/5-12-10; ③). The cabins, and the **restaurant** catering to tour groups, are owned and run by the San Miguel *ejido*; each cabin has a private bathroom and electricity, and some have kitchens.

Palenque

Set in thick jungle screeching with insects, **Palenque** is for many people the most extraordinary of the major Maya sites. It's not large – you can see everything in a morning – but it is hauntingly beautiful, strongly linked to the lost cities of Guatemala while keeping its own distinctive style. The **site**, in a beautiful **national park** 9km from the town of Palenque, occupies the top of an escarpment marking the northern limit of the Chiapas highlands. The **town** itself (officially Santo Domingo de Palenque) is of little intrinsic interest and is best viewed simply as a base for exploring the ruins and the waterfalls in the nearby hills. And, since there are a number of new camping and cabaña places near the ruins, you may prefer not to stay in town at all.

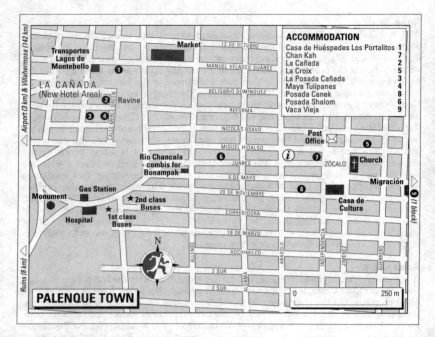

Arrival and information

Arriving at any of the **bus terminals**, you'll be on Juárez, where the highway comes into town. If you plan to leave the same day, particularly on a first-class bus, get your onward or return ticket on arrival. The **airport** is 5km north of town in a dusty settlement called Pakal Ná, a quick taxi-ride (US$1.50) into town.

Palenque's three **main streets**, Av Juárez, 5 de Mayo and Hidalgo, all run parallel to each other and lead straight up to the zócalo, the Parque Central. For a **map** and lots of useful information, call in at the helpful **tourist office** in the Plaza de Artesanías on Juárez, a block below the zócalo (Mon–Sat 8am–8pm, Sun 9am–1pm; ☎934/5-03-56). The staff know all the bus times and give out plenty of free leaflets. The **post office** is on Independencia, a block from the plaza; and there's a **laundry** on 5 de Mayo, opposite the *Hotel Kashlan*. Cibernet offers **email** from the small office on Independencia, near 20 de Noviembre (Mon–Sat 9am–2pm & 5–9pm; *cibernet@tnet.net.mx*)

The **banks** on Juárez are well used to changing travellers' cheques, but service is as slow as ever – you're better off using the **ATMs**. Alternatively, many of the **travel agencies**, also on Juárez, will change dollars or travellers' cheques; commission varies but it's considerably quicker than at the banks.

Accommodation

Palenque has seen a massive boom in **hotel** construction in recent years. There are plenty of places on the streets leading from the **bus stations** to the zócalo, especially Hidalgo (though the traffic noise makes these best avoided). **La Cañada rainforest area**, west of the town centre, set among the relative quiet of the remaining trees, is generally more upmarket, though with one excellent budget hotel. You'll also find

TOURS AND TRAVEL AGENCIES IN PALENQUE

The surge in the numbers of tourists visiting Palenque has encouraged a dozen or so travel agencies to offer **tours** to the surrounding attractions. Any of them can take you to the waterfalls at **Agua Azul** and **Misol-Há** (see p.485) and further afield to the ruins of **Bonampak** and **Yaxchilán** (p.492), but none can sell you an international air ticket. Guided **horse-riding** is also on offer, and some agencies can organize rafting, light air-craft flights and travel **to Guatemala** via the the the Usumacinta and San Pedro rivers. Sample prices are: US$5 per person for an all-day trip to Misol-Há and Agua Azul; US$50 for a one-day trip to the Maya ruins at Yaxchilán and Bonampak; and US$80 for an overnight trip to both sites, including a boat-trip to Yaxchilán and camping near Bonampak, then a guided walk to the site the next day. To visit both sites by plane will cost around US$120. A taxi to Bonampak costs around US$60. The agencies also offer transport to Flores (for Tikal) for US$35, via Bethél, but you can do the trip on your own *and* visit Yaxchilán on the way for less. Bear in mind that since the paving of the Frontier Highway, leading to Bonampak and Yaxchilán, and the opening of inexpensive accom-modation and restaurants nearby, it's easy enough to visit the sites on your own.

Recommended **tour agencies**, who'll usually speak English, include: Viajes Misol-Ha, Juárez 48 (☎934/5-04-88); Shumulhá, on Juárez next to the tourist office (☎934/5-03-56); and Viajes Yax-Ha, Juárez 123 (☎934/5-07-98). Colectivos Chambalu run to Palenque ruins from their office on Allende, near the corner with Juárez, every fifteen minutes from 6am to 6pm. They also have two daily trips to Agua Azul. (See "Moving on from Palenque" box, p.491, for details of how to get to Bonampak and Yaxchilán on your own.)

a host of new places, in addition to the *Mayabel* **campsite**, lining the **road to the ruins.**

IN TOWN

Casa de Huéspedes Los Portalitos, Mañuel Velasco Suárez, near the Transportes Lagos de Montebello bus station. Very ordinary place with rather less ordinary concrete beds, more com-fortable than they sound. Private showers. ②.

Chan Kah, corner of Juárez and Independencia (☎934/5-03-18). A touch of luxury right on the zócalo, this very comfortable small hotel is under the same ownership as the *Chan Kah Resort Village* near the ruins. ⑤.

La Croix, Hidalgo, on the corner of the zócalo (☎934/5-00-14). A long-established favourite and, though past its best, still worth trying. Rooms are arranged around a plant-filled courtyard whose walls are decorated with murals of Palenque. Popular with motorcyclists. ③.

Posada Canek, 20 de Noviembre 43 (☎934/5-11-13). One of the best-value hotels if you're travel-ling alone, and a popular travellers' place, with dorms (①) and private rooms (②), some with own bath. Good views from the balcony. ②.

Posada Shalom, Juárez 156 (☎934/5-09-44). New hotel, with clean rooms and tiled private bath-rooms: the best value in town at this price. Luggage storage. ②.

Vaca Vieja, 5 de Mayo 42 (☎934/5-03-77). A couple of blocks beyond the zócalo, this is a comfort-able hotel with private bathrooms, hot water and a decent restaurant. ②.

LA CAÑADA RAINFOREST AREA

La Cañada, Merle Green 14 (☎934/5-01-02). Spacious hotel rooms and cottages in quiet, tree-shaded grounds; excellent value at this price. Good restaurant. ④.

Maya Tulipanes, Merle Green 6 (☎934/5-02-01, fax 5-01-04). Very comfortable, a/c rooms with private bath. Shady grounds, a small pool and good restaurant. ⑤.

La Posada Cañada, behind the *Maya Tulipanes* (☎934/5-04-37). A very friendly place, popular with backpackers, *La Posada* is good for information about trips into the jungle. Rooms come with private bath and hot water, in a brightly painted two-storey building. Small new bar-restaurant. Discount for *Rough Guide* readers if staying more than one night. ③.

ON THE ROAD TO THE RUINS

The following hotels and campsites are listed in order of their distance from town.

Chan Kah Resort Village, 6km along on the left, just before the National Park entrance (☎934/5-03-18, fax 5-04-89). Luxury brick and stone cabañas in a lovely forest and river setting, humming with bird life.Three stone-lined swimming pools and a restaurant. ⑦.

El Panchan, at the National Park entrance, down a 200-metre track (3km from the ruins). Comfortable, inexpensive rooms and thatched cabins, some with private bath (③). Next to the cabins, but under different ownership, is a budget, laid-back camping spot with hammocks (①).

Camping Chaac, 2km from the site entrance. Rustic if basic, but very inexpensive, cabañas (②), plus camping (①) and small restaurant on the banks of two streams, with a friendly owner.

Mayabel Camping and Trailer Park, 2km from the site entrance (☎934/8-06-19). A great favourite with backpackers, *Mayabel* has a number of vehicle pads with electricity and water, and some cabañas (with hot water), in addition to palapa shelters for hammocks and tents. The site isn't crowded, and you can usually get a space. The path to the ruins through the back of the campsite is now closed, but magic mushroom aficionados continue to scour the fields in the morning mist. Lockers available. Hammock rental, tent or RV camping (①), cabaña (②).

Eating and drinking

Food in Palenque is fairly basic, and most restaurants serve up similar dishes, often pasta and pizza, to customers who've really only come for the ruins. Despite this, there are bargains to be had from the many **set menus** available; compare what's on offer from the boards outside. **Juárez** has several **budget places** between the bus stations and the zócalo. **Hidalgo** has more Mexican-style food, with several taco places, and at *Te'El*, a tiny café, a block below the plaza, you can drink delicious organic coffee. At the top of Hidalgo, on the corner of the **zócalo**, the *Restaurant Maya* has a wide choice and is popular though overpriced; *Virgo's*, across the street is better value. *Las Tinajas*, on 20 de Noviembre across from the *Posada Canek*, is a pleasant, family-run restaurant, with good food at fair prices. At *Granos Unidos*, on Guerrero, just behind the zócalo, you can get great cakes and wholewheat bread, ideal for taking on a trip, and there's a good Mexican **bakery**, *Flor de Palenque*, on Allende next to the colectivo terminal.

The ruins of Palenque

Palenque's style is unique. Superficially, it bears a closer resemblance to the Maya sites of Guatemala than to those of the Yucatán, but its **towered palace** and **pyramid tomb** are like nothing else, and the **setting**, too, is remarkable. Surrounded by hills covered in jungle, Palenque is at the same time right at the edge of the great Yucatán plain – climb to the top of any of the structures and you look out, across the dark green of the hills, over an endless stretch of low, pale-green flatland. The city flourished during the Classic period from around 300 to 900 AD, but its peak apparently came during a relatively short period of the seventh century, under two rulers – **Pacal** and **Chan-Bahlum**. Almost everything you can see (and that's only a tiny, central part of the original city) dates from this era.

Getting to the site is no problem. The most regular *combi* service is operated by Colectivos Chambalu, on Allende near the corner with Hidalgo, and you'll never have to wait more than fifteen minutes. The *combis* will stop anywhere along the road, useful if you're staying at one of the hotels or campsites, but they stop running at 6pm. After that it's either walk or take a taxi.

The ruins are in a **national park** (daily 8am–6pm; archeological zone daily 8am–5pm; US$2, free on Sun; admission includes museum). Arrive early, and climb the temples in the morning mist, if you want to avoid the worst of the heat and the crowds. There's a small **café** by the entrance, where for a fee you can leave bags while you explore, and a toilet by the ticket office. At the entrance to the site, there are ranks of souvenir stalls and you'll usually find a group of Lacandón in white robes (and gold watches) selling arrows and other artefacts.

The site

A prior visit to the **museum** (Tues–Sun 10am–4.30pm), on the road 1.5km before the site entrance, will give you a good idea of the scale of Palenque. The map of the site shows that only a quarter of the structures have been excavated and an intricate model of the palace complex shows how it would have appeared in the Classic period, with the tops of the buildings adorned with roof combs. There are also several carved panels removed from the site, and a good number of incense burners – large urns with elaborately stuccoed gods and mythological creatures – with explanations in Spanish and English. Signs inside the site are in English, Spanish and Tzeltal, though Chol is the language spoken by most modern Maya in this part of Chiapas.

As you enter **the site** itself, the great palace, with its extraordinary watch-tower (closed to visitors), stands ahead of you. To the right, at the end of a row of smaller structures, stands the **Templo de las Inscripciones**, an eight-stepped pyramid, 26m high, built up against a thickly overgrown hillside. The broad, extremely steep

stairway up the front, and paths up the hill, lead to a sanctuary on top that contains a series of stone panels carved with hieroglyphic inscriptions relating to Palenque's history. Most remarkable, though, is the **tomb** that lies at the heart of this pyramid. Discovered in 1952, this was the first such pyramid burial found in the Americas, and is still the most important and impressive. The smaller objects – the skeleton and the jade death mask – have been moved to the Anthropology Museum in México, but the crypt itself is still here, as is the massive, intricately carved stone sarcophagus. The **burial chamber**, and the narrow, vaulted stairway leading down to it (10am–4pm), are uncomfortably dank and eerie, but well worth the steep, slippery descent. You may not feel able to linger long at the bottom, however, as a long line of hot, claustrophobic visitors waits impatiently behind you. The deified king buried here was Pacal, and, in order that he should not be cut off from the world of the living, a hollow tube, in the form of a snake, runs up the side of the staircase from the tomb to the temple.

In June 1994 another remarkable tomb was discovered, in **Templo XIII**, in a pyramid similar to the Temple of the Inscriptions, located just to the west. This burial, of a man around forty years of age, is considered by archeologists to date from a similar period to that of Pacal. In addition to a number of jade and obsidian grave goods and food and drink vessels to sustain the deceased on his way to *Xibalba*, the Maya Underworld, the sarcophagus also contained the remains of two females, one adult and one adolescent. At present the tomb is not open to the public, but you can peer into the entrance through the bars.

The centrepiece of the site, **El Palacio**, is in fact a complex of buildings constructed at different times to form a rambling administrative or residential block. Its square **tower** (whose top floor was reconstructed in 1930) is quite unique, and no one knows exactly what its purpose was – perhaps a look-out post or an astronomical observatory. Bizarrely, the narrow staircase that winds up inside it starts only at the second level. Throughout you'll find delicately executed relief carvings, the most remarkable of which are the giant human figures on stone panels in the grassy courtyard.

From here, the lesser buildings of the **Grupo del Norte**, and the **Juego de Pelota** (ball-court), are slightly downhill across a cleared grassy area. On higher ground in the other direction, across the Río Otulúm – lined with stone and used as an aqueduct in the city's heyday – and half-obscured by the dense vegetation around them, lie the **Templo del Sol**, the **Templo de la Cruz** and the **Templo de la Cruz Foliada**. All are tall, narrow mounds surmounted by a temple with an elaborate stone roof-comb. Each, too, contains carved panels representing sacred rites – the cross found here is as important an image in Maya iconography as it is in Christian, representing the meeting of the heavens and the underworld with the land of the living.

The **Templo del Jaguar** is reached by a small path that follows the brook upstream – a delightful shaded walk. Beyond, more temples are being wrested from the jungle. If you want to penetrate a bit further, follow the path along the stream behind the Templo de las Inscripciones and you're in the jungle – or at least a pleasantly tame version of it. Tarzan creepers hang from giant trees, while all around there's the din of howler monkeys, strange bird calls and mysterious chatterings. The path leads to the *ejido* of Naranjo, a little over an hour's walk away. It's easy to believe you're walking over unexcavated pyramids: the ground is very rocky and some of the stones certainly don't look naturally formed.

Downstream, the river cascades through the forest and flows over beautiful limestone curtains and terraces into a series of gorgeous pools – the aptly named *El Baño de la Reina* (Bathing Pool of the Queen) is the most exquisite. The path leading down beside the river, past more recently excavated buildings and across the river over a sus-

---

MOVING ON FROM PALENQUE

Leaving Palenque by **bus**, there are surprisingly few direct services **to Mérida** (9hr): ADO has departures via **Campeche** at 8am and at 7pm and 10.30pm, and there are a couple of second-class services. **Cancún** (12hr) has two first-class departures, at 5pm and 8pm, and there are a couple of overnight buses to **México** (16hr). **Tuxtla** (7hr) has first-and second-class departures at least hourly, all calling at **Ocosingo** and **San Cristóbal** (5hr). ADO has plenty of buses to the main transport hub of **Villahermosa** (2hr 30min), and you may find it easier to get there and change for your onward journey.

Transportes Comitán y Lagos de Montebello, on Velasco Suárez, just past the market, has services down the Usumacinta valley (see below) for **Bonampak**, and **Frontera Corozal** (for Yaxchilán, and **Bethél** in Guatemala), as does Combis Río Chancala, on 5 de Mayo. If you're taking the boat from **La Palma** to **El Naranjo**, Guatemala, bear in mind the boat now usually leaves at 8am, so you may need to spend the night at **Tenosique**: if there's no direct bus take a Transportes Palenque colectivo from Allende near 20 Noviembre and change at **Emiliano Zapata**. Aerocaribe (and perhaps other airlines) fly from the recently extended airport 5km north of the town to San Cristóbal, Mérida, Cancún and Villahermosa, and to **Flores** (Guatemala). Check with one of the recommended travel agents on p.487.

---

pension bridge, eventually comes out on the main road opposite the museum and is an official **exit** but not an entrance.

The Usumacinta valley and the Frontier Highway south

The obvious starting point for trips to the Usumacinta valley sites of **Bonampak** and **Yaxchilán** is Palenque, where several agencies offer overland or plane trips to the sites – though you can also easily organize your own. If you do decide to head out on your own, you'll need to be prepared to walk, and possibly also to camp, though **accommodation** is becoming increasingly available.

The Usumacinta valley and the Lacandón forest form Mexico's last frontier: the **Frontier Highway** (Carretera Frontera) provides access to a number of new settlements whose inhabitants are rapidly changing the forest to farmland. The road is not yet complete all the way along the frontier, despite what some maps indicate, but it has reached **Chajúl** on the Río Lacantún. The only 'gap' is a 35-kilometre stretch of mountainous terrain between Chajúl and Flor de Café, at the other end of the Frontier Highway leading in from Comitán (see p.479), and even this may be complete by the time you read this. Several **buses** a day complete the nine-hour journey from Palenque **to Chajúl**, but you'll be discouraged from travelling beyond **Benemérito** by the Mexican army, and there is a real danger of armed robbery in this wild region. Plans for a series of **hydroelectric dams** on the Usumacinta, which would have inundated many archeological sites (as well as several new townships), appear to have been shelved, hopefully for good.

Exploring this route presents other options beyond Bonampak and Yaxchilán. From the riverbank settlement of Frontera Corozal, you can get a boat a short distance upstream to **Bethél** in Guatemala, and from the fast-expanding town of Benemérito you can take alonger trip on a trading boat upstream to **Sayaxché** (also in Guatemala), on the Río de la Pasión. The interior of this remote corner of Chiapas is the home of the **Lacandón Maya** and fortunately has some form of protection as the **Montes Azules Biosphere Reserve**.

THE LACANDÓN

You may already have encountered the impressively wild-looking **Lacandón Maya** selling exquisite (and apparently effective) bows and arrows at Palenque. Still wearing their simple, hanging white robes and with their hair uncut, the Lacandón were until recently the most isolated of all the Mexican tribes. The ancestors of today's Lacandónes are believed to have migrated to Chiapas from the Petén of Guatemala during the eighteenth century. Prior to that the Spanish had enslaved, killed or relocated the original inhabitants of the forest. The Lacandón refer to themselves as *Hach Winik* (true people); "Lacandón" was a label used by the Spanish to describe any native group outside colonial control who lived in the Usumacinta valley and western Petén. Appearances notwithstanding, some Lacandón families are quite wealthy, having sold timber rights in the jungle, though most of the timber money has now gone. This has led to a division in their society, and now most Lacandón live in one of two main communities: Lacanjá Chansayab, near Bonampak, with a village population predominantly made up of evangelical Protestants, some of whom are keenly developing low-impact tourist facilities (see below); and Nahá, where a small group still attempt to live a traditional life.

The best source of information on the Lacandón is the Casa Na Bolom in San Cristóbal de las Casas (see p.473), where you can find a manuscript of *Last Lords of Palenque* by Victor Perera and Robert Bruce (Little Brown & Co, 1982).

Bonampak

It's now possible to visit **Bonampak** on a day-trip from Palenque, and, as always, it's best to get an early start: Transportes Lagos de Montebello, on Velasco Suárez, and Combis Río Chancala, on 5 de Mayo in Palenque, have numerous departures to destinations along the Frontier Highway, beginning at 4.30am.

For Bonampak, you need to get off the bus at **San Javiér** (about 3hr), where there's a whitewashed government control hut on the left and on the right a hut where you can buy snacks and drinks.The large thatched visitors' centre here is not functioning. Take the side road bearing right to **Lacanjá Chansayab** (it may be signposted), and after 4km, at a right-hand bend in the road, fork left. This is where most tours **camp** for the night, at *Camping Margarito* (①), which also has a small restaurant, though no tents. If you can't face the two-hour walk to Bonampak, Lacandón taxi driver Chan Kin, who will probably be waiting outside the government control hut, will offer to take you in his taxi. The side road continues a few more kilometres to the Lacandón village, where you'll find several purpose-built **camping** shelters and hammocks available for rent. Ask for Kin Bor or Carlos Chan Bor, at the house where the paved road enters the village, either of whom will be able to fix you up with knowledgeable Lacandón guides to lead you through the forest. There are several rivers and waterfalls in the area, and you can reach the **Lacanjá ruins** in under two hours from here or Bonampak in three. If you can, pick up an information sheet in the **Casa Na Bolom** in San Cristóbal (see p.473) before you set off.

Lacandón boys may offer to guide you to the ruins and, though it's perfectly possible to follow the track on your own, you'll have a less apprehensive trip through the forest if you accept – and it won't cost much. The hike is wonderful in the dry season (Jan–April) – be prepared for mud other times.

After taking the **entrance fee** (US$2), the guard will probably not let you out of his sight. The guards usually have cold drinks for sale, but there's no food available. Once you've seen the ruins, head back to San Javiér junction, where you'll be able to catch a **bus** to Palenque until dusk – the road sees enough traffic to make hitching possible, too.

The site

The outside world first heard of the existence of Bonampak in 1946, when Charles Frey, an American conscientious objector taking refuge in the forest, was shown the site by the Lacandón, who apparently still worshipped at the ancient temples. Shortly after this, American photographer Giles Healey was also led to the site by the Lacandón, and was shown the famous **murals**; he was the first non-Maya ever to see these astonishing examples of Classic Maya art.

Set deep in the rainforest, the highlight of this superb site is the famed **Temple of the Frescoes**. Inside three separate chambers, on the temple walls and roof, are depicted vivid scenes of haughty Maya lords, splendidly attired in jaguar-skin robes and quetzal-plume headdresses, their equally well-dressed ladies, and bound prisoners, one with his fingernails ripped out, spurting blood. Musicians play drums, pipes and trumpets in what is clearly a celebration of victory.

The best way to view the paintings is to lie down on the floor of the chamber and allow your eyes to adjust to the dim light filtering in through the doorway. Though time and early cleaning attempts have taken their toll on the murals, recent work has restored some of their glory. That said, and however exciting it is to be here in person, try to see the reproductions in the National Museum of Anthropology in México (p.297) first, where you'll get a better impression of the whole scene.

The murals, dated to around 790 AD, show the Bonampak elite at the height of their power: unknown to them, the collapse of the Classic Maya civilization was imminent. Some details on the murals were never finished and Bonampak was abandoned shortly after the scenes in the temple were painted. In Room 1, the heir apparent, an infant wrapped in white cloth, is presented to assembled nobility under the supervision of the lord of Yaxchilán, while musicians play trumpets in the background. Room 2 contains a vivid, even gruesome, exhibition of power over Bonampak's enemies: tortured prisoners lie on temple steps, while above them lords in jaguar robes are indifferent to their agony. A severed head has rolled down the stairs and lord Chaan Muan, the king of Bonampak, grasps a prisoner (who appears to be pleading for mercy) by the hair – clearly about to deal him the same fate. Room 3 shows the price paid for victory: Chaan Muan's wife, Lady Rabbit, prepares to prick her tongue to let blood fall onto the paper in a clay pot in front of her. The smoke from burning the blood-soaked paper will carry messages to ancestor-gods. Other gorgeously dressed figures, their senses probably heightened by hallucinogenic drugs, dance on the temple steps.

Frontera Corozal and Yaxchilán

Twenty kilometres beyond San Javiér, the turning for **FRONTERA COROZAL** is marked by a comedor and shop selling basic supplies. Corozal itself, another 19km down the side road, and served by regular buses and *combis* from Palenque (last one back at 3pm), lies on the bank of the Usumacinta, where you need to catch a boat to get to Yaxchilán. There's a Mexican **immigration post**: visitors to Yaxchilán will always be asked to show their passports, despite the fact that the site is in Mexico. On the right past the immigration post are the new, thatched and brightly painted **cabañas** of *Escudo Jaguar* (☎934/5-03-56 in Palenque; ③), named after Jaguar Shield, a king of Yaxchilán. These have comfortable beds with mosquito nets, hot water in the tiled bathrooms and full-length windows open onto the porch – a touch of luxury at a bargain price. There's also a good **restaurant** here, and you can **camp** for less than US$2. More basic acommodation is available at Corozal's two **posadas** – the *Yani* (with fan; ①), on the right before the immigration post, is marginally the better – and there are a couple of *comedores*.

To reach the site, you need to get a ride in a boat heading downstream – ask around at the waterfront. It shouldn't prove too difficult as these are the boats used by tours from Palenque, and the boatmen will be pleased to make some extra money; bargain carefully, though, since you need to be picked up again. The trip takes about an hour and, unless you have to charter your own boat, should cost less than US$10 per person.

Yaxchilán: the site

A much larger site than Bonampak, **Yaxchilán** (daily 8am–4pm; US$2, free on Sun), strategically built on a bend in the river, was an important Classic-period centre. When the water is low, you can see (and climb) a pyramid built on a rock shelf on the river bed. Some archeologists suggest this was a bridge support, though this is unlikely as no corresponding structure has been found on the opposite bank, and the altar on top may indicate that it was used for religious ritual.

The first groups of numbered buildings and those around the **main plaza**, built on fairly level river terraces, are easy to view. The temples bear massive honeycombed roofs, now home to bats, and everywhere there are superb, well-preserved stucco carvings. These panels, on lintels above doorways and on stelae, depict rulers performing ritual events, often involving bloodletting to conjure up spirit visions of ancestors. Some of the very best lintels have been removed to the British Museum in London, but the number and quality of the remaining panels is unequalled at any other Maya site in Mexico. Yaxchilán's most famous kings (identified by their name-glyphs) were Shield Jaguar and his son Bird Jaguar, who ruled at the height of the city's power, from around 680 AD to 760 AD. Under their command Yaxchilán began the campaign of conquest that extended its sphere of influence over the other Usumacinta centres and enabled alliances with Tikal and Palenque.

A path behind Building 42 leads through the jungle, over several unrestored mounds, to three more tall temples. The guards won't always take you back here, as it's out of their way (and they insist you begin to return well before the 4pm closing time), but the climb is worth the effort for the view of distant mountain ridges. There's a real sense of a lost city as you explore the ancient, moss-covered stones, watched from the trees by toucans and monkeys. Butterflies flit around the forest glades, as, unfortunately, do mosquitoes.

On from Fontera Corozal and Yaxchilán

Entering Guatemala is relatively easy, as there's plenty of river traffic between Corozal and **Bethél**, a thirty-minute boat-ride upstream and on the opposite bank, where there's a Guatemalan immigration post. Buses leave Bethél at 5am and 1pm for **Flores** (for Tikal), an exhausting ride of at least five hours along a dirt road; or you can stay in the *Posada Maya* cabañas, set amid the ruins of Bethél (④), or camp (tent provided, ③), or get a bed at the basic *hospedaje* in the village. Heading **downstream from Yaxchilán** to the ruins of **Piedras Negras** on the Guatemalan bank is really only practicable as part of an organized whitewater rafting expedition, as there are rapids above and below the site, and beyond the river speeds through two massive canyons: the **Cañon de San José**, with fearsome rapids between cliffs 300m high, then the slightly less dramatic **Cañon de las Iguanas**.

The southern Usumacinta

Continuing south a further 35km brings you to **BOCA LACANTÚN**, where a bridge carries the road over the enormous Río Lacantún. You can expect any bus along this road to be stopped by immigration officials or army checkpoints, so keep your passport handy. At the confluence of the Lacantún and Usumacinta rivers is an unusual Maya remain, the **Planchon de Figuras**, a great limestone slab of unknown origin, carved with Maya glyphs, birds, animals and temples. If you're travelling by river, the beautiful **Chorro cascades** are just downstream.

Benemérito and onwards

The sprawling frontier town of **BENEMÉRITO**, 2km beyond Boca Lacantún, is the largest settlement in the Chiapas section of the Usumacinta valley, fast becoming an important centre for both river and road traffic. There's a hospital, market, shops, restaurants and a few basic **hotels**. The highway is the town's main street and in the centre, at the *Farmacía Arco Iris*, is the main road leading to the river, less than 2km away. **Arriving by boat** from Guatemala you'll find a restaurant and some none-too-cheap rooms by the dock. The other hotels, on the main street, are hardly any better: the *Hospedaje Montañero* (②) has rough beds with mattresses that feel like you're sleeping on a ploughed field, but there is electric light.

Getting to Palenque is no problem: buses and *combis* wait by the *Hospedaje El Tapanco*, and the restaurant opposite sells tickets. **Heading south**, a few buses a day go as far as the end of the road, which at the time of writing was Chajúl, on the Río Lacantún (5hr). A side road, used by buses, branching off to the southwest 8km beyond Benemérito, leads to **Pico de Oro**, an amazingly clean, pleasant village on the south bank of the Lacantún. There are a couple of **restaurants** but no hotels. Across the river, the huge **Montes Azules Biosphere Reserve** stretches for miles along the opposite bank, where you can hear the howler monkeys roaring. To experience the reserve, you can continue on by road to **Reforma Agraria**, where there's **accommodation** in *Las Guacamayas* (☎934/5-03-56; ③), new thatched cabañas on the bank of the Lacantún, and guides to show you the wonders of the rainforest.

By river to Sayaxché

If you hope to get by boat **from Benemérito to Sayaxché** in Guatemala (possibly 12hr), you'll need patience or a good deal of money. **Trading boats** are the cheapest method, but with no proper schedule you just have to ask. To reach Sayaxché in one day you'll need to leave early. Fast boats are now making the trip, stopping at the various sites en route, but you'll have to charter them at a cost of at least US$150, though the journey takes less than three hours. **Entering Guatemala**, you'll get your passport stamped at the army post at **Pipiles**, at the confluence with the Río de la Pasión. There's no Mexican immigration here (or at Benemérito); make sure you get an exit stamp in Frontera Corozal. Boats sometimes travel upriver beyond this point to Playa Grande in Guatemala, but this is an isolated area, with nothing like the traffic between Benemérito and Sayaxché. If you're **entering Mexico**, you'll cetainly be stopped at army checkpoints on the road.

TABASCO

The state of **Tabasco**, crossed by numerous slow-moving tropical rivers on their way to the Gulf, is at last making determined efforts to attract tourists. These rivers were used as trade highways by the ancient **Olmec** and **Maya** cultures, and the state boasts dozens of **archeological sites**. Few of these pre-Columbian cities have been fully excavated, though **Comalcalco**, north of Villahermosa, has been expertly restored and is certainly worth a visit.

Tabasco's **coast**, alternating between estuaries and sandbars, salt marshes and lagoons, is off the beaten track to most visitors. A road runs very close to the shore, however, enabling you to reach the deserted beaches. As yet these have somewhat limited facilities – even the main coastal town, **Paraíso**, is a tiny place.

Much of inland Tabasco is very flat, consisting of the flood plains of a dozen or so major rivers; indeed, most of the state's borders are waterways. Enterprising tour operators are running **boat trips** along the main rivers, the Grijalva and the Usumacinta, which are the best way to see remote ruins and to glimpse the region's abundant bird life. You can also travel by river into the Petén in **Guatemala**, leaving from La Palma, near Tenosique, in the far eastern corner of the state.

In the far south of the state, around **Teapa** and Villa Luz, the Chiapas highlands make their presence known in the foothills called the **Sierra Puana**. Overlooking the vast Gulf coast plain, these hills offer a retreat from the heat and humidity of the lowlands. Waterfalls spill down from the mountains, and a few small spas (*balnearios*) have developed. Village tracks provide some great **hiking trails** and, despite the proximity to Villahermosa, the state capital, you can enjoy a respite from the well-travelled tourist circuit. Nearby, in the remote **Sierra Huimanguillo**, southwest of Villahermosa, the **Agua Selva Project** is a superb example of ecotourism, aiming to bring small groups of visitors to enjoy these pristine mountains.

An almost unavoidable stop, **Villahermosa** itself has in recent years undergone an amazing transformation, with oil wealth financing the creation of spacious parks and several museums – the city at last lives up to its name. One excellent example is the **Parque Museo La Venta**, an outdoor archeological exhibition on the bank of a lagoon, which provides a glimpse of the otherwise barely accessible **Olmec** civilization.

Some history

Little is known about the **Olmec culture**, referred to by many archeologists as the mother culture of Mesoamerica. Its legacy of the Long Count calendar, glyphic writing, a rain god deity – and probably also the concept of zero and the ball game – influenced all subsequent civilizations in ancient Mexico, and the fact that it developed and flourished in the unpromising environment of the Gulf coast swamps 3200 years ago only adds to its mystery.

The Spanish Conquistador **Hernan Cortés** landed at the mouth of the Río Grijalva in 1519, and at first easily defeated the local Chontal Maya. However, the town he founded, Santa María de la Victoria, was beset first by indigenous attacks and then by pirates, eventually forcing a move to the present site and a change of name to "Villahermosa de San Juan Bautista" in 1596. For most of the colonial period, Tabasco remained a relative backwater, since the Spanish found the humid, insect-ridden swamps distinctly inhospitable. **Independence** did little to improve matters as local leaders fought among themselves, and it took the **French invasion** of 1862 and Napoleon III's imposition of the unfortunate Maximilian as Emperor of Mexico to bring some form of unity, with Tabasco offering fierce resistance to this foreign intrusion.

The industrialization of the country during the dictatorship of Porfirio Díaz passed agricultural Tabasco by, and even after the **Revolution** it was still a poor state, dependent on cacao and bananas. Though **Tomás Garrido Canabal**, Tabasco's governor in the 1920s and 1930s, is still respected as a reforming socialist whose implementation of laws regarding workers' rights and women's suffrage were decades ahead of the rest of the country, his period in office was also marked by intense **anticlericalism**. Priests were killed or driven out, all the churches were closed, and many of them, including the cathedral in Villahermosa, torn down. The region's **oil**, discovered in the 1930s but not fully exploited until the 1970s, provided the impetus to bring Tabasco into the modern world, enabling capital to be invested in the agricultural sector and Villahermosa to be transformed into the cultural centre it is today.

Villahermosa

VILLAHERMOSA, capital of the state, is a major and virtually unavoidable road junction: sooner or later you're almost bound to pass through here on the way from central Mexico to the Yucatán or back, especially if you hope to see Palenque (see p.488). It's

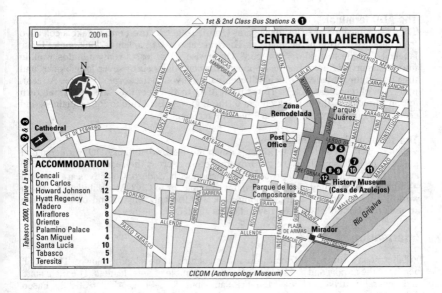

a large and prosperous city, and at first impression it can seem as bad a case of urban blight as any in Mexico. But the longer you stay, the more compensations you discover – quite apart from the **Parque La Venta**, there are the attractive plazas and quiet ancient streets, impressive ultra-modern buildings, and sudden unexpected vistas of the broad sweep of the **Río Grijalva**. In the evening, as the traffic disperses and the city cools down, its appeal is heightened, and strolling the pedestrianized streets around the *Zona Remodelada*, where everything stays open late, becomes a genuine pleasure. This lively area, between the two main squares, the **Parque Juárez** to the north and the **Plaza de Armas** just beyond the southern end, is also known as *Zona Luz* – or simply *La Zona*.

Arrival and orientation

The Aeropuerto Carlos A. Rovirosa, Carretera Villahermosa–Palenque Km 13, east of the centre, is a very busy regional **airport**, the nearest to Palenque. No buses run to the centre; a taxi will cost round US$7. Arriving at one of the two **bus stations**, you'll find things are pretty hectic as the highway thunders past through the concrete outskirts – the centre is a vast improvement. The two stations are pretty close to each other: the second-class a busy, ramshackle affair actually on the highway; first-class (known simply as El ADO – pronounced El *Ah-day-oh*) an efficient modern building just off the highway on Javier Mina. You'd be well advised to buy your outward ticket on arrival, partly because it can be hard to get on to departing buses (especially late afternoon and early morning ones to Palenque or Mérida), partly to avoid having to come back here more often than necessary. Villahermosa's humidity might make you consider taking **taxis** more frequently – worthwhile as the set fare in the city is only US$1, and plenty of *combis* ply the main streets. The city seems confusing at first, but you soon get to know the destinations, and the drivers and fellow passengers are helpful.

The ADO terminal

There's a guardería at ADO (daily 7am–11pm). To **get to the centre**, take a colectivo from outside the front of the terminal. There are also *combis* aplenty – look out for those labelled "Parque Juárez" or "Malecón". Otherwise, it's at least twenty minutes' walk to town: head up Merino or Fuentes, opposite the station, for six or seven long blocks, and then turn right at Madero, which will eventually get you to the zócalo (Plaza de Armas), past most of the cheap hotels. To get from ADO **to the second-class terminal**, turn left on Mina, walk three blocks down to the highway, Blvd Adolfo Ruíz Cortines, and cross it on the overpass – you can't miss the terminal.

The second-class terminal

Villahermosa's second-class terminal is much more crowded than ADO, with constant buses to main destinations. To **get into the centre**, cross the road by the footbridge and turn left, to follow the highway to its junction with Madero. Colectivos are plentiful – you want one heading along Madero, for example, or to CICOM – but it's not easy to work out where they're going. Asking a local is the only way to find out. **Taxis** are around, too, but not always as easy to find as at ADO.

Information

Villahermosa's **tourist information** infrastructure is developing slowly. The small booths at the airport and at ADO can offer only a jumble of hotel leaflets. The main state and federal **tourist office** (Mon–Fri 9am–3pm & 6–9pm; ☎93/16-36-33), Paseo Tabasco and Av de los Ríos, has some excellent booklets and maps, but it's not clearly signposted and, out near the modern Tabasco 2000 shopping and business complex, is too far away from the centre to be of much use. There are branches of all major **banks** (with ATMs) at the airport and in the centre, on Madero or Juárez, and you can easily change cash and travellers' cheques. The main **post office** is in the *Zona Remodelada* at the corner of Saenz and Lerdo (Mon–Fri 8am–7.30pm). **Travel agencies** are a boom industry here, with dozens in *La Zona* and at the bigger hotels, all of them arranging flights and trips to Palenque. Downtown, Viajes Villahermosa, 27 de Febrero 207 (☎93/12-54-56, fax 14-37-21), is recommended; while Creatur, Paseo Tabasco 715 (☎93/15-39-99, fax 15-39-88; *creatur@inforedmx.com.mx*), is the best in the region, with multi-lingual staff.

Accommodation

There are plenty of **budget hotels** in the centre, and, if you look around carefully, you can find somewhere both comfortable and reasonable in or near the *Zona Luz*, with some of the best options on Madero or Lerdo de Tejada, close to the heart of things. Many budget places have rooms on several floors but have no lift; bear this in mind as you're sweating with the humidity. Along Constitución, a block or so from the river, it's possible to find rooms for very little, though the very cheapest are distinctly dodgy. The most **upmarket** hotels are around the Tabasco 2000 complex.

Budget and mid-price

Madero, Madero 301 (☎93/12-05-16). The city's best value in this range, with features often not found in a budget hotel; ask for a room off the street. Private showers and some a/c rooms. ③.
Oriente, Madero 425 (☎93/12-11-01). Clean, tiled rooms with private bath, some with a/c. ②.
Palomino Palace, across from ADO (☎93/12-84-31). Decent hotel right by the bus station. Usually has rooms available with fan, private shower and TV. Bar and restaurant. ③.

Santa Lucía, Madero 418, next to the *Don Carlos* (☎93/12-24-99). Clean, well-furnished rooms with tiled bathrooms in a modern building – with a lift. ③.

San Miguel, Lerdo de Tejada 315 (☎93/12-15-06). Battered but serviceable rooms with clean sheets and private bath. ②.

Tabasco, Lerdo de Tejada 317 (☎93/12-05-64). Basic but good value, and plenty of room. ②.

Teresita, Constitución 224 (☎93/12-34-53). Easily the nicest budget accommodation along here, quite basic but friendly. Some rooms have private bath; the best are at the back, overlooking the river. ②.

More expensive

Cencali, Paseo Tabasco and Juárez (☎93/15-19-99, fax 15-66-00). Set in luxuriant gardens on the shore of a lagoon, this has a quiet location and a large inviting pool. ⑦.

Don Carlos, Madero 422 (☎93/12-24-92, fax 12-46-22). Thoroughly modern, comfortable a/c rooms that aren't outrageously expensive. Good restaurant and bar. ⑤.

Howard Johnson, Aldama 404 (☎ & fax 93/14-46-45). Just what you'd expect from the chain; modern, comfortable rooms with a/c and TV. Great views from the rooftop terrace. The pavement café right in the *Zona Luz* is a luxurious place to read the papers. ⑥.

Hyatt Regency, Pasao Tabasco and Juárez (☎93/15-12-34, fax 15-12-35). Extremely comfortable rooms in a luxurious setting, and great service, as befits Villahermosa's best hotel. The only drawback (apart from the price) is that the rooms don't have balconies to enjoy the view. ⑧.

Miraflores, Reforma 304 (☎93/12-00-22, fax 12-04-86). Excellent value on a pedestrian street in the heart of the *Zona Luz*. Colour TV and phone; a balcony café for people-watching; plus a restaurant and bar. Car rental in the lobby. ⑤.

The City

Though most visitors quite rightly head straight out to the **Parque La Venta**, the centre of Villahermosa warrants some exploration. The pedestrianized **Zona Remodelada**, with some vestiges of the colonial city, is as good a place as any to start your wandering. At its northern end, opposite the Parque Juárez, at the junction of Madero and Zaragoza, the **Centro Cultural de Villahermosa** (daily 10am–9pm; free) has changing exhibitions of art, photography and costume, as well as being a venue for films and concerts. The café here is excellent, too. The zócalo, **Plaza de Armas**, with its river views, is a pleasant places to while away some time, especially in the cool of the evening. Here, the imposing white-painted **Palacio del Gobierno**, with turrets at the corners, faces the pretty little church of La Concepción. The new footbridge at the corner of the Plaza de Armas allows you to stroll over the river and watch the fireflies glow in the bushes on the bank, and has an enormous *mirador* for splendid views.

The Casa de Azulejos and CICOM complex

Villahermosa's small **history museum**, at the corner of 27 de Febrero and Juárez (Tues–Sat 9am–8pm; US$0.70), gives a quirky, detailed account of Tabasco's history, illustrated by such diverse objects as an early X-ray machine, archeological pieces from Comalcalco and other information on the Maya sites, and the printing press of *El Disidente* newspaper from 1863. The turn-of-the-century museum building, which used to be a hotel, is popularly known as the "Casa de Azulejos" – and indeed there are tiles everywhere, forming an optical illusion in the lobby, with examples of patterns from all over Europe and the Middle East. Upstairs, wrought-iron balconies overlook the *Zona* – look up to see the statues of nymphs and classical figures perched on the railings around the roof.

An easy walk along the river from the *Zona Remodelada* brings you to Villahermosa's cultural centre, **CICOM** – Centro de Investigaciones de las Culturas Olmeca y Maya. At a couple of places small ferry boats cross the river. The complex includes a concert hall, a beautiful theatre, a research library and a fine restaurant, along with the **Centro de Estudios y Investigación de los Belles Artes** (Tues–Sun 10am–4pm; free), which hosts art and costume displays. The highlight for most visitors is undoubtedly the **Museo Regional de Anthropología Carlos Pellicer Cámara** (daily 9am–8pm; US$1.50), with artefacts and models displayed on four levels, proceeding chronologically downwards from the top floor. In addition to the Olmec and Maya displays, you can also view a reproduction of the Bonampak murals. Carlos Pellicer, a poet and anthropologist born in Villahermosa, and the driving force behind the rescue of the stone carvings from the original La Venta, is commemorated by a bronze statue outside the complex. His house, at C Narciso Sáenz 203, in the *Zona Remodelada*, has also been turned into a museum – the Casa Museo Carlos Pellicer (daily 9am–8pm; free).

Parque La Venta, the zoo and the Museo de Historia Natural

Soon after they were discovered by Pemex engineers draining a marsh, most of the important finds from the Olmec site of La Venta – some 120km west of the city, at the border with Veracruz state (see p.503) – were transferred to the **Parque La Venta**, set inside the much larger Parque Tomás Garrido Canabal. The Parque La Venta (which also contains a reasonable **zoo**) is on the shores of a large lake, the **Laguna de Ilusiones**; here you can rent boats or climb the Mirador de los Aguilas, a tower in the middle of the lake. Also in the park, opposite the La Venta entrance, the excellent **Museo de Historia Natural** (daily 9am–8pm; US$1) has good displays on the geography, geology, animals and plants of Tabasco.

   To get to the park hop on one of the *combis* that run along Madero in the city centre ("Tabasco 2000", "Circuito 1", "Parque Linda Vista" among others); they also run along the highway from the second-class bus terminal. Beyond La Venta, many of the *combis* continue to Tabasco 2000.

Visiting Parque La Venta

Although hardly the exact reproduction it claims to be, **Parque La Venta** (daily 9am–5pm, tickets sold 9am–4pm; US$2, including museum and zoo) does give you a chance to see a superb collection of artefacts from the earliest Mexican civilization in an appropriately jungly setting. You can enter through the **museum**, housed under an enormous thatched roof, where you can familiarize yourself with the known facts of the Olmec culture. The most significant and famous items in the park are, of course, the gigantic **basalt heads**, which present such a curious puzzle with their flattened, negroid features. There's a whole series of other Olmec stone sculptures; follow the numbers as the path winds through the park. In their zeal to re-create an authentic jungle setting, the designers have introduced deer and coatis (members of the racoon family) which wander around freely, while crocodiles, jaguars, monkeys and other animals from Tabasco are displayed in the zoo's sizeable enclosures. The mosquitoes are an authentic but unplanned touch.

Yumká

Villahermosa's latest ecological attraction, **Yumká** (daily 9am–5pm; US$4), is an ambitious combination of safari park and environmental studies centre, focusing on Tabasco's jungle and wetland habitats. Its formal name, Centro de Interpretación y Convivencia con la Naturaleza, is a bit of a mouthful, so most people simply call it Yumká, after the Chontal Maya god, a dwarf who looks after jungles. The park is large, covering more than six square kilometres, so after a guided walking tour of the Tabasco jungle, complete with crocodiles, you board a train for a tour round enormous paddocks representing the savannahs of Africa and Asia. Elephants, rhinos, giraffes and antelopes are rarely displayed in Mexico and almost never in such spacious surroundings. After a stop at the restaurant and souvenir shop, you're taken on a boat tour of the lagoon, where, in addition to hippos and monkeys, there are good bird-watching opportunities.

Yumká is 14km from the centre of Villahermosa, on the road to the airport. The Yumká **minibus** (US$1), decorated with a colourful jungle theme, departs from the car park near the *Restaurant La Venta*, on Av Ruíz Cortines, just before the entrance to the museums in the Parque La Venta.

Eating and drinking

The number of restaurants in Villahermosa has grown over the last few years, and some of the new ones are truly cosmopolitan. Most of the better hotels have improved their own dining rooms and, if you're staying near Tabasco 2000, your hotel restaurant will be among the best in the city.

Both **bus stations** have plenty of food joints nearby. Inside the second-class there are juice and coffee bars, a good bread shop and a less good restaurant. Across the street from ADO, there's a row of inexpensive places; the *Café Turistico* is best. The *Bar Neptuno*, half a block from ADO down Fuentes, is great to while away some time if you're waiting for a bus. The sign on the door says "Turistico", but the atmosphere is distinctly Mexican, with live music and slow service. Women are admitted, though it's probably best not to go alone. As ever, the **market** is good for fruit, bread and cheap tacos: you'll find it several blocks east of the *Zona Remodelada*, at Pino Suárez and Zozoya. *Aquarius*, Zaragoza 513, behind the Parque Juárez, is an excellent **vegetarian restaurant** and **health-food shop**, with delicious fresh wholemeal sandwiches and daily specials.

At the northern end of the *Zona,* the Parque Juárez is lively in the evenings as crowds swirl around watching the street entertainers. The pedestrian area fills with window-shoppers enjoying frozen yoghurts or eating out at open-fronted restaurants or one of the many *coctelerias*. The best place here for an inexpensive, filling meal at **lunchtime** is the buffet at *La Bodegita del Centro*, on Lerdo, near the corner with Madero, where you select from a variety of taco fillings, washed down with *horchata*, a vanilla or almond-flavoured rice drink. Or try the popular *El Tortito Valenzuela*, on the corner of 27 de Febrero and Madero, for filling tacos and tortas. The *Café La Cabaña*, at the end of Juárez near the *Cas de los Azulejos*, serves good but pricey coffee in a prime location. Even better, and less touristy, is the *Café Selecto*, round the corner on 27 de Febrero, past the corner with Hidalgo, where you get great *pan dulces* in an arty atmosphere.

MOVING ON FROM VILLAHERMOSA

Villahermosa being the state capital, you should have no problems getting an onward bus. To get to the first-class terminal take a 'Chedraui' *combi* – they go to a huge department store behind the terminal.

Between them, ADO and Cristóbal Colón operate dozens of services to all the main destinations: Tuxtla (7hr), Veracruz (7hr), Tenosique (3hr), Mérida (9hr), Campeche (6hr), Cancún (12hr), Chetumal (7hr), Oaxaca, (9hr) México (12hr), even the US border and Pacific coast. From ADO there are several departures to Palenque (2hr 30min), and you can also easily get there from the second-class terminal, from where there are constant departures to all the same destinations, plus Comalcalco, Paraíso and Frontera. For San Cristóbal (8–9hr), there are a few direct services; otherwise change at either Tuxtla or Palenque.

Beyond here, at the junction of Paseo Tabasco and the malecón, there are several taco **restaurants**, some of them quite fancy. More restaurants line Paseo Tabasco at intervals all the way up to the junction with Mina. Head up this way if you want to sample the best of comida Tabasqueña at the *Guaraguao*, on the corner of 27 de Febrero and Javier Mina (☎93/12-56-25). Specialities from the coasts and rivers of Tabasco include *pejelargarto*, a type of alligator gar (a pike-like fish, common to Tabasco's rivers), and great seafood. It closes early, though, about 8.30 or 9pm.

Comalcalco and the coast

The journey from Villahermosa along **the coast**, west to Veracruz or east to Campeche, is in many ways extraordinarily beautiful: the road hugs the shore so closely that in some places it's been washed away by storms, and it's never hard to find deserted beaches and lagoons. New bridges have replaced all but one of the ferries that used to cross the broad river mouths; the only one left is an ageing vessel carrying vehicles and passengers between Zacatal and **Ciudad del Carmen** (see p.518), at the western end of the huge Laguna de Terminos.

Attractive as the coastal route is, almost no tourists travel it, preferring the inland route to the Yucatán in order to visit Palenque en route. Even if this is your intention, you'll be well rewarded by spending a day north of Villahermosa, visiting the ruins of **Comalcalco**.

Comalcalco

The Classic-period site of **Comalcalco** (daily 8am–5pm; US$1.50) is an easy and worthwhile trip from Villahermosa, and you can be fairly sure of having the carefully tended ruins virtually to yourself. The westernmost Maya site, Comalcalco was occupied around the same time as Palenque, with which it shares some features, and may even have been ruled by some of the same kings.

The area's lack of building stone forced the Chontal Maya to adopt a distinctive, almost unique, form of construction – kiln-fired brick (the site's name means "house of bricks" in Nauhatl). As if the bricks themselves were not sufficient to mark this site as different, the builders added mystery to technology: each brick was stamped with a geometric or representational design before firing, and the design was deliberately placed facing inwards, so that it could not be seen in the finished building.

The site

There's a small **museum** at the site, and a restaurant. Take water with you, though, since the humidity is extremely high. If you're going to venture into the long grass or bushes, insect repellent is a must. Though there are dozens of structures, only around ten or so of the larger buildings have been subjected to any restoration. The first one you come to is the main structure of the **North Plaza Cluster**: Temple I, a tiered pyramid with a massive central stairway. Originally, the whole building (along with all of the structures here) would have been covered with stucco, sculpted into masks and reliefs of rulers and deities, and brightly painted. Now only a few of these features are left, the exposed ones protected from further erosion by thatched shelters, while some are deliberately left buried.

Opposite Temple I is the **Great Acropolis**: more mounds, mainly grass-covered, though there's a fine stucco mask of Kinich Ahau, the Maya sun god. Due to the fragile nature of the brick you're not allowed to climb most of the temples, but if you walk to the far end of the complex you'll come to **El Palacio**, where you can climb the mound and get a close view of the brickwork. There's a series of small arches here, faintly reminiscent of English Victorian railway architecture. You'll also get a good overview of the whole site, including many other mounds in the surrounding forest and farmland. **Cacao**, used as money by the Maya, and the main ingredient of their drinking chocolate, is grown in the area, and you'll pass cacao bushes on the way in, with huge green bean pods sprouting straight from their trunks.

Practicalities

The **bus from Villahermosa** takes an hour and a quarter: ADO has several departures a day, and Transportes Somellera runs a service every thirty minutes from the second-class station. Both bus stations in Comalcalco are on Gregorio Méndez; walk the 150m back to the highway and catch a *combi* heading north (left) towards Paraíso. The ruins are on the right (signposted) after about five minutes. Some *combis* go all the way there; otherwise, the site is fifteen minutes' walk up the track, past some houses and a cacao plantation. Should you get stuck in Comalcalco, there are a few basic **hotels** near the bus stations.

Paraíso and the coast road west

If you want to travel the coast route, catch one of the frequent buses passing the Comalcalco turn-off to **PARAÍSO**, a sleepy place thirty minutes away on the banks of the Río Seco. Everything you need is close to the pleasant, modern zócalo. Paraíso's ADO **bus station**, at the corner of Juárez and 2 de Abril, is just two blocks south of the zócalo. The second-class station, with far more departures, is less than fifteen minutes' walk north of the centre and well served by *combis*. If you're walking from the second-class to the centre, head south (left) and aim for the cathedral tower. Most **hotels** here are not up to much: *Hotel Hidalgo* (☎933/3-00-07; ③), on Degollado 206, at the corner of 2 de Abril, is the exception, with good, clean rooms with fan, private bathrooms with hot water, and drinking water. There are plenty of juice bars in and around the zócalo and a couple of decent, moderately priced **restaurants**: *La Galeria* serves inexpensive comedores, while *La Señorial* is a little more upmarket.

The Gulf coast beaches

The nearest beach, **Playa Limón**, is a twenty-minute *combi* ride north of Paraíso. East and west are more *playas* with thatched shelters and tiny seafood restaurants, but frankly the beaches are a bit of a disappointment. The sand is grey-brown and, though generally clean, you've always got the oil refinery in sight to the east. There are no hotels along this stretch, but plenty of spaces for camping – though you'll be attacked by swarms of mosquitoes and sandflies – and there are only second-class buses. Heading further **west** along the coast, you pass a few more tiny, rustic "resorts", some of them exhibiting signs of desolate poverty. At one estuary the road has fallen victim to the sea – the buses stop here and passengers have to cross in waiting boats. **Sánchez Magallanes** is the only town in the next hundred kilometres, but it's hardly worth staying here: the beaches aren't that clean, and there's only one **hotel**, the *Delia* (②), which is at least clean, along with lots of dilapidated seafood restaurants. Beyond here, the road heads away from the coast towards La Venta, forty minutes away.

La Venta

The small town of **LA VENTA**, on the border between Tabasco and Veracruz, would be of little interest were it not for the **archeological site** (daily 10am–4.30pm; US$1.50, free on Sun) where the huge Olmec heads displayed in Villahermosa were discovered. In the **museum** at the entrance, models show where the site was located, in a swamp surrounded by rivers, while glass cases are filled with unlabelled bits of pottery. Information panels on the wall give a good explanation of Olmec culture and history.

The site itself has a few weathered *stelae* or monuments, but the highlight is the huge grass-covered mound, about 30m high, clearly a pyramid, with fluted sides believed to represent the ravines on the flanks of a sacred volcano. The climb up is worth the effort for the views and the breeze. Paths below take you through the jungle – fascinating for its plants and butterflies but haunted by ferocious mosquitoes.

La Venta is served by a steady stream of **buses** to Villahermosa and Coatzalcoalcos, so there's no need to **stay**; the *Hotel del Sol* (②), on the corner of the small plaza, is a friendly, pleasant option if you get stuck.

Frontera and the coast road east

East of Paraíso, the road crosses several lagoons and rivers before reaching the junction with Hwy-180. Dirt roads head off left to numerous palm-shaded *playas*, each about five or six kilometres from the highway. If you're travelling light you could easily camp at any of these and get back to the main road in the morning. About 25km beyond Paraíso the bus will drop you in **FRONTERA**, a pleasant if uninspiring working town and port, little changed since Graham Greene landed here in 1938:

> Shark fins glided like periscopes at the mouth of the Grijalva River . . . three or four aerials stuck up into the blazing sky from among the banana groves and the palm-leaf huts; it was like Africa seeing itself in a mirror across the Atlantic. Little islands of lily plants came floating down from the interior, and the carcasses of old stranded steamers held up the banks. And then round a bend in the river Frontera . . . the Presidencia and a big warehouse and a white blanched street running off between wooden shacks.

The scene on the waterfront would still be familiar to Greene, but there's now a huge bridge over the Grijalva and the plaza, the **Parque Quintín Arauz**, has been tastefully modernized. **Arriving** by second-class bus, turn left out of the bus station and walk two blocks along Madero to get to the Parque or, from the first-class bus station, left along Zaragoza, then right, and walk three blocks down Madero from the other direction. Everything you'll need is around the plaza, including a couple of nondescript **hotels**; you're better off not staying if you have any choice. For tasty shrimp or a good-value comida corrida, try *El Conquistador*, in an old colonial building, at Juárez 8. Right by the wharf is a restaurant where the dock workers have their coffee served in tin mugs; as a visitor you'll get the chipped china cup and saucer, but the coffee's great. **Bars** in Frontera can exude a somewhat cosmopolitan atmosphere when the crew from a foreign ship is in port.

Thirteen kilometres away at the mouth of the river, on the eastern bank, is the rundown fishing settlement of **EL BOSQUE**. The beach is great for a lone, windswept walk, but is mainly left to the pelicans, except for on Sundays when it gets busy with holidaying Mexicans. The dirt road out here goes through lagoons and protected swamps, inhabited by a multitude of wildlife. Colectivos from Frontera are supposed to operate every ten minutes between 7am and 5pm, but they aren't reliable. If you get stranded, start to walk back along the dirt road: the further you walk, the more you improve your chances of catching a ride with someone heading back into town. **Buses leave Frontera** for Villahermosa or Ciudad del Carmen every one or two hours during daylight hours, and four buses daily go to Veracruz.

The Sierra Huimanguillo and the Agua Selva Project

More than 100km southwest of Villahermosa, between the borders of Veracruz and Chiapas, a narrow triangle of Tabasco thrusts into the mountains. Known as the **Sierra**

Huimanguillo, from the town in the lowlands just to the north, this little-visited corner of the state is the focus of the **Agua Selva Ecotourism Project**. Designed to bring the benefits of small-scale tourism to the *ejidos* of the area by building cabañas (*albergues*) in the villages, the project aims to bring economic benefits without sacrificing the abundant natural attractions. The mountains here are not that high, only up to 1000m, but they are rugged, and to appreciate them at their best you have to hike; not only to caves, canyons and waterfalls, but also to the **Zoque** ruins of Malpasito (near the *ejido* of the same name), with their astonishing **petroglyphs** – easily accessible by public transport from **Huimanguillo**.

Huimanguillo to Malpasito

Visiting the Agua Selva Project, you'll have to pass through **HUIMANGUILLO**, a mid-sized town 75km southwest of Villahermosa. Buses leave Villahermosa frequently during the day; if there isn't a direct one, go second-class to **Cárdenas** and change there. ADO buses stop right in the centre, on Escobar, half a block south of the plaza. Second-class buses arrive at the terminal on Gutiérrez, near the market, five blocks west along Libertad from the town centre. The bus for **Malpasito** leaves at 1pm (2hr 30min), returning from the village at 5am.

In the centre of town, the *Hotel del Carmen* on Morelos 39, two blocks south of the plaza (☎ and fax 937/5-09-15; ③), offers **information** and **accommodation**, with large well-furnished rooms, all with private bath. Downstairs, the *Cafetería Orquidias* serves good Mexican food, which you eat surrounded by photographs of the mountains and waterfalls in the sierra. The owner, George Pagole del Valle, a leading light in the Agua Selva project, will be able to supply information and may even give you a lift if he's heading to Malpasito.

Malpasito

Leaving Huimanguillo the road to Malpasito heads south, following the valley of the Río Grijalva (here called the **Mezcalapa**) for 60km, crossing into Chiapas at one point, before heading west onto a dirt road for 15km to reach the *ejido*.

By now you can see the peaks, with the great jungle-covered plateau of El Mono Pelón ("the bald monkey") dominating the skyline. This is the highest point in Tabasco, and the sheer sides look impossible to climb. In **MALPASITO** you can **stay** right by the river, in the simple, three-room *Albergue Ecológico* (②), managed by the Peréz Rincón family; you can eat with them or at the table by the river. Drinking and cooking water is piped in from a spring, pure and fresh, but you bathe in the river. Higher up, and nearer the **La Pava waterfalls**, the plusher *Albergue La Pava* (⑤, including meals) consists of large, oval thatched cabañas with bamboo sides, some with two storeys, giving you a bird's-eye view into the surrounding forest. The bus from Huimanguillo comes to within half a kilometre of the *albergue* in the village; to the *Albergue La Pava* cabañas it's a forty-minute walk up the side of gorge, stepping between moss-covered boulders, and crossing the river on a suspension bridge. This is an utterly beautiful, tranquil place, perfect for enjoying the abundant wildlife.

The Zoque ruins of Malpasito

A walk of just over 1km from the *albergue* in Malpasito brings you to the Post-Classic **Zoque** ruins of the same name, overlooked by jagged, jungle-covered mountains and reminiscent of Palenque (see p.488). Though the ruins bear resemblances, the Zoque were not a Maya group, and little is known about them today. On the way in you pass terraces and grass-covered mounds, eventually leading to the unusual **ball-court**. At the top of the stone terraces forming the south side of the court, a flight of steps leads down to a narrow room, with stone benches lining either side. Beyond this, and separate from the chamber, is a square pit more than 2m deep and 1.5m square. This room may have been used by the ball players, or at least one team, to effect a spectacular entrance as they emerged on to the top of the ball-court. Beyond the ball-court a grass-covered plaza leads to two flights of wide steps with another small plaza at the top, with stunning views of mountains all around.

Perhaps the most amazing feature of this site are the **petroglyphs**. More than three hundred have been discovered so far: animals, birds, houses and what are presumably religious symbols etched into the rock. One large boulder has the most enigmatic of all: flat-topped triangles surmounted by a square or rectangle, and shown above what look like ladders or steps. Stylized houses or launching platforms for the chariots of the gods? The trail leads on to a clear pool beneath a twelve-metre waterfall – too good to miss if the hike around the ruins has left you hot and dirty. More trails lead up into the mountains; a relatively easy one leads to the base of La Pava, an almost perpendicular pillar of rock, the top of which is said to resemble the head of a turkey.

Francisco J. Mujica and the Cascada Velo de Novia

Another *ejido* in the Agua Selva Project, **Francisco J. Mujica**, 18km northeast of Malpasito, has simple accommodation at the *Cabaña Raizes Zoque* (②). There's only intermittent public transport here, but it's connected by dirt road to Hwy-187 south from Huimanguillo, and you could get directions there from the tourist office in Villahermosa or in Malpasito. When you arrive, ask for Antonio Domínguez de Domínguez.

The hills around here are superb for walking and scrambling around canyons, but to venture to the most scenic parts you'll need a guide – easily arranged by the *ejido*. An **hour-long hike** from Mujica takes you over several rivers, beyond the *milpas*, to **Cascada Velo de Novia** (Bridal Veil Falls) and to the edge of an enormous canyon. The hike entails descending about 300m down an extremely steep slope – the guide will have a rope, but you'll still need to clutch at tree roots for support – then walking along a narrow rock ledge at the side of the river to get beneath the thundering cascade. Below the falls, the river winds between huge boulders before plunging over the edge of a sheer-sided, semicircular gorge. The only way out is to clamber up the way you came in. Few outsiders have been here, and you'll also have a chance to explore the hills, which are full of caves, many containing petroglyphs.

Teapa and the southern hills

An hour's bus ride through banana country to the south of Villahermosa, the small, friendly town of **TEAPA** is a lovely base for the spas and caves nearby. Cristóbal Colón **buses** leave Villahermosa for Tuxtla every couple of hours, calling at Teapa, though buses back are *de paso* and it may be difficult to get a seat. Though some second-class buses stop at the terminal on Méndez, right in the centre, most pull in at the **market** (plenty of good fruit stalls) near the edge of town. To get to the centre, walk a couple of blocks down the hill and turn left at the green clock onto Méndez, which takes you past the hotels and onto the plaza.

Teapa's **hotels** are good value: try the *Casa de Huéspedes Miye* (☎932/2-04-20; ②), a clean, family-run place with private showers and (sometimes) hot water, with rooms round a tiny plant-filled courtyard.

There's **swimming** in the Río Teapa here, but it's better at the *balneario* on the Río Puyacatengo, a few kilometres east (walk or take the bus for Tacotalpa). Six kilometres west of Teapa, almost on the Chiapas border, is the **El Azufre** spa, where for a small fee you can bathe in clear pools or take the waters in the sulphur pool. **Camping** is free and there's a small restaurant. Again you can get here on foot, or catch a second-class bus towards Pichucalco. Colectivos run from the plaza in Teapa to the spectacular **Grutas de Coconá** (daily 8am–4pm; US$0.35). Eight chambers are open to tourists, and some for spelunking only. A stroll through the caves takes about 45 minutes; in one chamber there's a supposedly miraculous representation of the face of Christ, carved by nature into the rock. You could also walk (45min) to the caves from Teapa; from Méndez, head for the Pemex station and turn right, following the sign. When you get near the forested hills, the road divides; head left over the railway track.

The Sierra Puana: Tapijulapa and Oxolotán

Southeast from Teapa, you can get further away from the humidity of the lowlands by taking day-trips up the valley of the Río Oxolotán to Tabasco's "hill country". This is an extraordinarily picturesque area, with unspoilt colonial towns set in beautiful wooded valleys, and a turquoise river laden with sulphur cascading over terraced cliff. You'll need to make a fairly early start to get the most out of the day. The 6.30am bus to **Tacotalpa** from the second-class station on Méndez in Teapa (20min) connects with one to **TAPIJULAPA**, the main settlement (45min), in time to have breakfast in the *Restaurant Mariquita*, in the corner of the shady plaza. The town is tiny, with narrow cobbled streets, red-tiled roofs, and unfortunately no accommodation. Turn right at the end of the main street, Av López Portillo, where steps lead down to the Río Oxolotán. Here you may find boats to take you upstream to visit the **Parque Natural Villa Luz**, with its spa pools, rivers, cascades and caves. Boats are more available on holidays, but it's easy enough to **walk** to the park: cross the tributary river on the suspension bridge, head left on the concrete path, across the football field, then follow the track over the hill, keeping close to the main river – about 35 minutes in all.

In the park (open daily; free), signed trails lead to caves, but the outstanding feature – not least for its powerful aroma – is the river, which owes its colour to dissolved minerals, especially sulphur. The river exits from a cave and meanders for 1km or so until it reaches the cliff marking the valley of the Río Oxolotán. Here it breaks up into dozens of cascades and semicircular pools. Thousands of butterflies settle on the riverbanks, taking nourishment from dissolved minerals, and jungle trees and creepers grow wherever they find a foothold: a truly primeval sight. The **caves** are not really open to the public, but you can peer into their precipitous entrances; in Maya cosmology the openings are believed to lead to the Underworld (*Xibalba*) and abode of the Lords of Death. Beyond the caves are a couple of open-air **swimming pools** said to have therapeutic properties.

Trucks and *combis* frequently make the trip (25min) from Tapijulapa to **OXOLOTÁN**. Here the ruins of a seventeenth-century Franciscan monastery host performances by the *Teatro Campesino y Indígena* (The Peasant and Indian Theatre), a company that has taken part in cultural festivals throughout Mexico and abroad. If you're in the area when a performance is scheduled, it's worth making an effort to go. **To get there** from Tapijulapa, climb the hill to the church, then descend to the road beyond, where there's a bus stop. The last bus back leaves at 6pm, but you're probably better off catching the 3pm bus if you're heading to Teapa.

East to the Usumacinta and Guatemala

Heading east from Villahermosa, Hwy-186 cuts across a salient of northern Chiapas before swinging north into **Campeche** to Francisco Escárcega, then east again as the only road across the base of the Yucatán peninsula to **Chetumal**. At Catazajá, in Chiapas, 110km from Villahermosa, is the junction for **Palenque**. If you've been there and want to see **Tikal** in Guatemala's Petén, the most direct route is via **Tenosique** and La Palma, then by boat up the Río San Pedro to El Naranjo. Several travel agencies in Palenque run minibuses to La Palma, but it's very easy to do it yourself, though the journey always involves at least one very early start.

Coming from either Palenque or Villahermosa, you'll pass through the dull town of **Emiliano Zapata**, hopefully only to change buses. The **bus stations** are in the same building on the edge of the town, and there are plenty of first- and second-class services to Villahermosa and Tenosique, tailing off rapidly in the evening. If you do get stuck, try the *Hotel Ramos* (☎934/3-07-44; ③), opposite the bus station, which is at least comfortable and saves you going into town. It also has the only proper **travel agent** for a long way: Creatur (☎ & fax 934/3-15-30).

Tenosique

The Río Usumacinta is crossed by the road and railway at Boca del Cerro, a few kilometres from **TENOSIQUE**, where the now placid river leaves some pretty impressive hills. **Buses** arrive at a small terminal close to the highway, just out of town. Inexpensive colectivos run frequently to the centre; get off when you see a large white church with blue trim on the right of the main street, C 26 (also known as "Pino Suárez"). If you have **to stay**, the *Azulejos* (②), opposite the church, has friendly staff; slightly better is the *Rome* (☎934/2-01-51; ②), a block closer to the plaza, on C 28.

If you're staying overnight and you've exhausted what limited sightseeing Tenosique has to offer (such as visiting the house where Pino Suárez was born and admiring his bust and monument), you'll want to head for the zócalo and Calles 26 and 28, the main areas for shopping and **eating**. The juice bar on the corner of the plaza prepares good licuados; there's also a good coffee shop just past the plaza on C 28, and the **market**, with a row of inexpensive comedores, is opposite. *La Palapa* restaurant overlooks the broad river, where the boat traffic heads constantly back and forth.

If you're going **to Guatemala** you'd be wise to stock up on provisions: there's a good **bakery** opposite the *Hotel Rome* and there are fruit stalls everywhere. The banks in Tenosique aren't interested in changing **money**, but Bancomer has an ATM; for Guatemalan quetzales ask around in the shops on C 28 where you should find someone who will give better rates than the boatmen. **Moving on**, there are plenty of bus services to Villahermosa during the day, a first-class service to México at 5pm and a 6pm bus to Escárcega and points east, with services finishing off around 7pm.

Pomoná

On the road from Emiliano Zapata, about 30km west of Tenosique, the ruins of **Pomoná** (daily 8am–4pm) are reached 4km down a signed track. Although the site, located in rolling countryside with views of forested hills to the south, makes a pleasant diversion, a visit is really only for the dedicated. The restored structures date from the Late Classic period; the site's largest building is a stepped pyramid with six levels. Pomoná was a subject site of the much larger city of Piedras Negras in Guatemala, further up the valley of the Usumacinta. The modern little **museum** houses some interesting carved panels and stelae, made even more mysterious by the omission of any explanations as to what you're seeing.

La Palma and the Río San Pedro to Guatemala

Buses for **LA PALMA** leave Tenosique every two hours from 4.30am to 4.30pm; there's no terminal, just follow C 31 down the side of the church for five blocks. They head due east through flat farming and ranching country and after an hour reach the

Río San Pedro, stopping at the *Parador Turístico* restaurant, by the dock, for the **boat-trip to El Naranjo** in Guatemala. The usual departure time is 8am, returning at 1pm from El Naranjo (4hr; US$20), but you may have to wait until sufficient passengers turn up. The trip is, frankly, overpriced, and you'll have a much more interesting time crossing to **Bethél**, visting Bonampak and Yaxchilán (see pp.492 and 494) en route to Flores. There are some basic **rooms** at La Palma; ask at the restaurant.

If you're **entering Mexico** here you might just be in time for the last bus to Tenosique; if not you'll probably be offered an overpriced truck ride. Bear in mind that the last buses onwards from Tenosique leave around 7pm. **Leaving for Guatemala**, you hand in your Mexican tourist card at the immigration post at El Pedregal, about halfway through the journey. **Border formalities** are hardly rigorous, though your luggage might be searched on leaving Mexico, and possibly again by the Guatemalan army on arrival at **EL NARANJO**, where the immigration official will usually demand an illegal fee. Entry to Guatemala is free for most Europeans; North Americans may be asked to buy a tourist card (US$5). There's a small, basic hotel and restaurant, the *Quetzal* (②), overlooking the river in El Naranjo, and 1km upstream from the ferry in the town proper, the *Posada San Pedro* has rustic bungalows (③); alternatively, no one will mind if you **camp**. Just up from the riverbank are some large, overgrown **ruins** with the bigger pyramids surmounted by machine gun posts. At least five daily **buses** leave El Naranjo for **Flores** (4hr 30min; US$4).

FIESTAS

The states of Chiapas and Tabasco are extremely rich in festivities. Local tourist offices should have more information on what's happening in your vicinity.

JANUARY

1 NEW YEAR'S DAY. **San Andres Chamula** (Chiapas) and **San Juan Chamula** (Chis), both near San Cristóbal, have civil ceremonies to install a new government for the year.

19 At **Tenosique** (Chis) the *El Pochó* dancers perform, dressed as jaguars and men to represent the struggle of good and evil. The celebration concludes on SHROVE TUESDAY with the burning of an effigy of El Pochó, god of evil.

20 DÍA DE SAN SEBASTIAN sees a lot of activity. In **Chiapa de Corzo** (Chis) a large fiesta with traditional dances lasts several days, with a re-enactment on the 21st of a naval battle on the Río Grijalva. Big, too, in **Zinacantán** (Chis), near San Cristóbal.

FEBRUARY

2 DÍA DE LA CANDELARIA. Colourful Indian celebrations at **Ocosingo** (Chis).

11 Religious fiesta in **Comitán** (Chis).

27 In **Villahermosa** (Tabasco), a fiesta commemorates the anniversary of a battle against the French.

CARNIVAL (the week before Lent – variable Feb–March) is at its most frenzied in the big cities – especially **Villahermosa** (Tab) – but is also celebrated in hundreds of villages throughout the area. **San Juan Chamula** (Chis) has a big fiesta.

MARCH

1 Anniversary of the foundation of **Chiapa de Corzo** (Chis) celebrated.

HOLY WEEK is widely observed – particularly big ceremonies in **San Cristóbal de las Casas** (Chis). **Ciudad Hidalgo** (Chis), at the border near Tapachula, has a major week-long market.

APRIL

1–7 A feria in **San Cristóbal de las Casas** (Chis) celebrates the town's foundation. A Spring Fair is generally held here later in the month.

Continues over

In the second half of the month **Villahermosa** (Tab) hosts its annual feria, with agricultural and industrial exhibits and the election of the queen of the flowers.

29 DÍA DE SAN PEDRO celebrated in several villages around San Cristóbal, including **Amatenango del Valle** and **Zinacantán** (Chis).

MAY

3 DÍA DE LA SANTA CRUZ celebrated in **San Juan Chamula** (Chis) and in **Teapa** (Tab), between Villahermosa and San Cristóbal.

8 DÍA DE SAN MIGUEL. Processions and traditional dances in **Mitontic** (Chis), near San Cristóbal.

15 DÍA DE SAN ISIDRO sees peasant celebrations everywhere – famous and picturesque fiestas in **Huistán** (Chis), near San Cristóbal.

Also, there's a four-day nautical marathon (variable dates) **from Tenosique to Villahermosa** (Tab), when crafts from all over the country race down 600km of the Usumacinta.

JUNE

13 DÍA DE SAN ANTONIO celebrated in **Zimojovel** (Chis), near San Cristóbal, and **Cárdenas** (Tab), west of Villahermosa.

24 DÍA DE SAN JUAN is the culmination of several days' celebration in **San Juan Chamula** (Chis).

JULY

7 Beautiful religious ceremony in **Comitán** (Chis), with candlelit processions to and around the church.

17 DÍA DE SAN CRISTóBAL celebrated enthusiastically in **San Cristóbal de las Casas** (Chis) and in nearby villages such as **Tenejapa** and **Amatenango del Valle** (Chis), and just one highlight in over a week of festivities.

20 Strongly indigenous festivities, heavily influenced by the Zapatista movement, in **Las Margaritas** (Chis), near Comitán.

25 DÍA DE SANTIAGO provokes widespread celebration – especially in **San Cristóbal de las Casas** (Chis), where they begin a good week earlier.

AUGUST

6 Images from the churches of neighbouring villages are brought in procession to **Mitontic** (Chis), for religious ceremonies there.

10 FIESTA DE SAN LORENZO in **Zinacantán** (Chis), with much music and dancing.

22–29 Feria in **Tapachula** (Chis).

24 Fiestas in **Venustiano Carranza** (Chis), south of San Cristóbal.

30 DÍA DE SANTA ROSA celebrated in **San Juan Chamula** (Chis).

SEPTEMBER

14–16 Throughout Chiapas, celebration of the annexation of the state to Mexico, followed by Independence celebrations everywhere.

29 DÍA DE SAN MIGUEL is celebrated in **Huistán** (Chis).

OCTOBER

On the first Sunday in October, the DÍA DE LA VIRGEN DEL ROSARIO is celebrated in **San Juan Chamula** and **Zinacantán** (Chis).

3 DÍA DE SAN FRANCISCO in **Amatenango del Valle** (Chis).

NOVEMBER

2 DAY OF THE DEAD is respected everywhere, with particularly strong traditions in **Chiapa de Corzo** (Chis).

29 DÍA DE SAN ANDRES celebrated in **San Andres Chamula** (Chis).

DECEMBER

12 DÍA DE LA VIRGEN DE GUADALUPE is an important one throughout Mexico. There are particularly good fiestas in **Tuxtla Gutiérrez** and **San Cristóbal de las Casas** (Chis), and the following day another in nearby **Amatenango del Valle** (Chis).

17–22 Pijijiapan (Chis), on the road to Tapachula, holds a feria and cheese expo.

travel details

Buses

Departures given are for direct first-class services; there are likely to be at least as many second-class buses (and often *combis* as well) to the same destinations.

Palenque to: Campeche (3 daily; 6hr); Cancún (3 daily; 12hr); Mérida (3 daily; 9hr); México (2 daily; 16hr); San Cristóbal (hourly; 5hr); Tuxtla Gutiérrez (hourly; 7hr); Villahermosa (at least 8 daily; 2hr 30min). Plenty of second-class buses run along the Frontier Highway for the junctions to **Bonampak** and **Yaxchilán**.

San Cristóbal to: Ciudad Cuauhtémoc, for Guatemala (at least 8 daily; 3hr 30min); Comitán, for Lagos de Montebello or the Guatemalan border (at least hourly; 2hr); México (5 daily; 20hr); Palenque (9 daily; 5hr); Tapachula (4 daily; 9hr); Tuxtla Gutiérrez (constantly; 2hr); Villahermosa, some direct, otherwise via Tuxtla or Palenque (6 daily; 8–9hr).

Tapachula to: Arriaga (12 daily; 4hr); México (10 daily; 18hr); Oaxaca (1 daily; 12hr); San Cristóbal (2 daily; 9hr); Tuxtla Gutiérrez (15 daily; 7hr); Veracruz (1 daily; 14hr); Villahermosa (2 daily; 13hr); Guatemala City (2 daily; 5–6hr).

Tuxtla Gutiérrez to: Ciudad Cuauhtémoc, for Guatemala (6 daily; 6hr); Comitán, for Lagos de Montebello or the Guatemalan border (hourly; 4hr); Mérida (4 daily; 14hr) México (at least 9 daily; 16hr); Palenque (hourly; 7hr); San Cristóbal (first-class hourly, others constantly; 2hr); Tapachula (15 daily; 7hr); Tonalá (hourly; 3hr 30min); Villahermosa (9 daily; 7hr).

Villahermosa to: Campeche (at least 12 daily; 6hr); Cancún (5 daily; 12hr); Chetumal (5 daily; 7hr), Mérida (at least 12 daily; 9hr), México (at least hourly; 11hr); Palenque (8 daily; 2hr 30min); San Cristóbal, some direct, otherwise via Tuxtla or Palenque (6 daily; 8–9hr); Tapachula (2 daily; 13hr); Tuxtla Gutiérrez (9 daily; 7hr); Veracruz (12 daily; 7hr).

International buses

Tapachula to: Guatemala: (2 daily at 9am & 2pm; 5–6hr).

International boats

La Palma (near Tenosique) to: El Naranjo, Guatemala (1 daily; 4hr)

Frontera Corozal (Yaxchilán) to: Bethél, Guatemala (several daily, no schedule; 30min)

Planes

Air services throughout the region are expanding as new airports open up, and services will almost certainly have increased from those listed in the text. For the latest information check with one of the recommended travel agents.

Villahermosa has several daily flights to the capital, but there are also daily direct services from Tuxtla Gutiérrez, Ciudad del Carmen, Coatzacoalcos and Tapachula. Aerocaribe (☎93/16-31-32 in Villahermosa) have scheduled services between Palenque, San Cristóbal, Flores, Mérida and Cancún.

Servicios Aéreos San Cristóbal, based in **Ocosingo** (☎967/3-10-88), operate light aircraft – from Palenque or San Cristóbal to Yaxchilán or Bonampak, for example.

CHAPTER TEN

THE YUCATÁN

T he three states that comprise the Yucatán peninsula – Campeche, Yucatán and Quintana Roo – are among the hottest and most tropical-feeling parts of Mexico, though they in fact lie further north than you might imagine: the sweeping curve of southern Mexico means that the Yucatán state capital, Mérida, is actually north of México. Until the 1960s, when proper road and train links were completed, the Yucatán lived out of step with the rest of the country – it had almost as much contact with Europe and the USA as with central Mexico. Tourism has since made major inroads, especially in the north around the great Maya sites and on the route from Mérida to the Quintana Roo coast, where development has centred on the "super-resort" of Cancún and the islands of Isla Mujeres and Cozumel. But away from the big centres, especially in the south, where townships are sparsely scattered in thick jungly forest, there's still a distinct pioneering feel.

Travelling around the peninsula, the changes in landscape are hard to miss. In Yucatán state, the shallow, rocky earth gives rise to stunted trees – here, underground wells known as *cenotes* are the only source of water. At the opposite end of the scale, Campeche boasts a huge area of **tropical forest**, the Calakmul Biosphere Reserve, though this is steadily shrinking with the growing demand for timber and land for cattle ranching. The entire peninsular coastline is great for spotting **wildlife** – notably turtles at the Si'an Ka'an Biosphere Reserve in Quintana Roo, and the flocks of flamingos at Celestún and Río Lagartos in Yucatán – but the most spectacular, white-sand **beaches** line the Caribbean coast, where magnificent offshore **coral reefs** form part of the second largest barrier reef system in the world.

Some history

The peninsula's modern boom is, in fact, a reawakening, for this has been the longest continuously civilized part of the country, with evidence of Maya inhabitants as early as 2500 BC, producing pottery and living in huts virtually identical to those you see in the villages today. **The Maya** are not a specifically Mexican culture – their greatest cities, indeed, were not in Mexico at all but in the lowlands of modern Guatemala, Belize and Honduras – but they did produce a unique style in the Yucatán and continued to flourish here long after the collapse of the "Classic" civilizations to the south. This they did in spite of natural handicaps – thin soil, heat, humidity and lack of water – and in the face of frequent invasion from central Mexico. And here the Maya peasantry still live, remarkably true to their old traditions and lifestyle, despite the hardships of the intervening years: ravaged by European diseases and forced to work on vast colonial *encomiendas*, or later, through the semi-slavery of debt peonage, on the *henequen* plantations or in the forests, hauling timber.

The florescence of Maya culture, throughout their extensive domains, came in the **Classic period** from around 300 to 900 AD: an age in which the cities grew up and Maya science and art apparently reached their height. The Maya calendar, a complex interaction of solar, lunar, astronomical and religious dates, was far more complicated and accurate than the Gregorian one, and they also developed a sophisticated mathematical and (still largely undeciphered) hieroglyphic system and perspective in art 500 or so years before Renaissance Europe. In the early ninth century AD, growing military tensions and a prolonged drought saw the abandonment of many of the southern lowland cities (Tikal and Calakmul among them), while the cities of the northern lowlands – such as Chichén Itzá, Uxmal and the Puuc sites – began to flourish. These in turn collapsed about 1200 AD, to be succeeded by Mayapán and a confederacy of other cities that probably included Tulum and Cozumel. By the time the Spanish arrived, Mayapán's power, too, had been broken by revolt, and the Maya had splintered into tribalism – although still with coastal cities and long-distance sea trade that awed the Conquistadors. It proved the hardest area of the country to pacify. Despite attempts to destroy all trace of the ancient culture, there was constant armed rebellion against the Spanish and later the Mexican authorities – the last the **Caste Wars** of the nineteenth century, during which the Maya, supplied with arms from British Honduras (Belize), gained brief control of the entire peninsula. Gradually, though, they were again pushed back into the wastes of southern Quintana Roo, where the final pockets of resistance held out until the beginning of this century.

CENTRAL YUCATÁN: THE GREAT MAYA SITES

There's really only one route around the Yucatán: the variation comes in where you choose to break the journey or to make side trips off the main trail. Whether from Palenque or by road and ferry along the beautiful coast from **Ciudad del Carmen**, Hwy-180 heads up to **Campeche**, from there to **Mérida**, and on via **Chichén Itzá** to the Caribbean coast. From Mérida the best of the **Maya sites** – Uxmal, Chichén Itzá and a trove of smaller, less visited ruins – are in easy reach.

The road that runs across **the south** of the peninsula, from **Francisco Escárcega** to Chetumal, is relatively new, passing through jungle territory rich in Maya remains, several of which have only recently been opened to the public. Though largely unexplored, these are beginning to see a trickle of visitors as access improves; you can get accommodation and arrange tours at **Xpujil**, a village named after the nearby archeological site, on the border between Campeche and Quintana Roo states.

Campeche

CAMPECHE, capital of the state that bears its name, is one of Mexico's less well-known colonial gems. Elegant eighteenth- and nineteenth-century houses painted in pastel shades and interspersed with the occasional church, give it a distinctly European feel. At its heart, relatively intact, lies a colonial port still surrounded by hefty defensive walls and fortresses; around, the trappings of a modern city that is once again becom-

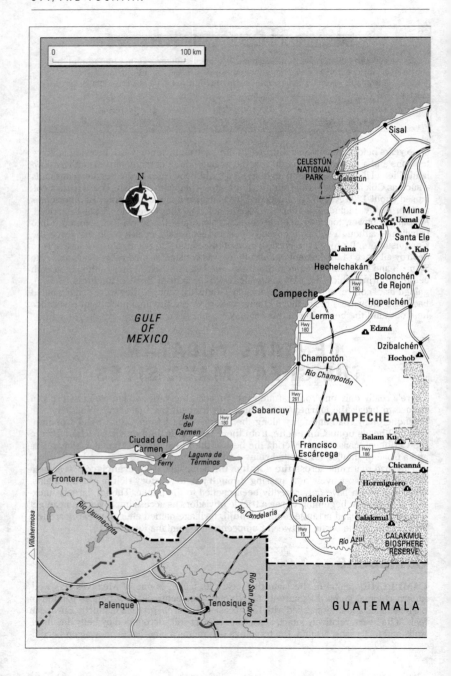

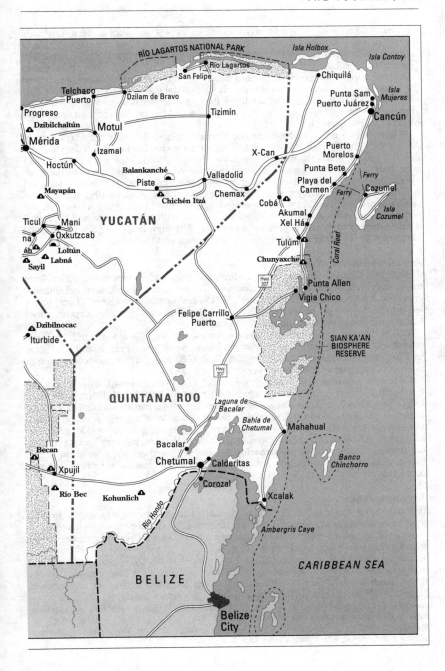

ing wealthy. The seafront is a bizarre mixture of ancient and ultra-modern: originally the city defences dropped straight into the sea, but now they face a reclaimed strip of land on which stand the spectacular new Palacio de Gobierno and State Legislature (spectacularly ugly in the eyes of most locals), and the big hotels. Few tourists stop here, preferring to sweep by en route to Escárcéga and Palenque or take Hwy-180 and the ferry along the beautiful coast route via Ciudad del Carmen to Villahermosa. This is strongly to Campeche's advantage (even if locals don't see it that way), for while the attractions in and around the city can't compare with Mérida's, it is at least spared the blight of tourist overkill.

A Spanish expedition under Francisco Hernandez landed outside the Maya town of Ah Kin Pech in 1517, only to beat a hasty retreat on seeing the forces lined up to greet them. It wasn't until 1540 that Francisco de Montejo founded the modern town, and from here set out on his mission to conquer the Yucatán. From then until the nineteenth century, it was the chief port in the peninsula, exporting mainly logwood (source of a red dye known as *hematein*) from local forests. It also became an irresistible target for the pirates who operated with relative impunity from bases on the untamed coast roundabout. Hence the fortifications, built between 1668 and 1704 after a particularly brutal massacre of the population. Although large sections of the walls have gone, seven of the eight original bulwarks (*baluartes*) survive.

Arrival and information

Campeche's **Central Camionera**, with first- and second-class terminals, is 2km from the colonial centre, along Av Gobernadores. To get to the centre, turn left outside, cross the road and take a city bus marked "Centro" or "Gobernadores". Local buses leave from the market just south of the city walls. If you arrive at the **airport**, about 10km southeast of town, you'll have to take a taxi.

Within the city, even-numbered **streets** run parallel with the sea, starting for some reason with C 8, just inside the ramparts; odd-numbered streets run inland. The zócalo, **Parque Principal**, is bordered by C 8, C 10, C 55 and C 57. Almost everything of interest is gathered within the old walls.

Campeche's **tourist office**, in the Plaza Moch Couoh on Av Ruiz Cortines, opposite the unsightly government palace (daily 9–8pm; ☎981/6-73-64 or 6-55-93, fax 6-67-67), is helpful and friendly and there's usually someone there who can speak English. Be sure to pick up the free tourist magazines, with articles about what's going on in and around town and in the state. They also have a list of independent **guides** (speaking various languages) who lead tours of the city and archeological zones; you may have to provide the transport. Other tourist **information booths** scattered around town at the major tourist sites and the bus station have a limited supply of maps and leaflets that you could just as easily pick up from the larger hotels.

Accommodation

Because Campeche is not on the tourist circuit, it boasts plenty of inexpensive **hotels**, though for the same reason they can be rather shabby. Avoid rooms overlooking the street, as Campeche's narrow lanes magnify traffic noise. The best bargains are to be found within a couple of blocks of the zócalo.

The **youth hostel**, on Av Agustín Melgar (☎981/1-18-08; ①), is clean and bustling, with single-sex dorms, and camping in the grounds, but it's a long way out. To get there, catch a bus ("Directo/Universidad") from the ADO station, or one marked "Lerma" or "Playa Bonita" heading west through the old walled city.

America, C 10 no. 252, between C 59 and C 61 (☎981/6-45-88). Elegant colonial building with comfortable rooms; the best ones overlook the courtyard. ④.

Baluartes, Av Ruíz Cortines, just south of the *Ramada* (☎981/6-24-10). The *Ramada*'s older and slightly cheaper rival, with a pool, TVs and a/c. ⑤.

Campeche, C 57 no. 2, opposite the cathedral (☎981/6-51-83). Basic rooms in a colonial house; the rooms overlooking the zócalo are noisy. ③.
Central, Av Gobernadores 462 (☎981/1-07-66). The name is hardly appropriate, as it's way out, opposite the bus stations, but it has perfectly adequate rooms. ③.
Colonial, C 14 no. 122 (☎981/6-22-22). The best value place in town, in an old colonial building. ③.
Posada del Ángel, C 10 no. 307, corner of C 55 (☎981/6-77-18). Modern hotel, centrally located by the corner of the cathedral. Some rooms have a/c. ③.
Ramada Inn, Av Ruíz Cortines 51 (☎981/6-22-33, fax 6-76-18). Comfortable, upmarket hotel with a pool, restaurant and nightclub. There's also a travel agency and car rental facilities. ⑦.

The City

Though your time is really as well spent wandering Campeche's old streets or seafront, you could pass some time at the **Baluarte San Carlos**, which has cannons on the battlement roof and, underneath, the beginnings of a network of ancient tunnels that undermines much of the town. Mostly sealed off now, the tunnels provided a place of refuge for the populace from pirate raids, and before that were probably used by the Maya.

Founded in 1540, the **Cathedral**, overlooking the zócalo, is one of the oldest churches on the peninsula. The bulk of the construction, though, took place much later, and what you see now is not particularly striking Baroque. **La Mansion Carvajal** on C 10 between C 51 and C 53 is also worth a visit – an elegant colonial house that once belonged to one of the city's richest families.

Fort San Miguel, which looks over the town from the southwest, houses Campeche's **archeological museum** (Tues–Sun 9am–2pm & 4–8pm; US$1). Maya artefacts from Edzná and Jaina predominate, including delicate Jaina figurines, many of which are cross-eyed – a feature that the Maya considered a mark of beauty. There's also some fine sculpture and some pre-Hispanic gold, but the highlight is the treasure from the tombs at Calakmul. The jade death masks are mesmerizing and every bit as impressive and beautiful as the death masks of Pacal from Palenque. Take a look at the views over the bulwarks, too, which are wonderful at sunset. **Fort San José**, on a hill on the opposite side of the city, is also a museum, this time housing armaments and a collection of items from the colonial era.

If you're desperate to be by the sea, a "Playa Bonita" bus, which goes along the waterfront, will take you past the fort museum and beyond to the reasonable **beaches** at **Playa Bonita** and **Lerma**, a fishing village just beyond the city.

Eating and drinking

Restaurants abound in the centre of Campeche, especially along C 8 and C 10. **Seafood**, served almost everywhere, is a good bet; try the shark or shrimps in spicy sauce.
Centro Manic, C 59 no. 22 between C 12 & C 14. Vegetarian restaurant, patisserie and bookshop that also organizes spiritual workshops.
El Gato Pardo, C 49, between C 10 and C 12, just outside the city wall. Pizzeria and video bar, serving excellent pizzas to young rock fans. Nightly until 1am.
Marganzo Regional, C 8 no. 262. Seafood and regional dishes served in relaxed surroundings. The breakfast buffet (US$5) is especially popular. Open daily 7am–midnight.
Nutri Vida, C 12 no. 167, near C 59. Good vegetarian restaurant serving fresh fruit, granola, yoghurt, juices, vegeburgers and other healthy food at reasonable prices. Closed Sat evening and Sun.
Restaurant del Parque, C 8 no. 251, corner of C 57 on the zócalo. Popular budget place for standard Mexican food. Daily 6am–midnight.
La Parroquia, C 55 no. 8. Traditional, family-run restaurant; good value and very popular with locals. Open 24hr.
Los Portales, C 55 no. 9. Across from *La Parroquia* and in much the same vein. Open 24hr.
Restaurant Miramar, C 8 and C 61. Campeche's best seafood; pricey, but worth it.

MOVING ON FROM CAMPECHE

Regular first-class ADO, Colon and second-class Autobuses del Sur **buses** (all from the same terminal – see p.516) leave for Ciudad del Carmen (hourly, 3hr), Mérida (more than 12 daily, 2hr), Chetumal via Escárcega and Xpujil (3 daily, 5–7hr), Villahermosa (10 daily, 6–7hr). There are also services to San Cristobal (via Palenque), Playa del Carmen, Veracruz, Mexico and Coatzalcoalcos (for Southern Veracruz) and second-class buses direct to Uxmal. Minibuses leave from the market just outside the southern end of the old city (C53 and Circuito Baluartes Este), for local villages like the craft centres Becal and Calkini, and for Edzná. Aeroméxico (☎938/6-56-78 or 6-49-25) operates a variety of internal flights; Calakmul (☎938/6-31-09 or 1-36-50) flies to México only. A taxi out to the **airport** costs around US$7.

Listings

American Express Next to the Banco del Atlantico, with an ADO bus booking office inside.

Banks Banco del Atlántico and Bancomer are next door to each other on Av 16 de Septiembre, opposite the Baluarte de la Soledad, both with ATMs. Banamex is on C 10, at the corner of C 53.

Car rental Autorent (☎981/6-27-14) in the *Ramada Inn*, or Hertz in the *Hotel Baluartes* (☎981/6-88-48).

Email and fax MultiPro (☎982/1-74-66, email *multipro41@hotmail.com*) C 63 no. 7 between C 12 and C 14 has internet facilities. You can fax from the Telecomm office on Av 16 de Septiembre (Mon–Fri 9am–8pm, Sat 9am–1pm).

Laundry The Tintoria Campeche (Mon–Sat 9am–4pm) on C 55, no. 26.

Post office Av 16 de Septiembre at C 53, in the Oficinas del Gobierno Federal (Mon–Fri 8am–8pm, Sat 9am–2pm).

Tours Destino Maya on Av Miguel Alemán, above the Cine Estelar (☎981/1-09-34 or 1-37-26), offers tours around the Maya sites in Campeche.

The Campeche coast

South of Campeche, Hwy 180 sweeps along the mostly deserted coast, passing several small resorts. Most tourists heading in this direction turn inland at **Champotón**, a growing fishing village and oil port at the mouth of the Río Champotón, on their way southeast towards Escárcega for Chetumal or Palenque. If you want to get anywhere reasonably quickly, even if you're heading to Villahermosa and beyond, this route is the best option. Alternatively, if you want to head towards Ciudad del Carmen and then into southern Veracruz, you could continue along the coast to **Sabancuy**, 83km before Ciudad del Carmen, a little village which has one of the best beaches in Campeche. There are few tourists and only one hotel, the *Posada Bellavista* (②). At **Isla Aguada**, the Puenta de la Unidad, said to be the longest road bridge in Mexico, crosses the eastern entrance to the **Laguna de Terminos**, joining the **Isla del Carmen** to the mainland.

Ciudad del Carmen

CIUDAD DEL CARMEN, the only town of any size on the 35-kilometre-long Isla del Carmen, doesn't merit a special trip except perhaps during its lively **fiesta** in July. It's not unpleasant, but it's hot and crowded and has much less historical atmosphere than Campeche. The conquistadors landed here in 1518, but the first settlers were pirates in 1633. Nowadays it's home to a fishing fleet, catching, among other things, giant prawns for export. The oil boom has created new industries and forced prices up, so you won't find any accommodation bargains here. The town's environs also suffer from oil industry pollution.

Just west of town is the **ferry dock** for Zacatal, where the road to Frontera (see p.504) continues. Buses don't necessarily make a direct connection. If you need to stay in Ciudad Del Carmen, try the *Casa de Huéspedes Bugambilias*, Av Periferica Nte 4 (☎938/2-49-28; ③), which has large clean rooms with baths and is away from the main road, though only five minutes from the bus station.

Practicalities

ADO (first-class) and Sur (second-class) buses use the same station on Av Periferica Ote. To get to the centre, take a taxi or colectivo (5am–11pm; about 20min). The **tourist office**, in the Palacio Municipal on the corner of C 22 and C 31 (Mon–Fri 8am–3pm), has plenty of information (English and Spanish) on Campeche state, but little about Ciudad del Carmen. The **post office** (Mon–Fri 7am–7pm, Sat 7am–1pm) is tucked away at C 22 no. 57, between C 25 and C 27, while Banamex, on the corner of C 24 at the edge of the Parque General Ignacio Zaragosa, and Bancomer, C 24 no. 42 at the corner with C 29 (both Mon–Fri 9am–1.30pm), have ATMs and cajeros.

Most of the **accommodation** is on C 20, C 22 and C 24 near the waterfront. At fiesta-time places fill up, so book ahead. Five minutes around the corner from the bus station, *Casa de Huéspedes Bugambilias*, Av Periferica Nte 4 (☎938/2-49-28; ③), has large clean rooms with baths away from the main road. The *Roma*, C 22 no. 110 (☎938/2-04-10; ②), is a good-value place across a small park from the waterfront; most luxurious of all is the *Hotel de Parque*, on the corner of C 33 between Parque General Ignacio Zaragosa and the waterfront (☎938/2-30-46 or 2-30-66; ⑦), where all rooms have a/c, TV and phone. **Food** in Ciudad del Carmen is a mixture of specialities from the Yucatán peninsula and the state of Tabasco, with a stress on shellfish. Many low-priced restaurants are grouped together along C 33 by the busy Parque General Ignacio Zaragosa, and there are two good places on the seafront opposite the *Roma*: *Cafetería La Fuente*, for basic Mexican snacks, and *La Ola Marina*, next door, which serves expensive, good seafood and shellfish in a relaxed atmosphere.

Edzná and the Chenes sites

Some 60km from Campeche lie the impressive ruins of **EDZNÁ** (daily 8am–5pm; US$2, free on Sun), the only local site practically accessible by bus. Though this is an area where the **Chenes** style of architecture (closely related to the Puuc of Uxmal; see p.535) dominated – *chen* means "well" and is a fairly common suffix to place names hereabouts – Edzná is far from a pure example of it, also featuring elements of Río Bec, Puuc and Classic Maya design. For the real thing, you have to venture further south.

Edzná was a large city, on the main trade route between the Maya of the highlands and the coast. The most important structure is the great **Templo de los Cinco Pisos** (Temple of the Five Storeys), a stepped palace/pyramid more than 20m high built on a vast acropolis. Unusually, each of the five storeys contains chambered "palace" rooms: while solid temple pyramids and multistorey "apartment" complexes are relatively common, it is rare to see the two combined in one building. At the front, a steep monumental staircase leads to a three-roomed temple, topped by a roof comb. The view from here is one of the most impressive in the Yucatán. It is easy to imagine the power that the high priest or king commanded as you look out over two plazas, the furthest of which must have been capable of holding tens of thousands of people. Beyond lie the unexcavated remains of other large pyramids, and behind them, the vast flat expanse of the Yucatán shelf. A stela of the God of maize positioned here was illuminated by the sun twice a year, on the dates for the planting and harvesting of maize, and the whole temple is orientated to the rising sun.

Lesser buildings surround the ceremonial precinct. The **Casa Grande**, a palace on the northwest side, and some of the buildings alongside it, were cleared by archeologists in late 1986. Some 55m long, the Casa Grande includes a room used as a *temezcal*, with stone benches and hearths over which water could be boiled. There are two haunting masks of the Gods of Day and Night in the **Templo de los Mascarones**. The rest of the site – including a large system of drainage (and possibly irrigation) canals – remains unexcavated.

Buses for Pich or Bon Fil leave from the huge market in Campeche (C 53 and Circuito Baluartes Este) every half-hour and will take you within 1km of the entrance at Edzná. Getting back is harder: there are passing buses but they are erratic; ask the driver of your bus on the way out. Alternatively, you could join an **organized trip** from Campeche. Some small **cabañas** are being built near the ruins; bookings can be made through the Campeche tourist office.

Other Chenes sites

The examples of true Chenes style are accessible only with a car or exceptional determination. The chief sites are reached on a poor road from **HOPELCHÉN**, a village about 100km from Campeche on the long route to Mérida. A bus follows this road as far as **Dzibalchen** and **Iturbide**, but it's not much use for visiting the sites as it turns straight round on arrival. If you choose to **stay** in Hopelchén, *Los Arcos*, C 17 on the corner of the plaza, near where the buses stop (☎982/2-00-37; ③), is the only option.

The best of the ruins are some way from the paved road and substantially buried in the jungle. **Hochob**, just outside Dzibalchen, has an amazing three-roomed temple (low and fairly small, as are most Chenes buildings), with a facade entirely covered in richly carved, stylized snakes and masks. The central chamber is surmounted by a crumbling roof-comb, and its decoration creates the effect of a huge mask, with the doorway as a gaping mouth. The remains of **Dzibilnocac**, 1km west of Iturbide, demonstrate the ultra-decorative facades typical of the Chenes style and its restored western temple pyramid makes a trip out here very worthwhile.

Francisco Escárcega to Xpujil

Heading south from Campeche on the inland route, Hwy-61 meets the east–west Hwy-186 at **FRANCISCO ESCÁRCEGA** (always referred to as Escárcega), a hot, dusty town straggling along the road and old train tracks for a couple of kilometres. There's little to detain you in town, but Escárcega does provide a jumping-off point for a number of relatively unexplored **Maya sites** that are now beginning to be developed for tourism. Known as the **Río Bec sites**, many of them are in the **Calakmul Biosphere Reserve**, a vast area of tropical forest, once heavily populated by lowland Maya, which stretches all the way into the Petén region of Guatemala. Though the region's most famous sites lies over the border at **Tikal**, others within Mexico, only recently accessible, are every bit as exciting as the sites of the northern Yucatán.

The ADO bus station is at the road junction; from there, walk 1500m east to the centre and the Sur bus station. If you need to **stay**, try the *Posada Escárcega* (☎981/4-00-79; ③), just two blocks from the second-class terminal; turn left and then second left. **Getting out of town** is relatively easy: at least ten buses run daily to Mérida, there's an hourly service to Campeche between 4am and 6pm, a 4.30am second-class bus to Palenque, and a couple to San Cristóbal; in addition, Escárcega is on the ADO first-class route between Chetumal and Villahermosa. Services to Xpujil and Chetumal run overnight or in the mornings only – nothing heads out in the afternoon.

However, the far from glamorous village of **XPUJIL** is a better place for exploring the region. Basically a one-street town straddling Hwy-186, it has a few simple places to stay. Try the *Hotel Calakmul* (☎983/2-91-62; ③) or the *Restaurant and Cabañas El Mirador Maya* (☎983/4-03-71; ③), which has simple, thatched cabañas with hammocks. There are a couple of restaurants, two Ladatel phones and a small post office.

Leaving Xpujil, there are, in theory, two ADO **buses** a day to Chetumal, and two to Escárcega and onward. Both of these are scheduled to leave in the morning, but staff at the bus station are not reliable with their timetable information. It is therefore best to buy your ticket first thing in the morning on the day you intend to leave. It is possible to catch a series of second-class buses through to Mérida via Dzibalchen, Hopelchen and the Ruta Puuc. This rough road passes through the northern half of the Calakmul Biosphere Reserve, and is an interesting and little travelled route north, if you have time to spare.

The Río Bec sites

The **Río Bec** style, characterized by long buildings with matching towers at each end and narrow roof-combs can be seen at a number of sites in this region. The most accessible is **Xpujil**, just 1500km back along the highway from Xpujil village (US$1, free on Sun). Dating from the Classic period, it is perhaps the least impressive of all the sites, though its three towers with almost vertical, and purely decorative stairways are very striking.

Trips to the sites and the forest are organized by Servidores Turisticos (☎983/2-33-04 or 2-44-88), a co-operative of locals, led by Fernando Sastre and Leticia Valensuela Santiago; ask for them at the *Calakmul* restaurant. Prices range from US$20 per person for a full day guided tour to Becán, Chicanná, Xpujil and the Grutas del Sol to US$75 for a tour to Calakmul (up to fifteen people). The guides are all local people from the cattle-ranching community, many of whom were once rapaciously cutting down the forest and killing the spotted cats for their pelts, but are now working to **preserve the forest**, which stands little chance of survival without initiatives such as this.

You can also take **taxis** to the sites. Expect to pay about US$40 for a taxi to Calakmul and Balam Ku, including waiting time and about US$15 to visit Chicanná and Becán.

Becán
Becán (US$2, free on Sun), 6km west of Xpujil then 500m north on a signed track, is unique among Maya sites in being entirely surrounded by a dry moat, 15m wide and 4m deep. This moat and the wall on its outer edge form one of the oldest known defensive systems in Mexico, and have led some to believe that this was the site of Tayasal, capital of the Itzá, rather than present-day Flores in Guatemala. The site was first occupied in 600 BC, reaching its peak between 600 and 1000 AD. Unlike many of the sites in the northern Yucatán, many of the buildings here seem to have been residential – note the unusual use of internal staircases.

Chicanná and Balam Ku
Chicanná (US$2, free on Sun), 3km further west than Becán, south of the highway, hosts the luxurious *Ramada Eco Village Resort* (☎91/535-24-66; ⑨). The buildings at the site recall the Chenes style in their elaborate decoration and repetitive masks of Chac; the great doorway in the **House of the Serpent Mouth** is especially impressive. **Balam Ku** (US$1, free on Sun), 50km beyond Chicanná, just after the turn-off to Calakmul, would be completely forgettable were it not for the two huge cross-eyed red masks that adorn its central temple. These are larger than any you'll see in the north, though less impressive than the masks at Kohunlich in nearby Quintana Roo. Their significance is unknown.

Río Bec and Hormiguero

Río Bec, which gives its name to the region's dominant architectural style, and **Hormiguero** are accessible only by dirt road. To see all the scattered buildings of Río Bec (free) you need to go on an organized expedition, but you can see one small group independently: head east 13km from Xpujil, then south 6km to the *ejido* of 20 de Noviembre. The site is protected within the **Reserva de Fauna U'Luum Chac Yuc**, so you need to sign in at the small museum that acts as the reserve headquarters (☎982/4-03-73), who will fix you up with a guide from the village. You'll see that, as with Xpujil, the "steps" on the twin towers were never meant to be climbed: the risers actually angle outwards. Hormiguero (US$2, free on Sunday), also fuses the Chenes style with the Río Bec. There are only two buildings excavated, the largest having a huge gaping mouth for its central doorway, surrounded by elaborate carving.

Calakmul

The most impressive of the Río Bec sites, **Calakmul** lies 60km off Hwy-186, which cuts across the bottom of the peninsula. Though it is only partially restored, its location in the heart of the jungle and its sheer size make this Classic Maya city irresistible. This is probably the biggest archeological area in Mesoamerica, extending for some 70km. It has seven thousand buildings in the central area alone and more stelae and pyramids than any other Maya city; the great pyramid here is the largest Maya building in existence, with a base covering five acres. The view of the rainforest from the top of the principal pyramids is stunning, bettered only at Tikal, and on a clear day you can even see the tallest Maya pyramid of all, Danta, at El Mirador in Guatemala. You're sure to see some wildlife too, especially if you arrive early – there are peccary, toucan, occasional howler monkeys and even jaguar here.

During the Classic period, the city had a population of about 200,000 people and was the regional capital of the southern part of Petén. A recently discovered *sacbe* (Maya road) running between Calakmul and El Mirador (another leads on to Tikal) has confirmed that these cities were in regular communication, as archeologists had long suspected. Calakmul reached its zenith between 500 and 850 AD but, like most cities in the area, it was abandoned about fifty years later. The site was discovered in 1931, but excavations only started taking place in 1982 and only a fraction of the buildings have been excavated so far, the rest being earthen mounds.

The treasures of Calakmul are on display in the archeological museum at Campeche (see p.517) and include two hauntingly beautiful jade masks. Another was found in a tomb in the main pyramid as recently as January 1998. You can also see the first mummified body to be found in Mesoamerica, from inside Structure no. 15, which was unearthed in 1995.

From Campeche to Mérida

From Campeche to Mérida there's a choice of two routes. First-class buses, and all *directo* services, take the shorter road via **Hwy-180** – the colonial Camino Real, lined with villages whose plazas are laid out on the traditional plan around a massive old church. **Hecelchakan**, about 80km from Campeche, has a small archeology museum on the main square (Mon–Sat 9am–6pm; free), with figures from Jaina and objects from other nearby sites. **Becal** (35km further) is one of the biggest centres for the manufacture of basketware and the ubiquitous Yucatecan **Jipis**, or "Panama" hats (real panama hats, as everyone knows, come from Ecuador). There's a Centro Artesanal by the road where you can buy them, but it's more interesting to go into the village and watch this cottage industry at work.

The longer route via Hopelchén and Muna, passing the great sites of **Sayil**, **Kabáh** and **Uxmal** (see p.535), is much better if you have the time. With a car you could easily visit all three, perhaps stopping also at **Bolonchén de Rejon**, with its nine wells, and the nearby **Grutas de Xtacumbilxunan**, 3km south, and still get to Mérida within the day. By bus it's slightly harder, but with a little planning – and if you set out early – you should be able to get to at least one. Kabáh is the easiest since its ruins lie right on the main road.

Mérida

Even if practically every road didn't lead to **MÉRIDA**, it would still be an inevitable stop. The "White City", capital of the state of Yucatán, is in every sense the leading town of the peninsula, and remarkably calm and likeable for all its thousands of visitors. Every street in the centre boasts a colonial church or mansion, while the plazas are alive with market stalls and free entertainment. You can live well here and find good beaches within easy reach, but above all it's the ideal base for excursions to the great Maya sites of Uxmal and Chichén Itzá (see p.535 and p.544).

Arrival, information and city transport

Mérida is laid out on a simple **grid** of numbered streets: even numbers run north–south, odd from east to west, with the zócalo, **Plaza Mayor**, bounded by C 60, C 61, C 62 and C 63. Mérida's **bus stations** lie around the corner from each other on the west side of town. The brand new first-class **Cameon**, C 70 no. 55, between C 69 and 71, is sparkling and air-conditioned, with a guardería. Some short-haul buses use minor terminals, but you're most likely to arrive at the busy **second-class** terminal, on C 69 between C 68 and C 70. Inside is a **tourist information** counter, a hotel reservations desk and some phones. You'll also find a small **post office** at the side on C 70, and a Banpais **bank** (Mon–Fri 9am–1.30pm) on the nearby corner.

City buses don't go all the way from the bus stations to the Plaza Mayor. To walk (about 20min), turn right outside the second-class bus station and you'll be on the corner of C 68 and C 69; the Plaza Mayor is three blocks north and four blocks east. Colectivos from the smaller places off the main highways terminate in Plaza de San Juan, on C 69 between C 62 and C 64. To get to the Plaza Mayor, leave Plaza de San Juan by the northeast corner and walk three blocks north up C 62.

Mérida's Manuel Crescencio Rejón **airport** is 7km southwest of the city. There's a **tourist office** (daily 8am–8pm), post office, long-distance phones and car rental desks. To get downtown, take a colectivo (buy a ticket at the desk) or bus #79 ("Aviación"), which drops off at the corner of C 67 and C 60.

Information

Mérida's main **tourist office** is in the Teatro Peón Contreras, on the corner of C 60 and C 57 (daily 8am–8pm; ☎99/24-92-90). Pick up a copy of *Yucatán Today*, in English and Spanish, to find out what's going on in and around town. *Discover Mérida of Yucatán* offers information on the areas outside Mérida, while *Restaurants of Yucatán* gives detailed reviews. There are also plenty of leaflets available and you'll usually find some English-speaking staff. The **federal tourist office** is in the pink building marked *Gobierno del Estado Secretaria de Desarrollo Economico*, C 59 no. 514, between C 62 and C 64 (Mon–Fri 8am–2pm). Pronatura, at C 1-D no. 254 (☎99/44-22-90), organize **tours** and also provide information on the ecology of the Yucatán.

City transport

As traffic in Mérida is so congested, and most of the places of interest are within walking distance, it really isn't worth the bother of using public transport to get around in

the centre – though it can be fun to hop onto one of the **horse-drawn carriages** that trot up and down the Paseo de Montejo; see p.527. However, to get out to some of the more far-flung sites (Palacio Cantón, for example), you may need to catch a bus. A number of buses leave from C 59 just east of the Parque Hidalgo; fares are around US$0.50. **Taxis** can be hailed all around town and from ranks at Parque Hidalgo, the post office, Plaza de San Juan and the airport. **Car rental** offices abound in Mérida, both at the airport and in the city (see "Listings" on p.531).

THE RUTA PUUC BUS

While at Mérida's second-class bus terminal you may want to buy a ticket for a transport-only **day-trip** by bus around the **Ruta Puuc** (see p.534), which can be difficult to visit without your own transport. Ask at the Autotransportes del Sur counter. The trip costs US$5 and leaves at 8am every morning, visiting Uxmal, Labná, Sayil, Kabáh and Xlapak. You get just long enough at each site to form a general impression, but there's no guide or lunch included in the price.

Accommodation

There are hundreds of **hotels** in Mérida, many in lovely colonial buildings very near the centre, so that although the city can get crowded at peak times you should always be able to find a room. The very cheapest hotels are concentrated **next to the bus station**, a noisy and grimy part of town, with a string of upmarket hotels along **Paseo de Montejo**, just north of the centre, most of them ultra-modern and lacking in charm or personality; the best hotels lie in between, both geographically and in terms of value. A luxurious alternative is to stay outside town in a colonial hacienda: try the seventeenth-century *Hacienda Katanchel*, at C 35 no. 520 (☎99/20-09-97 or 20-09-85; ⑨), which is set in 750 acres and boasts individual pavilions and fresh water wading pools; or ask at the tourist office for a full list of converted haciendas all over Yucatán. Finally, *Rainbow Maya* **trailer park**, 8km on the road to Progreso (☎99/28-04-48, fax 24-77-84; ②–③), has about 100 hook-ups, water and electricity. The head office is in the Canto Farmacía; to book ahead, write to C 61 no. 468.

Near the bus station

Casa Becil, C 67 no. 550-C, between C 66 and C 68 (☎99/24-67-64). Friendly place, popular with North Americans and convenient for the bus station. ③.

Casa Bowen, C 66 no. 521-B, between C 65 and C 67 (☎99/28-61-09). A travellers' favourite for years, this restored colonial house is set around a bright, pleasant courtyard. Spartan but acceptable rooms with baths (some with a/c), and two apartments with kitchens. ③–④.

Pantera Negra, C 67, no. 547-B, between C 68 and C 70 (☎ & fax 99/24-02-51). One of the most charming hotels in town for any budget, in an intimate and idiosyncratically decorated colonial house, just a block from the bus station. The owners make you feel very welcome and you may end up staying here for longer than you planned. Prices include breakfast. ④.

Posada del Ángel, C 67 no. 535, between C 66 and C 68 (☎99/23-27-54). Quiet and comfortable, with parking and restaurant. ④.

In the centre

Los Aluxes, C 60 no. 444 (☎99/24-21-99, fax 23-38-58). Big, modern and expensive luxury hotel with all anyone could possible want. ⑨.

Caribe, C 59 no. 500, Parque Hidalgo (☎99/24-90-22, fax 24-87-33; toll free: in Mexico ☎800/71-2-00-03, in US: ☎1-888/822-6431). In a small plaza a block from the Plaza Mayor, this place has a lovely patio restaurant and views of the cathedral and plaza from the rooftop pool. Travel agency; parking. ⑥.

Casa del Balam, C 60 no. 488 (☎99/24-88-44, fax 24-50-11; in US ☎1-800-624-8451). Luxury, ambience and beautifully furnished rooms, all with a/c, in a central locationl. The particularly pleasant bar has *mariachi* crooners in the evening. Travel agency and car rental; parking. ⑨.

Casa de Huéspedes Peniche, C 62 no. 507, just off the zócalo (☎99/28-55-18). Shambling but fascinating grand colonial house, with original paintings, a staircase out of *Gone with the Wind* and huge, bare rooms (bring a padlock). The shared bathroom looks like it hasn't been cleaned since the place was built. ②.

Flamingo, C 58, corner of C 59 (☎99/24-77-55). One of the cheapest in town with a pool. ③.

Gran Hotel, C 60 no. 496, Parque Hidalgo (☎99/24-77-30, fax 24-76-22). Colonnades, fountains, palms and statues all ensure that the *Gran* lives up to its name. Rooms, all with private shower, are well furnished, often with antiques. ⑥.

Hotel del Parque, C 60 no. 495, Parque Hidalgo (☎99/24-78-44, fax 28-19-29). Lovely old building just off the main plaza. Some rooms need improvement and those at the back are quieter. You can dine in intimate little balconies in the restaurant, *La Bella Epoca*. ⑥.

Margarita, C 66 no. 506, between C 61 and C 63 (☎99/23-72-36). Budget favourite; small but clean rooms and good rates for groups. ②.

Mucuy, C 57 no. 481, between C 56 and C 58 (☎99/28-51-93). Quiet, well-run and pleasant hotel, with clean, good-value rooms. English-speaking staff and a selection of books in English. ③.

Posada Toledo, C 58 no. 487 (☎99/23-16-90 or 23-22-56). Superb, beautifully preserved nineteenth-century building. The rooms, all with private shower and some with a/c, are filled with antiques and the courtyard is a delight. The food is good, too, served in a historic dining room. ⑤.

Reforma, C 59 no. 508 (☎99/24-79-22, fax 28-32-78). Long-established, recently restored hotel in a colonial building. Rooms are arranged around a cool courtyard and there's a relaxing poolside bar and parking. Good prices on guided day-trips to Uxmal and on the *Ruta Puuc*. ④.

San Juan, C 62 no. 545a between C 69 and C 71 (☎99/23-68-23). A variety of good-value rooms in a listed colonial house, run by a very knowledgeable and friendly Méridan. Free Internet, faxes, juice and coffee for guests plus fascinating tailor-made eco-tourist trips and archeological tours with professional archeologists working in the field. Prices include breakfast. ④.

San Luís, C 61, corner C 68 (☎99/24-75-88). Where the men from UNCLE would stay – fabulously kitsch, and deliberately so. The man on reception has worked there since it opened in the 1960s. A wonderfully retro pool, clean, spacious rooms with en-suite bathroom and a/c, and a restaurant. ④.

Trinidad, C 62 no. 46, between C 55 and C 57 (☎99/23-20-33). A wide range of rooms and a plant-filled courtyard. Decorated with modern paintings and antiques. Guests can use the pool at its sister hotel, the *Trinidad Galería* (☎99/21-09-35), nearby on the corner of C 60 and C 51. ③–④.

The City

Founded by Francisco de Montejo (the Younger) in 1542, Mérida is built over, and partly from, the ruins of a Maya city known as **Tihó**. Although, like the rest of the peninsula, it had little effective contact with central Mexico until the completion of road and rail links in the 1960s, trade with Europe brought wealth from the earliest days. In consequence the city looks more European than almost any other in Mexico – many of the older houses, indeed, are built with French bricks and tiles, brought over as tradeable ballast in the ships that exported henequen. Until the advent of artificial fibres, a substantial proportion of the world's rope was manufactured from Yucatecan henequen, a business that reached its peak during World War I.

In 1849, during the Caste Wars, the Maya armies besieging Mérida were within a hair's breadth of capturing the city and thus regaining control of the entire peninsula, when the Maya peasants left the fight in order to return to the fields to plant corn. It was this event, rather than the pleas of the inhabitants for reinforcements, that saved the élite from defeat and brought Yucatán under Mexican control. Around the turn of the century, Mérida was an extraordinarily wealthy city – or at least a city that had vast numbers of extremely rich landowners riding on the backs of a landless, semi-enslaved peonage – a wealth that went into the grandiose mansions of the outskirts (especially along the Paseo de Montejo) and into European educations for the children of the *haciendados*. Today, with that trade all but dead, it remains elegant and bustling, its streets filled with Maya going about their daily business.

Plaza Mayor

Any exploration of Mérida begins naturally in the **Plaza Mayor**. The hub of the city's life, it's ringed by some of Mérida's oldest buildings, dominated by the **Cathedral of San Idelfonso** (daily 6am–noon & 5–8pm), built in the second half of the sixteenth century. Although most of its valuables were looted in the Revolution, the **Cristo de las Ampillas** (Christ of the Blisters), in a chapel to the left of the main altar, remains worth seeing. This statue was carved, according to legend, from a tree in the village of Ichmul that burned for a whole night without showing the least sign of damage; later, the parish church at Ichmul burned down and the statue again survived, though blackened and blistered. The image is the focal point of a local fiesta at the beginning of October. Beside the cathedral, separated from it by the Pasaje San Alvarado, the old bishop's palace has been converted into shops and offices.

Next door to the cathedral is the new **Museo de Arte Contemperáneo de Yucatán** (daily 9am–5pm; US$1.50, free on Sun), the finest art museum in the state, with permanent displays of the work of internationally acclaimed Yucatecan artists such as Fernando Castro Pacheco, Gabriel Ramírez Aznar and Fernando García Ponce. Temporary exhibitions often include ceramics from around the region, Yucatecan embroidery and metallic art. On the south side of the plaza stands the **Casa de Montejo**, a palace built in 1549 by Francisco de Montejo himself and inhabited until 1980 by his descendants. It now belongs to *Banamex*, and much of the interior is open to the public (Mon–Fri 9am–5pm): the facade is richly decorated in the Plateresque style, and above the doorway Conquistadors are depicted trampling savages underfoot. The **Palacio Municipal**, on the third side, is another impressive piece of sixteenth-century design with a fine clock tower, but the nineteenth-century **Palacio de Gobierno** (daily 8am–10pm), completing the square, is more interesting to visit. Inside, murals depict the history of the Yucatán and, on the first floor, there's a small historical chamber devoted to the same subject.

North of the Plaza Mayor
Most of the remaining monuments in Mérida lie north of the zócalo, with C 60 and later the Paseo de Montejo as their focus. Calle 60 is one of the city's main commercial streets, lined with several of the fancier hotels and restaurants. It also boasts a series of colonial buildings, starting with the seventeenth-century Jesuit **Iglesia de Jesús**, between the Plaza Hidalgo and the Parque de la Madre. Beside it on C 59 is the **Cepeda Peraza Library**, full of vast nineteenth-century tomes; a little further down C 59, the **Pinacoteca Virreinal** houses a rather dull collection of colonial artworks and modern sculptures in a former church. Continuing up C 60, you reach the **Teatro Peón Contreras**, a grandiose Neoclassical edifice built by Italian architects in the heady days of Porfirio Díaz and recently restored. The **university** is opposite.

The **Museo de Arte Popular** (Tues–Sat 8am–8pm, Sun 8am–2pm; free) in the former monastery of La Mejorada, C 59 between C 50 and C 48, displays a fine collection of the different styles of indigenous dress found throughout Mexico. The rich wood and glass cases show *huipiles* (the long white dresses embroidered with colourful flowers at the neck, worn by Maya women), jewellery and household items, while old black-and-white photos provide glimpses of village life and ceremonials. At the rear of the museum you can stock up on souvenirs at the really good artesanía shop.

One block north of the Teatro Peón Contreras, the sixteenth-century **Iglesia Santa Lucía** stands on the elegant plaza of the same name – a colonnaded square that used to be the town's stagecoach terminus. Finally, three blocks further on, there's the **Plaza Santa Ana**, a modern open space where you turn right and then second left to reach the Paseo de Montejo.

Paseo de Montejo
The **Paseo de Montejo** is a broad, tree-lined boulevard lined with the magnificent, pompous mansions of the grandees who strove to outdo each other's style (or vulgarity) around the turn of the century. In one of the grandest, the Palacio Canton, at the corner of C 43, is Mérida's **Museo de Antropología** (Tues–Sat 8am–8pm, Sun 8am–2pm; US$5, free on Sun). The house was built for General Canton, state governor at the turn of the century, in a restrained but very expensive elegance befitting his position, and has been beautifully restored and maintained. Given the archeological riches that surround the city, the collection is perhaps something of a disappointment, but it's a useful introduction to the sites nonetheless, with displays covering everything from prehistoric stone tools to modern Maya life. Obviously there are sculptures and other objects from the main sites, but more interesting are the attempts to fill in the back-

ground and give some idea of what it was like to live in a Maya city; unfortunately, most labels are only in Spanish. Topographic maps of the peninsula, for example, explain how cenotes are formed and their importance to the ancient population; a collection of skulls demonstrates techniques of facial and dental deformation; and there are displays covering jewellery, ritual offerings and burial practices, as well as a large pictorial representation of the workings of the Maya calendar. The **bookshop** has leaflets and guidebooks in English to dozens of ruins in Yucatán and the rest of Mexico.

The walk out **to the museum** is quite a long one – you can get there on a "Paseo de Montejo" bus from C 59 just east of the Parque Hidalgo, or take a **calesa** (horse-drawn taxi) instead. This is not altogether a bad idea, especially if you fancy the romance of riding about in an open carriage, and if times are slack and you bargain well, it need cost no more than a regular taxi. Unfortunately, however, the horses are not always treated as well as they could be. Take some time to head a little further out on the Paseo de Montejo, to a lovely and very wealthy area where the homes are more modern and interspersed with big new hotels and pavement cafés. The **Monumento a la Patria**, about ten long blocks beyond the museum, is a titan, covered in neo-Maya sculptures relating to Mexican history – you'll also pass it if you take the bus out to Progreso. To do the Grand Tour properly, you should visit the **Parque de las Americas**, on Av Colón, which is planted with trees from every country on the American continent, and get back to the centre via the **Parque Centenario**, Av de los Itzaes and C 59, where there's a zoo, botanical gardens and a children's park.

Markets and handicrafts

Mérida's **market**, a huge place between calles 65, 67, 56 and 54, is for most visitors a major attraction. As far as quality goes, though, you're almost always better off buying in a shop – prices are no great shakes, either, unless you're an unusually skilful and determined haggler. Before buying anything, head for the **Casa de Artesanías** in the Edificio de Monjas, on C 63 west of the zócalo, where you'll get an idea of the potential quality and price of the goods. Run by the government-sponsored Fonapas organization, it sells crafts from the peninsula, which are of a consistently high quality, right down to the cheapest trinkets and toys.

The most popular purchase is a **hammock** – and Mérida is probably the best place in the country to buy one – but if you want something you can realistically sleep in, exercise a degree of care. There are plenty of cheap ones about, but comfort is measured by the tightness of the weave (the closer-packed the threads the better) and the breadth: since you're supposed to lie in them diagonally, in order to be relatively flat, this is far more crucial than the length (although obviously the central portion of the hammock should be at least as long as you are tall). A decent-sized hammock (*doble* at least, preferably *matrimonial*) with cotton threads (*hilos de algodon*, more comfortable and less likely to go out of shape than artificial fibres) will set you back at least US$20 – more if you get a fancy multicoloured version.

If you'd rather not mess about with vendors in the market, head for a **specialist dealer**. Tejidos y Cordeles Nacionales is one of the best, very near the market at C 56 no. 516-B. More of a warehouse than a shop, it has hundreds of the things stacked against every wall, divided up according to size, material and cost. Buy several and you can enter into serious negotiations over the price. Similar hammock stores nearby include El Campesino and El Aguacate, both on C 58, and La Poblana at C 65 no. 492.

Other good **buys** include tropical shirts (*guayaberas*), panama hats (known here as *jipis*) and *huipiles*, which vary wildly in quality, from factory-made, machine-stitched junk to hand-embroidered, homespun cloth. Even the best, though, rarely compare with the antique dresses that can occasionally be found: identical in style (as they have been for hundreds of years) but far better made and very expensive.

YUCATECAN CUISINE

Typical **Yucatecan specialities** include *puchero*, a stew of chicken, pork, carrot, squash, cabbage, potato, sweet potato and banana chunks with a delicious stock broth, garnished with radish, coriander and Seville orange; *poc-chuc*, a combination of pork with tomatoes, onions and spices; *sopa de lima* (not lime soup, exactly, but chicken broth with lime and tortilla chips in it); *pollo* or *cochinita pibil* (chicken or suckling pig wrapped in banana leaves and cooked in a *Pib*, basically a pit in the ground, though restaurants cheat on this); *papadzules* (tacos stuffed with hard-boiled eggs and covered in red and green pumpkin-seed sauce); and anything *en relleno negro*, a black, burnt-chile sauce. Little of this is hot, but watch out for the *salsa de chile habanero* that most restaurants have on the table – pure fire.

Eating

Good **restaurants** are plentiful in the centre of Mérida, though those on the Plaza Major can be quite expensive. Best head for the historic and atmospheric area around the **Plaza Hidalgo**, just north, along C 60 between C 61 and C 59, where you'll find plenty of good restaurants and pavement cafés, lively with crowds of tour groups and locals. Further afield, on **Paseo de Montejo**, the more expensive and sophisticated restaurants include lots of upmarket places popular with young locals.

There are a number of less expensive places around the junction of C 62 and C 61, at the northwest corner of the Plaza, but cheapest of all are the *loncherías* in the **market**, where you can get good, filling comidas corridas. Around the Plaza Mayor several wonderful **juice bars** – notably *Jugos California* – serve all the regular juices and licuados, as well as more unusual local concoctions: try mamey or guanabana. Other branches are dotted about the city. Combine these with something from the **bakery** Pan Montejo, at the corner of C 62 and C 63, to make a great breakfast.

Los Almendros, C 50, between C 57 and C 59, in the Plaza Mejorada. One of Mérida's most renowned restaurants, popular with locals and visitors. Delicious, moderately priced Yucatecan food, especially at Sunday lunchtime. The original *Los Almendros*, in Ticul, claims to have invented *poc-chuc* (see box above).

Restaurante Amaro, C 59 no. 507, between C 60 and C 62. Set in a lovely stone-flagged tree-shaded courtyard with a fountain. Some vegetarian menus, offering a welcome change for veggies who are tired of endless quesadillas.

La Bella Epoca, in *Hotel del Parque*. Intimate dining in a building full of period ambience with black-tie waiters and balconies for two overlooking the Plaza Hidalgo. Surprisingly cheap.

Lonchería Milly, C 59 no. 520, between C 64 and C 66. Tiny café serving basic, inexpensive dishes to a largely local crowd. Daily 7–11am & noon–5pm.

El Louvre, C 62 no. 499, corner of C 61. Popular eating place with tasty comidas corridas.

Marlin Azul, C 62 no. 488, near the zócalo. Best value breakfast in town – great if you're on a tight budget.

Las Mil Tortas, C 62, between C 67 and C 65. Great Mexican-style sandwiches and tortas.

El Patio Español, *Gran Hotel*, C 60, Parque Hidalgo. Historic restaurant offering good, surprisingly well-priced food, and great service. As the name indicates, Spanish dishes are a speciality.

Pizzería de Vito Corleone, C 59 no. 508, corner of C 62. Inexpensive pizza restaurant that also does takeaway.

El Rincón, in the *Hotel Caribe*, C 60, on the corner of Parque Hidalgo. Both this and the cheaper *Cafetería El Meson*, in the same building, are good, central places to eat in pleasant surroundings.

Entertainment and nightlife

Mérida is a lively city, and every evening you'll find the streets buzzing with revellers enjoying a variety of **free entertainment**. To find out what's happening, pick up a free copy of *Yucatán Today* from the tourist office or any hotel. **Venues** include the plazas, the garden behind the Palacio Municipal, the Teatro Peón Contreras (next to the tourist office) and the Casa de la Cultura del Mayas, C 63 between C 64 and C 66. Things can change, but typical performances might include energetic and fascinating **vaquerías** (vibrant Mexican folk dances, featuring different regional styles, to the rhythm of a *jaranera* band); Glen Miller-style **Big Band** music; the **Ballet Folklórico de la Universidad de Yucatán**, which performs a spectacular interpretation of Maya legends; **marimba** in the Parque Hidalgo; **classical music** concerts; and the very popular **Serenata Yucateca**, an open-air performance of traditional songs and music.

Perhaps the best time to see the Plaza Mayor and the surrounding streets is Sunday, when vehicles are banned from the area and day-long music, dancing, markets and festivities take over – a delight after the usual traffic roar. Street markets are set up along C 60 as far as the Plaza Santa Ana and there's a **flea market** in the Parque Santa Lucía.

There's plenty to do of a more commercial nature too, from **mariachi nights** in hotel bars to **Maya spectaculars** in nightclubs. Those aimed at tourists will be advertised in hotels, or in brochures available at the tourist office. Less obviously there are **video bars** and **discos** in most of the big hotels.

Apart from the hard-drinking *cantinas* (and there are plenty of these all over the city – including a couple of good ones on C 62, south of the plaza) – many of Mérida's **bars** double as restaurants.

Bars, discos and live music

La Ciudad Maya, C 84 no. 502, corner of C 59 (☎99/24-33-13). Floor shows with Yucatecan and Cuban music. Daily 1–10pm.

La Conquista, inside the *Paseo de Montejo* hotel, C 56 no. 482, near C 41. Quiet, dark, romantic disco.

Estudio 58, C 58, between C 55 and C 57, next to and underneath the *Hotel Maya Yucatán*. Central disco and nightclub with no cover charge. Live music and a happy hour 9.30–10.30pm.

Los Juglares, C 60 no. 500. Live jazz, blues and rock until 3am.

Kalia Rock House, C 22 no. 282, near C 37. Flavour of the month at the time of writing; noisy and fun; 9pm–3am.

Pancho's, C 59, opposite the *Hotel Reforma*. A steak restaurant with a pricey Tex-Mex menu and a disco later, *Pancho's* is a magnet for Americans homesick for "Mexican" food. The fun theme, with giant photos of Mexican Revolutionaries and bandolier-draped waiters in sombreros is ridiculously over the top. Try to hit the happy hour, 6–9pm.

La Prosperidad, C 56, corner of C 53. Earthier than the tourist bars, though becoming ever more popular. It's in a huge *palapa*, with live rock music in the afternoons and evenings. The beer's not cheap but it does come with substantial tasty snacks.

Listings

Airlines Aerocaribe/Aerocozumel/Mexicana Inter, Paseo de Montejo 500 (☎99/28-67-86; airport 46-16-78); Aeroméxico, Plaza Americana, Hotel Fiesta Americana (☎99/20-12-60; airport 46-14-00); Aviacsa, Prolongacion Montejo no. 130 (☎99/26-90-87; airport 46-13-78); Aviateca, Paseo de Montejo no. 475c (☎99/25-80-59; airport 46-13-12); Mexicana, Paseo de Montejo 493 (☎99/24-66-33; airport 46-13-92).

American Express Paseo de Montejo 95, between C 43 and C 45 (Mon–Fri 9am–2pm & 4–5pm, Sat 9am–noon; ☎99/28-42-22).

Banks and exchange Most banks are around C 65 between C 60 and C 64, and are open 9am–1.30pm. Banco Atlántico, C 65 no. 515, changes money 8am–1pm. Of the many casas de cambio around the cen-

San Cristobál de las Casas

Temple and beach at Tulum, Quintana Roo

Maya ruins at Palenque, Chiapas

Chichén Itzá, Yucatán

Río Tulijá, Agua Azul, Chiapas

Cobá, Quintana Roo

Calakmul, Campeche

Maya murals at Bonampak, Chiapas

Cenote, Valladolid, Yucatán

Coral and diver, Caribbean coast

Yaxchilán, Chiapas

tre, try Canto, C 61 no. 468, between C 54 and C 52 (Mon–Fri 8.30am–1.30pm & 4.30–7.30pm, Sat 8.30am–1pm), or Del Sureste, C 56 no. 491, between C 57 and C 59 (Mon–Sat 9am–5pm). Finex, C 60 and 59, in the corner of the Parque Hidalgo, is open longest (daily 8.30am–8pm).

Bookshops English-language guidebooks are sold at Dante Touristic Bookstore on the corner of C 57 and C 60. The *Holiday Inn*, Av Colón near the junction with Paseo de Montejo, has a small supply of English-language novels.

Car rental Hertz, at the airport (☎99/46-13-55); National, C 60 no. 486-F (☎99/23-24-93, airport 46-13-94); Thrifty, C 60 no.446-C (☎ & fax 99/23-34-40).

Consulates Opening hours are likely to be fairly limited, so it's best to phone ahead and check. Belize/UK, C 58 no. 450 (☎99/28-61-52); Cuba, C 1-C no. 277A between C 38 and C 40 (☎99/44-42-15); Spain C 3-A, no. 237 (☎99/44-83-50); USA, Paseo de Montejo at Av Colón 453 (☎99/25-50-11).

Laundry If your hotel doesn't do laundry, try Lavamatica, C 59 no. 508 (Mon–Fri 8am–6pm, Sat 8am–2pm), which offers full-service washes.

Post office C 65, between C 56 and C 56-A (Mon–Fri 7am–7pm, Sat 9am–1pm). Has a reliable *Lista de Correos* that keeps mail for ten days.

Telephones Use one of the ubiquitous Ladatels or one of the many casetas dotted around town: Caseta Condesa, C 59 near C 62; Computel, Paseo de Montejo on the corner with C 37; or TelPlus, C 61 no 497, between C 58 and C 60.

Travel agencies Mérida boasts dozens of travel agencies. The best for archeological, cultural and natural history tours in the peninsula are Ecoturismo Yucatán, C 3 no. 235 between C 32-A & C 34 (☎99/25-21-87, fax 25-90-47). For trips to Cuba, try Cubamex, C 17 no. 198, between C 18 & 20 (☎99/44-43-14), Cumex, C 61 no. 499 (☎99/23-91-99), or Viajes Crisal C 56 no. 483 (☎99/26-30-44, fax 23-79-13).

MOVING ON FROM MÉRIDA

Mérida is a major transport hub, especially if you're travelling on **by bus**. Most major destinations are served from the main first- and second-class stations, but some places are better served from the multitude of different little stations dotted around town.

From the first-class **Cameon**, the most important routes run by **ADO** are to Campeche, México, Palenque and Villahermosa. **Caribe Express** provides a comfortable, a/c service with videos to Campeche and Villahermosa, as well as Cancún, Escárcega, Playa del Carmen and a number of other destinations. There are also services to Akumal, Villahermosa, Tulum and Playa del Carmen run by **Autotransportes del Caribe**. Both Caribe Express and Autotransportes del Caribe also have desks in the main first- and second-class buildings.

Buses from the **second-class** station, on C 69 between C 68 and 70, leave for **Campeche** (Autotransportes de Sureste; 4hr); **Cancún** (Expreso de Oriente; 6hr); **Escárcega** (Autotransportes de Sureste; 6hr); **Palenque** (Autotransportes de Sureste; 10–11hr); **Playa del Carmen** (Expreso de Oriente; 7hr); **Tuxtla Gutiérrez** (Autotranportes de Sureste; 20hr); **Valladolid** (Expreso de Oriente; 3hr); and **Villahermosa** (Autotransportes de Sureste; 10hr).

Of Mérida's **smaller bus stations**, C 50 on the corner with C 67 serves Autobuses de Occidente en Yucatán, for destinations west of Mérida, and Lineas Unidos del Sur de Yucatán: buses leave for **Celestún** (5am–8pm; 2hr), **Oxkutzcab** (hourly) and **Sisal** (2hr). Autobuses del Noreste en Yucatán leave from C 50 no. 529, between C 65 and C 67, for **Río Lagartos** (6hr), San Felipe (7hr) and Tizimín (4hr). Directly opposite, Autotransportes de Oriente leave for **destinations inland and east of Mérida**, with hourly buses to Cancún (6hr) and to Izamal, Pisté and Valladolid.

In addition, **colectivos** depart Plaza de San Juan, C 69 between C 62 and C 64, for Dzibilchaltún, Oxkutzcab and Ticul, among other destinations. On the northern side of the plaza there are departures to Progreso (1hr) and to Dzibilchaltún, Sierra Papacal, Komchén and Dzitya.

Flights from Mérida leave for most Mexican cities and some international destinations; to get out to the airport, catch bus #79 ("Aviacion") going east on C 67.

North of Mérida: the coast

From Mérida to the port of **Progreso**, the closest point on the coast, is just 36km – thirty minutes on the bus. About halfway between the two, a few kilometres off the main road, lie the ancient ruins of **Dzibilchaltún**, with a cenote at the very middle of the city, fed with a constant supply of fresh water from a small spring, which you can swim in. The drive out of the city follows Paseo de Montejo through miles of wealthy suburbs and shopping malls before reaching the flat countryside where the henequen industry seems still to be flourishing. On the outskirts of Mérida there's a giant Cordemex processing plant, and a nearby shop run by the same company sells goods made from the fibre.

It's easy enough to visit both Dzibilchaltún and Progreso in one trip from Mérida: **buses** to Progreso leave from the terminal on C 62 between C 65 and C 67 and combis return to Mérida from the corner of C 80 and C 31 near the post office, on the north side of Progreso's parque central. Head out to the ruins early and from there either walk, hitch or wait for the lunchtime bus back to the main road, where you can flag down a Progreso bus. Alternatively, combis for Chablecal stop at Dzibilchaltún; they leave when full (about every half-hour) from the Parque de San Juan at Mérida (corner of C 62 and C 69).

Dzibilchaltún

The importance for archeologists of the ruins of the ancient city of **Dzibilchaltún** (daily 8am–5pm; US$1.50, free on Sun) is, unfortunately, hardly reflected in what you actually see. There was, apparently, a settlement here from 1000 BC right through to the Conquest, the longest continuous occupation of any known site; more than eight thousand structures have been mapped and the city's major points were linked by great causeways – but little has survived, in particular since the ready-dressed stones were a handy building material, used in several local towns and in the Mérida–Progreso road.

In addition to providing the ancient city with water, the 44-metre-deep **Cenote Xlacah** was of ritual importance to the Maya: more than six thousand offerings – including human remains – have been discovered in its depths. A causeway leads from the cenote to a ramshackle group of buildings around the **Templo de las Siete Muñecas** (Temple of the Seven Dolls). The temple itself was originally a simple square pyramid, subsequently built over with a more complex structure. Later still, a passageway was cut through to the original building and seven deformed clay figurines (dolls) buried, with a tube through which their spirits could commune with the priests. In conjunction with the buildings that surround it, the temple is aligned with various astronomical points and must have served in some form as an observatory. It is also remarkable for being the only known Maya temple to have windows and for having a tower in place of the usual roof-comb. The dolls, and many of the finds from the cenote, can be seen in a small museum by the site entrance. Around Dzibilchaltún, five and half square kilometres have been declared an **Eco-Archeological Park**, partly to protect a unique species of fish found in the cenote. Nature trails take you through the surrounding forest and it's a great place for bird-watching.

Progreso

First impressions of **PROGRESO** – a working port with a vast concrete pier – are unprepossessing, but the beach is long and broad with fine white sand (though the water's not too clean) and it makes for a pleasant day out from Mérida. The shorefront behind the beach is built up all the way to **Puerto Chicxulub**, an unattractive fishing village some 5km away, and a walk between the two takes you past the mansions of the old henequen exporters, interspersed with modern holiday villas.

Streets in Progreso are confusingly numbered using two overlapping systems: one has numbers in the 70s and 80s, the other in the 20s and 30s. However, it's a small place, and not difficult to find your way around. There are a few moderately priced **places to stay** on Av Malecón, which runs along the seafront between the beach and the hotels. The less expensive hotels are a few roads back. Best bets include *Hotel Miralmar*, C 27 no. 124, on the corner of C 76 (☎993/5-05-52; ③); *Real del Mar*, Av Malecón, near C 20 (☎993/5-07-98; ③), which has clean simple rooms with bathrooms; and *Tropical Suites*, Av Malecón 143 (☎993/5-12-63; ④), which has some suites with kitchens. As for **eating**, try the seafood snacks served at *Sol y Mar*, Av Malecón at C 80, or buy **picnic food** at the market on C 27 and C 80.

Beaches around Progreso

There are stretches of **beach** in either direction from Progreso and, though this coast is the focus of much new tourism development, it's never crowded. Indeed, in winter, when the holiday homes are empty (and the rates come down), you'll have miles of sand to yourself. Check the numbers posted outside the villas and you may find bargain **long-term accommodation**.

The road east from Progreso runs through Puerto Chicxulub and continues to **Telchac**, one hour away, and the luxury *Hotel Maya Beach Resort* (☎99/24-95-55; ⑨). Beyond, at **Chabihau**, there's a small, unnamed **hotel** (③). With more time and a little perseverance, it's possible to get even further east, to **DZILAM DE BRAVO**, a remote fishing village at the end of the road, with no beach because of its ugly, though functional, sea defence wall. Here the *Hotel Los Flamencos* (④), on the main road, about ten minutes' walk west of the main square, offers basic rooms. You can rent boats (at least US$65) at the dock to visit **Bocas de Dzilam**, 40km away in the **San Felipe Natural Park**. Set in 620 square kilometres of coastal forests, marshes and dunes, the *bocas* (Spanish for mouths) are freshwater springs on the seabed; the nutrients they provide help to encourage the wide biological diversity found here. Bird and wildlife-watching is superb: you'll see turtles, tortoises, crocodiles, spider monkeys and dozens of bird species.

A more direct way to get to Dzilam de Bravo is to catch a second-class bus in Mérida from the Autobuses del Noreste terminal. Four buses daily pass through on their way to and from Tizimín and Progreso, and one bus daily leaves for Izamal at 1pm.

Heading west, there are a number of new hotels and holiday homes along the road to **Yucalpetén**, a busy commercial port and naval base 4km from Progreso. Further west, the small but growing resorts of **Chelem** and **Chuburná**, respectively fifteen and thirty minutes from Progreso – and easy day-trips from Mérida – have clean, wide beaches and a few rooms and restaurants. It's hard to believe that the semi-deserted pueblo of **SISAL** was Mérida's chief port in colonial times. Change is in the air, though, as Sisal is earmarked for tourism. At present just a few North American duck-hunters come for the shooting in winter, staying at the *Club de Patos* ; the only other accommodation as yet is a couple of basic **budget hotels**, the *Los Corsarios* and the *Felicidades* (both ③) near the small zócalo. Beyond here the coast road is barely practicable, but there are empty beaches all the way round to Celestún.

Celestún

CELESTÚN, at the end of a sandbar on the peninsula's northwest coast, would be little more than a one-boat fishing village were it not for its amazing bird-filled lagoon that boasts a large flock of flamingos. To see them – as well as the blue-winged teals and shovellers that migrate here in the winter to take advantage of the plentiful fish in these warm, shallow waters – rent one of the boats from the bridge on the main road into Celestún. Get the bus driver to drop you off, as it's a twenty-minute walk from the main square. Launches cost US$33 and take up to six people. Bring your bathers with you as you may get the chance to swim in the rich red waters among the mangroves.

Nominally protected by inclusion in the 600-square-mile **Celestún Natural Park**, the flamingos are nevertheless harassed by boats approaching too close in order to give visitors a spectacular flying display, disturbing the birds' feeding. Try to make it clear to your boatman that you don't wish to interrupt the birds' natural behaviour; you will still get good photos from a respectable distance.

There are first-class **buses** from Mérida for Celestún every two hours from the Cameon. Second-class services, which also stop at Sisal, leave from the terminal on C 50, corner of C 67. There are half a dozen **lodgings** in the village: the *Hotel Gutiérrez*, C 12 no. 107 in Mérida (☎99/28-04-19; ④), which has some a/c rooms, and *Hotel Maria Carmen*, C 12 no. 111 (☎99/28-03-13; ④), are both on the beach not far from the main square. Further along the beach to the north is the *Hotel San Julio*, C 12 no. 93-A (no phone; ③), more basic than the others but clean and comfortable. Several **seafood restaurants** can be found on the dusty main street and on the beach – the *ceviche* in Celestún is invariably good – and there's also a market, a bakery, a bank and a filling station.

South of Mérida: Uxmal and the Ruta Puuc

About 80km south of Mérida in the **Puuc hills** lies a group of the peninsula's most important archeological sites. **Uxmal** (pronounced Oosh-mal) is chief of them, second only to Chichén Itzá in size and significance, but perhaps greater in its initial impact and certainly in the beauty and harmony of its extraordinary architectural style. Lesser sites include **Kabáh**, astride the main road not far beyond; **Sayil**, nearby down a rough side track; and **Labná**, further along this same track. Though related architecturally, each site is quite distinct from the others, and each is dominated by one major structure. From Labná you could continue to **Oxkutzcab**, on the road from Muna to Felipe Carillo Puerto, and head back to Mérida, via **Ticul** and **Mani,** or else take the longer route past the Maya ruins of **Mayapan**.

Like Chichén Itzá, the Puuc sites are now regarded as being as authentically Maya as Tikal or Palenque, rather than the product of invading Toltecs, as was once believed. Though there are new stylistic themes both in the Puuc sites and at Chichén Itzá, there are also marked continuities of architectural and artefactual technique, religious symbolism, hieroglyphic writing and settlement patterns. The newer themes are now believed to have been introduced by the **Chontal Maya** of the Gulf Coast lowlands, who had become the Yucatán's most important trading partner by the Terminal Classic period (800–1000 AD). The Chontal Maya themselves traded extensively with Oaxaca and central Mexico and are thought to have passed on their architectural styles and themes to the Yucatán.

Getting to the sites

The sites are far enough apart that it's impractical to do more than a fraction of the them by bus, unless you're prepared to spend several days and endure a lot of waiting around. The cheapest and most practical way to visit the sites is to take the **"Ruta Puuc" day-trip bus** (US$5), run by Autotransportes del Sur from the bus station (see p.524), and though you don't get much time at the ruins, Uxmal is the last visited and it is possible to stay later and pay for a different bus back. Scores of Mérida travel agencies offer pricier Puuc route trips.

It's better still to **rent a car**: in two days you can explore all the key sites, either returning overnight to Mérida or finding a room in Muna, Ticul or, more expensively, at Uxmal itself. This way you could even include the Uxmal *son et lumière* – better than the one at Chichén Itzá. For details of car rental agencies, see p.531.

Uxmal

UXMAL – "thrice-built" – represents the finest achievement of the **Puuc architectural style**, in which buildings of amazingly classical proportions are decorated with broad stone mosaic friezes of geometric patterns, or designs so stylized and endlessly repeated as to become almost abstract. As in every Maya site in the Yucatán, the face of **Chac**, the rain god, is everywhere. Chac must have been more crucial here than almost anywhere, for Uxmal and the other Puuc sites, almost uniquely, have no cenote or other natural source of water, relying instead on artificially created underground cisterns, jug-shaped and coated with lime, to collect and store rainwater. In recent years these have all been filled in, to prevent mosquitoes breeding.

Little is known of the city's history, but what is clear is that the chief monuments, and the city's peaks of power and population, fall into the Terminal Classic period, and

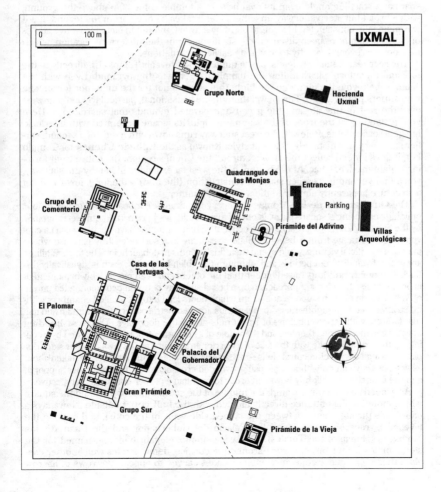

though there are indications of settlement long before this, most of the buildings that you see date from this period. Some time after 900 AD the city began to decline and by 1200 Uxmal and all the Puuc sites, together with Chichén Itzá, were all but abandoned. The reasons for this are unknown, although political infighting, ecological problems and loss of trade with Tula may have played a part. Later, the **Xiu dynasty** settled at Uxmal, which became one of the central pillars of the League of Mayapán, and from here, in 1441, the rebellion originated that finally overthrew the power of Mayapán and put an end to any form of centralized Maya authority over the Yucatán. All the significant surviving structures, though, date from the Classic period.

The site

Entering the site, the back of the great **Pirámide del Adivino** (Pyramid of the Magician) rises before you. The most remarkable-looking of all Mexican pyramids, it soars at a startling angle from its oval base to a temple some 30m above the ground, with a broad but steep stairway up either side. It takes its name from the legend that it was magically constructed in a single night by a dwarf, though in fact at least five stages of construction have been discovered – six if you count the modern restoration, which may not correspond exactly to any of its earlier incarnations.

The rear (east) stairway leads, past a tunnel which reveals Templo III, directly to the top, and a platform surrounding the temple that crowns the pyramid. Even with the chain to help you, the climb up the high, thin steps is not for the unfit, nor for anyone who suffers from vertigo. The views, though, are sensational, particularly looking west over the rest of the site and the green unexcavated mounds that surround it. Here you're standing at the front of the summit temple, its facade decorated with interlocking geometric motifs. Below it, the west stairway runs down either side of a second, earlier sanctuary in a distinctly different style. Known as the **Edificio Chenes** (or Templo IV), it does indeed reflect the architecture of the Chenes region, the entire front forming a giant mask of Chac. At the bottom of the west face, divided in half by the stairway, you'll find yet another earlier stage of construction (the first) – the long, low facade of a structure apparently similar to the so-called "Nunnery".

The **Quadrangulo de las Monjas** (Nunnery Quadrangle), a beautiful complex of four buildings enclosing a square plaza, is one of many buildings here named quite erroneously by the Spanish, to whom it resembled a convent. Whatever it may have been, it wasn't a convent; theories range from it being a military academy to a sort of earthly paradise where intended sacrificial victims would spend their final months in debauchery. The four buildings are in fact from different periods and, although they blend superbly, each is stylistically distinct. The **north building**, raised higher than the others and even more richly ornamented, is probably also the oldest. Approached up a broad stairway between two colonnaded porches, it has a strip of plain stone facade (from which doors lead into the vaulted chambers within) surmounted by a slightly raised panel of mosaics: geometric patterns and human and animal figures, with representations of Maya huts above the doorways. The **west building** boasts even more varied themes, and the whole of its ornamentation is surrounded by a coiling, feathered rattlesnake with the face of a warrior emerging from its jaws. All four sides display growing Maya architectural skills – the false Maya vaults of the interiors are taken about as wide as they can go without collapsing (wooden crossbeams provided further support), and the frontages are slightly bowed in order to maintain a proper horizontal perspective.

An arched passageway through the middle of the south building provided the square with a monumental entrance directly aligned with the **ball court** outside. Nowadays a path leads through here, between the ruined side walls of the court, and up onto the levelled terrace on which stand the Palacio del Gobernador and the **Casa de las Tortugas** (House of the Turtles). This very simple, elegant building, named for the stone turtles (or tortoises) carved around the cornice, demonstrates well another constant theme of Puuc architecture: stone facades carved to appear like rows of narrow columns. These probably represent the building style of the Maya huts still in use today – walls of bamboo lashed together. The plain bands of masonry that often surround them mirror the cords that tie the hut walls in place.

It is the **Palacio del Gobernador** (Governor's Palace), though, that marks the finest achievement of Uxmal's builders. John L. Stephens, arriving at the then virtually unknown site in June 1840, had no doubts as to its significance: "If it stood this day on its grand artificial terrace in Hyde Park or the Garden of the Tuileries," he later wrote, "it would form a new order . . . not unworthy to stand side by side with the remains of the Egyptian, Grecian and Roman art." The palace faces east, away from the buildings around it, probably for astronomical reasons – its central doorway aligns with the column of the altar outside and the point where Venus rises. Long and low, it is lent a remarkable harmony by the architect's use of light and shade on the facade, and by the strong diagonals that run right through its broad band of mosaic decorations – particularly in the steeply vaulted archways that divide the two wings from the central mass, like giant arrow-heads aimed at the sky. Close up, the mosaic is equally impressive, masks of Chac alternating with grid-and-key patterns and with highly stylized snakes. Inside, the chambers are, as ever, narrow, gloomy and unadorned; but at least the great central room, 20m long and entered by the three closer-set openings in the facade, is grander than most. At the back, the rooms have no natural light source at all.

Behind the palace stand the ruinous buildings of the **Grupo Sur** (South Group), with the partly restored Gran Pirámide (Great Pyramid), and El Palomar (Dovecote or Quadrangle of the Doves). You can climb the rebuilt staircase of the **Gran Pirámide** to see the temple on top, decorated with parrots and more masks of Chac, and look across at the rest of the site. **El Palomar** was originally part of a quadrangle like that of the Nunnery, but the only building to retain any form is this, topped with the great wavy, latticed roof-comb from which it takes its name.

Of the outlying structures, the **Pirámide de la Vieja** (Pyramid of the Old Woman), probably the earliest surviving building at Uxmal, is now little more than a grassy mound with a clearly man-made outline. The **Grupo del Cementerio** (Cemetery Group), too, is in a state of ruin – low altars in the middle of this square bear traces of carved hieroglyphs and human skulls.

Practicalities

Several **buses** a day run direct from Mérida to Uxmal, and any bus heading down the main road towards Hopelchén (or between Mérida and Campeche on the longer route) will drop you just a short walk from the entrance. Note that none runs late enough to get you back to Mérida after the *son et lumière*. At the modern **entrance to the site** (daily 8am–5pm; US$4, free on Sun) the **tourist centre** includes a small museum, a snack bar and a shop with guides to the site, souvenirs, film and suchlike. Uxmal's *son et lumière* (daily except Mon) is at 7pm in Spanish (US$2.50), 9pm in English (US$3); the commentary is pretty crass, but the lighting effects are undeniably impressive.

There are three expensive **hotels** nearby: the best value near the ruins is *Villas Arqueológicas* (✆ & fax 99/28-06-44; ⑦), right at the entrance, which has a/c rooms, a pool and a good library on the Maya; the colonial-style *Hacienda Uxmal* (✆99/23-47-44, fax 28-08-40; ⑨) and the less preicey but comfy *Rancho Uxmal* (✆99/2-02-77; ⑤), both 4km north towards Muna, are the other options, or else you can **camp** at the *Rancho* (①).

Travelling from Uxmal to Kabáh, you'll pass the **Sacbe campsite and trailer park** (②). It's about fifteen minutes' walk south from the main square in the village of Santa Elena; if you're travelling by bus, ask the driver to drop you off at the entrance. Run by a Mexican–French couple, who have maps and can provide accurate information about the area, the site is a haven for backpackers, with tent sites dotted among the shady fruit trees. There are also some new cabañas (②), and limited space for your own hammock. There's nowhere to **eat** here or in Santa Elena, so bring supplies.

Kabáh

Some 20km south of Uxmal, the extensive site of **KABÁH** (daily 8am–5pm; US$1.50, free on Sun) stretches across the road. Much of it remains unexplored, but the one great building, the **Codz Poop** or Palace of Masks, lies not far off the highway to the left. The facade of this amazing structure is covered all over, in ludicrous profusion, with goggle-eyed, trunk-nosed masks of Chac. Even in its present state – with most of the long, curved noses broken off – this is the strangest and most striking of all Maya buildings, decorated so obsessively, intricately and repetitively that it seems almost insane. Even the steps by which you reach the doorways and the interior are more Chac noses. There are a couple of lesser buildings grouped around the Codz Poop, and on the other side of the road an unusual circular pyramid – now simply a green, conical mound. Across the road a sort of triumphal arch marks the point where the ancient causeway from Uxmal entered the city.

Leaving Kabáh, you may have to virtually lie down in the road to persuade a bus to stop for you – ask the guards at the site for the bus times. Hitching a ride with other visitors, though, is generally pretty easy, and with luck you may even meet someone touring all the local sites.

Sayil

A sober, restrained contrast to the excesses of Kabáh, the ruined site of **Sayil** (daily 8am–5pm; US$1.50, free on Sun) lies some 5km along a minor road heading east from the highway, 5km beyond Kabáh. It is again dominated by one major structure, the extensively restored **Gran Palacio** (Great Palace), built on three storeys, each smaller than the one below, and some 80m long. Although there are several large masks of Chac in a frieze around the top of the middle level, the decoration mostly takes the form of bamboo-effect stone pillaring – seen here more extensively than anywhere. The interiors of the middle level, too, are lighter and airier than is usual, thanks to the use of broad openings, their lintels supported on fat columns. The upper and lower storeys are almost entirely unadorned, plain stone surfaces with narrow openings.

Few other structures have been cleared. From the Gran Palacio a path leads to the right to the large temple of **El Mirador**, and in the other direction to a stela, carved with a phallic figure and now protected under a thatched roof. On the opposite side of the road from all this, a small path leads uphill, in about ten minutes, to two more temples.

Xlapak and Labná

The minor road continues, paved but in poor condition, past the tiny Puuc site known as **XLAPAK** (daily 8am–5pm; US$1, free on Sun). Its proximity to the larger sites of Labná and Sayil means that Xlapak (Maya for "old walls") is seldom visited, but if you have the time, stop to see the recently restored buildings with their carvings of masks and yet more Chac noses. **LABNÁ** (daily 8am–5pm; US$1.50, free on Sun) is about 3km further. Near the entrance to this ancient city is a palace, similar to but less impressive than that of Sayil, on which you'll see traces of sculptures including the inevitable Chac, and a crocodile (or snake) with a human face emerging from its mouth – symbolizing a god escaping from the jaws of the underworld. Remnants of a raised causeway lead from here to a second group of buildings, of which the most important is the **Arco de Labná**. Originally part of a complex linking two great squares, like the Nunnery at Uxmal, it now stands alone as a sort of triumphal arch. Both sides are richly decorated: on the east with geometric patterns; on the west (the back) with more of these and niches in the form of Maya huts or temples. Nearby is El Mirador, a temple with the well-preserved remains of a tall, elaborate roof-comb.

Oxkutzcab and around

From the village of **OXKUTZCAB** (also known as Huerta del Estado) on Hwy-184, 20km from Labna, you can head north back to Mérida via Ticul and Mani. Though there's little reason to overnight in Oxkutzcab, it's as good a place as any to stop for a while, with a huge **fruit market**, bustling and lively in the mornings, selling most of its produce by the crate or sack. Calles 51 and 50 edge the main park and the mercado, with a large Franciscan church cornering them. There are also some remote Puuc ruins at Kuiuc and Xkichmook, both of which lie off a minor road that runs south from the village of Oxkutzcab.

    Buses to Mérida via Ticul (2hr), leave about every hour from the **bus station** at the corner of C 56 and C 51; colectivos come and go from beside the mercado on C 51. Of the two basic **hotels**, *Hospedaje "Trujeque"*, C 48, opposite the park (☎997/5-05-68; ③), is cleaner and more comfortable, though *Hospedaje Rosalia*, C 54 no. 103 (☎997/5-03-37; ③), has the advantage of being just around the corner from the bus station. The Banamex **bank** on C 50, opposite the park, can only exchange US dollars cash – not travellers' cheques. **Restaurants** and cafeterias skirt the market, but if you fancy a long, lazy lunch, try a few blocks back at the *Restaurante Su Cabaña Suiza*, C 54 no. 101, where comidas are served in the tranquillity of a spacious open-sided *palapa*.

The Grutas de Loltún

Just outside Oxkutzcab, hidden away near the road to Labná, the **Grutas de Loltún** (daily 9am–5pm; US$4, US$2 on Sun), studded with stalactites and stalagmites (one in the shape of a giant corn cob), were revered by the Maya as a source of water from a time long before they built their cities. At the entrance, a huge bas-relief of a Jaguar Warrior guards the opening to the underworld, and throughout there are traces of ancient paintings and carvings on the walls. Nowadays the caves are lit, and there are spectacular guided tours (officially at 9.30am, 11am, 12.30pm, 2pm & 3pm; in practice it depends on who turns up, and when). The surrounding jungle is visible through the collapsed floor of the last gallery and ten-metre-long tree roots long find an anchor on the cavern floor. The *Restaurante Guerrero*, by the entrance to the caves, is welcome but expensive.

    There's very little transport to the caves **from Oxkutzcab**: taxis exploit their monopoly by charging well over the odds for the short run. Colectivos and trucks that pass the caves leave from C 51 next to the market; if you get there by 8.30am you may be able to catch the truck taking the cave employees to work. Getting back is less easy, as the trucks are full of workers and produce, but, if you wait, something will turn up.

Ticul, Mayapán and Mani

Conveniently located 80km south of Mérida on Hwy-184, **TICUL** is another excellent base for exploring the Puuc region. You can head straight back to Mérida from here or else take the slightly longer route via the Maya sites of **Mani** and **Mayapan**. The town is an important centre of Maya shamanism as well as a pottery-producing centre and it's full of shops selling reproduction Maya antiquities, mostly too big to carry home. Visitors are welcome to watch the manufacturing process at the *fabricas*. Despite this, Ticul lives life at a slow pace, with more bicycles (and passenger-carrying *triciclos*) than cars.

    On the main road between Mérida and Felipe Carrillo Puerto in Quintana Roo, Ticul is an important transport centre, well served by **buses** to and from Mérida and with services to Cancún. If you're arriving by bus from Mérida, you'll be dropped in C 24 on the corner with C 25, behind the church. Buses **from Campeche** don't go through Ticul so you'll have to get off at Santa Elena to catch one of the colectivos that leave from the main square between about 6am and 7pm; the trip takes about thirty minutes. **Trucks** for Oxkutzcab and surrounding villages set off when they're full from the side of the plaza next to the church; **combis** for Mérida leave from further down the same street.

Even-numbered roads run north to south, odd numbers east to west. Calle 23 is the main street, with the plaza at its eastern end at C 26. Half a block from the plaza, the *Sierra Sosa*, C 26 no. 199-A (☎997/2-00-08; ④), has basic **rooms**, with shower and fan (upstairs is better), and a few new a/c rooms with TV. The English-speaking manager, Luis Sierra, is a good source of information, and you can make international calls from reception. Alternatives include the plusher *Motel Cerro Inn*, C 23 no. 292, at the western edge of town (☎997/2-02-60; ④), in its own tree-shaded spacious grounds with an on-site palapa restaurant; and the newer *Hotel Bugambilias*, C 23 between C 44 and C 46 (☎997/2-07-61; ④), slightly closer to town than the *Cerro*, but with less character.

The best of the **restaurants** is the original *Los Almendros*, C 23 no. 207, which serves superb local dishes in pleasant surroundings. The *Restaurant Colorín*, next door to *Hotel Sierra Sosa* on C 26, does an inexpensive comida, or, if you fancy a large satisfying pizza, try *La Gondolia Pizzeria*, C 23 on the corner of C 26. As usual, the least expensive places are the *loncherías* near the bus station.

Mayapán and Mani

Forty-nine kilometres north of Ticul are the ruins of **MAYAPÁN**, the most powerful city in the Yucatán from the eleventh to the fifteenth century. Its history is somewhat vague but, according to Maya chronicles, it formed (with Chichén Itzá and Uxmal) one of a triumvirate of cities that as the **League of Mayapán** exercised control over the entire peninsula from around 987 to 1185. However, these dates, based on surviving Maya chronicles, are controversial, since archeological evidence suggests that Mayapán was not a significant settlement until the thirteenth century. The rival theory has Mayapán founded around 1263, after the fall of Chichén Itzá.

The league broke up when the **Cocom** dynasty of Mayapán attacked and overwhelmed the rulers of an already declining Chichén Itzá, establishing themselves as sole controllers of the peninsula. Mayapán became a huge city by the standards of the day, with a population of some fifteen thousand in a site covering five square kilometres, in which traces of more than four thousand buildings have been found – here, rulers of subject cities were forced to live where they could be kept under control, perhaps even as hostages. This hegemony was maintained until 1441 when Ah Xupan, a Xiu leader from Uxmal, finally led a rebellion that succeeded in overthrowing the Cocom and destroying their city – thus paving the way for the disunited tribalism that the Spanish found on their arrival, which made their conquest so much easier.

What can be seen today is a disappointment – the buildings anyway were crude and small by Maya standards, at best poor copies of what had gone before. This has led to its widespread dismissal as a "decadent" and failing society, but a powerful case can be made for the fact that it was merely a changing one. Here the priests no longer dominated – hence the lack of great ceremonial centres – and what grew instead was a more genuinely urban society: highly militaristic, no doubt, but also far more centralized and more reliant on trade than anything seen previously.

After the fall of Mayapán, the Xiu abandoned Uxmal and founded **MANI**, 15km east of Ticul. It's hard to believe that what is now simply a small village was, at the time of the Conquest, the largest city the Spanish encountered. Fortunately for the Spanish, its ruler, Ah Kukum Xiu, converted to Christianity and became their ally. Here, in 1548, was founded one of the earliest and largest **Franciscan monasteries** in the Yucatán. This still stands, surrounded now by Maya huts, and just about the only evidence of Mani's past glories are the ancient stones used in its construction. In front of the church, in 1562, Bishop Diego de Landa held the notorious *auto-da-fé* in which he burned the city's ancient records (because they "contained nothing in which there was not to be seen the superstitions and lies of the devil"), destroying virtually all surviving original Maya literature.

Chichén Itzá

Chichén Itzá, the most famous, the most extensively restored, and by far the most visited of all Maya sites, lies conveniently astride the main road from Mérida to Cancún and the Caribbean, about 120km from Mérida and a little more than 200km from the coast. There's a fast and very regular bus service all along this road, making it perfectly feasible to visit as a day's excursion from Mérida, or en route from Mérida to the coast (or even as a day out from Cancún, as many tour buses do). The site, though, deserves better, and both to do the ruins justice and to see them when they're not entirely overrun by tourists, an overnight stop is well worth considering – either at the site itself or, less extravagantly, at the nearby village of **Pisté** or in Valladolid (see p.547).

The route from Mérida: Izamal and Aké

If your route to Chichén Itzá is fairly leisurely, **IZAMAL**, 72km from Mérida, is the one place that does merit a detour. The town is something of a quiet backwater whose colonial air is denied by its inhabitants' allegiance to their traditional dress and lifestyle. It was formerly an important Maya religious centre, where they worshipped **Itzamna**, mythical founder of the ancient city and one of the gods of creation, at a series of huge pyramid-temples of the same name. Most are now no more than low hillocks in the surrounding country, but two survive in the town itself. One, **Kinich Kakmo** (daily 8am–8pm; free), just a couple of blocks from the central plaza and dedicated to the sun god, has been partly restored. The other had its top lopped off by the Spanish and was replaced with a vast monastery, the **convent of St Anthony of Padua** (daily; free), which was painted a deep yellow, like much of the town, for the Pope's visit in 1993. The porticoed atrium is particularly beautiful and photogenic in the late afternoon, and inside it is a statue of the Virgin of Izamal, patron saint of the Yucatán.

There are a couple of very basic hotels in Izamal, both on the zócalo. Don't get caught out with no money here as there isn't a bank, though there is a **post office** on the main square. *Restaurant Portales* on the main square serves good Mexican **food**, as does the *Café Restaurant Los Norteños*, next to the bus station, one block back from the main square. **Buses to Izamal** leave every 45 minutes from Autotransportes de Oriente in Mérida (see p.531). They take a little over an hour and return to Mérida every 45 minutes. It's therefore possible to visit Izamal in a comfortable afternoon trip from Mérida.

The Maya city of **Aké**, which lies halfway between Izamal and Mérida on the highway, was probably in alliance with Izamal and is linked to it by one of the peninsula's largest *sacbes* (Maya roads). One of the most impressive buildings here is a large, pillared building on a platform, surrounded by a huge plaza of twenty thousand square metres. There is also a ruined henequen hacienda, San Lorenzo de Aké, on the same site, whose church is built over one of the temples.

Practicalities

Arriving at Chichén Itzá you'll find that the highway, which once cut straight through the middle of the ruins, has been re-routed around the site. If you're on a through bus it may drop you at the junction of the bypass and the old road, about ten minutes' walk from the entrance – most, though, drive right up to the site entrance. Although blocked off by gates at each side of the fenced-in site, the old road still exists, conveniently dividing the ruins in two: **Chichén Viejo** (Old Chichén) to the south, **Chichén Nuevo** (New or "Toltec" Chichén) to the north.

The main **entry to the site** (daily 8am–5pm, though the process of getting everyone out starts at least an hour earlier; US$4, extra with video camera or tripod, free on Sun) is to the west, at the Mérida end. Keep your ticket, which permits re-entry, and check the

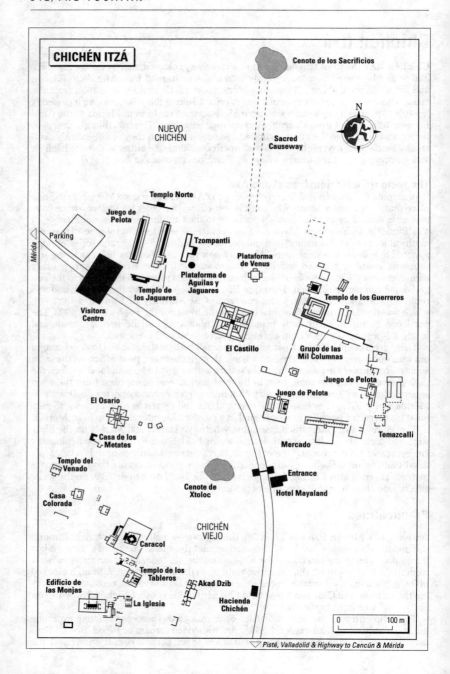

CHICHÉN ITZÁ

Cenote de los Sacrificios

NUEVO CHICHÉN

Sacred Causeway

N

Templo Norte

Juego de Pelota

Parking

Tzompantli

Plataforma de Venus

Plataforma de Aguilas y Jaguares

Templo de los Jaguares

Templo de los Guerreros

Visitors Centre

El Castillo

Grupo de las Mil Columnas

Juego de Pelota

Juego de Pelota

El Osario

Casa de los Metates

Mercado

Temazcalli

Templo del Venado

Casa Colorada

Cenote de Xtoloc

Entrance

Hotel Mayaland

Caracol

CHICHÉN VIEJO

Templo de los Tableros

Akad Dzib

Edificio de las Monjas

La Iglesia

Hacienda Chichén

0   100 m

Pisté, Valladolid & Highway to Cancún & Mérida

timetable for admissions to the various buildings – most open only for a couple of hours each day, and you'll want to plan your wanderings around their schedules. There are bus and car parks here, and a huge **visitor centre** (open until 10pm) with a museum, restaurant, and shops selling souvenirs, film, maps and guides (best are the Panorama series). **Guided tours** of the ruins can be arranged at the visitors centre. Group tours (9am–3.30pm) for six to eight people, in Spanish or English, cost around US$8 per person. Private tours (8am–2.30pm) cost around US$33 per guide. There's a nightly **son et lumière** in English (9pm; US$4) and Spanish (7pm; US$2): worth seeing if you're staying nearby – it's no great shakes, but there's nothing else to do in the evening.

You can also buy tickets and get in at the **smaller eastern gate** by the *Hotel Mayaland* (see below), where there are fewer facilities. Book at the hotel reception for two-hour **horseback riding trips** around Chichén Viejo.

To make your way to the Caribbean coast from Chichén Itzá, it's best to take any bus you can as far as Valladolid (see p.547), and if necessary change there for a first-class service.

Staying near Chichén Itzá

Chichén Itzá boasts some excellent **hotels** virtually on site. The *Hacienda Chichén* (☎985/1-00-45; in Mérida ☎99/24-88-44, fax 24-50-11; in US ☎1-800/624-8451; ⑨), which has a couple of small ruins within its grounds, is the best; write to C 60 no. 488, Mérida 97000. The even posher *Hotel Mayaland*, Carretera Mérida–Puerto Juárez Km 120 (☎985/1-01-28 or 1-00-77, fax 1-01-29; ⑨), has a gorgeous colonial-style dining room and rooms in luxurious thatched huts dotted about the gardens. Nearby Pisté has cheaper options.

Least aesthetically pleasing, but still pretty good, is *Villas Arqueologicas* (☎985/1-00-34, fax 1-00-18; ⑧), a modern place run by Club Med, with rooms set out round a patio enclosing a pool and cocktail bar: by night, its library of archeological and architectural tomes doubles as a disco (usually empty). All three hotels have pools, which are open to anyone who eats lunch there, though in the *Villas Arqueologicas* you could probably get away with just having a drink at the poolside bar.

Alternatively, you can take a taxi in the **other direction** (east) from the ruins and get to the tiny *Dolores Alba* (☎985/28-56-50; in Mérida ☎99/28-56-50; ⑤), just over 2km away, with a restaurant and rooms around a pool – the best value here if you don't mind being stuck by the road in the middle of nowhere (but still much less than an hour's walk from the site). The staff are very helpful and friendly and will provide transport to the site (but not back). Rooms can be booked in advance at the hotel of the same name in Mérida.

PISTÉ

Pisté is an unattractive village straddling the main road between Mérida and Valladolid, about twenty minutes' walk from the ruins. Its saving grace is that it enables visitors to get up early enough to miss the teeming hordes of package tourists who arrive at Chichén Itzá at about 10.30am. **Buses** pass Pisté every thirty minutes for Mérida and about every hour for Valladolid. There are also services to Cancún and Playa del Carmen.

Most **hotels** are on the main road, between the village and the ruins, so it's easy to shop around for the best deal. *Hotel Misión Chichén Itzá*, Km 118 (☎985/1-00-22, fax 1-00-23; ⑥), has a laid-back atmosphere and the best pool in Pisté. The *Piramide Inn and Trailer Park*, 2km from the ruins on the Mérida–Valladolid road (☎985/1-01-15; ⑥), is conveniently situated near the bus stop and the western entrance to the ruins – and there's a pool open to non-residents. The friendly *Posada Olalde* (⑤), Calle 6, off the main road, has basic, clean rooms with fans and hot water; coming from the bus terminal, turn left by *El Guayacan Artesenía*. The *Posada Maya*, calles 41 and 42, 20m down the road by the sign to Tizimín, is a new basic, concrete hotel, away from the village centre, with hammock space (US$3) for about five people (④). Budget travellers should head for the *Posada El Carrousel* (☎985/1-00-78; ③); the best rooms are at the back, away from the road.

There are **restaurants** lining the road, alongside the hotels. The best value are the *Posada El Carrousel* and *Las Mestizas*, which does some good value regional cuisine. The pricier hotels all have their own restaurants.

The site

Though in most minds **CHICHÉN ITZÁ** represents the very image of the Maya, in reality it is its very divergence from accepted Maya tradition that makes it so fascinating, and so important to archeologists. Today, its history remains hotly disputed. Archeologists are fairly certain that the city rose to power in the Terminal Classic period (between 800 and 1000 AD), and was probably established about five hundred years before that, but what they are undecided about is exactly who built the city. Much of the evidence at the site – an emphasis on human sacrifice, the presence of a huge ball court and the glorification of military activity – points to a strong Mexican influence; considering the dates of Chichén's ascendancy, it seemed that this was the result of the city's defeat by the Toltecs, a theory reinforced by the resemblance of the temple of the warriors to the L-shaped colonnade at Tula, along with numerous depictions of the Toltec god-king, the feathered serpent, **Quetzalcoatl** (Kukulkán to the Maya).

However, recent work at Chichén Itzá has revealed some continuity between Chichén Itzá and earlier Maya sites in the southern lowlands. It's now thought that Chichén Itzá was never invaded by the Toltecs, but occupied by Maya throughout its history, with the Mexican influence coming via its chief trading partner, the Chontal Maya or Putun of the Gulf Coast lowlands. The Chontal were themselves influenced by Mexico and Oaxaca through a thriving network of trade and political allegiances. This new theory is not without its own problems, though: while the **Itzá** kings who ruled Chichén Itzá were referred to by the contemporary Maya as "foreigners", the continuity of styles with the Maya sites of the southern lowlands suggests that the "foreigners" may actually have been Maya who moved north after droughts caused the abandonment of the forest cities.

Chichén Nuevo

If it's still reasonably early, head first for **El Castillo** (or the Pyramid of Kukulkán), the structure that dominates the site. This should allow you to climb it before the full heat of the day, and get a good overview of the entire area. It is a simple, relatively unadorned square building, with a monumental stairway climbing each face (though only two are restored), rising in nine receding terraces to a temple at the top. The simplicity is deceptive, however, as the building is in fact the **Maya calendar** made stone: each staircase has 91 steps, which, added to the single step at the main entrance to the temple, amounts to 365; other numbers relevant to the Maya calendar recur throughout the construction. Most remarkably, at sunset on the spring and autumn equinoxes, the great serpents' heads at the foot of the main staircase are joined to their tails (at the top) by an undulating body of shadow – an event of just a few hours that draws spectators, and awed worshippers, by the thousand.

Inside the present structure, an earlier pyramid survives almost wholly intact. An entrance has been opened at the bottom of El Castillo, through which you reach a narrow, dank and claustrophobic stairway (formerly the outside of the inner pyramid) that leads steeply to a temple on the top. In its outer room is a rather crude chac-mool, but in the **inner sanctuary**, now railed off, stands one of the greatest finds at the site: an altar, or throne, in the form of a jaguar, painted bright red and inset with jade "spots" and eyes – the teeth are real jaguar teeth. This discovery was one of the first to undermine the Toltec theory: though the sculpture is apparently Toltec in style, it predates their ostensible arrival.

THE "TOLTEC" PLAZA

The Castillo stands on the edge of the great grassy plaza that formed the focus of Nuevo Chichén Itzá: all its most important buildings are here, and from the northern edge a *sacbe*, or sacred causeway, leads to the great **Cenote de los Sacrificios**. The **Templo de los Guerreros** (Temple of the Warriors), and the adjoining **Grupo de las Mil Columnas** (Group of the Thousand Columns), take up the eastern edge of the plaza. These are the structures that most recall the great Toltec site of Tula, near México, both in design and in detail – in particular the colonnaded courtyard (which would originally have been roofed with some form of thatch) and the use of atlantean columns, representing warriors in armour, their arms raised above their heads. Throughout, the temple is richly decorated with carvings and sculptures (originally with paintings, too) of jaguars and eagles devouring human hearts, feathered serpents, warriors and, the one undeniably Maya feature, masks of Chac. On top are two superb **Chac-mools**: offerings were placed on the stomachs of these reclining figures, representing the messengers who would take the sacrifice to the gods, or perhaps the divinities themselves.

Once again, the Templo de los Guerreros was built over an earlier temple, in which (during set hours) some remnants of faded **murals** can be made out. The "thousand" columns alongside originally formed a square, on the far side of which is the building known as the **Mercado**, although there's no evidence that this actually was a marketplace. Near here, too, is a small, ruinous ball court.

Walking across the plaza towards the main ball court, you pass three small platforms. The **Plataforma de Venus** is a simple, raised, square block, with a stairway up each side guarded by feathered serpents. Here, rites associated with Quetzalcoatl in his role of Venus, the morning star, would have been carried out. Slightly smaller, but otherwise virtually identical in design, is the **Aquilas y Jaguares** platform, on which you'll see relief carvings of eagles and jaguars holding human hearts. Human sacrifices may even have been carried out here, judging by the proximity of the third platform, the **Tzompantli**, where victims' skulls were hung on display. This is carved on every side with grotesquely grinning stone skulls.

THE BALL COURT

Chichén Itzá's **Juego de Pelota** (ball court), on the western side of the plaza, is the largest known in existence – some 90m long. Its design is classically Maya: a capital I shape surrounded by temples, with the goals, or target rings, halfway along each side. Along the bottom of each side wall runs a sloping panel decorated in low relief with scenes of the game and its players. Although the rules and full significance of the game remain a mystery, it was clearly not a Saturday afternoon kick-about in the park. The players are shown processing towards a circular central symbol, the symbol of death, and one player (thought to be the winning captain – just right of the centre) has been decapitated, while another (to the left) holds his head and a ritual knife. Along the top runs the stone body of a snake, whose heads stick out at either end of this "bench".

At each end of the court stand small buildings with open **galleries** overlooking the field of play – the low one at the south may simply have been a grandstand, that at the north (the **Templo Norte**, also known as the Temple of the Bearded Man, after a sculpture inside) was almost certainly a temple – perhaps, too, the umpires' stand. Inside, there are several worn relief carvings and a whispering gallery effect that enables you to be heard clearly at the far end of the court, and to hear what's going on there.

The **Templo de los Jaguares** also overlooks the playing area, but from the side; to get to it, you have to go back out to the plaza. At the bottom – effectively the outer wall of the ball court – is a little portico supported by two pillars, between which a stone jaguar stands sentinel. Inside are some wonderful, rather worn, relief carvings of Maya priests, warriors, and animals, birds and plants. Beside this, a very steep, narrow staircase ascends to a platform overlooking the court and to the **Upper Temple** (restricted opening hours), with its fragments of a mural depicting battle scenes.

The **Cenote de los Sacrificios** lies at the end of the causeway that leads off through the trees from the northern side of the plaza – about 300m away. It's a remarkable phenomenon, an almost perfectly round hole in the limestone surface of the earth, some 60m in diameter and more than 40m deep, the bottom half full of water. It was thanks to the presence of this natural well (and perhaps another in the southern half of the site) that the city could survive at all, and it gives Chichén Itzá its present name "At the Edge of the Well of the Itzá". This well was regarded as a portal to the "otherworld" and Maya would throw offerings into it – incense, statues, jade and especially metal disks (a few of them gold), engraved and embossed with figures and glyphs – and also human sacrificial victims. People who were thrown in and survived emerged with the power of prophecy, having spoken with the gods. A new cafeteria now overlooks the well, a distraction for anyone contemplating the religious and mystical significance of the cenote.

Chichén Viejo

The southern half of the site is the most sacred part for contemporary Maya, though the buildings here are not, on the whole, in such good condition: less restoration work has been carried out so far, and the ground is not so extensively cleared. A path leads from the road opposite El Castillo to all the major structures, passing first the pyramid known as **El Osario** (aka the High Priest's Grave), currently undergoing restoration. Externally it is very similar to El Castillo, but inside, most unusually, a series of **tombs** was discovered. A shaft, explored at the end of the last century, drops down from the top through five crypts, in each of which was found a skeleton and a trap door leading to the next. The fifth is at ground level, but here too there was a trap door, and steps cut through the rock to a sixth chamber that opens onto a huge underground cavern – the burial place of the high priest. Sadly the shaft and cavern are not open to the public.

Near here, also very ramshackle, are the **Templo del Venado** (Temple of the Deer) and the **Casa Colorada** (Red House), with a cluster of ruins known as the Southwest Group beyond them. Follow the path round, however, and you arrive at **El Caracol** (the Snail, for its shape; also called the Observatory), a circular, domed tower standing on two rectangular platforms and looking remarkably like a twentieth-century observatory in outline. No telescope, however, was mounted in the roof, which instead has slits aligned with various points of astronomical observation. Four doors at the cardinal points lead into the tower, where there's a circular chamber and a spiral staircase leading to the upper level, from where sightings were made.

The so-called **Edificio de las Monjas** (the Nunnery) is a palace complex showing several stages of construction. It's in rather poor condition, the rooms mostly filled with rubble and inhabited by flocks of swallows, and part of the facade was blasted away by a nineteenth-century explorer, but is nonetheless a building of grand proportions. Its **annexe** has an elaborate facade in the Chenes style, covered in masks of Chac which combine to make one giant mask, with the door as a mouth. **La Iglesia** (the Church), a small building standing beside the convent, is by contrast a clear demonstration of Puuc design, with a low band of unadorned masonry around the bottom surmounted by an elaborate mosaic frieze and a roof-comb. Hook-nosed masks of Chac again predominate, but above the doorway are also the figures of the four **bacabs**, mythological creatures that held up the sky – a snail and a turtle on one side, an armadillo and a crab on the other.

Beyond Las Monjas, a path leads in about fifteen minutes to a further group of ruins – among the oldest on the site, but unrestored. Nearer at hand is the **Akad Dzib**, a relatively plain block of palace rooms which takes its name ("Obscure Writings") from some undeciphered hieroglyphs found inside. There are, too, red palm prints on the walls of some of the chambers – a sign frequently found in Maya buildings, whose significance is not yet understood. From here you can head back to the road past El Caracol and the Cenote de Xtoloc.

Valladolid and around

The second town of Yucatán state, **VALLADOLID** is around 40km from Chichén Itzá, still close enough to beat the crowds to the site on an early bus, and of interest in its own right. Although it took a severe bashing in the nineteenth-century Caste Wars, the town has retained a strong colonial feel, and centres on a pretty, peaceful zócalo. The most famous of the surviving churches is sixteenth-century **San Bernardino**, 1km southwest of the zócalo (daily 9am–11pm; mass daily at 6pm). Built over one of the town's **cenotes**, **Sis-Ha**, the church is currently under restoration: the buildings are very impressive, but there's little left inside as, like so many of the Yucatán's churches, San Bernardino was sacked by the local Indians in the Wars. Valladolid's other cenote, **Zací**, on C 36 between C 39 and C 37 (daily 8am–6pm; US$2), has become a tourist attraction, with a museum and an open-air restaurant at the entrance.

Arrival and information

Buses between Mérida and Cancún don't go into Valladolid, but stop at **La Isleta**, a small bus station on the highway, where you transfer to a local bus for the ten-minute into town. Valladolid's **bus station** is located on C 37 between C 54 and C 56, seven blocks to the west of the zócalo. *De paso* buses run at least hourly to both Mérida and Cancún and there are at least ten daily departures for Playa del Carmen, most of which are via Cancún, though a few take the road past Cobá and call at Tulum (see following chapter). Some local second-class buses begin their journey here, too, for the above destinations and the smaller towns, including Tizimín, for Río Lagartos.

To get to the centre from the bus station takes about ten minutes. Turn left onto C 37, then right after a couple of blocks, then left again, following C 39 to the pretty zócalo; you'll pass some of the cheaper **hotels** on the way. The **tourist office** is on the southeastern corner of the zócalo (daily 9am–noon & 4–6pm). Though in theory there's plenty of information available, including free maps of Valladolid, you'll be lucky to find the office attended. Best to head for **El Bazaar**, a collection of inexpensive restaurants on the corner of C 39 and C 40 on the zócalo; the souvenir shop here has maps and current information. The **post office** is on the zócalo, near the corner of C 39 on C 40 (Mon–Fri 8am–2.30pm), as is Bancomer, which changes travellers' cheques between 9.30am and 12.30pm. Banco de Sureste in Supermaz, a shopping plaza at C 39 no. 229, changes travellers' cheques every day (including weekends) until 8.30pm and cash until 9pm (closed 2–6.30pm). In the same plaza you'll find a shop with **Internet** facilities (*afa@mail.valladolid.net.mx*; US$5 an hour) and a **laundry**. For national and international **telephone calls** there are Ladatel casetas at the bus station and on the zócalo (daily 7am–10pm). You can **rent bikes** from Refaccionaría de Bicicletas Paulino Sliva at C 44 no. 191, between C 39 and C 41, for US$2 an hour.

Accommodation

Valladolid's budget hotels lie between the bus station and the centre, but for more atmosphere it's worth splashing out a bit to stay in colonial style on the zócalo.

María de la Luz, C 42, on the zócalo (☎ & fax 985/6-20-71). The rooms are less luxurious than the lobby, but comfortable and good value, with a/c. The restaurant, which serves huge inexpensive buffet breakfasts, opens onto the zócalo, and there's a pool. ④.

María Guadalupe, C 44 no. 198 (☎985/6-20-68). The best-value cheap hotel with clean, well-kept rooms with baths. Colectivos for the cenote at Dzitnup leave from outside. ③.

Maya, C 41 no. 231, four blocks west of the zócalo (no phone). Clean, cheap hotel, with rooms around a courtyard; some have a/c. ②–④.

El Mesón del Marqués, C 39 no. 203, on the zócalo (☎985/6-20-73 or 6-30-42, fax 6-22-80). Lovely hotel in a former colonial mansion, overlooking a courtyard with fountains and lush plants. There's a wonderful palm-fringed pool, and one of the best restaurants in town. ⑤.

Mendoza, C 39 no. 204, corner of C 46 (☎ & fax 985/6-20-02). The sole advantage of this place is its proximity to the bus station, but you'll find better quality if you press on towards the centre. ③–④.

San Clemente, C 42, corner of C 41 (☎985/6-31-61). Just off the zócalo, this very comfortable hotel has a restaurant and pool. Prices are similar to the *María de la Luz*, but the facilities are better. ④.

Zací, C 44 no. 193, between 39 and 37 (☎985/6-21-67). Pleasant hotel with a lovely, plant-filled courtyard and a small pool. Rooms have either a fan or, for a few dollars more, a/c and cable TV. ④.

Eating and drinking

Whatever your budget, to eat well in Valladolid you don't have to stray further than the zócalo, where you can get inexpensive snacks or treat yourself without going into debt.

El Bazaar, northeastern corner of the zócalo, C 39 and C 40. Inexpensive *loncherías* and pizzerias, always busy and open until late.

El Mesón del Marqués, C 39 no. 203, on the zócalo. Probably Valladolid's best restaurant, offering tranquillity in the centre of town and tables around the fountain of the hotel courtyard, though it's often packed with tour groups. Yucatecan specialities such as lime soup and *poc-chuc*.

Restaurante San Bernadino de Siena, C 49 no. 227, two blocks from Convento San Bernadino (☎985/6-27-20). Locally known as *Don Juanito's* and frequented mostly by Mexicans, this highly recommended, mid-price restaurant is a great place for a lazy lunch or dinner away from the hustle and bustle of the town centre.

Around Valladolid

From Valladolid the vast majority of traffic heads straight on to Cancún and the Caribbean beaches. There are a few places worth taking time out to explore, however, and, if you have more time, an alternative is to head north via Tizimín to **Río Lagartos** or **San Felipe**. You'll need to make an early start if you want to co-ordinate your buses, go on a flamingo trip and get back to Valladolid in the same day – the last bus for Tizimín from Río Lagartos leaves at 5.30pm and the last bus for Valladolid leaves Tizimín at 7pm. You'll have to return to Valladolid to head on to the Caribbean coast.

Cenote Dzitnup

Seven kilometres west of Valladolid, the remarkable **Cenote Dzitnup**, or X'Keken (daily 8am–5pm; US$1.50), is reached, by descending into a cave, where a nearly circular pool of crystal-clear, turquoise water is illuminated by a shaft of light from an opening in the roof. A swim in the ice-cold water is a fantastic experience, but take a sweater as the temperature in the cave is noticeably cooler than outside.

There are direct colectivos to Dzitnup from outside the *Hotel Maria Guadalupe* in Valladolid (see above). Alternatively, any westbound second-class bus will drop you at the turn-off, 5km from Valladolid, from where it's a 2km walk down a signed track. You could also take a taxi or, best of all, cycle from Valladolid.

Balankanché

Thirty-four kilometres from Valladolid, on the way to Chichén Itzá, you can visit the **Caves of Balankanché**, where in 1959 a sealed passageway was discovered leading to a series of caverns in which the ancient population had left offerings to Chac. "Guided tours" (in English daily 11am, 1pm & 3pm; US$7, US$2.50 on Sun) – in reality, a taped commentary – lead you past the usual stalactites and stalagmites, an underground pool and, most interestingly, many of the original Maya offerings still in situ. Be warned that in places the caves can be cold, damp and thoroughly claustrophobic. Charles Gallenkamp's book *Maya* has an excellent chapter devoted to the discovery of the caves, and to the ritual of exorcism that a local *h-man* (traditional priest) insisted on carrying out to placate the ancient gods and disturbed spirits. Buses between Valladolid and Mérida will drop you at *las grutas*.

Río Lagartos and Las Coloradas

Travelling by bus from Valladolid north to Río Lagartos, you have to change at the elegant colonial town of **TIZIMÍN**, 51km from Valladolid. There's little to see, but the small **Parque Zoológico de la Reina** has animals from all over the peninsula, and the pretty plaza is peaceful enough for whiling away a few hours. The best of the modest but overpriced hotels in the centre is *María Antonia*, C 50 (☎986/3-23-84; ④). Tizimín also has direct bus services to and from Mérida and Cancún.

RÍO LAGARTOS, 100km north of Valladolid, stands on a lagoon in marshy coastal flatland, inhabited by vast colonies of **pink flamingos**. Despite talk of turning the area into a new tourist centre, so far it remains a backwater fishing village. It's easy enough to visit on a day-trip from Valladolid, but if you want to stay, try the very comfortable *Cabañas dos Hermanos*, at the back of a family home, by the beach, which sleep two or three people and have private bathrooms and pay-as-you-view cable TV. From the bus station, turn right and continue on to the water's edge. You can also **camp** on the lagoon shore almost anywhere near town. A boat trip over to the seaward shore of the spit that encloses the lagoon will bring you to a couple of **beaches**, but they're not up to much, and in the end it's the flamingos alone that make a visit worthwhile.

You're likely to be swamped by offers to take you out to see the flamingos as soon get off the bus or out of your car. If not, the best place to start is the friendly *Restaurante Isla Contoy*, on the waterfront, where you can leaf though a book of photos and visitors' comments while waiting for your boat to turn up. A **boat** to visit the many feeding sites costs around US$35, with a maximum of seven people, but the price and length of the trip are infinitely negotiable. Make sure that your guide understands that you don't want to harass the flamingos, as some will get too close if they think their passengers would prefer to see some action. If you want to be certain that you are getting a knowledgeable guide, controlled by the syndicate that protects the flamingos, prearrange a trip with Adrian Marfil, C 16 no. 100 (☎98/3-26-68), or from Cancún with EcoloMex Tours (☎98/84-38-05, fax 84-38-49). As well as flamingos, you're likely to see fishing eagles, spoonbills and, if you're lucky, one of the very few remaining crocodiles for which Río Lagartos was named.

The most spectacular flamingo colony is at **Las Coloradas**, on the narrow spit that separates the lagoon from the sea about 16km east of Río Lagartos. There's a small village and salt factory here, but you'll need your own transport, as the bus timetable does not give you a chance to stay long enough to see anything.

San Felipe

If it's beaches you're after, **SAN FELIPE**, 12km west of Río Lagartos, is a much better bet – many of the buses from Valladolid to Río Lagartos come out here. There are a few cheap rooms for rent, above the Marufo cinema, and at least one good restaurant, the *El*

Payaso. However, most people get a boat across to the offshore spit to set up **camp** on one of a number of beaches. At Mexican holiday times these are positively crowded, the rest of the year quite deserted. If you do camp, be sure to bring protection against mosquitoes; if not, it's easy enough to arrange for the boat to collect you in the evening.

Isla Holbox

Although most traffic between Mérida and the coast heads directly east to Cancún, it is possible to turn north at Valladolid or Nuevo X-Can to **Chiquilá**, where you can board the ferry for **Isla Holbox**, a 25-kilometre-long island near the easternmost point of the Gulf coast. Sometimes touted as a new beach paradise to fill the place that Isla Mujeres once had in travellers' affections, it's by no means as attractive: the water is murkier than on the Caribbean coast and the sea can be rough. However, there are miles of empty beaches to enjoy, and anyone who's come from the more touristy resorts will find the island's relaxed, laid-back pace – and the genuinely warm welcome – something of a relief.

Practicalities

Buses for Chiquilá leave Valladolid (2hr 30min) and Tizimín (1hr 30min) a couple of times a day. Catch an early bus to make sure you get the afternoon ferry. Coming from the east, get a bus to the road junction just before Nuevo X-Can and wait for a colectivo (US$1) to Kantunilkin, about halfway to Chiquilá, where you can pick up the bus. The **Chiquilá ferry** for Holbox leaves twice a day, at 8am and 1pm (1hr; US$1.50), and returns at 5am and noon. Holbox is also served by a **car ferry**, leaving Chiquilá at 10am (daily except Thurs & Sun) and returning at 6am. Make sure you don't miss the boat: Chiquilá is not a place you want to get stranded. There's a restaurant and a store, but little else; if you need to stay the night in order to get the early ferry, you could camp under the *palapa* by the basketball court – mosquito netting is essential.

Isla Holbox has a few simple and inexpensive **hotels**; to contact them, call ☎988/7-16-68 and ask for the hotel by name or by its extension number. The first hotel you see, the *Posada Flamingo* (ext 102; ①), just to the right of the dock, has basic clean rooms with hot showers. It's handy for the early ferry and the friendly owners **rent scooters** and organize **boat trips**. To get nearer the **beach** you'll have to walk across the island, which takes about ten minutes. Here you'll find the *Posada Los Arcos* (①) on the plaza (ask at the *Tienda Dionora*), and, even nearer the sea, the cabañas at the *Posada Dingrid* (①). You'll also spot **houses for rent**, which can be worth it if you plan to stay a while. A couple of shops provide basic supplies and there are some good **seafood restaurants**, but little in the way of entertainment; have a drink and a chat with a fisherman, though, and you may get a chance to go fishing. Bring plenty of repellent as the mosquitoes here are some of the worst in Mexico.

QUINTANA ROO AND THE CARIBBEAN COAST

The coastal state of **Quintana Roo** was a forgotten frontier for most of modern Mexican history – its lush tropical forests exploited for their mahogany and *chicle* (from which chewing gum is made), but otherwise unsettled, a haven for outlaws and pirates, and for Maya living beyond the reach of central government. In the 1970s, however, the stunning palm-fringed white-sand **beaches** of the Caribbean coast and its magnificent offshore **coral reefs** began to attract **tourists**: the first highways were built, new townships settled, and the place finally became a full state (as opposed to an externally administered Federal Territory) in 1974.

REEF BEHAVIOUR

Coral reefs are the richest and most complex ecosystems on earth, but they are also very fragile. The colonies grow at a rate of only around 5cm per year, so they must be treated with care and respect if they are not to be damaged beyond repair. Remember to follow these **simple rules** while you are snorkelling, diving or in a boat.

- Never touch or stand on corals, as the living polyps on their surface are easily damaged.
- Avoid disturbing the sand around corals. Quite apart from spoiling visibility, the cloud of sand will settle over the corals and smother them.
- Don't remove shells, sponges or other creatures from the reef and avoid buying reef products from souvenir shops.
- Don't use suntan lotion in reef areas, as the oils remain on the surface of the water.
- Don't anchor boats on the reef: use the permanently secured buoys instead.
- Don't throw litter overboard.
- Check where you are allowed to go before going fishing.
- If you are an out-of-practice diver, make sure you revise your diving skills away from the reef first.

The stretch of **coast** beween Cancún and **Tulum** is the most heavily visited – and the focus of much recent, rapid hotel construction. Modern development is centred on the resorts of **Cancún** and **Playa del Carmen**, along with the islands of **Isla Mujeres** and **Cozumel**, which have become some of the world's most desirable package tour destinations and increasingly overdeveloped as a result. You'll see images of the Maya everywhere here, but while their culture is shamelessly used to promote tourism, little of this money ever reaches the Maya themselves, and where they haven't been forced out by developers, they continue to live in poverty in small communal villages in the scrub forest, growing maize and carving or weaving a few trinkets for tourists.

Further south things get quieter: the beaches within the **Si'an Ka'an Biosphere Reserve** are nesting sites for turtles, and behind them are areas of mangrove swamp, home to numerous animals including jaguar and even manatee. The vast and beautiful **Laguna de Bacalar** was an important stop on the Maya's pre-Columbian trade routes and was later used as an outpost for arms shipment from Belize during the Caste Wars. **Chetumal**, the state capital but otherwise a dull, duty-free border town, is of chief importance as a gateway to and from Belize. The southern coast, while rewarding for naturalists and adventurers, is difficult to visit: only a couple of roads offer access, and public transport is minimal.

Inland, Quintana Roo is little visited. There are some spectacular **Maya sites** here, though they are not as accessible or as well restored as the pristine open-air museums of Yucatán. **Cobá**, a lakeside Maya city just off the road to Valladolid, has some of the Maya World's tallest temples, but is only partially excavated, hidden in jungle swarming with mosquitoes. The early Classic site of **Kohunlich**, famous for its giant sculpted faces of the Maya sun god, lies in the heart of the Petén jungle that stretches into Guatemala and Belize; even more remote are the ruins of **Kinichna**, **Chacchoben** and **Dzibanche**.

Cancún

Hand-picked by computer, **CANCÚN** is, if nothing else, proof of Mexico's remarkable ability to get things done in a hurry if the political will is there. A fishing village of 120 people as recently as 1970, it's now a city with a resident population of half a million and receives almost two million visitors a year. To some extent the computer selected its

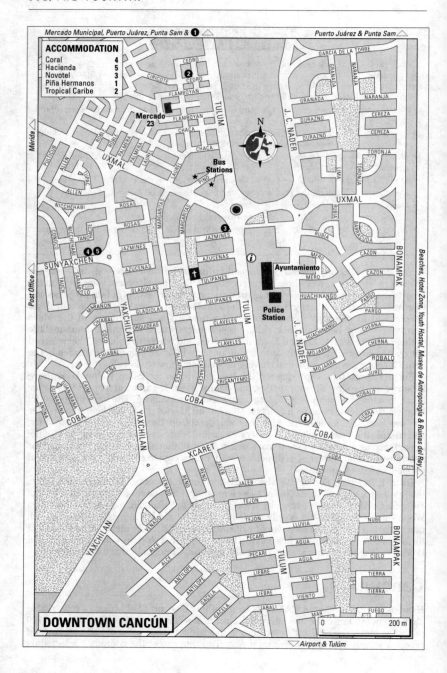

DOWNTOWN CANCÚN

location well. Cancún is marginally closer to Miami than it is to México, and if you come on an all-inclusive package tour the place has a lot to offer: striking modern hotels on white-sand beaches; high-class entertainment including parachuting, jet-skiing, scuba-diving and golf; a hectic nightlife; and from here much of the rest of the Yucatán is easily accessible. For the independent traveller, though, it is expensive, and can be frustrating and unwelcoming. You may well be forced to spend the night here, but without pots of money the true pleasures of the place will elude you.

There are, in effect, two quite separate parts to Cancún: the *zona commercial* downtown – the shopping and residential centre which, as it gets older, is becoming genuinely earthy – and the *zona hotelera*, a string of hotels and tourist amenities around "Cancún island", actually a narrow strip of sandy land connected to the mainland at each end by causeways. It encloses a huge lagoon, so there's water on both sides.

Arrival, information and city transport

Charter flights from Europe and South America, and direct scheduled flights from dozens of cities in Mexico and North and Central America, land at the **airport**, 15km south of the centre. Colectivos take you to any part of town for a fixed price (US$12 per person) – buy your ticket from the desk by the exit. Taxis cost more. Arriving by bus, you'll pull in at one of the two **bus stations**, next to each other in the heart of downtown, just by a roundabout at the major junction of Avenidas Tulum and Uxmal.

Avenida Tulum, Cancún's main street, is lined with the bulk of the city's shops, banks, restaurants and travel agencies, as well as many of the hotels – up side streets, but in view. The **state tourist office** is a couple of blocks from the bus station at Tulum 26 (daily 9am–9pm; ☎98/84-80-73). For the **federal tourist office** (daily 9am–9pm; ☎98/84-32-38 or 84-34-38), continue along Tulum until the roundabout at Av Cobá, turn left and the office is at the furthest corner of the block with Av J.C. Nader. Both have free maps and leaflets and copies of the ubiquitous promotional listings **magazines** *Cancún Tips* and *Cancún Nights*: all information you can pick up at just about every travel agency and hotel reception. There are several other tourist information kiosks on Tulum and in the *zona hotelera*; some are genuine, but if you're asked if you want "tourist information" as you pass, it's almost certain you're being selected for a time-share sales pitch. Many hotels arrange **trips** to the chief Maya ruins – most commonly Chichén Itzá, Tulum and Cobá. Check with the receptionist about the latest offers.

Downtown you'll be able to walk just about anywhere, but you need some sort of transport to get around the *zona hotelera*, which stretches for more than 20km. **Buses** marked "Tulum–Hoteles, Ruta 1" run along Av Tulum every few minutes. There's a fixed fare of US$0.50. Alternatively, **taxis** are plentiful and can be hailed almost anywhere – the trip between downtown and the *zona* costs around US$6. A car affords you more scope and makes day-trips as far as the ruins at Cobá perfectly feasible.

Accommodation

Cancún has plenty of accommodation, most of it very expensive for the casual visitor. **Downtown** holds the only hope of a decent budget room, while the glittering beachfront palaces of the **zona hotelera** offer exclusive luxury, many with extravagant interiors featuring waterfalls and cascades of tropical vegetation. All have excellent service, with colour TV and minibars in rooms, at least one immaculate pool, glitzy bars and restaurants, and, more often than not, shops and a travel agency. Many will also put on a show in the evening, a disco, or both. Of course, this is all rather expensive if you just drop by, but very much more reasonable as part of a **package**, and prices may be reduced considerably in the summer.

At the other end of the spectrum there is a 600-bed **youth hostel** out on the beach at the beginning of the *zona* on Av Kukulkán (☎98/83-13-37; ③). Single-sex dorms have bunks and lockers; the beach isn't great here, but there's a pool.

DOWNTOWN

Coral, Sunyaxchen 30, near Grosella (☎98/84-05-86, fax 84-45-69). Very reasonably priced for Cancún; away from the busiest traffic, clean rooms, some with a/c, and a pool. ④.

Hacienda, Sunyaxchen 39 (☎98/84-36-72, fax 84-12-08). Good location and good value; rooms all have a/c and colour TV and there's a pool, café, travel agency and beach club. ⑤.

Novotel, Tulum 27, corner of Azucenas and across from the bus station (☎98/84-29-99, fax 84-31-62). Centrally located, clean and secure; the best hotel in its class. Rooms, with fan or a/c, are very comfortable; try to get one at the back. The cool patio restaurant overlooks a small garden. ⑤.

Piña Hermanos, C 7 Ote (☎98/84-21-50). The best of three budget hotels in a row, and one of the city's best deals; from the bus station, head north along Tulum (by bus or about fifteen minutes' walk) almost to the junction with Av López Portillo. Turn right at C 10 Ote, then take the third on the right. Clean rooms with hot showers. ③.

Tropical Caribe, C Cedro 30, five blocks north along Tulum from the bus station (☎98/84-14-42). Large place with plenty of clean basic rooms with hot showers – the cheapest budget option. ②.

BEACH

Carisa y Palma, Km 9 (☎98/83-02-11). The cheapest of the beach hotels, but hardly a rock bottom price. All mod cons and pool. ⑧.

Club Las Velas, Blvd Kukulkán, Km 3.5 (☎98/83-22-22, fax 83-21-18; in US ☎1-800/223-9815). Overlooking the Nichupté Lagoon, this all-inclusive resort (the price covers meals and drinks, sports and evening entertainment) somehow manages to retain a village atmosphere. ⑨.

Kin Há, Blvd Kukulkán, Km 8 (☎98/83-23-77, fax 83-21-47). Near the main shopping and entertainment centres. Beautiful rooms and suites with spacious balconies. All the facilities and a great buffet breakfast at a reasonable price. ⑨.

Presidente Cancún, Blvd Kukulkán, Km 7.5 (☎98/83-02-00, fax 83-25-15; in US ☎1-800/468-3571). Luxury, first-class hotel with superb service. All rooms overlook the sea, and there are two pools and a jacuzzi. ⑨.

The Town and beaches

There's little to see in **downtown Cancún**. Most visitors head straight for the *zona hotelera* and the **beaches**. Though you're free to go anywhere, some of the hotels do their best to make you feel like a trespasser, and staff will certainly move you off the beach furniture if you're not a guest. To avoid being eyed suspiciously by hotel heavies, head for one of the dozen or so **public beaches**: all are free but you may have to pay a small charge for showers. Entertainment and expensive watersports are laid on all around the big hotels; if you venture further, where more sites await construction, you can find surprisingly empty sand and often small groups of nude sunbathers.

To catch a bit of culture while you're out here, the *Sheraton* boasts a small Maya ruin in its grounds, above the pool, while the **Museo de Antropología**, located behind the convention centre (Tues–Fri 9am–7pm, Sat & Sun 10am–5pm; US$2, free on Sun), has a small but absorbing outline of Mesoamerican and Maya culture and history, with information in English and Spanish. Cancún's largest Maya remains, the **Ruinas del Rey** (daily 8am–5pm; US$2, free on Sun), are at Km 17, overlooking the Nichupté Lagoon. They're not especially impressive – and, if you decide not to take one of the guides at the entrance, there's no information available to explain them – but the area is peaceful and very good for bird- and iguana-watching.

The best **snorkelling** in Cancún is at Punta Nizuc, next to *Club Med* territory. You aren't allowed to cross the grounds unless you're staying there, so you have to get off the bus at the *Westin Regina Resort*, cross their grounds to the beach, then turn right and walk for about twenty minutes until you reach the rocky point. Walk across the rocks and snorkel to your heart's content. To join a **snorkelling tour** or go **diving**, contact Aqua Tours (☎98/83-02-27) or Aquaworld (☎98/85-22-88). A one-tank dive costs about US$50 and a full PADI open-water certification course around US$400. To view the colourful underwater life in a more leisurely fashion, take a trip on Nautibus (☎98/83-10-04; US$38), a **glass-bottomed boat** that leaves from Playa Linda every ninety minutes from 8am until 3.30pm.

Eating

Cancún's **restaurants** outnumber hotels many times over, and competition is fierce. The bulk of the **tourist restaurants** line Av Tulum and its side streets: eat here and you can enjoy "fun" disco sounds with your meal. Though seafood and steak form the mainstay of many menus, you can also eat Arabic, Yucatecan, Italian, Chinese, French, Cajun and Polynesian, not to mention international fast food plus some local chains. All the **hotels** in the *zona* have at least one formal restaurant, some of which are very elegant indeed, surrounded by tropical foliage with fountains and music. Many also feature a more relaxed and relaxing beach or poolside dining room.

For **budget food**, follow the locals and make for the markets. From the bus station, walk a few blocks north along Tulum, turn down Flamboyan or Cerdo and you'll come to the **Mercado Municipal**, with plenty of food stalls and tiny restaurants. Further along, at the junction of Tulum and López Portillo, is a small plaza, complete with fountain, at the edge of another market. The little cafés here are packed with Mexican families and it's the nearest Cancún comes to having a zócalo.

DOWNTOWN

100 Percent Natural, Sunyaxchen 26, at the junction with Yaxchilán. Not entirely vegetarian, but it serves fruit drinks, salads, yoghurt and granola, as well as Mexican dishes, seafood and burgers. A pleasant enough place, if a little overpriced. There's also a branch in the Plaza Terramar in the *zona hotelera*.

Los Almendros, Bonampak 60, opposite the Plaza de Toros. This is the Cancún branch of the famous restaurant that originated in Ticul, and is justly renowned for its good-value Yucatecan specialities.

Gory Tacos, Tulipanes 26. Don't be put off by the name: this spotless and very friendly place serves good, inexpensive Mexican food, steaks, hamburgers and sandwiches, and a range of vegetarian meals.

La Habichuela, Margaritas 25, in front of the Parque Las Palapas. Long-established and fairly expensive restaurant set in a walled garden. The menu is excellent, featuring such dishes as *coco-bichuela*: half a coconut filled with lobster and shrimp in a curry sauce, accompanied by tropical fruits. Live jazz adds to the atmosphere.

La Placita, Yaxchilán 12. Highly recommended Mexican restaurant. Tacos, steaks and the like served in fairly authentic style.

El Tacolote, Cobá 19, across from the hospital. Popular with Mexicans and offering a wide range of good-value tacos.

THE ZONA HOTELERA

Doña Yola, inside the Plaza Terramar. Bargain all-you-can eat breakfast for US$4; the rest of the American-style menu is more expensive.

Faro's, Plaza Lagunas. Famed for fresh fish, lobster, shrimp, crab, mussels and clams; also serves steaks, pasta and *tapas*.

Mr Papa's, Terramar Plaza. Giant baked potatoes with dozens of fillings for around US$7.

Entertainment and nightlife

Since Cancún's whole rationale is to encourage almost two million visitors each year to have fun, the entertainment scene is lavish – or remorseless, depending on which way you look at it. There's everything from sports and gambling **bars** to romantic piano bars and fun bars, even just plain drinking bars: enough choice to ensure that you can find a place to have a good time without being ripped off. Most of the **nightclubs**, on the other hand, are pricey, with a "no shorts or sandals" dress code. A couple of **cinemas** show new American releases subtitled in Spanish: the largest downtown is the multi-screen Cine Royal on Tulum opposite the Amex Office; in the *zona*, there's a cinema in the Plaza Kukulkán.

BARS AND NIGHTCLUBS

La Boom, Blvd Kukulkán Km 3.5, at the front of the *Hotel Aquamarina Beach* (☎98/83-16-41). High-tech disco in an "English setting" with continuous videos. No cover charge on Mon; check *Cancún Tips* and *Cancún Nights* for other events.

Cats, Yaxchilán 12. Downtown club with live Jamaican bands. Daily 9pm–5am.

Christine's, in the *Krystal*, Blvd Kukulkán Km 9 (☎98/83-11-33, ext 499). The most sophisticated and expensive nightclub in town, famed for its light show. Thursday is 70s and 80s night: look in the free magazines or phone to check other weekly events. Don't turn up in shorts, jeans, sandals or without a shirt.

Daddy'o, Blvd Kukulkán Km 9, opposite the convention centre. A 21st-century nightclub with a high-tech sound system and a light and laser show. Casual dress but no shorts.

Fat Tuesday, Blvd Kukulkán Km 6.5, and in the Terramar Plaza in the *zona hotelera* (☎98/83-26-76 or 83-03-91). Restaurant-bar with an outside dance floor and a choice of sixty flavours of frozen drinks. Cover charge after 9pm; open until 4am.

Pat O'Brien's, Flamingo Plaza in the *zona hotelera* (☎98/83-08-32). Live rock, blues and jazz in a larger than life version of the famous New Orleans bar. Three bars: a piano bar, a video lounge and an outdoor patio. Open until 2am.

Señor Frogs, Blvd Kukulkán Km 5.5. Live reggae bands and karaoke nights.

Tequila Rock, in the *Party Centre*, Blvd Kukulkán Km 9 (☎98/84-81-32 or 90-98-45). Pop, rock and disco music with high-tech effects. Check for the daily events – open bar, two-for-one drinks, ladies night and the like. Casual dress, shorts allowed.

DINNER WITH LIVE MUSIC

Ballet Folklórico Nacional de México, at the *Continental Villas Plaza Hotel* in the *zona hotelera* (☎98/83-10-95). Buffet dinner nightly at 7pm with a professional ballet featuring 35 artists. Tickets cost around US$35.

La Fisheria, Plaza Caracol. Fresh seafood and pizza accompanied by live Caribbean music.

Iguana Wana, Plaza Caracol. Lively café with Mexican and seafood specialities. Live music every evening, happy hour from 5 to 7pm. Open until 2am.

Los Rancheros, Flamingo Plaza. Another Mexican restaurant with a lively atmosphere, *mariachi* and *marimba* music every night.

DINNER CRUISES

Cancún Queen, Blvd Kukulkán Km 10.5 (☎98/83-30-07 or 83-17-63). Fish and chicken dinner on a traditional Mississippi paddle boat. Live music followed by a fiesta and a variety of party games with prizes. Two daily departures at 6.30pm and 9.30pm, returning ninety minutes later.

Columbus, from the Royal Maya Marina at Blvd Kukulkán (☎98/83-32-68 or 83-32-71). Romantic cruise with lobster and steak dinners. Daily 4–7pm and 7.30–10.30pm.

Listings

American Express Tulum 208, two blocks beyond the *Hotel America* (☎98/84-19-99).

Banks Most banks are along Tulum and in the *zona hotelera* (9am–1.30pm; foreign exchange 10am–1pm) and many have 24hr ATMs. Banco del Atlántico, Tulum 15, offers good rates and credit card advances over the counter; the branch in the *zona hotelera*, on the corner of the convention centre at Km 9, has a money exchange booth (Mon–Fri 11am–2pm & 4–9pm). Banamex, Tulum 19, and in Plaza Terramar in the *zona hotelera*, and Bancomer, Tulum 26, have convenient ATMs. There are many casas de cambios which change cash (including currencies other than US$) and travellers' cheques faster than the banks, but generally offer worse rates.

Car rental Available at most hotels and at the airport, or try Avis, Mayfair Plaza (☎98/86-01-47), or Budget, Tulum 214 (☎98/84-69-55).

Consulates Canada, Plaza Mexico 312, Av Tulum (Mon–Fri 10am–2pm; ☎98/84-37-16); UK, *The Royal Caribbean*, *zona hotelera* (Mon–Fri 9am–5pm; ☎98/85-11-66 ext 462); US, Edificio Marruecos 31, Av Nader 40 (Mon–Fri 9am–2pm & 3–5.30pm; ☎98/84-24-11 or 84-63-99, fax 84-82-22).

Laundry Lavendería Las Palapas, on Gladiolas, at the far side of the park (Mon–Sat 7am–8pm, Sun 8am–2pm); Lavendería Alborada, Av Nader, just south of City Hall.

MOVING ON FROM CANCÚN

If you're heading west **by car** to Valladolid, Chichén Itzá and Mérida, you have a choice between the old road (*viejo*) or the new cuota highway, running a few kilometres north of the old road for most of its length. Drive north on Av Tulum then turn left to join López Portillo: after a few kilometres you will have the choice of which road to join. You pay in advance, at the booths on the highway, for the sections you intend to travel along. The trip all the way to Mérida costs US$30.

The first- and second-class **bus stations** are next to each other on the corner of Tulum and Uxmal. For Mérida, choices include the ADO Mercedes Benz; UNO; first-class, directo or second-class (5am–9pm; hourly). The journey takes between four and seven hours. Other destinations include Campeche on the deluxe ATS Plus (daily; 9.30am; 9hr); Chetumal on first-class (6.30am–midnight); first-class to México (6pm); Playa del Carmen on ADO Mercedes Benz (3 daily; 1hr), first-class (5 daily; 1hr) and second-class (every 30–45min; 1hr); Tizimín on first- and second-class (6 daily; 4hr); Tulum on first-class (5 daily; 2hr) and second-class (5 daily; 2hr); Valladolid on ADO Mercedes Benz and second-class (hourly; 3hr).

International **flights** leave regularly from Cancún; from downtown and the *zona hotelera* a taxi to the airport costs about US$8.

THE FERRY TO ISLA MUJERES

The passenger ferry for Isla Mujeres (see below) officially leaves from Puerto Juárez every thirty minutes between 8am and 8pm, the fast ferry (15min) on the hour and the slow ferry (30min) at thirty minutes past. However, in reality they simply leave when full, often at the same time. To get to the ferry terminal, catch a bus ("Puerto Juárez" or "Punta Sam") heading north from the stop on Tulum, opposite the bus station (20min), or take a taxi from Tulum (around US$3).

The car ferry (US$10 for car, plus US$1.50 for each passenger) leaves from Punta Sam, a few kilometres north of Puerto Juárez. There are six departures daily between 7.15am and 8.15pm, returning from Isla Mujeres between 6am and 7.15pm. However, it isn't really worth taking a car over to the island, which is small enough to cycle around and has plenty of bicycles and mopeds for rent.

Post office Av Sunyaxchen at the junction with Xel-Ha (Mon–Fri 8am–7pm, Sat 9am–1pm), with a reliable *Lista de Correos* (postcode 77501).

Shopping Mercado 23 (turn left off Avenida Tulum, three blocks north of the bus station), sells arts and crafts from all over the country and is a good place to pick up reasonably priced souvenirs.

Travel agents There's an abundance of tour operators and travel agency desks at most hotels, which can easily fix you up with the standard trips to Xel-Ha, the main ruins or sell tickets for a cruise. Marand Travel, Plaza Mexico, Av Tulum 200, Suite 208 (☎98/84-38-05, fax 84-38-49), owned by Martha and Richard Uscanga, who also run EcoloMex Tours, is the best travel agency if you want to see the wildlife of the Yucatán.

Isla Mujeres

ISLA MUJERES, just a couple of kilometres off the easternmost tip of Mexico in the startlingly clear Caribbean sea, is an infinitely more appealing prospect than Cancún. Its attractions are simple: first there's the beach, then there's the sea. And when you've tired of those, you can rent a bike or a moped to carry you around the island to more sea, more beaches, a coral reef and the tiny Maya temple that the conquistadors chanced upon, full of female figures, which gave the place its name. Unfortunately, however, Mujeres is no longer the desert island you may have heard about, and its natural attractions have been recognized and developed considerably in the last few years.

There are now several large hotels and regular day-trips from Cancún, and the once beautiful El Garrafón coral reef is now almost completely dead. Inevitably, too, prices have risen and standards (in many cases) have fallen. All that said, it can still seem a respite to those who've been slogging their way down through Mexico and around the Yucatán – everyone you've met along the way seems to turn up here eventually.

Arrival, information and island transport

The passenger **ferry** arrives downtown, at the main pier at the end of Av Morelos on Av Rueda Medina, which runs northeast to southwest; the car ferry comes in further east on Medina at the end of Bravo. Avenida Madero, one block north from the passenger ferry dock, cuts northeast straight across the island; as you walk away from the dock, the first street you cross is Juárez, the second Hidalgo and the third Guerrero, both of which lead north to the North Beach and south to the zócalo. The boats leave from Puerto Juárez (ten minutes in a taxi from central Cancún) every half hour, the last at 8pm. There's also a more expensive **hydrofoil**, which leaves from Playa Linda in Cancún's *zona hotelera* a few times a day, returning about an hour later. Aerocaribe and other airlines also occasionally fly out to Cancún or Cozumel from the small airstrip in the centre of the island.

The zócalo is skirted by Morelos, N. Bravo, Guerrero and Hidalgo. The **tourist office** (Mon–Fri 9am–2.30pm & 7–9pm) is on the top floor of the Plaza Isla Mujeres, Hidalgo 7 & 8, opposite *Hotel Xul Ha*. Here you can pick up leaflets, maps and copies of the free *Isla Mujeres* magazine (in Spanish and English). The **post office** (Mon–Fri 8am–7pm, Sat 9am–1pm) is at the corner of Guerrero and Mateos, about ten minutes' walk from the centre; mail is held at the *Lista de Correos* for up to ten days (postcode 77400). There are **long-distance phones** at Av Medina 6-B (9am–9pm). **Banks** are few: Banco del Atlántico, Medina 3 (Mon–Fri 9am–1pm), does currency exchange between 10am and noon, but to avoid the queues you could use the **casa de cambio** (daily 9am–9pm) on Hidalgo, opposite *Rolandis* restaurant between Madero and Abasolo. There's a **laundry** on Juárez at Abasolo.

The best way of getting around the island is by **moped or bicycle**: the island is a very manageable size with few hills. Operadora Turistica, Hidalgo 43 at Mateos (☎987/46-46-41), advertise "Golf Ears" for rent, which are very similar to golf carts. They also rent bikes, mopeds and snorkelling gear. Kan Kin, Absalo at Hidalgo, also rents out bikes and mopeds.

The only PADI-affiliated **dive shop** on the island is Coral on Matamoros no.13-A (☎987/7-07-63). It offers a range of trips including some to the "Cave of the Sleeping Sharks", where Tiger, Bull, Grey Reef, Lemon and Nurse Sharks are regularly encountered.

Accommodation

Isla Mujeres is short on good-value **budget places to stay**, and, though prices are lower than at Cozumel, so is the quality. Most of the reasonably priced options are on the northern edge of the island.

There is no official **campsite** on Isla Mujeres, but you can pitch your tent or hang your hammock under one of the *palapas* (US$2 per person paid to the restaurant) on Playa Indios, towards the southern end of the island, shortly before reaching El Garrafón National Park.

Hotel Berny, Juárez at Abasolo (☎987/84-36-72, fax 84-12-08). Good value with spacious, clean rooms and a swimming pool; near the centre and the seafront. ④.

El Caracol, Matamoros 5 (☎987/7-01-50). Two blocks from North Beach; rooms with or without a/c and a restaurant serving typical Mexican food. ④–⑤.

Caribe Maya, Av Francisco I Madero 9 (☎987/7-06-84). More character than the average budget hotel and good value. Some a/c rooms. ④.

Hotel Cabañas María del Mar, Av Carlos Lazo 1 (☎987/7-01-79, fax 7-01-56). Next to North Beach, with deluxe cabañas on the beach or hotel rooms with a/c, refrigerator and private balcony or terrace. Lively restaurant, tours and car rental. ⑧.

Posada del Mar, Medina 15-A (☎987/7-00-44 or 7-03-00, fax 7-02-66). Spacious rooms or bungalows with a/c, plus a restaurant and a pool with its own bar. ⑥.

María José, Madero 25 (☎987/70-24-44 or 70-24-45). Well-kept family-run hotel. Some of the back rooms open onto next door's roof, where you can hang your hammock. ④.

Osorio, Madero. Turn left from the ferry, take the first right, and the hotel is on your left (☎987/7-02-94). No frills, but clean and near the sea. ④.

Las Palmas, Guerrero 20 (no phone). The cheapest option on the island; basic but acceptable. ④.

Perla del Caribe, Madero 2 (☎987/7-01-20 or 7-05-07, fax 7-00-11). At the opposite side of town to the ferry, one of the smartest hotels on the island, with a pool, restaurant and sea-view rooms with verandahs. Car rental. ⑦.

Poc Na, Matamoros 15 (☎987/7-00-90), near the junction with Carlos Lazo, is a kind of private youth hostel, with small rooms with bunks and hammock space. It's a great place for meeting people, and has a reasonable restaurant. Rates include mattress and sheet or hammock. ①.

Roca Mar, corner of Guerrero and Bravo, behind the church next to the zócalo (☎987/7-01-01). One of the island's oldest hotels, well maintained, with a restaurant overlooking the Caribbean. ⑤.

Xul-ha, Hidalgo 23 Nte (☎987/7-00-75). Recently rebuilt next to the old hotel, this new hotel is clean and comfortable. ⑤.

The island

Isla Mujeres is no more than 8km long, and, at its widest point, barely a kilometre across. A lone road runs its length, past the dead calm waters of the landward coast – the other side, east-facing, is windswept and exposed. There's a small beach on this side in the town, but the currents even here can be dangerous. The most popular beach, just five minutes' walk from the town plaza, is **Playa Los Cocos** – at the northern tip of the island, but protected from the open sea by a little promontory on which stands what was the lone luxury hotel, the *El Presidente Zazil-Ha*. The hotel now stands abandoned, ravaged by one of the hurricanes that periodically wreck this coast.

If you've had enough of the beach, windsurfing and wandering round town (the Grand Tour takes little more than thirty minutes), rent a bike or moped to explore the south of the island. **El Garrafón National Park** (daily 8am–5pm; US$2), at the southern end of the island, is a tropical reef, just a few metres offshore, though, unfortunately, the crowds of day-trippers here have frightened away a lot of the fish here and the coral is virtually dead as a result of damage from divers and the anchors of the tourist boats. El Garrafón is almost at the southern end of the island – beyond, the road continues to the lighthouse, and from there a short rough track leads to the **Maya Temple** at the southernmost tip. It's not much of a ruin, but it is very dramatically situated on low rocky cliffs, below which you can often spot large fish basking.

On the way back, stop at **Playa Lancheros**, a palm-fringed beach that is virtually deserted except at lunchtimes when the day-trippers pile in. There's a small restaurant here, specializing in seafood, and a clutch of souvenir stalls. Inland, in the jungly undergrowth, lurk the decaying remains of the **Hacienda Mundaca**: an old house and garden to which scores of romantic (and quite untrue) pirate legends are attached.

You could also take a day-long boat trip to the island bird sanctuary of **Contoy** (some, with special permission, stay overnight), where you can see colonies of pelicans and cormorants and occasionally more exotic sea birds, as well as a sunken Spanish galleon.

Eating

The area along and around Hidalgo between Morelos and Abasolo, lined with **restaurants** and crafts shops, is the best place to spend an evening on Isla Mujeres. Simply wander through the laid-back music-filled streets and see what takes your fancy. For inexpensive, basic Mexican food and great low-priced fruit salads, head for the **loncherías** opposite *Las Palmas* hotel.

Le Bistro, Matamoros 29. Pseudo-French café with a varied menu at reasonable prices. Good breakfasts.

Restaurant Gomar, Hidalgo 5 on the corner with Madero. Good seafood and chicken, but not much atmosphere – and a very loud TV – in this rather expensive restaurant.

Miramar, Medina, next to the pier. Attractive place on the seafront, away from the centre. Seafood and meat dishes, a little on the expensive side.

Pizza Rolandis, Hidalgo, between Madero and Abasolo. One of a chain serving pizza, lobster, fresh fish and other Italian dishes with salads.

Tonyno's Pizza and Pasta, Hidalgo, between Madero and Morelos, opposite *Mexico Lindo*. The lowest-priced pizzas – delicious too.

The east coast: Cancún to Playa del Carmen

Resort development along the spectacular white-sand beaches south from Cancún to the marvellous seaside ruins of Tulum proceeds rapidly as landowners cash in on Cancún's popularity. The **Caribbean Barrier Reef** begins off **Puerto Morelos**, a quiet, though expensive, town with excellent beaches. Further south is **Punta Bete**, which is smaller and quieter, while the phenomenal growth of **Playa del Carmen**, the departure point for boats to Cozumel, has transformed a village with a ferry dock into a major holiday destination.

Finding a relatively deserted stretch of beach is increasingly difficult, though not impossible, and many visitors based in Cancún rent a car to explore the coast. Although a moped is feasible as far as Puerto Morelos, where the divided highway ends (and there's a filling station), it's a long trip for the underpowered bikes, and bus and truck drivers show scant respect as they pass. The bus is probably a better idea as the service along Hwy-307 is cheap and efficient.

Puerto Morelos and around

Leaving Cancún behind, the first town on the coast is **PUERTO MORELOS**, 20km south. Formerly of little interest except as the departure point for the car ferry to Cozumel, in recent years Puerto has seen a surge in popularity, becoming a base for tours and **diving trips**. The taxi ride from Cancún airport to Puerto Morelos is slightly cheaper than to Cancún itself, and many visitors on international flights bypass the city altogether, making this their first stop. It's as good a place as any to hang out for a while: despite a rash of new hotel and condo construction, it is a relaxing, laid-back alternative to the bustle of Cancún, with some lovely beaches and exceptionally fine watersports, though prices here have risen considerably in recent years.

Arrival and information

Interplaya **buses** leave Cancún's bus station every thirty to forty-five minutes between 5am and 10pm and drop you at the highway junction, where taxis wait to take you the 2km into town. There's a **long-distance telephone** by the police station on the corner of the plaza, a number of small shops, a supermarket and a **bank** (Mon–Fri 9.30am–1pm) that will cash travellers' cheques. The **car ferry to Cozumel** officially operates at 6am every day except Tuesday, when it goes at 9am, and Thursday, when it goes at 5am; on Monday an extra ferry is scheduled to leave at noon. You need to get to the terminal around three hours early to be sure of getting a space. The ferry returns from Cozumel at 2pm daily except for Monday, when it leaves at 10am and 5pm. The service is erratic, however, and it's best to check the times either in Cozumel or with the tourist office in Cancún.

Most of the town's **restaurants** are around the plaza. *Los Pelicanos* and *Las Palmeras* are good for seafood and the cosy restaurant at *Posada Amor* offers very good value in a friendly, informal atmosphere. It's also a great place to pick up information about what's going on in town. *Rancho Libertad* has some **vegetarian** food.

Accommodation

Almost all of the hotels in Puerto Morelos are right on the beach, but many of them are overpriced. You can **camp free** on the sand as long as you're not directly in front of a house or hotel, or try the *Acamaya Reef Trailer Park* (☎987/1-01-32), a couple of kilometres away from the centre, down the first turning on the left, 2km after the turn-off from the main highway, near the entrance to Crococun.

Amar Inn, north of the plaza, 500m along the seafront (☎987/1-00-26). The best place in town; pretty rooms and cabañas with kitchenettes around a shaded garden. The staff are very friendly and also run a shop selling handicrafts made by local Maya women (US$5 extra for breakfast). ⑥.

Caribbean Reef Club, fifteen minutes south of the plaza, beyond the car ferry dock (☎987/1-01-62). Luxury accommodation right on the beach, around a pool. Every room has a sea view and guests have free use of sailboats and windsurf boards. Prices soar in December and January. ⑧–⑨.

Hacienda Morelos, on the front, south of the plaza (☎ & fax 987/1-00-15). Bright, airy rooms. ⑥.

Ojo de Agua, north of the plaza (☎987/1-00-27). Sixteen beachfront rooms and a pool. ⑥.

Posada Amor, Rojo Romez, just south of the plaza (☎987/1-00-33). The least expensive option here. It's not on the beach, but it's friendly and comfortable, with plenty of character. ⑤.

Rancho Libertad, fifteen minutes south of the plaza, beyond the car ferry dock (☎987/1-01-81; in US ☎1-800/305-5225). Two-storey thatched cabañas in a beach and garden setting. Rates include substantial fruit and cereal breakfasts. Snorkel and bike rental and scuba instruction available. No children. ⑥.

The Town

The turn-off from Hwy- 307 ends at the small, modern **plaza** in the centre of Puerto Morelos: the only proper streets lead north and south for a few blocks, parallel to the beach. Ahead lies the **beach**, a wooden **dock** (the car ferry terminal is a few hundred metres south) and the **lighthouse**. There's a small wooden tourist booth in the plaza minded – sometimes – by Fernando during the mornings. You'll see signs advertising rooms, snorkelling, scuba-diving, and catamaran trips (US$40 per day, including lunch): with the reef only 600m offshore and in a very healthy condition, Puerto Morelos is a great place to learn to **dive**. *Rancho Libertad* (see above) offers two tank dives for US$60 as well as PADI certification. For **dive trips**, contact Fernando (☎987/1-02-44) at the little tourist hut on the ocean side of the town square.

If you want to learn more about the **natural and social history** of the area, contact Sandra Dayton (☎987/1-01-36, or leave a message at the *Amar Inn*), who runs **Maya Echo**, a group dedicated to the conservation of the area's natural beauty and the preservation of Maya culture and spirituality. They organize tailor-made, one-day tours into the forest and to local Maya villages, where the Maya will teach you about their way of life and their beliefs.

Just south of the turn-off for the *Acamaya Reef Trailer Park* (see above), the **Jardín Botanico Dr Alfredo Barrera** (daily 9am–5pm; US$2.50) features the native flora of Quintana Roo and is definitely worth a visit if you have the time. Exhibits are labelled in Spanish and English and there are also guides who can explain the medicinal uses of the plants. Trails lead to a small Maya site and a reconstruction showing how *chicle* was tapped from the sap of the *zapote* (sapodilla) tree before being used in the production of chewing gum.

Punta Bete

Tucked away between the more touristed resorts of Puerto Morelos and Playa del Carmen, the sedate **PUNTA BETE** is little more than a beach, a restaurant and a few cabañas, though there's now a big, expensive resort further down the beach towards Playa del Carmen. The beach is long, white and palm-fringed and not too crowded; it's also wonderful for **snorkelling** when the sea is calm. You can rent equipment from the restaurant *Xcalacoco*, which dishes up reasonably priced basic Mexican **food** and superb fish from 7.30am until 8pm. To get there, it's a slow, careful drive or a hot, dusty four-kilometre walk down the pot-holed dirt track from the highway. There's room for around thirty people in the **cabañas** (⑤), and **campers** with tents or trailers are welcome (US$3 per person), although there's no water or electricity hook-ups.

Playa del Carmen

PLAYA DEL CARMEN, once a soporific, very Mexican fishing village, has mushroomed in recent years and its streets are now packed with tourists – from cruise liners, on packages and on day-trips from Cancún. Prices have been forced up as a result and designer shops have started to move in. Nonetheless, it is lower key and on a smaller scale than Cancún, and attracts a predominantly younger crowd. Most of what happens here happens on the **beach**, where the sea is gloriously clear and the sand unfeasibly white; inland, the main centre of activity is one block back on Av 5, pedestrianized across five blocks from Playacar to C 6. Here, a multitude of dive shops offer diving and snorkelling trips and you can stock up on clothes, crafts and exquisite jewellery from all over Mexico and Guatemala – at a price.

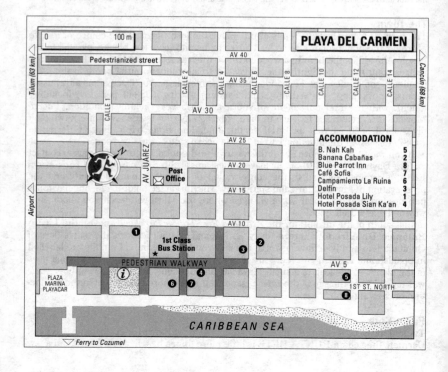

PLAYA DEL CARMEN

AV 40
AV 35
AV 30
AV 25
AV 20
AV 15
AV 10
AV 5

Tulum (63 km) / Cancún (68 km) / Airport

Pedestrianized street

Post Office

ACCOMMODATION
B. Nah Kah	5
Banana Cabañas	2
Blue Parrot Inn	8
Café Sofía	7
Campamiento La Ruina	6
Delfin	3
Hotel Posada Lily	1
Hotel Posada Sian Ka'an	4

1st Class Bus Station

PEDESTRIAN WALKWAY

PLAZA MARINA PLAYACAR

1ST ST. NORTH

CARIBBEAN SEA

Ferry to Cozumel

Arrival and information

Buses pull in at the corner of Av 5 and Av Juárez, the main street running east–west from the highway to the beach; some second-class buses stop one or two blocks further inland on Juárez. For **tourist information**, head for the wooden booth in the corner of the plaza (Mon–Sat 7am–midnight) at the end of Juárez. It's run by the multi-lingual Ramón Nuñez Díaz, who is there every day except August 31, when the booth is closed in celebration of his birthday. Pick up a copy of the useful *Destination Playa del Carmen*, which has a map, hotel and restaurant listings. Beware the other tourist information booths scattered around town, as they're mostly tied up with some ulterior motive – selling timeshares, for example.

Accommodation

You'll have no difficulty finding a room in Playa del Carmen – hotels are being built all the time. Budget travellers will find the town very expensive, though, as there's little under US$40. The **youth hostel**, on Av 30 near C 8, ten minutes' walk from the centre in a quiet part of town, is probably your best bet. Bunks in tightly packed dorms cost US$10 per person, with a ten percent discount with an IYH card. Lockers are provided.

B. Nah Kah, C 12 between the beach and Av 5 (☎987/3-00-48). Very popular and relaxed Italian-run bed and breakfast. Individual and charming. ⑦.

Banana Cabañas, C 6 Nte between Av 5 and 10 (☎987/3-00-36). Comfortable cabañas surrounding a leafy garden. Mosquito nets provided. ⑤.

Blue Parrot Inn, on and slightly back from the beach (☎987/3-00-83, fax 3-00-49). Wide range of cabañas and rooms; the new Tucan annexe has suites with one or two bedrooms and kitchenettes. Can be noisy at night when the hugely popular beachfront *Dragon* bar is hopping. ⑥–⑨.

Campamiento La Ruina, C 2 Nte, between Av 5 and the sea (☎987/3-04-05). Playa's most sociable and economical place to stay, on the beach with its own ruin in the grounds. There are a variety of options: a few hook-ups; cabañas with or without private bath; camping space, and a huge *palapa* with lockers and room for 34 hammocks. ②–④.

Café Sofia, C 2 Nte, between Av 5 and the sea. The cheapest option, opposite the Ruina. ①–④.

Delfin, Av 5 on corner with C 6 Nte (☎ & fax 987/3-01-76). Relatively new hotel; rooms with fans and private bathrooms. ⑥.

Hotel Posada Lily, Juárez, between Av 5 and 10 (☎987/3-01-16). Good budget option just one block back from the beach. ③.

Hotel Posada Sian Ka'an, corner of Av 5 and C 2 Nte (☎987/3-02-02, fax 3-02-04). Small hotel built around a dried-up cenote. Clean and comfortable rooms, some with kitchenettes, others with private terraces. ⑥.

Eating

Playa del Carmen is heaving with **restaurants**, whether you want a romantic candlelit dinner or a low-priced traditional Mexican meal. The pedestrianized section of **Avenida 5** is edged end-to-end with dining tables where you can eat pizza, pasta, French food, burgers and chips, veggie – you name it. Probably the nicest places, though, are the **beach restaurants** and bars, where your can sift sand between your toes while eating fresh fish and sipping icy margaritas. Keep an eye open for the various happy hours.

Da Gabi, C 12, half a block from the beach near the *Blue Parrot Inn*. Italian-run restaurant serving delicious fresh pasta and pizza. A little pricey but recommended.

Deli Café, Av 5, between C 4 and C 6. Fresh juices, pastries, ice-cream, burgers and other snacks. Great place for an inexpensive breakfast or to satisfy late-night munchies. Open all night.

Karen's, Av 5, between C 2 and C 4. Busy, moderately priced pizza restaurant in the heart of the pedestrianized zone. Live music on stage most nights and a happy hour 7–9pm.

Limones, Av 5, on the corner with C 6, just past the end of the pedestrianized area. Yucatecan and international specialities in romantic, leafy surroundings. Daily 6–11pm.

Mascaras, Juárez, near the beach. Thin-crust pizza, home-made pasta and seafood. Sip margaritas during the happy hour between noon and 6pm.

Media Luna, Av 5, opposite Plaza Rincon del Sol, near C 8. Vegetarian and seafood restaurant with delicious pasta and veg dishes. Hot crusty bread with fresh herb and garlic butter served with every meal. Small and popular; get there early. Daily except Tues; opens around 7pm.

Molcas, next to the pier. Pleasant setting for an expensive restaurant with an extensive menu. Live music Fri and Sat 6–9pm.

Sabor, Av 5, between C 2 and C 4. Great place for fresh juices, scrumptious cakes and vegetarian food at reasonable prices. The soya *tortas* are delicious.

Sergios, Av 5, on the corner of C 2. Good basic Mexican food in simple surroundings but still within the buzzy atmosphere of Av 5. Low prices for this part of town.

El Tacolote, Juárez, near the beach at the north edge of the plaza. Moderately priced restaurant serving barbecued meat with melted cheese.

Bars and nightlife

You can wander through Playa del Carmen well into the night, following the happy-hour trail and listening to all sorts of music from salsa and reggae to 1970s classics. Drinks aren't cheap if you pay the full price, but it's a great way to meet people.

Caribe Swing Bar and Restaurant, on the beach near C 4. Totally laid-back: swing in a hammock on the beach while listening to live reggae, calypso and soca. 9pm–12.30am.

New Calypso House Bar, Av 5, between C 4 and 6. Live Caribbean music on Fri and Sat, 5–11pm. Cosy atmosphere and a busy dance floor.

Siege's Disco, Juárez, near the beach. Popular disco that doesn't get going till after midnight. No cover charge most nights, except Saturday (US$5) and Wednesday, when US$15 buys unlimited drinks. Open 10pm–4am.

Listings

Banks Bital is on Juárez between Av 10 and Av 15 (Mon–Fri 8am–1pm) and Bancomer is on Juárez between Av 25 and Av 30 (Mon–Fri 9am–1.30pm) with a 24hr ATM. There are a few casas de cambio around town but they offer very poor rates.

Car and bike rental Executive on Av 5 (☎987/3-04-77) rent cars. Ciclissimo Sport (Mon–Sat only), opposite the ice factory on Juárez, near Av 30, and Copacabaña, Av 5 between C 10 and C 12, both rent bikes.

Email and fax There are a number of shops with Internet facilities on or around Av 5, including Caseta Telefonica (*phonefax@cancun.novenet.com.mx;* US$15 per hour) on C 4 Nte between Av 5 and Av 10.

Post office on Juárez, four blocks back from the beach (Mon–Fri 9am–7pm, Sat 9am–4pm); geared to dealing with tourists and has a stamp machine outside. The *Lista de Correos* (postcode 77710) keeps mail for ten days.

Telephones There are plenty of Ladatel phones and you can call long distance at Computel caseta (daily 7am–10pm) next to the bus station.

Travel agents and tours The small airstrip just south of town handles short jaunts, chiefly to Cozumel, but also to Chichén Itzá and other key Maya sites; operators include Aeroferinco (☎987/3-03-36), Aeroméxico (☎987/3-03-50) and Saab (☎987/3-08-04). Eurotravel at Rincon del Sol, Av 5 near C 8, or the travel agency at Molcas can organize tours to Maya ruins, along with horse riding, boat trips, sky diving and national and international flights.

Cozumel

ISLA COZUMEL is far larger than Mujeres and has, unfortunately, been developed beyond its potential. However, it offers the best **diving** in Mexico, with spectacular drop-offs, walls and swim-throughs, some beautiful **coral gardens** and a number of little-visited remote reefs where you can see larger pelagic fish and dolphins. The island is also good for **bird-watching** as it's a stopover on migration routes and has several species or variants endemic to Cozumel.

Before the Spanish arrived, the island appears to have been a major Maya centre, carrying on sea trade around the coasts of Mexico and as far south as Honduras and perhaps Panamá; after the Conquest it was virtually deserted for four hundred years. This ancient community – one of several around the Yucatán coast that survived the collapse of Classic Maya civilization – is usually dismissed as being the decadent remnant of a moribund society. But that was not the impression the Spanish received when they arrived, nor is it necessarily the right one. Architecture might have declined in the years from 1200 AD to the Conquest, but large-scale trade, specialization between centres and even a degree of mass production are all in evidence. Cozumel's rulers enjoyed a less grand style than their forebears, but the rest of an increasingly commercialized population were probably better off. And Cozumel itself may even have been an early free-trade zone, where merchants from competing cities could trade peaceably.

Whatever the truth, you get little opportunity to judge for yourself. A US air base, built here during World War II, has erased all trace of the ancient city, and the lesser ruins scattered across the roadless interior are mostly unrestored and inaccessible. The airfield did, at least, bring new prosperity – converted to civilian use, it remains the means by which most visitors arrive.

Arrival and information

Arriving by boat, you'll be right in the centre of town (officially **San Miguel**, but always known simply as Cozumel) with the zócalo just one block inland along Juárez; from the airport you have to take the VW combi service. The **tourist office** (Mon–Fri 9am–1pm) is upstairs inside the Plaza del Sol shopping centre on the zócalo; but there's nothing here that you can't get at hotels, restaurants and shop counters throughout the island. *Cozumel Tips* and the *Free Blue Guide to Cozumel* are crammed with discount cards and vouchers; the tabloid-sized, one-sheet *Insider's Guide to Diving and Snorkelling* can also be useful. The **post office** (Mon–Fri 8am–8pm, Sat 8am–5pm, Sun 9am–1pm) is about fifteen minutes' walk from the centre, on Av Melgar at the corner with C 7 Sur; for *Lista de Correos* use the postcode 77600. Cozumel has many **banks** (Mon–Fri 9am–1.30pm), most of them with ATMs; currency is exchanged between 10am and 12.30pm. Outside these hours, Banco del Atlántico on the southeast corner of the zócalo has a money exchange counter (Mon–Fri 9am–8pm) separate from the main banking hall, and there's also a **casa de cambio** on the south side of the main square (daily 9am–8pm).

There are dozens of **dive shops** in town. The better shops use experienced instructors and small, fast boats. Deep Blue, Av 10 at Salas (☎ & fax 987/2-56-53; in the US ☎214/343-3034; *www.ipp.unicomp.net/deepblue*) is one of the best on the island, offering tailor-made small-group tours to some of the most interesting and remote reefs on the island, and a full range of certification courses including PADI and IANTD (Nitrox) Certifications. They can also help find accommodation, including house rental.

Town transport

Cozumel town has been modernized and is easy enough to get around on foot – there's even a pedestrian zone. There's a distinct lack of buses, however, so to get further afield you'll have to go on a tour, take a taxi or rent a vehicle. **Cycling** is feasible on the tarmacked roads, but it can be a bit of an endurance test if you aren't used to long-distance pedalling, and positively unpleasant if you get caught in a sudden storm, likely from around July to October. **Mopeds** give you a bit more freedom and are easier to handle, and **jeeps** are available from numerous outlets (be sure to check the restrictions of your insurance if you want to go onto the dirt tracks). Prices vary little, but it's worth shopping around for special offers. Bikes cost around US$5 for 24 hours, mopeds three times that much, and jeeps around US$45 for a twelve-hour day.

Try Rentadora Cozumel, Av 10 Sur 172 (daily 8am–8pm; ☎987/2-11-20 or 2-14-29, fax 2-24-75), and in the lobby of *Hotel Flores*, Salas 72, which offers a full range of modern vehicles and will deliver the car to your hotel. Alternatively, try Rentadora Dorado, Juárez 181-C, which is a little cheaper.

Accommodation

Hotels in Cozumel are not cheap, most of them geared to divers. The affordable places are some way from the beaches, and you can find some bargains in the town centre, but the only truly budget option is to camp on the sands.

Aguilar, C 3 Sur 98, near the corner of Av 5 Sur (☎987/2-03-07, fax 2-07-69). Quiet rooms away from the road around a garden with pool and paddling pool. Fridges and cable TV are extra. ⑤.

Suites Colonial, Av 5 Sur 9, Aptdo 286 (☎987/2-05-42 or 2-05-06, fax 2-13-87). A/c rooms with baths, kitchenettes, cable TV and phones. ⑤–⑥.

Flores, Salas 72 (☎987/2-14-29). Basic rooms, fine for the price, and moped and bike rental in the lobby. ④.

Posada Letty, C 1 Sur, on the corner with Av 15 Sur (☎987/2-02-57). Clean, basic rooms; very light and airy on the first floor. ④.

El Marques, Av 5 Sur 180 (☎987/2-06-77, fax 2-05-37). Comfortable, a/c rooms with fridges, close to the zócalo. ⑤.

Maya Cozumel, C 5 Sur 4 (☎987/2-00-11, fax 2-07-81). Less expensive than the seafront hotels, but just as good, with spacious garden and pool. The a/c rooms have TV, refrigerators and phones. ⑥.

Pepita, Av 15 Sur, on the corner with C 1 Sur (☎987/2-00-98). Basic option with a small pool. ④.

Saolima, Salas 268 (no phone). Rooms away from the road around a plant-filled courtyard. ④.

Villablanca Garden Beach Hotel, about 2km east of the zócalo (☎987/2-01-30 or 2-45-88, fax 2-08-65). More spacious than the town hotels, with a pool, tennis court and dive shop. Dive packages offered and good snorkelling from just across the road. ⑥.

Vista del Mar, Melgar 45, near the corner with C 5 Sur (☎987/2-05-45, fax 2-04-45). Comfortable, modern a/c rooms with sea views, private terraces and refrigerators. Small pool, restaurant, cafeteria, bar, private parking, diving shop and car or scooter rental on the premises. ⑥.

The island

Downtown Cozumel is almost entirely devoted to tourism, packed with restaurants, souvenir shops, tour agencies and "craft markets". **Black coral**, a rare and beautiful product of the reefs, is sold everywhere. Don't buy it: until Jacques Cousteau discovered it off the island about twenty years ago, it was thought to be extinct. Even now there's not a great deal (it grows at little more than an inch every fifty years), so it's expensive and heavily protected – don't, under any circumstances, go breaking it off the reefs. A recent addition to the tourist attractions on the island is the **Archeological Park** (daily 8am–6pm; US$7) on Av 65 on the inland, southern edge of town. The fee includes a guided tour that lasts around an hour, depending on your own pace and interest, leading you along a shady path through a garden filled with replicas of relics from the various ancient Mesoamerican cultures. You can also see demonstrations of hammock- and tortilla-making, in a replica of a Maya home, by Maya in traditional dress.

Cozumel's eastern shoreline is often impressively wild but, as on Isla Mujeres, only the west coast is really suitable for **swimming**, protected as it is by a line of reefs and the mainland. The easiest **beaches** to get to are north of the town in front of the older resort hotels. Far better, though, to rent a vehicle and head off down to the less exploited places to the south.

Heading **south**, you pass first a clutch of modern hotels by the car ferry dock; offshore here, at the end of the Paraiso Reef, you can see a rather alarming wrecked airliner on the bottom – it's a movie prop. There's accessible snorkelling by *Hotel*

Barracuda and further along opposite the *Villablanca Garden Beach Hotel*. Carry on to the **Parque Chankanaab** or "Little Sea", recently designated a **National Park** (daily 7am–5.30pm; US$3), a beautiful if rather over-exploited lagoon full of turtles and lurid fish surrounded by botanical gardens. There's a beach and a tiny reef just offshore; also changing rooms, showers, diving and snorkelling equipment for rent, an expensive restaurant, and a protected children's beach. Further south, **Playa San Francisco** is the best spot for lounging and swimming, while at the southern tip, the **Laguna de Colombia** offers interesting snorkelling.

From here you can complete a circuit of the southern half of the island by following the road up the windswept eastern shoreline. There are a couple of good restaurants at **Punta Chiqueros** and **Punta Morena** and, on calm days, excellent deserted sands. The main road cuts back across the middle of the island to town, but if you have a jeep (not a moped, which probably won't have enough gas anyway) you could continue up a rough track to the northern point – off here is the small ruin of **Castillo Real**.

More accessible – halfway across the island from town, on the northern side of the road – the only excavated ruin on the island, **San Gervasio**, was built to honour Ixchel, the god of fertility. On the southern part of the island, the village of **Cedral** has a tiny Maya site near the old Spanish church; turn inland on the road shortly after passing San Francisco beach. If your vehicle is insured to go on dirt tracks, you can get to **Tumba de Caracol**, near the Punta Celarin Lighthouse on the southernmost point of the island. It may have been built by the Maya as a lighthouse, and is worth visiting to hear the music produced when the wind whistles through the shells encrusted in its walls.

Eating

Eating tends to be expensive wherever you go on Cozumel, but there's plenty of choice if you've got money to spend. Most of the restaurants are downtown or along the island's west coast, but for a more laid-back atmosphere you can enjoy long, lazy lunches in the **palapas** dotted every few kilometres along the rugged eastern coast. Keep your eyes peeled for **discount vouchers** such as the Promo Tips Card given away with *Cozumel Tips*.

La Choza, corner of Av 10 and C Salas. Busy and popular, mid-priced restaurant serving Mexican home cooking. Good service and a buzzing atmosphere.

El Foco, Av 5 Sur 13, near C Salas. Long-established, busy restaurant, serving moderately priced Mexican dishes.

Joe's Lobster Pub, Av 10, between C Salas and C 3. Touristy restaurant serving Mexican food; the house speciality is lobster in garlic sauce. Nightly live music. Open 6pm–2am.

La Laguna, inside Parque Chankanaab. Busy, expensive restaurant with an extensive menu including superb seafood, typical Mexican dishes and cocktails. The park closes at 5.30pm.

Las Palmeras, on the zócalo (☎987/2-05-32). Seafood and Mexican cuisine by the main pier. Busy but mediocre considering the prices. Open 7am–11pm.

Mi Chabelita, Av 10, between C 1 and Salas. One of the few lower-priced restaurants left near the downtown area. A basic Mexican menu in simple surroundings.

Paradise Café. On an anticlockwise circuit of the island, it's where the tarmac road meets the east coast. Palapa-roofed restaurant/bar in the middle of nowhere, dishing up moderately priced Mexican food to the accompaniment of reggae. Good place to swing in a hammock, sipping a margarita. Daily 10.30am–6.30pm.

Pepe's Grill, Av Melgar and C Salas (☎987/2-02-13). Seafood and steak in an elegant and relaxed atmosphere. Expensive but worth it. Daily 5–11pm.

Pizza Rolandi, Melgar 23. The best pizza on the island. Good service and great sangria.

Las Tortugas, Av 10 Nte, near C 2 Nte. Seafood, steaks and fajitas, as well as West Indian dishes, away from the hustle and bustle of the centre. Daily 11am–11pm.

From Playa south to Tulum

South of Playa del Carmen are a number of exquisite **beaches**, most of which have already been developed or are earmarked for exclusive hotels or condos within the next year or two. The first of note, 6km south of Playa, is **XCARET**, tagged the "Incredible Eco-Archeological Park", but in fact a huge, somewhat bizarre **theme park** (daily April–Sept 8.30am–6pm, Oct–March 8.30am–5pm; US$25, free for under-fives). There's a museum, tropical aquarium, aviary, "Maya village", botanical garden, small archeological ruins, pools and beaches, and more than a kilometre of subterranean rivers down which you can swim, snorkel or simply float – along with scores of others – with the help of neon rubber rings.

PUERTO AVENTURAS, 20km south of Playa, was originally planned to comple-ment Cancún, with the five-star hotels, tennis and golf clubs and first-class service to show for it. There's a wide white-sand beach, a marina and a dive centre, but little worth stopping for apart from the **Cedam Museum** (Mon–Fri 10am–5pm), which gives an insight into the lives of the ancient mariners and pirates of this coast, displaying arte-facts from ships wrecked on the reefs in the 1700s. Five kilometres south, the small fishing village of **XPU-HA** is known for its spectacular fresh-water lagoons, **El Cenote Azul** and **El Cenote**, both of which are popular swimming spots.

AKUMAL – "the place of the turtles" – is 11km on: another resort area with high-class accommodation and top-notch facilities. As you enter from the highway, you're greeted by an arch across the road, to the right of which is the reception for the swanky *Hotel Club Akumal Caribe Maya Villas* (☎987/3-05-96; in US ☎1-800/351-1622; ⑦–⑨). Apart from this, there's a variety of accommodation around the bay, ranging from beachfront bungalows to suites and condos, but none of it's cheap. Also on site are a couple of good, if expensive, restaurants and bars, limited shopping and The Akumal Dive Shop (☎987/4-12-59, fax 7-31-64).

Slightly further south, **AVENTURAS AKUMAL**, is dominated by the *Oasis Akumal* (☎987/2-28-28, fax 2-28-87; ⑨), an all-in resort with every facility you can think of. Also here is the *Villa de Rosa* (Postal 25, Tulum, Quintana Roo, 77780; ☎ & fax 987/4-12-71; ⑨), which specializes in **cave and cavern diving trips** along the Caribbean coast. A seven-night all-inclusive package starts at US$850 per person for a minimum of five people.

Six kilometres south of Akumal is another beautiful beach at **XCACEL** (US$2 fee), from where you can walk ten minutes south to a clean, cool cenote with a wooden plat-form for easy access (remember not to wear suntan lotion). Turtles lay their eggs here from May to September, when tourists are not encouraged: outside these times, you can see a few of the gentle creatures at the **turtle sanctuary**. The beach fills up occa-sionally with day-trippers from Playa del Carmen and Cancún, who flock to the large, expensive **restaurant** at the top of the beach (daily 10am–8pm), but otherwise this is a tranquil place to pitch your tent or park your trailer (no hook-ups), with clean show-ers and plenty of shade.

Xel-Ha Lagoon National Park (daily 8am–5.30pm; US$7), 13km north of Tulum, is somewhat overexploited, with expensive restaurants and souvenir shops, and a com-ments book full of complaints from disgruntled Mexicans who feel that too much of the information is in English rather than Spanish. That said, it's a beautiful place, but get here early as after 9.30am you'll be fighting for space. You can rent snorkelling equip-ment on the spot and lockers are available. Across the other side of the highway, the small and only partly excavated **ruins** of Xel-Ha are of little interest but for the Temple of the Birds, where faded paintings are still visible in places.

Tulum

Tulum, 130km south of Cancún, is one of the most picturesque of all Maya sites – small, but exquisitely poised on fifteen-metre-high cliffs above the turquoise Caribbean. When the Spanish first set eyes on the place in 1518, they considered it as large and beautiful a city as Seville. They were, perhaps, misled by their dreams of Eldorado, by the glory of the setting and by the brightly painted facades of the buildings, for architecturally Tulum is no match for the great cities. Nevertheless, thanks to the setting, it sticks in the memory like no other. It is also an important Maya spiritual and cultural centre, and is one of the villages in the **Zona Maya**.

If you want to take time out for a **swim**, you can plunge into the Caribbean straight from the beach on site. There are limitless further possibilities strung out along the sandy road that runs south along the beautiful and deserted coastline. This track continues, though practicable only in a sturdy (and preferably four-wheel drive) vehicle, all the way to Punta Allen at the tip of the peninsula. The beginning of the old road has been blocked to protect the ruins from traffic damage, so you have to join it further south.

The site

The site (daily 8am–5pm; US$4, free on Sun) is about 1km from the main road – be sure to get off the bus at the turn-off to the ruins and not at the village. **Entrance** is through a breach in the wall that protected the city on three sides; the fourth was defended by the sea. This wall, some five metres high with a walkway around the top, may have been defensive, but more likely its prime purpose was to delineate the ceremonial and administrative precinct (the site you see today) from the residential enclaves spread out along the coast in each direction. These houses – by far the bulk of the ancient city – were mostly constructed of perishable material, so little or no trace of them remains.

As you go through the walls, the chief structures lie directly ahead of you, with the Castillo rising on its rocky prominence above the sea. You pass first the tumbledown **Casa de Chultun**, a porticoed dwelling whose roof collapsed only in the middle of this century,

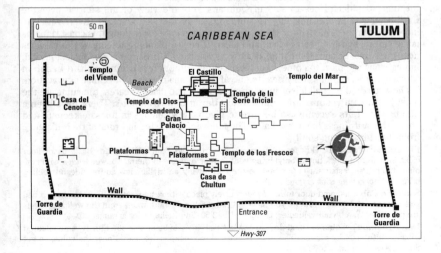

and immediately beyond it the **Templo de los Frescos**. The partly restored murals inside the temple depict Maya gods and symbols of nature's fertility: rain, corn and fish. They originally adorned an earlier structure and have been preserved by the construction around them of a gallery and still later (in the fifteenth century) by the addition of a second temple on top, with walls which, characteristically, slope outwards at the top. On the corners of the gallery are carved masks of Chac, or perhaps of the creator god Itzamna.

The **Castillo**, on the highest part of the site, commands imposing views in every direction. It may have served, as well as a temple, as a beacon or lighthouse – even without a light, it would have been an important landmark for mariners along an otherwise monotonously featureless coastline. You climb first to a small square, in the midst of which stood an altar, before tackling the broad stairway to the top of the castle itself. To the left of this plaza stands the **Templo del Dios Descendente**. The diving or descending god – depicted here above the narrow entrance of the temple – appears all over Tulum as a small, upside-down figure. His exact meaning is not known: he may represent the setting sun, or rain or lightning, or he may be the Bee God, since honey was one of the Maya's most important exports. Opposite is the **Templo de la Serie Inicial** (Temple of the Initial Series) – so called because in it was found a stela (now in the British Museum) bearing a date well before the foundation of the city, and presumably brought here from elsewhere. Right below the castle to the north is a tiny cove with a beautiful white beach, and on the promontory beyond it the **Templo del Viento** (Temple of the Wind), a small, single-roomed structure. This is reflected by a similar chamber – the **Templo del Mar** – overlooking the water at the southern edge of the site.

Staying near Tulum

There are a couple of hotels and restaurants in dusty Tulum village, though there's no reason to try them unless you're stuck without a beach place. You can **change money** at two casas de cambio in the village, one opposite the bus station and one next to it. Joys Car Rental (☎987/1-20-81), on the main street, rent cars and bikes at good rates.

By far the best places to stay, however, are in the **cabañas** and **campsites** scattered along the coast road to Punta Allen, south of the ruins, where you can rent huts or find space for a tent or a hammock. Dramatically situated on a cliff-top, these are some of the most popular places to stay in Quintana Roo: the view of the sunrise over the Caribbean sea in the morning is stunning, as is the sky at night. Even with the increased numbers of visitors, the gorgeous white-sand beach along this coast remains fairly empty, and the sea is warm and clear. If you're planning to stay at the cabañas near the ruins, be sure to turn up as early as you can – Christmas is the busiest period, but cabañas are hard to come by all year round. Although **camping on the beach** in Mexico is free, camping very near to one of the cabaña places could cause aggravation: it's best to pay the small fee or move further away. The places nearest the ruins are the most lively, with **restaurants**, and a **disco bar** at *Don Armando's*. There have been a number of **thefts** recently, so be sure to give your valuables in for safe-keeping and check the sturdiness of your cabaña. The following are listed in order of their distance from the ruins, going south.

El Mirador Cabañas, 1km from the ruins along the old Punta Allen road. Basic sandy-floor cabañas with hammock hooks only: bring your own or rent one of theirs. Shower *palapa* with running water. The restaurant is perched on the cliff, giving an idyllic view and wonderful cooling breezes. Snorkelling trips arranged. ③.

Santa Fe Cabañas, next door to *El Mirador*. Lively place with restaurant-bar. Cabañas have a bed and a hammock but no showers; you have to dredge your washing water from the well and toilets are primitive. Watch your valuables. Camping US$2.50. Snorkelling trips arranged. ③–④.

Don Armando's Cabañas, next door to *Santa Fe* (☎987/4-45-39 or 4-38-56). Sturdy, sandy-floored cabañas with security guards. The most popular of the inexpensive places near the ruins, so get there early. Camping US$3. ④.

Mar Caribe Cabañas, next to *Don's*. Rickety old cabañas for hammocks which were only intended for use by a fishing co-op, but there are plans to improve them. The restaurant does great fresh fish and has the broadest menu of all the cheaper places. ④.

Los Gatos Cabañas, 2km from the ruins. More laid-back than the places nearer the ruins; well-built thatched cabañas with mosquito-netted doubles and hammocks. A relatively private, shady spot, with a superb beach for swimming and snorkelling. Horseback riding can be arranged. Electricity in the restaurant and shower, and some cabañas have feeble battery light. ⑤.

La Perla Cabañas, the next along. Four basic cabañas and a restaurant with bar. ⑤–⑥.

Que Fresco, next to *La Perla*. Nice new cabañas, a restaurant and a shared shower with hot and cold water. ⑤–⑥.

Osho Oasis, 7km from the ruins (PO Box 99, Tulum, Quintana Roo; ☎ & fax 987/4-27-72). A comfortable retreat/resort with four standards of cabaña – some luxurious and spacious with private baths. The restaurant does a delicious veggie buffet, with fish by order. Electricity until about midnight. There's a meditation room and yoga classes, massage sessions, Zen sittings, Kundalini meditation, and a TV with video for occasional film shows. ⑦.

Casa de Maleo, the only cheaper place in this section. Very basic cabañas right on the beach. ④.

Los Arrecifes, 500m further south along the road. Established twenty years ago, this is one of the oldest places on this coast. Cabañas with or without private bath in an idyllic setting with its own stretch of palm-fringed beach and a restaurant. ⑥.

Ana y José, a little further south (call Cancún for reservations: ☎98/80-60-21, fax 80-60-22). A variety of comfortable rooms, some close to the beach with hot and cold water, others set back slightly with cold water only. Good restaurant with a sedate and intimate atmosphere. You can also rent bikes and organize day-trips into the Sian Ka'an Biosphere Reserve from here. ⑦.

Dos Ceibas, 9km from the ruins (☎987/1-20-92). The last on this stretch, and the best of the lot, with very beautiful cabañas almost in the Sian Ka'an Reserve, in front of a turtle egg-laying beach. ⑦.

Cobá

Set in muggy rainforest dotted with lakes, 50km northwest of Tulum, **COBÁ** is a fascinating, if little-visited site. Still only partly excavated, its most surprising characteristic is a resemblance not to the great ruins of the Yucatán, but to those of the Maya in lowland Guatemala and Honduras. This was clearly a very important centre in the Late Classic period (600–800 AD), and its remains, scattered between two lakes, are linked by more causeways than have been found at any other site. Seeing it all requires at least a couple of hours' wandering in the jungle, along sparsely signed paths. Most important of the structures is the part-restored **Pyramid of Nohoch Mul**, the tallest in the Yucatán and strikingly similar, in its long, narrow and precipitous stairway, to the famous Guatemalan ruins of Tikal.

Practicalities

There are four buses a day to Cobá from Tulum that continue on to Valladolid. They are all *de paso* once they reach Cobá – which means that you'll probably have to wait for a couple of hours. There are also four buses from Cobá to Tulum. Only three are *de paso* – a bus at 1.30pm leaves from Cobá itself.

The **village** of Cobá, where the bus stops, is little more than a collection of shacks a few hundred metres from the site entrance. Should you be in the mood to blow a lot of money, you could do little better than **stay** at the *Villas Arqueologicas* (☎98/84-25-74; in US ☎1-800/528-3100; ⑧), the only hotel anywhere near the site, and a wonderful bit of tropical luxury complete with swimming pool and archeological library. On the less expensive side, there are basic rooms to be had at *El Bocadito* (③), which also has a decent restaurant. Other than this, you have little choice but to grab a drink and something to eat from one of the stalls by the entrance to the site. Don't swim in the lake here – it's full of crocodiles.

The Sian Ka'an Biosphere Reserve

Created by presidential decree in 1986, the 5280-square-mile **Sian Ka'an Biosphere Reserve** is one of the largest protected areas in Mexico. The name means "the place where the sky is born" in the Maya language, and seems utterly appropriate when you experience the sunrise on this stunningly beautiful coast. It's a huge, sparsely populated region, with only around a thousand permanent inhabitants, mainly fishermen, *chicleros* and *milpa* farmers.

Approximately one-third of the area is **tropical forest**, one-third **fresh and salt water marshes and mangroves**, and one-third is marine environment, including a section of the longest **barrier reef** in the western hemisphere. The coastal forests and wetlands are particularly important feeding and wintering areas for North American migratory birds. Sian Ka'an contains examples of the principal ecosystems found in the Yucatán peninsula and the Caribbean: an astonishing variety of flora and fauna. All five species of Mexican **cat** – jaguar, puma, ocelot, margay and jaguarundi – are present, along with spider and howler **monkeys**, tapir, deer and the West Indian manatee. More than 300 species of **birds** have been recorded, including flamingo, roseate spoonbill, white ibis, crested guan, wood stork, osprey, and fifteen species of heron. The Caribbean beaches provide nesting grounds for four endangered species of **marine turtle**: the green, loggerhead, hawksbill and leatherback, while Morelet's and mangrove **crocodiles** inhabit the swamps and lagoons.

The Biosphere Reserve concept, developed since 1974 by UNESCO, is an ambitious attempt to combine the protection of natural areas and the conservation of their genetic diversity with scientific research and sustainable development. Reserves consist of a strictly protected **core area**, a designated **buffer zone** used for non-destructive activities, and an outer **transition zone**, merging with unprotected land, where traditional land-use and experimental research take place. The success of the reserve depends to a great extent on the co-operation and involvement of local people and the Sian Ka'an management plan incorporates several income-generating projects, such as improved fishing techniques, ornamental plant nurseries and, of course, tourism.

You can enter the reserve on your own (and at present there is no entrance fee) and there is accommodation at **Punta Allen**, the largest village in the reserve, but by far the best way to explore is on a **day-trip** with the **Amigos de Sian Ka'an**, a Cancún-based, non-profit organization formed to promote the aims for which the reserve was established. The Amigos support scientific research and produce a series of guide and reference books on the natural history of Sian Ka'an. You can either be picked up at your hotel **in Cancún, at Playa del Carmen** or at *Ana y José Cabañas* **in Tulum**. The weekly trip, led by bilingual Mexican biologists, begins at *Boca Paila Lodge*, where you will board a small launch and motor across the lagoon and upstream along through the mangroves canalized by the Maya. It's an amazing trip, with excellent opportunities for bird-watching and spotting crocodiles or manatees. At the inner lagoon you'll be shown where fresh water percolates up through the sandy lagoon floor. You'll also be given the choice to snorkel back along the channels through the mangroves, drifting with the current – that is, after a short talk on what to do if you meet a crocodile. Some day-trips include a visit to **Chunyaxche ruins** (see below), walking from the lagoon through the rainforest to the site. This is more likely if they start in Tulum rather than Cancún; ask when you're booking your trip.

To arrange a trip, for information on the work of the Amigos, or for details of how to receive their bulletin, call in at their office in Cancún at Av Cobá 5 between Nube and Brisa, on the third floor of the Plaza America (☎98/84-95-83, fax 87-30-80; *sian@cancun.rce.com.mx*), or write to Apartado Postal 770, Cancún 77500, Quintana Roo, Mexico.

Chunyaxche

The little-visited site of **Chunyaxche** (daily 8am–4pm; US$1.50, free on Sun) lies to the north of the reserve, about 25km south of Tulum. Some day-trips to the reserve include a trip to the ruins, but to **get there independently**, catch any second-class bus heading between Tulum and Chetumal and ask to be dropped at the entrance. A sign on the left of the highway points to a *palapa* that will one day be a visitor centre: for now you pay the caretaker.

Despite its size – probably the largest on the Quintana Roo coast – and proximity to Hwy-307, Chunyaxche is hardly developed for tourism, and you'll probably have the place to yourself. Archeological evidence indicates that Chunyaxche (also known as Muyil) was continuously occupied from the Preclassic period until after the arrival of the Spanish in the sixteenth century. There is no record of the inhabitants coming into direct contact with the conquistadors, but they were probably victims of depopulation caused by introduced diseases. Most of the buildings you see today date from the Postclassic period, between 1200 and 1500 AD. The tops of the tallest structures, just visible from the road, rise twenty metres from the forest floor. There are more than one hundred mounds and temples, none of them completely clear of vegetation, and it's easy to wander around and find dozens of buildings buried in the jungle; climbing them is forbidden, however.

The centre of the site is connected by a *sacbe* – a Maya road – to the small **Muyil lagoon** 500m away. This lagoon is joined to the large Chunyaxche lagoon and ultimately to the sea at **Boca Paila** by an amazing **canalized river**: the route used by Maya traders. If you travel along the river today you'll come across even less explored sites, some of which appear to be connected to the lagoon or river by **underwater caves**.

Leaving the site, particularly if you're making your way up to Tulum, should be easy enough, provided you don't leave it too late; continuing south could prove a little more difficult.

Punta Allen

Right at the tip of the peninsula, with a lighthouse guarding the northern entrance to the **Bahía de la Ascensión**, the Maya lobster-fishing village of **PUNTA ALLEN** is not a place you'd stumble across by accident. Some tourists from Cancún do get down this far in rented cars, but if you've only got one day virtually all you can do is turn around and head back.

Despite having a population of just four hundred, Punta Allen is the largest village within the reserve and is a focus of initiatives by both government departments and non-governmental organizations promoting sustainable development. During the summer, Earthwatch volunteers (see p.53) come here to assist scientists gathering data.

Entering the village, past the tiny naval station on the right and beached fishing boats on the left, you come to the first of the **accommodation** options: the *Cuzan Guest House* (☎983/4-03-58; ⑤), with tall conical cabañas and teepees, some with hot water. There's a **bar** and **restaurant** with information about the reserve, though you'll need to book meals if you're not staying there. On the beach, the *Let It Be Inn* (⑦) has three cabañas with private bath and a separate large thatched cabaña with a self-catering kitchen and dining room. *Chen Chomac Resort* (in Playa del Carmen: ☎987/2-20-20, fax 2-41-20; ⑦), a few kilometres north of the village, has some comfortable, modern thatched cabañas on the beach.

In theory there's a **long-distance phone** in the village shop, the Tienda Lili, but it can't be relied upon. A couple of small **restaurants**, the *Punta Allen* and the *Candy,* serve food. A **mobile shop** travels the length of the peninsula on Saturdays, selling meat, bread, fruit and vegetables, reaching Punta Allen about 2pm: useful if you're camping. Although there's no **dive shop**, the hotels generally have some form of watersport equipment for their guests and may let non-residents rent it. Fishermen can be persuaded to take you out into the reserve for a fee; they also go across the bay to the even tinier village of **Vigia Chico**, on the mainland.

From Tulum to Chetumal

The road from Tulum to Chetumal skirts around the Sian Ka'an Biosphere Reserve and heads inland, past Felipe Carrillo Puerto, a major crossroads on the routes to Valladolid and Mérida, the beautiful **Laguna Bacalar**, and on to **Chetumal**, the gateway to Belize and a good point from which to explore **Kohunlich** and other Maya sites.

Felipe Carillo Puerto

FELIPE CARILLO PUERTO, formerly known as **Chan Santa Cruz**, is the capital of the "Zona Maya" and an important spiritual centre for the Maya. During the Caste Wars, Maya from the north gathered forces here and looked for guidance from a miraculous talking cross that told them to fight on against their oppressors (such talking crosses and statues are common in Maya mythology as conduits through which disincarnate spirits speak, or as manifestations of a soul, usually that of a shaman, when it has left the body during the state of trance; they are known as *way'ob* by the Yucatek Maya). Presumably as an attempt to disguise its rebellious past, the town was renamed after a former governor of the Yucatán who was assassinated in 1924. However, a monument to the martyrs of the Caste Wars still stands in the town. There are several reasonable **hotels** around the main plaza – try the *Hotel Esquivel* (☎983/4-03-44; ③) on the zócalo, only 100m from the small bus station, but check the rooms first as some are significantly better than others.

Laguna Bacalar

Further south, some 35km north of Chetumal, is the beautiful **Laguna Bacalar**, the second largest lake in Mexico; 45km long and, on average, 1km wide, it links with a series of other lakes and eventually the Río Hondo and the sea. The village of Bacalar was a key point on the pre-Columbian trade route and unexcavated **Maya remains** surround the lake shore. The *Chilam Balam* of Chumayel, one of the Maya's sacred books, mentions it as the first settlement of the Itza, a Maya tribe originally from central Mexico. Near the village, there's a semi-ruinous **fort**: built by the Spanish for protection against British pirates from Belize (then British Honduras), it became a Maya stronghold in the Caste Wars, and was the last place to be subdued by the government, in 1901. There's a wide variety of **bird life**, as well as huge fish that reach nearly two metres long. Nearby is the **Cenote Azul**, an inky-blue "bottomless" well that is crowded with swimmers and picnickers at weekends.

There are several lakeshore restaurants in the village, a couple of very basic pensiones and the splendidly grand and imposing *Hotel Laguna* (☎983/2-35-17; ⑤). Other options are outside the town: *Rancho Encantado* (☎ & fax 983/8-04-27, in US ☎1-800/ 221-6509; ⑨ including breakfast and dinner) is a small resort on the lakeshore, with half a dozen cabañas, each with its own kitchen and dining room; it also organizes trips to Kohunlich and scuba-diving to Banco Chinchorro. *Paraiso Ranch* (☎983/7-10-26, fax 2-12-51; US$7 with their tent, US$5 with your own), 10km south of Bacalar (taxi US$3), is a family-owned **eco-tourism and conservation project** and one of the most beautiful places to stay in Quintana Roo. Facilities are basic – there are no showers, accommodation is in tents, there's no bar and only one little restaurant – but guests come to enjoy the breathtaking natural beauty and participate in the conservation work that the very hospitable family organize. They also arrange canoe expeditions and tours of the little-visited Maya ruins in the south of Quintana Roo.

Chetumal and around

If you're heading south to Belize or Guatemala, you can't avoid **CHETUMAL**, capital of the state of Quintana Roo. The city is beginning to assert itself after decades of virtual stagnation, but there are still no "sights" to speak of. The best is the new **Museo de la Cultura Maya** (Tues–Sun 9am–7pm; US$4) on Héroes, near the corner of Mahatma

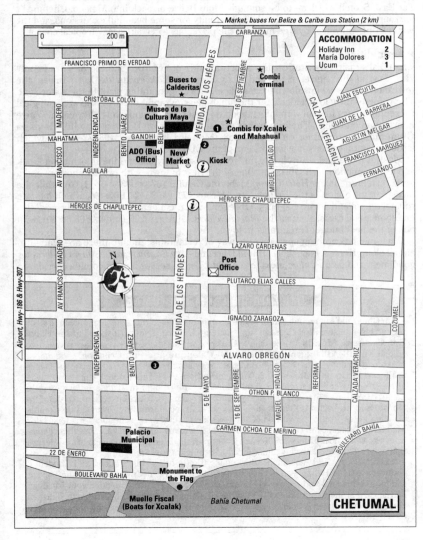

Gandhi. Although it has very few original artefacts, the numerous interactive displays and models provide a fascinating insight into ancient Maya society, mathematics and cosmology. The courtyard outside the museum often hosts free exhibitions and there's a good **bookshop** selling guides and maps. Chetumal's broad, modern streets (the town was levelled by Hurricane Janet just over thirty years ago) are lined with rather dull, overpriced hotels and restaurants, and with shops doing a brisk trade in **low-duty goods** – Dutch cheese, Taiwanese hi-fis, American peanuts, reproduction Levis from the Far East, Scotch whisky – to be smuggled into Belize or back into Mexico. Chetumal's surroundings, however, do offer the opportunity for some beautiful excursions, and the **waterfront**, enlivened by free music in the plaza, has a certain sleazy tropical charm.

Practicalities

Chetumal's main **bus station** is a short taxi ride out of town and the **airport** is only 2km west of the centre, at the end of Av Revolución. **Avenida de los Héroes**, the town's main street, runs down from a big electricity-generating plant to the waterfront. The **information kiosk** (look for the small glass pyramid opposite the archeological museum) is very helpful with information on buses, hotels and maps; they can also give information on Belize. The **bus ticket office** in town is on Belice at Gandhi. There's a **Guatemalan consulate** on Héroes 358 (Mon–Fri 9am–4pm; ☎983/2-65-65), which issues visas (not necessary for citizens of the EU or the USA).

Most of Chetumal's **hotels** are on Héroes, especially around the information kiosk and at the junction with Obregón. One of the best in town, with private showers and a good restaurant, is the *Hotel Ucum*, Mahatma Gandhi 167 (☎983/2-07-11; ③), while the nicest luxury option is the *Holiday Inn*, Héroes 171 (☎983/2-11-00; ⑦), which has a/c rooms, a pool and a travel agency. Obregón, which cuts east–west along Héroes, also has some good deals, such as the *María Dolores*, Obrégon 206 (☎983/2-05-08; ④), with one of the best budget restaurants in town.

Chetumal has nothing special in the way of restaurants, though there are **places to eat** all along Héroes, especially around Obregón – try *Sosilmar* at the *María Dolores* for good meat and fish. *Pantoja*, next to the *Hotel Ucum*, serves a good comida corrida – a

---

MOVING ON FROM CHETUMAL

From Chetumal's main bus station you'll be able to travel to most destinations on first- or second-class buses. First-class services include: **Cancún** (eight daily via **Tulum, Playa Del Carmen**); **Mérida** (three daily); **Campeche** (six daily, most via **Escarcega**, two stop at **Xpujil**); **Villahermosa** (three daily) **Palenque and San Cristóbal** (one daily); **México** (two daily). There are second-class services that follow the same routes. Buses to **Flores in Guatemala** (one daily) also leave from the main terminal. Buses for towns in **Belize** leave hourly from the Venus Bus Line (mornings) or Batty's (afternoons) in **Lázaro Cárdenas** market, in the city centre. Combis for **Bacalar** (every 30min), **Río Hondo** and **Mahahual/Xcalak** (one daily at 7am) leave from the Terminal de Combis on Hidalgo at Primo de Verdad. Other, smaller combis are scheduled to depart for Mahahual/Xcalak from C 16 de Septiembre at Mahatma Gandhi at 7am, but their departures are whimsical. **Boats for Xcalak** leave from the Muelle Fiscal (pier) off Boulevard Bahía every Friday, Saturday and Sunday at 8am and return at 3pm.

Taesa, Aviasca and Aeromexico have daily **flights** to Mérida, Cancún and Mexico; if you want to fly to Belize, you have to cross to Corozal, twenty minutes from the border, and take an internal flight. Crossing into Belize is straightforward: hand in your Mexican tourist card at the immigration office at the border and walk over the bridge to Belizean immigration; there's no charge. Moneychangers at the border offer fair rates and take travellers' cheques.

favourite with the locals. For budget food, stick to the area around the **markets**, or eat in one of the stalls in the market opposite the museum. Vegetarians, as is so often the case, have few options. The best is *Sergio's* on Obregon no. 182, which serves some veggie soups, pizzas and salads. There's a good **bakery** next to the *María Dolores*.

Around Chetumal

Near Chetumal are any number of refreshing escapes from the heat and dull modernity. At weekends, the town descends en masse on **CALDERITAS**, a small seaside resort just 6km north around the bay; there's a good campsite on the beach here, at *Amanacer en El Caribe*: they also have thatched cabañas, some with cooking facilities (⑤), and a trailer park. The **Laguna Milagros**, off the road towards Francisco Escárcega, is less spectacular than Bacalar, but is superb for bird-watching.

XCALAK is a tiny, very sleepy fishing community at the tip of the isthmus that stretches like a finger towards Belize on the other side of the huge Bahía de Chetumal. Boats leave from the Muelle Fiscal (pier) off Boulevard Bahía in Chetumal every Friday, Saturday and Sunday at 8am and return at 3pm.There are no spectacular beaches and nothing much to do in the village, but it is an excellent base for **bird-watching**, snorkelling and manatee safaris; contact the friendly and knowledgeable Carlos Vidal Batun, who organizes these trips. His house is at the southern end of the village or to book in advance, write in Spanish to him at domicilio conocido, Xcalak, Quintana Roo 77000. Adolfo Acevedo Young, a trained guide and conservationist (domicilio conocido, Xcalak, Quintana Roo 77940; ☎983/8-76-70) organizes **diving and boat trips** to the vast atoll of **Banco Chinchorro** and to Belize. There are few facilities in Xcalak: a couple of small restaurants and one basic but clean hotel, the *Caracol* (②).

MAHAHUAL, 25km north of Xcalak on an unpaved road, has more resident non-Mexicans, and a tiny beach. It's a very relaxing place, and is slightly closer to the Chinchorro atoll if you want to go diving. The Italian-owned cabañas, 400m after the *Piratos del Caribe* restaurant, 7km south of Mahahual village, are the best place to stay. Buses or combis will drop you there; otherwise you'll have to hitch as there are no taxis. If you want to **dive**, try Caribe Manaties Dive centre in town.

Local buses and combis run out to all of these frequently from the terminal at the junction of Verdad and Hidalgo, four blocks northwest of the information kiosk on Héroes. Buses to Calderitas leave from Cristóbal Colón, near the junction with Héroes. Travelling around this area, keep your passport and tourist card with you – as in all border zones, there are checkpoints on the roads.

Kohunlich and other Maya sites in the south

The most direct route from Chetumal back towards central Mexico is across the bottom of the peninsula via Francisco Escárcega (see p.520). This, on the whole, is virgin forest dotted only by sparse settlements with a desperately pioneer air, but in the Classic Maya era it was relatively populous. With a car you could visit several **sites** along the way – first, and most impressive, is **KOHUNLICH**, set in rainforest 60km from Chetumal, then another 9km off the road (daily 8am–5pm; US$4, free on Sun). Like Cobá, Kohunlich owes more to the traditions of Maya Guatemala than to the Yucatán. The ruins, dating from the late Pre-Classic to Early Classic (100–550 AD) are characteristic of sites in southern Campeche and Quintana Roo, featuring enormous monumental masks of deities. Its most impressive structure is the **Temple of the Masks**, with great sculpted faces of the Maya sun god.

There are other Maya sites in the south of Quintana Roo including the impressive Río Bec ruins at **Dzibanche**, **Chacchoben** and **Kinichna**. At present there is no transport to any of these ruins (or to Kohunlich), but plans are afoot and it's worth checking with the tourist office in Chetumal.

FIESTAS

JANUARY

The first week of January sees the festival of the Magi in **Tizimín** (Yucatán), an important religious and secular gathering.

6 FIESTA DE POLK KEKEN in **Lerma** (Campeche), near Campeche, with many traditional dances.

21 In **Dzitas** (Yuc), north of Chichén Itzá, an ancient festival with roots in Maya tradition.

In **Temax** (Yuc), between Mérida and Tizimín, the last Sunday of the month is celebrated with a fiesta – the culmination of a week's religious celebration.

FEBRUARY

CARNIVAL (the week before Lent, variable Feb–March) is at its most riotous in **Mérida**, though it's celebrated, too, in **Campeche** and **Chetumal** and on **Isla Mujeres** and **Cozumel**.

MARCH

20 FERIA DE LAS HAMACAS in **Tecoh** (Yuc), a hammock-producing village near Mérida.

21 EQUINOX Huge gathering to see the serpent shadow at **Chichén Itzá**.

APRIL

13 The traditional festival of honey and corn in **Hopelchén** (Cam) lasts until the 17th.

MAY

3 DÍA DE LA SANTA CRUZ is the excuse for another fiesta in **Hopelchén** (Cam); also celebrated in **Celestún** (Yuc) and **Felipe Carrillo Puerto** (Quintana Roo).

12–18 Fiesta in **Chankán Veracruz** (QR), near Felipe Carrillo Puerto, celebrating the Holy Cross which spoke to the Maya here.

20 FERIA DEL JIPI in **Becal** (Cam), the town where many of these hats are made.

JUNE

14–16 Fiestas for the patron saint of **Ciudad del Carmen** (Cam).

26–30 The Festival of San Pedro and San Pablo celebrated on **Cozumel** and in **Panaba** (Yuc), north of Tizimín.

JULY

At **Edzná** (Cam, date variable) a Maya ceremony to the god Chac is held, to encourage, or celebrate, the arrival of the rains.

AUGUST

10–16 Feria in **Oxkutzcab** (Yuc).

SEPTEMBER

14 DÍA DE SAN ROMAN. In **Dzan** (Yuc), near Ticul, the end of a four-day festival with fireworks, bullfights, dances and processions – in **Campeche** (Cam) the Feria de San Roman lasts until the end of the month.

21 EQUINOX Another serpent spectacle at **Chichén Itzá**.

29 DÍA DE SAN MIGUEL is celebrated with a major festival in **Maxcanu** (Yuc), on the road from Mérida to Campeche.

OCTOBER

The first two weeks of October in **Mérida** see processions and celebrations associated with the miraculous statue of Cristo de las Ampillas.

18 A pilgrimage centred on **Izamal** (Yuc) starts ten days of celebration, culminating in dances on the night of the 28th.

NOVEMBER

1–2 DAY OF THE DEAD celebrated almost everywhere.

8–13 Feria in **Tekax** (Yuc), on the road from Mérida to Felipe Carrillo Puerto, with dances and bullfights.

DECEMBER

3–8 Popular fiesta with traditional dances in **Kantunilkin** (QR).

8 DÍA DE LA INMACULADA CONCEPCIÓN is widely celebrated, but especially in **Izamal** (Yuc) and **Champotón** (Cam), each of which has a fiesta starting several days earlier.

travel details

Buses

There aren't many places that you can't get to by bus on the peninsula. Sometimes the timetabling isn't totally convenient but the service is generally efficient. The most useful services are between Mérida and Cancún and those provided by Interplaya, which run at least every thirty minutes between Cancún and Tulum. Some places aren't served by first-class buses, but second-class buses and combis will get you around locally and to the nearest major centre. Such places include: Oxkutzcab, Progreso, Ticul and Tizimín. The following frequencies and times are for first-class services. Second-class buses usually cover the same routes running ten to twenty percent slower.

Campeche to: Ciudad del Carmen (hourly; 3hr); Mérida (more than 12 daily; 2hr), Chetumal via Escarcega and Xpujil (3 daily; 5–7hr), Villahermosa (10 daily; 6–7hr). There are also services to San Cristobal (via Palenque), Cancún, Playa del Carmen, Veracruz, México and Coatzalcoalcos (for southern Veracruz).

Cancún to: Campeche (1 daily; 8hr); Chetumal (5 daily; 6hr); Mérida (frequently; 5–6hr); México (1 daily; 30hr+); Playa del Carmen (frequently; 1hr); Puerto Morelos (at least every 30min; 1hr); Tizimín (3 daily; 3hr); Tulum (at least every 30min; 2hr); Valladolid (6 daily; 2hr); Villahermosa (1 daily; 14hr).

Chetumal to: Cancún (8 daily via Tulum, Playa del Carmen; 5–8hr); Bacalar (every 30min; 30min); Merida (3 daily; 8–10hr); Campeche (daily; 10hr); Villahermosa (3 daily); Palenque & San Cristóbal (1 daily; 10hr); México (2 daily; 24hr); Mahahual/Xcalak (1 daily); Flores in Guatemala (1 daily; 12hr).

Mérida to: Campeche (every 30min; 3–4hr); Cancún (frequently; 5–6hr); Chetumal (7 daily; 9hr); México (6 daily; 28hr+); Palenque (2 daily; 10–11hr); Playa del Carmen (frequently; 8hr); Progreso (frequently; 45min); Tizimín (3 daily; 4hr); Tulum (8 daily; 6hr); Uxmal (13 daily; 2hr); Valladolid (hourly; 3hr); Villahermosa (6 daily; 10hr).

Playa del Carmen to: Cancún (frequently; 1hr); Chetumal (5 daily; 5–8hr); Cobá (4 daily; 2hr); Mérida (8 daily; 8hr); México (1 daily; 30hr+); Palenque (1 daily; 12hr); San Cristóbal de las Casas (1 daily; 14hr); Tulum (frequently; 1hr); Tuxtla Gutiérrez (1 daily; 16hr); Valladolid (3 daily; 4hr); Villahermosa (4 daily; 13hr).

Tizimín to: Mérida (3 daily; 4hr); Río Lagartos (5 daily; 1hr); Valladolid (hourly; 1hr).

Tulum to: Cancún (at least every 30min; 2hr); Chetumal (7 daily; 4–5hr); Cobá (4 daily; 1hr); Mérida (8 daily; 6hr); Playa del Carmen (frequently; 1hr); Valladolid (8 daily; 4hr); San Cristóbal (1 daily).

Valladolid to: Cancún (6 daily; 2hr); Chetumal (3 daily; 5hr); Cobá (4 daily; 2hr); Mérida (hourly; 3hr); Playa del Carmen (3 daily; 4hr); Tizimín (hourly; 1hr); Tulum (4 daily; 4hr).

Planes

Mérida, Cancún and Cozumel all have busy **international airports** with several daily flights to México and regular connections to Miami and many other cities in the southern USA. Campeche and Chetumal also have daily direct services to México. Around the Caribbean coast various small companies fly light planes – very frequently between Cancún and Cozumel, less often from these places to Isla Mujeres, Playa del Carmen and Tulum.

Ferries

There are frequent competitive ferry services to **Isla Mujeres** and **Cozumel**. On both routes there is a choice between a low-cost slow boat or a more luxurious fast boat, which generally halves the crossing time. Although there is a car ferry to Isla Mujeres, it is hardly worth taking a vehicle over as the island is so small.

Passenger Ferries

Chiquilá to: Isla Holbox (2 daily; 1hr).

Playa del Carmen to: Cozumel (every 1–2hr; 30min–1hr).

Punta Juárez to: Isla Mujeres (every 30min; 15–30min).

Car Ferries

Chiquilá to: Isla Holbox (1 daily, except Thurs & Sun; 1hr).

Puerto Morelos to: Cozumel – erratic, so check (1 daily, 2 on Mon; 2hr 30min).

Punta Sam to: Isla Mujeres (6 daily).

PART THREE

THE
CONTEXTS

THE HISTORICAL FRAMEWORK

Mexico as we know it, with its present borders, has been in existence for less than 150 years. Real history, and a political entity known as Mexico, can be traced back before that, to the Spanish Conquest – but anything which predates the sixteenth century is largely a matter of oral histories recorded long after the events, and of archeological conjecture, for the Spanish were assiduous in their destruction of traces of the cultures that preceded them.

Such cultures were not confined to Mexico, but must instead be considered as part of **Mesoamerica** which extends from the mid-north of Mexico well into Central America. To the north of this imaginary line the native tribes were essentially akin to those of North America, never abandoning their nomadic, hunter-gatherer existence; in the south, the Maya were spread all the way from south-eastern Mexico into what is now Honduras. Within Mesoamerica some of the world's most extraordinary societies grew up, creating – without the use of metal tools, draft animals or the wheel (used only in toys) – vast cities controlling millions of people, superb statuary and sculpture, and a mathematical and calendrical system more advanced than those known in the "civilized" world.

The **prehistory** set out below is based on the latest archeological theories which are generally, but by no means universally, accepted. There are still major puzzles – especially concerned with the extent and nature of the contact between the societies and their influence on each other – which, should they be solved, may overturn many existing notions.

And there remain those determined to prove some of the theories first coined in the eighteenth century when serious investigation began – that Mexico is Atlantis, or that its cities were founded by Egyptians, Assyrians or Indians (or more recently space travellers). Mormon expeditions, for instance, continue to dig for proof that ancient Mexicans were in fact the lost tribes of Israel.

PREHISTORY

Quite when the **first inhabitants** of the Americas crossed the Bering Straits is a subject that can keep archeologists going all day, but the earliest widely accepted date is around 15,000 years ago. Successive waves of nomadic, Stone-Age hunters continued to arrive until around 6000 BC, pushing their predecessors gradually farther south.

In the period known as **Archaic**, around 5000–2000 BC, come the first signs of settled habitation: the cultivation of corn, followed by the emergence of crude pottery, stone tools and even of trade between the regions. But the first real civilization was established in the **Preclassic** or **Formative** era (2500 BC–250 AD) with the rise of the Olmecs.

Still the least known of all the ancient societies, **Olmec** cities flourished in the low-lying coastal jungles of Tabasco and Veracruz. They are regarded by many as the inventors of almost every aspect of the cultures which are recognizably Mesoamerican. What you see of them in the museums today is a magnificent artistic style exemplified in their sculpture and in the famous colossal heads. These, with their puzzling "baby-faced" features, were carved from monolithic blocks of basalt and somehow transported over ninety kilometres from the quarries to their final settings – proof in itself of a hierarchical society commanding a sizeable workforce.

CLASSIC CIVILIZATIONS

The Olmec centres were already in decline by the end of the pre-Classic period – **La Venta**, the most important site, seems to have been abandoned about 400 BC, and the rest followed in the next few hundred years – but by this time other cities were growing up throughout central Mexico. The early phases of **Monte Albán**, near Oaxaca, show particularly strong Olmec influence, and in and around the great **Valley of México** itself (where México now stands; an area known in pre-Hispanic times as Anahuac) many small cities grew up. **Tlatilco** concealed a great hoard of Olmec objects, and all these cities must have had contact with the Olmecs through trade at least. Meanwhile there were hints of more important things to come; **Cuicuilco** (now in the capital's suburbs) was an important city until it was buried by a volcanic eruption around the beginning of the first century AD, and at the same time the first important buildings of **Teotihuacán** were being constructed.

Teotihuacán dominated the **Classic Period** (250–900 AD) in central Mexico as the first truly great urban society, and its architectural and religious influences are seen as far south as the Maya heartlands of Guatemala. Even today the city, with its great Pyramids of the Sun and Moon, is a vast and chillingly impressive testimony to an urban-based society ruled by a demanding religious elite. Historically, there's not a great deal to be said about Teotihuacán, for in the absence of written records we know almost nothing of its people or rulers, or even its true name (Teotihuacán was coined by the Aztecs – it means "the place where men became gods"). What is certain is that the city's period of greatness ended around 650 AD, and that within a century it had been abandoned altogether. Societies throughout Mesoamerica, and in particular the Maya, seem to have been disrupted at much the same time, and many other important sites were deserted.

The great **Maya** centres had also reached the peak of their artistic, scientific and architectural achievements in the Classic period, above all in their cities in the lowlands of Guatemala and Honduras. These survived longer than Teotihuacán, but by around 800 AD had also been abandoned. In the Yucatán the Maya fared rather better, their cities revived from about 900 by an injection of ideas (and perhaps invaders)

from central Mexico. The famous structures at **Chichén Itzá** mostly date from this later phase, around 900–1100 AD.

In general, the Classic era saw development everywhere – other important centres grew up on the **Gulf Coast** at El Tajín and in the Zapotec areas around **Monte Albán** – followed by very rapid decline. There are numerous theories to account for this – and certainly the fall of Teotihuacán must have affected its trading partners throughout Mexico severely – but none are entirely convincing. In all probability, once started, the disasters had a knock-on effect, and probably they were provoked by some sort of agricultural failure or ecological disaster which led to a loss of faith in the rulers, perhaps even rebellion.

TOLTECS AND AZTECS

At the same time, the start of the **post-Classic** era (900–1520 AD) saw the first of a series of invasions from the north which must have exacerbated any problems. Wandering tribes would arrive in the fertile valley of México, like what they saw, build a city adopting many of the styles and religions of their predecessors in the area, enjoy a brief period of dominance, and be subdued in turn by a new wave of Chichimeca. In general, all such tribes were known as **Chichimec**, which implies barbarian (even if many of them were at least semi-civilized before they arrived), and all claimed to have set out on their journeys from the legendary seven caves of Chicomoztoc. Many cities were founded in the valley, and many achieved brief ascendancy (or at least independence), but two names stand out in this new warlike era – the Toltecs and the Aztecs.

The **Toltec** people, who dominated the central valleys from around 950–1150 AD, were among the first to arrive – indeed some say that it was a direct attack by them which destroyed Teotihuacán. They assumed a mythical significance for the Aztecs, who regarded them as the founders of every art and science and claimed direct descent from Toltec blood. In fact, the Toltecs borrowed almost all their ideas from Teotihuacán, and their influence can never have been as pervasive as that city's.

Nevertheless there were developments under the Toltecs, and in particular the cult of **Quetzalcoatl** assumed new importance: the god is depicted everywhere at Tula, the Toltec capital (where he may have been embodied as a king or dynasty of kings), and it was from here that he was driven out by the evil god Texcatlipoca. The prediction of his return was later to have fatal consequences. The structure of Toltec society, too, was at least as militaristic as it was religious, and human sacrifice was practised on a far larger scale than had been seen before.

When the **Aztecs** (or Mexica) arrived in central Mexico around the end of the twelfth century they found numerous small city-states, more or less powerful, but none in anything like a position of dominance. Even so it wasn't until 1345 – a period spent scavenging and raiding, often in semi-slavery to local rulers or working as mercenaries – that they found sufficient peace and the prophesied sign (an eagle perched on a cactus devouring a snake) to build their own city.

This, **Tenochtitlán**, was to become the heart of the most formidable of all Mexican empires, but its birth was still not easy. The chosen setting, an island in a lake (now México) was hardly promising, and the new city was at first a subject of its larger neighbours. By forming reed islands anchored to the lake bed by trees, the Mexica became self-sufficient in agriculture and expanded their base; they rebelled successfully against their former rulers, and around 1429 formed a triple alliance with neighbouring Texcoco and Tlacopán to establish the basis of the **Aztec empire**. Its achievements were remarkable – in less than a hundred years the Aztecs had come to control, and demand tribute and taxes from, the whole of central and southern Mexico. Tenochtitlán became huge – certainly the invading Spanish could not believe its size and grandeur – but however it grew, the gods continued to demand more war: to suppress rebellious subjects, and to provide fresh victims for the constant rituals of human sacrifice.

Meanwhile, other societies had continued much as before. In Oaxaca the Zapotecs were subjected to invasions by **Mixtecs** from the mountains in much the same way as was happening in central Mexico. By war and alliance the Mixtecs came eventually to dominate all their lands – developing the crafts of the potter and goldsmith as never before – and fell to the Aztecs only in the last years before the Spanish Conquest. In the Yucatán, the **Maya** were never conquered, but their culture was in decline and any form of central authority had long since broken down. Nevertheless, they carried on trade all around the coasts, and Christopher Columbus himself (though he never got to Mexico) encountered a heavily laden boat full of Maya traders, plying between Honduras and the Yucatán. On the **Gulf Coast** Aztec dominance was total by the time the Spanish arrived, but they were still struggling to subdue the **West**.

THE SPANISH CONQUEST

Hernan Cortés landed on the coast near modern Veracruz on April 21, 1519 – Good Friday. With him there were just 550 men, a few horses, dogs and a cannon; yet in less than three years they had defeated the Aztecs and effectively established control over most of Mexico. Several factors enabled them to do so. First was Cortés himself, as ruthless a leader as any in history: he burned the expedition's boats within days of their arrival, so that there was literally no turning back. In addition his men had little to lose and much to gain, and their metal weapons and armour were greatly superior to anything the Aztecs had (although many Spaniards adopted Aztec-style padded cotton, which was warmer, lighter and almost as protective). Their gunpowder and cannon could also wreak havoc with opposing armies – if mainly psychologically. The horses, too, terrified the Aztecs as well as affording greater manoeuvrability, and the attack dogs, trained to kill, were almost as effective. None of these, though, in the end counted a fraction as much as Cortés' ability to form alliances with tribes who were fretting under Aztec subjugation and whose numbers eventually swelled his armies at least tenfold.

Even so, **Moctezuma**, had he chosen to do so, could certainly have destroyed the Spanish before they left their first camp, since his spies had brought news of their arrival almost immediately. Instead he sent a delegation bearing gifts of gold and jewels which he hoped would persuade them to leave in peace. They served only to inflame the imaginative greed of the Spanish. By all accounts Moctezuma was a morose, moody and indecisive man, but his failure to act against Cortés had deeper roots: he was also heavily influenced by religious omens, and the arrival of Cortés coincided with the predicted date for the return of **Quetzalcoatl**. The invaders were fair-skinned and bearded, as was Quetzalcoatl, and they had come from the east, whither he had vanished – moreover it seemed they bore a peaceful message like that of the god, for one of their first acts was always to ban human sacrifice. So although he put obstacles in their way, tried to dissuade them, and even persuaded his allies to fight them, when the Spanish finally reached Tenochtitlán in November 1519, Moctezuma welcomed them to the city as his guests. They promptly repaid this hospitality by making him a prisoner within his own palace.

This "phony war", during which Spanish troops skirmished with a number of other Indian tribes and made allies of many – most significantly the **Tlaxcalans** – lasted for about a year. In April 1520 news came of a second Spanish expedition, led by Panfilo Narvaez, which was under orders to capture Cortés and take him back to Cuba (the mission had always been unofficial, and many others hoped to seize the wealth of Mexico for themselves). Again, though, Cortés proved the more decisive commander – he marched back east, surprised Narvaez by night, killed him, and persuaded most of his troops to switch allegiance.

Meanwhile the Spaniards left behind in Tenochtitlán had finally provoked their hosts beyond endurance by killing a group of priests during a religious ceremony, and were under siege in their quarters. Cortés, with his reinforcements, fought his way back into the city on June 24, only to find himself trapped as well. On June 27, Moctezuma (still a prisoner) was killed – according to the Spanish, stoned to death by his own people while attempting to appeal for peace. Finally Cortés decided to break out on the night of the 30th – still commemorated as the **Noche Triste** – when the Spanish lost over half their number on the causeways across the lake. Most of them were so weighed down with gold and booty that they were barely able to move, let alone swim in the places where the bridges had been destroyed.

Once more, though, the Aztecs failed to follow up their advantage, and the Spanish survivors managed to reach the haven of their allies in Tlaxcala where they could regroup. The final assault on the capital began in January 1521, with more fresh troops and supplies, and more and more Indians throwing their lot in with the Spanish. Tenochtitlán was not only besieged (the Spanish built ships which could be sailed on the lake) but ravaged by an epidemic of smallpox among whose victims was Moctezuma's successor, Cuitlahuac. They held

out for several more months under **Cuauhtémoc** – the only hero of this long episode in Mexican eyes – but on August 13, 1521, Tenochtitlán finally fell to the Spanish.

Although much of the country remained to be pacified, the defeat of the Aztec capital made it inevitable that eventually it would be.

COLONIAL RULE

By dint of his success, Cortés was appointed Governor of **Nueva España** (New Spain) in 1522, although in practice he was watched over constantly by minders from Spain, and never therefore had much real freedom of action. There followed three hundred years of direct Spanish rule, under a succession of 61 viceroys personally responsible to the king in Spain. By the end of the sixteenth century the entire country had been effectively subjugated, and its boundaries stretched by exploration from Panama to the western states of the USA (although the area from Guatemala down, including the Mexican state of Chiapas, was soon under separate rule).

When the Spanish arrived, the **native population** of central Mexico was at least 25 million; by the beginning of the nineteenth century the total population of Nueva España was just six million, and at most half of these were pure-blooded natives. Some had been killed in battle, a few as a result of ill-treatment or simply from being left without homes or land to live on, but the vast majority died as a result of successive epidemics of European diseases to which the New World had no natural immunity. The effects were catastrophic, and not only for the Indians themselves. The few survivors found the burden of labour placed on them ever increasing as their numbers dwindled – for certainly no white man came to Mexico to do manual work – and became more and more like slaves.

The first tasks, in the Spanish mind, were of reconstruction, pacification and conversion. Tenochtitlán had already been destroyed in the war and subsequently pillaged, burned and its population dispersed. To complete matters – a conscious policy of destroying all reminders of Aztec power – the remaining stones were used to construct the new city, México. At first there was quite remarkable **progress**: hundreds of towns were laid out (on a plan, with a plaza surrounded by a grid of streets, as laid down in Spain); thousands of churches built, often in areas which had been sacred to the Indians, or on top of their pyramids (there were over 12,000 in Mexico by 1800); and with the first Franciscan monks arriving in 1524, mass conversions were the order of the day. In a sense the indigenous peoples were used to all this – the Aztecs and their predecessors had behaved in a similar manner – but they had never experienced a slavery like that which was to follow.

At the same time **the Church**, which at first had championed indigenous rights and attempted to record native legends and histories and educate the children, grew less interested, and more concerned with money. Any attempt to treat the Indians as human was in any case violently opposed by Spanish landowners, to whom they were rather less than machines (cheaper than machinery, and therefore more expendable). By the end of the colonial era the Church owned more than half of all the land and wealth in the country, yet most native villages would be lucky to see a priest once a year.

In a sense Mexico remained a wealthy nation – certainly the richest of the Spanish colonies – but that sense would only have been understood by the rulers, or by those back home in Spain. For the governing philosophy was that "what's good for Spain is good for Mexico", and to that end all **trade**, industry and profit was exclusively aimed. No local trade or agriculture which would compete with Spain was allowed, so the cultivation of vines or the production of silk was banned; heavy taxes on other products – coffee, sugar, tobacco, cochineal, silver and other metals – went directly to Spain or to still poorer colonies, and no trade except with Spain was allowed. Since the "Spanish Galleon" (actually more of a convoy) sailed from Veracruz just once a year and was even then subject to the vagaries of piracy, this was a considerable handicap.

It didn't prevent the growth of a small class of extraordinarily wealthy **hacendados** (owners of massive haciendas) and mine-owners – whose growing confidence is shown in the architectural development of the colonial towns, from fortress-like huddles at the beginning of the colonial era to the full flowering of baroque extravagance by its end – but it did stop the development of any kind of realistic economic infrastructure, even of decent roads linking the towns. Just about the only proper road in 1800 was the one which connected Acapulco with México and Veracruz, by which goods from the

Far Eastern colonies would be transported cross-country before shipment on to Spain.

Even among the wealthy there was growing **resentment**, fuelled by the status of Mexicans: only gachupines, Spaniards born in Spain, could hold high office in the government or church. There were about 40,000 of them in Mexico in 1800 out of the six million population, and some three million Indians – the rest were criollos (creoles, born in Mexico of Spanish blood) who were in general educated, wealthy and aristocratic; and mestizos (of mixed race) who dominated the lower ranks of the church, army and civil service, and worked as shopkeepers, small ranchers or even bandits and beggars.

INDEPENDENCE

By the beginning of the **nineteenth century** Spain's status as a world power was in severe decline. In 1796 British sea power had forced the Spanish to open their colonial ports to free trade, and in 1808 Spain itself was invaded by Napoleon, who placed his brother Joseph on the throne. At the same time new political ideas were transforming the world outside, with the French Revolution and the American War of Independence still fresh in the memory. Although the works of such political philosophers as Rousseau, Voltaire and Paine were banned in Mexico, the opening of the ports made it inevitable that their ideas would spread – especially as it was traders from the new United States who most took advantage of the opportunities. Literary societies set up to discuss these books quickly became centres of political dissent.

The spark, though, was provided by the French invasion of Spain, as colonies throughout Latin America refused to recognize the Bonaparte regime (and the campaigns of Bolívar and others in South America began). In Mexico, the gachupín rulers proclaimed their loyalty to Ferdinand VII (the deposed king) and hoped to carry on much as before, but creole discontent was not to be so easily assuaged. The literary societies continued to meet, and from one, in Querétaro, emerged the first leaders of the Independence movement: Father **Miguel Hidalgo y Costilla**, a creole priest, and **Ignacio Allende**, a disaffected junior army officer.

When their plans for a coup were discovered, the conspirators were forced into premature action, with Hidalgo issuing the famous *Grito* (cry) of Independence – *Méxicanos, viva México!* – from the steps of his parish church in Dolores on September 16, 1810. The mob of Indians and mestizos who gathered behind the banner swiftly took the major towns of San Miguel, Guanajuato and others to the north of the capital, but their behaviour – seizing land and property, slaughtering the Spanish – horrified the wealthy creoles who had initially supported the movement. In spring 1811, Hidalgo's army, huge but undisciplined, moved on the capital, but at the crucial moment Hidalgo threw away a clear chance to overpower the royalist army. Instead he chose to retreat, and his forces broke up as quickly as they had been assembled. Within months, Hidalgo, Allende and the other ringleaders had been captured and executed.

By this time most creoles, frightened at what had been unleashed, had rejoined the ranks of the royalists. But many mestizos and much of the indigenous population remained in a state of revolt, with a new leader in the mestizo priest **José María Morelos**. Morelos was not only a far better tactician than Hidalgo – instituting a highly successful series of guerrilla campaigns – he was also a genuine radical. By 1813 he controlled virtually the entire country, with the exception of the capital and the route from there to Veracruz, and at the **Congress of Chilpancingo** he declared the abolition of slavery and the equality of the races. But the royalists fought back with a series of crushing victories, Morelos was executed in 1815, and his forces, under the leadership of Vicente Guerrero, were reduced to carrying out the occasional minor raid.

Ironically, it was the introduction of liberal reforms in Spain, of just the type feared by the Mexican ruling classes, which finally brought about **Mexican Independence**. Worried that such reforms might spread across the Atlantic, many creoles once again switched their positions. In 1820 **Agustin de Iturbide**, a royalist general but himself a mestizo, threw in his lot with Guerrero; in 1821 he proposed the **Iguala Plan** to the Spanish authorities, who were hardly in a position to fight, and Mexico was granted independence. With Independence, though, came none of the changes which had been fought over for so long – the church retained its power, and one set of rulers had simply been changed for another, native set.

FOREIGN INTERVENTION

In 1822 Iturbide had himself proclaimed emperor; a year later he was forced to abdicate, a year after that he was executed. It was the first of many such events in a century which must rank among the most confused – and disastrous – in any nation's history. Not only had Independence brought no real social change, it had left the new nation with virtually no chance of successful government: the power of the Church and of the army was far greater than that of the supposed rulers; there was no basis on which to create a viable internal economy; and if the state hadn't already been bankrupted by the Independence struggle, it was to be cleaned out time and again by the demands of war and internal disruption. There were no less than 56 governments in the next forty years. In what approaches farce, the name of General **Santa Ana** stands out as the most bizarre figure of all, becoming president or dictator on eleven separate occasions and masterminding the loss of more than half of Mexico's territory.

Santa Ana's first spell in office followed immediately Iturbide – he declared Mexico a Republic (although he himself always expected to be treated as a king, and addressed as His Most Serene Majesty) and called a constitutional convention. Under the auspices of the new constitution, the Republic was confirmed, the country divided into thirteen states, and **Guadalupe Victoria**, a former guerrilla general, elected its first president. He lasted three years, something of a record. In 1829 the Spanish attempted a rather half-hearted invasion, easily defeated, after which they accepted the fact of Mexican Independence. In 1833 Santa Ana was elected president (officially) for the first time, the fifth to hold the post thus far.

In 1836 a rather more serious chain of events was set in motion when **Texas**, Mexican territory but largely inhabited by migrants from the USA, declared its independence. Santa Ana commanded a punitive expedition which besieged **the Alamo** in the famous incident in which Jim Bowie and Davy Crockett, along with 150 other defenders, lost their lives. Santa Ana himself, though, was promptly defeated and captured at the battle of San Jacinto, and rather than face execution he signed a paper accepting **Texan Independence**. Although the authorities in México refused to accept the legality of its claim, Texas was, de facto, independent. Meanwhile, in 1838, the French chose to invade Veracruz, demanding compensation for alleged damages to French property and citizens – a small **war** which lasted about four months, and during which Santa Ana lost a leg.

In 1845 the United States annexed Texas, and although the Mexicans at first hoped to negotiate a settlement, the redefinition of Texas to include most of Arizona, New Mexico and California made yet another war almost inevitable. In 1846 clashes between Mexican troops and US cavalry in these disputed western zones led to the declaration of the **Mexican-American War**. Following defeat for the Mexicans at Palo Alto and Resaca, three small US armies invaded from the north. At the same time General Winfield Scott took Veracruz after a long bombardment, and commenced his march on the capital. Santa Ana was roundly defeated on a number of occasions, and in September 1847, after heroic resistance by the Niños Heroes (cadets at the military academy) México itself was captured. In 1848, by the **Treaty of Guadalupe Hidalgo**, the US paid $15 million for most of Texas, New Mexico, Arizona and California, along with parts of Colorado and Utah: in 1854 the present borders were established when Santa Ana sold a further strip down to the Rio Grande for $10 million under the **Gadsen Purchase**.

REFORM

Mexico finally saw the back of Santa Ana when, in 1855, he left for exile in Venezuela. But its troubles were by no means at an end. A new generation had grown up who had known only an independent Mexico in permanent turmoil, who had lived through the American humiliation, and who espoused once more the liberal ideals of Morelos. Above all they saw their enemy as **the Church**: vast, self-serving, and far wealthier than any legitimate government, it had further sullied its reputation by refusing to provide funds for the American war. Its position enshrined in the constitution, it was an extraordinarily reactionary institution, bleeding the peasantry for the most basic of sacraments (few could afford official marriage, or burial) and failing to provide the few services it was charged with. All education was in church schools, which for 95 percent of the population meant no education at all.

Benito Juárez, a Zapotec Indian who had been adopted and educated by a priest, and later trained as a lawyer, became the leader of this liberal movement through several years of civil war in which each side became more bitterly entrenched in increasingly extreme positions. When the liberals first came to power following Santa Ana's exile they began a relatively mild attempt at reform: permitting secular education, liberating the press, attempting to distance the Church from government and instituting a new democratic Constitution. The Church responded by obstruction and by threatening to excommunicate anyone co-operating with the government. In 1858 there was a conservative coup, and for the next three years **internal strife** on an unprecedented scale. With each new battle the liberals proclaimed more drastic reforms, churches were sacked and priests shot; while the conservatives responded by executing anyone suspected of liberal tendencies.

In 1861 Juárez emerged, at least temporarily, triumphant. Church property was confiscated, monasteries closed, weddings and burials became civil affairs, and set fees were established for the services of a priest. It wasn't until 1867 that most of these **Reform Laws** were to be fully enacted – for the conservatives had one more card to play – but most are still in force today. Priests in Mexico, for example, are forbidden to wear their robes in public.

The conservatives' final chance was to appeal for outside help. At the end of the civil war, with the government bankrupt, Juárez had suspended payment of all foreign debts, and in 1861 a joint British, Spanish and French expedition occupied Veracruz to demand compensation. It rapidly became clear, however, that the French were after more than mere financial recompense. Britain and Spain withdrew their forces, and Napoleon III ordered his troops to advance on México. The aim, with the support of Mexican conservatives, was to place **Maximilian**, a Habsburg archduke, on the throne as emperor.

Despite a major defeat at Puebla on May 5, 1862 (now a national holiday), the French sent for reinforcements and occupied Mexico City in 1863. The new emperor arrived the following year. In many ways, Maximilian cuts a pathetic figure. He arrived in Mexico with almost no knowledge of its internal feuds (having gleaned most of his information from a book on court etiquette), expecting a triumphal welcome. Proving to be a liberal at heart – he refused to repeal any of Juárez's reforms – he promptly lost the support of even the small group which had initially welcomed him. While his good intentions seem undeniable, few believe that he would have been capable of putting them into practice even in the best of circumstances. And these were hardly ideal times. With Union victory in the **US Civil War**, the authorities there threw their weight behind Juárez, providing him with arms and threatening to invade unless the French withdrew (on the basis of the Monroe doctrine: America for the Americans). Napoleon, already worried by the growing power of Bismarck's Prussia back home, had little choice but to comply. After 1866, Maximilian's position was hopeless.

His wife, the **Empress Carlota**, sailed to Europe in a vain attempt to win fresh support, but Napoleon had taken his decision, the Vatican refused to contemplate helping a man who had continued to attack the church, and the constant disappointments eventually drove Carlota mad. She died, insane, in Belgium in 1927. Maximilian, meanwhile, stayed at the head of his hopelessly outnumbered troops to the end – May 15, 1867 – when he was defeated and captured at Querétaro. A month later, he faced the firing squad.

Juárez reassumed power, managing this time to ride the worst of the inevitable bankruptcy. The first steps towards economic reconstruction were taken, with the completion of a railway from Veracruz to the capital, encouragement of industry, and the development of a public education programme. Juárez died in office in 1872, having been re-elected in 1871, and was succeeded by his vice-president Lerdo de Tejada, who continued on the same road, though with few new ideas.

DICTATORSHIP

Tejada was neither particularly popular nor spectacularly successful, but he did see out his term of office. However, there had been several Indian revolts during his rule and a number of plots against him, the most serious of them led by a new radical liberal leader, **Porfirio Díaz**. Díaz had been a notably able military leader under Juárez, and in 1876, despite the re-election of Tejada, he proclaimed his own candidate

president. The following year he assumed the presidency himself, and was to rule as dictator for the next 34 years. At first his platform was a radical one – including full implementation of the Reform Laws and a decree of no re-election to any political office – but it was soon dropped in favour of a brutal policy of modernization. Díaz did actually stand down at the end of his first term, in 1880, but he continued to rule through a puppet president, and in 1884 resumed the presidency for an unbroken stretch until 1911.

In many ways the **achievements** of his dictatorship were remarkable: some 16,000 km of railway were built, industry boomed, telephones and telegraph were installed, and major towns, reached at last by reasonable roads, entered the modern era. In the countryside, Díaz established a police force – the notorious *rurales* – which finally stamped out banditry. Almost every city in Mexico seems to have a grandiose theatre and elegant public buildings from this era. But the costs were high: rapid development was achieved basically by handing over the country and its people to **foreign investors**, who owned the vast majority of the oil, mining rights, railways and natural resources. At the same time there was a policy of massive land expropriation: formerly communal village holdings being handed over to foreign exploitation or simply grabbed by corrupt officials.

Agriculture, meanwhile, was ignored entirely. The owners of vast haciendas could make more than enough money by relying on the forced labour of a landless peasantry, and had no interest in efficiency or production for domestic consumption. By 1900 the whole of Mexico was owned by some 3–4 percent of its population. Without land of their own, peasants had no choice but to work on the haciendas or in the forests, where their serfdom was ensured by wages so low that they were permanently in debt to their employers. The rich became very rich indeed; the poor had lower incomes and fewer prospects than they had a century earlier.

Once the *rurales* had done their job of making the roads safe to travel, they became a further burden – charging for the right to travel along roads they controlled and acting as a private police force for employers should any of their workers try to escape. In short, slavery had been reintroduced in all but name, and up to a quarter of the nation's resources came to be spent on internal security. The press was censored, too, education strictly controlled, and corruption rife.

REVOLUTION

With the onset of the **twentieth century**, Díaz was already old and beginning to lose his grip on reality. He had every intention of continuing in power until he dropped; but a real middle-class opposition was beginning to develop, concerned above all by the racist policies of their government (which favoured foreign investors above native ones) and by the lack of opportunity for themselves – the young educated classes. Their movement revived the old slogan of "*no reelección*", and in 1910 **Francisco Madero** stood against Díaz in the the presidential election. The old dictator responded by imprisoning his opponent and declaring himself victor at the polls by a vast majority. Madero, however, escaped to Texas where he proclaimed himself president, and called on the nation to rise in his support.

This was an entirely opportunist move, for at the time there were no revolutionary forces, but several small bands immediately took up arms. Most important were those in the northern state of Chihuahua, where **Pancho Villa** and **Pascual Orozco** won several minor battles, and in the southwest, where **Emiliano Zapata** began to arm Indian guerrilla forces. In May 1911 Orozco captured the major border town of Ciudad Juárez, and his success was rapidly followed by a string of Revolutionary victories. By the end of the month, hoping to preserve the system if not his role in it, Porfirio Díaz had fled into exile. On October 2, 1911, Madero was elected president.

Like the originators of Independence before him, Madero had no conception of the forces he had unleashed. He freed the press, encouraged the formation of unions and introduced genuine democracy, but failed to do anything about the condition of the peasantry or the redistribution of land. Zapata prepared to rise again.

Emiliano Zapata was perhaps the one true revolutionary in the whole long conflict to follow, and his battle cry of *Tierra y Libertad* (Land and Liberty) and insistence that "it is better to die on your feet than live on your knees" make him still a revered figure among the peasants – and revolutionaries – of the present day. By contrast, the rest were mostly out for personal gain: **Pancho Villa**, a cattle rustler and bandit in the time of

Díaz, was by far the most successful of the more orthodox generals, brilliantly inventive, and ruthless in victory. But his motivation, though he came from peasant stock, seems to have been personal glory – he appeared to love fighting, and at one stage, when a Hollywood film crew was travelling with his armies, would allegedly arrange his battles so as to ensure the best lighting conditions and most impressive fight scenes.

In any case Madero was faced by a more immediately dangerous enemy than his own erstwhile supporters – **US business interests**. Henry Lane Wilson, US ambassador, began openly plotting with **Victoriano Hurt**, a government general, and Felix Díaz, a nephew of the dictator, who was held in prison. Fighting broke out between supporters of Díaz and those of Madero, while Huerta refused to commit his troops to either side. When he did, in 1913, it was to proclaim himself president. Madero was shot in suspicious circumstances (few doubt an assassination sanctioned by Huerta) and opponents on the right, including Díaz, either imprisoned or exiled. The new government was promptly recognized by the United States and most other foreign powers, but not by the important forces within the country.

CONSTITUTION VS. CONVENTION

Villa and Zapata immediately took up arms against Huerta, and in the north Villa was joined by **Alvaro Obregón**, governor of Sonora, and **Venustiano Carranza**, governor of Coahuila. Carranza was appointed head of the Constitutionalist forces, though he was always to be deeply suspicious of Villa, despite Villa's constant protestations of loyalty. At first the Revolutionaries made little headway – Carranza couldn't even control his own state, although Obregón and Villa did enjoy some successes raiding south from Chihuahua and Sonora. But almost immediately the new US president, Woodrow Wilson, withdrew his support from Huerta and, infuriated by his refusal to resign, began actively supplying arms to the Revolution.

In 1914, the **Constitutionalists** began to move south, and in April of that year US troops occupied Veracruz in their support (though neither side was exactly happy about the foreign presence). Huerta, now cut off from almost every source of money or supplies, fled the country in July, and in August Obregón occupied the capital, proclaiming Carranza president.

Renewed fighting broke out straight away, this time between Carranza and Obregón, the Constitutionalists, on one side, and the rest of the Revolutionary leaders on the other, so-called **Conventionalists** whose sole point of agreement was that Carranza should not lead them. The three years of fighting which followed were the most bitter and chaotic yet, with petty chiefs in every part of the country proclaiming provisional governments, joining each other in factions and then splitting again, and the entire country in a state of anarchy. Each army issued its own money, and each press-ganged any able-bodied men they came across into joining. By 1920 it was reckoned that about one-eighth of the population had been killed.

Gradually, however, Obregón and Carranza gained ground – Obregón defeated Villa several times in 1915, and Villa withdrew to carry out border raids into the United States, hoping to provoke an invasion (which he nearly did: US troops pursued him across the border but were never able to catch up, and withdrew following defeat in a skirmish with Carranza's troops). Zapata, meanwhile, had some conspicuous successes – and occupied México for much of 1915 – but his irregular troops tended to disappear back to their villages after each victory. In 1919 he was tricked into a meeting with one of Carranza's generals and shot in cold blood; Villa retired to a hacienda in his home state, and was assassinated in 1923.

THE END OF THE REVOLUTION

Meanwhile Carranza continued to claim the presidency, and in 1917 set up a **Constitutional congress** to ratify his position. The document they produced – the present constitution – included most of the Revolutionary demands, among them workers' rights, a mandatory eight-hour day, national ownership of all mineral rights, and the distribution of large landholdings and formerly communal properties to the peasantry. Carranza was formally elected in May 1917 and proceeded to make no attempt to carry out any of its stipulations, certainly not with regard to land rights. In 1920 Carranza was forced to step down by **Obregón**, and was shot while attempting to escape the country with most of the contents of the treasury.

Obregón, at least, was well intentioned – but his efforts at real land reform were again stymied by fear of US reaction: in return for American support, he agreed not to expropriate land. In 1924 **Plutarco Elias Callés** succeeded him, and real progress towards some of the ideals of the Revolutionary Constitution began to be made. Work on large public works schemes began – roads, irrigation systems, village schools – and about eight million acres of land were given back to the villages as communal holdings. At the same time Calles instituted a policy of virulent anticlericalism, closing churches and monasteries, and forcing priests to flee the country or go underground.

These moves provoked the last throes of a backlash, as the Catholic **Cristero movement** took up arms in defence of the Church. From 1927 until about 1935 isolated incidents of vicious banditry and occasional full-scale warfare continued, eventually burning themselves out as the stability of the new regime became obvious, and religious controls were relaxed. In 1928 Obregón was re-elected, but assassinated three weeks later in protest at the breach of the "*no reelección*" clause of the Constitution. He was followed by Portes Gil, Ortiz Rubio and then Abelardo Rodriguez, who were controlled behind the scenes by Calles and his political allies, who steered national politics to the right in the bleak years of the 1930s depression.

MODERN MEXICO

By 1934 Mexico enjoyed a degree of peace, and a remarkable change had been wrought. A new culture had emerged – seen nowhere more clearly than in the great murals of Rivera and Orozco which began to adorn public buildings throughout the country – in which native heroes like Hidalgo, Morelos, Juárez and Madero replaced European ideals. Nowadays everyone in the Republic would claim Indian blood – even if the Indians themselves remain the lowest stratum of society – and the invasion of Cortés is seen as the usurpation of the nation's march to its destiny, a march which resumed with Independence and the Revolution. At the same time there was a fear in these early days that Callés was attempting to promote a dynasty of his own.

With the election of **Lázaro Cárdenas** in 1934, such doubts were finally laid to rest. As the spokesman of a younger generation, Cárdenas expelled Callés and his supporters from the country, at the same time setting up the single broad-based party which still rules today as the **PRI** (Party of the Institutionalized Revolution). Cárdenas set about an unprecedented programme of reform, redistributing land on a huge scale (170,000 square kilometres during his six-year term), creating peasant and worker organizations to represent their interests at national level, and incorporating them into the governing party. He also relaxed controls on the church to appease internal and international opposition.

In 1938 he nationalized the **oil** companies, an act which has proved one of the most significant in shaping modern Mexico and bringing about its industrial miracle. For a time it seemed as if yet more foreign intervention might follow, but a boycott of Mexican oil by the major consumers crumbled with the onset of World War II (apart from Neville Chamberlain, who cut off diplomatic relations and lost Great Britain an important investment market as a result), and was followed by a massive influx of money and a huge boost for Mexican industry as a result of the war. By the time he stood down in 1940, Cárdenas could claim to be the first president in modern Mexican history to have served his full six-year term in peace, and handed over to his successor without trouble.

Through the war **industrial growth** continued apace under Avila Camacho, and Mexico officially joined the Allies in 1942. Miguel Aleman (1946–52) presided over still faster development, and a further massive dose of public works and land reform – major prestige projects, like the University City in the capital, were planned by his regime. Over the next thirty years or so, massive oil incomes continued to stimulate industry, and the PRI maintained a masterly control of all aspects of public life without apparently losing the support of a great majority of the Mexican public. Of course it is an accepted fact of life that governments will line their own pockets first – a practice which apparently reached its height under **Lopez Portillo** (1976–82) – but the unrelenting populism of the PRI, its massive powers of patronage, and above all its highly visible and undoubted achievement of progress, maintained it in power with amazingly little dissent.

All this is not to say that there were no **problems**. The year 1959 saw the repression of a national railway strike where ten thousand workers lost their jobs and their leaders were placed in jail, and in **1968** hundreds of students were massacred in Tlatelolco square in México to stem an active pro-democracy student movement which threatened Mexico's image abroad as the Olympic games neared (Mexico's were the first Olympics to be held in the "Third World" and were seen as an opportunity to promote the regime abroad). The PRI was unable to buy off the students due to their rotating leadership, and unwilling to negotiate for fear of losing face. Although the massacre did put an end to student unrest, or at least any public manifestation of it, from Tlatelolco on the Mexican system lost a great deal of its legitimacy as the opposition saw fewer reasons for working within the system; guerrilla movements sprang up in Guerrero state, for example. The PRI was still, however, very much in control and had snuffed these movements out by the mid-Seventies. The government, who ran the union movement and the peasant organizations and delivered steady economic growth, appeared to have an unassailable hold on power as well as being genuinely popular across a wide spectrum of the population. In the mid-1990s, however, their sixty-year reign seems far less secure.

ECONOMIC CRISIS

The government of **Miguel de la Madrid** (1982–88) found itself faced with economic crisis on a national and international scale. Mexico's vast foreign debt (of almost $100 billion) had been run up in the heady days of the oil boom. Already a severe burden on the economy, the debt was greatly exacerbated by falling oil prices and revenues and rising international interest rates. At the same time the PRI seemed to be losing its populist touch: the twelve previous years, known as the "Docena Trágica" or tragic dozen, had seen flourishing corruption and economic mismanagement destroy the hopes brought about by the development of the oil industry. Also, de la Madrid was a US-educated financier who adopted the **austerity measures** imposed by the World Bank. Such policies won widespread acclaim from international bankers (Jesus Silva Herzog was voted "finance minister of the year" after his first year in office) but at home produced massive unemployment and drastically reduced standards of living – the average wage earner lost fifty percent of his or her purchasing power – while struggling to keep inflation down to 100 percent a year. An exploding population only added to the problems, and even the huge level of illegal emigration to the US had little impact on it. The business community suffered too. Outraged by the nationalization of the banks in 1982, they were further hit by a series of bankruptcies and by devaluation which made imported materials almost impossible to afford. With no sign of economic recovery, some of the vast panoply of interests covered by the PRI – from the all-powerful unions to the top businessmen – began to split off.

This movement against the PRI was exacerbated in 1985, when a huge **earthquake** hit the capital. The quake revealed widespread corruption, as the government attempted to prevent ordinary people from organizing their own rescue attempts to try and hide the inadequacy of official efforts. Furthermore, many of the buildings which collapsed were government-owned and although supposedly built to withstand earthquakes, turned out to have been constructed using inferior materials, with the profits siphoned off to construction companies and government officials. International relief aid was also diverted as the quake's victims were abandoned by the authorities.

Many grass-roots organizations were formed as the experience of the earthquake exposed the government's inability to provide anything other than rudimentary and poorly co-ordinated help; the beginning of a modern **civil society**. Independent tenant groups, neighbourhood and women's groups, and small scale trade unions began to press the government for specific rebuilding programmes and on wider social concerns such as lack of housing, basic services, police corruption and pollution.

Opposition also grew outside the capital. The right-wing opposition **PAN** won a string of minor election victories in the north (and were cheated out of the state governorship of Chihuahua by blatant fraud), while in the south a socialist/peasant alliance held power for a while in Juchitán (Oaxaca) before being ousted with traditional strong-arm tactics. These episodes highlighted a further danger – the increasing **polarization** of the country. In the north, life is heavily influenced by the USA and business and ranching interests hold sway. In the south, where peasants continue to press for more land redistribution, opposition is far more radical and left-wing: alternately inspired and intimidated by events in Central America.

De La Madrid's unpopularity was demonstrated at the 1986 World Cup final, when the crowd – mainly middle-class Mexicans – booed and jeered at him as he took his seat. Considering the traditional reverence which is usually accorded to the figure of the president, this was an unprecedented show of disrespect.

The **1988 election** was certainly dramatic, and may yet prove one of the most significant since the Revolution. Predictably, the PRI candidate, **Carlos Salinas de Gortari**, won. The extent of the opposition however, was significant, and into the traditional contest between PRI, PAN and a number of tiny splinter groups, a formidable new challenger emerged in the form of **Cuauhtémoc Cárdenas**, son of the legendary and much loved Lázaro. Cárdenas split from the PRI a year before the election and succeeded in uniting the Mexican left behind him (under the banner of the National Democratic Front, or FDN) for the first time since the Revolution.

The success of the **FDN** was spectacular, Cárdenas officially winning 32 percent of the vote, although the results took a week to appear after the "breakdown" of the electoral computer at a point when Cárdenas was clearly in the lead. Ballot rigging, voter intimidation and vote buying (typical of all Mexican elections), reached new heights. Cárdenas and his supporters claimed that he had won, and also claimed to have figures to support them. Salinas emerged from the tarnished contest with 50.36 percent of the vote and the PAN leader, Manuel Clouthier (previously the only serious challenger), came third with 17 percent Opposition parties won seats in the Senate for almost the first time since the PRI came to power.

Salinas undertook to pave the way for a new multi-party democracy in Mexico. As a relatively young, untried, internally chosen candidate, he had little in the way of a following either within the PRI itself or the country as a whole, and began by announcing a clean-up **campaign against corruption**. On Salinas' orders, the head of the official PEMEX oil workers' union (a notoriously corrupt figure known as "La Quina") was arrested. He also created a human rights commission to investigate abuses, and ended direct government control over PIPSA, the official monopoly newsprint supplier. Salinas also upheld mid-term electoral triumphs by the opposition PAN in the states of Baja California and Guanajuato, despite opposition from local PRI activists.

Early signs were thus encouraging. Despite the death in mysterious circumstances of the PAN leader Manuel Clouthier in **1989** and controversial victories by the PRI in various state elections, Salinas managed to secure widespread support through the radical nature of his economic programme, as well as through traditional political patronage. Initially Salinas maintained the economic policy of his predecessor, strategically timing Mexico's privatization programme to maximize revenue, tightening up on tax avoidance and the black economy, and reducing the foreign debt by almost half in three years through restructuring and co-operation with the IMF and private banks.

A compliant **television** media also helped foster the image of the president. This was not a new phenomenon, but Salinas benefited media barons through deregulation of the media and the sale of the state-owned station (now Televisión Azteca) and their support helped the PRI to sweep the board during the 1991 mid-term elections. Economic growth, falling inflation and a large influx of foreign capital seemed to confirm the success of the government's agenda.

In the meantime the opposition had been trying to mount a coherent challenge to the PRI. Cuauhtémoc Cárdenas, building from his success in 1988, founded a party to harness his popular support. The **PRD** (Party of the Democratic Revolution) had a very radical platform, reflecting much of its support base, but has moved increasingly to the centre, no longer opposing privatization in principle, and accepting the need for reform of the *ejido* system (see below). The PAN, with the PRI moving to the right, found its support base being eroded although it enjoyed unprecedented electoral gains.

The long-term consequences of the Salinas policy, however, were much less positive. **Social polarization** became even more extreme. By 1993, forty million Mexicans were living below the official poverty line (about half the population), while 24 Mexicans were listed in the Forbes list of the 500 richest men in the world. Most of these billionaires had acquired their wealth through buying privatized utilities. Salinas was committed to reducing the public debt and encouraging private investment, which he achieved by drastically cutting public spending and encouraging foreign companies by holding down wage levels. This involved expanding the "*maquiladora*" programme, which allowed

foreign companies to set up assembly plants along the US-Mexican border (enjoying substantial tax concessions), a ban on union activity and relaxed health and safety and environmental requirements; and pushing through the North American Free Trade Area (**NAFTA**; **TLC** in Spanish) which creates a free market between Canada, the USA and Mexico. This agreement has opponents in all the countries involved, with many in the USA and Canada fearing job losses and lax environmental standards. Theoretically, a free market, with each country benefiting from its own comparative advantage, should increase trade levels to a degree in which all the participants would gain, spurring the Mexican economy to expand to the level of its partners and allowing Mexico to enter the "First World". Most Mexicans, with good reason, suspected that the agreement would provide little benefit, allowing US companies to offload polluting industries in Mexico and to take advantage of cheap labour – Mexico's "comparative advantage".

Salinas' response to the problems was to intensify his programme of reform, while at the same time introducing a social programme to ameliorate the effects of his economic programme. The **national solidarity programme**, or PRONASOL, directed a billion-dollar budget towards self-help programmes for the poor. Communities would typically supply free labour, while PRONASOL would provide materials and technical expertise for such projects as supplying basic amenities – electricity, piped water, street lighting – or making up for cuts in other government services such as school and hospital building. PRONASOL was supported by a huge advertising campaign, and its logo (like the PRI insignia, in Mexico's national colours) was painted upon every available surface to advertise the achievements of the programme – and by implication of the PRI – in the community. Most of the PRONASOL budget went to areas with strong PRD support such as México, the southern states and Cárdenas' home state of Michoacán, in an attempt to buy off opposition and co-opt self-help groups.

Another plan of the Salinas strategy was to modify much of Mexico's Revolutionary legacy. Diplomatic relations with the Vatican, severed during the Revolution, were re-established, allowing the pope to visit Mexico for the first time. The national oil company PEMEX was split into smaller units to improve productivity, and foreign oil companies were allowed to prospect for new deposits, although the PEMEX monopoly was still more or less intact at the time of writing. The most important change in this direction was the Amendment to Article 27 of the Constitution, which deals with land reform.

Land reform, as enshrined in the original article of the Constitution, owed much to the legacy of Zapata. Land redistributed after the Revolution was parcelled out in communal holdings, known as **"ejidos"**, which could not be sold as they belonged to the state. At a local level the land was held in common, divided up by the communities themselves, following the pre-hispanic and Colonial tradition. Salinas changed all that by allowing the sale of *ejido* lands. Many peasants and indigenous communities feared that their landholdings were now vulnerable to speculators, especially as many poor communities exist in a state of almost permanent debt, and believed that their land would be seized to cover outstanding loans, worsening their economic plight still further.

Despite, and maybe because of, these unpopular moves, Salinas began to be seen as a strong presidential figure, with a dynamic agenda for change. The successful negotiation of the NAFTA treaty, on which he had staked his reputation, went smoothly despite having to deal with two very different US presidents (Bush and Clinton), and this enhanced his reputation as a statesman. Even the opposition had to concede that economic progress had been made, and that Salinas had a clear agenda for Mexico and would leave the presidency in a much better state than he found it, giving the PRI a new lease of life.

There seemed little doubt that the PRI would go on to win the presidential election scheduled for 1994 with a minimum of fuss. In many areas, it wouldn't even have to resort to fraud. The crisis and upheavals of earlier days finally seemed to have been left behind....

POLITICAL CRISIS

All this changed on New Year's Day 1994, when an armed guerrilla movement known as the **Zapatista Army of National Liberation** (EZLN), took control of San Cristóbal de las Casas and four other municipalities in the southernmost state of Chiapas. The guerrillas were mainly indigenous villagers: they demanded an end to the feudal system of land tenure in Chiapas, free elections, the repeal of NAFTA and the restoration of Article 27 of the Constitution. The army reacted with predictable use of force, committing human rights abuses along the way that included the bombing of civilians and the murder of prisoners. Long hidden from the world, the repressive side of the Mexican state – together with the plight of the indigenous peoples of Mexico – were suddenly front-page news throughout the world. To Salinas' credit, he rapidly prepared the ground for peace negotiations by ordering a cease-fire.

Negotiations progressed with remarkable speed to begin with. The government representative, Manuel Camacho Solís, ex-mayor of México and at one time potential PRI candidate for the presidency, made concessions to the guerrillas and upstaged the presidential candidate, Luis Donaldo Colosio, who remained silent about the conflict. Camacho was assisted by the Bishop of San Cristóbal, **Samuel Ruiz**, a champion of Indian rights in Chiapas and an advocate of liberation theology (many on the right have since accused the diocese of San Cristóbal of fostering the subversion, though with little apparent evidence: the Vatican even attempted to recall him in the middle of negotiations to explain himself and calls by the right have insisted on his excommunication). The real star of the negotiations was **Subcomandante Marcos** of the EZLN, the main spokesperson for the Zapatistas. The balaclava-clad, pipe-smoking guerrilla soon became a cult hero; his speeches and communiques were full of literary allusions and passionate rhetoric and also revealed a strong sense of humour. Talks ended in March, when an accord was put together. The EZLN then sent the accord back to its community bases for them to vote upon it. Decisions regarding whether to fight or negotiate were aggravated by the many different languages and dialects spoken and the inaccessibility of many villages and the results were not ready until June. An uneasy truce between army and guerrillas was maintained, and Mexicans were given ample time to dwell upon events in Chiapas.

As the Mexican saying goes, "Nothing happens in Mexico . . . until it does." Something happened on March 23, when the presidential candidate for the PRI, Luis Donaldo Colosio, was shot dead on the campaign trail in the border city of Tijuana. This was the first **assassination** of such a prominent government figure since 1928. The assassin, a former policeman, was allowed by Colosio's bodyguards to shoot him from almost point-blank range, fuelling conspiracy theories about the murder on a scale similar to the assassination of John F. Kennedy.

Despite the unexpected nature of the assassination, political violence in Mexico has a long history. This has been aggravated in recent years by a surge in **drug-related crime** among the Mexican cocaine cartels. In 1993, the archbishop of Guadalajara, Juan Jesús Ocampo, was shot dead at Guadalajara airport. He was reportedly caught in the crossfire between warring drug gangs, and some allege that drug cartels were also involved in the assassination of Colosio. Whatever the truth, and neither murder has been satisfactorily cleared up, it is clear that a huge amount of drugs are making their way across the Mexican border into the US, and that drug money has corrupted many in Mexican law enforcement and political circles. Although violence is nowhere near as widespread as in Colombia, say, the danger exists that the situation may deteriorate.

Another group suspected of carrying out drug murders are elements within the PRI itself. The so-called **"dinosaurs"** within the party, those committed to maintaining the status quo, felt threatened by moves to democratize the political system, which had been galvanized by the Chiapas negotiations. Colosio had pledged himself to democratic reforms, and his murder was calculated to remove this threat to the established system. The assassination of another prominent reformer in September 1994, José Francisco Ruiz Massieu (general secretary of the PRI), who was gunned down in México, seems also to have served as a warning against anyone trying to modify the system. Colosio's successor as presidential candidate, **Ernesto Zedillo Ponce de León**, was a minor PRI apparatchik, and in this climate of insecurity and violence, the **elections of August 1994** did not augur well.

In June the EZLN rejected the accord with the government, and in July the PRD candidate for the governorship of Chiapas, Amado Avendaño Figueroa, met with a suspicious "accident" when a truck with no number plates collided with his car, killing three passengers. Avendaño lost an eye as a result of the crash. It was no surprise when the PRI again triumphed in the presidential elections: Zedillo gained 48 percent of

the vote, Diego de Cevallos, the PAN candidate, 31 percent and Cárdenas for the PRD only 16 percent. The PRI also won all the senatorial races and the governorship of Chiapas. The scale of the vote (75 percent of voters participated, contrasting with traditionally high levels of absenteeism) and the presence of foreign observers at an election for the first time left little doubt that the PRI had managed yet again to defy all attempts to remove them; and despite high levels of fraud, it was clear that the governing party really had obtained popular backing. The Left were left in disarray as over 75 percent of votes cast were for the PRI and the PAN.

The results announced, the situation began almost immediately to deteriorate. In **Chiapas** the defeated Avendaño declared himself **"rebel governor"** after denouncing the elections as fraudulent. As many as half the municipalities in the state backed him, refusing to pay taxes to the official government, and both the PRD and the EZLN also supported his move. The EZLN warned that if the PRI candidate Eduardo Robledo was sworn in, the truce with the government would be at an end. Chiapas was anyway in a state of virtual **civil war**. Ranchers and landowners, who had long enjoyed the use of hired muscle to intimidate the peasantry, organized **death squads** to counter a massively mobilized peasantry. Land seizures and road blocks by one side were met with assassinations and intimidation by the other in a rapidly polarizing atmosphere. A build-up of Mexican troops in the state exacerbated the situation as Chiapas began to appear like an occupied Central American republic rather than a part of Mexico.

Post-electoral conflicts also developed after the governorship contests in **Veracruz** and **Tabasco**, both won in controversial circumstances by the PRI. Tabasco followed Chiapas' lead by declaring a "governor in rebellion". PRD supporters temporarily took over the centre of the state capital Villahermosa, and numerous PEMEX oil installations. In Veracruz, the PRD again claimed fraud in many of the municipalities in the south of the state. The PAN won in most of the urban centres, including the port of Veracruz itself.

On January 8, 1995, Zedillo attended the swearing in of the PRI governor of Chiapas. Ten days later, the EZLN deployed their forces, breaking the army cordon surrounding their positions and moving in to 38 municipalities (they had previously been confined to four). That they did it virtually undetected and later retreated, again without detection or a shot being fired, even under the watchful eyes of government troops, showed their familiarity with the terrain, the discipline of their troops and the folly of the "surgical strike" option contemplated by many in the military to wipe out the guerrillas.

The symbolic value of the EZLN action, combined with the apparent failure of the government to cope with either the worsening political or economic situation, triggered a massive **devaluation of the peso**. Foreign capital started to flood out of the country, and at a stroke Mexican wages were cut by almost half in real terms. Meantime, higher interest rates hit Mexican business hard, unemployment rose drastically, and IMF austerity measures were again imposed on Mexicans to pay for a debt run up by their government. Not surprisingly, public anger turned to the government, and especially Carlos Salinas, who was now said to have kept the peso artificially high to hide economic problems from view. On this tide of discontent, the PAN prosecutor arrested **Raúl Salinas**, brother of the president, in February, and Ruiz Massieu's brother Mario later in the year. Both were accused of complicity in the murder of José Francisco Ruiz Massieu.

In March 1995, apparently under pressure from the US, Zedillo launched an **offensive against the EZLN**. A small-arms cache was uncovered in Veracruz, and supposed members of the EZLN were arrested. In Chiapas, the EZLN retreated and major confrontation was avoided. Thousands of peasants, terrified both by the army's incursions and the violence of right-wing **paramilitary groups**, left their villages, becoming **internal refugees**. Although most of Chiapas' estimated 15,000 displaced people are Zapatista sympathizers, some are PRI supporters, and have fled from Zapatista controlled areas. Exercising the military option was a high-risk strategy for Zedillo, and one that didn't really come off: the EZLN enjoyed considerable public sympathy, especially in view of their largely non-violent methods. Even unmasking Subcomandante Marcos as **Rafael Guillén** failed to affect his popularity – indeed, cries of "Guillén for president" became common at opposition rallies. In a rapid U-turn, the government called off the army and set up **new negotiations**.

These proved to be even more protracted than the 1994 talks but eventually resulted in the **San Andrés Accords on Rights and Indigenous Cultures** (named for the village near San Cristóbal where they took place), signed in February 1996. Immediately prior to this agreement the Zapatistas proposed to establish a political front, the Zapatista Front of National Liberation (FZLN), at the same time stating that this political grouping would not contest elections. The San Andrés Accords guaranteed indigenous representation in national and state legislatures, but their implementation would require constitutional and legislative changes which Zedillo failed to push through Congress. Relations between the Zapatistas and the government negotiators, characterized by mutual distrust, were strained to breaking point, and in September the EZLN suspended further peace talks.

The spiral of armed political unrest was given a new twist in June 1996 with the appearance of the **Popular Revolutionary Army** (EPR) in Guerrero. During the rest of the year the EPR made its presence known, often by violent actions, in several states in the middle and south of the country. Despite the activities of the two guerrilla groups (and each appears to disassociate itself from the other), however, the likelihood of a revolutionary end to PRI's grip on power is extremely remote. The government's policy, in as far as one exists, appears to be one of containment and a gradual increase in military pressure rather than outright armed confrontation, in the expectation that public support for the romantic notion of guerrillas fighting for "land and liberty" will gradually fade as the old political institutions continue to undergo reform.

Political neglect, accompanied by a remorseless increase of the military presence on the Zapatistas' perimeter appeared also to give the paramilitary groups even greater freedom to operate, further escalating the level of violence. This culminated in the December 1997 **massacre at Acteal**: 45 displaced Tzotil Indians, 36 of them women and children, were murdered by paramilitary forces linked to PRI officials in Chiapas. The killings brought worldwide condemnation, and Zedillo had to act to show that the federal government writ still ran in Chiapas. He announced an official investigation into the killings and ordered the arrest of those suspected of taking part in the massacre.

Shortly after, in January 1998, interior minister Emiliano Chuayffet (and possible successor to Zedillo) and the Governor of Chiapas, César Ruiz Ferro, resigned.

The extra troops sent to Chiapas, ostensibly to stop more paramilitary killings, failed to prevent further violence and intimidation of Zapatista supporters, and the army even entered Zapatista strongholds on the pretext of searching for paramilitary arms. Emboldened by the militarily weak EZLN response to these incursions, the army began to move against the autonomous municipalities set up by the Zapatistas. This betrayal of the principles of a negotiated settlement finally provoked Bishop Ruiz to resign from his role as mediator in June 1998, causing the dissolution of the National Mediation Commission (CONAI). As this book goes to press, negotiations have broken down completely, leading some observers to conclude that the government has opted for a military strategy to overcome the Zapatistas by waging a "**low-intensity**" **war** in Chiapas.

One consequence of the increased international interest in Chiapas was the Mexican government's active campaign (supported by reports in some prominent sections of the media) against *simpatico* **foreigners**, whom it accuses of instigating political unrest in the state. Several dozen foreign journalists, church workers, human rights observers and even scientists have been detained and deported, and immigration officials subject anyone they suspect of being a Zapatista sympathiser to questioning and harassment.

POLITICAL REFORM

Despite the continuing crisis in Chiapas, Mexico's **political reforms** continued. In July 1996 new election rules imposing limits on campaign spending and the establishment of a fully independent federal electoral body (IFE) were agreed by the PRI and the main opposition parties. The new rules were brought into play for the first time in the July 1997 mid-term congressional elections, when the governorship of six states and México were also contested. The results were unprecedented: for the first time in its history PRI lost its majority in the Chamber of Deputies (the lower House of Congress) and lost control of México. Although the PRI has 239 of the 500

seats, the PRD, with 125 seats, is now the second largest party, closely followed by the PAN with 122 seats. The opposition – which also includes PT (Workers' Party) and PVEM (Green Party) representatives – could, if united, defeat the PRI, and have done so. The main opposition parties are separated by too wide an ideological gulf to form a permanent coalition, but the PRI government no longer can rely on congress to rubber-stamp Presidential decisions. The new congress began cutting its new-found teeth in the spring of 1998 by insisting on greater control over monetary policy, and even the PRI-dominated upper chamber, the Senate, is demanding – and receiving – more time to consider bills placed before it. The PRD leader, Cuauhtémoc Cárdenas, is a popular choice as **mayor of México** (previously always a presidential appointment), but he faces enormous obstacles in carrying out his manifesto of defeating crime and corruption in the capital.

Other dramatic changes are set to take place before the next **general election in 2000**. From the outset of his term, President Zedillo has promised to reform the selection of the PRI presidential candidate – and so far always the next president – by replacing the traditional *dedazo* (literally "fingering") whereby the ruling president picks his successor. In future the presidential candidate may be chosen by direct election by PRI members, with all other candidates chosen in US-style primaries. At the time of writing, two PRI candidates have declared their intention to run for nomination: **Manuel Bartlett**, governor of Puebla, and **Roberto Madrazo**, governor of Tabasco. **Vicente Fox Quesada**, the governor of Guanajuato, is likely to stand as the PAN candidate, and **Cuauhtémoc Cárdenas** (PRD), is certain to take what may be his last chance at the presidency.

The pace of change in the political landscape shows little sign of abating. With many mid-term elections still to contest before the general election, opposition parties will have plenty of opportunity to test the popularity of political reform, and they could even be in control of almost half the state governorships by then. All the opposition is firmly united in wanting to remove from the PRI its use of the colours of the national flag as party colours, and seems likely to achieve this before campaigning begins. Whether the PRI can hold out against the tide of opposition is uncertain, although they have overcome more than their share of problems in nearly seven decades in power. What seems certain is that the PRI will face ever greater pressures to reform, both from internal factions and from the growing power of a genuine opposition. Whether those reforms bring with them a democratic transition or a backlash remains to be seen.

And, while there is undoubtedly some form of economic crisis in progress alongside the political upheavals – the peso continues to slide in value against the dollar – Mexico's stock exchange was the most profitable in the world in 1997, throwing into sharp relief the enormous gulf between rich and poor and indicating the inequalities that need to be overcome before true democracy can be said to thrive in Mexico.

MONUMENTAL CHRONOLOGY

20,000 BC	First waves of Stone-Age migrants from the north.	Earliest evidence of man in the central valleys.
C6–C2 BC	Archaic period.	First evidence of settlement – cultivation, pottery and tools in the Valley of México.
1500 BC –300 AD	Pre-Classic period. Rise and dominance of the **Olmecs**.	The first simple pyramids and magnificent statuary at their Gulf Coast sites – San Lorenzo, La Venta and Tres Zapotes. Olmec influence on art and architecture everywhere, especially Monte Albán. Early evidence of new cultures in the Valley of México – Cuicuilco (buried by volcano) and Teotihuacán.
300–900 AD	Classic Period. **Teotihuacán** dominates Central Mexico, with evidence of its influence as far south as Kaminaljuyu in Guatemala. **Maya** cities flourish in the highlands of Guatemala and Honduras, as well as Mexican Yucatán.	Massive pyramids at Teotihuacán, decorated with stucco reliefs and murals. Monte Albán continues to thrive, while El Tajín on the Gulf Coast shows a new style in its Pyramid of the Niches. All the great sites – Uxmal, Palenque, Chichén Itzá, Edzná, Kabah – at their peak. Puuc, Chenes and Río Bec styles are perhaps the finest prehispanic architecture.
900–1500 AD	Post-Classic. In Central Mexico, a series of invasions by warlike tribes from the north.	**Toltecs** make their capital at Tula (c.900–1150), new use of columns and roofed space – chac-mools and Atlantean columns in decoration.
987	Toltec invasion of the Yucatán?	New Toltec-Maya synthesis especially evident at Chichén Itzá.
C10	**Mixtecs** gain control of Oaxaca area.	Mixtec tombs at Monte Albán, but seen above all at Mitla.
C11	League of Mayapán.	Maya architecture in decline, as Mayapán itself clearly demonstrates.
C13	Arrival of the Mexica in Central Mexico, last of the major "barbarian" invasions.	Many rival cities in the Valley of México, including Tenayuca, Texcoco and Culhuacán.
1345	Foundation of Tenochtitlán – rapid expansion of the **Aztec Empire**.	Growth of all the great Aztec cities, especially Tenochtitlán itself. In the east, cities such as Cholula and Zempoala fall under Aztec influence, and in the south, the Mixtecs are conquered. To the west, Purepecha (or Tarascan) culture developing, with their capital at Tzintzuntzan. Maya culture survives at cities such as Tulum.

1519	**Cortés** lands.	
1521	Tenochtitlán falls to Spanish.	Spanish destroy many ancient cities. Early colonial architecture is defensive and fortress-like; churches and mansions in México and elsewhere, monasteries with huge atriums for mass conversions. Gradually replaced by more elaborate renaissance and plateresque styles – seen above all in churches in the colonial cities north of the capital.
1524	First Franciscan monks arrive.	
1598	**Conquest** officially complete.	
C17–C18	**Colonial** rulers grow in wealth and confidence.	Baroque begins to take over religious building – great cathedrals at México and Puebla, lesser ones at Zacatecas. Towards the end the still more extravagant churrigueresque comes in: magnificent churches around Puebla and at Taxco and Tepotzotlán.
1810	Hidalgo proclaims **Independence**.	The development of the Neoclassical style through the influence of the new San Carlos art academy, but little building in the next fifty chaotic years.
1821	Independence achieved.	
1836	Texas declares independence – battles of the Alamo and San Jacinto.	
1838	Brief French invasion.	
1845	Texas joins USA – **Mexican-American War**.	
1847	US troops occupy México.	
1848	Half of Mexican territory ceded to US by treaty.	
1858-61	**Reform Wars** between liberals under Benito Juárez and Church-backed conservatives.	Many churches damaged or despoiled.
1861	Juárez triumphant; suspends payment of foreign debt. France, Spain and Britain send naval expedition.	
1862	Spain and Britain withdraw – invading French army defeated on May 5.	
1863	French take México. **Maximilian** becomes emperor.	Brief vogue for French styles. Paseo de la Reforma and Chapultepec Castle in the capital.
1866	French troops withdrawn.	

1867	Juárez defeats Maximilian.	
1876	**Porfirio Díaz** accedes to power.	The Porfiriano period sees a new outbreak of Neo-classical and grandiose public building. Palacio de las Bellas Artes and Post Office in México. Theatres and public buildings throughout the country.
1910	Madero stands for election, sparking the **Revolution**.	Another period of destruction rather than building.
1911	Díaz flees into exile.	
1911-17	Vicious revolutionary infighting continues.	
1920 on	Modern Mexico.	Modern architecture in Mexico is among the world's most original and adventurous, combining traditional themes with modern techniques. Vast decorative murals are one of its constant themes. The National Archeology Museum and University City in the capital are among its most notable achievements.

BALL GAMES & SACRIFICE: THE PRE-COLUMBIAN BELIEF SYSTEM

The Spanish conquest and subjugation of Mesoamerica saw the destruction of more than just the physical remains of what at the time were some of the most advanced societies in the world. Still more pressing for the Spanish were the suppression of "alien" cultures and the propagation of Catholicism. All traces of traditional religion and culture were to be rooted out and systematically dismantled. In the process, hundreds of thousands of books were burnt, priests executed, temples overturned. Even now, when the state profits from the huge interest in the pre-Columbian world and pays lip-service to multiculturalism, Mexican law forbids the teaching in schools of Yucatec Maya – the language of the people who built the pyramids. Such is the tenacity of traditional beliefs, though, that even five hundred years of effort have not been enough to eradicate them entirely: as anyone who has entered a rural Mexican church or witnessed the rituals of the Day of the Dead can attest.

Much of our knowledge of ancient Mesomerican beliefs, then, is derived from the surviving traditions of contemporary indigenous groups, which have been handed down through the generations. Further fragments are gleaned from the various Spanish accounts, from hieroglyphs and images carved into the ruins of buildings, from sculpture and pottery, jewellery retrieved from tombs and the few surviving written records.

SHAMANISM: THE ROOT OF MESOAMERICAN CULTURE

The great Mesoamerican civilizations comprised some of the purest **theocracies** the world has ever known. Every aspect of life was sacred and formed part of a huge cosmic interplay between the everyday, material world and the dream-like spirit world. This spirit world was home to a pantheon of gods, spirits and the souls of dead ancestors. The priests and kings who governed Mesoamerica so absolutely had privileged access to this realm, communicating with its denizens while in a state of trance, predicting the effect of the spiritual on the material from the motion of the stars, and maintaining the balance between the two worlds, thus avoiding misfortune or disaster. All was sacred – the days of the week, the cardinal points with their associated deities and spiritual properties – and every event from the planting of crops to the waging of war had to occur at the correct spiritual time.

This vast and elaborate belief system had its roots in **shamanism**, whose origins predate agriculture and settled village life. This is still the religion of the nomadic communities of Siberia, whose ancestors were the first to populate the Americas. In the shamanic universe everything is alive, not only in the material world but, more truly, in the spiritual. A rock has a soul every bit as much as a jaguar or a human being, and this soul can be separated from the physical form, a feat achieved by spiritually adept individuals known as shamans. The shaman's soul is able to travel through the spirit world, communing with gods, demons or ancestors or even appearing in the material world in another form, such as the shape of an animal. But the spirit world is an ambivalent place, containing both paradise and its opposite, inhabited by gods and demons and the souls of the evil as well as the good.

These malevolent and benevolent forces make the relationship between the **material and spiritual worlds** a delicate one. Disease, for instance, is not merely a physical condition, it is also a spiritual one which may result from the imprisoning of a soul by a malevolent spirit, or some other imbalance. The shaman, in a state of trance, can correct imbalances – journeying to free the soul from its prison, and thus making the material person well again. But in the shamanic universe, you rarely get something for nothing, and if a powerful spirit or a god is involved, sacrifice may be required to recompense that spirit.

The legacy of the shaman can be found in all Mexican religion. The Day of the Dead celebrations have their roots in a shamanic conception of the universe, as do the rituals of modern Mexican witchcraft. Nowadays, this legacy is most clearly seen in the belief systems of the tribes of northern Mexico, such as the **Yaqui** (whose shamanic traditions have been poetically immortalized by Carlos Castaneda) or the **Huichol**. It is worth taking a more detailed look at the practices and beliefs of the latter for the light it throws on ancient belief systems.

HUICHOL SHAMANISM

In the province of Nayarit in the desert of northern Mexico, the **Huichol** have survived the dominance of the Aztecs, Nuño de Guzman's bloody conquest of western Mexico, the subsequent Spanish exploitation, the Revolution and the technological leaps of the twentieth century. More than any other people in Mexico, they have remained faithful to the spiritual beliefs of their ancestors, and their way of life has changed little in thousands of years, never really moving beyond the first stages of village life that their cousins to the south abandoned in about 1300 BC.

Like all shamanic communities, Huichols see the material and spirit worlds as two poles of one universe. The border between the two is blurred; the communities are in regular communication with their dead ancestors, most of whom live in the underworld, and who often sneak back into the world of the living to steal their maize beer. The spirit world is used as a constant reference for occurrences in the material, with shamans, known as **Maracames**, providing the readings that inform the community. Two facets of their cosmology – an orientation of their sacred buildings to four cardinal points and a belief in a "first place" where their ancestors had been gods – stand out as distinctively Mesoamerican.

The most important Huichol buildings, **Xirikis**, are precisely oriented to the four cardinal points, each of which has a particular spiritual connotation. Each *Xiriki* is home to a disembodied ancestral shaman whose soul inhabits a quartz crystal attached to a ceremonial arrow lodged in its roof. Contemporary shamans use the spiritual strength of these crystals to travel to the Huichol spirit world, to confer with their ancestors, or with other spirits, and bring their wisdom into the community.

The centre of this spirit world is called **Wirikuta**. In the everyday, physical world, this is a dull stretch of desert in northwest Mexico, some 500km from Nayarit. In the spiritual world it is the Huichol womb of creation – the ground from which the sky and the stars emerged at the beginning of time, and the paradise where humans were created by the gods, and where for a while they lived with them as equals. The Huichol frequently visit *Wirikuta* in pilgrimages that involve taking peyote to induce trance-like states. A shaman guide orchestrates key rituals throughout the journey to protect the pilgrims from deceitful spirits, and interprets the landscape along the way: a waterhole becomes a spiritual gateway; shreds of cactus, the bones of ancestors. Plants, animals, rivers and mountains all have their associated spirits and their individual symbolic, sacred meaning.

Every aspect of Huichol life is filled with symbolism. Their bright weavings and intricate beaded masks reflect the spiritual reality behind the material, often depicting the three most sacred symbols of all – **corn**, the substance of creation, the **deer**, hunted for food but also revered, and **peyote**, the trance-inducing cactus. Gourds covered in brightly coloured beads, spelling out the wishes of their maker, are offered to the gods as sacrifices.

THE OLMECS: THE ROOTS OF MESOAMERICAN SHAMANISM

Archeological research at **Olmec** sites tells us that many of the Huichols' beliefs were common to the first great Mesoamerican civilization, whose cities and preoccupations formed a template to be traced by subsequent cultures. The Olmecs were the first Mesoamerican civilization literally to set their cosmology in stone, making a permanent record of their rulers, and the gods and spirits with whom they communed. Like the Huichol, they had a *Wirikuta*, but the Olmec place of creation was in the shape of the mighty volcano of **San Martín** in the south of modern Veracruz state. They built a replica – a sacred artificial mountain, complete with fluted sides – in their city at **La Venta**. This was the original Mesoamerican **pyramid**, a feature that recurs in virtually every subsequent culture: the Classic **Maya** conceived of their cities as a living landscape of sacred artificial mountains and trees, while the **Aztec** Templo Mayor was a dual pyramid representing the two sacred mountains of Coatepec and Tonacateptl.

Into the base of their volcano pyramid the Olmecs embedded huge stone **stelae**, one portraying ruling dignitaries communicating with gods and spirits – shamans, who, because of their crucial importance in maintaining the balance between the material and spiritual, had come to govern Olmec society. Such stelae, the equivalent of the Huichol rooftop arrowheads, were regarded as embodiments of the gods or kings they represented – spiritual telephones to the dead and the divine, whose users operated them in a trance state. These were the first stelae in Mesoamerica, and later versions fill the plazas of ruined cities all over Mexico and Central America.

One stela at La Venta depicts a **World Tree**, a symbol of the *axis mundi* at the centre of the Mesoamerican universe: its roots in the earth, its branches in the heavens, linking the underworld of the dead with the earth and sky. Though this was perhaps the first such representation, World Trees have been found in cities all over Mesoamerica and are portrayed in **Teotihuacán** mythology and in the **Codex Borgia**, one of the most beautiful of the few surviving Aztec books. At Maya **Palenque** there are several, including one on the lid of a ruler's sarcophagus: here key symbols and events of Maya mythology are written in the patterns and motion of the stars, and the ruler is shown falling through a World Tree inscribed in the night sky – the Milky Way.

Opposite Mexico's first pyramid, the Olmecs built a **gateway** to the shamanic spirit world in the form of a sunken, court-shaped plaza with an enormous pavement of serpentine blocks. They added two large platforms on either side of the entrance into the court and deposited huge quantities of sacred serpentine inside. These two platforms were topped with mosaics and patterns depicting aquatic plants, symbols of a gateway to the spirit world. Such symbols appeared all over Mesoamerica in the ensuing centuries, often decorating ball courts or ceramics.

Other surviving artefacts speak of stranger shamanic aspects to Olmec religion. Statuettes of half-jaguar, half-human babies probably depict the awakening of latent shamanic powers and associations with spirit animals – in the Mesoamerican pantheon each soul has its companion spirit animal. **Mirrors** found at Olmec cities were symbols of portals to the spirit world, an idea developed by the Aztecs, whose god, Tezcatlipoca ("Smoking Mirror") governs shamans and sorcerers in the Toltec and Aztec pantheon. In the Aztec creation myth, Tezcatlipoca assists Quetzalcoatl in the creation of the world.

The Olmec shaman-rulers also recompensed the gods and spirits through whom they kept the crucial balance between the material and the spiritual world. Human **sacrifice** and ritual bloodletting, those most Mesoamerican of practices, were probably developed by them for this purpose. And though there were different emphases, the basic structure of Olmec society – a theocracy ruled over by a priestly and regal elite who communicated with and propitiated the spirit world through sacrifice – would change little throughout Mesoamerica until the advent of Cortés. But there were some important developments. An increasing preoccupation with divining and balancing the material and the spirit world led to the invention of the calendar and writing, and the ball game and sacrifice became ever more crucial, particularly in central Mexico, where the appetites of the malevolent and bloodthirsty Mesoamerican gods increased with each new civilization.

THE CALENDAR

The Mesoamericans believed that the relationship between the spirit world and the material was recorded in the stars, and that certain astronomical configurations were ominous. For the Maya and Aztecs, the stars themselves were embodiments of gods, and the constellations re-enactments of cosmic events. The **Maya** version of *Wirikuta* was in the night sky – they regarded the three stars below the belt of Orion as the place of creation itself. This preoccupation led to the invention of the **calendar**, probably by the Zapotecs of Monte Albán in about 600 BC. Subsequent depictions of calendars can be seen across the spectrum of Mesoamerican art, notably on the Aztec Piedra del Sol, now in the Museum of Anthropology in México, and in the paintings in Maya codices.

By the time of the **Classic Maya** (300–900 AD), the 260-day calendar had become the fundamental map of the relationship between the spirit and material world, and the highest tool of prediction and divination outside the trance-state itself. Every number and day had its own significance; each of the twenty day-names had a specific supernatural god and a particular direction, passing in a continuous anticlockwise path from one day to the next until a cycle of time was completed. This calendar was used alongside a 365-day calendar, roughly matching the solar year, but lacking the leap days necessary to give it real accuracy. This was divided into eighteen groups of twenty days plus an unlucky additional five days. Each twenty-day grouping and each solar year also had a supernatural patron. When the two calendars were set in motion and were running concurrently, it took exactly 52 years for the cycle to repeat. In addition to these two calendars, the Pre-Classic Maya developed what is known as the **Long Count**, recording the total number of days elapsed since a mythological date when the first great cycle began. The mathematics required to administer this Long Count are advanced and complex – a stela at Copán in Honduras calculates the day of creation, recording it as a 29-figure number. For Mesoamerican civilizations, the ending of one cycle and the beginning of another heralded apocalypse and, afterwards, a new age and a reassertion of the ordered world from the disordered and demonic: one symbol of this new age was the construction of new temples over the old every 52 years. The Maya Long Count will end on December 23, 2012, and there are many who believe that this date will herald the end of the world that others predict for the millennium.

SACRIFICE

At the beginning of the 365-day cycle, the **Aztecs** extinguished all fires and smashed all ceramics throughout their empire. At midnight, if the stars passed overhead, priests ripped out the heart of a warrior and started a new fire in his chest – for the Aztecs, **sacrifice** was crucial in maintaining world harmony and the continuance of cosmic events. If the forces of the spirit world were not kept in balance with the proper appeasements, chaos and death would reign.

The ruling shaman/priests were vital to keep the world, and **life** itself, going, and sacrifice was one of their main tools: Mesoamericans believed that they were not so much living on borrowed time, but on time won

by trickery from the gods of death. Maya vases, buried with the dead, often depict scenes from the the the Popul Vuh, the creation epic of the Quiché Maya, in which the Hero Twins defeat the **Lords of the Underworld** through a series of shamanic tricks and their skill at playing the ball game. Central Mexican mythology went still further: life is not won from death by trickery, it is quite literally stolen. In one story, Quetzalcoatl and Xolotl descend to the underworld where they trick the god of death, Mictlantechutli, into giving them sacred bones left over from a previous creation. These bones are taken to the paradise of Tamoanchán – the central Mexican equivalent of the Huichol *Wirikuta*, or the Olmec San Martín – where they are ground into cornmeal. The gods then let their blood into the ground meal, and humans are born. After the creation of people, the gods convene in darkness at Teotihuacán, where they decide to create a new sun. This, too, depends on sacrifice, and the two gods hurl themselves into a fiery furnace to become the sun and the moon.

The bloody creation mythology of central Mexico is filled with the presence of the Lords of the Underworld trying to regain the life that was stolen from them; none were more preoccupied with this than the Aztecs. The Aztec empire was enslaved to Lords of the Underworld's seemingly insatiable appetite for **human hearts** – the price of continuing life and order. Bernal Díaz recounts the sacrifice of fattened children, women and captured warriors with horror, and concludes that the Aztec priests were slaves of the powers of darkness, an idea suggested even in their own mythology. The great Toltec prince Quetzalcoatl Topiltzin, renowned for his wisdom and holiness and founder of the great city of Tula, decided to make an end to human sacrifice and attempted to convince the inhabitants of Tula to give it up. He was unsuccessful, however, as the shamanic god, Tezcatlipoca, tricked the Toltecs and forced Quetzalcoatl Topiltzin into exile. Quetzalcoatl Topiltzin built a raft and left "for the east" from the Gulf coast, promising to return one day to banish false rulers and reinstate a higher order, where human sacrifice would play no part. It is a well known irony that Cortés landed on the Gulf Coast, where Quetzalcoatl Topiltzin was said to have left, at the time predicted for his return.

THE BALL GAME

Like sacrifice and bloodletting, the Mesoamerican **ball game**, once played all over prehispanic Mexico and Central America, and still played in some villages in the Oaxaca valleys and the northwest, was imbued with shamanic symbolism and the Mesoamerican mythology of death. For though many Mesoamerican peoples saw the ball travelling through the alley of the court as the sun journeying in and out of the underworld, the game was primarily seen as a metaphor for life, death and regeneration.

Like so much of Mesoamerican religious tradition, the game was developed by the Olmecs, probably from an earlier prototype. A carving dating back to 900 BC, found at the Olmec city of **San Lorenzo**, depicts a ball player kneeling to receive a ball; ball players were depicted at Dainzú outside Oaxaca, sometime after 150 BC, and ball-courts appear in the Pre-Classic Maya city of Izapa in the Chiapas mountains. The game was usually played in a ball-court shaped like a letter I. The players, in teams of two or three, would score points by hitting the ball with their upper arms or thighs, through hoops or at markers embedded in the walls of the court. Heavy bets were placed by supporters, and the penalty for losing the most important games was death (though there have been suggestion that the winners were sacrificed in some cities).

The **Classic Veracruz** civilization were obsessed with the ball game, and there are more than seventeen courts in their most important city, **El Tajín**. Most are covered with superbly carved bas-reliefs showing all aspects of the game, including sacrifice: one depicts a ball player having his chest cut open with an obsidian knife while a grinning skeleton rises from a pot. This figure appears in many of the carvings on the Tajín ball-courts, and is almost certainly an underworld lord – a personification of death. In Maya mythology, the ball game is played against the Lords of the Underworld, most famously by the Hero Twins of the Popul Vuh. The largest court of all at **Chichén Itzá** is covered in bas-reliefs of aquatic plants, symbolizing an opening to the underworld. Still more depict the game and the death rituals that were associated with it. One shows a player holding the severed head of a captive. The stump of his neck spouts serpents – symbols of the spiritual life force contained in blood – which transform into waterlilies, showing how the sacrifice opens the way to the spirit world.

Alex Robinson

ENVIRONMENT AND WILDLIFE

Mexico is one of the most biologically diverse countries in the world, with the second highest number of mammal species (450, after Indonesia), more than a thousand species of birds, at least 30,000 species of higher plants (including half of the world's pines), and more reptile species (700) than any other country. Many of these are endemic – found nowhere else – and this diversity, combined with its vast size (1,960,000 square kilometres) and tremendous range of natural environments make Mexico an ideal location for the visiting naturalist, irrespective of expertise.

Specific **wildlife highlights** include: the **gray whale calving grounds** off the west coast of Baja California (at their best in January and February); the arid interior plains of northern Mexico and their diverse collection of **cacti**; the semi-tropical forests which line the Gulf coast near Veracruz; the lush tropical forests of Chiapas and southern Yucatán, containing the remaining populations of **monkeys** and **large cats**, and full of vividly coloured **parakeets** and **toucans**; the Yucatán Peninsula, with its fabulous collection of migrating birds, including large flocks of **greater flamingo**, and the **barrier reef** and coastal islands in the Caribbean Sea, where the snorkelling reveals shoals of brilliantly coloured **fish**; the impressive colonies of sea birds along the southern Pacific coastline, including **frigate birds** and **boobies**. **Dolphins** are still commonly seen off all coastlines.

Unfortunately, as in many developing countries where economic hardship remains the prime concern, much of this natural beauty is **under threat** either from direct hunting or the indirect effects of deforestation and commercialization. It is imperative that we, as paying visitors, show a **responsible attitude** to the natural environment where it remains and endeavour to support the vital educational programmes which are seeking to preserve these remnants.

It should be stressed that not only is it extremely irresponsible, but it is also **illegal** to buy, even as souvenirs, most items which involves the use of wild animals or flowers in its production. This applies specifically to tortoiseshell, black coral, various species of butterfly, mussels and snails, stuffed baby crocodiles, cat skins and turtle shells. Trade in living animals, including tortoises, iguanas and parrots (often sold as nestlings) is also illegal, as is the uprooting of cacti.

GEOGRAPHY AND CLIMATE

The distinct geographical pattern seen in Mexico, in conjunction with the climatic variation from north to south, creates a series of isolated **biomes**, each with their individual flora and fauna. The **Tropic of Cancer** divides the country laterally, technically placing half the country inside and half outside the tropics.

The predominant geographical features tend to be southward continuations of North American counterparts; the **Sierra Madre Oriental** range which lies to the east is an extension of the Rocky Mountain range, and the **Sierra Madre Occidental** range to the west is an extension of the Sierra Nevada range. The interlying highlands and intermontane basins form the lofty **Northern Plateau**, which extends from México to the western tablelands of the United States.

Further south (between latitudes 18 and 20 degrees north) lies the range of volcanoes known as the **Sierra Volcanica Transversal**, which rises in altitude towards its southern edge and runs from the Pacific coast, almost as far as the Gulf of Mexico. The lands south of this range are extensive coastal plains and plateaus (the low-lying Yucatán), with intermittent higher ranges, such as the **Oaxaca** and **Chiapas Uplands**.

Most of the landmass is subject to the prevailing **trade winds** which blow from the northeast out across the Gulf of Mexico. Cool currents keep the Pacific coastal waters cooler and the air drier than the Atlantic coast, while the sharp escarpments of the Sierra Madre Oriental, creating a vast rain shadow, contribute to the aridity of the northern plateau.

Rainfall is variable across the landmass, scant in the arid deserts of the north Pacific and interior sierras and extremely heavy in the tropical cloud and rain forests of the southeastern slopes of the **Sierra Madre del Sur** and sections of the Gulf coast (the **rainy season** itself extends from late May to October or November).

VEGETATION

The influence of long-term **deforestation** for charcoal cutting or slash-and-burn agriculture has substantially denuded the original forest which covered large areas of Mexico. Today the northern mountains contain tracts of conifer, cedar and oak, especially around **Durango** where the largest pine forest reserves are to be found. At lower altitudes, the grass-covered **savannahs** are interrupted by the occasional palm or palmetto tree, and the riverbanks are graced with poplar and willow.

The tropical rainforests which border the Gulf of Mexico form a broad band which extends southward from **Tampico** across the base of the Yucatán peninsula and the northern part of Oaxaca, containing mahogany, cedar, rosewood, ebony and logwood, but these reserves are being ever reduced. Seasonal tropical forest and dry scrub cover the remaining areas of the Gulf coast and the lowlands of the Pacific coast. One particularly notable tree is a single **ahuehuetl** (or giant cypress) tree, believed to have a bore of more than 50m in circumference and rumoured to be the oldest living thing in the Americas. Extensive **mangrove forests** once lined much of the Gulf coast and the Caribbean, and grew along sheltered reaches of the Pacific shore, but these are being destroyed throughout their range, as coastlines are developed for tourism.

The flatter lands of the north, the north Pacific and portions of central Mexico are characterized by dry scrub and grassland. The most conspicuous of the vegetation in these drier areas however, are the **cacti**. Various species adorn these flat grasslands; the **saguaro** is a giant, tree-like growth which can exceed 15m in height, whereas the columns of the **cereus** cactus stand in lines, not dissimilar to fence posts, and can reach 8m in height. Another notable variety is the **prickly pear** (or *nopal*) which produces a fruit (*tuna*) that can either be eaten raw or used in the production of sweets. Other harvested varieties

THE 1998 FOREST FIRES

In the spring and summer of 1998, following an exceptionally long dry season and late arrival of the rains, both probably caused by the **El Niño** phenomenon – a cyclic rise in sea surface temperatures in the Pacific which diverts ocean currents and dramatically affects global weather patterns – devastating **forest fires** raged uncontrollably over huge areas of Mexico and neighbouring Guatemala. The pall of smoke from 10,000 fires, burning an area of 4000 square kilometres, darkened the skies as far north as Dakota and east to Florida in the USA. Pine forests in the Sierra Madre and the tropical forests of Oaxaca and Chiapas blazed in Mexico's worst environmental disaster since the Conquest. Over 95 percent of Mexico's original tree cover had been lost before the recent fires destroyed a quarter of the remaining forests.

Most fires began accidentally, often when the annual clearing of land on the forests' edge burned out of control, but some were set deliberately, often with the connivance of development interests, to reduce the conservation value of the land. Whatever their origin, the result is irreversible destruction to natural ecosystems and farmland alike. The mountains of Oaxaca have already been described in a UN report as the most eroded landscape on the planet, and when the fires eventually die down they will leave a legacy of ruined land, open to further erosion, driving *campesinos* to leave their farms for the overcrowded cities, and adding to Mexico's pressing social and environmental problems.

As the fires are still burning at the time of writing, it is impossible to document the full environmental cost of the tragedy, but many species of plants, some possibly unknown to science, and some animals will undoubtedly be driven over the brink of extinction, reducing Mexico's and the world's biodiversity.

include the pulpy-leaved **maguey** cactus (one of the Agave family), whose fermented juice forms the basis of tequila, mescal and pulque, and **henequen** (another Agave), which is grown extensively on the Yucatán Peninsula and used in the production of fibre.

The extensive **temperate grasslands** are composed primarily of clumped bunch grass and wiry, unpalatable Hilaria grass. Low-lying shrubs found amongst these grassy expanses include the spindly **ocotillo**, the **creosote bush**, the palm-like **yucca** with low-lying **mesquite** and **acacia** bushes in the more sheltered, damper areas. **Flowers** are commonplace throughout Mexico and form an integral part of day-to-day life. Two flowers, **frangipani** and **magnolia**, were considered to be of such value that they were reserved for the Aztec nobility. Today the blue blossoms of **jacaranda** trees and purple and red **bougainvillea** still adorn the walls of cities and towns during their spring and summer blooms. Even the harsh arid deserts of the north are carpeted with wild flowers during the brief Spring blooms which follow the occasional rains; the cacti blooms are particularly vivid. Many of these floral species are indigenous to Mexico, including cosmos, snapdragons, marigolds, dahlias and several species of wild **orchid** (over 800 species have been classified from the forests of Chiapas alone).

The **tropical forests** of Mexico provide supplies of both **chocolate** (from the cacao trees of the Chiapas) and vanilla, primarily for export. Also harvested is **chicle**, used in the preparation of chewing gum, from the latex of the sapodilla tree and wild rubber and sarsaparilla. Herbs, used in medicinal or pharmaceutical industries, include digitalis from wild foxgloves and various barks used in the preparation of purges and disinfectants. One plant, unique to Mexico, is *Discorea composita*, which is harvested in Veracruz, Oaxaca, Tabasco and Chiapas, and is used in the preparation of a vegetable hormone that forms an essential ingredient of the contraceptive pill.

INSECTS

Insect life is abundant throughout Mexico but numbers and diversity reach their peak in the tropical rain forests, particularly to the south of the country. Openings in the tree canopy attract a variety of colourful **butterflies**, gnats and locusts which swarm in abundance. For the

most part, insect life makes itself known mainly through the variety of bites and sores incurred whilst wandering through these areas: **mosquitoes** are a particular pest, with malaria still a risk in some areas. The **garrapata** is a particularly tenacious tick found everywhere livestock exists, and readily attaches itself to human hosts. A range of **scorpions**, whose sting can vary from extremely painful to definitively lethal, is found throughout the country.

Within the forests themselves, long columns of **leafcutter ants** criss-cross the floor in their search for food and surrounding tree trunks provide ideal shelter for the large, brown nests of **termites**. Further north in central Mexico, **army ants** have a direct bearing on the agricultural cycle; early cynicism by agronomists about the reluctance of peasant farmers to plant corn during certain phases of the moon has been forgotten with the realization that it is at these times that the ants are on the march. One species of ant, local to **Tlaxcala**, provides for seasonal labour not once but twice each year; firstly during the egg stage when it is harvested to produce a highly prized form of caviar and secondly during the grub stage, when it frequents the maguey cactus, which provides an equally prized food source. The most spectacular insect migration can be seen in winter in eastern **Michoacán**, where thousands of **monarch butterflies** hatch from their larval forms en masse, providing a blaze of colour and movement (see p.203).

FISH, AMPHIBIANS AND REPTILES

The diversity of Mexican inland and coastal habitats has enabled large numbers of both marine and freshwater species to remain mostly undisturbed. Among the freshwater species, **rainbow** and **brook trout**, silversides and catfish are particularly abundant (as are European carp in certain areas, where it has been introduced). The most highly regarded is a species of **whitefish** found in **Lake Chapala** and **Lake Patzcuaro**, where it forms the basis of a thriving local fishing industry.

Offshore, Mexican waters contain over one hundred marine species of significance, including varieties of tropical and temperate climates, coastal and deep waters, surface and ground feeders and sedentary and migratory lifestyles. Among the more important species are **jewfish**

(a type of giant sea bass), **swordfish, snapper, king mackerel, snook, tuna, mullet** and **anchovy**. Shrimp, crayfish and spiny lobster are also important commercial species. The marine fishing grounds on the **Pacific coast** are at their best off the coast of Baja California, where the warmer southern waters merge with sub-arctic currents from the north. Similarly, deep ocean beds and coastal irregularities provide correspondingly rewarding fishing in the waters of the **Campeche** bank on the Gulf of Mexico.

Reptiles are widely represented throughout Mexico. The lower river courses that flow through the southern forests are frequented by **iguana, crocodile** and its close relative, the **caiman**. Lizards range from the tiny nocturnal lizards along the Gulf coast to the tropical iguanas, which can reach up to 2m in length. **Marine turtles**, including the **loggerhead, green, hawksbill** and **leatherback**, are still found off many stretches of undeveloped waters and shores on both Atlantic and Pacific coasts. Hunting of both adults and eggs is now illegal, but numbers have been greatly reduced, as illegal hunting continues. Several kinds of **rattlesnake** are common in the deserts of northern Mexico, and farther south the rain-forests hold a substantial variety of other snakes, including the **boa constrictor, fer-de-lance, bushmaster** and the small **coral snake. Amphibian** life is similarly abundant; varieties include salamanders, several types of frog (including several **tree-frogs** in the southern forests) and one **marine toad** that measures up to 20cm in length.

BIRDS

More than five hundred species of tropical birds live in the rain and cloud forests of southern Mexico alone. Among these are resplendent **macaws, parrots** and **parakeets,** which make a colourful display as they fly amongst the dense tree canopy. The cereal-feeding habits of the parrot family have not endeared them to local farmers, and for this reason (and their continuing capture for sale as pets) their numbers have also been seriously depleted in recent times. In the lower branches, one can see large-billed **toucans** and on the ground, amongst the dense vegetation, it is also possible to see the occasional larger game birds, such as **curassow, crested guan, chachalaca** and **ocellated turkey**.

Particularly rare are the brilliantly coloured **trogons**, including the **resplendent quetzal**, inhabiting the cloud forests of the Sierra Madre de Chiapas (in the El Triunfo Reserve, p.468). The ancient Maya coveted its long, emerald green tail feathers which were used in priestly headdresses; its current status is severely endangered. To the east, the drier tropical deciduous forests of northern Yucatán, the Pacific coastal lowlands and the interior lowlands provide an ideal habitat for several carnivorous birds including owls and hawks. The most familiar large birds of Mexico, however, are the carrion-eating **black** and **turkey vultures** – locally *zopilote* – often seen soaring in large groups. The Yucatán is also one of the last remaining strongholds of the small **Mexican eagle**, which features in the country's national symbol.

Large numbers of coastal lagoons provide both feeding and breeding grounds for a wide variety of **aquatic birds** – some of them winter visitors from the north – including ducks, herons and grebes. Foremost amongst these are the substantial flocks of graceful **flamingo** which can be seen at selected sites along the western and northern coasts of the Yucatán peninsula. In the north of Mexico, the harsher and drier environment is less attractive; outlying towns and villages form a welcome sanctuary from this harshness for a variety of doves and pigeons and the areas with denser cover have small numbers of quail and pheasant. Any water feature in these drier zones, in addition to wetland areas further south, form attractive migration stopover sites for large flocks of North American species, including warblers, wildfowl and waders.

MAMMALS

Zoologists divide the animals of the Americas into two categories; the **Nearctic** region of the mid-latitudes in which the native animals are of North American affinity, and the **Neotropical** region of the lower latitudes, in which the fauna is linked to that of South American. The Isthmus of Tehuantepec marks the border between these two regions, serving as a barrier to many larger mammalian species.

The northern Nearctic region is predominantly composed of open steppe and desert areas and higher altitude oak and pine forests. Relatively few large mammals inhabit the highland forests, although one widespread species is the white-tailed deer, which is still overhunted as a source of food. The northern parts of the Sierra Madre Occidental mark the southernmost extent of several typically North American mammals, such as mountain sheep, and black and brown **bears**, though the latter are near extinction. Bears live in the **Cumbres de Monterrey National Park** (p.158) and wild horned sheep can be seen at the **San Pedro Martír National Park** in Baja California. Other mammals include deer, **puma**, **lynx**, **marten**, grey fox, mule sheep, porcupine, skunk, badger, rabbit and squirrel. A large array of smaller rodents, and their natural predators, the **coyote** and the **kit fox**, are also widespread throughout the forests. Nowadays the extensive grassland plains are frequented only by sporadic herds of **white-tailed deer**; the days of the pronghorn and even the bison have long passed under the burden of overhunting. Within the desert scrub, the **peccary** is still widely hunted and rodents, as ever, are in abundance forming an ample food supply for the resident **bobcats** and **ocelots**.

Baja California forms an outstanding wildlife sanctuary for marine mammals. **Guadalupe Island** is one of the few remaining breeding sites of the endangered **elephant seal** and the only known mating and nursery sites of the **gray whale** are around **Guerrero Negro** (p.76). Although some southern species (notably the **opossum** and **armadillo**) have succeeded in breaching the Tehuantepec line, and now thrive in northern Mexico and the southern United States, on the whole the Neotropical region holds a very different collection of mammals. The relationship between these species and the lush vegetation of the tropical rain forest and the highland cloud forests is particularly apparent. Many species are arboreal, living amongst the expansive tree canopies: these include **spider** and **howler monkeys**, opossums, tropical squirrels, the racoon-like **coati** and the gentle **kinkajou**.

Because of the paucity of grass on the shaded forest floors, ground-dwelling mammals are relatively scarce. The largest is the **tapir**, a distant relative of the horse, with a prehensile snout, usually never found far from water. Two species of **peccary**, a type of wild pig, wander the forest floors in large groups seeking their preferred foods (roots, palm nuts and even snakes), and there's the smaller **brocket deer**.

There are also large rodents, the **agouti** and the spotted **cavy**, which live in abundance along the numerous streams and river banks. These are hunted by the resident large cats, including **jaguar**, **puma** and **ocelot**.

The drier tropical and subtropical forests of northern Yucatán, the Pacific coastal lowlands and the interior basins produces a more varied ground cover of shrubs and grasses which supply food for the **white-tailed deer** and abundant small rodents, including the **spiny tree rat** and the **paca**, which in turn provide food for a variety of predators such as the **coyote**, **margay** and **jaguarundi**. Other large mammals which can still be found in small numbers are large and small **anteaters**, opossums and armadillos. The reefs and lagoons which run along the Quintana Roo coast have small colonies of the large aquatic **manatee** or sea cow, a gentle creature which feeds on sea grass.

WILDLIFE SITES

It would be almost impossible to compile a comprehensive list of sites of wildlife interest in Mexico, particularly as so much can be seen all over the country. The following is a selection of some of the outstanding areas, particularly ones that are easily accessible or close to major tourist centres. The few **zoos** that exist in Mexico are generally depressing places, but there is one outstanding exception – the conservation-oriented **Zoológico Miguel Alvárez del Toro** in Tuxtla Gutiérrez (p.465).

BAJA CALIFORNIA

Easily accessible from the west coast of the United States, the peninsula of **Baja California** is a unique part of the Mexican landmass. Its exceptional coastline provides sanctuaries for a wide variety of marine mammals, including the major wildlife attraction of the area, the migratory **gray whale** (see box). The lagoons where the whales gather can also offer superb views of other great whales, including **blue**, **humpback**, **fin**, **minke**, **sperm** and **orca** – killer whales.

Dolphins and **sea lions** and a variety of sea birds, including **pelicans**, **ospreys** and numerous waders such as plovers and sanderlings also inhabit the lagoons. The sparse vegetation provides roosting sites for both **jaegers** and **peregrines** and even the occasional **coyote** may be seen wandering over the sandy shores.

GRAY WHALE MIGRATION AND BREEDING

It is the **gray whales** and their well-documented migrations off the west coast of the peninsula which remain the outstanding spectacle of the region and continue to attract an estimated 250,000 visitors each year. Times have not always been so peaceful for these graceful leviathans; less than 150 years ago, the secret breeding grounds of the whales were discovered by Charles Melville Scammon. The Laguna Ojo de Liebre (renamed in recent times after the infamous whaler) was rapidly denuded of almost all of these magnificent beasts and it wasn't until the establishment of Scammon's Bay as the world's first whale sanctuary in 1972 that their numbers began to recover. The population in the area is currently estimated at about 20,000 – a dramatic recovery within the time span.

The whale's **migratory route** runs the length of the American Pacific seaboard, from Baja to the Bering Sea and back; this is a round trip of some 20,000km, which remains the longest recorded migration undertaken by any living mammal. They remain in the north for several months, feeding on the abundant krill in the high Arctic Summer, and building up body reserves for the long journey south to the breeding lagoons. The migration begins as the days begin to shorten and the pack ice starts to thicken, some time before the end of January.

Nowadays the human interest in the whales is purely voyeuristic, whale watching being a million-dollar industry, and in 1988 the Mexican government extended the range of the protected area to include the nearby San Ignacio Lagoon, forming the all-embracing National Park, the **Biosfera El Vizcaíno**. The San Ignacio Lagoon offers a daunting entrance of pounding surf and treacherous shoals, but once inside, its calmer waters flatten and spread inland for 15km towards the distant volcanic peaks of the Santa Clara mountains. Accessible points for land-based observation lie further north in the **Parque Natural de Ballena Gris** ("Gray Whale Natural Park"), 32km south of Guerrero Negro.

Offshore, there are several small islands whose protected status has encouraged colonization by highly diverse animal communities. Furthest north is the island of **Todos Santos** where the sandy beaches, festooned with the remnants of shellfish, are used as occasional sunning spots by the resident **harbour seals**. The atmosphere is ripe with an uncommon blend of guano, kelp and Californian sagebrush. The Pacific swell frequently disturbs the resting cormorants, which bask in the hot sunshine, and the skies are filled with wheeling **western gulls** (similar to the European lesser blackback gull) from the thriving colony on the island.

Farther south lies the island of **San Benito**, which lies just to the northeast of the much larger island of **Isla Cedros**. The island provides ideal nesting grounds for migrating **ospreys**, which travel south from the United States. The hillsides are covered by the tall **agave** (century plants) whose brief, once-in-a-lifetime blooms add an attractive splash of colour to the surrounding slopes. These towering succulents produce a broad rosette of golden florets, which provide a welcome supply of nectar for resident **hummingbirds**, and **ravens** wheel above, searching for carrion. The island,

along with Isla Cedros and the distant **Isla Guadalupe** (now a Biological Reserve) also provides a winter home to thousands of **elephant seals**, now happily recovering after years of overhunting. The large adult males arrive in December and the pebbly coves are soon crammed with the noisy and chaotic colony of mothers, calves and bachelor bulls, ruled by one dominant bull (or beach master) which can weigh up to two tonnes. The males make a terrible spectacle as, with necks raised and heads thrown back, they echo their noisy threats to any would-be rival who challenges the mating rights within their harem.

The interior of the peninsula has several areas of wildlife interest, many of which now have the protected status of nature reserve. Most significant of all are the National Parks of the **Sierra San Pedro Mártir** and the **Desierto Central**. Here the chaparral-covered hills cede to forests of Jeffrey pine and meadow tables, interspersed with granite *picachos* (peaks) and volcanic mesas. The **Constitución de 1857** National Park is another green oasis amongst the arid lowlands, where the coniferous woodlands form a picturesque border to the central **Laguna Hanson**. These sierras are renowned for the numerous palm-filled canyons which cut deep into the eastern escarpment; they make spectacular hiking areas with their miniature waterfalls, ancient **petroglyphs**, caves, **hot springs** and groves of **fan palms**.

DURANGO

Durango lies within a dry, hilly area where the intermittent oak and pine woodland is surrounded by large expanses of low-lying scrub. These areas are frequented by large numbers of **birds**, whose presence is an extension of their North American range. Typical species include **red-tailed hawk**, **American kestrel** and **mockingbird**. The denser, wooded areas provide the necessary cover for several more secretive varieties such as **Mexican jay**, **acorn woodpecker**, **Hepatic grosbeak** and the diminutive **Mexican chickadee**. This is also an occasional haunt of the **mountain lion** (or puma) and the coyote. In the dry scrub, **scorpions** abound. Other nearby sites worthy of investigation include El Salto and El Palmito.

THE MAZATLÁN ESTUARY

The **Mazatlán estuary** is an extensive area of estuarine sands with marshy margins: ideal feeding grounds for a variety of **waders and wildfowl**, including **marbled godwit**, **greater yellowlegs** and **willet**. Large numbers of herons and egrets feed in the shallow waters (including little green and **Louisiana heron** and **snowy** and **cattle egret**), while further out to sea passage birds include **laughing gull**, **gull-billed tern** and **olivaceous cormorant**. Most spectacular of all are the aptly named **magnificent frigate birds**, who make a dramatic sight with their long wings, forked tails and hooked bills, as they skim over the water's surface, in their search for fish.

The rocks offshore provide a suitable breeding site for both brown and blue-footed **booby** and the pools at the northern end of the town, behind the large hotels, have some interesting waterbirds, including **jacana**, **ruddy duck** and **canvasback**.

SAN BLAS

Immediately around **San Blas** are lagoons with wildlife very similar to that found in the Mazatlán estuary; boat tours from San Blas take you out to see herons, egrets and much more, with the possibility of a **caiman** the big attrac-

tion. Farther out the landscape forms areas of thicker scrub and dense forest at higher altitudes. Amongst this lower-lying scrub, it is possible to see the **purplish-backed jay**, **gila woodpecker** and **tropical kingbird**, whilst the skies above have the patrolling **white-tailed kite**. At higher altitudes, the bird life includes the locally named **San Blas jay**, **white-crowned parrot** and **cinnamon hummingbird**. The town itself provides sufficient scraps for scavengers such as black and **grey hawk** and various rodents.

VERACRUZ AND THE GULF COAST

The eastern coastline of Mexico has particular attractions of its own, and none is more rewarding to the visiting naturalist than the final remaining tract of **rainforest** on the Mexican Gulf coast, southeast of Veracruz. The surrounding vegetation is lush, the tended citrus orchards yielding to rolling tropical forest, with its dense growth of **ficus**, mango and banana trees and the occasional coconut palm. These trees provide cover for a colourful underlying carpet including **orchids**, lemon trees, camellias, fragrant **cuatismilla** and gardenias. Even the roadsides are lined with banks of **hibiscus**, oleander and the pretty, white-flowered shrub, known locally as "cruz de malta". At the centre of the whole area, **Lake Catemaco** is outstandingly beautiful.

The surrounding forest has suffered much in recent times and many of the larger mammals are no longer found in the region. One sanctuary which remains amongst this destruction is the ecological research station of **Los Tuxtlas**. Although the Institute's holding is fairly small, it adjoins a much larger state-owned reserve of some 25,000 acres on the flank of the San Martín volcano. Despite the problems of poaching and woodcutting, the area has the last remaining populations of brocket deer, **black howler monkey**, **ocelot**, **jaguarundi**, **kinkajous** and **coati**. It also boasts 92 species of reptile, fifty amphibians, thousands of insects and over three hundred species of birds.

With patience, it is possible to see such outstanding varieties as keel-billed toucan, black-shouldered kite, gold-crowned warbler, red-throated ant tanager, plain-breasted brush finch, red-lored parrot, ivory-billed woodpecker and the magnificent white hawk, to name but a few.

PALENQUE AND THE CHIAPAS UPLANDS

In the **Chiapas uplands,** the absence of climatic moderation by lower altitudes and coastal breezes creates dense, lush vegetation that is truly worthy of the name of tropical rainforest. The **Sierra Madre de Chiapas** is of particular interest to visiting naturalists, particularly the Pacific slope at altitudes between 1500 and 2500 metres, as these are the last sanctuary of the endangered **horned guan** and **azure-rumped tanager** and even the **quetzal**. **El Triunfo Reserve**, at 1800 metres in the very southeastern corner of the country, less than 50km from the Guatemalan border makes an excellent base camp for exploration of the area. The cloud forest is dense in this locality and the tall epiphyte-laden trees grow in profusion on the slopes and in the valleys, in the humid conditions which occur after the **morning fogs** have risen (generally by early afternoon).

Another area of interest in eastern Chiapas is the **Lagos de Montebello** National Park (p.481) where the more determined bird-watcher may be rewarded with views of **azure-hooded jay** and the **barred parakeet**. Human encroachment has substantially reduced the number of large mammals in the area, but small numbers of **howler monkey**, tapir and **jaguar** (known locally as "el tigre"), are a reminder of bygone days. Another speciality of the region is a vivid and diminutive **tree frog**, whose precise camouflage ensures that it is more often heard than seen.

At the archeological site of **Palenque** you're back among the tourists (and the howler monkeys) but the birding is unrivalled and local specialities include the **chestnut-headed oropendola**, **scaled ant pitta**, **white-whiskered puffbird**, **slaty-tailed trogon** and **masked tanager**.

In the area of marshland around the Río Usumacinta about 25km east of the junction between the main Palenque road and Highway 186, **pinnated bittern**, everglade kite and the rare **lesser yellow-headed vulture** have all been recorded.

THE YUCATÁN PENINSULA

The vegetation of the **Yucatán peninsula** is influenced by its low relief the ameliorating effects of its extensive coastline which brings regular and fairly reliable rain along with year-round high temperatures. In the north it's predominantly **dry scrub** and bush, although large areas have been cleared for the cultivation of crops such as maize, citrus fruits and henequen. To the south are lusher **tropical** and **sub-tropical** forest, where the effects of agriculture are less obvious, and the dense forest of **acacia**, **albizias**, widespread **gumbo limbo** and **ceiba** is in parts almost impenetrable. These form an ideal shelter for scattered populations of both the white-tailed and brocket deer. The whole peninsula is a unique wildlife area, with the bird life being particularly outstanding. Two specific sites worthy of thorough investigation are the archeological sites of **Cobá** (p.571) and **Chichén Itzá** (p.541). The abundant and spectacular birds which fill the treetops include **squirrel cuckoo**, **citreoline trogon** and **Aztec parakeet**, whilst circling in the skies above are the resident birds of prey such as **bat falcon**, **snail kite** and the ever-present black and turkey **vultures** (these can be distinguished, even at great heights, as the wings of the latter are clearly divided into two bands — the darker primaries and the lighter secondaries being quite distinct). It is also possible to see all three species of Mexican **toucan**; collared aracari, emerald toucanet and the spectacular keel-billed. The denser areas of forest also hold small remnants of the original **black howler** and **spider monkey** populations.

The village of Cobá borders a lake with extensive reed margins along its eastern edge, which attracts a variety of water birds. Typical visitors, either migratory or resident, include the grebe, the elusive **spotted rail, ruddy crake**, **northern jacana** and the occasional **anhinga** — a cormorant-like bird which captures fish by spearing them with its dagger-like bill. The reed beds provide cover for several more secretive species, including **mangrove vireo**, **ringed kingfisher** and **blue-winged warbler**, as well as several varieties of Hirundine such as **mangrove swallow** and grey-breasted martin.

Chichén Itzá is a must on the list of any visitor, but save a little time at the end of the day for an exploration of the forested areas which lie to the south of the "Nunnery". The drier climate and lower altitude in this part of the peninsula encourages a sparser vegetation, where the oaks and pines are less obvious. Other colours amongst this greenness come from a variety of splendid flowers, such as the multicoloured **bougainvillea**, the aromatic **frangipani** and the eye-catching blue and mauve blooms of the **jacaranda** tree. Occasional splashes are added by the striking red flowers of the **poinsettia** (or Christmas flower) and the brilliant yellows of **golden cups**, during their spring and summer blooms. The resident birds appear oblivious to the busy tourist traffic, and amongst the quieter areas, to the south and southwest of the main site, the abundant bird life includes **plain chachalaca** (surely a misnomer), **ferruginous pygmy owl**, cinnamon hummingbird, **turquoise-browed motmot** and numerous brilliant vireos, orioles and tanagers.

CANCÚN, COZUMEL AND THE CARIBBEAN COAST

Even the mega resort of **Cancún** has wildlife possibilities: the lagoons which line the outskirts have a variety of birds (such as great-tailed grackle and **melodious blackbird**). These wetland wastes form an ideal breeding ground for a number of brilliantly coloured **dragonflies** and **damselflies**, and the offshore scuba diving and snorkelling is quite stunning. More importantly the longest **barrier reef** in the Americas begins just south of the town. These extensive and spectacular reefs are formed by the limey skeletons of dozens of species of **coral**. The diversity of shape and form is spectacular, with varieties such as star, lettuce, gorgonian, elkhorn and staghorn being particularly widespread. The reefs provide food and shelter for over four hundred species of fish alone, including several species of **parrotfish** (which browse on the coral), butterfly fish, beau gregories, rock beauties and porkfish; the blaze of colour and feeling of abundance is unforgettable. The coral also provides protection for several other residents, such as **spiny lobster**, **sea urchins**, crabs and tentacled **anenomes**, but this fragile environment requires cautious exploration, if the effects of snorkellers and boat anchors are not to destroy the very thing that they seek to enjoy.

Puerto Juárez, where the ferries to **Isla Mujeres** leave from, and Isla Mujeres itself, offer a slightly less "touristy" environment in which to appreciate the natural beauty of the area. The bird life is also quite spectacular, with frequent views of frigate bird, **brown noddy**, laughing gull, **rufous-tailed hummingbird**, **tropical kingbird** and the **ubiquitous bananaquit**.

A series of offshore islands and coastal sites in Yucatán are worthy of special mention. **Natural Parks and nature reserves** include **Celestún** (p.533), on the west coast and **Río Lagartos** (p.549), to the north. Both parks have spectacular flocks of migratory **flamingos**, which winter here in the milder climate. **Isla Contoy** bird sanctuary off the northeastern tip of the peninsula is a worthwhile and popular day-trip from Cancún, and at **Puerto Morelos** (p.560), the largest **botanic garden** in Mexico provides a wonderful spot to observe numerous coastal and forest species.

Playa del Carmen is frequented by various wetland species including **American wigeon**, and the ferry trip to **Cozumel island** produces sightings of **sea birds** such as **royal** and **Caspian terns**, **black skimmer**, frigate birds and **Mexican sheartails**. On the island, the most rewarding sites are a couple of kilometres inland on the main road that runs across the island. The sparse woodland and hedgerows provide shelter for many typical **endemics**, such as **Caribbean dove**, **lesser nighthawk**, **Yucatán** and **Cozumel vireo**, the splendid **bananaquit** and a variety of **tanagers**. Elusive species which require more patient exploration (best through the **mangroves** which lie 3km north of San Miguel along the coast road) are the **mangrove cuckoo**, **yellow-lored parrot**, **Caribbean ealania** and **Yucatán flycatcher**.

The highlight of the peninsula's protected areas is the magnificent **Sian Ka'an Biosphere Reserve** (p.572), which includes coral reef, mangroves, fresh and saltwater wetlands and **littoral forest** – possibly the widest range of flora and fauna in the whole of Mexico.

Chris Overington with Peter Eltringham

MEXICAN MUSIC

As in Cuba, the international boom in Mexican music took place in the 1940s and 1950s, when classic songs like "Besame Mucho" and "Cielito Lindo" crooned out from cinema screens and radios and were played by "Latin-style" orchestras all over the world. This so-called "Golden Age" had died out by the 1960s when the boom in Mexican cinema ended, and the music retreated to within its borders. Here live music continues to thrive, whether performed by romantic trios or twenty-piece dance orchestras, responding to a country that loves to dance and sing.

As Buñuel was making cinema history in the capital, **Celia Cruz** came from Cuba to seek her fortune along with **Beny Moré**, **Bienvenido Granda** and **Damasio Pérez Prado**, the last of whom who developed the mambo rhythm between shifts as a session pianist at the Churrubusco film studios. These musicians were attracted by the bright lights of a city that didn't sleep: cosmopolitan and bohemian, México had long welcomed musicians from all over Latin America and taken their styles of music to heart. It's now the international capital of both **danzón**, originally from Cuba, and **cumbia**, from Colombia. Go to the *Salon Los Angeles* in the old centre of México on a Tuesday evening at 7pm, and you'll find 700 couples dancing, direct from the office. Sunday is the big night, however, when the enormous wooden floors carry the scent of shoe-polish and perfume, and three different fourteen-piece orchestras play *danzones* old and new.

Despite its history as a centre of Latin music, Mexico was closed to **rock** music until the late 1980s, when a change in import regulations and in laws that specifically banned rock concerts resulted in a flood of music from north of the border and from Europe. A result of this influx in international rock, and arguably the most important musical phenomenon of the last few years, has been the emergence of Mexican rock bands. The boom began in the 1980s with middle-class rockers like **Los Caifanes** playing to middle-class audiences who knew about the outside scene because they, or their parents, travelled regularly to Europe and the States. Ironically, the Caifanes' massive hit was with a cover of a traditional Cuban *son*, "La Negra Tomasa", which appealed to a public that understands *son* and salsa better than rock.

In the 1990s, **Café Tacuba** and **Maldita Vecindad** began to reach a bigger audience, both bands with an interest, to some extent, in exploring Mexican roots and reinterpreting Mexican son in their own way, as **Los Lobos** did so successfully a decade earlier. Then came **Maná** from Mexico's second city, Guadalajara, and Mexican rock entered the super-star level, albeit with a style that hovers rather too closely above the pop ballads so keenly promoted by the media giant Televisa. Most recently, the emergence of the **rap** band **Molotov** has challenged the polite pulp of Televisa, and they have become controversial cult heroes with a first CD that sold something like a million copies in Mexico alone. Rock, in its different guises, is booming, and new bands like **Plastelina Mosh**, **Control Machete** and **El Gran Silencio** are finding a home in the barrios of the world's biggest city.

SON

When Mexican rock bands like Café Tacuba look to their musical roots for the source of their inspiratation, they look to **Mexican son**. *Son* is a traditional music that grew out of the the eighteenth-century encounter between Spanish, indigenous and African cultures – a style first popularized by the **mariachi** bands – those extravagantly passionate musicians who came originally from Jalisco state. Though the same encounter produced Cuban *son* and other Latin American styles like the Venezuelan *joropo*, Mexican *son* fast developed its own distinct sound.

In fact, Mexican *son* describes eight or nine different styles of music, all of which share certain aspects: all are country styles that rely on the participation of their public to add counter-rhythms through **zapateado** foot-stamping dancing, and all are incredibly creative – a *son* musician has to be able to make up lyrics on the spot in response to a comment from the dance floor, and the lead musician has to be able to create new flights on his violin or guitar that will satisfy a public that demands nothing less than inspiration. *Son* is almost always played by a string band, with lyrics, sung in four-line *coplas*, that are witty, more sexual than sensual, poetic and proud.

Most internationally famous are the **sones jaliscienses**, the original repertoire of the *mariachi* bands, although, sadly, few of the commercial bands now play this music, preferring the more simple ballads and *cumbias* that their public know from the radio and TV. To hear the bands who still master the original sones, it's best to skip México's infamous Plaza Garibaldi and head off to southern Jalisco, where incredible twelve- or fourteen-piece *mariachis*, like **Los Reyes del Aserradero** and **Mariachi Tamazula** offer spectacular violins, plenty of trumpet and vocal harmonies in a sophisticated version of the country sones that were orignally played on a harp and three guitars. *Mariachis* became nationally and internationally popular following the cinema boom, when regional music was being recorded by major labels, notably RCA – a few of these treasures can be found on cassettes in markets, and there's a healthy trade among collectors looking for the original vinyls, but little has been re-released on CD.

Apart from the sones from Jalisco, the **sones jarochos** from Veracruz also received a lot of attention. Many Jarocho musicians like **Andres Huesca**, **Nicolás Sosa** and **Lino Chávez** tasted the big time in México before – as in the case of Nicolá's sosa – returning to the main square of Veracruz to play to the public whose taste was less subject to fashion. Today, there is a new interest in *son jarocho*, and the first lady of this style is without doubt **Graciana Silva**, "La Negra Graciana", who was offering her sones for ten pesos a piece to the people drinking

beers and eating fresh prawns in Veracruz's *zócalo* until one of such drinkers turned out to know more than she had expected about *son jarocho*. Eduardo Llerenas invited her to record for his staunchly independent label, Discos Corason, and the CD generated great interest in Europe. La Negra set off to play her sones at the Barbican Centre and Royal Festival Hall in London, at the Theatre de la Ville in Paris and at the Harbourfront Centre in Toronto.

Around the port of Veracruz, and in villages like Medellín de Bravo, where La Negra was born, the **African influence** has left its imprint on *son jarocho*, although further south the **indigenous** presence is much stronger and the harp virtually never played. Instead, the line-up consists exclusively of *requinto* and *jarana* guitars of different sizes and tunings. The sones are played more slowly and with a melancholy that is not so evident around the port. In the south of Veracruz, several young bands experimenting with fusions and creating new compositions gather annually on February 2 for the spectacular **Fiesta de la Candelaria** in **Tlacotalpan**. They set up a stage, and band after band is invited to play, several of whom invite the old soneros of the region to join their line-up. Leading this generation of Jarocho musicians is **Gilberto Gutiérrez** and his band, Mono Blanco, who recently recorded with the Mexican label Urtext.

Perhaps most vibrant today is the **Huastecan** style of *son*, in which a virtuoso violin is accompanied by a *huapanguera* and a *jarana* guitar, the two guitarrists singing falsetto vocals between flights of the violin. Each *son huasteco* is reinvented every time it's played: the singers compose new verses and the violinist creates new flourishes in response to the calls of a public who won't accept copies. There are literally hundreds of Huastecan *son* trios, the most outstanding being **Los Camperos de Valles**, **Trio Tamazunchale** and the youngsters **Dinastia Hidalguense**. Less-known bands play in cantinas and at country fiestas throughout the Huastecan region and participate in a growing number of festivals in Huastecan towns like Pahuatlán, Huejutla, Amatlán and, most recently, Xilitla. In the cafés of México's Coyocán barrio, trios sell their sones by the piece, offering impressive versions of "La Huasanga", "El llorar" and "El Fandanguito", amongst other sones, which are technically very demanding.

Seldom heard in the city but enormously popular back home in the villages of the Sierra Gorda, the **arribeño** style is the most poetic form of *son*. Here, the *trovador* – who seems to be the natural successor of the medieval troubadour – is a country poet, often with no formal education, who composes verses about local heroes, the planets, the earth and the continuing struggles for land. Usually two *trovadores*, both playing the *huapanguera* guitar and each accompanied by two violins and the small *vihuela* guitar, confront each other on tall bamboo platforms that are erected on two sides of the village square. The poets enter into musical combat, improvising verses which are interspersed with the *zapateado* dancing. Each year on December 31, probably the greatest living trovador, **Guillermo Velázquez**, organizes a festival in his village which pays homage to the old musicians before starting the *topada* musical combat that lasts all night.

Based in the Mexican west, in the hotlands of the Río Balsas basin, the legendary violinist **Juan Reynoso** recently won the prestigious National Prize for Arts and Science, never before offered to a country musician. Re-baptized by a local poet as "The Paganini of the Hotlands", Reynoso is an extraordinary violinist, even within the local tradition of **sones calentanos**, which are known for their complex melodies on the violin. Musicians find it hard to follow Don Juan, whose flights take unexpected turns, and whose genius, fortunately, has been recognized during his lifetime with a series of prestigious prizes, books, videos, concerts and tours.

Further west, in a region where the heat is so intense that it's known as "Hell's Waiting Room", **sones de arpa grande** (sones of the big harps) are one of Mexico's best-kept musical secrets. These bands – made up of a big harp, one or two violins and two guitars – don't thrive as they used to, but it's still possible to track down some great hair-raising harp by masters such as **Juan Pérez Morfín**, who plays with the legendary violinist **Beto Pineda**. In the brothels of Apatzingán and in the country fairs of the region, the sound boxes of the big harps are beaten in counter-rhythm by one of the musicians of the band or by a local fan who pays for the privilege. The harpist, meanwhile, must hold on to the melody – and his harp – with vocals that can sound something like a shout from the soul. Concerts are often organized by wealthy stable-owners who pride themselves on their dancing horses: although *norteño* music is very popular in this region, the horses will only dance to the big harp music, and they do so on wooden platforms, beating out the rhythm and counter-rhythm with their hooves.

Although *son* is basically mestizo music, several indigenous cultures play instrumental sones to accompany their ritual dances. **Sones abajeños** is the frenetic party music of the Purépecha of Michoacán, played on guitars, violins and a double bass. Between abajeños, the same musicians sing the hauntingly beautiful **Purépecha** love songs, *pirekuas*, which are composed in honour of a girlfriend or of some local event. Outstanding Purépecha *son* bands include **Atardecer** (Sunset), from the lake-village of Jarácuaro, and **Erandi** (Dawn). In the southern state of Oaxaca, the vibrant **Zapotec** culture has produced some of the country's great love songs and inspired mainstream Mexican romantic singers along the way. Sung in both Zapotec and Spanish, the **sones istmeños**, as they are known, are played to a slower 3/4 rhythm and are more melancholy than the *mestizo* sones. They boast some great solo passages on the *requinto* guitar and uniquely Zapotecan vocals, creating a very beautiful repertoire that has tempted some of Mexico's greatest urban vocalists to learn the Zapotecan lyrics and perform them in the big-city venues. **Lila Downs**, half-Mixtecan, half-American, is among the most successful and, typically, her repertoire also includes *rancheras*, *boleros* and jazz.

RANCHERA

It's interesting that the great **divas** of Mexican music, of which there is a long tradition, are currently turning to Mexican traditional and country music to develop their own repertoire. Singers like **Tania Libertad** and **Betsy Pecanins**, enormously popular throughout the 1980s as **nueva cancion** (new song) protest singers, are now singing their own versions of *norteñas*, *mariachi*, *sones istmeños* and Mexican *boleros* for a more mature public. Outstanding among this illustrious company is **Eugenia León**, whose vocal range and passion encompasses a broad range of music styles. This diva traditional has a direct line back to the early days of **ranchera** music, an urban style that emerged alongside the new towns and cities in the early decades of the century and that became massively popular with the growth of film and radio.

"Ranchera" comes from the word *rancho*, farm, although the music was composed in the towns and cities for a public that wanted to remember how it used to be. The wit and freshness of the original *son* lyrics were replaced by bitter words about loss and betrayal, while musically the intensity shifted from the complex melody and rhythms of *son* to the melodramatic style of singing *ranchera*.

The first great diva of ranchera music was **Lucha Reyes**, whose emotionally charged voice hinted at her own inner turmoil. She died tragically in the style of Billie Holiday and others, but her work has been resuscitated by the great Mexican cabaret singer **Astrid Hadad**, who offered a post-modern take on Reyes for the early 1990s, carried off so successfully because of her particular blend of humour and a very fine voice. Although Astrid now includes a breadth of Latin cabaret music in her repertoire, her great moments were captured in her first CD of *ranchera* songs called, quite simply, "¡Ay!"

Of the classic *ranchera* singers, the divas are now few and far between since the death of **Amalia Mendoza** and, more recently, of the great **Lola Beltrán** and of **María de Lourdes**. Today, fame and fortune has passed to a younger generation of male singers and, in particular, to **Alejandro Fernández**, a superstar who has left his father, the *ranchera* star Vicente Fernández, in the shade. Although musically there's little of the original *ranchera* left in Alejandro's repertoire, the melodrama and the association with ranch culture still exist − the *mariachi* trousers and sombrero hat are still in place, but Alejandro represents a different generation, more in the style of the new rock idols.

NORTEÑO

Apart from *ranchera*, the style that has had most popularity throughout the country is probably **norteño**. Known north of the border as Tex-Mex, *norteño* has its roots in the *corrido* ballads that retold the battles between Anglos and Meskins in the early nineteenth century. The war turned out badly for Mexico, which lost half its territory, and Mexicans living in what is now California, Arizona, New Mexico and Texas found themselves with a new nationality.

The late 1920s was the golden age of the *corrido*, when songs of the recent Revolution

---

**Cruce el Rio Grande
(I Crossed the Rio Grande)**

I crossed the Rio Grande
Swimming, not giving a damn!
The Border Patrol threw me back . . .
I disguised myself as a gringo
And tinted my hair blonde
But since I didn't know English
Back I go again.

Popular *norteño* ballad

---

were recorded in the hotels of San Antonio, Texas, and distributed on both sides of the border. The accordion, which had arrived with bohemian immigrants who came to work in the mines in the late nineteenth century, was introduced into the originally guitar-based groups by **Narciso Martinez** and **Santiago Jimenez** (father of the famous Flaco) in the 1930s, and the sound that they developed became the essence of *corrido* ensembles on both sides of the border.

When the accordion appeared, it brought the polka with it, and by the 1950s this had blended with the traditional duet singing of northern Mexico and with salon dances like the waltz, mazurka and the *chotis* (the central European *schottische* that travelled to Spain and France before arriving in northern Mexico) to produce the definitive *norteño* style. The accordion had already pepped up the songs with lead runs and flourishes between the verses, the *conjuntos norteños* needed to round out their sound to keep up with the big bands and so added bass and rolling drums − the basis of today's **conjuntos**.

Unlike most other regional styles, *norteño* is popular throughout the country. At a party in an isolated mountain community in central Mexico, the host takes out his accordion and plays *norteño corridos* until the dawn breaks. In an ice-cream parlour on the Pacific coast, the piped music is a *norteño* waltz. And waiting for darkness to cross the border at Tijuana, *norteños* are again the musical backdrop.

This country-wide popularity is most likely due to the **lyrics**. *Norteño* songs speak to people in words more real and interesting than the cozy pseudo-sophistication of Mexican pop music. The ballads tell of anti-heroes: small-time drug runners, illegal "wet-back" immigrants, a small-time thief with one blond eye-

El Gato Felix (Felix the Cat)

I'm going to sing a *corrido*
About someone who I knew
A distinguished journalist
Feared for his pen
From Tijuana to Madrid

They called him Felix the Cat
Because the story goes that
He was like those felines
He had seven lives
And he had to see them through

He came from Choi, Sinaloa
That was the place he was born
He stayed in Tijuana
Because it took his fancy
And he wanted to help in some way
With what he wrote in the paper

He made the government tremble
He went right through the alphabet
A whole rosary of threats
He made his paper Zeta popular

With his valiant pen
He pointed to corruption
He always helped the people
And more than two presidents
Had their eyes on him
In a treacherous way
the Cat met his end
Death, mounted on a racehorse
A real beast
Rode him down

Now Felix the Cat is dead
They are carrying him to his grave
He will be another one on the list
Of brave journalists
That they've wanted to silence

Candles burn for Felix Miranda
To you I dedicate my song
But don't you worry
There will be other brave people
To take your place.

Enrique Franco
(Los Tigres del Norte)

brow who defied the law. *Norteño* reflects the mood of a country that generally considers the government to be big-time thieves and hence has a certain respect for everyday people with the courage to stand up to a crooked system.

Groups like **Los Tigres del Norte** and **Los Cadetes del Norte** take stories from the local papers and convert them into ballads that usually begin "Voy a cantarles un corrido" (I'm going to sing you a *corrido*) before launching into a gruesome tale sung in a deadpan style as if it were nothing to go to a local dance and get yourself killed. One of the most famous *corridos*, "Rosita Alvírez", tells the story of a young girl who struck lucky: only one of the three bullets fired by her boyfriend hit and killed her.

Los Tigres are by far the most successful of all *norteño* groups – superstars, in fact – having won a Grammy and subsequently been adopted by Televisa. They now record in both the USA and Mexico, having achieved superstardom on both sides of the border. Quite early in their career, the band modified the traditional line-up by adding a sax and mixed the familiar rhythms with *cumbias*; however, their nasal singing style and the combination of instruments identifies the music very clearly as *norteño*.

THE BANDA BOOM

The enormous success of Los Tigres del Norte and their updated *norteño* sound resulted in a phenomenon that has changed the face of Mexican music in the 1990s: **banda music**. This is a fusion of the *norteño* style with the brass bands that have played at village fiestas all over the country for the last century. There are now hundreds of *bandas* in Mexico – ranging in size from four to twenty musicians – and all playing brass and percussion, with just an occasional guitar. Their repertoire includes *norteño* polkas, *ranchera* ballads, *cumbia*, *merengue* and *salsa* – all arranged for brass.

The most exciting of these groups is a fiery orchestra from Mazatlán, the **Banda del Recodo**. This is not a new band, indeed its former leader, Don Cruz Lizárraga, had been in the business for half a century, starting out in a traditional *tambora* marching band (the *tambora* is the huge, carried side drum) that played a straight repertoire of brass-band numbers. However, Don Cruz had always had an eye for musical fashions, adapting his material to *merengue*, *ranchera* or whatever anyone wanted to hear. His great banda hit was a version of Cuban bandleader Beny Moré's classic "La Culebra".

The *banda* boom currently dominates the TV music programmes and most places across the country except for the capital, where *cumbia* and *salsa* stay top of the bill. Elsewhere, it is the *bandas* that fill the stadiums and village halls, and it's their names you'll see painted in enormous multicoloured letters on any patch of white wall along the roads. The craze has brought with it a series of new dances, too, including the **quebradita** – a gymnastic combination of lambada, polka, rock'n'roll, rap and *cumbia*, which is danced with particular skill in all points north of Guadalajara.

In 1996, during a successful two-month tour of Europe, the band's founder Cruz Lizárraga died, and the Banda del Recodo passed into the hands of two of his musician sons, Germán, now in his late fifties, and the young Alfonso. Changes were afoot. The band left the independent label where they had made some 100 records and signed to the Televisa media empire. Several of the older musicians have been replaced with younger ones, and the original sound has suffered, although, ironically, record sales have never been better.

CUMBIA

Although the banda line-up dates back to the village band tradition and the *tambora* music of northwest Mexico, todays *bandas* rely heavily on **cumbia** for their repertoire, the simple dance music that came originally from Colombia but has taken deep root across Mexico.

Cumbia, now more popular in Mexico than in its native Colombia, has become simpler in its new home, more direct and danceable. For a long time, a national radio station used to call out "¡Tropi. . .Q!" – the last letter a "coooooooh" that could unblock traffic jams – and then launch into the latest cumbia hit, which was played without reprieve for a month and then forgotten. A song about cellular telephones replaced "No te metes con mi cucu" (Don't Mess With My Toot Toot), which in turn had

taken over from a song about fried chicken and chips – a thinly disguised treatise on how a macho likes his bird.

The flirtatious, addictive *cumbia* was the most popular music in Mexico in the 1980s, until *bandas* came along, and it remains a force throughout the country. Outside the capital, it tends to take on a more mellow, romantic tone, a sound closely associated with the band **Los Bukis**, who, before splitting up in the mid-1990s, made several albums, among them "Me volvi a acordar de tí", which sold 1.5 million legal copies and an estimated four million more in bootleg cassettes.

In the same line, an insipid mixture of *cumbia*, *norteño* and *ranchera*, which is sometimes known as **grupera** (or *onda grupera*), emerged in the late 1980s and continues to be enormously popular in small towns and villages – village populations have been known to swell four or five times over when a band like the **Yonics**, **Banda Machos** or the (now defunct) **Bronco** come to play. These musicians, like the *bandas* who share the same audience, arrive in a fleet of well-equipped coaches – one for them, one for the generator, one of lights and equipment and lavish leather suits and, quite often, one for their families. This music was despised by the media executives who, for many years, thought it common and continued to plug the familiar pretty faces of the pop idols that they manufactured. However, since the beginning of the 1990s, the phenomenal commercial success of the self-made *grupera*, banda and *norteña* musicians has forced the entertainment business to rethink. Groups like **Limite**, currently at the top of the lucrative country dance scene, are now regularly featured on TV shows and are invited to play in the hallowed halls of México's Auditorio Nacional, once the stronghold of protest singers and foreign ballet companies.

Mary Farquharson
A version of this article appears in the *Rough Guide to World Music*.

DISCOGRAPHY

Mexican recordings are widely available in the US – less so in Europe. A label to look out for is Corason, who are recording and releasing consistently excellent CDs and cassettes of traditional sounds from all over the country. They are distributed in the US by Rounder and by Topic in Britain.

COMPILATIONS

Various, *Anthology of Mexican Sones* (Corason, Mexico). This 3-CD set is the definitive survey of Mexican traditional music, featuring wonderful recordings of rural bands. Excellent accompanying notes plus lyrics in Spanish and English.

Various, *Mexico – Fiestas of Chiapas & Oaxaca* (Nonesuch Explorer, US). Atmospheric recordings from village festivities in southern Mexico. Marimba *conjuntos*, brass bands, some eccentric ensembles and great fireworks on the opening track. The next best thing to being there.

Various, *Mexique – Musiques Traditionnelles* (Ocora, France). For the more folklorically inclined, music from the many little-known indigenous communities of Mexico.

SONES AND MARIACHI

Conjunto Alma Jarochos, *Sones Jarochos* (Arhoolie, US). A fine disc, the first in a series of regional Mexican releases, featuring *sones* from Veracruz with harps and *jaranguitas*.

Los Camperos de Valles, *Sones de la Huasteca and El Triumfo* (Corason, Mexico). The Huasteca *sones* are considered by many to be the most beautiful music in Mexico. Played on violin, guitar and the small *vihuela* guitar, an important element is the falsetto singing of love songs that are both rowdy and romantic.

Juan Reynoso, *The Paganini of the Mexican Hotlands* (Corason, Mexico). The title is fair dues: Reynoso is Mexico's greatest country violinist, eighty years old now, but still in fine form on this recording, backed by vocal, guitars and drum.

Mariachi Coculense de Cirilo Marmolejo, *Mexico's Pioneer Mariachis Vol 1* (Arhoolie, US). Wonderful archive recordings from the 20s and 30s of one of the seminal groups. The disc also includes the first ever *mariachi* recording, from 1908.

Mariachi Reyes del Aserradero, *Sones from Jalisco* (Corason, Mexico). An excellent *mariachi* band from Jalisco state play the original *sones* from this region where *mariachi* was born.

Mariachi Tapatió de José Marmolejo, *The Earliest Mariachi Recordings: 1906–36* (Arhoolie, US). Archive recordings of a pioneer *mariachi* band, featuring the great trumpet playing of Jesús Salazar.

Mariachi Vargas, *20 Exitos* (Orfeon, Mexico). Big-band style *mariachi* from Silvestre Vargas, who has managed to stay at the top of his field for over fifty years. Always flexible, his band released one disastrous album of *mariachi*-rock but has otherwise had hits all the way. They work much of the year in the US.

La Negra Graciana, *Sones Jarochos* (Corason, Mexico). The first lady of Mexican harp plays solo and accompanied by her brother and sister-in-law. To be followed in 1998 by the release of La Negra recorded live in Paris (Buda, France).

Los Pregoneros del Puerto, *Music of Veracruz* (Rounder, US). Rippling *sones jaroches* from the Veracruz coast, where harp and *jarana* guitars still dominate. An enchanting album.

Various, *Pure Purépecha* (Corason, Mexico). A gem that brings together three duets of Purépecha peoples from Michoacán, singing sweet *pirecua* love songs, and some rowdy *abajeño sones* from Conjunto Atardecer.

RANCHERA AND NORTEÑO

Flaco Jimenez, *Ay te dejo en San Antonio* (Arhoolie, US). The best of Flaco's many recordings; he's a huge name in the Tex-Mex world north of the border.

José Alfredo Jimenez, *Homenaje a José Alfredo Jimenez* (Sony Discos, US). Jimenez was the king of *ranchera* and embodied the best and worst of Mexican machismo. As he predicted in one of his songs, everyone in Mexico missed him when he died.

Santiago Jimenez Snr, *Santiago Jimenez Snr* (Arhoolie, US). One of the great accordion players, recorded in 1979 with his son Flaco on *bajo sexto*. Earthy, authentic sound.

Los Lobos, *La Pistola y El Corazón* (Warner, US). The East LA band's brilliant 1991 tribute to their Mexican roots, with David Hidalgo pumping the accordion on their blend of *conjunto* and rock'n'roll.

Narciso Martínez, *Father of the Tex-Mex Conjunto* (Arhoolie, US). The title says it all: a collection of 1940s and 1950s numbers, some instrumental, others featuring the leading vocalists of the day.

Los Pingüinos del Norte, *Conjuntos Norteños* (Arhoolie, US). This album pairs up Tex and Mex *conjuntos*: Los Pingüinos, singing *corridos*, live in a *cantina* in northern Mexico, and Fred Zimmerle's Trio from San Antonio, Texas, performing typical polkas and *rancheras*.

Linda Ronstadt, *Canciones de mi Padre* and *Más Canciones* (Asylum, US). *Ranchera* classics sung very convincingly by the Mexican-American rocker, accompanied by Mariachi Vargas.

Los Tigres del Norte, *Corridos Prohibidos* (Fonovisa, US). A collection of *corridos* about Mexican low life and heroism from one of the best *norteño* groups in the business.

CUMBIA

Los Bukis, *Me Volvi a Acordar de Ti* (Melody, Mexico). The sound of soft *cumbia* – and the most popular Mexican record ever.

Sonora Dinamita, *Mi Cucu* (Discos Fuentes, Colombia). Mexican *cumbia* performed by a breakaway group of artists who took the name of the Colombian originals. Their lyrics, full of double meanings, are performed with a zest that has brought huge success in Mexico.

OTHERS

Agustín Lara, *Agustín Lara* (Orfeon, Mexico). The legendary crooner, the man who idolized prostitutes and married for love twelve times. One of Mexico's greatest composers of popular music, specializing in bolero ballads and music from Veracruz.

Various, *New Mexico: Hispanic Traditions* (Smithsonian Folkways, US). A good ethnographic recording from the Mexican diaspora in the US. Dances, songs, *corridos* and religious music in rustic style.

BOOKS

Mexico has attracted more than its fair share of famous foreign writers, and has inspired a vast literature and several classics. Until very recently, however, Mexican writers had received little attention: even now, when many new translations are being made available through small US presses, few are well known. Most big US bookshops will have an enormous array of books about, from, or set in Mexico, plus a few novels. In the rest of the English-speaking world there's far less choice, though the best known of the archeological and travel titles below should be available almost anywhere. In the lists below, the UK publisher is followed by the US one; where only one publisher is listed it's the same in both places, or we've specified; o/p means a book is out of print, but may still be found in libraries or secondhand bookstores.

For the less mainstream, and especially for contemporary Mexico, there are a few useful **specialist sources**. In the UK the **Latin America Bureau** (LAB), 1 Amwell St, London EC1R 1UL (☎0171/278-2829, fax 0171/278-0165; lab@gn.apc.org, www.lab.org.uk), publishes books covering all aspects of the region's society, current affairs and politics. Supporters receive a 25 percent discount off LAB books and a bi-annual copy of *Lab News*. In the US the **Resource Center**, PO Box 2178, Silver City NM 88062-2178 (☎505/388-0208, fax 388-0619), produces a wide range of publications, including a quarterly *Bulletin* (US$5 annually). In London you can freely visit **Canning House Library**, 2 Belgrave Square, SW1X 8PJ

(☎0171/235-2303), which has the UK's largest publicly accessible collection of books and periodicals on Latin America, though you have to be a member to take books out and receive the twice-yearly *Bulletin*, a review of recently published books on Latin America.

If you're travelling to the **Maya areas** of Mexico or Guatemala, visit the library and resource centre at **Maya – The Guatemalan Indian Centre**, 94A Wandsworth Bridge Rd, London SW6 2TF (call ☎0171/371-5291 for opening times; closed Jan, Easter and August; web.ukonline/jamie.marshall/index.html). Members (£5 annually) have access to the library (reference only) and video collection, and receive information of the monthly events and film shows held at the Centre. There is a particularly fine textile collection. The Centre's director, Krystyna Deuss, is the acknowledged English authority on Guatemalan life, dress and contemporary Maya rituals.

TRAVEL

Sybille Bedford *A Visit to Don Otavio* (NAL-Dutton, o/p/Eland). An extremely enjoyable, often hilarious, occasionally lyrical and surprisingly relevant account of Ms Bedford's travels through Mexico in the early 1950s.

Frances Calderon de la Barca *Life in Mexico* (U California). The diary of a Scotswoman who married the Spanish ambassador to Mexico and spent two years observing life there in the early nineteenth century.

Tom Owen Edmunds *Mexico: Feast and Ferment* (Hamish Hamilton/Viking Penguin). A coffee-table book of photographs, and a particularly good one, full of marvellous and unexpected images.

Charles Macomb Flandrau *Viva Mexico!* (Eland). First published in 1908, Flandrau's account of life on his brother's farm is something of a cult classic. Though attitudes are inevitably dated in places, it's extremely funny in others.

Thomas Gage *Travels in the New World* (U Oklahoma Press). Unusual account by an English cleric who became a Dominican friar as he travels through Mexico and Central America between 1635 and 1637, including fascinating insights into colonial life and some great attacks on the greed and pomposity of the Catholic Church abroad.

Graham Greene *The Lawless Roads* (Penguin). In the late 1930s Greene was sent to Mexico to investigate the effects of the persecution of the Catholic church. The result (see also his novel below) was this classic account of his travels in a very bizarre era of modern Mexican history.

Katie Hickman *A Trip to the Light Fantastic: Travels with a Mexican Circus* (Flamingo, UK). Enchanting, funny and uplifting account of a year spent travelling (and performing) with a fading Mexican circus troupe.

Aldous Huxley *Beyond the Mexique Bay* (Academy Chicago, o/p). Only a small part of the book is devoted to Mexico, but the descriptions of the archeological sites around Oaxaca, particularly, are still worth reading.

D.H. Lawrence *Mornings in Mexico* (Penguin/Peregrine Smith). A very slim volume, half of which is devoted to the Hopi Indians of New Mexico, this is an uncharacteristically cheerful account of Lawrence's stay in southern Mexico, and beautifully written.

John Lincoln *One Man's Mexico* (Century, o/p). Lincoln's travels in the late 1960s are an entertaining and offbeat read – travelling alone, often into the jungle, always away from tourists.

Patrick Marnham *So far from God...* (Penguin). A rather jaundiced view, but nevertheless a humorous and insightful one, as Marnham travelled from the US to Panama in 1984. About half the book is occupied with his journey through Mexico.

James O'Reilly and Larry Habegger, eds *Travelers' Tales Mexico* (O'Reilly, US). An anthology of Mexican travel writing. Disappointing considering the riches that are available: many here are reprinted magazine articles. Nonetheless there's something for everyone somewhere.

Nigel Pride *A Butterfly Sings to Pacaya* (Constable, UK, o/p). The author, accompanied by his wife and four-year-old *son*, travels south from the US border in a Jeep, heading through Mexico, Guatemala and Belize. Though the travels took place 25 years ago the pleasures and privations they experience rarely appear dated.

John Lloyd Stephens *Incidents of Travel in Central America, Chiapas, and Yucatán* (Dover). Stephens was a classic nineteenth-century traveller. Acting as American ambassador to Central America, he indulged his own enthusiasm for

archeology. His journals, told with superb Victorian pomposity punctuated with sudden waves of enthusiasm, make great reading. There have been many editions of the work: many include fantastic illustrations by Catherwood of the ruins overgrown with tropical rainforest; the Smithsonian edition combines some of these with modern photographs.

Paul Theroux *The Old Patagonian Express* (Pocket/Penguin). The epic journey from Boston to Patagonia by train spends just three rather bad-tempered chapters in Mexico, so don't expect to find out too much about the country. A good read nonetheless.

John Kenneth Turner *Barbarous Mexico* (U Texas). Turner was a journalist, and this account of his travels through nineteenth-century Mexico exposing the conditions of workers in the plantations of the Yucatán, serialized in US newspapers, did much to discredit the regime of Porfirio Díaz.

Ronald Wright *Time Among the Maya* (Henry Holt). A vivid and sympathetic account of travels from Belize through Guatemala, Chiapas and Yucatán, meeting the Maya of today and exploring their obsession with time. The book's twin points of interest are the ancient Maya and the recent violence.

MEXICAN FICTION

Mariano Azuela *The Underdogs* (U Pittsburgh). The first novel of the Revolution (finished in 1915), *The Underdogs* is told through the eyes of a group of peasants who form a semi-regular Revolutionary armed band: the story concerns their escapades, progress and eventual betrayal, ambush and massacre. Initially fighting for land and liberty, they end up caught up in a cycle of violence they cannot control and descend into brutal nihilism. The novel set many of the themes of post-revolutionary Mexican writing.

Carmen Boullosa *The Miracle Worker* (Jonathan Cape). One of Mexico's most promising contemporary writers, Boullosa's work focuses on traditional Mexican themes, often borrowing characters from history or myth. *The Miracle Worker* explores Mexican attitudes to Catholicism through the eyes of a messianic healer and her followers. The story can be seen as a parable on the Mexican political system, where ordinary Mexicans petition a distant and incomprehensible government machinery for favours, which are granted or refused in seemingly arbitrary decisions.

Laura Esquivel *Like Water for Chocolate* (Black Swan/Doubleday). Adapted to film, Laura Esquivel's novel has proved a huge hit in Mexico and abroad. The book is even better: sentimental (schmaltzy, even) it deals with the star-crossed romance of Tita, whose lover Pedro marries her sister. Using the magic of the kitchen, she sets out to seduce him back. The book is written in monthly episodes, each of which is prefaced with a traditional Mexican recipe. Funny, sexy, great.

Carlos Fuentes *The Death of Artemio Cruz* (Penguin/Farrar, Strauss & Giroux, o/p), *The Old Gringo* (Picador/HarperCollins). Fuentes is by far the best-known Mexican writer outside Mexico, influenced by Mariano Azuela and Juan Rulfo, and an early exponent of "magical realism". In *The Death of Artemio Cruz*, the hero, a rich and powerful man on his deathbed, looks back over his life and loves, from an idealist youth in the Revolution through disillusion to corruption and power; in many ways an indictment of modern Mexican society. Some of his other books are harder work: they include *Distant Relations* (Farrar, Strauss & Giroux/Abacus, o/p), *Where the Air is Clear* (Deutsch/Farrar, Strauss & Giroux), *A Change of Skin* (Deutsch/Farrar, Strauss & Giroux) and *Terra Nostra* (Penguin/Farrar, Strauss & Giroux). His latest offering, *The Crystal Frontier* (Bloomsbury), is a collection of stories examining the way personal contacts colour Mexicans' experiences of their unequal relationship with the USA.

Sergio Galindo *Otilia's Body* (U Texas). This prize-winning novel, published in Mexico as *Otilia Rauda*, traces the story of Otilia's passionate, tragic affair with an outlaw in post-revolutionary Mexico. Somewhat let down by an over-literal translation.

Jorge Ibargüengoitia *The Dead Girls, Two Crimes* and others (all Chatto/Avon, o/p). One of the first modern Mexican novelists translated into English, Ibargüengoitia was killed in a plane crash in 1983. These two are both blackly comic thrillers, superbly told, the first of them based on real events.

Octavio Paz, ed. *An Anthology of Mexican Poetry* (John Calder/Riverrun). Edited by Paz (perhaps the leading man of letters of the post-

revolutionary era) and translated by Samuel Beckett, this is as good a taste as you could hope for of modern Mexican poets. Some of Paz's own poetry is also available in translation.

Juan Rulfo *Pedro Páramo* (Serpent's Tail/Grove Atlantic). Widely regarded as the greatest Mexican novel of the twentieth century and a precursor of magic realism. The living and spirit worlds mesh when, at the dying behest of his mother, the narrator visits the deserted village haunted by the memory of his brutal patriarch father, Pedro Páramo. Dark, depressing and initially confusing but ultimately very rewarding. Rulfo's short-story collection *The Burning Plain and Other Stories* (U Texas), is rated by Gabriel García Marquez as the best in Latin America.

FOREIGN FICTION

There must be hundreds of novels by outsiders set in Mexico, all too many in the sex-and-shopping genre: apart from those below, others to look out for include a whole clutch of modern Americans, especially **Jack Kerouac's** *Desolation Angels* (Granton/Berkeley) and several of **Richard Brautigan's** novels. And of course there's **Carlos Castañeda's** *Don Juan* series (Penguin/Pocket Books) – a search for enlightenment through peyote.

Tony Cartano *After the Conquest* (Secker & Warburg, UK) An extraordinary fictional account of a fictional author who believes he is B. Traven's son and sets out to discover the truth about his father (see below). A psychological thriller which is also full of Mexican history and politics.

Eduardo Galeano *Genesis* and *Faces and Masks* (both Quartet/Pantheon). The opening parts of a trilogy by a Uruguayan writer, these anthologies of Indian legends, colonists' tales and odd snatches of history illuminate the birth of Latin America. Not specifically Mexican, but wonderful, relevant reading nonetheless.

Graham Greene *The Power and the Glory* (Penguin). Inspired by his investigative travels, this story of a doomed whisky priest on the run from the authorities makes a great yarn. It was a wonderful movie too.

Gary Jennings *Aztec* (Avon, US). Sex and sacrifice in ancient Mexico in this gripping bestseller. The narrator travels around the Aztec empire in search of his fortune, chancing upon almost every ancient culture along the way, and sleeping with most of them, until finally the Spanish arrive. Perfect beach or bus reading, and informative too.

D.H. Lawrence *The Plumed Serpent* (Penguin/McKay). One of Lawrence's own favourites, the novel reflects his intense dislike of the country which followed on the brief honeymoon period of *Mornings in Mexico*. Fans of his heavy spiritualism will love it.

Haniel Long *The Marvelous Adventure of Cabeza de Vaca* (Dawn Horse Press, US). Two short stories in one volume – the first the account of a shipwrecked Conquistador's journey across the new continent, the second the thoughts and hopes of Malinche, Cortés' interpreter.

Malcolm Lowry *Under the Volcano* (Pan/NAL-Dutton). A classic since its publication, Lowry's account of the last day in the life of the British Consul in Cuernavaca – passed in a Mescal-induced haze – is totally brilliant. His *Dark as the Grave Wherein my Friend is Laid* is also based on his Mexican experiences.

James A. Michener *Mexico* (Mandarin/Random House). Another doorstop from Michener. Fans will love it.

B. Traven Traven wrote a whole series of compelling novels set in Mexico. Among the best known are *Treasure of the Sierra Madre* (Picador/Farrar, Strauss & Giroux) and *The Death Ship* (Picador/L Hill Books, o/p), but of more direct interest if you're travelling are such works as *The Bridge in the Jungle* and the six books in the Jungle series: *Government*, *The Carreta*, *March to the Monteria*, *Trozas*, *The Rebellion of the Hanged* and *General from the Jungle* (all Allison & Busby/I R Dee, some o/p). These latter all deal with the state of the peasantry and the growth of Revolutionary feeling in the last years of the Díaz dictatorship, and if at times they're overly polemical, as a whole they're enthralling. Will Wyatt's *The Man who was B. Traven* (Cape, o/p in UK, published by Harcourt Brace in the US as *The Secret of the Sierra Madre*) is the best of the books on the quest for the author's identity.

HISTORY

The sources below are all entertaining and/or important references: more standard **general histories** include Henry Bamford Parkes' *History of Mexico* (Houghton Mifflin); *Fire and Blood: a History of Mexico* by T.R. Fehrenbach

(Da Capo, US); *A Concise History of Mexico from Hidalgo to Cárdenas* by Jan Bazant (CUP); and Judith Hellman, *Mexico in Crisis* (Holmes & Meier).

Inga Clendinnen *Ambivalent Conquests: Maya and Spaniard in Yucatán 1517 to 1570* (CUP). A product of meticulous research which documents the methods and consequences of the Spanish conquest of the Yucatán. The ambivalence in the title reflects doubts about the effectiveness of the conquest in subjugating the Maya, and the book provides insights into post-Conquest rebellions: over three hundred years after the conquest the Maya rose in revolt during the Caste War, and almost succeeded in driving out their white overlords, while in January 1994, Maya peasants in Chiapas stunned the world and severely embarrassed the Mexican government by briefly capturing and controlling cities in the southeastern area of the state.

Hernan Cortés *Letters from Mexico* (Yale UP). The thoughts and impressions of the Conquistador, first hand. Less exciting than Díaz, though.

Bernal Díaz *The Conquest of New Spain*, translated by JM Cohen (Penguin/Linnet Books). This abridged version is the best available of Díaz's classic *Historia Verdadera de la Conquista de la Nueva España*. Díaz, having been on two earlier expeditions to Mexico, accompanied Cortés throughout his campaign of Conquest, and this magnificent eye-witness account still makes compulsive reading.

Adolfo Gilly *The Mexican Revolution* (Verso/Routledge, Chapman & Hall, o/p). Written in México's notorious Lecumberri jail (Gilly was later granted an absolute pardon), this is regarded as the classic work on the Revolution. Heavygoing and highly theoretical though.

Michael Meyer and William Sherman *The Course of Mexican History* (OUP). Comprehensive and up-to-date general history.

William Prescott *History of the Conquest of Mexico* (Corona). Written in the mid-nineteenth century, and drawing heavily on Díaz, Prescott's history was the standard text for over a hundred years. It makes for pretty heavy reading and has now been overtaken by Thomas' account.

John Reed *Insurgent Mexico* (International Publications). This collection of his reportage of the Mexican Revolution was put together by Reed himself. He spent several months in 1913

and 1914 with various generals of the Revolution – especially Villa – and the book contains great descriptions of them, their men, and the mood of the times. It's far more anecdotal and easy to read than the celebrated *Ten Days that Shook the World.*

Hugh Thomas *Conquest: Montezuma, Cortés, and the Fall of Old Mexico* (Simon & Schuster, US); *The Conquest of Mexico* (Pimlico, UK). Same book, different title, but either way a brilliant narrative history of the Conquest by the British historian previously best known for his history of the Spanish Civil War. A massive work of real scholarship and importance – much of the archive material is newly discovered – but also humorous and readable, with appendices on everything from Aztec beliefs, history and genealogy to Cortés' wives and lovers.

James W. Wilkie and Albert L. Michaels, eds. *Revolution in Mexico* (U Arizona Press). A fascinating anthology of contemporary and more recent writing on the Revolution and the years which followed.

ANCIENT MEXICO

There are thousands of studies of ancient Mexico, many of them extremely academic and detailed, plus any number of big, highly illustrated coffee-table tomes on individual sites. Those below are of more general interest, and any of them will have substantial bibliographies to help you explore further.

Ignacio Bernal *Mexico Before Cortés* (Doubleday, US, o/p). The leading Mexican archeologist of the century, and one of the inspirations behind the National Museum of Anthropology, Bernal did important work on the Olmecs and on the restoration of Teotihuacán, and has written many important source works. This book covers much the same ground as Davies', though in less detail and more dated, but it has the advantage of being widely available in Mexico. A more scholarly version is available in *A History of Mexican Archeology: the Vanished Civilizations of Middle America* (Thames & Hudson, o/p).

Warwick Bray *Everyday life of the Aztecs* (P. Bedrick/Batsford). A volume full of information about Aztec warfare, music, games, folklore, religious ritual, social organization, economic and political systems and agricultural practice.

Although the book is now showing its age, and some of its conclusions are a bit dubious, its attractive comprehensiveness more than makes up for this. An excellent general introduction.

Inga Clendinnen *Aztecs: an interpretation* (CUP). A social history of the Aztec empire that seeks to explain the importance – and acceptance – of human sacrifice and other rituals. Fascinating, though best to know something about the Aztecs before you start.

Michael D. Coe *The Maya* (Thames & Hudson/Penguin). The updated fifth edition is the best available general introduction to the Maya: concise, clear and comprehensive. Coe has also written several more weighty, academic volumes. His *Breaking the Maya Code* (Penguin), a history of the decipherment of the Maya glyphs, owes much to the fact that Coe was present at many of the most important meetings leading to the breakthrough, demonstrating that the glyphs actually did reproduce Maya speech. Aside form anything else, it is a beautifully written, ripping yarn, though the slagging-off of Eric Thompson gets a bit wearisome.

Nigel Davies *The Ancient Kingdoms of Mexico* (Penguin). Although there's no single text which covers all the ancient cultures, this comes pretty close, covering the central areas from the Olmecs through Teotihuacán and the Toltecs to the Aztec Empire. An excellent mix of historical, archeological, social and artistic information, but it doesn't cover the Maya. Davies is also the author of several more detailed academic works on the Aztecs and Toltecs including *The Aztecs, A History* (U Oklahoma).

M.S. Edmonson, trans. *The Book of Chilam Balam of Chumayel* (Aegean, US). The Chilam Balam is a recollection of Maya history and myth, recorded by the Spanish after the Conquest. Although the style is not easy, it's one of the few keys into the Maya view of the world.

George Kubler *Art and Architecture of Ancient America* (Penguin/Yale UP). Exactly what it says: a massive and amazingly comprehensive work, covering not only Mexico but Colombia, Ecuador and Peru as well. It's rather old-fashioned, however, and fails to take into account the ground-breaking epigraphic findings in Maya scholarship.

Diego de Landa *Yucatán Before and After the Conquest* (Dover). A translation edited by

William Gates of the work written in 1566 as *Relación de las Cosas de Yucatán*. De Landa's destruction of almost all original Maya books as "works of the devil" leaves his own account as the chief source on Maya life and society in the immediate post-conquest period. Written during his imprisonment in Spain on charges of cruelty to the Indians (remarkable itself, given the institutional brutality of the time) the book provides a fascinating wealth of detail for historians.

Maria Longhena *Splendours of Ancient Mexico* (Thames & Hudson). Sumptuously illustrated coffee-table tome, with better than average text (translated from the Italian original) and excellent pictures and plans of all the major ancient sites.

Mary Ellen Miller *The Art of Mesoamerica: From Olmec to Aztec* (Thames & Hudson, UK). An excellent, wonderfully illustrated survey of the artisanship of the ancient cultures of Mexico, whose work reflects the sophistication of their civilizations.

Mary Ellen Miller and Karl Taube *The Gods and Symbols of Ancient Mexico and the Maya: An Illustrated Dictionary of Mesoamerican Religion* (Thames & Hudson). A superb modern reference on ancient Mesoamerica, written by two leading scholars. Taube's *Aztec and Maya Myths* (British Museum Press) is perfect as a short, accessible introduction to Mesoamerican mythology.

Jeremy A. Sabloff *Cities of Ancient Mexico* (Thames & Hudson). The best introduction to ancient Mexico currently available. Thoroughly up to date and easy to digest. Also worth checking is his *New Archeology and the Ancient Maya* (WH Freeman).

Linda Schele and David Freidel (and others). The authors, in the forefront of the "new archeology", have been personally responsible for decoding many of the glyphs, revolutionizing and popularizing Maya studies. Although their writing style, which frequently includes recreations of scenes inspired by their discoveries, is controversial to some fellow professionals it has also inspired a devoted following. *A Forest of Kings: The Untold Story of the Ancient Maya* (Quill, US) in conjunction with *The Blood of Kings*, by Linda Schele and Mary Miller, shows that far from being governed by peaceful astronomer-priests, the ancient Maya were ruled by hereditary kings, lived in populous, aggressive city-states, and engaged in a continuous entanglement of alliances and war. *The Maya Cosmos* (Quill, US), by Schele, Freidel and Joy Parker is perhaps more difficult to read, dense with copious notes, but continues to examine Maya ritual and religion in a unique and far-reaching way. *The Code of Kings* (Shribner, US), written in collaboration with Peter Matthews and illustrated with Justin Kerr's famous "rollout" photography of Maya ceramics, examines in detail the significance of the monuments at selected Maya sites. It's her last book – Linda Schele died in April 1998 – and sure to become a classic of epigraphic interpretation.

Robert Sharer *The Ancient Maya* (Stanford UP). The classic, comprehensive (and weighty) account of Maya civilization, now in a completely revised and much more readable fifth edition, yet as authoritative as ever. Required reading for archeologists, it provides a fascinating reference for the non-expert.

Dennis Tedlock, trans. *Popol Vuh* (Simon & Schuster). Translation of the Maya Quiché bible, a fascinating creation myth from the only ancient civilization to emerge from rainforest terrain. The Maya obsession with time can be well appreciated here, where dates are recorded with painstaking precision.

J. Eric S. Thompson *The Rise and Fall of Maya Civilization* (Pimlico/U Oklahoma, o/p). A major authority on the ancient Maya during his lifetime, Thompson produced many academic works; *The Rise and Fall...*, originally published in 1954, is one of the more approachable. Although more recent researchers have overturned many of Thompson's theories, his work provided the inspiration for the postwar surge of interest in the Maya, and he remains a respected figure.

Ptolemy Tompkins *This Tree Grows Out of Hell* (HarperCollins). An interesting attempt to piece together the mystery of Mesoamerican religion, which synthesizes and makes readable many of the recent findings in the area. The latter half of the book is a thoroughly unconvincing apology for the brutality of the Aztecs.

Richard F. Townsend *The Aztecs* (Thames & Hudson). Companion in the series to Coe's Maya book, this is a good introduction to all aspects of Aztec history and culture.

SOCIETY, POLITICS AND CULTURE

Tom Barry, ed. *Mexico: A Country Guide* (LAB/Resource Center). A comprehensive account of contemporary Mexico: Barry and ten other contributors impart their expertise to make this the best single volume survey on the issues facing Mexico in the 1990s.

Dan La Botz *Democracy in Mexico* (South End Press, US). Examines the political landscape of modern Mexico and puts it into historical context by equating the rise of civil society and political consciousness with the major defining events of recent decades — the 1968 student massacre, the 1985 earthquake, and the 1994 Zapatista uprising amongst others.

Harry Browne *For Richer, For Poorer* (LAB/Resource Center). A readable analysis of the background to NAFTA and the effects of and prospects for closer economic integration between the US and Mexico.

Miguel Covarrubias *Mexico South* (Routledge, Chapman & Hall; KPI). The people and popular culture of Veracruz and the Isthmus of Tehuantepec by the well-known Mexican artist and anthropologist. A good read, well illustrated.

Augusta Dwyer *On The Line* (LAB). A painstakingly detailed account of conditions on the US/Mexico border, where many of the most environmentally damaging factories on the continent poison lands and people on both sides of the frontier. The "line" is the only place in the world where the rich north directly borders the poorer south, and Dwyer documents the consequences of this economic discrepancy in case studies of *maquila* workers, legal and illegal immigrants and both victims and members of the US Border Patrol.

Judith Alder Hellman *Mexican Lives* (The New Press, US). A compilation of interviews with fifteen Mexicans on the eve of the signing of NAFTA, offering a poignant insight into how ordinary people, rich and poor alike, cope with everyday life on the brink of enormous political and social change, with the voices of the interviewees themselves speaking so clearly that their personalities and emotions stand out from the pages. Underlying all the accounts is the reality of institutional corruption, which affects every sector of society but falls heaviest on the poor. Worth reading by anyone who wants to understand what modern Mexico is like behind the headlines.

Oscar Lewis *The Children of Sanchez* (Vintage/Penguin, o/p). These oral histories of a working-class family in the México of the 1940s are regarded as a seminal work in modern anthropology. The book is totally gripping, though, and doesn't read in the least like an anthropological text. Lewis' other works, including *Pedro Martinez* (Vintage, o/p/Penguin, o/p), *A Death in the Sanchez Family* (Vintage, US, o/p) and *Five Families* (Souvenir, o/p), use the same first person narrative technique. All are highly recommended.

Octavio Paz *The Labyrinth of Solitude* (Penguin/Grove Atlantic). An acclaimed series of philosophical essays exploring the social and political state of modern Mexico. Paz, who died in 1998, won the Nobel prize for literature in 1990, and was universally regarded as the country's leading poet.

Elena Poniatowska A pioneer in the field of testimonial literature and one of Mexico's best-known essayists and journalists. In *Until We Meet Again Sweet Jesus* (Pantheon, US) Poniatowska turns her attentions on Jesusa, her cleaning lady. Jesusa's story of her marriage, involvement in the Revolution and postwar period include her views on life, love and society. Narrated in the first person, the text is compelling, lively and at times ribald: Jesusa herself is now a celebrity on the literary circuit. Other works available in English include *Massacre in Mexico* (U Missouri), a collage of testimonies of those present at the 1968 massacre of students in Tlatelolco; *Dear Diego* (Pantheon, US); and *Tinisima* (Farrar, Strauss & Giroux/Faber & Faber)

Gregory G. Reck *In the Shadow of Tlaloc* (Penguin/Waveland, o/p). Reck attempts a similar style to that of Oscar Lewis in his study of a Mexican village, and the effects on it of encroaching modernity. Often seems to stray over the border into sentimentality and even fiction, but interesting nonetheless.

Alan Riding *Mexico: Inside the Volcano* (IB Tauris, UK). In-depth analysis of modern Mexico by the British correspondent for the *New York Times*. Enlightening, though gloomy.

John Ross *Rebellion from the Roots* (Common Courage Press, US). A fascinating early account of the buildup to and first months of the 1994 Zapatista Rebellion, and still the definitive book on the subject. Ross's reporting style provides a really detailed and informative background, showing the uprising was no surprise to the

Mexican army. He's also the author of *Mexico in Focus* (LAB/Interlink), a short but authoritative guide to modern Mexican society, politics and culture – worth reading before a visit.

Chloë Sayer *The Arts and Crafts of Mexico* (Thames & Hudson/Chronicle). Sayer is the author of numerous books on Mexican arts, crafts and associated subjects (see below); all of them worth reading. *The Skeleton at the Feast* (British Museum Press, UK), written with Elizabeth Carmichael, is a wonderful, superbly illustrated insight into attitudes to death and the dead in Mexico.

Joel Simon *Endangered Mexico* (Sierra Club). Eloquent and compelling study documenting the environmental crisis facing Mexico at the end of the twentieth century. Accurate and very moving, it's essential reading for those wanting to know how and why the crisis exists – and why no one can offer solutions.

Mariana Yampolsky *The Traditional Architecture of Mexico* (Thames & Hudson). The enormous range of Mexico's architectural styles, from thatched peasant huts and vast *haciendas* to exuberant Baroque churches and solid, yet graceful public buildings is encompassed in this inspired book. While most of Mariana Yampolsky's superb photographs are in black and white, a chapter on the use of colour emphasizes its importance in every area of life; the text by Chloë Sayer raises it above the level of the average coffee-table book. (For guides to ecclesiastical architecture in Mexico see Richard Perry, below).

OTHER GUIDES

In Mexico itself, the best and most complete series of guides is that published by *Guías Panorama* – they have small books on all the main archeological sites, as well as more general titles ranging from *Wild Flowers of Mexico* to *Pancho Villa – Truth and Legend*.

Tim Burford *Backpacking in Mexico* (Bradt). Great on the practicalities of backpacking, with lots of information specifically relevant to Mexico, and a particularly good wildlife section. The hikes themselves cover all areas, including how to asecnd Popacatépetl.

Carl Franz *The People's Guide to Mexico* (John Muir). Not a guidebook as such, more of a series of anecdotes and words of advice for staying out of trouble and heading off the beaten track. Perennially popular, and deservedly so.

Joyce Kelly *An Archaeological Guide to Mexico's Yucatán Peninsula* (U Oklahoma). Detailed and practical guide to more than ninety Maya sites and eight museums throughout the peninsula, including many little-known or difficult-to-reach ruins; an essential companion for anyone travelling purposefully through the Maya World. Kelly's "star" rating – based on a site's archeological importance, degree of restoration and accessibility – may affront purists, but it does provide a valuable opinion on how worthwhile a particular visit might be.

Richard Perry *Mexico's Fortress Monasteries* (Espadaña Press, US). One in a series of expertly written guides to the sometimes overlooked treasures of Mexico's colonial religious architecture. This volume covers more than sixty cathedrals, churches and monuments in Central Mexico, from Hidalgo to Oaxaca; *Maya Missions* deals with colonial Yucatán and *More Maya Missions* covers Chiapas; all are illustrated by the author's simple but beautiful drawings. These specialist offerings, ideal for travellers who want more information than most guide books can provide, are not widely available, though you can find them in tourist bookshops in the areas they cover.

D.G. Schueler *Adventuring along the Gulf of Mexico* (Sierra Club Books, US). An entertaining read, with much general info on plants and animals along the Gulf coast.

R.J. Secor *Mexico's Volcanoes* (Mountaineers). Detailed routes up all the big volcanoes, and full of invaluable information for climbers.

WILDLIFE

Steve Howe and Sophie Webb *The Birds of Mexico and Northern Central America* (Oxford UP). A tremendous work, the result of years of research, this is the definitive book on the region's birds. Essential for all serious birders.

C. Kaplan *Coral reefs of the Caribbean and Florida* (Houghton Mifflin). Useful handbook on the abundant wildlife off the coasts off the Yucatán peninsula.

R.T. Peterson and E.L. Chalif *Mexican Birds* (Houghton Mifflin). The classic ornithological guide to Mexico. The text is excellent, but drawings are limited to indigenous examples only; migratory species are included in additional (North American) guides, which can be frustratingly impractical.

LANGUAGE

PHRASEBOOKS AND DICTIONARIES
Although we've listed a few essential words and phrases here, if you're travelling for any length of time some kind of dictionary or **phrasebook** is obviously a worthwhile investment: the *Rough Guide to Mexican Spanish* is the best practical guide, correct and colloquial, and will have you speaking the language faster than any other phrasebook. One of the best small, Latin-American Spanish dictionaries is the University of Chicago version (Pocket Books), widely available in Mexico. If you're using a **dictionary**, bear in mind that in Spanish CH, LL are traditionally counted as separate letters and are listed after the Cs, Ls and Ns respectively. This has recently changed, but many dictionaries won't have caught up.

Once you get into it, Spanish is the easiest language there is – and in Mexico people are desperately eager to understand and to help the most faltering attempt. English is widely spoken, especially in the tourist areas, but you'll get a far better reception if you at least try to communicate with people in their own tongue. You'll be further helped by the fact that Mexicans speak relatively slowly (at least compared with Spaniards in Spain) and that there's none of the difficult lisping pronunciation here.

The rules of **pronunciation** are pretty straightforward and, once you get to know them, strictly observed. Unless there's an accent, words ending in d, l, r and z are **stressed** on the last syllable, all others on the second last. All **vowels** are pure and short.

A somewhere between the A sound of back and that of father
E as in get
I as in police
O as in hot
U as in rule
C is soft before E and I, hard otherwise: *cerca* is pronounced serka.

G works the same way, a guttural H sound (like the *ch* in loch) before E or I, a hard G elsewhere: *gigante* becomes higante.
H is always silent
J the same sound as a guttural G: *jamon* is pronounced hamon.
LL sounds like an English Y: *tortilla* is pronounced torteeya.
Ñ is as in English unless it has a tilde (accent) over it, when it becomes NY: *mañana* sounds like manyana.
QU is pronounced like an English K.
R is rolled, RR doubly so.
V sounds more like B, *vino* becoming beano.
X is slightly softer than in English – some times almost S – except between vowels in place names where it has an H sound, like México (*meh*-hee-ko) or Oaxaca (wa-*ha*-ka). In Maya words, X sounds like *sh* – so Xel Ha is pronounced shel-ha.
Z is the same as a soft C, so *cerveza* becomes servesa.

BASICS

Yes, No	*Sí, No*	Open, Closed	*Abierto/a, Cerrado/a*
Please, Thank you	*Por favor, Gracias*	With, Without	*Con, Sin*
Where, When	*¿Dónde?, ¿Cuando?*	Good, Bad	*Buen(o)/a, Mal(o)/a*
What, How much	*¿Qué?, ¿Cuanto?*	Big, Small	*Gran(de), Pequeño/a*
Here, There	*Aquí, Allí*	More, Less	*Más, Menos*
This, That	*Este, Eso*	Today, Tomorrow	*Hoy, Mañana*
Now, Later	*Ahora, Más tarde*	Yesterday	*Ayer*

GREETINGS AND RESPONSES

Hello, Goodbye	*¡Hola!, Adiós*	What (did you say)?	*Mande?*
Good morning	*Buenos días*	My name is...	*Me llamo...*
Good afternoon/ night	*Buenas tardes/noches*	What's your name?	*¿Como se llama*
How do you do?	*¿Qué tal?*		*usted?*
See you later	*Hasta luego*	I am English	*Soy inglés(a)*
Sorry	*Lo siento/disculpeme*	...American*	*americano(a)*
Excuse me	*Con permiso/perdon*	...Australian	*australiano(a)*
How are you?	*¿Cómo está (usted)?*	...Canadian	*canadiense(a)*
Not at all/You're welcome	*De nada*	...Irish	*irlandés(a)*
I (don't) understand	*(No) Entiendo*	...Scottish	*escosés(a)*
Do you speak English?	*¿Habla (usted) Inglés?*	...Welsh	*galés(a)*
I don't speak Spanish	*(No) Hablo Español*	...New Zealander	*neozelandés(a)*

*Mexicans are Americans, too, so describing yourself as American can occasionally cause offence. Better to opt for "estadosunidense(a)" (from "Los Estados Unidos", Spanish for the United States) if you are a US American; and for Canadians, "canadiense".

NEEDS – HOTELS AND TRANSPORT

I want	*Quiero*	How do I get to...?	*¿Por dónde se va a...?*
Do you know...?	*¿Sabe...?*	Left, right, straight on	*izquierda, derecha,*
I'd like...	*Quisiera... por favor*		*derecho*
I don't know	*No sé*	Where is...?	*¿Dónde está...?*
There is (is there)?	*Hay (?)*	...the bus station	*...el camionera central*
Give me...	*Deme...*	...the railway station	*...la estación de*
(one like that)	*(uno asi)*		*ferrocarriles*
Do you have...?	*¿Tiene...?*	...the nearest bank	*...el banco más cercano*
...the time	*...la hora*	...the ATM	*...el cajero automático*
...a room	*...un cuarto*	...the post office	*...el correo*
...with two beds/	*...con dos camas/*		*(la oficina de correos)*
double bed	*cama matrimonial*	...the toilet	*...el baño/sanitario*
It's for one person	*Es para una persona*	Where does the bus	*¿De dónde sale el*
(two people)	*(dos personas)*	to...leave from?	*camión para...?*
...for one night	*...para una noche*	Is this the train for	*¿Es éste el tren para*
(one week)	*(una semana)*	Chihuahua?	*Chihuahua?*
It's fine, how much is it?	*¿Esta bien, cuánto es?*	I'd like a (return) ticket	*Quisiera un boleto*
It's too expensive	*Es demasiado caro*	to...	*(de ida y vuelta) para...*
Don't you have anything	*¿No tiene algo más*	What time does it leave	*¿A qué hora sale*
cheaper?	*barato?*	(arrive in...)?	*(llega en...)?*
Can one...?	*¿Se puede...?*	What is there to eat?	*¿Qué hay para comer?*
...camp (near) here?	*¿...acampar aquí (cerca)?*	What's that?	*¿Qué es eso?*
Is there a hotel nearby?	*¿Hay un hotel aquí*	What's this called in	*¿Cómo se llama este en*
cerca?		Spanish?	*español?*

NUMBERS AND DAYS

1	*un/uno/una*	13	*trece*	100	*cien(to)*	first	*primero/a*
2	*dos*	14	*catorce*	101	*ciento uno*	second	*segundo/a*
3	*tres*	15	*quince*	200	*doscientos*	third	*tercero/a*
4	*cuatro*	16	*dieciséis*	500	*quinientos*	fifth	*quinto/a*
5	*cinco*	20	*veinte*	700	*setecientos*	tenth	*decimo/a*
6	*seis*	21	*veintiuno*	1000	*mil*		
7	*siete*	30	*treinta*	2000	*dos mil*	Monday	*Lunes*
8	*ocho*	40	*cuarenta*			Tuesday	*Martes*
9	*nueve*	50	*cincuenta*	1999	*mil novocientos*	Wednesday	*Miércoles*
10	*diez*	60	*sesenta*		*noventa y nueve*	Thursday	*Jueves*
11	*once*	70	*setenta*			Friday	*Viernes*
12	*doce*	80	*ochenta*			Saturday	*Sábado*
		90	*noventa*			Sunday	*Domingo*

GLOSSARY OF COMMON MEXICAN TERMS AND ACRONYMS

AHORITA diminutive of *ahora* (now) meaning right now – usually an hour at least.

ALAMEDA city park or promenade; large plaza.

AYUNTAMIENTO town hall/government.

AZTEC the empire that dominated the central valleys of Mexico from the thirteenth century until defeated by Cortés.

BARRIO area within a town or city; suburb.

CAMIONETA small truck or van.

CANTINA bar, usually men-only.

CENOTE underground water source in the Yucatán.

CENTRAL CAMIONERA bus station.

CHAC Maya god of rain.

CHAC-MOOL recumbent statue, possibly a sacrificial figure or messenger to the gods.

CHARREADAS displays of horseman ship, rodeos.

CHARRO a Mexican cowboy.

COMAL large, round flat plate made of clay or metal used for cooking tortillas.

COMEDOR cheap restaurant, literally dining room.

CONVENTO either convent or monastery.

CTM Central Union organization.

CUAUHTÉMOC the last Aztec leader, commander of the final resistance to Cortés, and a national hero.

DESCOMPUESTO out of order.

DON/DOÑA courtesy titles (sir/madam), mostly used in letters or for professional people or the boss.

EJIDO communal farmland.

ENRAMADAS palapas-covered restaurants.

EZLN *Ejército Zapatista de Liberación Nacional*, the Zapatista Army of National Liberation. Guerrilla group in Chiapas.

EPR *Ejército Popular Revolutionario*, the Popular Revolutionary Army. Guerrilla group, not allied to the Zapatistas; their first appearance was in Guerrero in 1996.

FERIA fair (market).

FINCA ranch or plantation.

FONART government agency to promote crafts.

FONDA simple restaraunt or boarding house.

GRINGO not necessarily insulting, though it does imply North American – said to come from invading US troops, either because they wore green coats or because they sang *"Green grow the rushes oh!..."*

GUAYABERA embroidered shirt.

GÜERA/O blonde – very frequently used description of Westerners, especially shouted after women in the street; again, not intended as an insult.

HACIENDA estate or big house on it.

HENEQUEN hemp fibre, grown mainly in Yucatán, used to make rope.

HUIPIL Maya women's embroidered dress or blouse.

HUITZILOPOCHTLI Aztec god of war.

I.V.A. 15 percent value-added tax.

KUKULCAN Maya name for Quetzalcoatl.

LADINO applied to people, means Spanish-influenced as opposed to Indian: determined entirely by clothing (and culture) rather than physical race.

MALECÓN seafront promenade.

MALINCHE Cortés' Indian interpreter and mistress, a symbol of treachery.

MARIACHI quintessentially Mexican music, with lots of brass and sentimental lyrics.

MARIMBA xylophone-like musical instrument, also used of the bands based around it and the style of music.

MAYA tribe who inhabited Honduras, Guatemala and southeastern Mexico from earliest times, and still does.

MESTIZO mixed race.

METATE flat stone for grinding corn.

MIRADOR lookout point.

MIXTEC tribe from the mountains of Oaxaca.

MOCTEZUMA Montezuma, penultimate Aztec leader.

MUELLE jetty or dock.

NAFTA the North American Free Trade Agreement including Mexico, the USA and Canada; see also **TLC** below.

NAHUATL ancient Aztec language, still the most common after Spanish.

NORTEÑO literally northern – style of food and music.

PALACIO mansion, but not necessarily royal.

PALACIO DE GOBIERNO headquarters of state/federal authorities.

PALACIO MUNICIPAL headquarters of local government.

PALAPA palm thatch. Used to describe any thatched/palm-roofed hut.

PALENQUE cockpit (for cock fights).

PAN *Partido de Acción Nacional* (National Action Party), conservative opposition party; has gained several local election victories, mainly in the north.

PASEO a broad avenue, but also the ritual evening walk around the plaza.

PEMEX the Mexican national oil company, a vast and extraordinarily wealthy corporation, rumoured to be riddled with corruption, as is the powerful oil workers' union.

PLANTA BAJA ground floor – abbreviated PB in lifts.

PORFIRIANO the time of Porfirio Díaz's dictatorship – used especially of its grandiose neo-classical architecture.

PRD *Partido Revolucionario Democrático* (Party of the Democratic Revolution), the left-wing opposition formed and led by Cuauhtémoc Cárdenas; has the second largest number of seats in Congress.

PRI *Partido Revolucionario Institucional* (Party of the Institutional Revolution), the ruling party for the past eighty years.

PT *Partido del Trabajo* (Workers Party), small party but with opposition seats in Congress

PVEM *Partido Verde Ecologista de México* (Green Party), small opposition party.

QUETZALCOATL the plumed serpent, most powerful, enigmatic and widespread of all ancient Mexican gods.

ROMERÍA procession.

SACBE Maya road.

STELA free-standing carved monument.

TENOCHTITLÁN the Aztec capital, on the site of México.

TEOTIHUACÁN ancient city north of the capital – the first major urban power of central Mexico.

TIANGUIS Nahuatl word for market, still used of particularly varied marketplaces.

TLALOC Toltec/Aztec rain god.

TLC *Tratado de Libre Comercio*, NAFTA in Spanish.

TOLTEC tribe which controlled central Mexico between Teotihuacán and the Aztecs.

TULA Toltec capital.

TZOMPANTLI Aztec skull rack or "wall of skulls".

VIRREINAL from the period of the Spanish viceroys – ie colonial.

WETBACK illegal Mexican (or any Hispanic) in the US.

ZAPOTEC tribe which controlled the Oaxaca region to about 700 AD.

ZÓCALO the main plaza of any town.

GLOSSARY OF ART AND ARCHITECTURAL TERMS

ALFIZ decorative rectangular moulding over a doorway.

ARABESQUE elaborate geometric pattern of Islamic origin.

ARTESONADO intricate ceiling design, usually of jointed, inlaid wood.

ATLANTEAN prehispanic column in the form of a warrior – examples found at Tula.

ATRIUM enclosed forecourt of churchyard or monastery.

AZULEJO decorative glazed tile, usually blue and white.

CHURRIGUERESQUE highly elaborate, decorative form of Baroque architecture (usually in churches), named after the seventeenth-century Spanish architect.

CONVENTO monastery residence which includes the cloister.

DADO ornamental border on the lower part of an interior wall.

ESCUDO shield-shaped decoration.

ESCUTCHEON heraldic shield or coat-of-arms.

ESPADAÑA belfry, usually on top of the front wall of a church.

FLUTING vertical grooves in a column.

FRESCO technique of painting on wet or dry plaster.

GARITA ornamental pinnacle or battlement which looks like a sentry-box.

GROTESQUE ornamental style depicting fantastic birds, beasts and foliage.

HERRERIAN imperial style named after sixteenth-century Spanish architect Juan de Herrera.

LUNETTE crescent-shaped space above a doorway or beneath a vault.

MERLON decorative pyramidal battlement.

MUDÉJAR Spanish architectural style strongly influenced by Moorish forms.

OGEE curved, pointed arch.

PILA font or water basin; also commonly found in domestic buildings.

PILASTER flattened column used as decorative element.

PINJANTE glove-shaped decorative pendant, popular in eighteenth-century architecture.

PLATERESQUE elaborately decorative Renaissance architectural style.

PORTALES arcades.

PORTERÍA entry portico to a monastery.

PREDELLA base panel of an altarpiece.

PURISTA severe Renaissance architectural style, originating in sixteenth-century Spain.

RETABLO carved, painted wooden altarpiece.

TECALI translucent onyx, also called Mexican alabaster.

TEQUITQUI early colonial style of sculpture using Preconquest techniques.

ZAPATA wooden roof beam, often decoratively carved.

INDEX

Listen!

Stay in touch with us!

ROUGH*NEWS* is Rough Guides' free newsletter.
In three issues a year we give you news, travel
issues, music reviews, readers' letters and the
latest dispatches from authors on the road.

¿Qué pasa?

WHAT'S HAPPENING?
A ROUGH GUIDES SERIES –
ROUGH GUIDES PHRASEBOOKS

Rough Guide Phrasebooks
represent a complete shakeup
of the phrasebook format.
Handy and pocket sized, they
work like a dictionary to get you
straight to the point. With clear
guidelines on pronunciation,
dialogues for typical situations,
and tips on cultural issues, they'll
have you speaking the language
quicker than any other
phrasebook.

Czech, French, German, Greek,
Hindi & Urdu, Hungarian, Indonesian,
Italian, Japanese, Mandarin Chinese,
Mexican Spanish, Polish, Portuguese,
Russian, Spanish, Thai, Turkish,
Vietnamese

Further titles coming soon...

Introducing Tekware.
(What to wear when your biggest fashion concern is hypothermia.)

Lynn Hill climbing Three Sisters,
Photo: Clint Clemens

Made from advanced synthetic fabrics, **TEKWARE**® is clothing that dries faster, lasts longer and maintains overall comfort better than cotton. Its design combines the experience of world-class outdoor athletes and the expertise of our research and development teams. The result is a line of technologically superior outdoor equipment that makes cotton obsolete. For the dealer nearest you or to receive a free catalogue call: First Ascent, Units 2-5, Limetree Business Park, Matlock, Derbyshire, England DE4 3EJ, Freephone: 0800 146034.

NEVER STOP EXPLORING

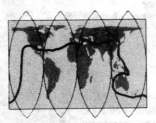

**HOSTELLING
INTERNATIONAL**

The last word in accommodation

Safe reliable accommodation
from $8 a night at over 4500 centres
in 60 countries worldwide

http://www.iyhf.org